95-27 A

WORLD
LITERATURE

Holt, Rinehart and Winston

Harcourt Brace Jovanovich HBJ

Austin • Orlando • San Diego • Chicago • Dallas • Toronto

ACKNOWLEDGMENTS

Field Test Participants

We wish to thank the following people, who participated in field testing of pre-publication materials:

Patricia L. Ely
Reading Senior High School
Reading, Pennsylvania

Carol H. Farthing
Bangor High School
Bangor, Maine

Art Garbosky
Corona del Sol High School
Tempe, Arizona

Delmas E. Hare
Westlake High School
Atlanta, Georgia

Leslie M. Moore
Jenks High School
Jenks, Oklahoma

Fred B. Myers
Katella High School
Anaheim, California

Wendell Schwartz
Adlai E. Stevenson
  High School
Prairie View, Illinois

Marian S. Sheidy
Wheaton Central High School
Wheaton, Illinois

Sandra R. Walter
Boston Latin High School
Boston, Massachusetts

John R. Williamson
Johnson Central Senior High School
Paintsville, Kentucky

COVER: PAUL GAUGUIN, *ANCESTORS OF TEHEMANA*, 1893, oil on canvas. 76.3 × 54.3 cm. Gift of Mr. and Mrs. Charles Deering McCormick. © 1992 The Art Institute of Chicago.

Acknowledgments: See page iv, which is an extension of the copyright page.

Printed in the United States of America

ISBN 0-03-053608-1

3456 040 96 95 94

WRITERS

Susan Wittig Albert has a Ph.D. in English from the University of California, Berkeley. She has taught at the University of Texas at Austin, Southwest Texas State University, and Tulane University. She is the author of *Stylistic and Narrative Structures in Middle English Verse Romances*.

Richard Cohen is the author of three novels, including *Say You Want Me*, which was nominated for the Pulitzer Prize. He has taught creative writing at the University of Wisconsin, Madison.

Rose Sallberg Kam received her M.A. in English from California State University, Sacramento, and taught English at the secondary level for seventeen years. She has been a freelance writer of educational materials since 1983. She is currently writing a book on biblical women.

David Adams Leeming is a professor of English and Comparative Literature at the University of Connecticut, Storrs. For several years, he taught English at Robert College in Istanbul, Turkey. He is the author of *Mythology: The Voyage of the Hero; Flights: Readings in Magic, Mysticism, Fantasy, and Myth; Mythology;* and *The World of Myth*.

Thomas Monsell has taught secondary English, including Shakespearean drama, for twenty years. He has directed many school productions of Shakespeare's plays and has acted in and directed stock and community theaters.

Carroll Moulton has a Ph.D. from Yale University and has taught Classical Studies at Princeton University and Duke University. He is the author of *Similes in the Homeric Poems* and the translator of Menander's *Dyskolos*. He has been writing and editing educational materials for nearly fifteen years.

Susanna Nied received her M.A. from San Diego State University. She teaches comparative literature at the university level and is the translator of several modern Scandinavian literary works.

Eileen Hillary Oshinsky has been a freelance writer and anthologist for more than fifteen years. She specializes in American, British, and World literatures as well as in grammar and composition.

REVIEWERS AND CONSULTANTS

ACKNOWLEDGMENTS

For permission to reprint copyrighted material, grateful acknowledgment is made to the following sources:

African Universities Press: "Telephone Conversation" by Wole Soyinka from *Reflections: Nigerian Prose and Verse,* edited by Frances Ademola. Copyright © 1962 by African Universities Press Ltd. Lagos.

Allied Books Limited: From *Out of My Later Years* by Albert Einstein. Copyright 1950 by the Philosophical Library, Inc.

The American-Scandinavian Foundation: From *The Life of Ibsen,* Vol. II, by Halvdan Koht. Copyright 1931 by The American-Scandinavian Foundation.

The Asia Society: "Thoughts of Hanoi" by Nguyen Thi Vinh, translated by Nguyen Ngoc Bich. Copyright © 1975 by The Asia Society.

Associated University Presses: "A Mother to Her First-Born" from *Initiation: Translations from Poems of the Didinga & Lango Tribes* by J. H. Driberg. Copyright 1932 by The Golden Cockerel Press, London.

Bantam Books, a division of Bantam Doubleday Dell Publishing Group, Inc.: "The White Snake" from *The Complete Fairy Tales of the Brothers Grimm,* Vol. 1, translated by Jack Zipes. Copyright © 1987 by Jack Zipes. From "The Second Teaching: Philosophy and Spiritual Decline" from *The Bhagavad-Gita,* translated by Barbara Stoler Miller. Translation copyright © 1986 by Barbara Stoler Miller.

Ben Belitt: From "A Pinecone, a Toy Sheep" by Pablo Neruda, translated by Ben Belitt from *Evergreen Review,* 1962.

Robert Bly: "The Guitar" by Federico García Lorca from *Lorca and Jiménez: Selected Poems,* translated by Robert Bly. Copyright © 1973 by Robert Bly. "Discoverers of Chile" by Pablo Neruda from *Neruda and Vallejo: Selected Poems,* translated by Robert Bly. Copyright © 1971 by Robert Bly.

George Braziller, Inc.: From "The Here and Now" from *Renaissance Culture: A New Sense of Order,* edited by Julian Mates and Eugene Cantelupe. Copyright © 1966 by Julian Mates and Eugene Cantelupe.

Cambridge University Press: "Ogun, god of war" translated by Ulli Beier and Bakare Gbadamosi from *Yoruba Poetry: An Anthology of Traditional Poems,* edited by Ulli Beier. Copyright © 1970 by Cambridge University Press.

John Cech: "Storytelling Stone," retold by John Cech, from *Parabola, The Magazine of Myth and Tradition,* vol. IV, no. 4, 1979. Copyright © 1979 by John Cech.

China Books & Periodicals, Inc.: "Love Must Not Be Forgotten" and from "Biographical Note—My Boat" by Zhang Jie, translated by Gladys Yang from *Love Must Not Be Forgotten,* edited by Gladys Yang. Copyright © 1986 by China Books.

City Lights Books: Chinese characters and literal translations, pp. 34–35, and "The moon's snow falls," p. 36, from *The Chinese Written Character as a Medium for Poetry* by Ernest Fenollosa, edited by Ezra Pound. Copyright © 1936 by Ezra Pound.

Columbia University Press: "Nieh Cheng" from *Records of the Historian: Chapters from the* Shih chi *of Ssu-ma Ch'ien,* translated by Burton Watson. Copyright © 1958, 1961, 1962, 1969 by Columbia University Press. From *The Pillow Book of Sei Shōnagon,* translated by Ivan Morris. Copyright © 1967 by Ivan Morris. From "Introduction" from *The Columbia Book of Chinese Poetry,* translated and edited by Burton Watson. Copyright © 1984 by Columbia University Press. Quote from "Kamo Mabuchi: Kokuikō," translated by Heinrich Dumoulin, and quote by Fujiwara no Teika, translated by Ryūsaku Tsunoda from *Sources of the Japanese Tradition,* compiled by Ryūsaku Tsunoda, Wm. Theodore de Bary, and Donald Keene. Copyright © 1958 by Columbia University Press.

The Condé Nast Publications Inc.: From Le Anne Schreiber's interview with Margaret Atwood from *Vogue,* January 1986. Courtesy *Vogue.* Copyright © 1986 by The Condé Nast Publications Inc.

Stanley Corngold: "The Metamorphosis" from *The Metamorphosis* by Franz Kafka, edited and translated by Stanley Corngold. Translation copyright © 1972 by Stanley Corngold.

The Crossroad/Continuum Publishing Group: "Trurl's Machine" from *The Cyberiad: Fables for the Cybernetic Age* by Stanislaw Lem, translated by Michael Kandel. Copyright © 1974 by The Crossroad/Continuum Publishing Group.

Joan Daves Agency: "I Am Not Lonely" from *Selected Poems of Gabriela Mistral,* translated by Langston Hughes. Copyright © 1957 by the Estate of Gabriela Mistral as author and Langston Hughes as translator.

(continued on page 1500)

CONTENTS

Unit 1

WORLD MYTHS AND FOLKTALES   1

WORLD MYTHS AND FOLKTALES   2

Introduction: **Tales About Beginnings**   8

How the World Was Made
(Cheyenne)   11

The Wooden People
from the Popol Vuh (Quiché Mayan)   18

Coyote and the Origin of Death
(Caddo)   23

Introduction: **The Hero and the Quest**   26

Theseus (Greek)   29

Osiris and Isis (Egyptian)   35

Green Willow (Japanese)   41

The White Snake (German)   47

     Behind the Scenes:
     The Brothers Grimm   52

Language and Culture: The Hero
and the Quest: Alive and Well   54

Language Skills: Using Transitions
for Comparison and Contrast   56

Critical Thinking and Writing:
Discovering Connections
in Literature   58

Unit 2

THE AFRICAN LITERARY TRADITION   61

TIME LINE   62

AFRICAN LITERATURE   64

The Great Hymn to the Aten
(Egyptian)   73

     Behind the Scenes:
     Daily Life in Ancient Egypt   78

New Kingdom Love Lyrics
(Egyptian)   81

     The Art of Translation:
     Egyptian Hieroglyphics   83

African Proverbs   85

     Elements of Literature:
     Features of African
     Oral Literature   88

**Song of a Mother to Her
Firstborn** (Didinga or Lango)   90

Ogun Kills on the Right (Yoruba)   95

Talk (Ashanti)   98

Introduction: **Sundiata: An Epic
of Old Mali**   102

from **Sundiata** (Mali)   105

Language and Culture: African
American Storytellers   118

Language Skills: Using Quotations
Effectively   120

Critical Thinking and Writing:
A Personal Response to Literature   122

Unit 3

THE ANCIENT MIDDLE EAST   125

TIME LINE   126

THE LITERATURE OF ANCIENT MESOPOTAMIA   128

Introduction: **The Epic of Gilgamesh**   136

from the **Epic of Gilgamesh**   139

> The Art of Translation: Comparing Translations of *Gilgamesh*   153

HEBREW LITERATURE   154

Introduction: **The Hebrew Bible**   160

In the Beginning
from Genesis   163

> Behind the Scenes: The King James Bible   169

Noah and the Flood
from Genesis   171

The Book of Ruth   178

> Seeing Connections: Biblical Allusions   185

from the **Book of Psalms**
Psalm 23   187
Psalm 104   188
Psalm 137   192

> Elements of Literature: Parallelism   195

Introduction: **The New Testament**   196

Parables
The Prodigal Son   199
The Sower   200
The Talents   202

Language and Culture: Deciphering Ancient Texts   204

Language Skills: Varying Sentence Beginnings and Avoiding Dangling Modifiers   206

Critical Thinking and Writing: Writing an Autobiographical Narrative   208

Unit 4

GREEK AND ROMAN LITERATURES   211

TIME LINE   212

GREEK LITERATURE   214

Introduction: **The Iliad**   224

from the **Iliad**
from Book 1   229
from Books 22 and 24   246

> The Art of Translation: A Recent Translation of Homer's *Iliad*   278

Sappho   279

You Are the Herdsman of Evening   281
Sleep, Darling   281
We Drink Your Health   281
To an Army Wife, in Sardis   282
You May Forget But   282
Tonight I've Watched   282
Don't Ask Me What to Wear   282

Thucydides   284

Funeral Speech of Pericles
from History of the Peloponnesian War   286

Plato   293

from the Apology
from the Dialogues   295

Sophocles   301

Introduction: **Oedipus Rex**   302

Oedipus Rex   307

  A Critical Comment:
Themes in *Oedipus Rex*   367

  Elements of Literature:
Tragedy and the
Tragic Hero   371

ROMAN LITERATURE   372

Virgil   379

Introduction: **The Aeneid**   380

***from the* Aeneid**
from Book 2, The Fall of Troy   383

  A Critical Comment: Themes
and Images in Book 2
of the *Aeneid*   406

Catullus   409

Wretched Catullus, Leave off
Playing the Fool   411
Lesbia Says She'd Rather
Marry Me   412
If Ever Anyone Anywhere   412
I Hate and I Love   412

Horace   414

The Golden Mean   416
Carpe Diem   417

  Primary Sources: Horace
and *The Art of Poetry*   419

Ovid   420

from Metamorphoses
The Creation   422
The Four Ages   425

Tacitus   428

The Burning of Rome
from The Annals   430

Language and Culture: Classical
Allusions in Modern English   436

Language Skills: Maintaining
Subject-Verb Agreement   438

Critical Thinking and Writing:
Creating an Epic Adventure   440

Unit 5

INDIAN LITERATURE   443

TIME LINE   444

INDIAN LITERATURE   446

The Rig Veda   454
Night   456

Introduction: **The Mahabharata**   458
Hundred Questions   461

The Bhagavad-Gita   467
Philosophy and Spiritual Discipline   469

  Seeing Connections:
The *Bhagavad-Gita*'s Influence
on Transcendentalism   477

The Panchatantra   478
Right-Mind and Wrong-Mind   480

The Ramayana   484
Rama and Ravana in Battle   486

  Behind the Scenes: The Tales
Behind India's Epics   495

Language and Culture: A God
with Universal Appeal   496

Language Skills: Avoiding Sentence
Fragments and Run-on Sentences   498

Critical Thinking and Writing:
Writing to Persuade   500

Unit 6

CHINESE AND JAPANESE LITERATURES 503

TIME LINE 504

THE LITERATURE OF CHINA 506

Introduction: **The Book of Songs** 512
Song 103: O Oriole, Yellow Bird 515
Song 130: What Plant Is Not Faded? 516

Li Po 518
Quiet Night Thoughts 520
Letter to His Two Small Children 520

The Art of Translation: Translating Chinese Poetry 523

Tu Fu 526
For Wei Pa, in Retirement 528
Night Thoughts Afloat 529
Jade Flower Palace 530

Li Ch'ing-chao 532
Peonies 534

Confucius 536
from the Analects 538

Lao-tzu 541
from the Tao Te Ching 543

Taoist Writers 546
Taoist Anecdotes
Wagging My Tail in the Mud 548
The Butterfly 548
Gold, Gold 548
The Missing Axe 549
The Lost Horse 549

Ssu-ma Ch'ien 551
Nieh Cheng
from Records of the Historian 553

THE LITERATURE OF JAPAN 558

Introduction: **Tanka Poetry** 564

Tanka Poets 566
Princess Nukada
I Waited and I 569
Oshikochi Mitsune
The End of My Journey 569
Ki Tsurayuki
Now, I Cannot Tell 569
Ono Komachi
How Helpless My Heart! 570
Priest Saigyo
Every Single Thing 570

Introduction: **Haiku** 572

Haiku Poets 574
Matsuo Bashō
On a withered branch 576
A village where they ring 576
No rice?— In that hour 576
Uejima Onitsura
Even stones in streams 576
Taniguchi Buson
Blossoms on the pear 576
Kobayashi Issa
A morning-glory vine 576

Primary Sources: A Glimpse into a Poet's Life 578

Sei Shōnagon 579
from The Pillow Book 581

Behind the Scenes: Lady Murasaki's Triumph 588

Zen Parables 589
Muddy Road 591
A Parable 591
Publishing the Sutras 592
The Thief Who Became a Disciple 593
The Taste of Banzo's Sword 593

Introduction: **Noh Plays** 596

Seami Motokiyo 598
Atsumori 600

Primary Sources: from *The Tale of the Heike:* ''The Death of Atsumori'' 610

Language and Culture: Senryu: Japan's Comic Verses 612

Language Skills: Maintaining Pronoun-Antecedent Agreement 614

Critical Thinking and Writing: Analyzing Imagery 616

Unit 7

PERSIAN AND ARABIC LITERATURES 619

TIME LINE 620
PERSIAN AND ARABIC LITERATURES 622

al-Khansa 630
On Her Brother 631

The Koran 633
The Exordium 635
The Cessation 635
Daylight 636
Comfort 636

The Thousand and One Nights 638
from The Third Voyage of Sindbad the Sailor 640

Behind the Scenes: A Thousand and One Nights of Inspiration 645

Introduction: **The *Shahname*: The Epic of Persia** 646
from The Tragedy of Sohráb and Rostám 649

Omar Khayyám 654
from the Rubáiyát 656

The Art of Translation: Two Translations of the *Rubáiyát* 660

Rumi 661
Unmarked Boxes 663

Saadi 665
Anecdotes and Sayings of Saadi 667

Language and Culture: Where the Mulla Goes, Laughter Follows 672

Language Skills: Maintaining Verb Tense Consistency 674

Critical Thinking and Writing: Observing and Analyzing a Process 676

Unit 8

THE MIDDLE AGES 679

TIME LINE 680
THE MIDDLE AGES 682

The Song of Roland 692
Lais 110, 130–134, 168–171, 173, 174, 176 694

Seeing Connections: *Poem of the Cid:* Spain's National Epic 703

Snorri Sturluson 704
Thor and Loki in Giantland *from the* Prose Edda 706

Behind the Scenes: Norse Mythology and Modern Fantasy Writers 714

Marie de France 715
Chevrefoil 717

Chrétien de Troyes 720
The Grail *from* Perceval 722

Introduction: **The Nibelungenlied** 730
How Siegfried Was Slain 733

Dante Alighieri   741

Introduction: **The Divine Comedy**   742

from the **Inferno**

from the Divine Comedy   747
- Canto 1   748
- Canto 3   751
- Canto 5   755
- Canto 33   761
- Canto 34   765

    Elements of Literature:
    Allegory   771

Geoffrey Chaucer   772

    The Wife of Bath's Tale
    from The Canterbury Tales   774

Language and Culture: Drama in the Middle Ages   786

Language Skills: Choosing Effective Diction   788

Critical Thinking and Writing: Writing a Character Sketch   790

Unit 9

FROM THE RENAISSANCE TO THE ENLIGHTENMENT   793

TIME LINE   794

RENAISSANCE LITERATURE   796

Introduction: **The Sonnet in the Renaissance**   804

Renaissance Sonnet Writers   806

    Francesco Petrarch
      Sonnet 61   808

    Pierre de Ronsard
      To Hélène   809

    William Shakespeare
      Sonnet 29   810
      Sonnet 64   810

    Elements of Literature:
    Enjambment   812

Giovanni Boccaccio   813

    The Tale of the Falcon
    from the Decameron   815

Miguel de Cervantes   821

    from Don Quixote   823

    Elements of Literature:
    Satire   838

William Shakespeare   839

Introduction: **The Elizabethan Theater**   840

The Tempest   845

    A Critical Comment:
    The Tempest and
    Shakespeare's Vision
    of the World   929

    Behind the Scenes:
    Shakespeare Around
    the World   933

LITERATURE OF THE ENLIGHTENMENT   934

Jean de La Fontaine   940

    from Fables
      The Council Held by the Rats   942
      The Cock and the Fox   943

Voltaire   945

    from Candide   947

    Elements of Literature:
    The Utopia as a
    Literary Genre   963

    Behind the Scenes: Drama
    in the Enlightenment   964

Language and Culture: The Print Revolution   966

Language Skills: Using Active and Passive Voices Effectively   968

Critical Thinking and Writing:
Resolving a Controversy   970

Unit 10

THE NINETEENTH CENTURY: ROMANTICISM TO REALISM   973

TIME LINE   974

THE NINETEENTH CENTURY   976

Johann Wolfgang von Goethe   986
from Faust, Part I   988

William Wordsworth   1002
The World Is Too Much with Us   1004

Alexander Pushkin   1006
I Have Visited Again   1008

Heinrich Heine   1011
The Lorelei   1013

Victor Hugo   1015
Russia 1812
from The Expiation   1017

Charles Baudelaire   1021
Invitation to the Voyage   1023

    Seeing Connections:
    The French Connection:
    Charles Baudelaire
    and Edgar Allan Poe   1026

**Paul Verlaine
and Arthur Rimbaud**   1027
The Sky Is Just Beyond the Roof   1029
The Sleeper of the Valley   1030

Guy de Maupassant   1032
The Jewels   1034

A Critical Comment:
The Short Story in the
Nineteenth Century   1042

Leo Tolstoy   1043
How Much Land Does
a Man Need?   1045

Anton Chekhov   1060
A Problem   1062

Henrik Ibsen   1069
A Doll's House   1071

    A Critical Comment:
    The Realistic Stage   1127

Language and Culture:
The Gothic Novel   1128

Language Skills: Keeping
Pronoun Reference Clear   1130

Critical Thinking and Writing:
Writing a Literary Review   1132

Unit 11

THE TWENTIETH CENTURY   1135

TIME LINE   1136

THE TWENTIETH CENTURY   1138

Europe

Rainer Maria Rilke
(Austria/Czechoslovakia)   1148
Black Cat   1150
The Swan   1151

    Primary Sources: Rilke's
    Letters to a Young Poet   1153

Franz Kafka (Austria/Czechoslovakia)   1154
The Metamorphosis   1156

The Art of Translation:
Two Translations of
The Metamorphosis 1194

Selma Lagerlöf (Sweden) 1196
The Rat Trap 1198

James Joyce (Ireland) 1207
Eveline 1209

Isak Dinesen (Denmark) 1214
The Ring 1216

Anna Akhmatova (Russia) 1223
Lot's Wife 1225

Behind the Scenes:
Pasternak's Tribute
to Akhmatova 1227

Federico García Lorca (Spain) 1228
The Guitar 1230

Elie Wiesel (Romania) 1232
from Night 1234

Primary Sources:
Elie Wiesel Accepts
the Nobel Peace Prize 1242

Albert Camus (Algeria/France) 1244
The Guest 1246

Italo Calvino (Italy) 1258
The Enchanted Garden 1259

Aleksandr Solzhenitsyn (Russia) 1264
Freedom to Breathe 1266
A Journey Along the Oka 1267

Primary Sources:
Solzhenitsyn Accepts
the Nobel Prize 1270

Stanislaw Lem (Poland) 1271
Trurl's Machine 1273

The Americas

**Joaquim Maria Machado
de Assis** (Brazil) 1281
A Canary's Ideas 1283

Gabriela Mistral (Chile) 1289
I Am Not Lonely 1290
The Little Girl That Lost a Finger 1291

Pablo Neruda (Chile) 1294
Discoverers of Chile 1296

Jorge Luis Borges (Argentina) 1298
Borges and Myself 1300

Seeing Connections:
The Divided Self 1302

Octavio Paz (Mexico) 1303
Wind and Water and Stone 1305

Gabriel García Márquez
(Colombia) 1307
The Handsomest Drowned
Man in the World 1309

Margaret Atwood (Canada) 1316
Elegy for the Giant Tortoises 1318

Jamaica Kincaid (Antigua) 1320
A Walk to the Jetty
from Annie John 1322

Seeing Connections:
Tales of the Islands
by Derek Walcott 1329

Africa and the Middle East

Léopold Sédar Senghor
(Senegal) 1330
And We Shall Be Steeped 1332

Abioseh Nicol (Sierra Leone) 1334
Life Is Sweet at Kumansenu 1336

Chinua Achebe (Nigeria) 1343
Marriage Is a Private Affair 1345

Wole Soyinka (Nigeria)   1351
Telephone Conversation   1353

Barbara Kimenye (Uganda)   1355
The Pig   1356

Mark Mathabane (South Africa)   1363
from Kaffir Boy   1365

Naguib Mahfouz (Egypt)   1375
Half a Day   1377

Yehuda Amichai (Israel)   1381
from Laments on the War Dead   1383

Asia

Santha Rama Rau (India)   1385
By Any Other Name   1387

Akutagawa Ryunosuke (Japan)   1393
The Nose   1395

Hwang Sun-won (Korea)   1402
Cranes   1404

Nguyen Thi Vinh (Vietnam)   1409
Thoughts of Hanoi   1411

Zhang Jie (People's Republic of China)   1414
Love Must Not Be Forgotten   1416

Language and Culture:
Conscience and Controversy   1428

Language Skills: Varying
Sentences   1430

Critical Thinking and Writing:
Identifying a Theme   1432

WRITING ABOUT LITERATURE   1434
Writing Answers to Essay
Questions   1434
Writing and Revising an Essay   1435
A Model Essay   1437
Documenting Sources for a
Research Paper   1439

**A HANDBOOK OF LITERARY
TERMS**   1440

**GRAMMAR, USAGE, AND
MECHANICS: A Reference Guide**   1455

GLOSSARY   1474

INDEX OF SKILLS   1488
Literary Skills   1488
Language and Vocabulary Skills   1491
Speaking and Listening Skills   1492
Composition Skills   1492
Critical Thinking Skills   1494

INDEX OF AUTHORS AND TITLES   1495

WORLD MYTHS AND FOLKTALES

▼ Literary Significance ▼

Myths and folktales are the world's oldest stories. People have told myths and folktales since language was created, keeping them alive and vital through the centuries by word of mouth.

Myths are stories about beginnings. They probably originally had a religious purpose, for they attempt to explain mysteries that people regard as sacred: how the world was created, why people must eventually die, why the world is imperfect.

Folktales are stories told by the common people. Most folktales are told for entertainment, although they may also teach values. Legends, tall tales, fables, and fairy tales are all forms of the folktale.

Myths and folktales are important in every world culture. A society without stories about its beginnings, its heroes, and its deepest values is like a person without a name, a family without roots.

WORLD MYTHS AND FOLKTALES

Myths and folktales are the world's oldest stories, passed on by word of mouth from generation to generation. Stories have always been important to people. The following story, "The Storytelling Stone," comes from the oral tradition of the Seneca Indians of North America. It explains, perhaps better than any book on mythology ever could, how stories came to be, and why people both value and need them.

In another time before this one, there was a boy who hunted every day in the forest. Once, late in the afternoon, he stopped beside a large rock and sat down near it to fix his bow and make new points on his arrows.

A man's voice spoke to him. "I will tell you a story," it said.

The boy was startled and a little afraid, but he searched all around the stone to find the source of the voice. It could only be the rock, he thought. It must have orenda, the magic power the old men talk about. So he spoke to it. "What did you say you wanted to tell me?"

"They are called stories; they are traditions. But first you must give me a present for telling it to you."

"Will this partridge do?" asked the boy, placing one of the birds he had hunted that day on the stone.

"Come back in the evening," the stone said, "and you will hear a legend about the world that was."

In the evening the boy sat on the stone again. The voice told him of the people who lived in the sky above, the "first people," the ones with great magic. Among them lived an old woman who dreamed that the large tree with the white blossoms that stood in the center of her village should be dug up by its roots. When she told her people about this, they followed the dream's instructions, uprooting the tree.

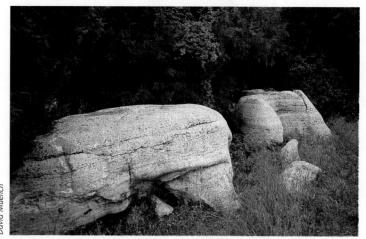

The stone has long been a symbol of strength and unity in the beliefs of many cultures, and it is often associated with foundations and with the origins of life.

❓ *Do any of these symbolic meanings come into play in this tale?*

They were frightened and angry over the hole it left and threw the old woman into it. She fell to earth, and the earth, which was completely under water then, had to be brought up from the depths by the animals and put upon the turtle's back and patted by the beavers' tails and allowed to grow before it could receive her who had fallen from the sky.

When he finished the tale, he noticed the boy had dozed off and so he said, "You must tell me if you become sleepy, and we can rest. If you sleep you will not hear. It is better that you come back tomorrow evening, and I will tell you more. Remember to bring my present."

Next day the boy hunted and in the evening returned to the rock with a string of birds. This time he did not miss a word. He came the next evening and the one after that.

"Where do you disappear to at night?" his friend asked him one day when they were out hunting together.

"I go to hear stories," he replied.

"What are they?"

"I don't know how to tell you about them, but come with me tonight and you will hear for yourself."

So he brought his friend to the stone, and its voice filled their ears with the tales of Genonsgwa and the stone coats, the Flying Heads, and the Porcupine people until the boys were sleepy and the stone sent them home to their beds.

The Pueblo Indians create story-teller dolls which depict grand-parent figures telling children stories of their ancestors and tales of the past.

Lawrence Migdale

Soon the whole village was buzzing with the news of the stone and the tales. The boys led the tribe to the place where the stone stood. The people carried fresh game with them which they left for the stone. They marveled over the things called tales that fell from its mouth. No one had ever heard about "The Master of Life" and "He Who Is Our Grandfather," or his enemy "He Who Is Clad In Ice." They did not know about such things as the songs of the corn or the prayer for the harvest, and the wisest among them knew then that they had known nothing until the stone had begun to speak. It took four years for the stone to tell all the tales, but the nights passed quickly.

The rock called the boy one evening after the others had left and said to him, "One day you will become old and be unable to hunt. These tales will help you in your old age. Tell the legends to others, but make sure that they give you something in return for them." And after it had told the boy the last story, the stone was silent and never spoke again.

The boy grew up and grew old. He did not forget the legends, and he told them to anyone who came to his lodge to listen. Many traveled from faraway tribes to hear the stories from the old man who had learned them from the stone when he was a boy. They gladly gave him tobacco, *meat, and pelts, for he knew the stories of their beginnings, too, and could tell them as well as the ones about his own tribe. There were few nights when his lodge did not have a crowd of listeners, enthralled and intent, catching the tales to take home with them to their own hearths.*

That is the way stories came to be and why there are many stories in the world where none had been before. The people from the other world before ours, the ones who had the strong and wonderful magic that the stone told about, are the ones we cannot stop telling stories about, even today.

—Retold by John Cech

"The Storytelling Stone" explains many of the most important things we need to know about myths and folktales. They tell about the beginnings of things. They include marvelous or supernatural events and tell of the deeds and adventures of gods and goddesses, heroes and heroines.

Myths and folktales remain vital to modern readers because they reveal common truths, patterns, and themes that are familiar to all ages and cultures.

They explain the origins of various rituals that people follow. They are passed down from generation to generation by word of mouth. Most important of all, however, they explain the human experience. They tell us, in poetic, imaginative terms, the most important things that we can communicate to one another: who we are, where we came from, and what we believe in. As mythologist Joseph Campbell once pointed out, myths and folktales are in some ways even "truer" than history.

What Is a Myth?

A **myth** is an anonymous, traditional story that explains a belief, a custom, or a mysterious natural phenomenon. The word *myth* comes from the Greek word *muthos*, which simply means "story."

❝ The study of mythology might be compared to the investigation of a sealed box. We do not know which is top or bottom, who sent it or why. ❞

—Mary Barnard

Lawrence Migdale

❝ Essentially, mythologies are enormous poems that are renditions of insights, giving some sense of the marvel, the miracle and wonder of life. ❞

—Joseph Campbell

CHINESE HORSE, from the Cave of Lascaux, Montignac, France. *These ancient cave paintings helped people to create a sense of order and belonging in the universe. Myths serve a similar function.*

Myths had specific purposes in their cultures. In every culture, however, the main functions of myths were:

1. To explain the creation of the world and the universe
2. To explain the human condition: how and why people were created, why they are flawed, why there is suffering in the world, why people must eventually die, and what happens to people after death
3. To explain natural phenomena, such as the setting of the sun and the phases of the moon
4. To explain the nature of gods and goddesses and how these deities and human beings interact
5. To explain the meanings behind religious rituals, customs, and beliefs
6. To explain historical events
7. To teach moral lessons

Myths were created out of a human need to make sense of the universe and explain how the world and its human inhabitants came to be.

Along with rituals, cave and rock paintings, songs, and prayers, myths were the means through which human beings in ancient times tried to find order and pattern in life. Myths helped people to feel a sense of harmony with a world that could be both beautiful and dangerous.

The Differences Between Myths and Folktales

As myths were told and retold over generations, they transformed. Not only their specific details, but also the purposes they served in their cultures, changed. One of the storytelling forms that arose from the myth was the folktale.

A **folktale** is a story that is created by the "folk"—the common people—and passed along orally from generation to generation. Folktales include legends, fables, tall tales, fairy tales, and ghost stories. Folktales differ from myths in several important ways:

1. Folktales, unlike myths, are secular, or nonreligious.
2. Folktales were created as much for their entertainment value as for the teaching of social or moral values.
3. Folktales feature magic, transformations, and enchantments, just as myths do. But although folktales may sometimes include gods or goddesses as characters, they are usually not central actors in the story.
4. Folktale heroes tend to be common, everyday folk who don't have special powers, unlike the heroes of myths, who are the superhuman offspring of gods or goddesses and human parents.
5. Folktales are not associated with religious rituals.

Title page to the first edition of Grimm's **Kinder- und Hausmärchen (Fairy Tales), 1815–1821.**

> Folktales are entertaining stories
> about ordinary people
> who survive by luck, by using their
> wits, and by relying on their own
> natural goodness.

The most important difference between a myth and a folktale concerns the purposes of each storytelling form. Myths are a direct expression of a culture's religious beliefs; folktales are not. But both myths and folktales explain important truths about life. They address our deepest needs and engage our sense of wonder. They are the stories of the human family.

*I*ntroduction

Tales About Beginnings

Probably the very first stories human beings told were **origin myths**—stories that explain how things came to be. Just as individual families have stories of where they came from, so do people all over the world have stories about their beginnings. Many of the great questions people had about their lives were answered by their origin myths: How was the world created? Why do people die? Is there life after death? Why is evil allowed to exist in the world? How did various animals, plants, and geographical features come to be?

---

origin myths: *stories that explain how things came to be.*

Most cultures have myths that explain how the universe was created. Many cultures also have stories about the end of a society, an era, or even of the world itself. Sometimes the end comes in the form of a great flood that cleanses the earth of evil and sets the stage for a new beginning. And many cultures have stories about a long-ago "Golden Age"—a time when the world enjoyed perfect peace, happiness, and prosperity. But this Golden Age is lost when evil, sickness, and death come into the world.

The Roles of Gods and Goddesses

Gods and goddesses are nearly always associated with origin myths. It is usually a god or goddess who forms the earth and the life on it.

Like human beings, gods and goddesses form family groups, or **pantheons**. Often, a culture's pantheon is ruled by a powerful "father" god and a "mother" goddess. There are usually offspring and other relatives. These other gods and goddesses are often associated with various aspects of life, from abstract values such as wisdom, fertility, love, and justice, to concrete forces of nature such as the wind, the sea, the moon, and earthquakes.

The Staying Power of Mythic Patterns

The more myths you read, the more you'll notice that certain themes, characters, and images keep recurring. These recurring patterns are called **archetypes**. They serve as basic models to which specific cultural details are added.

Archetypes are so powerful that they simply change a bit over time and reappear in different forms in other types of literature. Thus, the archetype of the

THE PEACEABLE KINGDOM, EDWARD HICKS.
The "peaceable kingdom" is a popular vision of a Golden Age.
❓ *What human hopes and yearnings do you think the idea of a peaceable kingdom symbolizes?*

lost Golden Age might appear today in a novel about a woman who remembers a happy childhood in her old home town but returns to it in middle age only to find that everything has changed and that the joy and innocence of that earlier time cannot be recaptured. The

———————◆———————

archetype (är′kə·tīp′): *a pattern or model that serves as the basis for different, but related, versions of a character, plot, or theme.*

————————————————

myth of a great flood might appear today in the form of a science-fiction

novel about the end of the world in which a war, disease, or alien invasion destroys almost everything, but leaves possibilities open for the world's rebirth.

The Purpose of Origin Myths

Origin myths gave the people who told them a sense of their place in the universe. Such myths told people who they were, where they came from, and what their destiny would be. The stories we tell today serve much the same purpose. All stories are outgrowths of myths; all stories ultimately deal with the *hows* and *whys* of human existence.

Reader's Guide

HOW THE WORLD WAS MADE

Background

The Cheyenne, a Native American people, have inhabited the North American continent for centuries. During the seventeenth century, the Cheyenne migrated from the Great Lakes region to the central plains. Their life on the plains was firmly linked with nature in general—and with the buffalo in particular. They came to depend upon the buffalo for their livelihood, and they made use of virtually every part of the animal: its flesh, its hide, and even its bones. Many Cheyenne religious rituals, such as the Sun Dance, were designed to insure the abundance of buffalo.

This Cheyenne myth is in many ways a "typical" creation story. It contains several common **motifs**, or recurring story features. Of special interest is the "earth-diver" motif. In this motif, a god sends a bird or animal to the depths of the ocean to bring back a bit of soil from which the entire earth can be created. This motif occurs among a variety of Native American peoples, but it occurs in remote parts of the world as well, such as Siberia. The turtle, too, is a recurring figure in the mythologies of many lands, from North America to China and India.

Oral Response

Many cultures view the earth as a female figure. The ancient Greeks, for example, personified the earth as a goddess called Gaia. The ancient Sumerians worshiped Ki, or Urash, the earth goddess. Today we often speak of "Mother Earth" and "the Earth Mother." As a class, discuss the feminine qualities of the earth. You may wish to record the class's ideas in the form of a word cluster on the chalkboard.

Literary Focus

An **origin myth** is a story that explains how something began. Origin myths provide explanations for mysteries that early peoples wanted to understand: why there are seasons, why we have day and night, why the moon has phases. Virtually every culture has an origin myth that explains the greatest mystery of all: the creation of the world.

How the World Was Made

A Cheyenne Myth

retold by

Alice Marriott and Carol K. Rachlin

 Do any of the details in this Cheyenne creation myth remind you of other stories you are familiar with?

In the beginning there was nothing, and Maheo, the All Spirit, lived in the void. He looked around him, but there was nothing to see. He listened, but there was nothing to hear. There was only Maheo, alone in nothingness.

Because of the greatness of his Power, Maheo was not lonesome. His being was a Universe. But as he moved through the endless time of nothingness, it seemed to Maheo that his Power should be put to use. What good is Power, Maheo asked himself, if it is not used to make a world and people to live in it?

With his Power, Maheo created a great water, like a lake, but salty. Out of this salty water, Maheo knew, he could bring all life that ever was to be. The lake itself was life, if Maheo so commanded it. In the darkness of nothingness, Maheo could feel the coolness of the water and taste on his lips the tang of the salt.

"There should be water beings," Maheo told his Power. And so it was. First the fish, swimming in the deep water, and then the mussels and snails and crawfish, lying on the sand and mud Maheo had formed so his lake should have a bottom.

The Granger Collection, New York

Let us also create something that lives on the water, Maheo thought to his Power.

And so it was. For now there were snow geese, and mallards and teal and coots and terns and loons living and swimming about on the water's surface. Maheo could hear the splashing of their feet and the flapping of their wings in the darkness.

I should like to see the things that have been created, Maheo decided.

And, again, so it was. Light began to grow and spread, first white and bleached in the east, then golden and strong till it filled the middle of the sky and extended all around the horizon. Maheo watched the light, and he saw the birds and fishes, and the shellfish lying on the bottom of the lake as the light showed them to him.

How beautiful it all is, Maheo thought in his heart.

Then the snow goose paddled over to where she thought Maheo was, in the space above the lake. "I do not see You, but I know that You exist," the goose began. "I do not know where You are, but I know You must be everywhere. Listen to me, Maheo. This is good water that You have made, on which we live. But birds are not like fish. Sometimes

Cheyenne shield, c. 1865.

we get tired swimming. Sometimes we would like to get out of the water."

"Then fly," said Maheo, and he waved his arms, and all the water birds flew, skittering along the surface of the lake until they had speed enough to rise in the air. The skies were darkened with them.

"How beautiful their wings are in the light," Maheo said to his Power, as the birds wheeled and turned, and became living patterns against the sky.

The loon was the first to drop back to the surface of the lake. "Maheo," he said, looking around, for he knew that Maheo was all about him, "You have made us sky and light

to fly in, and You have made us water to swim in. It sounds ungrateful to want something else, yet still we do. When we are tired of swimming and tired of flying, we should like a dry solid place where we could walk and rest. Give us a place to build our nests, please, Maheo."

"So be it," answered Maheo, "but to make such a place I must have your help, all of you. By myself, I have made four things: the water, the light, the sky air, and the peoples of the water. Now I must have help if I am to create more, for my Power will only let me make four things by myself."

"Tell us how we can help You," said all

the water peoples. "We are ready to do what You say."

Maheo stretched out his hand and beckoned. "Let the biggest and the swiftest try to find land first," he said, and the snow goose came to him.

"I am ready to try," the snow goose said, and she drove herself along the water until the white wake behind her grew and grew to a sharp white point that drove her up into the air as the feathers drive an arrow. She flew high into the sky, until she was only a dark spot against the clearness of the light. Then the goose turned, and down she plunged, faster than any arrow, and dived into the water. She pierced the surface with her beak as if it were the point of a spear.

The snow goose was gone a long time. Maheo counted to four four hundred times before she rose to the surface of the water and lay there floating, her beak half open as she gasped for air.

"What have you brought us?" Maheo asked her, and the snow goose sighed sadly, and answered, "Nothing. I brought nothing back."

Then the loon tried, and after him, the mallard. Each in turn rose until he was a speck against the light, and turned and dived with the speed of a flashing arrow into the water. And each in turn rose wearily, and wearily answered, "Nothing," when Maheo asked him what he had brought.

At last there came the little coot, paddling across the surface of the water very quietly, dipping his head sometimes to catch a tiny fish, and shaking the water beads from his scalp lock whenever he rose.

"Maheo," the little coot said softly, "when I put my head beneath the water, it seems to me that I see something there, far below. Perhaps I can swim down to it—I don't know. I can't fly or dive like my sisters and

brothers. All I can do is swim, but I will swim down the best I know how, and go as deep as I can. May I try, please, Maheo?"

"Little brother," said Maheo, "no man can do more than his best, and I have asked for the help of all the water peoples. Certainly you shall try. Perhaps swimming will be better than diving, after all. Try, little brother, and see what you can do."

"Hah-ho!" the little coot said. "Thank you, Maheo," and he put his head under the water and swam down and down and down and down, until he was out of sight.

An American coot.
Why is it significant that such a humble creature plays such a large role in the creation of the world?

The coot was gone a long, long, long, long time. Then Maheo and the other birds could see a little dark spot beneath the water's surface, slowly rising toward them. It seemed as if they would never see the coot himself, but at last the spot began to have a shape. Still it rose and rose, and at last

Maheo and the water peoples could surely see who it was. The little coot was swimming up from the bottom of the salty lake.

When the coot reached the surface, he stretched his closed beak upward into the light, but he did not open it.

"Give me what you have brought," Maheo said, and the coot let his beak fall open, so a little ball of mud could fall from his tongue into Maheo's hand, for when Maheo wanted to, he could become like a man.

"Go, little brother," Maheo said. "Thank you, and may what you have brought always protect you."

And so it was and so it is, for the coot's flesh still tastes of mud, and neither man nor animal will eat a coot unless there is nothing else to eat.

Maheo rolled the ball of mud between the palms of his hands, and it began to grow larger, until there was almost too much mud for Maheo to hold. He looked around for a place to put the mud, but there was nothing but water or air anywhere around him.

"Come and help me again, water peoples," Maheo called. "I must put this mud somewhere. One of you must let me place it on his back."

All the fish and all the other water creatures came swimming to Maheo, and he tried to find the right one to carry the mud. The mussels and snails and crawfish were too small, although they all had solid backs, and they lived too deep in the water for the mud to rest on them. The fish were too narrow, and their back fins stuck up

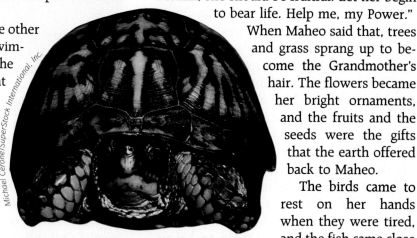

Michael Cerone/SuperStock International, Inc.

The box turtle.
Cheyenne culture is firmly linked with nature. How is this demonstrated in the myth?

through the mud and cut it to pieces. Finally only one water person was left.

"Grandmother Turtle," Maheo asked, "do you think that you can help me?"

"I'm very old and very slow, but I will try," the turtle answered. She swam over to Maheo, and he piled the mud on her rounded back, until he had made a hill. Under Maheo's hands, the hill grew and spread and flattened out, until the Grandmother Turtle was hidden from sight.

"So be it," Maheo said once again. "Let the earth be known as our Grandmother, and let the Grandmother who carries the earth be the only being who is at home beneath the water, or within the earth, or above the ground; the only one who can go anywhere by swimming or by walking as she chooses."

And so it was, and so it is. Grandmother Turtle and all her descendants must walk very slowly, for they carry the whole weight of the whole world and all its peoples on their backs.

Now there was earth as well as water, but the earth was barren. And Maheo said to his Power, "Our Grandmother Earth is like a woman; she should be fruitful. Let her begin to bear life. Help me, my Power."

When Maheo said that, trees and grass sprang up to become the Grandmother's hair. The flowers became her bright ornaments, and the fruits and the seeds were the gifts that the earth offered back to Maheo.

The birds came to rest on her hands when they were tired, and the fish came close to her sides. Maheo looked at the Earth

Woman and he thought she was very beautiful; the most beautiful thing he had made so far.

She should not be alone, Maheo thought. Let me give her something of myself, so she will know that I am near her and that I love her.

Maheo reached into his right side, and pulled out a rib bone. He breathed on the bone, and laid it softly on the bosom of the Earth Woman. The bone moved and stirred, stood upright and walked. The first man had come to be.

"He is alone with the Grandmother Earth as I once was alone with the void," said Maheo. "It is not good for anyone to be alone." So Maheo fashioned a human woman from his left rib, and set her with the man. Then there were two persons on the Grandmother Earth, her children and Maheo's. They were happy together, and Maheo was happy as he watched them.

After a year, in the springtime, the first child was born. As the years passed, there were other children. They went their ways, and founded many tribes.

From time to time, after that, Maheo realized that his people walking on the earth had certain needs. At those times, Maheo, with the help of his Power, created animals to feed and care for the people. He gave them deer for clothing and food, porcupines to make their ornaments, the swift antelopes on the open plains, and the prairie dogs that burrowed in the earth.

At last Maheo thought to his Power, Why, one animal can take the place of all the others put together, and then he made the buffalo.

Maheo is still with us. He is everywhere, watching all his people, and all the creation he has made. Maheo is all good and all life; he is the creator, the guardian, and the teacher. We are all here because of Maheo.

▲ First Thoughts

An **image** is a picture created by words. What was your favorite image in this myth?

Identifying Facts

1. Why does Maheo need the animals' help in order to complete the creation?
2. What is Grandmother Turtle's role in the creation?
3. Why does Maheo decide to create a human being? Describe how the first people are created.
4. What is the last thing Maheo creates?

Interpreting Meanings

1. An **origin myth** explains the beginnings of things. What beginnings, or origins, does this myth explain?
2. How would you **characterize** Maheo? What is his attitude toward his creations, including the earth and its inhabitants? Give three specific examples from the myth to support your views.
3. In this myth, all of the animals work together to help Maheo create the world. What does this suggest about the Cheyennes' view of nature?
4. How is the earth compared to a woman

in this myth? Find the **descriptive language** that characterizes the earth as feminine.

Applying Meanings

Think about Maheo's question, "What good is Power . . . if it is not used to make a world and people to live in it?" What do *you* think is the proper use of power? Explain your thoughts.

Creative Writing Response

Writing a Poem Based on a Myth. "How the World Was Made" is full of vivid **imagery**, or language that appeals to the senses of sight, hearing, smell, taste, and touch. Try writing your favorite part of this myth in the form of a poem, using some of the same imagery that occurs in the prose version. Your poem does not have to rhyme. If you wish, you may change the emphasis of the poem, telling the creation story from the point of view of one of the animals, such as Grandmother Turtle. Exchange your first-draft poem with a classmate for revision ideas. Then read your completed poem aloud to the class.

Critical Writing Response

Making Inferences. Myths and folktales represent a culture's traditions, values, and attitudes. Although this myth does not directly tell you about the Cheyenne people, you can make **inferences**, or educated guesses, about some of their attitudes and basic values concerning nature. How do you think the Cheyenne felt about nature and their relationship to it? Using a chart like the one below as a starting point, write a two- or three-paragraph essay about the Cheyenne view of nature as illustrated by the myth.

Evidence	Example from Myth	Inference
Maheo's reactions to his creations		
The role of animals in the creation of the world		

In the conclusion of your essay, describe how the Cheyenne view of nature is similar to or different from the view of nature held in your own time and culture.

Language and Vocabulary

Native American Words in the English Language

When European settlers first began colonizing North America, they found many places and things that they had no English names for. Native American languages supplied these names, and many American English words are direct "loans" from Native American languages. Below is a list of just a few of these words. Use a dictionary to find the words' contemporary meanings and the Native American language from which each word was borrowed.

1. raccoon
2. wigwam
3. hogan
4. coyote
5. toboggan
6. moose
7. pecan
8. hominy
9. chipmunk
10. bayou

Reader's Guide

THE WOODEN PEOPLE: *from the* POPOL VUH

Background

Popol Vuh (pō′pəl vu′), or The Book of Counsel, is the Quiché (kē·chā′) Mayan book of creation. Called the Mayan Bible by poet Carlos Fuentes, the Popol Vuh is one of the most important sources of pre-Columbian myth in Central America.

The Quiché Mayans settled in the highlands of Guatemala in about the ninth century A.D. Their great work, the Popol Vuh, tells the story of their origins and destiny. The Quiché Mayans believed that the Popol Vuh was a gift from the gods that could help people to see beyond the obvious and to become aware of mysteries and secrets that would otherwise be beyond the range of human insight.

The Quiché Mayan creation myth that follows, ''The Wooden People,'' comes from the first part of the Popol Vuh. This episode is the third creation story in a sequence of four. At this point in the mythic cycle, the gods have failed in two attempts to create suitable human beings. The first two attempts resulted in the creation of the animal kingdom and a being made of mud that disintegrated almost as soon as it was formed. Now the gods have made beings out of a more substantial material: wood. These wooden people, or manikins, become the world's first people.

Writer's Response

''The Wooden People'' includes an account of a devastating flood. Before you read this myth, write your ideas about why a flood might have been seen by early people as both a destructive and a creative force. In what ways can a flood be ''cleansing''?

Literary Focus

A **plot** is the series of connected events that make up a story. The most suspenseful or exciting point in a plot is the **climax**. In the climax, something happens to resolve the story's central conflict. The climax brings about a change in the situation presented in the story or results in a change in the main character or characters. As you read ''The Wooden People,'' determine what the climax of the story is.

THE WOODEN PEOPLE
from the Popol Vuh
A Quiché Mayan Myth
translated by
DENNIS TEDLOCK

Pay special attention to the behavior of the manikins—the wooden people. In what ways are they like us?

Mayan statuette.
Instituto Nacional de Antropologia E Historia

This was the peopling of the face of the earth:

They came into being, they multiplied, they had daughters, they had sons, these manikins, woodcarvings. But there was nothing in their hearts and nothing in their minds, no memory of their mason and builder. They just went and walked wherever they wanted. Now they did not remember the Heart of Sky.[1]

And so they fell, just an experiment and just a cutout for humankind. They were talking at first but their faces were dry. They were not yet developed in the legs and arms. They had no blood, no lymph. They had no sweat, no fat. Their complexions were dry, their faces were crusty. They flailed their legs and arms, their bodies were deformed.

And so they accomplished nothing before the Maker, Modeler[2] who gave them birth, gave them heart. They became the first numerous people here on the face of the earth.

Again there comes a humiliation, destruction, and demolition. The manikins, woodcarvings were killed when the Heart of Sky devised a flood for them. A great flood was made; it came down on the heads of the manikins, woodcarvings.

The man's body was carved from the wood of the coral tree by the Maker, Modeler. And as for the woman, the Maker, Modeler needed the pith of reeds for the woman's body. They were not competent, nor did they speak before the builder and sculptor who made them and brought them forth, and so they were killed, done in by a flood:

---

1. **Heart of Sky:** the father god of the Quiché Mayans.

2. **Maker, Modeler:** the Quiché Mayan god of creation.

Fragment of the Madrid codex, Mayan. *The Quiché Mayans recorded the myth of the wooden people in the* Popol Vuh, *or* Book of Counsel.

? *What counsel, or advice, does this myth give?*

There came a rain of resin from the sky.

There came the one named Gouger of Faces: he gouged out their eyeballs.

There came Sudden Bloodletter: he snapped off their heads.

There came Crunching Jaguar: he ate their flesh.

There came Tearing Jaguar: he tore them open.

They were pounded down to the bones and tendons, smashed and pulverized even to the bones. Their faces were smashed because they were incompetent before their mother and their father, the Heart of Sky, named Hurricane. The earth was blackened because of this; the black rainstorm began, rain all day and rain all night. Into their houses came the animals, small and great. Their faces were crushed by things of wood and stone. Everything spoke: their water jars, their tortilla griddles, their plates, their cooking pots, their dogs, their grinding stones, each and every thing crushed their faces. Their dogs and turkeys told them:

"You caused us pain, you ate us, but now it is *you* whom *we* shall eat." And this is the grinding stone:

"We were undone because of you.

Every day, every day,
in the dark, in the dawn, forever,
r-r-rip, r-r-rip,
r-r-rub, r-r-rub,
right in our faces, because of you.

This was the service we gave you at first, when you were still people, but today you will learn of our power. We shall pound and we shall grind your flesh," their grinding stones told them.

And this is what their dogs said, when they spoke in their turn:

"Why is it you can't seem to give us our food? We just watch and you just keep us down, and you throw us around. You keep a stick ready when you eat, just so you can hit us. We don't talk, so we've received nothing from you. How could you not have known? You *did* know that we were wasting away there, behind you.

"So, this very day you will taste the teeth in our mouths. We shall eat you," their dogs told them, and their faces were crushed.

And then their tortilla griddles and cooking pots spoke to them in turn:

"Pain! That's all you've done for us. Our mouths are sooty, our faces are sooty. By setting us on the fire all the time, you burn us. Since *we* felt no pain, *you* try it. We shall burn you," all their cooking pots said, crushing their faces.

The stones, their hearthstones were shooting out, coming right out of the fire, going for their heads, causing them pain. Now they run for it, helter-skelter.

They want to climb up on the houses, but they fall as the houses collapse.

They want to climb the trees; they're thrown off by the trees.

They want to get inside caves, but the caves slam shut in their faces.

Such was the scattering of the human work, the human design. The people were ground down, overthrown. The mouths and faces of all of them were destroyed and crushed. And it used to be said that the monkeys in the forests today are a sign of this. They were left as a sign because wood alone was used for their flesh by the builder and sculptor.

THE BONAMPOK FRESCO CYCLE, Mayan.
What non-human objects come to life in this myth? What do they do to the people?

SEF/Art Resource, New York

So this is why monkeys look like people: they are a sign of a previous human work, human design—mere manikins, mere wood-carvings.

First Thoughts

What is the most exciting or dramatic part of this myth to you?

Identifying Facts

1. **Describe** the wooden people. In what ways are they just a "cutout," or preliminary design, for human beings? In what ways are they like us?
2. Why does the god Heart of Sky punish the wooden people? How does he punish them?
3. What origin does this myth explain?

Interpreting Meanings

1. What do you consider the **climax**, or point of greatest suspense, in this story? Does the climax occur in a brief moment, or does it take up a longer portion of the story? Explain.
2. The word *competent* means "having the right qualities or abilities to fulfill a function." In what way were the wooden people "not competent"—that is, unable to act as the Mayan gods expected?
3. The gods in the Popol Vuh tried to create humans three times, and three

times they failed. What does this tell you about the way the Quiché Mayans viewed their gods?

Applying Meanings

How do the wooden people fail the gods? How might this myth have served to teach the Quiché Mayan people proper behavior?

Creative Writing Response

Narrating a Series of Events. One of the most amazing incidents in this myth is the revenge of the pots, pans, and tortilla griddles against the wooden people. Write a one- or two-paragraph narrative in which you describe an inanimate object or objects coming to life and interacting with people. For example, what might your television say about your viewing habits? Tell *what* happens, *where* it happens, *when* it happens, and *who* is involved. Include vivid **imagery** to bring the fantastic situation to life for your readers. What is the **climax** of your narrative?

Language and Vocabulary

Imagery

Imagery is language that appeals to the senses. Most images in literature are visual—that is, they create pictures in the reader's mind by appealing to the sense of sight. But imagery can also appeal to the senses of hearing, touch, taste, or smell. In fact, an effective image may appeal to several senses at once.

Dennis Tedlock's translation of the Popol Vuh is full of powerful imagery. Reread these passages from "The Wooden People." Then make a list of which sense each passage appeals to: sight, hearing, taste, touch, smell, or a combination of several.

1. "They were talking at first but their faces were dry. They were not yet developed in the legs and arms. They had no blood, no lymph. They had no sweat, no fat. Their complexions were dry, their faces were crusty."

2. "They were pounded down to the bones and tendons, smashed and pulverized even to the bones."

3. "The earth was blackened because of this; the black rainstorm began, rain all day and rain all night."

4. "Everything spoke: their water jars, their tortilla griddles, their plates, their cooking pots, their dogs, their grinding stones, each and every thing crushed their faces."

5. " 'Our mouths are sooty, our faces are sooty. By setting us on the fire all the time, you burn us.' "

Find other examples of imagery in this myth. How would you describe the overall effect of the imagery?

Reader's Guide

COYOTE AND THE ORIGIN OF DEATH

Background

Almost every culture has a story that explains the origin of death. In myths and folktales from different parts of the world, death comes into the world in a variety of ways. Sometimes death enters the world because people disobey the gods; sometimes there is a kind of gamble involved in which people must decide between two alternatives, and the one they unintentionally choose is death. In some stories, death comes into the world through the actions of a **trickster,** a universal figure in world myths and folktales, especially those from Africa and North America.

Tricksters are ambivalent figures who tend to leave trouble and chaos behind wherever they go. They rebel against any kind of authority or social convention. Tricksters are not necessarily evil. In fact, they often possess positive traits, such as cleverness, curiosity, and creativity. Many tricksters are simply mischievous, much like children are before they "know better." Others are less innocent in their intentions. The trickster archetype survives today in the form of comedians, clowns, and heroes of popular culture such as Bugs Bunny and the teenage film character Ferris Bueller.

The following myth comes from the Native American Caddo people. Coyote plays the role of the trickster in Caddo tales.

Writer's Response

In myths and folktales, tricksters are often animals. Note at least three animals that you think could be cast as tricksters, and three that probably wouldn't be cast as tricksters. Briefly explain your choices.

Literary Focus

Storytellers and writers usually try to provide a character's **motivation**—the reasons for a character's actions. A character's motivations set the **plot**, or sequence of events in a story, into motion. Try to figure out Coyote's motivation for doing what he does. Is the motivation stated, or do we have to **infer** it from the text?

COYOTE AND THE ORIGIN OF DEATH
A Caddo Myth
retold by
RICHARD ERDOES AND ALFONSO ORTIZ

◆ *Why does Coyote want to make certain that people stay dead forever?*

In the beginning of this world, there was no such thing as death. Everybody continued to live until there were so many people that the earth had no room for any more. The chiefs held a council to determine what to do. One man rose and said he thought it would be a good plan to have the people die and be gone for a little while, and then return.

As soon as he sat down, Coyote jumped up and said he thought people ought to die forever. He pointed out that this little world is not large enough to hold all of the people, and that if the people who died came back to life, there would not be food enough for all.

All the other men objected. They said that they did not want their friends and relatives to die and be gone forever, for then they would grieve and worry and there would be no happiness in the world. Everyone except Coyote decided to have people die and be gone for a little while, and then come back to life again.

The medicine men built a large grass house facing the east. When they had completed it, they called the men of the tribe together and told them that people who died

Carved wooden figure, Caddo.

Smithsonian Institution. Cat. # 378577

would be restored to life in the medicine house. The chief medicine man explained that they would sing a song calling the spirit of the dead to the grass house. When the spirit came, they would restore it to life. All the people were glad, because they were anxious for the dead to come and live with them again.

When the first man died, the medicine men assembled in the grass house and sang. In about ten days a whirlwind blew from the west and circled about the grass house. Coyote saw it, and as the whirlwind was about to enter the house, he closed the door. The spirit of the whirlwind, finding the door closed, whirled on by. In this way Coyote made death eternal, and from that time on, people grieved over their dead and were unhappy.

Now whenever anyone meets a whirlwind or hears the wind whistle, he says: "Someone is wandering about." Ever since Coyote closed the door, the spirits of the dead have wandered over the earth trying to find some place to go, until at last they discovered the road to the spirit land.

Coyote ran away and never came back, for when he saw what he had done, he was afraid. Ever after that, he has run from one place to another, always looking back first over one shoulder and then over the other to see if anyone is pursuing him. And ever since then he has been starving, for no one will give him anything to eat.

Tim Fitzharris/ALLSTOCK

The North American coyote.
? *What qualities of the coyote does this story explain?*

First Thoughts

Do you think that Coyote is an evil character? Why or why not?

Identifying Facts

1. What reasons does Coyote give for urging that people stay dead forever?
2. Describe the trick Coyote uses to prevent the dead from coming back to life.

3. What effect does Coyote's action have on society? What traits of the coyote does this tale explain?

Interpreting Meanings

1. Is Coyote selfish or wise? Explain. What do you think was his **motivation** for doing what he did?

2. In many myths and folktales, tricksters bring about sweeping changes in society, sometimes bringing order out of disorder. Why do you think the trickster is seen as an agent of change? How is this trickster quality brought out in this story?

3. Why do you think that the Caddo and many other Native American peoples chose the coyote to represent the trickster figure rather than some other animal?

Applying Meanings

If you had been at the council described at the beginning of this story, how would you have voted? Why?

Creative Writing Response

Writing a Television Script. Imagine the coyote of this tale as a cartoon character, like Wile E. Coyote, the troublemaker in the "Roadrunner" cartoons. Adapt this myth into a television script for a cartoon. You may need to give names to some of the characters, such as the chiefs and medicine men. Be sure to include teleplay (television script) directions in parentheses to describe the actions of the characters.

If you like to draw, you might try illustrating a few scenes from your cartoon adaptation.

Critical Writing Response

Comparing and Contrasting Two Myths. Read the following African tale from the Koikhoi people called "The Origin of Death." As you read, think about elements it shares with the Caddo tale. Think about the differences. Then write a two- or three-paragraph essay in which you compare and contrast the two stories.

The Origin Of Death
A Khoikhoi Myth
retold by
Paul Radin

The Moon, it is said, once sent an insect to men, saying, "Go to men and tell them, 'As I die, and dying live; so you shall also die, and dying live.'"

The insect started with the message, but, while on his way, was overtaken by the hare, who asked, "On what errand are you bound?"

The insect answered, "I am sent by the Moon to men, to tell them that as she dies and dying lives, so shall they also die and dying live."

The hare said, "As you are an awkward runner, let me go." With these words he ran off, and when he reached men, he said, "I am sent by the Moon to tell you, 'As I die and dying perish, in the same manner you also shall die and come wholly to an end.'"

The hare then returned to the Moon and told her what he had said to men. The Moon reproached him angrily, saying, "Do you dare tell the people a thing which I have not said?"

With these words the Moon took up a piece of wood and struck the hare on the nose. Since that day the hare's nose has been split, but men believe what Hare had told them.

Use a chart like the one below to organize your thoughts about the two stories.

	Khoikhoi	Caddo
1. Characterization of animal responsible for bringing death into the world		
2. Condition of world before deception		
3. Condition of world after deception		
4. Lesson of story		

*I*ntroduction

The Hero and the Quest

© Lucasfilm Ltd.

The heroic quest is a recurring archetype in American popular culture, as are heroes like Indiana Jones.
? *How is the heroic quest pattern played out in films like* **Raiders of the Lost Ark?**

Tales of the hero and the heroic quest occur in nearly every world culture. If we look closely at hero tales from all over the world and compare them, we find what the Irish novelist James Joyce and the American mythologist Joseph Campbell called the *monomyth*—literally, "the one story." This monomyth, or archetypal heroic quest story, has remarkably the same structure from culture to culture. It is as if each hero wears the particular "costume" of his or her culture, but is really the same hero underneath, facing the same kinds of challenges. Today, film heroes Luke Skywalker and Indiana Jones serve as modern versions of the quest hero.

The Nature of the Quest Hero

A **mythic hero** can be male or female. This hero usually has a remarkable birth or childhood. He or she is often the offspring of a god and a human being, and so possesses qualities of both immortals and mortals. Heroes may be born under unusual circumstances. Sometimes they are unaware of their origins and are raised by foster parents. The hero often shows early signs of being special, possessing either superhuman strength or supernatural powers.

The **folktale hero**, on the other hand, is often a very ordinary person, a stepchild or a neglected youngest child who is scoffed at by parents or older brothers and sisters. Although the folktale hero may not have superhuman abilities, he or she might be out of the ordinary in other ways. Many such heroes, for example, are exceptionally kind, clever, or resourceful.

Both mythic and folktale heroes are called to participate in an adventure or forced to face a series of challenges or tests. They may at first refuse to face their challenges, but they suffer greatly for their refusal. Eventually, they are forced by circumstances to accept their role and overcome the obstacles placed before them.

The Hero's Quest

A **quest** is a journey taken in search of something of value. The prize that is sought may be a specific person, such as a beautiful princess; an abstract concept, such as truth or the meaning of life; or a concrete object, such as a treasure or a magical charm. Sometimes the hero is simply searching for his or her "roots," such as a parent he or she has never known.

♦
quest: *a journey taken in search of a person or object of great value.*

Mythic heroes are often aided on their quests by loyal friends or by god or goddess benefactors. Folktale heroes are often helped by people, animals, or magical beings who are repaying them for good deeds done earlier. The quest itself does not always go smoothly. The hero may be tempted to leave the "true path" by succumbing to some temptation, such as a beautiful woman or the lure of an easier lifestyle. Sometimes a character flaw in the hero—usually overwhelming pride or impatience—causes him or her to falter on the quest.

The quest may involve a descent into the underworld or to some other dark and frightening place, such as an enchanted cave or forest, that ordinary human beings dare not enter. This is the ultimate stage of the hero's journey—"to boldly go where no one has gone before," as the prologue to *Star Trek* proclaims. Sometimes, the hero's final adventure may even involve the greatest sacrifice of all: giving up his or her life for others. If the hero survives the journey to the underworld, he or she returns to society, often with something to share: new knowledge, a renewed commitment, or greater compassion and wisdom. The hero may be rewarded by entering into a royal marriage and living "happily ever after."

What the Quest Means to Us

Perhaps the heroic quest tale is so universal because the challenges that the quest hero faces are symbolic of the challenges that each of us must face in life. "Killing monsters" may symbolize the individual fighting against social injustices or against inner conflicts that prevent happiness. The journey to the underworld might symbolize facing unpleasant realities, such as the existence of death, or looking inside ourselves to ask and answer tough questions.

As long as people feel the need to tell stories about the human journey, they will tell the enduring story of the hero and the quest.

Reader's Guide

THESEUS

Background

The story of Theseus, from ancient Greece, fits the general pattern of the hero and the quest in several ways. Theseus is secretly fathered by a king; he shows great strength as a boy; he kills a monster, wins a princess, and gains a kingdom; and he descends into the underworld.

The Greeks saw their gods as powerful beings who nevertheless had much in common with human beings, though on a grander scale. The Greek gods and goddesses could be generous and merciful, but they could also be petty and unfair. The ancient Greeks thought that their gods and goddesses played an active role in humans' lives.

Though all Greeks shared the same religion and language, their country was a group of separate, independent city-states. Among these were Athens, in central Greece, and Corinth, to the south. The island nation of Crete lay to the southeast. These three places form the setting of Theseus' story.

Writer's Response

Who is your favorite hero? Think of a superhuman character from books, television, or movies who appeals to you. Write a paragraph describing this hero and exploring what it is about him, her, or it that you admire.

Literary Focus

Characterization is the process by which an author reveals a character's personality. A writer can reveal character in the following ways:

1. By describing the character's appearance
2. By recording what the character says
3. By revealing the character's innermost thoughts and feelings
4. By showing the character's actions
5. By showing how other characters act toward the character
6. By telling us directly what the character is like: kind, untrustworthy, and so on

The first five methods are examples of **indirect characterization**. The last method is called **direct characterization**.

THESEUS
An Ancient Greek Myth
retold by
ROBERT GRAVES

When you come to the end of the third paragraph, identify the task that Theseus' mother gives him. Do you predict that Theseus will succeed or fail in his quest?

Temple of Apollo, overlooking the Aegean Sea on the Greek island of Naxos.

On a visit to Corinth, King Aegeus of Athens secretly married the Princess Aethra. She had grown tired of waiting for Bellerophon,[1] whose wife she should have been, to come home from Lydia. After a few pleasant days with Aethra, Aegeus told her: "I am afraid I must leave now, my dear. It will be safest, in case you have a son, to pretend that his father is the God Poseidon.[2] My eldest nephew might kill you if he knew of our marriage. He expects to be the next King of Athens. Goodbye!"

Once back, Aegeus never left Athens again.

Aethra had a son whom she named Theseus, and on his fourteenth birthday she asked him: "Can you move that huge rock?" Theseus, a remarkably strong boy, lifted the rock and tossed it away. Hidden underneath, he found a sword with a golden snake pattern inlaid on the blade, and a pair of sandals. "Those were left there by your father," Aethra said. "He is Aegeus, King of Athens. Take them to him and say that you found them under this rock. But mind, not a word to his nephews, who will be furious if they discover that you are the true heir to the throne of Athens. Because of them I have pretended all these years that Poseidon, not Aegeus, was your father."

Theseus went by the coast road to Athens. First he met a giant named Sinis, who had the horrible habit of bending two pine trees down towards each other, tying some poor

---

1. **Bellerophon** (bə·ler′ə·fän′): The Greek hero Bellerophon rode the winged horse Pegasus and killed a fire-breathing monster called the Chimera.

2. **Poseidon** (pō·sī′dən): One of the Olympians, the twelve major Greek gods and goddesses. Poseidon, called Neptune by the Romans, was the god of the sea and of horses.

traveler to their tops by his arms, and then suddenly letting go. The trees would fly upright and tear him in two. Theseus wrestled with Sinis, threw him senseless on the ground, and then treated him as he had treated others.

Next, Theseus faced and killed a monstrous wild sow, with tusks larger and sharper than sickles. Then he fought Procrustes, a wicked innkeeper who lived beside the main road and kept only one bed in his inn. If travelers were too short for the bed, Procrustes would lengthen them with an instrument of torture called "the rack"; if they were too tall, he would chop off their feet; and if they were the right size, he would smother them with a blanket. Theseus beat Procrustes, tied him to the bed, and cut off both his feet; but, finding him still too tall, cut off his head as well. He wrapped the dead body in a blanket and flung it into the sea.

King Aegeus had recently been married again: to a witch named Medea. Theseus did not know about this marriage, yet on his arrival at Athens, Medea knew by magic who he was; and decided to poison him—putting wolfbane[3] in a cup of wine. She wanted one of her own sons to be the next King. Luckily Aegeus noticed the snake pattern on Theseus' sword, guessed that the wine had been poisoned, and hastily knocked the cup from Medea's hand. The poison burned a large hole through the floor, and Medea escaped in a magic cloud. Then Aegeus sent a chariot to fetch Aethra from Corinth, and announced: "Theseus is my son and heir." The next day, Aegeus's nephews ambushed Theseus on his way to a temple; but he fought and killed them all.

Now, it had happened some years before that King Minos's son, Androgeus of Crete, visited Athens and there won all the competitions in the Athletic Games—running, jumping, boxing, wrestling, and throwing the discus. Aegeus's jealous nephews accused him of a plot to seize the throne, and murdered him. When Minos complained about this to the Olympians, they gave orders that Aegeus must send seven boys and seven girls from Athens every ninth year to be devoured by the Cretan Minotaur. The Minotaur was a monster—half bull, half man—which Minos kept in the middle of the Labyrinth, or maze, built for him by Daedalus. The Minotaur knew every twist and turn in the Labyrinth, and would chase his victims into some blind alley where he had them at his mercy.

So now the Athenians, angry with Theseus for killing his cousins, chose him as one of the seven boys sent to be eaten that year. Theseus thanked them, saying that he was glad of a chance to free his country of this horrid tribute. The ship in which the victims sailed carried black sails, for mourning, but Theseus took white sails along, too. "If I kill the Minotaur, I shall hoist these white sails. If the Minotaur kills me, let the black ones be hoisted."

Theseus prayed to the Goddess Aphrodite.[4] She listened to him and told her son Eros[5] to make Ariadne, Minos's daughter, fall in love with Theseus. That same night, she came to Theseus' prison, drugged the guards, unlocked the door of his cell with a key stolen from Minos's belt, and asked Theseus: "If I help you to kill the Minotaur, will you marry me?"

---

3. **wolfbane**, or wolfsbane: a poisonous plant of the buttercup family, with hoodlike yellow flowers.

4. **Aphrodite** (af′rə·dīt′ē): the Greek goddess of love and beauty, called Venus by the Romans.

5. **Eros** (er′äs′): the god of love, called Cupid by the Romans.

"With pleasure," he answered, kissing her hand.

Ariadne led the boys quietly from the prison. She showed them a magic ball of thread, given her by Daedalus before he left Crete. One need only tie the loose end of the thread to the Labyrinth door, and the ball would roll by itself through all the twisting paths until it reached the clear space in the middle. "The Minotaur lives there," Ariadne said. "He sleeps for exactly one hour in the twenty-four, at midnight; but then he sleeps sound."

Theseus' six companions kept guard at the entrance, while Ariadne tied the thread to the Labyrinth door. Theseus entered, ran his hand along the thread in the darkness and came upon the sleeping Minotaur just after midnight. As the moon rose, he cut off the monster's head with a razor-sharp sword lent him by Ariadne, then followed the thread back to the entrance where his friends stood anxiously waiting. Meanwhile, Ariadne had freed the seven girls, too, and all together they stole down to the harbor. Theseus and his friends, having first bored holes in the sides of Minos's ships, climbed aboard their own, pushed her off, and sailed for Athens. The Cretan ships which gave chase soon filled and sank; so Theseus got safely away, with the Minotaur's head and Ariadne.

Theseus beached his ship on the island of Naxos; he needed food and water. While Ariadne lay resting on the beach, the God Dionysus[6] suddenly appeared to Theseus. "I want to marry this woman myself," he said. "If you take her from me, I will destroy Athens by sending all its people mad."

Theseus dared not offend Dionysus and, since he had no great love for Ariadne anyway, he left her asleep and set sail. Ariadne wept with rage on waking, to find herself deserted; but Dionysus soon walked up, introduced himself, and offered her a large cup of wine. Ariadne drank it all, felt better at once, and decided that it would be far more glorious to marry a god than a mortal. Dionysus' wedding present to her was the splendid jeweled coronet which is now the constellation called "The Northern Crown." She bore several children to Dionysus, and eventually returned to Crete as Queen.

In the excitement, Theseus had quite forgotten to change the sails, and King Aegeus, watching anxiously from a cliff at Athens, saw the black sail appear instead of the white. Overcome by grief, he jumped into the sea and drowned. Theseus then became King of Athens and made peace with the Cretans.

A few years later, the Amazons, a fierce race of fighting women from Asia, invaded Greece and attacked Athens. Since Theseus listened to the Goddess Athene's[7] advice, he managed to defeat them; but never afterwards stopped boasting about his courage.

One day his friend Peirithous said to him: "I am in love with a beautiful woman. Will you help me to marry her?"

"By all means," Theseus answered. "Am I not the bravest king alive? Look what I did to the Amazons! Look what I did to the Minotaur! Who is the woman?"

"Persephone, Demeter's[8] daughter," Peirithous answered.

---

6. **Dionysus** (dī′ə·nī′səs): the Greek god of wine and celebration, called Bacchus by the Romans.

7. **Athene** (ə·thē′nē), also called Athena (-nə): the Greek goddess of wisdom, warfare, and crafts.

8. **Demeter** (di·mēt′ər): the Greek goddess of fruits, grains, and fertility; her daughter Persephone was abducted against her will by Hades, ruler of the underworld.

CERBERUS, WILLIAM BLAKE (1715–1827).

"Oh! Are you serious? Persephone is already married to King Hades, God of the Dead!"

"I know, but she hates Hades and wants children. She can have no living children by the God of the Dead."

"It seems rather a risky adventure," said Theseus, turning pale.

"Are you not the bravest king alive?"

"I am."

"Let us go, then!"

They buckled on their swords and descended to Tartarus[9] by the side entrance. Having given the dog Cerberus[10] three cakes dipped in poppy juice, to send him asleep, Peirithous rapped at the palace gate and entered.

Hades asked in surprise: "Who are you mortals, and what do you want?"

Theseus told him: "I am Theseus, the bravest king alive. This is my friend Peirithous, who thinks that Queen Persephone is far too good for you. He wants to marry her himself."

Hades grinned at them. Nobody had ever seen him grin before. "Well," he said, "it is true that Persephone is not exactly happy with me. I might even let her go, if you promise to treat her kindly. Shall we talk the matter over quietly? Please, sit down on that comfortable bench!"

Theseus and Peirithous sat down, but the bench Hades had offered them was a magic one. They became attached to it, so that they could never escape without tearing away part of themselves. Hades stood and roared for laughter, while the Furies[11] whipped the two friends; and ghostly spotted snakes stung them; and Cerberus, waking from his drugged sleep, gnawed at their fingers and toes.

"My poor fools," chuckled Hades, "you are here for always!"

---

9. **Tartarus** (tär'tə·rəs): the Greek underworld, ruled by Hades.
10. **Cerberus** (sur'bər·əs): a hideous three-headed dog that guards the gate of Tartarus.

---

11. **Furies:** three female spirits who punish wrong-doers; the Furies have hair made of snakes.

First Thoughts

Do you like Theseus? Does he fit your image of what a hero should be?

Identifying Facts

1. How does the young Theseus first prove his strength?
2. What is the Minotaur? What is his role in the story?
3. What finally happens to King Aegeus?
4. Why does Theseus journey to the underworld? What happens to him there?

Interpreting Meanings

1. List at least four **character traits**, or qualities, that Theseus shows in this story. Give examples of each. Then explain whether **direct** or **indirect characterization** is used to describe each trait.
2. Many mythic heroes, especially those in Greek and Roman mythology, develop excessive pride, or **hubris** (hyoo´bris). This pride results in the hero's downfall at the hands of the gods. At which point in the story does Theseus show the first signs of excessive pride? What is the result of his pride?
3. List at least three events or aspects of the story that seemed funny to you. What do the humorous touches add to the story?
4. One possible statement of the **theme** of this story can be found in this saying from the Book of Proverbs in the Hebrew Bible: ''Pride goeth before destruction, and an haughty spirit before a fall.'' In other words, pride and overconfidence can lead to failure. Do you agree that this is the theme of the story of Theseus, or can you think of another statement of theme that better fits this story?

Applying Meanings

Based on what you have learned about Theseus' character in this myth, do you think that he has learned anything by the end of this story? Use details from the story to support your answer.

Creative Writing Response

Extending the Story. In this version of the myth, Theseus' quest seems to end in Tartarus. In other versions of the story, however, Theseus is rescued by another Greek hero, Herakles (Hercules). Imagine that Theseus has been saved from the underworld. Write a brief story in which Theseus, newly released from his captivity, faces a new challenge. How does Theseus react to the challenge? Is he the same hero he was before the descent into the underworld, or has he somehow changed? Be sure to include **indirect characterization** (the character's own words and actions, and others' responses to the character) in your story to reveal how Theseus has or has not changed.

Language and Vocabulary

Using Dialogue

Author Robert Graves often uses **dialogue**, or quoted conversation between characters, as he retells the myth of Theseus. When you use dialogue, begin a new paragraph each time the speaker changes. Study the following example:

''It seems a rather risky adventure,'' said Theseus, turning pale.

''Are you not the bravest king alive?''

''I am.''

Write several lines of dialogue between two real or imagined characters. Use correct indentation and punctuation. You may refer to the grammar handbook at the back of this book to review punctuation.

Reader's Guide

OSIRIS AND ISIS

Background

The myth of Osiris and Isis, from ancient Egypt, tells the story of a god who dies and is brought back to life. Myths about dying gods were common in the ancient world and probably developed out of the sacrificial rites practiced by some ancient cultures. At the root of these ancient rites lies the notion that someone or something must die or be otherwise transformed before society can be renewed.

The ancient Egyptians associated Osiris' body with the Nile, the river that they depended on for their livelihood. They also believed that Osiris sat in judgment of the dead at the gates of the underworld. According to tradition, Osiris' attendants weighed the hearts of the dead against a feather. Only those whose hearts were lighter than the feather—that is, those who had led good lives—were granted the privilege of eternal life.

A key player in the myth of Osiris is his wife and sister, the goddess Isis. Like her Sumerian and Greek goddess counterparts Inanna and Demeter, Isis demonstrates persistence, strength, intelligence, and compassion. She uses these qualities to restore order to the world, serving as midwife in a new creation.

Writer's Response

Isis is one of the great female figures in mythology. Before you read, write a list of some other famous heroic female figures that you can think of. Describe their accomplishments. Are the roles of these female heroes different from the roles assigned to the men?

Literary Focus

Point of view is the vantage point from which a writer tells a story. In the **first-person point of view**, the narrator is a character in the story and we are limited to knowing only what that character sees and knows. In the **third-person limited point of view**, we can gain great insight into one character, but we can't know the inner workings of the other characters' minds except through inference. In the **omniscient**, or ''all-knowing,'' **point of view**, we get a ''god's-eye'' view of every character and every event, even the past and the future.

OSIRIS AND ISIS
An Ancient Egyptian Myth

retold by

PADRAIC COLUM

> *The myth of Osiris and Isis has been called one of the world's oldest and greatest love stories. As you read, consider how Isis' quest to save her husband reveals her deep love for him.*

When Osiris reigned death was not in the land. Arms were not in men's hands; there were not any wars. From end to end of the land music sounded; men and women spoke so sweetly and out of such depth of feeling that all they said was oratory and poetry.

Osiris taught men and women wisdom and he taught them all the arts. He it was who first planted the vine; he it was who showed men how and when to sow grain, how to plant and tend the fruit-trees; he caused them to rejoice in the flowers also. Osiris made laws for men so that they were able to live together in harmony; he gave them knowledge of the Gods, and he showed them how the Gods might be honored.

And this was what he taught them concerning the Gods: In the beginning was the formless abyss, Nuu. From Nuu came Re, the Sun. Re was the first and he was the most divine of all beings. Re created all forms. From his thought came Shu and Tefenet, the Upper and the Lower Air. From Shu and Tefenet came Qeb and Nut, the Earth and the Sky. The Earth and the Sky had been separated, the one from the other, but once they had been joined together. From the eye of Re, made out of the essence that is in that eye, came the first man and the first woman.

And from Qeb, the Father, and Nut, the Mother, Osiris was born. When he was born a voice came into the world, crying, "Behold, the Lord of all things is born!"

And with Osiris was born Isis, his sister. Afterwards was born Thout, the Wise One. Then there was born Nephthys. And, last, there was born Seth. And Seth tore a hole in his mother's side—Seth the Violent One. Now Osiris and Isis loved each other as husband and wife, and together they reigned over the land. Thout was with them, and he taught men the arts of writing and of reckoning. Nephthys went with Seth and was his wife, and Seth's abode was in the desert.

Seth, in his desert, was angered against Osiris, for everywhere green things that Seth hated were growing over the land—vine, and grain, and the flowers. Many times Seth tried to destroy his brother Osiris, but always his plots were baffled by the watchful care of Isis. One day he took the measurement of Osiris' body—he took the measurement from his shadow—and he made a chest that was the exact size of Osiris.

Soon, at the time before the season of drought, Seth gave a banquet, and to that banquet he invited all the children of Earth and the Sky. To that banquet came Thout, the Wise One, and Nephthys, the wife of Seth, and Seth himself, and Isis, and Osiris. And where they sat at banquet they could see the chest that Seth had made—the chest made of fragrant and diversified woods. All admired that chest. Then Seth, as though he would have them enter into a game, told all of them that he would give the chest to the one whose body fitted most closely in it. The children of Qeb and Nut went and laid themselves in the chest that Seth had made: Seth went and laid himself in it, Nephthys went and laid herself in it, Thout went and

Osiris enthroned in the domain of the Dead, 19th dynasty. *The ancient Egyptians worshiped Osiris as the ruler of the dead.* *In the beginning of this myth, what is Osiris' role on earth?*

laid himself in it, Isis went and laid herself in it. All were short; none, laid in the chest, but left a space above his or her head.

Then Osiris took the crown off his head and laid himself in the chest. His form filled it in its length and its breadth. Isis and Nephthys and Thout stood above where he lay, looking down upon Osiris, so resplendent of face, so perfect of limb, and congratulating him upon coming into possession of the splendid chest that Seth had made. Seth was not beside the chest then. He shouted, and his attendants to the number of seventy-two came into the banqueting hall. They placed the heavy cover upon the chest; they hammered nails into it; they soldered it all over with melted lead. Nor could Isis, nor Thout, nor Nephthys break through the circle that Seth's attendants made around the chest. And they, having nailed the cover down, and having soldered it, took up the sealed chest, and, with Seth going before them, they ran with it out of the hall.

Isis and Nephthys and Thout ran after those who bore the chest. But the night was dark, and these three children of Qeb and Nut were separated, one from the other, and from Seth and his crew. And these came to where the river was, and they flung the sealed chest into the river. Isis, and Thout, and Nephthys, following the tracks that Seth and his crew had made, came to the riverbank when it was daylight, but by that time the current of the river had brought the chest out into the sea.

Isis followed along the bank of the river, lamenting for Osiris. She came to the sea, and she crossed over it, but she did not know where to go to seek for the body of Osiris. She wandered through the world, and where she went bands of children went with her, and they helped her in her search. The chest that held the body of Osiris had drifted in the sea. A flood had cast it upon the land. It had lain in a thicket of young trees. A tree, growing, had lifted it up. The branches of the tree wrapped themselves around it; the bark of the tree spread itself around it; at last the tree grew there, covering the chest with its bark.

The land in which this happened was Byblos. The king and queen of the city, Melquart and Astarte, heard of the wonderful tree, the branches and bark of which gave forth a fragrance. The king had the tree cut down; its branches were trimmed off, and the tree was set up as a column in the king's house. And then Isis, coming to Byblos, was told of the wonderful tree that grew by the sea. She was told of it by a band of children who came to her. She came to the place: she found that the tree had been cut down and that its trunk was now set up as a column in the king's house.

She knew from what she heard about the wonderful fragrance that was in the trunk and branches of the tree that the chest she was seeking was within it. She stayed beside where the tree had been. Many who came to that place saw the queenly figure that, day and night, stood near where the wonderful tree had been. But none who came near was spoken to by her. Then the queen, having heard about the stranger who stood there, came to her. When she came near, Isis put her hand upon her head, and thereupon a fragrance went from Isis and filled the body of the queen.

The queen would have this majestical stranger go with her to her house. Isis went. She nursed the queen's child in the hall in which stood the column that had closed in it the chest which she sought.

She nourished the queen's child by placing her finger in its mouth. At night she would strip wood from the column that had grown as a tree, and throw the wood upon the fire. And in this fire she would lay the queen's child. The fire did not injure it at all; it burned softly around the child. Then Isis, in the form of a swallow, would fly around the column, lamenting.

One night the queen came into the hall where her child was being nursed. She saw no nurse there; she saw her child lying in the fire. She snatched the child up, crying out. Then Isis spoke to the queen from the column on which, in the form of a swallow, she perched. She told the queen that the child would have gained immortality had it been suffered to lie for a night and another night longer within the fire made from the wood of the column. Now it would be long-lived, but not immortal. And she revealed her own divinity to the queen, and claimed the column that had been made from the wonderful tree.

The king had the column taken down; it was split open, and the chest which Isis had sought for so long and with so many lamentations was within it. Isis wrapped the chest in linen, and it was carried for her out of the king's house. And then a ship was given to her, and on that ship, Isis, never stirring from beside the chest, sailed back to Egypt.

And coming into Egypt she opened the chest, and took the body of her lord and husband out of it. She breathed into his mouth, and, with the motion of her wings (for Isis, being divine, could assume wings), she brought life back to Osiris. And there, away from men and from all the children of Qeb and Nut, Osiris and Isis lived together.

But one night Seth, as he was hunting gazelles by moonlight, came upon Osiris and Isis sleeping. Fiercely he fell upon his brother; he tore his body into fourteen pieces. Then, taking the pieces that were the body of Osiris, he scattered them over the land.

Death had come into the land from the time Osiris had been closed in the chest through the cunning of Seth; war was in the land; men always had arms in their hands. No longer did music sound, no longer did men and women talk sweetly and out of the depths of their feelings. Less and less did grain, and fruit trees, and the vine flourish. The green places everywhere were giving way to the desert. Seth was triumphant; Thout and Nephthys cowered before him.

And all the beauty and all the abundance that had come from Re would be destroyed if the pieces that had been the body of Osiris were not brought together once more. So Isis sought for them, and Nephthys, her sister, helped her in her seeking. Isis, in a boat that was made of reeds, floated over the marshes, seeking for the pieces. One, and then another, and then another was found. At last she had all the pieces of his torn body. She laid them together on a floating island, and reformed them. And as the body of Osiris was formed once more, the wars that men were waging died down; peace came; grain, and the vine, and fruit trees grew once more.

And a voice came to Isis and told her that Osiris lived again, but that he lived in the Underworld where he was now the Judge of the Dead, and that through the justice that he meted out, men and women had life immortal. And a child of Osiris was born to Isis: Horus he was named. Nephthys and the wise Thout guarded him on the floating island where he was born. Horus grew up, and he strove against the evil power of Seth. In battle he overcame him, and in bonds he brought the evil Seth, the destroyer of his father, before Isis, his mother. Isis would not have Seth slain: still he lives, but now he is of the lesser Gods, and his power for evil is not so great as it was in the time before Horus grew to be the avenger of his father.

Giraudon/Art Resource, New York

Isis, from the sarcophagus of Ramses III, 20th dynasty. *Isis was the most popular and beloved Egyptian goddess. Among other things, she was regarded as a protector of children.*
❓ *What protective qualities does Isis demonstrate in this myth?*

Which **metamorphosis**, or transformation, strikes you as the most important one in this myth?

Identifying Facts

1. At the beginning of this myth, what is life like under Osiris' reign?
2. Why does Seth want to destroy Osiris?
3. Describe the actions Isis takes to save Osiris after each of his "deaths."

Interpreting Meanings

1. From what **point of view** is "Osiris and Isis" told? What are the advantages of telling the myth from this point of view? Can you see any disadvantages?
2. What explanation does this myth give for the introduction of death and evil into the world?
3. According to this myth, how did Osiris' "death" change the world? How is the natural balance finally restored?

Applying Meanings

In this myth we learn that Isis allowed the troublemaking Seth to be spared. Why do you suppose she did this? How would you have acted if you had been in Isis' place?

Creative Writing Response

Writing from a Different Point of View.
Rewrite your favorite portion of this narrative from the point of view of one of the following characters: Osiris, Isis, or Seth. Let the character speak in the first person, using the pronoun *I*. Be sure that the character reveals only what he or she could possibly know. For example, if you tell the story from Isis' point of view, you can only reveal her thoughts and feelings; you cannot know Osiris' thoughts while he is locked in the chest or Seth's thoughts as he is plotting his revenge.

Critical Writing Response

Evaluating a Statement of Theme. Below are some general statements of the **theme**, or central idea, of the myth "Osiris and Isis." In one or two paragraphs, discuss which, if any, of the statements of theme listed below best express what you think is the story's main theme. If you find all of the statements inadequate, form your own statement of the major theme and defend it.

1. True love can overcome any obstacle.
2. In order for society to experience renewal, the old must give way to the new.
3. Without evil, no one would appreciate the goodness in life.
4. Change and transformation are necessary aspects of life.

Reader's Guide

GREEN WILLOW

Background

Tomotada, the hero of this Japanese folktale, is a *samurai* (sam'ə·rī'), or warrior. During Japan's long feudal period (1200–1867), towns grew up around the castles of *daimyos* (dī'myōs'), feudal princes or lords. Each town was ruled by its daimyo, and each daimyo had many samurai at his command, much as feudal lords in England had knights. In this story, the Lord of Noto, Tomotada's prince, sends the samurai hero on an unspecified quest to the lord of the city of Kyoto.

One of the challenges of a questing hero is to resist distractions. In Tomotada's case, the distraction is a young woman named Green Willow. The tale "Green Willow" illustrates a particularly Japanese conflict. In Japanese culture, nature is valued, and the willow tree is especially admired because of its suppleness and grace, qualities important in Japanese tradition. Thus it is not only a particular woman, but also nature itself, that lures the hero away from the duties of his quest. Tomotada's conflict, then, shows a clash between the responsibilities of a samurai and the appeal of nature, a clash that appears often in Japanese folklore.

Writer's Response

Write a paragraph about a time when you chose to do something pleasant (perhaps watch television, go out with friends, or buy a treat) rather than complete a chore such as studying for a test or cleaning your room. Did you later regret your "distraction," or did you feel it was worth it?

Literary Focus

Conflict is a struggle or clash between opposing characters, forces, or emotions. In an **external conflict**, a character struggles against some outside force: another character, society, or a force of nature. An **internal conflict**, on the other hand, is a struggle between opposing desires or needs within a character's own mind. See if you can identify whether the conflicts Tomotada faces in this story are external, internal, or both.

GREEN WILLOW
A Japanese Folktale
retold by
PAUL JORDAN-SMITH

❚ *Read to the part of the story where Tomotada decides to ask to marry Green Willow (see page 43). Do you predict that Tomotada's decision will have a postive or negative effect on his life?*

The Granger Collection, New York

Mounted Samurai cleaning his sword, 16th–17th century.

In the era of Bummei there lived a young samurai, Tomotada, in the service of the daimyo of Noto. He was a native of Echizen, but had been accepted at a young age into the palace of the Lord of Noto, where he proved himself a good soldier and a good scholar as well, and enjoyed the favor of his prince. Handsome and amiable, he was admired also by his fellow samurai.

One day, the Lord of Noto called for Tomotada and sent him on a special quest to the Lord of Kyoto. Being ordered to pass through Echizen, Tomotada asked and was granted permission to visit his widowed mother. And so he set out on his mission.

Winter had already come; the countryside was covered with snow, and though his horse was among the most powerful in the Lord of Noto's stable, the young man was forced to proceed slowly. On the second day of his journey, he found himself in mountain districts where settlements were few and far between. His anxiety was increased by the onslaught of a heavy snowstorm, and his horse was showing signs of extreme fatigue. In the very moment of his despair, however, Tomotada caught sight of a cottage among the willows on a nearby hill. Reaching the dwelling, he knocked loudly on the storm doors which had been closed against the wind. Presently the doors opened, and an old woman appeared, who cried out with compassion at the sight of the noble Tomotada, "Ah, how pitiful! Traveling in such weather, and alone! Come in, young sir, come in!"

"What a relief to find a welcome in these lonely passes," thought Tomotada, as he led his horse to a shed behind the cottage. After seeing that his horse was well sheltered and fed, Tomotada entered the cottage, where he beheld the old woman and her husband, and a young girl as well, warming themselves by a fire of bamboo splints. The old couple respectfully requested that he be seated, and proceeded to warm some rice wine and prepare food for the warrior. The young girl, in the meantime, disappeared behind a screen, but not before Tomotada had observed with astonishment that she was extremely beautiful, though dressed in the meanest attire. He wondered how such a beautiful creature could be living in such a lonely and humble place. His thoughts, however, were interrupted by the old man, who had begun to speak.

"Honored Sir," he began. "The next village is far from here and the road is unfit for travel. Unless your quest is of such importance that it cannot be delayed, I would advise you not to force yourself and your horse beyond your powers of endurance. Our hovel is perhaps unworthy of your presence, and we have no comforts to offer; nevertheless, please honor us by staying under this miserable roof."

Tomotada was touched by the old man's words—and secretly, he was glad of the chance afforded him to see more of the young girl. Before long, a simple meal was set before him, and the girl herself came from behind the screen to serve the wine. She had changed her dress, and though her clothes were still of homespun, her long loose hair was neatly combed and smoothed. As she bent to fill his cup, Tomotada was amazed to see that she was even more beautiful than he had at first thought: she was the most beautiful creature he had ever seen. She moved with a grace that captivated him, and he could not take his eyes from her. The old man spoke apologetically, saying, "Please forgive the clumsy service of our daughter, Green Willow. She has been raised alone in these mountains and is only a poor, ignorant girl." But Tomotada protested that he considered himself lucky indeed to be served by so lovely a maiden. He saw that his admiring gaze made her blush, and he left his wine and food untasted before him. Suddenly struck by inspiration, he addressed her in a poem.

> As I rode through the winter
> I found a flower and thought,
> "Here I shall spend the day."
> But why does the blush of dawn
>   appear
> When the dark of night is still around
>   us?

Without a moment's hesitation, the girl replied:

> If my sleeve hides the faint color of
>   dawn,
> Perhaps when morning has truly come
> My lord will remain.

Then Tomotada knew that the girl had accepted his admiration, and he was all the more taken by the art of her verse and the feelings it expressed. "Seize the luck that has brought you here!" he thought to himself, and he resolved to ask the old couple to give

MAN AND WOMAN BY A HEDGE, HARUNOBO, 1725–1770.
? *What is the ideal of feminine beauty according to this folktale?*

him the hand of their daughter in marriage. Alas for the Lord of Noto's quest!

The old couple were astonished by the request of Tomotada, and they bowed themselves low in gratitude. After some moments of hesitation, the father spoke: "Honored master, you are a person of too high a degree for us to consider refusing the honor your request brings. Indeed our gratitude is unmeasurable. But this daughter of ours is merely a country girl, of no breeding and manners, certainly not fit to become the wife of a noble samurai such as yourself. But since you find the girl to your liking, and have condescended to overlook her peasant origins, please accept her as a gift, a humble handmaid. Deign, O Lord, to regard her

henceforth as yours, and act towards her as you will."

Now a samurai was not allowed to marry without the consent of his lord, and Tomotada could not expect permission until his quest was finished. When morning came, Tomotada resumed his journey, but his heart grew more apprehensive with every footfall of his horse. Green Willow rode behind her lord, saying not a word, and gradually the progress of the young man slowed to a halt. He could not tear his thoughts from the girl, and did not know whether he should bring her to Kyoto. He was afraid, moreover, that the Lord of Noto would not give him permission to marry a peasant girl, and afraid also that his daimyo might be likewise captivated by her beauty and take her for himself. And so he resolved to hide with her in the mountains, to settle there and become himself a simple farmer. Alas for the Lord of Noto's quest!

For five happy years, Tomotada and Green Willow dwelt together in the mountains, and not a day passed that did not bring them both joy and delight in each other and their life together. Forgotten was the time before Green Willow had come into his life. But one day, while talking with her husband about some household matter, Green Willow uttered a loud cry of pain, and became very white and still. "What is it, my wife?" cried Tomotada as he took her in his arms. "Forgive me, my lord, for crying out so rudely, but the pain was so sudden . . . My dear husband, hold me to you and listen—do not let me go! Our union has been filled with great joy, and I have known with you a happiness that cannot bear description. But now it is at an end: I must beg of you to accept it."

"Ah!" cried Tomotada, "It cannot be so. What wild fancies are these? You are only a

Green Willow **43**

little unwell, my darling. Lie down and rest, and the pain shall pass."

"No, my dearest, it cannot be. I am dying—I do not imagine it. It is needless to hide from you the truth any longer, my husband. I am not a human being. The soul of a tree is my soul, the heart of a tree my heart, the sap of a willow is my life. And some one, at this most cruel of moments, has cut down my tree—even now its branches have fallen to the ground. And this is why I must die! I have not even the strength left to weep, nor the time . . ."

With another cry of pain, Green Willow turned her head and tried to hide her face behind her sleeve. In the same moment, her form seemed to fold in upon itself, and before Tomotada's astonished and grief-stricken eyes, her robes crumpled in the air and fell empty to the ground.

Many years after this, an itinerant[1] monk came through the mountain passes on his way to Echizen. He stopped for water beside a stream, on the banks of which stood the stumps of three willow trees—two old and one young. Nearby, a rude stone memorial had been set up, which showed evidence of regular care unusual in such a remote place. He inquired about it from an old priest who lived in the neighborhood and was told the story of Green Willow.

"And what of Tomotada?" asked the mendicant,[2] when the priest had finished his tale. But the old man had fallen into a reverie and gazed at the shrine, oblivious of his guest.

"Alas for the Lord of Noto's quest!" the old man sighed to himself and fell silent.

The air grew chill as the evening drew on. At length, the old priest shook himself from his dreams.

"Forgive me!" he told his guest. "As age creeps upon me, I sometimes find myself lost in the memories of a young samurai."

The Granger Collection, New York

Eight Stallions (detail), Lang Shih-ning, Ch'ing Dynasty.

? *How does this folktale illustrate the Japanese regard for the beauties and value of nature?*

---

1. **itinerant** (ī·tin′ər·ənt): traveling from place to place.
2. **mendicant** (men′di·kənt): a monk or priest who lives mostly on charitable contributions.

First Thoughts

What is your *first* reaction to this folktale? What feelings or emotions did you experience as you read it?

Identifying Facts

1. Why does Tomotada stop at the cottage among the willows? Whom does he meet there?

2. Why doesn't Tomotada take Green Willow with him on his mission?

3. What does Tomotada learn about Green Willow as she is dying? What has caused her death?

Interpreting Meanings

1. In a word or phrase, sum up the **mood** created in the first half of the story. How does the **setting**—the time of year, the area, the weather, the cottage— contribute to the mood?

2. What qualities in Green Willow attract the samurai and distract him from his quest?

3. What is Tomotada's main **conflict** in this story? Is this conflict **external**, **internal**, or both?

4. The **crisis**, or **turning point**, is the point at which the main character makes a decision or commits an action that will affect the entire outcome of the story. What is the crisis in this story?

5. Who is the old priest at the end of the story? How do you know?

Applying Meanings

What do you think Tomotada should have done after Green Willow's death? Why do you say so?

Creative Writing Response

Writing a New Ending. Rewrite the second half of the tale so that Tomotada continues his quest and reaches Kyoto. Does he take Green Willow with him or leave her behind? Does the Lord of Noto allow Tomotada to marry Green Willow, or does the lord try to marry her himself? What new conflicts does Tomotada face? In your new ending, include an explanation of what Tomotada gains or loses by fulfilling the Lord of Noto's quest.

Language and Vocabulary

Transitional Expressions: Time Order

Words and phrases that link ideas, paragraphs, or sentences are known as **transitional expressions**. Some transitional expressions show the passage of time. Stories would be monotonous if the storyteller kept repeating, "and then . . . and then . . . and then. . . ." Instead, a good storyteller chooses from a variety of phrases that reflect time passages of varying lengths. In "Green Willow," such phrases as "Winter had already come," "For five happy years," and "Many years after this" give the reader a sense of the passing of time in the story.

Among the most common transitional words expressing the passing of time are: *after, as soon as, at first, during, earlier, later, finally, first, last, formerly, meanwhile, moments later, next, since, soon, then, until,* and *when.*

Write a one-paragraph **summary** of "Green Willow." In your summary, use transitions to express what happens first, next, and last in the story so that your reader can easily follow the sequence of events.

Reader's Guide

THE WHITE SNAKE

Background

This story comes from the Grimm brothers' famous collection of German fairy tales, collected and assembled during the nineteenth century. The tale is set several centuries earlier, however, in medieval times, when each German town had its own lord and castle.

The hero of the tale, who is never named, is the poor but trusted servant of a king. The hero sets out on a journey to see the world. It is not until he is well into his journey that he discovers what his goal is. He also discovers that three apparently trivial incidents early in his travels were really tests. His performance in these "practice tests" helps him to succeed at later, harder trials that he must pass to reach his goal.

The servant's story fits a questing hero archetype found in folklore everywhere. In this archetype, the boy or girl hero must be tested before he or she can make a royal marriage and "live happily ever after." The trials in these tales may test courage, wit, or spiritual or physical strength. The test **motif**, or pattern, suggests that by undergoing trials, the hero can gain maturity, and that in passing the tests he or she will emerge a stronger person.

Writer's Response

Write about a test in which you performed especially well. The test may have been academic, or it may have been a challenging situation in your life. What was responsible for your success? Did your view of yourself change as a result of your performance?

Literary Focus

The **fairy tale** is a particular kind of folktale that features supernatural elements such as spirits, talking animals, and magic. Good-hearted common people who triumph over evil are usually the heroes of fairy tales. Things and events in fairy tales often come in three's: three characters, three trials, three attempts to reach a goal. Many fairy tales point out a **moral lesson**—a message about how people ought to behave.

THE WHITE SNAKE
Jakob and Wilhelm Grimm
translated by
JACK ZIPES

The white snake is mentioned in the first paragraph, but it does not appear again in the fairy tale. As you read, decide what makes the white snake important enough to give the tale its title.

A long time ago there lived a king who was famous throughout the entire country for his wisdom. Nothing remained hidden from him, and it seemed as if he could obtain news of the most secret things through the air. However, he had one strange custom. Every day at noon, after the table was cleared of food and nobody else was present, a trusted servant had to bring him one more dish. This dish was always covered, and the servant himself did not know what was in it, nor did anyone else, for the king did not take the cover from the dish and eat until he was all alone. The king continued this custom for quite some time, until one day the servant, while removing the dish, was overcome by curiosity. He took it into his

room, and after he had carefully locked the door, he lifted the cover and found a white snake lying inside. Once he laid eyes on it, though, he had an irresistible desire to taste it. So he cut off a little piece and put it in his mouth. No sooner did his tongue touch it than he heard a strange whispering of exquisite voices outside his window. He went over to it to listen and noticed some sparrows talking to one another, telling what they had seen in the fields and forest. Tasting the snake had given him the power to understand the language of animals.

Now, it so happened that on this very day the queen lost her most beautiful ring, and the trusted servant was suspected of committing the theft because he had access to everything. The king summoned the servant and with harsh words threatened him, saying that if he was not able to name the

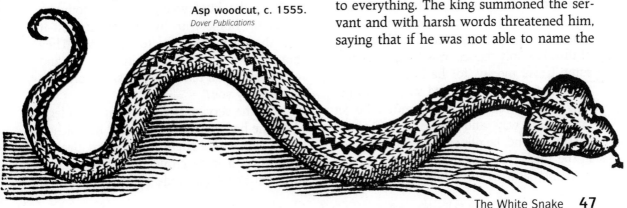

Asp woodcut, c. 1555.
Dover Publications

guilty person by morning, he himself would be considered the thief and would be executed. It was to no avail that the servant protested his innocence, for he was given a curt dismissal.

Distressed and afraid, he went down into the courtyard and tried to think of a way out of his predicament. Some ducks were peacefully sitting and resting by a running brook, preening themselves and chatting in a confidential tone. The servant stopped and listened to them as they told each other where they had been waddling about all morning and what good pickings they had found. But one of the ducks was irritable and said, "There's something heavy in my stomach. I was eating too fast and swallowed a ring that was lying under the king's window."

Right away the servant grabbed the duck by its neck, carried it into the kitchen, and said to the cook, "This one's well-fed. It's time you killed it!"

"All right," said the cook, weighing it in his hands. "It certainly hasn't been shy about stuffing itself. Besides, it's been waiting long enough for its roasting."

So he cut off the duck's neck, and when it was being cleaned, the queen's ring was found in its stomach. Now the servant could easily prove his innocence, and since the king wanted to make amends for having wronged his servant, he granted him a favor and promised him whatever royal post of honor he desired. The servant declined all of this. His only request was for a horse and some travel money, for he had a desire to travel about for a while and see the world.

When his wish had been granted, he set out on his way, and one day, as he was passing a pond, he noticed three fish trapped in the reeds and gasping for water. Though it is said that fish cannot talk, he heard them

crying in distress and wailing that they had to die so miserably. Since he felt sorry for them, he got down from his horse and put the three trapped fish back into the water. They wriggled for joy, stuck their heads out of the water, and cried out to him, "We'll remember you for saving our lives, and one day we'll repay you."

He rode on, and a while later it seemed to him that he heard a voice in the sand at his feet. He listened and heard an ant king complaining, "If only people with their clumsy beasts would keep away from us! That stupid horse is mercilessly trampling my people to death with his heavy hooves!"

The servant turned his horse onto a side path, and the ant king cried out to him, "We'll remember this, and one day we'll repay you."

The servant's path led into a forest, and there he saw a father and mother raven standing near their nest and pushing their young ones out of the nest.

"Get out! You're nothing but freeloaders!" they were exclaiming. "We can't find enough food to feed you anymore, and now you're big enough to feed yourselves."

The poor young birds lay on the ground, flapped their wings, and began crying, "We're just helpless children! How are we supposed to feed ourselves when we can't fly? All we can do is stay here and starve."

Then the kind young man dismounted, killed his horse with his sword, and left it for the young ravens to feed on. They hopped over to the horse, ate their fill, and cried out, "We'll remember this, and one day we'll repay you."

Now the servant had to use his own legs. After he had walked a long way, he reached a big city where there was a great deal of noise and a large crowd in the streets. A man on horseback rode by and announced

SAINT EUSTACE, DÜRER, 1500–1502.
Many folktales and fables feature the motif of a person being aided by an animal that he or she had earlier done a kindness for.
❓*What lesson about helpfulness and generosity do you think such stories teach?*

that the king's daughter was looking for a husband, but whoever declared himself a suitor would have to perform a difficult task, and if he did not complete it successfully, he would forfeit his life. Many men had already tried and had risked their lives in vain. When the young man saw the princess, he was so dazzled by her great beauty that he forgot all about the danger, went before the king, and declared himself a suitor. He was promptly led to the sea, and a gold ring was thrown into it before his eyes. The king told him that he was to fetch the ring from the depths of the sea, and he added, "If you come up without it, you'll be continually pushed back down until you perish in the waves."

Everyone felt sorry for the handsome young man and left him alone by the sea. He was standing on the shore thinking about what to do when he suddenly saw three fish swimming toward him. They were none other than the three fish whose lives he had saved. The one in the middle held a shell in its mouth, which it set down on the beach at the feet of the young man, who picked it up. When he opened the shell, he found the gold ring, and bursting with joy, he brought it to the king expecting that he would receive the promised reward. But when the proud king's daughter discovered that he was not her equal in birth, she scorned him and demanded that he first perform another task. She went down into the garden, and she herself scattered ten sacks full of millet in the grass.

"He must pick them all up before the sun rises tomorrow," she said.

"And not a single grain may be missing."

The young man sat down in the garden and tried to think of a way to accomplish the task, but nothing occurred to him, and he sat there quite sadly, expecting to be led to his death at the break of dawn. But when the first rays of the sun fell on the garden, he saw ten sacks all filled to the top and

Illustration by Walter Crane for an 1886 edition of *Household Stories from the Collection of the Brothers Grimm. Many tales from the folk tradition end "happily ever after." Do you think that such stories give people hope?*

standing side by side. Not a single grain was missing. The ant king had come during the night with thousands and thousands of ants, and the grateful insects had picked up the millet seeds with great diligence and gathered them into the sacks. The princess herself went down to the garden and was amazed to see that the young man had accomplished the task. But her proud heart could not be tamed, and she said, "Even if he has accomplished the first two tasks, he shall not become my husband until he has brought me an apple from the Tree of Life."

The young man did not know where the Tree of Life was. Therefore, he set out with the intention of going as far as his legs could carry him, even though he had no hope of finding it. One evening, after he had traveled through three kingdoms and reached a forest, he sat down beneath a tree and wanted to sleep. But he heard a noise in the tree, and a golden apple fell into his hand. At the same time three ravens flew down to him, landed on his knees, and said, "We're the three young ravens whom you saved from starvation. When we grew up, we heard you were looking for the golden apple. So we flew across the sea to the end of the world, where the Tree of Life is standing, and we've fetched the apple."

Now the young man was full of joy and started on his way home. He brought the golden apple to the beautiful princess, who no longer had any excuses to make. They divided the apple of life and ate it together, and her heart filled with love for him. In time they reached a ripe old age in peace and happiness.

First Thoughts

Does this fairy tale remind you of any other fairy tales you have heard? Name some of the characters and events in this tale that are familiar to you from other tales. How is this story different from the other tales?

Identifying Facts

1. How does the hero prove his innocence to the king?
2. What does the hero do for the animals he encounters on his journey?
3. How is the hero able to pass the "impossible" tests of the princess?

Interpreting Meanings

1. **Suspense** is the feeling of uncertainty and curiosity about what will happen next in a story. List three places in this story where the suspense builds. How is the situation resolved and the suspense relieved in each instance?

2. The young man in this fairy tale is an honest, good-hearted person, a "trusted servant." Yet, he gives in to temptation and discovers the king's secret, gaining the ability that only the king had before. How do you explain this seeming contradiction?

3. **Fairy tales** often teach a **moral lesson**—a lesson about how people ought to behave. What lesson or lessons do you think this fairy tale teaches? Name some other fairy tales you know and discuss the lessons they teach.

Applying Meanings

Fairy tales are simple tales without much character development. Their "happily ever after" endings may seem unrealistic to modern readers. Yet, fairy tales are still popular today. Why do you think this is so? What satisfactions do they give to readers?

Creative Writing Response

Writing a Fairy Tale.   Write a short original fairy tale. It may be humorous or serious, set in an imaginary time and place or set in contemporary times. Be sure to include as many features of the fairy tale as you can: a common person as the hero or heroine; supernatural elements; the triumph of good over evil; and a "happily ever after" ending. Try to make something in your fairy tale happen in three's: three characters or three similar incidents, for example. What moral lesson will your tale teach?

Critical Writing Response

Comparing Heroes.   In a three- to five-paragraph essay, compare the ideal of heroism shown in "The White Snake" to the ideal of heroism shown in "Theseus." How are the heroes of each story alike and different? Do you think the two notions of heroism demonstrated in each story are more similar than different? Use specific details from both selections to support your statements.

BEHIND THE SCENES

The Brothers Grimm

In Germany, one book has sold more copies than any other book except the Bible. The book is called *Kinder- und Hausmärchen*—literally, *Children's and Household Tales*. In English, the book is known as *Grimms' Fairy Tales*.

The Brothers Grimm were Jakob and Wilhelm. Born in Hanau, Germany, in the mid-eighteenth century, they were the eldest sons of a poor widow. The two brothers were close and shared a love of learning, but because they were not members of the upper class, they had to work hard to obtain their educations.

The first half of the nineteenth century was an era of enormous social change in Germany and throughout Europe. The growing middle and working classes in Germany were increasingly unhappy with the government, which was oppressive and disunified. The nineteenth century was also

the era of a European and American literary movement called **Romanticism**. Romantics believed in the values of passion and imagination. They rejected a slavish devotion to logic and reason. They were discontented with a society that had become urban and industrial. For artistic themes, they often turned to the folklore and the natural environment of the "common" people whose lifestyle they admired and idealized.

It was in this climate that the Grimms began to collect German folklore. They saw in it an opportunity to uncover the roots of the German heritage. They believed that folklore contained basic truths about the origins of civilization and that it recorded the only "true" laws and customs of the German people. They hoped that by publishing the folklore of Germany before the oral tradition was lost that they could

Jakob and Wilhelm Grimm.

provide German readers with a sense of national pride and purpose that was lacking in the chaotic social and political climate of the early nineteenth century.

The Grimms gathered stories from their middle-class neighbors, mostly educated women who had been told the stories by their nursemaids and servants. The brothers were determined to present the tales in as close to their original form as possible. But within their lifetimes, they revised their collection several times, hoping to appeal to an audience of middle-class Germans and their children. They added references to Christianity and the Protes-

tant work ethic. They also removed many of the gruesome elements that the middle-class Germans might not have wanted their children to read. This practice of ''cleaning up'' the tales continues to this day, for, as sanitized as they were, the Grimms' first edition of fairy tales is still far more graphic than twentieth-century retellings of the tales. Contrast, for example, the endings of the Walt Disney movie versions of *Snow White and the Seven Dwarves* and *Cinderella* with the Grimms' versions. According to the Brothers Grimm, the wicked queen in ''Snow White'' must dance to her death in slippers of molten lead, and pigeons peck out the eyes of Cinderella's evil step-sisters. The Disney versions leave out these grisly details.

Psychologists, educators, folklorists, and literary critics have kept up a lively debate about the Grimm brothers' contributions to folklore preservation. Some argue that the edited tales have been totally altered from their original form and purpose, so that they do not accurately reflect the oral tradition that the Grimms were supposedly trying to preserve. Others credit the Grimms with creating a new genre, the *Buchmarchen,* or ''book tale,'' a mixture of oral and literary traditions. The Grimms certainly added their own values to the tales. But they also preserved the spirit of social justice and collective pride that they felt all Germans, and perhaps all people everywhere, should claim as a part of their heritage.

LANGUAGE
—AND—
CULTURE

THE HERO AND THE QUEST: ALIVE AND WELL

Which of the following heroes was *not* featured in the unit you have just read?

a) the Greek hero Theseus

b) a Japanese samurai warrior

c) the Egyptian goddess Isis

d) Captain Picard of the starship *Enterprise*

If you answered *d,* you're right—but Captain Picard would not be out of place in such heroic company. The captain and crew of *Star Trek* have quite a bit in common with the heroes and heroines in the myths and folktales you have just read. They are the twentieth-century descendants of the archetypal heroes of old, undertaking twentieth-century equivalents of the heroic quest.

Updating the Archetypes

There are some differences between the heroes and quests of old and their contemporary versions, to be sure. These differences reflect the fact that popular entertainment today is more self-conscious than tales from the oral tradition, incorporating

The popular film Star Wars *and its sequels project the heroic quest archetype into another galaxy.*

? *Why do you think the quest story has endured for thousands of years?*

specifically contemporary concerns. For example, instead of relying on superhuman powers or the intervention of gods and goddesses, the captain and crew of the starship *Enterprise* rely on futuristic technology, scientific knowledge, and a sophisticated understanding of diverse alien cultures in order to succeed on their various quests. In this way, although the *Star Trek* adventures contain echoes of the heroic quest story, they are unmistakably a product of the twentieth century. They reflect our enthusiasm about technology and echo ongoing modern debates about the morality of interfering in the development of other cultures and using force to solve conflicts.

A Heroic Quest to the Stars

In recent years, perhaps the most successful testament to the enduring popularity of mythic and folktale archetypes appeared in the form of George Lucas's *Star Wars* trilogy, three of the most successful and beloved films of all time. Luke Skywalker, the hero of the trilogy, is cast in the mold of the archetypal folktale hero. Born a simple farm boy and raised by foster parents, Luke is kept from knowing his true heritage, which he slowly learns as he is swept up in a galactic adventure. He rescues a princess and defeats a superior enemy, using only his inherent goodness and intuition—the power of "the Force." During his adventures he is aided by a variety of friends and teachers who enable him to succeed on his quest. Like many heroes, Luke has flaws: impatience, pride, and impulsiveness. While training with his teacher, Yoda, he descends into an "underworld" and has a vision that gives him important clues to the seriousness of his quest. He is reluctant to face his destiny. But like Theseus in this unit, he is ultimately reunited with his true father—in this case, the evil Darth Vader. Only after many battles and hardships is Luke able to redeem his father and mature into the Jedi knight he is meant to be, becoming a hero of his culture.

An Appetite for Adventure

People of all ages are as fascinated by the hero and the quest today as they were thousands of years ago. Modern audiences stand in long lines at movie theaters to thrill to adventures that echo the heroic quest archetype: *Raiders of the Lost Ark, Back to the Future, The Dark Crystal, Aliens, Dances with Wolves, Willow.* They buy and collect comic books featuring such heroes as Spiderman, Wonder Woman, the Fantastic Four, and Batman. For over twenty-five years they have watched science-fiction adventures such as *Star Trek* and *Dr. Who* on television. And they have eagerly devoured the quest fantasy novels of J.R.R. Tolkien, Marion Zimmer Bradley, Anne McCaffrey, and a host of other science-fiction and fantasy writers.

Our modern heroes may look very different from their ancient counterparts, use different means to achieve their goals, and participate in different kinds of quests, but they are still heroic adventurers with sometimes superhuman abilities who embark on exciting journeys. They visit exotic places, meet strange beings, and battle awesome foes along the way, living out our fantasies and keeping alive the adventure-loving child within each of us.

USING TRANSITIONS FOR COMPARISON AND CONTRAST

Transitions, also called **linking expressions** and **connectives**, are words and phrases that show the relationships between ideas. You can use transitions to link ideas within a sentence, within a paragraph, or within a longer piece of writing. Transitions help your reader to follow your train of thought. Notice how the italicized transitions improve the following paragraph, which compares two tales.

Although "Green Willow" and "The White Snake" come from opposite sides of the world, the tales are similar in several ways. *Both* stories are set in feudal societies, and *both* feature heroes who face several trials. *In addition, both* tales deal with the importance of perseverance.

Transitions clarify the connections between ideas. *Although* alerts readers to a contrast between the ideas in the first part of a sentence and the ideas in the second part. *Both* and *in addition* link ideas that are alike. Note that transitions often are placed at the beginnings of clauses. Sometimes transitions serve to join sentences.

Transitions for Comparison and/or Contrast

Transitions can be grouped according to their uses. When you write about similarities and/or differences between ideas, you will find transitions from the groups below especially helpful.

Transitions that link similar ideas

again	furthermore
also	in addition
and	likewise
besides	moreover
both	similarly
each of	too

Transitions that contrast or limit ideas

although	instead
and yet	neither . . . nor
but	nevertheless
conversely	on the other hand
however	still
in spite of	yet

Exercise 1: Using Transitions for Comparison and/or Contrast

The numbered sentences in the paragraph below are followed by transitions in parentheses. Insert the transitions into the sentences to clarify similarities or differences between ideas.

The god Maheo and the goddess Isis have many traits in common. For example, Maheo uses his power to create the natural world.   **1)** Isis uses her power to restore the dead Osiris to life (on the other hand).   **2)** Both are creators of life (yet).   **3,4)** The deities are persis-

tent and caring (moreover, both). Maheo does not give up while struggling to create land.   5) He does his best to provide for his creatures (in addition).
6) Isis does not give up while searching for Osiris's body, and she does her best to shield Osiris from Seth's evil deeds (similarly). Maheo is the creator and preserver of the world.   7) Isis is a restorer and preserver (likewise).
8) Maheo and Isis do have differences; on the whole, both are kind and nurturing deities (however).

Transitions for Other Connections

Transitions can do more than indicate similarities and differences. Study the following groups of transitions.

Transitions that indicate time or position

above	meanwhile
afterward	nearby
before	next
eventually	opposite to
first (second, etc.)	

Transitions that indicate purpose, cause, or effect

as	since
because	so, so that
consequently	then
for	therefore
just as . . . so	

Transitions that indicate a summary, a conclusion, or an example

as a result	in other words
for example	on the whole
for instance	overall
in conclusion	therefore
in fact	

Exercise 2: Choosing Transitions

For each numbered sentence, choose an appropriate transition from the list specified in parentheses. Then insert the transition into the sentence. Join sentences if necessary when you are adding transitions.

Myths about death show how cultural attitudes can differ.

1. In a Khoikhoi myth, people are not originally supposed to die (transition indicating an example). The moon wants people to know this.

2. Hare, who carries the message, changes it (transition indicating contrast).

3. Death is brought into the world (transition indicating effect). Hare is punished for his actions. This myth stresses the unfairness of death.

4. In a Caddo myth, death is not inevitable (transition linking similar ideas). A medicine man wants to let the wandering souls of the dead come into a grass house.

5. They will be able to return to life (transition indicating purpose).

6. Coyote does not want the earth crowded (transition indicating contrast).

7. He secretly bars the door (transition indicating purpose).

8. Coyote is punished (transition linking similar ideas). This myth demonstrates a belief that death serves a purpose.

9. Cultural attitudes toward death may differ (transition indicating summary).

10. Death is never accepted without question or protest (transition indicating contrast).

Critical Thinking and Writing

DISCOVERING CONNECTIONS IN LITERATURE

What characteristics do your close friends have in common? What similar features do your favorite singing groups share? Whenever you compare two or more items, you can discover new relationships among people, places, events, or ideas you've always thought of as different.

Writing Assignment

Write an informative essay identifying and discussing connections, or similarities, between any two of the unit selections. Assume that your audience is familiar with the literature and wants to know more. In this essay, you'll use classification to develop your main idea.

Background

In this unit, you have read myths and folktales from a variety of cultures. Because these traditional narratives reflect basic questions about the world and the individual's place in it, many similarities link the tales. Here are some of the kinds of connections you can find:

- **Similar Subjects.** On the simplest level, two stories may deal with the same subject. You may have two stories about the origins of life, about bravery, or about death.

- **Similar Characters.** Similar characters may pop up in stories from dissimilar cultures. You may recognize such archetypes as the brave hero, the wise prophet, or the selfish trickster.

- **Similar Plots.** Throughout the world's literature, some plots occur again and again—with different characters and settings. For example, an average person receives unexpected rewards for acts of kindness, or a hero sacrifices something for the good of society.

- **Similar Imagery.** You may discover works that share strong images—for example, images of water, storms, mountains, forests, valleys, or animals.

- **Similar Themes.** Two different stories may convey similar insights about life or human nature.

Prewriting

Focused Reading and Questioning. To find common elements among works in this unit, answer the following questions:

1. Which works deal with the **subject** of loyalty to others and/or love for others?

2. In which works does the main **character** go on a quest?

3. In which works does the **plot** trace how something originates or how the world changes after a catastrophe?

4. Which works include **imagery** of a peaceful, fertile world?
5. Which works explore **themes** of love and marriage, or the loss of love?

Use one of these questions as the basis for your writing, or ask a question of your own.

Using Classification. One way to develop a main idea is to classify information. From your answers to the questions above, choose two works that have at least two elements in common. Then develop material for your essay by using a chart like the following one.

	Selection 1	Selection 2
Subject		
Main characters		
Minor characters		
Plot summary		
Imagery		
Theme		

Synthesize the charted information into a **thesis statement**, a sentence stating one main idea about the similarities in the two works.

Writing

Use the following plan as you draft your essay.

1. **Introductory Paragraph.** Cite the titles of the two works you'll examine, and identify the cultures they come from. Place your thesis statement at the end of this paragraph.

2. **Body Paragraphs.** Choose an order for presenting your ideas. Either discuss all the charted elements in the first work and then compare the second work to it (AABB order), or take each element separately and show the similarities in both works (ABAB order). In either case, use transitions to connect your points of comparison (see page 56). To illustrate the similarites, present specific details from each work.

3. **Concluding Paragraph.** Summarize the similarities you've discovered. In your final sentence, make an observation about how the similarities between the two works might be meaningful.

Evaluating and Revising

Use the following questions to evaluate and revise your draft.

1. Does your first paragraph include a thesis statement as well as the titles of the two works you've chosen?
2. In the body paragraphs, have you discussed at least two similarities between the works, including specifics to support your points?
3. Have you used transitions to clarify links between the ideas in your sentences and paragraphs?
4. Have you checked paragraph organization and sentence structure?

Proofreading and Publishing

Proofread to eliminate errors in grammar and mechanics, and make a final copy of your essay. Meet with a group of classmates, exchange papers, and discuss the connections that group members have discovered.

EUROPE

Mediterranean Sea

ASIA

Atlantic Ocean

SAHARA

EGYPT

Lower Egypt

Memphis

Thebes

Upper Egypt

ARABIAN DESERT

GHANA

MALI

SONGHAI

Timbuktu

KUSH

Meroë

Aksum

AKSUM

Rift Valley

Congo Zaire River

EAST AFRICAN CITY-STATES

CONGO

Zambesi River

KALAHARI DESERT

MADAGASC

ZULULAND

Niger River

Nile River

Red Sea

AFRICAN
KINGDOMS
AND
EMPIRES

c. 2700 B.C.–A.D. 1800

THE AFRICAN LITERARY TRADITION

▼ Time ▼
2700 B.C.–present

▼ Place ▼
Africa

▼ Literary Significance ▼

Africa's literary tradition begins in ancient Egypt. There, for the first time, people used paper and ink to record their thoughts and feelings. Ancient Egyptian literature is mainly a religious literature, but the Egyptians also wrote love poems and entertaining tales.

Although the written word has existed throughout Africa for centuries, the spoken word has remained the dominant form of creative expression in most African communities. For centuries, Africa's oral literature—its proverbs, chants, fables, folktales, and epics—has represented an ongoing creative process in which each reteller injects age-old themes with a fresh perspective.

TIME LINE

Africa

Detail of hieroglyphics from the Rosetta Stone.

The Granger Collection, New York

LITERARY EVENTS

▼

Egyptian *Pyramid Texts* are collected, **c. 2700–2200 B.C.**

Egyptian *Coffin Texts* are compiled, **c. 2000 B.C.**

Egyptian Book of the Dead is assembled, **c. 1580–1350 B.C.**

"Great Hymn to the Aten," attributed to Egyptian ruler Akhenaten, **c. 1375–1362 B.C.**

Egyptian New Kingdom lyrics are composed, **c. 1300–1100 B.C.**

| 3500 B.C. | 3000 B.C. | 2500 B.C. | 2000 B.C. | 1500 B.C | 1000 B.C |

Egyptians invent hieroglyphic writing, **c. 3500–3000 B.C.**

Old Kingdom in Egypt, **c. 2700–2181 B.C.**

The Pyramids and the Great Sphinx are built in Egypt, **c. 2500 B.C.**

Middle Kingdom in Egypt, **c. 2000–1780 B.C.**

New Kingdom in Egypt, **c. 1550–1085 B.C.**

Akhenaten institutes religious reforms in Egypt, **1375–1362 B.C.**

Moses leads Jews out of Egypt, **c. 1200 B.C.**

▲

CULTURAL AND HISTORICAL EVENTS

K. Scholz/SuperStock, Inc.

The Great Sphinx and the pyramid of Cheops.

Ethiopian painting of
King David, c. 1600s.

The Granger Collection, New York

Greek scholar
Herodotus writes
The Histories,
recounting his
travels in North
Africa, **c. A.D. 430** **B.C.**

Algerian-born Apuleius
writes *The Golden Ass*,
the oldest surviving Latin
novel, **c. A.D. 155**

St. Augustine, Bishop of
Hippo (in modern-day
Algeria) writes his
Confessions, **c. A.D. 400**

Carved
wooden
head of a
woman,
Ibo.

*Werner Forman Archiv/Musee Royale de L'Afrique
Centrale, Tervuren, Belgium/Art Resource*

Mali's great epic
Sundiata is composed,
c. 1200

Soninke oral
epic, *The Dausi*,
is composed,
c. 1600

500 B.C.	A.D. 1	500	1000	1500

Kushite kingdom
gains control of
Egypt, **751–
664 B.C.**

Last Egyptian dynasty,
378–342 B.C.

Alexander the Great
conquers Egypt,
c. 332 B.C.

Rise and fall of Kingdom
of Aksum, **c. 200 B.C.–
A.D. 500**

Bantu speakers begin
to move south and east
through Africa from the
Cameroon Highlands,
c. first century B.C.

Egypt becomes a Roman
province, **30 B.C.**

Christianity is
introduced into
Northern Africa
via the Roman
Empire,
c. A.D. 200

Rise and fall of the
Empire of Ghana,
c. A.D. 300–1100

Islam is brought
to West Africa,
c. 600

Swahili language
and culture develop
in East Africa,
c. 1000–1500

Rise and fall of
the Empire of
Mali, **c. 1200–
1400**

Rise and fall of
the Empire of
Songhai,
c. 1200–1592

Islam becomes
official religion
of Mali, **1235**

Kingdom of
Congo becomes
dominant
in the Zaire
Basin, **1300–
1540**

Rise of the
Zulu nation in
southern
Africa, **early
1800s**

Western
European
nations divide
Africa into
colonies, **late
1800s**

Werner Forman Archive

The mosque at Jenne, in Mali.

The border of this Time Line depicts Egyptian hieroglyphics, a form of
picture writing in which symbols represent words, syllables, or sounds.

AFRICAN LITERATURE

A frican literature is as old as the pyramids. Written literature on the African continent began with the ancient Egyptians, and many of their literary traditions have counterparts in African literature today.

The "Gift of the Nile"

The Greek historian Herodotus (hə·räd′ə·təs) (485–425 B.C.) called Egypt the "gift of the Nile," and it is not hard to understand why. The Nile itself provided settlers with water and, during the flood season, the fertilizing silt necessary for growing such crops as barley, wheat, vegetables, flax, and grapes. The Nile also provided the transportation that made ancient Egypt's thriving trade with neighbors possible. The Nile brought boats laden with gold, hardwood, and metals—all the resources that Egypt itself lacked. Without the Nile, Egypt would simply have been part of the vast and arid Sahara. With the Nile, Egypt was able to become a wealthy agricultural land and one of the most powerful civilizations the world has ever known.

The Nile provided another gift that enabled Egypt to grow into a remarkable and enduring civilization: the **papyrus** (pə·pī′rəs) reeds that grew along its banks. From these reeds the Egyptians developed paper, a far more convenient writing material than the clay tablets used by their neighbors in ancient Mesopotamia. (Our word *paper,* in fact, comes from *papyrus.*) Paper made centralized rule possible, enabling the Egyptians to keep written records, issue instructions, write histories, compute taxes, survey land, and carry out the other practical tasks of a complex society. In addition, ideas and literature could be shared far and wide and handed down to future generations.

❝ Truth is great and its effectiveness endures. **❞**
—*from* The Maxims of Ptahhotpe

Twenty-seven Centuries of Civilization

Under thirty-one **dynasties**, or successive ruling families, Egyptian civilization flourished for more than twenty-seven centuries. Its greatest years are divided into three main eras:

The Old Kingdom—from about 2700 to 2200 B.C. The great pyramids were built during this period.

The Middle Kingdom—from about 2000 to 1800 B.C. This period was characterized by Egypt's expanding economy and political power.

The New Kingdom—from about 1600 to 1100 B.C. Egypt was at the peak of its political power during this period. Its vast empire reached north to Syria, east to the Euphrates (yōō·frāt′ēz) River, and south to the East African kingdoms of Nubia and Kush.

A Highly Organized Society

The organization of Egyptian society resembled the shape of its pyramids. A single, powerful ruler, the **pharaoh**, was the pinnacle of the social pyramid. Priests and scribes formed the next level of the pyramid. Then came the upper class, consisting of merchants, doctors, engineers, lawyers, and other professionals. Forming the bottom of the pyramidic structure was the largest class: the workers, peasants, and slaves.

The pharaoh was not only a political leader but also a spiritual leader, representing the earthly incarnation of the god Horus (hō′rəs), son of Osiris (ō·sī′ris). It was the pharaoh's destiny to go and live with the gods after death, and in the afterlife to become identified with Osiris, god of the underworld. To ease the pharaoh's journey to the afterlife, the Egyptians built magnificent pyramids, which contained the pharaoh's mummified body and earthly possessions.

The Egyptian Pantheon

Religion was inseparable from everyday life in ancient Egypt. Because the Egyptians believed that their ruler, the pharaoh,

Statue of the falcon-headed god Horus, protecting the pharaoh, Ramses II. *The Egyptians believed that the pharaoh was the earthly incarnation of Horus.*

Thoth, the Egyptian god of learning.

66 I have not done iniquity. . . . I have not robbed with violence. . . . I have not stolen. . . . I have done no murder; I have done no harm. . . . I have not defrauded the offerings. . . . 99

—*Negative Confession from the Egyptian Book of the Dead*

was a god, service to the ruler was the same as religious worship. Yet the ancient Egyptians recognized and worshiped many other gods and goddesses besides the earthly one. These divine beings—numbering somewhere between eighty and eighty-nine—had different forms and represented different powers. Probably the most important group of gods was the *ennead* (en'ē·ad'), the nine creation gods. These were Atum, the creator; his children Shu and Tefnut; their children Geb and Nut; and Osiris, his wife/sister Isis, his brother Seth, and Seth's wife/sister Nephthys.

The Cult of the Dead

A fascination with death pervaded Egyptian culture. This "cult of the dead" largely dictated Egyptian morality and ethics. Starting in the Old Kingdom, the Egyptians wrote many works dedicated to the quest for life after death. These works contained magical spells for the protection of the dead, burial rites, and other funerary texts. The New Kingdom saw the ultimate expression of Egyptian funerary literature: the Book of the Dead, a kind of "traveler's guide" to the afterlife containing everything the deceased needed to have and know after death.

Religious literature did not stop with the Book of the Dead. Virtually everything the Egyptians wrote was in some way tied to their religious beliefs, written either to instruct people in morality or to praise the gods.

> Much of ancient Egyptian literature served to aid or instruct people in attaining the afterlife.

Strictly religious texts included **praise songs** and **hymns**. The most famous of these, "The Great Hymn to the Aten," is the earliest known praise song (see page 73). Other popular genres, or forms of literature, in ancient Egypt included **instructions**, sets of moral teachings often presented in the form of proverbs, and **autobiographies**, a form of secular literature intended to teach lessons in morality. Although the Egyptians told stories for entertainment, such as "The Tale of the Shipwrecked Sailor" and "King Cheops and the Magician," even these narratives were not without religious content. Finally, the Egyptians wrote **sacred** or **ritual dramas**—plays used in religious ceremonies.

During the New Kingdom, when the social structure and morality of the Egyptian culture had become less rigid, secular poetry was written. Much of this poetry was **pastoral**—that is, it portrayed everyday life in idyllic terms. Even today, the New Kingdom pastoral poetry delivers a fresh and honest view of romantic love.

Osiris (left) and Atum. *Osiris was the father of Horus, and the Egyptians believed that the pharaoh became Osiris after death.*

The Rise of Africa's Great Civilizations

By the close of the New Kingdom (about 1000 B.C.), Egypt had lost much of its status as a world power. Internally divided and supported by weak rulers, Egypt fell into decline. But ancient Egypt was not the only civilization in Africa. As Egyptian power was waning, the kingdom of Kush, at the southern end of the Nile River, was gaining strength and prominence. For centuries the Egyptians had struggled to contain the Kushites' power. Between 751 and 664 B.C., Kushite kings succeeded in conquering and ruling

Egypt. The Kushite kingdom continued to flourish long after Egypt's demise, and its capital city Meroë thrived as a major producer of iron well into the second century A.D.

In addition to Kush, smaller civilizations also existed around the edges of the Sahara, which was less extensive than it is today. These groups farmed and raised livestock in the fertile grasslands surrounding the desert. Among these were the Fasa of the northern Sudan, whose deeds are recalled today by the Soninke oral epic, *The Dausi.*

In the third century A.D., a rich kingdom in eastern Africa called Aksum (ăk′soom′) arose in what is now Ethiopia. Aksum thrived at the center of a trade route that extended as far west as Rome and as far east as India. The culture fell into decline in the sixth century A.D., but not before it developed its own writing system, called Ethiopic script. This writing system developed into several modern scripts still used in Ethiopia today.

As the Egyptian civilization in the north of Africa fell into decline, new civilizations to the east, west, and south began to rise.

Drought drove many migrants south and west. In western Africa, a series of great civilizations arose. The first of these, the kingdom of Old Ghana, was in place by A.D. 300. It was succeeded by the empires of Old Mali and Songhai, among others. The legendary city of Timbuktu was a center of trade and culture in both the Mali and Songhai empires.

New cultures sprang up throughout the South, including the Luba and Malawi (mä′lä·wē) empires in central Africa, the two Congo kingdoms, the Swahili (swä·hē′lē) culture of eastern Africa, the kingdom of Old Zimbabwe (zim·bä′bwä′), and the Zulu nation near the southern tip of the continent.

The period between A.D. 300 and A.D. 1600 marked Africa's long Golden Age. During this time, sculpture, music, metalwork, textiles, and oral literature flourished. African oral literature, like the literature of the ancient Egyptians, includes praise poems, love poems, tales, ritual dramas, and moral instructions distilled into the form of proverbs and fables. It also includes epics and more specific kinds of

Statue of a drummer, from the Mbala people of the Congo.

Timbuktu. *In the fifteenth century, Timbuktu—a center of trade and learning—was one of several bustling cities that dotted the kingdoms of West Africa.*

poems and narratives. From Africa's Golden Age came several oral epics, including the Mali epic *Sundiata* (see pages 102–117).

Foreign Influences in Africa

During the fourth century A.D., the Roman Empire had proclaimed Christianity as its state religion and taken control of the entire northern coast of Africa, including Egypt. This early Christian influence spread east to Aksum, eventually leading to the foundation of the Ethiopian Orthodox Church, still one of the largest religious groups in Ethiopia.

Around A.D. 700, Islam, the religion of the followers of Mohammed, was introduced into Africa. With Islam, the Arabic writing system was introduced as well. By 1235, Islam was the state religion of Old Mali. Somali and other eastern African nations were also largely Muslim.

Much later, near the close of Africa's Golden Age, Christianity and colonialism came hand in hand to sub-Saharan Africa. Ultimately, in the late 1800s, several European pow-

> **❝** . . . the singing that comes from your heart will echo in the ear of your son and live on in your people. **❞**
>
> —*from* The Dausi,
> *Soninke (Sudan)*

ers created colonized "countries." Social and political chaos reigned as traditional African nations were either split apart by European colonizers or joined with incompatible neighbors.

In the mid-1900s, a move toward independence gained force, and a rebirth of traditional cultures came with it. Literature written in African languages, rather than in English, French, or other European languages, gained popularity. This vital literature is clearly stamped with the tradition of African oral literature, or **orature**, as it has been called.

Kal Mueller/Woodfin Camp & Associates

A priest outside an Ethiopian Orthodox church. *Aksum, in modern-day Ethiopia, was a Christian kingdom by the sixth century* A.D.

> **46** What kind of people we become depends crucially on the stories we are nurtured on. . . . **99**
> —*Chinweizu, Nigeria*

Griots: Africa's Living Libraries

Traditionally, the keepers of oral literature in West Africa have been the **griots** (grē′ōz). In Africa today, a griot may be a professional storyteller, singer, or entertainer. In the past, though, the griot's role included all of these functions and more. Griots were skilled at creating and transmitting the many forms of African oral literature. Many also memorized their nations' histories and laws. Rather than consulting books or libraries, people in the kingdoms of Africa consulted griots. Elsewhere on the African continent, bards, storytellers, town criers, and oral historians also preserved and continued the oral tradition.

> **As storytellers, tutors to nobility, and living records of a culture's laws and customs, the griots were indispensable to African civilizations.**

The literary forms of Africa are many and varied. Yet they share certain features. Striking images of nature, poignant insights into the human condition, and subtle ironies allow these works to speak clearly to modern readers, thus transcending barriers of time and culture.

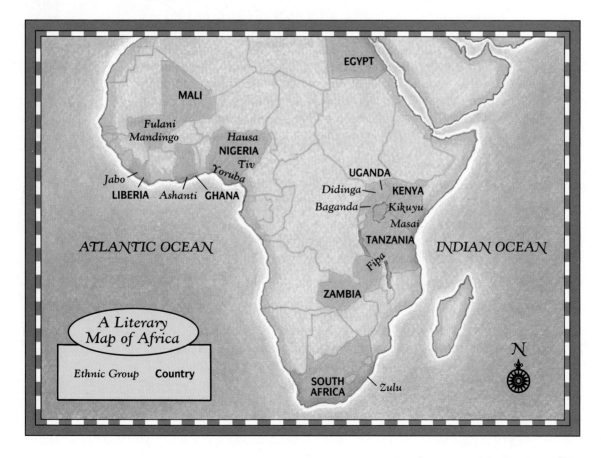

A Literary Map of Africa

Ethnic Group   Country

Reader's Guide

THE GREAT HYMN TO THE ATEN

Background

"The Great Hymn to the Aten" is the longest of several New Kingdom **hymns**, or **praise songs**, to the sun god Aten. This hymn was found on the wall of a tomb built for a royal scribe named Ay and his wife. It was intended to assure their safety in the afterlife.

The Egyptians had worshiped the sun—along with a host of other gods and goddesses—since the Old Kingdom. But during the Amarna period of the New Kingdom, the pharaoh Amenhotep IV, who later took the name Akhenaten (a name meaning "he who serves the Aten"), declared that the sun god, Aten, was the one true god. Thus, Egypt was introduced to **monotheism**, or a doctrine of belief in one god.

Akhenaten (ä′ke·nät′'n), who ruled from 1379 B.C. to 1362 B.C., was an unusual ruler. Under his reign, conservative, tradition-bound Egypt experienced a revolution that affected every aspect of life. Akhenaten was a talented poet, and this hymn, as well as several others, has been attributed to him. But Akhenaten's break with tradition must have seemed too risky for New Kingdom Egyptians, who for centuries had counted on the help of all the gods to keep them safe and happy after death. As soon as their radical pharaoh died, the people returned to worshiping their old gods.

Writer's Response

Imagine that an organization has commissioned you to write a "praise song" to the sun as part of its campaign to make people more aware of their environment. What features of the sun will you praise? Create a cluster of words and phrases that describe the sun's attributes, or qualities.

Literary Focus

An **epithet** is a descriptive name, adjective, phrase, or title that is used to describe a quality or characteristic of a person, place, or thing. We use epithets when we refer to "America the Beautiful," "Richard the Lionhearted," "Paris, the City of Lights," or "New Jersey, the Garden State." In "The Great Hymn to the Aten," epithets are used to show respect and honor for the attributes, or qualities, of the sun god.

THE GREAT HYMN
TO THE ATEN

translated by

MIRIAM LICHTHEIM

> *Note the specific words and phrases that are used to praise*
> *Aten. What kind of god is Aten? What is the speaker's*
> *attitude toward the god?*

Splendid you rise in heaven's lightland,°
O living Aten, creator of life!
When you have dawned in eastern lightland,
You fill every land with your beauty.

1. **lightland:** the sky.

5   You are beauteous, great, radiant,
High over every land;
Your rays embrace the lands,
To the limit of all that you made.
Being Re,° you reach their limits,

9. **Re** (rā): another name for the sun god.

10   You bend them ⟨for⟩ the son whom you love;
Though you are far, your rays are on earth,
Though one sees you, your strides are unseen.

When you set in western lightland,
Earth is in darkness as if in death;
15   One sleeps in chambers, heads covered,
One eye does not see another.
Were they robbed of their goods,
That are under their heads,
People would not remark it.
20   Every lion comes from its den,
All the serpents bite;
Darkness hovers, earth is silent,
As their maker rests in lightland.

Earth brightens when you dawn in lightland,
25   When you shine as Aten of daytime;
As you dispel the dark,

As you cast your rays,
The Two Lands° are in festivity.
Awake they stand on their feet,
30 You have roused them;
Bodies cleansed, clothed,
Their arms adore your appearance.
The entire land sets out to work,
All beasts browse on their herbs;
35 Trees, herbs are sprouting,
Birds fly from their nests,
Their wings greeting your *ka.*°
All flocks frisk on their feet,
All that fly up and alight,
40 They live when you dawn for them.
Ships fare north, fare south as well,
Roads lie open when you rise;
The fish in the river dart before you,
Your rays are in the midst of the sea. . . .

28. **The Two Lands:** Upper and Lower Egypt.

37. *ka:* life force.

HYMN TO AKHENATEN (DETAIL), ALI SELIM.
Do the images in this modern tapestry match the mood of the ancient poem? Why or why not?

Werner Forman Archive/Ramses Wissa Wassef School/Art Resource, New York

45 How many are your deeds,
    Though hidden from sight,
    O Sole God beside whom there is none!
    You made the earth as you wished, you alone,
    All peoples, herds, and flocks;
50 All upon earth that walk on legs,
    All on high that fly on wings,
    The lands of Khor and Kush,°
    The land of Egypt.
    You set every man in his place,
55 You supply their needs;
    Everyone has his food,
    His lifetime is counted.
    Their tongues differ in speech,
    Their characters likewise;
60 Their skins are distinct,
    For you distinguished the peoples.

    You made Hapy in *dat*,°
    You bring him when you will,
    To nourish the people,
65 For you made them for yourself.
    Lord of all who toils for them,
    Lord of all lands who shines for them,
    Aten of daytime, great in glory!
    All distant lands, you make them live,
70 You made a heavenly Hapy descend for them;
    He makes waves on the mountains like the sea,
    To drench their fields and their towns.
    How excellent are your ways, O Lord of eternity!
    A Hapy from heaven for foreign peoples,
75 And all lands' creatures that walk on legs,
    For Egypt the Hapy who comes from *dat.*

    Your rays nurse all fields,
    When you shine they live, they grow for you;
    You made the seasons to foster all that you
        made,
80 Winter to cool them, heat that they taste you.
    You made the far sky to shine therein,
    To behold all that you made;
    You alone, shining in your form of living Aten,
    Risen, radiant, distant, near.

52. **Khor and Kush:** Syria and Nubia.

62. **Hapy in *dat*:** Hapy is the river Nile; *dat* is the underworld. Ancient Egyptians thought that the Nile came from a river in the underworld.

85 You made millions of forms from yourself alone,
Towns, villages, fields, the river's course;
All eyes observe you upon them,
For you are the Aten of daytime on high. . . .

⟨Those on⟩ earth come from your hand as you
made them,
90 When you have dawned they live,
When you set they die;
You yourself are lifetime, one lives by you.
All eyes are on ⟨your⟩ beauty until you set,
All labor ceases when you rest in the west;
95 When you rise you stir [everyone] for the King,
Every leg is on the move since you founded the
earth.
You rouse them for your son who came from
your body,
The King who lives by Maat,° the Lord of the
Two Lands,
Neferkheprure, Sole-one-of-Re,
100 The Son of Re who lives by Maat,° the Lord of
crowns,
Akhenaten, great in his lifetime;
(And) the great Queen whom he loves, the Lady
of the Two Lands,
Nefer-nefru-Aten Nefertiti,° living forever.

98. **Maat:** The personification of truth, order, and moral law. The ancient Egyptians believed that only those who had followed Maat in life would achieve immortality.

103. **Nefertiti** (nef′ər·tē′tē): Akhenaten's wife, renowned for her beauty.

First Thoughts

Did the speaker's feelings about the sun seem strange to you, or could you understand and sympathize with them?

Identifying Facts

1. The speaker describes the sun's rising as a joyous occasion. How is the setting of the sun described?
2. Reread lines 45–88. Make a list of the things that Aten creates or makes possible.
3. A **hymn** is a song of praise. What attributes, or characteristics, of Aten does the speaker praise?

Interpreting Meanings

1. **Apostrophe** is a figure of speech in which a writer addresses some thing, concept, or absent person. Apostrophes are written in the **second person**, using the pronouns *you* and *yours*. Find three examples of apostrophe in "The Great Hymn to the Aten." How does the use of apostrophe convey respect to Aten?
2. An **epithet** is a brief descriptive name, title, or adjective that qualifies a person, place, or thing. An epithet appears in the second line of the hymn: "living Aten, creator of life!" Find two or three other epithets in the hymn. To what characteristics of Aten do they refer? What do they tell you about the relationship between Aten and his people?

3. This **hymn**, like other hymns and praise songs, was probably composed to be recited. What aspects of the poem make it particularly suitable for oral presentation? In your response, consider such features of the poem as **repetition**, **parallelism**, and the use of **apostrophe**. Read the poem aloud to hear its other oral characteristics.

Applying Meanings

"The Great Hymn to the Aten" is a celebration of an aspect of nature. Name some of the ways that people today celebrate or praise nature. How is our attitude toward nature similar to or different from the ancient Egyptians'?

Creative Writing Response

Writing a Hymn to the Sun. Refer to the cluster you made in your Writer's Response. In verse or prose, write a hymn in which you praise the sun's attributes and its contributions to life on earth. Remember that you are writing at the request of an environmental group and that your audience will be contemporary Americans, not ancient Egyptians. Don't hesitate to incorporate aspects of modern life in your hymn. Try to use several powerful **epithets**—descriptive words and phrases—in your hymn. If you wish, you may use **apostrophe** in your hymn, but be sure to maintain a consistent **second-person point of view**, addressing your subject, the sun, as *you*.

BEHIND THE SCENES

Daily Life in Ancient Egypt

Imagine yourself a New Kingdom Egyptian teenager, a member of the privileged upper classes. Your father, a high-ranking government worker, is wealthy. You live on an estate on the outskirts of Thebes, a center of government that lies on the banks of the Nile. Your colorfully decorated home has two stories plus a roof patio, a walled garden, and twenty rooms, counting guest rooms, toilets and baths, servants' quarters, and a shrine for daily worship. You may have a lotus pool filled with fish, and there is probably at least one pampered cat who shares your estate.

You wake up each morning in your slanted wooden bed, the head higher than the foot, with a brightly painted board at the lower end to keep you from sliding off. You don't use a pillow; instead, your head is supported by a wooden stand, made to measure for you and attached to the bedframe. You dress in a white, linen kilt; over this, you wear a short-sleeved robe, also of white linen. These fashions have not changed much over the years; in fact, your ancestors hundreds of years earlier probably wore similar garb. Whether you are male or female, you don jewelry: a head circlet, bracelets, anklets, and a necklace made of silver and semiprecious blue and red stones. You rub yourself with oil and use a black cosmetic, *kohl* (kōl), as eye makeup. Finally, you don a heavy wig, both for the sake of appearance and for protection from the sun. Then you hurry, barefoot, to join your family at the shrine just inside the gates of your home.

In the shrine, busts of your ancestors, as well as statues of gods and goddesses, line the walls. Among them are a likeness of Bast, the goddess of joy and love; a statue of Hathor, the cow-headed goddess of music, dance, and maternal love; and the statue of a local god, Bes, a lion-headed dwarf who wards off evil spirits. You and your family offer food and incense to the deities in the shrine as the busts of your ancestors look on from their honored positions in the holy place.

Afterwards, your family eats breakfast, older boys and men in one area, women and children in another. Sitting on cushions, people help themselves to plates of fruit, breads and cakes, and cheese or cold, spiced meat, eating with their fingers. After eating, your father goes to work. The younger children, wearing few or no clothes, run off to play with their balls, dolls, and toy animals. If you are a girl, you and your mother begin your daily tasks, working with your father's steward to supervise the buying, cooking, brewing, weaving, and other details of managing a large household. If you are a boy, you probably help oversee the crops and livestock raised on your parents' land.

At some point during the day, you join your brothers and sisters for a religion lesson from your mother. She tells you the story of Osiris and Isis, then explains that, centuries before, people believed that only the pharaoh and his family could have eternal life. Now, however, Egyptians believe that anyone can enter the afterlife by living virtuously and by having the correct rituals performed after death.

Your brother is preparing to enter your father's profession. As is customary, one of the sons in an Egyptian family is chosen to follow in his father's footsteps. Like the apprentices of all government workers, whether tax collectors, judges, administrators, or high officials, your brother began scribal training at the age of five. By copying words and texts and taking dictation, he has learned to read and write both hieroglyphics and cuneiform (see pages 83 and 204), for dealing with other countries. Now, at sixteen, he is almost ready to "graduate" and begin work in the branch of civil service he has chosen.

Your brother's best friend plans on entering the profession of his father, a priest. His training, however, will not even begin until he turns seventeen. Then he will be required to shave his head and enter a temple school, learning to read and write hieroglyphics and to perform the ritual chants, dramas, and activities associated with the worship of the gods.

Unlike your brother and his friend, you haven't had any formal schooling. But, if you are male, you are learning all you need to know to run an estate: mathematics for accounting, geometry for resurveying your family's land after the Nile's annual floodwaters subside, and natural sciences for plant and animal husbandry.

Your life is not all work, however. In your free time, you can choose from many recreational activities: board games, hunting, wrestling, dancing, swimming, and other sports. You enjoy life in this world, even though you spend a great deal of time preparing yourself for the next world. Your family is very important to you, and it is in the home that you learn the beliefs and values that will govern your adult life as an upper-class Egyptian. Although you may not realize it, you are one of the most privileged people alive in the ancient world, a member of a mighty civilization that will thrive, all told, for almost three thousand years.

Scala/Art Resource, New York

Egyptian Book of the Dead papyrus. *This scene shows the domestic tasks that must be carried out even in the afterlife.*

Reader's Guide

NEW KINGDOM LOVE LYRICS

Background

Lyric poems do not tell a story but instead, like songs, create a vivid, expressive testament to a speaker's thoughts or emotional state. Lyric poetry was already being composed in ancient Egypt during the Middle Kingdom period. However, love lyrics—a specific type of lyric poetry—come to us only from the New Kingdom. Most scholars think that these New Kingdom love poems were, in fact, written to be sung, perhaps accompanied by a harp or a set of reed pipes.

In both of the following poems, the speaker is someone quite different from the poet. Although the language in the poems is fresh and simple, conveying the heartfelt language of young lovers, the lyrics' complex figures of speech and careful meter suggest that the poets were highly skilled and well educated, probably wealthy male members of the pharaoh's court.

Oral Response

Think of some love songs you have heard. As a class, brainstorm a list of common characteristics of popular love songs: the feelings they address, the figures of speech they use, the situations they describe. What qualities do these songs emphasize? What emotions do they celebrate? Write these characteristics on the chalkboard. What common features did you discover?

Literary Focus

The **speaker** of a poem is the voice that addresses us. The speaker expresses emotions or ideas that may or may not be those of the poet. It is helpful to think of the speaker as a character who may be very different from the poet: a different age, race, or gender, for example. Readers should not assume that the speaker and the poet are one and the same.

New Kingdom Love Lyrics

translated by
William Kelley Simpson

> *As you read, note how these ancient poems express themes that are common to the love poetry of all ages and cultures. Could these poems have been written in modern times?*

The Voice of the Wild Goose

The voice of the wild goose,
caught by the bait, cries out.
Love of you holds me back,
and I can't loosen it at all.

5   I shall set aside my nets.
But what can I tell my mother
to whom I return every day
when I am laden with catch?

     I did not set my traps today;
10   love of you has thus entrapped me.

Ray Richardson/Animals Animals

Most Beautiful Youth Who Ever Happened

Most beautiful youth who ever happened,
I want to take your house as housekeeper;
we are arm in arm,
and love of you goes round and round.

5   I say to my heart within me in prayer:
if far away from me is my lover tonight,
then I am like someone already in the grave.
Are you not indeed well-being and life?

     Joy has come to me through your well-being,
10   my heart seeks you out.

How would you describe the feelings of the speakers? Did you identify with them at all?

Identifying Facts

1. What does the speaker in the first poem do every day? Why is this day different?
2. What does the speaker in the second poem want to do?

Interpreting Meanings

1. How would you describe the speakers in these poems?
2. What is the speaker's **tone**, or attitude, toward love in each poem?
3. In "The Voice of the Wild Goose," love serves as a kind of trap. How is this **metaphor**, or comparison, appropriate? How does the metaphor comment on the notion of "true love"?

Applying Meanings

Each poem mentions a negative aspect of love. State these aspects in a few words. In your experience, do you think negative aspects are inevitable consequences of love? Why or why not?

Creative Writing Response

Writing as a Different Speaker. Try writing a love poem or love letter in which you create a speaker who is quite different from yourself. You might wish to write as a historical or literary figure, or even as a popular media figure such as an actor, a football player, or a politician. Let your imagination run wild, and be sure that your poem or letter is a convincing expression of the feelings of someone who is very different from you.

Critical Writing Response

Comparing Love Poems. Emily Dickinson was a reclusive American poet (1830–1886) whose poems expressed tremendous feelings of love and desire, often using strikingly original images and metaphors. Compare the following poem by Dickinson to the two Egyptian love poems you have read. In two or three paragraphs, explain the similarities and differences you see in these poems. Consider the speaker in each, the emotions that are expressed, and the imagery.

> It's All I Have to Bring Today—
> Emily Dickinson
>
> It's all I have to bring today—
> This, and my heart beside—
> This, and my heart, and all the fields—
> And all the meadows wide—
> Be sure you count—should I forget
> Some one the sum could tell—
> This, and my heart, and all the Bees
> Which in the Clover dwell.

Language and Vocabulary

Clichés

Clichés (klē·shāz′) are words or phrases, often figures of speech, that have been used so often that they have become lifeless and almost meaningless. "Love makes the world go round," "The language of love," and "Love is blind" are only a few of the dozens of clichés associated with the topic of love.

See if you can identify the clichés in the following sentences. Then, challenge yourself by rewriting them, removing all clichés and replacing them with original language.

1. I've been wearing my heart on my sleeve ever since you first looked at me.
2. I'm just a loser at the game of love.
3. Even though she broke my heart, love still has me in its clutches.
4. My heart pounds and my palms sweat every time I see him.

THE ART OF TRANSLATION

Egyptian Hieroglyphics

The ancient Egyptians were among the earliest civilizations to create a written language and literature. They called their writing "the words of the god" and believed that it was invented by Thoth, god of wisdom and patron of scribes. Only the Sumerians, who lived in what is now Iraq, developed a writing system as early—probably between 4000 and 3000 B.C. The literature of the Old Kingdom period, including the *Pyramid Texts* and the *Instructions of Wisdom*, dates from the middle of the third millenium B.C.

Hieroglyphics (hī′ər·ō′glif′iks) is a form of written language in which pictures represent ideas. Hieroglyphic writing was beautiful and ornamental, and it was often painted or carved into wood or stone, although the Egyptians did much of their writing on papyrus scrolls, using pen and ink. Over time, hieroglyphic symbols began to represent syllables and sounds, rather than ideas. In addition, two simplified, cursive forms of hieroglyphics evolved: **hieratic** (hī′ər·at′ik) and **demotic** (dē·mät′ik).

Around the fourth century A.D., when alphabetical writing began to replace hieroglyphics in Egypt, the knowledge needed to unlock the meaning of hieroglyphics was lost. By the Middle Ages, scholars took little interest in hieroglyphics

The Granger Collection, New York

The Rosetta Stone

and believed that they represented a mystical code intelligible only to ancient Egyptian priests. This was far from the truth. The hieroglyphic writings translated so far record everything from laundry lists to love poems.

Interest in hieroglyphics revived somewhat during the Renaissance, and a number of European scholars made it their lives' work to translate the cryptic writing. But none could make the mysteriously beautiful pictures "talk." Hieroglyphics would have kept their stony silence had not an officer in Napoleon's army discovered the Rosetta Stone near Rashid, Egypt, in 1799. This famous stone records a decree of King Ptolemy V (circa 196 B.C.) in three different scripts: one in hieroglyphics, one in demotic script, and one in Greek. By comparing the three texts, a French scholar, Jean François Champollion (shän·pô·lyōn′), was able to break the "code" of hieroglyphic writing in 1822. Because of Champollion's work, hieroglyphics can now be understood relatively easily with help from a hieroglyphic dictionary. But because hieroglyphics represent only consonants, without vowel sounds, scholars today are not sure how to pronounce the ancient Egyptian tongue.

Reader's Guide

AFRICAN PROVERBS

Background

In the oral literatures of the various peoples of Africa, proverbs are much more than quaint old sayings. Instead, they represent a poetic form that uses few words but achieves great depth of meaning. In cultures that have no written literature, proverbs function as the distilled essence of a people's values and knowledge. They are used to settle legal disputes, resolve ethical problems, and teach children the philosophy of their people. Because proverbs often contain puns, rhymes, and clever allusions, they also provide entertainment. Speakers who know and use such proverbs have power within the community; their eloquence makes others want to listen to them, and their ability to apply the proverbs to appropriate circumstances demonstrates an understanding of social and political realities. More than one modern African leader has turned to the wisdom of proverbs in order to make decisions and to gain popular support and respect.

Proverbs are memorable not only because they are so brief (usually no more than a sentence) but also because, like poetry, they compress sometimes complicated ideas into a few thoughtfully crafted words. And unlike many other forms of literature, they can be easily translated into another language.

Oral Response

As a class, brainstorm as many English proverbs as you can: "It's no use crying over spilled milk," "A penny saved is a penny earned," and so on. Write the proverbs on the chalkboard. Then choose a proverb that is particularly meaningful to you and tell how you have experienced the truth of that proverb in your everyday life.

Literary Focus

A **proverb** is a short saying that expresses a common truth or experience, usually about human failings and the ways that people interact with one another. Proverbs often incorporate such literary elements as **metaphor** ("An ounce of prevention is worth a pound of cure"), **alliteration** ("He who laughs last laughs best"), **parallelism** ("Where there's a will, there's a way"), and **rhyme** ("When the cat's away, the mice will play").

AFRICAN PROVERBS

The proverbs of several African groups are presented in this selection. The proverbs are listed by ethnic group, with the name of the country of origin in parentheses. Sometimes two groups have proverbs whose meaning is the same, but whose wording and imagery are different. Look for examples of these as you read. Do any of these proverbs remind you of proverbs you already know? What is specifically African about them?

Jabo (Liberia)

One does not embrace the leopard.

It is not only giants that do great things.

If you have nothing you are anxious to please.

The man who listens is the one who understands.

Ashanti (Ghana)

One bird in your hand is better than ten birds in the sky.

When a nation is about to come to ruin, the cause begins in the homes of its people.

What is bad luck for one man is good luck for another.

Ashanti gold weight illustrating the proverb, "The bird's relation is the one he sits next to."

Marc & Evelyne Bernheim/Woodfin Camp & Associates

No one knows the story of tomorrow's dawn.

When you do not know how to dance, then you say, "The drum is not sounding sweetly."

If one finger tries to pick up something from the ground, it cannot.

Yoruba (Nigeria)

One who asks never loses his way.

A person who has only one set of clothing does not play in the rain.

However large the ear, it cannot hear seven speeches at once.

He whom one loves never does anything wrong.

A delicious stew does not last long in the pot.

A river does not flow so far that it forgets its source.

The path does not close on a man with a machete.[1]

---

1. **machete** (mə·shet′ē): a large, curved knifelike instrument used as a weapon and for cutting through bushes or underbrush.

Baganda (Uganda)

Those who love each other need only a small place.

Loose teeth are better than no teeth.

One who refuses you beans saves you from indigestion.

The man who has not carried loads himself does not know how heavy they are.

A tree does not fall on one who is not there.

Wherever the snail goes, there also goes the shell.

Where there are no dogs, the weasels play.

Words are easy, but real friendship is difficult.

Silence finishes the argument.

Masai (Tanzania/Kenya)

Best of all advisors is the one who says what you would say.

The polite lie is better than the forceful truth.

The zebra does not despise its stripes.

Don't fight a lion with a stick.

The elephant is not burdened by its own tusks.

The eye with hatred in it can bore through stone.

There is no hill that never ends.

Yoruba fetish. *A fetish is an object believed to have magical powers.*

Zulu (Zululand, South Africa)

Do not speak of a rhinoceros if there is no tree nearby.

Even when there is no cock, day dawns.

One does not follow a snake into its hole.

One gets drowned even in shallow water.

The house of the talkative person lets in rain.

No snake ever forgot its hole.

Magic takes time.

First Thoughts

Which of these proverbs would you most like to remember and use in your everyday life? Which ones did you have difficulty understanding?

Interpreting Meanings

1. Which Masai proverb tells you that the Masai value courtesy and diplomacy?
2. Which Baganda proverb is similar to the American expression "When the cat's away, the mice will play"?
3. The Yoruban "A river does not flow so far that it forgets its source" has much the same meaning as the Zulu "No snake ever forgot its hole." Locate another example of proverbs from different groups that have a similar meaning. Explain the meaning.

Applying Meanings

Decide which of the African proverbs you liked best. Did you prefer the humorous ones, the direct ones, or the political ones? Compare them with the proverbs you thought of in the Oral Response. Explain how your choices reflect your own values, principles, and sense of humor.

Creative Writing Response

1. **Dramatizing a Proverb.** Proverbs are similar to **morals**—the brief statements that appear at the end of many fables. A moral directly states the lesson the fable has taught. Choose a favorite African proverb and imagine that it is attached to the end of a fable. With a partner or a small group, write the fable that would dramatize the meaning of the proverb you have selected. Then act out the fable and have the class guess what the proverb is.

2. **Creating Your Own Proverbs.** Proverbs have stood the test of time because they address general truths. Is there some common truth of modern life that has not, as far as you know, been made the subject of a proverb? Think of an example and create a proverb that addresses it. Don't hesitate to use modern language or slang. If you can't think of a new topic, try updating or modernizing a well-known proverb.

ELEMENTS OF LITERATURE

Features of African Oral Literature

African orature, like other oral literature, is distinguished by its use of **repetition** and **parallel structure**. These techniques involve the repetition of words, phrases, lines, and sentence structures throughout a poem or tale. Such repetitions probably serve foremost as memory aids for griots and other storytellers. But repetition has other uses as well. It creates rhythm, builds suspense, and adds emphasis to parts of a poem or narrative. Repeated lines, or **refrains**, often mark places where an audience can join in the oral performance.

Another feature of African oral literature is the **repeat-and-vary** technique, in which lines or phrases are repeated with slight variations—sometimes just by changing a single word. In addition, African oral poems employ the sound device of **tonal assonance**. Most of the languages of Africa, like many Asian languages, are **tonal**; that is, the tones in which syllables are spoken determine the meanings of words. For example, in a Bantu language spoken in Cameroon, one word can mean "payment" if spoken in a high tone, and "crossroads" if spoken in a low tone. Though English is not tonal, we can get some idea of tonality if we think of the way we say "Uh, huh" for "Yes," "Uh, uh" for "No," and "Uh, oh" as a warning. In fact, linguists believe that these three expressions may have come to America with the African slave trade.

The tradition of African orature involves much more than the delivery of memorized words. Presentations of oral literature almost always include spirited audience participation. In certain types of oral poetry, such as chants (see page 95), the listeners join in the chorus or chime in at other key points, underscoring lines and phrases with feeling. In addition, songs and tales sometimes use the **call-and-response** format, in which the leader calls out a line or phrase and the audience responds with an answering line or phrase, becoming performers themselves. Audiences listening to oral tales participate freely in singing the songs and shouting the proverbs that accompany the tales, as well as providing cheers, catcalls, and advice to the performer. This kind of audience involvement can even alter the form and content of a tale. In ways not immediately apparent to readers, then, Africa's orature is truly a living, dynamic literature.

Werner Forman Archive/Art Resource, New York

Musicians of the court of Temi of Ede (Nigeria) use talking drums to announce the arrival of a dignitary.

Reader's Guide

SONG OF A MOTHER TO HER FIRSTBORN

Background

This **cradle song** represents an important type of oral poetry. For centuries, African women have created poems like this to be chanted or sung. While the tender words and lulling repetitions express the mother's love, they also entertain and soothe the baby.

In the Didinga and Lango cultures of Uganda, as in many others, children are seen as a kind of immortality for the parents. The naming of a child involves a ceremony—mentioned in this poem—which does not occur until a certain number of days after the birth. The poem also mentions the traditions of a neighboring group, who believe that their gods will try to harm a child if it seems valuable. This neighboring group gives children names like ''Worthless One'' in order to trick the gods into sparing the child. But the mother who sings this poem reassures her baby that the gods of his own people are kind and wish him well. She refers, as well, to the positive changes the baby has made in her life and in his father's life, and she predicts that the baby will one day become a father in his turn and a great leader. In these ways, the poem places the new baby firmly within his family and within the social and religious traditions of his people.

Writer's Response

What do you think children need to know? In a paragraph, summarize what you would tell your children if you were a parent. Explain why it would be important to communicate those things.

Literary Focus

The narrator in this poem uses **figurative language** to show her love for her child. As you read, look for **similes** (indirect comparisons using the words *as* or *like*: *free as a bird*) and **metaphors** (direct comparisons made without the use of the words *as* or *like*: *time is money*).

SONG OF A MOTHER TO HER FIRSTBORN

A Didinga or Lango Cradle Song (Uganda)

translated by

JACK H. DRIBERG

> Have you ever seen a newborn baby? Many people find babies, with their small, puckered faces, far from beautiful. After reading to line 33, stop and notice how the speaker in this poem has described her baby's appearance. What does her choice of words tell you about her and her response to her child?

Speak to me, child of my heart.
Speak to me with your eyes, your round laughing
    eyes,
Wet and shining as Lupeyo's bull-calf.

Speak to me little one,
5 Clutching my breast with your hand,
So strong and firm for all its littleness.
It will be the hand of a warrior, my son,
A hand that will gladden your father.
See how eagerly it fastens on me:
10 It thinks already of a spear.
O son, you will have a warrior's name and be a
    leader of men.
And your sons, and your sons' sons, will
    remember you long after you have slipped into
    darkness.
But I, I shall always remember your hand
    clutching me so.
I shall recall how you lay in my arms,
15 And looked at me so, and so,
And how your tiny hands played with my bosom.
And when they name you great warrior, then will
    my eyes be wet with remembering.

Ugandan women walking to work in the fields.

And how shall we name you, little warrior?
See, let us play at naming.
20 It will not be a name of despisal, for you are my
firstborn.
Not as Nawal's son is named will you be named.
Our gods will be kinder to you than theirs.
Must we call you "Insolence" or "Worthless One"?
Shall you be named, like a child of ill fortune,
after the dung of cattle?
25 Our gods need no cheating, my child:
They wish you no ill.
They have washed your body and clothed it with
beauty.
They have set a fire in your eyes.
And the little puckering ridges of your brows—
30 Are they not the seal of their fingerprints when
they fashioned you?
They have given you beauty and strength, child of
my heart,
And wisdom is already shining in your eyes,
And laughter.
So how shall we name you, little one?
35 Are you your father's father, or his brother, or yet
another?

Song of a Mother to Her Firstborn **91**

Whose spirit is it that is in you, little warrior?
Whose spear-hand tightens round my breast?
Who lives in you and quickens to life, like last
    year's melon seed?
Are you silent, then?
40 But your eyes are thinking, thinking, and glowing
    like the eyes of a leopard in a thicket.
Well, let be.
At the day of the naming you will tell us.

O my child, now indeed I am happy.
Now indeed I am a wife—
45 No more a bride, but a Mother-of-one.
Be splendid and magnificent, child of desire.
Be proud as I am proud.
Be happy as I am happy.
Be loved as now I am loved.
50 Child, child, child, love I have had from my man.
But now, only now, have I the fullness of love.
Now, only now, am I his wife and the mother of
    his firstborn.
His soul is safe in your keeping, my child, and it
    was I, I, I who have made you.
Therefore am I loved.
55 Therefore am I happy.
Therefore am I a wife.
Therefore have I great honor.

You will tend his shrine when he is gone.
With sacrifice and oblation you will recall his
    name year by year.
60 He will live in your prayers, my child,
And there will be no more death for him, but
    everlasting life springing from your loins.
You are his shield and his spear, his hope and
    redemption from the dead.
Through you he will be reborn, as the saplings in
    the Spring.
And I, I am the mother of his firstborn.
65 Sleep, child of beauty and courage and fulfillment,
    sleep.
I am content.

Robert Harding Picture Library

Ugandan woman working in the field.
*What kind of life does the mother in
this poem want for her child?*

As you read this poem, you probably formed mental images of both the baby and the mother. How did you visualize them in your mind?

Identifying Facts

1. What have the gods done for the baby?
2. What does the mother finally decide about the baby's name?
3. How has the baby brought "great honor" to his mother?

Interpreting Meanings

1. Much of the **imagery** in this poem centers on the baby's eyes. How are they described throughout the poem? What does this imagery tell you about the mother's feelings for her baby?
2. In lines 29–30, to what are the baby's wrinkled brows compared? What kind of **figure of speech** is used in this comparison?
3. List all the things to which the child is compared. What characteristics and strengths do these things suggest?
4. How will the child fulfill his father's immortality?

Applying Meanings

Think about the hopes that parents today have for their children and for their children's future positions in society. How do you think these hopes are like those expressed in the poem? How are they different?

Creative Writing Response

Composing a Chant. Reread the paragraph you wrote for the Writer's Response on page 89, about what you would like to tell your children. Compose a song or chant, perhaps similar in form to "Song of a Mother to Her Firstborn," in which you restate some of the ideas from your paragraph. In your chant, use **metaphors** and **similes** to create vivid images and to make your meaning clear.

Critical Writing Response

Making and Supporting a Generalization. Based on the evidence in this poem, what can you generalize about the roles of men and women in the Didinga and Lango cultures, and the expectations that are held for their lives? Consider especially the mother's hopes and expectations for her son and the effect that his birth will have on her own life. In a three-paragraph essay, support your generalization with at least three examples from the poem. In your final paragraph, explain the limitations of making such generalizations about an entire culture based on only one poem. You may use a chart like the one below to organize your essay.

	Generalized Role	Lines in Poem that Support Generalization
Male		
Female		

Reader's Guide

OGUN KILLS ON THE RIGHT

Background

There are more than twenty million Yoruba (yō'rōō·bə) speakers in West Africa. Folklorist Roger D. Abrahams describes them as "a nation within a nation, with important 'colonies' in Haiti, Brazil, Cuba, and Trinidad . . . An ancient city society [with] one of the most fully documented expressive cultures in the Old World." In the complex Yoruba society, hunters, fishermen, and farmers all have their own guilds or trade groups, and each trade group has its own lore and traditions. These traditions include oral poems chanted at group gatherings such as meetings, festivals, or funerals. "Ogun Kills on the Right" is an example of the oral poetry of the hunters' group. Such oral poems are usually accompanied by drumming.

Ogun, the god of iron and war, is a central figure in all hunters' poetry. Whether or not he is mentioned in a poem, he is considered the moving force behind the poem. Just as the jungle is unrelenting, Ogun too is unrelenting: a god of iron, bloodshed, war, vengeance, and fury, but also of heroism and great generosity.

Oral Response

Think of any community organizations, such as the Boy Scouts, Girl Scouts, or a local church, that you might be familiar with. What kinds of ceremonies do these groups perform at their gatherings? Share your knowledge with the class. Discuss what the meaning or function of these ceremonies might be.

Literary Focus

Repetition and **parallelism** create rhythm and build suspense in this poem. Repetition is used to create emphasis. If a certain word or phrase is repeated often enough, the reader is more likely to pay attention and remember it. Parallelism—the repetition of words, phrases, or sentences that have the same grammatical structure or state a similar idea—is used for its poetic effects and its ability to build suspense. Repetition and parallelism are especially important in oral literature because repeating sounds and phrases helps the process of memorization and builds audience anticipation.

OGUN KILLS ON THE RIGHT
A Yoruban Oral Poem (Nigeria)
translated by

ULLI BEIER AND BAKARE GBADAMOSI

At a certain point, this poem turns, or changes, from a list of the god's attributes, or personal qualities, to a plea for his protection. Which line marks the turn?

Ogun kills on the right and destroys on the right.
Ogun kills on the left and destroys on the left.
Ogun kills suddenly in the house and suddenly in
    the field.
Ogun kills the child with the iron with which it
    plays.
5   Ogun kills in silence.

Ogun kills the thief and the owner of stolen
    goods.
Ogun kills the owner of the house,
and paints the hearth with his blood.

Ogun is the forest god.
10   He gives all his clothes to the beggars.
He gives one to the woodcock—who dyes it in
    indigo.°
He gives one to the coucal—who dyes it in
    camwood.°
He gives one to the cattle egret°—who leaves it
    white.

Ogun's laughter is no joke.
15   His enemies scatter in all directions.
The butterflies do not have to see the leopard . . .
they scatter in all directions!

Master of iron, chief of robbers,
you have water, but you bathe in blood.

Ogboni staff.

Collection High Museum of Art, Atlanta: The Fred and Rita Richman Collection. 1980.500.74

11. **woodcock:** a large, long-beaked bird mottled in bluish black and grey. **indigo:** a plant yielding a deep blue-black dye.
12. **coucal:** a long-tailed, reddish brown and black bird, resembling a pheasant. **camwood:** an African hardwood tree yielding a red-brown dye.
13. **cattle egret:** a long-necked, white-plumed bird.

20 The light shining in your face
   is not easy to behold:
   Ogun, with the bloody cap,
   let me see the red of your eye.

   Ogun is not like pounded yam:
25 do you think you can knead him in your hand
   and eat of him until you are satisfied?
   Do you think Ogun is something you can throw
      into your cap
   and walk away with it?

   Ogun is a mad god
30 who will ask questions after seven hundred and
      eighty years.
   Ogun have pity on me:
   whether I can reply, or whether I cannot reply:
   Ogun don't ask me anything!

   The lion never allows anybody to play with his
      cub.
35 Ogun will never allow his child to be punished.
   Ogun do not reject me!
   Does the woman who spins ever reject a spindle?
   Does the woman who dyes ever reject a cloth?
   Does the eye that sees ever reject a sight?
40 Ogun, do not reject me.

Indiana University Art Museum 70.50. Photo by Michael Cavanagh, Kevin Montague

Nigerian shrine figure. *Objects and poems are often used in ritual ceremonies.*
What function do you think this poem served in the Yoruban hunters' ceremonies?

First Thoughts

Based on the list of his attributes, or qualities, listed in this poem, what do you think of Ogun? Why do you think the speaker wants Ogun's protection?

Identifying Facts

1. How does Ogun deal with thieves?
2. According to the speaker in the poem, what is Ogun *not* like?

Interpreting Meanings

1. **Repetition** can be used to emphasize certain words, as well as to create rhythm. In the first stanza, which words and phrases are repeated? What do they emphasize?
2. What can you **infer** about the god's character from this statement: "Ogun's laughter is no joke"?
3. In the last three stanzas of this chant, **parallelism** is used to create rhythm and to group similar ideas. Find two sets of questions that are parallel in structure. What ideas are expressed by each set of questions?

Applying Meanings

Ogun is a god of contradictions. He is vengeful as well as generous. How do you think Ogun reflects his people's understanding of the forces of nature?

Creative Response

Drawing a Character in the Poem. Write a list of Ogun's characteristics, both **concrete**, or tangible, and **abstract**, or intangible. Then sketch Ogun as you visualize him. If you wish, use colored pencils, pastels, paints, or even make a collage to complete the likeness.

Critical Writing Response

Comparing Poems. The following fragment of a hunters' poem comes from Gabon, on Africa's west coast. In what ways is it similar to "Ogun"?

> from The Elephant II
> translated by
> C. M. Bowra
>
> In the frightened forest the tree sleeps, the
>   leaves are dead,
> the monkeys have closed their eyes, hanging
>   from the branches above us:
> the antelopes slip past us with silent steps,
> eat the fresh grass, prick their ears,
> lift their heads and listen frightened:
> the cicada is silent, stops his grinding song.
> Elephant hunter, take your bow!
> *Elephant hunter, take your bow!*
>
> In the forest where no one passes but you,
> hunter, lift up your heart, leap and walk:
> meat in front of you, the huge piece of meat,
> the meat that walks like a hill,
> the meat that makes the heart glad,
> the meat that we'll roast on our coals,
> the meat into which our teeth sink,
> the fine red meat and the blood we drink
>   smoking.
>
> Elephant hunter, take your bow!
> *Elephant hunter, take your bow!*

Write a two- or three-paragraph essay explaining the similarities between "The Elephant II" and "Ogun Kills on the Right." Compare the uses of **parallelism**, **repetition**, and **imagery** in the two poems. A chart similar to the following may help you.

	"Ogun Kills . . ."	"The Elephant II"
Parallel structure		
Repetition		
Imagery		

TALK
An Ashanti Tale (Ghana)
retold by
HAROLD COURLANDER

Reader's Guide

Background The following tale comes from the Ashanti, whose traditional homeland is the dense and hilly forest beyond the city of Kumasi in south-central Ghana. There the Ashanti cleared the jungle for small farms, fished the rivers, hunted, and pursued their skills in weaving, metalworking, and other arts. Ghana was colonized by the British in the mid-nineteenth century and exploited for its gold and other natural resources. But the Ashanti, protected in their geographical stronghold, were able to maintain their ancient culture. Ghana regained its independence in 1960. Today Ashanti people live in all parts of the country.

Writer's Response Imagine that some inanimate object you use often, such as this textbook or your pen, could talk. What might it tell you? Write several lines of dialogue between yourself and the object.

Literary Focus **Irony** is the contrast between expectation and reality. In **situational irony**, what happens is very different from what we expect to happen. Ironic contrast can be very humorous, as this African tale shows.

TALK

The first sentence in this tale establishes the setting as real and specific, leading the reader to expect a realistic story. What happens to your expectations in the second sentence?

A farmer went out to his field one morning to dig up some yams. While he was digging, one of the yams said to him: "Well, at last you're here. You never weeded me, but now you come around with your digging stick. Go away and leave me alone!"

The farmer turned around and looked at his cow in amazement. The cow was chewing her cud and looking at him.

"Did you say something?" he asked.

The cow kept on chewing and said nothing, but the man's dog spoke up.

"It wasn't the cow who spoke to you," the dog said. "It was the yam. The yam says leave him alone."

The man became angry, because his dog had never talked before, and he didn't like his tone besides. So he took his knife and cut a branch from a palm tree to whip his dog. Just then the palm tree said, "Put that branch down!"

The man was getting very upset about the way things were going, and he started to throw the palm branch away, but the palm branch said, "Man, put me down softly!"

He put the branch down gently on a stone, and the stone said, "Hey, take that thing off me!"

This was enough, and the frightened farmer started to run for his village. On the way he met a fisherman going the other way with a fish trap on his head.

"What's the hurry?" the fisherman asked.

"My yam said, 'Leave me alone!' Then the dog said, 'Listen to what the yam says!' When I went to whip the dog with a palm branch the tree said, 'Put that branch down!' Then the palm branch said, 'Do it softly!' Then the stone said, 'Take that thing off me!' "

"Is that all?" the man with the fish trap asked. "Is that so frightening?"

"Well," the man's fish trap said, "did he take it off the stone?"

"Wah!" the fisherman shouted. He threw the fish trap on the ground and began to run with the farmer, and on the trail they met a weaver with a bundle of cloth on his head.

"Where are you going in such a rush?" he asked them.

"My yam said, 'Leave me alone!' " the farmer said. "The dog said, 'Listen to what the yam says!' The tree said, 'Put that branch down!' The branch said, 'Do it softly!' And the stone said, 'Take that thing off me!' "

"And then," the fisherman continued, "the fish trap said, 'Did he take it off?' "

"That's nothing to get excited about," the weaver said, "no reason at all."

"Oh, yes it is," his bundle of cloth said. "If it happened to you you'd run too!"

"Wah!" the weaver shouted. He threw his bundle on the trail and started running with the other men.

They came panting to the ford in the river and found a man bathing.

Gold insignia worn by the Ashanti king's high servants.

"Are you chasing a gazelle?" he asked them.

The first man said breathlessly: "My yam talked at me, and it said, 'Leave me alone!' And my dog said, 'Listen to your yam!' And when I cut myself a branch the tree said, 'Put that branch down!' And the branch said, 'Do it softly!' And the stone said, 'Take that thing off me!' "

The fisherman panted, "And my trap said, 'Did he?' "

The weaver wheezed, "And my bundle of cloth said, 'You'd run too!' "

"Is that why you're running?" the man in the river asked.

"Well, wouldn't you run if you were in their position?" the river said.

The man jumped out of the water and began to run with the others. They ran down the main street of the village to the house of the chief. The chief's servants brought his stool out, and he came and sat on it to listen to their complaints. The men began to recite their troubles.

"I went out to my garden to dig yams," the farmer said, waving his arms. "Then everything began to talk! My yam said, 'Leave me alone!' My dog said, 'Pay attention to your yam!' The tree said, 'Put that branch down!' The branch said, 'Do it softly!' And the stone said, 'Take it off me!' "

"And my fish trap said, 'Well, did he take it off?' " the fisherman said.

"And my cloth said, 'You'd run too!' " the weaver said.

"And the river said the same," the bather said hoarsely, his eyes bulging.

Ashanti mask.
How does the repetition in this story increase the humor?

The chief listened to them patiently, but he couldn't refrain from scowling.

"Now this is really a wild story," he said at last. "You'd better all go back to your work before I punish you for disturbing the peace."

So the men went away, and the chief shook his head and mumbled to himself, "Nonsense like that upsets the community."

"Fantastic, isn't it?" his stool said. "Imagine, a talking yam!"

First Thoughts

A "punch line" is the final line of a joke. Usually, the punch line is surprising and contains the point of the joke. Did the final line of this story act as a punch line for you?

Identifying Facts

1. What are the yam's reasons for speaking to the farmer?
2. Why does the farmer begin to run?
3. Who joins the farmer as he runs?
4. How does the chief settle the matter?

Interpreting Meanings

1. The storyteller uses **dialogue** as a means of **indirect characterization**. What do the farmer's words reveal about his personality? Name one of the farmer's strengths and one of his weaknesses.
2. This story is based on **situational irony**. What is the first ironic occurrence in the story? What is the main effect of the story's irony?
3. Explain why the story's **title** is, or is not, appropriate. Does it accurately sum up what the story is about, or would you have given the story another title?

Applying Meanings

Did you find that this story became funnier to you as it went along? What would the effect have been if the joke had been shorter?

Critical Writing Response

Identifying a Main Idea. Many folktales from Africa—as well as from other parts of the world—warn about the dangers of talking too much or saying foolish things. Read "The Talking Skull" and, in two or three well-developed paragraphs, compare and contrast it to "Talk." Consider the two stories in terms of action and plot, situational irony, and surprise endings. Does "The Talking Skull" end with a punch line? Does it have a moral? Does "Talk" have a moral, or is it simply an entertaining story?

The Talking Skull
A Nigerian Folktale
translated by
Leo Frobenius and Douglas G. Fox

A hunter goes into the bush. He finds an old human skull. The hunter says: "What brought you here?" The skull answers: "Talking brought me here." The hunter runs off. He runs to the king. He tells the king: "I found a dry human skull in the bush. It asks you how its father and mother are."

The king says: "Never since my mother bore me have I heard that a dead skull can speak." The king summons the Alkali, the Saba, and the Degi, and asks them if they have ever heard the like. None of the wise men has heard the like and they decide to send a guard out with the hunter into the bush to find out if his story is true, and, if so, to learn the reason for it. The guard accompany the hunter into the bush with the order to kill him on the spot should he have lied. The guard and the hunter come to the skull. The hunter addresses the skull: "Skull, speak." The skull is silent. The hunter asks as before: "What brought you here?" The skull does not answer. The whole day long the hunter begs the skull to speak, but it does not answer. In the evening the guard tell the hunter to make the skull speak, and when he cannot they kill him in accordance with the king's command. When the guard are gone the skull opens its jaws and asks the dead hunter's head: "What brought you here?" The dead hunter's head replies: "Talking brought me here!"

Introduction

from Sundiata: An Epic of Old Mali

"I teach kings the history of their ancestors . . . for the world is old, but the future springs from the past."

—Djeli Mamoudou Kouyaté, *Sundiata*

These words of the griot who narrates the Mali epic *Sundiata* (soōn·dyä′tə) could also apply to the epic itself. An **epic**, or long narrative poem, is like a bridge from the past to the future. Epic tales of vanished heroes—partly human, partly superhuman, who embody the highest values of a society—do more than entertain. They also carry a culture's history, values, and traditions forward to future generations.

The Oral Epic

Most ancient epics began as **oral epics**, also known as **primary epics**. Researchers in all parts of the world—from Eastern Europe to Africa—have found oral epics that have yet to be recorded in writing. From listening to these performances, they have learned that an oral epic includes much more than words. Traditional repetitions, gestures, sound effects, songs, and proverbs play an important role in the "live" performance of epics. An oral epic, in fact, is an exciting blend of narrative, poetry, and drama.

It is usually not until long after its form is more-or-less fixed that an epic is written down. As it is written and translated into foreign languages, the epic undergoes another kind of change. Many

---

legend: *a story about extraordinary deeds, based to some extent on fact.*

---

elements of oral epics do not carry over well into writing. Repetition, for example, enlivens an oral performance, but tends to deaden written works. Translators find it difficult to carry over the original poetic elements such as rhyme and meter into foreign languages. But the narrative, or storytelling, elements of epics *do* carry over into writing, and they survive translation easily.

The African Epic Tradition

The African literary tradition boasts of several oral epics. Among them are *The Dausi*, from the Soninke of Sudan; *Monzon and the King of Kore*, from the Bambara of western Africa; the epic of

Askia the Great, medieval ruler of the Songhai empire in western Africa; and the epic of Shaka Zulu, eighteenth-century founder of the Zulu empire of southern Africa. Some African epics have been lost over time. Others survive as fragments. A few African epics have even provided the inspiration for modern African novels. To date, however, the best-preserved, best-known African epic is *Sundiata*, from the Mandingo people of western Africa. This epic is known to several peoples of West Africa and exists in several versions. Like other African epics, *Sundiata* has been preserved and passed on by **griots**, Africa's oral historians and "living libraries."

Sundiata: Fact and Legend

Like most of the world's epics, *Sundiata* is a fascinating blend of fact and legend. Sundiata Keita, the story's hero, really existed. He was a powerful leader who, in 1235, defeated the Sosso nation of western Africa and reestablished the Mandingo Empire of Old Mali. Under Sundiata, Mali expanded from the Atlantic coast to the northern border of present-day Nigeria, including the lands today called Guinea, Gambia, Senegal, Mali, and western Niger. Arts and trade flourished during his reign, and the empire he founded lasted more than 250 years. Sundiata's empire

Marc & Evelyne Bernheim/Woodfin Camp & Associates

Ceremonial mask from Mali.

finally fell to the Songhai, under Askia the Great, in 1493.

But *Sundiata* is not a historical document. Rather, the story of Sundiata, over time, became transmuted into **legend**—a story about extraordinary deeds that has been passed on from one generation to the next. Like all legends, the story of Sundiata is based to some extent on fact, but it is fact that has become greatly embellished over time. Supernatural powers are attributed to Sundiata, and he is involved in a mighty conflict between good and evil.

Sundiata in Written Form

The epic of Sundiata was first recorded in Guinea during the 1950s, when it was told by the griot Djeli Mamoudou Kouyaté (djä′lē mä′mōo·dōo kōo·yä′tā) to folklorist D. T. Niane. No one knows how many centuries old this version of the epic is. Niane edited the epic as he heard it and translated it from Mandingo into French. His version was later translated into English. Because the epic is now "twice removed" from its original source, it has lost many of the features of the original language: its meter, assonance, and alliteration. However, it still contains some of the original songs, repetition, and proverbs that accompanied the oral performance.

Reader's Guide

from SUNDIATA: AN EPIC OF OLD MALI

Background

The hero Sundiata, like other epic heroes, has an unusual childhood
and shows signs of greatness even in these early years. As he grows
up, he endures many trials. He undertakes a long journey into exile
and back before emerging as a leader of his people, one who embodies many of his culture's highest values. The supernatural plays a major role in the epic: Sundiata, as well as his mother, sister, and
enemies, all possess supernatural powers. His story is told in a formal,
elevated style, and the "stage" on which the action takes place is
broad. The events of the epic, including its many detailed battle
scenes, have a wide-ranging significance. All these aspects of *Sundiata*
reflect patterns common to epics throughout the world.

However, the setting and characters in *Sundiata* also reveal the
unique history and traditions of the culture from which the epic
sprang. Mali in the thirteenth century was a powerful kingdom, enriched by alliances with many neighboring nations. Its civilization was
complex and wealthy, its leaders well-educated. But its king, Sundiata's father, died when Sundiata was still a child, leaving Mali vulnerable. An invasion by enemies, the Sossos, is the event that tests
Sundiata's heroism.

Writer's Response

Whom do you consider heroic? Think of a man, woman, or fictional
character whom you consider a hero. In a paragraph, describe your
hero, explaining which qualities make him or her heroic.

Literary Focus

An **epic** is a long narrative work that relates the deeds of a larger-
than-life hero who embodies the values of his or her society. Epics
blend history, legend, and myth and are often told orally for generations before finally being written down.

from SUNDIATA
An Epic of Old Mali
D. T. Niane
translated by

G. D. PICKETT

 These excerpts from Sundiata show the hero in his first childhood triumph and end with his great triumph in adulthood. As you read, note Sundiata's qualities as a leader and hero to his people.

CHARACTERS IN THE EPIC

Maghan Sundiata: the hero of the epic. He is also called "Mari Djata" and "Sogolon Djata."

King Maghan Kon Fatta: Sundiata's father, the king of Mali.

Sogolon Kedjou: Sundiata's mother.

Balla Fasséké: Sundiata's griot.

Sassouma Bérété: the queen mother; the first wife of the king.

Dankaran Touman: Sassouma Bérété's son. He is King Maghan Kon Fatta's successor and Sundiata's half brother.

Soumaoro Kanté: the sorcerer-king of Sosso; Sundiata's nemesis.

from The Lion's Awakening

Maghan Sundiata, also called Mari Djata, is the son of King Maghan Kon Fatta of Mali and his second wife, Sogolon Kedjou. A mysterious hunter has predicted that the boy will one day be a mightier leader than Alexander the Great, the legendary Greek conqueror. Few people believe this prophecy, however, because Mari Djata is already seven years old and has still not learned how to walk. He seems an unlikely candidate for emperor.

King Maghan Kon Fatta dies and his first wife, Sassouma Bérété, makes her own son the king. Always jealous of Mari Djata and his mother, she banishes them to the backyard of the palace, forcing them to live a life of poverty.

Sogolon Kedjou and her children lived on the queen mother's leftovers, but she kept a little garden in the open ground behind the village. It was there that she passed her brightest moments looking after her onions and gnougous.[1] One day she happened to be short of condiments and went to the queen mother to beg a little baobab[2] leaf.

1. **gnougous:** root vegetables.
2. **baobab** (bā'ō·bab'): a tropical tree whose leaves are used as a cooking herb.

Baobab landscape.

? *What role does the baobab tree play in the conflict between Sassouma and Mari Djata (Sundiata)?*

"Look you," said the malicious Sassouma, "I have a calabash[3] full. Help yourself, you poor woman. As for me, my son knew how to walk at seven and it was he who went and picked these baobab leaves. Take them then, since your son is unequal to mine." Then she laughed derisively with that fierce laughter which cuts through your flesh and penetrates right to the bone.

Sogolon Kedjou was dumbfounded. She had never imagined that hate could be so strong in a human being. With a lump in her throat she left Sassouma's. Outside her hut Mari Djata, sitting on his useless legs, was blandly eating out of a calabash. Unable to contain herself any longer, Sogolon burst into sobs and seizing a piece of wood, hit her son.

---

3. **calabash:** a hollowed-out gourd used as a bowl.

"Oh son of misfortune, will you never walk? Through your fault I have just suffered the greatest affront of my life! What have I done, God, for you to punish me in this way?"

Mari Djata seized the piece of wood and, looking at his mother, said, "Mother, what's the matter?"

"Shut up, nothing can ever wash me clean of this insult."

"But what then?"

"Sassouma has just humiliated me over a matter of a baobab leaf. At your age her own son could walk and used to bring his mother baobab leaves."

"Cheer up, Mother, cheer up."

"No. It's too much. I can't."

"Very well then, I am going to walk today," said Mari Djata. "Go and tell my father's smiths to make me the heaviest possible iron rod. Mother, do you want just the leaves of the baobab or would you rather I brought you the whole tree?"

"Ah, my son, to wipe out this insult I want the tree and its roots at my feet outside my hut."

Balla Fasséké, who was present, ran to the master smith, Farakourou, to order an iron rod.

Sogolon had sat down in front of her hut. She was weeping softly and holding her head between her two hands. Mari Djata went calmly back to his calabash of rice and began eating again as if nothing had happened. From time to time he looked up discreetly at his mother who was murmuring in a low voice, "I want the whole tree, in front of my hut, the whole tree."

All of a sudden a voice burst into laughter behind the hut. It was the wicked Sassouma telling one of her serving women about the scene of humiliation and she was laughing loudly so that Sogolon could hear. Sogolon fled into the hut and hid her face under the blankets so as not to have before her eyes this heedless boy, who was more preoccupied with eating than with anything else. With her head buried in the bedclothes Sogolon wept and her body shook violently. Her daughter, Sogolon Djamarou, had come and sat down beside her and she said, "Mother, Mother, don't cry. Why are you crying?"

Mari Djata had finished eating and, dragging himself along on his legs, he came and sat under the wall of the hut for the sun was scorching. What was he thinking about? He alone knew.

The royal forges were situated outside the walls and over a hundred smiths worked there. The bows, spears, arrows and shields of Niani's warriors came from there. When Balla Fasséké came to order the iron rod, Farakourou said to him, "The great day has arrived then?"

"Yes. Today is a day like any other, but it will see what no other day has seen."

The master of the forges, Farakourou, was the son of the old Nounfaïri, and he was a soothsayer like his father. In his workshops there was an enormous iron bar wrought by his father Nounfaïri. Everybody wondered what this bar was destined to be used for. Farakourou called six of his apprentices and told them to carry the iron bar to Sogolon's house.

When the smiths put the gigantic iron bar down in front of the hut the noise was so frightening that Sogolon, who was lying down, jumped up with a start. Then Balla Fasséké,[4] son of Gnankouman Doua, spoke.

"Here is the great day, Mari Djata. I am speaking to you, Maghan, son of Sogolon. The waters of the Niger can efface the stain from the body, but they cannot wipe out an insult. Arise, young lion, roar, and may the bush know that from henceforth it has a master."

The apprentice smiths were still there, Sogolon had come out and everyone was watching Mari Djata. He crept on all fours and came to the iron bar. Supporting himself on his knees and one hand, with the other hand he picked up the iron bar without any effort and stood it up vertically. Now he was resting on nothing but his knees and held the bar with both his hands. A deathly silence had gripped all those present. Sogolon Djata closed his eyes, held tight, the muscles in his arms tensed. With a violent jerk he

---

4. **Balla Fasséké:** Before he died, the king had named Balla Fasséké as Mari Djata's griot. As griots traditionally served kings, this apppointment indicated Maghan Kon Fatta's faith in the prophecy that Sundiata would one day become king. Here, Balla Fasséké is playing the role of the town crier for Sundiata.

threw his weight on to it and his knees left the ground. Sogolon Kedjou was all eyes and watched her son's legs which were trembling as though from an electric shock. Djata was sweating and the sweat ran from his brow. In a great effort he straightened up and was on his feet at one go—but the great bar of iron was twisted and had taken the form of a bow!

Then Balla Fasséké sang out the "Hymn to the Bow," striking up with his powerful voice:

"Take your bow, Simbon,
Take your bow and let us go.
Take your bow, Sogolon Djata."

When Sogolon saw her son standing she stood dumb for a moment, then suddenly she sang these words of thanks to God who had given her son the use of his legs:

"Oh day, what a beautiful day,
Oh day, day of joy;
Allah[5] Almighty, you never created
a finer day.
So my son is going to walk!"

Standing in the position of a soldier at ease, Sogolon Djata, supported by his enormous rod, was sweating great beads of sweat. Balla Fasséké's song had alerted the whole palace and people came running from all over to see what had happened, and each stood bewildered before Sogolon's son. The queen mother had rushed there and when she saw Mari Djata standing up she trembled from head to foot. After recovering his breath Sogolon's son dropped the bar and the crowd stood to one side. His first steps were those of a giant. Balla Fasséké fell into step and pointing his finger at Djata, he cried:

"Room, room, make room!
The lion has walked;
Hide antelopes,
Get out of his way."

Behind Niani there was a young baobab tree and it was there that the children of the town came to pick leaves for their mothers. With all his might the son of Sogolon tore up the tree and put it on his shoulders and went back to his mother. He threw the tree in front of the hut and said, "Mother, here are some baobab leaves for you. From henceforth it will be outside your hut that the women of Niani will come to stock up."

Ceremonial headdresses from Mali.

---

5. **Allah:** the Muslim name for God.

Sogolon Djata walked. From that day forward the queen mother had no more peace of mind. But what can one do against destiny? Nothing. Man, under the influence of certain illusions, thinks he can alter the course which God has mapped out, but everything he does falls into a higher order which he barely understands. That is why Sassouma's efforts were vain against Sogolon's son, everything she did lay in the child's destiny. Scorned the day before and the object of public ridicule, now Sogolon's son was as popular as he had been despised. The multitude loves and fears strength. All Niani talked of nothing but Djata; the mothers urged their sons to become hunting companions of Djata and to share his games, as if they wanted their offspring to profit from the nascent glory of the buffalo-woman's son. The words of Doua on the name-giving day[6] came back to men's minds and Sogolon was now surrounded with much respect; in conversation people were fond of contrasting Sogolon's modesty with the pride and malice of Sassouma Bérété. It was because the former had been an exemplary wife and mother that God had granted strength to her son's legs for, it was said, the more a wife loves and respects her husband and the more she suffers for her child, the more valorous will the child be one day. Each is the child of his mother; the child is worth no more than the mother is worth. It was not astonishing that the king Dankaran Touman was so colorless, for his mother had never shown the slightest respect to her husband and never, in the presence of the late king, did she show that humility which every wife should show before her husband.

---

6. **The words . . . name-giving day:** Doua, King Maghan's griot, had repeated the hunter's prophecy at the infant Sundiata's ceremonial naming.

People recalled her scenes of jealousy and the spiteful remarks she circulated about her co-wife and her child. And people would conclude gravely, "Nobody knows God's mystery. The snake has no legs yet it is as swift as any other animal that has four."

While still a child, Sundiata becomes a great hunter. He becomes friends with Manding Bory, the son of his father's third wife. When an attempt to kill Sundiata fails, Sassouma and her son Dankaran Touman drive Sundiata into exile. The hero and his family find refuge in the kingdom of Mema.

As Sundiata grows to manhood, the evil Soumaoro Kanté, sorcerer-king of a neighboring kingdom, gains power and conquers many nations. When Sundiata hears that Soumaoro has invaded Mali, he decides to challenge the sorcerer-king and gain control of his rightful kingdom. Sundiata thus makes his way to Sosso, Soumaoro's capital city, to meet Soumaoro face to face. Sundiata fights and wins several battles along the way and becomes a popular leader. Many new soldiers gladly join his ranks.

from Krina

Sundiata went and pitched camp at Dayala in the valley of the Niger. Now it was he who was blocking Soumaoro's road to the south. Up till that time, Sundiata and Soumaoro had fought each other without a declaration of war. One does not wage war without saying why it is being waged. Those fighting should make a declaration of their grievances to begin with. Just as a sorcerer ought not to attack someone without taking him to task for some evil deed, so a king should not wage war without saying why he is taking up arms.

Soumaoro advanced as far as Krina, near the village of Dayala on the Niger and decided to assert his rights before joining battle. Soumaoro knew that Sundiata also was a sorcerer, so, instead of sending an embassy, he committed his words to one of his owls. The night bird came and perched on the roof of Djata's tent and spoke. The son of Sogolon in his turn sent his owl to Soumaoro. Here is the dialogue of the sorcerer-kings:

"Stop, young man. Henceforth I am the king of Mali. If you want peace, return to where you came from," said Soumaoro.

"I am coming back, Soumaoro, to recapture my kingdom. If you want peace you will make amends to my allies and return to Sosso where you are the king."

"I am king of Mali by force of arms. My rights have been established by conquest."

"Then I will take Mali from you by force of arms and chase you from my kingdom."

"Know, then, that I am the wild yam of the rocks;[7] nothing will make me leave Mali."

"Know, also that I have in my camp seven master smiths who will shatter the rocks. Then, yam, I will eat you."

"I am the poisonous mushroom that makes the fearless vomit."

"As for me, I am the ravenous cock, the poison does not matter to me."

"Behave yourself, little boy, or you will burn your foot, for I am the red-hot cinder."

"But me, I am the rain that extinguishes the cinder; I am the boisterous torrent that will carry you off."

"I am the mighty silk-cotton tree that looks from on high on the tops of other trees."

"And I, I am the strangling creeper that climbs to the top of the forest giant."

"Enough of this argument. You shall not have Mali."

"Know that there is not room for two kings on the same skin, Soumaoro; you will let me have your place."

"Very well, since you want war I will wage war against you, but I would have you know that I have killed nine kings whose heads adorn my room. What a pity, indeed, that your head should take its place beside those of your fellow madcaps."

"Prepare yourself, Soumaoro, for it will be long before the calamity that is going to crash down upon you and yours comes to an end."

Balla Fasséké, Sundiata's griot, and Nana Triban, Sundiata's half-sister, have been imprisoned in Soumaoro's palace, but they finally escape. They join Sundiata on the eve of the battle of Krina. Fakoli Koroma, Soumaoro's nephew, also arrives at the camp. Because Soumaoro kidnapped his

Statue of ancestral couple from Mali.

---

7. . . . **the wild yam of the rocks:** When the vines of these yams grow in boulder-strewn areas, their underground tubers anchor them among the rocks and make them very difficult to uproot.

wife, Fakoli has vowed revenge. Nana Triban and Fakoli pledge their loyalty to Sundiata, and Nana Triban tells Sundiata that the way to insure Soumaoro's defeat is to touch him with a cock's spur. On the morning of the battle, Sundiata and Manding Bory, his half-brother, devise a plan to strip Soumaoro of his power.

"Brother," said Manding Bory, "have you got the bow ready?"

"Yes," replied Sundiata. "Look."

He unhooked his bow from the wall, along with the deadly arrow. It was not an iron arrow at all, but was made of wood and pointed with the spur of a white cock. The cock's spur was the Tana of Soumaoro,[8] the secret which Nana Triban had managed to draw out of the king of Sosso.

"Brother," said Nana Triban, "Soumaoro now knows that I have fled from Sosso. Try to get near him for he will avoid you the whole battle long."

These words of Nana Triban left Djata worried, but Balla Fasséké, who had just come into the tent, said to Sundiata that the soothsayer had seen the end of Soumaoro in a dream.

The sun had risen on the other side of the river and already lit the whole plain. Sundiata's troops deployed from the edge of the river across the plain, but Soumaoro's army was so big that other sofas[9] remaining in Krina had ascended the ramparts to see the battle. Soumaoro was already distinguishable in the distance by his tall headdress, and the wings of his enormous army brushed the river on one side and the hills on the other. As at Neguéboria,[10] Sundiata did not deploy all his forces. The bowmen of Wagadou[11] and the Djallonkés stood at the rear ready to spill out on the left towards the hills as the battle spread. Fakoli Koroma and Kamandjan[12] were in the front line with Sundiata and his cavalry.

With his powerful voice Sundiata cried "*An gnewa.*"[13] The order was repeated from tribe to tribe and the army started off. Soumaoro stood on the right with his cavalry.

Djata and his cavalry charged with great dash but they were stopped by the horsemen of Diaghan and a struggle to the death began. Tabon Wana[14] and the archers of Wagadou stretched out their lines towards the hills and the battle spread over the entire plain, while

---

8. **the Tana of Soumaoro:** The cock's spur (the spiny projection on the leg of a rooster) is Soumaoro's Tana, that is, the taboo, or prohibition, imposed on him by his ancestors. In breaking this taboo, Soumaoro will incur the wrath of his ancestors who will then withdraw the magic powers that have made him invincible.
9. **sofas:** warriors.
10. **Neguéboria:** an earlier battle fought and won by Sundiata.
11. **Wagadou:** a name for Old Ghana.
12. **Kamandjan:** king of Sibi; one of Sundiata's childhood friends.
13. ***An gnewa:*** Forward.
14. **Tabon Wana:** King of Tabon; also called Fran Kamara.

an unrelenting sun climbed in the sky. The horses of Mema were extremely agile, and they reared forward with their forehooves raised and swooped down on the horsemen of Diaghan, who rolled on the ground trampled under the horses' hooves. Presently the men of Diaghan gave ground and fell back towards the rear. The enemy center was broken.

It was then that Manding Bory galloped up to announce to Sundiata that Soumaoro, having thrown in all his reserve, had swept down on Fakoli and his smiths. Obviously Soumaoro was bent on punishing his nephew. Already overwhelmed by the numbers, Fakoli's men were beginning to give ground. The battle was not yet won.

His eyes red with anger, Sundiata pulled his cavalry over to the left in the direction of the hills where Fakoli was valiantly enduring his uncle's blows. But wherever the son of the buffalo passed, death rejoiced. Sundiata's presence restored the balance momentarily, but Soumaoro's sofas were too numerous all the same. Sogolon's son looked for Soumaoro and caught sight of him in the middle of the fray. Sundiata

Werner Forman Archive/Fuhrman Collection, New York/Art Resource, New York

struck out right and left and the Sossos scrambled out of his way. The king of Sosso, who did not want Sundiata to get near him, retreated far behind his men, but Sundiata followed him with his eyes. He stopped and bent his bow. The arrow flew and grazed Soumaoro on the shoulder. The cock's spur no more than scratched him, but the effect was immediate and Soumaoro felt his powers leave him. His eyes met Sundiata's. Now trembling like a man in the grip of a fever, the vanquished Soumaoro looked up towards the sun. A great black bird flew over above the fray and he understood. It was a bird of misfortune.

"The bird of Krina," he muttered.

The king of Sosso let out a great cry and, turning his horse's head, he took to flight. The Sossos saw the king and fled in their turn. It was a rout. Death hovered over the great plain and blood poured out of a thousand wounds. Who can tell how many Sossos perished at Krina? The rout was complete and Sundiata then dashed off in pursuit of Soumaoro.

Sundiata and Fakoli pursue Soumaoro, who has fled with his son Sosso Balla. They succeed in capturing Sosso Balla, but Soumaoro escapes into a cave. He is never heard from again. Sundiata heads for the nearby village of Koulikoro, where he waits for his army.

Werner Forman Archive/Dallas Museum of Fine Art/Art Resource, New York

The victory of Krina was dazzling. The remains of Soumaoro's army went to shut themselves up in Sosso. But the empire of Sosso was done for. From everywhere around kings sent their submission to Sundiata. The king of Guidimakhan sent a richly furnished embassy to Djata and at the same time gave his daughter in marriage to the victor. Embassies flocked to Koulikoro, but when Djata had been joined by all the army he marched on Sosso. Soumaoro's city, Sosso, the impregnable city, the city of smiths skilled in wielding the spear.

In the absence of the king and his son, Noumounkeba, a tribal chief, directed the defense of the city. He had quickly amassed all that he could find in the way of provisions from the surrounding countryside.

Sosso was a magnificent city. In the open plain her triple rampart with awe-inspiring towers reached into the sky. The city comprised a hundred and eighty-eight fortresses and the palace of Soumaoro loomed above the whole city like a gigantic tower. Sosso had but one gate; colossal and made of iron, the work of the sons of fire. Noumounkeba hoped to tie Sundiata down outside of Sosso, for he had enough provisions to hold out for a year.

The sun was beginning to set when Sogolon Djata appeared before Sosso the

Magnificent. From the top of a hill, Djata and his general staff gazed upon the fearsome city of the sorcerer-king. The army encamped in the plain opposite the great gate of the city and fires were lit in the camp. Djata resolved to take Sosso in the course of a morning. He fed his men a double ration and the tam-tams[15] beat all night to stir up the victors of Krina.

At daybreak the towers of the ramparts were black with sofas. Others were positioned on the ramparts themselves. They were the archers. The Mandingoes[16] were masters in the art of storming a town. In the front line Sundiata placed the sofas of Mali, while those who held the ladders were in the second line protected by the shields of the spearmen. The main body of the army was to attack the city gate. When all was ready, Djata gave the order to attack. The drums resounded, the horns blared and like a tide the Mandingo front line moved off, giving mighty shouts. With their shields raised above their heads the Mandingoes advanced up to the foot of the wall, then the Sossos began to rain large

---

15. **tam-tams:** small drums.
16. **Mandingoes:** the inhabitants of Old Mali.

stones down on the assailants. From the rear, the bowmen of Wagadou shot arrows at the ramparts. The attack spread and the town was assaulted at all points. Sundiata had a murderous reserve; they were the bowmen whom the king of the Bobos had sent shortly before Krina. The archers of Bobo are the best in the world. On one knee the archers fired flaming arrows over the ramparts. Within the walls the thatched huts took fire and the smoke swirled up. The ladders stood against the curtain wall and the first Mandingo sofas were already at the top. Seized by panic through seeing the town on fire, the Sossos hesitated a moment. The huge tower surmounting the gate surrendered, for Fakoli's smiths had made themselves masters of it. They got into the city where the screams of women and children brought the Sossos' panic to a head. They opened the gates to the main body of the army.

Then began the massacre. Women and children in the midst of fleeing Sossos implored mercy of the victors. Djata and his cavalry were now in front of the awesome tower palace of Soumaoro. Noumounkeba, conscious that he was lost, came out to fight. With his sword held aloft he bore down on Djata, but the latter dodged him and, catching hold of the Sosso's braced arm, forced him to his knees whilst the sword dropped to the ground. He did not kill him but delivered him into the hands of Manding Bory.

Soumaoro's palace was now at Sundiata's mercy. While everywhere the Sossos were begging for quarter,[17] Sundiata, preceded by Balla Fasséké, entered Soumaoro's tower. The griot knew every nook and cranny of the palace from his captivity and he led Sundiata to Soumaoro's magic chamber.

When Balla Fasséké opened the door to the room it was found to have changed its appearance since Soumaoro had been touched by the fatal arrow. The inmates of the chamber had lost their power. The snake in the pitcher was in the throes of death, the owls from the perch were flapping pitifully about on the ground. Everything was dying in the sorcerer's abode. It was all up with the power of Soumaoro. Sundiata had all Soumaoro's fetishes[18] taken down and before the palace were gathered together all Soumaoro's wives, all princesses taken from their families by force. The prisoners, their hands tied behind their backs, were already herded together. Just as he had wished, Sundiata had taken

Werner Forman Archive/Dallas Museum of Fine Art/Art Resource, New York

Stool used in religious ceremonies, from Mali. *The base and seat represent the earth and sky, connected by a central tree. Images of nature play an important role in Sundiata.*

❓ *How does the narrator use nature imagery to describe the downfall of Sosso?*

---

17. **quarter:** mercy.

18. **fetishes:** objects believed to have magical powers.

Sosso in the course of a morning. When everything was outside of the town and all that there was to take had been taken out, Sundiata gave the order to complete its destruction. The last houses were set fire to and prisoners were employed in the razing of the walls. Thus, as Djata intended, Sosso was destroyed to its very foundations.

Yes, Sosso was razed to the ground. It has disappeared, the proud city of Soumaoro. A ghastly wilderness extends over the places where kings came and humbled themselves before the sorcerer-king. All traces of the houses have vanished and of Soumaoro's seven-story palace there remains nothing more. A field of desolation, Sosso is now a spot where guinea fowl and young partridges come to take their dust baths.

Many years have rolled by and many times the moon has traversed the heaven since these places lost their inhabitants. The bourein,[19] the tree of desolation, spreads out its thorny undergrowth and insolently grows in Soumaoro's capital. Sosso the Proud is nothing but a memory in the mouths of griots. The hyenas come to wail there at night, the hare and the hind come and feed on the site of the palace of Soumaoro, the king who wore robes of human skin.

Sosso vanished from the earth and it was Sundiata, the son of the buffalo, who gave these places over to solitude. After the destruction of Soumaoro's capital the world knew no other master but Sundiata.

---

19. **bourein:** a dwarf shrub.

First Thoughts

Which episode from this epic stands out most clearly in your mind? Why? Did any portion of the epic remind you of any other stories you have read?

Identifying Facts

1. How are Mari Djata (Sundiata) and his family mistreated after his father dies?

2. How does Mari Djata avenge his mother's humiliation at the hands of Sassouma?

3. Why do Sundiata and Soumaoro have a "dialogue" at the beginning of "Krina"? What **metaphors** do they use to describe themselves?

4. What is the outcome of the **conflict** between Sundiata and Soumaoro?

5. What does Sosso look like before the battle of Krina? What does it look like afterward?

Interpreting Meanings

1. The incident in which Mari Djata (Sundiata) begins to walk reveals a great deal about his **character**. From that incident, what can you infer about Sundiata's sense of justice? What does the incident reveal about his physical strength and determination?

2. Three brief songs occur in "The Lion's Awakening." What events do these songs accompany? What purpose do you think these songs serve in the narrative?

3. An exchange of boasts before battle, like Sundiata's and Soumaoro's dialogue, occurs frequently in epics. Scholars think that *Sundiata* was often performed for the Mandingo army before battles. What effect do you think the boastful exchange might have had on such an audience?

4. How does Soumaoro's secret chamber look after he is wounded by Sundiata's arrow? What does the room's appearance imply about the sorcerer's fate?

5. Why do you think Sundiata chose to completely destroy the city of Sosso rather than make it a part of his kingdom?

6. An **epic**, with its blend of history and legend, reflects a society's values. Based on your reading of these excerpts from *Sundiata,* what values do you think were honored by the Mandingo culture? Can you tell what kinds of behaviors they found despicable?

Applying Meanings

Sundiata, like many epics, glorifies war. War is depicted in the epic as colorful, even spectacular. Explain how modern views of war are similar to those expressed in *Sundiata* and how they differ. Consider the media of modern culture, such as television, literature, and movies. Which changes might be responsible for the differences?

Creative Writing Response

Recording an Oral History.   Begin an oral history of your own family, school, or community. Interview someone about a historical event, large or small, that that person witnessed. Perhaps the person you interview will remember details about a famous leader or other celebrity. Or perhaps he or she participated in a war or some large group effort, or witnessed a natural disaster. Ask the person to recall details about

the event. Write up your interview, and share it with the class.

Critical Writing Response

Explicating the Theme.   An epic, like any longer piece of literature, may contain several **themes**, or messages, that give central insights into human life. In a sentence, state one or more of the themes that you see in *Sundiata.* One of the following questions, or some questions of your own, may lead you to some possible statements of theme from the epic:

1. How much control do people have over fate?

2. Does strength alone constitute power, or must strength be combined with virtue?

3. What makes a just, strong leader?

4. What are the duties of a leader to his or her country or community?

5. What is a true "national hero"?

From the answer to the question, formulate a statement of the theme that you believe is a central theme of *Sundiata.* Then, in a three- or four-paragraph essay, explain how the epic illustrates that theme. Use specific details from the epic to support your statements.

Speaking and Listening

Telling the Story of an Unlikely Hero. Sundiata has an unpromising start in life. He is serious, seldom speaks, doesn't play with other children, and, at the age of seven, still hasn't learned to walk. Do you think it is likely that a child who starts out like Sundiata could become a great leader? Think of another hero of history, myth, or folklore who was at first considered insignificant, or even "backward," but who went on to do great things. (Remember that a hero can be either male or female.) Briefly recount the hero's story to the class. End your story with your own opinions about why people all over the world like stories about people who overcome hardship and triumph in the end.

Language and Vocabulary

Context Clues

You can often guess the meaning of an unfamiliar word by examining its **context**—the other words, phrases, and sentences that surround it. There are several main types of context clues:

1. **Synonyms**—The sentence may contain a word or phrase that is similar in meaning to the word you do not know.
2. **Antonyms**—The sentence may contain a word or phrase that means the opposite of the word you do not know.
3. **Definitions**—The sentence may contain a direct definition of the word.
4. **Restatements**—The word's meaning may be clarified by a restatement that is signaled by dashes, parentheses, or even a phrase such as *that is* or *in other words*. Sometimes the meaning of a word is revealed by an **appositive**—a restatement set off by commas.

In the following sentences, words from *Sundiata* are shown in italics. (In the text, these words are footnoted.) What type of context clue can help you to determine the meaning of each italicized word?

1. The hungry child looked inside the *calabash* carefully, checking the hollowed-out gourd bowl for remnants of food.
2. The *sofas* stood outside the castle walls, ready with their bows to face the enemy warriors' attack.
3. The *gnougous,* a root vegetable, was a common part of the diet of the people of Old Mali.
4. The *baobab* is a tropical tree with edible fruit and leaves that can be used as an herb for cooking.

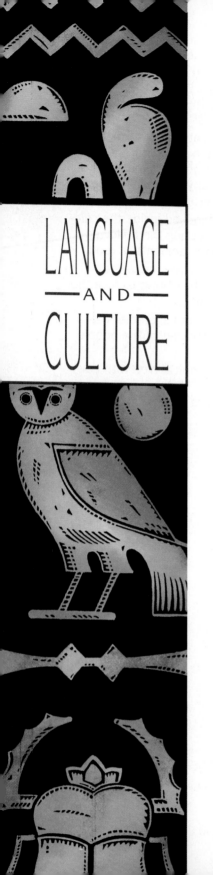

AFRICAN AMERICAN STORYTELLERS

"Hey, ever'body. I'm Brother Blue, a street cat callin' you. Come close. . . ." So begins a tale by Brother Blue, really Dr. Hugh Morgan Hill, African American storyteller. Blue performs at hospitals and prisons, preschools and libraries. But just as often, he simply stands on the Boston sidewalks, wearing his bright clothes and a knit cap decorated with ribbons, flowers, and balloons, telling stories to passers-by. He chants his tales in a blend of rap and poetry, moving to the beat as he talks.

Brother Blue has been performing for almost fifty years. He grew up poor, the only black child in a white school. He was below average as a student, and he had a severe stammer. But somehow he discovered that when he told a story, recited poetry, or sang, his stammering stopped. When he began telling stories to his classmates and at school assemblies, he didn't know that he was stepping into a tradition thousands of years old.

Encouraged by a caring teacher, Blue overcame his academic difficulties. He went on to graduate from both Harvard and Yale, where he studied drama, theology, and the oral tradition. In 1972, he launched Brother Blue's Soul Theater, a forum for his unique blend of storytelling, chanting, singing, dancing, and acting. He had realized by then that oral literature was his calling.

The African American Storytelling Tradition

Brother Blue, like all storytellers, gets his tales from many sources. Some come from his own experiences or from his imagination; some come from books or from other storytellers. Some, however, are stories he heard as a child, tales from the African American tradition. Traditional African American stories show many links to the oral tradition of Africa. For example, most African groups tell animal tales. In many African animal tales, a hare appears as a trickster figure. When African slaves were brought to America, the hare became Brer Rabbit. He was joined by Brer Fox, Brer Bear, Brer Possum, and others based on animals native to the North American continent. Among the peoples of Africa, animal tales had been used to dramatize, in a tactful way, personality quirks and social issues affecting the community. In fact, the Ewe (ā'wā) people of Togo have a saying: "Because I tell tales about animals, I have never been named in a libel suit."

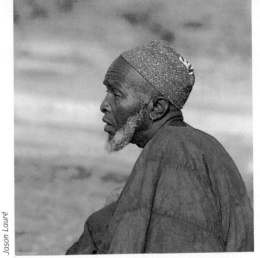

Jason Lauré

Dogon griot.
❓ *How has the role of the griot been transported to African American culture?*

An American Griot

Some modern storytellers work to strengthen the connections between African and African American storytelling traditions. One of these storytellers is Mary Carter Smith, who has been called an urban American griot. Born in Alabama, she worked for thirty-one years as a teacher and a librarian in inner-city Baltimore. She shared with her students the stories and songs she had learned as a child in the South, and she began writing her own poetry as well. Eventually, Smith began performing her tales and songs at other schools and colleges. Today she travels widely throughout America, dressed in flowing robes and scarves made from African textiles, telling tales.

Entertainment—and More

Because it lets performers and listeners work together, storytelling has been called a "co-creative" process; between the words of the storyteller and the imagination of the audience, the story comes alive. The satisfaction of this shared effort is one of the main reasons that storytelling entertains.

In sharing enjoyment, of course, other benefits occur. Among the peoples of Africa, storytelling provides a chance to communicate social rules and values and an indirect way to resolve community conflicts. In the African American tradition, too, storytelling has served as a means of passing on values and making social comments. Modern African American storytellers also notice other positive effects. Brother Blue explains, "When you're there in the streets, you meet the street people. The people who are suffering, dying, lost, some going mad, some drunk. . . . You know, you can sober up a man with a story. Stories are healing." Mary Carter Smith offers a similar viewpoint. She sees her stories as tearing down walls between people and building bridges of understanding. "I have committed myself," she explains, ". . . to truth, freedom, justice, and peace for all peoples, black or white, young or old, free or in bondage. My stories are my message."

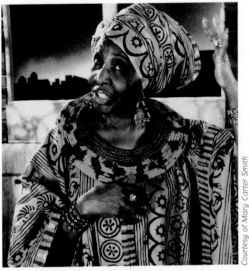

Courtesy of Mary Carter Smith

African American storyteller Mary Carter Smith.

USING QUOTATIONS EFFECTIVELY

To avoid confusing your readers, punctuate quotations correctly, and work them smoothly into your writing. Punctuation shows your readers which words you have written and which you have **quoted**—taken directly from sources. Note how a lack of proper punctuation causes confusion.

CONFUSING

My experience bears out what the griot knew: that growth is not always easy, and it is not as quick as you would like it.

CLEAR

My experience bears out what the griot knew: that "growth is not always easy. . . ." and "[it] is not as quick as you would like it."

In the second sentence, quotation marks tell the reader which words come from a literary work. Ellipses (. . .) show where material has been omitted from the quotation, and brackets ([ ]) show where a word has been added.

Punctuating Brief Quotations

Notice how the boldface commas, quotation marks, upper- and lower-case letters, and other marks are used in the examples that follow.

QUOTING A SENTENCE

The poet tries to flatter the sun god when he writes, "**Y**ou made the earth as you wished, you alone."

QUOTING A FRAGMENT

An Ashanti proverb states that the cause of a country's ruin "**b**egins in the homes of its people."

QUOTING A QUOTATION

Like the chief in the Ashanti tale, my cousin Jarrel said, " '**N**ow this is really a wild story.' "

SHOWING OMISSIONS (USING ELLIPSES)

According to a Yoruban poem, the god Ogun "**k**ills . . . the owner of stolen goods."

SHOWING INSERTIONS (USING BRACKETS)

The man grew angry not with the yam, but with the dog, because he didn't like "**[t**he dog's] tone."

QUOTING LINES OF POETRY

The Egyptians' tolerance of cultural differences is reflected in the lines, "**T**heir tongues differ in speech, / Their characters likewise; / Their skins are distinct, / For you distinguished the peoples."

(For over three lines of poetry or prose, separate the quotation from the text and indent each line ten spaces from the left margin.)

Exercise 1: Punctuating Brief Quotations

Use part or all of each quotation in a sentence. Use correct punctuation.

1. "The snake has no legs yet it is as swift as any other animal that has four." (*Sundiata*)

2. "One who asks never loses his way." (Yoruba proverb)

3. "Though you are far, your rays are on earth, / Though one sees you, your strides are unseen." ("The Great Hymn to the Aten")

4. "Do not speak of a rhinoceros if there is no tree nearby." (Zulu proverb)

Integrating Brief Quotations

When you are using brief quotations, you must **integrate** them—work them smoothly into your sentences and show their relevance to your ideas.

DISJOINTED
Like a knife, Ogun is useful but dangerous. "Ogun's laughter is no joke." He is bloodthirsty.

INTEGRATED
Like a knife, Ogun is useful but dangerous. *Ironically, even* "Ogun's laughter is no joke," *for* he is bloodthirsty even when he is happy.

In the second passage, an introductory phrase and a subordinate clause work the quotation smoothly into the writing. They also show how the writer has interpreted the quotation.

Methods for Inserting Brief Quotations

You can place quotations in various positions in your sentences. Study these examples.

Final Position
For several reasons, "Ogun's laughter is no joke."

Beginning Position
"Ogun's laughter is no joke"; instead, it inspires fear.

Middle Position
Just as "Ogun's laughter is no joke," so is his justice almost unjust.

Interrupted
"Ogun's laughter," warns the singer, "is no joke."

Exercise 2: Integrating Quotations

Choose four quotations from works in this unit, and use a different method for inserting each into a sentence you write. Use correct punctuation.

Critical Thinking and Writing

A PERSONAL RESPONSE TO LITERATURE

"I think I know what this poet's talking about—I've had days like that." "I'm not sure I get the point of the story." "That character's a lot like my crazy cousin." All these comments reflect personal connections between readers and literary works. By exploring your personal responses to what you read, you can discover new depths, both in literature and in yourself.

Writing Assignment

Write an essay expressing your feelings about one of the works in this unit. You might explain how some aspect of the work relates to your own life. You might explore your thoughts or feelings about some aspect of the work. Or you might trace your reading process, recalling your initial responses to the work and recounting how your responses changed as you reread the work and thought about it or discussed it. Assume that your audience is familiar with the literature and is curious about your opinion. In this essay, you'll develop and support a generalization.

Background

In this unit, you've found examples of ancient written literature as well as timeless oral literature. Each selection speaks to readers in a unique way, and each

reader brings to the literature a unique set of responses. For your essay, consider the range of your personal responses. As you read, you may have felt amusement or boredom, sorrow or delight, puzzlement or deep understanding. Consider, too, the range of elements that evoked your responses. Works in this unit rely especially upon:

- **Imagery** drawn from daily life, in which words evoke for readers the sights, sounds, smells, tastes, and textures familiar to the writer
- **Figurative language**, in which a striking comparison can deepen readers' insights
- **Irony**, in which readers' expectations are reversed, creating surprise or humor
- **Repetition** and **parallel structure**, in which words, phrases, or sentence structures recur, creating patterns that underscore ideas
- **Onomatopoeia** and **dialogue**, in which sound effects and speech patterns communicate subtleties of emotion

Prewriting

Focused Reading and Questioning. To generate ideas, first choose the work that you liked most (or least) in this unit. Then freewrite answers to these questions.

1. Did you like or dislike the selection? Why?
2. Which image or idea from the work is most memorable to you? Why?
3. In what ways does the work relate to your own experience?
4. What was the author trying to accomplish?
5. What questions do you have about the work?

Developing a Generalization. Look over your freewriting and group responses that can be connected. Choose the set of responses you'd like to write about. Next, draft a **generalization**, a broad statement covering the responses in the set. Fill in a chart like the one below to be sure you have enough specific material to support your generalization.

Generali-zation	Support 1	Support 2	Support 3
	Example	Example	Example
	Example	Example	Example

Writing

Use the following plan as you draft your essay.

1. **Introductory Paragraph.** Catch your readers' interest by quoting, from the work you have chosen, a line or phrase that is especially relevant to your response. Explain how the quotation relates to your response. Then use your generalization as a thesis statement. Be sure to cite the title of the work you have chosen and specify the culture from which it comes.

2. **Body Paragraphs.** Referring to your chart, present the material that supports your generalization. From your freewriting, draw examples that will help you express your response. Use quotations from the work, as well. If you are tracing your response process, arrange paragraphs chronologically. Otherwise, move from your simplest response to your most complicated, or from your least powerful point to your most powerful.

3. **Concluding Paragraph.** Restate your generalization in new terms. Leave readers with a strong impression of your main response.

Evaluating and Revising

Use these questions to evaluate and revise your essay.

1. Does your introduction catch your readers' attention and clearly state your general response?
2. Is your generalization valid? Does it cover all the specifics you've cited?
3. Have you explained your generalization with enough specifics (including examples and quotations)?
4. Do your paragraphs follow a logical order?
5. Have you worked your quotations smoothly into your sentences?

Proofreading and Publishing

Proofread to eliminate errors in grammar and mechanics. Then make a final copy of your essay. Organize the response essays into a class literary journal for everyone to read.

ANCIENT MIDDLE EAST

☐ Fertile Crescent

— Kingdom of David
and Solomon in the
10th Century B.C.

Black Sea

ASIA MINOR

Mt. Ararat

ASSYRIA

Nineveh

MESOPOTAMIA

CYPRUS

Euphrates River

Mediterranean
Sea

SYRIA

GALILEE

Sea of
Galilee

Nazareth

KINGDOM
OF ISRAEL

Samaria

Jordan River

Jerusalem

PHILISTIA

Gaza

Bethlehem

Dead
Sea

ARABIAN DESERT

KINGDOM
OF JUDAH

EGYPT

Nile River

Sinai
Peninsula

THE ANCIENT MIDDLE EAST

▼ **Time** ▼

c. 3000 B.C.–A.D. 100

▼ **Place** ▼

The Ancient Middle East

▼ **Literary Significance** ▼

Mesopotamian Literature: Sumerian and Babylonian literature consists of hymns, laments, dirges, proverbs, essays, rules of conduct, fables, myths, and epic tales. The most famous surviving work from the ancient cultures of Mesopotamia is a long narrative poem about a king named Gilgamesh, which may be the world's oldest epic.

Hebrew Literature: The Hebrew Bible, known to Christians as the Old Testament, is both the great sacred text of the Hebrews and the chronicle of their history. It contains examples of many diverse literary forms, from psalms, or sacred hymns, to historical narratives and proverbs.

TIME LINE
The Ancient Middle East

LITERARY EVENTS

▼

Cuneiform tablet, c. 1980 B.C.

The Granger Collection, New York

The Granger Collection, New York

Alabaster head of a
Sumerian prince, c. 2100 B.C.

Cuneiform tablets
are inscribed with
Sumerian writings,
3000–2500 B.C.

Legends about
Gilgamesh begin to
appear on cuneiform
tablets, **c. 2500 B.C.**

4500 B.C.	4000 B.C.	3500 B.C.	3000 B.C.	2500 B.C.

Sumerians settle
in Mesopotamia,
c. 4500 B.C.

Floods ravage
Mesopotamia,
4000–3500 B.C.

Sumerians develop
cuneiform writing,
3500–3000 B.C.

Gilgamesh is king in Uruk,
c. 2750 B.C.

Sumerians build
temples at Eridu,
Ur, and Uruk,
3500–3000 B.C.

The Hanging Gardens of Babylon. Colored
engraving, nineteenth century.

The Granger Collection, New York

▲

**CULTURAL AND
HISTORICAL EVENTS**

Thirteenth-century illuminated manuscript of the Book of Ruth.

The Granger Collection, New York

Hammurabi's Code is set down in Babylon, **c. 1700 B.C.**

The *Epic of Gilgamesh* is written down by Babylonians in Mesopotamia, **c. 1300 B.C.**

Time setting of the Hebrew Bible Book of Ruth, **c. 1300–1000 B.C.**

The Torah is assembled from earlier texts; many Psalms are written, **c. 1010–925 B.C.**

The writings of the Hebrew Bible prophets, **c. 925–587 B.C.**

The Book of Ruth is written, **c. 600 B.C.**

The Hebrew Bible in its entirety is assembled, **c. 300 B.C.**

The books of the New Testament are written, **c. A.D. 70–100**

| 2000 B.C. | 1500 B.C. | 1000 B.C. | 500 B.C. | A.D. 1 |

Abraham and Sarah migrate from Mesopotamia to Canaan; Jewish history begins, **c. 1900 B.C.**

Babylon under Hammurabi reaches its cultural and artistic peak, **c. 1792 B.C.**

Hittites invade Babylon, **c. 1600 B.C.**

Babylonians conquer Sumeria, **c. 2000 B.C.**

Moses leads Jews out of Egypt, **c. 1200 B.C.**

King David reigns in Israel, **c. 1010–970 B.C.**

King Solomon reigns in Israel, **970–925 B.C.**

Israel splits into Samaria and Judah, **925 B.C.**

Assyrians rise to power in Mesopotamia, **c. 900 B.C.**

Neo-Babylonian empire replaces Assyrians, **c. 612 B.C.**

Many Jews are taken into exile by Babylonian King Nebuchadnezzar II, **586 B.C.**

Persians capture Babylon; some Jews return to Israel, **c. 539 B.C.**

Alexander the Great conquers Mesopotamia and neighboring peoples, **c. 330 B.C.**

Jews gain independence from the Seleucids during the Maccabee Rebellion, **c. 168–142 B.C.**

Romans come to power; establish provinces in Galilee, Samaria, and Judea, **c. 30 B.C.**

The life of Jesus of Nazareth, **c. A.D. 1–33**

Mesopotamia falls under Roman rule, **c. A.D. 50**

Romans destroy Jerusalem, **A.D. 70**

Jews expelled from the Holy Land; beginning of the Diaspora, **A.D. 132–135**

Solomon's Temple in Jerusalem. German woodcut, 1486.

The Granger Collection, New York

This time line border depicts images derived from Sumerian cuneiform. Invented around 3500 B.C., cuneiform is considered the world's oldest system of writing.

THE LITERATURE OF ANCIENT MESOPOTAMIA

Mesopotamia (mes′ə·pə·tā′mē·ə), a word that means "the land between the rivers," is the name given by the Greeks to an ancient area of the Middle East. Today, the region corresponds roughly to a large part of present-day Iraq as well as to parts of Iran, Turkey, and Syria. This region is also known as the **Fertile Crescent**, an agriculturally rich land watered by the **Tigris** and **Euphrates** (yoo·frāt′ēz) rivers.

A Civilization Built on Mud

Mesopotamia proved attractive to a series of people who successively dominated the region. The **Sumerians** (sōō·mer′ē·ənz) were the first of these peoples. They were probably a wandering people who settled in Sumer, in the marshlands of the delta formed by the Tigris and Euphrates rivers, sometime between 5000 and 4000 B.C.

The Sumerians dug canals to drain the marshlands and irrigate their crops. There was no stone in the delta region, and virtually no timber, so the Sumerians used mud to build their houses and to make an excellent grade of pottery. Mud also provided the raw material for the clay tablets on which the Sumerians wrote their laws, financial transactions, and literature. The entire Sumerian civilization, one might say, was fashioned out of river mud.

How the Sumerians Lived

The Sumerians made their living mainly by growing crops, such as wheat and barley, and by raising cattle, goats, and sheep. They developed a reputation as successful merchants

> *❝ May there be floodwater in the Tigris and Euphrates,/ May the plants grow high on their banks and fill the meadows,/ May the Lady of Vegetation pile the grain in heaps and mounds. ❞*
>
> —from ''The Courtship of Inanna and Dumuzi'' translated by Diane Wolkstein and Samuel Noah Kramer

Sumerian bronze lintel. *This lintel—the top part of a doorframe—was mounted over the main entrance of a temple, c. 2500 B.C.*

and traders, and they were known for their beautiful stonework, metalwork, and sculpture. They had many goods to trade with their neighbors on the Persian Gulf.

> The Sumerians achieved a high level of culture. With farming and trade as their economic base, they were able to turn their energies to artistic accomplishments.

The Sumerians lived in **city-states**, each consisting of a large town or city and its surrounding lands. These city-states were walled for protection against invaders. Archaeological finds show that the city-states were laid out around great pyramidlike temples called **ziggurats** (zig′oo·rats′). The ziggurats were six or seven stories high, layered rather like a wedding cake, and probably brightly decorated, with each story, or layer, painted a different color. In each city, the ziggurat was presided over by a priest-king, whom the people regarded as the earthly representative of the local god. Some of the ancient ziggurats are still standing in Iraq today.

Female Worshiper, Sumerian. Early Dynasty III, c. 2800–2550 B.C.

Scala/Art Resource, New York

Statue of a woman, Sumerian.

In fact, during the Persian Gulf Conflict in 1991, allied pilots were instructed not to bomb these ancient structures. The Iraqi Air Force, knowing that allied bombers would be reluctant to bomb anywhere near these sites, parked their own jets under the protective shadow of these ancient archaeological treasures.

The largest Sumerian city-states, such as Ur, Uruk, and Lagash, had populations in the tens of thousands. Many of the city-states were within sight of one another. Yet, the Sumerians seem never to have developed a central, unifying government. Because of this lack of a unifying political force, the city-states often competed against one another for land and precious resources.

Sumerian Society and Cultural Achievements

Sumerian society was based on a strict, three-level class system. At the top of the social ladder were the nobles, who mainly consisted of the priests and government officials. Below them were the members of the Sumerian "middle class," the merchants and artisans, as well as professional people such as doctors. At the bottom of the Sumerian social structure were the peasants—most of whom were farmers—and the slaves.

The Sumerians achieved a high level of culture. They had an advanced knowledge of architecture, as their ziggurats and other buildings show. Their knowledge of science and mathematics enabled them to develop a mathematical system based on a unit of sixty. They also created a remarkably precise twelve-month calendar based on cycles of the moon.

Sumerian Cuneiform: "Wedge-Writing"

Of all their innovations, the development of one of the world's first systems of writing was probably the Sumerians' chief cultural achievement. They wrote on clay tablets using a type of writing that we call **cuneiform** (kyoo·nē′ə·fôrm′), from the Latin word *cuneus*, meaning "wedge." Cuneiform was a system of wedge-shaped markings made with a pointed stick, or **stylus**.

THE ROYAL STANDARD OF UR, c. 2500 B.C. *This portion of the standard depicts a military victory.*

Tens of thousands of clay tablets have been excavated since the end of the last century, and many more tablets may still be awaiting discovery. The majority of tablets

> The Sumerians developed one of the world's first writing systems, called *cuneiform*, a system of wedge-shaped markings.

contain financial transactions and other examples of practical record keeping. But thousands more of the tablets contain imaginative literature, including myths, epics, hymns, laments, proverbs, and fables.

Waves of Invaders

Perhaps because the Sumerians failed to form a unified government of all their city-states, they were vulnerable to invaders. A succession of different peoples dominated Mesopotamia after the Sumerians. First came the **Akkadians** (ə·kā′dē·ənz), a Semitic people. Under their king, **Sargon**, the Akkadians established a great empire that lasted nearly a century. Thanks mostly to a famous Sumerian ruler named **Gudea**, Sumerian culture managed to rebound for a short

Sumerian bronze of a harnessed chariot, c. 3000–2000 B.C.
*Disunity among the various city-states left the
Sumerians vulnerable to invasion by neighboring
peoples.*
*How did elements of Sumerian culture survive in
spite of the arrival of successive waves of invaders?*

Inscribed relief of Assurbanipal.

time after the Akkadian empire ended. But then a second
wave of Semitic invaders arrived on the scene. These new-
comers established a magnificent new capital city on the
banks of the Euphrates River and called it **Babylon**, meaning
"gate of the gods."

The Rise of Babylon

The Babylonians, as the builders of Babylon came to be
called, suppressed the Sumerians politically, removing all
their power. By 2000 B.C. the Sumerians no longer existed
as an independent people. But the Babylonians recognized the
value of Sumerian culture and adopted it as their own. They
adapted the Sumerian cuneiform script to their own Semitic
language and translated many of the Sumerian writings,
including the fragmented story of a great king called Gilgamesh, who searched the world for the secret of eternal life.
The Babylonians continued to use Sumerian as a literary language, much as Europeans used Latin during the Middle Ages.

In addition to the *Epic of Gilgamesh*, the literature of
Babylon included creation myths, hymns, and stories of the

Great Flood. The Babylonian style was known for its use of parallelism (see page 195), which resulted in a balanced literary structure similar to the Hebrew, or biblical, style.

In about 1792 B.C., under the reign of **Hammurabi** (hä′moo·rä′bē), the sixth Babylonian ruler, Babylon reached the peak of its glory, becoming the religious and cultural center of western Asia. Today, Hammurabi is most famous for creating a set of laws known as the **Code of Hammurabi**, a collection of 282 laws that regulated every aspect of Babylonian life, from building codes to marriage and divorce. The Code of Hammurabi was highly detailed and harshly punitive. It was based on the unyielding concept of "an eye for an eye, a tooth for a tooth."

The Great Library of Nineveh

In about 1600 B.C., the **Hittites**, a warlike group of conquerors from Asia Minor, invaded Mesopotamia and looted Babylon. Although they did not hold on to Babylon permanently, the Hittites left behind their laws, which were less drastic than the Code of Hammurabi. After the Hittites, Babylon suffered invasion after invasion by mountain peoples looking for a better life in the rich Tigris-Euphrates Valley. Then, in about 900 B.C., the **Assyrians** (ə·sir′ē·ənz) came into Mesopotamia.

The Assyrians were fiercely warlike and feared throughout the ancient world. However, like many conquerors

> 66 I will proclaim to the world the deeds of Gilgamesh. This was the man to whom all things were known; this was the king who knew the countries of the world. He was wise, he saw mysteries and knew secret things. . . . 99
>
> —*from the* Epic of Gilgamesh, *translated by N. K. Sandars*

Founders Society Purchase, Detroit Institute of Arts

THE DRAGON OF MARDUK **from the Ishtar Gate, Babylonian.**

throughout history, they appreciated the accomplishments of the culture they had conquered, and they preserved its richness. The Assyrians built their capital, **Nineveh** (nin'ə·və), on the banks of the Tigris, about 230 miles north

The University Museum, University of Pennsylvania. #T4-109

Front of a lyre, Mesopotamian. *This ornately decorated lyre features mythological figures, including the epic hero Gilgamesh (top).*

> The Babylonians and Hittites left their cultural imprint on the civilization established by the Sumerians. But it was the brutal and warlike Assyrians who ultimately preserved the Mesopotamian literary legacy.

of present-day Baghdad. There, by decree of **King Assurbanipal**, they created a magnificent library in which they carefully stored and preserved the clay tablets containing Sumerian and Babylonian literature. Archaeologists uncovered the remains of this library in the ruins of Nineveh. Tablets containing the priceless remains of Sumerian/Babylonian writings were excavated from these ruins in the middle of the eighteenth century. In fact, it was through the ruins of the Assyrian civilization that archaeologists got their very first glimpse of Mesopotamia's rich and ancient past.

The Rebirth and Final Fall of Babylon

In 612 B.C. the Assyrians' combined enemies, led by the **Chaldeans** (kal·dē'ənz), overthrew them. After the Chaldeans took control of Mesopotamia, Babylon rose once again to enjoy a period of further glory. The Chaldean ruler **Nebuchadnezzar** (neb'yə·kəd·nez'ər) rebuilt the city, creating spectacular palaces and temples of glazed multicolored bricks. Under Nebuchadnezzar's reign, Babylon became known for its Hanging Gardens, one of the Seven Wonders of the World recognized by the ancient Greeks. (According to legend, the king built the huge tiered "mountain"—really a ziggurat—that supported the hanging gardens as a gift to his wife, Amytis, who longed for her wooded and mountainous homeland.) Babylon was also known for a great ziggurat that some historians have identified as the "Tower of Babel," mentioned in the Hebrew Bible as the tower built by the survivors of the Great Flood. ("Babel" was the Hebrew name for Babylon.) Nebuchadnezzar was the king who destroyed Jerusalem and kept the Jews captive in Babylon for seventy years.

Babylon, which once flourished on the site of the modern-day Iraqi city of al Hillah, fell to **Cyrus the Great** of Persia in 539 B.C. It remained a center of trade and culture for several centuries, until a new port was dug at a more favorable site on the Euphrates. After that, Babylon, the last of the great ancient Mesopotamian empires, fell into ruins.

❝ The Pyramids first, which in Egypt were laid;/Next Babylon's Garden, for Amytis made. . . . ❞

—from "Seven Wonders of the Ancient World," Anonymous

Robert Harding Picture Library

THE TOWER OF BABEL. *From a fifteenth-century illuminated manuscript. The legend of the tower may have been inspired by the architectural wonders of ancient Babylon.*

*I*ntroduction

The Epic of Gilgamesh

Written 4,000 years ago, the *Epic of Gilgamesh* is at least a thousand years older than the Greek epics the *Iliad* and the *Odyssey*, as well as most of the books of the Hebrew Bible. This tale of a superhuman Sumerian king was popular in ancient times throughout the Middle East. Today, its story of the king's painful search for everlasting life still touches readers deeply. Yet the epic lay forgotten for almost 2,500 years, until an amateur archaeologist stumbled upon it in 1839.

The Story of King Gilgamesh

Like most epics, the *Epic of Gilgamesh* is based on at least some grains of fact. Many scholars believe that Gilgamesh was an actual king who reigned over the city-state of Uruk, in Sumer, sometime between 2700 and 2500 B.C. Gradually, over the centuries, King Gilgamesh became a legendary figure of mythic proportions, rather like King Arthur in the European Middle Ages. Tales of Gilgamesh's exploits grew and were probably recited in verse for centuries before being recorded in writing. The earliest written fragments date from about 3000 B.C. Later, the tale was repeated and reworked by writers from the Sumerian,

Babylonian, and Assyrian cultures. Some scholars believe that the epic was finally put into its most complete form by a scribe in 1300 B.C.

◆

epic: *a long narrative that recounts the deeds of a larger-than-life hero who embodies the values of a particular society.*

The Gilgamesh of the epic is a superhuman hero, two parts god and one part human. He thus possesses both supernatural powers and human weaknesses, and in many ways it is his human weaknesses that make him so interesting to us and to the ancient peoples who eagerly listened to and learned from his exploits. He is the leader of his people and the builder of a great city, yet he suffers from excessive pride. In fact, it is because he rejects the love of Ishtar, the goddess of love and war, and insults the gods that he suffers the death of his dear friend, Enkidu. Refusing to accept death, "the common lot of man," Gilgamesh embarks on a quest for immortality. With superhuman strength, courage, and persistence, he confronts obstacles along the way, but he must ultimately accept human limitations.

Relief of Gilgamesh from the Temple of Sargon II, eighth century B.C.

Versions of the *Epic of Gilgamesh* have now been found at sites almost as far north as the Black Sea and as far south as Jerusalem, and from the Mediterranean coast eastward to the Persian Gulf. The epic was so widely known that many scholars believe it served as an **archetype**, or model, for hero myths that would appear later in Greece, India, and Persia.

The *Epic of Gilgamesh* reveals a great deal about the ancient Mesopotamians' sometimes pessimistic views of existence. But it also shows us the sensitivity and humanity of these ancient peoples, who are not unlike us in their joys, sorrows, and strivings.

Statue of the Sumerian king Gudea of Lagash, 2200 B.C.

Versions of the Epic

The selections from *Gilgamesh* presented here are based on twelve clay tablets of cuneiform script. These tablets were among 25,000 discovered in modern Iraq, at Nineveh, in the buried ruins of the library of King Assurbanipal of Assyria (669–626 B.C.). Nineveh was razed by Persian invaders in 612 B.C., and the original tablets were broken and marred. But the recent discovery of older versions of the epic has helped scholars to clarify many parts of the story that once were missing or vague.

Reader's Guide

from the EPIC OF GILGAMESH

Background

Though the Sumerian and Babylonian civilizations were advanced for their time and offered their citizens certain comforts and pleasures, the people were powerless against ever-present threats of devastating floods, severe droughts, and belligerent neighbors who sought "the good life" in the Tigris and Euphrates Valley. It is no wonder, then, that the religious beliefs of the ancient Mesopotamians were somewhat pessimistic. The people worshiped a pantheon, or family, of unpredictable gods and goddesses who could bring about misfortune as well as favor. Regardless of one's status or how one lived one's life, there was no joyful afterlife to look forward to. The end of life offered no consolation, only emptiness.

These beliefs are evident in the epic, as the hero Gilgamesh, in spite of his great powers, suffers a life-changing loss. When the person who means the most to him dies, the proud Gilgamesh must come to terms with the reality that he will not live forever. And because, in the Sumerian view, death offers only emptiness, Gilgamesh rebels against it, and sets off on a quest to attain immortality.

Writer's Response

The search for everlasting life is a common theme in world literature. Think of stories you have read or films you have seen that deal with this theme. What is the usual outcome of people's search for immortality? What do you think is the point of such stories?

Literary Focus

Gilgamesh is the earliest known **epic hero**, and he may have been the model for many later epic heroes, including Homer's Odysseus. All epic heroes are superior human beings. All have supernatural strength and spiritual powers, and all are mighty leaders of their people. But most of them, like Gilgamesh, are of mixed divine and human birth, and thus possess human weaknesses. We admire these heroes for their divine, superhuman qualities. At the same time, we sympathize with them because their weaknesses and difficulties remind us of our own. If even they must accept human limitations, what of us?

from the EPIC OF GILGAMESH

N. K. SANDARS

> Read to the end of the first paragraph of the section entitled
> "The Search for Everlasting Life." What is Gilgamesh's
> motivation for seeking out Utnapishtim? Do you predict that
> Gilgamesh will succeed or fail in his quest?

CHARACTERS IN THE EPIC

Anu (ā′nōō): the god of the
heavens; the father-god.

Ea (ā′ə): the god of wisdom;
usually a friend to humans.

Enkidu (en′kē·dōō): Gilgamesh's friend; a wild man
whom the gods created
out of clay.

Enlil (en·lil′): the god of the
air, the wind, and the
earth.

Gilgamesh (gēl′gə·mesh′, or
gil′gə·mesh′): the king
of Uruk and the epic's
hero.

Ishtar (ish′tär): the goddess
of love and war; the queen
of heaven.

Ninurta (nə·nʉr′tə): the god of
war and of irrigation.

Shamash (shä′mäsh): a god
associated with the sun
and human laws.

Siduri (sə·doo′rē): goddess of
wine and brewing.

Urshanabi (ʉr′shə·nä·bē): the
ferryman who travels daily
across the sea of death to
the home of Utnapishtim.

Utnapishtim (oot·nə·pēsh′təm):
the survivor of a flood
sent by the gods to de-
stroy humanity; the gods
granted him eternal life.

The epic opens with an introduction to Gilgamesh, king of the city-state of Uruk.
Gilgamesh, who is two-thirds god and one-
third man, is handsome, courageous, and
powerful. But he is also arrogant, and he
continually oversteps his bounds as a ruler.
His people, upset over the liberties Gilgamesh takes with them, pray to the gods for
relief. In response, the gods send a match
for Gilgamesh: the wild man Enkidu, reared
by wild animals and unfamiliar with civilization. When the two men meet, they engage
in a fierce wrestling match, which Gilgamesh
wins. But the two men become close friends,

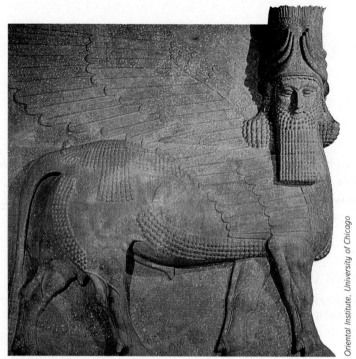

Winged, human-headed bull that once flanked the entrance to the throne room of King Sargon II's palace, 721–705 B.C.

? *How is the Sumerian underworld described in Enkidu's dream?*

and Enkidu, now civilized, joins Gilgamesh on a series of adventures. First they destroy Humbaba, the demon who guards the great Cedar Forest, and then they level the forest. When they dare to criticize the goddess Ishtar, who makes romantic overtures to Gilgamesh, she sends the Bull of Heaven to ravage the land as punishment. Gilgamesh and Enkidu destroy the bull. The gods cannot tolerate such disrespect, and they decree that one of the heroes must die. In this section of the epic, Enkidu has fallen mortally ill.

The Death of Enkidu

As Enkidu slept alone in his sickness, in bitterness of spirit he poured out his heart to his friend. "It was I who cut down the cedar, I who leveled the forest, I who slew Humbaba and now see what has become of me. Listen, my friend, this is the dream I dreamed last night. The heavens roared, and earth rumbled back an answer; between them stood I before an awful being, the somber-faced man-bird; he had directed on me his purpose. His was a vampire face, his foot was a lion's foot, his hand was an eagle's talon. He fell on me and his claws were in my hair, he held me fast and I smothered; then he transformed me so that my arms became wings covered with feathers. He turned his stare towards me, and he led me away to the palace of Irkalla,[1] the Queen of Darkness, to the house from which none who enters ever returns, down the road from which there is no coming back.

---

1. **Irkalla** (ir·kä′lə): also called Ereshkigal; goddess of the underworld.

"There is the house whose people sit in darkness; dust is their food and clay their meat. They are clothed like birds with wings for covering, they see no light, they sit in darkness. I entered the house of dust and I saw the kings of the earth, their crowns put away forever; rulers and princes, all those who once wore kingly crowns and ruled the world in the days of old. They who had stood in the place of the gods like Anu and Enlil, stood now like servants to fetch baked meats in the house of dust, to carry cooked meat and cold water from the water skin. In the house of dust which I entered were high priests and acolytes,[2] priests of the incantation and of ecstasy; there were servers of the temple, and there was Etana, that king of Kish whom the eagle carried to heaven in the days of old. I saw also Samuqan, god of cattle, and there was Ereshkigal, the Queen of the Underworld; and Belit-Sheri squatted in front of her, she who is recorder of the gods and keeps the book of death. She held a tablet from which she read. She raised her head, she saw me and spoke: 'Who has brought this one here?' Then I awoke like a man drained of blood who wanders alone in a waste of rushes; like one whom the bailiff has seized and his heart pounds with terror."

Gilgamesh had peeled off his clothes, he listened to his words and wept quick tears, Gilgamesh listened and his tears flowed. He opened his mouth and spoke to Enkidu: "Who is there in strong-walled Uruk who has wisdom like this? Strange things have been spoken, why does your heart speak strangely? The dream was marvelous but the terror was great; we must treasure the dream whatever the terror; for the dream has shown that misery comes at last to the healthy man, the end of life is sorrow." And

Gilgamesh lamented, "Now I will pray to the great gods, for my friend had an ominous dream."

This day on which Enkidu dreamed came to an end and he lay stricken with sickness. One whole day he lay on his bed and his suffering increased. He said to Gilgamesh, the friend on whose account he had left the wilderness, "Once I ran for you, for the water of life, and I now have nothing." A second day he lay on his bed and Gilgamesh watched over him but the sickness increased. A third day he lay on his bed, he called out to Gilgamesh, rousing him up. Now he was weak and his eyes were blind with weeping. Ten days he lay and his suffering increased, eleven and twelve days he lay on his bed of pain. Then he called to Gilgamesh, "My friend, the great goddess cursed me and I must die in shame. I shall not die like a man fallen in battle; I feared to fall, but happy is the man who falls in the battle, for I must die in shame." And Gilgamesh wept over Enkidu. . . .

Gilgamesh laments Enkidu's death for seven days and nights. Finally, he has the people of Uruk fashion a magnificent statue of Enkidu as a memorial. Then the grieving Gilgamesh leaves Uruk.

The Search for Everlasting Life

Bitterly Gilgamesh wept for his friend Enkidu; he wandered over the wilderness as a hunter, he roamed over the plains; in his bitterness he cried, "How can I rest, how can I be at peace? Despair is in my heart. What my brother is now, that shall I be when I am dead. Because I am afraid of death I will go as best I can to find Utnapishtim whom

---

2. **acolytes** (ak′ə·līts′): priests' assistants.

they call the Faraway, for he has entered the assembly of the gods." So Gilgamesh traveled over the wilderness, he wandered over the grasslands, a long journey, in search of Utnapishtim, whom the gods took after the deluge; and they set him to live in the land of Dilmun,[3] in the garden of the sun; and to him alone of men they gave everlasting life.

At night when he came to the mountain passes Gilgamesh prayed: "In these mountain passes long ago I saw lions, I was afraid and I lifted my eyes to the moon; I prayed and my prayers went up to the gods, so now, O moon god Sin,[4] protect me." When he had prayed he lay down to sleep, until he was woken from out of a dream. He saw the lions round him glorying in life; then he took his axe in his hand, he drew his sword from his belt, and he fell upon them like an arrow from the string, and struck and destroyed and scattered them.

So at length Gilgamesh came to Mashu,[5] the great mountains about which he had heard many things, which guard the rising and the setting sun. Its twin peaks are as high as the wall of heaven and its paps reach down to the underworld. At its gate the Scorpions stand guard, half man and half dragon; their glory is terrifying, their stare strikes death into men, their shimmering halo sweeps the mountains that guard the rising sun. When Gilgamesh saw them he shielded his eyes for the length of a moment only; then he took courage and approached. When they saw him so undismayed the Man-Scorpion called to his mate, "This one who comes to us now is flesh of the gods."

The mate of the Man-Scorpion answered, "Two thirds is god but one third is man."

Then he called to the man Gilgamesh, he called to the child of the gods: "Why have you come so great a journey; for what have you traveled so far, crossing the dangerous waters; tell me the reason for your coming?" Gilgamesh answered, "For Enkidu; I loved him dearly, together we endured all kinds of hardships; on his account I have come, for the common lot of man has taken him. I have wept for him day and night, I would not give up his body for burial, I thought my friend would come back because of my weeping. Since he went, my life is nothing; that is why I have traveled here in search of Utnapishtim my father; for men say he has entered the assembly of the gods, and has found everlasting life. I have a desire to question him concerning the living and the dead." The Man-Scorpion opened his mouth and said, speaking to Gilgamesh, "No man born of woman has done what you have asked, no mortal man has gone into the mountain; the length of it is twelve leagues of darkness; in it there is no light, but the heart is oppressed with darkness. From the rising of the sun to the setting of the sun there is no light." Gilgamesh said, "Although I should go in sorrow and in pain, with sighing and with weeping, still I must go. Open the gate of the mountain." And the Man-Scorpion said, "Go, Gilgamesh, I permit you to pass through the mountain of Mashu and through the high ranges; may your feet carry you safely home. The gate of the mountain is open."

---

3. **Dilmun:** the land beyond the seas (the Persian Gulf); the paradise of the Sumerians.
4. **Sin:** father of Shamash, the sun god, and Ishtar, the goddess of love; son of Enlil, the chief god.
5. **Mashu:** in the Lebanon ranges.

Gilgamesh successfully makes his way through the twelve leagues of darkness. When he comes out on the other side of Mashu, he is greeted with an astounding sight.

Copper statue of a Sumerian goddess,
c. 2100–2000 B.C.

There was the garden of the gods; all round him stood bushes bearing gems. Seeing it he went down at once, for there was fruit of carnelian with the vine hanging from it, beautiful to look at; lapis lazuli leaves hung thick with fruit, sweet to see. For thorns and thistles there were hematite and rare stones, agate, and pearls from out of the edge of the sea. While Gilgamesh walked in the garden by the edge of the sea Shamash saw him, and he saw that he was dressed in the skins of animals and ate their flesh. He was distressed, and he spoke and said, "No mortal man has gone this way before, nor will, as long as the winds drive over the sea." And to Gilgamesh he said,

"You will never find the life for which you are searching." Gilgamesh said to glorious Shamash, "Now that I have toiled and strayed so far over the wilderness, am I to sleep, and let the earth cover my head forever? Let my eyes see the sun until they are dazzled with looking. Although I am no better than a dead man, still let me see the light of the sun."

Beside the sea she lives, the woman of the vine, the maker of wine; Siduri sits in the garden at the edge of the sea, with the golden bowl and the golden vats that the gods gave her. She is covered with a veil; and where she sits she sees Gilgamesh coming towards her, wearing skins, the flesh of the gods in his body, but despair in his heart, and his face like the face of one who has made a long journey. She looked, and as she scanned the distance she said in her own heart, "Surely this is some felon; where is he going now?" And she barred her gate against him with the cross-bar and shot home the bolt. But Gilgamesh, hearing the sound of the bolt, threw up his head and lodged his foot in the gate; he called to her, "Young woman, maker of wine, why do you bolt your door; what did you see that made you bar your gate? I will break in your door and burst in your gate, for I am Gilgamesh who seized and killed the Bull of Heaven, I killed the watchman of the cedar forest, I overthrew Humbaba who lived in the forest, and I killed the lions in the passes of the mountain."

Then Siduri said to him, "If you are that Gilgamesh who seized and killed the Bull of Heaven, who killed the watchman of the cedar forest, who overthrew Humbaba that lived in the forest, and killed the lions in the passes of the mountain, why are your cheeks so starved and why is your face so drawn? Why is despair in your heart and your face like the face of one who has made a long journey? Yes, why is your face burned from heat and cold, and why do you come here wandering over the pastures in search of the wind?"

Gilgamesh answered her, "And why should not my cheeks be starved and my face drawn? Despair is in my heart and my face is the face of one who has made a long journey, it was burned with heat and with cold. Why should I not wander over the pastures in search of the wind? My friend, my younger brother, he who hunted the wild ass of the wilderness and the panther of the plains, my friend, my younger brother who seized and killed the Bull of Heaven and overthrew Humbaba in the cedar forest, my friend who was very dear to me and who endured dangers beside me, Enkidu my brother, whom I loved, the end of mortality has overtaken him. I wept for him seven days and nights till the worm fastened on him. Because of my brother I am afraid of death, because of my brother I stray through the wilderness and cannot rest. But now, young woman, maker of wine, since I have seen your face do not let me see the face of death which I dread so much."

She answered, "Gilgamesh, where are you hurrying to? You will never find that life for which you are looking. When the gods created man they allotted to him death, but life they retained in their own keeping. As for you Gilgamesh, fill your belly with good things; day and night, night and day, dance and be merry, feast and rejoice. Let your clothes be fresh, bathe yourself in water, cherish the little child that holds your hand, and make your wife happy in your embrace; for this too is the lot of man."

But Gilgamesh said to Siduri, the young woman, "How can I be silent, how can I rest, when Enkidu whom I love is dust, and I too

The University Museum, University of Pennsylvania, #T4-278

Lyre with bull's head, Sumerian, c. 2500 B.C.
❓ *What role did the Bull of Heaven play in the events leading to Gilgamesh's quest?*

shall die and be laid in the earth. You live by the seashore and look into the heart of it; young woman, tell me now, which is the way to Utnapishtim, the son of Ubara-Tutu? What directions are there for the passage; give me, oh, give me directions. I will cross the Ocean if it is possible; if it is not I will wander still farther in the wilderness."

Siduri sends Gilgamesh into the woods to find Urshanabi, the ferryman, who is building a boat. In anger and ignorance, Gilgamesh smashes some sacred stones that Urshanabi is fashioning into a prow to protect his boat. Gilgamesh then builds another boat, and Urshanabi guides him across the ocean and over the waters of death.

So Urshanabi the ferryman brought Gilgamesh to Utnapishtim, whom they call the Faraway, who lives in Dilmun at the place of the sun's transit, eastward of the mountain. To him alone of men the gods had given everlasting life.

Now Utnapishtim, where he lay at ease, looked into the distance and he said in his heart, musing to himself, "Why does the boat sail here without tackle and mast; why are the sacred stones destroyed, and why does the master not sail the boat? That man who comes is none of mine; where I look I see a man whose body is covered with skins of beasts. Who is this who walks up the shore behind Urshanabi, for surely he is no man of mine?" So Utnapishtim looked at him and said, "What is your name, you who come here wearing the skins of beasts, with your cheeks starved and your face drawn? Where are you hurrying to now? For what reason have you made this great journey, crossing the seas whose passage is difficult? Tell me the reason for your coming."

He replied, "Gilgamesh is my name. I am from Uruk, from the house of Anu." Then Utnapishtim said to him, "If you are Gilgamesh, why are your cheeks so starved and your face drawn? Why is despair in your heart and your face like the face burned with heat and cold; and why do you come here, wandering over the wilderness in search of the wind?"

Gilgamesh explains his quest and asks Utnapishtim for the secret of eternal life. The old man's reply is not what Gilgamesh expects.

Utnapishtim said, "There is no permanence. Do we build a house to stand forever, do we seal a contract to hold for all time? Do brothers divide an inheritance to keep forever, does the flood time of rivers endure? It is only the nymph of the dragonfly who sheds her larva and sees the sun in his glory. From the days of old there is no permanence. The sleeping and the dead, how alike they are, they are like a painted death. What is there between the master and the servant when both have fulfilled their doom? When the Anunnaki,[6] the judges, come together, and Mammetun the mother of destinies, together they decree the fates of men. Life and death they allot but the day of death they do not disclose."

Then Gilgamesh said to Utnapishtim the Faraway, "I look at you now, Utnapishtim, and your appearance is no different from mine; there is nothing strange in your features. I thought I should find you like a hero prepared for battle, but you lie here taking your ease on your back. Tell me truly, how was it that you came to enter the company of the gods and to possess everlasting life?" Utnapishtim said to Gilgamesh, "I will reveal to you a mystery, I will tell you a secret of the gods."

The Story of the Flood

"You know the city Shurrupak,[7] it stands on the banks of Euphrates? That city grew old and the gods that were in it were old. There was Anu, lord of the firmament, their father, and warrior Enlil their counselor, Ninurta the helper, and Ennugi watcher over canals; and with them also was Ea. In those days the world teemed, the people multiplied, the world bellowed like a wild bull, and the great god was aroused by the clamor. Enlil heard

---

6. **Anunnaki** (ä·nōō·nä′kē): underworld gods who serve Ereshkigal by judging the dead.
7. **Shurrupak** (shə·roop′ak): the ancient city of Sumer.

the clamor and he said to the gods in council, 'The uproar of mankind is intolerable and sleep is no longer possible by reason of the babel.' So the gods agreed to exterminate mankind. Enlil did this, but Ea because of his oath warned me in a dream. He whispered their words to my house of reeds, 'Reed-house, reed-house! Wall, O wall, hearken reed-house, wall reflect; O man of Shurrupak, son of Ubara-Tutu; tear down your house and build a boat, abandon possessions and look for life, despise worldly goods and save your soul alive. Tear down your house, I say, and build a boat. These are the measurements of the bark as you shall build her: let her beam equal her length, let her deck be roofed like the vault that covers the abyss; then take up into the boat the seed of all living creatures."

"When I had understood I said to my lord, 'Behold, what you have commanded I will honor and perform, but how shall I answer the people, the city, the elders?' Then Ea opened his mouth and said to me, his servant, 'Tell them this: I have learned that Enlil is wrathful against me, I dare no longer walk in his land nor live in his city; I will go down to the Gulf to dwell with Ea my lord. But on you he will rain down abundance, rare fish and shy wildfowl, a rich harvest-tide. In the evening the rider of the storm will bring you wheat in torrents.'

"In the first light of dawn all my household gathered round me, the children brought pitch and the men whatever was necessary. On the fifth day I laid the keel and the ribs, then I made fast the planking. The ground-space was one acre, each side of the deck measured one hundred and twenty cubits, making a square. I built six decks below, seven in all, I divided them into nine sections with bulkheads between. I drove in wedges where needed, I saw to the punt-poles, and laid in supplies. The carriers

Courtesy of The Oriental Institute of the University of Chicago

Sumerian votive statues. *These statues, whose eyes are wide with awe of the gods, were installed in temples to worship in place of their human counterparts.*
❓ *Based on Utnapishtim's story, how would you characterize the Sumerian gods?*

brought oil in baskets, I poured pitch into the furnace and asphalt and oil; more oil was consumed in caulking, and more again the master of the boat took into his stores. I slaughtered bullocks for the people and every day I killed sheep. I gave the shipwrights wine to drink as though it were river water, raw wine and red wine and oil and white wine. There was feasting then as there is at the time of the New Year's festival; I myself anointed my head. On the seventh day the boat was complete.

"Then was the launching full of difficulty; there was shifting of ballast above and below till two thirds was submerged. I loaded into her all that I had of gold and of living things, my family, my kin, the beast of the field both wild and tame, and all the craftsmen. I sent them on board, for the time that Shamash had ordained was already fulfilled when he said, 'In the evening, when the rider of the storm sends down the destroying rain, enter the boat and batten her down.' The time was fulfilled, the evening came, the rider of the storm sent down the rain. I looked out at the weather and it was terrible, so I too boarded the boat and battened her down. All was now complete, the battening and the caulking; so I handed the tiller to Puzur-Amurri the steersman, with the navigation and the care of the whole boat.

"With the first light of dawn a black cloud came from the horizon; it thundered within where Adad, lord of the storm was riding. In front over hill and plain Shullat and Hanish, heralds of the storm, led on. Then the gods of the abyss rose up; Nergal[8] pulled out the dams of the nether waters, Ninurta the warlord threw down the dikes, and the seven judges of hell, the Annunaki, raised their torches, lighting the land with their livid flame. A stupor of despair went up to heaven when the god of the storm turned daylight to darkness, when he smashed the land like a cup. One whole day the tempest raged, gathering fury as it went, it poured over the people like the tides of battle; a man could not see his brother nor the people be seen from heaven. Even the gods were terrified at the flood, they fled to the highest heaven, the firmament of Anu; they crouched against the walls, cowering like curs. Then Ishtar the sweet-voiced Queen of Heaven cried out like a woman in travail: 'Alas the days of old are turned to dust because I commanded evil; why did I command this evil in the council of all the gods? I commanded wars to destroy the people, but are they not my people, for I brought them forth? Now like the spawn of fish they float in the ocean.' The great gods of heaven and of hell wept, they covered their mouths.

"For six days and six nights the winds blew, torrent and tempest and flood overwhelmed the world, tempest and flood raged together like warring hosts. When the seventh day dawned the storm from the south subsided, the sea grew calm, the flood was stilled; I looked at the face of the world and there was silence, all mankind was turned to clay. The surface of the sea stretched as flat as a rooftop; I opened a hatch and the light fell on my face. Then I bowed low, I sat down and I wept, the tears streamed down my face, for on every side was the waste of water. I looked for land in vain, but fourteen leagues distant there appeared a mountain, and there the boat grounded; on the mountain of Nisir[9] the boat held fast, she held fast and did not budge. One day she held, and a second day on the mountain

---

8. **Nergal:** god of plagues of the underworld.

9. **Nisir:** sometimes identified with Ararat.

of Nisir she held fast and did not budge. A third day, and a fourth day she held fast on the mountain and did not budge; a fifth day and a sixth day she held fast on the mountain. When the seventh day dawned I loosed a dove and let her go. She flew away, but finding no resting-place she returned. Then I loosed a swallow, and she flew away but finding no resting-place she returned. I loosed a raven, she saw that the waters had retreated, she ate, she flew around, she cawed, and she did not come back. Then I threw everything open to the four winds, I made a sacrifice and poured out a libation on the mountain top. Seven and again seven cauldrons I set up on their stands, I heaped up wood and cane and cedar and myrtle. When the gods smelled the sweet savor, they gathered like flies over the sacrifice. Then, at last, Ishtar also came, she lifted her necklace with the jewels of heaven that once Anu had made to please her. 'O you gods here present, by the lapis lazuli round my neck I shall remember these days as I remember the jewels of my throat; these last days I shall not forget. Let all the gods gather round the sacrifice, except Enlil. He shall not approach this offering, for without reflection he brought the flood; he consigned my people to destruction.'

"When Enlil had come, when he saw the boat, he was wroth[10] and swelled with anger at the gods, the host of heaven, 'Has any of these mortals escaped? Not one was to have survived the destruction.' Then the god of the wells and canals Ninurta opened his mouth and said to the warrior Enlil, 'Who is there of the gods that can devise without Ea? It is Ea alone who knows all things.' Then Ea opened his mouth and spoke to warrior Enlil, 'Wisest of gods, hero Enlil, how could you so senselessly bring down the flood?

Lay upon the sinner his sin,
Lay upon the transgressor his transgression,
Punish him a little when he breaks loose,
Do not drive him too hard or he perishes;
Would that a lion had ravaged mankind
Rather than the flood,
Would that a wolf had ravaged mankind
Rather than the flood,
Would that famine had wasted the world
Rather than the flood,
Would that pestilence had wasted mankind
Rather than the flood.

It was not I that revealed the secret of the gods; the wise man learned it in a dream. Now take your counsel what shall be done with him.'

"Then Enlil went up into the boat, he took me by the hand and my wife and made us enter the boat and kneel down on either side, he standing between us. He touched our foreheads to bless us saying, 'In time past Utnapishtim was a mortal man; henceforth he and his wife shall live in the distance at the mouth of the rivers.' Thus it was that the gods took me and placed me here to live in the distance, at the mouth of the rivers."

The Return

Utnapishtim said, "As for you, Gilgamesh, who will assemble the gods for your sake, so that you may find that life for which you are searching? But if you wish, come and put it to the test: only prevail against sleep for six days and seven nights." But while Gilgamesh sat there resting on his haunches, a mist of sleep like soft wool teased from the fleece drifted over him, and Utnapishtim said to his wife, "Look at him now, the

---

10. **wroth** (rôth): (British) angry.

Seated couple, Sumerian.

and roused me." But Utnapishtim said, "Count these loaves and learn how many days you slept, for your first is hard, your second like leather, your third is soggy, the crust of your fourth has mold, your fifth is mildewed, your sixth is fresh and your seventh was still over the glowing embers when I touched and woke you." Gilgamesh said, "What shall I do, O Utnapishtim, where shall I go? Already the thief in the night has hold of my limbs, death inhabits my room; wherever my foot rests, there I find death."

Then Utnapishtim spoke to Urshanabi the ferryman: "Woe to you Urshanabi, now and forevermore you have become hateful to this harborage; it is not for you, nor for you are the crossings of this sea. Go now, banished from the shore. But this man before whom you walked, bringing him here, whose body is covered with foulness and the grace of whose limbs has been spoiled by wild skins, take him to the washing-place. There he shall wash his long hair clean as snow in the water, he shall throw off his skins and let the sea carry them away, and the beauty of his body shall be shown, the fillet[11] on his forehead shall be renewed, and he shall be given clothes to cover his nakedness. Till he reaches his own city and his journey is accomplished, these clothes will show no sign of age, they will wear like a new garment." So Urshanabi took Gilgamesh and led him to the washing-place, he washed his long hair as clean as snow in the water, he threw off his skins, which the sea carried away, and showed the beauty of his body. He renewed the fillet on his forehead, and to cover his nakedness gave him clothes which would show no sign of age, but would wear like a new garment till he reached his own city, and his journey was accomplished.

strong man who would have everlasting life, even now the mists of sleep are drifting over him." His wife replied, "Touch the man to wake him, so that he may return to his own land in peace, going back through the gate by which he came." Utnapishtim said to his wife, "All men are deceivers, even you he will attempt to deceive; therefore bake loaves of bread, each day one loaf, and put it beside his head; and make a mark on the wall to number the days he has slept."

So she baked loaves of bread, each day one loaf, and put it beside his head, and she marked on the wall the days that he slept; and there came a day when the first loaf was hard, the second loaf was like leather, the third was soggy, the crust of the fourth had mold, the fifth was mildewed, the sixth was fresh, and the seventh was still on the embers. Then Utnapishtim touched him and he woke. Gilgamesh said to Utnapishtim the Faraway, "I hardly slept when you touched

---

11. **fillet** (fil′it): a narrow headband.

Relief of King Assurbanipal's armed guard, Assyrian, c. 800 B.C.

Then Gilgamesh and Urshanabi launched the boat on to the water and boarded it, and they made ready to sail away; but the wife of Utnapishtim the Faraway said to him, "Gilgamesh came here wearied out, he is worn out; what will you give him to carry him back to his own country?" So Utnapishtim spoke, and Gilgamesh took a pole and brought the boat in to the bank. "Gilgamesh, you came here a man wearied out, you have worn yourself out; what shall I give you to carry you back to your own country? Gilgamesh, I shall reveal a secret thing, it is a mystery of the gods that I am telling you. There is a plant that grows under the water, it has a prickle like a thorn, like a rose; it will wound your hands, but if you succeed in taking it, then your hands will hold that which restores his lost youth to a man."

When Gilgamesh heard this he opened the sluices so that a sweet-water current might carry him out to the deepest channel; he tied heavy stones to his feet and they dragged him down to the water-bed. There he saw the plant growing; although it pricked him he took it in his hands; then he cut the heavy stones from his feet, and the sea carried him and threw him on to the shore. Gilgamesh said to Urshanabi the ferryman, "Come here, and see this marvelous plant. By its virtue a man may win back all his former strength. I will take it to Uruk of the strong walls; there I will give it to the old men to eat. Its name shall be 'The Old Men Are Young Again'; and at last I shall eat it myself and have back all my lost youth." So Gilgamesh returned by the gate through which he had come, Gilgamesh and Urshanabi went together. They traveled their twenty leagues and then they broke their fast; after thirty leagues they stopped for the night.

Gilgamesh saw a well of cool water and he went down and bathed; but deep in the pool there was lying a serpent, and the serpent sensed the sweetness of the flower. It rose out of the water and snatched it away, and immediately it sloughed its skin and returned to the well. Then Gilgamesh sat down and wept, the tears ran down his face, and he took the hand of Urshanabi; "O Urshanabi, was it for this that I toiled with my hands, is it for this I have wrung out my heart's blood? For myself I have gained nothing; not I, but the beast of the earth has joy of it now. Already the stream has carried it twenty leagues back to the channels where I found it. I found a sign and now I have lost it. Let us leave the boat on the bank and go."

After twenty leagues they broke their fast, after thirty leagues they stopped for the night; in three days they had walked as much as a journey of a month and fifteen days. When the journey was accomplished they arrived at Uruk, the strong-walled city. Gilgamesh spoke to him, to Urshanabi the ferryman, "Urshanabi, climb up on to the wall of Uruk, inspect its foundation terrace, and examine well the brick work; see if it is not of burnt bricks; and did not the seven wise men lay these foundations? One third of the whole is city, one third is garden, and one third is field, with the precinct of the goddess Ishtar. These parts and the precinct are all Uruk."

This too was the work of Gilgamesh, the king, who knew the countries of the world. He was wise, he saw mysteries and knew secret things, he brought us a tale of the days before the flood. He went a long journey, was weary, worn out with labor, and returning engraved on a stone the whole story.

First Thoughts

What do you think Gilgamesh has learned by the end of the epic?

Identifying Facts

1. Why does Gilgamesh want to find Utnapishtim?
2. According to the story of the flood, why do the gods decide to destroy humanity? How do the gods react when they see the effects of the flood?
3. What extraordinary power does Utnapishtim claim the magical plant possesses? What does Gilgamesh want to do with the plant?
4. What happens to the plant, and what is Gilgamesh's reaction to this event?

Interpreting Meanings

1. According to Enkidu's dream, what is the underworld like? Why is this dream important for an understanding of Gilgamesh's **motivations** in seeking immortality?
2. What pleasures does Siduri tell Gilgamesh to content himself with? Why do you think Gilgamesh is unwilling to take Siduri's advice at this point in his journey?
3. Summarize Utnapishtim's response to Gilgamesh when Gilgamesh asks him for the secret of eternal life. Do you think Utnapishtim's argument is convincing? In what ways is Utnapishtim not what Gilgamesh expected?
4. Some scholars believe that the story of the flood was originally a separate **myth** that was later woven into the story of Gilgamesh. Do you think that the flood story interrupts the narrative, or does it add something to the meaning of the story? Explain.

5. Utnapishtim asks his wife to bake a loaf of bread to mark each day that Gilgamesh sleeps, because "all men are deceivers." Is Gilgamesh deliberately deceiving Utnapishtim by claiming that he hardly slept? Is it possible that Gilgamesh himself has been somehow deceived? Explain.

6. **Irony** is the contrast between what is expected to happen and what actually does happen. Explain what is ironic about what happens to the plant of eternal youth. What does this irony teach Gilgamesh?

7. An **epic hero** always in some way represents the highest values of his or her culture and acts with his or her people in mind. In what ways is Gilgamesh's quest selfish? In what ways is he undertaking his quest not only for himself, but for all the people of Uruk? What does he ultimately bring back to his people?

Applying Meanings

Some people feel that an awareness of the inevitability of death makes people more aware that life is precious and that they should make the most of time. Other people feel that knowing life must eventually come to an end makes it impossible to fully enjoy life's pleasures. What do you think about this issue? How do you think the ancient Sumerians felt about it, based on the epic you have just read?

Creative Writing Response

Creating a New Episode of the Epic. What if, after he had lost the magic flower, Gilgamesh had tried to retrieve it again, and succeeded? How will Gilgamesh use the plant? Will he share it with others? Will he try to bring Enkidu back to life? Will he discover that eternal youth has its drawbacks? Write an account of Gilgamesh's retrieval of the plant and its results. Show both the actions and the feelings of Gilgamesh. If you wish, you may continue your episode into a new ending for the epic.

Speaking and Listening

Defending a Position. Imagine that you are one of the following students who has just finished reading the *Epic of Gilgamesh*.

Student #1: That was the stupidest story I've ever read. Gilgamesh obviously had the brain of a flea, or he would never have gone off on such a wild-goose chase in the first place. Everyone knows there's no such thing as immortality. It's a totally unrealistic story and a waste of time. I want to read something that I can relate to my life.

Student #2: Well, most myths and epics are unrealistic. I mean, no one literally goes out and fights monsters or descends to the underworld. But I think the story rings true in some way. It's like Gilgamesh had to find out that people aren't meant to live forever, just so that he could make peace with Enkidu's death and accept his own mortality. I really sympathized with his situation.

Which student's views are most similar to your own? Pair off with a classmate who holds the opposite view and, in front of the class, defend the position of Student #1 or #2. Use specific examples from the epic to defend your position.

THE ART OF TRANSLATION

Comparing Translations of Gilgamesh

The original *Epic of Gilgamesh* was presented in verse rather than prose. Several fine verse translations of the epic are available. Some are direct translations from cuneiform tablets. One of the most successful versions of the epic, however, is Herbert Mason's very personal translation. Mason was a student at Harvard when he was first introduced to the epic. Because Mason had suffered a deep loss—the death of his father—when he was a child, he sympathized strongly with Gilgamesh's grief over the loss of Enkidu and with Gilgamesh's quest. Mason created a new retelling of the Gilgamesh epic, freely reshaping material from several sources.

Sumerian cuneiform tablet.

Trustees of the British Museum

Compare the following passage from the Mason translation with the same passage from the Sandars prose translation you have just read (see page 142). Then discuss the differences you see between the two versions.

When he arrived at the mountains of Mashu,
Whose peaks reach to the shores of
    Heaven
And whose roots descend to Hell, he saw
The Scorpion people who guard its gate,
Whose knowledge is awesome, but whose
    glance is death.

When he saw them, his face turned ashen
    with dismay,
But he bowed down to them, the only way
    to shield himself
Against effusions of their gaze.
The Scorpion man then recognized
In Gilgamesh the flesh of gods and told his
    wife:
This one is two-thirds god, one-third man
And can survive our view, then spoke to
    him:
Why have you come this route to us?
The way is arduous and long
And no one goes beyond.

I have come to see my father,
Utnapishtim,
Who was allowed to go beyond.
I want to ask him about life and death,
To end my loss. My friend has died.
I want to bring him back to life.

—*translated by Herbert Mason, 1971*

HEBREW LITERATURE

For much of their history, the Hebrews were wanderers. Instead of building great monuments or far-reaching empires like the Egyptians and many of their neighbors in Mesopotamia, the Hebrews, or Jews, forged a rich cultural life based on their religious beliefs. These beliefs are given form in the **Hebrew Bible**, known to Christians as the **Old Testament**. In a way, the Hebrew Bible is the great "monument" left behind by the ancient Hebrews, for it is the record of their spiritual, literary, and historical experience.

The Early Hebrew Patriarchs

Moses holding the Ten Commandments, from a fourteenth-century illuminated manuscript.

Hebrew history begins in Mesopotamia with **Abraham**, the first Hebrew patriarch, or "founding father." According to the Hebrew Bible, Abraham and his wife Sarah left the Babylonian city of Ur and crossed the Jordan River to the land of **Canaan**, the part of the Fertile Crescent that lay between the Jordan River and the Mediterranean Sea. The descendants of Abraham and Sarah came to be called *Hebrews*, which means "people from across the river."

The Hebrews lived in Canaan for four generations under the Hebrew patriarchs: Abraham, his son Isaac, and his grandson Jacob. Jacob, who was later named Israel, lent his name to the Hebrews, who came to be called the **Israelites**. The Book of Genesis in the Hebrew Bible tells the story of Joseph, Jacob's favorite son, who was betrayed and sent into slavery in Egypt by his eleven jealous brothers. Joseph won the favor of the pharaoh in Egypt by predicting a famine, thus enabling Egypt to store grain in preparation for a severe drought to come. When the famine struck, Egypt was well prepared, but Canaan was caught unaware. Joseph saved the Israelites from starvation by bringing them into Egypt.

The Egyptians drowning in the Red Sea. *Colored engraving after Gustave Doré.*

❓ *What aspect of early Hebrew history does this engraving depict?*

Captivity and the Flight from Egypt

In Egypt, the Israelites organized themselves into twelve tribes. But years after Joseph had led the Israelites to salvation in Egypt, a new Egyptian pharaoh enslaved them. Various historical sources indicate that around 1200 B.C. a leader named **Moses** led the Hebrews on an *exodus*, or "going forth," to freedom across an arm of the Red Sea and into the Sinai Desert. In the Hebrew Bible, the **Book of Exodus** tells how God aided Moses in this daring escape from slavery in Egypt.

The Book of Exodus also relates an event that has become central to the Hebrew faith. While traveling through the desert toward Canaan, called "the Promised Land," Moses received from God the **Ten Commandments**, a code of ethics, or moral conduct. God promised to lead the Hebrews to the Promised Land on the condition that they obey these Commandments. The Ten Commandments laid the foundation for what has come to be known as **Mosaic law**.

Moses died during the difficult years in the Sinai desert. But one of his followers, **Joshua**, eventually led the Israelites back into Canaan.

> " He that is slow to anger is better than the mighty; and he that ruleth his spirit than he that taketh a city. "
>
> —*Proverbs 16:32*
> *King James Bible*

The Promised Land

When the Israelites arrived in Canaan, it was already inhabited by other peoples, among them the Canaanites and the Philistines. The Israelites struggled to make a place for themselves over the next two hundred years. Their task was difficult because of disagreements among the twelve tribes of Israel. This period in Hebrew history is recounted in the book called **Judges**, because judges were the only unifying political and military power within the twelve tribes.

Eventually, around 1020 B.C., a Hebrew leader named **Saul** succeeded in unifying the twelve tribes, becoming the first king of Israel. The Israelites flourished under his rule

THE GIVING OF THE TABLETS OF THE LAW, RAPHAEL (1483–1520).
? *In exchange for following his commandments, what did God promise Moses and his followers?*

Scala/Art Resource, New York

and became the most powerful group of people in Canaan. However, the Hebrews were never able to gain complete and lasting control over the Philistines, who inhabited the coastal area of Canaan. (The Romans, in fact, called Canaan Palestine, after the Philistines.)

An Interlude of Peace and Stability

For almost one hundred years, the Hebrews enjoyed an era of prosperity and stability. Saul's successor, **King David**, who reigned from 1010 to 970 B.C., was able to break the Philistine's control of coastal lands and capture the city of the Jebusites (jeb′yə·sīts). Under David, this small hill town was transformed into the Hebrew capital city of **Jerusalem**. David's son **Solomon**, who reigned until about 925 B.C., launched many ambitious projects to beautify Jerusalem. His greatest contribution was the construction of the magnificent **Temple of Jerusalem**, a central place of worship which became an important symbol of the Hebrews' spiritual unity. Today, all that remains of this once-splendid structure is its western wall, now known as the Wailing Wall because of the many tearful prayers said there over the centuries by people mourning the Temple's destruction.

Conflict and Division

After Solomon's death, Israel again entered a period of political and economic turmoil. Internal conflicts drove the twelve tribes apart. To the south, the tribes of Benjamin and Judah founded **Judah**, or Judea, from which the word *Jew*,

> With Solomon's death, disagreements among the twelve tribes split the Hebrew kingdom in two: Israel to the north and Judah to the south.

used interchangeably with the word *Hebrew*, comes. Judah contained the city of Jerusalem. To the north, the remaining ten tribes founded **Israel**, later called Samaria. Although the twelve tribes had split politically into two kingdoms, they continued to think of themselves as one people spiritually.

> ❝ In those days there was no king in Israel; every man did that which was right in his own eyes. ❞
>
> —*Judges 21:25*

The National Gallery of Art, Washington. Widener Collection

THE YOUTHFUL DAVID, ANDREA DEL CASTAGNO (1423–57).

Mesopotamian Invaders

Although Israel was larger and wealthier than Judah, its internal weaknesses made it vulnerable to attack from invaders. In 722 B.C., the Assyrian rulers of Mesopotamia conquered Israel. The ten tribes of Israel scattered, and they were gradually absorbed into the surrounding cultures. Hebrew tradition refers to these groups as the "Ten Lost Tribes."

In 586 B.C., after the Chaldeans had supplanted the Assyrians as the dominant power in Mesopotamia, the Chaldean king **Nebuchadnezzar** conquered Israel's stronger neighbor, Judah. He destroyed the Temple of Jerusalem and took many Hebrews into slavery in Babylon. Thus began one of the most bitter periods in Hebrew history, the **Babylonian Exile**.

Despite their separation from their homeland, the exiled Hebrews remembered their culture and kept it alive.

The Holy Land

•••• Kingdom of David and Solomon in the 10th Century B.C.

SYRIA

N

GALILEE

Sea of Galilee

Nazareth

Samaria

Jerusalem

Bethlehem

Gaza

Jordan River

MEDITERRANEAN SEA

KINGDOM OF ISRAEL

Dead Sea

SYRIAN DESERT

PHILISTIA

EGYPT

Nile River

KINGDOM OF JUDAH

RED SEA

SINAI PENINSULA

MEDITERRANEAN SEA

MIDDLE EAST

PERSIAN GULF

RED SEA

ARABIAN PENINSULA

AFRICA

When the Persian leader **Cyrus the Great** conquered Babylon and freed the Hebrew slaves in 539 B.C., many Hebrews returned to Jerusalem to rebuild the temple and reestablish their society. Some Hebrews, however, stayed in Babylon. Thus were sown the first seeds of the *Diaspora* (dī·as′pə·rə)—literally, the "scattering"—that would come to characterize the state of the Hebrew nation.

> For almost eight hundred years, the tiny kingdom of Judah withstood conquest, slavery, and domination at home by a series of foreign rulers.

Although Cyrus allowed the Hebrews to return to Jerusalem, he did not grant them independence. Instead, for the next three-and-a-half centuries the Hebrews lived under the domination of a series of foreign rulers, including Alexander the Great of Macedonia. None of these rulers seriously threatened the Hebrews until 167 B.C., when the Seleucid King Antiochus (an·tī′ə·kəs) IV tried, ultimately unsuccessfully, to suppress Judaism.

The Hebrew Identity: A Covenant with God

The experience of living in a state of exile left the Hebrews vulnerable in many ways, but also provided inspiration for remarkable cultural creativity and spiritual unity. Since ancient times, the Hebrew people have focused on their God, **Yahweh**, as their source of unity. Unlike most of their neighbors in the Middle East, the Hebrews were **monotheists**—that is, they worshiped one god. They viewed Yahweh as a guiding entity who was always with them and rejected the notion that a human king could also be divine.

Yahweh differed from other gods in many ways, but especially in establishing with his people a special agreement, or **covenant**. The terms of this covenant meant that he would always guide Hebrew history, protecting his people if they fulfilled his law. Thus, even when the Hebrew people lost their homeland, they found a sense of belonging in their ongoing relationship with Yahweh.

> **❝** Now therefore, if ye will obey my voice indeed, and keep my covenant, then ye shall be a peculiar treasure unto me above all people. . . . **❞**
>
> —*Exodus 19:5*

*I*ntroduction

The Hebrew Bible

For good reason, the Hebrews have often been referred to as the "people of the book." The "book" is the Hebrew Bible, the great document of Jewish historical, literary, and spiritual experience.

The History of the Hebrew Bible

The Hebrew Bible tells the history of the Jewish people and presents the basic laws and teachings of their faith. The contents of the Hebrew Bible existed first in oral tradition. Then, over a period of centuries lasting from approximately 1000 to 100 B.C., the various parts of the Hebrew Bible were written and assembled. The Hebrew Bible was mostly written in Hebrew and Aramaic, another Semitic language that had replaced Hebrew as the language spoken by the Jews in about 400 B.C.

What Is the Hebrew Bible?

The Hebrew Bible is not one book, but many. In fact, the very name "Bible" comes from *biblia*, the plural of the Greek word *biblion*, "a book." The Hebrew Bible consists of twenty-four separate books, beginning with the Book of Genesis and ending with Chronicles. Christians refer to the Hebrew Bible as the Old Testament and accept it as sacred, but unlike the Jews they accept a second book of sacred writings, the New Testament (see page 196), as part of their Bible as well.

The Books of the Hebrew Bible

The Jewish people call their Bible **Tanakh,** an acronym formed from the first letters of the Hebrew words for the three categories of books contained in it: **Torah** (Law), **Nevi'im** (Prophets), and **Ketuvim** (Writings).

The Torah, or Law, is the first and oldest part of the Hebrew Bible. Sometimes called the Five Books of Moses—for, according to tradition, Moses wrote them—the Torah consists of five books that contain the earliest historical narratives of the Jewish people: Genesis, Exodus,

◆

narrative: *a kind of writing that tells a story or relates an event.*

Leviticus, Numbers, and Deuteronomy. It also contains the basic tenets, or beliefs, and laws of Jewish faith, with detailed instructions on worship practices and conduct for daily life. The Torah is also known by the Greek word *Pentateuch*, meaning "five scroll jars," referring to the fact that at one time the five scrolls on which the Torah was written were kept in jars. The Torah is held in such reverence by Jewish people that no copy of it, no matter how old or worn, is ever destroyed. In cases of serious damage, it must be given a full funeral and buried as a beloved member of the family.

Nevi'im, or Prophets, contains the powerful words of the prophets: Isaiah, Jeremiah, and Ezekiel, among others. The prophets were not "fortunetellers" but social and spiritual reformers who were believed to be divinely inspired. The prophets called on the people of Israel to repent and lead purer lives, in keeping with God's covenant. These books also include the historical narratives of Joshua, the Judges, and the succession of Hebrew rulers that began with Saul, David, and Solomon.

Finally, Ketuvim, or Writings, consists of a rich variety of **genres**, or types, of literature, from Psalms and Proverbs to the Song of Songs (or Song of Solomon), Ecclesiastes, the Book of Job, and the Book of Ruth. The Book of Psalms contains lyrical hymns of praise that overflow with poignant emotions and imagery.

◆

psalm (säm): *a sacred song or hymn.*

The Book of Ruth is a tender work about compassion, loyalty, and tolerance that is sometimes described as a "short story." And the Book of Job features a dramatic dialogue between God and a man named Job, in which the question

The Jewish Museum, New York/Art Resource, New York

Torah ark curtain, late eighteenth century.

of human suffering is deeply and movingly probed.

The Themes of the Hebrew Bible

The Hebrew Bible is concerned above all with exploring the Hebrews' developing relationship with God. In the Hebrew Bible, God, or Yahweh, makes promises to people, but he also makes constant demands of them. Human beings are often tested, and they do not always pass their tests. They make mistakes and suffer the consequences of their actions. But they also experience the mercy of God and the constant promise of spiritual renewal, for the power to fulfill the covenant with God is within the power of each individual.

Reader's Guide

IN THE BEGINNING
from Genesis

Background

The Book of Genesis is the first of the Five Books of Moses, or the Torah. Genesis reflects the Hebrew people's beliefs about the origins of things, and it contains the core teachings of Jewish belief. Genesis begins with the birth of the universe and goes on to explain the emergence of evil, the cause of the Great Flood, the origin of languages, and the development of God's covenant with the Hebrew people.

Most scholars today believe that Genesis is actually a composite of separate narratives by different writers collected over a period of several hundred years. This may explain why Genesis contains two accounts of the creation of human beings. The first narrative tells us that God created the universe in six days and that man and woman were created at the same time. The second story, set in the Garden of Eden, tells us that Adam was created first and that Eve was created from his rib. Taken together, the two creation stories give us a fuller picture of the Hebrews' concept of God and humanity's relationship with God. We also come to understand their answers to some of the questions that concern all humankind: how and why people were created, why there is pain and conflict on earth, and why there is death.

Writer's Response

What do you already know, or think you know, about the story of creation in Genesis? Jot down some of the details you remember about Adam and Eve and the story of creation. As you read, see if you have remembered those details correctly, or if there are any details that you have forgotten. Does anything in the story of creation surprise you?

Literary Focus

Repetition—the repeating of words, phrases, or even entire sentences or passages—is an important feature of the Hebrew, or biblical, style. Repetition can serve several functions in a work of literature. It can create rhythm and build suspense and dramatic intensity. It can also help to emphasize important words and ideas.

IN THE BEGINNING
from Genesis
King James Bible

The Greek word genesis means "coming into being" or "originating." What beginnings, or origins, do these portions of the Book of Genesis explain?

The Creation

In the beginning God created the heaven and the earth. And the earth was without form, and void; and darkness was upon the face of the deep. And the Spirit of God moved upon the face of the waters.[1]

And God said "Let there be light": and there was light. And God saw the light, that it was good: and God divided the light from the darkness. And God called the light Day, and the darkness he called Night. And the evening and the morning were the first day.

And God said, "Let there be a firmament[2] in the midst of the waters, and let it divide the waters from the waters." And God made the firmament, and divided the waters which were under the firmament from the waters which were above the firmament: and it was so. And God called the firmament Heaven. And the evening and the morning were the second day.

And God said, "Let the waters under the heaven be gathered together unto one place, and let the dry land appear": and it was so.

And God called the dry land Earth; and the gathering together of the waters he called Seas: and God saw that it was good. And God said, "Let the earth bring forth grass, the herb[3] yielding seed, and the fruit tree yielding fruit after his[4] kind, whose seed is in itself, upon the earth": and it was so. And the earth brought forth grass, and herb yielding seed after his kind, and the tree yielding fruit, whose seed was in itself, after his kind: And God saw that it was good. And the evening and the morning were the third day.

And God said, "Let there be lights in the firmament of the heaven to divide the day from the night; and let them be for signs, and for seasons, and for days, and years. And let them be for lights in the firmament of the heaven to give light upon the earth": and it was so. And God made two great lights; the greater light to rule the day, and the lesser light to rule the night: he made the stars also. And God set them in the firmament of

---

1. **waters:** According to Hebrew belief, only water existed before the creation began.
2. **firmament:** the sky, seen as an arch or a vault.

3. **herb:** vegetation.
4. **his:** its (*Its*, the neuter form of the pronoun, did not come into common use until late in the seventeenth century, after the King James Bible was published).

THE GARDEN OF EDEN, ERASTUS S. FIELD (1805–1900).
How does this painting compare with your own image of the Garden of Eden?

SuperStock International, Inc.

the heaven to give light upon the earth, and to rule over the day and over the night, and to divide the light from the darkness: and God saw that it was good. And the evening and the morning were the fourth day.

And God said, "Let the waters bring forth abundantly the moving creature[5] that hath life, and fowl that may fly above the earth in the open firmament of heaven." And God created great whales, and every living creature that moveth, which the waters brought forth abundantly, after their kind,[6] and every winged fowl after his kind: and God saw that it was good. And God blessed them, saying, "Be fruitful, and multiply, and fill the waters in the seas, and let fowl multiply in the earth." And the evening and the morning were the fifth day.

And God said, "Let the earth bring forth the living creature after his kind, cattle, and creeping thing, and beast of the earth after his kind": and it was so. And God made the beast of the earth after his kind, and cattle after their kind, and every thing that creepeth upon the earth after his kind: and God saw that it was good.

And God said, "Let us make man in our image, after our likeness: and let them have dominion over the fish of the sea, and over the fowl of the air, and over the cattle, and over all the earth, and over every creeping thing that creepeth upon the earth." So God created man in his own image, in the image of God created he him; male and female created he them. And God blessed them, and

---

5. **creature:** an old plural form without the *s*.
6. **their kind:** their nature.

God said unto them, "Be fruitful, and multiply, and replenish the earth, and subdue it: and have dominion over the fish of the sea, and over the fowl of the air, and over every living thing that moveth upon the earth."

And God said, "Behold, I have given you every herb bearing seed, which is upon the face of all the earth, and every tree, in the which is the fruit of a tree yielding seed; to you it shall be for meat. And to every beast of the earth, and to every fowl of the air, and to every thing that creepeth upon the earth, wherein there is life, I have given every green herb for meat":[7] and it was so. And God saw every thing he had made, and, behold, it was very good. And the evening and the morning were the sixth day.

Thus the heavens and the earth were finished, and all the host[8] of them. And on the seventh day God ended his work which he had made; and he rested on the seventh day from all his work which he had made. And God blessed the seventh day, and sanctified it: because that in it he had rested from all his work which God created and made.

The Garden of Eden

These are the generations of the heavens and of the earth when they were created, in the day that the Lord God made the earth and the heavens, and every plant of the field before it was in the earth, and every herb of the field before it grew: for the Lord God had not caused it to rain upon the earth, and there was not a man to till the ground. But there went up a mist from the earth, and watered the whole face of the ground. And the Lord God formed man of the dust of the ground, and breathed into his nostrils the breath of life; and man became a living soul.

And the Lord God planted a garden eastward in Eden; and there he put the man whom he had formed. And out of the ground made the Lord God to grow every tree that is pleasant to the sight, and good for food; the tree of life also in the midst of the garden, and the tree of knowledge of good and evil. And a river went out of Eden to water the garden; and from thence it was parted, and became into four heads. The name of the first is Pison: that is it which compasseth the whole land of Havilah,[9] where there is gold; and the gold of that land is good: there is bdellium[10] and the onyx stone. And the name of the second river is Gihon: the same is it that compasseth the whole land of Ethiopia. And the name of the third river is Hiddekel:[11] that is it which goeth toward the east of Assyria. And the fourth river is Euphrates.[12] And the Lord God took the man, and put him into the garden of Eden to dress it and to keep it. And the Lord God commanded the man, saying, "Of every tree of the garden thou mayest freely eat. But of the tree of the knowledge of good and evil, thou shalt not eat of it: for in the day that thou eatest thereof thou shalt surely die."

And the Lord God said, "It is not good that the man should be alone; I will make him an help meet[13] for him." And out of the

---

7. **meat:** In the King James Bible, meat simply means food in general. Animal meat is called flesh.
8. **host:** multitude.

9. **Pison** (pē′sən) . . . **Havilah** (hav′ə·lə): land rich in gold, perhaps located in Arabia.
10. **bdellium** (del′ē·əm): a kind of jewel—either a crystal, a pearl, or a deep-red gem such as a garnet.
11. **Gihon** (gē′hän) . . . **Hiddekel** (hid′ə·kəl): *Hiddekel* is the biblical name for the Tigris River.
12. **Euphrates** (yoo·frāt′ēz): longest river in western Asia.
13. **help meet:** mate.

ground the Lord God formed every beast of the field, and every fowl of the air; and brought them unto Adam to see what he would call them: and whatsoever Adam called every living creature, that was the name thereof. And Adam gave names to all cattle, and to the fowl of the air, and to every beast of the field; but for Adam there was not found an help meet for him. And the Lord God caused a deep sleep to fall upon Adam, and he slept: and he took one of his ribs, and closed up the flesh instead thereof; and the rib, which the Lord God had taken from man, made he a woman, and brought her unto the man. And Adam said, "This is now bone of my bones, and flesh of my flesh: she shall be called Woman, because she was taken out of Man." Therefore shall a man leave his father and his mother, and shall cleave unto his wife: and they shall be one flesh.

The Fall

And they were both naked, the man and his wife, and were not ashamed.

Now the serpent[14] was more subtil[15] than any beast of the field which the Lord God had made. And he said unto the woman, "Yea, hath God said, 'Ye shall not eat of every tree of the garden'?" And the woman said unto the serpent, "We may eat of the fruit of the trees of the garden. But of the fruit of the tree which is in the midst of the garden, God hath said, 'Ye shall not eat of it, neither shall ye touch it, lest ye die.'" And the serpent said unto the woman, "Ye shall not surely die. For God doth know that in

EVE, LUCAS CRANACH THE ELDER, c. 1530. Eve's temptation has been a popular subject in European art for centuries.

---

14. **the serpent:** traditionally understood to be, or to be possessed by, Satan; formerly the angel Lucifer, Satan was cast out of heaven because he set himself up as God's enemy.

15. **subtil:** subtle, meaning here crafty or sly.

the day ye eat thereof, then your eyes shall be opened, and ye shall be as gods, knowing good and evil." And when the woman saw that the tree was good for food, and that it was pleasant to the eyes, and a tree to be desired to make one wise, she took of the fruit thereof, and did eat, and gave also unto her husband with her; and he did eat. And the eyes of them both were opened, and they knew that they were naked; and they sewed fig leaves together, and made themselves aprons. And they heard the voice of the Lord God walking in the garden in the cool of the day: and Adam and his wife hid themselves from the presence of the Lord God amongst the trees of the garden. And the Lord God called unto Adam, and said unto him, "Where art thou?" And he said, "I heard thy voice in the garden, and I was afraid, because I was naked; and I hid myself." And he said, "Who told thee that thou wast naked? Hast thou eaten of the tree, whereof I commanded thee that thou shouldest not eat?" And the man said, "The woman whom thou gavest to be with me, she gave me of the tree, and I did eat." And the Lord God said unto the woman, "What is this that thou hast done?" And the woman said, "The serpent beguiled me, and I did eat." And the Lord God said unto the serpent, "Because thou hast done this, thou are cursed above all cattle,[16] and above every beast of the field; upon thy belly shalt thou go, and dust shalt thou eat all the days of thy life. And I will put enmity between thee and the woman, and thy seed and her seed; it shall bruise thy head, and thou shalt bruise his heel." Unto the woman he said, "I will greatly multiply thy sorrow and thy conception;[17] in sorrow thou shalt bring forth children; and thy desire shall be to thy husband, and he shall rule over thee." And unto Adam he said, "Because thou hast hearkened unto[18] the voice of thy wife, and hast eaten of the tree, of which I commanded thee, saying, Thou shalt not eat of it: cursed is the ground for thy sake; in sorrow shalt thou eat of it all the days of thy life; thorns also and thistles shall it bring forth to thee; and thou shalt eat the herb of the field; in the sweat of thy face shalt thou eat bread, till thou return unto the ground: for out of it wast thou taken, for dust thou art, and unto dust shalt thou return." And Adam called his wife's name Eve; because she was the mother of all living. Unto Adam also and to his wife did the Lord God make coats of skins, and clothed them.

And the Lord God said, "Behold, the man[19] is become as one of us, to know good and evil: and now, lest he put forth his hand, and take also of the tree of life,[20] and eat, and live for ever": therefore the Lord God sent him forth from the garden of Eden, to till the ground from whence he was taken. So he drove out the man; and he placed at the east of the garden of Eden, Cherubims[21] and a flaming sword which turned every way, to keep the way of[22] the tree of life.

---

16. **cattle:** a general term for all animals.

17. **conception:** childbearing pains.
18. **hearkened unto:** listened to and obeyed.
19. **man:** man and woman.
20. **tree of life:** a second tree in Eden, apparently a source of immortality.
21. **Cherubims** (cher'yoo·bimz): warrior angels who act as guardian spirits and support the throne of God.
22. **keep the way of:** prevent access to.

The story of creation answers many questions about the human condition, but it also raises some tantalizing questions. What questions does the account of the creation leave you with?

Identifying Facts

1. What responsibilities or privileges does God give to humans in the first account of creation?

2. In the second creation account, how is man created? Why is woman created, and how does God create her?

3. In "The Fall," how do Adam and Eve change after they eat the forbidden fruit?

4. How does God punish Adam, Eve, and the serpent?

5. What problems that still plague humanity are explained in "The Fall"?

Interpreting Meanings

1. **Repetition** occurs in the first account of the creation with the phrases "God said . . . and it was so" and "God saw that it was good." Why do you think these phrases are repeated so often? How do they help to characterize God?

2. In "The Garden of Eden," how does Adam's naming of the birds and the beasts assert his "dominion," or authority?

3. Does God seem to consider Adam and Eve equally guilty, or does he punish one of them more than the other? Explain your answer.

4. In the first creation account, God approves of all his creations. Men and women seem to be created equal, and no mention is made of the Fall. Why do you think that people tend to forget this story, and focus instead on Eve's creation from Adam's rib and the subsequent temptation and Fall?

Applying Meanings

Artists often use the story of the Fall as a **metaphor** for a person's loss of innocence, or for passing from childhood into adulthood. What kinds of temptations does the world present to people your age today? Who or what could be cast in the role of the serpent? If you were Adam or Eve, would you accept or reject the fruit the serpent urged you to take? Explain.

Creative Writing Response

Writing from the First-Person Point of View. Absent from the creation stories of Genesis are personal details—glimpses into the psychology of the characters. Rewrite the account of the Fall from the **first-person point of view** of Adam, Eve, or the serpent, using the pronoun *I*. Reveal as much about the character of your narrator as possible, describing the setting and interactions with the other characters in a way you believe he, she, or it would describe them.

Critical Writing Response

Establishing a Theme. Many scholars say that the moral struggle of men and women is a central **theme** of the Hebrew Bible. The first book of the Hebrew Bible plays a critical role in "setting the stage" for that theme. Find examples from the accounts from Genesis that you have just read—episodes, conflicts, characterization—that anticipate or illustrate this theme. Then write a three-paragraph essay showing how your examples support this theme. You might want to use a chart like the one below to organize your evidence.

Creation	The Garden of Eden	The Fall

BEHIND THE SCENES

The King James Bible

Frontispiece to the King James Bible,
(1611). *Engraving.*

The King James Bible, published in 1611, is a product of Renaissance England. In 1604, the newly crowned English king, King James, called a conference of clergymen and scholars to discuss a new English translation of the Bible. Several translations of the Bible already existed, but during the Renaissance people began to be more aware of history and more sensitive to the idea that translations could be inaccurate. King James decided to gather together a group of some of the finest scholars and clergymen in England and commission them to assemble the most faithful translation of the Bible ever published. This translation, he decided, would draw upon the best Hebrew and Greek texts available, and it would leave out the interpretive—and generally inaccurate and biased—comments so common in English translations of the time.

Seven years later, fifty-four scholars and a team of bishops published their results. Their work has come to be known as the King James Bible, also known as the Authorized Version (after the Anglican Church that approved it), and the English Bible.

Modern English literature—especially the literature of the seventeenth through the nineteenth centuries—would be very different had the King James Bible not existed. In fact, the English language itself owes the popularization of many everyday expressions to the King James Bible: "loving kindness," "tender mercy," and "the wisdom of Solomon."

Even in its own day, however, the language of the King James Bible was considered old-fashioned. For example, even though by 1611 the English were beginning to use the pronoun *you,* the King James Bible continued to use the archaic form, *thou.* But in spite of its archaic-sounding language, many believe that the King James Bible ranks with the works of Shakespeare as a model of the English language at its most expressive and poetic.

Reader's Guide

NOAH AND THE FLOOD
from Genesis

Background

The Hebrew story of Noah and the Flood preserves the memory of a terrifying deluge that occurred in Mesopotamia some time in the distant past. By the time the Book of Genesis was assembled, Hebrew storytellers knew many different versions of the ancient story. Instead of discarding any version, the people who assembled the various accounts in Genesis combined the different stories into one long narrative.

Even with various story strands braided into one story, however, the basic ideas are clear: God sends the flood to punish humanity for wickedness, but he saves one good man and his family. God then invites this family into a special pact, or **covenant**, in which God promises never again to destroy the entire earth. God makes the rainbow a symbol of this promise.

Like the creation stories of Genesis, the story of Noah explains beginnings. For example, it explains the appearance of rainbows after a storm. It also explains the development of the covenant, the ongoing pact between the Hebrews and God.

Writer's Response

The story of Noah and the Flood is so famous that most people know something about it, even if they have not read it. List all the features of the story that you are already familiar with. After you have read the story, check your list. Were all of your items accurate?

Literary Focus

Theme is the central idea or insight of a work of literature. Most themes are **implied**—that is, a reader must determine the theme based on details given in the story. A theme is usually the view of a particular writer, but in the Hebrew Bible, themes are expressive of the Hebrew people's deepest beliefs and concerns. The story of Noah and the Flood is the first occurrence in the Hebrew Bible of what is perhaps the most important theme in the Book of Genesis: the theme of the covenant, of the solemn promise that God makes with humankind, binding God and his creation together for eternity.

NOAH AND THE FLOOD
from Genesis
Jewish Publication Society of America

 As you read, note any details that help to characterize God and Noah. What kind of person is Noah? What is God's attitude toward his creation before and after the Flood?

The Lord saw how great was man's wickedness on earth, and how every plan devised by his mind was nothing but evil all the time. And the Lord regretted that He had made man on earth, and His heart was saddened. The Lord said, "I will blot out from the earth the men whom I created—men together with beasts, creeping things, and birds of the sky; for I regret that I made them." But Noah found favor with the Lord.

This is the line of Noah. Noah was a righteous man; he was blameless in his age; Noah walked with God. Noah begot three sons: Shem, Ham, and Japheth.

The earth became corrupt before God; the earth was filled with lawlessness. When God saw how corrupt the earth was, for all flesh had corrupted its ways on earth, God said to Noah, "I have decided to put an end to all flesh, for the earth is filled with lawlessness because of them: I am about to destroy them with the earth. Make yourself an ark of gopher wood;[1] make it an ark with compartments, and cover it inside and out with pitch.[2] This is how you shall make it: the length of the ark shall be three hundred cubits,[3] its width fifty cubits, and its height thirty cubits. Make an opening for daylight in the ark, and terminate it within a cubit of the top. Put the entrance to the ark in its side; make it with bottom, second, and third decks.

"For My part, I am about to bring the Flood waters upon the earth to destroy all flesh under the sky in which there is breath of life; everything on earth shall perish. But I will establish My covenant with you, and you shall enter the ark, with your sons, your wife, and your sons' wives. And of all that lives, of all flesh, you shall take two of each into the ark to keep alive with you; they shall be male and female. From birds of every kind, cattle of every kind, every kind of creeping thing on earth, two of each shall come to you to stay alive. For your part, take of everything that is eaten and store it away, to serve as food for you and for them." Noah did so; just as God commanded him, so he did.

Then the Lord said to Noah, "Go into the ark, with all your household, for you alone have I found righteous before Me in this

---

1. **gopher wood:** an unidentified type of wood.
2. **pitch:** a gummy, tar-like substance used for waterproofing.

3. **cubit** (kyoo′bit): a measure of 17 to 22 inches.

generation. Of every clean[4] animal you shall take seven pairs, males and their mates, and of every animal which is not clean, two, a male and its mate; of the birds of the sky also, seven pairs, male and female, to keep seed alive upon all the earth. For in seven days' time I will make it rain upon the earth, forty days and forty nights, and I will blot out from the earth all existence that I created." And Noah did just as the Lord commanded him.

Noah was six hundred years old when the Flood came, waters upon the earth. Noah, with his sons, his wife, and his sons' wives, went into the ark because of the waters of the Flood. Of the clean animals, of the animals that are not clean, of the birds, and of everything that creeps on the ground, two

---

4. **clean:** The Hebrews made a distinction between animals that were clean—that is, fit for eating and free from ceremonial defilement—and those that were unclean.

NOAH'S ARK, EDWARD HICKS, 1846.

Philadelphia Museum of Art: Bequest of Lisa Norris Elkins

of each, male and female, came to Noah into the ark, as God had commanded Noah. And on the seventh day the waters of the Flood came upon the earth.

In the six hundredth year of Noah's life, in the second month, on the seventeenth day of the month, on that day

All the fountains of the great deep burst apart,

And the floodgates of the sky broke open.

The rain fell on the earth forty days and forty nights. That same day Noah and Noah's sons, Shem, Ham, and Japheth, went into the ark, with Noah's wife and the three wives of his sons—they and all beasts of every kind, all cattle of every kind, all creatures of every kind that creep on the earth, and all birds of every kind, every bird, every winged thing. They came to Noah into the ark, two each of all flesh in which there was breath of life. Thus they that entered comprised male and female of all flesh, as God had commanded him. And the Lord shut him in.

The Flood continued forty days on the earth, and the waters increased and raised the ark so that it rose above the earth. The waters swelled and increased greatly upon the earth, and the ark drifted upon the waters. When the waters had swelled much more upon the earth, all the highest mountains everywhere under the sky were covered. Fifteen cubits higher did the waters swell, as the mountains were covered. And all flesh that stirred on earth perished—birds, cattle, beasts, and all the things that swarmed upon the earth, and all mankind. All in whose nostrils was the merest breath of life, all that was on dry land, died. All existence on earth was blotted out—man, cattle, creeping things, and birds of the sky; they were blotted out from the earth. Only Noah was left, and those with him in the ark.

And when the waters had swelled on the earth one hundred and fifty days, God remembered Noah and all the beasts and all the cattle that were with him in the ark, and God caused a wind to blow across the earth, and the waters subsided. The fountains of the deep and the floodgates of the sky were stopped up, and the rain from the sky was held back; the waters then receded steadily from the earth. At the end of one hundred and fifty days the waters diminished, so that in the seventh month, on the seventeenth day of the month, the ark came to rest on the mountains of Ararat.[5] The waters went on diminishing until the tenth month; in the tenth month, on the first of the month, the tops of the mountains became visible.

At the end of forty days, Noah opened the window of the ark that he had made and sent out the raven; it went to and fro until the waters had dried up from the earth. Then he sent out the dove to see whether the waters had decreased from the surface of the ground. But the dove could not find a resting place for its foot, and returned to him to the ark, for there was water over all the earth. So putting out his hand, he took it into the ark with him. He waited another seven days, and again sent out the dove from the ark. The dove came back to him toward evening, and there in its bill was a plucked-off olive leaf! Then Noah knew that the waters had decreased on the earth. He waited still another seven days and sent the dove forth; and it did not return to him any more.

In the six hundred and first year, in the first month, on the first of the month, the waters began to dry from the earth; and when Noah removed the covering of the ark, he saw that the surface of the ground was

---

5. **Ararat** (ar'ə·rat'): the highest mountain in Turkey.

drying. And in the second month, on the twenty-seventh day of the month, the earth was dry.

God spoke to Noah, saying, "Come out of the ark, together with your wife, your sons, and your sons' wives. Bring out with you every living thing of all flesh that is with you: birds, animals, and everything that creeps on earth; and let them swarm on the earth and be fertile and increase on earth." So Noah came out, together with his sons, his wife, and his sons' wives. Every animal, every creeping thing, and every bird, everything that stirs on earth came out of the ark by families.

Then Noah built an altar to the Lord and, taking of every clean animal and of every clean bird, he offered burnt offerings on the altar. The Lord smelled the pleasing odor, and the Lord said to Himself: "Never again will I doom the earth because of man, since the devisings of man's mind are evil from his youth; nor will I ever again destroy every living being, as I have done.

> So long as the earth endures,
> Seedtime and harvest,
> Cold and heat,
> Summer and winter,
> Day and night
> Shall not cease."

God blessed Noah and his sons, and said to them, "Be fertile and increase, and fill the earth. The fear and the dread of you shall be upon all the beasts of the earth and upon all the birds of the sky—everything with which the earth is astir—and upon all the fish of the sea; they are given into your hand. Every creature that lives shall be yours to eat; as with the green grasses, I give you all these. You must not, however, eat flesh with its life-blood in it. But for your own life-blood I will require a reckoning: I will re-quire it of every beast; of man, too, will I require a reckoning for human life, of every man for that of his fellow man!

> Whoever sheds the blood of man,
> By man shall his blood be shed;
> For in His image
> Did God make man.

Be fertile, then, and increase; abound on the earth and increase on it."

And God said to Noah and to his sons with him, "I now establish My covenant with you and your offspring to come, and with every living thing that is with you—birds, cattle, and every wild beast as well—all that have come out of the ark, every living thing on earth. I will maintain My covenant with you: never again shall all flesh be cut off by the waters of a flood, and never again shall there be a flood to destroy the earth."

God further said, "This is the sign that I set for the covenant between Me and you, and every living creature with you, for all ages to come. I have set My bow[6] in the clouds, and it shall serve as a sign of the covenant between Me and the earth. When I bring clouds over the earth, and the bow appears in the clouds, I will remember My covenant between Me and you and every living creature among all flesh, so that the waters shall never again become a flood to destroy all flesh. When the bow is in the clouds, I will see it and remember the ev-erlasting covenant between God and all liv-ing creatures, all flesh that is on earth. That," God said to Noah, "shall be the sign of the covenant that I have established between Me and all flesh that is on earth."

The sons of Noah who came out of the ark were Shem, Ham, and Japheth—Ham

---

6. **bow** (bō): rainbow.

being the father of Canaan. These three were the sons of Noah, and from these the whole world branched out.

Noah, the tiller of the soil, was the first to plant a vineyard. He drank of the wine and became drunk, and he uncovered himself within his tent. Ham, the father of Canaan, saw his father's nakedness and told his two brothers outside. But Shem and Japheth took a cloth, placed it against both their backs and, walking backwards, they covered their father's nakedness; their faces were turned the other way, so that they did not see their father's nakedness. When Noah woke up from his wine and learned what his youngest son had done to him, he said,

> "Cursed be Canaan;
> The lowest of slaves
> Shall he be to his brothers."

And he said,

> "Blessed be the Lord,
> The God of Shem;
> Let Canaan be a slave to them.
> May God enlarge Japheth,
> And let him dwell in the tents of Shem;
> And let Canaan be a slave to them."

Noah lived after the Flood 350 years. And all the days of Noah came to 950 years; then he died.

THE FLOOD, NICOLAS POUSSIN, 1664.

? *Why do you think "Noah and the Flood" is one of the most popular stories from the Bible?*

Scala/Art Resource, New York

Noah and the Flood   **175**

First Thoughts

How did you feel when you read about the destruction of all living things except for the creatures on the ark?

Identifying Facts

1. Why does God destroy the earth with a flood? Why are Noah and his family spared?

2. Why does Noah send a dove out of the ark? What does the return of the dove with an olive branch tell Noah?

3. What is the first thing Noah does after the ark is unloaded?

Interpreting Meanings

1. Water can symbolize rebirth as well as destruction. How are both destruction and rebirth involved in the flood story?

2. What clues can you find in the story of the Flood that show the virtuous side of Noah's **character**? What can you infer about Noah's personality from the final section of the story?

3. Paraphrase the **theme** of God's covenant with all living things. What does the making of this covenant tell you about God's attitude toward his creation?

4. Compare the story of Noah to the story of creation. Is God characterized the same way in both stories? Is he portrayed as more forgiving or more vengeful in the story of Noah than in the story of Adam and Eve?

Applying Meanings

According to the story of Noah, God is discouraged by the corruption and wickedness of his creation. Do you think that the best way to fix a mistake is usually to obliterate it and start over? Or do you believe that there is something redeeming about everything that is created?

Creative Writing Response

Writing and Acting Out a Dramatic Sketch. Stories in the Hebrew Bible often do not include the background and details that we have come to associate with modern narratives. How do you suppose Noah's neighbors reacted to his building of the ark? With a partner or small group, write a short dramatic sketch, one to two pages long, in which Noah explains to his neighbors why he is building an enormous ark. How do his neighbors respond to his project? Are they understanding, alarmed, or mocking? How does Noah deal with his neighbors' reactions? As a group, present your sketch to the class.

Critical Writing Response

Comparing and Contrasting Accounts of the Flood. The story of the flood in the *Epic of Gilgamesh* (see page 145) is strikingly similar to the story of "Noah and the Flood." In each story a man is warned of a flood and is saved from destruction by building an ark for himself, his family, and a number of animals. Think of other ways that the two flood stories resemble each other, and ways in which they are different. What do you think these two cultures—Mesopotamian and Hebrew—have in common? What differences exist between the cultures? Write a two- to three-paragraph essay in which you explore these questions. You might want to use a diagram like the one below to plan your essay.

Reader's Guide

THE BOOK OF RUTH

Background

The story of Ruth is set about 1100 B.C., approximately the same time that the Trojan War was taking place in Asia Minor. But it was probably not written down until nearly seven hundred years later, when the Hebrew people returned to Israel after their seventy-year captivity in Babylon. This was a time of turmoil when Hebrew leaders perceived foreign customs as a threat to the identity of the Jewish people.

Ruth was a woman from Moab (mō′ab′), a kingdom east of the Dead Sea. The religion of Moab involved the worship of idols—a practice the Hebrews condemned. Ruth married a Jewish man, Mahlon, but was soon left widowed and childless. In 1100 B.C., a woman who had no husband or son could expect to experience dire poverty. Fortunately, the ancient Israelites practiced a custom called "levirate" (lev′ə·rit) marriage (from *levir,* meaning "husband's brother"). According to this custom, a close male relative of the dead husband, such as a brother, was obliged to marry the widow if the husband had left no son. The firstborn son of this second marriage would be raised in the dead husband's name and would be considered his legal heir. Despite being an outsider, Ruth went to Israel with her mother-in-law Naomi and ultimately married Boaz (bō′az′), a relative of her husband's.

Oral Response

Most of us have felt like outsiders at one time or another. Hold a class discussion in which each of you describes an experience in which you felt as if you "didn't belong." What was the cause of this feeling? Who or what helped you overcome this feeling? Or does something—society or yourself—still need to change in order for you to stop feeling this way?

Literary Focus

The Book of Ruth is sometimes called the first **short story** ever written. Unlike the poetry of the Book of Psalms or the narratives in the Book of Genesis, the Book of Ruth contains developed **characters**, a specific **setting**, a definite **plot**, or course of events, and an underlying **theme** about loyalty and acceptance.

THE BOOK OF RUTH

King James Bible

> *The Book of Ruth is an entertaining story, but it is also a lesson about devotion, tolerance, and compassion. Pay attention to the message of the story of Ruth and note the rewards received by characters who express devotion.*

Chapter 1

Now it came to pass in the days when the judges ruled that there was a famine in the land. And a certain man of Bethlehem-Judah[1] went to sojourn in the country of Moab,[2] he, and his wife, and his two sons.

And the name of the man was Elimelech, and the name of his wife Naomi, and the names of his two sons Mahlon and Chilion, Ephrathites[3] of Bethlehem-Judah. And they came into the country of Moab and continued there.

And Elimelech, Naomi's husband, died; and she was left, and her two sons.

And they took them wives of the women of Moab; the name of the one was Orpah, and the name of the other Ruth: and they dwelled there about ten years.

And Mahlon and Chilion died also, both of them; and the woman was left of her two sons and her husband.

Then she arose with her daughters-in-law, that she might return from the country of Moab: for she had heard in the country of Moab how that the Lord had visited his people in giving the bread.

Wherefore she went forth out of the place where she was, and her two daughters-in-law with her; and they went on the way to return unto the land of Judah.

And Naomi said unto her two daughters-in-law, "Go, return each to her mother's house: the Lord deal kindly with you, as ye have dealt with the dead and with me. The Lord grant you that ye may find rest, each of you in the house of her husband." Then she kissed them; and they lifted up their voice and wept.

And they said unto her, "Surely we will return with thee unto thy people."

And Naomi said, "Turn again, my daughters: why will ye go with me? Are there yet any more sons in my womb, that they may be your husbands?

"Turn again, my daughters, go your way; for I am too old to have a husband. If I should say I have hope, if I should have a husband also tonight and should also bear sons, would ye tarry for them till they were

---

1. **Bethlehem-Judah:** that is, Bethlehem in Judah; Judah was a region in southern Palestine that eventually became a kingdom rivaling Israel to the North.
2. **Moab:** a kingdom of the Dead Sea, in what is today called Jordan.
3. **Ephrathites** (ef'rə·thīts): natives of Bethlehem, once known as Ephrath; members of the clan of Ephrah.

RUTH AND NAOMI, WILLEM DROST. Ruth's famous quote, "Wither thou goest, I will go," is often used in wedding ceremonies.
? *What quality in Ruth does this speech demonstrate?*

grown? Would ye stay for them from having husbands? Nay, my daughters; for it grieveth me much for your sakes that the hand of the Lord is gone out against me."

And they lifted up their voice and wept again: and Orpah kissed her mother-in-law, but Ruth clave unto[4] her.

And she said, "Behold, thy sister-in-law is gone back unto her people and unto her gods: Return thou after thy sister-in-law."

And Ruth said, "Entreat me not to leave thee or to return from following after thee:

for whither thou goest, I will go; and where thou lodgest, I will lodge: thy people shall be my people, and thy God my God: where thou diest, will I die, and there will I be buried: the Lord do so to me, and more also, if ought[5] but death part thee and me."

When she saw that she was steadfastly minded to go with her, then she left speaking unto her.

So they two went until they came to Bethlehem. And it came to pass, when they were come to Bethlehem, that all the city was moved about them, and they said, "Is this Naomi?" And she said unto them, "Call me not Naomi, call me Mara:[6] for the almighty hath dealt very bitterly with me. I went out full, and the Lord hath brought me home again empty: Why then call ye me Naomi, seeing the Lord hath testified against me, and the Almighty hath afflicted me?"

So Naomi returned, and Ruth the Moabitess, her daughter-in-law, with her, which returned out of the country of Moab: and they came to Bethlehem in the beginning of barley harvest.

Chapter 2

And Naomi had a kinsman of her husband's, a mighty man of wealth, of the family of Elimelech; and his name was Boaz.

And Ruth the Moabitess said unto Naomi, "Let me now go to the field and glean ears of corn after him in whose sight I shall find grace."[7] And she said unto her, "Go, my daughter."

---

4. **clave unto:** clung to; was faithful to (archaic form of *cleaved*).

5. **ought** (archaic): aught, meaning "anything."

6. **Naomi . . . Mara:** Naomi means "pleasantness" or "my pleasant one," in Hebrew, and Mara means "bitterness" or "the bitter one."

7. **glean. . . grace:** According to biblical law, the poor were entitled to glean in the fields—that is, to gather the bits of grain left or dropped by the reapers. The corners of the fields were also left for the poor to reap.

And she went, and came, and gleaned in the field after the reapers: and her hap[8] was to light on a part of the field belonging unto Boaz, who was of the kindred of Elimelech.

And, behold, Boaz came from Bethlehem and said unto the reapers, "The Lord be with you." And they answered him, "The Lord bless thee."

Then said Boaz unto his servant that was set over the reapers, "Whose damsel is this?"

And the servant that was set over the reapers answered and said, "It is the Moabitish damsel that came back with Naomi out of the country of Moab. And she said, 'I pray you, let me glean and gather after the reapers among the sheaves': so she came, and hath continued even from the morning until now, that she tarried a little in the house."

Then said Boaz unto Ruth, "Hearest thou not, my daughter? Go not to glean in another field, neither go from hence, but abide here fast by my maidens. Let thine eyes be on the field that they do reap, and go thou after them. Have I not charged the young men that they shall not touch thee? And when thou art athirst, go unto the vessels, and drink of that which the young men have drawn."

Then she fell on her face and bowed herself to the ground and said unto him, "Why have I found grace in thine eyes, that thou shouldest take knowledge of me, seeing I am a stranger?"

And Boaz answered and said unto her, "It hath fully been showed me all that thou hast done unto thy mother-in-law since the death of thine husband: and how thou hast left thy father and thy mother, and the land of thy nativity and art come unto a people which thou knewest not heretofore. The Lord recompense thy work, and a full reward be given thee of the Lord God of Israel, under whose wings thou art come to trust."

Then she said, "Let me find favor in thy sight, my lord; for that thou hast comforted me, and for that thou hast spoken friendly unto thine handmaid, though I be not like unto one of thine handmaidens."

And Boaz said unto her, "At mealtime come thou hither, and eat of the bread, and dip thy morsel in the vinegar." And she sat beside the reapers: and he reached her

Dover Publications

RUTH AND BOAZ, GUSTAVE DORÉ.

---

8. **hap:** luck.

parched corn, and she did eat, and was sufficed, and left.

And when she was risen up to glean, Boaz commanded his young men, saying, "Let her glean even among the sheaves, and reproach her not. And let fall also some of the handfuls on purpose for her, and leave them, that she may glean them, and rebuke her not."

So she gleaned in the field until even, and beat out that she had gleaned: and it was about an ephah[9] of barley.

And she took it up and went into the city: and her mother-in-law saw what she had gleaned: and she brought forth and gave to her what she had reserved after she was sufficed.

And her mother-in-law said unto her, "Where hast thou gleaned today? and where wroughtest thou? Blessed be he that did take knowledge of thee." And she showed her mother-in-law with whom she had wrought, and said, "The man's name with whom I wrought today is Boaz."

And Naomi said unto her daughter-in-law, "Blessed be he of the Lord, who hath not left off his kindness to the living and to the dead." And Naomi said unto her, "The man is near of kin unto us, one of our next kinsmen."

And Ruth the Moabitess said, "He said unto me also, 'Thou shalt keep fast by my young men, until they have ended all my harvest.'"

And Naomi said unto Ruth her daughter-in-law, "It is good, my daughter, that thou go out with his maidens, that they meet thee not in any other field."

So she kept fast by the maidens of Boaz to glean unto the end of barley harvest and of wheat harvest; and dwelt with her mother-in-law.

Chapter 3

Then Naomi her mother-in-law said unto her, "My daughter, shall I not seek rest for thee,[10] that it may be well with thee? And now is not Boaz of our kindred, with whose maidens thou wast? Behold, he winnoweth barley tonight in the threshing floor. Wash thyself therefore, and anoint thee, and put thy raiment upon thee, and get thee down to the floor: but make not thyself known unto the man, until he shall have done eating and drinking. And it shall be, when he lieth down, that thou shalt mark the place where he shall lie, and thou shalt go in and uncover his feet and lay thee down; and he will tell thee what thou shalt do."

And she said unto her, "All that thou sayest unto me I will do."

And she went down unto the floor and did according to all that her mother-in-law bade her.

And when Boaz had eaten and drunk and his heart was merry, he went to lie down at the end of the heap of corn: and she came softly and uncovered his feet and laid her down.

And it came to pass at midnight, that the man was afraid and turned himself: and, behold, a woman lay at his feet.

And he said, "Who art thou?" And she answered, "I am Ruth thine handmaid: Spread therefore thy skirt[11] over thine handmaid; for thou art a near kinsman."

And he said, "Blessed be thou of the Lord, my daughter: for thou hast showed more kindness in the latter end than at the beginning, inasmuch as thou followedst not young

---

9. **ephah** (ē'fə): a little more than a bushel.

10. **seek rest for thee:** that is, seek a husband; Naomi is trying to fulfill the responsibility of a parent for arranging the marriage of a child.

11. **Spread therefore thy skirt:** a formal act of betrothal.

men,[12] whether poor or rich. And now, my daughter, fear not; I will do to thee all that thou requirest: for all the city of my people doth know that thou art a virtuous woman. And now it is true that I am thy near kinsman: howbeit, there is a kinsman nearer than I. Tarry this night, and it shall be in the morning that if he will perform unto thee the part of a kinsman, well; let him do the kinsman's part: but if he will not do the part of a kinsman to thee, then will I do the part of a kinsman to thee, as the Lord liveth: lie down until the morning."

And she lay at his feet until the morning: and she rose up before one could know another. And he said, "Let it not be known that a woman came into the floor."

Also he said, "Bring the veil that thou hast upon thee, and hold it." And when she held it, he measured six measures of barley and laid it on her: and she went into the city.

And when she came to her mother-in-law, she said, "Who art thou, my daughter?" And she told her all that the man had done to her.

And she said, "These six measures of barley gave he me; for he said to me, 'Go not empty unto thy mother-in-law.'"

Then said she, "Sit still, my daughter, until thou know how the matter will fall: for the man will not be in rest until he have finished the thing this day."

Chapter 4

Then went Boaz up to the gate and sat him down there and, behold, the kinsman of whom Boaz spake came by; unto whom he said, "Ho, such a one! turn aside, sit down here." And he turned aside and sat down.

And he took ten men of the elders of the city and said, "Sit ye down here." And they sat down.

And he said unto the kinsman, "Naomi, that is come again out of the country of Moab, selleth a parcel of land, which was our brother Elimelech's. And I thought to advertise thee, saying, Buy it before the inhabitants and before the elders of my people. If thou wilt redeem it, redeem it: but if thou wilt not redeem it, then tell me, that I may know: for there is none to redeem it beside thee; and I am after thee." And he said, "I will redeem it."

Then said Boaz, "What day thou buyest the field of the hand of Naomi, thou must buy it also of Ruth the Moabitess, the wife of the dead, to raise up the name of the dead upon his inheritance."

And the kinsman said, "I cannot redeem it for myself, lest I mar mine own inheritance:[13] Redeem thou my right to thyself; for I cannot redeem it."

Now this was the manner in former time in Israel concerning redeeming and concerning changing, for to confirm all things; a man plucked off his shoe, and gave it to his neighbor: and this was a testimony in Israel.

Therefore the kinsman said unto Boaz, "Buy it for thee." So he drew off his shoe.

And Boaz said unto the elders and unto all the people, "Ye are witnesses this day, that I have bought all that was Elimelech's, and all that was Chilion's and Mahlon's, of the hand of Naomi. Moreover, Ruth the

---

12. **thou followedst not young men:** Boaz, who is eighty years old, is praising Ruth for her willingness to fulfill the levirate marriage obligation by marrying him even though he is old.

13. **lest I mar mine own inheritance:** in other words, by spending money on property that will go to the son legally regarded as Mahlon's, rather than his own.

RUTH AND BOAZ WITH THE REAPERS, French miniature, c. 1250.

Moabitess, the wife of Mahlon, have I purchased to be my wife, to raise up the name of the dead upon his inheritance, that the name of the dead be not cut off from among his brethren and from the gate of his place: Ye are witnesses this day."

And all the people that were in the gate and the elders said, "We are witnesses. The Lord make the woman that is come into thine house like Rachel and like Leah,[14] which two did build the house of Israel: and do thou worthily in Ephrath, and be famous in Bethlehem. And let thy house be like the house of Pharez, whom Tamar bare unto Judah,[15] of the seed which the Lord shall give thee of this young woman."

So Boaz took Ruth, and she was his wife: and when he went in unto her, the Lord gave her conception, and she bare a son.

And the women said unto Naomi, "Blessed be the Lord, which hath not left thee this day without a kinsman, that his name may be famous in Israel. And he shall be unto thee a restorer of thy life and a nourisher of thine old age: for thy daughter-in-law, which loveth thee, which is better to thee than seven sons, hath born him."

And Naomi took the child and laid it in her bosom and became nurse unto it.

And the women her neighbors gave it a name, saying, "There is a son born to Naomi;"[16] and they called his name Obed: He is the father of Jesse, the father of David.

Now these are the generations of Pharez: Pharez begat Hezron, and Hezron begat Ram, and Ram begat Amminadab, and Amminadab begat Nahshon, and Nahshon begat Salmon, and Salmon begat Boaz, and Boaz begat Obed, and Obed begat Jesse, and Jesse begat David.

---

14. **like Rachel and like Leah:** two sisters who were Jacob's wives, their sons were among the twelve sons of Jacob who founded the twelve tribes of Israel.

15. **Pharez . . . Judah:** Judah was the fourth son of Jacob and Leah. After his daughter-in-law Tamar had twice been left a childless widow after two of his sons died, she tricked Judah into becoming the father of her twin sons, Pharez and Zarah.

16. **son born to Naomi:** not literally, but rather a son in the sense of a legal heir to both her dead husband and dead sons; some biblical scholars suggest that the child may have been legally regarded as Naomi's.

How did you feel about the conclusion of the Book of Ruth? Did you find it satisfying and appropriate, or did you expect a different ending?

Identifying Facts

1. How does Naomi try to persuade Ruth and Orpah not to follow her?
2. How do Ruth and Naomi manage to survive in Bethlehem?
3. How does Ruth come to the attention of Boaz? Why does he admire her?
4. Why does Boaz first ask another relative to "redeem" the property and wife of Elimelech?

Interpreting Meanings

1. Ruth's decision to forsake her people and follow Naomi is celebrated as a shining example of selfless devotion. Her virtue is best expressed in the famous line, "Whither thou goest, I will go." Go back to the story and list the details that emphasize each of the following values: hospitality, courtesy, modesty, acceptance, and respect for custom and tradition.
2. The relationship between Ruth and Boaz is sometimes spoken of as a "love story." Do you think this is a good way to describe it? If so, what attitudes toward love and marriage does their relationship represent?
3. **Irony** is the contrast between what is expected and what actually takes place. At the end of the story, it is said that David, the greatest king of Israel, will be descended from Ruth. What is **ironic** about this detail?
4. The Book of Ruth is often called a **short story**. Discuss the specific differences between the story of Ruth and the stories you have read from the Book of

Genesis. Consider the elements that make the Book of Ruth a short story: **character development**, **setting**, **plot**, and **theme**.

Applying Meanings

After her husband's death, Ruth has the opportunity to stay in her homeland and live with her own family, yet she decides to go with Naomi to Israel. Have you ever willingly or unwillingly found yourself an outsider in a strange or foreign place or among people you didn't know well? Describe your situation, how you felt about it, and the choices you made.

Creative Writing Response

Writing a Letter. Imagine that you are Ruth and that a day or two has passed since you married Boaz. Write a letter to your sister-in-law, Orpah. Summarize for her the experiences you have had since you and Naomi left Moab. Tell Orpah what you have found difficult and what you have enjoyed. Be sure to share your hopes for the future.

Critical Writing Response

Analyzing Characterization. Ruth is a strong, complex **character**. Characters can be drawn in several different ways. A writer can reveal a character directly by telling what he or she is like. On the other hand, a writer can sketch a character indirectly by describing the character's appearance and dress, letting the character speak to others, revealing the character's thoughts and feelings, showing how the character affects other people, and showing the character's actions. Write a two- to three-paragraph essay exploring the characterization of Ruth in the Book of Ruth. Provide examples of **direct** and **indirect characterization** from the story.

SEEING CONNECTIONS

Biblical Allusions

A **literary allusion** is a reference made in one work of literature to another work of literature. Such an allusion is only effective when the reader recognizes the reference and sees how the two works are associated. Literature abounds with allusions to the Bible. John Keats, an English poet, found inspiration in the story of Ruth. In his "Ode to a Nightingale" (1819), he speaks of the immortality of the poetic melody in the bird's song:

Thou wast not born for death, immortal
        Bird!
    No hungry generations tread thee down;
The voice I hear this passing night was
        heard
    In ancient days by emperor and clown:
Perhaps the selfsame song that found a path
    Through the sad heart of Ruth, when,
        sick for home,
        She stood in tears amid the alien corn;
        The same that ofttimes hath
    Charmed magic casements, opening on
        the foam
    Of perilous seas, in faery lands forlorn.

Keats expects his readers to recognize the biblical allusion and to associate it with a specific context. Explain Keats's allusion to the story of Ruth. Is the allusion accurate, or has Keats taken liberties with Ruth's story? Is the allusion effective?

Frequently, the titles of books, plays, songs, and movies contain biblical allusions. In the following list, each title is a phrase (or paraphrase) from the King James version of the Hebrew Bible. Look in a copy of a King James Bible for the context of the following titles. Read the original passage and identify the person, place, thing, event, or phrase used in each of the following titles.

1. *Adam's Rib,* a movie by James Cukor (Genesis 2:21)
2. *East of Eden,* a novel by John Steinbeck (Genesis 3:24)
3. "Adam Raised a Cain," a song by Bruce Springsteen (Genesis 4:1)
4. *Exodus,* a novel by Leon Uris (Book of Exodus)
5. *Absalom! Absalom!,* a novel by William Faulkner (2 Samuel 19:4)
6. *By the Skin of Our Teeth,* a play by Thornton Wilder (Job 19:20)
7. *The Sun Also Rises,* a novel by Ernest Hemingway (Ecclesiastes 1:5)
8. *Song of Solomon,* a novel by Toni Morrison (Song of Solomon)

See if you can locate other works whose titles are allusions to the Hebrew Bible.

What other biblical persons, places, or events could be used as allusions in current films you have seen or in stories, novels, and plays with which you are familiar?

Reader's Guide

PSALMS 23, 104, AND 137
from the Book of Psalms

Background

The Book of Psalms contains 150 poems. The poems were combined into a single collection around the fourth century B.C. or even later, and the book now appears in the section of the Hebrew Bible called Writings. Nearly half the psalms carry the title "Song of David," but this does not mean that every poem was composed personally by King David, who lived around 1000 B.C. Some psalms were performed in sacred rituals long before David ruled, and others, such as Psalm 137, were composed after his reign.

The Greek word *psalmos,* which means "a plucking of strings," tells us that the poems were sung to musical accompaniment. The Hebrew title *Tehillim* means "songs of praise." Many psalms, like Psalm 104, sing praise to God. But adoration is not the only emotion the psalms express. They are lyric poems, and, like other lyric poems, they range in emotion from bitter anger to joyous exultation. The Book of Psalms features laments, personal meditations, and even battle songs. Much of the Hebrew Bible is devoted to the narration of the ancient history of the Hebrews, but the psalms' emphasis on personal responses to God makes them unique.

Writer's Response

What are some songs you especially like? From the lyrics of one or more songs, write down a few lines or phrases that mean a great deal to you. How do they express or arouse your feelings?

Literary Focus

Parallelism is the repetition of words, grammatically similar phrases, or ideas. Rather than relying on poetic devices like rhyme and meter, the psalms use parallelism to create a sense of balance and order and to show the relationship between similar ideas.

PSALM 23
King James Bible

The Twenty-third Psalm is probably the most often recited of all the psalms. It compares God to a shepherd who loves his flock and to a host who lavishes hospitality on his guests. People often find comfort in this psalm. Which lines do you find especially comforting?

The Lord is my shepherd;
I shall not want.[1]

He maketh me to lie down in green pastures:
He leadeth me beside the still waters.

5 He restoreth my soul:
He leadeth me in the paths of righteousness for
his name's sake.

Yea, though I walk through the valley of the
shadow of death, I will fear no evil: for thou art
with me;
Thy rod and thy staff they comfort me.

Thou preparest a table before me in the presence
of mine enemies:
10 Thou anointest my head with oil;[2] my cup
runneth over.

Surely goodness and mercy shall follow me all the
days of my life:
And I will dwell in the house of the Lord for ever.

THE GOOD SHEPHERD.
Marble statue, fourth century.

---

1. **want:** lack the necessities of life.
2. **anointest . . . oil:** It was a Jewish custom to show respect or hospitality toward a man by pouring oil on his head, since his hair and beard might be dusty from the roads or fields.

PSALM 104
King James Bible

> *As you read the following psalm, imagine the scenes the psalmist creates in words. What can you see? What can you hear? What specific details appeal to the senses of smell and taste and touch?*

Bless the Lord, O my soul.
O Lord my God, thou art very great;
Thou art clothed with honor and majesty:

Who coverest thyself with light as with a garment:
5   Who stretchest out the heavens like a curtain:

Who layeth the beams of his chambers in the
   waters:
Who maketh the clouds his chariot:
Who walketh upon the wings of the wind:

Who maketh his angels spirits;
10   His ministers a flaming fire:

Who laid the foundations of the earth,
That it should not be removed for ever.

Thou coverest it with the deep as with a garment:
The waters stood above the mountains.

15   At thy rebuke they fled;
At the voice of thy thunder they hasted away.

They go up by the mountains;
They go down by the valleys unto the place which
   thou hast founded for them.

Thou hast set a bound that they may not pass
   over;
20   That they turn not again to cover the earth.

He sendeth the springs into the valleys,
Which run among the hills.

They give drink to every beast of the field:
The wild asses quench their thirst.

25 By them shall the fowls of the heaven have their
  habitation,
Which sing among the branches.

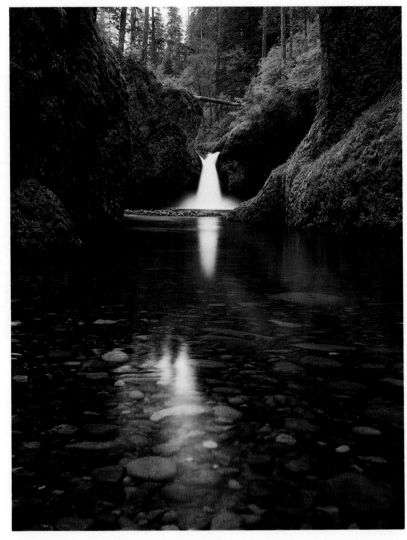

David Muench Photography

He watereth the hills from his chambers:
The earth is satisfied with the fruit of thy works.

He causeth the grass to grow for the cattle,
30   And herb for the service of man:
That he may bring forth food out of the earth;

And wine that maketh glad the heart of man,
And oil to make his face to shine,
And bread which strengtheneth man's heart.

35   The trees of the Lord are full of sap;
The cedars of Lebanon, which he hath planted;

Where the birds make their nests:
As for the stork, the fir trees are her house.

The high hills are a refuge for the wild goats;
40   And the rocks for the conies.[1]

He appointed the moon for seasons:
The sun knoweth his going down.

Thou makest darkness, and it is night:
Wherein all the beasts of the forest do creep
      forth.

45   The young lions roar after their prey,
And seek their meat from God.

The sun ariseth, they gather themselves together,
And lay them down in their dens.

Man goeth forth unto his work
50   And to his labor until the evening.

O Lord, how manifold are thy works!
In wisdom hast thou made them all:
The earth is full of thy riches.

The young David with pipe, bell, and harp. *From a thirteenth-century illuminated manuscript.*

---

1. **conies:** probably rabbits.

So is this great and wide sea,
55 Wherein are things creeping innumerable, both
        small and great beasts.

There go the ships:
There is that leviathan,[2] whom thou hast made to
        play therein.

These wait all upon thee;
That thou mayest give them their meat in due
        season.

60 That thou givest them they gather:
Thou openest thine hand, they are filled with
        good.

Thou hidest thy face, they are troubled:
Thou takest away their breath, they die, and
        return to their dust.

Thou sendest forth thy spirit, they are created:
65 And thou renewest the face of the earth.

The glory of the Lord shall endure for ever:
The Lord shall rejoice in his works.

He looketh on the earth, and it trembleth:
He toucheth the hills, and they smoke.

70 I will sing unto the Lord as long as I live:
I will sing praise to my God while I have my
        being.

My meditation of him shall be sweet:
I will be glad in the Lord.

Let the sinners be consumed out of the earth,
75 And let the wicked be no more.
Bless thou the Lord, O my soul.
Praise ye the Lord.

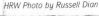
HRW Photo by Russell Dian

On what kinds of images does this psalm focus? What is the overall effect of the imagery?

---

2. **leviathan** (lə·vī′ə·thən): probably a whale.

PSALM 137

King James Bible

*The following psalm expresses the sorrow of the Jews during
their exile in Babylon after King Nebuchadnezzar destroyed
Jerusalem. The opening verses immediately capture the
Hebrews' emotional pain. At what point does the psalmist's
extreme sorrow turn to a bitterness that causes him to start
cursing his captors?*

By the rivers of Babylon, there we sat down,
Yea, we wept, when we remembered Zion.[1]

We hanged our harps upon the willows in the
    midst thereof.

For there they that carried us away captive
    required of us a song;
5 And they that wasted us required of us mirth,
    saying, Sing us one of the songs of Zion.

How shall we sing the Lord's song in a strange
    land?

If I forget thee, O Jerusalem, let my right hand
    forget her cunning.

If I do not remember thee, let my tongue cleave
    to the roof of my mouth;
If I prefer not Jerusalem above my chief joy.

10 Remember, O Lord, the children of Edom[2] in the
    day of Jerusalem;

---

1. **Zion** (zī′ən): the Jewish homeland; also, the hill in Jerusalem on
which the temple was built.
2. **Edom** (ē′dəm): a country south of the Dead Sea.

Who said, Raze it, raze it, even to the foundation
  thereof.

O daughter of Babylon, who art to be destroyed;
Happy shall he be, that rewardeth thee as thou
  hast served us.

Happy shall he be, that taketh and dasheth thy
  little ones against the stones.

KING DAVID, PETER PAUL RUBENS (1577–1640).

Which of the psalms did you find most moving and memorable? Why?

Identifying Facts

1. According to the Twenty-third Psalm, how is the Lord like a shepherd?
2. How is God portrayed in Psalm 104?
3. In Psalm 137, what have the Babylonians asked the exiled Hebrews to do? How do the Hebrews respond?

Interpreting Meanings

1. The Twenty-third Psalm is often read at funeral services as a consolation to mourners, and people recite it to give themselves courage and hope in troubled times. What kind of consolation might this psalm offer people? Do you find it consoling?
2. Find at least one example of **imagery** in Psalm 104 that appeals to each of the five senses. What is the effect of the imagery?
3. At what point in Psalm 137 does the **mood**, or emotional atmosphere, change sharply? How would you describe the mood of the psalm before the shift? How would you describe it after? What is the emotional effect of the final line of Psalm 137?
4. Each of the psalms contains many examples of **parallelism**, or parallel structure—places where actual words and phrases are repeated, or an idea is restated in slightly different words. Find at least one example of parallelism in each of the psalms you have read. Then describe the effect of this use of parallelism.

Applying Meanings

Think of contemporary poems or song lyrics—even sung advertisements or political speeches—that use parallelism or other forms of repetition. What is the purpose and effect of the parallelism in each case?

Critical Writing Response

Comparing Translations of the Twenty-third Psalm. The following version of the Twenty-third Psalm is from the Psalms of the Anchor Bible, published in 1965. The Anchor Bible is designed to convey the meaning of the original Hebrew to contemporary readers. Read this version, and compare it to the King James translation you have just read. Which version do you find more literal? More beautiful? Which version do you like better? Which details of vocabulary or figurative language affect your conclusions? Present your answers to these questions in a two- or three-paragraph essay.

Psalm 23
The Anchor Bible Translation (1965)

Yahweh is my shepherd,
　　I shall not lack.
In green meadows he will make me lie
　　down;
Near tranquil waters will he guide me,
5　　to refresh my being.
He will lead me into luxuriant pastures,
　　as befits his name.
Even though I should walk
　　in the midst of total darkness,
10　I shall fear no danger
　　since you are with me.
Your rod and your staff—
　　behold, they will lead me.
You prepare my table before me,
15　　in front of my adversaries.
You generously anoint my head with oil,
　　my cup overflows.
Surely goodness and kindness will attend
　　me
　　all the days of my life;
20　And I shall dwell in the house of Yahweh
　　for days without end.

ELEMENTS OF LITERATURE

Parallelism

Parallelism, or **parallel structure**, is the repetition of words, phrases, or sentences that have the same grammatical structure or that restate a similiar idea. Parallelism is used frequently in literature that is meant to be read aloud, such as poetry and speeches. The technique of parallelism occurs often in the Hebrew, or biblical, style. It is especially striking in the Book of Psalms. The psalms do not rely on rhyme, meter, or other obvious poetic devices. Instead, they use the rhythm created by parallel structure to unify ideas, emphasize images, and heighten the emotional effect of the words.

Parallelism often occurs in the repetition of a word or an entire sentence pattern. This is called **structural parallelism**, and it can be seen in the following example:

> If I forget thee, O Jerusalem, let my
> right hand forget her cunning.
> If I do not remember thee, let my
> tongue cleave to the roof of my
> mouth.
>
> (Psalm 137:7–8)

Parallelism can also take the form of a **restatement** of an entire idea in different words. This restatement can occur in a single line or in successive lines:

> Lord, my heart is not haughty,
> nor mine eyes lofty;
> neither do I exercise myself in great
> matters,
> or in things too high for me.
>
> (Psalm 131:1)

Note that the lines above do not rely on repeated words or sentence patterns, but instead on the restatement of ideas. By presenting two versions of the same idea, the psalmist adds a layer of meaning to the psalm. In addition, the repetition creates emotional intensity.

Another form of parallelism involves **antithesis** (an·tith′ə·sis), or contrast. In antithesis, ideas are tied together because they are complementary, or opposite, rather than similar, as in the following example:

> Weeping may endure for a night,
> but joy cometh in the morning.
>
> (Psalm 30:5)

Read each of the psalms in this unit aloud. Listen for examples of parallelism. Does the parallelism occur in the repetition of words or sentence structure, in the restatement of ideas, or in the use of contrasting ideas? What is the effect of the parallelism in each case?

The New Testament

The Christian Bible includes both the Hebrew Bible and the New Testament. Like the Hebrew Bible, the New Testament is a collection of books: twenty-seven books written within the relatively short time span of the first two centuries A.D. Because Greek was the most commonly spoken language around the Mediterranean at that time, the New Testament was written in everyday Greek. But because the writers of the New Testament were Hebrews, they wrote from the perspective of the Hebrew culture and tradition.

The Four Gospels

The Hebrew Bible opens with the Five Books of Moses, which explain the origins of the Hebrew people and their beliefs. Similarly, the New Testament opens with four Gospels, which explain the origins and key beliefs of Christianity. The word *Gospel* comes from the Old English word *godspel* or "good news," a direct translation of *euangelion*, the Greek name for these books. The "good news" of the Gospels is that of the life and message of Jesus Christ, a wandering Jewish teacher who attracted a great deal of attention during the era of Roman rule in Jerusalem. The word

Christ, meaning "the anointed one," implies divinity, and Jesus' followers believe that he is the divine son of God. According to Christian belief, God established a new covenant, or testament, with humanity by sending his only son to die for people's sins. Thus, Christians see the New Testament as a continuation of the Hebrew covenant with God.

Gospels: *the teachings of Jesus and the Apostles, which appear as the first four books of the New Testament.*

The four Gospels are attributed to Matthew, Mark, Luke, and John, but scholars do not know the exact identity of these writers. Mark's Gospel was the first one written. Matthew and Luke based their Gospels partly on Mark's work. As a result, these three Gospels parallel each other closely enough to be called the synoptic (si·näp′tik) gospels. The word *synoptic* comes from the Greek word *syn*, meaning "same," and *optic*, meaning "vision." Even the synoptic Gospels, however, differ somewhat from one another, for each writer wrote for a different audience and emphasized different aspects of Christ's life and works.

Illumination from the Irish *Book of Kells*, eighth century. *Medieval art often uses the symbols of the angel, the lion, the bull, and the eagle to represent the four evangelists, Matthew, Mark, Luke, and John, respectively.*

The Other Books of the New Testament

After the Gospels, the other books of the New Testament are, in order, the Acts of the Apostles, the Epistles, and Revelation. The Acts of the Apostles, written by Luke, continues Luke's gospel. It covers events from about A.D. 30 to A.D. 50 and features the deeds of the missionary Paul. Paul, originally named Saul, was a dogged persecutor of Christians who converted to Christian-ity—and changed his name—after receiving a vision. Paul contributed to the next section of the New Testament, the Epistles. Epistles are letters written to various people and communities to spread the teachings of Christ. Paul wrote seven of the Epistles, and scholars believe that his disciples wrote another seven in his name. These epistles explain the Gospels in more detail, especially as they apply to concrete problems faced by early Christians.

◆

epistle (ē·pis′əl): *(1) a long, formal letter giving instruction to the recipient; (2) a letter in the New Testament written by a follower of Christ to spread the word of Christianity.*

The final book of the New Testament, Revelation, was written in about A.D. 95, probably by a prophet identified by some scholars as John of Patmos. The name *Revelation* is a direct translation of the Greek word *apokalypsis*, "apocalypse" (ə·päk′ə·lips′). The apocalypse, a popular form of literature, was full of symbols and visions, and Revelation, like other apocalyptic literature of its time, vividly recounts the age-old struggle between good and evil and the ultimate triumph of good. Through the writer's choice of symbols, Revelation also brings the Bible full circle. It unites the Hebrew Bible with the New Testament through the use of images associated with the creation accounts of Genesis: "a new heaven and a new earth" and a new "tree of life" (Revelation 21:1 and 22:2).

Reader's Guide

THE PRODIGAL SON, THE SOWER, THE TALENTS

Background

A **parable** is a short narrative that teaches a moral, or lesson about life. It is like a fable, except that its characters are humans rather than animals. The message of the parable does not need to be directly stated, for it can usually be inferred, or guessed from the text itself.

The New Testament contains about forty parables, and they occur in all four Gospels. They are attributed to Jesus, who, like other Jewish teachers, used them to make his messages clear. The parables tend to be down-to-earth and easy to grasp on a literal level, involving ordinary events that people of Jesus' time could relate to: a shepherd searching for a sheep that has strayed from the flock; bridesmaids who are asleep and unprepared when the bridal party arrives; a poor woman who loses a coin. The underlying messages of the parables concern deep truths such as conduct in life and moral laws.

Oral Response

One of the most famous and often-quoted parables in the New Testament is "The Good Samaritan." It is about a traveler who is robbed, beaten, and left to die on a road between Jericho and Jerusalem. Two "upstanding citizens" ignore the victim, but a Samaritan—a member of a despised ethnic and religious minority—tends the man's wounds and pays an innkeeper to take care of him until he is well. How would you state the moral of this parable?

Literary Focus

The word **parable** comes from a Greek word meaning "comparison" or "analogy." Parables convey morals, or lessons about life, through the use of **allegory**—a story with an underlying message that can be understood on both a literal and a symbolic level. Because symbols can be interpreted in more than one way, even a brief allegory can yield more than one meaning. All the New Testament parables use characters, objects, and events to symbolize, or stand for, abstract concepts.

THE PRODIGAL SON
New English Bible

The word prodigal *usually means "recklessly extravagant" or "wasteful," but it can also imply great generosity. As you read the parable, try to determine to which son the word applies. Could the word* prodigal *apply to the father as well?*

THE RETURN OF THE PRODIGAL SON, REMBRANDT (1609–1669).

Scala/Art Resource, New York

Again he[1] said: "There was once a man who had two sons; and the younger said to his father, 'Father, give me my share of the property.' So he divided his estate between them.[2] A few days later the younger son turned the whole of his share into cash and left home for a distant country, where he squandered it in reckless living. He had spent it all, when a severe famine fell upon that country and he began to feel the pinch. So he went and attached himself to one of the local landowners, who sent him on to his farm to mind the pigs.[3] He would have been glad to fill his belly with the pods that the pigs were eating; and no one gave him anything. Then he came to his senses and said, 'How many of my father's paid servants have more food than they can eat, and here am I, starving to death! I will set off and go to my father, and say to him, "Father, I have sinned, against God and against you; I am no longer fit to be called your son; treat me as one of your paid servants."' So he set out for his father's house. But while he was still a long way off his father saw him, and his heart went out to him. He ran to meet him, flung his arms round him, and kissed him. The son said, 'Father, I have sinned, against God and against you; I am no longer fit to be called your son.' But the father said to his servants, 'Quick! fetch a robe, my best one, and put it on him; put a ring on his finger

---

1. Jesus
2. **So he divided his estate between them:** The younger son's share would be one third.

3. **mind the pigs:** Because the Jews considered pigs to be unclean animals, tending pigs was considered degrading work.

and shoes on his feet. Bring the fatted calf and kill it, and let us have a feast to celebrate the day. For this son of mine was dead and has come back to life; he was lost and is found.' And the festivities began.

"Now the elder son was out on the farm; and on his way back, as he approached the house, he heard music and dancing. He called one of the servants and asked what it meant. The servant told him, 'Your brother has come home, and your father has killed the fatted calf because he has him back safe and sound.' But he was angry and refused to go in. His father came out and pleaded with him; but he retorted, 'You know how I have slaved for you all these years; I never once disobeyed your orders; and you never gave me so much as a kid, for a feast with my friends. But now that this son of yours turns up, after running through your money with his women, you kill the fatted calf for him.' 'My boy,' said the father, 'you are always with me, and everything I have is yours. How could we help celebrating this happy day? Your brother here was dead and has come back to life, was lost and is found.'"

Luke 15:12–30

THE SOWER
New English Bible

 In Jesus' time, farmers planted their fields by hand. With sacks of seed hung around their necks, they walked along, scattering the seed in wide arcs. How does this practice help to explain the situation described in the parable?

On another occasion he[1] began to teach by the lake-side. The crowd that gathered round him was so large that he had to get into a boat on the lake, and there he sat, with the whole crowd on the beach right down to the water's edge. And he taught them many things by parables.

As he taught he said:

"Listen! A sower went out to sow. And it happened that as he sowed, some seed fell along the footpath; and the birds came and ate it up. Some seed fell on rocky ground, where it had little soil, and it sprouted quickly because it had no depth of earth; but when the sun rose the young corn was scorched, and as it had no proper root it

1. **he**: Jesus.

withered away. Some seed fell among thistles; but the thistles shot up and choked the
corn, and it yielded no crop. And some of
the seed fell into good soil, where it came
up and grew, and bore fruit; and the yield
was thirtyfold, sixtyfold, even a hundredfold." He added, "If you have ears to hear,
then hear."

When he was alone, the Twelve[2] and
others who were round him questioned him
about the parables. He replied, "To you the
secret of the kingdom of God has been given;
but to those who are outside everything
comes by way of parables, so that (as Scripture says) they may look and look, but see
nothing; they may hear and hear, but understand nothing; otherwise they might turn
to God and be forgiven."

So he said, "You do not understand this
parable? How then are you to understand
any parable? The sower sows the word.[3]
Those along the footpath are people in
whom the word is sown, but no sooner have
they heard it than Satan[4] comes and carries
off the word which has been sown in them.
It is the same with those who receive the
seed on rocky ground; as soon as they hear
the word, they accept it with joy, but it
strikes no root in them; they have no stay-
ing-power; then, when there is trouble or
persecution on account of the word, they fall
away at once. Others again receive the seed

Courtesy of the Museum of Fine Arts, Boston. Bridgeman/Art Resource, N.Y.

THE SOWER, JEAN FRANÇOIS MILLET (1814–1875).
*In this parable, who or what does the sower
represent?*

among thistles; they hear the word, but
worldly cares and the false glamour[5] of
wealth and all kinds of evil desire come in
and choke the word, and it proves barren.
And there are those who receive the seed in
good soil; they hear the word and welcome
it; and they bear fruit thirtyfold, sixtyfold,
or a hundredfold."

Mark 4:1–20

---

2. **the Twelve:** the twelve disciples of Jesus; also
   called the Apostles.
3. **the word:** the word of God; the Gospels.
4. **Satan:** the devil.

---

5. **glamour:** (British) glamor.

THE TALENTS

New English Bible

*This parable is called "The Talents" because earlier translations used the name of a valuable gold coin, the **talent**, instead of the phrase "bags of gold." What does the word **talent** usually mean today? How does the parable apply to both meanings of **talent**?*

"It is like a man going abroad, who called his servants and put his capital in their hands; to one he gave five bags of gold, to another two, to another one, each according to his capacity. Then he left the country. The man who had the five bags went at once and employed them in business, and made a profit of five bags, and the man who had the two bags made two. But the man who had been given one bag of gold went off and dug a hole in the ground, and hid his master's money. A long time afterwards their master returned, and proceeded to settle accounts with them. The man who had been given the five bags of gold came and produced the five he had made: 'Master,' he said, 'you left five bags with me; look, I have made five more.' 'Well done, my good and trusty servant!' said the master. 'You have proved trustworthy in a small way; I will now put you in charge of something big. Come and share your master's delight.'[1] The man with the two bags then came and said, 'Master, you left two bags with me; look, I have made two more.' 'Well done, my good and trusty servant!' said the master. 'You have proved trustworthy in a small way; I will now put

you in charge of something big. Come and share your master's delight.' Then the man who had been given one bag came and said, 'Master, I knew you to be a hard man: you reap where you have not sown, you gather where you have not scattered; so I was afraid, and I went and hid your gold in the ground. Here it is—you have what belongs to you.' 'You lazy rascal!' said the master. 'You knew that I reap where I have not sown, and gather where I have not scattered? Then you ought to have put my money on deposit, and on my return I should have got it back with interest. Take the bag of gold from him, and give it to the one with the ten bags. For the man who has will always be given more, till he has enough and to spare; and the man who has not will forfeit even what he has. Fling the useless servant out into the dark, the place of wailing and grinding of teeth!'"

---

1. **share your master's delight:** enjoy the same prosperity as the master.

Matthew 25:14–31

First Thoughts

Which of the parables could you most easily apply to your own life?

Identifying Facts

1. In "The Prodigal Son," why does the younger son want to return home? What is his father's reaction to his return? What is his brother's reaction?

2. In what four places do the seeds land in "The Sower"? What happens to the seeds in each location?

3. In "The Talents," what does each servant do with the gold he receives? Why is the master angry with the third servant?

Interpreting Meanings

1. What did you think of the father's reaction to his son's return in "The Prodigal Son"? On an **allegorical** level, what might this **parable** be saying about God's love for sinners?

2. In "The Sower," some seeds fall among thistles, which Jesus identifies as "worldly cares and the false glamour of wealth and all kinds of evil desire." What are some of the "thistles" in today's world?

3. In "The Talents," the third servant simply hides his gold rather than risk investing it. On an allegorical level, what has he done? If the master symbolizes God, what does this parable say about what God expects people to do with their "talents"?

4. Choose one of the three **parables**, and state its **moral**, or lesson, in a sentence. Then think of a situation in your everyday life to which the parable could apply.

Applying Meanings

At different times in your life, have you been—or could you be—the younger son who returns, the older son who feels cheated, or the father who forgives in "The Prodigal Son"? Discuss how a person could identify with each of these characters at different times in his or her life. In what ways is this parable universal—that is, applicable to both Christians and non-Christians alike?

Creative Writing Response

Updating a Parable. Take any one of the three parables, and rewrite it using language, situations, and references that a modern reader would understand. To plan your updated parable, make a chart that shows the details of the original parable and the allegorical meaning of those details. Then decide how you will change the details in your parable. The allegorical meaning should remain the same. You might want to use a chart similar to the following example—for "The Prodigal Son"—to plan your parable.

Original Details (characters, places, things)	Allegorical Meaning	Updated Details (characters, places, things)
the father	forgiveness; God	school principal
the younger son	recklessness; sinner	high-school student who ditches classes
the older son	obedience; faithful follower who is jealous	honors student who never misses a day of class

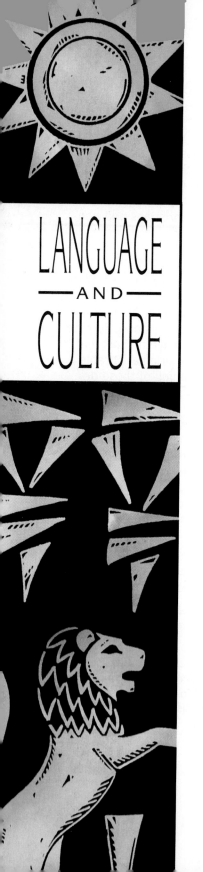

DECIPHERING ANCIENT TEXTS

The study of ancient literatures is part art, part science, and part adventure. While not all archaeologists are cast in the mold of an Indiana Jones, many do risk life and limb—facing treacherous weather, dangerous terrain, and hostile governments—in their efforts to recover ancient writings. No less taxing are scholars' efforts to understand the meaning of the long-lost texts. Ancient scripts can be as baffling as codes or ciphers. In fact, linguists often do employ the principles of modern cryptography, or the art of writing and deciphering codes, to "break the code" of ancient texts.

Once "decoded," ancient texts must be translated into modern language. The translator tries to preserve both the spirit and the form of the ancient language. Occasionally, the translator must reconstruct parts of the text that are unreadable, never recovered, or simply too obscure to understand. To recreate missing text, the translator needs a thorough understanding of the historical and cultural context in which the work was written. Sometimes so much of an ancient text has been lost that any attempts to reconstruct it would be futile.

The Discovery of Sumerian Cuneiform

Cuneiform is a system of writing based on the precise arrangement of wedge-shaped markings. Our knowledge of the long-extinct Sumerian culture comes from clay tablets inscribed in cuneiform between 3500 B.C. and 2000 B.C. But until excavation of Sumerian cuneiform tablets began in the mid-nineteenth century, there had been no knowledge of the Sumerian culture for thousands of years.

Sumerian, a non-Semitic language, has little in common with other ancient languages of Mesopotamia and the surrounding regions. But Babylonian and Assyrian conquerers of Sumer adopted the Sumerian script and language as their own literary language. The *Epic of Gilgamesh* that appears in this unit is in fact a Babylonian version of earlier Sumerian epics. Babylonian scribes recorded many of their own texts twice: once in Sumerian and once in Akkadian, the Babylonians' own language. Linguists found the earlier, solely Sumerian texts difficult, if not impossible, to translate. They were able to decipher the meaning of Sumerian cuneiform only when they compared it to corresponding Akkadian texts. In addition, because archaeologists usually found the cuneiform tablets in fragments, like the pieces of a jigsaw puzzle, they had few complete texts to work from.

Cuneiform in "Triplicate"

Fortunately for translators, the diligent Sumerian and Babylonian scribes tended to copy texts several times. Scholars were able to reconstruct many broken tablets from multiple copies. Scholars were also aided by an important feature of Sumerian literary style: the repetition of key passages. For example, in one narrative, a messenger is sent with a message, and the message is recorded both as he receives it and as he delivers it. Modern readers would find this kind of repetition tiresome and boring, but thanks to this stylistic tendency, a missing fragment from a passage of text could be filled in when the same passage was repeated later on.

Still, neither the Sumerians' taste for repetition nor the Babylonians' careful copying could completely prevent the ravages of time. Many cuneiform tablets have been lost—either disintegrated or buried under four thousand years' accumulation of soil.

The Dead Sea Scrolls

Unlike the long-lost Sumerian texts, the languages of the Bible have been "alive" continuously for about 2,000 years. The text that we call the Hebrew Bible was first passed on orally, then written down in Hebrew, Aramaic, and Greek. Questions about biblical texts are caused not so much by missing or undecipherable material as by conflicting interpretations.

An exciting archaeological advance in biblical interpretation occurred in 1947, however, when a Bedouin shepherd, out looking for his herd, stumbled upon some ancient scrolls in a cave near the Dead Sea. Many more scrolls were eventually found in the same area. Some of the scrolls dated from 200 B.C. The Dead Sea Scrolls, as they have been named, probably belonged to a Jewish sect called the Essenes.

DEAD SEA SCROLL: THE MANUAL OF DISCIPLINE, COLUMN 2–4.

These scrolls, which contain most of the contents of the Hebrew Bible, represent the oldest written fragments of the Bible ever discovered. They demonstrate that there existed a unified Hebrew Bible by A.D. 70. Surprisingly, the first translations released show that later versions of the Hebrew Bible (those in circulation from antiquity until now) were fairly faithful transcriptions of the earliest sources. It was not until late in 1991 that the Huntington Library in California, amid much controversy, released the complete Dead Sea Scrolls to the public. Thus, the mystery behind the scrolls is still unfolding.

VARYING SENTENCE BEGINNINGS AND AVOIDING DANGLING MODIFIERS

Caught up in the flow of writing a narrative, you may find yourself composing sentence after sentence with the same basic structure. One way to correct this tendency is to use introductory elements to achieve sentence variety and to add information. An **introductory element**—any word, phrase, or clause that comes before the subject of a sentence—lets you vary sentence rhythms. In addition, it offers a concise way to include facts and details. Compare the examples below.

MONOTONOUS

Boaz is impressed by Ruth's beauty, loyalty, and dignity. He makes generous offers. He also takes practical steps to clear the way for their marriage. Boaz guards her reputation with these steps, which demonstrate his love.

IMPROVED

Impressed by Ruth's beauty, loyalty, and dignity, Boaz makes generous offers. He also takes practical steps to clear the way for their marriage. *By guarding her reputation with these steps,* he demonstrates his love.

Notice how the introductory elements, italicized in the second passage, allow the writer to vary and condense sentences without losing important details.

Types of Introductory Elements

In the following examples, each introductory element is followed directly by the subject of the sentence.

Adjectives
Simple and rhythmic, the psalms express intense emotions.

Adverb
Frequently, psalms employ parallel structure and contrast.

Prepositional Phrase
In the parable, one servant hides his master's money.

Present Participial Phrase
Begging forgiveness, the prodigal son returns to his father.

Past Participial Phrase
Reared among animals, Enkidu is shaggy-haired and wild.

Appositive Phrase
A very human hero, Gilgamesh suffers from excessive pride.

Adverbial Clause
Although they are simple stories, parables convey complex thoughts.

Exercise 1: Using Introductory Elements

Restructure each of the following sentences, making the italicized portion an introductory element. Be sure that the subject of the sentence comes directly after each introductory element.

1. Gilgamesh constructs a magnificent wall *around Uruk.* (prepositional phrase)
2. Gilgamesh and Enkidu insult the gods *shamelessly.* (adverb)
3. Gilgamesh seeks immortality *because he hopes to avoid his friend's fate.* (adverbial clause)
4. Utnapishtim, *warming to his tale,* tells the story of the flood. (present participial phrase)
5. Gilgamesh, *a wiser person now,* returns to his tasks in Uruk. (appositive phrase)

Dangling Modifiers

A **dangling modifier**—an introductory element that does not refer clearly to the word it modifies—can be either amusing or confusing. To correct a dangling modifier in your writing, reword the sentence so that the introductory element appears as close as possible to the word it modifies.

DANGLING MODIFIERS
Tempted by the serpent, the apple is irresistible to Eve. (Is the apple tempted by the serpent?)

Handsome and brave, everyone's admiration focuses on Gilgamesh. (Is admiration handsome and brave?)

CORRECTED SENTENCES
Tempted by the serpent, Eve finds the apple irresistible.

Handsome and brave, Gilgamesh attracts everyone's admiration.

Notice that correcting the sentence can involve choosing new words to convey the same meaning.

An introductory element cannot modify the possessive form of a noun or a possessive adjective.

DANGLING MODIFIER
Tamed by civilization, Enkidu's friendship with Gilgamesh costs him his life. ("Enkidu's friendship" was not tamed.)

CORRECTED SENTENCE
Tamed by civilization, Enkidu loses his life because of his friendship with Gilgamesh.

Exercise 2: Correcting Dangling Modifiers

Reword the sentences below to correct each dangling modifier. Try to avoid changing the introductory elements.

1. Ashamed and guilty, God punishes Adam and Eve.
2. Growing in the once-fruitful ground, Adam and Eve now find thorns and thistles.
3. With their bleak mud and shadows, Sumerians expected no joy in the caves of the afterlife.
4. By treating the goddess disrespectfully, Enkidu's doom is sealed.
5. Like Noah, Utnapishtim's boat is built according to divine specifications.
6. Taught to act unselfishly, biblical parables show how ordinary people can achieve extraordinary things.
7. Admiring epic heroes for their superhuman abilities, their human failings also help us to empathize with them.

Critical Thinking and Writing

WRITING AN AUTOBIOGRAPHICAL NARRATIVE

Now that you've read the *Epic of Gilgamesh* and several biblical tales and parables, it's your turn to be a storyteller. By delving into ancient literature, you have found reflections of a variety of human experiences: the loss of a loved one, failure to reach a goal, and leaving one's home for new surroundings, among others. You can find similar reflections by narrating incidents, either large or small, from your own life.

Writing Assignment

In a narrative essay, tell the story of an incident in your life: a success or failure, a realization about yourself, a special time with a friend. Bring the event to life for your audience, and show how it has affected you. Assume that you are writing for teen and adult readers of a general-interest magazine. For this assignment, you will analyze causes and effects.

Background

Characters in this unit respond to their experiences in realistic ways. Some, like Gilgamesh, gain insight from adversity. Others, like Adam and Eve, the prodigal son, and the lazy servant, suffer because of their actions. Still others, like Noah and Ruth, are rewarded for their choices. Think of your experiences, large and small. Which have most affected your attitudes, feelings, and behavior?

Prewriting

Recalling an Incident. The incident you choose needn't be dramatic; simple, every-day events can also have lasting effects. Think of two or three different experiences that changed you or brought new discoveries about yourself, about another person, or about life in general. Choose the incident most meaningful to you. Then free-write about it, focusing on sensory details (sights, sounds, scents, tastes, and tex-tures) and on your thoughts and feelings during the incident.

Analyzing Causes and Effects. Reflect on causes and effects of your incident, and fill out a diagram based on the one below. Decide which effects have, in turn, created further effects.

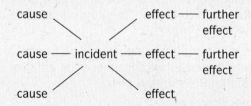

Next, sum up in one or two sentences the significance your experience had for you.

Writing

Follow these guidelines for drafting a narrative.

1. **Introductory Paragraph.** Draw readers in immediately by beginning with action. Your freewriting may provide strong, sensory verbs that will be useful here. Go on to work in any background information (about setting or characters, for example) that readers will need to understand the incident. End the paragraph with a reference to the significance this incident has for you.

2. **Body Paragraphs.** Again, pull the most vivid details out of your freewriting, and bring your narrative to life by showing rather than telling. Well-chosen details describing sights, sounds, textures, and so on can convey your experiences more effectively than whole paragraphs of explanation could.

   Organize your narrative chronologically, beginning with the causes of the incident, then recounting the incident, and finally showing its effects on you. Or, if appropriate, use flashback: begin with the effects, and then move backward in time to show how and why they occurred. In either case, refer to your cause-and-effect diagram as you write, so that you can include details showing not only what happened, but also why it happened and what resulted from it. Use transitions (see page 56) to keep both the time order and the cause-and-effect relationships clear.

3. **Concluding Paragraph.** Your conclusion should communicate your reflections about the incident. Leave readers with a definite idea of how this incident affected your life.

Evaluating and Revising

Use these questions to evaluate and revise your draft.

1. Does your introductory paragraph show action and refer to the significance of the incident?

2. Do you use enough specific, sensory details? Are all details relevant to your focus?

3. Have you recounted the incident from beginning to end in a clear and logical way?

4. Have you shown causes and results of the incident? Have you clearly stated its significance and its effect on your life?

5. Are your sentences varied in structure and grammatically correct?

Proofreading and Publishing

Proofread your work, correcting errors in spelling and mechanics, and make a final copy. With your teacher's guidance, select a local or national periodical that features personal-experience articles, and submit your essay for publication.

ANCIENT GREECE AND ROME

- Ancient Greece
- Roman Empire, c. A.D. 120

Atlantic Ocean

BRITAIN

GAUL

Alps

Pyrenees Mountains

Rubicon R.

IBERIA

Tiber R.

Rome

ITALY

MAGNA GRAECIA

Carthage

SICI

MACEDONIA

Byzantium

Troy

ASIA MINOR

Delphi

Thebes

Corinth

Athens

GREECE

Sparta

PELOPONNESUS

CYPRUS

CRETE

Black Sea

Mediterranean Sea

PALES

Alexandria

Jeru

NORTH AFRICA

Memphis

EGYPT

SAHARA

Nile River

Thebes

ARABIAN
DESERT

GREEK AND ROMAN LITERATURES

▼ **Time** ▼
800 B.C.—A.D. 200

▼ **Place** ▼
The Ancient Mediterranean

▼ **Literary Significance** ▼

Ancient Greece: The literature of ancient Greece includes the Homeric epics the *Iliad* and the *Odyssey,* lyric poetry, drama, philosophical works, and histories. The fourth and fifth centuries B.C. are considered the classical period of ancient Greece, a period in which Greece, especially the city-state of Athens, made outstanding cultural and political achievements. After Athens' decline, Alexander the Great conquered many lands, spreading Greek cultural influences—including political, literary, and philosophical traditions—throughout much of the Mediterranean, western Asia, and North Africa.

Ancient Rome: After the death of Alexander the Great, the Romans continued to spread and preserve the legacy of Greek civilization. Eventually, however, the Romans developed a rich culture of their own. Among the treasures of the Roman literary legacy are the *Aeneid*—an epic describing the legend of the founding of Rome—lyric poetry, high comedy, oratory, and history. The Roman Empire steadily expanded its territory through military conquest until its decline in the fifth century A.D.

TIME LINE
Ancient Greece and Rome

LITERARY EVENTS ▼

Sappho. Detail of Greek vase, c. 440 B.C.

The Granger Collection, New York

Sappho **(500s B.C.)** composes lyrics

Aesop **(500s B.C.)** composes fables

Pindar **(518–438 B.C.)** composes odes

Herodotus **(485–425 B.C.)**, called the "Father of History"

Classical era of Greek drama; Aeschylus, Sophocles, and Euripide write tragedies, **c. 480–400 B.C.**

Thucydides **(c. 460–401 B.C.)**, *History of the Peloponnesian War*

Aristophanes **(c. 450–386 B.C.)**, *Lysistrata*

Homer **(c. 700 B.C.)**, *Iliad, Odyssey*

Lyric poetry flourishes, **600s–400s B.C.**

Plato **(c. 429–347 B.C.)**, *The Republic*

BEFORE 800 B.C.	700 B.C.	600 B.C.	500 B.C.	400 B.C.

Minoan civilization, **c. 3000–1000 B.C.**

Mycenaeans gain control of Crete, **c. 1400 B.C.**

Mycenaeans destroy rival city of Troy, **c. 1250 B.C.**

Dorians invade Greece; period known as the Greek Dark Ages begins, **c. 1100 B.C.**

Olympic games in honor of Zeus begin, **776 B.C.**

Emergence of Greek city-states, **700–500 B.C.**

Rome is founded, **c. 700 B.C.**

Roman Republic is established, **509 B.C.**

Classical period in Greek history, **499–338 B.C.**

Greek city-states fight invaders in the Persian Wars, **499–448 B.C.**

Roman law is codified in the Twelve Tablets, **451–450 B.C.**

Epidemic of bubonic plague strikes Athens, **430 B.C.**

Athens loses to Sparta in the Peloponnesian War, **431– 404 B.C.**

Giraudon/Art Resource, New York

Head of a bull, Minoan, 1500 B.C.

▲ **CULTURAL AND HISTORICAL EVENTS**

Wall painting of a father's mask used in comedies.

Catullus **(c. 84–c. 54 B.C.)**, *Poems*

Terence **(c. 190–159 B.C.)**, former slave from North Africa, writes comedies

Virgil **(70–19 B.C.)**, *Aeneid*

Horace **(65–8 B.C.)**, *Odes*

Ovid **(43 B.C.–A.D. 17)**, *Metamorphoses*

Julius Caesar.

Plautus **(c. 250–184 B.C.)** writes comedies

Cato **(234–149 B.C.)** writes prose in Latin

Cicero **(106–43 B.C.)**, greatest orator of classical Roman literature, *Orations*

Martial **(c. A.D. 40–104)**, *Poems*

Tacitus **(c. A.D. 56–117)**, *Annals*

Juvenal **(c. A.D. 60–140)**, *Satires*

Aristotle **(384–322 B.C.)**, *Poetics*

Theocritus **(c. 300–260 B.C.)**, *Idylls*

| 300 B.C. | 200 B.C. | 100 B.C. | A.D. 1 | A.D. 100 |

Plato founds the Academy in Athens, **387 B.C.**

Philip II becomes king of Macedonia; conquers Greece, **359–336 B.C.**

Alexander the Great conquers Mesopotamia, Persia, and part of India, spreading Greek culture throughout these regions, **336–323 B.C.**

First Punic War between Rome and Carthage, **264–241 B.C.**

Second Punic War, **218–201 B.C.**

Third Punic War; Carthage is destroyed, **149–146 B.C.**

Julius Caesar becomes dictator for life, **48 B.C.**

Julius Caesar is assassinated, **44 B.C.**

Octavian and Marc Antony defeat Brutus and Cassius, **42 B.C.**

Octavian defeats Antony and Cleopatra at Battle of Actium, **31 B.C.**

Roman Empire is established with Augustus Caesar as emperor, **27 B.C.**

Rome is destroyed by fire under the emperor Nero, **A.D. 64**

Reign of Marcus Aurelius, **161–180**

Alexander the Great in battle.

Roman aqueduct in Segovia, Spain.

This time line border is decorated with images found on ancient Greek pottery.

GREEK LITERATURE

Draped warrior, bronze, 6th century B.C.

The achievements of the ancient Greeks flowed mainly from their ability to wonder, to ask the question, "Why?" The Greeks sought to know the basic truths of human nature, and they believed in the pursuit of excellence in all aspects of life. "Man is the measure of all things," declared the philosopher and teacher Protagoras (prō·tag′ə·rəs) (c. 485–410 B.C.). The Greeks' efforts to understand themselves and the peoples around them produced an intense love of intellectualism and rational thought and gave rise to historical writings, political and philosophical theories, and literature that have endured for centuries.

The Heroic Age

Greek civilization began in Crete. By 2000 B.C., a remarkable culture had developed on this rugged, mountainous island, sixty miles south of mainland Greece. This civilization is called **Minoan** (mi·nō′ən), after the legendary King Minos (mī′näs′) of Crete, who supposedly sacrificed twelve young men and women each year to feed a half-man, half-bull monster called the Minotaur.

Minoan civilization directly influenced the rise of the **Mycenaean** (mī′sə·nē′ən) culture which flourished between 1500 and 1200 B.C. on the Greek mainland. But while the Minoans were peaceful, the Mycenaeans were both enterprising and aggressive. Scholars believe that around 1250 B.C., under the leadership of King Agamemnon (ag′ə·mem′nän′), the Mycenaeans organized an expedition against the city of Troy in Asia Minor. Four centuries later, the poet Homer immortalized the heroes of this "Trojan War" in the *Iliad*, one of the earliest epics in Western literature. To the Greeks of Homer's time, the Mycenaean era was known as the **Heroic Age.**

Fresco of Knossos. *The fresco depicts the ritual of bull-jumping practiced by Minoan youths, both male and female. The figure of the bull was worshiped as a symbol of strength and fertility.*

The Dark Age in Greece

Less than fifty years after the Trojan War, Mycenaean culture began a mysterious decline. This decline accelerated when a wave of invaders called the **Dorians** (dôr′ē·ənz) swept across the Greek peninsula in 1100 B.C. The Dorians burned the Mycenaean palace centers, and Greek culture entered a so-called **Dark Age** that lasted several centuries. During the Dark Age, writing apparently fell out of use, and there is no record of cultural development during this long period.

The Epic Age

The earliest surviving works of Greek poetry are the **epics** the *Iliad* and the *Odyssey* by Homer (see page 224). Around 750 B.C., shortly after Homer composed his epics, the Greeks developed a script for their language, based on a system borrowed from the Phoenicians. This system became what we know as the alphabet, named for its two initial letters, *alpha* and *beta.* Whether its purpose was to aid commercial dealings or, as one theory holds, to record Homer's epics for posterity, the Greek invention of the alphabet opened the door to a remarkable age of literary achievement.

> ❝ Our way is to consider each separate thing alone by itself; the Greeks always saw things as parts of a whole, and this habit of mind is stamped upon everything they did. ❞
>
> —Edith Hamilton

The Rise of the City-States

Between 700 and 500 B.C., Greek life became more organized and institutional. Small, fragmented settlements banded together to form communities. Soon a number of **city-states** emerged. The typical city-state, called a *polis* (from which the word *politics* is derived) was ruled by a king.

Tzovaras/Art Resource, New York

Delphi, Athenian temple to Apollo. *Apollo was one of the Greek gods worshiped universally in ancient Greece and its territories.*

In this period of city-states, the Greeks still did not think of themselves as a single nation. However, they did feel some common cultural bonds. They called themselves **Hellenes** (hel´ēnz´), believing themselves direct descendants of Hellen, the son of Deucalion (dōō·kāl´ē·ən), who, according to a Greek myth, was the sole survivor of a great flood and thus the ancestor of all Greeks. This cultural identity set the Greeks apart from their "barbarian" neighbors, and

> Although the Greeks did not think of themselves as a unified nation, they forged a cultural identity based on shared athletic contests, religious worship, and a belief in their mythological origins.

the resulting sense of unity found expression in various social and religious institutions. A regular series of athletic contests brought the main Greek city-states in contact with one another and fostered a sense of Greek identity. The most important games were those held at Olympia every four years in honor of the god Zeus. A number of religious shrines, chief among them that of the god Apollo (ə·päl′ō) at Delphi (del′fī), were universal centers of worship.

Greek Gods and Goddesses

We have our first glimpses of Greek religion in the epics of Homer, since the gods play important roles in both the *Iliad* and the *Odyssey.* The ancient Greeks saw their gods as being very human. In fact, they often possessed the worst traits of humans: jealousy, irrational anger, and pettiness. There

The Gods and Goddesses of Ancient Greece

Greek Name	Roman Name	Area of Activity or Power
Kronos (krō′nəs) also Cronus	Saturn	Head of the Titans; agriculture; father of Zeus
Zeus (zyōōs)	Jupiter	King of the gods; ruler of the sky; weather; upholder of oaths; hospitality
Hera (hir′ə)	Juno	Wife of Zeus and queen of the gods; upholder of marriage
Poseidon (pō·sī′dən)	Neptune	Brother of Zeus; ruler of the sea; horses; earthquakes
Hades (hā′dēz′)	Pluto	Brother of Zeus; ruler of the underworld
Demeter (di·mēt′ər)	Ceres (sir′ēz′)	Goddess of the earth; corn and crops
Persephone (pər·sef′ə·nē)	Proserpina (prō·sʉr′pi′nə)	Daughter of Demeter and wife of Hades; queen of the underworld
Ares (er′rēz′)	Mars	God of war
Apollo (ə·päl′ō)	Apollo	Prophecy; light; youth; music; archery; both healing and plague; the sun; poetry
Athena (ə·thē′nə)	Minerva	Wisdom; warfare; crafts
Artemis (är′tə·mis)	Diana	Hunting and wild animals; childbirth; the moon
Hephaestus (hē·fes′təs)	Vulcan	Fire; smelting; crafts; blacksmith for the gods
Hermes (hʉr′mēz′)	Mercury	Messenger of the gods; travelers; trickery; theft; commerce; science
Aphrodite (af′rə·dīt′ē)	Venus	Love; beauty; pleasure
Eros (er′äs′)	Cupid	Love
Dionysus (dī′ə·nī′səs)	Bacchus (bak′əs)	Liberation; wine; music; theater; fertility

Relief of a soldier of Darius, 518–460 B.C.

were two fundamental differences that distinguished the gods from humanity. First, gods and goddesses were ageless and immortal. Second, they were immensely more powerful than human beings. But the gods were not puppet masters who controlled human beings. Rather, the Greeks believed that everyone had his or her own destiny, or fate. A god could help you or hinder you, depending on your relationship with the god, your own character and talents, and the trouble you took to give the god proper respect through rituals of prayer and offerings.

The Lyric Age

From about the seventh to the fifth centuries B.C., **lyric poetry** began to flourish among the Greeks. Unlike the epic, this new poetry did not recount heroic deeds of men and gods. Instead, lyric poetry used relatively few lines to express the personal emotions of a single speaker. Only a small fraction of this poetry has survived. The odes of **Pindar** (pin'dər) (518–438 B.C.) celebrated the victors in the major athletic contests, while the lyrics of **Sappho** (saf'ō) (early sixth century B.C.) comprise some of the finest and most honest love poems ever written (see page 279).

Sparta and Athens

Despite their cultural bonds, bitter rivalries often occurred between the Greek city-states. By the start of the fifth century B.C., two rival states—**Sparta** and **Athens**—had emerged

> By the early fifth century B.C., Athens and Sparta were the two chief city-states. Sparta was noted for its discipline and conservatism. Athens experimented with political democracy and became a brilliant center of ancient Greek culture.

from these conflicts as the most powerful in Greece. Sparta owed its prominence to an extremely militaristic and conservative culture, where, according to popular legends, all

SEF/Art Resource, New York

Leonides at Thermopyles, Jacques-Louis David (1748–1825). Leonides was a Spartan ruler during the Persian Wars who made a heroic but unsuccessful stand against the Persians at the Battle of Thermopylae, 480 B.C.

boys and girls underwent years of rigorous physical training, and frail infants were left on mountaintops to die.

Athens emerged as a power to be reckoned with when the city played a leading role in the **Persian Wars**, which began in 499 B.C. and ended in 448 B.C. The Persian emperor Darius launched these wars when the Greek cities in Asia Minor revolted against Persian rule. At one point, the Persians entered Athens and nearly destroyed the city, but the Athenians finally defeated the Persian invaders.

Pericles and the Golden Age of Athens

Athens was the main beneficiary of the Persian Wars in Greece. The important victories of the Athenians at Marathon (490 B.C.) and Salamis (480 B.C.) marked the beginning of the great age of Athens, in which Athens took its place

> ❝ Ritual and myth are the two forms in which Greek religion presents itself to the historian. . . . There are no founding figures and no documents of revelation, no organizations of priests and no monastic orders. ❞
>
> —*Walter Burkert*

Parthenon frieze. *The Parthenon was a temple dedicated to the goddess Athena, built between 447 and 432 B.C.*

> **❝** Sophocles' *Oedipus* is not only the greatest creation of a major poet and the classic representative figure of his age: he is also one of the long series of tragic protagonists who stand as symbols of human aspiration and despair. . . . **❞**
>
> —*Bernard Knox*

as the wartime leader of all the city-states and the chief naval power of Greece. Despite the power that Athens had acquired as a result of the wars, at home the Athenians established a **democratic government**, or rule by the people (or free adult males, at least—women and slaves could not vote), rather than a dictatorship. Athenian democracy was one of the earliest democratic governments, and it had a tremendous influence on the formation of both the Roman Republic and American democracy.

Starting in the late 460s B.C., during the height of the Athenian "Golden Age," the great general and statesman **Pericles** (per′i·klēz′) (c. 494–429 B.C.) guided the fortunes of Athens for over three decades. Pericles was a skillful politician who steered a middle course between extremist views in the democratic assembly. He was also a patron of literature, philosophy, and the arts. It was Pericles who organized the campaign to build Athens's most famous temple, the Parthenon, dedicated to the city's patron goddess, Athena.

The Rise of Greek Drama

Three of the greatest authors of **tragedy** in the history of Western literature—**Aeschylus** (es'ki·ləs), **Sophocles** (säf'ə-klēz'), and **Euripides** (yoo·rip'ə·dēz')—all lived during the intellectual ferment of Athens in the fifth century B.C. Their plays posed profound questions about the limits of knowledge, individual free will, moral responsibility, and human suffering.

> The Age of Pericles, or the Golden Age of Athens, fostered the rise of Greek drama. Playwrights such as Aeschylus, Sophocles, and Euripides were encouraged to explore and question in their works the wide range of human emotions.

Sophocles (c. 496–406 B.C.) was the most admired playwright of his day and the winner of over twenty prizes for his dramas. As a general and a friend of the statesman Pericles, he was involved in many of the great events of his time. He explores the issues of pride, loyalty, and personal responsibility in works such as *Oedipus Rex* (see page 302) and *Antigone.*

In addition to tragedy, the Athenian stage was also the site for the production of great **comedies**. One of the best-loved authors of comedy in ancient Greece was **Aristophanes** (ar'i·stäf'ə·nēz') (c. 450–c. 386 B.C.). Aristophanes' comedies used farce and satire to deal with such serious issues as education and war.

The Historians: Herodotus and Thucydides

During the fifth and fourth centuries B.C., the Greek search for knowledge also resulted in the flourishing of historical writings. **Herodotus** (hə·räd'ə·təs) (c. 485–c. 425 B.C.) is considered—in the West, at least—the first historian. He not only wrote a chronicle of the Persian Wars but also reported on many foreign lands and customs of peoples he met in

Bust of Aeschylus. *Aeschylus (525–456 B.C.) was the first great Greek playwright. His tragedies expanded dramatic form and considered the conflict of individual will and the greater forces of the world. Only seven of his eighty plays survive.*

his travels. **Thucydides** (thoo·sid′i·dēz′) (c. 460–401 B.C.) analyzed the Athenian rise to power and the conflict with Sparta in his *History of the Peloponnesian War* (see page 284). Unlike Herodotus, who filled his narrative with colorful character sketches and interesting digressions, Thucydides' work stressed rigorous research and objective reporting. Like Herodotus, however, Thucydides also conceived his role as that of a moral teacher. In this respect, the Greek historians resembled the philosophers and the playwrights.

The Great Greek Philosophers: Socrates, Plato, and Aristotle

The Golden Age of Greek history also saw the emergence of great philosophical thinkers and writers. According to tradition, the Greek philosopher **Socrates** (säk′rə·tēz′) (469–399 B.C.) once asked a young Athenian boy whether he thought a great deal. The boy modestly replied no, but at least, he said, he had wondered a great deal. The response Socrates gave the boy has become proverbial: "Wisdom," he replied, "begins in wonder." Socrates called himself a "philosopher," a Greek word meaning "lover of wisdom."

> The Greek philosophers' efforts to ask questions, record ideas, devise methods, and teach moral principles have had an enormous and lasting impact on Western culture.

Socrates' pupil **Plato** (plā′tō) (c. 429–c. 347 B.C.) preserved his mentor's method of questioning in a series of dialogues, or conversations, in which the "character" Socrates would pose and answer philosophical questions. Plato's writings examined such concepts as freedom of conscience, the nature of reality, the existence of the soul, ideal government, and how to lead a virtuous and happy life.

Plato's greatest pupil was **Aristotle** (ar′is·tät′l) (384–322 B.C.), who studied in Athens and later became tutor to the young Alexander the Great. Aristotle wrote numerous treatises on such subjects as logic, ethics, political theory,

Bronze bust of Aristotle.
Aristotle was founder of a school called the Lyceum, and he served as teacher to Alexander the Great.

rhetoric, and biology. In the *Poetics*, one of his most influential works, he set forth the principles of Greek tragic drama (see page 371). Aristotle's systematic inquiry into numerous branches of knowledge had an enormous impact on the development of Western philosophy. Even modern students of philosophy and literature must acquaint themselves with the works of Plato and Aristotle.

The Decline of Athens

The increasing resentment toward and envy of Athenian expansion led to clashes and then to full-scale war between Athens and its chief rival, Sparta. The **Peloponnesian War**, which involved other city states on each side, lasted from 431 to 404 B.C. Sparta was victorious, and Athens spiraled into a decline from which it never recovered.

In the middle of the fourth century B.C., the kingdom of Macedon, ruled first by Philip and then by his son **Alexander the Great**, emerged as the most powerful state in the Greek-speaking world. Alexander, in particular, conquered lands from Egypt to India. By the time of Alexander's death in 323 B.C., Greek language and culture had spread throughout the Mediterranean, North Africa, and Western Asia. This continuation of Greek culture by Alexander, and later by the Romans who would conquer the Macedonians in 197 B.C., is called the **Hellenistic Age** because it emulated, or imitated, the Hellenic Age, the age of the Greeks. The Romans would be greatly responsible for the preservation and spread of Greek knowledge in the West.

> **❝** The absence of romance in my history will, I fear, detract somewhat from its interest; but if it be judged useful by those inquirers who desire an exact knowledge of the past as an aid to the interpretation of the future, which in the course of human things must resemble if it does not reflect it, I shall be content. **❞**
>
> —*Thucydides*

Scala/Art Resource, New York

Battle of Alexander, mosaic. *Alexander the Great was responsible for the revival of the waning Greek culture, spreading it far beyond the reaches of the original Greek territories.*

Introduction

The Iliad

Europe's first, and most enduring, literary epics, the *Iliad* (il'ē·əd) and the *Odyssey* (äd'i·sē), were composed sometime between 900 and 700 B.C. We know little about Homer, the author of these epics. Homer was probably a native of the Greek district of Ionia on the western coast of Asia Minor. The name *Homer* means "hostage," indicating that the poet may have been a slave or descended from slaves. Tradition says Homer was blind, a detail probably based more on convention than on fact:

SEF/Art Resource, New York

Bust of Homer.

In Greek culture, physical blindness was often a metaphor for profound insight.

Homer belonged to a class of bards called **rhapsodes**. Like the griots of African oral tradition (see page 70), the rhapsodes played a vitally important role in Greek society, serving as both oral historians and entertainers.

The written versions of the epics became a staple of Greek education during the Athenian Golden Age, from the sixth to the fourth centuries B.C. The *Iliad* and the *Odyssey* were the "Bibles" of Greek civilization: they gave coherence to a chaotic pantheon of gods and goddesses, and their heroes embodied the ideal of *arete* (ä·re'tā), or excellence, for which the ancient Greeks strived.

The Legend of the Trojan War

Both the *Iliad* and the *Odyssey* tell stories about the heroes and events of the Trojan War. According to oral tradition, the war began with a beauty contest. Three goddesses—Aphrodite, Athena, and Hera—decided to compete for a golden apple that was inscribed "To the Fairest." The gods, smart enough not to get involved in a potentially hazardous situation, chose a mortal man to judge who was the most beautiful goddess. Paris, a young and handsome but naive prince of Troy, was selected. He was offered bribes by each goddess in turn. The bribe he accepted was Aphrodite's, for she offered him the most appealing gift: marriage with the world's most beautiful woman, Helen, the wife of King Menelaus of Greece. Paris took Helen from Menelaus, and the two sailed for Troy. As a result of the abduction of Helen, the various Greek chieftains, bound by oaths of loyalty, banded together under the leadership of Menelaus's brother, Agamemnon, and attacked Troy. The war party laid seige to Troy, beginning a conflict that would drag on for ten years, until the Greeks, thanks to the wiles of the clever hero Odysseus, finally succeeded in sacking Troy and recapturing Helen.

Scala/Art Resource, New York

PARNASSUS, RAPHAEL (1483–1520). Detail. *The medieval poet Dante, an admirer of Homer, stands to the right of the Greek bard.*

The Conventions of the Homeric Epics

Certain features of Homer's work were so widely imitated in later written epics, such as Virgil's *Aeneid* (see page 380) and Milton's *Paradise Lost* that they became recognizable characteristics, or **conventions**, of the epic genre. Yet the origins of many of these conventions lie in the oral tradition that gave birth to the *Iliad* and the *Odyssey*. The oral poets used formulas that allowed them to rapidly summarize past events or quickly sketch characters in the epic. Following are some of the epic conventions that occur in the *Iliad*:

1. Invocation. The *Iliad* begins with an **invocation**, or formal plea for aid, to the Muse Calliope (kə·lī′ə·pē′), one of the nine goddesses who presided over the arts and sciences. The Greeks believed that this "immortal one" spoke through mortal epic poets:

Anger be now your song, immortal one,
Achilles' anger, doomed and ruinous,
that caused the Achaeans loss on bitter loss
and crowded brave souls into the undergloom....

The invocation also serves to state the epic's subject and theme.

2. *In medias res.* The epic plunges us into the middle of the action—that is, *in medias res* (in mä′dē·äs′ res′), a Latin term meaning "into the midst of things." **Flashbacks** are then used to inform the

APOTHEOSIS OF HOMER, JEAN-AUGUSTE-DOMINIQUE INGRES, 1827.
Apotheosis *means exaltation or deification. Why do you think Homer was represented in this way centuries after his death?*

Giraudon/Art Resource, New York

audience of events that took place before the narrative's current time setting.

3. Epic similes. One of the most striking features of the language of the *Iliad* is Homer's use of extended, elaborate comparisons called **epic** or **Homeric similes**. Some epic similes are developed over many lines. These similes compare heroic events to simple, everyday events—events that Homer's audience could easily understand. For example, when, in Book 9, Achilles feels all his heroic deeds have gone unrewarded, he says "A bird will give her fledglings every scrap/she comes by, and go hungry, foraging./That is the case with me." Homer's listeners would have been familiar with the image of the bird; this simile would help them to understand the epic hero's feelings.

4. Metrical Structure. The *Iliad* was originally composed in dactylic hexameter, a meter consisting of six stressed syllables per line. This meter probably closely imitated the speech patterns of the Greeks during Homer's time. But the meter is also formulaic, or fixed and conventional. The use of a conventional, predictable metrical structure would have given the rhapsodes a standard pattern to follow, thereby aiding memorization of lines and passages.

5. Stock epithets. Another figure of speech that occurs frequently in the *Iliad* is the **stock epithet**, a descriptive adjective or phrase that is repeatedly used with—or in place of—a noun or proper name. Thus, the audience repeatedly hears of "Andromache of the ivory-white arms" and "the pale-gold goddess Aphrodite." The repetition of these epithets helped the audience to follow the narrative and also helped the rhapsode as he improvised the poem in performance.

The Characters of the *Iliad*

The Greeks

Achilles (ə·kil′ēz′): the son of a mortal king, Peleus, and the sea-goddess Thetis. King of the Myrmidons, Achilles is the mightiest of the Greek warriors.

Agamemnon (ag′ə·mem′nän′): king of Mycenae and commander of the Greek forces. He is Menelaus's older brother.

Ajax (ā′jaks′): one of the strongest Greek warriors.

Calchas (kal′kəs): a seer or prophet who counsels the Greeks.

Clytemnestra (klī′təm·nes′trə): Agamemnon's wife; Helen's sister.

Helen (hel′ən): the wife of Menelaus, whose abduction by Paris is the cause of the legendary war.

Menelaus (men′ə·lā′əs): king of Sparta; husband of Helen.

Nestor (nes′tər): king of Pylos. The oldest of the Greek leaders at Troy, he serves as a counselor.

Odysseus (ō·dis′ē·əs): a wily, middle-aged Greek warrior. He is the protagonist of Homer's *Odyssey.*

Patroclus (pə·trō′kləs): Greek warrior and dearest friend of Achilles.

The Trojans

Andromache (an·dräm′ə·kē): faithful wife of Hector.

Astyanax (as·tī′ə·naks′): youngest son of Hector and Andromache.

Briseis (brī′si·əs): a girl captured from the Trojans by Achilles as a prize of war.

Chryseis (kri′si·əs): a girl captured by Agamemnon during the plunder of Chrysa. Her father, Chryses, is a priest of the god Apollo.

Hector (hek′tər): the son of King Priam and Queen Hecuba and commander of the Trojan forces.

Hecuba (hek′yoo·bə): the queen of Troy; Priam's wife.

Paris (par′is): son of King Priam and Queen Hecuba. He is also known as Alexandros.

Priam (prī′əm): the king of Troy; the father of Hector and Paris.

Gods and Goddesses

Aphrodite (af′rə·dīt′ē): the goddess of love. She sides with the Trojans during the war.

Apollo (ə·päl′ō): the god of poetry, music, and prophecy; he also sides with the Trojans. He is often referred to only as the son of Zeus and Leto, the daughter of Titans.

Athena (ə·thē′nə): the goddess of wisdom; she takes the Greeks' side in the conflict.

Hera (hir′ə): wife of Zeus; enemy of the Trojans.

Hermes (hur′mēz′): messenger of the gods, also called the Wayfinder.

Thetis (thēt′is): a sea-goddess; mother of Achilles.

Zeus (zyoos): the father-god; he remains more or less neutral throughout the conflict.

Reader's Guide

from the ILIAD

Background

As the *Iliad* begins, the war between the Greeks and the Trojans has been a stalemate for nearly ten years. The Greek forces face a crisis: A deadly plague has swept through their army. On the tenth day of the plague, the hero Achilles calls an assembly of the entire army to discuss the crisis. This meeting leads to the great quarrel between Achilles and Agamemnon that opens the epic.

As you read the *Iliad,* keep in mind the following facts about the beliefs held by the Greeks of Homer's time:

1. A warrior's material possessions—the spoils of war won in combat—were a direct measure of his honor and prestige in the community. The loss of these possessions was equivalent to being publicly shamed, the worst insult a hero could suffer.

2. The Greeks believed that their gods and goddesses played an active role in the affairs of human beings. Although people are the actual combatants in the war, the gods take sides in the conflict and have a profound effect on its outcome.

3. Respect for the dead was considered a sacred duty, for an unburied corpse was considered an offense to the gods. The soul of a person whose body was not buried was doomed to wander the earth forever.

Writer's Response

The Greek warriors strove to achieve *arete,* or personal honor and excellence. What does personal excellence mean to you? How can an ideal of excellence help to make a better society? Can the pursuit of excellence actually harm a society? Freewrite your ideas.

Literary Focus

Foreshadowing is the use of clues to hint at what is going to happen later in a plot. Foreshadowing arouses the reader's curiosity and increases suspense. A **flashback** is a scene that interrupts the present action of a plot to narrate the events of an earlier time. Watch for foreshadowing and flashbacks throughout the *Iliad.*

from the ILIAD
from Book 1
Homer
translated by

ROBERT FITZGERALD

Notice how Homer characterizes Agamemnon and Achilles, the two central figures in Book 1. What do you think of these two men? How do you think Homer wants you to view them?

BOOK 1: The Quarrel

Anger be now your song, immortal one,
Achilles' anger, doomed and ruinous,
that caused the Achaeans° loss on bitter loss
and crowded brave souls into the undergloom,

5 leaving so many dead men—carrion
for dogs and birds; and the will of Zeus was done.
Begin it when the two men first contending
broke with one another—

the Lord Marshal
Agamemnon, Atreus' son, and Prince Achilles.

10 Among the gods, who brought this quarrel on?
The son of Zeus by Leto.° Agamemnon
angered him, so he made a burning wind
of plague rise in the army: rank and file
sickened and died for the ill their chief had done

15 in despising a man of prayer.
This priest, Chryses, had come down to the ships
with gifts, no end of ransom for his daughter;
on a golden staff he carried the god's white bands
and sued for grace from the men of all Achaea

20 the two Atridae° most of all:

"O captains

Menelaus and Agamemnon, and you other
Achaeans under arms!
The gods who hold Olympus, may they grant you

3. **Achaeans** (ə·kē′ənz): one of the names used in the *Iliad* for the Greeks.

11. **The son . . . Leto** (lē′tō): Apollo.

20. **Atridae** (ə·trī′dē): Agamemnon and Menelaus are the sons of Atreus (ā′trē·əs), the king of Mycenae. At the time of the Trojan War, and in Homer's own day, Greece was not a unified country but an amalgam of diverse kingdoms. The *Atridae* refers to one of many families of kings.

plunder of Priam's town and a fair wind home,
25   but let me have my daughter back for ransom
as you revere Apollo, son of Zeus!"

Then all the soldiers murmured their assent:
"Behave well to the priest. And take the ransom!"

But Agamemnon would not. It went against his desire,
30   and brutally he ordered the man away:

"Let me not find you here by the long ships
loitering this time or returning later,
old man; if I do,
the staff and ribbons of the god will fail you.
35   Give up the girl? I swear she will grow old
at home in Argos, far from her own country,
working my loom and visiting my bed.
Leave me in peace and go, while you can, in safety."

So harsh he was, the old man feared and obeyed him,
40   in silence trailing away
by the shore of the tumbling clamorous whispering sea,
and he prayed and prayed again, as he withdrew,
to the god whom silken-braided Leto bore:

"O hear me, master of the silver bow,
45   protector of Tenedos and the holy towns,
Apollo, Sminthian,° if to your liking
ever in any grove I roofed a shrine
or burnt thighbones in fat upon your altar—
bullock or goat flesh—let my wish come true:
50   your arrows on the Danaans° for my tears!"

Now when he heard this prayer, Phoebus Apollo
walked with storm in his heart from Olympus's crest,
quiver and bow at his back, and the bundled arrows
clanged on the sky behind as he rocked in his anger,
55   descending like night itself. Apart from the ships
he halted and let fly, and the bowstring slammed
as the silver bow sprang, rolling in thunder away.
Pack animals were his target first, and dogs,
but soldiers, too, soon felt transfixing pain
60   from his hard shots, and pyres burned night and day.
Nine days the arrows of the god came down
broadside upon the army. On the tenth,
Achilles called all ranks to assembly. Hera,

46. **Sminthian** (smin′thē·ən): epithet for Apollo, probably in reference to his role as destroyer of mice; the Greek for *mouse* is *sminthos*.

50. **Danaans** (dān′ənz): one of the names for the Greeks.

whose arms are white as ivory, moved him to it,
65   as she took pity on Danaans dying.
All being mustered, all in place and quiet,
Achilles, fast in battle as a lion,
rose and said:

                    "Agamemnon, now, I take it,
the siege is broken, we are going to sail,
70   and even so may not leave death behind:
if war spares anyone, disease will take him . . . .
We might, though, ask some priest or some diviner,
even some fellow good at dreams—for dreams
come down from Zeus as well—

Fresco of the *Iliad*,
showing the Greek
gods, by Sabatelli. *Many
of the gods are painted
here with clues to their
identities. Zeus and Hera, for
instance, are seated in their
thrones at the top of the painting.
Can you identify Ares, the god of
war, or Aphrodite, the goddess of love?*

from The Iliad, Book 1   **231**

75　why all this anger of the god Apollo?

Has he some quarrel with us for a failure
in vows or hecatombs?° Would mutton burned
or smoking goat flesh make him lift the plague?"

Putting the question, down he sat. And Calchas,
80　Calchas Thestorides, came forward, wisest
by far of all who scanned the flight of birds.
He knew what was, what had been, what would be,
Calchas, who brought Achaean's ships to Ilion°
by the diviner's gift Apollo gave him.
85　Now for their benefit he said:

　　　　　　　　　　　　　　　　　　"Achilles,

dear to Zeus, it is on me you call
to tell you why the Archer God° is angry.
Well, I can tell you. Are you listening? Swear
by heaven that you will back me and defend me,
90　because I fear my answer will enrage
a man with power in Argos, one whose word
Achaean troops obey.

　　　　　　　　　A great man in his rage is formidable
for underlings: though he may keep it down,
he cherishes the burning in his belly
95　until a reckoning day. Think well
if you will save me."

Said Achilles:

　　　　　　　　　　　　　　　　　　"Courage.

Tell what you know, what you have light to know.
I swear by Apollo, the lord god to whom
100　you pray when you uncover truth,
never while I draw breath, while I have eyes to see,
shall any man upon this beachhead dare
lay hands on you—not one of all the army,
not Agamemnon, if it is he you mean,
105　though he is first in rank of all Achaeans."

The diviner then took heart and said:

　　　　　　　　　　　　　　　　　"No failure

in hecatombs or vows is held against us.
It is the man of prayer whom Agamemnon
treated with contempt: he kept his daughter,
110　spurned his gifts: for that man's sake the Archer

77. **hecatombs** (hek′ə·tōmz′):
sacrifices to the gods; originally a hecatomb consisted of
a hundred oxen.

83. **Ilion** (il′ē·ən): another name
for Troy; the founder of Troy
was Ilus, who named the city
for his father, Tros.

87. **the Archer God:** Apollo.

Greek vase.

visited grief upon us and will again.
Relieve the Danaans of this plague he will not
until the girl who turns the eyes of men°
shall be restored to her own father—freely,
115 with no demand for ransom—and until
we offer up a hecatomb at Chryse.
Then only can we calm him and persuade him."

He finished and sat down. The son of Atreus,
ruler of the great plain, Agamemnon,
120 rose, furious. Round his heart resentment
welled, and his eyes shone out like licking fire.
Then, with a long and boding look at Calchas,
he growled at him:

                              "You visionary of hell,
never have I had fair play in your forecasts.
125 Calamity is all you care about, or see,
no happy portents; and you bring to pass
nothing agreeable. Here you stand again
before the army, giving it out as oracle
the Archer made them suffer because of me,
130 because I would not take the gifts
and let the girl Chryseis go; I'd have her
mine, at home. Yes, if you like, I rate her
higher than Clytemnestra, my own wife!
She loses nothing by comparison
135 in beauty or womanhood, in mind or skill.

For all of that, I am willing now to yield her
if it is best; I want the army saved
and not destroyed. You must prepare, however,
a prize of honor for me, and at once,
140 that I may not be left without my portion—
I, of all Argives.° It is not fitting so.
While every man of you looks on, my girl
goes elsewhere."

Prince Achilles answered him:

145 "Lord Marshal, most insatiate of men,
how can the army make you a new gift?
Where is our store of booty? Can you see it?
Everything plundered from the towns has been
distributed; should troops turn all that in?
150 Just let the girl go, in the god's name, now;

113. **the girl . . . of men:** He is referring to Chryseis.

Plate of Apollo crowned with myrtle. *Myrtle is a small, wild evergreen that the ancient Greeks considered sacred to the goddess Aphrodite.*

141. **Argives** (är'gīvz'): Greeks from Argos, in the northeastern part of the Peloponnesus.

we'll make it up to you, twice over, three
times over, on that day Zeus gives us leave
to plunder Troy behind her rings of stone."

Agamemnon answered:

"Not that way
155   will I be gulled, brave as you are, Achilles.
Take me in, would you? Try to get around me?
What do you really ask? That you may keep
your own winnings, I am to give up mine
and sit here wanting her? Oh, no:
160   the army will award a prize to me
and make sure that it measures up, or if
they do not, I will take a girl myself,
your own, or Ajax's, or Odysseus' prize!
Take her, yes, to keep. The man I visit
165   may choke with rage; well, let him.
But this, I say, we can decide on later.

Look to it now, we launch on the great sea
a well-found ship, and get her manned with oarsmen,
load her with sacrificial beasts and put aboard
170   Chryseis in her loveliness. My deputy,
Ajax, Idomeneus,° or Prince Odysseus,
or you, Achilles, fearsome as you are,
will make the hecatomb and quiet the Archer."
Achilles frowned and looked at him, then said:

175   "You thick-skinned, shameless, greedy fool!
Can any Achaean care for you, or obey you,
after this on marches or in battle?
As for myself, when I came here to fight,
I had no quarrel with Troy or Trojan spearmen:
180   they never stole my cattle or my horses,
never in the black farmland of Phthia°
ravaged my crops. How many miles there are
of shadowy hills between, and foaming seas!
No, no, we joined for you, you insolent boor,
185   to please you, fighting for your brother's sake
and yours, to get revenge upon the Trojans.
You overlook this, dogface, or don't care,
and now in the end you threaten to take my girl,
a prize I sweated for, and soldiers gave me!

190   Never have I had plunder like your own

**Detail of a vase handle depicting
Ajax.**

171. **Idomeneus** (ī·däm′i·nōōs′,
-nyōōs′): king of Crete and
leader of the Cretan forces
against Troy.

181. **Phthia** (thī′ə): Achilles' home
in northern Greece.

from any Trojan stronghold battered down
by the Achaeans. I have seen more action
hand to hand in those assaults than you have,
but when the time for sharing comes, the greater
195 share is always yours. Worn out with battle
I carry off some trifle to my ships.
Well, this time I make sail for home.
Better to take now to my ships. Why linger,
cheated of winnings, to make wealth for you?"

200 To this the high commander made reply:

"Desert, if that's the way the wind blows. Will I
beg you to stay on my account? I will not.
Others will honor me, and Zeus who views
the wide world most of all.

No officer

Marble bust of Zeus, c. 131 B.C.

205 is hateful to my sight as you are, none
given like you to faction, as to battle—
rugged you are, I grant, by some god's favor.
Sail, then, in your ships, and lord it over
your own battalion of Myrmidons.° I do not
210 give a curse for you, or for your anger.
But here is warning for you:

209. **Myrmidons** (mʉr′mə·dänz′):
warriors from Thessaly, in
northern Greece; followers of
Achilles.

Chryseis

being required of me by Phoebus Apollo,
she will be sent back in a ship of mine,
manned by my people. That done, I myself
215 will call for Briseis at your hut, and take her,
flower of young girls that she is, your prize,
to show you here and now who is the stronger
and make the next man sick at heart—if any
think of claiming equal place with me."

220 A pain like grief weighed on the son of Peleus,°
and in his shaggy chest this way and that
the passion of his heart ran: should he draw
longsword from hip, stand off the rest, and kill
in single combat the great son of Atreus,
225 or hold his rage in check and give it time?
And as this tumult swayed him, as he slid
the big blade slowly from the sheath, Athena
came to him from the sky. The white-armed goddess,
Hera, sent her, being fond of both,

220. **son of Peleus:** Achilles.

230 concerned for both men. And Athena, stepping
   up behind him, visible to no one
   except Achilles, gripped his red-gold hair.

   Startled, he made a half turn, and he knew her
   upon the instant for Athena: terribly
235 her gray eyes blazed at him. And speaking softly
   but rapidly aside to her he said:

   "What now, O daughter of the god of heaven
   who bears the stormcloud,° why are you here? To see
   the wolfishness of Agamemnon?
240 Well, I give you my word: this time, and soon,
   he pays for his behavior with his blood."

   The gray-eyed goddess Athena said to him:

   "It was to check this killing rage I came
   from heaven, if you will listen. Hera sent me,
245 being fond of both of you, concerned for both.
   Enough: break off this combat, stay your hand
   upon the sword hilt. Let him have a lashing

237–238. **god . . . who bears the
stormcloud:** Zeus.

ATHENA RESTRAINING THE ANGER OF ACHILLES IN BATTLE WITH AGAMEMNON.
GIOVANNI BATTISTA TIEPOLO (1696–1770).
*Why has Hera sent Athena? What is Athena's promise to
Achilles?*

236 Greek and Roman Literatures

with words, instead: tell him how things will be.
Here is my promise, and it will be kept:
250 winnings three times as rich, in due season,
you shall have in requital for his arrogance.
But hold your hand. Obey."

The great runner,
Achilles, answered:
"Nothing for it, goddess,
but when you two immortals speak, a man
255 complies, though his heart burst. Just as well.
Honor the gods' will, they may honor ours."
On this he stayed his massive hand
upon the silver pommel,° and the blade
of his great weapon slid back in the scabbard.
260 The man had done her bidding. Off to Olympus,
gaining the air, she went to join the rest,
the powers of heaven in the home of Zeus.

But now the son of Peleus turned on Agamemnon
and lashed out at him, letting his anger ride
265 in execration:
"Sack of wine,
you with your cur's eyes and your antelope heart!
You've never had the kidney to buckle on
armor among the troops, or make a sortie
with picked men—oh, no; that way death might lie.
270 Safer, by god, in the middle of the army—
is it not?—to commandeer the prize
of any man who stands up to you! Leech!
Commander to trash! If not, I swear,
you never could abuse one soldier more!

275 But here is what I say: my oath upon it
by this great staff: look: leaf or shoot
it cannot sprout again, once lopped away
from the log it left behind in the timbered hills;
it cannot flower, peeled of bark and leaves;
280 instead, Achaean officers in council
take it in hand by turns, when they observe
by the will of Zeus due order in debate:
let this be what I swear by then: I swear
a day will come when every Achaean soldier
285 will groan to have Achilles back. That day
you shall no more prevail on me than this

258. **pommel:** the knob on the end of the hilt of a sword or dagger.

dry wood shall flourish—driven though you are,
and though a thousand men perish before
the killer, Hector. You will eat your heart out,
290 raging with remorse for this dishonor
done by you to the bravest of Achaeans."

He hurled the staff, studded with golden nails,
before him on the ground. Then down he sat,
and fury filled Agamemnon, looking across at him.
295 But for the sake of both men Nestor arose,
the Pylians'° orator, eloquent and clear;
argument sweeter than honey rolled from his tongue.
By now he had outlived two generations
of mortal men, his own and the one after,
300 in Pylos land, and still ruled in the third.
In kind reproof he said:

                "A black day, this.
Bitter distress comes this way to Achaea.
How happy Priam and Priam's sons would be,
and all the Trojans—wild with joy—if they
305 got wind of all these fighting words between you,
foremost in council as you are, foremost
in battle. Give me your attention. Both
are younger men than I, and in my time
men who were even greater have I known
310 and none of them disdained me. Men like those
I have not seen again, nor shall: Peirithous,
the Lord Marshal Dryas, Caereus, Exadius,
Polyphemus, Theseus°—Aegeus's son,
a man like the immortal gods. I speak
315 of champions among men of earth, who fought
with champions, with wild things of the mountains,
great centaurs° whom they broke and overpowered.
Among these men I say I had my place
when I sailed out of Pylos, my far country,
320 because they called for me. I fought
for my own hand among them. Not one man
alive now upon earth could stand against them.
And I repeat: they listened to my reasoning,
took my advice. Well, then, you take it too.
325 It is far better so.

                Lord Agamemnon,
do not deprive him of the girl, renounce her.

296. Pylians (pīl′ē·ənz): people from Pylos (pī′los), a town in the Peloponnesus.

311–313. Peirithous . . . Theseus: heroes of Nestor's generation.

317. centaurs: legendary creatures, half-man and half-horse.

Mycenaean death mask, once thought to be the mask of Agamemnon.
❓ What is Agamemnon's attitude toward Achilles?

The army had allotted her to him.
Achilles, for your part, do not defy
your King and Captain. No ones vies in honor
330 with him who holds authority from Zeus.
You have more prowess, for a goddess bore you;
his power over men surpasses yours.

But, Agamemnon, let your anger cool.
I beg you to relent, knowing Achilles
335 a sea wall for Achaeans in the black waves of war."

Lord Agamemnon answered:

                        "All you say

is fairly said, sir, but this man's ambition,
remember, is to lead, to lord it over
everyone, hold power over everyone,
340 give orders to the rest of us! Well, one
will never take his orders! If the gods
who live forever made a spearman of him,
have they put insults on his lips as well?"

Achilles interrupted:

"What a poltroon,°

344. **poltroon** (päl·trōōn'): coward.

345 how lily-livered I should be called, if I
knuckled under to all you do or say!
Give your commands to someone else, not me!
And one more thing I have to tell you: think it
over: this time, for the girl, I will not
350 wrangle in arms with you or anyone,
though I am robbed of what was given me;
but as for any other thing I have
alongside my black ship, you shall not take it
against my will. Try it. Hear this, everyone:
355 that instant your hot blood blackens my spear!"

They quarreled in this way, face to face, and then
broke off the assembly by the ships. Achilles
made his way to his squadron and his quarters,
Patroclus by his side, with his companions.

Photo Nimatallah/Art Resource, New York

A scene of sacrifice.

360 Agamemnon proceeded to launch a ship,
assigned her twenty oarsmen, loaded beasts
for sacrifice to the god, then set aboard
Chryseis in her loveliness. The versatile
Odysseus took the deck, and, all oars manned,
365 they pulled out on the drenching ways of sea.
The troops meanwhile were ordered to police camp
and did so, throwing refuse in the water;
then to Apollo by the barren surf
they carried out full-tally hecatombs,
370 and the savor curled in crooked smoke toward heaven.

That was the day's work in the army.

Agamemnon
had kept his threat in mind, and now he acted,
calling Eurybates and Talthybios,
his aides and criers:

"Go along," he said,
375 "both of you, to the quarters of Achilles
and take his charming Briseis by the hand
to bring to me. And if he balks at giving her
I shall be there myself with men-at-arms
in force to take her—all the more gall for him."

380 So, ominously, he sent them on their way,
and they who had no stomach for it went

along the waste sea shingle° toward the ships
and shelters of the Myrmidons. Not far
from his black ship and hut they found the prince
385 in the open, seated. And seeing these two come
was cheerless to Achilles. Shamefast, pale
with fear of him, they stood without a word;
but he knew what they felt and called out:

                              "Peace to you,
criers and couriers of Zeus and men!
390 Come forward. Not one thing have I against you:
Agamemnon is the man who sent you
for Briseis. Here then, my lord Patroclus,
bring out the girl and give her to these men.
And let them both bear witness before the gods
395 who live in bliss, as before men who die,
including this harsh king, if ever hereafter
a need for me arises to keep the rest
from black defeat and ruin.

                                    Lost in folly,
the man cannot think back or think ahead
400 how to come through a battle by the ships."
Patroclus did the bidding of his friend,
led from the hut Briseis in her beauty
and gave her to them. Back along the ships
they took their way, and the girl went, loath to go.

405 Leaving his friends in haste, Achilles wept,
and sat apart by the gray wave, scanning the endless sea.
Often he spread his hands in prayer to his mother:°

"As my life came from you, though it is brief,
honor at least from Zeus who storms in heaven
410 I call my due. He gives me precious little.
See how the lord of the great plains, Agamemnon,
humiliated me! He has my prize,
by his own whim, for himself."

                                    Eyes wet with tears,
he spoke, and her ladyship his mother heard him
415 in green deeps where she lolled near her old father.
Gliding she rose and broke like mist from the inshore
gray sea face, to sit down softly before him,
her son in tears; and fondling him she said:

382. **shingle:** beach covered with large, coarse gravel.

407. **mother:** the goddess Thetis (thē′tis), a daughter of Nereus, the old man of the sea.

from The Iliad, Book 1 **241**

Fresco of Agamemnon carrying away Briseis, by Giovanni Battista Tiepolo.
How is Briseis important to the plot of the Iliad?

"Child, why do you weep? What grief is this?
420 Out with it, tell me, both of us should know."
Achilles, fast in battle as a lion,
groaned and said:

                    "Why tell you what you know?
We sailed out raiding, and we took by storm
that ancient town of Eetion° called Thebe,
425 plundered the place, brought slaves and spoils away.
At the division, later,
they chose a young girl, Chryseis, for the king.
Then Chryses, priest of the Archer God, Apollo,
came to the beachhead we Achaeans hold,
430 bringing no end of ransom for his daughter;

424. **Eetion** (ē·ē′tē·än): king of Thebe (thē′bē), a city near Troy.

he had the god's white bands on a golden staff
and sued for grace from the army of Achaea,
mostly the two Atridae, corps commanders.
All of our soldiers murmured in assent:
435 'Behave well to the priest. And take the ransom!'
But Agamemnon would not. It went against his desire,
and brutally he ordered the man away.
So the old man withdrew in grief and anger.
Apollo cared for him: he heard his prayer
440 and let black bolts of plague fly on the Argives.

One by one our men came down with it
and died hard as the god's shots raked the army
broadside. But our priest divined the cause
and told us what the god meant by the plague.

445 I said, 'Appease the god!' but Agamemnon
could not contain his rage; he threatened me,
and what he threatened is now done—
one girl the Achaeans are embarking now
for Chryse beach with gifts for Lord Apollo;
450 the other, just now, from my hut—the criers
came and took her, Briseus' girl, my prize,
given by the army.
                            If you can, stand by me:
go to Olympus, pray to Zeus, if ever
by word or deed you served him—
455 and so you did, I often heard you tell it
in Father's house: that time when you alone
of all the gods shielded the son of Cronus°
from peril and disgrace—when other gods,
Pallas Athena, Hera, and Poseidon,
460 wished him in irons, wished to keep him bound,
you had the will to free him of that bondage,
and called up to Olympus in all haste
Aegaeon, whom the gods call Briareus,°
the giant with a hundred arms, more powerful
465 than the sea-god, his father. Down he sat
by the son of Cronus, glorying in that place.
For fear of him the blissful gods forbore
to manacle Zeus.

                    Remind him of these things,
cling to his knees and tell him your good pleasure

457. **son of Cronus:** Zeus; Cronus ruled over the Titans until his son, Zeus, dethroned him and became ruler over the Olympians.

463. **Briareus** (brī·är′ē·əs): a giant who helped Zeus and the Olympians overcome the Titans.

470 if he will take the Trojan side
and roll the Achaeans back to the water's edge,
back on the ships with slaughter! All the troops
may savor what their king has won for them,
and he may know his madness, what he lost
475 when he dishonored me, peerless among Achaeans."

Her eyes filled, and a tear fell as she answered:

"Alas, my child, why did I rear you, doomed
the day I bore you? Ah, could you only be
serene upon this beachhead through the siege,
480 your life runs out so soon.
Oh early death! Oh broken heart! No destiny
so cruel! And I bore you to this evil!

But what you wish I will propose
To Zeus, lord of the lightning, going up
485 myself into the snow-glare of Olympus
with hope for his consent.

                              Be quiet now
beside the long ships, keep your anger bright
against the army, quit the war.

                              Last night
Zeus made a journey to the shore of Ocean
490 to feast among the Sunburned,° and the gods
accompanied him. In twelve days he will come
back to Olympus. Then I shall be there
to cross his bronze doorsill and take his knees.
I trust I'll move him."

                              Thetis left her son
495 still burning for the softly belted girl
whom they had wrested from him. . . .

Scala/Art Resource, New York

Vase depicting Thetis bringing armor to Achilles.
? What is the relation of Thetis to Achilles? Why would she bring him his armor?

490. **the Sunburned:** Ethiopians.

Fresco from the isle of Crete.

Photo Nimatallah/Art Resource, New York

First Thoughts

Which character do you think was more in the right, Agamemnon or Achilles? Explain.

Identifying Facts

1. What crisis in the Greek camp confronts the leaders at the opening of the epic? How does this crisis lead to a conflict between Achilles and Agamemnon?
2. What action does Agamemnon take to appease Apollo? What does he take from Achilles?
3. What oath does Achilles swear? Why does he withdraw from the battle?
4. What does Thetis promise to do for her son Achilles?

Interpreting Meanings

1. What impression do you form of Agamemnon's **character** from his own words and actions and the reactions of Calchas and Achilles?

2. What ominous, or threatening, images can you identify in the first fifteen lines of Book 1 of the *Iliad*? What future events do these images **foreshadow**?
3. In the scene between Achilles and his mother Thetis, there is a **flashback** to an earlier time when Thetis helped to defend Zeus. What purpose does this flashback serve?
4. What role do the gods and goddesses play in Book 1? Are they aloof observers, fair intermediaries, or meddling nuisances? Describe the roles played by Apollo, Athena, and Thetis in this book of the *Iliad*.

Applying Meanings

Do you think that Achilles is justified in his wrath against Agamemnon and his subsequent withdrawal from battle? Imagine that Achilles is a modern-day military officer. Would a modern general be justified in withdrawing from combat if his personal honor were at stake? If so, under what circumstances?

Parthenon frieze (477–432 B.C.). *This frieze depicts Ares, the god of war, at right, and Dionysus, the god of agriculture and wine, facing Demeter, the goddess of fertility.*

The Bridgeman Art Library/Art Resource, New York

from the ILIAD
from Books 22 and 24
Homer
t r a n s l a t e d   b y
ROBERT FITZGERALD

Based on what you have learned about Achilles in the epic thus far, how do you predict he will behave toward his enemy, the Trojan hero Hector, when the two men finally meet in battle?

Without Achilles' help, the Greeks are at a serious disadvantage against the Trojans, who are led by their great warrior Hector, the son of the Trojan king, Priam. In Book 6, we glimpse Hector's humanity as he shares a loving moment with his wife Andromache and his son Astyanax. Book 6 also reveals to us Hector's pride, for we learn that although he believes Troy is doomed, honor will not allow him to surrender.

Hector returns to battle, fighting fiercely for the Trojans. As fear grows in the Greek camp, Agamemnon admits that he has wronged Achilles. He sends a delegation of ambassadors to offer amends and to ask Achilles and his comrades to return to battle. Achilles' immense pride is revealed as he stubbornly refuses to accept Agamemnon's gifts. He tells the delegates that he has decided to return to his kingdom and live out his life in comfort, forgoing the honor of dying a hero's death in battle.

When the Trojans break through the Greek defenses, Achilles' best friend Patroclus pleads with the hero to permit him to rejoin the fighting. Achilles reluctantly agrees (Books 11–15). As the battle rages, the god Apollo strikes Patroclus from his horse, giving Hector the opportunity to slay the warrior and strip the corpse of its armor.

On hearing of Patroclus's death, Achilles is overcome with grief and rage. Vowing to avenge his friend, he finally returns to the battle, mercilessly slaying the Trojan forces (Books 19–21). As Book 22 opens, the exhausted Trojans take refuge behind the high walls of the city. One Trojan remains outside the walls: Hector.

Fresco from the isle of Crete.

BOOK 22: The Death of Hector

Once in the town, those who had fled like deer
wiped off their sweat and drank their thirst away,
leaning against the cool stone of the ramparts.°
Meanwhile Achaeans with bright shields aslant
5 came up the plain and nearer. As for Hector,
fatal destiny pinned him where he stood
before the Scaean Gates, outside the city.

Now Achilles heard Apollo calling
back to him:

                "Why run so hard, Achilles
10 mortal as you are, after a god?
Can you not comprehend it? I am immortal.
You are so hot to catch me, you no longer
think of finishing off the men you routed.
They are all in the town by now, packed in
15 while you were being diverted here. And yet
you cannot kill me; I am no man's quarry."

Achilles bit his lip and said:

"Archer of heaven, deadliest
of immortal gods, you put me off the track,
20 turning me from the wall this way. A hundred
might have sunk their teeth into the dust
before one man took cover in Ilion!
You saved my enemies with ease and stole
my glory, having no punishment to fear.
25 I'd take it out of you, if I had the power."

Then toward the town with might and main he ran,
magnificent, like a racing chariot horse
that holds its form at full stretch on the plain.
So light-footed Achilles held the pace.
30 And aging Priam was the first to see him
sparkling on the plain, bright as that star
in autumn rising, whose unclouded rays
shine out amid a throng of stars at dusk—
the one they call Orion's° dog, most brilliant,
35 yes, but baleful as a sign: it brings
great fever to frail men. So pure and bright
the bronze gear blazed upon him as he ran.
The old man gave a cry. With both his hands

3. **ramparts:** defensive embankments surrounding a town.

Statue of Apollo.

34. **Orion:** a constellation named after a hunter who was loved and accidentally killed by the goddess Artemis.

thrown up on high he struck his head, then shouted,
40 groaning, appealing to his dear son. Unmoved,
Lord Hector stood in the gateway, resolute
to fight Achilles.

                Stretching out his hands,
old Priam said, imploring him:

                          "No, Hector!
Cut off as you are, alone, dear son,
45 don't try to hold your ground against this man,
or soon you'll meet the shock of doom, borne down
by the son of Peleus. He is more powerful
by far than you, and pitiless. Ah, were he
but dear to the gods as he is dear to me!
50 Wild dogs and kites would eat him where he lay
within the hour, and ease me of my torment.
Many tall sons he killed, bereaving me,
or sold them to far islands. Even now
I cannot see two sons of mine, Lycaon°
55 and Polydorus,° among the Trojans massed
inside the town. A queen, Laothoe,
conceived and bore them. If they are alive
amid the Achaean host, I'll ransom them
with bronze and gold: both I have, piled at home,
60 rich treasures that old Altes, the renowned,
gave for his daughter's dowry. If they died,
if they went under to the homes of Death,
sorrow has come to me and to their mother.
But to our townsmen all this pain is brief,
65 unless you too go down before Achilles.
Come inside the wall, child; here you may
fight on to save our Trojan men and women.
Do not resign the glory to Achilles,
losing your own dear life! Take pity, too,
70 on me and my hard fate, while I live still.
Upon the threshold of my age, in misery,
the son of Cronus° will destroy my life
after the evil days I shall have seen—
my sons brought down, my daughters dragged away,
75 bedchambers ravaged, and small children hurled
to earth in the atrocity of war,
as my sons' wives are taken by Achaeans'
ruinous hands. And at the end, I too—
when someone with a sword-cut or a spear

54. **Lycaon** (lī·kā′än)
55. **Polydorus** (pôl·i·dō′rəs)

72. **son of Cronus:** Zeus.

80 has had my life—I shall be torn apart
on my own doorstep by the hounds
I trained as watchdogs, fed from my own table.
These will lap my blood with ravenous hearts
and lie in the entranceway.

                        Everything done
85 to a young man killed in war becomes his glory,
once he is riven° by the whetted bronze:
dead though he be, it is all fair, whatever
happens then. But when an old man falls,
and dogs disfigure his gray head and cheek
90 and genitals, that is most harrowing
of all that men in their hard lives endure."

    The old man wrenched at his gray hair and pulled out
hanks of it in both hands, but moved
Lord Hector not at all. The young man's mother
95 wailed from the tower across, above the portal,
streaming tears, and loosening her robe
with one hand, held her breast out in the other,
saying:

                  "Hector, my child, be moved by this,
and pity me, if ever I unbound
100 a quieting breast for you. Think of these things,
dear child; defend yourself against the killer
this side of the wall, not hand to hand.
He has no pity. If he brings you down,
I shall no longer be allowed to mourn you
105 laid out on your bed, dear branch in flower,
born of me! And neither will your lady,
so endowed with gifts. Far from us both,
dogs will devour you by the Argive ships."

    With tears and cries the two implored their son,
110 and made their prayers again, but could not shake him.
Hector stood firm, as huge Achilles neared.
The way a serpent, fed on poisonous herbs,
coiled at his lair upon a mountainside,
with all his length of hate awaits a man
115 and eyes him evilly: so Hector, grim
and narrow-eyed, refused to yield. He leaned
his brilliant shield against a spur of wall
and in his brave heart bitterly reflected:
"Here I am badly caught. If I take cover,

86. **riven:** split or torn apart.

Hector Taking Leave from Andromache, Angelica Kauffmann (1741–1807).

Stone etching of a battle of the Trojan War.

? *Why does Hector refuse to back down? How does he talk himself into facing Achilles?*

120 slipping inside the gate and wall, the first
to accuse me for it will be Polydamas,°
he who told me I should lead the Trojans
back to the city on that cursed night
Achilles joined the battle. No, I would not,

125 would not, wiser though it would have been.
Now troops have perished for my foolish pride,
I am ashamed to face townsmen and women.
Someone inferior to me may say:
'He kept his pride and lost his men, this Hector!'

130 So it will go. Better, when that time comes,
that I appear as he who killed Achilles
man to man, or else that I went down
fighting him to the end before the city.
Suppose, though, that I lay my shield and helm

135 aside, and prop my spear against the wall,
and go to meet the noble Prince Achilles,
promising Helen, promising with her
all treasures that Alexandros° brought home
by ship to Troy—the first cause of our quarrel—

121. **Polydamas** (pō·lid′ə·məs): a Trojan leader.

138. **Alexandros:** another name for Paris. *Alexandros* means "champion."

250 Greek and Roman Literatures

140 that he may give these things to the Atridae?
Then I might add, apart from these, a portion
of all the secret wealth the city owns.
Yes, later I might take our counselors' oath
to hide no stores, but share and share alike
145 to halve all wealth our lovely city holds,
all that is here within the walls. Ah, no,
why even put the question to myself?
I must not go before him and receive
no quarter, no respect! Aye, then and there
150 he'll kill me, unprotected as I am,
my gear laid by, defenseless as a woman.
No chance, now, for charms from oak or stone
in parley with him—charms a girl and boy
might use when they enchant each other talking!
155 Better we duel, now at once, and see
to whom the Olympian awards the glory."

These were his shifts of mood. Now close at hand
Achilles like the implacable god of war
came on with blowing crest, hefting the dreaded
160 beam of Pelian ash° on his right shoulder.
Bronze light played around him, like the glare
of a great fire or the great sun rising,
and Hector, as he watched, began to tremble.
Then he could hold his ground no more. He ran,
165 leaving the gate behind him, with Achilles
hard on his heels, sure of his own speed.
When that most lightning-like of birds, a hawk
bred on a mountain, swoops upon a dove,
the quarry dips in terror, but the hunter,
170 screaming, dips behind and gains upon it,
passionate for prey. Just so, Achilles
murderously cleft the air, as Hector
ran with flashing knees along the wall.
They passed the lookout point, the wild fig tree
175 with wind in all its leaves, then veered away
along the curving wagon road, and came
to where the double fountains well, the source
of eddying Scamander.° One hot spring
flows out, and from the water fumes arise
180 as though from fire burning; but the other
even in summer gushes chill as hail

160. **Pelian** (pēl′ē·ən) **ash:** wood cut from trees on Mount Pelion, one of the highest mountains in Greece.

178. **Scamander** (skə·man′dər): river of Troy.

or snow or crystal ice frozen on water.
Near these fountains are wide washing pools
of smooth-laid stone, where Trojan wives and daughters
185 laundered their smooth linen in the days
of peace before the Achaeans came. Past these
the two men ran, pursuer and pursued,
and he who fled was noble, he behind
a greater man by far. They ran full speed,
190 and not for bull's hide or a ritual beast
or any prize that men compete for: no,
but for the life of Hector, tamer of horses.
Just as when chariot-teams around a course
go wheeling swiftly, for the prize is great,
195 a tripod° or a woman, in the games
held for a dead man, so three times these two
at full speed made their course round Priam's town,
as all the gods looked on. And now the father
of gods and men° turned to the rest and said:

200 "How sad that this beloved man is hunted
around the wall before my eyes! My heart
is touched for Hector; he has burned thigh flesh
of oxen for me often, high on Ida,°
at other times on the high point of Troy.
205 Now Prince Achilles with devouring stride
is pressing him around the town of Priam.
Come, gods, put your minds on it, consider
whether we may deliver him from death
or see him, noble as he is, brought down
210 by Peleus' son, Achilles."

                      Gray-eyed Athena
said to him:

                  "Father of the blinding bolt,
the dark stormcloud, what words are these? The man
is mortal, and his doom fixed, long ago.
Would you release him from his painful death?
215 Then do so, but not all of us will praise you."

Zeus who gathers cloud replied:

                       "Take heart,
my dear and honored child. I am not bent
on my suggestion, and I would indulge you.
Act as your thought inclines, refrain no longer."

195. **tripod:** a bronze altar used in sacrifices.

198–199. **father of gods and men:** Zeus.

203. **Ida:** Mount Ida, in Phrygia, the source of many rivers, including the Scamander.

220 So he encouraged her in her desire,
     and down she swept from ridges of Olympus.
     Great Achilles, hard on Hector's heels,
     kept after him, the way a hound will harry
     a deer's fawn he has startled from its bed
225 to chase through gorge and open glade, and when
     the quarry goes to earth under a bush
     he holds the scent and quarters till he finds it;
     so with Hector: he could not shake off
     the great runner, Achilles. Every time
230 he tried to spring hard for the Dardan gates°
     under the towers, hoping men could help him,
     sending missiles down, Achilles loomed
     to cut him off and turn him toward the plain,
     as he himself ran always near the city.
235 As in a dream a man chasing another
     cannot catch him, nor can he in flight
     escape from his pursuer, so Achilles
     could not by his swiftness overtake him,
     nor could Hector pull away. How could he
240 run so long from death, had not Apollo
     for the last time, the very last, come near
     to give him stamina and speed?

                                        Achilles
     shook his head at the rest of the Achaeans,
     allowing none to shoot or cast at Hector—
245 none to forestall him, and to win the honor.
     But when, for the fourth time, they reached the springs,
     the Father poised his golden scales.

                                        He placed
     two shapes of death, death prone and cold, upon them,
     one of Achilles, one of the horseman, Hector,
250 and held the midpoint, pulling upward. Down
     sank Hector's fatal day, the pan went down
     toward undergloom, and Phoebus Apollo left him.
     Then came Athena, gray-eyed, to the son
     of Peleus, falling in with him, and near him,
255 saying swiftly:

                        "Now at last I think
     the two of us, Achilles loved by Zeus,
     shall bring Achaeans triumph at the ships
     by killing Hector—unappeased
     though he was ever in his thirst for war.

230. **Dardan gates:** gates of Troy; Dardania, a city built near the foot of Mount Ida, became part of Troy.

Bust of Athena.

from The Iliad, Book 22   **253**

260 There is no way he may escape us now,
not though Apollo, lord of distances,
should suffer all indignity for him
before his father Zeus who bears the stormcloud,
rolling back and forth and begging for him.

265 Now you can halt and take your breath, while I
persuade him into combat face to face."

These were Athena's orders. He complied,
relieved, and leaning hard upon the spearshaft
armed with its head of bronze. She left him there

270 and overtook Lord Hector—but she seemed
Deiphobus° in form and resonant voice,
appearing at his shoulder, saying swiftly:
"Ai! Dear brother, how he runs, Achilles,
harrying you around the town of Priam!

275 Come, we'll stand and take him on."

To this,

great Hector in his shimmering helm replied:

"Deiphobus, you were the closest to me
in the old days, of all my brothers, sons
of Hecuba and Priam. Now I can say

280 I honor you still more
because you dared this foray for my sake,
seeing me run. The rest stay under cover."

Again the gray-eyed goddess spoke:

"Dear brother, how your father and gentle mother

285 begged and begged me to remain! So did
the soldiers round me, all undone by fear.
But in my heart I ached for you.
Now let us fight him, and fight hard.
No holding back. We'll see if this Achilles

290 conquers both, to take our armor seaward,
or if he can be brought down by your spear."

This way, by guile, Athena led him on.
And when at last the two men faced each other,
Hector was the first to speak. He said:

295 "I will no longer fear you as before,
son of Peleus, though I ran from you
round Priam's town three times and could not face you.
Now my soul would have me stand and fight,

271. **Deiphobus** (de·if′ō·bəs): one of Hector's brothers.

Vase depicting Achilles.

whether I kill you or am killed. So come,
300 we'll summon gods here as our witnesses,
none higher, arbiters° of a pact: I swear
that, terrible as you are,
I'll not insult your corpse should Zeus allow me
victory in the end, your life as prize.
305 Once I have your gear, I'll give your body
back to Achaeans. Grant me, too, this grace."

But swift Achilles frowned at him and said:

"Hector, I'll have no talk of pacts with you,
forever unforgiven as you are.
310 As between men and lions there are none,
no concord between wolves and sheep, but all
hold one another hateful through and through,
so there can be no courtesy between us,
no sworn truce, till one of us is down
315 and glutting with his blood the wargod Ares.
Summon up what skills you have. By god,
you'd better be a spearman and a fighter!
Now there is no way out. Pallas Athena
will have the upper hand of you. The weapon
320 belongs to me. You'll pay the reckoning
in full for all the pain my men have borne,
who met death by your spear."
                                        He twirled and cast
his shaft with its long shadow. Splendid Hector,
keeping his eye upon the point, eluded it
325 by ducking at the instant of the cast,
so shaft and bronze shank passed him overhead
and punched into the earth. But unperceived
by Hector, Pallas Athena plucked it out
and gave it back to Achilles. Hector said:

330 "A clean miss. Godlike as you are,
you have not yet known doom for me from Zeus.
You thought you had, by heaven. Then you turned
into a word-thrower, hoping to make me lose
my fighting heart and head in fear of you.
335 You cannot plant your spear between my shoulders
while I am running. If you have the gift,
just put it through my chest as I come forward.
Now it's for you to dodge my own. Would god
you'd give the whole shaft lodging in your body!

HECTOR KILLED BY ACHILLES, PETER PAUL RUBENS (1577–1640).

How do Hector and Achilles differ as heroes? With which hero do you most identify? Why?

340 War for the Trojans would be eased
     if you were blotted out, bane° that you are."

     With this he twirled his long spearshaft and cast it,
     hitting his enemy mid-shield, but off
     and away the spear rebounded. Furious
345 that he had lost it, made his throw for nothing,
     Hector stood bemused. He had no other.
     Then he gave a great shout to Deiphobus
     to ask for a long spear. But there was no one
     near him, not a soul. Now in his heart
350 the Trojan realized the truth and said:

     "This is the end. The gods are calling deathward.
     I had thought
     a good soldier, Deiphobus, was with me.
     He is inside the walls. Athena tricked me.
355 Death is near, and black, not at a distance,
     not to be evaded. Long ago
     this hour must have been to Zeus's liking
     and to the liking of his archer son.°
     They have been well disposed before, but now

341. **bane:** the cause of distress, death, or ruin.

358. **archer son:** Apollo.

256 Greek and Roman Literatures

360 the appointed time's upon me. Still, I would not
die without delivering a stroke,
or die ingloriously, but in some action
memorable to men in days to come."

With this he drew the whetted blade that hung
365 upon his left flank, ponderous and long,
collecting all his might the way an eagle
narrows himself to dive through shady cloud
and strike a lamb or cowering hare: so Hector
lanced ahead and swung his whetted blade.
370 Achilles with wild fury in his heart
pulled in upon his chest his beautiful shield—
his helmet with four burnished metal ridges
nodding above it, and the golden crest
Hephaestus° locked there tossing in the wind,
375 Conspicuous as the evening star that comes,
amid the first in heaven, at fall of night,
and stands most lovely in the west, so shone
in sunlight the fine-pointed spear
Achilles poised in his right hand, with deadly
380 aim at Hector, at the skin where most
it lay exposed. But nearly all was covered
by the bronze gear he took from slain Patroclus,
showing only, where his collarbones
divided neck and shoulders, the bare throat
385 where the destruction of a life is quickest.
Here, then, as the Trojan charged, Achilles
drove his point straight through the tender neck,
but did not cut the windpipe, leaving Hector
able to speak and to respond. He fell
390 aside into the dust. And Prince Achilles
now exulted:

                              "Hector, had you thought
that you could kill Patroclus and be safe?
Nothing to dread from me; I was not there.
All childishness. Though distant then, Patroclus's
395 comrade in arms was greater far than he—
and it is I who had been left behind
that day beside the deep-sea ships who now
have made your knees give way. The dogs and kites
will rip your body. His will lie in honor
400 when the Achaeans give him funeral."

374. **Hephaestus** (hē·fes'təs): the blacksmith of the gods, who forged new arms for Achilles after Patroclus, wearing Achilles' armor, was slain by Hector.

Hector, barely whispering, replied:

"I beg you by your soul and by your parents,
do not let the dogs feed on me
in your encampment by the ships. Accept
405 the bronze and gold my father will provide
as gifts, my father and her ladyship
my mother. Let them have my body back,
so that our men and women may accord me
decency of fire when I am dead."

410 Achilles the great runner scowled and said:

"Beg me no beggary by soul or parents,
whining dog! Would god my passion drove me
to slaughter you and eat you raw, you've caused
such agony to me! No man exists
415 who could defend you from the carrion pack—
not if they spread for me ten times your ransom,
twenty times, and promise more as well;
aye, not if Priam, son of Dardanus,
tells them to buy you for your weight in gold!
420 You'll have no bed of death, nor will you be
laid out and mourned by her who gave you birth.
Dogs and birds will have you, every scrap."

Then at the point of death Lord Hector said:

"I see you now for what you are. No chance
425 to win you over. Iron in your breast
your heart is. Think a bit, though: this may be
a thing the gods in anger hold against you
on that day when Paris and Apollo
destroy you at the Gates,° great as you are."

428–429. **Paris . . . Gates:**
Achilles is later slain by Paris,
who shoots an arrow into
Achilles' heel, the only part
of his body that is vulnerable.

430 Even as he spoke, the end came, and death hid him;
spirit from body fluttered to undergloom,
bewailing fate that made him leave his youth
and manhood in the world. And as he died
Achilles spoke again. He said:

435 "Die, make an end. I shall accept my own
whenever Zeus and the other gods desire."
At this he pulled his spearhead from the body,
laying it aside, and stripped
the bloodstained shield and cuirass° from his shoulders.
440 Other Achaeans hastened round to see

439. **cuirass** (kwi·ras'): armor protecting the breast and back.

Hector's fine body and his comely face,
and no one came who did not stab the body.
Glancing at one another they would say:

"Now Hector has turned vulnerable, softer
445 than when he put the torches to the ships!"

And he who said this would inflict a wound.
When the great master of pursuit, Achilles,
had the body stripped, he stood among them,
saying swiftly:

                  "Friends, my lords and captains
450 of Argives, now that the gods at last have let me
bring to earth this man who wrought
havoc among us—more than all the rest—
come, we'll offer battle around the city,
to learn the intentions of the Trojans now.
455 Will they give up their strongpoint° at this loss?
Can they fight on, though Hector's dead?

                              But wait:

why do I ponder, why take up these questions?
Down by the ships Patroclus's body lies
unwept, unburied. I shall not forget him

455. strongpoint: Troy.

The funeral of Patroclus.
*What effect does Patroclus's death have on
the events of the Trojan War?*

460 while I can keep my feet among the living.
If in the dead world they forget the dead,
I say there, too, I shall remember him,
my friend. Men of Achaea, lift a song!
Down to the ships we go, and take this body,
465 our glory. We have beaten Hector down,
to whom as to a god the Trojans prayed."

Indeed, he had in mind for Hector's body
outrage and shame. Behind both feet he pierced
the tendons, heel to ankle. Rawhide cords
470 he drew through both and lashed them to his chariot,
letting the man's head trail. Stepping aboard,
bearing the great trophy of the arms,°
he shook the reins, and whipped the team ahead
into a willing run. A dustcloud rose
475 above the furrowing body; the dark tresses
flowed behind, and the head so princely once
lay back in dust. Zeus gave him to his enemies
to be defiled in his own fatherland.
So his whole head was blackened. Looking down,
480 his mother tore her braids, threw off her veil,
and wailed, heartbroken to behold her son.
Piteously his father groaned, and round him
lamentation spread throughout the town,
most like the clamor to be heard if Ilion's
485 towers, top to bottom, seethed in flames.
They barely stayed the old man, mad with grief,
from passing through the gates. Then in the mire
he rolled, and begged them all, each man by name:
"Relent, friends. It is hard; but let me go
490 out of the city to the Achaean ships.
I'll make my plea to that demonic heart.
He may feel shame before his peers, or pity
my old age. His father, too, is old.
Peleus, who brought him up to be a scourge
495 to Trojans, cruel to all, but most to me,
so many of my sons in flower of youth
he cut away. And, though I grieve, I cannot
mourn them all as much as I do one,
for whom my grief will take me to the grave—
500 and that is Hector. Why could he not have died
where I might hold him? In our weeping, then,
his mother, now so destitute, and I

472. **great trophy of the arms:**
Hector's armor.

Dallas Museum of Art, Munger Fund

**Black-figured panel amphora
depicting dueling figures.**

might have had surfeit° and relief of tears."

503. **surfeit:** an excess of.

These were the words of Priam as he wept,
505 and all his people groaned. Then in her turn
Hecuba led the women in lamentation:

"Child, I am lost now. Can I bear my life
after the death of suffering your death?
You were my pride in all my nights and days,
510 pride of the city, pillar to the Trojans
and Trojan women. Everyone looked to you
as though you were a god, and rightly so.
You were their greatest glory while you lived.
Now your doom and death have come upon you."

515 These were her mournful words. But Hector's lady
still knew nothing; no one came to tell her
of Hector's stand outside the gates. She wove
upon her loom, deep in the lofty house,
a double purple web with rose design.
520 Calling her maids in waiting,
she ordered a big caldron on a tripod
set on the hearthfire, to provide a bath
for Hector when he came home from the fight.
Poor wife, how far removed from baths he was
525 she could not know, as at Achilles' hands
Athena brought him down.

                              Then from the tower
she heard a wailing and a distant moan.
Her knees shook, and she let her shuttle° fall,
and called out to her maids again:

528. **shuttle:** as used here, an instrument that carries thread back and forth; used in the craft of weaving.

                              "Come here.
530 Two must follow me, to see this action.
I heard my husband's queenly mother cry.
I feel my heart rise, throbbing in my throat.
My knees are like stone under me. Some blow
is coming home to Priam's sons and daughters.
535 Ah, could it never reach my ears! I die
of dread that Achilles may have cut off Hector,
blocked my bold husband from the city wall,
to drive him down the plain alone! By now
he may have ended Hector's deathly pride.
540 He never kept his place amid the chariots
but drove ahead. He would not be outdone
by anyone in courage."

Saying this, she ran

like a madwoman through the megaron,°
her heart convulsed. Her maids kept at her side.
545 On reaching the great tower and the soldiers,
Andromache stood gazing from the wall
and saw him being dragged before the city.
Chariot horses at a brutal gallop
pulled the torn body toward the decked ships.
550 Blackness of night covered her eyes; she fell
backward swooning, sighing out her life,
and let her shining headdress fall, her hood
and diadem,° her plaited band and veil
that Aphrodite once had given her,
555 on that day when, from Eetion's house,
for a thousand bridal gifts, Lord Hector led her.
Now, at her side, kinswomen of her lord
supported her among them, dazed and faint
to the point of death. But when she breathed again
560 and her stunned heart recovered, in a burst
of sobbing she called out among the women:

"Hector! Here is my desolation. Both
had this in store from birth—from yours in Troy
in Priam's palace, mine by wooded Placus
565 at Thebe in the home of Eetion,
my father, who took care of me in childhood,
a man cursed by fate, a fated daughter.
How I could wish I never had been born!
Now under earth's roof to the house of Death
570 you go your way and leave me here, bereft,
lonely, in anguish without end. The child
we wretches had is still in infancy;
you cannot be a pillar to him, Hector,
now you are dead, nor he to you. And should
575 this boy escape the misery of the war,
there will be toil and sorrow for him later,
as when strangers move his boundary stones.
The day that orphans him will leave him lonely,
downcast in everything, cheeks wet with tears,
580 in hunger going to his father's friends
to tug at one man's cloak, another's chiton.°
Some will be kindly: one may lift a cup
to wet his lips at least, though not his throat;
but from the board some child with living parents

543. **megaron** (meg′ə·rän): the central hall of the house.

553. **diadem:** ornamental head-band.

Albright-Knox Art Gallery, Buffalo, New York. Charles W. Goodyear Fund, 1933. Attributed to the "Athena Master"; Panathenaic Athena and two Heiropoioi, c. 500–485 B.C. White-ground terra cotta, 11³/₄″ × 4¹/₈″ × 2⁵/₈″.

Vase showing a black-figured Lekythos, c. 500–485 B.C. *This vase is attributed to the "Athena Master," an unknown Greek sculptor thought to be responsible for many surviving renderings of Athena.*

581. **chiton** (kī′tən): a tunic.

585 gives him a push, a slap, with biting words:
      'Outside, you there! Your father is not with us
      here at our feast!' And the boy Astyanax
      will run to his forlorn mother. Once he fed
      on marrow only and the fat of lamb,

590 high on his father's knees. And when sleep came
      to end his play, he slept in a nurse's arms,
      brimful of happiness, in a soft bed.
      But now he'll know sad days and many of them,
      missing his father. 'Lord of the lower town'

595 the Trojans call him. They know, you alone,
      Lord Hector, kept their gates and their long walls.
      Beside the beaked ships now, far from your kin,
      the blowflies' maggots in a swarm will eat you
      naked, after the dogs have had their fill.

600 Ah, there are folded garments in your chambers,
      delicate and fine, of women's weaving.
      These, by heaven, I'll burn to the last thread
      in blazing fire! They are no good to you,
      they cannot cover you in death. So let them

605 go, let them be burnt as an offering
      from Trojans and their women in your honor."

Thus she mourned, and the women wailed in answer.

BOOK 24: Priam and Achilles

After he slays Hector in Book 22, Achilles prepares for Patroclus's ceremonial funeral. When the Greeks burn Patroclus's body, they also hold elaborate athletic contests, a custom in funeral services for distinguished men (Book 23).

  As Book 24 opens, Achilles is still so enraged at Hector's killing of Patroclus that he refuses to give up Hector's body for burial. This is a particularly offensive form of revenge, for both the Greeks and Trojans believed that certain funeral rites were necessary before the soul of a dead person could find rest. Achilles' shameful treatment of Hector's body offends Zeus, and he finally orders Achilles to give up the body to Priam. The aged king, bowed with grief and bearing a rich ransom to exchange for his son's corpse, is escorted to the Greek camp by the god Hermes, who is disguised as a young man.

Greek vase depicting Achilles and Ajax playing dice.

Scala/Art Resource, New York

                              Now night had fallen,
     bringing the sentries to their supper fire,
     but the glimmering god Hermes, the Wayfinder,
     showered a mist of slumber on them all.
5   As quick as thought, he had the gates unbarred
     and open to let the wagon enter, bearing
     the old king and the ransom.
                                        Going seaward
     they came to the lofty quarters of Achilles,
     a lodge the Myrmidons built for their lord
10   of pine trees cut and trimmed, and shaggy thatch
     from mowings in deep meadows. Posts were driven
     round the wide courtyard in a palisade,
     whose gate one crossbar held, one beam of pine.
     It took three men to slam this home, and three
15   to draw the bolt again—but great Achilles
     worked his entryway alone with ease.
     And now Hermes, who lights the way for mortals,
     opened for Priam, took him safely in
     with all his rich gifts for the son of Peleus.
20   Then the god dropped the reins, and stepping down
     he said:

                         "I am no mortal wagoner,
     but Hermes, sir. My father° sent me here
     to be your guide amid the Achaean men.

22. **father:** Zeus.

Now that is done, I'm off to heaven again
25 and will not visit Achilles. That would be
to compromise an immortal's dignity—
to be received with guests of mortal station.
Go take his knees, and make your supplication:
invoke his father, his mother, and his child;
30 pray that his heart be touched, that he be reconciled."

Now Hermes turned, departing for Olympus,
and Priam vaulted down. He left Idaeus°
to hold the teams in check, while he went forward
into the lodge. He found Achilles, dear
35 to Zeus, there in his chair, with officers
at ease across the room. Only Automedon°
and Alcimus° were busy near Achilles,
for he had just now made an end of dinner,
eating and drinking, and the laden boards
40 lay near him still upon the trestles.

                                          Priam,
the great king of Troy, passed by the others,
knelt down, took in his arms Achilles' knees,
and kissed the hands of wrath that killed his sons.

When, taken with mad Folly in his own land,
45 a man does murder and in exile finds
refuge in some rich house, then all who see him
stand in awe.
So these men stood.

                                          Achilles
gazed in wonder at the splendid king,
50 and his companions marveled too, all silent,
with glances to and fro. Now Priam prayed
to the man before him:

                    "Remember your own father,
Achilles, in your godlike youth: his years
like mine are many, and he stands upon
55 the fearful doorstep of old age. He, too,
is hard pressed, it may be, by those around him,
there being no one able to defend him
from bane of war and ruin. Ah, but he
may nonetheless hear news of you alive,
60 and so with glad heart hope through all his days
for sight of his dear son, come back from Troy,
while I have deathly fortune.

32. **Idaeus** (ī'dē'əs): the herald of the Trojans.

36. **Automedon** (ô·täm'ə·dän): Achilles' charioteer.
37. **Alcimus** (al·sī'məs): son of Ares, the god of war.

Alinari/Art Resource, New York

Vase with detail of Hermes. *Hermes—the messenger god as well as the god of travelers—is identified by the staff he carries and the wings on his feet.*

Noble sons
I fathered here, but scarce one man is left me.
Fifty I had when the Achaeans came,
65 nineteen out of a single belly, others
born of attendant women. Most are gone.
Raging Ares cut their knees from under them.
And he who stood alone among them all,
their champion, and Troy's, ten days ago
70 you killed him, fighting for his land, my prince,
Hector.

     It is for him that I have come
among these ships, to beg him back from you,
and I bring ransom without stint.°

        Achilles,
be reverent toward the great gods! And take
75 pity on me, remember your own father.
Think me more pitiful by far, since I
have brought myself to do what no man else
has done before—to lift to my lips the hand
of one who killed my son."

       Now in Achilles
80 the evocation of his father stirred
new longing, and an ache of grief. He lifted
the old man's hand and gently put him by.
Then both were overborne as they remembered:
the old king huddled at Achilles' feet
85 wept, and wept for Hector, killer of men,
while great Achilles wept for his own father
as for Patroclus once again; and sobbing
filled the room.

      But when Achilles' heart
had known the luxury of tears, and pain
90 within his breast and bones had passed away,
he stood then, raised the old king up, in pity
for his gray head and graybeard cheek, and spoke
in a warm rush of words:

        "Ah, sad and old!
Trouble and pain you've borne, and bear, aplenty.
95 Only a great will could have brought you here
among the Achaean ships, and here alone
before the eyes of one who stripped your sons,

Detail of vase depicting Priam.

your many sons, in battle. Iron must be
the heart within you. Come, then, and sit down.
100 We'll probe our wounds no more but let them rest,
though grief lies heavy on us. Tears heal nothing,
drying so stiff and cold. This is the way
the gods ordained the destiny of men,
to bear such burdens in our lives, while they
105 feel no affliction. At the door of Zeus
are those two urns° of good and evil gifts
that he may choose for us; and one for whom
the lightning's joyous king dips in both urns
will have by turns bad luck and good. But one
110 to whom he sends all evil—that man goes
contemptible by the will of Zeus; ravenous
hunger drives him over the wondrous earth,
unresting, without honor from gods or men.
Mixed fortune came to Peleus. Shining gifts
115 at the gods' hands he had from birth: felicity,
wealth overflowing, rule of the Myrmidons,
a bride immortal at his mortal side.
But then Zeus gave afflictions too—no family
of powerful sons grew up for him at home,
120 but one child, of all seasons and of none.
Can I stand by him in his age? Far from my country
I sit at Troy to grieve you and your children.
You, too, sir, in time past were fortunate,
we hear men say. From Macar's isle of Lesbos
125 northward, and south of Phrygia and the Straits,°
no one had wealth like yours, or sons like yours.
Then gods out of the sky sent you this bitterness:
the years of siege, the battles and the losses.
Endure it, then. And do not mourn forever
130 for your dead son. There is no remedy.
You will not make him stand again. Rather
await some new misfortune to be suffered."

The old king in his majesty replied:

"Never give me a chair, my lord, while Hector
135 lies in your camp uncared for. Yield him to me
now. Allow me sight of him. Accept
the many gifts I bring. May they reward you,
and may you see your home again.
You spared my life at once and let me live."

106. **urns:** vases with feet or pedestals.

125. **the Straits:** the Dardanelles, narrow waterway between the Aegean Sea and the Sea of Marmara.

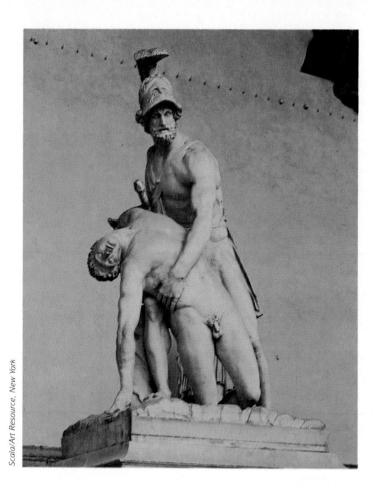

Menelaus and the dead Patroclus.
Based on events in the Iliad, *what can you infer about the Greek warrior code? What values were Greek warriors willing to die for? What actions did they consider dishonorable?*

140 Achilles, the great runner, frowned and eyed him
under his brows:

                    "Do not vex me, sir," he said.
"I have intended, in my own good time,
to yield up Hector to you. She who bore me,°
the daughter of the Ancient of the sea,

143. **She who bore me:** Thetis.

145 has come with word to me from Zeus. I know
in your case, too—though you say nothing, Priam—
that some god guided you to the shipways here.
No strong man in his best days could make entry
into this camp. How could he pass the guard,
150 or force our gateway?

                    Therefore, *let me be.*
Sting my sore heart again, and even here,
under my own roof, suppliant though you are,
I may not spare you, sir, but trample on
the express command of Zeus!"

When he heard this,
155 the old man feared him and obeyed with silence.
Now like a lion at one bound Achilles
left the room. Close at his back the officers
Automedon and Alcimus went out—
comrades in arms whom he esteemed the most
160 after the dead Patroclus. They unharnessed
mules and horses, led the old king's crier
to a low bench and sat him down.
Then from the polished wagon
they took the piled-up price of Hector's body.
165 One chiton and two capes they left aside
as dress and shrouding for the homeward journey.
Then, calling to the women slaves, Achilles
ordered the body bathed and rubbed with oil—
but lifted, too, and placed apart, where Priam
170 could not see his son—for seeing Hector
he might in his great pain give way to rage,
and fury then might rise up in Achilles
to slay the old king, flouting Zeus's word.
So after bathing and anointing Hector
175 they drew the shirt and beautiful shrouding over him.
Then with his own hands lifting him, Achilles
laid him upon a couch, and with his two
companions aiding, placed him in the wagon.
Now a bitter groan burst from Achilles,
180 who stood and prayed to his own dead friend:

                              "Patroclus,
do not be angry with me, if somehow
even in the world of Death you learn of this—
that I released Prince Hector to his father.
The gifts he gave were not unworthy. Aye,
185 and you shall have your share, this time as well."

The Prince Achilles turned back to his quarters.
He took again the splendid chair that stood
against the farther wall, then looked at Priam
and made his declaration:

                              "As you wished, sir,
190 the body of your son is now set free.
He lies in state. At the first sight of Dawn
you shall take charge of him yourself and see him.
Now let us think of supper. We are told

that even Niobe in her extremity
195 took thought for bread—though all her brood had perished,
her six young girls and six tall sons. Apollo,
making his silver longbow whip and sing,
shot the lads down, and Artemis with raining
arrows killed the daughters—all this after
200 Niobe had compared herself with Leto,
the smooth-cheeked goddess.

                              She has borne two children,
Niobe said, How many have I borne!
But soon those two destroyed the twelve.

                                        Besides,
nine days the dead lay stark, no one could bury them,
205 for Zeus had turned all folk of theirs to stone.
The gods made graves for them on the tenth day,
and then at last, being weak and spent with weeping,
Niobe thought of food. Among the rocks
of Sipylus' lonely mountainside, where nymphs
210 who race Achelous's° river go to rest,
she, too, long turned to stone, somewhere broods on
the gall immortal gods gave her to drink.°

Like her we'll think of supper, noble sir.
Weep for your son again when you have borne him
215 back to Troy; there he'll be mourned indeed."
In one swift movement now Achilles caught
and slaughtered a white lamb. His officers
flayed it, skillful in their butchering
to dress the flesh; they cut bits for the skewers,
220 roasted, and drew them off, done to a turn.
Automedon dealt loaves into the baskets
on the great board; Achilles served the meat.
Then all their hands went out upon the supper.
When thirst and appetite were turned away,
225 Priam, the heir of Dardanos, gazed long
in wonder at Achilles' form and scale—
so like the gods in aspect. And Achilles
in his turn gazed in wonder upon Priam,
royal in visage° as in speech. Both men
230 in contemplation found rest for their eyes,
till the old hero, Priam, broke the silence:

"Make a bed ready for me, son of Thetis,
and let us know the luxury of sleep.

210. **Achelous** (ə·kel'ō·əs): a river god.

194–212. **Niobe** (nī'ō·bə') . . . **drink:** a woman whose children were killed by the goddess Artemis and the god Apollo because she boasted of her superiority to their mother, Leto; Niobe was then turned into a pillar of stone, from which her tears are still said to flow. This pillar of stone is on a mountain called Sipylus (si'pil·əs) in Asia Minor.

229. **visage:** face, expression.

From that hour when my son died at your hands
235 till now, my eyelids have not closed in slumber
over my eyes, but groaning where I sat
I tasted pain and grief a thousandfold,
or lay down rolling in my courtyard mire.
Here for the first time I have swallowed bread
240 and made myself drink wine.

                      Before, I could not."

Achilles ordered men and serving women
to make a bed outside, in the covered forecourt,
with purple rugs piled up and sheets outspread
and coverings of fleeces laid on top.
245 The girls went out with torches in their hands
and soon deftly made up a double bed.
Then Achilles, defiant of Agamemnon,
told his guest:

                     "Dear venerable sir,
you'll sleep outside tonight, in case an Achaean
250 officer turns up, one of those men
who are forever taking counsel with me—
as well they may. If one should see you here
as the dark night runs on, he would report it
to the Lord Marshal Agamemnon. Then
255 return of the body would only be delayed.
Now tell me this, and give me a straight answer:
How many days do you require
for the funeral of Prince Hector?—I should know
how long to wait, and hold the Achaean army."

260 Old Priam in his majesty replied:

"If you would have me carry out the burial,
Achilles, here is the way to do me grace.
As we are penned in the town, but must bring wood
from the distant hills, the Trojans are afraid.
265 We should have mourning for nine days in hall,
then on the tenth conduct his funeral
and feast the troops and commons;
on the eleventh we should make his tomb,
and on the twelfth give battle, if we must."

270 Achilles said:

              "As you command, old Priam,

Giraudon/Art Resource, New York

PRIAM BEFORE HECTOR'S TOMB IN THE TEMPLE OF APOLLO, from the studio of Colombe, c. 1500. *This scene is a medieval rendering of the story of Troy.*

the thing is done. I shall suspend the war
for those eleven days that you require."
He took the old man's right hand by the wrist
and held it, to allay his fear.

                                                  Now crier

275 and king with hearts brimful retired to rest
in the sheltered forecourt, while Achilles slept
deep in his palisaded lodge. Beside him,
lovely in her youth, Briseis° lay.
And other gods and soldiers all night long,
280 by slumber quieted, slept on. But slumber
would not come to Hermes the Good Companion,
as he considered how to ease the way
for Priam from the camp, to send him through
unseen by the formidable gatekeepers.
285 Then Hermes came to Priam's pillow, saying:

278. **Briseis:** In order to appease Achilles, Agamemnon had had Briseis returned to him.

272 Greek and Roman Literatures

"Sir, no thought of danger shakes your rest,
as you sleep on, being great Achilles' guest,
amid men fierce as hunters in a ring.
You triumphed in a costly ransoming,
290 but three times costlier your own would be
to your surviving sons—a monarch's fee—
if this should come to Agamemnon's ear
and all the Achaean host should learn that you are here."

The old king started up in fright, and woke
295 his herald. Hermes yoked the mules and horses,
took the reins, then inland like the wind
he drove through all the encampment, seen by no one.
When they reached Xanthus,° eddying and running
god-begotten river, at the ford,
300 Hermes departed for Olympus. Dawn
spread out her yellow robe on all the earth,
as they drove on toward Troy, with groans and sighs,
and the mule-team pulled the wagon and the body.
And no one saw them, not a man or woman,
305 before Cassandra.° Tall as the pale-gold
goddess Aphrodite, she had climbed
the citadel of Pergamus° at dawn.
Now looking down she saw her father come
in his war-car, and saw the crier there,
310 and saw Lord Hector on his bed of death
upon the mulecart. The girl wailed and cried
to all the city:

                    "Oh, look down, look down,
go to your windows, men of Troy, and women,
see Lord Hector now! Remember joy
315 at seeing him return alive from battle,
exalting all our city and our land!"

Now, at the sight of Hector, all gave way
to loss and longing, and all crowded down
to meet the escort and body near the gates,
320 till no one in the town was left at home.
There Hector's lady and his gentle mother
tore their hair for him, flinging themselves
upon the wagon to embrace his person
while the crowd groaned. All that long day
325 until the sun went down they might have mourned
in tears before the gateway. But old Priam

298. **Xanthus** (zan'thəs): also called *Scamander*.

305. **Cassandra** (kə·san'drə): a daughter of Priam and Hecuba; in Greek mythology, Apollo gives her the gift of prophecy, but when she rejects his advances, he decrees that no one will believe her predictions. She figures more prominently in other versions of the Trojan War legend, such as in Euripides' drama *The Trojan Women*.

307. **Pergamus** (pur'gə·məs): the citadel, or fortress, of Troy.

spoke to them from his chariot:

                         "Make way,
let the mules pass. You'll have your fill of weeping
later, when I've brought the body home."

330   They parted then, and made way for the wagon,
allowing Priam to reach the famous hall.
They laid the body of Hector in his bed,
and brought in minstrels, men to lead the dirge.°

°333. **dirge:** funeral hymn.

While these wailed out, the women answered, moaning.
335   Andromache of the ivory-white arms
held in her lap between her hands
the head of Hector who had killed so many.
Now she lamented:

                  "You've been torn from life,
my husband, in young manhood, and you leave me
340   empty in our hall. The boy's a child
whom you and I, poor souls, conceived; I doubt
he'll come to manhood. Long before, great Troy
will go down plundered, citadel and all,
now that you are lost, who guarded it
345   and kept it, and preserved its wives and children.
They will be shipped off in the murmuring hulls
one day, and I along with all the rest.
You, my little one, either you come with me
to do some grinding labor, some base toil
350   for a harsh master, or an Achaean soldier
will grip you by the arm and hurl you down
from a tower° here to a miserable death—

°351–352. **hurl you down from a tower:** Indeed, after the fall of Troy, Astyanax *was* thrown by the Greek conquerors from the walls of the city.

out of his anger for a brother, a father,
or even a son that Hector killed. Achaeans
355   in hundreds mouthed black dust under his blows.
He was no moderate man in war, your father,
and that is why they mourn him through the city.
Hector, you gave your parents grief and pain
but left me loneliest, and heartbroken.
360   You could not open your strong arms to me
from your deathbed, or say a thoughtful word,
for me to cherish all my life long
as I weep for you night and day."

                      Her voice broke,
and a wail came from the women. Hecuba
365   lifted her lamenting voice among them:

"Hector, dearest of sons to me, in life
you had the favor of the immortal gods,
and they have cared for you in death as well.
Achilles captured other sons of mine
370 in other years, and sold them overseas
to Samos, Imbros, and the smoky island,
Lemnos.° That was not his way with you.
After he took your life, cutting you down
with his sharp-bladed spear, he trussed and dragged you
375 many times round the barrow° of his friend,
Patroclus, whom you killed—though not by this
could that friend live again. But now I find you
fresh as pale dew, seeming newly dead,
like one to whom Apollo of the silver bow
380 had given easy death with his mild arrows."

Hecuba sobbed again, and the wails redoubled.
Then it was Helen's turn to make lament:

"Dear Hector, dearest brother to me by far!
My husband is Alexandros,
385 who brought me here to Troy—God, that I might
have died sooner! This is the twentieth year
since I left home, and left my fatherland.
But never did I have an evil word
or gesture from you. No—and when some other
390 brother-in-law or sister would revile me,
or if my mother-in-law spoke to me bitterly—
but Priam never did, being as mild
as my own father—you would bring her round
with your kind heart and gentle speech. Therefore
395 I weep for you and for myself as well,
given this fate, this grief. In all wide Troy
no one is left who will befriend me, none;
they all shudder at me."

                              Helen wept,
and a moan came from the people, hearing her.
400 Then Priam, the old king, commanded them:

"Trojans, bring firewood to the edge of town.
No need to fear an ambush of the Argives.
When he dismissed me from the camp, Achilles
told me clearly they will not harass us,
405 not until dawn comes for the twelfth day."

371–372. **Samos** (sä′mäs), **Imbros** (im′bräs) . . . **Lemnos** (lem′näs): islands in the Aegean Sea.

375. **barrow:** a mound of earth and stones built over a grave.

Then yoking mules and oxen to their wagons
the people thronged before the city gates.
Nine days they labored, bringing countless loads
of firewood to the town. When Dawn that lights
410 the world of mortals came for the tenth day,
they carried greathearted Hector out at last,
and all in tears placed his dead body high
upon its pyre, then cast a torch below.
When the young Dawn with finger tips of rose
415 made heaven bright, the Trojan people massed
about Prince Hector's ritual fire.
All being gathered and assembled, first
they quenched the smoking pyre with tawny wine
wherever flames had licked their way, then friends
420 and brothers picked his white bones from the char
in sorrow, while the tears rolled down their cheeks.
In a golden urn they put the bones,
shrouding the urn with veiling of soft purple.
Then in a grave dug deep they placed it
425 and heaped it with great stones. The men were quick
to raise the death-mound, while in every quarter
lookouts were posted to ensure against
an Achaean surprise attack. When they had finished
raising the barrow, they returned to Ilion,
430 where all sat down to banquet in his honor
in the hall of Priam king. So they performed
the funeral rites of Hector, tamer of horses.

Helen and Priam. *The abduction of the Greek Helen by the Trojan Paris eventually led to the deaths of his brother Hector and his father Priam by the vengeful Greek forces.*

First Thoughts

How did you feel about Achilles' behavior toward Hector and Priam in these two books?

Identifying Facts

1. What advice do Priam and Hecuba give to Hector as he stands outside the walls of the city?

2. In lines 119–156 of Book 22, what courses of action does Hector consider and reject before fighting Achilles?

3. How does Athena deceive Hector? Why is Zeus unable to save Hector?

4. What is Hector's dying request, and how does Achilles respond to it?

5. What does Achilles agree to do to allow Hector a proper burial?

Interpreting Meanings

1. The meeting of Hector and Achilles in Book 22 is the dramatic **climax** of the *Iliad*. At this climactic confrontation, Hector trembles and then runs away. How does Homer prepare you for Hector's flight by his revelation of the Trojan's thoughts and by his description of Achilles' advance? Does Hector's action

diminish your respect for him, or could you sympathize with his reaction? Explain your response.

2. An **epic simile** is an extended simile in which an event of epic proportions is compared to something from everyday life that would be familiar to the audience. Reread the description in Book 22 of the duel between Achilles and Hector and identify all the epic similes Homer uses to describe their final clash.

3. What new aspects of Achilles' character are revealed by the scene with Priam in Book 24? How would your perception of Achilles have been affected if the *Iliad* had ended with Hector's death in Book 22?

4. Consider the role of the Olympian gods and goddesses in the *Iliad* as a whole. List at least three incidents in the epic in which the Olympians direct or influence events. Do you think the mortal characters in the epic are puppets manipulated by the Olympians, or do they exercise freedom of choice or action? Give reasons for your answer.

5. Some critics see the central **theme** of the *Iliad* as concerned with the idea that people must exercise generosity with one another—that if people behaved with reason, they might be able to live together in peace and harmony. Which portions of the epic support this view of the theme? Do you agree that it is a central theme of the work? Why or why not?

Applying Meanings

The *Iliad* is primarily a war epic. In your view, is the *Iliad* a condemnation of the brutality of war, a celebration of the heroism that war can inspire, or an evenly developed examination of both of these aspects? Justify your answer.

Creative Writing Response

Writing a Screenplay. One of the most enjoyable aspects of the *Iliad* is its vivid portrayal of character and action. Select one of the scenes you have read from Homer's *Iliad* and write a screenplay for a film version of the scene. Your script should include not only dialogue but notes on costumes, casting choices, and special effects that you think would contribute to an effective film version of the scene. Experiment with different settings in place and time. For example, you might set your film during World War II, the Vietnam War, or even imagine a similar conflict between aliens on another planet.

Critical Writing Response

Comparing and Contrasting Heroes. Consider Achilles and Hector as ideals of the hero in ancient Greece. What special qualities does each hero exhibit? In what ways do they mirror one another? Are their limitations and weaknesses the same, or are they different? Is one more ''human'' than the other? Write a brief essay in which you compare and contrast Achilles and Hector as heroes. Cite evidence from the epic to support your findings. You may use a chart like the one below to organize your ideas.

	Achilles	Hector
Similarities		
Differences		
Strengths		
Weaknesses		

THE ART OF TRANSLATION

A Recent Translation of Homer's Iliad

There are many English translations of Homer's Iliad, *both in prose and in verse. Below is an excerpt from Book 22 of Robert Fagles's recent translation of the* Iliad. *Read the lines of verse below; then, on page 251, reread lines 157 through 173 of the Fitzgerald translation.*

                So he wavered,
waiting there, but Achilles was closing on
   him now
like the god of war, the fighter's helmet
   flashing,
over his right shoulder shaking the Pelian
   ash spear,
that terror, and the bronze around his
   body flared
like a raging fire of the rising, blazing sun.
Hector looked up, saw him, started to
   tremble,
nerve gone, he could hold his ground no
   longer,
he left the gates behind and away he fled
   in fear—
and Achilles went for him, fast, sure of his
   speed

as the wild mountain hawk, the quickest
   thing on wings,
launching smoothly, swooping down on a
   cringing dove
and the dove flits out from under, the
   hawk screaming
over the quarry, plunging over and over,
   his fury
driving him down to break and tear his
   kill—
so Achilles flew at him, breakneck on in
   fury
with Hector fleeing along the walls of Troy,
fast as his legs would go.

What different images does each translator emphasize in showing Hector's fear, Achilles' wrath and determination, and the speed with which Hector flees? What are the differences in the way each translator handles the epic simile that compares Achilles' pursuit of Hector to a hawk hunting its prey? Which version do you prefer? Why?

Sappho
Early Sixth Century B.C.

Lee Boltin Picture Library

Sappho (saf'ō) was born on the Greek island of Lesbos toward the end of the seventh century B.C. She wrote nine books of lyric verse—more than five hundred poems—but only a few fragments survive. Nevertheless, she is still considered a supreme Greek lyric poet of this period. In fact, Plato admiringly dubbed her "the tenth Muse":

> Some say nine Muses—but count again.
> Behold the tenth: Sappho of Lesbos.

This remark is fitting because the Muses, or spirits of poetic inspiration, like Sappho, were women, and because few Greek poets, male or female, achieved Sappho's stature.

Most scholars believe that Sappho was an educated woman who at some point in her life was exiled to Sicily. She may have returned to Lesbos to become the head of a group of priestesses who worshiped Aphrodite. We know that Sappho married and had a daughter, Cleis (klā'əs). Sappho's love for her daughter is the subject of some of her most moving lyric poems. According to one legend, Sappho killed herself for the love of a ferryman by throwing herself from a cliff. Another source, however, suggests that she died of old age in her bed, tended by her daughter.

Sappho composed most of her poems in a style called *monody*—that is, the poems were meant to be sung by a single voice, rather than by a chorus. Although it is clear that Sappho wrote for public occasions such as marriage ceremonies, most of her verse is intensely private and personal. In most of the poems that survive, Sappho speaks to the women who were her companions and friends.

Sappho's poetry exists today in fragmentary form. Many of these fragments were found on papyrus strips carelessly thrown away or wadded up into the mummified bodies of crocodiles. In many cases, all that remains of an original poem is two or three lines. In addition, the poems were copied, recopied, and translated by many different people over the centuries. Nevertheless, the genius of Sappho's poetic expression shines brightly in a handful of glittering fragments.

Reader's Guide

SAPPHO'S LYRIC POEMS

Background

Greek lyric verse resulted from a move away from the epic tradition to a poetry that expressed more intimate and personal themes. The word *lyric* is derived from *lyre,* the stringed instrument on which poets, including Sappho, accompanied themselves. These poet/singers addressed a variety of themes and topics. Some other prominent masters of Greek lyric poetry included Archilochus (är·kil′ə·kəs), Alcaeus (al·sē′əs), Simonides (sī·män′ə·dēz′), and Pindar, all of whom flourished from the seventh to the fifth centuries B.C.

The speaker of a lyric poem is not always the poet but a **persona**, or character whose voice and concerns do not necessarily reflect those of the poet. For example, the speaker in "Don't Ask Me What to Wear" may be Sappho herself speaking to her daughter Cleis, but the speaker in "To an Army Wife, in Sardis" is clearly an army officer stationed far from home.

Writer's Response

Lyric poets often write to express their feelings about the people closest to them. Think about the people you care most about, and jot down one or two words that express your feelings about each person.

Literary Focus

The power of **lyric poetry** lies in its immediacy and its ability to quickly and fully describe a strong emotion. This is done through the first-person speaker, the "I" telling the poem, and through the use of sensory **imagery**—that is, images that appeal to the senses and trigger memories and emotional responses. For instance, the purple ribbon in "Don't Ask Me What to Wear" evokes for the speaker memories of her mother and of her youth. The reader is invited to share the speaker's wistfulness, if not her memories.

LYRIC POEMS
Sappho
translated by
MARY BARNARD

❦ *As you read the following lyrics, note how the poet uses simple words and strong, vivid images.*

You Are the Herdsman of Evening

You are the herdsman of evening

Hesperus,[1] you herd
homeward whatever
Dawn's light dispersed

You herd sheep—herd
goats—herd children
home to their mothers

Sleep, Darling

Sleep, darling

I have a small
daughter called
Cleis,[2] who is

like a golden
flower
    I wouldn't
take all Croesus'[3]
kingdom with love
thrown in, for her

PARNASSUS, RAPHAEL (1483–1520). *Detail depicting Sappho.*

We Drink Your Health

We drink your health

Lucky bridegroom!
Now the wedding you
asked for is over

and your wife is the
girl you asked for;
she's a bride who is

---

1. **Hesperus** (hes'pər·əs): the evening star.
2. **Cleis** (klā'əs)
3. **Croesus** (krē'səs): Lydian king famous for his great wealth.

5

charming to look at,
with eyes as soft as
10　honey, and a face

that Love has lighted
with his own beauty
Aphrodite has surely

outdone herself in
15　doing honor to you!

To an Army Wife, in Sardis

To an army wife, in Sardis:[4]

Some say a cavalry corps,
some infantry, some, again,
will maintain that the swift oars

5　of our fleet are the finest
sight on dark earth; but I say
that whatever one loves, is.

This is easily proved: did
not Helen—she who had scanned
10　the flower of the world's manhood—

choose as first among men one
who laid Troy's honor in ruin?
Warped to his will, forgetting

love due her own blood, her own
15　child, she wandered far with him.
So Anactoria, although you

being far away forget us,
the dear sound of your footstep
and light glancing in your eyes

20　would move me more than glitter
of Lydian horse or armored
tread of mainland infantry

You May Forget But

You may forget but

Let me tell you
this: someone in
some future time
will think of us

Tonight I've Watched

Tonight I've watched

The moon and then
the Pleiades[5]
go down

The night is now
half-gone; youth
goes; I am

in bed alone

Don't Ask Me What to Wear

Don't ask me what to wear

I have no embroidered
headband from Sardis to
give you, Cleis, such as
5　I wore
　　　and my mother
always said that in her
day a purple ribbon
looped in the hair was thought
to be high style indeed

10　but we were dark:
　　　　　a girl
whose hair is yellower than
torchlight should wear no
headdress but fresh flowers

---

4. **Sardis** (sär′dis): capital of the ancient kingdom of
Lydia; of strategic importance in the ancient world.

5. **Pleiades** (plē′ə·dēz′): a star cluster in the constellation Taurus.

First Thoughts

Which of the seven poems that you read was your favorite? Why?

Identifying Facts

1. In "You Are the Herdsman of Evening," what is the function of Hesperus, the evening star? What is the function of "Dawn's light"?
2. What is the occasion of the poem "We Drink Your Health"? Whom does the speaker address?
3. What prediction does the speaker make in "You May Forget But"?
4. In "Don't Ask Me What to Wear," why does the speaker not give Cleis the ribbon she wants?

Interpreting Meanings

1. What **personification**, or treatment of an inanimate object as human, is developed in "You Are the Herdsman of Evening"? How is this comparison extended throughout the poem?
2. In "Sleep, Darling," what **image** does the speaker use to show how valuable her daughter is? How is that image similar to the one in "To an Army Wife, in Sardis"?
3. How do you imagine the speaker in "You May Forget But"? For what do you think he or she will be remembered?
4. Which of the poems seems most lyrical to you, that is, which one speaks the most intensely and eloquently of an emotion? Explain.

Applying Meanings

Were you able to relate to Sappho's poems? Have you ever had feelings similar to those expressed by the speakers in these poems? Explain why you think it is —or is not—possible to identify with these poems from ancient Greece.

Creative Writing Response

Writing a Lyric. Look again at the list of people and feelings you made in the Writer's Response on page 280. Then write a brief lyric poem about your feelings for one of those people. Remember to use the first-person singular—the pronoun "I"— and to include images that help convey how you feel about your subject.

Critical Writing Response

Comparing Lyric Poetry. The American poet H. D. (Hilda Doolittle, 1886–1961), who was at the center of the Imagist movement of the early twentieth century, was influenced by the stark imagery and symbolism of ancient Greek poetry. Read H. D.'s poem "Moonrise," and compare it to the poems of Sappho that you have read. Consider both poets' use of the first-person speaker, the kind of emotion that is expressed, and the images used to express these emotions. You might want to make a chart like the one below.

	Sappho	H. D.
Speaker		
Emotions		
Images		

Moonrise
H. D.

Will you glimmer on the sea?
will you fling your spear-head
on the shore?
what note shall we pitch?
we have a song,
on the bank we share our arrows;
the loosed string tells our note:

O flight,
bring her swiftly to our song.
She is great,
we measure her by the pine trees.

Thucydides
c. 460–401 B.C.

Scala/Art Resource, New York

As a young man, Thucydides (thōō·sid′ i·dēz′) enjoyed wealth and privilege, and he went on to become a leading participant in the brilliant flowering of culture during the later fifth century B.C. in Athens. He had a bright future ahead of him as a military officer and a statesman. All that changed, however, during the Peloponnesian War between Athens and Sparta, which broke out in 431 B.C.

The war, which involved nearly every Greek city-state, lasted twenty-seven years, ending with the bitter defeat of Athens. The conflict was personally catastrophic for Thucydides. In 424 B.C. he was placed in charge of a fleet in the northern Aegean Sea. His failure to relieve the town of Amphipolis, which was under siege by the Spartans, cost him his post. He was sentenced to twenty years of exile from Athens.

Even before his exile, Thucydides had conceived the idea of writing a history of the Peloponnesian War. Now it became his all-consuming passion. By seeking out information from *both* Athenians and Spartans and keeping his narrative focused on his chosen topic, he set standards for himself that have defined the historian's craft down to the present day.

Thucydides viewed human beings as caught up in endless, predictable conflicts of self-interest. An accurate chronicle of the war, he believed, could provide invaluable lessons for future conduct. Time has proved him correct: even now, one of the basic texts at the U. S. Naval War College in Newport, Rhode Island, is Thucydides' *History of the Peloponnesian War.*

In his description of warfare, Thucydides turned away from the vision of heroic glory presented in earlier Greek works such as Homer's *Iliad.* For Thucydides, warfare was brutal and destructive—in his own phrase, "a violent teacher." Thucydides' *History* is filled with a sense of tragic destiny not far removed from that of his contemporary, the dramatist Sophocles (see page 301). In fact, some critics read the *History* as a kind of tragic drama of the pride and fall of Athens.

Reader's Guide

FUNERAL SPEECH OF PERICLES
from History of the Peloponnesian War

Background

The greatest Athenian statesman of Thucydides' day was Pericles (per'i·klēz'). The occasion for the famous speech reproduced here was the annual public funeral for the Athenian war dead of the previous year—in this instance the first year of the Peloponnesian War (431–430 B.C.). In Thucydides' day, **rhetoric**—the use of language, especially oratory, for persuasion—was considered the highest form of prose. It was common practice for historians to present history through the "speeches" of famous figures. These speeches were a valued means of showing a particular viewpoint. Thus Pericles' speech embodies not only Pericles' opinions, but the views of patriotic Athenians in general. Of course, Thucydides was not able to capture Pericles' address word for word, but no historian put this practice of recording speeches to better use than Thucydides.

Oral Response

In part of his speech, Pericles describes the Athenian form of government. Ancient Athens is often called the "cradle" of democracy. What are some of the characteristic features of a democracy? As a class, discuss what the word **democracy** means to you.

Literary Focus

Persuasion is a kind of writing that tries to convince the reader or listener to think or act in a certain way. Examples of persuasion include political speeches, newspaper editorials, and advertisements, as well as many essays and longer works of literature. Persuasion often appeals to the emotions as, for example, in advertisements that promise consumers greater attractiveness or increased popularity. The kind of persuasive writing that appeals primarily to reason rather than to emotion is called **argument**.

FUNERAL SPEECH OF PERICLES

from History of the Peloponnesian War
Thucydides
translated by
BENJAMIN JOWETT

> *Some of the more difficult passages in this selection have been paraphrased within the text. As you read, try to identify the goal of Pericles' persuasion in this speech. How does he want his listeners to think about their city?*

"Most of those who have spoken here before me have commended the lawgiver who added this oration to our other funeral customs; it seemed to them a worthy thing that such an honor should be given at their burial to the dead who have fallen on the field of battle. But I should have preferred that, when men's deeds have been brave, they should be honored in deed only, and with such an honor as this public funeral, which you are now witnessing. Then the reputation of many would not have been imperiled on the eloquence or want of eloquence of one, and their virtues believed or not as he spoke well or ill. For it is difficult to say neither too little nor too much; and even moderation is apt not to give the impression of truthfulness. The friend of the dead who knows the facts is likely to think that the words of

The law which enjoins this oration has been often praised. But I should prefer to praise the brave by deeds only, not to imperil their reputation on the skill of an orator. Still, our ancestors approved the practice, and I must obey.

the speaker fall short of his knowledge and of his wishes; another who is not so well informed, when he hears of anything which surpasses his own powers, will be envious and will suspect exaggeration. Mankind are tolerant of the praises of others so long as each hearer thinks that he can do as well or nearly as well himself, but, when the speaker rises above him, jealousy is aroused and he begins to be incredulous. However, since our ancestors have set the seal of their approval upon the practice, I must obey, and to the utmost of my power shall endeavor to satisfy the wishes and beliefs of all who hear me.

"I will speak first of our ancestors, for it is right and seemly that now, when we are lamenting the dead, a tribute should be paid to their memory. There has

I will first commemorate our predecessors, who gave us freedom and empire. And before praising the dead, I will describe how Athens has won her greatness.

never been a time when they did not inhabit this land, which by their valor they have handed down from generation to generation, and we have received from them a free state. But if they were worthy of praise, still more were our fathers, who added to their inheritance, and after many a struggle transmitted to us their sons this great empire. And we ourselves assembled here today, who are still most of us in the vigor of life, have carried the work of improvement further, and have richly endowed our city with all things, so that she is sufficient for herself both in peace and war. Of the military exploits by which our various possessions were acquired, or of the energy with which we or our fathers drove back the tide of war, Hellenic or barbarian, I will not speak; for the tale would be long and is familiar to you. But before I praise the dead, I should like to point out by what principles of action we rose to power, and under what institutions and through what manner of life our empire became great. For I conceive that such thoughts are not unsuited to the occasion, and that this numerous assembly of citizens and strangers may profitably listen to them.

"Our form of government does not enter into rivalry with the institutions of others. We do not copy our neighbors, but are an example to them. It is true that we are called a democracy, for the administration is in the hands of the many and not of the few. But while the law secures equal justice to all alike in their private disputes, the claim of excellence is also recognized; and when a citizen is in any way distinguished, he is preferred to the public service, not as a matter of privilege, but as the reward of merit. Neither is poverty a bar, but a man may benefit his country whatever be the obscu-

Our government is a democracy, but we honor men of merit, whether rich or poor. Our public life is free from exclusiveness, our private from suspicion; yet we revere alike the injunctions of law and custom.

rity of his condition. There is no exclusiveness in our public life, and in our private intercourse we are not suspicious of one another, nor angry with our neighbor if he does what he likes; we do not put on sour looks at him which, though harmless, are not pleasant. While we are thus unconstrained in our private intercourse, a spirit of reverence pervades our public acts; we are prevented from doing wrong by respect for the authorities and for the laws, having an especial regard to those which are ordained for the protection of the injured as well as to those unwritten laws which bring upon the transgressor of them the reprobation of the general sentiment.

"And we have not forgotten to provide for our weary spirits many relaxations from toil; we have regular games and sacrifices throughout the year; our homes are beautiful and elegant; and the delight which we daily feel in all these things helps to banish melancholy. Because of the greatness of our city the fruits of the whole earth flow in upon us; so that we enjoy the goods of other countries as freely as of our own.

We find relaxation in our amusements, and in our homes; and the whole world contributes to our enjoyment.

"Then, again, our military training is in many respects superior to that of our adversaries. Our city is thrown open to the world, and we never expel a foreigner or prevent him from seeing or learning anything of which the secret if revealed to an enemy might profit him. We rely not upon management or trickery, but upon our own hearts and hands. And in the matter of education, whereas they from early youth are always undergoing laborious exercises which are to make them brave, we live at ease, and yet are equally ready to face

In war we singly are a match for the Peloponnesians united; though we have no secrets and undergo no laborious training.

the perils which they face. And here is the proof. The Lacedaemonians[1] come into Attica[2] not by themselves, but with their whole confederacy following; we go alone into a neighbor's country; and although our opponents are fighting for their homes and we on a foreign soil, we have seldom any difficulty in overcoming them. Our enemies have never yet felt our united strength; the care of a navy divides our attention, and on land we are obliged to send our own citizens everywhere. But they, if they meet and defeat a part of our army, are as proud as if they had routed us all, and when defeated they pretend to have been vanquished by us all.

"If then we prefer to meet danger with a light heart but without laborious training, and with a courage which is gained by habit and not enforced by law, are we not greatly the gainers? Since we do not anticipate the pain, although, when the hour comes, we can be as brave as those who never allow themselves to rest; and thus too our city is equally admirable in peace and in war. For we are lovers of the beautiful, yet simple in our tastes, and we cultivate the mind without loss of manliness. Wealth we employ, not for talk and ostentation, but when there is a real use for it. To avow poverty with us is no disgrace; the true disgrace is in doing nothing to avoid it. An Athenian citizen does not neglect the state because he takes care of his own household; and even those of us

We are not enervated by culture or vulgarized by wealth. We are all interested in public affairs, believing that nothing is lost by free discussion. Our goodness to others springs not from interest, but from the generous confidence of freedom.

who are engaged in business have a very fair idea of politics. We alone regard a man who takes no interest in public affairs, not as a harmless, but as a useless character; and if few of us are originators, we are all sound judges of a policy. The great impediment to action is, in our opinion, not discussion, but the want of that knowledge which is gained by discussion preparatory to action. For we have a peculiar power of thinking before we act and of acting too, whereas other men are courageous from ignorance but hesitate upon reflection. And they are surely to be esteemed the bravest spirits who, having the clearest sense both of the pains and pleasures of life, do not on that account shrink from danger. In doing good, again, we are unlike others; we make our friends by conferring, not by receiving favors. Now he who confers a favor is the firmer friend, because he would fain by kindness keep alive the memory of an obligation; but the recipient is colder in his feelings, because he knows that in requiting another's generosity he will not be winning gratitude but only paying a debt. We alone do good to our neighbors not upon a calculation of interest, but in the confidence of freedom and in a frank and fearless spirit. To sum up: I say that Athens is the school of Hellas,[3] and that the individual Athenian in his own person seems to have the power of adapting himself to the most varied forms of action with the utmost versatility and grace. This is no passing and idle word, but truth and fact; and the assertion is verified

In fine,[4] Athens is the school of Hellas. She alone in the hour of trial rises above her reputation. Her citizens need no poet to sing their praises: for every land bears witness to their valor.

---

1. **Lacedaemonians** (las′ə·di·mō′nē·ənz): Spartans.
2. **Attica** (at′i·kə): the region of Greece surrounding Athens.
3. **Hellas** (hel′əs): Greece; *Hellenes* (hel′ēnz′) are Greeks.
4. **In fine** (fīn): in conclusion.

The Acropolis in Athens. *The Athenian Acropolis was the religious center of Athens; the Parthenon, or temple to Athena, was built there.*

by the position to which these qualities have raised the state. For in the hour of trial Athens alone among her contemporaries is superior to the report of her. No enemy who comes against her is indignant at the reverses which he sustains at the hands of such a city; no subject complains that his masters are unworthy of him. And we shall assuredly not be without witnesses; there are mighty monuments of our power which will make us the wonder of this and of succeeding ages; we shall not need the praises of Homer or of any other panegyrist[5] whose poetry may please for the moment, although his representation of the facts will not bear the light of day. For we have compelled every land and every sea to open a path for our valor, and have everywhere planted eternal memorials of our friendship and of our enmity. Such is the city for whose sake these men nobly fought and died; they could not bear the thought that she might be taken from them; and every one of us who survive should gladly toil on her behalf.

"I have dwelt upon the greatness of Athens because I want to show you that we are contending for a higher prize than those who enjoy none of these privileges, and to establish by manifest proof the merit of these men

The praise of the city is the praise of these men, for they made her great. Good and bad, rich and poor alike, preferred death to dishonor.

---

5. **panegyrist** (pan′ə·jir′ist, -jī′rist): someone who gives a formal speech or written tribute of great praise.

whom I am now commemorating. Their loftiest praise has been already spoken. For in magnifying the city I have magnified them, and men like them whose virtues made her glorious. And of how few Hellenes can it be said as of them, that their deeds when weighed in the balance have been found equal to their fame! Methinks that a death such as theirs has been gives the true measure of a man's worth; it may be the first revelation of his virtues, but is at any rate their final seal. For even those who come short in other ways may justly plead the valor with which they have fought for their country; they have blotted out the evil with the good, and have benefited the state more by their public services than they have injured her by their private actions. None of these men were enervated by wealth or hesitated to resign the pleasures of life; none of them put off the evil day in the hope, natural to poverty, that a man, though poor, may one day become rich. But, deeming that the punishment of their enemies was sweeter than any of these things, and that they could fall in no nobler cause, they determined at the hazard of their lives to be honorably avenged, and to leave the rest. They resigned to hope their unknown chance of happiness; but in the face of death they resolved to rely upon themselves alone. And when the moment came they were minded to resist and suffer, rather than to fly and save their lives; they ran away from the word of dishonor, but on the battlefield their feet stood fast, and in an instant, at the height of their fortune, they passed away from the scene, not of their fear, but of their glory.

"Such was the end of these men; they were worthy of Athens, and the living need not desire to have a more he-

Contemplate and love Athens, and you will know how to value them. They were united in their deaths, but their glory is separate

roic spirit, although they may pray for a less fatal issue. The value of such a spirit is not to be expressed in words. Anyone can discourse to you forever about the advantages of a brave defense,

and single. Their sepulcher is the remembrance of them in the hearts of men. Follow their example without fear: it is the prosperous, not the unfortunate, who should be reckless.

which you know already. But instead of listening to him I would have you day by day fix your eyes upon the greatness of Athens, until you become filled with the love of her; and when you are impressed by the spectacle of her glory, reflect that this empire has been acquired by men who knew their duty and had the courage to do it, who in the hour of conflict had the fear of dishonor always present to them, and who, if ever they failed in an enterprise, would not allow their virtues to be lost to their country, but freely gave their lives to her as the fairest offering which they could present at her feast. The sacrifice which they collectively made was individually repaid to them; for they received again each one for himself a praise which grows not old, and the noblest of all sepulchers—I speak not of that in which their remains are laid, but of that in which their glory survives, and is proclaimed always and on every fitting occasion both in word and deed. For the whole earth is the sepulcher of famous men; not only are they commemorated by columns and inscriptions in their own country, but in foreign lands there dwells also an unwritten memorial of them, graven not on stone but in the hearts of men. Make them your examples, and, esteeming courage to be freedom and freedom to be happiness, do not weigh too nicely the perils of war. The unfortunate who has no hope of a change for the better has less reason to throw away his life than the prosperous who, if he survives, is always liable to a change for the worse, and to whom any accidental fall makes the most serious difference. To a man of spirit, cowardice and disaster coming together are far more bitter than death striking him unperceived at a time when he is full of courage and animated by the general hope.

"Wherefore I do not now commiserate the parents of the dead who stand here; I would rather comfort them. You know that your life has been passed amid manifold vicissitudes; and that they may be deemed fortunate who have gained most honor, whether an honorable death like theirs, or an honorable sorrow like yours, and whose days have been so ordered that the term of their happiness is likewise the term of their life. I know how hard it is to make you feel this, when the good fortune of others will too often remind you of the gladness which once lightened your hearts. And sorrow is felt at the want of those blessings, not which a man never knew, but which were a part of his life before they were taken from him. Some of you are of an age at which they may hope to have other children, and they ought to bear their sorrow better; not only will the children who may hereafter be born make them forget their own lost ones, but the city will be doubly a gainer. She will not be left desolate, and she will be safer. For a man's counsel cannot have equal weight or worth, when he alone has no children to risk in the general danger. To those of you who have passed their prime, I say: Congratulate yourselves that you have been happy during the greater part of your days; remember that your life of

The parents of the dead are to be comforted rather than pitied. Some of them may yet have children who will lighten their sorrow and serve the state; while others should remember how large their share of happiness has been, and be consoled by the glory of those who are gone.

sorrow will not last long, and be comforted by the glory of those who are gone. For the love of honor alone is ever young, and not riches, as some say, but honor is the delight of men when they are old and useless.

"To you who are the sons and brothers of the departed, I see that the struggle to emulate them will be an arduous one. For all men praise the dead, and, however preeminent your virtue may be, hardly will you be thought, I do not say to equal, but even to approach them. The living have their rivals and detractors, but when a man is out of the way, the honor and good will which he receives is unalloyed. And, if I am to speak of womanly virtues to those of you who will henceforth be widows, let me sum them up in one short admonition: To a woman not to show more weakness than is natural to her sex is a great glory, and not to be talked about for good or for evil among men.

Sons and brothers will find their example hard to imitate, for men are jealous of the living, but envy follows not the dead. Let the widows restrain their natural weakness, and avoid both praise and blame.

"I have paid the required tribute, in obedience to the law, making use of such fitting words as I had. The tribute of deeds has been paid in part; for the dead have been honorably interred, and it remains only that their children should be maintained at the public charge until they are grown up: this is the solid prize with which, as with a garland, Athens crowns her sons living and dead, after a struggle like theirs. For where the rewards of virtue are greatest, there the noblest citizens are enlisted in the service of the state. And now, when you have duly lamented, everyone his own dead, you may depart."

So have I paid a due tribute of words to the dead. The city will pay them in deeds, as by this funeral, so too by the maintenance of their children.

Which single emotion in his listeners do you think Pericles wanted to appeal to most in this speech? Explain your answer.

Identifying Facts

1. When Pericles speaks about the Athenian form of government, how does he define a democracy?

2. How does Pericles contrast the Athenians' military training with the training of the Spartans? What proof does he offer of the Athenians' superiority?

3. Why does Pericles feel that the parents of the dead should not be pitied? What advice does he offer the widows who mourn their dead?

Interpreting Meanings

1. Explain how Pericles gains the sympathetic attention of his listeners in the introduction to his speech.

2. Pericles' funeral oration is an outstanding example of the rhetorical art of **persuasion**. What do you think is Pericles' purpose in praising Athens and Athenian democracy? What is he trying to persuade his listeners to do or believe?

3. Identify at least one example of **argument**, or persuasion that appeals to reason. Then identify a part of the speech that seems designed to appeal primarily to emotion.

4. Athens in Pericles' day was a man's world as far as public life was concerned. How do Pericles' words to the women of Athens reflect this situation?

5. Briefly summarize the values praised by Pericles in the funeral oration.

Applying Meanings

Imagine that the United States is at war, and that the President delivers a speech similar to that of Pericles' funeral oration.

Would such a speech repel or inspire you? Why or why not? Explain your answer.

Critical Writing Response

Comparing Democracies.   Many of the claims made by Pericles sound remarkably similar to descriptions of the American democratic system given in speeches by political leaders today. In a brief essay, analyze the ways in which American democracy reflects the ancient Greek ideal of democracy. What ideals were held in high esteem by the Greeks? In what ways does American democracy diverge from these ideals? Completing a chart like the one below may help you to plan your essay.

Ideals	Athens	U.S.A.
Freedom of speech		
Promotion on merit		

Language and Vocabulary

Antithesis

Antithesis (an·tith′ə·sis) is the use of language to express sharply contrasting ideas in parallel phrases or structures. The saying "Whoever is not with us is against us" is an example of antithesis. Pericles often uses this device to make his speech more pointed and effective, as in these examples:

> We do not copy our neighbors, but are an example to them.

> We rely not upon management or trickery, but upon our own hearts and hands.

1. What other examples of antithesis can you find in Pericles' speech? List at least three examples.

2. Why do you think that antithesis—the juxtaposition of directly contrasting ideas—is such an effective device of persuasion?

Plato

c. 429–c. 347 B.C.

SEF/Art Resource, New York

Plato was the preeminent philosopher of the Golden Age. As a young student of rhetoric from an aristocratic family, Plato's destiny was sealed when he met Socrates (469–399 B.C.). The older man was a teacher whose unorthodox style and uncompromising pursuit of the truth appealed to many prominent young men of Plato's time.

Most of what we know about Socrates comes from Plato's works, for the older philosopher left no writings of his own. Socrates was an eccentric. Pretending to be ignorant, he wandered the streets of Athens, a shabby and unkempt figure who questioned people about concepts such as virtue, truth, and wisdom. He never preached or offered his own solutions, but he would demonstrate by his ceaseless questioning that no argument was infallible. The technique of questioning that he developed is known as the **Socratic method**.

Socrates' pointed criticism of official authorities earned him a reputation as a public nuisance. The controversy over his teaching methods and his belief that an "unexamined life is not worth living" led to a vicious persecution. In 399 B.C., he was tried and executed on false charges of corrupting the minds of his young students.

Plato recorded much of Socrates' philosophy and many of his speeches in his *Dialogues*. Nearly all of Plato's thirty-four philosophical works are written in the form of such **dialogues**, in which two or more characters debate with the principal speaker and challenger, Socrates. Plato used the dialogues as a vehicle to present a comprehensive philosophical system known as **Platonism**. According to the Platonic system, ideas are the only reality, and people should rely on reason, not on their senses, to comprehend the world.

In 387 B.C., Plato founded a school called the Academy, a center of philosophical learning. He wrote a number of famous works, including *The Republic*, which sets forth in brilliant detail his theory of an ideal state ruled by philosopher-kings. When he was sixty years old, during a sea voyage, Plato's ship was raided by pirates, and he was sold as a slave to a former student, who helped him return to Athens. Plato never left the city again.

Reader's Guide

from the APOLOGY
from the Dialogues

Background

The term *apology* did not have the same meaning for the Greeks as it does for modern readers. Socrates' apology at his trial was not an expression of regret or shame; it was a defense of his philosophy and way of life as well as a bitingly sarcastic attack on his judges. At the conclusion of Socrates' speech, the jury of 501 Athenian citizens voted, found him guilty, and condemned him to death by poison.

Although the *Apology* is among Plato's *Dialogues,* it is itself a **monologue**, or a speech given at length by one person. In Socrates' case, the monologue was his opportunity to explain himself and to honor the letter of the law. He even went so far as to suggest ironically that his services to Athens merited a pension. At this point, the jury reconfirmed the death penalty by an even larger majority. The selection below includes Socrates' final address to the court.

Writer's Response

In this speech to the court, Socrates refuses to compromise his loyalty to the pursuit of truth, even at the cost of his life. How do you feel about people who refuse to compromise their beliefs? Are some beliefs worth dying for? Freewrite your answers for a few minutes.

Literary Focus

An **analogy** is a comparison of two things to show that they are alike in certain respects. We use analogies to show how something unfamiliar is like something well known or widely experienced. One famous example of analogy is Benjamin Franklin's *Epitaph on Himself:*

> The body of Benjamin Franklin, Printer (like the cover of an old book, its contents torn out and stripped of its lettering and gilding), lies here, food for worms; but the work shall not be lost, for it will (as he believed) appear once more in a new and more elegant edition, revised and corrected by the Author.

Socrates uses several analogies in the *Apology* to make his points clearer to his listeners and to strengthen his arguments.

from the APOLOGY
from the Dialogues
Plato
translated by
BENJAMIN JOWETT

As you read the following speech, try to determine why Socrates has been so highly admired throughout the ages as both a philosopher and a teacher.

SCHOOL OF ATHENS, RAPHAEL. *Plato, the older figure in the center (left) stands next to Aristotle. Socrates, in the upper left, debates with the youth of Athens.*

Not much time will be gained, O Athenians, in return for the evil name which you will get from the detractors of the city, who will say that you killed Socrates, a wise man; for they will call me wise, even although I am not wise, when they want to reproach you. If you had waited a little while, your desire would have been fulfilled in the course of nature. For I am far advanced in years, as you may perceive, and not far from death. I am speaking now not to all of you, but only to those who have condemned me to death. And I have another thing to say to them: You think that I was convicted because I had no words of the sort which would have procured my acquittal—I mean, if I had thought fit to leave nothing undone or unsaid. Not so; the deficiency which led to my conviction was not of words—certainly not. But I had not the boldness or impudence or inclination to address you as you would have liked me to do, weeping and wailing and lamenting, and saying and doing many things which you have been accustomed to hear from others, and which, as I maintain, are unworthy of me. I thought at the time that I ought not to do anything common or mean when in danger: nor do I now repent of the style of my defense; I would rather die having spoken after my manner, than speak in your manner and live. For neither in war nor yet at law ought I or any man to use every way of escaping death. Often in battle there can be no doubt that if a man will throw away his arms, and fall on his knees before his pursuers, he may escape death; and in other dangers there are other ways of escaping death, if a man is willing to say and do anything. The difficulty, my friends, is not to avoid death, but to avoid unrighteousness; for that runs faster than death. I am old and move slowly, and the slower runner has overtaken me, and my accusers are keen and quick, and the faster runner, who is unrighteousness, has overtaken them. And now I depart hence condemned by you to suffer the penalty of death—they too go their ways condemned by the truth to suffer the penalty of villainy and wrong; and I must abide by my award—let them abide by theirs. I suppose that these things may be regarded as fated—and I think that they are well.

And now, O men who have condemned me, I would fain prophesy to you; for I am about to die, and in the hour of death men are gifted with prophetic power. And I prophesy to you who are my murderers, that immediately after my departure punishment far heavier than you have inflicted on me will surely await you. Me you have killed because you wanted to escape the accuser, and not to give an account of your lives. But that will not be as you suppose: far otherwise. For I say that there will be more accusers of you than there are now; accusers whom hitherto I have restrained: and as they are younger they will be more inconsiderate with you, and you will be more offended at them. If you think that by killing men you can prevent some one from censuring your evil lives, you are mistaken; that is not a way of escape which is either possible or honorable; the easiest and the noblest way is not to be disabling others, but to be improving yourselves. This is the prophecy which I utter before my departure to the judges who have condemned me.

Friends, who would have acquitted me, I would like also to talk with you about the thing which has come to pass, while the magistrates are busy, and before I go to the place at which I must die. Stay then a little, for we may as well talk with one another while there is time. You are my friends, and I should like to show you the meaning of this event which has happened to me. O my

Bust of Socrates.

has happened to me is a good, and that those of us who think that death is an evil are in error. For the customary sign would surely have opposed me had I been going to evil and not to good.

Let us reflect in another way, and we shall see that there is great reason to hope that death is a good; for one of two things— either death is a state of nothingness and utter unconsciousness, or, as men say, there is a change and migration of the soul from this world to another. Now, if you suppose that there is no consciousness, but a sleep like the sleep of him who is undisturbed even by dreams, death will be an unspeakable gain. For if a person were to select the night in which his sleep was undisturbed even by dreams, and were to compare with this the other days and nights of his life, and then were to tell us how many days and nights he had passed in the course of his life better and more pleasantly than this one, I think that any man, I will not say a private man, but even the great king will not find many such days or nights, when compared with the others. Now, if death be of such a nature, I say that to die is gain; for eternity is then only a single night. But if death is the journey to another place, and there, as men say, all the dead abide, what good, O my friends and judges, can be greater than this? If, indeed, when the pilgrim arrives in the world below, he is delivered from the professors of justice in this world, and finds the true judges who are said to give judgment there, Minos and Rhadamanthus and Aeacus and Triptolemus,[2] and other sons of

judges—for you I may truly call judges—I should like to tell you of a wonderful circumstance. Hitherto the divine faculty of which the internal oracle[1] is the source has constantly been in the habit of opposing me even about trifles, if I was going to make a slip or error in any matter; and now as you see there has come upon me that which may be thought, and is generally believed to be, the last and worst evil. But the oracle made no sign of opposition, either when I was leaving my house in the morning, or when I was on my way to the court, or while I was speaking, at anything which I was going to say; and yet I have often been stopped in the middle of a speech, but now in nothing I either said or did touching the matter in hand has the oracle opposed me. What do I take to be the explanation of this silence? I will tell you. It is an intimation that what

---

1. **oracle:** Socrates believed that he was constantly guided by a divine inner voice which warned him against evil acts and wrong choices.

---

2. **Minos** (mī'näs): king of Crete. **Rhadamanthus** (rad'ə·man'thəs): brother of Minos. **Aeacus** (ē'ə·kəs): according to one legend, the father of Achilles. **Triptolemus** (trip·tōl'ə·məs): priest of Demeter; after death, all were made judges in Hades, the world of the dead.

Roman mosaic of the School of Plato.

God who were righteous in their own life, that pilgrimage will be worth making. What would not a man give if he might converse with Orpheus and Musaeus and Hesiod[3] and Homer? Nay, if this be true, let me die again and again. I myself, too, shall have a wonderful interest in there meeting and conversing with Palamedes,[4] and Ajax[5] the son

3. **Orpheus** (ôr′fē·əs): a famous musician and poet of Greek mythology. **Musaeus** (mo͞o·zē′əs): Greek poet who lived around 1400 B.C. **Hesiod** (hē′sē·əd): Greek poet of the eighth century B.C.

4. **Palamedes** (pal′ə·mē′dēz): a Greek hero who fought in the Trojan War; he was accused of treachery and stoned to death.

5. **Ajax:** a Greek hero in the Trojan War; feeling that the armor of Achilles was unjustly awarded to Odysseus and not to himself, Ajax went mad.

of Telamon, and any other ancient hero who has suffered death through an unjust judgment; and there will be no small pleasure, as I think, in comparing my own sufferings with theirs. Above all, I shall then be able to continue my search into true and false knowledge; as in this world, so also in the next; and I shall find out who is wise, and who pretends to be wise, and is not. What would not a man give, O judges, to be able to examine the leader of the great Trojan expedition; or Odysseus[6] or Sisyphus,[7] or numberless others, men and women too! What infinite delight would there be in conversing with them and asking them questions! In another world they do not put a man to death for asking questions: assuredly not. For besides being happier than we are, they will be immortal, if what is said is true.

Wherefore, O judges, be of good cheer about death, and know of a certainty, that no evil can happen to a good man, either in life or after death. He and his are not neglected by the gods; nor has my own approaching end happened by mere chance. But I see clearly that the time had arrived when it was better for me to die and be released from trouble; wherefore the oracle gave no sign. For which reason, also, I am not angry with my condemners, or with my accusers; they have done me no harm, although they did not mean to do me any good; and for this I may gently blame them.

Still, I have a favor to ask of them. When my sons are grown up, I would ask you, O my friends, to punish them; and I would have you trouble them, as I have troubled you, if they seem to care about riches, or anything, more than about virtue; or if they pretend to be something when they are really nothing—then reprove them, as I have reproved you, for not caring about that for which they ought to care, and thinking that they are something when they are really nothing. And if you do this, both I and my sons will have received justice at your hands.

The hour of departure has arrived, and we go our ways—I to die, and you to live. Which is better God only knows.

---

6. **Odysseus** (ō·dis′ē·əs): cleverest of the Greek warriors; hero of Homer's *Odyssey*.
7. **Sisyphus** (sis′ə·fəs): After his death, Sisyphus was punished in Hades by eternally having to roll up a hill a huge stone that always rolled down just as it got to the top.

First Thoughts

Do you think Socrates acts heroically, or is his decision to die for his beliefs foolish? Explain.

Identifying Facts

1. What prophecy does Socrates make in the opening of his speech to those who voted to condemn him?

2. When he addresses those friends who voted to acquit him, how does Socrates explain the silence of his internal oracle?

3. Why does Socrates say he is not angry with his condemners and accusers? For what does he gently blame them?

4. Why does Socrates say he is not afraid of death?

5. At the conclusion of his speech, what favor does Socrates ask of his judges?

Interpreting Meanings

1. Toward the end of the first paragraph, Socrates uses the **analogy** of two runners to argue that pleading for his life would be dishonorable. Explain what is being compared in this analogy. How does this comparison help to strengthen Socrates' argument?
2. What **analogies** does Socrates draw when he argues that it is reasonable to hope that death is a good thing?
3. Socrates was renowned for his use of sarcasm, or **verbal irony**: saying one thing but meaning another. Given the circumstances, what is ironic about his remark at the end of his speech that "in another world they do not put a man to death for asking questions"?
4. What adjective would you use to describe Socrates' **tone** in this speech?
5. Socrates was an observer of the best and the worst in human nature, and he also experienced bitter injustice in his own life. Yet he says that "no evil can happen to a good man, either in life or after death" (see page 299). How do you explain this apparent contradiction?

Applying Meanings

How do you think a man like Socrates would be regarded today? Would you enjoy him as one of your own teachers? What do you think you could learn from him? Explain.

Creative Writing Response

Judging Socrates. Imagine that you are one of the judges who voted against Socrates and that you have just heard his final speech. How do you feel now? Are you likely to change your vote in his favor? Write a three-paragraph essay in which you explain why you were or were not persuaded by Socrates' speech. You may want to refer to the notes you took in Writer's Response (see page 294).

Then, as a class, take a vote. Will you allow Socrates to live, or is he still condemned to die?

Critical Writing Response

Understanding Analogies. On one level, an **analogy** is a simple comparison of two unlike things, but analogies can be more complicated. Not only are unlike things compared to one another, but the relationship between two things or ideas can in turn be compared to the relationship between two other things or ideas. The typical construction of this kind of analogy is: "*a* is to *b* as *c* is to *d*," often written in this form: "a:b::c:d." For example:

1. Socrates is to Plato as a teacher is to a student. (Socrates:Plato::teacher:student)
2. A speech is to an orator as a poem is to a poet. (speech:orator::poem:poet)
3. A microscope is to a biologist as a hammer is to a carpenter. (microscope:biologist::hammer:carpenter)

In the first analogy, the comparison of teacher to student actually describes the relationship between Socrates and Plato. In the second analogy, the first part of each comparison is something made by each of the second parts: orators make speeches and poets make poems. Finally, in the third analogy, the first part of each comparison is a tool used by the second: biologists use microscopes and carpenters use hammers.

Try to construct at least two analogies of your own. For example, you could begin with "Inexperience is to youth as. . . ." Then, in a few sentences, explain the relationship between the parts of your analogies.

Sophocles
c. 496–406 B.C.

Lee Boltin Picture Library

The tragedies of Sophocles probe the depth of human suffering and despair as profoundly as the works of any writer in world literature. The playwright himself, in contrast to the misery he portrayed in his works, lived a long, comfortable, and happy life. He grew up in a well-to-do family in Athens, enjoyed a carefree childhood and education, and eventually became a distinguished public official as well as an outstanding dramatist.

Sophocles first achieved recognition in the theater at the age of twenty-eight, when he defeated Aeschylus—another great Greek playwright—in an annual dramatic competition. He went on to win twenty-four first prizes over the next six decades—the best record of any Greek playwright. He produced 123 plays, of which only seven survive today.

The artistic fulfillment of Sophocles' long life reflects the spirit of the age in which he lived. The first half of the fifth century B.C. in Athens was a time of political expansion and social optimism, following the great victories of the Greeks over the invading Persians at Marathon (490 B.C.) and Salamis (480 B.C.). In the second half of the century, the Athenians experienced tremendous intellectual and cultural developments. This was the brilliant era of the statesman Pericles, the historians Herodotus and Thucydides, and the philosopher Socrates. It was the age that raised the majestic temple called the Parthenon on the Acropolis high above the city and developed democracy as a political system. The age of Sophocles was indeed a time when anything seemed possible through human effort and reason.

Toward the end of Sophocles' life, however, this expansive spirit began to dwindle, largely because of the costly investment of Athenian lives and resources in the long Peloponnesian War (431–404 B.C.). This conflict pitted Athens and her allies against the rival city of Sparta and various other allied city-states for twenty-seven years. Perhaps this is one of the reasons that Sophocles' surviving plays—most of which were written after 440 B.C.—are so deeply troubling. They depict characters caught up in unsolvable dilemmas that test their faith in divine and human justice.

Oedipus Rex

Oedipus Rex is considered one of the world's greatest tragedies. A **tragedy** is a serious drama featuring a noble, dignified main character—often a member of royalty—who strives to achieve something and is ultimately defeated. The defeat of the hero may appear to be brought about by forces beyond his or her control, and the outcome, or fate, seems almost predetermined. But often the main character's downfall is brought about by his or her own character flaw or weakness—the **tragic flaw.** In spite of defeat and even death, however, the tragic hero is ennobled by his or her newly gained self-knowledge and wisdom.

The Greek Theater

The second half of the fifth century B.C. was the golden age of Greek drama, especially of tragedy, which grew out of religious ritual drama. In Athens, the dramatic festivals and contests were the center of cultural life. The annual festival in honor of the god Dionysus, called the Dionysia, was a four-day extravaganza held in March or April, during which fifteen thousand spectators witnessed a variety of plays in the open-air Theater of Dionysus. Tragedies were usually presented in trilogies, or cycles of three linked plays, together with comedies or other forms of lighter drama. The dramatic festival was so important to civic life that the city magistrates selected the playwrights for each annual competition, and wealthy citizens with political ambitions subsidized the production fees. Judges ranked the competing playwrights and awarded prizes to the winners.

The Theater of Dionysus was carved out of a stone hillside and resembled a semicircle with steeply rising tiers of seats. At the bottom was the rounded **orchestra**, or performance area, where the chorus sang and danced. Behind the orchestra was an open, practically bare stage, where the actors spoke their lines from behind huge masks. These masks were often decorated to suggest character types familiar to the audience: for example, a king, a messenger, a prophet, a queen, or a nurse. All the roles in Greek plays were performed by male actors. By switching masks, one actor could play a number of roles—both male and female—in a single play.

Theater of Dionysus.
❓ *How is this ancient Greek theater like or unlike the theater today? How do you think the Greeks might have compensated for a lack of amplified sound and artificial lighting?*

The Oedipus Trilogy

Oedipus Rex is one of Sophocles' three "Theban plays"—three tragedies about King Oedipus (ed′i·pəs) of Thebes and his family. Sophocles did not write these three plays to be performed at a single festival, as was a common practice in his day. Instead, he composed them over a 36-year period—actually beginning with the tragedy *Antigone*, the third and last part of the story, which was first performed in 442 B.C. This play, which takes place after the death of Oedipus, dramatizes a fateful struggle between Oedipus's daughter Antigone and his

successor as the ruler of Thebes, King Creon. In *Antigone*, Sophocles explored a timeless conflict: the clash between individual conscience and established authority, or the law of the state.

The middle part of the story—the death and redemption of Oedipus in exile and old age—became the subject of Sophocles' last tragedy, *Oedipus at Colonus*. This play, produced in 406 B.C., was written when the playwright was nearing the age of ninety. Remarkably, the play does not reflect any decline in Sophocles' poetic powers.

The Story of Oedipus

Oedipus Rex—chronologically the first part of the Theban trilogy—was actually written second. The tale of King Oedipus would have been familiar to the Greek audience of the time. Oedipus is the ill-fated king of Thebes whose mysterious past catches up with him and wreaks havoc on himself and his family. Oedipus won the hand of Queen Jocasta after the death of her husband, King Laius, by solving a riddle posed by the Sphinx, a monster that was terrorizing the city of Thebes.

Oedipus had been traveling to Thebes from Corinth, having run away from his home there because of a divine prediction that he would someday murder his father and marry his mother. Oedipus did not know that he was not the child of the king and queen of Corinth, but was in fact the child of Jocasta and Laius of Thebes. They, too, had heard the prophecy when he was born and had made arrangements for a shepherd to leave the infant, with its ankles pinned together, on the side of a mountain to die. The shepherd, however, took pity on the child and gave him to a Corinthian messenger, who in turn brought him to the king and queen of Corinth. They named him Oedipus, which means "swollen foot," and raised him as their son. Years later, as Oedipus traveled to Thebes, he unknowingly met King Laius, his real father, on the road and killed him, thus setting the prophecy into motion.

Oedipus earned his reputation of deliverer of the Thebans by solving the riddle of the Sphinx and saving the city of Thebes from disaster. The Sphinx was a monster in the shape of a lion with the wings of an eagle and the head of a woman. It lay waiting outside the city and would challenge passersby to solve the riddle: "What walks on four legs in the morning, on two legs at noon, and on three legs in the evening?" If they could not answer, they were killed immediately. Until Oedipus, no one had the answer to the riddle— "Man"—and the city was suffering. After solving the riddle of the Sphinx, Oedipus marries Jocasta, has four children with her, and rules with her and Creon, her brother, for twenty years.

As the play begins, the city of Thebes is suffering again, this time from a terrible plague. Creon reports from the oracle, or priestess, of Apollo that the plague will not end until the murderer of King Laius is found and punished. Oedipus commits himself to locating the

Detail of Oedipus and the Sphinx.

murderer and suffers terrible consequences as he discovers the truth about
himself and his identity.

The Structure and Themes of the Play

Because the story of Oedipus was well
known to the fifth-century B.C. audience,
Sophocles was able to focus his play on
the discovery of deeds committed before
the action of the play begins. All the violence takes place offstage, and what the
audience sees are the responses of those
who must live with the truth or perish.

The play maintains a tight dramatic
framework. All the action takes place in
a single location and involves a small
number of characters interacting with
the central figure Oedipus, who remains
on stage for nearly the entire play. In
addition, the Chorus, who serve simply
as nameless onlookers and commenta-
tors in other Greek tragedies, are turned
by Sophocles into a collective "actor"
within the drama itself.

The play consists almost entirely of
dramatic dialogue. But in this work what
is left unsaid is often more powerful
than what is explicitly expressed. Practically every line contains a possible double meaning or an ambiguity. This verbal
irony serves to reinforce the dramatic
irony of the play, as the main characters
and even the Chorus only gradually
come to grips with what is evident to
the audience at the very start. The
razor-sharp irony in *Oedipus Rex* is one
of the elements that has given the play
its power to spellbind audiences for
thousands of years—and has also made
updated versions of the story popular

Roman mosaic of actors preparing for a
performance with masks.

Scala/Art Resource, New York

from Roman times to the present day.

The themes, or underlying messages,
of *Oedipus Rex* are crucial to the play's
long-lasting appeal. Audiences for generations have recognized and been affected
by the issues that lead to Oedipus's
downfall. The themes explored include:

1. The quest for identity
2. The nature of innocence and guilt
3. The nature of moral responsibility
4. Human will versus fate
5. The abuse of power

The structure of most Greek tragedies
presents a tight, formal arrangement of
parts. These parts include the **prologue**
(opening scene), the ***parodos*** (the first of
the Chorus's lyric songs or choral odes),
a regular alternation of scenes in **dialogue** and **choral odes**, and finally the
exodos (concluding scene). These terms
have been retained in this translation of
Oedipus Rex.

Reader's Guide

OEDIPUS REX

Background

During the early years of the Peloponnesian War, when *Oedipus Rex* was first produced, Athens was suffering from both political instability and a devastating plague that was taking its toll on the population. Thus, Sophocles opens his play with a situation that the Athenians could readily identify with: The city of Thebes is beset by a terrible plague, and there is no end in sight. According to the oracle of Apollo, the plague will continue until the murderer of King Laius, still living in Thebes, is caught and punished for his crime. Oedipus, casting himself in the role of savior of Thebes, as he did once before with the deadly Sphinx, vows to do everything in his power to apprehend the murderer and save his people. Little does he realize that his vow will relentlessly lead him to an encounter with himself and his darkest secrets.

Writer's Response

The ancient Greeks cited the myth of Oedipus as a striking example of how human fortunes can suffer unexpected drastic reversals—how even good and noble people can suffer at the hands of fate or the will of the gods. Can you think of other examples from literature or real life in which people suddenly experience a sharp reversal of fortune? What were the circumstances? Were the people involved responsible for what happened, or were they innocent victims? How do people explain and cope with such tragedies? Freewrite your answer.

Literary Focus

Irony is the difference between what is expected to happen and what actually happens. **Dramatic irony** occurs when the reader or audience knows something important that a character in a story or drama does not know. The fundamental irony in *Oedipus Rex* stems from the fact that the audience knows King Oedipus's true identity, while he is unaware of it. Sophocles ingeniously creates numerous variations on this central irony throughout the play, increasing the audience's suspense and heightening their pity and horror.

OEDIPUS REX
Part 1
Sophocles
translated by

DUDLEY FITTS AND ROBERT FITZGERALD

> The action of **Oedipus Rex** *may be described as a search for the truth. As you read, pay attention to the role each character plays in either fulfilling or further complicating this search.*

CHARACTERS

Oedipus (ed'i·pəs, ē'di-), King of Thebes

A Priest

Creon (krē'än'), brother of Jocasta

Teiresias (tī·rē'sē·əs), a blind seer

Jocasta (jō·kas'tə), wife of Oedipus and widow of Laius (lā'yəs), former King of Thebes

Messenger, from Corinth

Shepherd of Laius

Second Messenger, from the palace

Chorus of Theban Elders

Choragos (kə·rā'gəs), the leader of the Chorus

Antigone (an·tig'ə·nē) and **Ismene** (is·mē'nē), daughters of Oedipus and Jocasta

Suppliants

Page

Servants and Attendants

SCENE

Before the palace of OEDIPUS, *King of Thebes. A central door and two lateral doors open onto a platform which runs the length of the facade. On the platform, right and left, are altars; and three steps lead down into the "orchestra," or chorus-ground. At the beginning of the action these steps are crowded by suppliants who have brought branches and chaplets of olive leaves and who lie in various attitudes of despair.* OEDIPUS *enters.*

Stratford Festival, Stratford, Ontario Canada; Photo by Don McKague

═ PROLOGUE ═══════════════

Oedipus.

My children, generations of the living
In the line of Cadmus,° nursed at his ancient hearth:
Why have you strewn yourselves before these altars
In supplication, with your boughs and garlands?

5 The breath of incense rises from the city
With a sound of prayer and lamentation.

                                Children,

I would not have you speak through messengers,
And therefore I have come myself to hear you—
I, Oedipus, who bear the famous name.

10 (*to a* PRIEST) You, there, since you are eldest in the
    company,
Speak for them all, tell me what preys upon you,
Whether you come in dread, or crave some blessing:
Tell me, and never doubt that I will help you
In every way I can; I should be heartless

2. **Cadmus** (kad'məs): in Greek mythology, a prince who killed a dragon and sowed its teeth, which turned into an army of men who fought one another; with the five survivors of the battle, Cadmus founded Thebes.

6 **?** Try to visualize the despairing postures of the suppliants as Oedipus addresses the people. Together with the details of the incense and the sounds of lamentation, what mood does the scene suggest at the opening of the play?

9 **?** Do you think Oedipus is boasting here? Or is he merely being objective about his own status as the King of Thebes?

15   Were I not moved to find you suppliant here.
Priest.
      Great Oedipus, O powerful King of Thebes!
      You see how all the ages of our people
      Cling to your altar steps: here are boys
20   Who can barely stand alone, and here are priests
      By weight of age, as I am a priest of God,
      And young men chosen from those yet unmarried;
      As for the others, all that multitude,
      They wait with olive chaplets in the squares,
      At the two shrines of Pallas, and where Apollo
25   Speaks in the glowing embers.
                                    Your own eyes
      Must tell you: Thebes is tossed on a murdering sea
      And cannot lift her head from the death surge.
      A rust consumes the buds and fruits of the earth;
      The herds are sick; children die unborn,
30   And labor is vain. The god of plague and pyre
      Raids like detestable lightning through the city,
      And all the house of Cadmus is laid waste,
      All emptied, and all darkened: Death alone
      Battens upon the misery of Thebes.

35   You are not one of the immortal gods, we know;
      Yet we have come to you to make our prayer
      As to the man surest in mortal ways
      And wisest in the ways of God. You saved us
      From the Sphinx, that flinty singer,° and the tribute
40   We paid to her so long; yet you were never
      Better informed than we, nor could we teach you:
      It was some god breathed in you to set us free.

      Therefore, O mighty King, we turn to you:
      Find us our safety, find us a remedy,
45   Whether by counsel of the gods or men.
      A king of wisdom tested in the past
      Can act in a time of troubles, and act well.
      Noblest of men, restore
      Life to your city! Think how all men call you
50   Liberator for your triumph long ago;
      Ah, when your years of kingship are remembered,
      Let them not say *We rose, but later fell—*
      Keep the State from going down in the storm!
      Once, years ago, with happy augury,

22 ❓ What gestures might the Priest make as he says these lines?

39. **Sphinx . . . singer:** The Sphinx was a winged monster that killed anyone who could not answer her riddle: "What walks on four legs in the morning, two legs at noon, and three legs in the evening?" Oedipus gave the correct answer: "A man crawls as an infant, walks erect as a man, and uses a staff in old age." The Sphinx then killed herself.

42 ❓ What qualities or personality traits in Oedipus does the Priest single out as the ruler's special virtues?

53 ❓ What familiar metaphor for a state or kingdom is suggested by this line? How does the Priest refer again to this metaphor in line 58?

55 You brought us fortune; be the same again!
    No man questions your power to rule the land:
    But rule over men, not over a dead city!
    Ships are only hulls, citadels are nothing,
    When no life moves in the empty passageways.

Oedipus.

60 Poor children! You may be sure I know
    All that you longed for in your coming here.
    I know that you are deathly sick; and yet,
    Sick as you are, not one is as sick as I.
    Each of you suffers in himself alone
65 His anguish, not another's; but my spirit
    Groans for the city, for myself, for you.

    I was not sleeping, you are not waking me.
    No, I have been in tears for a long while
    And in my restless thought walked many ways.
70 In all my search, I found one helpful course,
    And that I have taken: I have sent Creon,
    Son of Menoeceus,° brother of the Queen,
    To Delphi, Apollo's place of revelation,°
    To learn there, if he can,
75 What act or pledge of mine may save the city.
    I have counted the days, and now, this very day,
    I am troubled, for he has overstayed his time.
    What is he doing? He has been gone too long.
    Yet whenever he comes back, I should do ill
80 To scant whatever duty God reveals.

Priest.

    It is a timely promise. At this instant
    They tell me Creon is here.

Oedipus.   O Lord Apollo!
    May his news be fair as his face is radiant!

Priest.

    It could not be otherwise: he is crowned with bay,
85 The chaplet is thick with berries.

Oedipus.   We shall soon know;
    He is near enough to hear us now.

[*Enter* CREON.]

                                        O Prince:

    Brother: son of Menoeceus:
    What answer do you bring us from the god?

60 ❓ Notice how Oedipus repeatedly refers to the Thebans as "children." What does this suggest about the way he regards them?

72. **Menoeceus** (me·nē′sus)
73. **Delphi** (del′fī) . . . **revelation:** Delphi was the seat of the most famous oracle of the god Apollo.

Creon.

90   A strong one. I can tell you, great afflictions
      Will turn out well, if they are taken well.

Oedipus.

      What was the oracle? These vague words
      Leave me still hanging between hope and fear.

Creon.

      Is it your pleasure to hear me with all these
      Gathered around us? I am prepared to speak,
95   But should we not go in?

Oedipus.   Let them all hear it.

      It is for them I suffer, more than for myself.

Creon.

      Then I will tell you what I heard at Delphi.
      In plain words
      The god commands us to expel from the land of Thebes
100   An old defilement we are sheltering.
      It is a deathly thing, beyond cure;
      We must not let it feed upon us longer.

Oedipus.

      What defilement? How shall we rid ourselves of it?

Creon.

      By exile or death, blood for blood. It was
105   Murder that brought the plague-wind on the city.

Oedipus.

      Murder of whom? Surely the god has named him?

Creon.

      My lord: long ago Laius was our king,
      Before you came to govern us.

Oedipus.   I know;

      I learned of him from others; I never saw him.

Creon.

110   He was murdered; and Apollo commands us now
      To take revenge upon whoever killed him.

Oedipus.

      Upon whom? Where are they? Where shall we
         find a clue
      To solve that crime, after so many years?

Creon.

      Here in this land, he said.

                              If we make enquiry,

90 ❓ In what different ways could the actor playing Creon deliver these lines?

95 ❓ These two short speeches about where to hold their discussion suggest a contrast between Oedipus's and Creon's attitudes toward the people. What is this contrast?

109 ❓ What is dramatically ironic about Oedipus's line here?

115 We may touch things that otherwise escape us.

Oedipus.

Tell me: Was Laius murdered in his house,
Or in the fields, or in some foreign country?

Creon.

He said he planned to make a pilgrimage.
He did not come home again.

Oedipus. And was there no one,
120 No witness, no companion, to tell what happened?

Creon.

They were all killed but one, and he got away
So frightened that he could remember one thing only.

Oedipus.

What was that one thing? One may be the key
To everything, if we resolve to use it.

Creon.

125 He said that a band of highwaymen attacked them,
Outnumbered them, and overwhelmed the King.

Oedipus.

Strange, that a highwayman should be so daring—
Unless some faction here bribed him to do it.

Creon.

We thought of that. But after Laius' death
130 New troubles arose and we had no avenger.

Oedipus.

What troubles could prevent your hunting down
    the killers?

Creon.

The riddling Sphinx's song
Made us deaf to all mysteries but her own.

Oedipus.

Then once more I must bring what is dark to light.
135 It is most fitting that Apollo shows,
As you do, this compunction for the dead.
You shall see how I stand by you, as I should,
To avenge the city and the city's god,
And not as though it were for some distant friend,
140 But for my own sake, to be rid of evil.
Whoever killed King Laius might—who knows?—
Decide at any moment to kill me as well.
By avenging the murdered king I protect myself.

127 ❓ Notice how Oedipus refers to a single "highwayman" in this line, whereas Creon had just mentioned a "band of highwaymen" in the plural in line 125. Do you think this is just a casual change from the plural to the singular? What might this slip on Oedipus's part (if it is a slip) suggest? Explain.

143 ❓ These lines are dramatically ironic, since the audience knows that Oedipus himself is the murderer. In addition to the dramatic irony, what does Oedipus's speculation about his own danger suggest about the nature of ancient Greek kingship?

Come, then, my children: leave the altar steps,
145   Lift up your olive boughs!
                            One of you go
And summon the people of Cadmus to gather here.
I will do all that I can; you may tell them that.

[*Exit a* PAGE.]

So, with the help of God,
We shall be saved—or else indeed we are lost.

Priest.

150   Let us rise, children. It was for this we came,
And now the King has promised it himself.
Phoebus° has sent us an oracle; may he descend
Himself to save us and drive out the plague.

[*Exeunt* OEDIPUS *and* CREON *into the palace by the central door. The* PRIEST *and the* SUPPLIANTS *disperse right and left. After a short pause the* CHORUS *enters the orchestra.*]

152. **Phoebus** (fē′bəs): a name for Apollo as sun god; here, alluding to him as the god of prophecy.

═ PARADOS° ═══════════

Strophe 1

Chorus.
    What is God singing in his profound
155   Delphi of gold and shadow?
    What oracle for Thebes, the sunwhipped city?

    Fear unjoints me, the roots of my heart tremble.

    Now I remember, O Healer,° your power, and wonder:
    Will you send doom like a sudden cloud, or
        weave it
160   Like nightfall of the past?

    Speak, speak to us, issue of holy sound:
    Dearest to our expectancy: be tender!

Antistrophe 1

    Let me pray to Athena, the immortal daughter of Zeus,
    And to Artemis her sister
165   Who keeps her famous throne in the market ring,
    And to Apollo, bowman at the far butts of heaven—

Parados (par′ə·dōs′): the entrance song of the Chorus. Song and speech alternate throughout the play. In this choral song, the *strophe* (strō′fē) was sung as the Chorus turned from one side of the orchestra to the other. The *antistrophe* (an·tis′trə·fē) was sung while the Chorus moved in a direction opposite from that of the strophe.

158. **Healer:** Apollo, the god of medicine.

O gods, descend! Like three streams leap against
The fires of our grief, the fires of darkness;
Be swift to bring us rest!

170   As in the old time from the brilliant house
Of air you stepped to save us, come again!

Strophe 2

Now our afflictions have no end,
Now all our stricken host lies down
And no man fights off death with his mind;

175   The noble plowland bears no grain,
And groaning mothers cannot bear—
See, how our lives like birds take wing,
Like sparks that fly when a fire soars,
To the shore of the god of evening.

Antistrophe 2

180   The plague burns on, it is pitiless,
Though pallid children laden with death
Lie unwept in the stony ways,

And old gray women by every path
Flock to the strand about the altars

185   There to strike their breasts and cry
Worship of Phoebus in wailing prayers:
Be kind, God's golden child!

Strophe 3

There are no swords in this attack by fire,
No shields, but we are ringed with cries.
190   Send the besieger plunging from our homes
Into the vast sea room of the Atlantic
Or into the waves that foam eastward of Thrace°—

For the day ravages what the night spares—

Destroy our enemy, lord of the thunder!
195   Let him be riven by lightning from heaven!

Antistrophe 3

Phoebus Apollo, stretch the sun's bowstring,
That golden cord, until it sing for us,

170 ❓ The Chorus says that Apollo saved the city of Thebes once before. To what previous crisis do you think they are alluding?

187 ❓ How does the mood of Strophe 2 and Antistrophe 2 contrast with the mood of the first strophe and antistrophe? What images in the second pair of stanzas focus on death and decay?

192. **Thrace** (thrās): a region lying between the Aegean Sea, the Danube River, and the Black Sea.

196 ❓ What physical activity does the Chorus associate with Apollo? In the Chorus's imagination, is Apollo primarily a healer or a destroyer? Or is he both at once? Explain.

Flashing arrows in heaven!
                              Artemis, Huntress,
Race with flaring lights upon our mountains!

200   O scarlet god, O golden-banded brow,
        O Theban Bacchus in a storm of Maenads,°

[*Enter* OEDIPUS, *center.*]

        Whirl upon Death, that all the Undying hate!
        Come with blinding torches, come in joy!

201. **Theban Bacchus** (bak′əs): Bacchus, also known as Dionysus, was the god of revelry and of brutality. He came to Thebes accompanied by women who sang and danced wildly. When Pentheus, the king of Thebes, mocked the god and his followers, he was punished by being torn limb from limb. **Maenads** (mē′nadz): priestesses of Bacchus.

SCENE 1

Oedipus.

Is this your prayer? It may be answered. Come,

205 Listen to me, act as the crisis demands,
And you shall have relief from all these evils.

Until now I was a stranger to this tale,
As I had been a stranger to the crime.
Could I track down the murderer without a clue?

210 But now, friends,
As one who became a citizen after the murder,
I make this proclamation to all Thebans:
If any man knows by whose hand Laius, son
of Labdacus,
Met his death, I direct that man to tell me everything.

215 No matter what he fears for having so long withheld it.
Let it stand as promised that no further trouble
Will come to him, but he may leave the land
in safety.

Moreover: If anyone knows the murderer to
be foreign,
Let him not keep silent: he shall have his
reward from me.

220 However, if he does conceal it; if any man
Fearing for his friend or for himself disobeys this edict,
Hear what I propose to do:

I solemnly forbid the people of this country,
Where power and throne are mine, ever to
receive that man

225 Or speak to him, no matter who he is, or let him
Join in sacrifice, lustration,° or in prayer.
I decree that he be driven from every house,
Being, as he is, corruption itself to us: the Delphic
Voice of Zeus has pronounced this revelation.

230 Thus I associate myself with the oracle
And take the side of the murdered king.

As for the criminal, I pray to God—
Whether it be a lurking thief, or one of a number—
I pray that that man's life be consumed in evil
and wretchedness.

235 And as for me, this curse applies no less

207 **?** What is unintentionally
ironic about Oedipus's
statement here?

226. **lustration** (lus·trā′shən): purification through ritual.

316 Greek and Roman Literatures

If it should turn out that the culprit is my guest here,
Sharing my hearth.

                You have heard the penalty.
I lay it on you now to attend to this
For my sake, for Apollo's, for the sick
240   Sterile city that heaven has abandoned.
Suppose the oracle had given you no command:
Should this defilement go uncleansed forever?
You should have found the murderer: your king,
A noble king, had been destroyed!

                      Now I,
245   Having the power that he held before me,
Having his bed, begetting children there
Upon his wife, as he would have, had he lived—
Their son would have been my children's brother,
If Laius had had luck in fatherhood!
250   (But surely ill luck rushed upon his reign)—
I say I take the son's part, just as though
I were his son, to press the fight for him
And see it won! I'll find the hand that brought
Death to Labdacus' and Polydorus' child,°
255   Heir of Cadmus' and Agenor's line.°
And as for those who fail me,
May the gods deny them the fruit of the earth,
Fruit of the womb, and may they rot utterly!
Let them be wretched as we are wretched, and
      worse!

260   For you, for loyal Thebans, and for all
Who find my actions right, I pray the favor
Of justice, and of all the immortal gods.

Choragos.
Since I am under oath, my lord, I swear
I did not do the murder, I cannot name
265   The murderer. Might not the oracle
That has ordained the search tell where to find him?

Oedipus.
An honest question. But no man in the world
Can make the gods do more than the gods will.

Choragos.
There is one last expedient—

Oedipus.   Tell me what it is.
270   Though it seem slight, you must not hold it back.

235 **?** How does Sophocles deepen the irony of Oedipus's curse in these lines?

251 **?** The irony in this long speech now reaches an almost unbearable intensity. What tone of voice might an actor playing Oedipus use for these lines?

254. **Labdacus** (lab′də·kəs): king of Thebes and father of Laius. **Polydorus' child:** Polydorus (päl·i·dō′rəs) was the grandfather of Laius.

255. **Agenor's** (ə·jē′nôr) **line:** Agenor, father of Cadmus, the founder of Thebes.

Choragos.

    A lord clairvoyant° to the lord Apollo,
    As we all know, is the skilled Teiresias.
    One might learn much about this from him, Oedipus.

Oedipus.

    I am not wasting time:
275   Creon spoke of this, and I have sent for him—
    Twice, in fact; it is strange that he is not here.

Choragos.

    The other matter—that old report—seems useless.

Oedipus.

    Tell me. I am interested in all reports.

Choragos.

    The King was said to have been killed by highwaymen.

Oedipus.

280   I know. But we have no witnesses to that.

Choragos.

    If the killer can feel a particle of dread,
    Your curse will bring him out of hiding!

Oedipus.   No.
    The man who dared that act will fear no curse.

    [*Enter the blind seer* TEIRESIAS, *led by a* PAGE.]

Choragos.

    But there is one man who may detect the criminal.
285   This is Teiresias, this is the holy prophet
    In whom, alone of all men, truth was born.

Oedipus.

    Teiresias: seer: student of mysteries,
    Of all that's taught and all that no man tells,
    Secrets of Heaven and secrets of the earth:
290   Blind though you are, you know the city lies
    Sick with plague; and from this plague, my lord,
    We find that you alone can guard or save us.

    Possibly you did not hear the messengers?
    Apollo, when we sent to him,
295   Sent us back word that this great pestilence
    Would lift, but only if we established clearly
    The identity of those who murdered Laius.
    They must be killed or exiled.
                      Can you use
    Birdflight or any art of divination°

271. **clairvoyant** (kler·voi'ənt): capable of perceiving through intuition things that cannot be seen.

276. ❓ Compare Oedipus's statement here with lines 76-80. How does this passage resemble his earlier speech?

Stratford Festival, Stratford, Ontario Canada; Photo by Don McKague; Donald Davis as Teiresias

299. **Birdflight . . . divination:** The flight of birds was observed by prophets and used in interpreting the future.

300 To purify yourself, and Thebes, and me
From this contagion? We are in your hands.
There is no fairer duty
Than that of helping others in distress.

Teiresias.
How dreadful knowledge of the truth can be
305 When there's no help in truth! I knew this well,
But made myself forget. I should not have come.

Oedipus.
What is troubling you? Why are your eyes so cold?

Teiresias.
Let me go home. Bear your own fate, and I'll
Bear mine. It is better so: trust what I say.

Oedipus.
310 What you say is ungracious and unhelpful
To your native country. Do not refuse to speak.

Teiresias.
When it comes to speech, your own is neither temperate
Nor opportune. I wish to be more prudent.

Oedipus.
In God's name, we all beg you—

Teiresias.   You are all ignorant.
315 No; I will never tell you what I know.
Now it is my misery; then, it would be yours.

Oedipus.
What! You do know something, and will not tell us?
You would betray us all and wreck the State?

Teiresias.
I do not intend to torture myself, or you.
320 Why persist in asking? You will not persuade me.

Oedipus.
What a wicked old man you are! You'd try a stone's
Patience! Out with it! Have you no feeling at all?

Teiresias.
You call me unfeeling. If you could only see
The nature of your own feelings . . .

Oedipus.   Why,
325 Who would not feel as I do? Who could endure
Your arrogance toward the city?

Teiresias.   What does it matter!

321 ❓ Is Oedipus's annoyed reaction here understandable, in your opinion? Or is Oedipus prematurely angry with Teiresias?

Whether I speak or not, it is bound to come.

Oedipus.

Then, if "it" is bound to come, you are bound to
   tell me.

Teiresias.

No, I will not go on. Rage as you please.

Oedipus.

330   Rage? Why not!

And I'll tell you what I think:
You planned it, you had it done, you all but
Killed him with your own hands: if you had eyes,
I'd say the crime was yours, and yours alone.

Teiresias.

So? I charge you, then,

335   Abide by the proclamation you have made:
From this day forth
Never speak again to these men or to me;
You yourself are the pollution of this country.

Oedipus.

You dare say that! Can you possibly think you have

340   Some way of going free, after such insolence?

Teiresias.

I have gone free. It is the truth sustains me.

Oedipus.

Who taught you shamelessness? It was not your craft.

Teiresias.

You did. You made me speak. I did not want to.

Oedipus.

Speak what? Let me hear it again more clearly.

Teiresias.

345   Was it not clear before? Are you tempting me?

Oedipus.

I did not understand it. Say it again.

Teiresias.

I say that you are the murderer whom you seek.

Oedipus.

Now twice you have spat out infamy. You'll pay
   for it!

Teiresias.

Would you care for more? Do you wish to be
   really angry?

331 ❓ How do you react to Oedipus's accusation in these lines?

Greek vase showing preparations
for a play.

Oedipus.

350   Say what you will. Whatever you say is worthless.

Teiresias.

I say you live in hideous shame with those
Most dear to you. You cannot see the evil.

Oedipus.

It seems you can go on mouthing like this forever.

Teiresias.

I can, if there is power in truth.

Oedipus.   There is:

355   But not for you, not for you,
You sightless, witless, senseless, mad old man!

Teiresias.

You are the madman. There is no one here
Who will not curse you soon, as you curse me.

Oedipus.

You child of endless night! You cannot hurt me

360   Or any other man who sees the sun.

Teiresias.

True: it is not from me your fate will come.
That lies within Apollo's competence,
As it is his concern.

Oedipus.   Tell me:

Are you speaking for Creon, or for yourself?

Teiresias.

365   Creon is no threat. You weave your own doom.

Oedipus.

Wealth, power, craft of statesmanship!
Kingly position, everywhere admired!
What savage envy is stored up against these,
If Creon, whom I trusted, Creon my friend,

370   For this great office which the city once
Put in my hands unsought—if for this power
Creon desires in secret to destroy me!

He has bought this decrepit fortuneteller, this
Collector of dirty pennies, this prophet fraud—

375   Why, he is no more clairvoyant than I am!

Tell us:

Has your mystic mummery° ever approached the
    truth?
When that hellcat the Sphinx was performing here,

364 **?** Why should Oedipus
suddenly connect Creon
with Teiresias here? Look
back to see if line 275 gives
you a clue.

376. **mummery:** pretentious or
hypocritical rites.

What help were you to these people?
Her magic was not for the first man who came along:
380 It demanded a real exorcist. Your birds—
What good were they? or the gods, for the matter of that?
But I came by,
Oedipus, the simple man, who knows nothing—
I thought it out for myself, no birds helped me!
385 And this is the man you think you can destroy,
That you may be close to Creon when he's king!
Well, you and your friend Creon, it seems to me,
Will suffer most. If you were not an old man,
You would have paid already for your plot.

Choragos.

390 We cannot see that his words or yours
Have been spoken except in anger, Oedipus,
And of anger we have no need. How can God's will
Be accomplished best? That is what most
            concerns us.

Teiresias.

You are a king. But where argument's concerned
395 I am your man, as much a king as you.
I am not your servant, but Apollo's.
I have no need of Creon to speak for me.

Listen to me. You mock my blindness, do you?
But I say that you, with both your eyes, are blind:
400 You cannot see the wretchedness of your life,
Nor in whose house you live, no, nor with whom.
Who are your father and mother? Can you tell me?
You do not even know the blind wrongs
That you have done them, on earth and in the
            world below.
405 But the double lash of your parents' curse will whip you
Out of this land some day, with only night
Upon your precious eyes.
Your cries then—where will they not be heard?
What fastness of Cithaeron° will not echo them?
410 And that bridal-descant° of yours—you'll know it
            then,
The song they sang when you came here to Thebes
And found your misguided berthing.
All this, and more, that you cannot guess at now,
Will bring you to yourself among your children.

383 🅠 This line furnishes a complex illustration of Sophoclean irony. As he mocks Teiresias, Oedipus tries deliberately to be ironic when he says he is a "simple man, who knows nothing." Explain how this line contains another, unintentional level of dramatic irony.

391 🅠 Choragos speaks for the entire Chorus. Do you agree with the Chorus's reaction to Oedipus here?

409. **Cithaeron** (si·thē′rän): a mountain in Boeotia (bē·ō′shə), where Oedipus as an infant was left to die.
410. **descant** (des′kant′): melody.

415   Be angry, then. Curse Creon. Curse my words.
    I tell you, no man that walks upon the earth
    Shall be rooted out more horribly than you.

Oedipus.
    Am I to bear this from him?—Damnation
    Take you! Out of this place! Out of my sight!

Teiresias.
420   I would not have come at all if you had not asked me.

Oedipus.
    Could I have told that you'd talk nonsense, that
    You'd come here to make a fool of yourself, and of me?

Teiresias.
    A fool? Your parents thought me sane enough.

Oedipus.
    My parents again!—Wait: who were my parents?

Teiresias.
425   This day will give you a father, and break your heart.

Oedipus.
    Your infantile riddles! Your damned abracadabra!

Teiresias.
    You were a great man once at solving riddles.

Oedipus.
    Mock me with that if you like; you will find it true.

Teiresias.
    It was true enough. It brought about your ruin.

Oedipus.
430   But if it saved this town?

Teiresias (*to the* PAGE).   Boy, give me your hand.

Oedipus.
    Yes, boy; lead him away.
                   —While you are here
    We can do nothing. Go; leave us in peace.

Teiresias.
    I will go when I have said what I have to say.
    How can you hurt me? And I tell you again:
435   The man you have been looking for all this time,
    The damned man, the murderer of Laius,
    That man is in Thebes. To your mind he is foreign-born,
    But it will soon be shown that he is a Theban,
    A revelation that will fail to please.
                       A blind man,

427 **?** Explain Teiresias' mocking irony in this line. To what achievement of Oedipus does the prophet refer?

440 Who has his eyes now; a penniless man, who is
    rich now;
And he will go tapping the strange earth with his staff
To the children with whom he lives now he will be
Brother and father—the very same; to her
Who bore him, son and husband—the very same

445 Who came to his father's bed, wet with his father's
    blood.

Enough. Go think that over.
If later you find error in what I have said,
You may say that I have no skill in prophecy.

[*Exit* TEIRESIAS, *led by his* PAGE. OEDIPUS
goes into the palace.]

446 ❓ What gestures might Teiresias make as he says these lines?

═ ODE° 1 ═

Strophe 1

Chorus.

    The Delphic stone of prophecies
450 Remembers ancient regicide
And a still bloody hand.
That killer's hour of flight has come.
He must be stronger than riderless
Coursers of untiring wind,

455 For the son of Zeus armed with his father's thunder
Leaps in lightning after him;
And the Furies° follow him, the sad Furies.

Antistrophe 1

Holy Parnassus'°° peak of snow
Flashes and blinds that secret man,
460 That all shall hunt him down:
Though he may roam the forest shade
Like a bull gone wild from pasture
To rage through glooms of stone.
Doom comes down on him; flight will not avail him;
465 For the world's heart calls him desolate,
And the immortal Furies follow, forever follow.

Strophe 2

But now a wilder thing is heard

Ode: a song chanted by the Chorus. An ode separates one scene from the next.

455 ❓ To whom does the Chorus allude when they mention "the son of Zeus"? (The "Delphic stone" in line 449 and "Holy Parnassus' peak of snow" in line 458 are clues.)

457. **Furies:** avenging spirits.

458. **Parnassus** (pär·nas′əs): the mountain where Apollo's oracle was located.

467 ❓ What does the Chorus mean by a "wilder thing" in this line? Who is the "old man skilled at hearing Fate" who has appeared in the previous scene?

Stratford Festival, Stratford, Ontario Canada; Photo by Don McKague

From the old man skilled at hearing Fate in the
    wingbeat of a bird.
Bewildered as a blown bird, my soul hovers and
    cannot find
470   Foothold in this debate, or any reason or rest of mind.
But no man ever brought—none can bring
Proof of strife between Thebes' royal house,
Labdacus' line, and the son of Polybus;
And never until now has any man brought word
475   Of Laius' dark death staining Oedipus the King.

Antistrophe 2

Divine Zeus and Apollo hold
Perfect intelligence alone of all tales ever told;
And well though this diviner works, he works in
    his own night;
No man can judge that rough unknown or trust in
    second sight,

480   For wisdom changes hands among the wise.
Shall I believe my great lord criminal
At a raging word that a blind old man let fall?
I saw him, when the carrion woman° faced him of
    old,
Prove his heroic mind! These evil words are lies.

483. **carrion woman:** the Sphinx.

484 ❓ Why does the Chorus refuse to believe Teiresias' accusations against Oedipus?

═ Scene 2 ═

Creon.
485   Men of Thebes:
I am told that heavy accusations
Have been brought against me by King Oedipus.

I am not the kind of man to bear this tamely.

If in these present difficulties
490   He holds me accountable for any harm to him
Through anything I have said or done—why, then,
I do not value life in this dishonor.
It is not as though this rumor touched upon
Some private indiscretion. The matter is grave.
495   The fact is that I am being called disloyal
To the State, to my fellow citizens, to my friends.

Choragos.
He may have spoken in anger, not from his mind.

Creon.
But did you not hear him say I was the one
Who seduced the old prophet into lying?

Choragos.
500   The thing was said; I do not know how seriously.

Creon.
But you were watching him! Were his eyes steady?
Did he look like a man in his right mind?

Choragos.   I do not know,
I cannot judge the behavior of great men.
But here is the King himself.

    [*Enter* OEDIPUS.]

Oedipus.   So you dared come back.
505   Why? How brazen of you to come to my house,

486 ❓ What are the accusations to which Creon refers here?

503 ❓ Is the Chorus noncommittal here because they want to play the peacemaker, or are they "passing the buck," in your opinion?

You murderer!
                    Do you think I do not know
That you plotted to kill me, plotted to steal my throne?
Tell me, in God's name: am I a coward, a fool,
That you should dream you could accomplish this?
510   A fool who could not see your slippery game?
A coward, not to fight back when I saw it?
You are the fool, Creon, are you not? hoping
Without support or friends to get a throne?
Thrones may be won or bought: you could do neither.

Creon.
515   Now listen to me. You have talked; let me talk, too.
You cannot judge unless you know the facts.

Oedipus.
You speak well: there is one fact; but I find it hard
To learn from the deadliest enemy I have.

Creon.
That above all I must dispute with you.

Oedipus.
520   That above all I will not hear you deny.

Creon.
If you think there is anything good in being stubborn
Against all reason, then I say you are wrong.

Oedipus.
If you think a man can sin against his own kind
And not be punished for it, I say you are mad.

Creon.
525   I agree. But tell me: what have I done to you?

Oedipus.
You advised me to send for that wizard, did you not?

Creon.
I did. I should do it again.

Oedipus.   Very well. Now tell me:
How long has it been since Laius—

Creon.   What of Laius?

Oedipus.
Since he vanished in that onset by the road?

Creon.
530   It was long ago, a long time.

Oedipus.   And this prophet,
Was he practicing here then?

Creon.   He was; and with honor, as now.

Oedipus.

Did he speak of me at that time?

Creon.   He never did;

At least, not when I was present.

Oedipus.   But . . . the inquiry?

I suppose you held one?

Creon.   We did, but we learned nothing.

Oedipus.

535 Why did the prophet not speak against me then?

Creon.

I do not know; and I am the kind of man

Who holds his tongue when he has no facts to go on.

Oedipus.

There's one fact that you know, and you could tell it.

Creon.

What fact is that? If I know it, you shall have it.

Oedipus.

540 If he were not involved with you, he could not say

That it was I who murdered Laius.

Creon.

If he says that, you are the one that knows it!—

But now it is my turn to question you.

Oedipus.

Put your questions. I am no murderer.

Creon.

545 First, then: You married my sister?

Oedipus.   I married your sister.

Creon.

And you rule the kingdom equally with her?

Oedipus.

Everything that she wants she has from me.

Creon.

And I am the third, equal to both of you?

Oedipus.

That is why I call you a bad friend.

Creon.

550 No. Reason it out, as I have done.

Think of this first: Would any sane man prefer

Power, with all a king's anxieties,

537 **?** What tone of voice might the actor playing Creon use for this line?

To that same power and the grace of sleep?
Certainly not I.

555 I have never longed for the king's power—only his rights.
Would any wise man differ from me in this?
As matters stand, I have my way in everything
With your consent, and no responsibilities.
If I were king, I should be a slave to policy.

560 How could I desire a scepter more
Than what is now mine—untroubled influence?
No, I have not gone mad; I need no honors,
Except those with the perquisites I have now.
I am welcome everywhere; every man salutes me,

565 And those who want your favor seek my ear,
Since I know how to manage what they ask.
Should I exchange this ease for that anxiety?
Besides, no sober mind is treasonable.
I hate anarchy

570 And never would deal with any man who likes it.

Test what I have said. Go to the priestess
At Delphi, ask if I quoted her correctly.
And as for this other thing: if I am found
Guilty of treason with Teiresias,

575 Then sentence me to death! You have my word
It is a sentence I should cast my vote for—
But not without evidence!
                    You do wrong
When you take good men for bad, bad men for good.
A true friend thrown aside—why, life itself

580 Is not more precious!
                    In time you will know this well:
For time, and time alone, will show the just man,
Though scoundrels are discovered in a day.

Choragos.

This is well said, and a prudent man would ponder it.
Judgments too quickly formed are dangerous.

Oedipus.

585 But is he not quick in his duplicity?
And shall I not be quick to parry him?
Would you have me stand still, hold my peace,
      and let
This man win everything, through my inaction?

560 ❓ What do you think of Creon's reasoning in these lines? Is his argument convincing, or is it sophistic—that is, fair-seeming, but logically faulty?

582 ❓ Explain the contrast that Creon draws between just men and scoundrels in these lines.

587 ❓ Whom does Oedipus address in these lines?

Creon.

And you want—what is it, then? To banish me?

Oedipus.

590   No, not exile. It is your death I want,

So that all the world may see what treason means.

Creon.

You will persist, then? You will not believe me?

Oedipus.

How can I believe you?

Creon.   Then you are a fool.

Oedipus.

To save myself?

Creon.   In justice, think of me.

Oedipus.

595   You are evil incarnate.

Creon.   But suppose that you are wrong?

Oedipus.

Still I must rule.

Creon.   But not if you rule badly.

Oedipus.

O city, city!

Creon.   It is my city, too!

Choragos.

Now my lords, be still. I see the Queen,

Jocasta, coming from her palace chambers;

600   And it is time she came, for the sake of you both.

This dreadful quarrel can be resolved through her.

[*Enter* JOCASTA.]

Jocasta.

Poor foolish men, what wicked din is this?

With Thebes sick to death, is it not shameful

That you should rake some private quarrel up?

605   (*to* OEDIPUS) Come into the house.

                          —And you, Creon, go now:

Let us have no more of this tumult over nothing.

Creon.

Nothing? No, sister: what your husband plans for me

Is one of two great evils: exile or death.

Oedipus.

He is right.

596 ❓ Why do you think Oedipus says that he *must* rule? Is it the tyrant in him, or a belief in fate?

Why, woman, I have caught him squarely
610 Plotting against my life.

                Creon.   No! Let me die
Accursed if ever I have wished you harm!

Jocasta.
Ah, believe it, Oedipus!
In the name of the gods, respect this oath of his
For my sake, for the sake of these people here!

Strophe 1

Choragos.
615 Open your mind to her, my lord. Be ruled by her,
    I beg you!

Oedipus.
What would you have me do?

Choragos.
Respect Creon's word. He has never spoken like a fool,
And now he has sworn an oath.

Oedipus.   You know what you ask?

Choragos.   I do.

Oedipus.   Speak on, then.

Choragos.
A friend so sworn should not be baited so,
620 In blind malice, and without final proof.

Oedipus.
You are aware, I hope, that what you say
Means death for me, or exile at the least.

Strophe 2

Choragos.
No, I swear by Helios,° first in Heaven!
    May I die friendless and accursed,
625 The worst of deaths, if ever I meant that!
    It is the withering fields
        That hurt my sick heart:
    Must we bear all these ills,
        And now your bad blood as well?

Oedipus.
630 Then let him go. And let me die, if I must,
Or be driven by him in shame from the land of
    Thebes.

623. **Helios** (hē′lē·äs′): one of the Titans; sun god often confused with Apollo. He was associated with the truth.

It is your unhappiness, and not his talk,
That touches me.
                    As for him—
Wherever he goes, hatred will follow him.

Creon.

635   Ugly in yielding, as you were ugly in rage!
Natures like yours chiefly torment themselves.

Oedipus.

Can you not go? Can you not leave me?

Creon.   I can.

You do not know me; but the city knows me,
And in its eyes I am just, if not in yours.

[*Exit* CREON.]

Antistrophe 1

Choragos.

640   Lady Jocasta, did you not ask the King to go to
        his chambers?

Jocasta.

First tell me what has happened.

Choragos.

There was suspicion without evidence; yet it rankled
As even false charges will.

Jocasta.   On both sides?

Choragos.   On both.

Jocasta.   But what was said?

Choragos.

Oh let it rest, let it be done with!
645   Have we not suffered enough?

Oedipus.

You see to what your decency has brought you:
You have made difficulties where my heart saw none.

Antistrophe 2

Choragos.

Oedipus, it is not once only I have told you—
You must know I should count myself unwise
650   To the point of madness, should I now forsake you—
        You, under whose hand,
           In the storm of another time,

632 **?** Why does Oedipus yield to the Chorus's request not to punish Creon?

New York Public Library/Stratford Festival/Photo by: Don McKague

Our dear land sailed out free.
    But now stand fast at the helm!

Jocasta.

655   In God's name, Oedipus, inform your wife as well:
    Why are you so set in this hard anger?

Oedipus.

    I will tell you, for none of these men deserves
    My confidence as you do. It is Creon's work,
    His treachery, his plotting against me.

Jocasta.

660   Go on, if you can make this clear to me.

Oedipus.

    He charges me with the murder of Laius.

661 ❓ Think carefully: Has Creon
    in fact charged Oedipus
    with the murder of Laius?

Oedipus Rex, Scene 2   **333**

Jocasta.

>Has he some knowledge? Or does he speak from
>>hearsay?

Oedipus.

>He would not commit himself to such a charge,
>But he has brought in that damnable soothsayer

665 >To tell his story.

Jocasta.   Set your mind at rest.

>If it is a question of soothsayers, I tell you
>That you will find no man whose craft gives knowledge
>Of the unknowable.

>>Here is my proof:

>An oracle was reported to Laius once

670 >(I will not say from Phoebus himself, but from
>His appointed ministers, at any rate)
>That his doom would be death at the hands of his
>>own son—
>His son, born of his flesh and of mine!

>Now, you remember the story: Laius was killed

675 >By marauding strangers where three highways meet;
>But his child had not been three days in this world
>Before the King had pierced the baby's ankles
>And left him to die on a lonely mountainside.

>Thus, Apollo never caused that child

680 >To kill his father, and it was not Laius' fate
>To die at the hands of his son, as he had feared.
>This is what prophets and prophecies are worth!
>Have no dread of them.

>>   It is God himself

>Who can show us what he wills, in his own way.

Oedipus.

685 >How strange a shadowy memory crossed my mind,
>Just now while you were speaking; it chilled my heart.

Jocasta.

>What do you mean? What memory do you speak of?

Oedipus.

>If I understand you, Laius was killed
>At a place where three roads meet.

Jocasta.   So it was said;

690 >We have no later story.

Oedipus.   Where did it happen?

Jocasta.

    Phocis,° it is called: at a place where the Theban Way
    Divides into the roads toward Delphi and Daulis.°

Oedipus.

    When?

Jocasta.   We had the news not long before you
    came
    And proved the right to your succession here.

Oedipus.

695   Ah, what net has God been weaving for me?

Jocasta.

    Oedipus! Why does this trouble you?

Oedipus.   Do not ask me yet.
    First, tell me how Laius looked, and tell me
    How old he was.

Jocasta.   He was tall, his hair just touched
    With white, his form was not unlike your own.

Oedipus.

700   I think that I myself may be accursed
    By my own ignorant edict.

Jocasta.   You speak strangely.
    It makes me tremble to look at you, my King.

Oedipus.

    I am not sure that the blind man cannot see.
    But I should know better if you were to tell me—

Jocasta.

705   Anything—though I dread to hear you ask it.

Oedipus.

    Was the King lightly escorted, or did he ride
    With a large company, as a ruler should?

Jocasta.

    There were five men with him in all: one was a herald,
    And a single chariot, which he was driving.

Oedipus.

710   Alas, that makes it plain enough!
                      But who—
    Who told you how it happened?

Jocasta.   A household servant,
    The only one to escape.

Oedipus.   And is he still

691. **Phocis** (fō′sis): country in which Mount Parnassus was located.

692. **Daulis** (dô′lis): in Phocis, east of Delphi.

692 ❓ Try to visualize the place where the "three roads" meet, and then draw a diagram.

695 ❓ What sudden change of tone might Oedipus use in this line?

703 ❓ As Oedipus starts to question Jocasta more carefully, what might he begin to suspect?

A servant of ours?

Jocasta.　　　　　No; for when he came back at last
And found you enthroned in the place of the dead king,

715　He came to me, touched my hand with his, and begged
That I would send him away to the frontier district
Where only the shepherds go—
As far away from the city as I could send him.
I granted his prayer; for although the man was a
　　slave,

720　He had earned more than this favor at my hands.

Oedipus.
Can he be called back quickly?

Jocasta.　　　　　　　　Easily.
But why?

Oedipus.　I have taken too much upon myself
Without inquiry; therefore I wish to consult him.

Jocasta.
Then he shall come.

　　　　　But am I not one also
725　To whom you might confide these fears of yours?

Oedipus.
That is your right; it will not be denied you,
Now least of all; for I have reached a pitch
Of wild foreboding. Is there anyone
To whom I should sooner speak?

730　Polybus° of Corinth is my father.
My mother is a Dorian: Merope.°
I grew up chief among the men of Corinth
Until a strange thing happened—
Not worth my passion, it may be, but strange.

735　At a feast, a drunken man maundering in his cups°
Cries out that I am not my father's son!

I contained myself that night, though I felt anger
And a sinking heart. The next day I visited
My father and mother, and questioned them.
　　They stormed,
740　Calling it all the slanderous rant of a fool;
And this relieved me. Yet the suspicion
Remained always aching in my mind;
I knew there was talk; I could not rest;
And finally, saying nothing to my parents,

720　**?** How did Jocasta behave toward the lone witness to the attack on her husband?

729　**?** How would you describe Oedipus's feelings toward Jocasta?
730. **Polybus** (päl'i·bəs): king of Corinth.
731. **Merope** (mer'ə·pē): The Dorians were descended from Dorus, a son of Apollo.

735. **maundering** (môn'dər·ing) **in his cups:** talking aimlessly while under the influence of wine.

745 I went to the shrine at Delphi.
The god dismissed my question without reply;
He spoke of other things.
                    Some were clear,
Full of wretchedness, dreadful, unbearable:
As, that I should lie with my own mother, breed
750 Children from whom all men would turn their eyes;
And that I should be my father's murderer.

I heard all this, and fled. And from that day
Corinth to me was only in the stars
Descending in that quarter of the sky,
755 As I wandered farther and farther on my way
To a land where I should never see the evil
Sung by the oracle. And I came to this country
Where, so you say, King Laius was killed.

I will tell you all that happened there, my lady.

760 There were three highways
Coming together at a place I passed;
And there a herald came towards me, and a chariot
Drawn by horses, with a man such as you describe

Seated in it. The groom leading the horses
765 Forced me off the road at his lord's command;
But as this charioteer lurched over towards me
I struck him in my rage. The old man saw me
And brought his double goad down upon my head
As I came abreast.
                    He was paid back, and more!
770 Swinging my club in this right hand I knocked him
Out of his car, and he rolled on the ground.
                    I killed him.

I killed them all.
Now if that stranger and Laius were—kin,
Where is a man more miserable than I?
775 More hated by the gods? Citizen and alien alike
Must never shelter me or speak to me—
I must be shunned by all.
                    And I myself
Pronounced this malediction upon myself!

Think of it: I have touched you with these hands,
780 These hands that killed your husband. What defilement!

773 **?** Why do you think Oedipus
hesitates before the word
kin in this line?

New York Public Library/Stratford Festival/Peter Smith & Company

Oedipus Rex, Scene 2   **337**

Am I all evil, then? It must be so,
Since I must flee from Thebes, yet never again
See my own countrymen, my own country,
For fear of joining my mother in marriage
785 And killing Polybus, my father.

Ah,

If I was created so, born to this fate,
Who could deny the savagery of God?

Oh holy majesty of heavenly powers!
May I never see that day! Never!
790 Rather let me vanish from the race of men
Than know the abomination destined me!

Choragos.

We too, my lord, have felt dismay at this.
But there is hope: you have yet to hear the shepherd.

Oedipus.

Indeed, I fear no other hope is left me.

Jocasta.

795 What do you hope from him when he comes?

Oedipus.   This much:
If his account of the murder tallies with yours,
Then I am cleared.

Jocasta.   What was it that I said
Of such importance?

Oedipus.   Why, "marauders," you said,
Killed the King, according to this man's story.
800 If he maintains that still, if there were several,
Clearly the guilt is not mine: I was alone.
But if he says one man, single-handed, did it,
Then the evidence all points to me.

Jocasta.

You may be sure that he said there were several;
805 And can he call back that story now? He cannot.
The whole city heard it as plainly as I.
But suppose he alters some detail of it:
He cannot ever show that Laius' death
Fulfilled the oracle: for Apollo said
810 My child was doomed to kill him; and my child—
Poor baby!—it was my child that died first.

No. From now on, where oracles are concerned,
I would not waste a second thought on any.

785 ❓ Oedipus now suspects that he has unwittingly cursed himself as the true murderer of Laius. However, given the fact that he still calls Polybus of Corinth his father in this line, what dreadful truth does he *not* yet suspect?

803 ❓ Jocasta referred to "marauding strangers" in the plural at line 675, and Oedipus now distinguishes between plural and singular. Where was the issue of plural vs. singular assailants hinted at earlier in the play?

Oedipus.

You may be right.

                    But come: let someone go
815 For the shepherd at once. This matter must be settled.

Jocasta.

I will send for him.
I would not wish to cross you in anything,
And surely not in this.—Let us go in.

817 ❓ What does the word *cross* mean in this line?

[*Exeunt into the palace.*]

ODE 2

Strophe 1

Chorus.

Let me be reverent in the ways of right,
820 Lowly the paths I journey on;
Let all my words and actions keep
The laws of the pure universe
From highest Heaven handed down.
For Heaven is their bright nurse,
825 Those generations of the realms of light;
Ah, never of mortal kind were they begot,
Nor are they slaves of memory, lost in sleep:
Their Father is greater than Time, and ages not.

Antistrophe 1

The tyrant is a child of Pride
830 Who drinks from his great sickening cup
Recklessness and vanity,
Until from his high crest headlong
He plummets to the dust of hope.
That strong man is not strong.
835 But let no fair ambition be denied;
May God protect the wrestler for the State
In government, in comely policy,
Who will fear God, and on His ordinance° wait.

838. **ordinance** (ôrd''n·əns): de-cree or command.

Strophe 2

Haughtiness and the high hand of disdain
840 Tempt and outrage God's holy law;
And any mortal who dares hold

No immortal Power in awe
Will be caught up in a net of pain:
The price for which his levity is sold.
845   Let each man take due earnings, then,
And keep his hands from holy things,
And from blasphemy stand apart—
Else the crackling blast of heaven
Blows on his head, and on his desperate heart;
850   Though fools will honor impious men,
In their cities no tragic poet sings.

Antistrophe 2

Shall we lose faith in Delphi's obscurities,
We who have heard the world's core
Discredited, and the sacred wood
855   Of Zeus at Elis° praised no more?
The deeds and the strange prophecies
Must make a pattern yet to be understood.
Zeus, if indeed you are lord of all,
Throned in light over night and day,
860   Mirror this in your endless mind:
Our masters call the oracle
Words on the wind, and the Delphic vision blind!
Their hearts no longer know Apollo,
And reverence for the gods has died away.

844 **?** What fate does the Chorus predict for the haughty man?

855. **Elis** (ē′lis): city in the Peloponnesus.

856 **?** What does the Chorus insist will happen?

First Thoughts

How did you react to Oedipus in the first scenes of the play? Does he strike you as a proud tyrant, as a sympathetic ruler, or as something in between? Explain your answer.

Identifying Facts

1. What conflict or problem do the people of the city of Thebes face as the play opens?

2. According to Ode 1, which god will inevitably punish the murderer of Laius? What misgiving disturbs the Chorus's confidence in this ode, and how do they deal with this misgiving?

3. What argument does Jocasta use to persuade Oedipus to ignore the soothsayers or oracles? In the course of her argument, what minor detail motivates Oedipus to pursue a new line of investigation?

4. Explain why Oedipus left Corinth. What chance remark caused him to question Polybus and Merope? What was he afraid of?

Interpreting Meanings

1. In line 35, the Priest says that the Thebans know that Oedipus is not "one of the immortal gods." How *do* the Thebans regard Oedipus? What reasons do they have for their opinion of him?

2. When Oedipus questions Creon about the murder of Laius, what **dramatic irony** does the playwright begin to develop?

3. It is significant that the seer, or prophet, Teiresias, is blind. Explain how this is ironic. Also, explain the irony of Oedipus's angry and arrogant response to the prophet.

4. In the course of Ode 1, the Chorus expresses both confident optimism and nervous apprehension. How is the Chorus's indecision a comment on the basic conflict of the play so far? What possible resolutions to the conflict can you predict?

5. What personality trait in Oedipus's character do you think drives him on to insist at lines 814–815 that the shepherd be summoned? If you were Oedipus, would you let well enough alone at this point, or would you insist on probing further to get at the truth?

6. In Ode 2, the Chorus comments harshly on those who defy prophecy. What in the previous scene is the Chorus responding to? What does this say about where the Chorus stands in the play—in other words, whose side is the Chorus on? Explain your answer.

Applying Meanings

Oedipus's hot-tempered reactions to Teiresias and Creon in Scenes 1 and 2 contrast strongly with his sympathy and compassion for the people of Thebes in the Prologue. Sophocles portrays Oedipus as a complex ruler with many conflicting character traits. Do you think a complex personality is likely to prove an advantage or a liability for a leader? Explain your answer.

Critical Writing Response

Analyzing Form. Each scene in *Oedipus Rex* is followed by an ode, performed by the Chorus. Reread the Parodos (the Chorus's entrance scene), Ode 1, and Ode 2. What seems to be the function of each ode in response to the preceding scene? Is the function similar in each ode? Explain your answer in a one- to two-page essay.

OEDIPUS REX
Part 2
Sophocles
translated by

DUDLEY FITTS AND ROBERT FITZGERALD

> As you read, look for the turning point, the moment at which
> Oedipus and others begin to suspect the truth of the situation.
> Watch how the various characters respond to or cover up their
> growing doubts.

SCENE 3

[*Enter* JOCASTA.]

Jocasta.

865 Princes of Thebes, it has occurred to me
To visit the altars of the gods, bearing
These branches as a suppliant, and this incense.
Our King is not himself: his noble soul
Is overwrought with fantasies of dread,

870 Else he would consider
The new prophecies in the light of the old.
He will listen to any voice that speaks disaster,
And my advice goes for nothing.

[*She approaches the altar, right.*]

      To you, then, Apollo,
Lycian° lord, since you are nearest, I turn in prayer.

875 Receive these offerings, and grant us deliverance
From defilement. Our hearts are heavy with fear
When we see our leader distracted, as helpless sailors
Are terrified by the confusion of their helmsman.

[*Enter* MESSENGER.]

Messenger.

Friends, no doubt you can direct me:

880 Where shall I find the house of Oedipus,
Or, better still, where is the King himself?

871 **❓** What does Jocasta mean by "the new prophecies in the light of the old"? Explain what the new prophecies are. What were the old ones? What does Jocasta think of these prophecies?

874. **Lycian** (lish′ē·ən): One of Apollo's names is Lycius, which has been explained variously as "wolf-god," "god of light," and "god of Lycia."

878 **❓** Explain Jocasta's simile here. Who is being compared to whom?

Choragos.
　It is this very place, stranger; he is inside.
　This is his wife and mother of his children.

Messenger.
　I wish her happiness in a happy house,
885　Blest in all the fulfillment of her marriage.

Jocasta.
　I wish as much for you: your courtesy
　Deserves a like good fortune. But now, tell me:
　Why have you come? What have you to say to us?

Messenger.
　Good news, my lady, for your house and your
　　husband.

Jocasta.
890　What news? Who sent you here?

Messenger.　　　　　　　　I am from Corinth.
　The news I bring ought to mean joy for you,
　Though it may be you will find some grief in it.

Jocasta.
　What is it? How can it touch us in both ways?

Messenger.
　The word is that the people of the Isthmus°
895　Intend to call Oedipus to be their king.

Jocasta.
　But old King Polybus—is he not reigning still?

Messenger.
　No. Death holds him in his sepulcher.

Jocasta.
　What are you saying? Polybus is dead?

Messenger.
　If I am not telling the truth, may I die myself.

Jocasta.
900　(*to a* MAIDSERVANT) Go in, go quickly; tell this
　　to your master.

　O riddlers of God's will, where are you now!
　This was the man whom Oedipus, long ago,
　Feared so, fled so, in dread of destroying him—
　But it was another fate by which he died.

[*Enter* OEPIDUS, *center.*]

894. **Isthmus:** Corinth is located on a narrow strip of land connecting the Peloponnesus with eastern Greece.

901 ❓ What tone of voice might Jocasta use here?

Oedipus.

905 Dearest Jocasta, why have you sent for me?

Jocasta.

Listen to what this man says, and then tell me
What has become of the solemn prophecies.

Oedipus.

Who is this man? What is his news for me?

Jocasta.

He has come from Corinth to announce your
father's death!

Oedipus.

910 Is it true, stranger? Tell me in your own words.

Messenger.

I cannot say it more clearly: the King is dead.

Oedipus.

Was it by treason? Or by an attack of illness?

Messenger.

A little thing brings old men to their rest.

Oedipus.

It was sickness, then?

Messenger.   Yes, and his many years.

Oedipus.

915 Ah!
Why should a man respect the Pythian hearth,° or
Give heed to the birds that jangle above his head?
They prophesied that I should kill Polybus,
Kill my own father; but he is dead and buried,
920 And I am here—I never touched him, never,
Unless he died of grief for my departure,
And thus, in a sense, through me. No. Polybus
Has packed the oracles off with him underground.
They are empty words.

Jocasta.   Had I not told you so?

Oedipus.

925 You had; it was my faint heart that betrayed me.

Jocasta.

From now on never think of those things again.

Oedipus.

And yet—must I not fear my mother's bed?

Jocasta.

Why should anyone in this world be afraid,

916. **Pythian** (pith′ē·ən) **hearth:**
Delphi was also known as
Pythia. The priestess of
Apollo was called Pythia.

Since Fate rules us and nothing can be foreseen?
930   A man should live only for the present day.

Have no more fear of sleeping with your mother:
How many men, in dreams, have lain with their
    mothers!
No reasonable man is troubled by such things.

Oedipus.
    That is true; only—
935   If only my mother were not still alive!
    But she is alive. I cannot help my dread.

Jocasta.
    Yet this news of your father's death is wonderful.

Oedipus.
    Wonderful. But I fear the living woman.

Messenger.
    Tell me, who is this woman that you fear?

Oedipus.
940   It is Merope, man; wife of King Polybus.

Messenger.
    Merope? Why should you be afraid of her?

Oedipus.
    An oracle of the gods, a dreadful saying.

Messenger.
    Can you tell me about it or are you sworn to silence?

Oedipus.
    I can tell you, and I will.
945   Apollo said through his prophet that I was the man
Who should marry his own mother, shed his
    father's blood
With his own hands. And so, for all these years
I have kept clear of Corinth, and no harm has come—
Though it would have been sweet to see my
    parents again.

Messenger.
950   And is this the fear that drove you out of Corinth?

Oedipus.
    Would you have me kill my father?

Messenger.   As for that
    You must be reassured by the news I gave you.

Oedipus.
    If you could reassure me, I would reward you.

939 The Corinthian Messenger, who has been listening to the dialogue between Oedipus and Jocasta since line 915, now joins in for a crucial exchange that moves Oedipus several steps further toward the truth. How might the actor playing the messenger behave in the interval between lines 915 and 939?

Messenger.
955   I had that in mind, I will confess: I thought
       I could count on you when you returned to Corinth.

Oedipus.
       No: I will never go near my parents again.

Messenger.
       Ah, son, you still do not know what you are doing—

Oedipus.
       What do you mean? In the name of God tell me!

Messenger.
       —If these are your reasons for not going home.

Oedipus.
960   I tell you, I fear the oracle may come true.

Messenger.
       And guilt may come upon you through your parents?

Oedipus.
       That is the dread that is always in my heart.

Messenger.
       Can you not see that all your fears are groundless?

Oedipus.
       How can you say that? They are my parents, surely?

Messenger.
965   Polybus was not your father.

Oedipus.   Not my father?

Messenger.
       No more your father than the man speaking to you.

Oedipus.
       But you are nothing to me!

Messenger.   Neither was he.

Oedipus.
       Then why did he call me son?

Messenger.   I will tell you:
       Long ago he had you from my hands, as a gift.

Oedipus.
970   Then how could he love me so, if I was not his?

Messenger.
       He had no children, and his heart turned to you.

Oedipus.
       What of you? Did you buy me? Did you find me
           by chance?

967 **?** What do you imagine is Oedipus's emotional state at this point: one of growing relief, confusion, or despair?

Messenger.

I came upon you in the crooked pass of Cithaeron.

Oedipus.

And what were you doing there?

Messenger.   Tending my flocks.

Oedipus.

975   A wandering shepherd?

Messenger.   But your savior, son, that day.

Oedipus.

From what did you save me?

Messenger.   Your ankles should tell you that.

Oedipus.

Ah, stranger, why do you speak of that childhood
        pain?

Messenger.

I cut the bonds that tied your ankles together.

Oedipus.

I have had the mark as long as I can remember.

Messenger.

980   That was why you were given the name you bear.

Oedipus.

God! Was it my father or my mother who did it?
Tell me!

Messenger. I do not know. The man who gave you
        to me
Can tell you better than I.

Oedipus.

It was not you that found me, but another?

Messenger.

985   It was another shepherd gave you to me.

Oedipus.

Who was he? Can you tell me who he was?

Messenger.

I think he was said to be one of Laius' people.

Oedipus.

You mean the Laius who was king here years ago?

Messenger.

Yes; King Laius; and the man was one of his herdsmen.

Oedipus.

990   Is he still alive? Can I see him?

980 ❓ This line refers to the
        derivation of the name
Oedipus from words meaning
"swollen" and "foot." The first
part of Oedipus's name,
however, may also be related
to a Greek word meaning "to
know." Why would this
etymology also be ironically
appropriate?

Messenger.   These men here
     Know best about such things.

Oedipus.   Does anyone here
     Know this shepherd that he is talking about?
     Have you seen him in the fields, or in the town?
     If you have, tell me. It is time things were made plain.

Choragos.

995   I think the man he means is that same shepherd
     You have already asked to see. Jocasta perhaps
     Could tell you something.

Oedipus.   Do you know anything
     About him, Lady? Is he the man we have
          summoned?
     Is that the man this shepherd means?

Jocasta.   Why think of him?

1000   Forget this herdsman. Forget it all.
     This talk is a waste of time.

Oedipus.   How can you say that,
     When the clues to my true birth are in my hands?

Jocasta.
     For God's love, let us have no more questioning!
     Is your life nothing to you?

1005   My own is pain enough for me to bear.

Oedipus.
     You need not worry. Suppose my mother a slave,
     And born of slaves: no baseness can touch you.

Jocasta.
     Listen to me, I beg you: do not do this thing!

Oedipus.
     I will not listen; the truth must be made known.

Jocasta.

1010   Everything that I say is for your own good!

Oedipus.   My own good
     Snaps my patience, then; I want none of it.

Jocasta.
     You are fatally wrong! May you never learn who you are!

Oedipus.
     Go, one of you, and bring the shepherd here.
     Let us leave this woman to brag of her royal name.

Jocasta.

1015   Ah, miserable!

999 **?** Now it is Jocasta's turn to rejoin the dialogue after a long silence since line 937. Between lines 938 and 999, what gestures or facial expressions might Jocasta use to register her reactions to the revelations of the Corinthian Messenger?

1014 **?** What does Oedipus assume about Jocasta in this bitter remark? Why is this assumption ironic?

New York Public Library/Stratford Festival/Peter Smith & Company

That is the only word I have for you now.
That is the only word I can ever have.

[*Exit into the palace.*]

Choragos.
    Why has she left us, Oedipus? Why has she gone
    In such a passion of sorrow? I fear this silence:
1020   Something dreadful may come of it.

Oedipus.   Let it come!
    However base my birth, I must know about it.
    The Queen, like a woman, is perhaps ashamed
    To think of my low origin. But I
    Am a child of Luck; I cannot be dishonored.
1025   Luck is my mother; the passing months, my
        brothers,
    Have seen me rich and poor.
                    If this is so,
    How could I wish that I were someone else?
    How could I not be glad to know my birth?

1025 **?** What metaphors does Oedipus use in these lines for his parentage and family relationships?

ODE 3

Strophe

Chorus.

If ever the coming time were known
1030 To my heart's pondering,
Cithaeron, now by Heaven I see the torches
At the festival of the next full moon,
And see the dance, and hear the choir sing
A grace to your gentle shade:
1035 Mountain where Oedipus was found,
O mountain guard of a noble race!
May the god who heals us lend his aid,
And let that glory come to pass
For our king's cradling-ground.

Antistrophe

1040 Of the nymphs that flower beyond the years,
Who bore you, royal child,
To Pan° of the hills or the timberline Apollo,
Cold in delight where the upland clears,
Or Hermes for whom Cyllene's° heights are piled?
1045 Or flushed as evening cloud,
Great Dionysus, roamer of mountains,
He—was it he who found you there,
And caught you up in his own proud
Arms from the sweet god-ravisher°
1050 Who laughed by the Muses' fountains?°

SCENE 4

Oedipus.

Sirs: though I do not know the man,
I think I see him coming, this shepherd we want:
He is old, like our friend here, and the men
Bringing him seem to be servants of my house.
1055 But you can tell, if you have ever seen him.

[*Enter* SHEPHERD *escorted by servants.*]

Choragos.

I know him, he was Laius' man. You can trust him.

1042. **Pan:** son of Hermes; part goat, part man; associated with woodlands, forests, and mountains. Shepherds loved the music he played on his reed pipes.

1044. **Cyllene** (sə·lē′nē): the mountain where Hermes was born.

1045. What fantasy does the Chorus briefly indulge about Oedipus's infancy in these lines? How does the mood of the ode deepen the irony of the play at this point?

1049. **god-ravisher:** the presumed mother of Oedipus.

1050. **Muses' fountains:** The Muses were born at a spring on the slopes of Mount Olympus.

Oedipus.

Tell me first, you from Corinth: is this the shepherd
We were discussing?

Messenger.   This is the very man.

Oedipus.

(*to* SHEPHERD) Come here. No, look at me. You
must answer

1060   Everything I ask.—You belonged to Laius?

Shepherd.

Yes: born his slave, brought up in his house.

Oedipus.

Tell me: what kind of work did you do for him?

Shepherd.

I was a shepherd of his, most of my life.

Oedipus.

Where mainly did you go for pasturage?

Shepherd.

1065   Sometimes Cithaeron, sometimes the hills nearby.

Oedipus.

Do you remember ever seeing this man out there?

Shepherd.

What would he be doing there? This man?

Oedipus.

This man standing here. Have you ever seen him
before?

Shepherd.

No. At least, not to my recollection.

Messenger.

1070   And that is not strange, my lord. But I'll refresh
His memory: he must remember when we two
Spent three whole seasons together, March to
    September,
On Cithaeron or thereabouts. He had two flocks;
I had one. Each autumn I'd drive mine home

1075   And he would go back with his to Laius' sheepfold.—
Is this not true, just as I have described it?

Shepherd.

True, yes; but it was all so long ago.

Messenger.

Well, then: do you remember, back in those days,
That you gave me a baby boy to bring up as my own?

1059 **❓** How would Oedipus indicate his reaction to a movement or gesture by the Shepherd as he speaks this line? What tone of voice might Oedipus use?

Bust of Bacchus, god of wine and vegetation, c. 131–115. *Bacchus is the Roman version of the Greek god Dionysus.*

Lee Boltin Picture Library

Shepherd.

1080   What if I did? What are you trying to say?

Messenger.

King Oedipus was once that little child.

Shepherd.

Damn you, hold your tongue!

Oedipus.   No more of that!

It is your tongue needs watching, not this man's.

Shepherd.

My King, my Master, what is it I have done wrong?

Oedipus.

1085   You have not answered his question about the boy.

Shepherd.

He does not know . . . He is only making

    trouble . . .

Oedipus.

Come, speak plainly, or it will go hard with you.

Shepherd.

In God's name, do not torture an old man!

Oedipus.

Come here, one of you; bind his arms behind him.

Shepherd.

1090   Unhappy king! What more do you wish to learn?

Oedipus.

Did you give this man the child he speaks of?

Shepherd.   I did.

And I would to God I had died that very day.

Oedipus.

You will die now unless you speak the truth.

Shepherd.

Yet if I speak the truth, I am worse than dead.

Oedipus.

1095   Very well; since you insist upon delaying—

Shepherd.

No! I have told you already that I gave him the boy.

Oedipus.

Where did you get him? From your house? From

    somewhere else?

Shepherd.

Not from mine, no. A man gave him to me.

> 1082 **?** Why do you think the Shepherd bursts in so angrily here?

> 1090 **?** Who else in the play so far has called Oedipus "unhappy" because of his desire to learn more?

Oedipus.

    Is that man here? Do you know whose slave he was?

Shepherd.

1100   For God's love, my King, do not ask me any more!

Oedipus.

    You are a dead man if I have to ask you again.

Shepherd.

    Then . . . Then the child was from the palace of Laius.

Oedipus.

    A slave child? or a child of his own line?

Shepherd.

    Ah, I am on the brink of dreadful speech!

Oedipus.

1105   And I of dreadful hearing. Yet I must hear.

Shepherd.

    If you must be told, then . . .

                      They said it was Laius' child;

    But it is your wife who can tell you about that.

Oedipus.

    My wife!—Did she give it to you?

Shepherd.   My lord, she did.

Oedipus.

    Do you know why?

Shepherd.   I was told to get rid of it.

Oedipus.

1110   An unspeakable mother!

Shepherd.   There had been prophecies . . .

Oedipus.

    Tell me.

Shepherd. It was said that the boy would kill his
    own father.

Oedipus.

    Then why did you give him over to this old man?

Shepherd.

    I pitied the baby, my King,

    And I thought that this man would take him far
    away

1115   To his own country.

                He saved him—but for what a fate!

    For if you are what this man says you are,

    No man living is more wretched than Oedipus.

1110 Who is the "mother"? Explain why you think Oedipus uses the adjective "unspeakable" to describe her here.

Oedipus.

Ah God!

It was true!

　　　All the prophecies!

　　　　　—Now,

1120　O Light, may I look on you for the last time!

I, Oedipus,

Oedipus, damned in his birth, in his marriage
　　damned,

Damned in the blood he shed with his own hand!

[He rushes into the palace.]

1123 **❓** What do you predict
Oedipus will do as he
rushes offstage after this
speech?

═ ODE 4 ═══════

Strophe 1

Chorus.

Alas for the seed of men.

1125   What measure shall I give these generations
That breathe on the void and are void
And exist and do not exist?

Who bears more weight of joy
Than mass of sunlight shifting in images,
1130   Or who shall make his thought stay on
That down time drifts away?

Your splendor is all fallen.

O naked brow of wrath and tears,
O change of Oedipus!
1135   I who saw your days call no man blest—
Your great days like ghosts gone.

Antistrophe 1

That mind was a strong bow.

Deep, how deep you drew it then, hard archer,
At a dim fearful range,
1140   And brought dear glory down!

You overcame the stranger—
The virgin with her hooking lion claws°—
And though death sang, stood like a tower
To make pale Thebes take heart.

1145   Fortress against our sorrow!

True king, giver of laws,
Majestic Oedipus!
No prince in Thebes had ever such renown,
No prince won such grace of power.

Strophe 2

1150   And now of all men ever known
Most pitiful is this man's story:
His fortunes are most changed, his state
Fallen to a low slave's
Ground under bitter fate.

1138 **?** Who is the "archer" addressed by the Chorus in these lines?

1142. **virgin . . . claws:** The Sphinx was depicted as having the paws of a lion.

1155 O Oedipus, most royal one!
The great door that expelled you to the light
Gave at night—ah, gave night to your glory:
As to the father, to the fathering son.

All understood too late.

1160 How could that queen whom Laius won,
The garden that he harrowed at his height,
Be silent when that act was done?

Antistrophe 2

But all eyes fail before time's eye,
All actions come to justice there.
1165 Though never willed, though far down the deep past,
Your bed, your dread sirings,
Are brought to book at last.
Child by Laius doomed to die,
Then doomed to lose that fortunate little death,
1170 Would God you never took breath in this air
That with my wailing lips I take to cry:

For I weep the world's outcast.

I was blind, and now I can tell why:
Asleep, for you had given ease of breath
1175 To Thebes, while the false years went by.

═ EXODOS° ═══════════════

[*Enter, from the palace,* SECOND MESSENGER.]

Second Messenger.
Elders of Thebes, most honored in this land,
What horrors are yours to see and hear, what weight
Of sorrow to be endured, if, true to your birth,
You venerate the line of Labdacus!
1180 I think neither Istros nor Phasis,° those great rivers,
Could purify this place of the corruption
It shelters now, or soon must bring to light—
Evil not done unconsciously, but willed.

The greatest griefs are those we cause ourselves.

Choragos.
1185 Surely, friend, we have grief enough already;
What new sorrow do you mean?

Exodos (eks′ə·dəs): the final scene.

1180. **Istros** (is′trəs) **nor Phasis** (fā′sis)

1183 ❓ What distinction does the Second Messenger draw in this line? How is this contrast important to the action of the play as a whole?

Second Messenger.   The Queen is dead.

Choragos.

Jocasta? Dead? But at whose hand?

Second Messenger.   Her own.
The full horror of what happened you cannot know,
For you did not see it; but I, who did, will tell you

1190   As clearly as I can how she met her death.

When she had left us,
In passionate silence, passing through the court,
She ran to her apartment in the house,
Her hair clutched by the fingers of both hands.

1195   She closed the doors behind her; then, by that bed
Where long ago the fatal son was conceived—
That son who should bring about his father's death—
We heard her call upon Laius, dead so many years,
And heard her wail for the double fruit of her
          marriage,

1200   A husband by her husband, children by her child.

Exactly how she died I do not know:
For Oedipus burst in moaning and would not let us
Keep vigil to the end: it was by him
As he stormed about the room that our eyes
          were caught.

1205   From one to another of us he went, begging a sword,
Cursing the wife who was not his wife, the mother
Whose womb had carried his own children and
          himself.
I do not know: it was none of us aided him,
But surely one of the gods was in control!

1210   For with a dreadful cry
He hurled his weight, as though wrenched out of
          himself,
At the twin doors: the bolts gave, and he rushed in.
And there we saw her hanging, her body swaying
From the cruel cord she had noosed about her neck.

1215   A great sob broke from him, heartbreaking to hear,
As he loosed the rope and lowered her to the
          ground.

I would blot out from my mind what happened next!
For the King ripped from her gown the golden
          brooches

1200 ❓ Explain what the Messenger means by this apparently contradictory line.

That were her ornament, and raised them, and
    plunged them down

1220   Straight into his own eyeballs, crying, "No more,
No more shall you look on the misery about me,
The horrors of my own doing! Too long you
    have known
The faces of those whom I should never have seen,
Too long been blind to those for whom I was
    searching!

1225   From this hour, go in darkness!" And as he spoke,
He struck at his eyes—not once, but many times;
And the blood spattered his beard,
Bursting from his ruined sockets like red hail.

So from the unhappiness of two this evil has sprung,
1230   A curse on the man and woman alike. The old
Happiness of the house of Labdacus
Was happiness enough: where is it today?
It is all wailing and ruin, disgrace, death—all
The misery of mankind that has a name—
1235   And it is wholly and forever theirs.

Choragos.
    Is he in agony still? Is there no rest for him?

Second Messenger.
    He is calling for someone to lead him to the gates
So that all the children of Cadmus may look upon
His father's murderer, his mother's—no,
1240   I cannot say it!
              And then he will leave Thebes,
Self-exiled, in order that the curse
Which he himself pronounced may depart from
    the house.
He is weak, and there is none to lead him,
So terrible is his suffering.
              But you will see:
1245   Look, the doors are opening; in a moment
You will see a thing that would crush a heart
    of stone.

[*The central door is opened;* OEDIPUS, *blinded, is
led in.*]

Choragos.
    Dreadful indeed for men to see.

1246 ❓ Stage direction: Describe the way you visualize the stage action and the entrance of Oedipus here.

Never have my own eyes
Looked on a sight so full of fear.

1250   Oedipus!
What madness came upon you, what daemon°
Leaped on your life with heavier
Punishment than a mortal man can bear?
No: I cannot even
1255   Look at you, poor ruined one.
And I would speak, question, ponder,
If I were able. No.
You make me shudder.

1251. **daemon** (dē′mən): evil spirit.

Oedipus.

God.   God.
1260   Is there a sorrow greater?
Where shall I find harbor in this world?
My voice is hurled far on a dark wind.
What has God done to me?

1259–1263 ❓ How would you read these lines?

Choragos.

Too terrible to think of, or to see.

Strophe 1

Oedipus.

1265   O cloud of night,
Never to be turned away: night coming on,
I cannot tell how: night like a shroud!

My fair winds brought me here
                                    O God. Again
The pain of the spikes where I had sight,
1270   The flooding pain
Of memory, never to be gouged out.

1271 ❓ Do you read Oedipus's act of self-blinding as a punishment, an attempt to "shut out" the truth, or something else?

Choragos.

This is not strange.
You suffer it all twice over, remorse in pain,
Pain in remorse.

Antistrophe 1

Oedipus.

1275   Ah dear friend
Are you faithful even yet, you alone?
Are you still standing near me, will you stay
        here,

Patient, to care for the blind?

                            The blind man!

Yet even blind I know who it is attends me,

1280   By the voice's tone—

Though my new darkness hide the comforter.

Choragos.

Oh fearful act!

What god was it drove you to rake black

Night across your eyes?

Strophe 2

Oedipus.

1285   Apollo. Apollo. Dear

Children, the god was Apollo.

He brought my sick, sick fate upon me.

But the blinding hand was my own!

How could I bear to see

1290   When all my sight was horror everywhere?

Choragos.

Everywhere; that is true.

Oedipus.

And now what is left?

Images? Love? A greeting even,

Sweet to the senses? Is there anything?

1295   Ah, no, friends: lead me away.

Lead me away from Thebes.

                          Lead the great wreck

And hell of Oedipus, whom the gods hate.

Choragos.

Your fate is clear, you are not blind to that.

Would God you had never found it out!

Antistrophe 2

Oedipus.

1300   Death take the man who unbound

My feet on that hillside

And delivered me from death to life! What life?

If only I had died,

This weight of monstrous doom

1305   Could not have dragged me and my darlings down.

Choragos.

I would have wished the same.

1290 ❓ According to Oedipus, who is responsible for his blindness?

Oedipus.

Oh never to have come here
With my father's blood upon me! Never
To have been the man they call his mother's
    husband!

1310   Oh accursed! Oh child of evil,
To have entered that wretched bed—
                      the selfsame one!
More primal than sin itself, this fell to me.

Choragos.

I do not know how I can answer you.
You were better dead than alive and blind.

Oedipus.

1315   Do not counsel me any more. This punishment
That I have laid upon myself is just.
If I had eyes,
I do not know how I could bear the sight
Of my father, when I came to the house of Death,

1320   Or my mother: for I have sinned against them both
So vilely that I could not make my peace
By strangling my own life.
              Or do you think my children,
Born as they were born, would be sweet to my
    eyes?
Ah never, never! Nor this town with its high walls,

1325   Nor the holy images of the gods.
                  For I,
Thrice miserable!—Oedipus, noblest of all the line
Of Cadmus, have condemned myself to enjoy
These things no more, by my own malediction
Expelling that man whom the gods declared

1330   To be a defilement in the house of Laius.
After exposing the rankness of my own guilt,
How could I look men frankly in the eyes?
No, I swear it,
If I could have stifled my hearing at its source,

1335   I would have done it and made all this body
A tight cell of misery, blank to light and sound:
So I should have been safe in a dark agony
Beyond all recollection.
             Ah Cithaeron!
Why did you shelter me? When I was cast upon
    you,

1328 **?** What is the "malediction" to which Oedipus refers in this line?

1334 **?** What gesture might Oedipus make as he speaks these lines?

1340   Why did I not die? Then I should never
          Have shown the world my execrable birth.

          Ah Polybus! Corinth, city that I believed
          The ancient seat of my ancestors: how fair
          I seemed, your child! And all the while this evil
1345   Was cancerous within me!

                              For I am sick
          In my daily life, sick in my origin.

          O three roads, dark ravine, woodland and way
          Where three roads met: you, drinking my father's
             blood,
          My own blood, spilled by my own hand: can you
             remember
1350   The unspeakable things I did there, and the things
          I went on from there to do?

                       O marriage, marriage!
          The act that engendered me, and again the act
          Performed by the son in the same bed—

                         Ah, the net
          Of incest, mingling fathers, brothers, sons,

1355   With brides, wives, mothers: the last evil
That can be known by men: no tongue can say
How evil!
        No. For the love of God, conceal me
Somewhere far from Thebes; or kill me; or hurl
    me
Into the sea, away from men's eyes forever.

1360   Come, lead me. You need not fear to touch me.
Of all men, I alone can bear this guilt.

[*Enter* CREON.]

Choragos.

    We are not the ones to decide; but Creon here
May fitly judge of what you ask. He only
Is left to protect the city in your place.

Oedipus.

1365   Alas, how can I speak to him? What right have I
To beg his courtesy whom I have deeply wronged?

1366 ❓ Explain why Oedipus feels that he can hardly face speaking to Creon.

Creon.

    I have not come to mock you, Oedipus,
Or to reproach you, either.
(*to* ATTENDANTS)   —You, standing there:
If you have lost all respect for man's dignity,
1370   At least respect the flame of Lord Helios:
Do not allow this pollution to show itself
Openly here, an affront to the earth
And Heaven's rain and the light of day. No, take
    him
Into the house as quickly as you can.
1375   For it is proper
That only the close kindred see his grief.

1371 ❓ Do you think that Creon's comment about Oedipus as an example of "pollution" contradicts his earlier statement that he has not come to "mock" or "reproach" Oedipus? Or can you reconcile these two statements? Explain.

Oedipus.

    I pray you in God's name, since your courtesy
Ignores my dark expectation, visiting
With mercy this man of all men most execrable:
1380   Give me what I ask—for your good, not for mine.

Creon.

    And what is it that you would have me do?

Oedipus.

    Drive me out of this country as quickly as may be
To a place where no human voice can ever greet me.

Creon.

1385
I should have done that before now—only,
God's will had not been wholly revealed to me.

Oedipus.
But his command is plain: the parricide°
Must be destroyed. I am that evil man.

Creon.
That is the sense of it, yes; but as things are,
We had best discover clearly what is to be done.

Oedipus.
1390
You would learn more about a man like me?

Creon.
You are ready now to listen to the god.

Oedipus.
I will listen. But it is to you
That I must turn for help. I beg you, hear me.

The woman in there—
1395
Give her whatever funeral you think proper:
She is your sister.
                    —But let me go, Creon!
Let me purge my father's Thebes of the pollution
Of my living here, and go out to the wild hills,
To Cithaeron, that has won such fame with me,
1400
The tomb my mother and father appointed for me,
And let me die there, as they willed I should.
And yet I know
Death will not ever come to me through sickness
Or in any natural way: I have been preserved
1405
For some unthinkable fate. But let that be.

As for my sons, you need not care for them.
They are men, they will find some way to live.
But my poor daughters, who have shared my table,
Who never before have been parted from their
        father—
1410
Take care of them, Creon; do this for me.
And will you let me touch them with my hands
A last time, and let us weep together?
Be kind, my lord,
Great prince, be kind!
                    Could I but touch them,

1386. **parricide** (par′ə·sīd′): one who murders his or her parent.

1415   They would be mine again, as when I had my eyes.

[*Enter* ANTIGONE *and* ISMENE, *attended.*]
    Ah, God!
    Is it my dearest children I hear weeping?
    Has Creon pitied me and sent my daughters?

Creon.
    Yes, Oedipus: I knew that they were dear to you
1420   In the old days, and know you must love them still.

Oedipus.
    May God bless you for this—and be a friendlier
    Guardian to you than he has been to me!

    Children, where are you?
    Come quickly to my hands: they are your
        brother's—
1425   Hands that have brought your father's once clear
        eyes
    To this way of seeing—
                  Ah dearest ones,
    I had neither sight nor knowledge then, your father
    By the woman who was the source of his own life!
    And I weep for you—having no strength to see
        you—,
1430   I weep for you when I think of the bitterness
    That men will visit upon you all your lives.
    What homes, what festivals can you attend
    Without being forced to depart again in tears?
    And when you come to marriageable age,
1435   Where is the man, my daughters, who would dare
    Risk the bane that lies on all my children?
    Is there any evil wanting? Your father killed
    His father; sowed the womb of her who bore him;
    Engendered you at the fount of his own existence!
1440   That is what they will say of you.
                     Then, whom
    Can you ever marry? There are no bridegrooms
        for you,
    And your lives must wither away in sterile
        dreaming.

    O Creon, son of Menoeceus!
    You are the only father my daughters have,

1416 ❓ Antigone and Ismene have no lines. How could you best make use of their presence on the stage?

1440 ❓ Why is Oedipus convinced that his daughters' futures will be all suffering? Why must they pay for his sins?

1445   Since we, their parents, are both of us gone
            forever.
        They are your own blood: you will not let them
        Fall into beggary and loneliness;
        You will keep them from the miseries that are mine!
        Take pity on them; see, they are only children,
1450   Friendless except for you. Promise me this,
        Great Prince, and give me your hand in token of it.

[CREON *clasps his right hand.*]
        Children:
        I could say much, if you could understand me,
        But as it is, I have only this prayer for you:
1455   Live where you can, be as happy as you can—
        Happier, please God, than God has made your
            father!
Creon.
        Enough. You have wept enough. Now go within.
Oedipus.
        I must; but it is hard.
Creon.   Time eases all things.
Oedipus.
        But you must promise—
Creon.   Say what you desire.
Oedipus.
1460   Send me from Thebes!
Creon.   God grant that I may!
Oedipus.
        But since God hates me . . .
Creon.   No, he will grant your wish.
Oedipus.
        You promise?
Creon.   I cannot speak beyond my knowledge.
Oedipus.
        Then lead me in.
Creon.   Come now, and leave your children.
Oedipus.
        No! Do not take them from me!
Creon.   Think no longer
1465   That you are in command here, but rather think

1462 ❓ Explain the irony of this
         line, given all that has
      gone before in the play.

How, when you were, you served your own
    destruction.

1466 ❓ What tone of voice might Creon use for this line?

[*Exeunt into the house all but the* CHORUS; *the* CHORAGOS *chants directly to the audience:*]
Choragos.
    Men of Thebes: look upon Oedipus.

    This is the king who solved the famous riddle
    And towered up, most powerful of men.
1470   No mortal eyes but looked on him with envy,
    Yet in the end ruin swept over him.

    Let every man in mankind's frailty
    Consider his last day; and let none
    Presume on his good fortune until he find
1475   Life, at his death, a memory without pain.

1475 ❓ What moral lesson does the Chorus draw from the action of the play?

A CRITICAL COMMENT

Themes in Oedipus Rex

Many readers have wondered about the theme or message that Sophocles intended to convey in *Oedipus Rex*. Some critics say that the play is nothing more than an ingenious detective story, in which the detective himself turns out to be the hated culprit. Others assume that the play must mask hidden references to Sophocles' own time, so that Oedipus's pride and downfall mirror the figure of the Athenian statesman Pericles, or perhaps the fortunes of Athens itself. While each of these theories may represent part of the truth, many readers have recognized that the implications of the tragedy go far beyond its structure as a detective story or its relevance to real life in the playwright's own time.

One of the main questions of the drama has to do with the degree of guilt to be assigned to the fallen king. In one view, Oedipus must be held fully responsible for his actions. Even if his monumental crimes were committed unintentionally, critics say, Oedipus might have avoided them through greater vigilance. Others insist that the very process of discovery shows the great king's tragic flaw: his own self-confidence and pride as revealed in his arrogant treatment of Teiresias and Creon. The actual Greek title of the play is, in fact, *Oedipus Tyrannos* (the title *Oedipus Rex* is Latin for "Oedipus the King"). The term *tyrant* in ancient Greek refers more to a powerful, self-made ruler than to an evil despot, and Oedipus, as portrayed by Sophocles, does

Themes in *Oedipus Rex*   **367**

not seem to be particularly tyrannical. Still, the flaw of pride in Oedipus cannot be lightly dismissed.

On the other hand, we also see from numerous touches of characterization in the play that Oedipus is basically a sincere ruler, a good man, and a loving father. We are therefore forced to consider even larger questions of divine justice and the individual's place in the world. Are human beings creatures of free will, or are their actions, for good or ill, determined by forces beyond their control? In interpreting this play, it is difficult to say exactly where Sophocles stands on this issue. Certainly we can hear the faith and reverence for the gods reflected in most of the choral odes. On the other hand, Sophocles also carefully removes any direct divine intervention from the action of the play itself. Moreover, he allows Oedipus and Jocasta to serve occasionally as spokespersons for the religious skepticism that was in the air in Athens during the later fifth century B.C. At several points in the play, Oedipus defines himself as "a child of luck," also suggesting a denial of the power of the gods.

In the final moments of the drama, this issue emerges in a new light. Throughout the play, the idea that the individual is a completely self-sufficient creature is undermined by irony and doubt. But in the end, it is Oedipus's self-knowledge, in fulfillment of the injunction to "know thyself," that gives him the strength to face the truth and to go out to meet his fate.

First Thoughts

How did you react to the end of the tragedy? What emotions did you experience?

Identifying Facts

1. What news does the Corinthian Messenger announce? After this announcement, what does the Messenger reveal about Oedipus's true parentage?
2. After Oedipus threatens him with torture, what crucial facts does the Shepherd disclose?
3. According to the Chorus in lines 1150–1154, how have Oedipus's fortunes changed? What comparison do they use for their king in these lines?
4. Summarize the news announced by the Second Messenger. What actions by Oedipus and Jocasta does he describe?

Interpreting Meanings

1. In lines 891–892, the Corinthian Messenger indicates that his news may contain both joy and grief. Explain how this comment turns out to be a classic example of **irony** as the scene progresses.
2. In line 1000, what conclusion has Jocasta evidently reached? What information supplied by the Messenger has enabled her to reach this conclusion?
3. Explain how lines 1104–1105 might be regarded as the **climax**, or turning point, of the play.
4. In lines 1320–1322, Oedipus says that he has sinned so vilely against both his parents that he could not bear to see them even in the house of Death. Yet we know that Oedipus acted in ignorance. By most modern standards, would Oedipus be judged guilty? Judging from his portrayal of Oedipus's reaction to the discovery of his deeds, how do you think Sophocles felt about Oedipus's crimes?
5. In your opinion, does Sophocles succeed in maintaining **suspense** in the play right up to the end? Explain your answer.

Applying Meanings

Consider the closing speech made by the Chorus in lines 1467–1475. They speak sadly of Oedipus's pride and stature and pronounce:

> and let none
> Presume on his good fortune until he find
> Life, at his death, a memory without pain.

What do you think this means? Do you think it is possible to live a life that will be a "memory without pain"?

The Play as a Whole
Interpreting Meanings

1. Do you think that Oedipus is an admirable character, or do you think that he is significantly flawed? If he is admirable, what are some of the positive qualities you admire in him? If he is flawed, what are some of his negative traits?

2. Sophocles' play raises some very difficult questions regarding guilt and responsibility for unintentional crimes. Can you think of any other examples of unforgivable acts committed in ways that make the assignment of responsibility almost impossible?

3. The **plot** of *Oedipus Rex* builds with irresistible force to a climax when Oedipus discovers the truth about his identity and his past actions. Why do you think that the play does not end with the revelation of the truth and Oedipus's self-blinding? What is the dramatic function of the final meeting between Oedipus and Creon?

4. Compare the first song of the Chorus in the Parodos with their lament in Ode 4. How has the attitude of the Chorus changed in the course of the drama? Do you think the Chorus reflects the point of view of the author, the audience, or any of the characters? Explain the reasons for your answer.

5. In Greek drama the most violent actions, such as Jocasta's suicide and Oedipus's self-blinding, customarily occurred offstage and were reported by messengers. How might this treatment of violence differ in a modern version of the play for the stage or the screen? Could one argue that the secondhand reporting of violence might in fact produce a more chilling impression on an audience than an actual presentation of the violent actions themselves?

6. Based on your reading of *Oedipus Rex*, can you understand why the experience of an audience observing the suffering of a character in a **tragedy** may be, in fact, uplifting and exhilarating?

Creative Writing Response

Extending the Myth. At the end of *Oedipus Rex*, several issues are left unresolved. Will Creon agree to exile Oedipus from Thebes? What will happen to Oedipus's children? Will the plague be lifted from the city of Thebes? What special fate is reserved for the hero himself (see lines 1403–1405)? Using either prose narrative or dramatic dialogue, write a short sequel to *Oedipus Rex*. Then compare the plot of your sequel with the plot line of Sophocles' play, *Oedipus at Colonus*.

Critical Writing Response

Analyzing Oedipus as a Tragic Hero. Consider the character of Oedipus in the light of Aristotle's theory of tragedy as this theory is explained on page 371. Do you agree that Oedipus's misfortune is brought about by "some error of judgment or frailty," or do you have a different interpretation? Write a three- to four-paragraph essay in which you analyze Oedipus as a tragic hero. Use evidence from the play to support your ideas.

Language and Vocabulary

Figures of Speech

A **figure of speech** is a word or phrase that describes one thing in terms of another and is not meant to be understood on a literal level. The most common figures of speech are:

1. The **simile**, which compares one thing to another with the use of connective words such as *like* or *as*
2. The **metaphor**, which makes a comparison between two seemingly unlike things without using any connective words
3. **Personification**, in which a nonhuman thing or quality is referred to as if it were human

Sophocles' play abounds with figurative language. Identify the figures of speech in the passages below as **similes**, **metaphors**, or **personification**. Then explain what things are being compared or personified in each passage. Some passages may contain more than one figure of speech.

1. **Priest.** Your own eyes
   Must tell you: Thebes is tossed on a
     murdering sea
   And cannot lift her head from the
     death surge (lines 25–27)
2. **Chorus.** Now I remember, O Healer,
     your power, and wonder:
   Will you send doom like a sudden
     cloud, or weave it
   Like nightfall of the past? (lines 158–
   160)
3. **Chorus.** See, how our lives like birds
     take wing,
   Like sparks that fly when a fire soars,
   To the shore of the god of evening.
   (lines 177–179)

4. **Teiresias.** But the double lash of your
     parents' curse will whip you
   Out of this land some day, with only
     night
   Upon your precious eyes. (lines 405–
   407)
5. **Chorus.** Holy Parnassus' peak of snow
   Flashes and blinds that secret man,
     That all shall hunt him down:
   Though he may roam the forest shade
   Like a bull gone wild from pasture
   To rage through glooms of stone.
   (lines 458–463)
6. **Choragos.** Oedipus, it is not once only
   I have told you—
   You must know I should count myself
     unwise
   To the point of madness, should I now
     forsake you—
   You, under whose hand,
   In the storm of another time,
   Our dear land sailed out free.
   But now stand fast at the helm! (lines
   648–654)
7. **Oedipus.** Ah, what net has God been
     weaving for me? (line 695)
8. **Chorus.** Haughtiness and the high
     hand of disdain
   Tempt and outrage God's holy law.
   (lines 839–840)
9. **Oedipus.** Luck is my mother; the
     passing months, my brothers,
   Have seen me rich and poor. (lines
   1025–1026)
10. **Chorus.** I who saw your days call no
     man blest—
   Your great days like ghosts gone.
   (lines 1135–1136)

11. **Oedipus.** O cloud of night,
    Never to be turned away: night com-
        ing on,
    I cannot tell how: night like a shroud!
    (lines 1265–1267)
12. **Oedipus.** O three roads, dark ravine,
        woodland and way
    Where three roads met: you, drinking
        my father's blood,

My own blood, spilled by my own
    hand: can you remember
The unspeakable things I did there,
    and the things
I went on from there to do? (lines
1347–1351)

ELEMENTS OF LITERATURE

Tragedy and the Tragic Hero

The Greek philosopher Aristotle (384–322 B.C.) pays special attention to tragedy in his treatise *The Poetics*. He explains that tragic dramas should be tightly unified constructions based on a single action and featuring a single protagonist, or hero. Tragedies generally deal with characters who are neither exceptionally virtuous nor exceptionally evil. According to Aristotle, the hero should have "a character between these two extremes—that of a man [or a woman] who is not preeminently good and just, yet whose misfortune is brought about not by vice or depravity, but by some error of judgment or frailty." This weakness is known as *hamartia*, (hä′mär·tē′ə) which is often translated as "tragic flaw." Typically, this flaw takes the form of excessive pride or arrogance, called *hubris* (hyoo′bris).

As a tragedy unfolds, according to Aristotle, the tragic hero goes through one or more reversals of fortune leading up to a final recognition of a truth that has remained hidden from him. In the process he experiences profound suffering. Aristotle supplements his theory by observing that as the members of an audience witness this deep suffering, their emotions of pity and fear lead them to experience a feeling of *catharsis* (kə·thär′sis), or purgation, that leaves them with a new sense of self-awareness and renewal. Paradoxically, then, the experience of watching a tragedy and being purged of upsetting emotions brings a kind of pleasure to the spectator.

In his analysis of tragedy in *The Poetics*, Aristotle cites Sophocles' play *Oedipus Rex* several times as a supreme example of tragic drama. Were you moved to pity and fear by this tale of Oedipus's suffering? Did you also feel a final sense of renewal through the experience?

ROMAN LITERATURE

After the death of Alexander the Great in 323 B.C., the center of power in the Mediterranean world gradually shifted westward to Rome. With this shift, the legacy of Greek civilization also passed into Roman hands. When the Romans emerged as the undisputed masters of a vast empire, they began to produce literary and artistic works that could rival those of their Greek teachers.

The Founding of Rome

The Romans' own ideas about their origins appear in legends about the founding of the city. One such legend was the basis for the *Aeneid* (ē·nē′id), the national epic of Rome written by the poet Virgil (vur′jəl) (70–19 B.C.). According to the epic, when the Greeks sacked Troy, the hero Aeneas fled from the flaming ruins of the city, carrying his aged father on his back and leading his young son by the hand. Together with his followers, Aeneas established a colony of the Trojan people on Italian soil (see page 380).

In reality, the founding of Rome was less dramatic. The city of Rome began in the year 753 B.C. as an agricultural settlement on the east bank of the river Tiber in the region known as Latium.

In the late sixth century B.C., the Romans set up a republican government, that is, a government in which voters elect representatives to make political decisions for them. This republican form of government lasted nearly five centuries and was looked to as a model by the framers of the American Constitution in the eighteenth century.

The Romans were a practical people. They valued order, thrift, ambition, and loyalty. Three Latin words sum up traditional Roman values: *pietas* (pē′ā·täs), or religious observance; *gravitas* (grav′i·täs′), or seriousness of conduct and purpose; and *fides* (fē′dās), or patriotism and loyalty.

> ❝ One of the great strengths of their empire was their willingness . . . to borrow and to adapt freely from others whatever they found useful. This made possible the transmission of religions, ideas, and ideals from older cultures, and it helped them construct . . . a respectable literature, an efficient military machine, a formidable bureaucracy, and the world's greatest legal system. ❞
>
> —Frank C. Bourne

THE FORUM, GIUSEPPE BECCHETTI
(1724–1794). *Watercolor.*

The Republic and Roman Expansion

By 270 B.C., all Italy south of the river Rubicon was in Roman hands. During the centuries that followed, the Romans conquered Spain and waged three costly and lengthy conflicts,

The Romans steadily expanded their territory through military conquest, first in Italy and then overseas in Spain, North Africa, and Greece.

known as the **Punic** (pyoo′nik) **Wars**, with their rival city Carthage, situated across the Mediterranean in North Africa (see the map on page 381). During these wars, a daring attack by the Carthaginian general Hannibal, who led a troop of African elephants across Spain and the Alps, nearly brought the terrified Romans to their knees. In 146 B.C., however, the Romans finally prevailed and reduced Carthage to ruins. In the same year, the Romans assured their conquest of Greece with a decisive victory over the city of Corinth.

Julius Caesar and the Breakdown of the Republic

As Roman armies pushed farther from home, full-time professional troops replaced citizen soldiers. These men were loyal primarily to their personal commander, rather than to the state. Far from home, an army commander could make major decisions entirely on his own and could acquire enormous personal wealth. By far the most successful of these army commanders was **Julius Caesar** (102–44 B.C.).

> **❝ *Veni, vidi, vici* — I came, I saw, I conquered. ❞**
>
> —*Julius Caesar*

ASSASSINATION OF CAESAR, H. F. FUGER.

Photo Nimatallah/Art Resource, New York

In a power struggle for the control of Rome, Caesar was the victor in 48 B.C. He became dictator for life—but he did not grow old in office. On March 15 (the "Ides of March" in the Roman calendar) in 44 B.C., a conspiracy of senators who disliked Caesar's reforms and feared his power assassinated him in the senate house. The assassins, however, had underestimated Caesar's great popularity with the people, and angry crowds forced the leaders of the conspiracy, Brutus and Cassius, to flee from Rome. Two years later, in 42 B.C., the conspirators lost a decisive battle to Mark Antony and **Octavian**, Caesar's great-nephew, as well as his adopted son and heir. The victors, however, soon became enemies, and more years of civil war ensued. Antony withdrew to the East, where he joined forces with Queen Cleopatra of Egypt. Octavian defeated them at the battle of Actium in 31 B.C. Antony and Cleopatra committed suicide, leaving Octavian, at the age of thirty-two, the undisputed leader of the Roman world.

Early Latin Literature

Early Roman writings were highly dependent in style and content on Greek literary models. But by the middle of the third century B.C., the Romans accepted the challenge of producing a national literature. Roman literary genius first

Roman coins, c. 60–44 B.C.
These coins depict figures such as Julius Caesar, Venus, Mark Antony, an elephant, and trophies.

> Roman literature flowered first in the genres of comedy and oratory, and then in lyric and philosophical poetry.

flourished in drama, specifically witty **comedies** about human follies and misadventures. The popular playwright **Plautus** (plôt′əs) (c. 250–184 B.C.) established the outlines of Roman comedy in his raucous farces. His successor **Terence** (c. 190–c. 159 B.C.), a freed black slave from North Africa, produced polished comedies that appealed to the sophisticated urban elite.

A second literary genre in which the Romans excelled was **oratory**, or speech. From the earliest days, legal disputes and political debates were intense and required a logical and sophisticated speaking style. It was natural, then, for the

Bust of Augustus surrounded by the coins of his reign (63 B.C.– A.D. 14). *These coins depict the emperor's zodiac sign, his grandsons, and the Roman conquest of Egypt.*

Lee Boltin Picture Library

Romans to adapt Greek rhetorical styles and practices to their own needs. **Cicero** (sis′ə·rō) (106–43 B.C.), an orator of the late Roman republic, was a master of rhetoric as well as the author of distinguished philosophical essays.

Poetry was also a favorite literary form in the last years of the Republic. Many Roman poets, like **Lucretius** (lŏŏ· krē′shəs) (c. 96–55 B.C.), wrote philosophical poems, while **Catullus** (kə·tul′əs) (c. 84–54 B.C.) wrote intensely personal lyric verse (see page 409).

Roman Religion and Philosophy

The earliest Roman gods and goddesses were local deities associated with the earth, the rain, the harvest, and other phenomena related to farming. As the modest village of Rome expanded its boundaries and incorporated new territories and larger populations, these rural deities rose in status and became organized into a state cult. This "official" religion revolved around major gods such as Jupiter, the principal god of heaven, and Mars, the god of war. The Roman pantheon gradually assimilated many of the Greek gods and goddesses, changing their names but keeping their essential attributes (see the chart on page 217).

After about 150 B.C., various philosophical schools competed with religious movements in the search for ways to live in the world. The **Epicureans** (ep′i·kyŏŏ′rē·ənz), for example, held that the object of life was to seek pleasure, avoid pain, and value true friendship. The **Stoics** (stō′iks) disagreed, arguing that the goal of the wise individual was to seek tranquility through moderation in all things.

Augustus and the Early Empire

After he had defeated Antony and Cleopatra in 31 B.C., Julius Caesar's adopted son and heir Octavian took control of the Roman Empire. Octavian carefully maintained the forms of republican rule, but he steadily directed all power into his own hands. The Roman Republic formally became an empire in 27 B.C., when Octavian was given the name *Augustus* (meaning "of good omen") and the title *imperator* ("emperor"). Augustus spent much of his vast wealth rebuilding the city of Rome. In a popular phrase, he "found Rome brick, and left it marble." During his long reign (27 B.C.–A.D. 14) peace returned at last to the Roman world. Roman propaganda of the age celebrated Augustus as the heroic restorer of a Golden Age, and even during his lifetime cults sprang up dedicated to his worship as a god.

The reign of Augustus marked the transition from republic to empire in Rome.

During the **Age of Augustus**, Rome essentially became a *monarchy*, meaning that the emperor ruled for life and chose his successor, usually from his own family. The cruelty and incompetence of Augustus' successors—Tiberius, Caligula, Claudius, and Nero—were amply detailed by Roman historians. One outstanding example is the account of Nero's behavior during the great fire of Rome in A.D. 64 by Cornelius **Tacitus** (tas′i·təs), a historian who revealed ironic and sometimes extreme disgust for imperial rule (see page 428).

By contrast with Augustus' immediate successors, a line of capable rulers upheld order and prosperity throughout the empire in the second century A.D. At the start of this period, the Roman Empire reached its greatest geographical extent, stretching from Spain and Britain in the west to the borders of Persia in the east.

❝ When that the poor have cried, Caesar hath wept; /
Ambition should be made of sterner stuff: /
Yet Brutus says he was ambitious; /
And Brutus is an honorable man. ❞

—*from* Julius Caesar,
William Shakespeare

Scala/Art Resource, New York

The Roman Forum today.

Latin Literature of the Empire

After he consolidated his power in the late first century B.C., Augustus gathered around his court the most gifted writers to celebrate the achievements of their age. Chief among them was the poet **Virgil**. His epic, the *Aeneid*, depicts the story of Aeneas's legendary founding of Rome. Virgil deliberately wove the emperor Augustus into the epic by linking him through family lines to Aeneas (see page 380). In this way, Virgil gave Rome a national epic that connected history to contemporary life. Other writers who enjoyed the patronage of Augustus were the historian **Livy** (59 B.C.–A.D. 17), who devoted forty years of his life to writing a massive chronicle of events from the founding of Rome to his own times, and the poets **Horace** (65–8 B.C.) and **Ovid** (43 B.C.–A.D. 17) (see pages 414 and 420).

The Later Empire: Rome's Decline and Fall

During the late second and third centuries A.D., the Roman Empire began its slow decay. Poor supervision of the empire resulted in corruption and inefficiency. The military began to dominate the process of finding new rulers.

In the late third century A.D., the emperor Diocletian (ruled 284–305) tried to solve the problem of governing the enormous Roman Empire by dividing it into two administrative units. Rome remained the capital of the western region, while the eastern part was ruled from Byzantium. In the fourth century, Byzantium became Constantinople (modern Istanbul in Turkey) in honor of the emperor Constantine (ruled 306–337). This ruler's conversion to Christianity and his efforts to install the Christian religion throughout the empire had far-reaching effects on the history of medieval Europe. Latin became the language of the Western church and remained the principal language of rulers, scholars, scientists, and the clergy throughout the Middle Ages.

During the later fourth and fifth centuries, a weakened Rome became increasingly vulnerable to the invasions of tribes such as the Germans, the Visigoths, and the Huns. The date usually given for the fall of Rome is A.D. 476, when it was overrun by the forces of the German chief, Oadacer. The eastern empire continued to exist until 1453, when the Ottoman Turks besieged and conquered Constantinople.

> **❝** At home all was tranquil, and there were magistrates with the same titles; there was a younger generation, sprung up since the victory of Actium, and even many of the older men had been born during the civil wars. How few were left who had seen the republic! **❞**
>
> *—Tacitus*

Virgil
70–19 B.C.

Alinari/Art Resource, New York

Publius Vergilius Maro, known as Virgil (vur′jəl), lived most of his life under the shadow of political turmoil. During his youth and early adult years, various political factions struggled for control of Rome in a series of bloody civil wars. Only when Virgil was nearly forty did Julius Caesar's great-nephew Octavian finally restore order by becoming Rome's sole ruler. The reign of Octavian, who used the honorary title *Augustus* (meaning "revered one"), ushered in one of the longest eras of peace and order in the history of Rome. It was during this time that Virgil composed his epic history of the founding of Rome.

Born near the northern town of Mantua, Virgil had deep roots in the Italian countryside. His father was a farmer who found the means to provide Virgil with a good education. This was the first opportunity for the shy young Virgil to experience the sophisticated life of the city. In Rome, like youths of nobler birth, Virgil studied widely in Greek law, philosophy, and literature. He tried life in the court system but found it too nerve-racking. With the outbreak of another war, Virgil retired to his country home. There he began to write pastoral poetry, or poetry that idealizes rural life.

During the war, the land owned by Virgil's family was confiscated. It was returned later through the influence of Octavian's minister of propaganda, who had taken an interest in Virgil's work. With the publication of the pastoral *Eclogues*, Virgil's reputation was fully established, and he turned away from the pastoral form to write the epic story of Aeneas, called the *Aeneid.* He worked slowly and methodically on the *Aeneid* during the last ten years of his life. In a letter, he complained that the project was driving him "almost out of his mind." When the poem was nearly complete, Virgil became ill during a voyage to Greece. With his dying breath he begged his friends to burn the manuscript, for he was not satisfied with it. Fortunately, the emperor Augustus, who recognized the value of Virgil's poem both as literature and as favorable propaganda for his own rule, refused to comply with the poet's last wish and preserved the *Aeneid* for future generations.

The Aeneid

At an early point in his career, Virgil resolved to devote his poetic powers to composing a great national epic of Rome that would put recent Roman achievements on a par with those of the Greeks. In writing a long epic about the wanderings of a refugee from Troy, Virgil consciously imitated Homer (see page 224). The first six books of the *Aeneid* contain many episodes and scenes inspired by Homer's *Odyssey*, while the last six books are roughly modeled on scenes from the *Iliad*. On one level, the story of Aeneas is not so different from that of Odysseus, who, returning from the Trojan wars, traveled far and met with much adventure.

The Story of Aeneas

Aeneas's travels begin when he goes into exile after the fall and burning of Troy. The ghost of his dead wife, Creusa, has told him to sail to Italy, where he will found an empire. Over the following six years, Aeneas travels by sea, often blown off course. At one point he lands in Carthage, where he meets Queen Dido. They fall in love and plan to marry, but the gods push Aeneas on towards Italy. As he sails from Carthage, Dido curses him and dramatically commits suicide out of grief at his departure. In Cumae, Aeneas consults the priestess Sibyl who takes him to the underworld, where he meets the ghost of his father, Anchises. There Aeneas receives a fuller prophecy of the founding of Rome. He sees a long line of Roman leaders who will descend from him. The line culminates with Augustus, Virgil's own patron. The concluding books of the *Aeneid* describe Aeneas's arrival in Italy and the conquests and battles he undergoes in order to establish a settlement for his people and to begin the Roman culture.

A New Kind of Epic Hero

Virgil, being thoroughly Roman, could not help but transform everything he borrowed from his Greek epic model. Most importantly, he refashioned the characterization of the Homeric heroes, adjusting them to fit a concept of the ideal Roman character. It is significant, for example, that the first time Virgil presents his hero in Book 1, Aeneas is weeping in frustration and envying the dead who fell at Troy. Virgil's Aeneas is no machine-like, larger-than-life warrior like Homer's Achilles; he is complex and enigmatic. He is courageous and valiant,

The Voyages of Aeneas

ADRIATIC SEA

Corsica
Trojan Camp
LATIUM
Caieta
Cumae
TYRRHENIAN SEA
ITALY
Sardinia
Temple of Minerva
Buthrotum
AEGEAN SEA
GREECE
IONIAN SEA
Actium
Charybdis
Eryx
Ithaca
Drepanum
Sicily
Scylla
Strophades
Delos
Carthage
Cyclopes' Harbor
Syracuse
Aenos
Troy
Pergamea
AFRICA
N
MEDITERRANEAN SEA
Mt. Ida
Crete

but also deeply sensitive and often divided by the conflict between duty and passion. The *Aeneid* marks the passing of an older heroic ideal and its replacement with a more complex hero sharply constricted by adverse fate and human limitations. Virgil repeatedly stresses that Aeneas's greatness involves his ability to sacrifice his own will for the public good. Aeneas achieves great things, but he is also acutely aware that no achievement is possible without pain and loss.

Virgil's Influence

Virgil is a classical writer who has had a great influence on Western literature not only because of the quality of his work, but also because of the time in which he lived and the values he admired. The Age of Augustus, which the poet celebrated, was one of the high points of Roman civilization. Virgil created his epic of Rome shortly before the birth of Christ and the founding of the Christian religion, whose history would be affected by the Roman Empire for the next four centuries. One reason for Virgil's remarkable impact on later literature was his appeal to Christian authors and educators during the early centuries and later in the Middle Ages. Christianity condemned many pagan authors as unsuitable reading, but the moral virtues of duty, moderation, and piety that Virgil emphasized made him acceptable to Christians, and his poems were used as school texts. Literary critics eventually recognized Virgil's poetry as the fullest development of classical epic and pastoral poetry. The *Aeneid* became a model that inspired the works of Dante Alighieri (see page 741), Edmund Spenser, and John Milton, among others.

Reader's Guide

from the AENEID
from Book 2, The Fall of Troy

Background

Like Homer before him, Virgil chose to begin his long tale not at the beginning, but at a point in the thick of the story: *in medias res,* literally "in the middle of things." Book 1 opens with Aeneas's shipwreck at Carthage on the shores of North Africa and with his fateful encounter with the tragic queen Dido. Books 2 and 3 provide an extended flashback in which Aeneas recounts his earlier suffering and adventures, just as Odysseus does in Books 9-12 of the *Odyssey.* (Odysseus is called by his Roman name, Ulysses, in the *Aeneid.*)

At the start of Book 2, a great banquet is in progress, at which Dido asks Aeneas to describe his experiences during the fall of Troy. The banquet hall at Carthage is hushed as Aeneas summons the inner strength to recount in this lengthy flashback the "unspeakable" suffering of his people during the seige of the Greeks. Aeneas will speak firsthand of the infamous Trojan horse, the death of King Priam, and his encounters with Helen of Troy, his mother (the goddess Venus), and the ghost of his wife, Creusa.

Writer's Response

Do you think the lives of great leaders show a mixture of triumph and tragedy, achievements and setbacks? Think of one or two great leaders, either living or dead, whom you admire. Freewrite on the theme of triumph and tragedy in the lives of these leaders.

Literary Focus

Conflict is a struggle or clash between opposing characters, forces, or emotions. In an **external conflict**, a character struggles against some outside force: another character, society as a whole, or some natural force. For example, during much of Book 2, Aeneas must fight the invading Greeks. An **internal conflict**, on the other hand, is a struggle between opposing needs, desires, or emotions within a single character. In Book 2, Virgil depicts Aeneas as suffering from internal conflicts at several points in the narrative. One example is his desire to destroy Helen despite Venus's warning to him.

from the AENEID
from Book 2: The Fall of Troy
Virgil
translated by
ROBERT FITZGERALD

As you read, note how Virgil uses many of the elements of the Homeric epic, such as elaborate similes, epithets—or repeated, concise descriptions—and dramatic speeches.

CHARACTERS IN THE *AENEID*

Aeneas (i·nē′əs): ancestor of the Roman rulers; son of the goddess Venus and Anchises, the king of Dardanus.

Anchises (an·kī′sēz′): father of Aeneas; king of Dardanus; ally of Priam—the king of Troy.

Ascanius (as·kā′nē·əs): son of Aeneas and Creusa, also called Iulus.

Creusa (krē·yōō′sə): Priam's daughter; wife of Aeneas; first to tell him to journey to Italy.

Dido (dī′dō): queen of Carthage; lover of Aeneas who kills herself when he leaves her for Italy.

The Sibyl (sib′əl): the priestess of Apollo who leads Aeneas through the underworld.

"Knowing their strength broken in warfare, turned
Back by the fates, and years—so many years—
Already slipped away, the Danaan° captains
By the divine handicraft of Pallas° built
A horse of timber, tall as a hill,
And sheathed its ribs with planking of cut pine.
This they gave out to be an offering
For a safe return by sea, and the word went round.

3. **Danaan** (dān′ə·ən): a name for the Greeks.

4. **Pallas** (pal′əs): a name for the goddess Athena, here called Minerva.

But on the sly they shut inside a company
10 Chosen from their picked soldiery by lot,
Crowding the vaulted caverns in the dark—
The horse's belly—with men fully armed.
Offshore there's a long island, Tenedos,°
Famous and rich while Priam's kingdom lasted,
15 A treacherous anchorage now, and nothing more.
They crossed to this and hid their ships behind it
On the bare shore beyond. We thought they'd gone,
Sailing home to Mycenae° before the wind,
So Teucer's town° is freed of her long anguish,
20 Gates thrown wide! And out we go in joy
To see the Dorian° campsites, all deserted,
The beach they left behind. Here the Dolopians°
Pitched their tents, here cruel Achilles lodged,
There lay the ships, and there, formed up in ranks,
25 They came inland to fight us. Of our men
One group stood marveling, gaping up to see
The dire gift of the cold unbedded goddess,°
The sheer mass of the horse.
                                        Thymoetes° shouts
It should be hauled inside the walls and moored
30 High on the citadel—whether by treason
Or just because Troy's fate went that way now.
Capys° opposed him; so did the wiser heads:
'Into the sea with it,' they said, 'or burn it,
Build up a bonfire under it,
35 This trick of the Greeks, a gift no one can trust,
Or cut it open, search the hollow belly!'

Contrary notions pulled the crowd apart.
Next thing we knew, in front of everyone,
Laocoon with a great company
40 Came furiously running from the Height,
And still far off cried out: 'O my poor people,
Men of Troy, what madness has come over you?
Can you believe the enemy truly gone?
A gift from the Danaans, and no ruse?
45 Is that Ulysses'° way, as you have known him?
Achaeans° must be hiding in this timber,
Or it was built to butt against our walls,
Peer over them into our houses, pelt
The city from the sky. Some crookedness

13. **Tenedos** (ten'ə·däs): an island sacred to Apollo.

18. **Mycenae** (mī·sē'nē): capital of the kingdom ruled by Agamemnon.
19. **Teucer's town:** Teucer (tū'sər) was a former king of Troy.
21. **Dorian** (dôr'ē·ən): one of the peoples of Greece.
22. **Dolopians** (dôl·ō'pē·ənz): people from Thessaly.

27. **cold . . . goddess:** Minerva.

28. **Thymoetes** (thī·mō'tēz)

32. **Capys** (ka'pəs): Aeneas's comrade.

45. **Ulysses** (yōo·lis'ēz): the Roman's name for the Greek hero Odysseus.
46. **Achaeans** (ə·kē'ənz): a name for the Greeks.

50 Is in this thing. Have no faith in the horse!
Whatever it is, even when Greeks bring gifts
I fear them, gifts and all.'
                              He broke off then
And rifled his big spear with all his might
Against the horse's flank, the curve of belly.
55 It stuck there trembling, and the rounded hull
Reverberated groaning at the blow.
If the gods' will had not been sinister,
If our own minds had not been crazed,
He would have made us foul that Argive° den
60 With bloody steel, and Troy would stand today—
O citadel of Priam, towering still!
But now look: hillmen, shepherds of Dardania,°
Raising a shout, dragged in before the king
An unknown fellow° with hands tied behind—
65 This all as he himself had planned,
Volunteering, letting them come across him,
So he could open Troy to the Achaeans.

59. **Argive** (är'gīv): a name for the Greeks.

62. **Dardania** (där·dā'nē·ə): Troy. The founder of the city was Dardanus.
64. **unknown fellow:** Sinon.

THE PROCESSION OF THE TROJAN HORSE INTO TROY, GIOVANNI BATTISTA TIEPOLO.

Sure of himself this man was, braced for it
Either way, to work his trick or die.
70 From every quarter Trojans run to see him,
Ring the prisoner round, and make a game
Of jeering at him. Be instructed now
In Greek deceptive arts: one barefaced deed
Can tell you of them all.

*The spy Sinon puts on a convincing performance to
persuade the Trojans that he has escaped from the
Greeks after being betrayed and condemned to
death. Having gained the Trojans' confidence, he
easily makes them believe that the Greeks have
abandoned the siege of the city, leaving the strange
wooden horse behind to appease the angry gods.*

75 And now another sign, more fearful still,
Broke on our blind miserable people,
Filling us all with dread. Laocoon,
Acting as Neptune's priest that day by lot,
Was on the point of putting to the knife
80 A massive bull before the appointed altar,
When ah—look there!
From Tenedos, on the calm sea, twin snakes—
I shiver to recall it—endlessly
Coiling, uncoiling, swam abreast for shore,
85 Their underbellies showing as their crests
Reared red as blood above the swell; behind
They glided with great undulating backs.
Now came the sound of thrashed seawater foaming;
Now they were on dry land, and we could see
90 Their burning eyes, fiery and suffused with blood,
Their tongues a-flicker out of hissing maws.
We scattered, pale with fright. But straight ahead
They slid until they reached Laocoon.
Each snake enveloped one of his two boys,
95 Twining about and feeding on the body.
Next they ensnared the man as he ran up
With weapons: coils like cables looped and bound him
Twice round the middle; twice about his throat
They whipped their back-scales, and their heads
    towered,
100 While with both hands he fought to break the knots,

Laocoon and his two sons battle the twin snakes.
❓ *How do the snakes serve as an omen to the Trojans?*

Photo Nimatallah/Art Resource, New York

Drenched in slime, his headbands black with venom,
Sending to heaven his appalling cries
Like a slashed bull escaping from an altar,
The fumbled axe shrugged off. The pair of snakes
105 Now flowed away and made for the highest shrines,
The citadel of pitiless Minerva,
Where coiling they took cover at her feet
Under the rondure° of her shield. New terrors
Ran in the shaken crowd: the word went round
110 Laocoon had paid, and rightfully,
For profanation of the sacred hulk
With his offending spear hurled at its flank.
'The offering must be hauled to its true home,'
They clamored. 'Votive prayers to the goddess
115 Must be said there!'
                    So we breached the walls
And laid the city open. Everyone

108. **rondure** (rän′dyo͞or′): circle.

Pitched in to get the figure underpinned
With rollers, hempen lines around the neck.
Deadly, pregnant with enemies, the horse
120 Crawled upward to the breach. And boys and girls
Sang hymns around the towrope as for joy
They touched it. Rolling on, it cast a shadow
Over the city's heart. O Fatherland,
O Ilium,° home of gods! Defensive wall
125 Renowned in war for Dardanus's people!
There on the very threshold of the breach
It jarred to a halt four times, four times the arms
In the belly thrown together made a sound—
Yet on we strove unmindful, deaf and blind,
130 To place the monster on our blessed height.
Then, even then, Cassandra's lips unsealed
The doom to come: lips by a god's command
Never believed or heeded by the Trojans.
So pitiably we, for whom that day
135 Would be the last, made all our temples green
With leafy festal boughs throughout the city.

As heaven turned, Night from the Ocean stream
Came on, profound in gloom on earth and sky
And Myrmidons° in hiding. In their homes
140 The Teucrians lay silent, wearied out,
And sleep enfolded them. The Argive fleet,
Drawn up in line abreast, left Tenedos
Through the aloof moon's friendly stillnesses
And made for the familiar shore. Flame signals
145 Shone from the command ship. Sinon, favored
By what the gods unjustly had decreed,
Stole out to tap the pine walls and set free
The Danaans in the belly. Opened wide,
The horse emitted men; gladly they dropped
150 Out of the cavern, captains first, Thessandrus,
Sthenelus and the man of iron, Ulysses;
Hand over hand upon the rope, Acamas, Thoas,
Neoptolemus and Prince Machaon,°
Menelaus and then the master builder,
155 Epeos,° who designed the horse decoy.
Into the darkened city, buried deep
In sleep and wine, they made their way,
Cut the few sentries down,

124. **Ilium** (il'ē·əm): another name for Troy.

139. **Myrmidons** (mʉr'mə·dänz'): followers of Achilles.

150–153. **Thessandrus** (thə·san'drəs); **Sthenelus** (sthen'ə·ləs); **Acamas** (ak'ə·məs); **Thoas** (thō'əs); **Machaon** (ma·kā'on)

155. **Epeos** (e·pē'əs).

Wall carving of a Roman ship and its warriors.

Let in their fellow soldiers at the gate,
160 And joined their combat companies as planned.

That time of night it was when the first sleep,
Gift of the gods, begins for ill mankind,
Arriving gradually, delicious rest.
In sleep, in dream, Hector appeared to me,
165 Gaunt with sorrow, streaming tears, all torn—
As by the violent car on his death day—
And black with bloody dust,
His puffed-out feet cut by the rawhide thongs.
Ah god, the look of him! How changed
170 From that proud Hector who returned to Troy
Wearing Achilles' armor, or that one
Who pitched the torches on Danaan ships;
His beard all filth, his hair matted with blood,
Showing the wounds, the many wounds, received
175 Outside his father's city walls. I seemed
Myself to weep and call upon the man
In grieving speech, brought from the depth of me:

'Light of Dardania, best hope of Troy,
What kept you from us for so long, and where?
180 From what far place, O Hector, have you come,
Long, long awaited? After so many deaths
Of friends and brothers, after a world of pain
For all our folk and all our town, at last,
Boneweary, we behold you! What has happened
185 To ravage your serene face? Why these wounds?'

He wasted no reply on my poor questions
But heaved a great sigh from his chest and said:
'Ai! Give up and go, child of the goddess,°
Save yourself, out of these flames. The enemy
190 Holds the city walls, and from her height
Troy falls in ruin. Fatherland and Priam
Have their due; if by one hand our towers
Could be defended, by this hand, my own,
They would have been. Her holy things, her gods
195 Of hearth and household° Troy commends to you.
Accept them as companions of your days;
Go find for them the great walls that one day
You'll dedicate, when you have roamed the sea.'

As he said this, he brought out from the sanctuary
200 Chaplets and Vesta, Lady of the Hearth,
With her eternal fire.
                                    While I dreamed,
The turmoil rose, with anguish, in the city.
More and more, although Anchises' house
Lay in seclusion, muffled among trees,
205 The din at the grim onset grew; and now
I shook off sleep, I climbed to the roof top
To cup my ears and listen. And the sound
Was like the sound a grassfire makes in grain,
Whipped by a Southwind, or a torrent foaming
210 Out of a mountainside to strew in ruin
Fields, happy crops, the yield of plowing teams,
Or woodlands borne off in the flood; in wonder
The shepherd listens on a rocky peak.
I knew then what our trust had won for us,
215 Knew the Danaan fraud: Deiphobus'°
Great house in flames, already caving in
Under the overpowering god of fire;
Ucalegon's° already caught nearby;

188. child of the goddess: Aeneas is the son of Venus.

194–195. gods . . . household: Romans had household and domestic gods called Lares (lā'rēz) and Penates (pē·nā'tēz').

HRW Photo By Barb

Temple of Vesta in Rome. *Vesta was the goddess of the hearth and home.*

215. Deiphobus (dē'ə·fō'bəs)

218. Ucalegon (yōo·kal'ə·gän)

The glare lighting the straits beyond Sigeum;°
220 The cries of men, the wild calls of the trumpets.

To arm was my first maddened impulse—not
That anyone had a fighting chance in arms;
Only I burned to gather up some force
For combat, and to man some high redoubt.°
225 So fury drove me, and it came to me
That meeting death was beautiful in arms.
Then here, eluding the Achaean spears,
Came Panthus, Othrys'° son, priest of Apollo,
Carrying holy things, our conquered gods,
230 And pulling a small grandchild along: he ran
Despairing to my doorway.

                                        'Where's the crux,
Panthus,' I said. 'What strongpoint shall we hold?'
Before I could say more, he groaned and answered:
'The last day for Dardania has come,
235 The hour not to be fought off any longer.
Trojans we have been; Ilium has been;
The glory of the Teucrians is no more;
Black Jupiter has passed it on to Argos.°
Greeks are the masters in our burning city.
240 Tall as a cliff, set in the heart of town,
Their horse pours out armed men. The conqueror,
Gloating Sinon, brews new conflagrations.
Troops hold the gates—as many thousand men
As ever came from great Mycenae; others
245 Block the lanes with crossed spears; glittering
In a combat line, swordblades are drawn for slaughter.
Even the first guards at the gates can barely
Offer battle, or blindly make a stand,'

Impelled by these words, by the powers of heaven,
250 Into the flames I go, into the fight,
Where the harsh Fury, and the din and shouting,
Skyward rising, calls. Crossing my path
In moonlight, five fell in with me, companions:
Ripheus, and Epytus, a great soldier,
255 Hypanis, Dymas, cleaving to my side
With young Coroebus, Mygdon's ° son. It happened
That in those very days this man had come
To Troy, aflame with passion for Cassandra,

219. **Sigeum** (si·jē′əm)

224. **redoubt** (ri·dout′): defense.

228. **Panthus** (pan′thəs); **Othrys** (ôth′ris)

238. **Argos** (är′gôs, -gəs): a town in the Peloponnesus.

254–256. **Ripheus** (rif′o͞os); Epytus (e′pi·təs); **Hypanis** (hī′pan·əs); **Dymas** (dī′məs); **Mygdon** (mig′dän)

Bringing to Priam and the Phrygians°
260 A son-in-law's right hand. Unlucky one,
To have been deaf to what his bride foretold!
Now when I saw them grouped, on edge for battle,
I took it all in and said briefly,
                                    'Soldiers,
Brave as you are to no end, if you crave
265 To face the last fight with me, and no doubt of it,
How matters stand for us each one can see.
The gods by whom this kingdom stood are gone,
Gone from the shrines and altars. You defend
A city lost in flames. Come, let us die,
270 We'll make a rush into the thick of it.
The conquered have one safety: hope for none.'

The desperate odds doubled their fighting spirit:
From that time on, like predatory wolves
In fog and darkness, when a savage hunger
275 Drives them blindly on, and cubs in lairs
Lie waiting with dry famished jaws—just so
Through arrow flights and enemies we ran
Toward our sure death, straight for the city's heart,
Cavernous black night over and around us.
280 Who can describe the havoc of that night
Or tell the deaths, or tally wounds with tears?
The ancient city falls, after dominion
Many long years. In windrows° on the streets,
In homes, on solemn porches of the gods,
285 Dead bodies lie. And not alone the Trojans
Pay the price with their heart's blood; at times
Manhood returns to fire even the conquered
And Danaan conquerors fall. Grief everywhere,
Everywhere terror, and all shapes of death.

*Aeneas and his small band of friends overcome a
detachment of Greek soldiers and put on their armor
and insignia. Thus disguised, they are able to cut
down a number of the invaders.*

290   When gods are contrary
They stand by no one. Here before us came
Cassandra, Priam's virgin daughter, dragged
By her long hair out of Minerva's shrine,
Lifting her brilliant eyes in vain to heaven—

Wall carving of a soldier in armor.

Scala/Art Resource, New York

259. **Phrygians** (frij′ē·ənz): people
of Phrygia, a country in Asia
Minor where Troy was located.

283. **windrows:** rows of hay or
grain that have been raked
together.

295 Her eyes alone, as her white hands were bound.
Coroebus, infuriated, could not bear it,
But plunged into the midst to find his death.
We all went after him, our swords at play,
But here, here first, from the temple gable's height,
300 We met a hail of missiles from our friends,
Pitiful execution, by their error,
Who thought us Greek from our Greek plumes and
    shields.
Then with a groan of anger, seeing the virgin
Wrested from them, Danaans from all sides
305 Rallied and attacked us: fiery Ajax,
Atreus'° sons, Dolopians in a mass—
As, when a cyclone breaks, conflicting winds
Will come together, Westwind, Southwind, Eastwind
Riding high out of the Dawnland; forests
310 Bend and roar, and raging all in spume
Nereus with his trident churns the deep.
Then some whom we had taken by surprise
Under cover of night throughout the city
And driven off, came back again: they knew
315 Our shields and arms for liars now, our speech
Alien to their own. They overwhelmed us.

306. **Atreus** (ā′trē·əs): father of Agamemnon and Menelaus.

One by one the remaining Trojan warriors are killed in a hail of missiles from their own side. Aeneas is drawn by the cry of battle to Priam's castle, where a great massacre is about to take place.

                    Mars gone berserk, Danaans
In a rush to scale the roof; the gate besieged
By a tortoise shell of overlapping shields.
320 Ladders clung to the wall, and men strove upward
Before the very doorposts, on the rungs,
Left hand putting the shield up, and the right
Reaching for the cornice. The defenders
Wrenched out upperworks and rooftiles: these
325 For missiles, as they saw the end, preparing
To fight back even on the edge of death.
And gilded beams, ancestral ornaments,
They rolled down on the heads below. In hall

Others with swords drawn held the entrance way,
330 Packed there, waiting. Now we plucked up heart
To help the royal house, to give our men
A respite, and to add our strength to theirs,
Though all were beaten. And we had for entrance
A rear door, secret, giving on a passage
335 Between the palace halls; in other days
Andromache,° poor lady, often used it,
Going alone to see her husband's parents
Or taking Astyanax° to his grandfather.
I climbed high on the roof, where hopeless men
340 Were picking up and throwing futile missiles.
Here was a tower like a promontory
Rising toward the stars above the roof:
All Troy, the Danaan ships, the Achaean camp,
Were visible from this. Now close beside it
345 With crowbars, where the flooring made loose joints,
We pried it from its bed and pushed it over.
Down with a rending crash in sudden ruin

336. **Andromache** (an·dräm′ə·kē): Hector's wife.

338. **Astyanax** (as·tī′ə·naks′)

Attic cup, c. 5th century B.C. *This vase depicts Cassandra, a wounded Trojan, and Andromache protecting her son Astyanax.*

Wide over the Danaan lines it fell;
But fresh troops moved up, and the rain of stones
350 With every kind of missile never ceased.

Just at the outer doors of the vestibule
Sprang Pyrrhus, all in bronze and glittering,
As a serpent, hidden swollen underground
By a cold winter, writhes into the light,
355 On vile grass fed, his old skin cast away,
Renewed and glossy, rolling slippery coils,
With lifted underbelly rearing sunward
And triple tongue a-flicker. Close beside him
Giant Periphas and Automedon,°
360 His armorbearer, once Achilles' driver,
Besieged the place with all the young of Scyros,°
Hurling their torches at the palace roof.
Pyrrhus shouldering forward with an axe
Broke down the stony threshold, forced apart
365 Hinges and brazen doorjambs, and chopped through
One panel of the door, splitting the oak,
To make a window, a great breach. And there
Before their eyes the inner halls lay open,
The courts of Priam and the ancient kings,
370 With men-at-arms ranked in the vestibule.
From the interior came sounds of weeping,
Pitiful commotion, wails of women
High-pitched, rising in the formal chambers
To ring against the silent golden stars;
375 And, through the palace, mothers wild with fright
Ran to and fro or clung to doors and kissed them.
Pyrrhus with his father's brawn stormed on,
No bolts or bars or men availed to stop him:
Under his battering the double doors
380 Were torn out of their sockets and fell inward.
Sheer force cleared the way: the Greeks broke through
Into the vestibule, cut down the guards,
And made the wide hall seethe with men-at-arms—
A tumult greater than when dikes are burst
385 And a foaming river, swirling out in flood,
Whelms every parapet and races on
Through fields and over all the lowland plains,
Bearing off pens and cattle. I myself
Saw Neoptolemus furious with blood

359. **Periphas** (pur'ə·fəs); **Auto-medon** (ô·tä'mə·dən)

361. **Scyros** (sī'rəs): an island in the Aegean Sea.

390 In the entrance way, and saw the two Atridae;°
Hecuba I saw, and her hundred daughters,
Priam before the altars, with his blood
Drenching the fires that he himself had blessed.
Those fifty bridal chambers, hope of a line
395 So flourishing; those doorways high and proud,
Adorned with takings of barbaric gold,
Were all brought low: fire had them, or the Greeks.
What was the fate of Priam, you may ask.
Seeing his city captive, seeing his own
400 Royal portals rent apart, his enemies
In the inner rooms, the old man uselessly
Put on his shoulders, shaking with old age,
Armor unused for years, belted a sword on,
And made for the massed enemy to die.
405 Under the open sky in a central court
Stood a big altar; near it, a laurel tree
Of great age, leaning over, in deep shade
Embowered the Penates.° At this altar
Hecuba and her daughters, like white doves
410 Blown down in a black storm, clung together,
Enfolding holy images in their arms.
Now, seeing Priam in a young man's gear,
She called out:

          'My poor husband, what mad thought
Drove you to buckle on these weapons?
415 Where are you trying to go? The time is past
For help like this, for this kind of defending,
Even if my own Hector could be here.
Come to me now: the altar will protect us,
Or else you'll die with us.'

                        She drew him close,
420 Heavy with years, and made a place for him
To rest on the consecrated stone.

                           Now see
Polites, one of Priam's sons, escaped
From Pyrrhus' butchery and on the run
Through enemies and spears, down colonnades,
425 Through empty courtyards, wounded. Close behind
Comes Pyrrhus burning for the death-stroke: has him,
Catches him now, and lunges with the spear.
The boy has reached his parents, and before them
Goes down, pouring out his life with blood.

390. **Atridae** (ə·trī′dē): Agamemnon and Menelaus.

408. **Penates** (pē·nā′tēz′): Roman household gods.

430 Now Priam, in the very midst of death,
    Would neither hold his peace nor spare his anger.

    'For what you've done, for what you've dared,' he said,
    'If there is care in heaven for atrocity,
    May the gods render fitting thanks, reward you
435 As you deserve. You forced me to look on
    At the destruction of my son: defiled
    A father's eyes with death. That great Achilles
    You claim to be the son of—and you lie—
    Was not like you to Priam, his enemy;
440 To me who threw myself upon his mercy
    He showed compunction, gave me back for burial
    The bloodless corpse of Hector, and returned me
    To my own realm.'
                        The old man threw his spear
    With feeble impact; blocked by the ringing bronze,
445 It hung there harmless from the jutting boss.°
    Then Pyrrhus answered:
                        'You'll report the news
    To Pelides,° my father; don't forget
    My sad behavior, the degeneracy
    Of Neoptolemus. Now die.'

445. **boss:** here, an architectural protuberance.

447. **Pelides** (pē′li·dēz): Achilles, son of Peleus.

Bowl depicting soldiers in battle.

Alinari/Art Resource, New York

With this,
450 To the altar step itself he dragged him trembling,
Slipping in the pooled blood of his son,
And took him by the hair with his left hand.
The sword flashed in his right; up to the hilt
He thrust it in his body.
That was the end
455 Of Priam's age, the doom that took him off,
With Troy in flames before his eyes, his towers
Headlong fallen—he that in other days
Had ruled in pride so many lands and peoples,
The power of Asia.
On the distant shore
460 The vast trunk headless lies without a name.

For the first time that night, inhuman shuddering
Took me, head to foot. I stood unmanned,
And my dear father's image came to mind
As our king, just his age, mortally wounded,
465 Gasped his life away before my eyes.
Creusa came to mind, too, left alone;
The house plundered; danger to little Iulus.
I looked around to take stock of my men,
But all had left me, utterly played out,
470 Giving their beaten bodies to the fire
Or plunging from the roof.
It came to this,
That I stood there alone. And then I saw
Lurking beyond the doorsill of the Vesta,
In hiding, silent, in that place reserved,
475 The daughter of Tyndareus.° Glare of fires
Lighted my steps this way and that, my eyes
Glancing over the whole scene, everywhere.
That woman, terrified of the Trojans' hate
For the city overthrown, terrified too
480 Of Danaan vengeance, her abandoned husband's
Anger after years—Helen, that Fury
Both to her own homeland and Troy, had gone
To earth, a hated thing, before the altars.
Now fires blazed up in my own spirit—
485 A passion to avenge my fallen town
And punish Helen's whorishness.
'Shall this one

475. **daughter of Tyndareus** (tin·der'ē·əs): Helen.

Look untouched on Sparta and Mycenae
After her triumph, going like a queen,
And see her home and husband, kin and children,
490 With Trojan girls for escort, Phrygian slaves?
Must Priam perish by the sword for this?
Troy burn, for this? Dardania's littoral°

Be soaked in blood, so many times, for this?
Not by my leave. I know
495 No glory comes of punishing a woman,
The feat can bring no honor. Still, I'll be
Approved for snuffing out a monstrous life,
For a just sentence carried out. My heart
Will teem with joy in this avenging fire,
500 And the ashes of my kin will be appeased.'

So ran my thoughts. I turned wildly upon her,
But at that moment, clear, before my eyes—
Never before so clear—in a pure light
Stepping before me, radiant through the night,
505 My loving mother came: immortal, tall,

BURNING OF TROY, STEFANO DELLA BELLA
(1610–1664).

Scala/Art Resource, New York

from The Aeneid, Book 2 **399**

And lovely as the lords of heaven know her.
Catching me by the hand, she held me back,
Then with her rose-red mouth reproved me:

                                'Son,

Why let such suffering goad you on to fury

510   Past control? Where is your thoughtfulness
For me, for us? Will you not first revisit
The place you left your father, worn and old,
Or find out if your wife, Creusa, lives,
And the young boy, Ascanius—all these

515   Cut off by Greek troops foraging everywhere?
Had I not cared for them, fire would by now
Have taken them, their blood glutted the sword.
You must not hold the woman of Laconia,°
That hated face, the cause of this, nor Paris.

520   The harsh will of the gods it is, the gods,
That overthrows the splendor of this place
And brings Troy from her height into the dust.

518. **woman of Laconia** (lə·kō′nē·ə): Helen.

Aeneas Recounting to Dido the Fall of Troy, Baron Pierre-Narcisse Guérin (1774–1833).

Look over there: I'll tear away the cloud
That curtains you, and films your mortal sight,
525 The fog around you.—Have no fear of doing
Your mother's will, or balk at obeying her.—
Look: where you see high masonry thrown down,
Stone torn from stone, with billowing smoke and dust,
Neptune is shaking from their beds the walls
530 That his great trident pried up, undermining,
Toppling the whole city down. And look:
Juno in all her savagery holds
The Scaean Gates,° and raging in steel armor
Calls her allied army from the ships.
535 Up on the citadel—turn, look—Pallas Tritonia°
Couched in a stormcloud, lightening, with her
    Gorgon!°
The Father° himself empowers the Danaans,
Urges assaulting gods on the defenders.
Away, child; put an end to toiling so.
540 I shall be near, to see you safely home.'

She hid herself in the deep gloom of night,
And now the dire forms appeared to me
Of great immortals, enemies of Troy.
I knew the end then: Ilium was going down
545 In fire, the Troy of Neptune going down,
As in high mountains when the countrymen
Have notched an ancient ash, then make their axes
Ring with might and main, chopping away
To fell the tree—ever on the point of falling,
550 Shaken through all its foliage, and the treetop
Nodding; bit by bit the strokes prevail
Until it gives a final groan at last
And crashes down in ruin from the height.

Now I descended where the goddess guided,
555 Clear of the flames, and clear of enemies,
For both retired; so gained my father's door,
My ancient home.

*Arriving home, Aeneas finds his father, Anchises,
resolved to die in the carnage of Troy. Unable to
convince him to flee, he swears, despite his wife's
piteous pleas, that he will join his father in death.
Then he sees an omen that changes his mind.*

533. **Scaean** (skē′ən) **Gates:** the northwest entry to Troy.

535. **Pallas Tritonia** (trə·tō′nē·ə): a name for Minerva; she was supposed to have been born near Lake Tritonis in Libya.

536. **Gorgon** (gôr′gən): Medusa, a terrifying monster slain by Perseus; her head was given to the goddess Minerva, who carried it upon her father's shield.

537. **Father:** Jupiter.

from The Aeneid, Book 2 **401**

She went on, and her wailing filled the house.
But then a sudden portent came, a marvel:

560 Amid his parents' hands and their sad faces
A point on Iulus' head seemed to cast light,
A tongue of flame that touched but did not burn him,
Licking his fine hair, playing round his temples.
We, in panic, beat at the flaming hair

565 And put the sacred fire out with water;
Father Anchises lifted his eyes to heaven
And lifted up his hands, his voice, in joy:

'Omnipotent Jupiter, if prayers affect you,
Look down upon us, that is all I ask,

570 If by devotion to the gods we earn it,
Grant us a new sign, and confirm this portent!'
The old man barely finished when it thundered
A loud crack on the left. Out of the sky
Through depths of night a star fell trailing flame

575 And glided on, turning the night to day.
We watched it pass above the roof and go
To hide its glare, its trace, in Ida's° wood;
But still, behind, the luminous furrow shone
And wide zones fumed with sulphur.

                       Now indeed

580 My father, overcome, addressed the gods,
And rose in worship of the blessed star.

'Now, now, no more delay. I'll follow you.
Where you conduct me, there I'll be.

                  Gods of my fathers,
Preserve this house, preserve my grandson. Yours

585 This portent was. Troy's life is in your power.
I yield. I go as your companion, son.'
Then he was still. We heard the blazing town
Crackle more loudly, felt the scorching heat.

'Then come, dear father. Arms around my neck:

590 I'll take you on my shoulders, no great weight.
Whatever happens, both will face one danger,
Find one safety. Iulus will come with me,
My wife at a good interval behind.
Servants, give your attention to what I say.

595 At the gate inland there's a funeral mound
And an old shrine of Ceres the Bereft;°

577. **Ida** (ī′də): a mountain near Troy, the setting for the Judgment of Paris.

596. **Ceres the Bereft:** the mother of Proserpina (prō·sur′pi·nə); who was fated to spend part of the year in the underworld.

Near it an ancient cypress, kept alive
For many years by our fathers' piety.
By various routes we'll come to that one place.
600 Father, carry our hearthgods, our Penates.
It would be wrong for me to handle them—
Just come from such hard fighting, bloody work—
Until I wash myself in running water.'

When I had said this, over my breadth of shoulder
605 And bent neck, I spread out a lion skin
For tawny cloak and stooped to take his weight.
Then little Iulus put his hand in mine
And came with shorter steps beside his father.
My wife fell in behind. Through shadowed places
610 On we went, and I, lately unmoved
By any spears thrown, and squads of Greeks,
Felt terror now at every eddy of wind,
Alarm at every sound, alert and worried
Alike for my companion and my burden.
615 I had got near the gate, and now I thought
We had made it all the way, when suddenly
A noise of running feet came near at hand,
And peering through the gloom ahead, my father
Cried out:
   'Run, boy; here they come; I see
620 Flame light on shields, bronze shining.'
        I took fright,
And some unfriendly power, I know not what,
Stole all my addled wits—for as I turned
Aside from the known way, entering a maze
Of pathless places on the run—
        Alas,
625 Creusa, taken from us by grim fate, did she
Linger, or stray, or sink in weariness?
There is no telling. Never would she be
Restored to us. Never did I look back
Or think to look for her, lost as she was,
630 Until we reached the funeral mound and shrine
Of venerable Ceres. Here at last
All came together, but she was not there;
She alone failed her friends, her child, her husband.
Out of my mind, whom did I not accuse,
635 What man or god? What crueler loss had I

AENEAS AND ANCHISES, **GIOVANNI LORENZO BERNINI (1598–1680).** *Anchises holds a statue of the penates, or gods who protected household supplies in individual homes.*

from The Aeneid, Book 2   **403**

THE BURNING OF TROY, SIENA. The figure in the center of the painting is Creusa, or her ghost.

How is Creusa significant to Aeneas's adventures?

Beheld, that night the city fell? Ascanius,
My father, and the Teucrian Penates,
I left in my friends' charge, and hid them well
In a hollow valley.
           I turned back alone
640 Into the city, cinching my bright harness.
Nothing for it but to run the risks
Again, go back again, comb all of Troy,
And put my life in danger as before:
First by the town wall, then the gate, all gloom,
645 Through which I had come out—and so on backward,
Tracing my own footsteps through the night;
And everywhere my heart misgave me: even

Stillness had its terror. Then to our house,
Thinking she might, just might, have wandered there.
650 Danaans had got in and filled the place,
And at that instant fire they had set,
Consuming it, went roofward in a blast;
Flames leaped and seethed in heat to the night sky.
I pressed on, to see Priam's hall and tower.
655 In the bare colonnades of Juno's shrine
Two chosen guards, Phoenix° and hard Ulysses,
Kept watch over the plunder. Piled up here
Were treasures of old Troy from every quarter,
Torn out of burning temples: altar tables,
660 Robes, and golden bowls. Drawn up around them,
Boys and frightened mothers stood in line.
I even dared to call out in the night;
I filled the streets with calling; in my grief
Time after time I groaned and called Creusa,
665 Frantic, in endless quest from door to door.
Then to my vision her sad wraith° appeared—
Creusa's ghost, larger than life, before me.
Chilled to the marrow, I could feel the hair
On my head rise, the voice clot in my throat;
670 But she spoke out to ease me of my fear:

'What's to be gained by giving way to grief
So madly, my sweet husband? Nothing here
Has come to pass except as heaven willed.
You may not take Creusa with you now;
675 It was not so ordained, nor does the lord
Of high Olympus give you leave. For you
Long exile waits, and long sea miles to plow.
You shall make landfall on Hesperia°
Where Lydian Tiber° flows, with gentle pace,
680 Between rich farmlands, and the years will bear
Glad peace, a kingdom, and a queen for you.
Dismiss these tears for your beloved Creusa.
I shall not see the proud homelands of Myrmidons
Or of Dolopians, or go to serve
685 Greek ladies, Dardan lady that I am
And daughter-in-law of Venus the divine.
No: the great mother of the gods detains me
Here on these shores. Farewell now; cherish still
Your son and mine.'

656. **Phoenix** (fē′niks)

666. **wraith** (rāth): ghost.

678. **Hesperia** (hes·pir′ē·ə): name given to Italy by Aeneas.

679. **Lydian** (lid′ē·ən) **Tiber:** The Etruscans were supposed to have come from Lydia, a region in Asia Minor.

With this she left me weeping,
690 Wishing that I could say so many things,
And faded on the tenuous air. Three times
I tried to put my arms around her neck,
Three times enfolded nothing, as the wraith
Slipped through my fingers, bodiless as wind,
695 Or like a flitting dream.
                    So in the end
As night waned I rejoined my company.
And there to my astonishment I found
New refugees in a great crowd: men and women
Gathered for exile, young—pitiful people
700 Coming from every quarter, minds made up,
With their belongings, for whatever lands
I'd lead them to by sea.
                    The morning star
Now rose on Ida's ridges, bringing day.
Greeks had secured the city gates. No help
705 Or hope of help existed.
So I resigned myself, picked up my father,
And turned my face toward the mountain range."

A CRITICAL COMMENT

Themes and Images in Book 2 of the Aeneid

The full force of Virgil's narrative lies not in its focus on descriptive details, but rather in the personal response of Aeneas to the advancing tragedy. Aeneas's thirst for revenge comes into conflict with his duties as a survivor and with the pronouncements of fate. These conflicts recur throughout the *Aeneid,* constituting central themes of the epic.

At the beginning of the enemy attack, the sleeping Aeneas has a vision of the slain Trojan hero Hector, who urges him to escape the holocaust and save the sacred treasures of the city. However, it is only when Aeneas climbs to the roof of his house and sees the fires engulfing the homes of his friends that he grasps the full magnitude of the Greek assault. His first reaction is blind rage: he can think only of throwing himself into the flames or giving himself over to revenge to quench his own fury.

In what follows, Virgil repeatedly emphasizes the idea of wasted valor. First the young Coroebus throws away his life in a failed attempt to save his beloved Cassandra. Then, in the ensuing fight, Aeneas's small band of warriors are cut down by the missiles of their own countrymen. Finally, Aeneas returns to the palace of Priam and witnesses in helpless outrage the brutal killing of the feeble, broken king.

At this point, Aeneas's thoughts turn to his own family, and he begins to accept the awesome responsibility of the survivor as something greater than his overpowering desire for revenge. Virgil here emphasizes another central theme of his epic: the problem of fate and free will. On his way back to save his family, Aeneas comes face to face with Helen—the cause, from his point of view, of the entire war. He is about to vent his fury on her when his mother Venus stays his hand. Venus gives Aeneas a powerful display of the divine forces orchestrating the destruction of Troy—forces that are far beyond any factors of human guilt and retribution.

The debate over individual responsibility is resumed when Aeneas returns to his family. This time it is his father Anchises who nearly melts Aeneas's own resolve, until he is swayed by a startling portent: the image of flickering flames around the head of his own son, followed by a meteor pointing the way to safety. Aeneas is now ready to shoulder the burden of his past and future destiny as he sets off, carrying his father on his back and leading his young son by the hand.

As we begin to understand as early as Book 2, the power of "destiny" or "fate" is not simply a matter of resignation by Aeneas to the rule of unseen powers. Instead, destiny calls forth even greater force of will and commitment on the part of the hero. This is precisely the idea of self-mastery that is expressed by the epithet *pius* (variously translated as "pious," "responsible," "dutiful," "conscientious") attached to the name of Aeneas throughout the poem. This heroic quality occasionally gives Aeneas the strength to overcome external enemies, but more often it puts him into conflict with himself. Aeneas's internal conflicts set up some of the emotional high points of the poem. These conflicts come into focus as the hero gives himself over to indulgence of his love for Dido in Book 4, his weariness in Book 5, and his obsessive revenge in Book 12.

Many of the themes and images developed in Book 2 reverberate throughout the whole epic. For example, the shared tragedy of fathers and sons is a pattern that repeatedly unfolds in Books 9 to 12. The sense of the awesome power of fate recurs with particular force in the prophetic vision in the underworld in Book 6, and again in the pageant of Roman history engraved on Aeneas's divine shield in Book 8.

First Thoughts

How did you react to the violence in Aeneas's account of the fall of Troy?

Identifying Facts

1. Why do the Trojans assume that the Greeks have sailed for home? How do they interpret the death of Laocoon?
2. What is Priam's fate? How is Helen saved from Aeneas's fury?
3. What signs convince Aeneas and Anchises that they must leave Troy?
4. At what point does Aeneas realize that his wife is gone? What is Creusa's parting message to Aeneas?

Interpreting Meanings

1. What strengths make Aeneas a leader of his people? What weaknesses does Virgil reveal in his epic hero?
2. The narrative in Book 2 clearly portrays Aeneas's **external conflicts** with the Greeks. He experiences **internal conflict** when he witnesses Priam's death. Find at least two other examples of internal conflict. What is the outcome of each conflict?
3. Although the title character of Virgil's epic is a man, the poem is deeply concerned with female characters. How do Cassandra, Hecuba, Venus, and Creusa play important roles in the poem?
4. Like Homer, Virgil uses **epic similes**, or extended comparisons in which epic events are likened to ordinary events in order to make them more accessible or interesting to the reader. Identify two examples of epic similes and explain what makes them vivid and exciting.

Applying Meanings

How do you rate Aeneas as a leader? If you were a Trojan refugee, would you follow him? Why or why not?

Critical Writing Response

Comparing Heroes. In a three- to four-paragraph essay, compare and contrast Aeneas with one of the heroes you have read about in this book or with a modern hero from television or film. Consider:

1. The nature of their quests
2. The use of their intelligence, physical strength, or special powers
3. Their acceptance of aid from others
4. Their loyalties
5. Their attitudes toward violence

Language and Vocabulary

Analyzing an Epic Simile

Reread lines 273–279 from Book 2, in which Aeneas describes his companions' and his own desperation as they rush to make a final stand against the Greeks. Then compare these lines with the following paraphrase:

> From that time on, while black night enveloped us, we ran straight for the heart of the city, toward our certain death, moving through flights of arrows and enemy troops, in the same way that preying wolves run in fog and darkness when they are driven recklessly on by fierce hunger and their starving cubs lie waiting in lairs.

This paraphrase conveys the meaning of the passage from the epic, but not its emotional impact.

1. How does Virgil organize the elements of the comparison so that his simile builds to a climax?
2. Which images are particularly effective in communicating the desperate emotional state of Aeneas and his small band of Trojans?

Catullus
c. 84–c. 54 B.C.

Quintus Catulus orator et Poeta.

After 60 B.C., the maneuverings for power by Julius Caesar and his principal rival, Pompey, threatened to bring an end to the Roman Republic and to drag Rome into civil war. Most writers at this time were chiefly concerned with politics and public debate. One voice, the personal, lyric voice of Gaius Valerius Catullus (kə·tul′əs), stood out among them. Catullus turned away from the models of the Roman epics, which focused on war and politics. Instead, he found inspiration in the lyric poetry of the ancient Greeks, particularly the love lyrics of Sappho. Despite the personal nature of his poetry, Catullus won many admirers, including Julius Caesar himself. Ironically, Catullus's only attempt at public satire was a number of poems that showed his opposition to the ambitions of Julius Caesar. Fortunately, the Roman leader seemed not to take the satires to heart.

As a young man, Catullus left the home of his prosperous family in Verona and headed for Rome. He soon joined the fashionable social and literary circles of the capital. His love affair with a wealthy Roman woman named Clodia (klō′dē·ə) is the subject of a long series of poems that explore the range of his feelings for her. Around 57 B.C., when he was disillusioned with love, Catullus left Rome to travel and to visit the tomb of his brother who had recently died. During his travels, he wrote much about his feelings of love and loss.

Catullus occupies an important place in the history of Latin poetry, not only for the excellence of his lyrics, but also for his experimentation with form. He popularized the use of the elegiac couplet—a pair of lines consisting of a hexameter (six metrical feet) and a pentameter (five metrical feet). This meter later became standard for an entire genre of Latin poetry called the "love elegy."

Centuries later, Catullus became one of the most popular of the Roman poets rediscovered in the Renaissance. Leading European writers such as the Italian Petrarch (see page 806) and the British Ben Jonson imitated the lyrics of Catullus. Since the era of the Renaissance, Catullus's short "book" of 116 poems has been universally admired for its passion, sophistication, and charm.

Reader's Guide

LYRIC POEMS OF CATULLUS

Background

A large number of Catullus's poems are addressed to a Roman woman named Clodia with whom he had a passionate affair. She was ten years older than the poet and was married to a prominent Roman politician. Her brother, Publius Clodius, was a notorious troublemaker in Roman politics and the bitter enemy of the famous orator, Cicero. Clodia herself seems to have been both beautiful and faithless.

In his poems, Catullus calls Clodia by the name Lesbia, a reference to the great Greek lyric poet Sappho (see page 279), who lived on the island of Lesbos and whose love poetry Catullus admired. Catullus's poems to and about Lesbia cover a range of emotions—from hope at the beginning of their relationship to anger and disillusionment at the end. At its best, his poetry is direct and intensely emotional.

Oral Response

Have you ever been in a relationship where you have felt difficult, strong emotions for another person? For instance, have you ever had a friend or a relative whom you loved one day and were angry with the next? In your journal make a list of the possible feelings you had for this person. Are these feelings confusing or contradictory? How do you express and resolve these feelings?

Literary Focus

Hyperbole is a figure of speech which uses exaggeration or overstatement for emphasis, often for comic effect. For example, when a friend tells you that she heard a joke so funny that she nearly died of laughter, she is demonstrating hyperbole. You believe the joke was very funny, but you know your friend could not have died from it.

LYRIC POEMS
Catullus
translated by
RENEY MYERS, ROBERT J. ORMSBY, AND PETER WHIGHAM

 As you read, make a list of the range of emotions expressed in each lyric poem. Do you think that Catullus is accurately describing the variety and changeability of human emotion?

Wretched Catullus, Leave off Playing the Fool

Wretched Catullus, leave off playing the fool:
Give up as lost what is forever past.
But once, bright, golden suns beamed down
    and cast
A happiness on you when she would rule
5   Your steps and lead you into joyous play.
How much you loved her! More than any man
Can ever love. With her, what joy began!
That sunny world seemed yours in every way.
Yet now she does not want you, and alas,
10 You must not chase her nor live wretchedly,
Thus make your heart as hard as it can be.
So goodbye, baby! Catullus now will pass
You up, won't need you, nor will entertain
A thought of you nor seek your company.
15 Oh wicked thing, I'm tough as I can be!
Now who'll invite you? Where will you obtain
Praise of your beauty? Who'll make sorrows
    blisses?
Who'll love you now? Or bite your lips in kisses?
Not Catullus! He's determined to abstain.

—*translated by Reney Myers and*
  Robert J. Ormsby

Roman depiction of Spring as a woman picking flowers.

Scala/Art Resource, New York

Lesbia Says She'ld Rather Marry Me

Lesbia says she'ld rather marry me
than anyone,
    though Jupiter himself came asking
or so she says,
    but what a woman tells her lover in desire
should be written out on air & running water.

        —translated by Peter Whigham

If Ever Anyone Anywhere

If ever anyone anywhere, Lesbia, is looking
    for what he knows will not happen
and then unexpectedly it happens
    the soul is astonished,
as we are now in each other,
    an event dearer than gold,
for you have restored yourself, Lesbia, desired
restored yourself, longed for, unlooked for,
    brought yourself back
to me. White day in the calendar!
    Who happier than I?
What more can life offer
than the longed for unlooked for event
   when it happens?

        —translated by Peter Whigham

Roman fresco of a poet or scribe.

I Hate and I Love

I hate and I love. And if you ask me how,
I do not know: I only feel it, and I'm torn in two.

        —translated by Peter Whigham

First Thoughts

In which of these poems does Catullus seem to be happiest? In which does he seem most miserable?

Identifying Facts

1. "Wretched Catullus, Leave off Playing the Fool" is divided into two sections. What advice does Catullus give himself in the first eleven lines? Whom does he address in lines 12–19, and what does he say?

2. In "Lesbia Says She'ld Rather Marry Me," what attitude does Catullus express toward women in general?

3. What is the "unlooked for event" that the poet celebrates in "If Ever Anyone Anywhere"?

Interpreting Meanings

1. What does the last line of "Lesbia Says She'ld Rather Marry Me" imply about Lesbia's sincerity? How would you describe the **tone**, or attitude, of the speaker of this poem? Is it bitter, accepting, or indifferent? Explain.

2. "I Hate and I Love" is a brief statement of ambivalence, or the feeling of two strong, contradictory emotions at once. How is the speaker's tone in this poem different from that in "Lesbia Says She'ld Rather Marry Me"?

3. What examples of **hyperbole**, or deliberate overstatement, can you find in Catullus's poetry? What effect does the hyperbole have in each case?

4. Describe the contrast between the first part (lines 1–11) and the second part (lines 12–19) of "Wretched Catullus, Leave Off Playing the Fool." Is the speaker's "toughness" in the second part convincing? Give reasons for your answer.

Applying Meanings

One critic has suggested that the Romans may have considered Catullus's poetry frivolous or trivial. How do you feel about Catullus's poetry? Do you think it is frivolous? Or do you think the expression of personal feelings is a valid and important use of literature? Explain.

Creative Writing Response

Writing a Dramatic Scene. Catullus's lyrics give readers many insights into his own personality, as well as that of his beloved Lesbia. Using these hints as a point of departure for characterization and dialogue, write a short dramatic scene that involves Catullus and Lesbia. Feel free to use one of the situations implied by the poems (for example, a quarrel or a reconciliation), or create a dramatic situation of your own. Try to include at least one example of **hyperbole**, or deliberate exaggeration, in your scene.

Critical Writing Response

Comparing Lyric Poems. In a brief essay, compare and contrast one of Catullus's love lyrics with a lyric written by Sappho (see page 279). In your essay, be sure to include a discussion of how the speaker in each poem conveys emotion through imagery, figures of speech, and the careful control of tone.

Horace
65–8 B.C.

Quintus Horatius Flaccus, better known as Horace, lived during the Augustan Age, one of the most creative periods of Roman civilization. Horace, who was to become one of the greatest of Roman poets, had humble beginnings as the child of a father who was a freed slave. Nevertheless, his father was determined to give his son a first-rate education. Thus, as a boy, Horace was sent to study rhetoric and philosophy both in Rome and in Athens, Greece—a great privilege usually reserved only for the sons of the wealthiest upper classes.

As a young man, Horace made the mistake of fighting with Brutus on the losing side of the civil war that followed Julius Caesar's assassination in 44 B.C. Though his small landholdings were confiscated after the war, Horace proved to be a survivor. He started to write poetry in order to make a place for himself in Roman society. His poetic gifts, combined with a sense of humor that prevented him from taking himself too seriously, made Horace a favorite of the rich literary patrons who surrounded the new emperor Augustus. Horace remained at the center of sophisticated Roman literary society for the rest of his comfortable life.

Horace tended to moralize, and some critics feel that his poetry is not very profound. His poems are known more for their style than for their substance. He wrote on a wide variety of subjects, both light and serious. He is best known for his humorous *Satires*, his poetic *Epistles* (letters in verse to various friends), and his *Epodes* (lyric lampoons). His work about the poet's craft, *The Art of Poetry*, had a profound effect on poets and critics during the Age of Rationalism in the seventeenth and eighteenth centuries in Europe.

Reader's Guide

THE GOLDEN MEAN AND CARPE DIEM

Background

Horace's greatest literary achievement may be his collection called *Odes*. An **ode** is a complex, songlike poem devoted to a serious subject. Before Horace, the typical ode was written for ceremonial or public occasions. Horace perfected a more personal and reflective type of ode.

"The Golden Mean" and "Carpe Diem," both from the *Odes*, express messages that can be put in the form of **maxims**, or short sayings. A "mean" is a middle position between two extremes. The idea of a harmonious "golden mean" occurs throughout classical Greek and Roman literature. Indeed, the motto said to have been inscribed on the ancient temple of Apollo at Delphi in Greece was *mēden agan* — "Nothing to excess." The concept of the golden mean also appears in other cultures: in the *Analects* of Confucius, in the Indian *Panchatantra,* and in the comedies of the French dramatist Molière. *Carpe diem* means "Seize the day," or "Enjoy life fully while you can." This is another philosophy of life that appears commonly throughout world literature.

Writer's Response

Before you read these poems, think about these two maxims: "Nothing to excess" and "Seize the day." Do you agree, for example, that people should avoid extremes, or do you believe that it's impossible to have too much of a good thing? Do you believe in "seizing the day," or do you think that it's wiser to put off enjoyment today in order to assure greater rewards in the future? How does the way you live your life reflect either of these maxims? Briefly freewrite your response.

Literary Focus

Tone is the attitude a writer takes toward the reader, a subject, or a character. It is conveyed through the writer's choice of words and details. A tone can be described as satirical, tender, comic, awed, ironic, passionate, wistful, melancholy, or by any of a number of other adjectives. As you read "The Golden Mean" and "Carpe Diem," pay attention to the tone of each. Does Horace seem to approve of living by "the golden mean"? Does he believe in "seizing the day"?

THE GOLDEN MEAN
Horace
translated by
WILLIAM COWPER

As you read this poem, try to decide what Horace's ideal of a "golden mean" is.

Receive, dear friend, the truths I teach;
So shalt thou live beyond the reach
   Of adverse fortune's power;
Not always tempt the distant deep,
5   Nor always timorously creep
Along the treacherous shore.

He that holds fast the golden mean,
And lives contentedly between
   The little and the great,
10   Feels not the wants that pinch the poor,
Nor plagues that haunt the rich man's door,
   Embittering all his state.

The tallest pines feel the most power
Of winter blasts; the loftiest tower
15   Comes heaviest to the ground;
The bolts that spare the mountain's side,
His cloud-capped eminence divide,
   And spread the ruin round.

The well-informed philosopher
20   Rejoices with a wholesome fear
   And hopes, in spite of pain;
If winter bellows from the north,
Soon the sweet spring comes dancing forth,
   And nature laughs again.

25   What if thine heaven be overcast,
The dark appearance will not last;
   Expect a brighter sky.
The God that strings the silver bow,°

The Metropolitan Museum of Art, Rogers Fund, 1903 (03.14.5)

Roman wall painting, mid-first century B.C.

28. **God . . . bow:** Apollo, who was god of music and poetry and who played a golden lyre. In his destructive aspect, Apollo used the bow to slay his enemies.

Awakes sometimes the Muses° too,
30   And lays his arrows by.

If hindrances obstruct thy way,
Thy magnanimity display,
    And let thy strength be seen;
But Oh! if fortune fill thy sail
35 With more than a propitious° gale,
    Take half thy canvas in.

29. **Muses:** nine goddesses who presided over the arts.

35. **propitious** (prō·pish'əs): favorable.

CARPE DIEM
Horace
translated by
THOMAS HAWKINS

 Carpe diem *is a recurring theme throughout world literature. Is Horace's idea of* **carpe diem** *best expressed by the saying "Eat, drink, and be merry," or is Horace expressing a deeper view of the theme?*

Strive not, Leuconoe,° to know what end
The gods above to me or thee will send:
Nor with astrologers consult at all,
That thou mayst better know what can befall;
5 Whether thou liv'st more winters, or thy last
Be this, which Tyrrhen waves° 'gainst rocks do cast.
Be wise! Drink free, and in so short a space
Do not protracted hopes of life embrace:
Whilst we are talking, envious time doth slide;
10 This day's thine own; the next may be denied.

1. **Leuconoe** (lyōō·kō'nō·ē): an intimate friend of the poet.

6. **Tyrrhen** (tir'ēn) **waves:** a reference to the Tyrrhenian Sea, a part of the Mediterranean, southwest of Italy.

First Thoughts

What were the strongest impressions you had after reading these poems? Did you agree or disagree with their messages?

Identifying Facts

1. According to the second stanza of "The Golden Mean," what advantage is gained by someone who "holds fast the golden mean"?
2. In lines 1–6 of "Carpe Diem," what does the speaker advise Leuconoe *not* to do?

Interpreting Meanings

1. What **metaphors** does Horace use to present the idea of moderation in the first two stanzas of "The Golden Mean"?
2. Line 28 of "The Golden Mean" is an **allusion**, or reference, to the god Apollo, the patron of musicians, poets, and healers whom the Greeks and Romans viewed as an embodiment of beauty and reason. But Apollo could also be cruel and unforgiving. How does this allusion add to the meaning of the poem?
3. Describe the **tone** of the last four lines of "Carpe Diem." Would you say that it is enthusiastic and high-spirited, urging Leuconoe to go out and have a good time? Or is it thoughtful and even melancholy, urging Leuconoe to make the best use of time and not take life for granted? Explain.

Applying Meanings

Is Horace's advice in these poems valuable as a practical guide to life today, or are there some situations in which you would reject the speaker's philosophy? Explain your answer.

Creative Writing Response

Writing an Advice Column. Imagine that you are a writer of a newspaper advice column. Adopt the philosophy that Horace promotes in either "The Golden Mean" or "Carpe Diem" in one of your responses to a reader needing personal advice. For example, perhaps your reader wants to quit high school and travel around the country. You might advise him or her to follow a philosophy of moderation instead. Your advice to a shy and timid person who is afraid of taking risks might be quite different, however. In your response, summarize the reader's problem, give your advice, and explain why you think the philosophy of either "The Golden Mean" or "Carpe Diem" offers the best approach to dealing with the reader's problem.

Critical Writing Response

Comparing Poetic Themes. In a two- or three-paragraph essay, compare and contrast the themes of "The Golden Mean" and "Carpe Diem." Do you see any potential conflicts between the philosophies expressed in each poem? How do you think Horace would have resolved any apparent conflict?

Language and Vocabulary

Latin Word Roots

Many words in Modern English have Latin roots. Use a good dictionary to identify the **etymology**, or word origin, of the following words from "The Golden Mean." In addition to tracing the Latin word roots, identify any prefixes and suffixes that you discover.

1. fortune
2. timorously
3. contentedly
4. eminence
5. obstruct
6. magnanimity
7. propitious
8. adverse

PRIMARY SOURCES

Horace and The Art of Poetry

PARNASSUS, RAPHAEL.
Do you agree with Horace that the poet's aim should be "to blend in one the delightful and the useful"?

Scala/Art Resource, New York

Horace's The Art of Poetry *was published in 13 B.C., when the author was in his early fifties. It was probably the last work that he wrote. Although his ideas were directed mainly to writers of dramatic poetry, much of his advice is useful for any writer—and can even speak to us today. Read the following excerpts from his brief work. If you were giving advice to writers today, which of these quotations would you find useful? Which quotations do you think give good advice for your own writing?*

You writers, choose a subject that is within your powers, and ponder long what your shoulders can and cannot bear. He who makes every effort to select his theme aright will be at no loss for choice of words or lucid arrangement.

The secret of all good writing is sound judgment. . . . I shall bid the clever imitator to look to life and morals for his real model, and draw thence language true to life.

The poet's aim is either to profit or to please, or to blend in one the delightful and the useful. Whatever the lesson you would convey, be brief, that your hearers may catch quickly what is said and faithfully retain it. Every superfluous word is spilled from the too-full memory.

A kind and sensible critic will censure verses when they are weak, condemn them when they are rough; ugly lines he will score in black, will lop off pretentious ornaments, force you to clear up your obscurities, criticize a doubtful phrase, and mark what needs a change. . . .

Ovid
43 B.C.–A.D. 17

Like his older contemporary, Horace, Publius Ovidius Naso, better known as Ovid (äv'id), thrived in Rome's high society. But unlike Horace, who moved in a circle that enjoyed the approval of the emperor Augustus, Ovid was attracted to Rome's more freewheeling fast set, a clique that included the emperor's unruly granddaughter, Julia. Ovid's poetry—much of which celebrated women—was considered witty and elegant, but not very serious. However, it caused the emperor Augustus a great deal of outrage, for Augustus, whose own rise to power was accomplished with much underhandedness and bloodshed, decided late in life that Rome was becoming dangerously immoral. He worried that Ovid's poetry encouraged infidelity in married women. Worse, he feared that his own granddaughter, Julia, had fallen under Ovid's influence.

In an effort to fend off Rome's decline—and a family scandal—the emperor accused Ovid of irreverence toward the state and sent him into exile. Ovid, whose only true crime may have been the possession of knowledge about Julia's promiscuous behavior, was forced to leave Rome for a remote town on the Black Sea. The Latin poet and lover of the Latin languge lived out his life among foreigners.

Among Ovid's most famous surviving works are his daring *Ars Amatoria* ("The Art of Love"), a poem that graphically outlines the techniques of amorous conquest, and its tongue-in-cheek sequel, *Remedia Amoris* ("The Cures of Love"). These works reinforced the impression of Ovid as a spokesman for decadence and pleasure-seeking. In spite of this reputation, however, Ovid's works present a balanced view of both the creative and the destructive forces of human passion. These two sides of Ovid's literary concern also underlie his greatest poetic masterpiece, *Metamorphoses* (met'ə·môr'fə·sēz'). Ovid's popularity experienced a revival during the Middle Ages, when he enjoyed the reputation of a wise professor of love. His teachings contributed to the medieval concept of courtly love.

Reader's Guide

from METAMORPHOSES

Background

In *Metamorphoses,* Ovid uses the same verse form, the dactylic hexameter, employed by Homer and Virgil. The dactylic hexameter, a meter consisting of six stressed syllables per line, was traditional for Greek and Roman epics, suggesting that Ovid intended his huge collection of tales to be read as a grand epic. Unlike the epics of Homer and Virgil, however, *Metamorphoses* does not feature a central epic hero. Instead, it presents the whole range of Roman mythology—roughly two hundred poems in all—woven together in a continuous narrative sequence from the creation of the world down to the assassination of Julius Caesar.

    Metamorphoses, which means "transformations," had a tremendous influence on later European literature, providing countless source-stories for writers such as Chaucer (see page 772), Boccaccio (see page 813), and Shakespeare (see page 839). Many still regard *Metamorphoses* as a model of tight narrative structure. In fact, Ovid's brief verse narratives about the transformations—seldom longer than two or three pages each—resemble short stories. Each narrative moves swiftly to establish the characters, the setting, and a central conflict, which then, more often than not, leads directly to the metamorphosis that is the heart of the story.

Writer's Response

Metamorphosis, or transformation, serves as the unifying theme of Ovid's work. Briefly describe the stages of your own life in terms of a series of metamorphoses.

Literary Focus

An **allegory** is a poem or story in which characters, settings, or events stand for other people or events, or for abstract qualities or ideas. For example, some readers have interpreted the myth of the Four Ages as an allegory for the general decline of civilization from a state of innocence to a state of strife and discord.

from METAMORPHOSES
Ovid
translated by
ROLFE HUMPHRIES

As you read the following selections, think about how they illustrate Ovid's central theme of transformation.

My intention is to tell of bodies changed
To different forms; the gods, who made the
   changes,
Will help me—or I hope so—with a poem
That runs from the world's beginning to our
   own days.

The Creation

5   Before the ocean was, or earth, or heaven,
Nature was all alike, a shapelessness,
Chaos, so-called, all rude and lumpy matter,
Nothing but bulk, inert, in whose confusion
Discordant atoms warred: there was no sun
10 To light the universe; there was no moon
With slender silver crescents filling slowly;
No earth hung balanced in surrounding air;
No sea reached far along the fringe of shore.
Land, to be sure, there was, and air, and ocean,
15 But land on which no man could stand, and water
No man could swim in, air no man could breathe,
Air without light, substance forever changing,
Forever at war: within a single body
Heat fought with cold, wet fought with dry,
   the hard
20 Fought with the soft, things having weight
   contended
With weightless things.
             Till God, or kindlier Nature,

Settled all argument, and separated
Heaven from earth, water from land, our air
From the high stratosphere, a liberation
25   So things evolved, and out of blind confusion
Found each its place, bound in eternal order.
The force of fire, that weightless element,
Leaped up and claimed the highest place in
        heaven;
Below it, air; and under them the earth
30   Sank with its grosser portions; and the water,
Lowest of all, held up, held in, the land.

Whatever god it was, who out of chaos
Brought order to the universe, and gave it
Division, subdivision, he molded earth,
35   In the beginning, into a great globe,
Even on every side, and bade the waters
To spread and rise, under the rushing winds,
Surrounding earth; he added ponds and marshes,
He banked the river-channels, and the waters
40   Feed earth or run to sea, and that great flood

Giraudon/Art Resource, New York

Celestial Atlas: Southern Hemisphere, **Gerard Valk and Pieter Schenk,** 1708

Washes on shores, not banks. He made the plains
Spread wide, the valleys settle, and the forest
Be dressed in leaves; he made the rocky
    mountains
Rise to full height, and as the vault of Heaven
45 Has two zones, left and right, and one between
        them
Hotter than these, the Lord of all Creation
Marked on the earth the same design and pattern.
The torrid zone too hot for men to live in,
The north and south too cold, but in the middle
50 Varying climate, temperature and season.
Above all things the air, lighter than earth,
Lighter than water, heavier than fire,
Towers and spreads; there mist and cloud
    assemble,
And fearful thunder and lightning and cold winds,
55 But these, by the Creator's order, held
No general dominion; even as it is,
These brothers brawl and quarrel; though
        each one
Has his own quarter, still, they come near tearing
The universe apart. Eurus is monarch
60 Of the lands of dawn, the realms of Araby,
The Persian ridges under the rays of morning.
Zephyrus holds the west that glows at sunset,
Boreas, who makes men shiver, holds the north,
Warm Auster governs in the misty southland,
65 And over them all presides the weightless ether,
Pure without taint of earth.
                                These boundaries given,
Behold, the stars, long hidden under darkness,
Broke through and shone, all over the spangled
    heaven,
Their home forever, and the gods lived there,
70 And shining fish were given the waves for
        dwelling
And beasts the earth, and birds the moving air.

But something else was needed, a finer being,
More capable of mind, a sage, a ruler,
So Man was born, it may be, in God's image,
75 Or Earth, perhaps, so newly separated

From the old fire of Heaven, still retained
Some seed of the celestial force which fashioned
Gods out of living clay and running water.
All other animals look downward; Man,
80 Alone, erect, can raise his face toward Heaven.

The Four Ages

The Golden Age was first, a time that cherished
Of its own will, justice and right; no law,
No punishment, was called for; fearfulness
Was quite unknown, and the bronze tablets held
85 No legal threatening; no suppliant throng
Studied a judge's face; there were no judges,
There did not need to be. Trees had not yet
Been cut and hollowed, to visit other shores.
Men were content at home, and had no towns
90 With moats and walls around them; and no
        trumpets
Blared out alarums; things like swords and
        helmets
Had not been heard of. No one needed soldiers.
People were unaggressive, and unanxious;
The years went by in peace. And Earth,
        untroubled,
95 Unharried by hoe or plowshare, brought forth all
That men had need for, and those men were
        happy,
Gathering berries from the mountainsides,
Cherries, or blackcaps, and the edible acorns.
Spring was forever, with a west wind blowing

100 Softly across the flowers no man had planted,
And Earth, unplowed, brought forth rich grain;
        the field,
Unfallowed, whitened with wheat, and there were
        rivers
Of milk, and rivers of honey, and golden nectar
Dripped from the dark-green oak-trees.

**Medieval manuscript page of
Metamorphoses depicting
Jupiter's revolt against Saturn.**

                                After Saturn°
105 Was driven to the shadowy land of death,
And the world was under Jove, the Age of Silver
Came in, lower than gold, better than bronze.
Jove made the springtime shorter, added winter,

104. **Saturn:** the Roman god of
the seasonal cycle, loosely
associated with Cronus the
Titan, who was overthrown
by his son Zeus (Jove, or Jupiter).

Ovid **425**

Summer, and autumn, the seasons as we know
    them.
110   That was the first time when the burnt air glowed
White-hot, or icicles hung down in winter.
And men built houses for themselves; the caverns,
The woodland thickets, and the bark-bound
    shelters
No longer served; and the seeds of grain were
    planted
115   In the long furrows, and the oxen struggled
Groaning and laboring under the heavy yoke.
Then came the Age of Bronze, and dispositions
Took on aggressive instincts, quick to arm,
Yet not entirely evil. And last of all
120   The Iron Age succeeded, whose base vein
Let loose all evil: modesty and truth
And righteousness fled earth, and in their place
Came trickery and slyness, plotting, swindling,
Violence and the damned desire of having.
125   Men spread their sails to winds unknown to
    sailors,
The pines came down their mountainsides,
    to revel
And leap in the deep waters, and the ground,
Free, once, to everyone, like air and sunshine,
Was stepped off by surveyors. The rich earth,
130   Good giver of all the bounty of the harvest,
Was asked for more; they dug into her vitals,
Pried out the wealth a kinder lord had hidden
In Stygian shadow,° all that precious metal,
The root of evil. They found the guilt of iron,
135   And gold, more guilty still. And War came forth
That uses both to fight with; bloody hands
Brandished the clashing weapons. Men lived on
    plunder.
Guest was not safe from host, nor brother from
    brother,
A man would kill his wife, a wife her husband,
140   Stepmothers, dire and dreadful, stirred their brews
With poisonous aconite, and sons would hustle
Fathers to death, and Piety lay vanquished,
And the maiden Justice, last of all immortals,
Fled from the bloody earth.

**The god Mars, or a
fighting warrior.
Etruscan statue, 5th
century B.C.**

133. **Stygian** (stij′ē·ən) **shadow:**
the netherworld, through
which the River Styx is said
to flow.

First Thoughts

How did you visualize the Golden Age as described by Ovid?

Identifying Facts

1. What was nature like before the creation? After the creation, what warring pairs of elements continued to threaten to "tear the universe apart"?
2. According to "The Creation," how do human beings differ from the animals?
3. Identify the Four Ages. What are the characteristics of each age?

Interpreting Meanings

1. Ovid's poetic treatment of the process of creation bears a number of striking similarities to the biblical account in the Book of Genesis (see page 163). What are some of these similarities?
2. An **allegory** is a work in which characters, setting, or events stand for more general ideas. How can "The Four Ages" be read as an allegory for the decline of humanity from a state of innocence? Find three or four examples from the text that contribute to this allegorical interpretation. Decide whether the last age, the age of iron, can be read as an allegory for our own day.
3. During the Golden Age, only one of the four seasons exists. What is this season, and why is it appropriate?
4. What, if anything, motivates each of the stages of decline in "The Four Ages"? Does a human action precede each stage of degeneration, or is the decline beyond human control? Discuss.

Applying Meanings

Allegories about the decline of civilization accept as a premise that there was once a Golden Age—that civilization was indeed once nearer to paradise than it is now. Do you believe that this premise is true? Do you think that there literally was a time when life on earth was peaceful and harmonious? Argue your opinion.

Creative Writing Response

Writing a Myth. Make up your own brief myth that explains the development of American culture from some point in the past to the present. Where your myth begins is up to you: You could, for example, choose to begin thousands of years before the arrival of Columbus, the Pilgrims' landing at Plymouth Rock in 1620, or the American Revolution of 1776. Like Ovid, you may want to designate a certain number of "ages" or "stages" for your myth. For each age, give a few notable characteristics or events, or provide a description which helps to distinguish that era from the others.

Critical Writing Response

Comparing Allegorical Interpretations of Myths. The characters, settings, and events in an **allegory** may stand for other people or events, or for abstract qualities or ideas. In a brief essay, discuss how "The Creation" and "The Four Ages" might be interpreted as contrasting allegorical stories. How does "The Creation" suggest an optimistic point of view about the inevitability of progress? How does "The Four Ages" suggest a pessimistic viewpoint about the inevitability of decline? In your essay, be sure to support your points with specific references to the stories. A chart like the one below might help you to organize your ideas.

	Creation	Four Ages
Characterization of humans		
Characterization of gods		

Tacitus
c. A.D. 56–c. A.D. 117

The Bettmann Archive

If Cornelius Tacitus (tas'i·təs) had lived in another age, he might have become a great statesman. He was an exceptionally skilled orator, and he served Rome in a variety of public offices. He spent a good part of his life, however, under the tyrannical rule of unusually cruel and corrupt emperors. He grew up, for example, during the reign of Nero (nir'ō), who ruled A.D. 54–68, and spent most of his adult years under the reign of the sadistic Domitian (də·mish'ən), who ruled A.D. 81–96.

Tacitus' firsthand observations of the injustice and cruelty of the Roman emperors of his time drove him to take up the pen. Nearly all of Tacitus' writing shows a spirit of defiance. His first published work, *Agricola*, was a defense of his father-in-law, a public official who had been treated unjustly.

Tacitus is best known for his two histori-cal works, of which only fragments have survived. The *Annals* depicts the troubled reigns of Tiberius, Caligula, Claudius, and Nero, which took place between the years A.D. 14 and A.D. 68. The *Histories* continues the chronicle up to the death of Domitian in A.D. 96. Tacitus also wrote an important treatise on rhetoric, or the art of persuasive speaking, called *Dialogues of the Orators.*

Modern readers expect histories to be complete, accurate, and "objective," that is, written without directly revealing the writer's bias or point of view. Objective writing allows the reader to form his or her own opinions and conclusions. The notion of objective historical writing dates back to the earliest Greek historians, particularly Thucydides. But Tacitus seems to have felt differently. He often allowed his emotions and personal convictions to appear in his narrative. His contempt for the emperors' abuses of power and for those Romans who hypocritically flattered the rulers is also clear.

Tacitus thought history should be used for moral purposes: He believed that the evil deeds of powerful people should not be forgotten after their deaths; he also believed that good deeds should be recorded and praised. Whether or not Tacitus exaggerated or distorted details to suit his own purposes, as some of his critics have claimed, he contributed perhaps more than any other source to the shaping of our picture of the early Roman Empire.

Reader's Guide

THE BURNING OF ROME

Background

This selection, which describes a disastrous fire that swept through Rome in A.D. 64, is drawn from Book XV of Tacitus' *Annals*. It offers a fine example of the historian's preoccupation with moral bankruptcy and general ruin. Nero, whose actions lie at the center of Tacitus' account, became emperor of Rome in A.D. 54 at the age of seventeen. Although the young ruler and his advisers initiated some enlightened programs during his first five years in power, the emperor became steadily more vain, corrupt, and violent. In addition to revealing Tacitus' bitterness and disgust toward Nero's irresponsibility during the crisis of the fire, this account also records for the first time the reaction of first-century pagan Rome toward the new religion of Christianity.

Writer's Response

Why would it be important for a historian to distinguish between fact and opinion? Is it even possible to write objectively about history? Freewrite your answer.

Literary Focus

Style is the way a writer expresses his or her thoughts through language. All writers have some idea about how they can best convey their ideas. As a result, they make decisions about which words to use, how long or short the sentences and paragraphs should be, and what images and figures of speech are appropriate and fitting. Style is often viewed separately from content, but often the style is what makes the content memorable.

THE BURNING OF ROME
from The Annals
Tacitus
translated by
GEORGE GILBERT RAMSAY

As you read, note how effectively Tacitus suits his style to his subject. Notice his choice of language and the way he forms his sentences in his description of a traumatic time in Roman history.

Bust of Nero, emperor of Rome.

And now came a calamitous fire—whether it was accidental or purposely contrived by the Emperor remains uncertain for on this point authorities are divided—more violent and destructive than any that ever befell our city. It began in that part of the Circus[1] which adjoins the Palatine and Caelian hills.[2] Breaking out in shops full of inflammable merchandise, it took hold and gathered strength at once; and being fanned by the wind soon embraced the entire length of the Circus, where there were no mansions with protective walls, no temple-enclosures, nor anything else to arrest its course. Furiously the destroying flames swept on, first over the level ground, then up the heights, then again plunging into the hollows, with a rapidity which outstripped all efforts to cope with them, the ancient city lending itself to their progress by its narrow tortuous streets and its misshapen blocks of buildings. The

---

1. **Circus:** Circus Maximus, a great arena used for chariot races.
2. **Palatine** (pal′ə·tīn′) **and Caelian** (sē′lē·ən) **hills:** two of the seven hills of ancient Rome.

shrieks of panic-stricken women; the weakness of the aged, and the helplessness of the young; the efforts of some to save themselves, of others to help their neighbors; the hurrying of those who dragged their sick along, the lingering of those who waited for them—all made up a scene of inextricable confusion.

Many persons, while looking behind them, were enveloped from the front or from the side; or having escaped to the nearest place of safety, found this, too, in possession of the flames, and even places which they had thought beyond their reach in the same plight with the rest. At last, not knowing where to turn, or what to avoid, they poured into the roads or threw themselves down in the fields; some having lost their all, not having even food for the day; others, though with means of escape open to them, preferred to perish for love of the dear ones whom they could not save. And none dared to check the flames; for there were many who threatened and forced back those who would extinguish them, while others openly flung in torches, saying that *they had their orders;*—whether it really was so, or only that they wanted to plunder undisturbed.

At this moment Nero was at Antium.[3] He did not return to the city until the flames were approaching the mansion which he had built to connect the Palatine with the Gardens of Maecenas;[4] nor could they be stopped until the whole Palatine, including the palace and everything around it, had been consumed. Nero assigned the Campus Martius[5] and the Agrippa[6] monuments for the relief of the fugitive and houseless multitude. He threw open his own gardens also, and put up temporary buildings for the accommodation of the destitute; he brought up provisions from Ostia and the neighboring towns; and he reduced the price of corn to three sesterces[7] the peck. But popular as these measures were, they aroused no gratitude; for a rumor had got abroad that at the moment when the city was in flames Nero had mounted upon a stage in his own house, and by way of likening modern calamities to ancient, had sung the tale of the sack of Troy.

Not until the sixth day was the fire got under, at the foot of the Esquiline hill,[8] by demolishing a vast extent of buildings, so as to present nothing but the ground, and as it were the open sky, to its continued fury. But scarcely had the alarm subsided, or the populace recovered from their despair, when it burst out again in the more open parts of the city; and though here the loss of life was less, the destruction of temples and porticoes of pleasance was still more complete. And the scandal attending this new fire was the greater that it broke out in property owned by Tigellinus,[9] in the Aemilian[10]

---

3. **Antium** (ant'i·əm): a seaside town about thirty-two miles south of Rome, and Nero's birthplace; it is now called Anzio.

4. **Gardens of Maecenas** (mī·sē'nəs): a luxurious pleasure palace built by Maecenas, an intimate supporter of the Emperor Augustus and an important patron of literary men, including Horace and Virgil.

5. **Campus Martius** (mär·shəs): the Field of Mars, an area of central Rome, originally the site of a temple of Mars; it was later expanded to include a great many buildings, including baths, temples, and gardens constructed for Agrippa around 25 B.C.

6. **Agrippa** (ə·grip'ə): Marcus Vipsanius Agrippa (63–12 B.C.), a Roman military leader.

7. **sesterces** (ses·tûr'sēz): silver pieces, each worth about five cents.

8. **Esquiline** (es'kwə·līn') **hill:** one of the seven hills of ancient Rome.

9. **Tigellinus** (tij'ə·lī'nəs): Nero's worthless friend, who joined and encouraged the emperor in his cruelties and debaucheries.

10. **Aemilian** (i·mē'li·ən)

THE EMPEROR PLAYING HIS LYRE WHILE ROME BURNED, nineteenth-century engraving.
Why do you think the subject of Nero and the burning of Rome would be interesting to modern audiences and modern artists?

The Granger Collection, New York

quarter; the general belief being that Nero had the ambition to build a new city to be called after his own name. For of the fourteen regions into which Rome was divided only four remained intact. Three were burnt to the ground; in the other seven, nothing remained save a few fragments of ruined and half-burnt houses.

To count up the number of mansions, of tenements, and of temples that were destroyed would be no easy matter. Among the oldest of the sacred buildings burnt was that dedicated by Servius Tullius to the Moon, and the Great Altar and fane[11] raised by Evander to the Present Hercules. The temple vowed by Romulus[12] to Jupiter, the Stayer of Flight; the Royal Palace of Numa;[13] the Temple of Vesta,[14] with the Household Gods[15] of the Roman people, were all destroyed; added to these were the treasures won in numerous battles, and masterpieces of Greek art, as well as ancient and genuine monuments of Roman genius which were remembered by the older generation amid all the splendor of the restored city, and which could never be replaced. Some noted that the nineteenth of July, the day on which the fire began, was also the day on which the Senonian Gauls[16] had taken and burnt the

---

11. **fane** (fān): sanctuary or temple.
12. **Romulus** (räm′yo͞o·ləs): the legendary founder of Rome.

13. **Numa:** Numa Pompilius (no͞o′mə päm·pil′i·əs): second king of Rome; he succeeded Romulus.
14. **Vesta** (ves′tə): goddess of the hearth.
15. **Household Gods:** the Lares (lā′rez′) and Penates (pē·nā′tēz′), minor deities that presided over family and home.
16. **Senonian Gauls** (sə·nō′ni·ən gôlz): barbarians from northern Italy who captured and burned Rome about 390 B.C.

city; others were so curious in their calculations as to discover that the two burnings were separated from one another by exactly the same number of years, of months, and of days.

Nero profited by the ruin of his country to erect a palace in which the marvels were not to be gold and jewels, the usual and common-place objects of luxury, so much as lawns and lakes and mock-wildernesses, with woods on one side and open glades and vistas on the other. His engineers and masters-of-works were Severus and Celer; men who had the ingenuity and the impudence to fool away the resources of the Empire in the attempt to provide by Art what Nature had pronounced impossible.

For these men undertook to dig a navigable canal, along the rocky shore and over the hills, all the way from Lake Avernus to the mouths of the Tiber.[17] There was no other water for supplying such a canal than that of the Pontine marshes;[18] and even if practicable, the labor would have been prodigious, and no object served. But Nero had a thirst for the incredible, and traces of his vain attempt to excavate the heights adjoining Lake Avernus are to be seen to this day.

The parts of the city unoccupied by Nero's palace were not built over without divisions, or indiscriminately, as after the Gallic fire, but in blocks of regular dimensions, with broad streets between. A limit was placed to the height of houses; open spaces were left; and colonnades were added to protect the fronts of tenements, Nero undertaking to build these at his own cost, and to hand over the building sites, cleared of rubbish, to the proprietors. He offered premiums also, in proportion to the rank and means of owners, on condition of mansions or tenements being completed within a given time; and he assigned the marshes at Ostia for the reception of the rubbish, which was taken down the Tiber in the same vessels which had brought up the corn. Certain parts of the houses were to be built without beams, and of solid stone, Gabian or Alban, those stones being impervious to fire. Then as water had often been improperly intercepted by individuals, inspectors were appointed to secure a more abundant supply, and over a larger area, for public use; owners were required to keep appliances for quenching fire in some open place; party walls were forbidden, and every house had to be enclosed within walls of its own.

These useful provisions added greatly to the appearance of the new city; and yet there were not wanting persons who thought that the plan of the old city was more conducive to health, as the narrow streets and high roofs were a protection against the rays of the sun, which now beat down with double fierceness upon broad and shadeless thoroughfares.

Such were the measures suggested by human counsels; after which means were taken to propitiate the Gods. The Sibylline books[19] were consulted, and prayers were offered, as prescribed by them, to Vulcan, to Ceres, and to Prosperine. Juno[20] was supplicated by

---

17. **Lake Avernus** (ə·vur'nəs): a small lake near Cumae, in the center of an extinct volcano; **Tiber**: The Tiber River runs through Rome.
18. **Pontine** (pän'tēn) **marshes**: a swampy region between Rome and Naples.

19. **Sibylline** (sib'ə·līn') **books**: nine ancient books, supposedly written by the Sybil, or prophetess; these books reveal the destiny of Rome.
20. **Vulcan** (vul'kən): god of fire and metalworking; **Ceres** (sir'ēz): goddess of grain and harvest; **Proserpine** (prō·sur'pi·nə): wife of Pluto, king of Hades; **Juno** (jōō'nō): queen of the gods and goddess of marriage.

the matrons, in the Capitol first, and afterwards at the nearest point upon the sea, from which water was drawn to sprinkle the temple and image of the Goddess; banquets to the Goddesses and all-night festivals were celebrated by married women.

But neither human aid, nor imperial bounty, nor atoning-offerings to the Gods, could remove the sinister suspicion that the fire had been brought about by Nero's order. To put an end therefore to this rumor, he shifted the charge onto others, and inflicted the most cruel tortures upon a body of men detested for their abominations, and popularly known by the name of Christians. This name came from one Christus, who was put to death in the reign of Tiberius by the Procurator Pontius Pilate; but though checked for the time, the detestable superstition broke out again, not in Judaea only, where the mischief began, but even in Rome, where every horrible and shameful iniquity, from every quarter of the world, pours in and finds a welcome.

First those who acknowledged themselves of this persuasion were arrested; and upon their testimony a vast number were condemned, not so much on the charge of incendiarism as for their hatred of the human race. Their death was turned into a diversion. They were clothed in the skins of wild beasts, and torn to pieces by dogs; they were fastened to crosses, or set up to be burned, so as to serve the purpose of lamps when daylight failed. Nero gave up his own gardens for this spectacle; he provided also Circensian games,[21] during which he mingled with the populace, or took his stand upon a chariot, in the garb of a charioteer. But guilty as these men were and worthy of direst punishment, the fact that they were being sacrificed for no public good, but only to glut the cruelty of one man, aroused a feeling of pity on their behalf.

Meanwhile Italy was ransacked for contributions. The provinces and allied peoples were rifled, as well as the states which are called 'free.' Even the Gods had to submit to being plundered. The temples in the city were despoiled, and emptied of the gold consecrated at triumphs, or vowed by past generations of Romans in times of panic or prosperity. As for Asia and Achaia,[22] not offerings only, but the very images of the Gods were carried off by Acratus and Secundus Carrinas, who were sent out to those provinces for the purpose. The former was a freedman ready for any kind of villainy; the latter was a man whose lips were tinged with Greek learning, but who had no real culture in his heart.

We are told that Seneca[23] craved leave to withdraw to a remote country retreat to avoid the odium of such sacrilege; on this being denied him, he pretended to be suffering from some muscular ailment, and shut himself up in his own chamber. Other accounts say that Nero ordered poison to be administered to him by one of his own freedmen, called Cleonicus; but that Seneca escaped the trap, either by the man's avowal, or by his own precaution in adopting a simple diet of natural fruits, and slaking his thirst from running water.

---

21. **Circensian** (sûr·ken′si·ən) **games:** games held in the Circus, or arena.

22. **Asia and Achaia** (ə·kā′ə): Asia Minor and Greece.

23. **Seneca** (sen′i·kə): Nero's minister of state, a Stoic philosopher; he retired from office in A.D. 62. He was forced to commit suicide as the result of a court intrigue in A.D. 65.

First Thoughts

Do you think this is an eyewitness report of the burning of Rome, rather than a secondhand account of the disaster?

Identifying Facts

1. According to Tacitus, why was nothing done to stop the burning of Rome?
2. When a second fire broke out in the open parts of the city, what rumor about the emperor was circulated? What steps did Nero take to squelch this rumor?
3. How did Nero pay for the rebuilding of Rome?

Interpreting Meanings

1. Locate the details that describe Nero. What impression do these details create of the emperor? Which details might have led another historian to a different conclusion?
2. Consider Tacitus' description of the first outbreak of the fire in Rome in the first paragraph (see page 430). Judging from his use of language, his tone, and his images, how would you describe his **style**? For example, is it concise, impassioned, or detached? Support your answer with examples from the selection.
3. Tacitus' famous passage about the Christians is one of the earliest historical references to Christianity by a non-Christian writer. How does Tacitus show that he is prejudiced against the Christians? On what grounds does he express anger about their persecution?

Applying Meanings

If you were the editor in chief of a major daily newspaper, and Tacitus put in an application for a job as a reporter, would you give him the job? Why or why not?

Creative Writing Response

Rewriting an Account. You are one of the historical "authorities" whom Tacitus mentions on page 430. You believe the fire at Rome was accidental, and that Nero did his best to relieve the people's hardship and to rebuild the city. Write a short account of the fire, changing the tone toward the emperor from negative to positive.

Language and Vocabulary

Exploring Connotations

The **connotations** of words—as distinct from their literal meanings or **denotations**—are their associations or emotional overtones. Tacitus uses words whose connotations seem calculated to have an emotional impact on the reader. Such a style, of course, influences the reader indirectly. By using **loaded language**, language that appeals to readers' emotions, Tacitus reveals his own prejudices.

Reread the following passages. Then explain how the connotations of the italicized words or phrases differ from those of the words or phrases given in parentheses.

1. "But Nero had *a thirst for the incredible,* and traces of his *vain* attempt to excavate the heights adjoining Lake Avernus are to be seen to this day." (a taste for the unusual; unsuccessful)
2. "To put an end therefore to this rumor, he shifted the charge on to others; and inflicted the most cruel tortures upon a body of men detested for their *abominations,* and popularly known by the name of Christians." (crimes)
3. " . . . but though checked for the time, the *detestable superstition* broke out again, not in Judaea only, where the *mischief* began, but even in Rome. . . ." (religious belief; trouble)

LANGUAGE
—AND—
CULTURE

CLASSICAL ALLUSIONS IN MODERN ENGLISH

An **eponym** (ep'ə·nim') is a person—either mythical or real—from whose name the name of a nation, idea, or term has been derived. Classical Greek and Roman myth and literature have lent English dozens of eponymous expressions. See how many of the following expressions you know.

Achilles' Heel

According to Homer's *Iliad*, the hero Achilles was fated to win great glory but to die an early death. Achilles' mother, the sea nymph Thetis, tried to forestall her son's destiny when he was still an infant by dipping every part of his body in the waters of the Styx, a river in the underworld. The magic waters were supposed to protect Achilles against all wounds in battle. However, Thetis forgot to immerse one part of her son's body: the heel by which she held him. Years later, the Trojan prince Paris slew Achilles with an arrow that pierced him—you guessed it—in the heel. Nowadays an "Achilles' heel" is used to refer to any vulnerable point in a plan or in a person's character.

Midas Touch

The Greeks told several legends about Midas, who ruled the kingdom of Phrygia (frij'ē·ə) in Asia Minor (now Turkey). In the most famous story, the god Dionysus granted Midas one wish. Midas wished that everything he touched would turn to gold. Dionysus took him literally, and Midas became the original "Goldfinger" and an instant billionaire. Unfortunately, the king's food, wine, and even his daughter were also transformed into gold as soon as he touched them. Today, the expression "Midas touch" applies to anyone who easily acquires riches.

Pandora's Box

Hesiod (hē'sē·əd), a poet who was roughly contemporary with Homer, tells the story of Zeus's creation of the first woman, Pandora. Before he sent Pandora to live on earth, Zeus gave her a mysterious box, instructing her never to open it. Once on earth, however, Pandora's curiosity got the better of her. When she opened the box, war, plague, and famine escaped and took up permanent residence in the world. Only hope remained inside the box, as a consolation prize to mortals. The expression "opening a

The Bridgeman Art Library/Art Resource, New York

PANDORA, DANTE GABRIEL ROSSETTI, 1869.
❓ *How would you describe Pandora's expression in Rossetti's painting? Is it fitting to her mythological role?*

Pandora's box'' now refers to an action likely to lead to unforeseen—and unpleasant—consequences.

Pyrrhic Victory

In 279 B.C., King Pyrrhus (pir'əs) fought the Romans for control of his territories in northwestern Greece. Pyrrhus hoped to panic the Romans by sending a herd of trained battle elephants charging against them, but his strategy failed. The Romans fought back fiercely, and Pyrrhus's army suffered heavy losses. Although Pyrrhus was technically victorious, he is said to have remarked after the battle that another such victory would ruin him. A "Pyrrhic (pir'ik) victory'' still refers to any victory that is too costly to be worthwhile.

Scylla and Charybdis

During his ten-year return voyage home from Troy in Homer's *Odyssey,* the hero Odysseus had to navigate a perilous strait. The six-headed monster Scylla (sil'ə) guarded the strait on one side. To the other side was a churning whirlpool, Charybdis (kə·rib'dis). If Odysseus sailed too near, Charybdis would suck his ship down into the abyss. Odysseus chose to sail near the Scylla, who promptly reached down from her rocky perch on a cliff into Odysseus' ship, seizing and eating six men, one for each of her ghastly jaws. Even now, ''to be caught between Scylla and Charybdis'' is to be forced to choose between two unattractive options. It's the classical equivalent of being caught between a rock and a hard place.

Siren's Song

This expression also comes from the *Odyssey,* where the sirens were seductive sea nymphs, each one part bird and part woman. They sang so beautifully that all the sailors who passed near their rock longed to hear them. Those who yielded to this temptation, however, were drawn toward the Sirens' island and died on its rocky coast. The curious—and wily—Odysseus managed to have his cake and eat it, too. He ordered his men to plug their ears with beeswax and to lash him to the mast so that he could listen to the Sirens' song. Nowadays, a ''siren song'' refers to any irresistible attraction. The danger associated with the ancient sirens is reflected in another meaning of the word *siren* that surfaced in the nineteenth century: a loud signal meant as an alert or a warning, as in a police or ambulance siren.

MAINTAINING SUBJECT-VERB AGREEMENT

As you enrich your writing with details of character and action, your sentences grow more complex. Making verbs agree with subjects in sentences can be tricky, even for experienced writers. Yet errors in **subject–verb agreement** distract readers and reduce your credibility. By learning to double-check certain constructions, you can keep your writing credible and clear.

Subject-Verb Agreement

Make each verb agree in number with its subject. In many English sentences and clauses, the subject comes right before the verb. Subject-verb agreement is easy then: a singular verb for a singular subject (A Greek fights a Trojan.), a plural verb for a plural subject (Greeks fight the Trojans.). However, variations on the standard sentence pattern can increase agreement problems. Study the following five types.

Problems in Subject-Verb Agreement

1. Intervening Words

INCORRECT
   The tone of Sappho's verses remind me of Amy Lowell's poetry.

CORRECT
   The *tone* of Sappho's verses *reminds* me of Amy Lowell's poetry.

Even if other nouns come between subject and verb, a verb still must agree with its subject.

2. Compound Subjects

INCORRECT
   In the end, Achilles or Hector have to die.

CORRECT
   In the end, Achilles or Hector *has* to die.

Most compound subjects take a plural verb: Achilles and Hector *have* great strength. But compound subjects joined by *or* or *nor* take a singular verb.

3. Linking Verbs

INCORRECT
   The best selection were two odes by Horace.

CORRECT
   The best *selection was* two odes by Horace.

A linking verb must agree with its subject, not with the complement (the complement in this case is "two odes"). This is true even if the subject is singular and the complement plural.

4. Indefinite Pronouns

INCORRECT
   Despite the two men's boasting, neither help the victim.

CORRECT
   Despite the two men's boasting, *neither helps* the victim.

The indefinite pronouns listed below always take singular verbs.

anyone	nobody
everyone	somebody
no one	each
someone	either
anybody	neither
everybody	

5. Adjective Clauses

INCORRECT

Tacitus is among the many historians who loves to digress.

Oedipus is the only one of all the travelers who answer the riddle correctly.

CORRECT

Tacitus is among the many *historians* who *love* to digress.

Oedipus is the only *one* of all the travelers who *answers* the riddle correctly.

In clauses with relative pronouns (*who, which,* or *that*) as subjects, the verb may be either singular or plural. It should agree with the relative pronoun's antecedent (*historians* and *one* in the above examples).

Exercise 1: Subject-Verb Agreement

Choose the correct verb form.

1. Only a slim volume of Sappho's poems (survive, survives) today.
2. Patroclus, respecting Achilles' feelings, (justify, justifies) his hero's actions.
3. Careful reporting and perceptive political analysis (mark, marks) Thucydides' *History of the Peloponnesian War.*
4. Neither Jocasta nor Oedipus (realize, realizes) that they are related.
5. A horrific sight in the underworld (was, were) the three snarling mouths of Cerberus.
6. Plato's *Dialogues* are many and varied, but each (teach, teaches) an aspect of Plato's philosophy.
7. Achilles is typical of many epic heroes who knowingly (face, faces) death rather than live without glory.
8. The writings of Tacitus, which (is, are) rich in historical detail and gossip, make fascinating reading.
9. (Is/Are) Herodotus or Thucydides considered the "father of Greek history"?
10. Anyone who (read, reads) the *Aeneid* finds Aeneas a complex hero.

Exercise 2: Revising for Subject-Verb Agreement

Scan a story or an essay you have written, underlining the following kinds of sentences:

1. those in which words intervene between subject and verb
2. those with compound subjects
3. those with linking verbs and complements
4. those containing indefinite pronouns
5. those containing relative clauses

Check your sentences for subject-verb agreement, and correct any such errors that you find.

Critical Thinking and Writing

CREATING AN EPIC ADVENTURE

Today's heroes are usually people like us, fallible but capable of courageous acts. Heroes of Greek and Roman antiquity, however, are far larger than life, superhuman in bravery and prowess. Which kind of hero makes a more appealing role model?

Writing Assignment

Write a brief adventure featuring a hero of your own invention. Your audience is fourth- and fifth-graders, and you want to offer them a new way of looking at the world, as well as to entertain them. In this assignment, you will use the literary elements that you have become familiar with: setting, characters, plot, and theme.

Background

Though they represent different time periods and cultures, the tales of Achilles, Oedipus, and Aeneas share a number of **epic conventions**. Consider the following points as you invent your hero. (You don't have to pattern your hero after the Greek or Roman models, however.)

- **Lineage.** The hero is the offspring of a mortal and a deity. (Oedipus, the exception, is of royal birth.) Heroes have divine powers but human weaknesses.
- **Childhood.** The hero shows early signs of unusual wisdom, strength, or courage.

- **Character.** Heroes are virtuous, determined, passionate, valiant, and noble. Their strength of character lets them endure pain and loss to achieve their goals.
- **Journeys.** The hero goes on a quest, endures trials, and emerges as a leader. Heroes are helped and hindered by gods and goddesses.

Prewriting

Brainstorming. Brainstorm background information about a hero. Decide which time period and place the hero comes from, what his or her society values, and what the hero hopes to accomplish. Also, consider the epic conventions listed above.

Planning. Drawing on the material you have brainstormed, plan a single adventure featuring your hero. Use a story map like the one on the following page.

Writing

1. **Introductory Paragraphs.** You might begin by showing the hero involved in an action or a dialogue that initiates the **conflict.** However you choose to begin, capture your readers' attention and provide enough detail to get them involved in the story.

2. **Body Paragraphs.** Include events that advance the plot, reveal char-

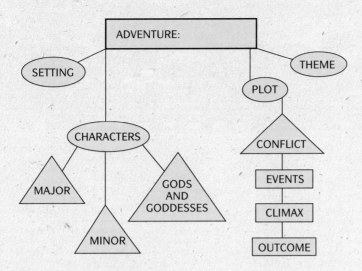

acter, and underscore the conflict or the theme. You might experiment with the use of **foreshadowing** to hint at the climax to come, or with the use of **flashback** to fill in background information.

Combine dialogue, description, and action to bring your adventure to life. Use **epic similes** (extended, grandiose comparisons) and **stock epithets** (descriptive phrases that take the place of names) to create special effects.

3. **Concluding Paragraph.** By the end of your adventure, the conflict should be resolved. The theme of your adventure should emerge from the whole story, but emphasize it now by your choice of details for the ending.

Evaluating and Revising

Use these questions to evaluate and revise your draft.

1. Does the **setting** help readers to picture the action and grasp the mood? Do vivid details bring the setting to life?

2. Does a **conflict** set the chain of events in motion? Is the order of events clear? Does the action have a plausible climax and resolution?

3. Are the **characters'** personalities revealed through the use of dialogue and other indirect forms of characterization?

4. Have you provided enough clues for your readers to grasp the **theme**— the central idea you want your story to convey?

5. Are your sentences varied and grammatically correct?

Proofreading and Publishing

Proofread to eliminate errors in mechanics, and make a final copy of your adventure. Work with your classmates to present your adventures to elementary-school students.

ANCIENT INDIA

About A.D. 450

☐ Gupta Empire

Hindu Kush

• Harappa

Indus River

• Mohenjo-Daro

THAR DESERT

Himal.

Kapilavastu

Ganges

ARABIAN PENINSULA

Vindhya Mountains

Arabian Sea

INDIA

Eastern Ghats

Western Ghats

Indian Ocean

INDIAN LITERATURE

▼ Time ▼
2500 B.C.–A.D. 1500

▼ Place ▼
India

▼ Literary Significance ▼

India boasts a rich, diverse, and long-lasting literary tradition. Most Westerners are surprised to discover that the Indian literary tradition contains more texts than the ancient Greek and Roman traditions combined.

The earliest Indian literature has survived from the Aryan migrations that occurred around 1500 B.C. The literature of this period is called Vedic literature, after the Vedas, collections of sacred hymns.

In the sixth century B.C., Indian literature entered its classical period, which lasted until about A.D. 1000. The literature of this period, which includes epics, court poems, and dramas, was written in Sanskrit, an elite language known for its formality and richness of expression.

Both the Vedic and classical literatures reflect the beliefs of India's dominant religion, Hinduism. Such central Hindu concepts as *dharma, karma,* and reincarnation feature prominently in the literature of the classical period. This literature includes the Indian epics the *Mahabharata* and the *Ramayana,* as well as the less lofty but thoroughly entertaining beast fables represented in the *Panchatantra* and other collections.

TIME LINE

India

LITERARY EVENTS

▼

Bronze female dancer from the Indus Valley civilization. c. 2500 B.C.

The Granger Collection, New York

Later Vedas, Upanishads, and Brahmanas are comp[ ] **c. 900–c. 500 B.C.**

Earliest hymns from the *Rig Veda* are written down, **c. 1000 B.C.**

Vedic period, **1500–500 B.C.**

2500 B.C.	2000 B.C.	1500 B.C.	1000 B.C.

Indus Valley civilization in northwest India reaches its height, **c. 2500 B.C.**

Invasions of Indo-European-speaking nomads coincide with decay of Indus Valley civilization, **c. 1500 B.C.**

Hinduism develops; groups move across India and develop stable kingdoms, **c. 1500–c. 500 B.C.**

Lions from the column of Ashoka, 240 B.C.

Krishna *(center)*, an important Hindu god.

The Granger Collection, New York

▲

CULTURAL AND HISTORICAL EVENTS

Head of Buddha,
c. A.D. 100–200.

Museum of Art, Rhode Island School of Design: Helen M. Danforth Fund, Photography by Cathy Carver

Panchatantra is composed,
c. A.D. 300

Kalidasa, great Sanskrit poet and dramatist, writes drama *Shakuntala*, **c. A.D. 400**

Mahabharata, including *Bhagavad-Gita*, is written down, **c. 300 B.C.– c. A.D. 300**

Classical period of Indian literature,
500 B.C.–A.D. 1000

Ramayana is compiled,
c. 200 B.C.–c. A.D. 200

Illustration from a sixteenth-century manuscript of the *Ramayana*.

Courtesy of the Freer Gallery of Art, Smithsonian Institution, Washington, D.C.: 07.271v38 – Indian Manuscript: late 16th century; Mughal, Akbar school; Persian translation of "Ramayana of Valmiki: 130 miniatures in opaque colors and gold; 27.5 x 15.2 cm (10 7/8 x 6") average leaf size

500 B.C.	A.D. 1	500	1000

Life of Gautama Buddha,
c. 536–483 B.C.

Written form of Sanskrit develops, **c. 500 B.C.**

Buddhism and Jainism develop, **c. 500 B.C.**

Gupta dynasty rules,
A.D. 320–467

Rival Indian rulers fight for power; invading Arabs bring first Muslim rule to India, **c. 600–1000**

Portuguese explorer Vasco da Gama arrives in Calcutta, signaling the beginning of European presence in Indian history, **1498**

Alexander the Great invades India, **326 B.C.**

Maurya dynasty builds an empire; King Ashoka (**c. 272–232 B.C.**) spreads Buddhism throughout India, **321–185 B.C.**

Shiva, one of the principal Hindu gods.

Nelson-Atkins Museum, Kansas City, MO

Muslim Turks invade India, eventually establishing a sultanate in Delhi, **c. 1000–c. 1300**

This time line border shows characters from the still-undeciphered Indus Valley script, developed in ancient India between 2500 and 1500 B.C.

Time Line   **445**

INDIAN LITERATURE

Indra, the Vedic god of war, accompanied by the celestial nymphs, fresco from the Ajanta Caves, C. A.D. 580. *The Hindus eventually incorporated Indra into their own pantheon as a sky god.*

66 So far as I am able to judge, nothing has been left undone, either by man or Nature, to make India the most extraordinary country that the sun visits on his round. Nothing seems to have been forgotten, nothing overlooked. 99

—*Mark Twain*

Scholars are not sure who the first settlers of India were, but they do know that an advanced civilization flourished in northern India between 2500 and 1500 B.C. This was the so-called **Indus Valley** civilization, whose remaining artifacts—undiscovered by archaeologists until the early nineteenth century—show some interesting similarities to the art of later Hindu (hin'dōō') culture in India.

Around 1500 B.C., a wave of migrations into India began that would continue into the seventeenth century A.D. The earliest known migrants called themselves **Aryans** (ar′ē·ənz). They were a group of nomadic, or wandering, warriors and herders. Many scholars believe that the Aryans, like other Indo-European peoples, probably originated in central Asia. Although the Aryans were not city-builders like their predecessors in the Indus Valley, they brought with them a well-developed language and literature, as well as a set of religious beliefs.

The Vedic Period in India

The first literary period in India is known as the **Vedic** period, lasting from 1500 B.C. to approximately 500 B.C. This period is named for the **Vedas** (vā′dəz), a set of hymns that formed the cornerstone of the Aryan culture. Hindus still consider the Vedas to be the most sacred of all literature, for they believe that these sacred hymns were revealed to humans directly by the gods. The oldest existing Vedic hymns are collected in the *Rig Veda* (rig′ vā′də), featuring poems of praise to the beauty of the earth and the wonder of existence. (The word *veda* and our word *video* both come from the Indo-European root *weid-*, meaning "to see" or "to know.") For centuries, the Vedas were transmitted orally by priests who had memorized every syllable. Even after a system for writing literature had been introduced in the sixth century B.C., the Vedas were still passed on orally by priests.

The Classical Period: The Legacy of Sanskrit

After the Vedic period ended, and until about A.D. 1000, Indian literature entered its **classical** period. The main literary language of northern India during this period was **Sanskrit** (san′skrit′), an Indo-European language. Most languages of northern India tend, like Sanskrit itself, to belong to the Indo-European family of languages. The main languages of southern India, by contrast, come from an independent family of languages with ancient roots in the Indian subcontinent: the **Dravidian** (drə·vid′ē·ən) languages, such as Tamil (tam′əl) and Kannada (kä′nə·də). But even the "higher,"

Statue of a man recovered from the ruins of Mohenjo-Daro, a center of the Indus Valley civilization.

Pakistan Government, Department of Archaeology

Sanskrit inscriptions on the interior walls of a dome, India.

or elite, forms of the Dravidian languages often borrowed the cultural concerns and vocabularies of Sanskrit texts.

One of the most fascinating facts about Sanskrit is that by 600 B.C. it had become a "frozen" literary language. In other words, over long periods of time written Sanskrit barely changed to reflect evolutions in everyday speech, and it remained much the same in its grammar and syntax for centuries. An analogy to this situation would be if we today spoke contemporary English but wrote everything in Old English, the language used in Anglo-Saxon literary works such as *Beowulf.*

> By 600 B.C., Sanskrit had become a fixed and frozen literary language that would change very little over the centuries to come.

Sanskrit, which means "perfect speech," is one of the most important legacies of India's ancient literary tradition. It is considered a sacred language, the language spoken by the gods and goddesses. As such, Sanskrit was seen as the only appropriate form of expression for the noblest literary works—epics, court poems, and dramas, among others. Although India claims more than fourteen major languages and hundreds of regional dialects, Sanskrit has given an amazing cohesiveness to Indian literature over the past 3500 years. Poets, novelists, and dramatists, writing in various Indian languages, have drawn much of their inspiration from the classical tradition represented by Sanskrit texts, which are known for their beauty and intellectual subtlety.

> **"** When doubts haunt me, when disappointments stare me in the face, and I see not one ray of light on the horizon, I turn to the *Bhagavad-Gita,* and find a verse to comfort me; and I immediately begin to smile in the midst of overwhelming sorrow. **"**
>
> —*Mahatma Gandhi*

Literature During the Classical Period

Like the ancient Greeks, the Indians had two great epics—the **Mahabharata** (mə·hä′bä′rə·tə) and the **Ramayana** (rä·mä′yə·nə). These works had been part of India's oral tradition for centuries, but they were finally written down in a more-or-less fixed form during the classical period. Poetry and drama reached a high point during this period. Beast fables were also immensely popular and often used by religious teachers to illustrate moral points. During the classical period, many beast fables from the oral tradition were finally put together in collections, the most famous of which was the **Panchatantra**, a world classic that has appeared in some two hundred versions in many different languages.

Hinduism: The Key to Indian Culture

It is tempting for a Westerner to stereotype all of India's literature as essentially religious or mythological, whereas in fact India boasts a wide array of literary types, from the love and war poems of the classical Tamil tradition to the deeply personal lyric poems of such women poets as Mira Bai. Nevertheless, it is impossible to understand the Indian literary tradition—which claims more texts than the ancient Greek and Latin traditions combined—without speaking of the religion that claims the majority of India's 900 million people as followers: **Hinduism**.

Hinduism evolved from the beliefs of the ancient Aryans of the Vedic period. More than a religion, Hinduism is a way of life, with a seemingly endless variety of beliefs, rituals, and gods. It has no single written doctrine or set of rules, and no single prophet or religious leader, such as Jesus Christ or Mohammed. Its pantheon, or assembly of gods and goddesses, consists of (by some counts) 330 million different deities. Nevertheless, three particular deities stand out in the Hindu pantheon: Brahma (brä´mə) the Creator, Vishnu (vish´n$\overline{oo}$) the Protector, and Shiva (shē´və) the Destroyer.

Despite the enormous number of different cults and sects in Hinduism, many Hindus believe that all the gods—and indeed, everything in the universe—are aspects of a single essence, or immortal spirit. This belief in the ultimate oneness of existence serves as a counterweight to the diversity of India's enormous population and its many different classes of people and methods of worship.

The earliest texts of Hinduism are the Vedic hymns and an entire body of sacred prose literature, including the **Upanishads** ($\overline{oo}$·pan´i·shadz´), that serve as commentaries on, or philosophical extensions of, the hymns. The two great Hindu epics, the *Mahabharata* and the *Ramayana*, vividly illustrate the lessons of Hinduism, focusing on the Hindu concepts of *dharma*, *karma*, and reincarnation.

THE GODLY PAIR (KRISHNA AND RAHDA) ON THE BIRD GARUDA

A SCRIBE, c. 1625.

Lessons of Indian Literature: Following One's Dharma

Dharma (där′mə) comes from a Sanskrit verb meaning "to hold." The closest word in English that begins to define dharma is "religion." Dharma is also close in meaning to such concepts as duty, righteousness, ethics, morality, law, and order.

According to Hindu belief, every individual is born with a unique dharma, which unfolds throughout a lifetime according to the individual's choices. Most of the lessons of dharma—what to do or not to do in a given situation—must be determined by the individual on a moment-by-moment basis. There are times when even the most righteous person, such as the god Krishna in the *Mahabharata*, must lie or act in other seemingly unrighteous ways in order to act in accordance with his or her dharma. Ultimately, dharma requires that a person fulfill the duties of his or her station in life, however lofty or humble it might be.

The Caste System in India

A person's dharma depends upon his or her **caste** (kast), or social standing. In Indian tradition, people are not created equal. Rather, they are categorized at birth into one of four groups, or ranks of society. Hindu religious law uses the word **varna** (vär′nə), meaning "color" or "rank," to refer to the order of the various castes in society. The origin of the varnas goes back at least to the *Rig Veda*. One Vedic hymn speaks of the four varnas resulting from the sacrifice of the primal man, called Purusa. His body was divided into the fourfold varna system: from his head came the *Brahmans* (brä′mənz), the scholars, priests, and teachers; from his torso came the *Kshatriyas* (kə·shat′rē·yəz), the rulers and warriors; from his thighs came the *Vaisyas* (vīs′yəz), the merchants, farmers, and artisans; and from his feet came the *Sudras* (soo̅′drəz), those who clean up after all the others and do much of life's unpleasant work.

The caste system is also a key element of Indian literature. In the *Bhagavad-Gita* (bug′ə·vəd gē′tä), part of the *Mahabharata*, the god Krishna (krish′nə) continually appeals to the warrior Arjuna's sense of his varna. As a warrior, it is Arjuna's dharma to fight. If he does not fight as a warrior should, he will violate his dharma, harming not only himself, but also his family, his society, and ultimately the world order. Arjuna knows all this. The question that baffles Arjuna, and other epic heroes and heroines, is not what dharma is supposed to be, but how it can be successfully carried out with the greatest happiness and least hardship.

The caste system in India finds its origins in the Vedic hymns of the ancient Aryans.

Karma and Reincarnation

Hindus also believe in the concepts of karma and reincarnation. **Karma** (kär′mə) is a Sanskrit word meaning "action." **Reincarnation**, also known as the "transmigration of souls," is a process in which one's soul is reborn in another body. One's actions, or karma, in this life influence one's rebirth and future life. For example, good karma in this life leads to rebirth in a higher form and social position. When a soul is sufficiently purified, it is united with Brahma, the ultimate spiritual reality.

Buddhism—The Search for Spiritual Peace

Great religious and political ferment marked the close of the Vedic Age. It was during this time that a major religion, **Buddhism** (bood′iz′əm), came into being. Buddhism was founded by **Siddharta Gautama** (sid·där′tə gout′ə·mə) (563–483 B.C.), a young prince who renounced his life of wealth and ease in order to discover the key to spiritual peace. ("Buddha" means "Enlightened One," a title given to Siddharta by his followers.) As a result of intense spiritual contemplation, he came to believe that life was suffering, that the cause of suffering was a wrongheaded desire for individual fulfillment, and that the path to mastering this desire was a life of honesty, nonviolence, willpower, continual self-examination, and profound meditation. In contrast to the social stratification of the Hindu caste system, Buddhism insists that all people are potentially equal.

Statue of Buddha, second century A.D., Indian. *Buddhism was born in India but found its greatest following in Southeast Asia.*

Spread of *Buddhism and Hinduism* by A.D. 750

Hinduism and Buddhism

Buddhism

Ashoka, the "Righteous" Emperor

The **Maurya empire** (322–230 B.C.) was the first Indian empire; through warfare and iron-fisted rule, it claimed at its height most of northern India. Yet its greatest ruler, **Ashoka** (d. 232 B.C.), preached goodness, nonviolence, and "righteousness." He also promoted Buddhism, closely monitoring the ethics of his officials' behavior, encouraging vegetarianism, and outlawing hunting for sport. Most significantly, he made Buddhism a religion of missionaries, sending teachers as far away as Southeast Asia, where Buddhism still thrives.

After Ashoka's death in 232 B.C., Buddhism fell into decline, and by the end of the first century A.D. it had nearly disappeared in India. But Buddhism's effect on Hinduism has never been erased. Many Hindus practice some degree of vegetarianism, and the contemplative life preached by Buddha remains a key aspect of Hinduism.

The Gupta Empire

The next great political power in India was the **Gupta dynasty**, which controlled most of northern India from A.D. 320 to 467. Under the Guptas, Hinduism reached a full flowering, and a fertile ground was provided for the expression of Hindu culture through the arts. During this time, Hindu sculpture flourished, and the classical period of Indian literature reached its height.

> Hinduism reached a full flowering during the Gupta empire (A.D. 320–467).

Unity Through Diversity

Indian culture may be characterized as a struggle to achieve unity in the face of enormous diversity. In many ways, it has been the geography of India—the land itself—that has ultimately unified India's multitude of languages, customs, and beliefs. Certainly Indian politics have only periodically achieved this unity. Indian literature, especially classical Sanskrit literature, has fared better. For it is in the classical literature of India—the epics, dramas, poems, and tales—that we see, again and again, expressions of the Hindu belief in the connection between all living things and their oneness in the divine unity.

ASVATTHAMAN SHOOTS AN ARROW OF FIRE AT THE PANDAVAS. Illustration from the **Razm-nama.**

> **66** OM. This eternal Word is all: what was, what is and what shall be, and what beyond is in eternity. All is OM. **99**
> —*from* Mandukya Upanishad

Detail of the Meenakshi Temple wall, India.

The Rig Veda
c. 1000 B.C.

A yakshi, Indian, c. A.D. 150.

The *Rig Veda* (rig′ vä′də) is a collection of more than one thousand hymns that have come to be revered as the sacred texts of the Hindu religion. The original hymns are in an archaic form of Sanskrit, an ancient Indo-European language brought to India by the Aryans, who migrated from the west around 1500 B.C.

The *Rig Veda*, which has come to mean "hymns of supreme sacred knowledge," began as part of sacred rituals in the lives of the Aryan people. Because the Hindus regarded the *Rig Veda* as being divinely inspired, or "heard" directly from the gods, they thought it only fitting that later generations also "hear" the hymns. Thus, even after Sanskrit became a written language, the hymns were transmitted orally by Vedic priests.

Generations of Hindu priests, or *brahmans* (brä′mənz), learned the hymns according to a strict method of memorization. Today, we can appreciate how effective this method was by comparing written versions of the *Rig Veda* made by different scribes: The hymns appear in practically the same words in each manuscript.

The Vedas reveal a great deal about early Indo-European civilizations. We know that the Aryans who came to India were nomads, people with no permanent home. According to the Vedic hymns, the Aryans eventually settled down and became farmers who raised crops and livestock, built simple huts, wore woven wool clothing, made iron tools, and developed communities. The hymns also tell us that the Aryan settlers had their share of social problems, including drunkenness, gambling, and fighting. But most of all, the hymns reveal that the Aryans were a highly poetic people who worshiped the forces of nature.

The Aryans laid the foundation for a powerful religious faith: Hinduism. Hindu worship today generally departs a great deal from the rituals outlined in the ancient texts. On occasions such as weddings and funerals, however, brahman priests in modern India still solemnly chant hymns from the Vedas.

Reader's Guide

NIGHT
from the Rig Veda

Background

The *Rig Veda* contains not only the oldest Vedic hymns but also the most lyrical ones. In their beauty and simplicity, these hymns have been compared to the psalms of the Hebrew Bible.

In the Vedic literature, a god or goddess was assigned to nearly every aspect of nature: For example, the god Surya was associated with the sun, while the god Agni was associated with fire. The hymns were songs of praise for the beauty and wonders of nature. They were also prayers used to seek protection and cooperation from the forces of nature. "Night," like many of the hymns, reveals that the ancient nomads who sang these songs both loved and feared the natural world around them.

"Night" is the only hymn in the ten books of the *Rig Veda* that is dedicated to Ratri (rä'trē), the goddess of night. Night was thought to be a sister of Dawn, a bright goddess. Instead of being depicted as simply dark, Night is also described as a bright deity whose eyes, the stars, drive away the darkness.

Writer's Response

In everyday life and in many literary works, night is often associated with danger or evil. The ancient Aryans, however, believed that night also had some beneficial and beautiful aspects. What qualities do you associate with night? Freewrite your response.

Literary Focus

A **hymn** is a lyric poem, or song, that is addressed to a divine being. Through hymns, people praise the power and wisdom of their deities. Hymns are also often a way of asking for divine help or mercy. Usually intended to be sung during ceremonies or religious worship, most hymns are formal and dignified in tone. The hymn "Night" achieves two purposes: It sings the praises of the goddess and enlists her help in protecting the singer's community.

NIGHT

from the Rig Veda

translated by

WENDY DONIGER O'FLAHERTY

As you read this hymn, make a list of the qualities that are attributed to the goddess of night. Why do you think that the night is seen as feminine?

1. The goddess Night has drawn near, looking about on many sides with her eyes. She has put on all her glories.

2. The immortal goddess has filled the wide space, the depths and the heights. She stems the tide of darkness with her light.

3. The goddess has drawn near, pushing aside her sister the twilight. Darkness, too, will give way.

4. As you came near to us today, we turned homeward to rest, as birds go to their home in a tree.

5. People who live in villages have gone home to rest, and animals with feet, and animals with wings, even the ever-searching hawks.

6. Ward off the she-wolf and the wolf; ward off the thief. O night full of waves, be easy for us to cross over.

7. Darkness—palpable, black, and painted—has come upon me. O Dawn, banish it like a debt.

8. I have driven this hymn to you as the herdsman drives cows. Choose and accept it, O Night, daughter of the sky, like a song of praise to a conqueror.

LADY WAITING, Indian, c. 1800.
Does this painting strike you as a good illustration for the hymn? Why or why not?

First Thoughts

What image in this poem struck you as the most powerful or memorable? Why?

Identifying Facts

1. Find the verse in which Night is spoken of in terms not of darkness but of light.
2. In verse 6, what request does the speaker make of Night?
3. In the last verse of this hymn, what offering does the speaker ask Night to "choose and accept"?

Interpreting Meanings

1. What positive or beneficial qualities of night are suggested in this **hymn**?
2. **Personification** is a figure of speech in which a nonhuman thing is talked about as though it were human. In this hymn, Night is referred to as "she," as if it were alive. What other details personify Night?
3. A **simile** is a figure of speech that makes a comparison between two unlike things using a word such as *like, as,* or *than*. Find at least three similes in this hymn. Explain what is being compared in each.

Applying Meanings

Although this hymn is set in an ancient world very different from ours, many of its details seem timeless. Which details mean the most to you? Which would probably not mean much to a modern reader?

Creative Writing Response

Writing a Description. Review your free-writing about the qualities you associate with night. Then use the associations as the basis for a paragraph in which you vividly describe night. You may imitate the form of the hymn and address your description to night as if it were a living being or deity.

Critical Writing Response

Comparing and Contrasting Two Hymns. In a two- or three-paragraph essay, compare and contrast the hymn "Night" from the *Rig Veda* to the New Kingdom Egyptian hymn "The Great Hymn to the Aten" (see page 73). In your essay, you may wish to consider the following points of each hymn:

1. The **subject**
2. The **purpose** (to praise the deity; to ask for divine help or mercy)
3. The **imagery** and **figures of speech** (**apostrophe, epithets, similes, metaphors**)
4. The **tone** (dignified, informal)

Explore any other points of similarity or difference that you can find in the two hymns. In your concluding paragraph, speculate on the similarities and differences between the New Kingdom Egyptians' and the ancient Aryans' views of their deities as revealed in their hymns.

Language and Vocabulary

Apostrophe

Apostrophe is a figure of speech in which a speaker directly addresses an absent or dead person, an abstract quality, or something nonhuman as if it were present. This technique is typically employed in hymns that address a divine being.

1. Which lines of the hymn contain examples of apostrophe? Who is addressed?
2. Apostrophe can serve as a way to "get a handle on" cosmic forces beyond our control. Addressing such forces directly seems to make them more approachable, as in the nursery rhyme, "Rain, rain, go away!" Can you name two more examples?

Introduction

The Mahabharata

The *Mahabharata* (mə·hä′bä′rə·tə), which may well be the longest poem ever composed in any language, is one of the two great epics of ancient India. Hundreds of millions of people regard this ancient poem as a rich source of religious, philosophical, and practical wisdom.

The Scope of the Epic

The word *Mahabharata* means "great story of Bharata's descendants." The epic poem tells about two rival families descended from a legendary king named Bharata: the Kauravas (kou′rä·vəz) and the Pandavas (pän′də·vəz). The main story takes up less than half the poem.

◆

conflict: *a struggle or clash between opposing characters, forces, or emotions.*

The remainder of this vast narrative is composed of independent texts and digressions, or asides, into other subjects. The most famous of these digressions is the religious and philosophical dialogue known as the *Bhagavad-Gita* (bug′ə·vəd gē′tä) (see page 467).

Historians believe that some of the events and settings depicted in the epic have a basis in fact, referring to events that took place as long ago as 1000 B.C. For example, the epic's central battle between the rival families may reflect a historical struggle for control of lands bordering the upper Ganges and Yamuna rivers, near what is now the city of Delhi, the capital of modern India.

The Author of the *Mahabharata*

The *Mahabharata* in its present form was composed sometime between the fourth century B.C. and the fourth century A.D. According to tradition, the author of the epic was a sage named Vyasa, meaning "compiler" or "arranger." Whether Vyasa actually existed or not, the name is appropriate, for the epic is a collection of works gathered from many sources. The work is probably the result of many hands.

A Struggle for Power

The central conflict of the epic is the rivalry between two families, or sets of cousins, over the kingdom of Kurukshetra (koo·roo·kshä′trə). Both sets of cousins are partly divine—that is, they were fathered by gods. The quarrel between the two families is ignited by Duryo-dhana (door·yō′də·nə), the eldest of the Kaurava branch of the family.

After his father gives a piece of the Kaurava kingdom to his cousins the Pandavas, Duryodhana, whose name means "Mr. Dirty Fighter," becomes jealous. On the advice of his uncle, a gambler, Duryodhana challenges Yudhistira (yoo·də·stē·rə), the eldest of the Pandava brothers, to a game of chance using loaded dice. At a climactic moment early in the epic, Yudhistira blindly stakes all of the Pandavas' worldly goods on the game. By the end of the game, he has lost not only his wealth but also his freedom and that of his brothers and their wife. Duryodhana then sentences the Pandavas to twelve years of exile in the forest. A final provision of the sentence is that, after the final year of exile, the Pandavas must leave the forest and live for a year in disguise, undetected by anyone. If they can fulfill this condition, they can regain all that they lost.

The Pandavas are accompanied in exile by their common wife, a woman of breathtaking beauty and inner strength named Draupadi (drou′pə·dē). Won by the warrior Arjuna (är′ joo·nə) in a contest, Draupadi lives with each Pandava brother in turn—an arrangement resulting from an order of the Pandavas' mother that all the brothers should share in whatever good comes to one.

When the Pandavas return from exile and demand their rightful share of the kingdom, the Kauravas refuse. The Pandavas feel they have no choice but to go to war with their cousins. Although they emerge victors from the great epic battles of the *Mahabharata*, the cost of the Pandavas' victory is immense destruction and suffering.

The Continuing Appeal of the *Mahabharata*

The *Mahabharata* is both a popular entertainment and a treasure trove of wisdom and philosophy. As a testament to its popularity, the *Mahabharata* has been translated into nearly all the languages of India, and it has also been absorbed

Scene from *The Mahabharata*, a film by Peter Brook.

into the various cultural traditions of Southeast Asia. Such popular entertainments as Indian folk theater and Indonesian shadow-puppet theater have taken their plot elements from episodes of the *Mahabharata*. A highly rated Indian television series based on the epic has drawn millions of hooked viewers. An internationally acclaimed stage and film adaptation by English director Peter Brook has proven appealing to American and European audiences. Even today, the *Mahabharata* speaks to a large and diverse audience.

Reader's Guide

HUNDRED QUESTIONS
from the Mahabharata

Background

The episode "Hundred Questions" comes from Book 2 of the *Maha-bharata,* near the end of the Pandava brothers' twelve-year exile in the forest. At first glance, this episode seems a far cry from sacred matters. Yet the *Mahabharata* is an important text of the Hindu religion.

The Hindu concept of *dharma* (där'mə), or sacred duty, is central to the *Mahabharata*. In Hinduism, each person has prescribed responsibilities and duties that make up his or her dharma. By performing these duties, each individual contributes to a universal order. Thus, a devout Hindu servant will try to be as loyal as possible, and a devout leader will strive to embody the highest qualities of leadership: wisdom, humility, and respect for his or her parents and the gods. Thus, heroism in the *Mahabharata,* unlike heroism depicted in many other world epics, depends less on physical prowess or great cleverness and more on the proper fulfillment of dharma.

In this episode, Yudhistira, the eldest Pandava brother, must respond to a series of questions that test his character and challenge him to fulfill his dharma.

Writer's Response

Two of the questions that Yudhistira must answer in this episode are "Who is really happy?" and "What is the greatest wonder of the world?" Freewrite your own answers to both these questions. As you read the selection, compare your answers to those the hero gives.

Literary Focus

The **theme** is the central idea of a work of literature. A theme is not the same as the subject of a work. The theme is the idea the writer wishes to convey *about* the subject. For example, in the poem "Carpe Diem" (see page 417), Horace's *subject* is the passage of time, but his *theme* is that we must make the most of each moment.

While the themes of some works are directly stated, most themes are implied. It is up to the reader to piece together all the clues the writer has provided about the work's underlying meaning.

HUNDRED QUESTIONS
from the Mahabharata
translated by
R. K. NARAYAN

❖ *Read to the end of the paragraph that begins "He wept and lamented aloud," on page 463. Do you predict that Yudhistira will suffer the same fate as his brothers?*

Yudhistira (right), in a scene from *The Mahabharata*, a film by Peter Brook.

G. Abegg/Sygma Photo News

THE FIVE PANDAVA BROTHERS

Yudhistira (yōō·dē′stē·rə): the eldest and most capable brother.

Bhima (bē′mə): second son of Pandu.

Arjuna (är′jōō·nə): the third son and greatest warrior of the epic.

Nakula (nä′kōō·lə): one of the twins born to Madri, second wife of Pandu.

Sahadeva (sä·hä·dā′və): the other twin born to Madri.

The Pandavas were in a hopeful mood when they came back to their original starting point, Dwaitavana,[1] after their prolonged pilgrimage. Dwaitavana was rich in fruits and roots, and the Pandavas lived on sparse diets, performing austerities[2] and practicing rigid vows.

They managed to live, on the whole, a

---

1. **Dwaitavana** (dwā·ta′və·nə): a place in the forest.
2. **austerities** (ô·ster′ə·tēz): practices of self-denial and self-discipline.

tranquil life—until one day a brahmin[3] arrived in a state of great agitation. He had lost a churning staff and two faggots[4] of a special kind, with which he produced the fire needed for his religious activities. All his hours were normally spent in the performance of rites. But that day, he wailed, "A deer of extraordinary size, with its antlers spreading out like the branches of a tree, dashed in unexpectedly, lowered its head, and stuck the staff and the faggots in its horns, turned round, and vanished before I could understand what was happening. I want your help to recover those articles of prayer, for without them I will not be able to perform my daily rites. You can see its hoof marks on the ground and follow them."

As a *kshatriya*,[5] Yudhistira felt it his duty to help the brahmin, so with his brothers, he set out to chase the deer. They followed its hoof marks and eventually spotted it, after a long chase. But when they shot their arrows, the deer sprang away, tempted them to follow it here and there, and suddenly vanished without a trace. They were by this time drawn far into the forest and, feeling fatigued and thirsty, they sat under a tree to rest.

Yudhistira told his youngest brother, Nakula, "Climb this tree and look for any sign of water nearby."

Presently, Nakula cried from the top of the tree, "I see some green patches and also hear the cries of cranes . . . must be a water source." He came down and proceeded towards a crystal-clear pond, sapphire-like, reflecting the sky. He fell down on his knees and splashed the water on his face. As he did this, a loud voice, which seemed to come from a crane standing in the water, cried, "Stop! This pond is mine. Don't touch it until you answer my questions. After answering, drink or take away as much water as you like." Nakula's thirst was so searing that he could not wait. He bent down and, cupping his palms, raised the water to his lips. He immediately collapsed, and lay, to all purposes, dead.

After a while, Yudhistira sent his brother, Sahadeva, to see what was delaying Nakula's return. He too rushed forward eagerly at the sight of the blue pond, heard the warning, tasted the water, and fell dead.

Arjuna followed. On hearing the voice, he lifted his bow, shot an arrow in the direction of the voice, and approached the water's edge. The voice said, "Don't be foolhardy. Answer me first before you touch the water."

Arjuna, surveying with shock and sadness the bodies of his younger brothers, replied, "When you are silenced with my arrows, you will cease to question. . . ." Driven to desperation with thirst and enraged at the spectacle of his dead brothers, he sent a rain of arrows in all directions. As the voice continued to warn, "Don't touch," he stooped and took the water to his lips and fell dead.

Next came Bhima. He saw his brothers lying dead, and swung his mace and cried back when he heard the voice, "O evil power, whoever you may be, I will put an end to you presently, but let me first get rid of this deadly thirst. . . ." Turning a deaf ear to the warning, he took the water in the cup of his palm and with the first sip fell dead, the mace rolling away at his side.

Yudhistira himself presently arrived, passing through the forest where no human being had set foot before except his brothers. He was struck by the beauty of the

---

3. **brahmin** (brä'min): person of the highest, priestly caste; also, **brahman**.

4. **faggots:** bundles of sticks.

5. *kshatriya* (kə·shat'rē·yə): person of the warrior caste.

Yudhistira's brothers Arjuna, Bhima, Nakula, and Sahadeva, and their wife Draupadi. From *The Mahabharata*, a film by Peter Brook.

? *What happens to Yudhistira's brothers when they drink from the lake?*

What was the meaning of the gods' statement at Arjuna's birth that no one could vanquish him?" How was he to explain this calamity to Kunthi?[7]

A little later he said to himself, "This is no ordinary death. I see no marks of injury on any of them. What is behind it all?" Could it be that Duryodhana had pursued them, and had his agents at work? He observed the dead faces; they bore no discoloration or sign of decay. He realized that his brothers could not have been killed by mortals, and concluded that there must be some higher power responsible. Resolving not to act hastily, he considered all the possibilities, and stepped into the lake to perform the rites for the dead.

The voice now said, "Don't act rashly; answer my questions first and then drink and take away as much water as you like. If you disregard me, you will be the fifth corpse here. I am responsible for the deaths of all these brothers of yours; this lake is mine and whoever ignores my voice will die. Take care!"

Yudhistira said humbly, "What god are you to have vanquished these invincible brothers of mine, gifted and endowed with inordinate strength and courage? Your feat is great and I bow to you in homage, but please explain who you are and why you have slain these innocent slakers of thirst? I do not understand your purpose, my mind is agitated and curious. Please tell me who you are."

At this request he saw an immense figure materializing beside the lake, towering over the surroundings. "I am a yaksha.[8] These brothers of yours, though warned, tried to force their way in and have paid for it with

surroundings—enormous woods, resonant with the cry of birds, the occasional grunt of a bear, or the light tread of a deer on dry leaves—and then he came upon the magnificent lake, looking as if made by heavenly hands. There on its bank he saw his brothers.

He wept and lamented aloud. Both the poignancy and the mystery of it tormented him. He saw Arjuna's bow and Bhima's mace lying on the ground, and reflected, "Where is your promise to split Duryodhana's thigh?[6]

---

6. **Duryodhana's thigh:** a promise made by Bhima at the end of the game of dice after the Pandavas had lost everything to their cousins.

7. **Kunthi** (ko͞on'tē): the mother of Yudhistira, Arjuna, and Bhima.

8. **yaksha** (yak'shə): forest divinity or nature spirit.

their lives. If you wish to live, don't drink this water before you answer my questions."

Yudhistira answered humbly, "O yaksha, I will not covet what is yours. I will not touch this water without your sanction, in spite of my thirst. I will answer your questions as well as I can."

The yaksha asked, "What makes the sun rise? . . . What causes him to set?"

Yudhistira answered, "The Creator Brahma[9] makes the sun rise, and his dharma[10] causes the sun to set. . . ."

Yudhistira had to stand a grueling test. He had no time even to consider what to say, as the questions came in a continuous stream. Yudhistira was afraid to delay an answer or plead ignorance. Some of the questions sounded fatuous, some of them profound, some obscure but packed with layers of significance. Yudhistira was constantly afraid that he might upset the yaksha and provoke him to commit further damage, although one part of his mind reflected, "What worse fate can befall us?"

Without giving him time to think, the questions came, sometimes four at a time in one breath. Their range was unlimited, and they jumped from one topic to another.

"What is important for those who sow? What is important for those who seek prosperity?" Before Yudhistira could complete his sentence with "Rain," he also had to be answering the next question with "Offspring. . . ."

The yaksha went on to ask, "What is weightier than the earth?"

"Mother."[11]

"Higher than the heavens?"

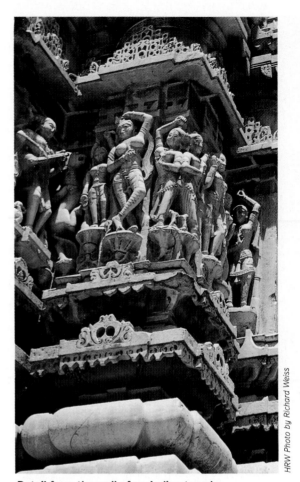

Detail from the wall of an Indian temple.

HRW Photo by Richard Weiss

"Father."[12]

"Faster than the wind?"

"Mind."

"What sleeps with eyes open?"

"Fish."

"What remains immobile after being born?"

"Egg."

"Who is the friend of the exile?"

"The companion on the way."

---

9. **Brahma** (brä´mə): a Hindu creator god.

10. **dharma** (där´mə): rule or law.

11. **Mother:** possibly because "mother Earth" personified is thought to live deep inside the earth.

---

12. **Father:** possibly because "Father" is conceived of here as a sky-god.

"Who is the friend of one about to die?"

"The charity done in one's lifetime."

"Who is that friend you could count on as God given?"

"A wife."

"What is one's highest duty?"

"To refrain from injury."

To another series of questions on renunciation, Yudhistira gave the answers: "Pride, if renounced, makes one agreeable; anger, if renounced, brings no regret; desire, if renounced, will make one rich; avarice, if renounced, brings one happiness. True tranquility is of the heart. . . . Mercy may be defined as wishing happiness to all creatures. . . . Ignorance is not knowing one's duties. . . . Wickedness consists in speaking ill of others."

"Who is a true brahmin? By birth or study or conduct?"

"Not by birth, but by knowledge of the scriptures and right conduct. A brahmin born to the caste, even if he has mastered the Vedas,[13] must be viewed as of the lowest caste if his heart is impure."

There were a hundred or more questions in all. Yudhistira felt faint from thirst, grief, and suspense, and could only whisper his replies. Finally, the yaksha said, "Answer four more questions, and you may find your brothers—at least one of them—revived. . . . Who is really happy?"

"One who has scanty means but is free from debt; he is truly a happy man."

"What is the greatest wonder?"

"Day after day and hour after hour, people die and corpses are carried along, yet the onlookers never realize that they are also to die one day, but think they will live for ever. This is the greatest wonder of the world."

"What is the Path?"

"The Path is what the great ones have trod. When one looks for it, one will not find it by study of scriptures or arguments, which are contradictory and conflicting."

At the end of these answers, the yaksha said, "From among these brothers of yours, you may choose one to revive."

Yudhistira said, "If I have only a single choice, let my young brother, Nakula, rise."

The yaksha said, "He is after all your stepbrother. I'd have thought you'd want Arjuna or Bhima, who must be dear to you."

"Yes, they are," replied Yudhistira. "But I have had two mothers. If only two in our family are to survive, let both the mothers have one of their sons alive. Let Nakula also live, in fairness to the memory of my other mother Madri."[14]

The yaksha said, "You have indeed pleased me with your humility and the judiciousness of your answers. Now let all your brothers rise up and join you."

The yaksha thereafter revived all his brothers and also conferred on Yudhistira the following boon: "Wherever you may go henceforth, with your brothers and wife, you will have the blessing of being unrecognized." The yaksha was none other than Yama,[15] the God of Justice, and father of Yudhistira, who had come to test Yudhistira's strength of mind and also to bless him with the power to remain incognito—a special boon in view of the conditions laid down for the last year of exile.[16]

---

13. **Vedas** (vā'dəz): sacred collection of Hindu wisdom.

14. **Madri** (mä'drē): The twins Nakula and Sahadeva were born to Madri, second wife of Pandu. Madri was thus the "other mother" of the three elder brothers.

15. **Yama** (yä'mə): In most versions of the epic, the father of Yudhistira is Dharma ("right" or "law" personified), and Yama is the god of death.

16. **conditions . . . exile:** The Pandavas had agreed to spend the last year of their exile outside the forest and in disguise.

First Thoughts

What did you think of Yudhistira's answers? Which ones did you agree or disagree with most?

Identifying Facts

1. Explain how the Pandava brothers came to find themselves, tired and thirsty, deep in the forest.

2. How does Yudhistira respond when the yaksha questions him? List two of the yaksha's questions and Yudhistira's responses.

3. What is the real identity of the yaksha, and why has he come to the lake? How does the yaksha reward Yudhistira for his correct answers?

Interpreting Meanings

1. How does Yudhistira's character differ from the characters of his four brothers?

2. An **epic hero** must often endure a test or trial of his physical strength or of his ethical values. What qualities in Yudhistira do you think are being tested in the question-and-answer challenge? How and why does Yudhistira succeed in this challenge?

3. Describe the **setting** of this episode. (See especially the fifth and tenth paragraphs.) How does the setting contribute to the **mood** of the episode?

4. What **theme,** or message, about human behavior does this episode from the *Mahabharata* suggest? Support your answer with evidence from the selection.

Applying Meanings

In one of his answers, Yudhistira tells the yaksha what the greatest wonder of the world is. Do you agree with his answer? If not, what do you consider the greatest wonder?

Creative Writing Response

Creating Riddles. Some of the questions that the yaksha asks Yudhistira are **riddles,** in that some twist of logic must be unraveled to answer them. For example, one part of a question seems to contradict another: ''What remains immobile after being born?'' (Answer: ''Egg.'') Work with a partner to create your own sets of riddles and answers. Then pose your riddles to the class, and see how other students respond.

Critical Writing Response

Analyzing Theme. In a three-paragraph essay, identify and analyze the **theme,** or underlying meaning, of this episode in the epic. Pay special attention to these aspects of the story: the contrast between Yudhistira and his brothers; Yudhistira's answers to the yaksha's questions; and the resurrection of the brothers from death to life as a result of Yudhistira's correct answers. Completing a chart like the one below may help you to organize the material for your essay.

Yudhistira's traits	Brothers' traits
Caution	Foolhardiness

Questions	Answers
What is highest duty?	Refrain from injury.

The Bhagavad-Gita
c. 300 B.C.–c. A.D. 300

ARJUNA AND HIS CHARIOTEER, LORD KRISHNA.

If you ask any devout Hindu what passage in the *Mahabharata* is the most sacred, the answer will probably be the *Bhagavad-Gita* (bug′ə·vəd gē′tä), literally, "Song of the Lord." The *Gita*, as it is affectionately known, is an episode that interrupts the epic *Mahabharata* (see page 458). By the beginning of Book 6 of the main epic, the five Pandava brothers have returned from exile and are seeking to regain their share of the kingdom. The leader of the Kauravas, Duryodhana, decides to destroy his cousins, the Pandavas, whom he regards as dangerous rivals. The armies of each side then mass for battle.

The *Gita* episode consists of a dialogue between the Pandava brother Arjuna and his charioteer, Krishna, just before the great battle begins. The hero Arjuna sits weeping because he does not want to spill the blood of his relatives, the Kauravas. Krishna urges Arjuna to forget his doubts and to fight.

Krishna plays a double role in the epic. He is at once Arjuna's human brother-in-law and, unbeknownst to the hero, the embodiment of Vishnu (vish′no͞o), one of the most important gods in the Hindu pantheon.

The *Bhagavad-Gita* is divided into eighteen sections, or "teachings." The poem is a fine example of **didactic verse**, or poetry meant to convey a philosophy. The *Gita* deals with the nature of the body and the soul, the relationship of human beings to the divine, and the ways the individual can attain "the pure calm of infinity." The *Gita* has been called the bedside book of every pious Hindu. Many Hindus believe that they will attain instant salvation if they hear the *Gita* recited just before they die.

The teachings of this ancient poem also played a major role in shaping the philosophy of Mahatma Gandhi (1869–1948), the charismatic leader who guided India to independence from Britain in 1947. Gandhi called the *Gita* his "spiritual dictionary," a book that taught him to free himself of money, property, and ambition.

Gandhi's philosophy of nonviolent protest profoundly influenced Dr. Martin Luther King, Jr., when he led the Civil Rights movement in the 1960s. The teachings of the ancient *Bhagavad-Gita* have thus indirectly but critically affected modern American society.

Reader's Guide

PHILOSOPHY AND SPIRITUAL DISCIPLINE
from the Bhagavad-Gita

Background

In this selection from the *Bhagavad-Gita,* Krishna urges the warrior-hero Arjuna to fulfill his *dharma,* or "sacred duty," by waging battle. Krishna argues that since it is the fate of every soul to be reincarnated after death—that is, to assume another bodily form—Arjuna need not feel guilty about killing his enemies. The wise warrior should fulfill his dharma as a faithful Hindu and not care about pleasure or pain, profit or loss, success or failure. The narrator who reports this conversation between Krishna and Arjuna is Sanjaya, an attendant to Arjuna's blind uncle, King Dhritarashtra.

Oral Response

Recall one or two specific examples from your own experience, or that of someone you know, when fulfilling a duty created an internal conflict. A diagram like the following may help you explain to the class the source of the conflict in these situations:

Literary Focus

A **paradox** is an apparent contradiction that is actually true. For example, in this selection Krishna states a paradox when he tells Arjuna, "Our bodies are known to end,/but the embodied self is enduring,/indestructible and immeasurable. . . ." How can something be "embodied" and still live forever? In Hindu beliefs, the "embodied self" is the spirit that inhabits the living body. The spirit endures; the physical body does not. As you read Krishna's words in the *Bhagavad-Gita,* you will find many such paradoxes.

PHILOSOPHY AND SPIRITUAL DISCIPLINE

from the Bhagavad-Gita

translated by

BARBARA STOLER MILLER

As you read the dialogue below, try to identify the different arguments Krishna uses to persuade Arjuna. How effective is each argument, in your opinion?

PRINCIPAL CHARACTERS IN THE *BHAGAVAD-GITA*

Sanjaya (sän·jī′ä): attendant to King Dhritarashtra.

Arjuna (är′jōō·nə): the third of the five Pandava brothers.

Krishna (krish′nə): Arjuna's charioteer, who is really a god.

Bhishma (bēsh′mə): great-uncle to the Pandava brothers.

Drona (drō′nə): Arjuna's teacher in archery.

Dhritarashtra (drē·tə·räsh′trə): Arjuna's uncle and father of the Pandavas' enemies, the Kauravas.

Sanjaya

1   Arjuna sat dejected,
    filled with pity,
    his sad eyes blurred by tears.
    Krishna gave him counsel.

Lord Krishna

2   Why this cowardice
    in time of crisis, Arjuna?

The coward is ignoble, shameful,
foreign to the ways of heaven.

3   Don't yield to impotence!
    It is unnatural in you!
    Banish this petty weakness from your heart.
    Rise to the fight, Arjuna!

Arjuna

4   Krishna, how can I fight
    against Bhishma and Drona
    with arrows
    when they deserve my worship?

5   It is better in this world
    to beg for scraps of food
    than to eat meals
    smeared with the blood
    of elders I killed
    at the height of their power
    while their goals
    were still desires.

6   We don't know which weight
    is worse to bear—
    our conquering them
    or their conquering us.

Arjuna and Krishna, from Peter Brook's film version of the *Mahabharata*.
? What is Krishna's true identity?

We will not want to live
if we kill
the sons of Dhritarashtra
assembled before us.

7   The flaw of pity
blights my very being;
conflicting sacred duties
confound my reason.
I ask you to tell me
decisively—Which is better?
I am your pupil.
Teach me what I seek!

8   I see nothing
that could drive away
the grief

that withers my senses;
even if I won kingdoms
of unrivaled wealth
on earth
and sovereignty over gods.

Sanjaya

9   Arjuna told this
to Krishna—then saying,
"I shall not fight,"
he fell silent.

10 Mocking him gently,
Krishna gave this counsel
as Arjuna sat dejected,
between the two armies.

Lord Krishna

11 You grieve for those beyond grief,
    and you speak words of insight;
    but learned men do not grieve
    for the dead or the living.

12 Never have I not existed,
    nor you, nor these kings;
    and never in the future
    shall we cease to exist.

13 Just as the embodied self
    enters childhood, youth, and old age,
    so does it enter another body;
    this does not confound a steadfast man.

14 Contacts with matter make us feel
    heat and cold, pleasure and pain.
    Arjuna, you must learn to endure
    fleeting things—they come and go!

15 When these cannot torment a man,
    when suffering and joy are equal
    for him and he has courage,
    he is fit for immortality.

16 Nothing of nonbeing comes to be,
    nor does being cease to exist;
    the boundary between these two
    is seen by men who see reality.

17 Indestructible is the presence
    that pervades all this;
    no one can destroy
    this unchanging reality.

18 Our bodies are known to end,
    but the embodied self is enduring,
    indestructible, and immeasurable;
    therefore, Arjuna, fight the battle!

19 He who thinks this self a killer
    and he who thinks it killed,

both fail to understand;
it does not kill, nor is it killed.

20 It is not born,
    it does not die;
    having been,
    it will never not be;
    unborn, enduring,
    constant, and primordial,
    it is not killed
    when the body is killed.

21 Arjuna, when a man knows the self
    to be indestructible, enduring, unborn,
    unchanging, how does he kill
    or cause anyone to kill?

22 As a man discards
    worn-out clothes
    to put on new
    and different ones,
    so the embodied self
    discards
    its worn-out bodies
    to take on other new ones.

23 Weapons do not cut it,
    fire does not burn it,
    waters do not wet it,
    wind does not wither it.

24 It cannot be cut or burned;
    it cannot be wet or withered;
    it is enduring, all-pervasive,
    fixed, immovable, and timeless.

25 It is called unmanifest,
    inconceivable, and immutable;
    since you know that to be so,
    you should not grieve!

26 If you think of its birth
    and death as ever-recurring,

then too, Great Warrior,
you have no cause to grieve!

27 Death is certain for anyone born,
and birth is certain for the dead;
since the cycle is inevitable,
you have no cause to grieve!

28 Creatures are unmanifest in origin,
manifest in the midst of life,
and unmanifest again in the end.
Since this is so, why do you lament?

29 Rarely someone
sees it,
rarely another
speaks it,
rarely anyone
hears it—
even hearing it,
no one really knows it.

30 The self embodied in the body
of every being is indestructible;
you have no cause to grieve
for all these creatures, Arjuna!

31 Look to your own duty;
do not tremble before it;
nothing is better for a warrior
than a battle of sacred duty.

32 The doors of heaven open
for warriors who rejoice
to have a battle like this
thrust on them by chance.

33 If you fail to wage this war
of sacred duty,
you will abandon your own duty
and fame only to gain evil.

34 People will tell
of your undying shame,
and for a man of honor
shame is worse than death.

35 The great chariot warriors will think
you deserted in fear of battle;
you will be despised
by those who held you in esteem.

36 Your enemies will slander you,
scorning your skill
in so many unspeakable ways—
could any suffering be worse?

37 If you are killed, you win heaven;
if you triumph, you enjoy the earth;
therefore, Arjuna, stand up
and resolve to fight the battle!

38 Impartial to joy and suffering,
gain and loss, victory and defeat,
arm yourself for the battle,
lest you fall into evil.

39 Understanding is defined in terms of
  philosophy;
now hear it in spiritual discipline.
Armed with this understanding, Arjuna,
you will escape the bondage of action.

40 No effort in this world
is lost or wasted;
a fragment of sacred duty
saves you from great fear.

41 This understanding is unique
in its inner core of resolve;
diffuse and pointless are the ways
irresolute men understand.

42 Undiscerning men who delight
in the tenets of ritual lore

utter florid speech, proclaiming,
"There is nothing else!"

43 Driven by desire, they strive after
    heaven
and contrive to win powers and
    delights,
but their intricate ritual language
bears only the fruit of action in rebirth.

44 Obsessed with powers and delights,
their reason lost in words,
they do not find in contemplation
this understanding of inner resolve.

45 Arjuna, the realm of sacred lore
is nature—beyond its triad of qualities,
dualities, and mundane rewards,
be forever lucid, alive to your self.

46 For the discerning priest,
all of sacred lore
has no more value than a well
when water flows everywhere.

47 Be intent on action,
not on the fruits of action;
avoid attraction to the fruits
and attachment to inaction!

48 Perform actions, firm in discipline,
relinquishing attachment;
be impartial to failure and success—
this equanimity is called discipline.

49 Arjuna, action is far inferior
to the discipline of understanding;
so seek refuge in understanding—pitiful
are men drawn by fruits of action.

50 Disciplined by understanding,
one abandons both good and evil deeds;

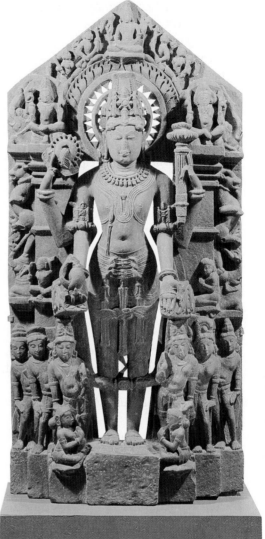

Vishnu with attendants, Indian, c. A.D. 1026.
*The Hindu god Vishnu has many incarnations,
one of whom is Krishna.*

so arm yourself for discipline—
discipline is skill in actions.

51 Wise men disciplined by understanding
relinquish the fruit born of action;
freed from these bonds of rebirth,
they reach a place beyond decay.

from the Bhagavad-Gita   **473**

52 When your understanding passes
        beyond
    the swamp of delusion,
    you will be indifferent to all
    that is heard in sacred lore.

53 When your understanding turns
    from sacred lore to stand fixed,
    immovable in contemplation,
    then you will reach discipline.

Arjuna

54 Krishna, what defines a man
    deep in contemplation whose insight
    and thought are sure? How would he
        speak?
    How would he sit? How would he
        move?

Lord Krishna

55 When he gives up desires in his mind,
    is content with the self within himself,
    then he is said to be a man
    whose insight is sure, Arjuna.

56 When suffering does not disturb his
        mind,
    when his craving for pleasures has
        vanished,
    when attraction, fear, and anger are
        gone,
    he is called a sage whose thought is
        sure.

57 When he shows no preference
    in fortune or misfortune
    and neither exults nor hates,
    his insight is sure.

58 When, like a tortoise retracting
    its limbs, he withdraws his senses
    completely from sensuous objects,
    his insight is sure.

59 Sensuous objects fade
    when the embodied self abstains from
        food;
    the taste lingers, but it too fades
    in the vision of higher truth.

60 Even when a man of wisdom
    tries to control them, Arjuna,
    the bewildering senses
    attack his mind with violence.

61 Controlling them all,
    with discipline he should focus on me;
    when his senses are under control,
    his insight is sure.

62 Brooding about sensuous objects
    makes attachment to them grow;
    from attachment desire arises,
    from desire anger is born.

63 From anger comes confusion;
    from confusion memory lapses;
    from broken memory understanding is
        lost;
    from loss of understanding, he is
        ruined.

64 But a man of inner strength
    whose senses experience objects
    without attraction and hatred,
    in self-control, finds serenity.

65 In serenity, all his sorrows
    dissolve;
    his reason becomes serene,
    his understanding sure.

66 Without discipline,
    he has no understanding or inner
        power;
    without inner power, he has no peace;
    and without peace where is joy?

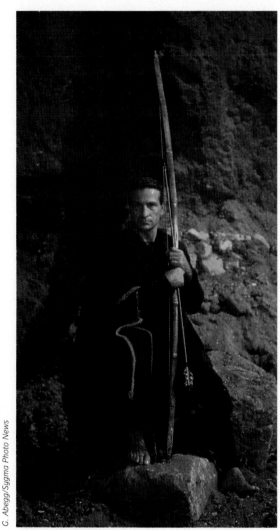

Arjuna with his bow, from Peter Brook's film version of the *Mahabharata*.

67 If his mind submits to the play
of the senses,
they drive away insight,
as wind drives a ship on water.

68 So, Great Warrior, when withdrawal
of the senses
from sense objects is complete,
discernment is firm.

69 When it is night for all creatures,
a master of restraint is awake;
when they are awake, it is night
for the sage who sees reality.

70 As the mountainous depths
of the ocean
are unmoved when waters
rush into it,
so the man unmoved
when desires enter him
attains a peace that eludes
the man of many desires.

71 When he renounces all desires
and acts without craving,
possessiveness,
or individuality, he finds peace.

72 This is the place of the infinite spirit;
achieving it, one is freed from delusion;
abiding in it even at the time of death,
one finds the pure calm of infinity.

First Thoughts

Do you agree with Krishna's teachings concerning worldly success? Why or why not?

Identifying Facts

1. In stanzas 30–31, what argument does Krishna use to persuade Arjuna to fight? According to Krishna in stanzas 33–36, what are the dangers to Arjuna's reputation if he fails to fight?

2. In stanzas 47–48, what outlook toward failure and success does Krishna recommend to Arjuna? On what should Arjuna be "intent"? On what should he *not* be intent?

from the Bhagavad-Gita   **475**

3. In stanza 67, what does Krishna say happens to a man who gives in to his senses? In stanza 71, what does Krishna say happens when a man gives up all desires?

Interpreting Meanings

1. From stanzas 4–8, what can you infer about Arjuna's values? How have these values contributed to his dilemma? Give specific examples to support your points.

2. The technique of **parallelism** is the repetition of words or phrases that have the same grammatical structure. For example, the four lines of stanza 23 illustrate a parallel arrangement of words in each line. How does the poet use parallelism in stanza 29?

3. In "Hundred Questions," the hero Yudhistira, Arjuna's brother, says that one's highest duty is to refrain from injury (see page 465). In the *Bhagavad-Gita,* however, Krishna tells Arjuna that it is his sacred duty to fight. How do stanzas 18–21 help to resolve this **paradox**, or apparent contradiction?

4. What do you think is the most important teaching, or lesson, in Krishna's advice to Arjuna? Possible answers might include the importance of self-control, the need to do one's duty, the importance of living in the present, the importance of knowing oneself, and the need to protect one's reputation. Briefly explain your choice.

Applying Meanings

The *Bhagavad-Gita* states that someone who "renounces all desires and acts without craving, possessiveness, or individual- ity" will achieve inner peace. Do you believe this? How relevant is this advice in today's world? Explain the reasons for your answer.

Creative Writing Response

Writing a Rebuttal. Imagine that you are in the Pandavas' camp and you have an opportunity to talk to Arjuna after Krishna finishes. Write a brief impassioned speech in which you rebut, or maintain a point of view opposite to, Krishna's argument that Arjuna should fight his cousins. In your argument, you might mention the love you have for your own family and the fear you and your comrades have of dying a futile death. If you wish, you may act out the speech with classmates.

Critical Writing Response

Examining Paradox. Santha Rama Rau, a contemporary Indian writer, has said that the *Bhagavad-Gita* is "full of philosophical and moral paradox. It can, for instance, be interpreted as pacifist doctrine or as a call to war." The nature of paradox is that it reveals a kind of truth, although it seems at first to be self-contradictory and untrue. In a brief essay, examine the element of paradox in the dialogue between Krishna and Arjuna. Does Krishna resolve the seeming contradictions of his argument? If so, how? Some of the main topics of Krishna's paradoxical arguments you may want to consider include the following: the nature of duty, the purposes of action, the role of reincarnation in the universe, and the consequences of desire. In your essay, be sure to refer to specific passages in the poem.

SEEING CONNECTIONS

The Bhagavad-Gita's Influence on Transcendentalism

The philosophy of Transcendentalism flourished in New England between 1830 and 1860. American writers Ralph Waldo Emerson (1803–1882) and Henry David Thoreau (1817–1862) were the leaders of the Transcendentalist movement. Transcendentalists taught that the most profound realities go beyond, or *transcend,* everyday human experience. They believed human beings needed to look beyond surfaces to a deeper reality, and that in this way they could find signs of God everywhere, in nature and in individuals.

The *Bhagavad-Gita* in New England

When the Sanskrit classics of ancient India started to appear in English translation in the first half of the nineteenth century, the Transcendentalists eagerly pored over the Indian texts. Thoreau was profoundly impressed by the *Bhagavad-Gita* and the Indian tradition. As he wrote in *Walden*—his most famous work—''The pure Walden water mingled with the sacred water of the Ganges [India's most sacred river].''

Cosmic Unity

The Transcendentalists were especially attracted to the concept in the *Gita* of an eternal, cosmic unity called *brahman,* similar to Emerson's concept of the ''Over-Soul.'' According to the *Gita,* the *atman,* or individual soul, of every human being

merges again with the *brahman* of the universe.

In 1857, Emerson published ''Brahma,'' a poem that expressed many Transcendentalist ideas. The poem's speaker, Brahma, is the embodiment of a universal, creative force.

> If the red slayer thinks he slays,
>   Or if the slain think he is slain,
> They know not well the subtle ways
>   I keep, and pass, and turn again.
>
> Far or forgot to me is near;
>   Shadow and sunlight are the same;
> The vanished gods to me appear;
>   And one to me are shame and fame.
>
> They reckon ill who leave me out;
>   When me they fly, I am the wings;
> I am the doubter and the doubt,
>   And I the hymn the Brahman sings.
>
> The strong gods pine for my abode,
>   And pine in vain the sacred Seven;
> But thou, meek lover of the good!
>   Find me, and turn thy back on
>   heaven.

The words ''sacred Seven'' in the last stanza refer to the greatest Hindu saints. Note how the first stanza in the selection above strikingly resembles stanza 19 from the *Bhagavad-Gita* (see page 471).

The Panchatantra

C. A.D. 300

Illustration from an Arabic version of the Panchatantra.

The *Panchatantra* (pun'chə·tän'trə) began in ancient India as a tool for teaching statecraft to young princes. The anonymous work consists of a series of fables, or brief stories that teach practical lessons about life. The stories are contained within a larger outer story, a narrative framework that gives the tales a thematic unity.

In the outer story, called the "frame," a brahman priest named Vishnusharman (vish'nōō·shär'mən) tries to teach the art of rulership to two rather dimwitted young princes. The lessons take the form of a series of fables, presented in five sections: how one loses friends, how one wins friends, how one should handle international relations, how one may lose profits and possessions, and how hasty actions can have harmful consequences.

The central theme that runs through the *Panchatantra* is the idea of *niti* (ni'tē), which means "worldly wisdom." A person needs five things in order to achieve *niti*: physical security, freedom from want, resolute action, good friends, and the use of intelligence. A person with *niti* is the sort of person who can get the better of evil or unscrupulous rivals or plotters by turning the tables on them.

The *Panchatantra* is among the most well-known collections of fables in the world. It was translated into Persian as early as the sixth century A.D. During the Middle Ages, it was translated into Arabic, Greek, Hebrew, Latin, German, and Italian. The classical Indian fables have influenced works as diverse as *The Thousand and One Nights* (see page 638), Geoffrey Chaucer's *Canterbury Tales* (see page 772), and Giovanni Boccaccio's *Decameron* (see page 813). All three of these works, like the *Panchatantra*, rely on a frame story to establish overall unity.

Reader's Guide

RIGHT-MIND AND WRONG-MIND
from the Panchatantra

Background

The fable "Right-Mind and Wrong-Mind" and the second fable it contains, "A Remedy Worse Than the Disease," illustrate two of the main literary elements of the *Panchatantra*. One of these is the use of the story-within-a-story device to emphasize different aspects of the lesson being taught by the main fable. In this case, "A Remedy Worse Than the Disease" casts light on the lesson being taught by "Right-Mind and Wrong-Mind." Another prominent literary element of the *Panchatantra* is an intermingling of prose and **epigrams**—brief, clever verses that often contain a moral. Epigrams are effective devices for summarizing the message of the story line. The frequent use of epigrams gives the *Panchatantra* much of its special flavor and appeal.

This selection is taken from "The Loss of Friends," the first section of the *Panchatantra*. Like many of the fables in the section, "Right-Mind and Wrong-Mind" shows how greed and malice can destroy a friendship.

Oral Response

If you wanted to teach a friend a moral or practical lesson about life, do you think it would be more effective to use the direct method of a lecture or the indirect method of telling a fable? Discuss the reasons for your opinion with the rest of the class.

Literary Focus

A **fable** is a brief story in prose or verse that teaches a moral or a practical lesson about life. The characters in most fables are animals that behave and speak like human beings. Occasionally, however, the characters—whether humans or humanlike animals—represent abstract qualities. The following selection features both types of characters. The young man named Right-Mind, for example, is not so much a fully developed character as he is a symbol of the quality of virtue. The heron, on the other hand, is more like a real person, since he is neither all good nor all bad.

RIGHT-MIND AND WRONG-MIND

from the Panchatantra

translated by

ARTHUR WILLIAM RYDER

> **As you read, pay attention to the epigrams—short verses that present a moral—that appear throughout the tale. Do you think these epigrams unnecessarily interrupt the story, or do they serve a useful purpose?**

In a certain city lived two friends, sons of merchants, and their names were Right-Mind and Wrong-Mind. These two traveled to another country far away in order to earn money. There the one named Right-Mind, as a consequence of favoring fortune, found a pot containing a thousand dinars,[1] which had been hidden long before by a holy man. He debated the matter with Wrong-Mind, and they decided to go home, since their object was attained. So they returned together.

When they drew near their native city, Right-Mind said: "My good friend, a half of this falls to your share. Pray take it, so that, now that we are at home, we may cut a brilliant figure before our friends and those less friendly."

But Wrong-Mind, with a sneaking thought of his own advantage, said to the other: "My good friend, so long as we two hold this treasure in common, so long will our virtuous friendship suffer no interruption. Let us each take a hundred dinars, and go to our homes after burying the remainder. The decrease or increase of this treasure will serve as a test of our virtue."

Now Right-Mind, in the nobility of his nature, did not comprehend the hidden duplicity of his friend, and agreed to the proposal. Each then took a certain sum of money. They carefully hid the residue in the ground, and made their entrance into the city.

Before long, Wrong-Mind exhausted his preliminary portion because he practiced the vice of unwise expenditure and because his predetermined fate offered vulnerable points. He therefore made a second division with Right-Mind, each taking a second hundred. Within a year this, too, had slipped in the same way through Wrong-Mind's fingers. As a result, his thoughts took this form: "Suppose I divide another two hundred with him, then what is the good of the remainder, a paltry four hundred, even if I steal it? I

---

1. **dinars** (di·närz′): A dinar was originally a Roman coin (*decenarium*). This currency of varying values was used in many parts of the Mediterranean and the Middle East.

think I prefer to steal a round six hundred." After this meditation, he went alone, removed the treasure, and leveled the ground.

A mere month later, he took the initiative, going to Right-Mind and saying: "My good friend, let us divide the rest of the money equally." So he and Right-Mind visited the spot and began to dig. When the excavation failed to reveal any treasure, that impudent Wrong-Mind first of all smote his own head with the empty pot, then shouted: "What

Page from the dictionary of Sāhāngīr, Mughal, 17th century.
Why do you think fables have been used as teaching tools?

became of that good lucre?[2] Surely, Right-Mind, you must have stolen it. Give me my half. If you don't, I will bring you into court."

"Be silent, villain!" said the other. "My name is Right-Mind. Such thefts are not in my line. You know the verse:

> A man right-minded sees but trash,
> Mere clods of earth, in others' cash;
> A mother in his neighbor's wife;
> In all that lives, his own dear life."

So together they carried their dispute to court and related the theft of the money. And when the magistrates learned the facts, they decreed an ordeal[3] for each. But Wrong-Mind said: "Come! This judgment is not proper. For the legal dictum runs:

> Best evidence is written word;
> Next, witnesses who saw and heard;
> Then only let ordeals prevail
> When witnesses completely fail.

In the present case, I have a witness, the goddess of the wood. She will reveal to you which one of us is guilty, which not guilty." And they replied: "You are quite right, sir. For there is a further saying:

> To meanest witnesses, ordeals
>   Should never be preferred;
> Of course much less, if you possess
>   A forest goddess' word.

Now we also feel a great interest in the case. You two must accompany us tomorrow morning to that part of the forest." With this they accepted bail from each and sent them home.

Then Wrong-Mind went home and asked his father's help. "Father dear," said he, "the

---

2. **lucre** (lōō'kər): riches; money.
3. **ordeal:** here, a form of trial in which guilt or innocence was determined by subjecting the accused to painful or dangerous tests.

dinars are in my hand. They only require one little word from you. This very night I am going to hide you out of sight in a hole in the mimosa tree that grows near the spot where I dug out the treasure before. In the morning you must be my witness in the presence of the magistrates."

"Oh, my son," said the father, "we are both lost. This is no kind of scheme. There is wisdom in the old story:

> The good and bad of given schemes
> Wise thought must first reveal:
> The stupid heron saw his chicks
> Provide a mongoose meal."

"How was that?" asked Wrong-Mind. And his father told the story of

A Remedy Worse Than the Disease

A flock of herons once had their nests on a fig tree in a part of a forest. In a hole in the tree lived a black snake who made a practice of eating the heron chicks before their wings sprouted.

At last one heron, in utter woe at seeing the young ones eaten by a snake, went to the shore of the pond, shed a flood of tears, and stood with downcast face. And a crab who noticed him in this attitude, said: "Uncle, why are you so tearful today?" "My good friend," said the heron, "what am I to do? Fate is against me. My babies and the youngsters belonging to my relatives have been eaten by a snake that lives in a hole in the fig tree. Grieved at their grief, I weep. Tell me, is there any possible device for killing him?"

On hearing this, the crab reflected: "After all, he is a natural-born enemy of my race. I will give him such advice—a kind of true lie—that other herons may also perish. For the proverb says:

Tree of life, Indian, c. 1600–1700.
What is the meaning of the title, "A Remedy Worse Than the Disease"?

> Let your speech like butter be;
> Steel your heart remorselessly:
> Stir an enemy to action
> That destroys him with his faction."

And he said aloud: "Uncle, conditions being as they are, scatter bits of fish all the way from the mongoose burrow to the snake's hole. The mongoose will follow that trail and will destroy the villainous snake."

When this had been done, the mongoose followed the bits of fish, killed the villainous snake, and also ate at his leisure all the herons who made their home in the tree.

"And that is why I say:

> The good and bad of given schemes, . . .

and the rest of it."

But Wrong-Mind disdained the paternal warning, and during the night he hid his father out of sight in the hole in the tree. When morning came, the scamp took a bath, put on clean garments, and followed Right-Mind and the magistrates to the mimosa tree, where he cried in piercing tones:

"Earth, heaven, and death, the feeling mind,
Sun, moon, and water, fire and wind,
Both twilights, justice, day and night
Discern man's conduct, wrong or right.

O blessed goddess of the wood, which of us two is the thief? Speak."

Then Wrong-Mind's father spoke from his hole in the mimosa: "Gentlemen, Right-Mind took that money." And when all the king's men heard this statement, their eyes blossomed with astonishment, and they searched their minds to discover the appropriate legal penalty for stealing money, in order to visit it on Right-Mind.

Meanwhile, Right-Mind heaped inflammable matter about the hole in the mimosa and set fire to it. As the mimosa burned, Wrong-Mind's father issued from the hole with a pitiful wail, his body scorched and his eyes popping out. And they all asked: "Why, sir! What does this mean?"

"It is all Wrong-Mind's doing," he replied. Whereupon the king's men hanged Wrong-Mind to a branch of the mimosa, while they commended Right-Mind and caused him satisfaction by conferring upon him the king's favor and other things.

First Thoughts

Did you feel that Right-Mind was doing the right thing by setting the fire? Did his action surprise you?

Identifying Facts

1. Why does Wrong-Mind want Right-Mind to bury most of the treasure? What does Wrong-Mind then do on his own?
2. Why does Wrong-Mind want to hide his father in the mimosa tree?
3. How does Right-Mind expose Wrong-Mind's scheme?

Interpreting Meanings

1. What lessons about rulership can be learned from "Right-Mind and Wrong-Mind"?
2. How does the second **fable**, "A Remedy Worse Than the Disease," shed light on, or reinforce, the **moral** of "Right-Mind and Wrong-Mind"?
3. An **epigram** is a brief, clever, and usually memorable statement. Which of the four-line epigrammatic verses in each fable best sums up the story's **moral**?

Applying Meanings

Do you think "Right-Mind and Wrong-Mind" has any relevance to modern readers? How might the moral of the fable be applied today to such fields as business and law?

Creative Writing Response

Writing a Fable. "Right-Mind and Wrong-Mind" is taken from the first part of the *Panchatantra,* which features tales under the heading "Loss of Friends." Make a list of the behaviors that could cause a person to lose a friend. Choose one behavior in particular that you think is the most destructive to friendship. Then think of a brief fable of your own that would illustrate that behavior and its effects. You may create characters who represent specific traits. Try to write at least one **epigram** to include in your tale.

The Ramayana

c. 200 B.C.–C. A.D. 200

TWO SPIES DISGUISED AS MONKEYS APPROACH THE ARMY OF RAMA.

The *Ramayana* (rä·mä′yə·nə) is one of India's great Hindu epics. The main character Rama (rä′mə) is, like Krishna, an incarnation of the Hindu god Vishnu (vish′noo). Rama and his wife Sita (sē′tə) are semidivine figures, but their story in the epic is a moving, human tale of love and jealousy, loss and recovery, separation and return.

The *Ramayana* is a long poem of some 25,000 couplets. As in the case of the *Mahabharata*, the authorship of the *Ramayana* is attributed to a shadowy figure, the poet-sage Valmiki (väl·mē′kē), who composed the epic in Sanskrit.

The main plot of the epic begins with Prince Rama, who, having won his bride Sita through a miraculous trial of strength, is ready to inherit his rightful throne. Rama, however, is banished from his father's kingdom as the result of an evil court intrigue, and for many years he wanders in exile, accompanied by Sita and by his loyal brother Lakshmana (läk′shmə·nə).

In the first half of the epic, Sita is abducted by the fierce Ravana (rä′və·nə), the many-headed king of the demons, and brought to Ravana's island fortress, the kingdom of Lanka. During their quest to rescue Sita, Rama and Lakshmana ally themselves with the monkey-king Hanuman (hän′oo·män′). Rama finally conquers Ravana, wins back his bride, and returns in triumph to his kingdom.

During her captivity, Sita has proved to be as faithful as she is beautiful and wise. But despite the fact that Sita has passed through an ordeal of fire to prove her purity, Rama harbors lingering doubts about her fidelity. These doubts lead, in the end, to Sita's tragic despair and departure from the earth to assume her place as a goddess.

The image of Sita as a flesh-and-blood woman of saintly devotion and great physical endurance reflects the ideal portrait of many classic Indian heroines. Similarly, the loving description of the lush forests, cool hermitages, and other holy places gives us insight into the "geography" of Indian consciousness. The *Ramayana*, like all national epics, holds up a mirror to a rich and complex culture.

Reader's Guide

RAMA AND RAVANA IN BATTLE
from the Ramayana

Background

The following selection, which describes the climax of the titanic battles between Rama and Ravana, is drawn from Book 6 of the *Ramayana*. R. K. Narayan's retelling of the narrative is based on a medieval version of the *Ramayana* by the south Indian poet Kamban. Kamban, who drew upon the Sanskrit original of Valmiki, composed his version of the epic in the Tamil language. In this climactic episode, the magic weapons and supernatural powers make for an exciting sequence. More important, however, is the sense we get of a blurring of reality and illusion, and of a conflict that goes beyond the simple opposition between good and evil.

Writer's Response

Thousands of years before such films as *Star Wars,* the struggle between good and evil in the *Ramayana* was imagined as a battle unfolding on a cosmic scale, involving fantastic weapons that could destroy the whole universe. Freewrite for a few minutes your ideas for a science-fiction film that would present an epic struggle between good and evil.

Literary Focus

An **epic** is a long narrative poem that relates the great deeds of a larger-than-life hero who embodies the values of a particular society. Most epics include elements of myth, legend, folklore, and history. The tone is serious and the language grand. Most epic heroes undertake quests to achieve something of tremendous value to themselves or their society.

RAMA AND RAVANA IN BATTLE

from the Ramayana

translated by

R. K. NARAYAN

 As you read this account of the final confrontation between the epic hero Rama and his enemy Ravana, try to identify the values and character traits that make Rama an ideal epic hero.

Every moment, news came to Ravana of fresh disasters in his camp. One by one, most of his commanders were lost. No one who went forth with battle cries was heard of again. Cries and shouts and the wailings of the widows of warriors came over the chants and songs of triumph that his courtiers arranged to keep up at a loud pitch in his assembly hall. Ravana became restless and abruptly left the hall and went up on a tower, from which he could obtain a full view of the city. He surveyed the scene below but could not stand it. One who had spent a lifetime in destruction now found the gory spectacle intolerable. Groans and wailings reached his ears with deadly clarity; and he noticed how the monkey hordes[1] reveled in their bloody handiwork. This was too much for him. He felt a terrific rage rising within him, mixed with some admiration for Rama's valor. He told himself, "The time has come for me to act by myself again."

He hurried down the steps of the tower, returned to his chamber, and prepared himself for the battle. He had a ritual bath and performed special prayers to gain the benediction of Shiva;[2] donned his battle dress, matchless armor, armlets, and crowns. He had on a protective armor for every inch of his body. He girt his swordbelt and attached to his body his accouterments[3] for protection and decoration.

When he emerged from his chamber, his heroic appearance was breathtaking. He summoned his chariot, which could be drawn by horses or move on its own if the horses were hurt or killed. People stood aside when he came out of the palace and entered his chariot. "This is my resolve," he said to himself: "Either that woman Sita, or my wife Mandodari,[4] will soon have cause to cry and roll in the dust in grief. Surely, before this day is done, one of them will be a widow."

---

1. **monkey hordes:** a tribe of spirits aiding Rama in his battle with Ravana.

2. **Shiva** (shē′və): a god of destructive forces; originally a storm god; he carries a trident.

3. **accouterments** (ə·kōōt′ər·mənts): a soldier's equipment, not including clothes or arms.

4. **Mandodari** (mən·dō′də·rē)

Courtesy of the Freer Gallery of Art, Smithsonian Institution, Washington, D.C.; 07.271-297v—Indian Manuscript; late 16th century; Mughal; Akbar school; Persian translation of "Ramayana" of Valmiki; 130 miniatures in opaque colors and gold; 27.5 × 15.2 cm. (10 7/8 × 6") average leaf size

RAVANA WITH CHARIOT. Ravana is typically portrayed as having numerous heads and arms.

The gods in heaven noticed Ravana's determined move and felt that Rama would need all the support they could muster. They requested Indra[5] to send down his special chariot for Rama's use. When the chariot appeared at his camp, Rama was deeply impressed with the magnitude and brilliance of the vehicle. "How has this come to be here?" he asked.

"Sir," the charioteer answered, "my name is Matali.[6] I have the honor of being the charioteer of Indra. Brahma, the four-faced god and creator of the Universe, and Shiva, whose power has emboldened Ravana now to challenge you, have commanded me to bring it here for your use. It can fly swifter than air over all obstacles, over any mountain, sea, or sky, and will help you to emerge victorious in this battle."

Rama reflected aloud, "It may be that the rakshasas[7] have created this illusion for me. It may be a trap. I don't know how to view it." Whereupon Matali spoke convincingly to dispel the doubt in Rama's mind. Rama, still hesitant, though partially convinced, looked at Hanuman[8] and Lakshmana[9] and asked, "What do you think of it?" Both answered, "We feel no doubt that this chariot is Indra's; it is not an illusory creation."

Rama fastened his sword, slung two quivers full of rare arrows over his shoulders, and climbed into the chariot.

The beat of war drums, the challenging cries of soldiers, the trumpets, and the rolling chariots speeding along to confront each other, created a deafening mixture of noise. While Ravana had instructed his charioteer to speed ahead, Rama very gently ordered his chariot-driver, "Ravana is in a rage; let him perform all the antics he desires and

---

5. **Indra** (in′drə): important Hindu god appearing in various forms; sometimes considered the god of war, sometimes the chief of all the minor gods.

6. **Matali** (mə·təl·ē′)

7. **rakshasas** (räk′shə·səz): malevolent spirits capable of assuming various shapes.

8. **Hanuman** (hän′oo·män′): a form of the name Hanumat; he is a monkey-king and the principal ally of Rama in his war with Ravana.

9. **Lakshmana** (läk′shmə·nə): half brother of Rama; known as the embodiment of loyalty.

exhaust himself. Until then be calm; we don't have to hurry forward. Move slowly and calmly, and you must strictly follow my instructions; I will tell you when to drive faster."

Ravana's assistant and one of his staunchest supporters, Mahodara[10]—the giant among giants in his physical appearance—begged Ravana, "Let me not be a mere spectator when you confront Rama. Let me have the honor of grappling with him. Permit me to attack Rama."

"Rama is my sole concern," Ravana replied. "If you wish to engage yourself in a fight, you may fight his brother Lakshmana."

Noticing Mahodara's purpose, Rama steered his chariot across his path in order to prevent Mahodara from reaching Lakshmana. Whereupon Mahodara ordered his chariot-driver, "Now dash straight ahead, directly into Rama's chariot."

The charioteer, more practical-minded, advised him, "I would not go near Rama. Let us keep away." But Mahodara, obstinate and intoxicated with war fever, made straight for Rama. He wanted to have the honor of a direct encounter with Rama himself in spite of Ravana's advice; and for this honor he paid a heavy price, as it was a moment's work for Rama to destroy him, and leave him lifeless and shapeless on the field. Noticing this, Ravana's anger mounted further. He commanded his driver, "You will not slacken now. Go." Many ominous signs were seen now—his bow strings suddenly snapped; the mountains shook; thunders rumbled in the skies; tears flowed from the horses' eyes; elephants with decorated foreheads moved along dejectedly. Ravana, noticing them, hesitated only for a second, saying, "I don't care. This mere mortal Rama

10. **Mahodara** (mə·hō′də·rə)

RAMA IN COUNSEL WITH SHIVA AND BRAHMA, Indian, c. 1610.
What do Shiva and Brahma send to help Rama?

National Gallery of Canada, Ottawa, Gift of Max Tanenbaum, Toronto, 1979

is of no account, and these omens do not concern me at all." Meanwhile, Rama paused for a moment to consider his next step; and suddenly turned towards the armies supporting Ravana, which stretched away to the horizon, and destroyed them. He felt that this might be one way of saving Ravana. With his armies gone, it was possible that Ravana might have a change of heart. But it had only the effect of spurring Ravana on; he plunged forward and kept coming nearer Rama and his own doom.

Rama's army cleared and made way for Ravana's chariot, unable to stand the force of his approach. Ravana blew his conch[11] and its shrill challenge reverberated through space. Following it another conch, called "Panchajanya,"[12] which belonged to Mahavishnu[13] (Rama's original form before his present incarnation), sounded of its own accord in answer to the challenge, agitating the universe with its vibrations. And then Matali picked up another conch, which was Indra's, and blew it. This was the signal indicating the commencement of the actual battle. Presently Ravana sent a shower of arrows on Rama; and Rama's followers, unable to bear the sight of his body being studded with arrows, averted their heads. Then the chariot horses of Ravana and Rama glared at each other in hostility, and the flags topping the chariots—Ravana's ensign of the Veena[14] and Rama's with the whole universe on it—clashed, and one heard the stringing and twanging of bowstrings on both sides, overpowering in volume all other sound. Then followed a shower of arrows from Rama's own bow. Ravana stood gazing at the chariot sent by Indra and swore, "These gods, instead of supporting me, have gone to the support of this petty human being. I will teach them a lesson. He is not fit to be killed with my arrows but I shall seize him and his chariot together and fling them into high heaven and dash them to destruction." Despite his oath, he still strung his bow and sent a shower of arrows at Rama, raining in thousands, but they were all invariably shattered and neutralized by the arrows from Rama's bow, which met arrow for arrow. Ultimately Ravana, instead of using one bow, used ten with his twenty arms, multiplying his attack tenfold; but Rama stood unhurt.

Ravana suddenly realized that he should change his tactics and ordered his charioteer to fly the chariot up in the skies. From there he attacked and destroyed a great many of the monkey army supporting Rama. Rama ordered Matali, "Go up in the air. Our young soldiers are being attacked from the sky. Follow Ravana, and don't slacken."

There followed an aerial pursuit at dizzying speed across the dome of the sky and rim of the earth. Ravana's arrows came down like rain; he was bent upon destroying everything in the world. But Rama's arrows diverted, broke, or neutralized Ravana's. Terror-stricken, the gods watched this pursuit. Presently Ravana's arrows struck Rama's horses and pierced the heart of Matali himself. The charioteer fell. Rama paused for a while in grief, undecided as to his next step. Then he recovered and resumed his offensive. At that moment the divine eagle Garuda[15] was seen perched on Rama's flagpost, and the gods who were watching felt that this could be an auspicious sign.

After circling the globe several times, the dueling chariots returned, and the fight continued over Lanka.[16] It was impossible to be very clear about the location of the battleground as the fight occurred here, there, and everywhere. Rama's arrows pierced Ravana's armor and made him wince. Ravana was so insensible to pain and impervious to attack that for him to wince was a good sign, and the gods hoped that this was a turn for the better. But at this moment, Ravana suddenly changed his tactics. Instead of merely shooting his arrows, which were powerful in

---

11. **conch** (känch): a shell used as a trumpet.
12. **Panchajanya** (pän·chə·jän′yə)
13. **Mahavishnu** (mə·hä·vish′nŏŏ)
14. **ensign of the Veena:** banner with the image of an ancient stringed instrument.

---

15. **Garuda** (gə·rŏŏ′də)
16. **Lanka** (läng′kə): Ravana's kingdom.

from the Ramayana **489**

themselves, he also invoked several supernatural forces to create strange effects: he was adept in the use of various asthras[17] which could be made dynamic with special incantations. At this point, the fight became one of attack with supernatural powers, and parrying of such an attack with other supernatural powers.

Ravana realized that the mere aiming of shafts with ten or twenty of his arms would be of no avail because the mortal whom he had so contemptuously thought of destroying with a slight effort was proving formidable, and his arrows were beginning to pierce and cause pain. Among the asthras sent by Ravana was one called "Danda,"[18] a special gift from Shiva, capable of pursuing and pulverizing its target. When it came flaming along, the gods were struck with fear. But Rama's arrow neutralized it.

Now Ravana said to himself, "These are all petty weapons. I should really get down to proper business." And he invoked the one called "Maya"[19]—a weapon which created illusions and confused the enemy.

With proper incantations and worship, he sent off this weapon and it created an illusion of reviving all the armies and its leaders—Kumbakarna[20] and Indrajit[21] and the others—and bringing them back to the battlefield. Presently Rama found all those who, he thought, were no more, coming on with battle cries and surrounding him. Every man in the enemy's army was again up in arms. They seemed to fall on Rama with victorious cries. This was very confusing and

Rama asked Matali, whom he had by now revived, "What is happening now? How are all these coming back? They were dead." Matali explained, "In your original identity you are the creator of illusions in this universe. Please know that Ravana has created phantoms to confuse you. If you make up your mind, you can dispel them immediately." Matali's explanation was a great help. Rama at once invoked a weapon called "Gnana"[22]— which means "wisdom" or "perception." This was a very rare weapon, and he sent it forth. And all the terrifying armies who seemed to have come on in such a great mass suddenly evaporated into thin air.

Ravana then shot an asthra called "Thama,"[23] whose nature was to create total darkness in all the worlds. The arrows came with heads exposing frightening eyes and fangs, and fiery tongues. End to end the earth was enveloped in total darkness and the whole of creation was paralyzed. This asthra also created a deluge of rain on one side, a rain of stones on the other, a hailstorm showering down intermittently, and a tornado sweeping the earth. Ravana was sure that this would arrest Rama's enterprise. But Rama was able to meet it with what was named "Shivasthra."[24] He understood the nature of the phenomenon and the cause of it and chose the appropriate asthra for counteracting it.

Ravana now shot off what he considered his deadliest weapon—a trident endowed with extraordinary destructive power, once gifted to Ravana by the gods. When it started on its journey there was real panic all round. It came on flaming toward Rama, its speed

---

17. **asthras** (ä′strəs): weapons endowed with supernatural powers.
18. **Danda** (dän′də)
19. **Maya** (mä′yä′)
20. **Kumbakarna** (kum·bə·kär′nə)
21. **Indrajit** (in·drə·jit′)

22. **Gnana** (gnä′nə)
23. **Thama** (tä′mə)
24. **Shivasthra** (shi·vä′strə)

or course unaffected by the arrows he flung at it.

When Rama noticed his arrows falling down ineffectively while the trident sailed towards him, for a moment he lost heart. When it came quite near, he uttered a certain mantra[25] from the depth of his being and while he was breathing out that incantation,

---

25. **mantra** (man'trə): a formula believed to have magical power; used in incantation.

RAMA IS PRESENTED WITH THE CELESTIAL WEAPONS.
❓ *How are these weapons, or* asthras, *special?*

an esoteric syllable in perfect timing, the trident collapsed. Ravana, who had been so certain of vanquishing Rama with his trident, was astonished to see it fall down within an inch of him, and for a minute wondered if his adversary might not after all be a divine being although he looked like a mortal. Ravana thought to himself, "This is, perhaps, the highest God. Who could he be? Not Shiva, for Shiva is my supporter; he could not be Brahma,[26] who is four faced; could not be Vishnu, because of my immunity from the weapons of the whole trinity. Perhaps this man is the primordial being, the cause behind the whole universe. But whoever he may be, I will not stop my fight until I defeat and crush him or at least take him prisoner."

With this resolve, Ravana next sent a weapon which issued forth monstrous serpents vomiting fire and venom, with enormous fangs and red eyes. They came darting in from all directions.

Rama now selected an asthra called "Garuda" (which meant "eagle"). Very soon thousands of eagles were aloft, and they picked off the serpents with their claws and beaks and destroyed them. Seeing this also fail, Ravana's anger was roused to a mad pitch and he blindly emptied a quiverful of arrows in Rama's direction. Rama's arrows met them half way and turned them round so that they went back and their sharp points embedded themselves in Ravana's own chest.

Ravana was weakening in spirit. He realized that he was at the end of his resources. All his learning and equipment in weaponry were of no avail and he had practically come to the end of his special gifts of destruction. While he was going down thus, Rama's own

---

26. **Brahma** (brä'mə): the god of creation.

from the Ramayana   **491**

spirit was soaring up. The combatants were now near enough to grapple with each other and Rama realized that this was the best moment to cut off Ravana's heads.[27] He sent a crescent-shaped arrow which sliced off one of Ravana's heads and flung it far into the sea, and this process continued; but every time a head was cut off, Ravana had the benediction of having another one grown in its place. Rama's crescent-shaped weapon was continuously busy as Ravana's heads kept cropping up. Rama lopped off his arms but they grew again and every lopped-off arm hit Matali and the chariot and tried to cause destruction by itself, and the tongue in a new head wagged, uttered challenges, and cursed Rama. On the cast-off heads of Ravana devils and minor demons, who had all along been in terror of Ravana and had obeyed and pleased him, executed a dance of death and feasted on the flesh.

Ravana was now desperate. Rama's arrows embedded themselves in a hundred places on his body and weakened him. Presently he collapsed in a faint on the floor of his chariot. Noticing his state, his charioteer pulled back and drew the chariot aside. Matali whispered to Rama, "This is the time to finish off that demon. He is in a faint. Go on. Go on."

But Rama put away his bow and said, "It is not fair warfare to attack a man who is in a faint. I will wait. Let him recover," and waited.

When Ravana revived, he was angry with his charioteer for withdrawing and took out his sword, crying, "You have disgraced me. Those who look on will think I have retreated." But his charioteer explained how Rama suspended the fight and forebore to attack when he was in a faint. Somehow, Ravana appreciated his explanation and patted his back and resumed his attacks. Having exhausted his special weapons, in desperation Ravana began to throw on Rama all sorts of things such as staves,[28] cast-iron balls, heavy rocks, and oddments he could lay hands on. None of them touched Rama, but glanced off and fell ineffectually. Rama went on shooting his arrows. There seemed to be no end of this struggle in sight.

Now Rama had to pause to consider what final measure he should take to bring this campaign to an end. After much thought, he decided to use "Brahmasthra,"[29] a weapon specially designed by the Creator Brahma on a former occasion, when he had to provide one for Shiva to destroy Tripura,[30] the old monster who assumed the forms of flying mountains and settled down on habitations and cities, seeking to destroy the world. The Brahmasthra was a special gift to be used only when all other means had failed. Now Rama, with prayers and worship, invoked its fullest power and sent it in Ravana's direction, aiming at his heart rather than his head; Ravana being vulnerable at heart. While he had prayed for indestructibility of his several heads and arms, he had forgotten to strengthen his heart, where the Brahmasthra entered and ended his career.

Rama watched him fall headlong from his chariot face down onto the earth, and that was the end of the great campaign. Now one noticed Ravana's face aglow with a new quality. Rama's arrows had burnt off the layers of dross, the anger, conceit, cruelty, lust, and egotism which had encrusted his real self, and now his personality came through in its

---

27. **Ravana's heads:** Ravana is a demon-king usually depicted with ten heads and ten pairs of arms.

28. **staves:** staffs.
29. **Brahmasthra** (brä·mä′strə)
30. **Tripura** (trip′oo·rə)

pristine form—of one who was devout and capable of tremendous attainments.[31] His constant meditation on Rama, although as an adversary, now seemed to bear fruit, as his face shone with serenity and peace. Rama noticed it from his chariot above and commanded Matali, "Set me down on the ground." When the chariot descended and came to rest on its wheels, Rama got down and commanded Matali, "I am grateful for your services to me. You may now take the chariot back to Indra."

Surrounded by his brother Lakshmana and Hanuman and all his other war chiefs, Rama approached Ravana's body, and stood gazing on it. He noted his crowns and jewelry scattered piecemeal on the ground. The decorations and the extraordinary workmanship of the armor on his chest were blood covered. Rama sighed as if to say, "What might he not have achieved but for the evil stirring within him!"

At this moment, as they readjusted Ravana's blood-stained body, Rama noticed to his great shock a scar on Ravana's back and said with a smile, "Perhaps this is not an episode of glory for me, as I seem to have killed an enemy who was turning his back and retreating. Perhaps I was wrong in shooting the Brahmasthra into him." He looked so concerned at this supposed lapse on his part that Vibishana,[32] Ravana's brother, came forward to explain. "What you have achieved is unique. I say so although it meant the death of my brother."

"But I have attacked a man who had turned his back," Rama said. "See that scar."

Vibishana explained, "It is an old scar. In ancient days, when he paraded his strength around the globe, once he tried to attack the

Courtesy of the Freer Gallery of Art, Smithsonian Institution, Washington, D.C.; 07.271-270 – Indian Manuscript; late 16th century; Mughal; Akbar school; Persian translation of "Ramayana" of Valmiki; 130 miniatures in opaque colors and gold; 27.5 × 15.2 cm. (10 7/8 × 6") average leaf size

THE DEATH OF RAVANA.

divine elephants that guard the four directions. When he tried to catch them, he was gored in the back by one of the tuskers and that is the scar you see now; it is not a fresh one though fresh blood is flowing on it."

Rama accepted the explanation. "Honor him and cherish his memory so that his spirit may go to heaven, where he has his place. And now I will leave you to attend to his funeral arrangements, befitting his grandeur."

---

31. **attainments:** accomplishments.
32. **Vibishana** (vi′bē·shä′nə)

from the Ramayana   **493**

First Thoughts

Does this episode from the *Ramayana* call to mind any scenes from other epics you have read?

Identifying Facts

1. At the beginning of this episode, what does Ravana resolve after he has put on his armor and summoned his chariot?

2. What support do the gods give Rama? What doubts does Rama have about the chariot, and who reassures him?

3. How does Mahodara disobey Ravana's orders, and what is the result of this disobedience?

4. What kinds of weapons are used in the battle between Rama and Ravana? How is Ravana finally killed?

Interpreting Meanings

1. How do the details in the first paragraph establish the main **external conflict** of this episode? Which details show Ravana's **internal conflict**?

2. **Suspense** is the uncertainty or anxiety we feel about what is going to happen next in a story. How does the author of the *Ramayana* create suspense in this episode?

3. What role is played by the gods in the *Ramayana*?

4. What values does Rama, the hero of this national **epic**, embody? How does Rama's treatment of the defeated Ravana emphasize these values?

Applying Meanings

Rama is portrayed as extremely cautious when he uses his ultimate weapon, the "Brahmasthra," to defeat Ravana. This weapon is not described in the text; it is simply said to be "a special gift to be used only when all other means had failed." How do you envision this weapon?

Creative Writing Response

Writing a Sequel. Rama's victory over Ravana in the epic is followed by his rescue of Sita, who had been abducted and imprisoned by the demon. Using clues from the introduction to this selection (see page 484) and from the characterization of Rama, write your own version of the reunion between the hero and his wife.

Critical Writing Response

Comparing Aspects of Two Indian Epics. The *Bhagavad-Gita* (see page 467) and the *Ramayana* represent very different kinds of epic narratives, but the selections you have read express some common views of the nature of human struggle and death. In an essay, consider how aspects of Krishna's teaching to Arjuna are similar to the treatment of Rama's final confrontation with Ravana. Before you begin writing, list details from both selections in a chart like the following one.

	Arjuna	Rama
How do the gods help each hero?		
What is the hero's "sacred duty" in each epic?		
What moments of doubt does each hero have?		
What is the importance of self-control and self-discipline for each hero?		

BEHIND THE SCENES

The Tales Behind India's Epics

Who *are* the two shadowy figures who created the *Ramayana* and the *Mahabharata?* No one knows. But, as you may expect, there are stories about each.

According to tradition, the sage Valmiki wrote the *Ramayana* after being inspired by a god and a bird. Valmiki had been listening to Narada, the messenger god, tell the tale of Rama's life. Later, bathing in the Ganges and pondering all he had heard, Valmiki noticed two herons soaring and diving along the banks of the river. Suddenly a hunter shot one of the pair. The other heron cried out in grief. Valmiki, filled with pity, cursed the hunter and was surprised to find that his angry words emerged as poetry. Then the god Brahma appeared. He explained that the poetry was a gift; Valmiki must use it to write the story of Rama's life. Valmiki was eager to obey, and the *Ramayana* was the result.

The story of the *Mahabharata*'s origin, like the *Mahabharata* itself, is longer. The tale behind this epic begins with an unwise king, a wise man, and a snake. It ends with a time-warp twist worthy of modern science fiction.

King Pariksit, a descendant of the family whose final victory the *Mahabharata* recounts, was hunting deer when he offended a meditating wise man. The wise man's son cursed Pariksit, dooming the king to die within seven days from the poison of Taksaka, a huge, black cobra. The wise man, horrified, warned the king but could not avert the curse. King Pariksit built himself

Vyasa *(right)* dictating the story of the *Mahabharata* to the god Ganesha *(center)*.

a tower, set guards around its base, and climbed aloft, armed with doctors, priests, and magical remedies. But the wily Taksaka transformed himself into a basket of fruit and, changing several of his helpers into messengers, had himself delivered to King Pariksit. Pariksit died before anyone could intervene.

Pariksit's son, Janamejaya, then ascended the throne. He began a campaign to burn all snakes, hoping to destroy Taksaka. However, a sage begged the young king to have pity on the serpent, and Janamejaya spared Taksaka. It was then that Vyasa appeared. This wise man was a reincarnation of Janamejaya's ancestor, one of the heroic Pandavas who had participated in the battles with the Kauravas. Janamejaya begged Vyasa to tell the whole story of the struggle. Vyasa complied, and the *Mahabharata* was born.

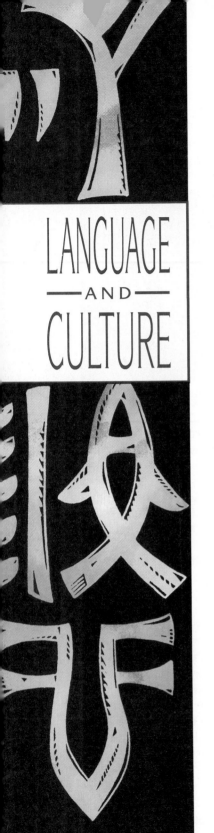

A GOD WITH UNIVERSAL APPEAL

Who's super-strong, irresistibly attractive, and blue? If you guessed the Hindu god Krishna, the Highest Soul, the Infinite One, you're right. As an incarnation of the blue-skinned Vishnu, Krishna is usually shown with skin of the same hue. Krishna uses his superhuman strength to fight demons and monsters, and his powers, combined with his good looks and high spirits, endear him to men as well as women of all ages.

The Metropolitan Museum of Art, Purchase, Edward C. Moore, Jr. Gift, 1928 (28.63.1)

KRISHNA LIFTS MOUNT GOUARDHAN.
What are Krishna's special characteristics?

Krishna, Mischief-Maker

According to legend, Krishna was secretly placed in the care of a cowherd and his wife immediately after birth. This trick was necessary to protect the baby from a demon, Kamsa, who was bent on destroying him. So Krishna grew up in a rural village, playing in the mud and pulling cows' tails like the other boys, his identity disguised. As he grew older, he was known throughout the village as a mischief-maker, often pilfering food or breaking things and then lying about it. Yet his beauty was so great that his parents, and everyone else in the village, saw his pranks as charming and loved him for them.

One story tells of Krishna's being reproved by his mother for eating dirt. Lying, he denies the accusation, inviting her to look into his mouth and see for herself. When she looks into his mouth, she sees "the whole universe in all its variety, with all the forms of life and time and nature and action and hopes, and her own village, and herself." She realizes that her son is a god. She instantly forgets all she has seen, but she is filled with even greater love for the boy.

A Very Human God

Krishna was a latecomer to the Hindu pantheon. He appeared when emphasis was shifting away from the worship of the raw forces of nature (fire or storms, for example) toward the worship of human qualities. The young Krishna's very human faults, and his parents' and neighbors' tolerant, even delighted, response to them, underscore this shift.

Some of Krishna's dealings with monsters illustrate another aspect of the Krishna cult: the idea that vengeance should be tempered with mercy. Legend has it that Krishna was still a baby when he killed his first monster. She was an ogress sent to destroy Krishna. She had transformed herself into a beautiful, godlike woman, but had smeared herself with poison. She visited the baby's hut and held him to her poisoned breast to kill him. Using his superhuman strength, Krishna killed her instead. Then, mercifully, he wiped out her sins, so that her soul reached "the heaven of the good."

Krishna's charming personality and good looks made him irresistible to women. When Krishna played his flute at night, any woman who heard it was compelled to join him. In Hindu religious thought, the women's attraction to Krishna symbolized the soul's longing for holiness. The fact that even married women left their homes to follow Krishna's flute signified that Krishna's worshipers were expected to leave their worldly concerns and follow the ways of the god.

As the cult of Krishna spread, it sometimes conflicted with the worship of the older gods. One tale reflecting this conflict describes how the resentful Agni, god of fire, started a brushfire to kill Krishna and the other cowherds. Krishna calmly sucked the fire into his mouth, extinguishing it. In the same way, the cult of Krishna extinguished the cults of many of the older gods.

Krishna has been portrayed in many ways in Hindu art and literature. Whether he appears as a plump baby or a mighty slayer of monsters, as a simple cowherd or a dazzling prince, he is above all a god who loves humanity. And, for many centuries, this charming, blue-skinned trickster god has been devoutly loved in return.

AVOIDING SENTENCE FRAGMENTS AND RUN-ON SENTENCES

Sentence Fragments

Unclear sentences make your writing hard to follow. Sentence fragments leave readers hanging, missing half the substance of your thought. Run-on sentences leave readers struggling to sort out too many piled-up concepts.

Each sentence must contain a **subject** and a **verb** and express a complete thought. A **sentence fragment** is a phrase or a dependent clause used as an independent sentence. To correct it, add the missing parts to make a complete sentence.

SENTENCE FRAGMENT (No verb)
Hymns praising the earth's beauty.

(Note that a word ending in -*ing*, by itself, is not a verb.)

COMPLETE SENTENCE (Verb phrase added)
Hymns praising the earth's beauty *make up* the *Rig Veda*.

SENTENCE FRAGMENT (No subject)
Receive the attention of poets.

COMPLETE SENTENCE (Subject added)
Natural wonders receive the attention of poets.

SENTENCE FRAGMENT (No verb or subject)
All the wonders of creation.

COMPLETE SENTENCE (Subject and verb added)
The Vedic hymns celebrate all the wonders of creation.

SENTENCE FRAGMENT (Subordinate clause)
Because the hymns were a way to ask for divine help and mercy.

COMPLETE SENTENCE (Joined to independent clause)
Because the hymns were a way to ask for divine help and mercy, *they were viewed as religious poems*.

Notice how the italicized words complete each thought. In informal writing, you may use fragments on purpose for emphasis or tone. Unintentional fragments, however, weaken your writing.

Exercise 1: Correcting Sentence Fragments

Correct each fragment, using the most appropriate method.

1. Indra, sending a chariot for Rama.
2. Are part of the literature of India.
3. When his brothers drink from the lake.
4. The war between the sons of royal brothers.
5. A compilation of Hindu legend and thought.
6. As a result of Yudhistira's answers.
7. Krishna, who serves as Arjuna's trusted charioteer.
8. Lived and farmed in the Indus Valley thousands of years ago.
9. The Vedic period in India.
10. The poets writing in Sanskrit.

Run-on Sentences

Independent clauses—word groups that contain subjects and verbs and express complete thoughts—cannot be joined indiscriminately. They must be joined with an appropriate connector or punctuation mark. Incorrectly joined, two or more independent clauses create a **run-on sentence**.

RUN-ON SENTENCES

No punctuation
Krishna reminds Arjuna that it is his sacred duty to wage battle he urges him to rise above the pain and suffering of war.

Comma splice
Krishna reminds Arjuna that it is his sacred duty to wage battle, he urges him to rise above the pain and suffering of war.

(A comma alone is not enough to join two independent clauses.)

METHODS FOR CORRECTING RUN-ON SENTENCES

1. **Use a semicolon.** Krishna reminds Arjuna that it is his sacred duty to wage battle; he urges him to rise above the pain and suffering of war.

2. **Use a comma and coordinating conjunction.** Krishna reminds Arjuna that it is his sacred duty to wage battle, *and* he urges him to rise above the pain and suffering of war.

3. **Subordinate one clause.** Krishna reminds Arjuna that it is his sacred duty to wage battle, *though he urges him to rise above the pain and suffering of war.*

Subordinating one clause can give it less weight or emphasis in the sentence. Note that conjunctive adverbs—words like *however, in addition, furthermore, then, next*—cannot be used to subordinate a clause unless they are correctly punctuated.

RUN-ON SENTENCE
Krishna reminds Arjuna that it is his sacred duty to wage battle, *however* he urges him to rise above the pain and suffering of war.

CORRECTED SENTENCE
Krishna reminds Arjuna that it is his sacred duty to wage battle; *however,* he urges him to rise above the pain and suffering of war.

A conjunctive adverb between two independent clauses must be preceded by a semicolon.

Exercise 2: Correcting Run-on Sentences

Correct each run-on sentence in all three of the ways illustrated above.

1. In the *Panchatantra,* a story contained within another story emphasizes different aspects of a lesson being taught, the lesson is emphasized by the use of epigrams.

2. Much of the *Ramayana* concerns Rama's attempts to win back his wife Sita, then he banishes her because he fears she has been unfaithful.

3. Ralph Waldo Emerson's poem ''Brahma'' echoes the philosophy and even the wording of the *Bhagavad-Gita* this is not surprising since he was fascinated by ancient Indian literature.

Critical Thinking and Writing

WRITING TO PERSUADE

What's the best way to talk you into doing something? Does coaxing work better than coercion? Is logic more convincing than manipulation? Whether you want to convert others to your viewpoint or encourage them to act in support of a cause, persuasive techniques will help you to build plausible and convincing arguments.

Writing Assignment

Write a letter about a national, local, school, or personal issue that you consider important. Your audience is a friend or group of friends whose position differs from yours, and your purpose is to persuade your audience to accept your viewpoint or to take action. In this assignment, you will develop an argument with specific reasons and evidence.

Background

In this unit you have encountered several kinds of persuasion. In the *Bhagavad-Gita,* Krishna uses argument and counterargument to urge Arjuna into battle. The fables of the *Panchatantra* rely on analogies to convince readers to accept certain morals. In these selections, as in all effective persuasion, opinions are directly or indirectly justified and evidence is presented. As you choose your topic and plan your letter, think about the kinds of persuasion that will be most compelling.

Prewriting

Analyzing Your Audience. Answer these questions in detail about the friends you hope to convince.

1. What do they already know about the issue?
2. How and why is their opinion different from yours?
3. What concerns do they share with you?
4. What will make it difficult to persuade them?
5. What will be their strongest counterargument?

Generating Evidence and Organizing Support

In one sentence, sum up the opinion you hope to convince your audience of or the action you want your audience to take. Beneath that sentence, list the reasons for your opinion. Next, begin generating facts and examples that can support your reasons; brainstorm for evidence based on your personal experience and observation. Then research books, periodicals, and media presentations, filling in the gaps in your knowledge with expert testimony.

Finally, familiarize yourself with opposing points of view and the reasons people hold those points of view, and look for evidence that disproves their reasons.

To organize your material, complete a chart like the one below. Use your brainstorming material, your research notes, and your answers to the audience analysis questions.

	My Position	Opponent's Position
Reason A		
Evidence		
Reason B		
Evidence		
Reason C		
Evidence		

Writing

Use these steps to draft your letter.

1. **Introductory Paragraph.** Follow the standard conventions for beginning a letter. Then introduce your topic with a question, a quotation, or an unusual fact. Explain key terms if necessary. End with your position statement, the sentence that sums up your opinion.
2. **Body Paragraphs.** Treat your points in order of importance (least important first). Explain each point, supported by facts and examples, in a separate paragraph. In each paragraph, you may also cite opposing views and counter them. Or you may cover all opposing views in one paragraph. In either case, use the kinds of persuasion that will be most effective for your audience: direct, logical argument; emotional appeals; or argument by analogy. Use transitions to link ideas.
3. **Concluding Paragraph.** Restate your opinion and briefly sum up your main points. End with a strong call to action, whether literal action or the acceptance of a new viewpoint. Add an appropriate closing and signature.

Evaluating and Revising

Use these questions to evaluate and revise your letter.

1. Does your introduction catch readers' attention and state your position clearly?
2. Have you provided enough reasons, facts, and examples?
3. Have you dealt fairly with opposing views?
4. Are your main points and support logically organized?
5. Have you used effective persuasive techniques and transitions?
6. Have you followed standard letter form?

Proofreading and Publishing

Proofread to eliminate errors in grammar and mechanics, and make a final copy of your letter. As your teacher directs, exchange letters with classmates. Use discussion or role-playing to explore each letter's effectiveness.

RUSSIA

Mongolia

Inner Mongo

AFGHANISTAN

CHINA

GREAT WALL

Beijing

Kufow

Huang He River

Indus River

INDIA

Tibet

Himalayas

Ganges River

Chang Jiang River

TAIWA

CHINA
AND
JAPAN

☐ Chinese Empire, c. 1775
☐ Japan, c. 1850

Bay of
Bengal

South China
Sea

HOKKAIDO

a of
ban

HONSHU

JAPAN

Edo (Tokyo)

Mt. Fuji

Osaka

SHIKOKU

KYUSHU

Pacific Ocean

East China Sea

N

CHINESE AND JAPANESE LITERATURES

▼ **Time** ▼

2000 B.C.—A.D. 1900

▼ **Place** ▼

China and Japan

▼ **Literary Significance** ▼

China: Perhaps no other world culture has produced as much superb poetry as China, which reveres poetry as the highest art form. Influenced by Confucianism, Taoism, and Buddhism, Chinese poetry often focuses on the contemplation of nature and the search for harmony. China also boasts a strong tradition of philosophical and historical prose writings. Chinese storytelling grew from an oral tradition to a written tradition of moral tales, supernatural tales, and, by the eighteenth century, the novel.

Japan: The earliest Japanese writings were written in Chinese, but between the fifth and eighth centuries A.D., the Japanese adapted the Chinese system of writing to fit their own language. Japanese poetry is distinguished by such forms as the **tanka** and the **haiku**. The prose tradition in Japan reached a height during the Heian Period (794–1185), when diaries, journals, and other forms of narrative were given a high polish by aristocrats, many of them women. By the eleventh century, a Japanese writer, Lady Murasaki, had composed the world's first novel, *The Tale of Genji*. Japanese literature is also known for its unique dramatic forms, particularly the subtle and mysterious Noh plays.

TIME LINE
China and Japan

LITERARY EVENTS

▼

Chinese sage Confucius **(551–479 B.C.)** teaches ethical principles known as Confucianism, recorded in his *Analects*

Teachings of Lao-tzu **(c. 500s B.C.)** give rise to Taoism in China

The Book of Songs is compiled in China, **c. 1000–600 B.C.**

Ssu-ma Ch'ien (China) **(c. 145–c. 90 B.C.)**, *Records of the Historian*

Chinese gilt bronze Buddh[a], T'ang dynasty, A.D. 618–907

BEFORE 1000 B.C.   **600 B.C.**   **200 B.C.**   A.D. **200**

Art of writing develops in China during the Shang dynasty, **c. 1500–1122 B.C.**

Feudal system develops in China during the Chou dynasty; the Hundred Schools period sees a profusion of teachers and philosophers, **1122–256 B.C.**

Southeast Asians may have arrived in Japan, **c. 1000 B.C.**

Warring States period in China, **c. 400–221 B.C.**

Chinese and Korean immigrants introduce rice paddy agriculture into Japan, **c. 250 B.C.– A.D. 250**

Ch'in dynasty unifies China; Great Wall is built, **221–207 B.C.**

Han dynasty in China; Confucianism becomes the official state doctrine; Buddhist teachings arrive from India, **206 B.C.– A.D. 220**

Japanese Noh robe.

Museum of Art, Rhode Island School of Design, Gift of Lucy T. Aldrich

The Great Wall of China.

▲

CULTURAL AND HISTORICAL EVENTS

Sei Shōnagon (Japan) **(late 900s–early 1000s)**, *The Pillow Book*

Murasaki Shikibu (Japan) **(c. 978–c. 1026)**, *The Tale of Genji*

Man'yoshu, an anthology of poetry, and the *Kojiki,* chronicles of the legendary origins of Japan, are compiled, **c. 700**

Li Po **(701–762)** and Tu Fu **(712–770)** (China) compose poetry

The aristocrats of Japan's Heian court compose tanka, **c. 800–1200**

Kokinshu, Imperial anthology of Japanese poetry, **905**

Li Ch'ing-chao (China) **(1084–1151)** composes poetry

The Tale of Heike, Japanese epic, **c. 1225**

Yoshida Kenko (Japan) **(c. 1283–c. 1352)**, *Essays in Idleness*

Development of Noh drama in Japan, **c. 1338–1568**; Seami Motokiyo **(c. 1363–1442)** writes *Atsumori* and other dramas

Matsuo Bashō **(1644–1694)**, and Uejima Onitsura **(1660–1738)** are among the earliest poets to write haiku

Ts'ao Hsueh-ch'in **(c. 1700–1764)** writes *Dream of the Red Chamber*, one of China's most famous novels

Taniguchi Buson **(1715–1783)** and Kobayashi Issa **(1762–1826)** write haiku

600 1000 1400 1800

Japanese Prince Shotoku encourages the adoption of Chinese culture, **593–622**

mato clan emerges as e dominant political force Japan, **c. A.D. 400**

ddhism and Chinese tings are introduced to an, **400s–500s**

Sung dynasty in China sees the development of Neo-Confucianism, **960–1279**

T'ang dynasty, called China's "Golden Age," **618–907**

Japan's Heian era witnesses a cultural flowering and the rise of feudalism, **c. 794–1185**

The shogun becomes the supreme power in Japan, **1192**

Zen sect of Buddhism develops in Japan, **c. 1200s**

Mongol leader Genghis Khan conquers China; his grandson Kubla Khan establishes the Yuan dynasty, **1279–1368**

Period of civil war and turmoil in Japan, **1338–1568**

Ming dynasty in China, **1368–1644**

Boxer Rebellion ignites revolutionary spark in China, **1900**

Portuguese merchants and Christianity reach Japan, **1540s**

Shogun closes Japan to foreigners, **1639**

Ch'ing (Manchu) dynasty in China, **1644–1911**

Treaty of Nanking gives Britain control of Hong Kong, signaling the rise of Western imperialism in China, **1842**

Commodore Perry ends Japanese isolationist policy, **1853**

Meiji Restoration; Japan begins industrialization, **1868**

Travelpix/FPG International

Japanese shrine, Hiroshima.

This time line border features a form of Chinese writing known as "seal style," which had developed by the third century B.C. and is still in use today.

THE LITERATURE OF CHINA

> **❝** Learning without thought is labor lost; thought without learning is perilous. **❞**
>
> —*from* The Confucian Analects

Ritual wine vessel, Shang dynasty, c. 1200–c. 1000 B.C.

Chinese civilization as a distinct and continuous culture has existed for nearly four thousand years—longer than any other world culture. The art of writing, using a unique "alphabet" of over three thousand characters, developed in the second millennium B.C. (2000–1000) in China, and with it came the beginning of a literary tradition that continues to this day. The nature of Chinese literature reflects the political and social history of China and the impact of powerful religions that came from within and outside the country.

Chinese History: Dynastic Rule

The political profile of China over the centuries is one of periods of stability, enforced by a strong central authority, followed by struggles between warring local princes and rival families trying to wrest control from the ruling family.

The **Shang** (shäng) **dynasty**, which came to power in China around the year 1766 B.C. and continued until 1122 B.C., is the first period of family rule about which there is historical evidence. It was during the Shang reign that the unique system of Chinese writing began to develop. Unlike our modest alphabet of twenty-six letters representing a limited number of sounds, the thousands of Chinese characters represent complete words or units of meaning.

The **Chou** (jō) **dynasty** overthrew the Shang and held power until about 256 B.C.—the longest dynastic rule in Chinese history. The Chou established a structure of imperial rule that became the model of government for China until the early twentieth century. The emperor, usually the oldest son of the ruling family, controlled a vast territory by

Chinese jade, large dark green mountain, 19th century.

Art Resource, New York

Sample of Chinese calligraphy.

creating a network of local government officials whose advancement depended on their loyalty to the imperial family.

In 221 B.C., the **Ch'in dynasty** overpowered the Chou. (Some believe the name *China* was derived from *Ch'in.*) The Ch'in rulers connected and fortified their empire by building roads and completing a long wall across their northern border, the famous Great Wall of China.

The Han (hän), T'ang (täng), and Sung (sōong) dynasties that followed were periods of expansion and greater contact with the outside world. Literature, the arts, technology, and trade flourished; yet each dynasty, eventually weakened by corruption and infighting, was succeeded in turn by a more vigorous force.

Outside Influences

The **Mongols**, a warlike, semi-nomadic people from northeastern Asia, conquered imperial China in the late twelfth century A.D. Mongol rule was overthrown and Chinese rule restored in 1368 with the accession of the **Ming dynasty**. The Ming and later dynasties sought to reassert Chinese culture by limiting contact with foreign influences.

Despite centuries of Chinese efforts to limit outside influence, the expanding nations of nineteenth-century Europe (Great Britain, France, Germany, and Russia) forced the imperial Chinese authority to grant them large areas of China that they could run for their economic advantage.

Twentieth-century China has seen civil war and the installation of a harsh Communist regime. But even the last four decades of Communist rule have run true to the age-old pattern of Chinese political history. There have been alternating periods of stability and unrest, revolutionary fervor followed by greater ideological flexibility, and periodic demands for more democracy brutally crushed by a totalitarian central government.

Chinese Religion and Philosophy

Chinese literature, and indeed all of Chinese culture, has been profoundly influenced by three great schools of thought, all originating in the sixth and fifth centuries B.C.: the philosophies of **Confucianism** and **Taoism**, and the religion of **Buddhism**.

The Granger Collection, New York

Chinese glazed earthenware tomb figure of a lion, T'ang dynasty, early eighth century A.D.

Confucius (551–479 B.C.) was the first great Chinese teacher, and since his time, the profession of teaching has commanded great respect in China. His teaching emphasized ethical values such as honesty, loyalty, respect for elders, love of learning, and moral restraint. Confucius did not write down any of his teachings, but after his death they were compiled by his disciples in books now called the *Analects* (see page 538).

THE THIRTEEN EMPERORS (detail), ATTRIBUTED TO YEN LI-PEN (d. A.D. 673), T'ang dynasty, Silk handscroll.

The sixth and fifth centuries B.C. gave rise to three belief systems that have influenced Chinese culture: Confucianism, Taoism, and Buddhism.

The next great teacher to influence Chinese thinking was **Lao-tzu** (lou′dzə′), sometimes spelled Lao-tze. He was born around 570 B.C., but little is known of his personal life and background. However, the values expressed in his book

PEACOCK AND APRICOT BLOSSOMS, LÜ CHI, Ming Dynasty.

Tao Te Ching (see page 543) have deeply affected Chinese thought and expression. Above all, the Taoist (dou'ist) philosophy reveres nature as the great teacher and urges people to seek wisdom by contemplating the simplicity and power of natural forces.

Confucianism and Taoism were enriched by the arrival of a third powerful system of belief, Buddhism (see page 451), imported from India during the Han dynasty. Buddhist thought stresses the importance of ridding oneself of earthly desires and of seeking ultimate peace and enlightenment through detachment. With its stress on living ethically and its de-emphasis on material concerns, Buddhism appealed to both Confucians and Taoists.

The Balance of Opposites

Unlike Western religions, Chinese religions are based on the perception of life as a process of continual change in which opposing forces, such as heaven and earth or light and dark, balance one another. These opposites are symbolized by the *yin* and the *yang*. *Yin*, the passive and feminine force, counterbalances *yang*, the active and masculine force, and each contains a "seed" of the other, as represented in the traditional *yin-yang* symbol.

Chinese Literature

In terms of sheer volume, Chinese literature dwarfs all other literatures of the world. It has been estimated that more than half of all the books ever written have been Chinese. Moreover, literature and learning have been among the highest cultural values. Indeed, for centuries the main avenue to power and prestige for ambitious young men in China was passing the imperial examinations. These exams for entrance into the imperial bureaucracy tested a candidate's knowledge of the classic Chinese texts and his ability to compose poetry.

Chinese Poetry

To the Chinese, poetry has always been an exercise for the mind and the spirit rather than a purely literary pursuit. In keeping with Confucian, Taoist, and Buddhist thought,

66 Chinese poetry is of all poetry I know the most human and the least symbolic or romantic. **99**

—*Goldsworthy Lowes Dickinson*

Chinese poetry often involves the contemplation of nature and the search for harmony between the inner and outer worlds. Chinese poetry is almost exclusively lyrical. Its essence is the exploration of passing feelings and impressions.

> The Chinese have traditionally valued poetry above all genres, seeing it as a vehicle for spiritual attainment and the cultivation of wisdom.

The Book of Songs, or *Shih Ching* (see page 512), first compiled in the sixth century B.C., is the oldest collection of Chinese poetry and has been revered and studied for centuries as a model of poetic expression and moral insight. Chinese lyrical poetry reached its height, however, during the T'ang dynasty (A.D. 618–907). Inspired by scenes of natural beauty, T'ang poets such as **Li Po** and **Tu Fu** wrote about the fragile blossoms in spring, the falling of leaves in autumn, or the changing shape of the moon.

Chinese Prose and Drama

Although the Chinese have traditionally revered poetry above all other literary forms and have viewed fiction and drama as lesser art forms, Chinese prose has a long and distinguished history. Chinese writers have always admired their ancient prose literature for its style, particularly the clear, unadorned expression of the Confucian *Analects* and the biographical writings of the great historian **Ssu-ma Ch'ien** (see page 551).

Chinese storytelling began with oral folktales and Buddhist parables, but over the centuries, a tradition of written narrative developed, including cycles of heroic adventures, tales of the supernatural, and monumental family chronicles, such as the immensely popular eighteenth-century novel, *Dream of the Red Chamber.*

Sophisticated stage art emerged late in China, around the eleventh or twelfth century. It developed from popular entertainment or court performances into a full-length dramatic medium. Today, Chinese drama is famous for its gorgeous costumes, raucous music, and lively acrobatics.

> **❝** The [Chinese] poem is the voice of the poet not self-consciously addressing posterity or the world at large, but speaking quietly to a few close friends, or perhaps simply musing to himself. **❞**
>
> —Burton Watson

NARCISSUS AND PLUM, CH'IU YING. **Ming dynasty.**

The Granger Collection, New York

The Book of Songs

Tuning the Lute and Drinking Tea, attributed to Chou Fang (fl. A.D. 780–810). *Artists of the T'ang dynasty, such as Chou Fang, set the standard for Chinese figure composition.*

The Nelson-Atkins Museum of Art, Kansas City, Missouri

*T*he *Book of Songs* is a collection of 305 of the earliest recorded poems in Chinese history. First compiled in the sixth century B.C., these poems were actually meant to be sung, although their melodies have long been lost. Regarded as the foundation of Chinese literature, *The Book of Songs* provides a lyrical record of the people who lived in northern China and the feudal states surrounding the Yellow River during the early centuries of the Chou (jō) dynasty (1122–249 B.C.). It is fitting that the Chinese word for poetry, *shih* (shə), is rooted in the *Songs'* Chinese title *Shih Ching* (shə jing).

A Record of the Chinese Past

The Book of Songs includes court songs that entertained the aristocracy, story songs that recounted Chou dynasty legends, and hymns that were sung in the temples, accompanied by dance. Many of the poems are brief folk songs or ballads.

◆

ballad: *a simple, traditional song, particularly one that tells a romantic or sentimental story.*

In the *Songs*, unknown singers created images of people farming and hunting, courting and marrying, performing rituals, and fighting in battles. We hear their happiness as they describe a well-to-do lover or celebrate the planting season and hear their bitterness and suffering as they complain of a rejecting lover or the hardships of war.

Traditional Interpretations of the *Songs*

By the seventh century B.C., the *Songs* had already achieved a legendary status in the Chou dynasty. They were well known in the feudal courts and were often performed as court entertainment. Because the *Songs* were so familiar, scholars began quoting lines or verses out of context, and often inaccurately, applying them to new situations. Interpreters wrote commentaries that cast new light on the poems' social and political significance. Eventually, many songs acquired interpretations probably never intended by the ancient singers.

Around 500 B.C., the Chinese philosopher and teacher Confucius (see page 536) reinterpreted many of the *Songs* to make them into models of his moral teachings, although there is no evidence to support the legend that he himself compiled the *Songs*. However, Confucius did have strong feelings about the importance of the poems. He felt that the *Songs* described a wide range of emotion and experience and that to not study them would be like closing one's eyes to the world.

A Revered Place in Chinese History

The Book of Songs became one of the "Five Classics" of Confucianism—texts that embodied Confucian ideals in the five areas of metaphysics, politics, history, society, and poetry. As an expression of the Confucian poetic vision, the *Book of Songs* became part of the basic educational curriculum in China when Confucianism was adopted as the official state doctrine during the Han dynasty (206 B.C.–A.D. 220). Each poem was accompanied by an official interpretation that explained the poem's relationship to the moral and social fabric of the period in which it was written. Until recent times, Chinese schoolchildren studied *The Book of Songs* as both poetry and moral lessons and were required to memorize all 305 songs.

Today, however, scholars are laying aside such traditional interpretations to see *The Book of Songs* simply as a classic work of literature that expresses a people's humanity. In the *Songs*, the people of Chou still sing to us across time, revealing the inner and outer worlds they lived in and, in the process, establishing the strong lyrical tradition that has shaped Chinese poetry.

Standing warrior, T'ang dynasty.

The Art Institute of Chicago, Chinese Armored guardian, earthenware with polychrome pigments and gilding, Tang dynasty, 1st half 8th century, ht: 96.5 cm, Gift of Russell Tyson, 1943.1139. 3/4 view. Photograph by Bob Hashimoto.

Reader's Guide

from The Book of Songs

Background

The two selections from *The Book of Songs* come from a collection of 160 folk songs attributed to the feudal states of the Chou empire. Among the earliest of the *Songs,* these folk songs have apparently been revised and refined since they were written centuries ago.

Like many selections in *The Book of Songs,* these folk songs tend to have strong, regular rhythms that echo the gongs, drums, bronze bells, and stone chimes of early Chinese music. These compact lyrics also feature repeated words and phrases, although there are often subtle changes in the repetition. The folk songs are best known, however, for their direct outpourings of human feeling, especially on the themes of separation, hardship, and love.

According to Chinese tradition, Song 103 expresses the feelings of a young princess of the state of Wei (wā). Long ago she was separated from her family by an unhappy marriage to the Lord of Hsü (shoo), the ruler of a small, nearby state. When she tried to return to her people, the men of Hsü detained her against her will. Song 130 probably expresses the lament of a Chinese peasant, one who represents the common man forced to take up arms for a war lord. *The Book of Songs* contains some of history's earliest antiwar songs.

Oral Response

The speakers in both of these poems are far from home. How have you felt when you have been separated from your home, family, and friends? Discuss your experiences with the class.

Literary Focus

Repetition is a literary device that consists of repeated sounds, words, phrases, or other elements in prose and poetry. Writers use repetition to unify a work, build rhythm, and add emphasis to particular feelings and ideas. In folk songs and ballads, repetition often appears in the form of a recurring word or group of words called a **refrain**. For example, the refrain "For I'm weary with hunting, and fain would lie down" appears at the end of several stanzas in the Scottish ballad "Lord Randall." Like many refrains, this one also repeats with a slight variation: "For I'm sick at the heart, and fain would lie down."

from The Book of Songs

translated by

ARTHUR WALEY

 As you read, notice how repeated words and phrases emphasize the speakers' concerns. What feelings are conveyed by this repetition?

O Oriole, Yellow Bird

103

O oriole, yellow bird,
Do not settle on the corn,
Do not peck at my millet.°
The people of this land
5   Are not minded to nurture me.
I must go back, go home
To my own land and kin.

O oriole, yellow bird,
Do not settle on the mulberries,
10 Do not peck my sorghum.°
With the people of this land
One can make no covenant.
I must go back, go home
To where my brothers are.

15 O oriole, yellow bird
Do not settle on the oaks,
Do not peck my wine-millet.
With the people of this land
One can come to no understanding.
20 I must go back, go home
To where my own men° are.

3. **millet** (mil'it): in Asia, a cereal grass with small grain used for food.

10. **sorghum** (sôr'gəm): a tropical grass grown for its food products, such as syrup or grain.

21. **men:** here, the speaker's adult kinsmen, such as her father and uncles.

What Plant Is Not Faded?
130

What plant is not faded?
What day do we not march?
What man is not taken
To defend the four bounds?

5 What plant is not wilting?
What man is not taken from his wife?
Alas for us soldiers,
Treated as though we were not fellow-men!

Are we buffaloes, are we tigers
10 That our home should be these desolate wilds?
Alas for us soldiers,
Neither by day nor night can we rest!

The fox bumps and drags
Through the tall, thick grass.
15 Inch by inch move our barrows
As we push them along the track.

Wall painting, T'ang dynasty, c. A.D. 618–906.

? What feelings does the speaker in Song 130 express about the life of a soldier?

K. Scholz/SuperStock, In

First Thoughts

What kinds of emotions do these ancient Chinese poems express?

Identifying Facts

1. To whom is Song 103 addressed? What are the speaker's three complaints about "the people of this land"?
2. What great desire does the speaker of Song 103 express?
3. Point out three lines in Song 130 that state the speaker's concerns.

Interpreting Meanings

1. In Song 103, why does the speaker tell the oriole of her desire to go home?
2. The first four sentences of Song 130 are all questions. What is the significance of the speaker's many questions? What feelings do they evoke?
3. Choose an example of **repetition** in each poem. What emotion is expressed by the repeated phrase?

Applying Meanings

In what ways do these poems remind you of songs you know? Could they be set to music and still be relevant today?

Creative Writing Response

Composing a Rap Song. Like these poems from *The Book of Songs,* rap music is a direct expression of feelings. Rap also uses strong, repetitive rhythms and, often, a refrain. With a partner or small group, compose a two- to three-verse rap song that expresses your feelings about love, war, or some other subject. Include a refrain that echoes your main idea. Be ready to perform your rap song for the class.

Critical Writing Response

Comparing and Contrasting Two Folk Songs. In a two- to three-paragraph essay, compare and contrast Song 130 ("What Plant Is Not Faded?") with the classic folk song "Where Have All the Flowers Gone?" by Pete Seeger, below.

Where Have All the Flowers Gone?
Pete Seeger

Where have all the flowers gone,
    Long time passing?
Where have all the flowers gone,
    Long time ago.
Where have all the flowers gone?
The girls have picked them every one.
When will they ever learn?
When will they ever learn?

Where have all the young men gone,
    Long time passing?
Where have all the young men gone,
    Long time ago.
Where have all the young men gone?
Gone for soldiers every one.
When will they ever learn?
When will they ever learn?

Where have all the soldiers gone,
    Long time passing?
Where have all the soldiers gone,
    Long time ago.
Where have all the soldiers gone?
Gone to graveyards every one.
When will they ever learn?
When will they ever learn?

Where have all the graveyards gone,
    Long time passing?
Where have all the graveyards gone,
    Long time ago.
Where have all the graveyards gone?
Gone to flowers every one.
When will they ever learn?
When will they ever learn?

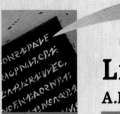

Li Po
A.D. 701–762

New York Public Library Picture Collection

Chinese poet Li Po (lē bō) lived during the T'ang (täng) dynasty (618–907), an age of great prosperity and cultural achievement. Two of China's greatest poets, Li Po and his friend Tu Fu (dōō fōō), wrote during this golden age of poetry. These two poets of contrasting dispositions and styles embody the highest poetic achievements of the T'ang dynasty. Tu Fu, a melancholy wanderer, wrote innovative poetry known for its elegance, realism, and social consciousness. Li Po, a free-spirited vagabond, wrote traditional lyric poetry characterized by its sense of playfulness, fantasy, and grace.

Although Li Po was probably born in central Asia, he grew up in the province of Szechwan (se'chwän') in southwestern China. He was a well-educated youth from a good family who chose to forego the test for imperial service taken by many young men of the upper classes. Instead, the young Li Po lived as a hermit and served as a wandering knight, a sword-wielding avenger of wrongs against women and children. At the age of twenty-five he became a vagabond who wandered for most of his days.

As he traveled throughout China, Li Po wrote poetry and made many friends of government officials, fellow poets, and even hermits. He also married four times and fathered several children, although he never seems to have settled down in a home of his own.

Li Po's travels in China served to spread his fame as a poet. Even the emperor admired him. In fact, Li Po abandoned his nomadic life for a time to serve the emperor as an imperial court poet. There Li Po delighted in a life of unaccustomed luxuries.

Some time afterward, Li Po entered into the service of a rebel prince. When the prince's bid for power failed, however, Li Po was imprisoned and then banished, a sentence that was revoked just as he was on his way to exile. Three years later, the poet died suddenly. An appropriately romantic Chinese legend tells that he drowned one night as he leaned from his boat to embrace the watery reflection of the moon.

Reader's Guide

POEMS OF LI PO

Background

Like most of his contemporaries, Li Po wrote in a wide range of poetic forms, of which the brief verse "Quiet Night Thoughts" and the longer "Letter to His Two Small Children" are two examples. Many of his masterpieces are "old style" verses that imitate the rhythms and flow of rambling folk songs. According to Chinese critics, however, Li Po was at his best in concise four-line poems with five to seven words per line. His poem *Yeh-ssu* (ye sə), translated here as "Quiet Night Thoughts," is a masterpiece of this form. It has been memorized by virtually all Chinese schoolchildren for centuries. The English translation provided here has eight lines, twice as many as the original, in order to accommodate the rhythms of English verse.

A lifelong observer of nature, Li Po created vivid images of China's best-known mountains and streams, often recalled in a mood of solitude. "Quiet Night Thoughts" and "A Letter to His Two Small Children," though different in form, both resonate with images of nature and the thoughts and emotions of the solitary poet. Traditional Chinese poets like Li Po were often inspired by watching the moon, visiting the mountains, or viewing spring blossoms. By writing poems they completed their experiences.

Writer's Response

Imagine yourself far away from home, like Li Po, dreaming of the people and places left behind. Using specific word pictures, write a few phrases describing the sights and sounds you would miss most.

Literary Focus

Alliteration is the repetition of consonant sounds in words that appear close together. Alliteration usually occurs at the beginning of words, as in *broken bottle*. But alliteration may also occur within words, as in *He was always wide-awake*. Poets may use alliteration to give their poems greater unity, to achieve special rhythmic and musical effects, or to emphasize particular words. Alliteration is a commonly used sound device in traditional Chinese poetry.

QUIET NIGHT THOUGHTS
Li Po
translated by
ARTHUR COOPER

 What is the central image in this poem?

Before my bed
there is bright moonlight
So that it seems
like frost on the ground:

5   Lifting my head
I watch the bright moon,
Lowering my head
I dream that I'm home.

LETTER TO HIS TWO SMALL CHILDREN
Li Po
translated by
ARTHUR COOPER

 What mood and experience do the poet's images create?

Here in Wu° Land mulberry leaves are green,
Silkworms in Wu have now had three sleeps:

My family, left in Eastern Lu,
Oh, to sow now Turtle-shaded fields,

1. **Wu** (wōō): a river in central China.

5   Do the Spring things I can never join,
Sailing Yangtze° always on my own—

Let the South Wind blow you back my heart,
Fly and land it in the Tavern court
Where, to the East, there are sprays and leaves
10 Of one peach tree, sweeping the blue mist;

This is the tree I myself put in
When I left you, nearly three years past;
A peach tree now, level with the eaves,
And I sailing cannot yet turn home!

15 Pretty daughter, P'ing-yang is your name,
Breaking blossom, there beside my tree,
Breaking blossom, you cannot see me
And your tears flow like the running stream;

And little son, Po-ch'in you are called,
20 Your big sister's shoulder you must reach
When you come there underneath my peach,
Oh, to pat and pet you too, my child!

I dreamt like this till my wits went wild,
By such yearning daily burned within;
25 So tore some silk, wrote this distant pang
From me to you living at Wen Yang . . .

6. **Yangtze** (yangk'sē): the longest river in China, flowing from Tibet to the East China Sea.

POET WANDERING IN THE MOONLIGHT, TU CHIN.
What does the growth of a peach tree measure in this poem?

What dominant feelings do these two poems evoke? Which images communicate these feelings most effectively?

Identifying Facts

1. What word or words suggesting a season does Li Po use in each poem?

2. What dreams does Li Po describe in his poems?

3. Which repeated consonants create **alliteration** in the lines, "Before my bed/ there is bright moonlight" and "I dreamt like this till my wits went wild"?

Interpreting Meanings

1. What is the overall **mood**, or feeling, of "Quiet Night Thoughts"? How does the poet use **imagery**, or word pictures, to convey that mood?

2. Like many Chinese poets, Li Po uses a form of **parallelism** in which pairs of lines follow the same basic sentence structure. Point out the parallelism in the last four lines of "Quiet Night Thoughts." What two ideas are contrasted in these two parallel pairs of lines?

3. How does the poet use images of nature to emphasize his solitude in "Letter to His Two Small Children"? What emotions are evoked in this poem?

4. In which of Li Po's two poems is **alliteration** used more frequently? How do these repeated consonants add to the poem's effect?

Applying Meanings

The poems' speakers chose to express their feelings by using images of nature and the seasons. If you felt as lonely as the speakers, what season would you use to express your emotions? Why?

Creative Writing Response

Writing a Poem in Letter Form. Imagine that you are far away and thinking of family members or friends and how much you miss them. As Li Po did, write a letter in the form of a poem that expresses your feelings. To help convey your emotion, use at least two **images**, or word-pictures, that suggest the appropriate seasons or aspects of nature. For example, a flock of migrating birds might convey the idea of yearning to head home. Try to use the sound device of **alliteration** in some of your lines.

Speaking and Listening

Planning and Performing a Choral Reading. With a partner or a small group, prepare and perform a choral reading of either "Quiet Night Thoughts" or "Letter to His Two Small Children." You might want to accompany your reading with a recording of appropriate Chinese music or the live sounds of a flute and drums, if class musicians are available. Use the following list as a guide to prepare and perform your reading for the class.

1. Decide which lines will be read by each solo, or single, voice and which lines might be read by a chorus. For example, "Quiet Night Thoughts" could be read by two solo voices reading alternating pairs of lines.

2. Make a copy of the poem and mark the reading parts you've decided upon.

3. For your part, underline the words you particularly want to stress and note the punctuation where you will pause or stop.

4. Practice your choral reading before performing it for the class.

THE ART OF TRANSLATION

Translating Chinese Poetry

Many masterpieces of world literature would be unavailable to us if it were not for **translation**, the rendering of spoken or written words from one language into another. Literary translators practice a complex art. To begin with, they must be able to understand the meaning, structure, and style of the original work. Then they must convey these elements artfully in a second language, striking a balance between the two extremes of upholding form over content or content over form.

The best translators are often themselves writers, such as the poets Witter Bynner and Ezra Pound, who produced different translations of the same poem by Li Po. Such poetic translations may begin with a ''word-for-word'' rendering like the following literal translation of another classical Chinese verse. In the classical Chinese language, each character usually stands for a single syllable that also represents a one-syllable Chinese word.

月　耀　如　晴　雪

Moon rays like pure snow

梅　花　似　照　晃

Plum flowers resemble bright stars

可　憐　金　鏡　轉

Can admire gold disc turn

庭　上　玉　芳　馨

Garden high above jewel weeds fragrant

Here is Ezra Pound's more graceful rendering of the moon poem, based on the literal translation you have just read:

> The moon's snow falls on the plum tree;
> Its boughs are full of bright stars.
> We can admire the bright turning disc;
> The garden high above there, casts its
>   pearls to our weeds.

Classical Chinese poetry is open to wide-ranging interpretations because of the unique grammatical structure of the Chinese language. In classical Chinese, there are no indications of pronoun gender, verb tenses, or noun number. Connecting words and even the subjects of sentences are often omitted. Translators must therefore rely on clues given in the poem's context and imagery.

Two very different translations of the same Li Po poem appear on the following pages. In preparing his translation of the Li Po poem that appears on page 524, Pound worked from an English prose translation of a Japanese version. Bynner, for his translation on page 525, worked from the original Chinese poem. In both versions of the poem, a young woman whose marriage was undoubtedly arranged by her parents describes how her feelings toward her husband blossomed into love.

The River Merchant's Wife: A Letter
Li Po
translated by
Ezra Pound

While my hair was still cut straight across my forehead
I played about the front gate, pulling flowers.
You came by on bamboo stilts, playing horse,
You walked about my seat, playing with blue plums.
And we went on living in the village of Chokan:
Two small people, without dislike or suspicion.

At fourteen I married My Lord you.
I never laughed, being bashful.
Lowering my head, I looked at the wall.
Called to, a thousand times, I never looked back.

At fifteen I stopped scowling,
I desired my dust to be mingled with yours
Forever and forever and forever.
Why should I climb the look out?

At sixteen you departed,
You went into far Ku-to-yen, by the river of swirling eddies,
And you have been gone five months.
The monkeys make sorrowful noise overhead.

You dragged your feet when you went out.
By the gate now, the moss is grown, the different mosses,
Too deep to clear them away!
The leaves fall early this autumn, in wind.
The paired butterflies are already yellow with August
Over the grass in the West garden;
They hurt me. I grow older.
If you are coming down through the narrows of the river Kiang,
Please let me know beforehand,
And I will come out to meet you
                    As far as Cho-fu Sa.

THE NORTH SEA *(left section)*, CHOU CH'EN (c. 1455–c. 1537).

A Song of Ch'ang-Kan
Li Po
translated by
Witter Bynner

My hair had hardly covered my forehead.
I was picking flowers, playing by my door,
When you, my lover, on a bamboo horse,
Came trotting in circles and throwing green plums.
We lived near together on a lane in Ch'ang-kan,
Both of us young and happy-hearted.
. . . At fourteen I became your wife,
So bashful that I dared not smile,
And I lowered my head toward a dark corner
And would not turn to your thousand calls;
But at fifteen I straightened my brows and laughed,
Learning that no dust could ever seal our love,
That even unto death I would await you by my post
And would never lose heart in the tower of silent watching.
. . . Then when I was sixteen, you left on a long journey
Through the Gorges of Ch'ü-t'ang, of rock and whirling water.
And then came the fifth month, more than I could bear,
And I tried to hear the monkeys in your lofty far-off sky.
Your footprints by our door, where I had watched you go,
Were hidden, every one of them, under green moss,
Hidden under moss too deep to sweep away.
And the first autumn wind added fallen leaves.
And now, in the eighth month, the yellowing butterflies
Hover, two by two, in our west-garden grasses. . . .
And because of all this, my heart is breaking
And I fear for my bright cheeks, lest they fade.
. . . Oh, at last, when you return through the three Pa districts,
Send me a message home ahead!

Eighteenth-century Chinese print from a series depicting women's occupations.

SEF/Art Resource, New York

1. Pound calls Li Po's poem a letter and includes its "writer" in the title. Bynner calls the poem a "song." How do these different titles affect your reading of each poem?
2. What are the main differences in imagery in each poem?
3. Which translator's version of the poem do you prefer? Why?

Tu Fu
A.D. 712–770

SuperStock International

Tu Fu (dōō fōō) was born into a noble family of scholar-officials. As a youth, he was confident of securing one of the imperial appointments that was the dream of every young aristocrat in the T'ang (täng) dynasty. So it was a bitter blow when, at the age of twenty-four, he failed the writing examinations in prose and poetry that were the means of gaining imperial positions.

Having failed the tests, Tu Fu spent most of his days wandering and moving in and out of minor government positions throughout the empire. Although he passed the imperial examinations much later in life, he did so without distinction. His failure kept him from realizing his youthful dream of becoming an advisor to the emperor.

Tu Fu's family connections and modest wealth nonetheless assured him of relative comfort until 755, when a violent rebellion ended the T'ang dynasty's days of glory. After that, Tu Fu was often on the road, searching for a way to make a living. In 757, while Tu Fu was away seeking work, his young son died, possibly from starvation or a plague. During the remaining years of his life, Tu Fu lived in hardship and poor health. He died in 770 on a houseboat on a river near Hangchow.

The uncertain course of Tu Fu's life is reflected in his poetry, which is often marked by bitterness and melancholy. As a young man, he wrote mainly about the beauty of nature and his own sorrows. But as he grew older, Tu Fu's poems turned to more humanitarian themes. He became sensitive to people's sufferings and was the first Chinese poet to write at length about current social concerns. After the bloody rebellion of 755, he wrote many poems condemning the folly of war—a common theme in Chinese poetry.

Although Tu Fu was neither well known nor especially well regarded as a poet during his own lifetime, he wrote in an elegant style that influenced later Chinese poets for centuries after his death. His poetry is even more polished than that of Li Po (lē bō), the friend and fellow poet with whom he is often linked. To the Chinese, "Li Po is the people's poet, Tu Fu is the poets' poet."

Reader's Guide

POEMS OF TU FU

Background

Perhaps the most respected of all the ancient Chinese poets, Tu Fu focused on the affairs of the world and the sufferings of his people. In stating his goal as a poet, Tu Fu once said, "If my words aren't startling, death itself has no rest."

Like many Chinese poets of his time, Tu Fu wrote in a variety of forms, but he was unequaled in his mastery of the difficult eight-line classical verse form called the *lü-shih* (lyōo'shi), meaning "regulated verse." This demanding form, somewhat like the Western poetic form the *sonnet*, (see page 804), was considered a showcase for a Chinese poet's classical technique.

The poems included here represent the poet's realistic and sometimes ironic outlook on life. As you read these poems, notice the vivid images and the concrete details that were a hallmark of Tu Fu's poetry.

Writer's Response

Tu Fu often wrote poems about the social concerns of his time. List five pressing social concerns that might inspire a contemporary Tu Fu to write poetry today.

Literary Focus

Mood is the overall feeling or atmosphere of a work of literature. A poem's mood might be cheerful or gloomy, defiant or accepting. Writers usually establish a mood by using descriptive details and evocative language—words that call up particular images or feelings. In the traditional Chinese poetry of Tu Fu's time, a single mood usually characterized each poem. But Tu Fu broke new ground by including shifting moods within a single poem.

FOR WEI PA, IN RETIREMENT

Tu Fu

translated by
ARTHUR COOPER

In this poem, Tu Fu seems to celebrate a friend's retirement. What are Tu Fu's feelings about being retired from the world's affairs?

Our livelong days we never meeting
Move as do stars in other clusters,
Yet this evening ("And what an evening!")
We're sharing this lamp and candlelight;
5   But youth and strength, how briefly it lasts
For both our heads have become grizzled
And half of those we ask about, ghosts,
Till cries of shock pierce our very breasts:
How could we know twenty years would pass
10   Before I came again to your house?
Though in those days you were unmarried
Suddenly sons and daughters troop in,
"Greet merrily Papa's Companion,"
Ask from what parts it is that I come?
15   But such exchange remains unfinished:
You chase them off to get out the wine
"And in night rain pull up spring onions"
To be steamed fresh with yellow millet . . .
Now (with your "Come, we can meet seldom")
20   You've charged my glass ten times in sequence:
Ten times and still I'm not quite tipsy
But filled with sense of old acquaintance;
For tomorrow the hills divide us,
Both out of sight in the world's affairs!

ENJOYING FRESH AIR IN A MOUNTAIN RETREAT, SHENG MOU (c. 1330–1369).

The Nelson-Atkins Museum of Art, Kansas City, Missouri

NIGHT THOUGHTS AFLOAT

Tu Fu

translated by

ARTHUR COOPER

As you read this poem, jot down two possible meanings for the word **drifting** *in line 13.*

By bent grasses
in a gentle wind
   Under straight mast
I'm alone tonight,

5   And the stars hang
above the broad plain
   But moon's afloat
in this Great River:

    Oh, where's my name
10 among the poets?
    Official rank?
"Retired for ill health."

    Drifting, drifting,
what am I more than
15   A single gull
between sky and earth?

THE NORTH SEA (right section), CHOU CH'EN (C. 1455–1537).
The goal of much of Chinese painting is to capture spirit through form.
What spirit does this painting seem to express? Do you think it suits the spirit of the poem?

JADE FLOWER PALACE

Tu Fu

translated by
KENNETH REXROTH

What does this poem reveal about Tu Fu's perspective on imperial wealth and power?

The stream swirls. The wind moans in
The pines. Gray rats scurry over
Broken tiles. What prince, long ago,
Built this palace, standing in
5   Ruins beside the cliffs? There are
Green ghost fires in the black rooms.
The shattered pavements are all
Washed away. Ten thousand organ
Pipes whistle and roar. The storm
10   Scatters the red autumn leaves.

His dancing girls are yellow dust.
Their painted cheeks have crumbled
Away. His gold chariots
And courtiers are gone. Only
15   A stone horse is left of his
Glory. I sit on the grass and
Start a poem, but the pathos of
It overcomes me. The future
Slips imperceptibly away.
20   Who can say what the years will bring?

WHILING AWAY THE SUMMER, LIU KUAN-TAO (c. 1279–1300).
How does this poem contrast the past and the present?

The Nelson-Atkins Museum of Art, Kansas City, Missouri

First Thoughts

What concerns seem to preoccupy Tu Fu?

Identifying Facts

1. Describe the **setting** (time and place) of "For Wei Pa, in Retirement." What specific **details** bring the setting to life?
2. To what does Tu Fu compare himself in "Night Thoughts Afloat"?
3. What did Tu Fu try to do after he had looked at the Jade Flower Palace? Why did he fail?

Interpreting Meanings

1. Tu Fu's poem "For Wei Pa, in Retirement" is both a celebration and a kind of **lament**, or expression of sorrow. What experiences does the poem celebrate? What experiences does it mourn?
2. The first two stanzas of "Night Thoughts Afloat" describe a scene and the last two express the poet's feelings. What is the **mood** of the first two stanzas? Of the last two?
3. In Tu Fu's time, a poem was expected to represent only one **mood**, **tone**, and **setting**. Tu Fu broke with tradition and often shifted moods, tones, and images within a poem. Find at least two shifts in any of Tu Fu's poems. How do these shifts affect your reading of each poem?

Applying Meanings

Which of Tu Fu's poems has the most meaning for you in terms of your own personal experience? Why?

Critical Writing Response

Comparing and Contrasting Two Poems. Tu Fu's poem "Jade Flower Palace" is similar in **theme** to the following poem, "Ozymandias," by Percy Bysshe Shelley, a nineteenth-century English Romantic poet.

Ozymandias
Percy Bysshe Shelley

I met a traveler from an antique land
Who said—"Two vast and trunkless legs of
  stone
Stand in the desert. . . . Near them, on the
  sand,
Half sunk a shattered visage lies, whose
  frown,
And wrinkled lip, and sneer of cold com-
  mand,
Tell that its sculptor well those passions
  read
Which yet survive, stamped on these lifeless
  things,
The hand that mocked them and the heart
  that fed;
And on the pedestal these words appear:
'My name is Ozymandias, king of kings:
Look on my works, ye Mighty, and despair!'
Nothing beside remains. Round the decay
Of that colossal wreck, boundless and bare
The lone and level sands stretch far away."

In two or three paragraphs, compare and contrast "Jade Flower Palace" and "Ozymandias." Consider the similarities and differences in **mood**, **tone**, and **setting** between the two poems. How do the poets use **imagery** and concrete **details**? In the final paragraph, state which poem you prefer and why. You may organize your ideas in a chart like the one below.

	Jade Flower Palace	Ozymandias
Setting (concrete details)		
Mood and tone		
Images in poem		
Theme		

Li Ch'ing-chao
C. A.D. 1084–1151

Art Resource, New York

For hundreds of years, many women in China have excelled at composing classical poetry. But no one is the equal of Li Ch'ing-chao (lē ching jou), long regarded as China's greatest woman poet of any period. A gifted and versatile writer, Li Ch'ing-chao was also one of the most liberated women of her day.

Li Ch'ing-chao grew up in a literary-minded family of noted scholars and officials. Her mother wrote poetry and her father belonged to a powerful literary circle. Because of her father's position as an imperial scholar-officer, Li Ch'ing-chao was brought up in court society and was trained in the arts and classical literature. This was an unusual upbringing for a woman of the Sung dynasty.

When Li Ch'ing-chao was seventeen, she competed with a friend of her father's in writing poetry. She also dared to criticize the friend's views in her poems. In doing so, she violated the Confucian code of conduct for aristocratic women. But instead of being punished for her immodesty, Li Ch'ing-chao gained admiration for her talents.

At the age of eighteen, Li Ch'ing-chao married the son of a powerful minister from an illustrious family. It was a happy marriage in which Li Ch'ing-chao and her husband wrote poems to each other and shared common interests in literature and the arts. Over time, they amassed one of the largest art collections in China. In 1129, Li Ching-chao's whole world collapsed when her husband died, possibly of typhoid, just before the imperial capital was invaded by barbarians from the north. During the next few years, Li Ch'ing-chao fled for her life, following the Sung court's retreat south of the Yangtze (yangk'sē) River.

In her later years as a widow, Li Ch'ing-chao remained a target of court intrigue. She lost many of her precious possessions and lived the last years of her life in misery.

Only about fifty poems remain of the six volumes of lyric poetry Li Ch'ing-chao wrote in her lifetime. Many of her poems celebrate her happy marriage or express her loneliness when her husband was away. The aim of her poetry, she said, was to capture a single moment in time.

Reader's Guide

PEONIES

Background

Li Ch'ing-chao composed many poems in the *tz'u* (tsə), or "lyric meter" form, which requires that the poet supply words to pre-established musical patterns. Chinese poets, in fact, never say that they "write a tz'u." Instead, they "fill in a tz'u," keeping to the precise patterns of well-known Chinese songs.

Originally, the tz'u were lyrics written to songs from Central Asia sung by popular musical entertainers. Later, the elite poets of China wrote tz'u by following the songs' different metrical patterns, including the number and length of lines and specific rhyme schemes. Along with the title of their tz'u, Chinese poets often included the original tune title to indicate the metrical pattern they followed. Later tz'u were usually not intended to be sung.

Li Ch'ing-chao is regarded as the greatest writer of tz'u poetry from any period. Her poem "Peonies" reflects the special poetic qualities of ambiguity, delicacy, and indirectness that distinguish tz'u from other forms of Chinese verse.

Writer's Response

Peonies (pē'ə·nēz) are large, fragrant flowers that have been a favorite in Chinese gardens for centuries. The Chinese view the peony as a symbol of female beauty and love, as well as a sign of spring. It is the queen of flowers, and it is often used as a symbol of the emperor's favorite lady.

Write the name of your favorite flower or plant in the center of a sheet of paper. Around the name, make a word cluster of whatever images the flower or plant brings to your mind: its color, scent, the time of year you associate with it, and so on.

Literary Focus

Personification is a figure of speech in which a nonhuman thing or quality is described as if it were human. The phrase "Mother Earth," for example, personifies our home planet by associating it with the nurturing human qualities of motherhood. In traditional Chinese poetry, poets often personify elements in nature, such as the wind, clouds, and flowers.

Li Ch'ing-chao   **533**

PEONIES

Li Ch'ing-chao

translated by

KENNETH REXROTH AND LING CHUNG

Li Ch'ing-chao's poems are complex in feeling. As you read this poem, note places where the mood shifts subtly.

You open the low curtains of the women's quarter
   in the palace.
And carefully the carved railings guard you.
You stand alone in the middle of the balcony in
   the end of Spring.
Your flowerlike face is clear and bright as flowing water.
5   Gentle, modest, your natural innocence is apparent to all.
All flowers have withered except you.
In the morning breeze, in glittering dew,
You make your morning toilet
And become still more splendid and bewitching.
10 The wind envies you as you laugh at the moon.
The God of Spring falls in love with you forever.
Over the east side of the city the sun rises
And shines on the ponds and the gardens
And teahouses of the courtesans in the south side.
15 The perfumed carriages run home.
The banquet tables are cleared of scattered flowers
   and silks.
Who will succeed you when you have become
   perfumed dust?
The Palace of Brilliant Light° was not more beautiful,
As the sun rises through the branches of your
   blossoms.
20 I pledge my love to you in a gold cup.
As the painted candles gutter and die,
I for one do not welcome the yellow twilight.

The Granger Collection, New York

18. **Palace of Brilliant Light:** an allusion to the emperor's palace, whose golden staircases and inlaid-pearl walls glowed in the dark with a brilliant light.

First Thoughts

Which image in this poem struck you as being the most vivid and memorable? Why?

Identifying Facts

1. What do the opening lines of the poem tell you about the place and time of year in which the poem is set?
2. How is twilight described in "Peonies"? What words express the speaker's feelings about that time?

Interpreting Meanings

1. What does the **personification** of the peonies reveal about the poet's feelings toward nature?
2. What **mood** is suggested in the first and middle parts of "Peonies"? What contrasting mood is expressed in the last part of the poem? Which particular lines express the subtle change in mood?
3. Is "Peonies" simply a celebration of a very beautiful woman, or does it express other concerns? Before you answer, consider the meaning implied in lines 6 and 17.

Applying Meanings

In this poem springtime evokes somber thoughts as well as feelings of delight. Why might spring be regarded as a melancholy as well as a happy season?

Creative Writing Response

Writing Song Lyrics. "Peonies" was originally composed to fit a popular melody. Choose a song that you like, and write new lyrics for it. Write about any subject, but make sure that the words you write fit the rhythmic pattern and the rhyme scheme of the song you have selected. You may want to record your song or perform it for the class when you have finished.

Critical Writing Response

Analyzing the Poem's Effect. In a two-paragraph essay, identify how "Peonies" affected you and why it had that effect. Use your answers to the following questions to stimulate prewriting ideas.

1. What were my feelings about the poem? Did it intrigue, bore, puzzle, or move me?
2. How did the poem's imagery affect me? Were the images colorful? interesting? confusing?
3. From its name, what did I expect the poem to be about? How did my expectations affect my response?

Language and Vocabulary

Ambiguity

Ambiguity is the expression of an idea in language that suggests more than one meaning. Poet Li Ch'ing-chao uses ambiguity in "Peonies" when she says, "I for one do not welcome the yellow twilight." Is the poet referring to the time just after sunset or to any developing darkness? Or does she intend "twilight" to mean a gradual period of decline in her youth and beauty? The poet's ambiguity deliberately leads us into different streams of thought, all of which make sense in the context of the poem.

Answer the following questions to analyze the poet's use of ambiguity in "Peonies."

1. Identify the lines that suggest the poet is addressing a flower in this poem. Which lines suggest that she is addressing a woman?
2. Toward the end of the poem, the speaker says, "I pledge my love to you in a gold cup." Who might "I" be if "you" refers to a woman? If "you" refers to a flower?

Confucius
551–479 B.C.

His family name was K'ung, and he is known in Chinese history by the title K'ung-fu-tzu (koon'foo·dzə'), which means Master K'ung. In the West he is known as Confucius (kən·fyoo'shəs).

Confucius grew up in a poor family of possibly noble heritage. He lived an ordinary life that was marked by an extraordinary love for learning. When he married at the age of nineteen, Confucius had already distinguished himself as a young scholar. By the time he died in 479 B.C. at the age of seventy-three, this largely self-educated man had become the most learned teacher in China.

Confucius was the first person in recorded Chinese history to believe in education for all and to regard teaching as a life's work. He gave private lessons to young men, train-ing them in the moral character he saw as proper and necessary to the ruling classes. But he longed for a more public position in government that would allow him to reform society according to the ancient "Way of Goodness," a traditional code of personal ethics and honor which contemporary rulers had discarded in favor of personal gain. For a decade or more, Confucius traveled from state to state seeking a ruler who would put this traditional moral code into practice. But his notions were out of step with the rulers' ways of oppression and violence. Finally, at the age of sixty-seven, Confucius returned home to teach a small band of followers in the practice of the Way.

Confucius left no writings. The only written record of his teachings was put together by his followers long after his death. This record of conversations with Confucius, the Master, is known in English as the *Analects*, which means "selected sayings," or "selections from a group of works." The *Analects* is divided into twenty books. Only six or seven of them may be Confucius' actual teachings. The other books were probably added by later disciples of the Confucian school. Generations after Confucius' death, Confucian thought took hold in China and profoundly influenced all of East Asia, including Japan and Korea. In traditional China, the *Analects* was essential reading for every educated person for more than two thousand years.

Reader's Guide

from the ANALECTS

Background

The sayings in the *Analects* range from brief statements to more extended dialogues between Confucius and his students. The sayings express ideas based on Chinese traditions as well as on the ways of the Chinese kings Confucius admired. In fact, Confucius declared that he was "a transmitter rather than a creator of ideas," a man who was "not born with any superior knowledge, only a lover of past tradition." He believed that studying the wisdom of the ancients enabled people to join the continuous chain of minds from the past to their own time.

In the *Analects,* Confucius, called "the Master," speaks about the inherent goodness people should cultivate within themselves. The true self of every person—marked by unselfishness, courage, and honor—is a reflection of *chung-yung,* usually translated as "the Golden Mean," an ideal of universal moral and social harmony. The *Analects* instructs the individual on how to achieve "moderation in all things" through moral education, the building of a harmonious family life, and the development of virtues such as loyalty, obedience, and a sense of justice.

Throughout the *Analects,* Confucius also emphasizes "filial piety," the carrying out of basic obligations to one's living parents or dead ancestors. In addition, the *Analects* stresses Confucius' concern with social and religious rituals. To Confucius, a person's inner virtues can be fully realized only through concrete acts of "ritual propriety," proper behavior toward other human beings.

Writer's Response

Confucius believed that all people could develop good moral character. List five qualities that you admire in people you know. How do these qualities reflect good moral character?

Literary Focus

A **maxim** is a brief, direct statement that expresses a basic rule of human conduct or a general truth about human behavior, as in the statement: "Success is getting what you want; happiness is wanting what you get." Familiar proverbs such as "The early bird catches the worm" are also maxims. A maxim provides a simple and direct way to capture a profound, complex truth about human conduct and behavior.

from the ANALECTS
Confucius
translated by
ARTHUR WALEY

As you read these sayings from the **Analects,** *make a list of the attitudes or beliefs that Confucius appears to be against. Make a separate list of the ideals he is striving to teach.*

Portrait of Confucius, seventeenth century.

The Master said, "He who rules by moral force is like the polestar,[1] which remains in its place while all the lesser stars do homage to it." (II, 1)

The Master said, "If out of the three hundred *Songs*[2] I had to take one phrase to cover all my teaching, I would say 'Let there be no evil in your thoughts.'" (II, 2)

---

1. **polestar:** the North Star, toward which the earth's axis points; also, a directing principle.

2. ***Songs:*** *The Book of Songs.*

The Master said, "At fifteen I set my heart upon learning. At thirty, I had planted my feet firm upon the ground. At forty, I no longer suffered from perplexities. At fifty, I knew what were the biddings of Heaven. At sixty, I heard them with docile ear. At seventy, I could follow the dictates of my own heart; for what I desired no longer overstepped the boundaries of right." (II, 4)

Tzu-yu[3] asked about the treatment of parents. The Master said, " 'Filial sons nowadays are people who see to it that their parents get enough to eat. But even dogs and horses are cared for to that extent. If there is no feeling of respect, wherein lies the difference?" (II, 7)

The Master said, "Yu,[4] shall I teach you what knowledge is? When you know a thing, to recognize that you know it, and when you do not know a thing, to recognize that you do not know it. That is knowledge." (II, 17)

The Master said, "He who seeks only coarse food to eat, water to drink, and bent arm for pillow, will without looking for it find happiness to boot. Any thought of accepting wealth and rank by means that I know to be wrong is as remote from me as the clouds that float above." (VII, 15)

The Duke of She[5] asked Tzu-lu[6] about Master K'ung (Confucius). Tzu-lu did not reply. The Master said, "Why did you not say 'This is the character of the man: so intent upon enlightening the eager that he forgets his hunger, and so happy in doing so that he forgets the bitterness of his lot and does not realize that old age is at hand.' That is what he is." (VII, 18)

Tzu-kung[7] asked about government. The Master said, "Sufficient food, sufficient weapons, and the confidence of the common people." Tzu-kung said, "Suppose you had no choice but to dispense with one of these three, which would you forgo?" The Master said, "Weapons." Tzu-kung said, "Suppose you were forced to dispense with one of the two that were left, which would you forgo?" The Master said, "Food. For from of old, death has been the lot of all men; but a people that no longer trusts its rulers is lost indeed." (XII, 7)

Someone said, "What about the saying 'Meet resentment with inner power'?" The Master said, "In that case, how is one to meet inner power? Rather, meet resentment with upright dealing and meet inner power with inner power." (XIV, 36)

The Master said, "A gentleman is distressed by his own lack of capacity; he is never distressed at the failure of others to recognize his merits." (XV, 18)

Tzu-kung asked saying, "Is there any single saying that one can act upon all day and every day?" The Master said, "Perhaps the saying about consideration: 'Never do to others what you would not like them to do to you.' " (XV, 23)

---

3. **Tzu-yu** (dzə yō): one of Confucius' principal disciples, often credited with sayings of his own.
4. **Yu** (yō): a disciple of humble birth.
5. **Duke of She** (shu): an adventurer and self-styled nobleman, a contemporary of Confucius.
6. **Tzu-lu** (dzə lōo): a disciple of Confucius, known for his outgoing personality.

---

7. **Tzu-kung** (dzə gōong): a disciple of Confucius, who also served as a government official.

Which of the statements in the *Analects* do you find most meaningful? Why? Which would you find the most difficult to put into action in your own life?

Identifying Facts

1. According to the Master, Confucius, what simple rule of conduct summarizes his teaching?
2. To the Master's way of thinking, what is wrong with the "filial sons" of the day?

Interpreting Meanings

1. In Book II, Analect 7, Confucius speaks of filial piety (honoring one's parents) as more than just a form of good behavior. Why do you think he emphasizes such conduct in his teachings?
2. Which of the Master's sayings is most like the Bible's Golden Rule: "Do unto others as you would have them do unto you"? What is the main difference between Confucius' saying and the Golden Rule?
3. One of the **maxims** in the *Analects* states: "A gentleman is distressed by his own lack of capacity; he is never distressed at the failure of others to recognize his merits." Translate this maxim into your own words. Do you agree or disagree with it? Why?

Applying Meanings

Many people still quote traditional sayings that state rules of conduct, such as "Look before you leap" and "A penny saved is a penny earned." Why do you think such **maxims** have stood the test of time?

Creative Writing Response

Writing Maxims. Think of one or more rules of conduct and one or more general truths about human experience that you feel are important. Then write these rules or simple truths in the form of maxims, such as: "The more things you own, the more they own you." Take your favorite maxim and design it as a bumper sticker.

Critical Writing Response

Comparing and Contrasting Maxims. In America, one of the most popular writers of often-quoted maxims was none other than Benjamin Franklin, the great inventor, diplomat, and politician. Franklin wrote humorous but wise maxims. Many of them were taken from proverbs in other languages, folk sayings, and the words of other writers. Here is a sampling of Franklin's wit and wisdom:

> If a man empties his purse into his head, no man can take it away from him. An investment in knowledge always pays the best interest.
>
> Glass, china, and reputation are easily cracked and never well mended.
>
> He that composes himself is wiser than he that composes books.
>
> 'Tis hard for an empty bag to stand upright.
>
> Nothing brings more pain than too much pleasure; nothing more bondage than too much liberty.
>
> None preaches better than the ant, and she says nothing.

Compare Franklin's maxims to those you have just read by Confucius. What are the similarities and differences in the two writers' views, as expressed in their maxims? Do you think that the two men would agree with each other, or would they have grounds for dispute? Do both of them seem to follow the idea of a Golden Mean—that is, of moderation in all things? Write your ideas in a paragraph or two. Be sure to support your views with specific examples from each writer's works.

Lao-tzu
c. 571 B.C. – ?

New York Public Library Picture Collection

According to Chinese legend, Lao-tzu (lou′dzə′) had a miraculous birth: He was born as an old, bearded, white-haired man, who was thereafter called "The Old Philosopher" or "The Old Boy" and lived to the age of 160. As the legend suggests, Lao-tzu, the reputed founder of the Chinese philosophy of Taoism (dou′iz′əm), is a shadowy figure, more of a legend than a historical reality.

In his biography of Lao-tzu, China's Grand Historian Ssu-ma Ch'ien (sə mä chen) recounts a legendary meeting between Lao-tzu and the much younger philosopher Confu-

cius, who supposedly came seeking Lao-tzu's advice about rituals. Instead, Lao-tzu counseled Confucius to rid himself of excessive enthusiasm, arrogance, and other traits that Lao-tzu said were of no use to Confucius' "true person."

Whether or not this meeting between Confucius and Lao-tzu actually occurred, it does serve to highlight the differences between their two contrasting schools of thought. Broadly defined, Taoism consists of the joyful acceptance of life and a willingness to yield to the natural world, becoming one with it. Confucianism, on the other hand, emphasized the individual's responsibility to act purposefully and sensibly, always consciously carrying out prescribed duties to family and society. Both philosophies, however, are rooted in ancient Chinese tradition, and the Chinese people see them as complementary, rather than opposing, views.

In defining the essence of his philosophy, Lao-tzu said, "He who knows does not speak. He who speaks does not know." Chinese poet Po Chü-i (bō jü ē) underscored the irony of this statement when he wrote:

"He who talks doesn't know,
he who knows doesn't talk":
that is what Lao-tzu told us,
in a book of five thousand words.
If he was the one who knew,
how could he have been such
a blabbermouth?

Reader's Guide

from the TAO TE CHING

Background

The *Tao Te Ching* (dou deh jing) is a brief collection of sayings and poetry that teach the nature of Taoism. According to the Grand Historian Ssu-ma Ch'ien, Lao-tzu wrote the *Tao Te Ching* when, fed up with the decay he saw in government, he retired from his work as an archivist. The result of his retirement was the *Tao Te Ching,* or "Classic of the Way of Power," which, among other things, was intended to provide guidance for rulers who wished to govern according to *Tao,* or the Way. After the Bible, the *Tao Te Ching* has been the most translated book in history.

These passages from the *Tao Te Ching,* like those in the Confucian *Analects,* often teach through **maxims**, or brief sayings about life, and use parallel language and other repetitive devices to unify the text and enhance oral reading and memorization. The heart of the *Tao Te Ching,* however, is the presence of a central figure called "the Master." According to the translator of this version, "the Master" is a man or woman "whose life is in perfect harmony with the way things are" and who has become one with "the Tao, the Truth, the Life." Although traditional translations refer to the Master as *he,* the translator here often uses *she,* for "the Master" could mean anyone—including you.

Writer's Response

According to Lao-tzu, water symbolizes, or stands for, a model of Tao. Write the word *water* in the center of a piece of paper. Around it, create clusters of words and phrases that describe water's essential qualities and benefits to the world.

Literary Focus

A **paradox** is an apparently contradictory phrase or statement that is actually true. For example, in the New Testament, Saint Paul uses a paradox when he declares, "For when I am weak, then I am strong" (2 Corinthians). The statement challenges us to find an underlying truth that resolves the apparent contradiction. Saint Paul means that when he is weak in worldly terms, he is strong in his spirit. Lao-tzu uses paradoxes to focus attention on important points in his text. Reconciling these paradoxes is a key to understanding Taoist philosophy.

from the TAO TE CHING

Lao-tzu

translated by
STEPHEN MITCHELL

As you read these passages about Taoism, jot down the phrases or lines that have the greatest meaning for you. Also jot down the lines you find the most mysterious or puzzling.

2

When people see some things as beautiful,
other things become ugly.
When people see some things as good,
other things become bad.

Being and non-being create each other.
Difficult and easy support each other.
Long and short define each other.
High and low depend on each other.
Before and after follow each other.

Therefore the Master
acts without doing anything
and teaches without saying anything.
Things arise and she lets them come;
things disappear and she lets them go.
She has but doesn't possess,
acts but doesn't expect.
When her work is done, she forgets it.
That is why it lasts forever.

Founders Society Purchase, General Membership and Donations Fund, The Detroit Institute of Arts

EARLY AUTUMN, CH'IEN HSUAN.
How might the teachings of the first four lines of Passage 2 be applied to the viewing of this painting? How do you feel about the painting?

8

The supreme good is like water,
which nourishes all things without trying to.
It is content with the low places that people
disdain.
Thus it is like the Tao.

In dwelling, live close to the ground.
In thinking, keep to the simple.
In conflict, be fair and generous.
In governing, don't try to control.
In work, do what you enjoy.
In family life, be completely present.

When you are content to be simply yourself
and don't compare or compete,
everybody will respect you.

29

Do you want to improve the world?
I don't think it can be done.

The world is sacred.
It can't be improved.
If you tamper with it, you'll ruin it.
If you treat it like an object, you'll lose it.

There is a time for being ahead,
a time for being behind;
a time for being in motion,
a time for being at rest;
a time for being vigorous,
a time for being exhausted;
a time for being safe,
a time for being in danger.

The Master sees things as they are,
without trying to control them.
She lets them go their own way,
and resides at the center of the circle.

MOUNTAINS, STREAMS, AND AUTUMN-TINTED TREES,
WANG HUI (1632–1717), Ch'ing dynasty.

First Thoughts

In what circumstances might Taoism be helpful as an approach to life? In what circumstances might it be ineffective as an approach to life?

Identifying Facts

1. In passage 2, what is the Master's approach to acting and teaching? What happens when she forgets her work?
2. In passage 8, in what two ways is water like the Tao? What must one do to gain people's respect?
3. In passage 29, what will happen if you mistreat the world? How does the Master act toward the world?

Interpreting Meanings

1. In passage 2, point out one **paradox**, or apparent contradiction, that actually makes sense. What does Lao-tzu mean in these lines?
2. In passage 29, what does Lao-tzu mean when he says the world cannot be improved? How does the rest of this passage support this idea?
3. What is the message of passage 8? Do you agree or disagree with it? Why or why not?

Applying Meanings

Confucian thought is most often directed to social situations and conduct in everyday life, while Taoist thought applies to a broad relationship between people and nature. Suppose that you had to choose either Confucianism or Taoism as a guide to life. Which philosophy would you feel more comfortable living by? Why?

Creative Writing Response

Creating a Dialogue. Create an imaginary dialogue between a modern high-school student and Lao-tzu in which the philosopher tries to answer a question the student has raised. Focus your dialogue on a concrete problem with a friendship, schoolwork, or a career choice that a modern student might actually face. Be sure that your answer is in harmony with Lao-tzu's beliefs.

Critical Writing Response

Comparing and Contrasting Two Passages. Lines 7–14 of passage 29 from the *Tao Te Ching* are similar in theme and form to the biblical poem "To Every Thing There Is a Season" from Chapter 3 of Ecclesiastes. In a two- or three-paragraph essay, compare and contrast "There is a time for being ahead . . ." with "To Every Thing There Is a Season." In your essay, consider similarities and differences in style, language, and theme or message.

To Every Thing There Is a Season
King James Bible

To every thing there is a season,
And a time to every purpose under the
   heaven:
A time to be born, and a time to die;
A time to plant, and a time to pluck up that
   which is planted;
A time to kill, and a time to heal;
A time to break down, and a time to build
   up;
A time to weep, and a time to laugh;
A time to mourn, and a time to dance;
A time to cast away stones, and a time to
   gather stones together;
A time to embrace, and a time to refrain
   from embracing;
A time to get, and a time to lose;
A time to keep, and a time to cast away;
A time to rend, and a time to sew;
A time to keep silence, and a time to speak;
A time to love, and a time to hate;
A time of war, and a time of peace.

—Ecclesiastes 3:1–8

Taoist Writers
Fourth through Second Centuries B.C.

Landscape (left half), Ming dynasty.

Chuang Tzu (fourth century B.C.)

The Chinese philosopher Chuang Tzu (jwäng dzə) was the most important early interpreter of the philosophy of Taoism (dou'iz'əm). Very little is known of Chuang Tzu's life except that he served as a minor court official.

What we do know about Chuang Tzu comes mainly from the fictional stories about him in the final chapters of *Chuang Tzu*, a book of stories that contains his teachings, although it was written by others. In these stories, Chuang Tzu appears as a quirky character who cares little for either public approval or material possessions.

Content to live humbly, this wise man wears patched clothing and shabby shoes tied on with string. In one tale, Chuang Tzu even insists to his protesting disciples that they should not bury him when he dies. He wants nature as his only coffin and the heavenly bodies as his only jewels.

Lieh Tzu (fourth century B.C.)

Some scholars doubt that Lieh Tzu (lē'ə dzə) ever existed. Much of the *Lieh Tzu*, the book that bears his name, has been shown to be a forgery. Nevertheless, most experts believe that there was a real Lieh Tzu, a Taoist teacher who had many philosophical differences with his forebears Lao-tzu and Chuang Tzu. Lieh Tzu argued that a sequence of causes predetermines everything that happens, including one's choice of action. Since no one can change the unchangeable Way, or Tao, people should pursue their own self-interests.

Lui An (172–122 B.C.)

Lui An (lə än) was not only a Taoist scholar but the grandson of the founder of the Han dynasty (206 B.C.–A.D. 221). Lui An's royal title was the Prince of Haui-nan (hwī nan). The prince surrounded himself with a circle of philosophers, and under his patronage they produced a collection of essays on metaphysics, cosmology, politics, and conduct. Lui An took his own life after organizing a failed coup against his cousin, the emperor.

Reader's Guide

TAOIST ANECDOTES

Background

Chinese philosophers, whether followers of Taoism or Confucianism, have long used **anecdotes**, or brief stories, to convey indirectly the teachings of their philosophy. These anecdotes are the works of three Taoist philosophers. The stories are intended to impart the spiritual teachings of Taoism, with its focus on oneness with the world and the unchangeable nature of the Way.

These anecdotes often reflect different approaches to Taoist philosophy. Chuang Tzu, for example, tends to point directly to the Tao, or the Way, at work in the universe, while Lieh Tzu emphasizes the folly of those who don't see beyond the obvious to the underlying patterns that Taoists believe govern all action. But the anecdotes also have much in common. To make their philosophical points easier to accept, the philosophers convey their ideas in a single, colorful incident intended to amuse their readers. The anecdotes often use witty dialogue and light-hearted humor to "sugar coat" the philosophical point of their tales.

Writer's Response

Many of these ancient Chinese anecdotes can be boiled down to a **maxim**, a saying that states a truth about human experience or a rule for human conduct, such as "You can't tell a book by its cover" or "All is fair in love and war." Make a list of other popular maxims that could be illustrated in brief stories.

Literary Focus

An **anecdote** is a brief story that focuses on a single interesting incident or event, often an event that reveals the character of an important person. The writer of an anecdote surrounds this incident with just enough details to make the point of the anecdote clear and vivid for readers. Many anecdotes, like the ones you are about to read, are witty as well as instructive.

TAOIST ANECDOTES

translated by

MOSS ROBERTS

As you read these different anecdotes, try to discover the Taoist "point" that is hidden in each story.

Wagging My Tail in the Mud

The hermit poet Chuang Tzu was angling[1] in the River Pu. The king of Ch'u sent two noblemen to invite Chuang to come before him. "We were hoping you would take on certain affairs of state," they said. Holding his pole steady and without looking at them, Chuang Tzu said, "I hear Ch'u has a sacred tortoise that has been dead three thousand years, and the king has it enshrined in a cushioned box in the ancestral hall. Do you think the tortoise would be happier wagging its tail in the mud than having his shell honored?" "Of course," replied the two noblemen. "Then begone," said Chuang Tzu. "I mean to keep wagging my tail in the mud."

—*Chuang Tzu*

The Butterfly

Chuang Tzu said, "Once upon a time I dreamed myself a butterfly, floating like petals in the air, happy to be doing as I pleased, no longer aware of myself! But soon enough I awoke and then, frantically clutching myself, Chuang Tzu was I! I wonder: Was Chuang Tzu dreaming himself the butterfly,

BUTTERFLY, DIANE ONG.

or was the butterfly dreaming itself Chuang Tzu? Of course, if you take Chuang Tzu and the butterfly together, then there's a difference between them. But that difference is only due to their changing material forms."

—*Chuang Tzu*

Gold, Gold

Many, many years ago there was a man of the land of Ch'i who had a great passion for gold. One day at the crack of dawn he went to the market—straight to the gold dealers'

---

1. **angling:** fishing.

Horseman, late Han dynasty.

stalls, where he snatched some gold and ran. The market guards soon caught him. "With so many people around, how did you expect to get away with it?" a guard asked.

"When I took it," he replied, "I saw only the gold, not the people."

—*Lieh Tzu*

The Missing Axe

A man whose axe was missing suspected his neighbor's son. The boy walked like a thief, looked like a thief, and spoke like a thief. But the man found his axe while he was digging in the valley, and the next time he saw his neighbor's son, the boy walked, looked, and spoke like any other child.

—*Lieh Tzu*

The Lost Horse

A man who lived on the northern frontier of China was skilled in interpreting events.

One day for no reason, his horse ran away to the nomads across the border. Everyone tried to console him, but his father said, "What makes you so sure this isn't a blessing?" Some months later his horse returned, bringing a splendid nomad stallion. Everyone congratulated him, but his father said, "What makes you so sure this isn't a disaster?" Their household was richer by a fine horse, which the son loved to ride. One day he fell and broke his hip. Everyone tried to console him, but his father said, "What makes you so sure this isn't a blessing?"

A year later the nomads came in force across the border, and every able-bodied man took his bow and went into battle. The Chinese frontiersmen lost nine of every ten men. Only because the son was lame did the father and son survive to take care of each other. Truly, blessing turns to disaster, and disaster to blessing: the changes have no end, nor can the mystery be fathomed.

—*Lui An*

First Thoughts

Which of these anecdotes contained a message that you could apply to your own life?

Identifying Facts

1. How does Chuang Tzu defy society's expectations in "Wagging My Tail in the Mud"?

2. In Lieh Tzu's tale "The Missing Axe," what causes a man to change his views of his neighbor's son?

3. In "Gold, Gold," why does the thief attempt a robbery in broad daylight?

4. In "The Lost Horse," is the frontiersman's broken hip good luck or a disaster? Why?

Interpreting Meanings

1. What does "Wagging My Tail in the Mud" reveal about Chuang Tzu's character? How does the tale reflect Taoist beliefs concerning oneness with nature and the need to be true to oneself?

2. What does Lui An's tale "The Lost Horse" teach about how people tend to interpret the events of their lives?

3. Many **anecdotes** can be reduced to a simple observation about human nature. Sum up the points of "Gold, Gold" and "The Missing Axe," each in a single sentence. In what way are the points of these two anecdotes similar?

4. What is Chuang Tzu's purpose in comparing himself to a tortoise in "Wagging My Tail in the Mud"? In imagining himself a butterfly in "The Butterfly"?

Applying Meanings

Of the five anecdotes told here, choose one or two that seem to mirror most closely your own observations about human nature. What human strengths or weaknesses do these anecdotes praise or criticize?

Critical Writing Response

Comparing Views. Some of the anecdotes you have just read might express attitudes toward life that you find surprising, baffling, or in conflict with your own views and beliefs. Choose one anecdote that expresses a view quite different from your own. Then write two or three well-developed paragraphs explaining the difference between the way you would be likely to approach a particular situation and the way the philosopher to whom the anecdote is attributed would approach it. What are the advantages of your attitude? What truth and value do you find in the view expressed in the anecdote?

Speaking and Listening

Telling an Anecdote. Everyone has a story to tell—something humorous, strange, frightening, important, or silly that has happened to them. Think of an anecdote from your own life that you would be willing to share with the rest of the class. It could be a story about something funny that you did when you were younger, an adventure you had one summer vacation, or an embarrassing incident at a family get-together. Be sure that your anecdote makes a point, even if it is a general point such as "Truth is stranger than fiction." Present your anecdote to the class orally. End your anecdote with a maxim that tells what point the anecdote is making.

Ssu-ma Ch'ien
c. 145–90 B.C.

CH'EN YUAN ADMONISHING LIU TSUNG, **Ming dynasty, artist unknown.**

Washington, D.C., 11.233—Chinese painting, Ming dynasty, 15th century; "Admonishing in Chains"; color on silk makimono: 207.9 × 36.9 cm (81 7/8 × 14 1/2")

Ssu-ma Ch'ien (sə mä chen) was the greatest of China's "Grand Historians." The son of the court historian to the Han (hän) dynasty, he succeeded his father in that important position. Ssu-ma Ch'ien then dedicated himself to completing the first history of China, a project his father had begun. This sweeping historical record would cover the whole world known to him—that is, the Han empire and the surrounding areas of East and Central Asia. It would extend from the dawn of Chinese history to the dramatic events of his own day: the founding of the first central university, the expansion of the empire into Central Asia, and the creation of overland trade routes, like the great Silk Road, that for the first time joined China with the European world.

But a personal tragedy interrupted Ssu-ma Ch'ien's work on this monumental project. He incurred the wrath of the reigning ruler, Emperor Wu, by defending a disgraced general accused of treason. As a result, Ssu-ma Ch'ien was imprisoned and condemned to the cruel punishment of castration for his crime.

According to Chinese custom, a gentleman sentenced to such a humiliating punishment was expected to commit suicide and die unscarred. However, Ssu-ma Ch'ien, by submitting to the mutilation, chose a life of bitterness and shame instead. As he explained years later in a letter to a friend, "If I concealed my feelings and clung to life, . . . it was because I could not bear to leave unfinished my deeply cherished project, because I rejected the idea of dying without leaving to posterity my literary work. . . . When it finally becomes known in the world, I shall have paid the debt of my shame; nor will I regret a thousand deaths."

After eighteen years of work, Ssu-ma Ch'ien fulfilled his dream. He completed the *Records of the Historian* a few years before he died at the age of fifty-five. In this historic chronicle, Ch'ien covers almost three thousand years of Chinese history in more than half a million written characters painstakingly etched onto bamboo tablets. Considered a masterpiece of historical writing, the *Records* established a structure for all the dynastic histories of China to come.

Reader's Guide

NIEH CHENG
from Records of the Historian

Background

The story of Nieh Cheng (nye jung) is taken from a section of Ssu-ma Ch'ien's biographies devoted to "assassin-retainers," wandering avengers of injustice who were an ancient tradition in China. Although the assassins' vengeful acts were strictly illegal, they were, paradoxically, also considered honorable, especially if they were undertaken on behalf of women and children who had been victims of wrongdoing. According to the Confucian code of conduct, revenge against wrongdoings was a duty, and, like many Chinese customs of the time, this duty far outweighed the rules of law.

In choosing to immortalize such subjects as assassin-retainers, Ssu-ma Ch'ien is recognizing the value of human beings who hold a low station in life. The assassins he wrote about are worthy men, he explains, even though "some succeeded in carrying out their duty and some did not. But it is perfectly clear that they had all determined upon the deed. They were not false to their intentions. Is it not right, then, that their names should be handed down to later ages?" Given this outlook, it is not surprising that many of Ssu-ma Ch'ien's biographies memorialize individuals whose defiant spirits struggled against hopeless odds to uphold a personal ideal or principle, as Ssu-ma Ch'ien himself did.

Writer's Response

What do you predict a hired assassin will be like? Think of images you know from movies and TV. Then write a brief description to convey your impressions of a paid assassin.

Literary Focus

Tone is the attitude a writer takes toward the reader, a subject, or a character. Like a speaker's tone of voice, a writer's tone may be described as lighthearted, melancholy, serious, ironic, or as reflecting any number of other emotions. Tone is conveyed through the writer's choice of words and details. The tone of the historian Ssu-ma Ch'ien's writings reveals his views of the people whose lives he recorded.

NIEH CHENG
from Records of the Historian
Ssu-ma Ch'ien
translated by
BURTON WATSON

As you read this biography, ask yourself why Nieh Cheng chose to act as he did. Do you agree with the choices he made? Could he have avoided his fate?

Chinese sword. *The introduction of the iron sword into China enabled the Ch'in dynasty to unify the numerous, smaller Chinese states in 221 B.C.*

Scala/Art Resource

Nieh Cheng

Some forty years later there was the affair of Nieh Cheng in Chih.[1] Nieh Cheng was from the village of Deep Well in Chih. He killed a man and, in order to escape retaliation, went with his mother and elder sister to the state of Ch'i,[2] where he made a living as a butcher. Some time later Yen Chung-tzu of P'u-yang,[3] an official in the service of Marquis Ai of Han, had a falling-out with Han Hsia-lei,[4] the prime minister of Han. Fearful that he might be put to death, Yen Chung-tzu fled from the state and traveled about to other states searching for someone who would be willing to get back at Hsia-lei for him.

When he arrived in Ch'i, someone told him that Nieh Cheng was a man of valor and daring who, fleeing from his enemies, was hiding out among the butchers. Yen Chung-tzu went to his door and requested an interview, but was several times turned away. He then prepared a gift of wine which he asked to be allowed to offer in the presence of Nieh Cheng's mother. When the drinking was well underway, Yen Chung-tzu brought forth a hundred taels[5] of yellow gold which he laid before Nieh Cheng's mother with wishes for a long life. Nieh Cheng was astounded at such generosity and firmly re-

---

1. **Nieh Cheng** (nye jung) **in Chih** (jər)
2. **Ch'i** (chē)
3. **Yen Chung-tzu** (yen joong dzə) **of P'u-yang** (po͞o yang)
4. **Han Hsia-lei** (hän shä lä)

---

5. **tael** (tāl): a monetary unit roughly equivalent to 1 1/3 ounces of silver.

fused the gift. When Yen Chung-tzu just as firmly pressed it on him, Nieh Cheng repeated his refusal, saying, "I am fortunate enough to have my old mother with me. Though our family is poor and I am living in a strange land and earning my way as a dog butcher,[6] I am still able, come morning and evening, to find some sweet or tasty morsel with which to nourish her. She has everything she needs for her care and comfort—I could not be so bold as to accept your gift."

Yen Chung-tzu asked the others present all to withdraw and spoke to Nieh Cheng in private. "I have an enemy," he said, "and I have already traveled about to a great many states. When I reached Ch'i, however, I was privileged to learn that you, sir, are a man of extremely high principles. Therefore I have presented these hundred taels of gold, hoping that you may use them to purchase some trifling gift of food for your honored parent and that I may have the pleasure of your friendship. How would I dare hope for anything more?"

Nieh Cheng replied, "I have been content to humble my will and shame my body, living as a butcher here by the marketplace and well, only because I am fortunate enough to have my old mother to take care of. While she lives, I dare not promise my services to any man!"

Yen Chung-tzu continued every effort to persuade him, but to the end Nieh Cheng was unwilling to accept the gift. Yen Chung-tzu nevertheless did all that etiquette demands of a proper guest before taking his leave.

Some time later Nieh Cheng's mother died and, when she had been buried and the mourning period was over, Nieh Cheng said to himself, "Ah! I am a man of the marketplace and well, swinging a knife and working as a butcher, while Yen Chung-tzu is chief minister to one of the feudal lords. And yet he did not consider it too far to come a thousand miles, driving far out of his way just to make friends with me. I treated him very shabbily indeed! I have accomplished no great deeds for which I might be praised, yet Yen Chung-tzu presented a hundred taels of gold to my mother with wishes for her continued good health. Though I did not accept it, it is clear that he did so simply because he has a profound appreciation of my worth. Now a worthy gentleman, burning with anger and indignation, has offered friendship and trust to a poor and insignificant man. Can I bear to remain silent and let it end there? Earlier, when he made his request of me, I refused only because my mother was still alive. Now that her years have come to a close, I shall offer my services to one who truly understands me!"

Thereupon he journeyed west to P'u-yang in Wey[7] and went to see Yen Chung-tzu. "The reason I would not agree earlier," he said, "was simply that my mother was still alive. Now, unfortunately, the years Heaven gave her have come to a close. Who is this enemy that you wish to take revenge on? I request permission to undertake the task!"

Yen Chung-tzu then related to him the whole story. "My enemy is Han Hsia-lei, the prime minister of Han. He is also the younger uncle of the ruler of Han. His clan is numerous and powerful and there are many armed guards stationed wherever he happens to be.

---

6. **dog butcher:** Dog meat was considered acceptable to eat in China during this time.

7. **Wey** (wā)

YANG KUEI-FEI MOUNTING A HORSE (detail), CH'IEN HSUAN. *In Chinese painting, the line is the basic element of the painting, in contrast to light and shadow, which serve as the foundations for much of Western art.*

I had hoped to send someone to stab him to death, but so far no one has been able to accomplish it. Now if you are so kind as not to reject my plea for help, I hope you will allow me to give you additional carriages and men to assist you in the job."

But Nieh Cheng said, "Han and Wey are near neighbors. Now if one is going to murder the prime minister of another state, and the prime minister also happens to be a close relative of the ruler, then the circumstances make it unwise to send a large party of men. If you try to use a lot of men, then there are bound to be differences of opinion on how best to proceed; if there are differences of opinion, then word of the undertaking will leak out; and if word leaks out, then the whole state of Han will be up in arms against you! What could be more dangerous?"

Nieh Cheng therefore declined to accept any carriages or attendants, but instead took leave and set off alone, disguising his sword as a walking stick, until he reached Han. When he arrived, the Han prime minister Hsia-lei happened to be seated in his office, guarded and attended by a large body of men bearing lances and other weapons. Nieh Cheng walked straight in, ascended the steps, and stabbed Hsia-lei to death. Those about the prime minister were thrown into great confusion, and Nieh Cheng, shouting loudly, attacked and killed thirty or forty of them. Then he flayed the skin of his face, gouged out his eyes, and, butchering himself as he had once done animals, spilled out his bowels and in this way died.

The ruler of Han had his corpse taken and exposed in the marketplace, offering to re-

Ssu-ma Ch'ien   **555**

ward anyone who could identify him, but no one knew who he was. The ruler then hung up the reward, promising to give a thousand pieces of gold to anyone who could say who it was that had killed Prime Minister Hsia-lei. A long time passed but no one came forward with the answer.

Meanwhile Nieh Cheng's elder sister Jung[8] heard that someone had stabbed and killed the prime minister of Han, but that the blame could not be fixed since no one knew the culprit's name. His corpse had been exposed in the marketplace with a reward of a thousand pieces of gold hanging above it, she was told. Filled with apprehension, she said, "Could it be my younger brother? Ah— Yen Chung-tzu certainly knew what he was capable of!"

Then she set off at once and went to the marketplace of Han, where she found that the dead man was indeed Nieh Cheng. Throwing herself down beside the corpse, she wept in profound sorrow, crying, "This man is called Nieh Cheng from the village of Deep Well in Chih!"

The people passing back and forth through the market all said to her, "This man has committed an act of violence and treachery against the prime minister of our state and our king has posted a reward of a thousand gold pieces for anyone who can discover his name—have you not heard? How dare you come here and admit that you were acquainted with him?"

Jung replied, "Yes, I have heard. But Cheng was willing to accept shame and disgrace,

throwing away his future and making a living in the marketplace, because our mother was still in good health and I was not yet married. After our mother had ended her years and departed from the world, and I had found a husband, then Yen Chung-tzu, recognizing my brother's worth, lifted him up from hardship and disgrace and became his friend, treating him with kindness and generosity. So there was nothing he could do. A gentleman will always be willing to die for someone who recognizes his true worth. And now, because I am still alive, he has inflicted this terrible mutilation upon himself so as to wipe out all trace of his identity. But how could I, out of fear that I might be put to death, allow so worthy a brother's name to be lost forever?"

Having astounded the people of the marketplace with these words, she cried three times in a loud voice to Heaven and then died of grief and anguish by the dead man's side. When the inhabitants of Chin, Ch'u, Ch'i, and Wey heard of this, they all said, "Cheng was not the only able one—his sister too proved herself a woman of valor!"

If Cheng had in fact known that his sister would be unwilling to stand by in silence but, heedless of the threat of execution and public exposure, would make her way a thousand miles over the steep passes, determined to spread his fame abroad, so that sister and brother would both end as criminals in the marketplace of Han, then he would surely never have agreed to undertake such a mission for Yen Chung-tzu. And as for Yen Chung-tzu, it can certainly be said that he knew how to recognize a man's ability and win others to his service.

---

8. **Jung** (roong)

First Thoughts

How did you feel about what Nieh Cheng did? How did you feel about what his sister did? In your opinion, were their actions moral?

Identifying Facts

1. Why is Yen Chung-tzu searching for an assassin?
2. Why does Nieh Cheng refuse Yen Chung-tzu's request at first? Why does he later have a change of heart?
3. After he assassinates the prime minister, why does Nieh Cheng mutilate and kill himself?
4. Why do the people finally declare Cheng's sister to be ''a woman of valor''?

Interpreting Meanings

1. In this biography of Nieh Cheng, what seems to be the author's attitude toward his subject? For example, is the author's **tone** admiring, scornful, pitying, disinterested, respectful, or severe? Give examples from the text to support your view.
2. Was Yen Chung-tzu's cause necessarily a noble one? How do you account for Nieh Cheng's decision to lay down his life for a man he hardly knew?

3. **Irony** refers to a contrast between what is expected and what actually happens. Think about Cheng's reasons for killing himself as he did. In what way is his sister's behavior ironic?

Applying Meanings

Would you do anything for someone who alone seemed to recognize your inner worth? Why or why not?

Speaking and Listening

Enacting a Courtroom Trial. Imagine that Nieh Cheng has not committed suicide but has decided to stand trial instead. As directed by your teacher, stage Nieh Cheng's courtroom trial using the ancient details of his story but trying him according to twentieth-century American views of justice. Choose members of the class to be the judge, jury, defendant (Cheng), defense attorney, prosecuting attorney, and witnesses for both sides. Include Cheng's sister Jung, imagining that she, too, is alive. Have a student record the proceedings on videotape, if possible, or make a sound recording of the trial. Play back the proceedings later and critique your performances.

THE LITERATURE OF JAPAN

The Art Institute of Chicago, Japanese, Figure of Sogyo Hachiman in the Guise of a Buddhist Monk, wood, 9th century, ht: 53.3 × w: 46 × d: 31.7 cm, Gift of Joseph and Helen Regenstein Foundation, 1960.755

❝ It was in fact the widespread adoption of Chinese culture, including the wholly unsuitable Chinese method of writing, which was to determine the course of Japanese literature over the centuries. **❞**

—Donald Keene

Hachiman, the Shinto god of war, in the guise of a Buddhist monk. Late Heian period, ninth century A.D. *When Buddhism was introduced into Japan, Shintoism was temporarily pushed into the background. However, the two religions eventually became intermingled.*

Although early Japan borrowed much from Chinese culture, including the Chinese system of writing, Japanese culture evolved its own character and style over time. The distinctiveness of Japanese culture grew out of the unique social arrangements and world view developed by a people who, living on a starkly beautiful chain of mountainous islands, were largely isolated from their neighbors.

Early Japan

Japan's early political structure was based on clan, or family, divisions. Each clan developed a well-defined hierarchy of classes, with aristocrats, warriors, and priests at the top and peasants and workers at the bottom. Without any central authority, the clans constantly fought one another. Finally, in the fourth century A.D., one family group, the **Yamato**, grew powerful enough to subdue the others.

The Yamato admired Chinese culture, political organization, and philosophy and took steps to introduce these Chinese forms to Japan. The Yamato prince **Shotoku** (shô·tô·kōō) actually imposed the Chinese imperial system on Japan, creating an emperor, an imperial bureaucracy, and a grand capital city. In Japan, however, the emperor for the most part remained a figurehead.

The Feudal Era: Warlords and Samurai

In the eighth century A.D. ambitious aristocrats began to assemble huge private estates in the countryside, beyond the reach of the imperial authority. These local landowning lords surrounded themselves with professional warriors, called **samurai** (sam′ə·rī′). The samurai lived by a very strict code of behavior, somewhat like the chivalric code of the knights of medieval Europe but based more on absolute loyalty to one's overlord and on concepts of personal honor than on religious ideals.

> The Yamato clan in the fourth century A.D. introduced Chinese culture, political structures, and ideas into Japanese society.

In the latter part of the twelfth century, a strongman named Yoritomo seized effective control of the empire and had himself declared **shogun**, or "general." Over the next five centuries, a series of shoguns ruled Japan, but none could ever completely control the feuding warlords, who kept the country in a state of constant warfare.

The Granger Collection, New York

Samurai suit of armor, c. 1515.

The Downfall of Feudalism

Finally, in the late 1500s, a powerful shogun crushed the warring feudal lords and the **Tokugawa shogunate**, or shogun-ruled regime, controlled all of Japan from a new capital at Edo, later called Tokyo. At about this time, the Western world was seeking contact with Japan. These contacts alarmed the shogunate, which feared revolt at home or invasion from abroad. By 1630, Japan was a closed society: all foreigners were expelled, Japanese Christians were persecuted, and foreign travel was forbidden under penalty of death.

Opening to the West

This government-imposed isolation continued for two centuries. Then, in 1853, Commodore Matthew Perry of the United States Navy steamed into Tokyo Bay with demands that Japan open its doors to the West. Treaties were negotiated and Japan began to trade with the Western powers. As feared, outside influences did cause changes in Japan. The shogunate was ended in 1868, and Japan, under a new and more powerful emperor, rapidly acquired the latest technological knowledge, introduced universal education, and created an impressive industrial economy.

Shintoism and Buddhism

Shintoism, the ancient religion of Japan, reveres indwelling divine spirits called *kami,* found in natural places and objects. Later, divinity was ascribed to revered ancestors and

> The native Japanese Shinto religion, which regarded both nature and dead ancestors as divine, easily accommodated the arrival of new religions such as Buddhism.

finally to the emperor himself. The native Shinto tradition easily accommodated the various strains of Buddhism that

YOUNG WOMAN ATTENDED BY A MAID,
SUZUKI HARUNOBU, C. 1766.
Woodblock print.

Statue of Japan's first Shogun, Minamoto Yorimoto, thirteenth century.

Tokyo National Museum, Kodansha International

had been adopted by the Japanese from the Chinese and the Koreans, beginning in the fifth and sixth centuries A.D.

Although Buddhism originated in India, it was elaborated by many Chinese monks and scholars and developed into a series of schools or sects quite distinct from its Indian counterparts. Although all schools of Buddhism sought the attainment of spiritual freedom and inner tranquility, the various sects stressed different paths to this goal. **Zen Buddhism**, for example, emphasized the importance of meditation, concentration, and self-discipline as the way to enlightenment.

Japanese Literature: Pride in Poetry

Although originally inspired by Chinese models and preceded by a long oral tradition, Japanese written literature came into its own after the fifth century A.D., when the Japanese adapted the Chinese system of writing to the needs of their own language.

> **"** Japanese poetry has as its subject the human heart. It may seem to be of no practical use and just as well left uncomposed, but when one knows poetry well, one understands also without explanation the reasons governing order and disorder in the world. **"**
>
> —*Kamo Mabuchi (1697–1769)*

> 66 There are no teachers of Japanese poetry. But they who take the old poems as their teachers, steep their minds in the old style, and learn their words from the masters of former time—who of them will fail to write poetry? 99
>
> —*Fujiwara no Teika (1162–1241)*

M. Howell/SuperStock, Inc.

PORTRAIT OF A WOMAN, KITAGAWA UTAMARO, **late eighteenth century.** *Kitagawa's rich and sensuous composition influenced European artists such as Toulouse-Lautrec.*

As in China, composing poetry has always been a highly respected activity in Japan. From the beginnings of imperial government to the present day, poetry writing has been encouraged by official competition and rewarded by publication in collections, or anthologies. Beginning with the five-line **tanka** form in the eighth century A.D., Japanese poetry has been known for its brief lyrical bursts of feeling and the extreme compression of its verse. The culmination of the Japanese poets' tendency to compress meaning into a few

> Early Japanese literature was influenced by Chinese models, but after the fifth century A.D., literature in Japan developed its own distinctive style.

words came in the seventeenth century with the development of the **haiku** (hī′koō) form.

Japanese Prose

The greatest flowering of classical Japanese prose occurred during the **Heian** (hā′än) **period** (A.D. 794–1185), when a leisurely life at court made it possible for well-educated women to chronicle the hothouse atmosphere in which they lived. In the long and detailed *Tale of Genji*, considered by many scholars to be the world's first true novel, the aristocrat, **Lady Murasaki Shikibu**, traces the life of a gifted and charming prince. Her accomplishment led her to become as highly regarded in Japan as William Shakespeare (see page 839) is in English-speaking countries. Another tenth-century court lady, **Sei Shōnagon**, also immortalized the Heian age by writing witty and revealing journal entries about court life in *The Pillow Book*.

UKIYOE SCHOOL, KATSUKAWA SHUNSHO (1726–1792).

Japanese Drama

The most distinctive form of Japanese drama is called *Noh* (nō), which literally means "talent" or "skill." The purpose of Noh dramas is the invocation of a moment of wisdom or truth in the tradition of Zen Buddhism. **Kabuki** (kä·boō′kē) is another form of Japanese drama. The Kabuki drama appeals to a more general audience than Noh drama and makes use of stock characters and stylized situations, but the acting is broadly melodramatic and the emotions portrayed are easily understood. Colorful costumes and lively music and dance also please Kabuki audiences.

> **"** . . . Nō [Noh] does not make a frontal attack on the emotions. It creeps at the subject warily. **"**
>
> —Arthur Waley

*I*ntroduction

Tanka Poetry

The **tanka** (täng′kə) may be the most beloved form of Japanese poetry. Invented more than a thousand years ago, tanka are still being composed by Japanese poets. Even today, the Emperor of Japan holds an annual tanka-writing competition to celebrate the New Year.

Tanka Form

Tanka, meaning "short songs," are brief and lyrical poems. The traditional tanka consists of exactly thirty-one syllables divided among five lines. Three of the poem's lines have seven syllables, and the other two have five syllables. Within this rigid form the

Poem cards by Shinsai Ga, c. 1805. *In the Japanese tradition, poetry and illustration are often combined in cards like these.*

---

tanka (täng′kə): *a traditional form of Japanese poetry consisting of thirty-one syllables divided among five lines.*

---

great tanka poets managed to compress an entire world of beauty and emotion. Eventually, tanka provided the inspiration for an even more condensed poetic form—the **haiku**, a three-line poem of seventeen syllables (see page 572).

The Origin of Tanka

The earliest known tanka appeared in a collection of poems that was written in the eighth century A.D. Called the *Man-yōshū* (män·yō′shoo), or *Collection of Ten Thousand Leaves*, this anthology, which features a variety of poetic forms, is still widely quoted and praised.

At the time that the *Manyōshū*

appeared, Japanese poets were just beginning to break away from the powerful influence of Chinese literary tradition. In early times, Japanese was exclusively a spoken language; there was no system for writing it down. The earliest Japanese poets wrote in Chinese. Between the fifth and the eighth centuries, a system for writing Japanese was developed, adapting Chinese characters to describe Japanese sounds. These phonetic characters came to be known as *kana* (kä′nä), meaning "borrowed names."

By the time the *Manyōshū* was compiled, Japanese poets had begun to appreciate the lyrical power of their own language. Historically, the Japanese view the *Manyōshū* as the beginning of a written literature that they could call entirely their own. Many of the tanka in the Manyōshū describe nature, the impermanence of life, solitude, and love—themes that are echoed in modern tanka.

Tanka and Medieval Court Life

Tanka continued to thrive throughout the medieval period. During the Heian (hā′än) period (A.D. 794–1185), writing tanka was a common ritual of court life. A prince would dash off a tanka and send it to his loved one, who would reply with her own poem. Aristocrats amused themselves by playing a game in which one person would invent the first three lines of a tanka and another would finish it.

In 905 a second great anthology featuring tanka verse, the *Kokinshū* (kō·kēn′shoō), appeared. The poems in the *Kokinshū*, numbering more than a thousand, are subtle and sophisticated. Many rely on repetition of a sound to create an emotional effect. In a poem by Ki nō Tomonori (kē nō tō·mō·nō′rē), for example, the consonant *h* is repeated to reinforce the poem's tranquil mood:

Hisakata no	This perfectly still
Hikari nodokeki	Spring day bathed in the soft light
Haru no hi ni	From the spread-out sky,
Shizu kokoro naku	Why do the cherry blossoms
Hana no chiruramu	So restlessly scatter down?

Ki nō Tsurayuki (kē nō tsoō·rä·yoō′kē), one of the editors of the *Kokinshū*, summarized the essence of Japanese tanka in his preface:

Poetry has its seeds in man's heart. . . . Man's activities are various and whatever they see or hear touches their hearts and is expressed in poetry. When we hear the notes of the nightingale among the blossoms, when we hear the frog in the water, we know that every living being is capable of song. Poetry, without effort, can move heaven and earth, can touch the gods and spirits . . . it turns the hearts of man and woman to each other and it soothes the soul of the fierce warrior.

Though his comments were written over a thousand years ago, they still hold true for much of Japanese verse.

Tanka Poets
Seventh through Twelfth Centuries A.D.

THE POETESS ONO KOMACHI, early 1820s.

The poets who wrote tanka centuries ago are still widely read in Japan. In fact, their poems are so familiar that they are the basis of a popular "poem-card" game traditionally played in Japan at the New Year. In this game, one player reads the first half of a poem from the thirteenth-century anthology, *The Verses of a Hundred Poets.* The other players must then choose the correct ending to the poem from among the hundred cards spread on the floor. Yet ironically, very few facts are known about these early masters whose words have become so deeply ingrained in Japanese culture.

Princess Nukada
(seventh century A.D.)

One of the earliest composers of tanka, the Princess Nukada (nōō·kä′dä), was a favorite at the court of two emperors and was the most accomplished female poet of her time. We know little else about her, however. The only clues we have to her character are her poems, which are delicate and passionate. Some of them, including the one reproduced here, were written for her elder sister, the Princess Kagami (kä·gä′mē).

Oshikochi Mitsune
(late ninth century A.D.)

Oshikochi Mitsune (ō′shē·kō′chē mē·tsōō′nä) was among the greatest poets of the early Heian era. He was one of the editors of the *Kokinshū,* and some of his verses appear in that anthology. Many of his poems are melancholy, but they are never sentimental.

Ki Tsurayuki (A.D. 884–946)

Another editor of the *Kokinshū,* Ki Tsurayuki (kē′ tsōō·rä·yōō′kē), was a high court official as well as an accomplished writer and calligrapher. In addition to his fine tanka poems, he also wrote a travel diary that interwove poetry with prose. At the time, most cultured Japanese men chose to write prose in Chinese. Generally, only women and those men who could not afford a classical education wrote in Japanese. Be-

Courtesy of the Freer Gallery of Art, Smithsonian Institution, Washington, D.C.; 70.22—Japanese Painting; Edo Period, 19th century; Rimpa School; by Sakai Hoitsu "The Thirty-six Poets"; ink and colors on paper: 150.90 × 163.0 cm (59 1/2 × 64 1/8")

THE THIRTY-SIX MASTER POETS, SAKAI HOITSU, **Edo period.** *Although the "master poets" depicted here are all men, much of the best Japanese poetry was composed by women. Men tended to use the Chinese system of writing, which did not lend itself to poetic composition in Japanese.*

cause Ki Tsurayuki preferred to write in Japanese, and did not want to invite ridicule, he wrote his diary under a woman's name.

Ono Komachi (mid-tenth century A.D.)

Of all the poets whose tanka appeared in the *Kokinshū,* Ono Komachi (ō′nō kō·mä′chē) is perhaps the most revered. Her great physical beauty and the emotional power of her verse made her a celebrated figure in her time. More than three centuries after her death, Kan'ami Kiyotsugu, a Noh dramatist, wrote a play about Ono Komachi, whom he described as:

The brightest flower long ago
Her dark brows arched
Her face bright-powdered always
When cedar-scented halls could scarce
    contain
Her damask robes.

Saigyo (A.D. 1118–1190)

Among the most accomplished twelfth-century tanka poets was Saigyo (sä′ē·gyō), who abandoned his position as a royal bodyguard at the age of twenty-three to become a priest. His tanka were written during his years of wanderings through the Japanese countryside.

Reader's Guide

TANKA POEMS

Background

The tanka you are about to read were composed by five different poets over a period of more than five centuries, yet they share similar forms and techniques. All are brief, all evoke strong images and emotions, and all are subtle and indirect. The themes of the poems reflect each author's age, social position, and philosophy. In the art of tanka, what the poet does *not* say is often just as important as what he or she *does* say. It is up to the reader to make the connections between what is stated directly and what is implied.

In certain ways, the translations you are about to read differ notably from the original poems. Only one of the translated poems follows the traditional tanka form of thirty-one syllables. Nor do the translated poems have the same rhythm and cadence as the originals. Yet in other respects the translated poems are faithful to traditional Japanese style. None of the lines in the translated poems rhyme, for instance, which is in keeping with classical tanka tradition.

Writer's Response

Many tanka poems describe a scene that evokes a sense of loneliness or quiet reflection. Imagine that you were going to take a photograph to convey a similar mood. Freewrite for five minutes, describing in detail what you would include in your photograph.

Literary Focus

Assonance is the repetition of similar vowel sounds in words that are close together. For example, listen to the assonance in this line: "The breeze stirred the green leaves." The Japanese language lends itself to assonance, for Japanese has fewer vowel sounds than English. Thus, it is easy to create words or phrases that repeat the same vowel sound. In classical tanka, assonance was used to create certain moods or ideas. The vowel sound *a,* for instance, was linked with the idea of brilliance or clarity. The vowel sound *o,* on the other hand, evoked a sense of gloominess or obscurity, as in the phrase *oboro-zuki,* which means "pale, clouded moon." In the tanka translated in the Introduction (see page 565), the vowel sounds *a* or *o* occur in all except three of the original Japanese words.

TANKA POEMS

translated by

GEOFFREY BOWNAS AND ANTHONY THWAITE

> *Each of these five poems contains at least one example of assonance—similar vowel sounds. As you read, look for the words in each poem that are linked by assonance.*

I Waited and I

I waited and I
Yearned for you.
My blind
Stirred at the touch
Of the autumn breeze.

—*Princess Nukada*

The End of My Journey

The end of my journey
Was still far off,
But in the tree-shade
Of the summer mountain
I stood, my mind floating.

—*Oshikochi Mitsune*

Now, I Cannot Tell

Now, I cannot tell
What my old friend is thinking:
But the petals of the plum
In this place I used to know
Keep their old fragrance.

—*Ki Tsurayuki*

The Granger Collection, New York

PLUM GARDEN, ANDŌ HIROSHIGE (1797–1858).
Andō Hiroshige is noted for the lyrical vision of his paintings.
? **What mood does** Plum Garden *evoke?*

How Helpless My Heart!

How helpless my heart!
Were the stream to tempt,
My body, like a reed
Severed at the roots,
Would drift along, I think.

—*Ono Komachi*

Every Single Thing

Every single thing
Changes and is changing
Always in this world.
Yet with the same light
The moon goes on shining.

—*Priest Saigyo*

Tanka poet Ki Tsurayuki.

First Thoughts

Which image in these tanka was most memorable for you? Did the image create a distinctive mood?

Identifying Facts

1. List one **image** of nature used in each tanka to help convey its theme.
2. Point out examples of **assonance**, or similar vowel sounds, in two different poems.

Interpreting Meanings

1. In Princess Nukada's poem, what is the relationship between the idea of waiting and the autumn breeze stirring the blind?
2. In the poem by Oshikochi Mitsune, what state of mind is suggested by the phrase "my mind floating"? Does it seem to be a pleasant or unpleasant state of mind?
3. In Ki Tsurayuki's poem, what parallel does the speaker seem to be drawing between his old friend and the scent of the plum blossoms? Does the speaker draw comfort from this comparison, or does it make him sad?
4. In the poem by Ono Komachi, what might the stream symbolize? Is the speaker's attitude toward the stream active or passive? Point out specific words in the poem to support your answer.
5. What views of permanence and change are expressed in the poem by Priest Saigyo through the image of the moon? Explain how the use of **assonance** in the poem links the ideas of permanence and change.

Applying Meanings

Reread the five poems. If you were asked to make a generalization about the subjects and themes of tanka poetry based on these five poems, what would your conclusion be? What do tanka poems say about the relationship between people and nature, for example? What is their attitude toward the idea of time and change?

Creative Writing Response

Coauthoring a Tanka. Play the traditional Japanese game of writing a tanka with a partner (see page 566). On a 3" x 5" note card, write the first three lines of a tanka. Then exchange your card with a partner, who will write the last two lines on another card. Identify the two "halves" of the tanka by writing the same number on the back of each card. Then spread all the cards tanka-side up on a table or on the floor and let students decide which "halves" go together. Remember that the tanka should have thirty-one syllables—three lines of seven syllables each and two lines of five syllables each. You might look back at your description of the imaginary photograph (see page 568) for ideas of tanka to write.

Critical Writing Response

Comparing Two Translations. Reread Ono Komachi's tanka on page 570. Then read the following translation of the same poem:

> ### So Lonely Am I
> Ono Komachi
> translated by
> Donald Keene
>
> So lonely am I
> My body is a floating weed
> Severed at the roots.
> Were there water to entice me
> I would follow it, I think.

Write a two-paragraph essay comparing and contrasting the two translations. Consider the following points:

- Which translation seems more romantic or sentimental? Cite details to support your answer.
- In which translation does the speaker seem more helpless? Point out words in each poem that create an impression of passiveness or free choice.
- How does the translation affect the **theme** of the poem?

River Landscape with Fireflies (DETAIL)

Haiku

A **haiku** (hī′kōō) is a brief, unrhymed poem three lines long. In Japanese, the first and last lines have five syllables each and the middle line has seven. This strict, condensed form challenges poets to convey their feelings and observations in a few vivid images.

The History of Haiku

Examples of short verses similar to haiku have been found in thirteenth- or fourteenth-century Japanese literature. However, the art of haiku was not perfected until later in the seventeenth century, when the greatest of the classical haiku poets, Bashō (ba′shō), lived. When English authors such as John Milton were composing vast and intricate poems, Bashō and his pupils were writing strikingly pure, compressed verses only a few words long. In the centuries since Bashō, the haiku form has been adopted by poets the world over. The haiku's emphasis on familiar images from nature, presented in compact form, has given the form a lasting appeal.

The Art of Haiku

Unlike many Western poets, the classical haiku masters do not present sensory images with similes, metaphors, or other figures of speech. Rather, haiku poets simply present unadorned images, and the reader must make an imaginative leap to understand the connection between them.

---◆---

haiku (hī′kōō): *a brief, unrhymed, three-line poem in which the first and third lines have five syllables each and the middle line has seven.*

The Japanese language differs greatly from English. For example, it has no articles and rarely uses pronouns. To accommodate these differences, the English translators of the haiku in this section have made some changes. In some cases, the translators have chosen to make the English haiku rhyme, though this is not in keeping with Japanese tradition. In other cases, the poems do not have exactly seventeen syllables, or the syllables are not divided among the three lines of the poem according to the classical formula.

Japanese haiku, even in their original form, leave much unsaid, compounding the challenges of translation. As a result, one haiku may have numerous translations with subtle differences. Consider, for example, the following well-known haiku by Bashō:

Furu-ike ya
  kawazu tobi-komu
    mizu-no-oto

Harold G. Henderson's literal translation of this haiku reads:

Old pond:
  Frog jump-in.
    Water-sound.

Harry Behn's translation retains the seventeen-syllable structure of the original Japanese:

An old silent pond . . .
A frog jumps into the pond,
splash! Silence again.

A looser translation by Asatarō Miyamori captures the image and abandons the three-line form:

The ancient pond!
A frog plunged—splash!

The Lasting Appeal of Haiku

Some haiku contain allusions to Zen philosophy and Japanese history and customs. These references might be lost on non-Japanese readers. Yet most haiku can be understood and appreciated by readers from any culture. Consider this early haiku:

If to the moon
  one puts a handle—what
    a splendid fan!
      —Sokan (1465–1553)
        —translated by Harold G. Henderson

THE CAP FOR THE COMING OF AGE CEREMONY, RYŪRYŪKYO SHINSAI, 1800s.
Spencer Museum of Art, The University of Kansas, William Bridges Thayer Memorial

In a few words, the author manages to create a vivid picture of the full moon seen behind the branch of a tree.

A more subtle comparison of images appears in the following haiku, composed almost two centuries after Sokan's:

On top of skeletons
  they put a gala dress, and then—
    the flower-viewing!
      —Onitsura (1660–1738)
        —translated by Harold G. Henderson

The poem alludes to a Japanese tradition that signals the beginning of spring. Families dress in their finest clothes and walk through the cherry orchards to see the cherry trees covered in the first blossoms of the year. Yet both the fashionable people and the cherry trees have only temporarily disguised their "skeletons." Onitsura's haiku may have reminded his audience of the Buddhist teaching that what is beautiful today may wither and die tomorrow.

Haiku Poets
Seventeenth through Nineteenth Centuries

Matsuo Bashō, Watanahe Kwasan.

Matsuo Bashō (1644–1694)

The son of a samurai, Matsuo Bashō spent his youth in the service of a local lord. He began writing verses when he was nine and soon showed remarkable promise. Before he was thirty, he had won acclaim as a poet and had started his own poetry school.

Two things shaped Bashō's poetry: his devotion to Zen Buddhism and his travels. In 1684, at the age of forty, Bashō set out on the first of his many journeys through Japan. Traveling alone, Bashō endured great discomforts and loneliness. Yet some of his best haiku were composed on these lonely journeys.

Uejima Onitsura (1660–1738)

One of Bashō's greatest admirers was Uejima Onitsura (ō·nēt·sōo′ra). Like Bashō, Onitsura came from a samurai background and began writing poetry at an early age. Though Onitsura admired Bashō, he did not imitate Bashō's style. His poems are more joyful and exuberant than Bashō's and somewhat less philosophical.

Taniguchi Buson (1715–1783)

Taniguchi Buson (bōo′sän′), a younger contemporary of Onitsura, soon established his own poetic style. His haiku are generally regarded as second only to Bashō's. Buson was an accomplished painter, and his poems reflect his fascination with light and color.

Kobayashi Issa (1762–1826)

Kobayashi Issa (ē′sä′) is one of the most beloved of Japan's haiku masters. His life was extraordinarily sad. His mother died when he was an infant, and his relations with his stepmother were so poor that his father sent him away from home to study when he was only fourteen. His first wife bore him five children, but all of them died in infancy before his wife succumbed to an illness. Possibly because of these many sorrows, Issa's verses are taut with emotion, though they are rarely sentimental.

Reader's Guide

HAIKU

Background

The six poems that follow were written by four different poets over a span of two centuries. In spite of this, the poems have a great deal in common. All adhere to haiku's strict form. Each poem combines two or more images in vivid and sometimes surprising ways. However, all the poems vary greatly in mood. Some are philosophical or somber, while others are romantic or fanciful.

The first three selections are by Bashō. In all three poems, Bashō finds beauty in seemingly insignificant or ordinary objects or events. This insight is inspired by the Buddhist belief that, through contemplation, a person can find significance in even the humblest of things. In most haiku, the meaning is present in the images themselves. The haiku master stands back from the images he creates and allows his readers to draw their own conclusions.

Writer's Response

Many haiku describe subtle signs of the changing seasons and the emotions that these changes arouse. Which season of the year makes you the most happy? Which signs—sights, sounds, odors—tell you that that season is approaching? Freewrite for five minutes about the approach of your favorite season.

Literary Focus

Imagery is language that appeals to the senses—sight, hearing, smell, touch, and taste. The imagery a writer selects helps readers imagine a scene and respond emotionally to it. For example, a writer might describe an ocean as ''a crashing gray tide'' to build a feeling of fear or as ''rippling blue waves'' to suggest tranquility. Haiku poets rarely state an emotion; instead, they challenge the reader to extract the meaning of the poem by looking closely at the images.

HAIKU

translated by

HAROLD G. HENDERSON, PETER BEILENSON, AND HARRY BEHN

As you read the following haiku, decide how the images in each shape your emotional response.

Matsuo Bashō

On a withered branch
  A crow has settled—
    autumn nightfall.

A village where they ring
  no bells!—Oh, what *do* they do
    at dusk in spring?

No rice?—In that hour
  we put into the gourd
    a maiden-flower.
        —translated by Harold G. Henderson

Uejima Onitsura

Even stones in streams
  of mountain water compose
    songs to wild cherries.
      —translated by Peter Beilenson and Harry Behn

Taniguchi Buson

Blossoms on the pear;
  and a woman in the moonlight
    reads a letter there. . . .
        —translated by Harold G. Henderson

Kobayashi Issa

A morning-glory vine
  all blossoming, has thatched
    this hut of mine.
      —translated by Harold G. Henderson

MORNING GLORIES, IKEGAMI SHŪBO.
? *How has a vine "thatched" the speaker's hut in Issa's poem?*

The University of Michigan Museum of Art, Gift of Mr. and Mrs. Frederic R. Smith, Acc. no. 1973/2.89

First Thoughts

Which haiku made you feel most joyful? Which one is the saddest?

Identifying Facts

1. Images of nature are central to traditional Japanese haiku. List the elements of nature mentioned in the haiku that you have just read.

2. What seasons do the images in these haiku suggest?

Interpreting Meanings

1. Does nature seem to be a positive or a negative force in the haiku? Give examples to support your opinion.

2. In many haiku, the poet surprises and delights the reader by showing a relationship between two dissimilar things. In Bashō's first haiku, what relationship does he establish between the image in the third line and the image in the first two lines?

3. **Tone** is the attitude a writer takes toward the reader, a subject, or a character. What is the tone of Onitsura's haiku? What makes you say so?

4. What **imagery** occurs in Buson's haiku?

5. What two things are contrasted in Issa's poem? What might each of these two things symbolize or stand for?

Applying Meanings

In Issa's poem, nature transforms something plain into something beautiful. What experiences have you had in which nature transformed something ugly into something delightful—for example, raindrops transforming a spider's web into shimmering lace or flowers growing in a junkyard?

Creative Writing Response

Writing a Haiku. Reread Bashō's haiku "On a Withered Branch." According to translator and critic Harold G. Henderson, at the time Bashō wrote this famous poem, he was "consciously looking for the poetic beauty to be found in things not in themselves particularly beautiful." Look through the haiku you have just read. Which other haiku seem to find beauty in ordinary things? How does the poet manage to make these ordinary things seem beautiful and meaningful?

Try writing your own haiku about an everyday object or event that might not seem very beautiful or interesting: a tin can lying on a sidewalk, a moss-covered rock, the reflection of light on an old brick wall, or an insect skittering across a log. Jot down a list of possible images and some descriptions that occur to you. Then compose a haiku based on your favorite image. Remember that a haiku is unrhymed and three lines long. The first and last lines should have five syllables each, and the middle line should have seven. Revise your haiku until it is as simple and compressed as you can possibly make it. Then read it aloud to the class.

PRIMARY SOURCES

A Glimpse into a Poet's Life

Matsuo Bashō is still the most beloved Japanese poet, admired for mixing sorrow and humor in his haiku. A wanderer who gave up the comforts of home, Bashō led an active life, but in his later years he was more and more drawn to solitude. This excerpt from his biographical work "Prose Poem on the Unreal Dwelling" gives us a firsthand insight into Bashō's love of both solitude and nature.

My body, now close to fifty years of age, has become an old tree that bears bitter peaches, a snail which has lost its shell, a bagworm separated from its bag; it drifts with the winds and clouds that know no destination. Morning and night I have eaten traveler's fare, and have held out for alms a pilgrim's wallet. On my last journey my face was burnt by the sun of Matsushima, and I wetted my sleeve at the holy mountain. I longed to go as far as that shore where the puffins cry and the Thousand Islands of the Ainu can be seen in the distance, but my companion drew me back, telling how dangerous so long a journey would be with my sickness. I yielded. Then I bruised my heels along the rough coast of the northern sea, where each step in the sand dunes is painful. This year I roamed by the shores of the lake in quest of a place to stay, a single stalk of reed where the floating nest of the grebe might be borne to rest by the current. This is my Unreal Dwelling, and it stands by the mountain called Kokubu. An ancient shrine is near, which so purifies my senses that I feel cleansed of the dust of the world. . . .

The man who used to live here had most refined tastes, and did not clutter up the hut even with objects of art. Apart from the household shrine there is just the little alcove for hanging nightclothes. Once, when he heard that the High Priest of Mount Kora was in the capital, he asked him for a plaque to decorate the alcove. The priest nonchalantly took his brush in hand and wrote the words "Unreal Dwelling." On the back he inscribed his name to serve as a memento to later people who might see it.

In this hut where I live as a hermit, as a passing traveler, there is no need to accumulate household possessions. All I have is a broadbrimmed hat of nettle wood and a rush raincoat, which I hang on a post above my pillow. During the day the old gentleman who looks after the shrine or villagers from the foot of the mountain come here and pass the day in stories of a kind to which I am unaccustomed, how boars are grubbing up the rice seedlings, or about rabbits infesting the bean fields. Or when, as very rarely happens, visitors come from afar, we sit calmly at night, the moonlight our companion, arguing with our shadows.

—*translated by Donald Keene*

Sei Shōnagon
c. 965–?

Heibonsha Ltd.

Some of the liveliest female voices in Japanese literature are nearly a thousand years old. One of the most vital belongs to Sei Shōnagon (sā′ē shō′nä·gōn′), who served as a lady-in-waiting to the Empress Sadako (sä′dä·kō) in the late tenth century.

We know very little about Shōnagon's life. She was born around 965 into the Kiyowara (kē·yō·wä′rä) clan. Her father, a minor government official, had earned a modest reputation as a poet. Sometime around 990, Shōnagon went to Kyoto, where she served in the royal court for about ten years. What became of her after she left the court remains a mystery.

The little knowledge we have of Shōnagon's life comes from her writings. During her ten years in Kyoto, Shōnagon jotted down various ideas and impressions and tucked the papers away in her room. Part diary, part random notes, these writings came to be known as the *Notes of the Pillow*. In Shōnagon's day, "pillows" were made of wood, and some had drawers in which letters or journals could be stored. Men and women at court may have amused themselves by scribbling their thoughts in a notebook in the evenings and hiding the notes in these "pillow books."

Lady Shōnagon wrote prose so clear and expressive that it is still held up as a model to Japanese schoolchildren. It is therefore hard to imagine that she did not intend *The Pillow Book* to be published. Nevertheless, she claimed to be dismayed after her book was discovered:

> I wrote these notes at home, when I had a good deal of time to myself and thought no one would notice what I was doing. Everything that I have seen and felt is included. Since much of it might appear malicious and even harmful to people, I was careful to keep my book hidden. But now it has become public, which is the last thing I expected. . . .

Some scholars claim that this passage was added long after Shōnagon died. Despite centuries of exhaustive research, many mysteries surround Shōnagon's life and her manuscript. Shōnagon probably would have enjoyed that irony.

Reader's Guide

from THE PILLOW BOOK

Background

In Japan, forms of personal writing such as the diary have been a major literary genre for centuries. *The Pillow Book* represents a unique form of the diary genre. More a collection of inspired jottings than a diary, Shōnagon's masterpiece contains vivid sketches of people and places, sly anecdotes and witticisms, snatches of poetry, and 164 lists. Every phrase is stamped with Shōnagon's personality. She was quick to praise an elegant turn of phrase or a beautiful kimono, but, like all aristocrats of her time, she seldom took notice of ordinary working people. When she did it was usually to note their rough and—to her—unseemly ways.

The Pillow Book provides a vivid picture of court life during the Heian (hā'än) period (794–1185). Through Shōnagon we learn that the Japanese calendar dictated everything from coronations to cutting toenails; that royal cats had a higher rank than some governors; and that musicians were forbidden to walk in the emperor's presence. Aristocratic women let their long straight hair sweep down past their ankles, colored their teeth black, and wore clothes dyed to match the colors of the seasons. They spent most of their lives behind decorative screens even though they, like Shōnagon, were often highly educated, talented, and influential.

Oral Response

According to Lady Shōnagon, *The Pillow Book* was intended to be a private journal, yet it was discovered and eventually printed. The last words of *The Pillow Book* state Shōnagon's views of this breach of privacy: "Whatever people may think of my book, I still regret that it ever came to light." How would you react if someone read and made public a letter or diary that you had intended to be private? Discuss the topic of personal writing and privacy.

Literary Focus

Wit is a quality of speech or writing that combines verbal cleverness with keen perception, especially of contradictory elements. Lady Shōnagon's writing sparkles with clever word play, puns, sharp observations, and descriptions of humorous situations.

from THE PILLOW BOOK
Sei Shōnagon
translated by
IVAN MORRIS

> *Nothing, it seems, escaped Sei Shōnagon's sharp eye—or her sharp wit. As you read these excerpts from* The Pillow Book, *pay attention not only to what Shōnagon reveals about her society, but also to what she reveals about herself.*

RIVER LANDSCAPE WITH FIREFLIES *(detail).*
What specific details does Sei Shōnagon use to describe each of the four seasons?

In Spring It Is the Dawn

In spring it is the dawn that is most beautiful. As the light creeps over the hills, their outlines are dyed a faint red and wisps of purplish cloud trail over them.

In summer the nights. Not only when the moon shines, but on dark nights too, as the fireflies flit to and fro, and even when it rains, how beautiful it is!

In autumn the evenings, when the glittering sun sinks close to the edge of the hills and the crows fly back to their nests in threes and fours and twos; more charming still is a file[1] of wild geese, like specks in the distant sky. When the sun has set, one's heart is moved by the sound of the wind and the hum of the insects.

---

1. **file** (fīl): a single line or row.

Sei Shōnagon   **581**

In winter the early mornings. It is beautiful indeed when snow has fallen during the night, but splendid too when the ground is white with frost; or even when there is no snow or frost, but it is simply very cold and the attendants hurry from room to room stirring up the fires and bringing charcoal, how well this fits the season's mood! But as noon approaches and the cold wears off, no one bothers to keep the braziers[2] alight, and soon nothing remains but piles of white ashes.

from Hateful Things

One is in a hurry to leave, but one's visitor keeps chattering away. If it is someone of no importance, one can get rid of him by saying, "You must tell me all about it next time"; but, should it be the sort of visitor whose presence commands one's best behavior, the situation is hateful indeed.

One finds that a hair has got caught in the stone on which one is rubbing one's inkstick, or again that gravel is lodged in the inkstick, making a nasty, grating sound.

Someone has suddenly fallen ill and one summons the exorcist.[3] Since he is not at home, one has to send messengers to look for him. After one has had a long fretful wait, the exorcist finally arrives, and with a sigh of relief one asks him to start his incantations. But perhaps he has been exorcizing too many evil spirits recently; for hardly has he installed himself and begun praying when his voice becomes drowsy. Oh, how hateful!

A man who has nothing in particular to recommend him discusses all sorts of subjects at random as though he knew everything.

Things That Cannot Be Compared

Summer and winter. Night and day. Rain and sunshine. Youth and age. A person's laughter and his anger. Black and white. Love and hatred. The little indigo plant[4] and the great philodendron. Rain and mist.

When one has stopped loving somebody, one feels that he has become someone else, even though he is still the same person.

In a garden full of evergreens the crows are all asleep. Then, towards the middle of the night, the crows in one of the trees suddenly wake up in a great flurry and start flapping about. Their unrest spreads to the other trees, and soon all the birds have been startled from their sleep and are cawing in alarm. How different from the same crows in daytime!

Embarrassing Things

While entertaining a visitor, one hears some servants chatting without any restraint in one of the back rooms. It is embarrassing to know that one's visitor can overhear. But how to stop them?

A man whom one loves gets drunk and keeps repeating himself.

To have spoken about someone not knowing that he could overhear. This is embarrassing even if it be a servant or some other completely insignificant person.

---

2. **braziers** (brā′zhərz): metal pans or bowls used to hold burning coals or charcoal.

3. **exorcist** (eks′sôr·sist): a person who drives away an evil spirit or spirits through ritual prayers or incantations.

4. **indigo** (in′di·gō′) **plant**: a plant that yields a deep blue dye. Dyeing was an important art form of the aristocratic women of the Heian period.

Crows and Plum Tree, and Rabbits and Pine Trees in Snow; (Detail) Katsu Jagyoku, Shin'enkan Collection, Los Angeles County Museum of Art

RABBITS AND CROWS IN THE NIGHT SNOW (one half of a screen), DAGYOKU SANJIN (1733–1778).

? *What imagery does Sei Shōnagon use to contrast crows at night with crows during the day?*

To hear one's servants making merry. This is equally annoying if one is on a journey and staying in cramped quarters or at home and hears the servants in a neighboring room.

Parents, convinced that their ugly child is adorable, pet him and repeat the things he has said, imitating his voice.

An ignoramus[5] who in the presence of some learned person puts on a knowing air and converses about men of old.

A man recites his own poems (not especially good ones) and tells one about the praise they have received—most embarrassing.

Lying awake at night, one says something to one's companion, who simply goes on sleeping.

In the presence of a skilled musician, someone plays a zither[6] just for his own pleasure and without tuning it.

A son-in-law who has long since stopped visiting his wife runs into his father-in-law in a public place.

Masahiro Really Is a Laughing-Stock

Masahiro really is a laughing-stock. I wonder what it is like for his parents and friends. If people see him with a decent-looking servant, they always call for the fellow and laughingly ask how he can wait upon such a master and what he thinks of him. There are skilled dyers and weavers in Masahiro's household, and when it comes to dress, whether it be the color of his under-robe or

---

5. **ignoramus** (ig′nə·rā′məs): an ignorant and stupid person.

6. **zither** (zith′ər): an inaccurate translation. The instrument being referred to here is really a *koto*, a Japanese instrument with thirteen strings.

Sei Shōnagon   **583**

the style of his cloak, he is more elegant than most men; yet the only effect of his elegance is to make people say, "What a shame someone else isn't wearing these things!"

And how strangely he expresses himself! Once, when he was due to report for night duty at the Palace, he ordered that the clothes and other things he would need should be brought from his house. "Send *two* servants," he said. One man came and said that he could easily carry everything. "You're an odd fellow," said Masahiro. "How can one man bring the things of two people? After all, can you put two measures in a one-measure jar?" No one had the slightest idea what he meant; but there was loud laughter.

On another occasion a messenger brought Masahiro a letter from someone, asking for an immediate reply. "You hateful fellow!" said Masahiro. "Has someone been putting peas on the stove?[7] And who's stolen the ink and brush I had in this residence? Very odd! I could understand people taking rice or wine . . ." And again everyone laughed.

When the Empress Dowager was ill, Masahiro was sent from the Palace to inquire after her. When he came back, people asked which of her gentlemen-in-waiting had been present. He named a few people, four or five in all. "Was no one else there?" "Well, there were some others," replied Masahiro, "but they had all left." It is amazing that we could still laugh at him—so accustomed were we to hearing his foolishness.

One day when I was alone he came up to me and said, "My dear lady, I have something I must tell you at once—something that I've just heard." "And what may that be?" I asked. He approached my curtain.[8] "I heard someone who instead of saying, 'Bring your body closer,' used the phrase 'Bring up your five parts.'"[9] And again I burst into laughter.

On the middle night during the period of official appointments Masahiro was responsible for filling the lamps with oil. He rested his foot on the cloth under the pedestal of one of the lamps, and since the cloth happened to have been freshly oiled, his foot stuck to it. As soon as he started to walk off, the lamp fell over and, as he hurried along with the cloth stuck to his foot, the lamp dragged after him, making a terrible clatter.

One day when he thought he was alone in the Table Room, neither of the First Secretaries having reported for duty, Masahiro took a dish of beans that was lying there and went behind the Little Screen.[10] Suddenly someone pulled aside the screen—and there was Masahiro, stealthily munching away at the beans. Everyone who saw him was convulsed with laughter.[11]

---

7. **peas on the stove:** In Shōnagon's time, the image of peas popping in a stove was used to describe people in a hurry, but Masahiro's use of the expression is peculiar.

8. **curtain:** Masahiro is speaking to Shōnagon through a curtain. In feudal Japan, women of high society spent much of their time behind wooden screens hung with heavy curtains. The screens protected the women from being seen by men and strangers.

9. **five parts:** a Buddhist term referring to the knees, elbows, and head. When a person bowed and touched all "five parts" to the ground, it implied utmost respect.

10. **Little Screen:** In the royal palace in Kyoto, this separated the Imperial Dining Room from the Imperial Washing Room. It had a cat painted on one side, and birds and bamboo on the other.

11. **saw him . . . laughter:** Eating was a private business in Heian Japan—most aristocrats ate alone. Thus, Masahiro's behavior would seem strange and ludicrous to Shōnagon and other court members—almost like being caught without his clothes on.

Pleasing Things

Finding a large number of tales that one has not read before. Or acquiring the second volume of a tale whose first volume one has enjoyed. But often it is a disappointment.

Someone has torn up a letter and thrown it away. Picking up the pieces, one finds that many of them can be fitted together.

One has had an upsetting dream and wonders what it can mean. In great anxiety one consults a dream-interpreter, who informs one that it has no special significance.

A person of quality is holding forth about something in the past or about a recent event that is being widely discussed. Several people are gathered round him, but it is oneself that he keeps looking at as he talks.

A person who is very dear to one has fallen ill. One is miserably worried about him even if he lives in the capital and far more so if he is in some remote part of the country. What a pleasure to be told that he has recovered!

I am most pleased when I hear someone I love being praised or being mentioned approvingly by an important person.

A poem that someone has composed for a special occasion or written to another person in reply is widely praised and copied by people in their notebooks. Though this is something that has never yet happened to me, I can imagine how pleasing it must be.

A person with whom one is not especially intimate refers to an old poem or story that is unfamiliar. Then one hears it being mentioned by someone else and one has the pleasure of recognizing it. Still later, when one comes across it in a book, one thinks, "Ah, this is it!" and feels delighted with the person who first brought it up.

I feel very pleased when I have acquired some Michinoku paper, or some white, decorated paper, or even plain paper if it is nice and white.

A person in whose company one feels awkward asks one to supply the opening or

RABBITS AND CROWS IN THE NIGHT SNOW (one half of a screen), DAGYOKU SANJIN (1733–1778).

closing line of a poem. If one happens to recall it, one is very pleased. Yet often on such occasions one completely forgets something that one would normally know.

I look for an object that I need at once, and I find it. Or again, there is a book that I must see immediately; I turn everything upside down, and there it is. What a joy!

When one is competing in an object match[12] (it does not matter what kind), how can one help being pleased at winning?

I greatly enjoy taking in someone who is pleased with himself and who has a self-confident look, especially if he is a man. It is amusing to observe him as he alertly waits for my next repartee;[13] but it is also interesting if he tries to put me off my guard by adopting an air of calm indifference as if there were not a thought in his head.

I realize that it is very sinful of me, but I cannot help being pleased when someone I dislike has a bad experience.

It is a great pleasure when the ornamental comb that one has ordered turns out to be pretty.

I am more pleased when something nice happens to a person I love than when it happens to myself.

Entering the Empress's room and finding that ladies-in-waiting are crowded round her in a tight group, I go next to a pillar which is some distance from where she is sitting. What a delight it is when Her Majesty summons me to her side so that all the others have to make way!

---

12. **object match:** a kind of game in which teams of players competed to solve riddles about objects, such as flowers, seashells, birds, insects, and fans.

13. **repartee** (rep′ər·tē′): a quick, witty reply.

First Thoughts
Is Lady Shōnagon the sort of person you would like to have as a friend? Why or why not?

Identifying Facts
1. Point out two passages from "Things That Cannot Be Compared" and "In Spring It Is the Dawn" that highlight the beauty of the natural world. Which images are especially striking?
2. What three actions does Shōnagon offer as proof that Masahiro "really is a laughing-stock"?
3. In "Embarrassing Things," what conduct does Shōnagon find embarrassing in servants?

Interpreting Meanings
1. In "Pleasing Things," what role do reading and writing seem to play in Shōnagon's life? Cite at least four examples to support your view.
2. What is Shōnagon's attitude toward people of very high rank? Give two examples to support your opinion.
3. Give three examples of Shōnagon's **wit**, or verbal cleverness. In each example, identify what the wit reveals about Shōnagon's insightfulness, playfulness, or even spitefulness.
4. What are two positive and two negative aspects of human nature implied in "Pleasing Things" and "Hateful Things"?

5. Which contrasts in "Things That Cannot Be Compared" are most obvious? Why? Which contrasts might be the least obvious to observers? Why?

Applying Meanings

For centuries, people in many different cultures have used journals and other forms of private writing to express thoughts and beliefs that they may not have been able to convey in any other way. What do you think are the values of keeping a journal or some other form of private writing? What could a person learn by keeping some form of diary or journal?

Creative Writing Response

Creating a List. *The Pillow Book* is full of Shōnagon's lists of everything from "Different Ways of Speaking" and "Things That Fall from the Sky" to "Depressing Things" and "Things That Should Be Large." Create your own list of things, people, or situations that are connected in some way. For example, you could write a list of habits that annoy you, jobs you'd never want to take, things that look better in the dark, or situations that make you squirm. Write spontaneously and light-heartedly, as Shōnagon did. Try to make some of your entries witty and clever by using sarcasm, humor, or wordplay. Don't be afraid to show your personality and opinions in your writing.

Critical Writing Response

Writing a Character Sketch. *The Pillow Book* reveals as much about Lady Shōnagon as it does about Japanese court life. Write a two- or three-paragraph essay describing what kind of person you think Shōnagon was, based on inferences you have drawn from the excerpts you have read. Be sure to support your assessment of her character with specific examples from *The Pillow Book*.

Language and Vocabulary

The Active Voice

A sentence may be written in either the **active** or the **passive** voice. In a sentence written in the active voice, the subject performs the action, as in "Masahiro filled the lamps." In a sentence written in the passive voice, the subject receives the action of the verb, as in "The lamps were filled by Masahiro."

Most writers prefer the active voice because it is more direct than the passive voice. It emphasizes the role of the person or thing performing the action. It is also usually more concise than the passive voice.

Rewrite the following sentences in the active voice:

1. A light was seen by them in the distance.
2. Anna was told by the music teacher that she had great talent.
3. The ground is covered by fallen snow.
4. The letter was snatched from her hand by Thomas.
5. The blueberry pie had been eaten by the dog.

BEHIND THE SCENES

Lady Murasaki's Triumph

Sei Shōnagon's contemporary and rival was Lady Murasaki Shikibu (mōō·rä·sä′kē shē·kē·bōō′), one of the most celebrated writers of the Heian era. Murasaki wrote what is widely regarded as the world's first true novel, *The Tale of Genji.* The sprawling epic recounts the adventures of Genji, the handsome, sensitive, and talented young son of a Japanese emperor. The genius of the tale lies in the author's deep insight into human emotions and motivations. Lady Murasaki's novel is one of the earliest examples of psychological realism ever written. Her achievement is all the more remarkable considering that, at the time she lived, very little prose was written in Japan, as poetry was the favored form.

By all accounts, Lady Murasaki was an extraordinary woman, far more educated than most upper-class men of her generation. Her father, a minor government official and member of a powerful clan, lamented the fact that his brilliant child seemed destined to waste her talents because she was not born a man. He need not have worried. When Murasaki was in her late twenties, she was appointed to serve in the royal court of the reigning emperor. While at court, her skills blossomed in the presence of a brilliant circle of painters, dancers, and poets, many of them women. Murasaki's observations of Heian court intrigues feature prominently in *Genji,* the most vivid prose work to come from medieval Japan.

THE LADY FUJITSUBO WATCHING PRINCE GENJI DEPARTING IN THE MOONLIGHT, ANDŌ HIROSHIGE (1797–1858) AND U. TOYOKUNI (1769–1825).

Bridgeman Art Library/SuperStock, Inc.

Zen Parables

Elliot Erwit/Magnum Photos, Inc.

Zen Monk, Japan.

Zen is difficult to describe. It is a sect of Buddhism, but it is less a religion than a form of Buddhist meditative practice. It has no holy book, no ornate church, no complicated ritual. Zen monks do not preach sermons about right and wrong behavior. Zen focuses on the inner self, rather than on the outer self that acts in the world. Yet for eight hundred years, Zen has exerted a strong appeal to Japanese warriors as well as monks, to politicians as well as artists. Today, it is practiced by businesspeople who use its principles to relieve stress and focus their minds on essential priorities.

The Philosophy of Zen

The object of Zen is to free the mind from everyday, conventional logic through medi-tation. Followers of Zen believe that meditation empties the mind and suppresses the ego, leading to a clearer understanding of one's own nature. According to one legend, Bodhidharma, a famous Zen monk, gazed at a blank wall for nine years before achieving inner enlightenment.

Monks and Warriors

Originating in India and spreading to China, Zen Buddhism was introduced to Japan in 1191. Zen monasteries were soon founded in Kamakura and Kyoto. During the Kamakura period (1185–1333), the samurai, the warriors who served the aristocracy, were attracted to Zen by its discipline and simplicity. They applied Zen principles to martial arts such as archery and fencing.

Virtually every aspect of Japanese culture was influenced by Zen. Because Zen monks drank bitter green tea in order to stay awake during meditation, tea drinking grew into a lengthy and symbol-laden ritual. The arts also felt the impact of Zen, as manifested in the stylized formality of the Noh drama (see page 596) and the conciseness of haiku poetry (see page 572). Nearly every art form of classical Japan—painting, poetry, dance, architecture, drama, and gardening—has been influenced by Zen, with its emphasis on simplicity, self-discipline, and meditation. Even the expressions of everyday speech in Japan draw from this austere religion.

Reader's Guide

ZEN PARABLES

Background

Zen parables are deceptively simple stories originally used to teach aspiring monks about Buddhism. The relationship between a Zen monk and his teacher is an extraordinary one. Instead of imparting facts in a clear and logical way, the Zen master first tries to confuse his students, to force them to abandon all preconceived notions of what knowledge is. This technique prepares them to understand the parables.

To intimidate his students, the master may assume a fierce expression and a cold demeanor. He may ask a pupil a question and then interrupt the pupil halfway through his answer. He may pose what appear to be ridiculous questions, such as "What did your face look like before you were born?" Or he may command students to perform seemingly impossible tasks: "Pull a bird out of your sleeve." (An advanced student might respond by folding a sheet of paper into the shape of a bird.) The master might answer a serious question with an absurd response. If the pupil asks, "What is the nature of the Buddha?" his master might reply, "Pass me that fan!" or "Pork dumpling!"

A Zen master behaves this way in part to make a student wary of language. Words, according to Zen, are dangerous, for they can prevent people from experiencing the world directly.

Oral Response

As a class, compile a list of stories that you are familiar with that teach a lesson—perhaps parables from the Bible or fables. How did you determine their messages? Do any have similar messages?

Literary Focus

A **parable** is a brief allegorical story that teaches a moral, or lesson about life. Parables are a form of didactic literature. The most famous parables in Western literature are those told by Jesus in the New Testament (see page 198). Jesus presented moral lessons in short tales about events in everyday life—for example, a stray sheep or a spendthrift son. Many Zen stories, like the biblical parables, are also deceptively simple tales that contain profound truths.

ZEN PARABLES

translated by

PAUL REPS

In addition to their entertainment value, each of these Zen parables contains a moral lesson. After each story, see if you can write the moral in a sentence or two.

Art Resource, New York

Painting of a Zen monk, Japanese.

Muddy Road

Tanzan and Ekido[1] were once traveling together down a muddy road. A heavy rain was still falling.

Coming around a bend, they met a lovely girl in a silk kimono[2] and sash, unable to cross the intersection.

"Come on, girl," said Tanzan at once. Lifting her in his arms, he carried her over the mud.

Ekido did not speak again until that night when they reached a lodging temple. Then he no longer could restrain himself. "We monks don't go near females," he told Tanzan, "especially not young and lovely ones. It is dangerous. Why did you do that?"

"I left the girl there," said Tanzan. "Are you still carrying her?"

A Parable

Buddha told a parable in a sutra:[3]

A man traveling across a field encountered a tiger. He fled, the tiger after him. Coming to a precipice, he caught hold of the root of

---

1. **Tanzan** (tän′zän′) **and Ekido** (e·kē′dō)
2. **kimono:** a wide-sleeved robe, fastened with a sash; part of the traditional costume for men and women in Japan.
3. **sutra** (sōō′trə): one of a collection of stories that describe the teachings of the Buddha.

Ryoanji Temple's rock garden. *The Japanese rock garden, carefully created out of rock and sand, is an expression of the Zen concept of God.*

a wild vine and swung himself down over the edge. The tiger sniffed at him from above. Trembling, the man looked down to where, far below, another tiger was waiting to eat him. Only the vine sustained him.

Two mice, one white and one black, little by little started to gnaw away the vine. The man saw a luscious strawberry near him. Grasping the vine with one hand, he plucked the strawberry with the other. How sweet it tasted!

Publishing the Sutras

Tetsugen,[4] a devotee of Zen in Japan, decided to publish the sutras, which at that time were available only in Chinese. The books were to be printed with wood blocks in an edition of seven thousand copies, a tremendous undertaking.

Tetsugen began by traveling and collecting donations for this purpose. A few sympathizers would give him a hundred pieces of gold, but most of the time he received only small coins. He thanked each donor with equal gratitude. After ten years Tetsugen had enough money to begin his task.

It happened that at that time the Uji River[5] overflowed. Famine followed. Tetsugen took the funds he had collected for the books and spent them to save others from starvation. Then he began again his work of collecting.

Several years afterwards an epidemic spread over the country. Tetsugen again gave away what he had collected, to help his people.

For a third time he started his work, and after twenty years his wish was fulfilled. The printing blocks which produced the first edi-

---

4. **Tetsugen** (tet·sōō′gen)

---

5. **Uji** (ōō′jē′) **River:** a minor river near Kyoto on the Japanese island of Honshu.

tion of sutras can be seen today in the Obaku[6] monastery in Kyoto.

The Japanese tell their children that Tetsugen made three sets of sutras, and that the first two invisible sets surpass even the last.

The Thief Who Became a Disciple

One evening as Shichiri Kojun[7] was reciting sutras a thief with a sharp sword entered, demanding either his money or his life.

Shichiri told him: "Do not disturb me. You can find the money in that drawer." Then he resumed his recitation.

A little while afterwards he stopped and called: "Don't take it all. I need some to pay taxes with tomorrow."

The intruder gathered up most of the money and started to leave. "Thank a person when you receive a gift," Shichiri added. The man thanked him and made off.

A few days afterwards the fellow was caught and confessed, among others, the offense against Shichiri. When Shichiri was called as a witness he said: "This man is no thief, at least as far as I am concerned. I gave him the money and he thanked me for it."

After he had finished his prison term, the man went to Shichiri and became his disciple.

The Taste of Banzo's Sword

Matajuro Yagyu[8] was the son of a famous swordsman. His father, believing that his son's work was too mediocre to anticipate mastership, disowned him.

So Matajuro went to Mount Futara[9] and there found the famous swordsman Banzo.[10] But Banzo confirmed the father's judgment. "You wish to learn swordsmanship under my guidance?" asked Banzo. "You cannot fulfill the requirements."

"But if I work hard, how many years will it take me to become a master?" persisted the youth.

"The rest of your life," replied Banzo.

"I cannot wait that long," explained Matajuro. "I am willing to pass through any hardship if only you will teach me. If I become your devoted servant, how long might it be?"

"Oh, maybe ten years," Banzo relented.

"My father is getting old, and soon I must take care of him," continued Matajuro. "If I work far more intensively, how long would it take me?"

"Oh, maybe thirty years," said Banzo.

"Why is that?" asked Matajuro. "First you say ten and now thirty years. I will undergo any hardship to master this art in the shortest time!"

"Well," said Banzo, "in that case you will have to remain with me for seventy years. A man in such a hurry as you are to get results seldom learns quickly."

"Very well," declared the youth, understanding at last that he was being rebuked for impatience, "I agree."

Matajuro was told never to speak of fencing and never to touch a sword. He cooked for his master, washed the dishes, made his bed, cleaned the yard, cared for the garden, all without a word of swordsmanship.

Three years passed. Still Matajuro labored on. Thinking of his future, he was sad. He

---

6. **Obaku** (ō·bä′kōō)
7. **Shichiri Kojun** (shē·chē′rē Kō′jun)
8. **Matajuro Yagyu** (mä·tä·jōō′rō yäg′ū)

---

9. **Mount Futara** (fōō·ta′ra)
10. **Banzo** (bän′zō)

had not even begun to learn the art to which he had devoted his life.

But one day Banzo crept up behind him and gave him a terrific blow with a wooden sword.

The following day, when Matajuro was cooking rice, Banzo again sprang upon him unexpectedly.

After that, day and night, Matajuro had to defend himself from unexpected thrusts. Not a moment passed in any day that he did not have to think of the taste of Banzo's sword.

He learned so rapidly he brought smiles to the face of his master. Matajuro became the greatest swordsman in the land.

SWORDSMAN AND SPEARMAN FIGHTING, ANDŌ HIROSHIGE (1797–1858).
Do you agree with Banzo's observation that someone in a hurry to learn will **not** *learn quickly?*

First Thoughts

Would you prefer these parables to have explicitly stated meanings or morals? Why or why not?

Identifying Facts

1. Who are Tanzan and Ekido? For what does Ekido criticize Tanzan in "Muddy Road"?
2. Name all the dangers that the man in "A Parable" faces.
3. What events slow the monk Tetsugen's attempts to publish a Japanese edition of the sutras in "Publishing the Sutras"?
4. In "The Thief Who Became a Disciple," what does Shichiri testify in court?
5. In "The Taste of Banzo's Sword," why does Matajuro become sad working with the master, Banzo?

Interpreting Meanings

1. In "Muddy Road," what does Tanzan mean when he asks Ekido if he is still carrying the girl?
2. In "A Parable," what might the precipice, the tigers, and the mice **symbolize**, or stand for? What is the significance of the man eating the strawberry? What lesson about life do you think this **parable** teaches?
3. According to "Publishing the Sutras," the Japanese tell their children that Tetsugen's two "invisible" editions of the sutras were superior to the actual books. What point do you think this statement makes?
4. Why do you think the thief becomes the disciple of Shichiri Kojun? What values does this **parable** teach?
5. Describe Banzo's unconventional teaching methods. What do you think he is teaching Matajuro about the art of swordsmanship?

Applying Meanings

Each of the parables you have just read teaches a lesson about life. Which parable seems most relevant to a situation in your own life? Explain. Do you disagree with the lessons taught by any of these parables?

Creative Writing Response

Writing a Parable. Many Zen parables contain a **paradox**, an apparent contradiction that is actually true. For instance, the notion that the best way to reform a thief is to thank him for stealing is a paradox. Think for a few minutes about how a seeming contradiction can ultimately prove true, keeping in mind some of the Zen parables you have read. Then write a brief parable of your own about one of the following paradoxical situations:

1. A person who becomes rich by giving something away
2. A competition that is won through losing
3. An enemy who becomes a friend when he or she is trusted
4. A dangerous situation that changes when a person stops feeling fear
5. A difficult task that becomes easy when a person stops trying hard

Speaking and Listening

Acting Out a Parable. Many Zen parables express universal truths. Pair off with another student and choose a Zen parable that you have read and enjoyed. See if you can adapt it to a modern setting and situation without losing the moral. For instance, you could adapt "The Taste of Banzo's Sword" by making Banzo a baseball coach who teaches his students by throwing balls at them when they least expect it. Then, with your partner, create a script in which you enact the parable. Perform your parable for the rest of the class.

Introduction

Noh Plays

Noh (nō) is the great dramatic art of medieval Japan. In Japanese, Noh is written with a Chinese character,

お・能. which signifies "talent." Indeed, the actors who perform Noh plays must be talented mimes and dancers as well as skilled interpreters of character. They must also be able to convey a mood or feeling in a single word or gesture. The power of Noh, with its emphasis on the spiritual, lies in its ability to convey emotions subtly and create a mood of otherworldly silence.

The Noh Tradition

Noh was developed in fourteenth-century Japan, at about the same time that the Italian poet Dante Alighieri was writing *The Divine Comedy* (see page 742). Like Dante's poems, Noh plays have religious sources. They are strongly influenced by Zen, the meditative Buddhist religion.

◆

Noh (nō): *a classic Japanese dramatic form that incorporates music, dance, and mime.*

By the mid-fourteenth century, Noh had become popular with the Japanese royalty. Under the patronage of powerful

shoguns and samurai, Noh texts became increasingly complex. They were embroidered with so many historical and literary allusions that they became almost unintelligible to common folk. Yet the best Noh plays, particularly those composed by the actor, critic, and playwright Seami Motokiyo (zā·ä'mē mō·tō·kē'yō), strike deep chords and are still performed today.

The Granger Collection, New York

Japanese Noh mask, c. 1400s. *The wearing of masks is traditional in Japanese Noh drama.*

Noh robe. *Artisans had to innovate to produce the elaborate cloth used for Noh robes.*

Masks, Flutes, and Drums

Noh plays are formal and stylized. They are performed on a small stage, about eighteen square feet. The stage is bare, save for a symbolic pine tree and pillars. Musicians and a chorus flank the main stage. The actors are few, and they are always male. Most of them wear heavy robes and hand-painted wooden masks that represent a particular character or emotion: a vengeful ghost, a holy man, a beautiful girl, a warrior, a wrathful serpent-woman. The masks muffle the voices of the actors, giving them an unreal, otherworldly quality. The chorus consists of eight or ten singers who never take part in the action of the play. Instead, they echo a principal actor's words or speak for him as he dances or mimes an action.

Priests and Ghosts

Each Noh drama involves two principal actors. The first is a restless ghost, or spirit, called the *shite* (shtā), who has assumed the form of an ordinary person. The second actor is a bystander, or *waki* (wä′kē′), who is often a wandering priest. The *waki* poses some questions to the spirit, who is typically plagued by disturbing memories of passion or injustice from his or her past life. The *waki*'s questions inspire the *shite* to unburden his soul and reveal his true identity. One of the most common themes in Noh drama involves the *shite*'s release from the suffering he or she is feeling in death.

A Stylized Dramatic Form

Noh plays were traditionally staged in groups of five, with the first performance beginning in the morning and the last ending long after dark.

Unlike most Western plays, Noh dramas have sketchy plots, the characters are flat and one-dimensional, and time and space are treated in an unrealistic way. A span of several years may be distilled into one motion of a fan, or a single moment of joy or pain may be expressed in a lengthy dance. Noh thrives on such contradictions. Indeed, some of the most acclaimed moments in Noh plays are those in which nothing happens at all. The most difficult role in Noh drama is that of a *shite* who sits—masked, silent, and motionless—for an hour and a half. Somehow the actor must convey his emotions through the sheer force of his will.

Seami Motokiyo
c. 1363–1443

Two Japanese Noh masks. *Noh masks, which represent certain emotions or supernatural qualities, are often masterpieces of sculpture.*

Seami Motokiyo had acting in his blood, for his father Kanami (kä′nä·mē′), a priest, was one of the finest performers of his day. At the time of Seami's birth in 1363, Noh was still an unrefined art—more chants and dances than true drama. Under the patronage of the shogun Ashikaga Yoshimitsu (äsh·ē·kä′gä yō·shē·mē′tsoo), this began to change. Ashikaga, a Zen convert and passionate devotee of the arts, brought various performers, including Seami's father, to live at his palace in Kyoto. He was particularly fond of young Seami and personally supervised the boy's education.

Seami's training in Noh began very early, probably around the time he was seven years old. Five years later, he was performing at court. At the age of twenty, not long after his father's death, he took over his father's acting school and began to write plays. At least two dozen of the best Noh dramas are attributed to Seami.

We know very little of Seami's personal life. Some say he became a Zen priest late in life; others say he had two sons, both of them actors. After Ashikaga's death in 1408, Seami lost favor at court and was eventually exiled for a period of time in 1434. According to legend, this brilliant and versatile figure of Noh drama died alone at the age of eighty-one in a Buddhist temple near Kyoto.

Seami was the main theorist and a noted critic of Noh drama in his time. In fact, many of the scant details we know of Seami's life come from the treatises on the Noh theater he wrote for his students. By all accounts, Seami, like his father, was a brilliant actor. His performances were said to have been graceful, restrained, and mysterious. He strove to invest his students with the same qualities, encouraging them to act purely for the fun of it in the beginning of their training at the age of six or seven, then work hard for the next fifteen or twenty years to achieve mastery of three basic roles: the warrior, the woman, and the old man. Like the practice of Zen, mastery of Noh was a lifelong task requiring immense discipline.

Reader's Guide

ATSUMORI

Background

Atsumori (ä·tsōō·mō'rē) is one of Seami's most famous plays. It is drawn from an episode of *The Tale of the Heike* (hā'kə), a medieval Japanese epic based on historical fact that tells the story of the rise and fall of the Taira family, otherwise known as the Heike. The epic describes how the Taira are vanquished by a rival clan, the Minamoto (or Genji) family, the same Genji family of Lady Murasaki's *The Tale of Genji* (see page 588).

The Heike suffered one of their most terrible defeats at a place by the sea called Ichi no tani. The play takes place many years after this battle. A priest named Rensei, who was once a warrior with the Genji clan, has decided to return to the scene of the battle to pray for a sixteen-year-old named Atsumori, whom he killed on the beach that terrible day. Rensei had taken pity on Atsumori and had almost refrained from killing him. He realized, though, that if he did not kill the boy, his fellow warriors would. He explained to Atsumori that he must kill him, and promised to pray for his soul.

When Rensei reaches Ichi no tani years later, he meets two peasants who are returning home from their fields. It is dusk, and one of them is playing a flute. This reminds the priest of Atsumori, who was carrying a flute when he died. Rensei soon makes an astonishing discovery about one of the peasants.

Writer's Response

Rensei regrets his slaying of Atsumori so much that he spends the rest of his life trying to atone for his deed. Think of a time in your life when you regretted something you did. How did you try to make up for it?

Literary Focus

The characters in *Atsumori* are **flat**—that is, they possess only one or two visible traits. **Flat characters** contrast with **round characters**, who, like real people, gradually reveal complex, often conflicting qualities. Flat characters do not seem realistic to us, and yet in some cases a writer may have a good reason for creating them. Some one-dimensional characters, for instance, may function as symbols of emotions or universal human qualities, such as repentance, anger, or wisdom.

ATSUMORI

Seami Motokiyo

translated by

ARTHUR WALEY

As you read this play, pay attention to the techniques of the Noh drama that were described in the introduction. Try to imagine what effect these techniques would have on the audience watching the play.

NIGHT ATTACK ON THE SANJO PALACE, c. 1250, artist unknown.

Fenollosa-Weld Collection. Courtesy of Museum of Fine Arts, Boston

PERSONS

The Priest Rensei (ren'sā), formerly the warrior Kumagai of the Genji clan

A Young Reaper, who turns out to be the ghost of

Atsumori (ä·tso͞o·mō′rē), a young warrior of the (Taira) Heike clan

His Companion

Chorus

Priest.

    Life is a lying dream, he only wakes
    Who casts the world aside.

    I am Kumagai no Naozane, a man of the country of
        Musashi. I have left my home and call myself the
        priest Rensei; this I have done because of my grief
        at the death of Atsumori, who fell in battle by my
        hand. Hence it comes that I am dressed in priestly
        guise.

    And now I am going down to Ichi no tani[1] to pray
        for the salvation of Atsumori's soul.

[*He walks slowly across the stage, singing a song descriptive of his journey.*]

    I have come so fast that here I am already at Ichi no
        tani, in the country of Tsu.

    Truly the past returns to my mind as though it were
        a thing of today.

    But listen! I hear the sound of a flute coming from a
        knoll of rising ground. I will wait here till the
        flute-player passes, and ask him to tell me the
        story of this place.

Reapers *(together).*

    To the music of the reaper's flute
    No song is sung
    But the sighing of wind in the fields.

Young Reaper.

    They that were reaping,
    Reaping on that hill,
    Walk now through the fields
    Homeward, for it is dusk.

Reapers *(together).*

    Short is the way that leads
    From the sea of Suma back to my home.
    This little journey, up to the hill
    And down to the shore again, and up to the hill—
    This is my life, and the sum of hateful tasks.
    If one should ask me
    I too would answer
    That on the shore of Suma

---

1. **Ichi no tani** (ē′chē nō tä′nē): the location of a battle lost by the Taira (Heike) clan, of which Atsumori was a member.

I live in sadness.
Yet if any guessed my name,
Then might I too have friends.
But now from my deep misery
Even those that were dearest
Are grown estranged. Here must I dwell abandoned
To one thought's anguish:
That I must dwell here.[2]

Priest.

Hey, you reapers! I have a question to ask you.

Young Reaper.

Is it to us you are speaking? What do you wish to know?

Priest.

Was it one of you who was playing on the flute just now?

Young Reaper.

Yes, it was we who were playing.

Priest.

It was a pleasant sound, and all the pleasanter because one does not look for such music from men of your condition.

Young Reaper.

Unlooked for from men of our condition, you say!
Have you not read:
"Do not envy what is above you
Nor despise what is below you"?
Moreover the songs of woodmen and the flute-playing of herdsmen,
Flute-playing even of reapers and songs of wood-fellers
Through poets' verses are known to all the world.
Wonder not to hear among us
The sound of a bamboo flute.

Priest.

You are right. Indeed it is as you have told me.
Songs of woodmen and flute-playing of herdsmen . . .

---

2. The reapers are speaking as one person. It is common in Noh theater for a chorus to speak a leading character's lines, often while the lead character is dancing.

Reaper.

Flute-playing of reapers . . .

Priest.

Songs of wood-fellers . . .

Reapers.

Guide us on our passage through this sad world.

Priest.

Song . . .

Reaper.

And dance . . .

Priest.

And the flute . . .

Reaper.

And music of many instruments . . .

Chorus.

These are the pastimes that each chooses to his taste.
Of floating bamboo wood
Many are the famous flutes that have been made;
Little Branch and Cicada Cage,
And as for the reaper's flute,
Its name is Green Leaf;
On the shore of Sumiyoshi
The Korean flute they play.
And here on the shore of Suma
On Stick of the Salt-kilns[3]
The fishers blow their tune.

Priest.

How strange it is! The other reapers
have all gone home, but you alone
stay loitering here. How is that?

Reaper.

How is it, you ask? I am seeking for a
prayer in the voice of the evening waves. Perhaps
you will pray the Ten Prayers for me?

Priest.

I can easily pray the Ten Prayers for you, if you will
tell me who you are.

Scene from a Noh play performance.

The Granger Collection, New York

---

3. **Little Branch**, **Cicada Cage**, **Green Leaf**, and **Stick of the Salt-kilns** are all names of flutes; a cicada is a type of insect.

Reaper.

To tell you the truth—I am one of the family of Lord
Atsumori.

Priest.

One of Atsumori's family? How glad I am!
Then the priest joined his hands *(he kneels down)*
and prayed:

Namu Amidabu.[4]

Praise to Amida Buddha![5]
"If I attain to Buddhahood,
In the whole world and its ten spheres
Of all that dwell here none shall call on my name
And be rejected or cast aside."

Chorus.

"Oh, reject me not!
One cry suffices for salvation,
Yet day and night
Your prayers will rise for me.
Happy am I, for though you know not my name,
Yet for my soul's deliverance
At dawn and dusk henceforward I know that you
will pray."
So he spoke. Then vanished and was seen no more.

[*Here follows the Interlude between the two Acts, in
which a recitation concerning* ATSUMORI*'s death takes
place. These interludes are subject to variation and are
not considered part of the literary text of the play.*]

Priest.

Since this is so, I will perfom all night the rites of
prayer for the dead, and calling upon Amida's
name will pray again for the salvation of Atsumori.

[*The ghost of* ATSUMORI *appears, dressed as a young
warrior.*]

Atsumori.

Would you know who I am

---

4. *Namu Amidabu* (nä′mōō ä′mə·dä′bōō): The prayer by which followers of the Amida Buddha obtained salvation.

5. **Amida Buddha** (ä′mē′dä bōō′də): an enlightened being worshiped
by followers of a Buddhist sect in medieval Japan.

That like the watchmen at Suma Pass
Have wakened at the cry of sea birds roaming
Upon Awaji shore?
Listen, Rensei. I am Atsumori.

Priest.

How strange! All this while I have never stopped
beating my gong and performing the rites of the
Law.[6] I cannot for a moment have dozed, yet I
thought that Atsumori was standing before me.
Surely it was a dream.

Atsumori.

Why need it be a dream? It is to clear the karma[7]
of my waking life that I am come here in visible
form before you.

Priest.

Is it not written that one prayer will wipe away ten
thousand sins? Ceaselessly I have performed the
ritual of the Holy Name[8] that clears all sin away.
After such prayers, what evil can be left? Though
you should be sunk in sin as deep . . .

Atsumori.

As the sea by a rocky shore,
Yet should I be saved by prayer.

Priest.

And that my prayers should save you . . .

Atsumori.

This too must spring
From kindness of a former life.[9]

Priest.

Once enemies . . .

Atsumori.

But now . . .

Noh mask.
*How do you envision the speech and
movements of the characters?*

---

6. **the rites of the Law:** the doctrines of Buddhism, or of a Buddhist sect.
7. **karma** (kär'mə): a person's actions, which Buddhists believe influence the fate of a person in this and future lives.
8. **the ritual of the Holy Name:** the recitation of the prayer ''Namu Amidabu.''
9. **From kindness of a former life:** Atsumori must have done Rensei some kindness in a former incarnation. This would account for Rensei's remorse.

Seami Motokiyo   **605**

Priest.

In truth may we be named . . .

Atsumori.

Friends in Buddha's Law.

Chorus.

There is a saying, "Put away from you a wicked
   friend; summon to your side a virtuous enemy."
   For you it was said, and you have proven it true.
And now come tell with us the tale of your confession, while the night is still dark.

Chorus.

He[10] bids the flowers of spring
Mount the treetop that men may raise their eyes
And walk on upward paths;
He bids the moon in autumn waves be drowned
In token that he visits laggard men
And leads them out from valleys of despair.

Atsumori.

Now the clan of Taira,[11] building wall to wall,
Spread over the earth like the leafy branches of a
   great tree:

Chorus.

Yet their prosperity lasted but for a day;
It was like the flower of the convolvulus.[12]
There was none to tell them
That glory flashes like sparks from flint-stone,
And after—darkness.
Oh wretched, the life of men!

Atsumori.

When they were on high they afflicted the humble;
When they were rich they were reckless in pride.
And so for twenty years and more
They ruled this land.
But truly a generation passes like the space of a
   dream.
The leaves of the autumn of Juyei[13]

---

10. **He:** Buddha.
11. **Taira** (tä·ē′rä): the clan of the Heike.
12. **convolvulus** (kən·väl′vyoo·ləs): a flower of the morning-glory
    family.
13. **Juyei** (joo·yā′): The Taira evacuated the capital in the second
    year of Juyei, 1188.

Japanese Noh actor. *Most Noh plays
contain the "Three Roles" of the old
person, the woman, and the warrior. To
achieve* yugen, *a mark of high
accomplishment in the arts, Seami says
that the three roles must be acted
beautifully.*

? *How does* Atsumori *deviate from the
traditional three-role Noh drama?*

Were tossed by the four winds;
Scattered, scattered (like leaves too) floated their
    ships.
And they, asleep on the heaving sea, not even in
    dreams
Went back to home.
Caged birds longing for the clouds—
Wild geese were they rather, whose ranks are broken
As they fly to southward on their doubtful journey.
So days and months went by; spring came again
And for a little while
Here dwelt they on the shore of Suma
At the first valley.[14]
From the mountain behind us the winds blew down
Till the fields grew wintry again.
Our ships lay by the shore, where night and day
The sea gulls cried and salt waves washed on our
    sleeves.
We slept with fishers in their huts
On pillows of sand.
We knew none but the people of Suma.
And when among the pine trees
The evening smoke was rising,
Brushwood, as they called it,
Brushwood we gathered
And spread for carpet.
Sorrowful we lived
On the wild shore of Suma,
Till the clan Taira and all its princes
Were but villagers of Suma.

Atsumori.

But on the night of the sixth day of the second
    month
My father Tsunemori[15] gathered us together.
"Tomorrow," he said, "we shall fight our last fight.
Tonight is all that is left us."
We sang songs together, and danced.

Priest.

Yes, I remember; we in our siege-camp

---

14. **the first valley:** Ichi no tani.
15. **Tsunemori** (tsü′nə·mō′rē): one of the lords of the Taira clan.

Heard the sound of music
Echoing from your tents that night;
There was the music of a flute . . .

Atsumori.

The bamboo flute! I wore it when I died.

Priest.

We heard the singing . . .

Atsumori.

Songs and ballads . . .

Priest.

Many voices

Atsumori.

Singing to one measure.

[ATSUMORI *dances.*]

First comes the royal boat.

Chorus.

The whole clan has put its boats to sea.
He[16] will not be left behind;
He runs to the shore.
But the royal boat and the soldiers' boats
Have sailed far away.

Atsumori.

What can he do?
He spurs his horse into the waves.
He is full of perplexity.
And then

Chorus.

He looks behind him and sees
That Kumagai pursues him;
He cannot escape.
Then Atsumori turns his horse
Knee-deep in the lashing waves,
And draws his sword.
Twice, three times he strikes; then, still saddled,
In close fight they twine; roll headlong together
Among the surf of the shore.
So Atsumori fell and was slain, but now the Wheel
    of Fate
Has turned and brought him back.

Samurai warrior.

---

16. **He:** Atsumori; the passage is mimed throughout.

[ATSUMORI *rises from the ground and advances toward the Priest with uplifted sword.*]

"There is my enemy," he cries, and would strike,
But the other is grown gentle
And calling on Buddha's name
Has obtained salvation for his foe;
So that they shall be reborn together
On one lotus[17] seat.
"No, Rensei is not my enemy.
Pray for me again, oh pray for me again."

---

17. **lotus** (lōt′əs): a water lily sacred to Buddhists.

First Thoughts

What dominant feeling did this play leave you with?

Identifying Facts

1. What discovery does Rensei make about the Young Reaper?
2. Read the final eight lines of the play, in which the chorus speaks with the voice of Atsumori. How does Atsumori feel about Rensei?

Interpreting Meanings

1. What is the essential **conflict** between Rensei and Atsumori? How do they bring this conflict to a resolution?
2. Both Rensei and Atsumori are **flat characters**. Nevertheless, the character of Rensei is more developed than that of Atsumori. What conflicting feelings does Rensei have that bring him to life as a character?
3. In the middle of the play, Atsumori makes a long speech comparing warriors to images from nature. Name some of these images, and explain what they reveal about Atsumori's view of war.

4. Very near the end of the play, Atsumori almost attacks Rensei, then changes his mind. He declares, "No, Rensei is not my enemy," and pleads, "Pray for me again, oh pray for me again." What impression of Atsumori's state of mind does this line create?
5. Do you think the music the reapers play on their flutes is happy or sad? Why? Support your conclusion with quotations from the play.

Applying Meanings

Think about the saying on page 606: "Put away from you a wicked friend: summon to your side a virtuous enemy." In the play, Rensei is the "virtuous enemy." Have you ever had someone or something you thought was an enemy do something good for you? How did you react?

Critical Writing Response

Comparing Dramatic Forms. Think of three aspects of a Noh drama—such as the unusual treatment of time and space—that are different from conventional plays performed in the West. Write a

Seami Motokiyo **609**

three-paragraph essay explaining how these aspects illustrate the ways in which classical Japanese theater differs from our own. To help you formulate your ideas, use a chart like the one below. Part of the chart has been filled in for you.

Dramatic Features	Japanese Noh Drama	Western Drama
Characterization	Characters are flat, showing only one or two traits	Main characters are usually round; secondary characters may be flat
Conflict		
Setting: time and space		
Other		

Language and Vocabulary

Oxymorons

An **oxymoron** is a figure of speech that combines apparently contradictory or opposing ideas, as in the phrases "deafening silence" and "living death." In *Atsumori,* the chorus recites a saying that contains two oxymorons: "Put away from you a wicked friend; summon to your side a virtuous enemy." The oxymoronic phrases "wicked friend" and "virtuous enemy" are striking and powerful because they challenge our conventional ideas about friends and enemies.

Many oxymorons challenge our conventional notions of a thing or idea. For instance, the oxymoron "cruel kindness" suggests that an apparent kindness may actually be wounding.

What adjectives can be paired with the following nouns to create oxymorons?

1. law   3. dream   5. loneliness
2. sorrow   4. love   6. duty

PRIMARY SOURCES

from The Tale of the Heike: "The Death of Atsumori"

Many Noh plays were based on dance-ballads or poems that would have been familiar to the audiences of the time. The Noh play Atsumori *is based on an episode from* The Tale of the Heike, *a Japanese epic from the thirteenth century.*

Unlike many medieval epics composed in the West, The Tale of the Heike *does not glorify war. Its tone is melancholy, and it portrays glory as a mixed blessing. Here, Kumagai Naozane, who later becomes the priest Rensei, meets the young Atsumori on the battlefield at Ichi no tani and reluctantly kills him.*

The Death of Atsumori

When the Heike were routed at Ichi no tani, and their nobles and courtiers were fleeing to the shore to escape in their ships, Kumagai Naozane came riding along a narrow path onto the beach, with the intention of intercepting one of their great captains. Just then his eye fell on a single horseman who was attempting to reach one of the ships in the offing. The horse he rode was dappled-gray, and its saddle glittered with gold mounting. Not doubting that he was one of the chief captains, Kumagai beckoned to him with his war fan, crying out: "Shameful! to show an enemy your back. Return! Return!"

The warrior turned his horse and rode back to the beach, where Kumagai at once engaged him in mortal combat. Quickly hurling him to the ground, he sprang upon him and tore off his helmet to cut off his head, when he beheld the face of a youth of sixteen or seventeen, delicately powdered and with blackened teeth, just about the age of his own son and with features of great beauty. "Who are you?" he asked. "Tell me your name, for I would spare your life."

"Nay, first say who you are," replied the young man.

"I am Kumagai Naozane of Musashi, a person of no particular importance."

"Then you have made a good capture," said the youth. "Take my head and show it to some of my side, and they will tell you who I am."

"Though he is one of their leaders," mused Kumagai, "if I slay him it will not turn victory into defeat, and if I spare him, it will not turn defeat into victory. When my son Kojirō was but slightly wounded at Ichi no tani this morning, did it not pain me? How this young man's father would grieve to hear that he had been killed! I will spare him."

Just then, looking behind him, he saw Doi and Kajiwara coming up with fifty horsemen. "Alas! look there," he exclaimed, the tears running down his face, "though I would spare your life, the whole countryside swarms with our men, and you cannot escape them. If you must die, let it be by my hand, and I will see that prayers are said for your rebirth in Paradise."

"Indeed it must be so," said the young warrior. "Cut off my head at once."

Kumagai was so overcome by compassion that he could scarcely wield his blade. His eyes swam and he hardly knew what he did, but there was no help for it; weeping bitterly he cut off the boy's head. "Alas!" he cried, "what life is so hard as that of a soldier? Only because I was born of a warrior family must I suffer this affliction! How lamentable it is to do such cruel deeds!" He pressed his face to the sleeve of his armor and wept bitterly. Then, wrapping up the head, he was stripping off the young man's armor when he discovered a flute in a brocade bag. "Ah," he exclaimed, "it was this youth and his friends who were amusing themselves with music within the walls this morning. Among all our men of the Eastern Provinces I doubt if there is any one of them who has brought a flute with him. How gentle the ways of these courtiers!"

When he brought the flute to the Commander, all who saw it were moved to tears; he discovered then that the youth was Atsumori, the youngest son of Tsunemori, aged sixteen years. From this time the mind of Kumagai was turned toward the religious life.

SENRYU: JAPAN'S COMIC VERSES

> After he's scolded
> His wife too much,
> He cooks the rice.

> Zen priest,
> Meditation finished,
> Looking for fleas.

> "Don't worry!" he says,
> And then tells you something
> That really gets you worried.

Do you notice anything funny about these "haiku"? Do they sound more like a comedian than like Bashō? Well, you're right: the poems above are not haiku but *senryu* (sen·r̄oo). Similar in form, senryu and haiku differ in tone and purpose. Most senryu are intended to be funny—some seem the poetic equivalent of cartoons—but they have a deeper purpose as well. These small verses focus on everyday events in order to point out the humor and irony inherent in the human condition.

> Workmen eating lunch,
> With a side order
> Of gripes.

> First childbirth—
> Her husband feels like
> He did half the work.

> Off to work,
> The burglar to his wife:
> "Lock up tight when you go to bed!"

Both haiku and senryu contain seventeen Japanese syllables, usually grouped in a 5-7-5 pattern. However, a traditional haiku relies on nature imagery for part of its impact, and it must contain a word referring to a season of the year. Most haiku are serious, even mystical, in tone. Senryu, by contrast, need not include nature imagery or refer to the seasons. Instead, they emphasize the small but telling dramas played out in daily life. And the tone of senryu ranges from playful to irreverent to ribald:

> Judging from the pictures,
> Hell looks the more
> Interesting place.

> Home from work,
> The bachelor sniffs
> At the leftover rice.

> One bite
> And I'm doing a dance—
> Red peppers.

SHOKI AND DEMON, YOSA (TANIGUCHI) BUSON, 1777.

Christie, Manson & Woods International, Inc.

Senryu means "River Willow," which was the pen name of Karai Hachiemon (1718–1790), the poet who made senryu famous. Before Hachiemon's time, the verse form had been called *maeku-zuke* (mā'ē·kōo·zōo'kē), and it had first appeared during the late 1600s. The tradition of Japanese humorous verse, from which senryu developed, is older still: humorous poetry has been a part of Japanese literature for over a thousand years.

Karai "Senryu" Hachiemon was trained as a writer of haiku. He had little success as a poet; he may have been a bit too down-to-earth for haiku. He did much better as an editor, publishing several popular collections of poems in the genre that came to bear his name. Many of the senryu in his collections are anonymous, though a number are thought to be the work of Hachiemon himself.

Some early senryu poke fun at more serious Japanese literature. One poet, Kenkabô, slyly ridicules Sei Shōnagon, tenth-century author of *The Pillow Book* (see page 579):

> *Sei Shōnagon*
> *Makes her dictionary*
> *A pillow.*

The implication here is that Shōnagon was too lazy to consult her dictionary and write proper Japanese; instead, she dozed at her writing, using her dictionary as a literal "pillow book."

One virtue of senryu is that, unlike much other classical literature, it never takes itself too seriously. As a result, it's doubtful that anyone, no matter how intimidated by poetry in general, has ever approached a senryu verse thinking, "This stuff is too deep for me." Modern senryu writers tackle modern subjects:

> *"Do take out your teeth*
> *Once more!"*
> *Begs the grandchild.*
> —*Shunu*

> *On a bicycle,*
> *Lifting up both legs,*
> *Through a puddle.*
> —*Shukei*

But the underlying tone, realistic and emphatically human, remains the same. Is it any wonder that this unpretentious verse form has stayed popular for almost three hundred years?

Language and Culture **613**

MAINTAINING PRONOUN-ANTECEDENT AGREEMENT

Making pronouns agree with **antecedents**—the words they refer to—can be a difficult challenge. However, a few basic rules can help you to keep your writing clear.

Pronoun-Antecedent Agreement

Choose pronouns that agree in number and gender with their **antecedents**. A **pronoun**—a word that stands for a noun or another pronoun—can be singular or plural, masculine or feminine. In general, singular nouns call for singular pronouns, and plural nouns call for plural pronouns. But be alert for problems in the four areas listed below.

1. Compound Antecedents

INCORRECT
    Lao-tzu and Buddha explained *his* ideas.

CORRECT
    Lao-tzu and Buddha explained *their* ideas.

Compound antecedents joined by *and* take a plural pronoun. Compound antecedents joined by *or* or *nor* take a singular pronoun.

INCORRECT
    Did Sei Shōnagon or Murasaki Shikibu record *their* observations in *The Pillow Book*?

CORRECT
    Did Sei Shōnagon or Murasaki Shikibu record *her* observations in *The Pillow Book*?

2. Indefinite Pronouns as Antecedents

INCORRECT
    Among the Japanese empress's handmaidens, everyone had *their* own rank in the hierarchy.

CORRECT
    Among the Japanese empress's handmaidens, everyone had *her* own rank in the hierarchy.

The following indefinite pronouns, used as antecedents, are singular.

anyone	nobody
everyone	somebody
no one	each
someone	either
anybody	neither
everybody	

Their gender depends on sentence context. If you are unsure, use *his or her,* or reword the sentence. The following indefinite pronouns can be singular or plural, depending on sentence sense.

any	enough
more	none
plenty	most
some	

INCORRECT

Of all Li Ch'ing-chao's poems, none took *their* theme from politics.

CORRECT

Of all Li Ch'ing-chao's poems, none took *its* theme from politics.

None is used here in the sense of "not one," so it needs a singular pronoun.

3. Abstract and Collective Nouns

INCORRECT

Bashō's imagery achieved *their* effects through a succession of vivid flashes.

CORRECT

Bashō's imagery achieved *its* effects through a succession of vivid flashes.

Some abstract nouns seem to name clusters of things: imagery, poetry. Still, they take singular pronouns. **Collective nouns** name groups: series, set, collection, group, majority, amount, number. These may take plural pronouns if your sentence refers to individual items within the group.

INCORRECT

These poets' works were rich in imagery, and a number reflected specifics from *its* authors' daily lives.

CORRECT

These poets' works were rich in imagery, and a number reflected specifics from *their* authors' daily lives.

Here *number* refers to several works being considered individually.

4. Titles

INCORRECT

Confucius' *Analects* conveyed *their* message in a way anyone could understand.

CORRECT

Confucius' *Analects* conveyed *its* message in a way anyone could understand.

The title of a literary work, even if it is plural, takes a singular pronoun.

Exercise: Making Pronouns Agree with Antecedents

Revise each sentence so that pronouns agree with their antecedents.

1. Each haiku poet can express their emotions simply and unpretentiously.
2. The *Analects* and the *Tao Te Ching* taught its lessons through maxims.
3. Everyone will probably have their own interpretation of "Gold, Gold."
4. Striking images used by Shōnagon include the series that may reflect their creator's malice.
5. Through poetry, either Li Ch'ing-chao or Princess Nukada will work their magic on the reader.
6. Lao-tzu and Ssu-ma Ch'ien did not write merely to entertain; instead, he wanted to convey serious points about life.
7. Though over a thousand years old, Li Po's "Quiet Night Thoughts" will never lose their place of honor in Chinese literature.
8. Tu Fu left behind a poetry collection that still can touch their readers today.
9. Li Ch'ing-chao wrote love poems for their readers.
10. Li Ch'ing-chao's artistry is evident in the poem "Peonies"; they contain complex imagery.

ANALYZING IMAGERY

Has the sound of music or the sight of a child's toy ever transported you back to an earlier time in your life? Do the words *concert* and *storm* conjure up pictures in your mind? These **images**, or representations of sensory experiences, stimulate the imagination and engage the emotions. Whether they occur in real life or in literature, images call forth personal associations.

Writing Assignment

Choose a work from this unit and write an informative essay about it. In your essay, examine the ways in which the work's imagery contributes to its mood and theme. Assume that your audience has read the work and is interested in your interpretation. For this assignment, you will use techniques of literary analysis.

Background

In many cases, works in this unit are word paintings, celebrating nature or recreating the total experience of a moment in life. Some make imaginative comparisons using the following figures of speech.

- **Similes** are comparisons using the word *like* or *as*: "... bright moonlight ... like frost on the ground."—Li Po, "Quiet Night Thoughts."

- **Metaphors** are comparisons without the word *like* or *as*: "His dancing girls are yellow dust."—Tu Fu, "Jade Flower Palace."
- **Personification** assigns human qualities to animals, objects, or ideas: "Were the stream to tempt, / My body. . . ."—Ono Komachi.

Notice such figures of speech as you choose a work and interpret its imagery.

Prewriting

Focused Reading. Choose a work (or several, if you are using tanka or haiku verses) and reread it at least twice—once aloud. To begin your analysis, complete a chart like this one.

Image	
Figure(s) of speech used to create image	
Emotions/ mood image produces	
Image's relation to theme	

Interpreting Imagery. Referring to your chart, answer the following questions to determine how the imagery functions in the poem as a whole.

1. What are the main images in this work?
2. How do the images relate to one another?
3. What emotions do the images convey?
4. Why might the author have chosen these particular images?
5. How would you state the theme of the work?
6. How do the images relate to the theme?

From your answers, synthesize one idea that you can explain in detail about the imagery in this work. Sum up your idea into a thesis sentence.

Writing

Use the following plan as you draft your essay.

1. **Introductory Paragraph.** Consider beginning with a personal response to this work, perhaps explaining why you have chosen it. Cite the title and the author. End with your thesis sentence.
2. **Body Paragraphs.** Each body paragraph should contain one point about the imagery, supported with explanations and quotations from the work. Arrange your points logically, perhaps from simplest to most complicated.

3. **Concluding Paragraph.** Restate your thesis in light of the points you've explained. Consider ending with another personal response to the work. Try to entice readers to revisit the work and make their own analysis.

Evaluating and Revising

Use these questions to evaluate and revise your essay.

1. Does the first paragraph catch readers' interest and state your thesis?
2. Do details and quotations support your points about the imagery? Are quotations well chosen and well integrated?
3. Are your ideas in a logical order?
4. Does your conclusion reinforce your thesis, leaving readers with something to think about?
5. Are your sentences varied and grammatically correct?

Proofreading and Publishing

Proofread carefully to eliminate errors in mechanics. Share your analysis with classmates who have selected the same work, and plan a panel discussion to explore the variations in your interpretations.

Atlantic
Ocean

EUROPE

SPAIN

• Cordova
• Granada

ITALY

MACEDONIA

Black Sea

GREECE

Mediterranean Sea

SYRIA

Baghdad

• Damascus

NORTH AFRICA

LIBYA

Cairo •

EGYPT

ARABIA

Medina

• Mecca

Nile River

Red Sea

ISLAMIC
EMPIRE

C. A.D. 900

SAHARA

PERSIAN AND ARABIC LITERATURES

▼ Time ▼
(700 B.C.–A.D. 1400)

▼ Place ▼
The Middle East

▼ Literary Significance ▼

In A.D. 641, Arabs invaded the Persian Empire, which had flourished in the Middle East since about 700 B.C. The Arabs converted much of the Middle East to Islam, the religion founded by the prophet Mohammed. The Koran, which Muslims believe to be the direct word of Allah, or God, still inspires the millions of Muslims around the world. In addition to the Koran, Arabic writings include lyric poetry, philosophy, religion, history, and science. The Arabic work best known in the West is *The Thousand and One Nights,* a collection of fabulous tales from the Arab oral tradition.

Since the Islamic conquest in the seventh century, native Persian language and literary forms had been all but eclipsed by Arabic language and culture. But in the ninth century A.D., a renaissance of Persian culture began. The poet Ferdowsi completed a national epic of Persia (now Iran), the *Shahname.* Later, Omar Khayyám wrote the *Rubáiyát,* a famous collection of brief poems that evolved from traditional Persian poetic forms. This same period in Persian literature saw the rise of Sufism, a sect of Islam. The mystical works of Sufi writers and poets are still cherished by readers throughout the world.

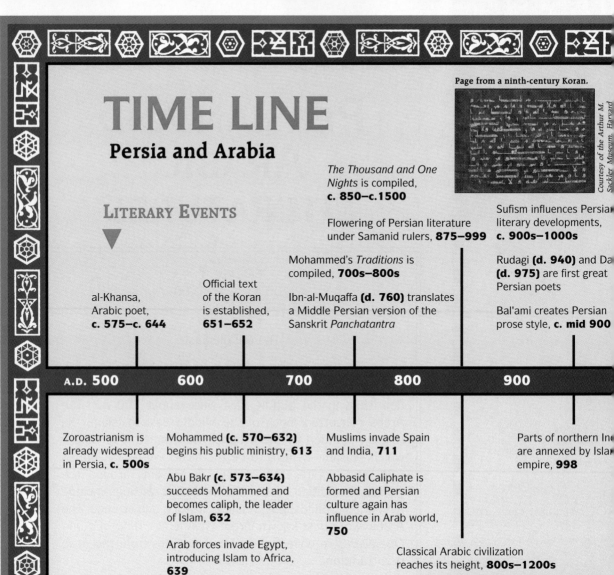

TIME LINE
Persia and Arabia

Page from a ninth-century Koran.

Courtesy of the Arthur M. Sackler Museum, Harvard

LITERARY EVENTS ▼

The Thousand and One Nights is compiled, **c. 850–c.1500**

Flowering of Persian literature under Samanid rulers, **875–999**

Sufism influences Persian literary developments, **c. 900s–1000s**

Mohammed's *Traditions* is compiled, **700s–800s**

Ibn-al-Muqaffa **(d. 760)** translates a Middle Persian version of the Sanskrit *Panchatantra*

Rudagi **(d. 940)** and Da **(d. 975)** are first great Persian poets

Bal'ami creates Persian prose style, **c. mid 900**

al-Khansa, Arabic poet, **c. 575–c. 644**

Official text of the Koran is established, **651–652**

A.D. 500   600   700   800   900

Zoroastrianism is already widespread in Persia, **c. 500s**

Mohammed **(c. 570–632)** begins his public ministry, **613**

Abu Bakr **(c. 573–634)** succeeds Mohammed and becomes caliph, the leader of Islam, **632**

Arab forces invade Egypt, introducing Islam to Africa, **639**

Arab forces conquer Persia; most Persians become Muslims, **640–650**

Muslims invade Spain and India, **711**

Abbasid Caliphate is formed and Persian culture again has influence in Arab world, **750**

Classical Arabic civilization reaches its height, **800s–1200s**

Parts of northern In are annexed by Isla empire, **998**

▲ CULTURAL AND HISTORICAL EVENTS

Cupola of a mosque in Ishfahan, Iran.

Art Resource, New York

Scheherazade amusing the sultan, from *The Thousand and One Nights.*

The Granger Collection, New York

Silk medallion rug, Persian.

National Gallery of Art, Washington. Widener Collection

Rumi **(1207–1273)**, Sufi poet, *Masnavi*

Works of Baha ud-Din Zuhair **(d. 1258)** represent height of classical elegance in Arabic poetry

Saadi **(c. 1213–1292)**, Sufi poet and prose writer, *Gulistan*

Ferdowsi completes the national epic *Shahname* in **1010**

Omar Khayyám **(c.1048–1131)**, *Rubáiyát*

Hafiz **(c. 1326–1389)**, Sufi poet

| 1000 | 1100 | 1200 | 1300 | 1400 |

Muslims defeat Christian crusaders and take Jerusalem, **1187**

Christians begin driving Muslims out of Spain, **1085**

Muslims establish Timbuktu in West Africa as a center of trade and learning, **1087**

Muslim Turks establish a sultanate at Delhi, laying the foundations for modern-day Pakistan and Bangladesh, **c. 1200s**

Mongol conqueror Genghis Khan devastates centers of Muslim-Persian culture, **1221**

Miniature of Mecca, Ottoman Empire.

Giraudon/Art Resource, New York

This border contains designs derived from ceramic tiles produced by Persian and Arabic artisans. Such tiles were a basic element of decorative architecture throughout the Islamic world.

PERSIAN AND ARABIC LITERATURES

❝ Neither snow nor rain nor heat nor gloom of night stays these couriers from the swift completion of their appointed rounds. ❞

—Inscription on the New York City Post Office, adapted from a comment by Herodotus on the Persian postal system

Sometime around 1500 B.C., a massive migration out of central Asia took place. Some of these people, known as the **Aryans**, settled in India, where they founded the Vedic culture (see page 447). In the centuries that followed, other Aryan groups moved west, settling in what is now the Middle Eastern country of Iran. (*Iran* comes from the word "Aryan.") One of these Aryan communities was called **Persian**, after the Greek name for the part of Iran they settled, Persis. This group, which arrived around 700 B.C., gave its name to the Persian language. It also gave birth to two great leaders: **Cyrus the Great** (d. 529 B.C.) and **Darius I** (520–486 B.C.). These rulers built the largest empire the world had yet seen. At its height, the **Persian Empire** stretched from northern India to North Africa. An efficient administration governed the extensive empire, and a remarkably modern postal system allowed communications to travel swiftly between remote regions.

Religious Beliefs in the Persian Empire

When the Aryan settlers arrived in the Middle East, they, like the Aryan settlers of India, worshiped many gods. But a prophet from eastern Iran named **Zarathustra** ("Zoroaster" in Greek) revolutionized religious practices in the Middle East during the Persian Empire. Zarathustra founded a religion called **Zoroastrianism** (zō′rō·as′trē·ən·iz′əm). Zoroastrians believed in two gods. One was the good and kind Ahura Mazda, or Ormazd, "the Wise Lord." Ormazd embodied the virtues of truth and law. His enemy was the evil god Ahriman. Zoroastrians believed that the good Ormazd and the evil Ahriman were engaged in an ongoing struggle, and that one day Ormazd would triumph. People who fol-

Ahura Mazda, the chief god of Zoroastrianism, the
religion of ancient Persia. *Ahura Mazda, a benevolent
god, was usually represented as a winged figure.*

Erich Lessing/Magnum Photos, Inc.

lowed Ormazd during their lifetimes would live in paradise
after death.

As the Persians conquered their neighbors, they spread
the practice of Zoroastrianism. In 331 B.C., the Greek emperor **Alexander the Great** conquered the Persian Empire.
But the Persians continued to fight fiercely, first with the
Greeks, then with the Romans, to preserve their religious

> The mighty Persian Empire spread
> the practice of Zoroastrianism, which
> would influence the development of
> later religions throughout the Middle
> East and beyond.

and cultural practices. The struggle would continue until the
seventh century A.D. At this time, another people, the **Arabs**,
would sweep through the region with the force of a whirlwind, bringing with them a new religion—**Islam**.

The Birth of Islam

The Arabs were largely sheltered from world events on the
Arabian peninsula, which they called "the Arab island." Although some Arabs lived in cities, most led a nomadic, or
wandering, lifestyle. No central power dominated the peninsula. Some Arab rulers held power locally along stretches

A *mihrab* from the temple of
Ishfahan in Iran. *The mihrab, a
prayer niche that faces Islam's
holy city of Mecca, is a feature
of every mosque.*

of sea coast or interior desert passages, but the nomadic
tribes lived in continual movement, following the lines of
desert wells. Into the vast region of scattered tribes came a
man who preached a faith called **Islam** that would unify the
peninsula politically and spiritually.

The founder of Islam was a native Meccan named **Mohammed** (c. A.D. 570–632). In Mohammed's day, Mecca was
a city plagued by poverty. The lot of the poor so upset
Mohammed that he often retreated to the hills to seek
spiritual peace through meditation. Muslims believe that
during one of these retreats, Mohammed was visited by the
angel Gabriel, who revealed to him the word of God. Mohammed continued to witness these revelations throughout
his life. Later, Mohammed gained many followers, to whom
he dictated the revelations of *Allah,* the one god. These
revelations were later compiled into the holy book of Islam,
the **Koran,** which means "recitation." (see page 633).

Many of the traditions familiar to Christians and Jews
continue in Islam. For example, the Hebrew laws from the
time of Moses are fundamental to the teachings of Islam.
And, like Christians, **Muslims**—the followers of Islam—
believe in the hierarchy of the angels and the day of judgment. Islam also teaches that God, all-powerful, acts through
prophets and believers. Muslims are taught the traditions
of the prophets, from Abraham to Jesus, and believe that
Mohammed was the last in a long line of prophets. Although
Islam rejects some of the key beliefs of Christianity, such as
the concept of the trinity, the Koran requires Muslims to
respect the other believers of "the books," Jews and Christians. One of the main requirements of Islam is that believers submit their will to Allah. The word *Islam,* in fact, means
"submission."

The Rise of the Islamic Empire

Islam, which stresses community and charity, held a strong
appeal for Mecca's poor, and Mohammed quickly made
scores of converts. However, after the first congregation of
believers in Mecca, powerful men sought to silence Mohammed permanently. He narrowly escaped and fled north
to Medina, where he officially founded his ministry in 613.
Later, outside Medina, Mohammed's followers defeated

Meccan forces, returning to Mecca in triumph. Thirty years after Mohammed's death, Arab armies, with the sword in one hand and the Koran in the other, swarmed across the Persian Empire as far east as Afghanistan and as far west as Spain. The influence of Islam proved lasting, and the word of Allah eventually spread to parts of Africa and the Far East. Today, Islam claims more than 800 million followers around the world.

The Abbasid Caliphate

Following Mohammed's death, Islamic political and spiritual leadership was placed in the hands of a *caliph* (kā'lif), or "successor." The seat of the caliph's power was the Caliphate. In A.D. 750, a powerful Muslim leader named Abbas and his followers, the **Abbasids**, founded a Caliphate in Baghdad (the capital of modern Iraq). Here, Arabic influences mixed freely with Persian traditions. This marriage of cultures produced splendid results. Although most Persians converted to Islam, Persian literary and governmental practices were maintained. Intellectual activity blossomed. Well before Europe opened its first university, the "House of Wisdom" had been established in Baghdad. The **Abbasid Caliphate** sparked a cultural explosion that swept across the empire. Classical Arabic civilization reached a peak between the ninth and thirteenth centuries. New stability and order allowed for developments in the sciences and the arts.

The Abbasid Caliphate marked the cultural high point of the Islamic empire. Sciences and the arts flourished.

After Europe emerged from the Middle Ages, it received the fruit of the Arab cultural legacy. In addition to developing the Arabic system of numerals, the Arabs had made great strides in the sciences, especially algebra, chemistry, and astronomy. Arabic treatises on music theory and philosophy also influenced Europeans. Europe would also receive, via Arab libraries, the classical Greek and Roman works that fueled the European Renaissance.

> **❝** Doubtless Mohammed had no idea of world conquest. He conceived it his duty to give all his fellow countrymen the chance of embracing Islam. If the summons was resisted by violence, then he must fight back. **❞**
>
> —*J. J. Saunders,*
> History Today, *Vol. XI, No. 3*

Arabic Literature

The Arabs have a long oral tradition in literature. One center of oral literature in pre-Islamic Arabia was Souk Ozak (sook' ō·zäk'), "Ozak market." Here, once a year, poets gathered to sing in bardic contests. The oral tradition is still alive in Arabic cities today. From the Arab proverbs, the most an-

ASCENT OF THE PROPHET MOHAMMED TO HEAVEN, **Persian illustration.**

cient of Arabic literature, to the Koran, the streets of Arab cities and towns buzz with the poetry of the Arabic tongue. While Christians traditionally use bells to call the faithful to worship, Muslims use the human voice. Throughout the day, Arabic communities echo with the various calls to communal prayer.

The Arabs have a long written tradition as well. The language of the Koran became the model of classical Arabic, which still unites Muslims worldwide in spite of numerous languages and local dialects. The study of the Koran led to the composition of the *Hadith*, "Traditions of the Prophet." The *Hadith* is a vast collection of sayings and actions attributed to Mohammed. Together, the Koran and the *Hadith* provided a sturdy foundation for the development of a thriving Arabic literary tradition.

Poetry was highly valued from the beginnings of Arabic literature. Poets were greatly respected among pre-Islamic Arabs, and they continued to be throughout the Islamic period. The Arabic word for poet is *sha'er*, literally, "he who knows." Not all poets were men, however. One type of verse, a lament for the deceased, was composed exclusively by women. In pre-Islamic Medina, early in the seventh century, a woman named **al-Khansa** wrote strikingly poignant verse about the deaths of her two brothers (see page 630).

In the classical era, many Arabic poets created sensual lyrics that stood in sharp contrast to the puritanical prose written by interpreters of the Koran. These love lyrics overflowed with courtly love conventions similar to those found in later medieval European poetry.

Much of Arabic prose dealt with interpretations of the Koran, but influential prose writers appeared in secular fields as well. The travel writings of Ibn Battuta gave birth to the modern science of sociology, and the Arab historical tradition became a model for European imitations. But Arabic prose writers also aimed at sheer, delightful entertainment: *The Thousand and One Nights*, composed in Baghdad from the ninth through the sixteenth centuries, still provides surprises to modern readers (see page 638). Perhaps the greatest gift of Arabic culture, however, was translation. The vast library of Alexandria, which housed myriad volumes of Greek and Roman literature in translation, inspired awe in Arabs and foreigners alike.

> ❝ O serene soul! Return to your Lord, joyful, and pleasing in His sight. Join My servants and enter My Paradise. ❞
>
> —*from the Koran, translated by N. J. Dawood*

Persian Poetry

Classical Persian literature flourished under Arab occupation in Persia. Under the enormous momentum of its initial conquests, the Islamic empire made hundreds of thousands of converts, not only to Islam but also to the Arabic language. But eventually the cultures and languages of the conquered peoples made a comeback. Less well-controlled reaches of the empire produced their own ruling dynasties. In Iran, for example, the **Samanid dynasty** held considerable power from 875 to 999. Although it upheld Islamic law, this dynasty, a family of rulers descended from Persians, encouraged the use of Persian forms for artistic pursuits.

NOMADIC ENCAMPMENT, MIR SAYYID-'ALI, c. 1540. At first, the Arabic conquerors of the Middle East attempted to impose their culture throughout the empire.

Did this project succeed? Why or why not?

Courtesy of The Arthur M. Sackler Museum Harvard University, Cambridge, Massachusetts, Gift of John Goelet

The first great Persian poets and prose writers arose under Samanid patronage. **Dakiki** (d. 975) was the first important poet of this Persian revival. His work emphasized Persian history, including Zoroastrian ideas. Later, **Ferdowsi** (c. 940–1020) used Dakiki's material in the composition of the Persian epic *Shahname*, or *Book of Kings* (see page 646).

> Persian culture made a comeback under the Samanid dynasty. The use of the Persian language in poetry, initially suppressed by the Islamic empire, was revived.

The poet **Omar Khayyám** (c. 1048–1131) wrote in a traditional Persian form, the *rubá'i*. The *rubá'i* was not considered "high art" by Khayyám's contemporaries; in fact, the poet was immortalized not by Persians but by the nineteenth-century translator Edward FitzGerald. FitzGerald's fabulously popular translation of the *Rubáiyát* (see page 654) has made Khayyám the most famous Persian poet in the West.

Some of the greatest works of Persian poetry were a product of **Sufism**, a sect of Islam that attracted many Persian followers. A mystical sect, Sufism teaches that a direct experience with Allah can be achieved through intuition. Sufis developed a popular poetic form called the *ghazal*, a type of ode. The Sufi poet **Hafiz** (1326–1389) was a master of this form. **Rumi** (1207–1273) wrote the *Masnavi*, a book of mystical poetry that crowns the literary masterpieces of Sufi poetry (see page 661).

Persian Prose

Most Persian prose works were produced in the fields of philosophy and history. Animal fables, however, were also a great favorite among Persian audiences. In fact, the *Panchatantra*, a collection of fables from ancient India (see page 478), came to the West by way of a Persian translation. The Sufis produced Persian prose works in the form of sayings, anecdotes, and didactic stories. The *Gulistan* of **Saadi** (see page 665), a thirteenth-century Sufi sage, stands as a masterpiece of Persian prose.

Binder of the *Divan (Poetical Works)* of Hafiz. *Hafiz was a fourteenth-century Sufi poet.*

al-Khansa
c. A.D. 575–c. 644

FIGURE OF A WOMAN WRITING, TCHÉHEL SOLOUN, seventeenth century, Persian.

Her full name was Tumadir bint Amr, but this Arabian poet is best known by her nickname, *Khansa*, which means "snub-nosed." Only a few facts about her have survived the centuries since she lived. She was born about A.D. 575 and belonged to the Sulyam tribe and the Sharid clan. She was married to a kinsman and bore six children. Around 630, when she was in her mid-fifties, her community accepted the then-new religion of Islam. She joined them and may even have been part of the delegation that went to Medina to offer its submission directly to Mohammed. The exact date of her death is unknown, but she lived into old age, dying around 644 or, as some reports assert, perhaps as late as 660.

Only a thousand or so lines of al-Khansa's poetry remain, but that fragment is enough to assure her place in Arabic literature. Her work is technically brilliant, emotionally rich, and highly eloquent. Among her poems is "On Her Brother," an elegy, or poem composed to lament one who is dead. Even in al-Khansa's day, the elegy was an ancient form. But she gave it a new degree of refinement. Her poem is richly textured with pride and sorrow that resonate through time. The poem conveys a sense of the characters of both the subject and the poet.

As a poet, al-Khansa enjoyed respect and high status in her community. Pre-Islamic clans such as hers felt themselves blessed when one of their members proved to have the poetic gift, because through poetry the memory of their accomplishments could endure beyond their lifetimes. A talented poet like al-Khansa thus helped to insure the community's immortality. Her poems have not only kept her name and those of her brothers alive, but have also preserved the memory of her clan.

ON HER BROTHER

al-Khansa

translated by

WILLIS BARNSTONE

Reader's Guide

Background Although al-Khansa died a Muslim, her poetry belongs to the pre-Islamic era. Pre-Islamic Arab society in general did not believe in an afterlife; for them, the only possible immortality was an enduring reputation. Since the Arabs of al-Khansa's time had no tradition of historical writing, it was the poets who preserved the memory of esteemed community members and their deeds.

Writer's Response To the pre-Islamic Arabs, immortality meant being remembered by the living. Do you agree that this is a form of immortality? In what other ways can people be "immortalized"? Freewrite your ideas.

Literary Focus Usually, an **elegy** is a poem that memorializes the death of a person or laments something lost. Elegies may express sorrow over the passing of life and beauty, or they may be meditations on the nature of death. An elegy is usually formal in language and structure, and its tone is usually solemn or melancholy.

ON HER BROTHER

In this poem al-Khansa honors a brother lost in battle. What aspects of his character does she emphasize most?

My brother was not a camel driver,
a coward, shallow-hearted like a beast.

His sword glittered like a pool
under roaming night clouds.

5   He ran faster
than any of his men.

What good is life—even if he were
happy—since he ran out of time?

Each man whose family was happy in him
10 will visit his grave.

You saw a knight
on a horse running with its tail floating

in the wind, a brown warrior wrapped
in a coat of thin iron.

15 When they overtook him they shouted
like shepherds at daybreak.

Battle scene, Persian, c. 1530.
*How do you think the speaker
of the poem feels about war?*

Courtesy of the Freer Gallery of Art, Smithsonian Institution, Washington, D.C., 54.4—Battle Scene. Persian painting. Attributed to
Muhmud Musawwir. Safavid period. Tabriz school or Qazvin, 16th
century. Color and gold on paper: 32.2 × 20.6 cm.

First Thoughts

What emotions are expressed in "On Her
Brother"? Is the speaker sad, angry, or
indifferent? What makes you say so?

Interpreting Meanings

1. What **figures of speech**, or comparisons, does al-Khansa use to make her
   opinion of her brother's worth clear?
2. Which lines in al-Khansa's **elegy** convey
   her sorrow? What feelings besides sorrow does she express? Explain.

Applying Meanings

What human needs do you think are met
by a memorial such as an elegy?

Creative Writing Response

Writing an Elegy. Write a brief elegy in
remembrance of someone who has died
whose loss you keenly felt. You need not
write about someone you knew personally;
you might choose someone famous, like
Martin Luther King, Jr. Use figures of
speech and images that fittingly express
your sadness.

The Koran
C. A.D. 651–652

Courtesy of The Arthur M. Sackler Museum Harvard University, Cambridge, Massachusetts, Discretionary Fund of the Islamic Department

Page from a Koran, c. 1100.

To more than eight hundred million Muslims, the Koran (kə·ran′) is the word of Allah, the Arabic name for God. According to Muslim belief, the Koran comes from tablets kept in heaven, dictated by the angel Gabriel to the prophet Mohammed.

Mohammed was born into a prominent family in the Arabian city of Mecca around A.D. 570. Despite his family's social position, Mohammed's childhood was filled with hardship and sorrow. By the age of six he was an orphan. Nevertheless, by adulthood he had managed to become a worldly and successful merchant.

When he was about forty, this prosperous businessman, possibly troubled by civil unrest in Mecca, began to meditate at night in a hillside cave near his home. It was here that, according to Islamic belief, the angel Gabriel appeared to Mohammed and announced, "You are the messenger of God." Mohammed received numerous visions, or revelations, in the years that followed, and he dedicated his life to preaching the oneness of God and rejecting the beliefs that many Arabs followed in his day.

Mohammed recognized similarities between the messages he had received and the doctrines of Christianity and Judaism. However, more than these religions, Mohammed's preaching emphasized the power of divine judgment and the need for pious submission to the will of Allah. Hence, the name given to Mohammed's religion, *Islam*, means "submission." One who accepts Islam is a *Muslim*—"one who submits to God."

According to tradition, Mohammed could neither read nor write, so his followers memorized his utterances or jotted them down on whatever they could find—a leaf, a scrap of leather, a rock. After Mohammed died, his followers feared that his words would be lost forever if they did not gather all these versions and record them in a single authoritative Arabic text. Within twenty years, a group of scribes had accomplished this goal and had ordered the destruction of all other versions of Mohammed's revelations. They called this scripture the *Koran*, an Arabic word meaning "recitation," and decreed it the official scripture of Islam.

Reader's Guide

from the KORAN

Background

Because of the Koran's divine authority, as well as the grace and power of its language, orthodox Muslims consider it perfect and unalterable. Consequently, when readers recite the Koran on public occasions, precise rules govern their tone and pronunciation. In addition, Muslims consider that translations can lead to distortion and can only approximate the words of Allah. Although the Koran appears in Turkish, Urdu, English, and many other languages, these translations are considered paraphrases and cannot be used for rituals or ceremonies.

Because of the Koran's importance in Islam, Muslim scholars have devoted their lives to the study of the text. This practice, known as *tafsir,* involves interpreting classical Arabic words and writing commentaries on various passages of the holy book. The purpose of *tafsir* is to ensure that Muslims understand Allah's revelation, but the scholars' work has served, as well, to confirm the Koran as the perfect model of Arabic grammar and diction.

The central theme of the Koran is that there is only one all-powerful God—Allah—who created the world. This God is merciful and compassionate, but he is also the God of Judgment Day. The proper response to Allah is to submit to his will, be generous to the poor, and lead an upright life. Every individual has a choice between following the good, which leads to an afterlife of eternal bliss, or giving in to evil, which leads to eternal damnation.

Oral Response

Discuss with your classmates the idea of an eternal struggle between good and evil. When have you been aware of such a struggle, either in your own life or in the world around you?

Literary Focus

Antithesis is a form of parallelism in which sharply contrasting ideas are expressed in grammatically balanced sentences. For example, the English poet Alexander Pope wrote ''To err is human; to forgive, divine.'' The statement presents the antithesis between humans who err (sinners) and a divine God who forgives.

from the KORAN

translated by

N. J. DAWOOD

> *The Koran consists of 114 Surahs, or chapters. Notice that each of the following Surahs begins in the same way, with the line "In the name of Allah, the Compassionate, the Merciful." Why do you think this is done?*

THE EXORDIUM

*IN THE NAME OF ALLAH
THE COMPASSIONATE
THE MERCIFUL*

*Praise be to Allah, Lord of the Creation,
The Compassionate, the Merciful,
King of Judgment-day!
You alone we worship, and to You alone
we pray for help.
Guide us to the straight path
The path of those whom You have favored,
Not of those who have incurred Your wrath,
Nor of those who have gone astray.*

THE CESSATION

*In the Name of Allah,
the Compassionate, the Merciful*

When the sun ceases to shine; when the stars fall down and the mountains are blown away; when camels big with young are left untended and the wild beasts are brought together; when the seas are set alight and men's souls are reunited; when the infant girl, buried alive, is asked for what crime she was slain; when the records of men's deeds

The Metropolitan Museum of Art, Rogers Fund, 1910 (10.218)

Koran stand from Turkestan, eighth to fourteenth century.

from the Koran   **635**

the utterance of an accursed devil.

Whither then are you going?

This is an admonition to all men: to those among you that have the will to be upright. Yet you cannot will, except by the will of Allah, Lord of the Creation.

DAYLIGHT

In the Name of Allah,
the Compassionate, the Merciful

By the light of day, and by the fall of night, your Lord has not forsaken you, nor does He abhor you.

The life to come holds a richer prize for you than this present life. You shall be gratified with what your Lord will give you.

Did He not find you an orphan and give you shelter?

Did He not find you in error and guide you?

Did He not find you poor and enrich you?

Therefore do not wrong the orphan, nor chide away the beggar. But proclaim the goodness of your Lord.

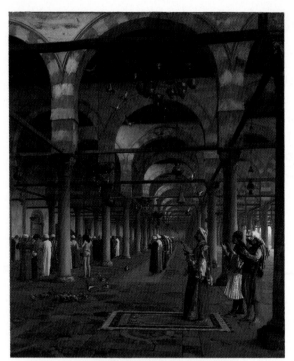

PRAYER IN THE MOSQUE OF 'AMR, JEAN-LÉON GÉRÔME (1824–1904).
? *What attitude toward Allah do these selections urge?*

The Metropolitan Museum of Art,
Bequest of Catharine Lorillard Wolfe, 1887.
Catharine Lorillard Wolfe Collection (87.15.130)

are laid open and the heaven is stripped bare; when Hell burns fiercely and Paradise is brought near: then each soul shall know what it has done.

I swear by the turning planets and by the stars that rise and set; by the fall of night and the first breath of morning: this is the word of a gracious and mighty messenger, held in honor by the Lord of the Throne, obeyed in heaven, faithful to his trust.

No, your compatriot is not mad. He saw him[1] on the clear horizon. He does not grudge the secrets of the unseen; nor is this

COMFORT

In the Name of Allah,
the Compassionate, the Merciful

Have We[2] not lifted up your heart and relieved you of the burden which weighed down your back?

Have We not given you high renown?

Every hardship is followed by ease. Every hardship is followed by ease.

When your task is ended resume your toil, and seek your Lord with all fervor.

---

1. **He saw him:** a reference to the Prophet's vision of Gabriel.

2. **We:** Allah.

First Thoughts

Do these excerpts from the Koran remind you of any other examples of sacred literature that you have read elsewhere in this book? Explain.

Identifying Facts

1. In "The Exordium," what does the speaker ask Allah to do?
2. What does "The Cessation" say souls will learn when the earth ends?
3. According to "Daylight," what three things should a person do to show gratitude for the Lord's goodness?
4. What reassuring words does "Comfort" offer?

Interpreting Meanings

1. In "The Exordium," Mohammed seeks guidance to "the path of those whom You have favored,/Not of those who have incurred Your wrath." The righteous, described in the first prepositional phrase, stand in **antithesis** to the sinful, described in the second prepositional phrase. Find and explain one or two other examples of antithesis in these excerpts from the Koran.
2. Many of the sentences in "Daylight" and "Comfort" are punctuated as questions. How does the use of questions reinforce the point being made in these passages?
3. Which of the images in these excerpts do you find most striking? What impact do you think these images are intended to have on readers?

Applying Meanings

In "The Cessation," Mohammed admonishes his followers to be "upright." In "Daylight," he instructs them not to "wrong the orphan, nor chide away the beggar." How might modern Muslims apply these teachings to decisions in their daily lives?

Creative Writing Response

Composing and Delivering a Sermon. Create a brief **sermon**—a speech that addresses morals or responsibility—to deliver to your classmates. Begin by choosing for your theme some moral lesson: the necessity for personal responsibility; the need to consider the rights of others; the importance of working cooperatively. Decide how you want to motivate your friends—through fear of punishment, hope for reward, an appeal to their sense of fairness, or some other means. Then write your sermon. You might want to practice delivering your sermon at home before presenting it to the class.

The Thousand and One Nights
c. 850–c. 1500

The Granger Collection, New York

Frontispiece by Edmund Dulac from
Sinbad the Sailor and Other Stories.

Ever since the writer Antoine Galland translated *The Thousand and One Nights*—or *The Arabian Nights' Entertainments*—into French in the early eighteenth century, this collection of tales has been the best-known and most widely read work of Arabic literature in the West. The often fantastic adventures of the characters Ali Baba, Aladdin, and Sindbad are known throughout the world today.

The Thousand and One Nights probably developed over several centuries. The original stories came from many oral and written sources, including such collections as the Indian *Panchatantra* (see page 478) and tales brought by travelers from China, India, and every part of the Middle East. Scholars have identified sources for many of the stories, but the true origins of many others remain unknown because they exist in more than one version and in more than one language.

The earliest references to *The Thousand and One Nights* appear in manuscripts from as early as the ninth century A.D. Kept alive by Arab storytellers throughout the Middle Ages, the collection grew and changed. By the mid-sixteenth century, the stories had been put into the form we know today by an unknown Egyptian compiler. The group of tales was first published in Arabic in 1548.

The tales in the collection are loosely held together by an element that was common in medieval literature—a **frame story**. In the frame story, a sultan, Shahriyar, is enraged at his wife's unfaithfulness and orders her executed. He then takes a new wife each day but has her killed at dawn the next day because he believes that no woman can ever be faithful. The supply of potential wives is running low when the sultan takes Scheherazade (shə·her′ə·zä′də) as his wife.

Scheherazade is a spellbinding storyteller. Each night, she entertains the sultan with a new tale but delays revealing the ending until the following night. The captivated sultan keeps postponing her execution in order to hear the stories. After one thousand and one nights of tales, he abandons his plans to kill Scheherazade, and the couple remains happily married.

Reader's Guide

from THE THIRD VOYAGE OF SINDBAD THE SAILOR
from The Thousand and One Nights

Background

Sindbad, one of the heroes in *The Thousand and One Nights,* is a rich young man from Baghdad (now the capital of Iraq) who becomes a sea merchant after recklessly spending all of his wealth. Sindbad's marvelous adventures during the several voyages he makes to regain his fortune are the subject of this story cycle. The stories of Sindbad the Sailor are almost certainly Arabic in origin, but no one knows from which part of the Arab world they come. Some scholars believe that the tales originated in Baghdad. Others argue persuasively that the stories originated in Oman (a country on the southeast coast of the Arabian peninsula) and became associated with Baghdad only later.

Every seafaring culture—ancient Greece, medieval Arabia, and post-Renaissance Europe, to name a few—has produced imaginative literature about adventures at sea. In seafaring literature, the voyage becomes an opportunity to show courage and ambition, the shipwreck is a symbol of ultimate misfortune and loneliness, and the threatening monster represents the universal fear of the unknown.

Writer's Response

Even if you have never read a Sindbad story before, you might know something about Sindbad and his adventures or about other seafaring adventure stories such as *Treasure Island* or *Robinson Crusoe.* Write down some of the words, phrases, and images that you associate with such stories. What do you predict will be some of the features of the story you are about to read?

Literary Focus

Most **plots** follow the same basic pattern. They begin with a situation in which there is a **conflict**, or a problem, that the characters have to solve. As they try to solve the problem, the characters encounter a series of **complications** that usually make their problem worse. This part of the plot is called the **rising action**. The rising action builds to a high point, which is called the **climax**. After the climax comes the **resolution**, the part of the plot in which the problem is finally resolved.

from THE THIRD VOYAGE OF SINDBAD THE SAILOR

from The Thousand and One Nights

translated by

N. J. DAWOOD

> *Who is narrating this story? List everything you learn about the narrator in the first paragraph. Then read on to the end of the third paragraph. How do you predict the narrator will respond to the dangerous situation in which he finds himself?*

Astrolabe, Yemeni, 1296–1297. *Astrolabes, which calculate the altitudes of stars, were an invaluable tool to early navigators.*

Know, my friends, that for some time after my return I continued to lead a happy and tranquil life, but I soon grew weary of my idle existence in Baghdad and once again longed to roam the world in quest of profit and adventure. Unmindful of the dangers of ambition and worldly greed, I resolved to set out on another voyage. I provided myself with a great store of goods and, after taking them down the Tigris,[1] set sail from Basrah,[2] together with a band of honest merchants.

The voyage began prosperously. We called at many foreign ports, trading profitably with our merchandise. One day, however, whilst we were sailing in midocean, we heard the captain of our ship, who was on deck scanning the horizon, suddenly burst out in a loud lament. He beat himself about the face, tore his beard, and rent his clothes.

"We are lost!" he cried, as we crowded round him. "The treacherous wind has

---

1. **Tigris** (tī'gris): river in southwest Asia, flowing from Turkey through Iraq.
2. **Basrah** (bus're): port at the head of the Shatt-al-Arab Channel, where the Tigris and Euphrates rivers join.

driven us off our course towards that island which you see before you. It is the Isle of the Zughb, where dwell a race of dwarfs more akin to apes than men, from whom no voyager has ever escaped alive!"

Scarcely had he uttered these words when a multitude of apelike savages appeared on the beach and began to swim out towards the ship. In a few moments they were upon us, thick as a swarm of locusts. Barely four spans[3] in height, they were the ugliest of living creatures, with little gleaming yellow eyes and bodies thickly covered with black fur. And so numerous were they that we did not dare to provoke them or attempt to drive them away, lest they should set upon us and kill us to a man by force of numbers.

They scrambled up the masts, gnawing the cables with their teeth and biting them to shreds. Then they seized the helm and steered the vessel to their island. When the ship had run ashore, the dwarfs carried us one by one to the beach, and, promptly pushing off again, climbed on board and sailed away.

Disconsolately we set out to search for food and water, and by good fortune came upon some fruit trees and a running stream. Here we refreshed ourselves, and then wandered about the island until at length we saw far off among the trees a massive building, where we hoped to pass the night in safety. Drawing nearer, we found that it was a towering palace surrounded by a lofty wall, with a great ebony door which stood wide open. We entered the spacious courtyard, and to our surprise found it deserted. In one corner lay a great heap of bones, and on the far side we saw a broad bench, an open oven,

pots and pans of enormous size, and many iron spits for roasting.

Exhausted and sick at heart, we lay down in the courtyard and were soon overcome by sleep. At sunset we were awakened by a noise like thunder. The earth shook beneath our feet and we saw a colossal black giant approaching from the doorway. He was a fearsome sight—tall as a palm tree, with red eyes burning in his head like coals of fire; his mouth was a dark well, with lips that drooped like a camel's loosely over his chest, whilst his ears, like a pair of large round discs, hung back over his shoulders; his fangs were as long as the tusks of a boar and his nails were like the claws of a lion.

The sight of this monster struck terror to our hearts. We cowered motionless on the ground as we watched him stride across the yard and sit down on the bench. For a few moments he eyed us one by one in silence; then he rose and, reaching out towards me, lifted me up by the neck and began feeling my body as a butcher would a lamb. Finding me little more than skin and bone, however, he flung me to the ground and, picking up each of my companions in turn, pinched and prodded them and set them down until at last he came to the captain.

Now the captain was a corpulent fellow, tall and broad-shouldered. The giant seemed to like him well. He gripped him as a butcher grips a fatted ram and broke his neck under his foot. Then he thrust an iron spit through his body from mouth to backside and, lighting a great fire in the oven, carefully turned his victim round and round before it. When the flesh was finely roasted, the ogre tore the body to pieces with his fingernails as though it were a pullet, and devoured it limb by limb, gnawing the bones and flinging them against the wall. The monster then stretched himself out on the bench and soon

---

3. **spans:** A span was a measurement equal to nine inches, based on the distance between the extended thumb and little finger.

fell fast asleep. His snores were as loud as the grunts and gurgles that issue from the throat of a slaughtered beast.

Thus he slept all night, and when morning came he rose and went out of the palace, leaving us half-crazed with terror.

As soon as we were certain that the monster had gone, we began lamenting our evil fortune. "Would that we had been drowned in the sea or killed by the apes!" we cried. "That would surely have been better than the foul death which now awaits us! But that which Allah has ordained must surely come to pass."

Illustration by Edmund Dulac from *Sinbad the Sailor and Other Stories*.

We left the palace to search for some hiding place, but could find no shelter in any part of the island, and had no choice but to return to the palace in the evening. Night came, and with it the black giant, announcing his approach by a noise like thunder. No sooner had he entered than he snatched up one of the merchants and prepared his supper in the same way as the night before. Then, stretching himself out to sleep, he snored the night away.

Next morning, when the giant had gone, we discussed our desperate plight.

"By Allah," cried one of the merchants, "let us rather throw ourselves into the sea than remain alive to be roasted and eaten!"

"Listen, my friends," said another. "We must kill this monster. For only by destroying him can we end his wickedness and save good Muslims from his barbarous cruelty."

This proposal was received with general approbation; so I rose in my turn and addressed the company. "If we are all agreed to kill this monster," I said, "let us first build a raft on which we can escape from this island as soon as we have sent his soul to damnation. Perchance our raft will take us to some other island, where we can board a ship bound for our country. If we are drowned, we shall at least escape roasting and die a martyr's death."

"By Allah," cried the others, "that is a wise plan."

Setting to work at once, we hauled several logs from the great pile of wood stacked beside the oven and carried them out of the palace. Then we fastened them together into a raft, which we left ready on the seashore.

In the evening the earth shook beneath our feet as the black giant burst in upon us, barking and snarling like a mad dog. Once more he seized upon the stoutest of my companions and prepared his meal. When he had eaten his fill, he stretched himself upon the bench as was his custom and soon fell fast asleep.

Noiselessly we now rose, took two of the great iron spits from the oven, and thrust them into the fire. As soon as they were red-hot we carried them over to the snoring monster and plunged their sharpened ends deep into his eyes, exerting our united weight from above to push them home. The giant gave a deafening shriek which filled our hearts with terror and cast us back on the ground many yards away. Totally blinded, he leapt up from the bench groping for us with outstretched hands, while we nimbly dodged his frantic clutches. In despair he felt his way to the ebony door and

THE COLOSSUS, FRANCISCO JOSÉ DE GOYA Y LUCIENTES. *Goya was one of the greatest painters of nineteenth-century Spain and, indeed, of Europe.*
Does Goya's Colossus match your own image of the giant in this tale? Why or why not?

staggered out of the yard, groaning in agonies of pain.

Without losing a moment we made off towards the beach. As soon as we reached the water we launched our raft and jumped aboard; but scarcely had we rowed a few yards when we saw the blind savage running towards us, guided by a foul hag of his own kind. On reaching the shore they stood howling threats and curses at us for a while, and then caught up massive boulders and hurled them at our raft with stupendous force. Missile followed missile until all my companions, save two, were drowned; but we three who escaped soon contrived to paddle beyond the range of their fury.

from the Third Voyage of Sindbad the Sailor   **643**

First Thoughts

What did you think of Sindbad as a hero? Does he rely more on strength or on intelligence? Did any of his actions surprise you?

Identifying Facts

1. How do Sindbad and his companions happen to land on the island?

2. What does the giant do to the captain and two other companions of Sindbad?

3. How do the sailors render the giant helpless to pursue them?

4. How do the survivors finally escape from the island?

Interpreting Meanings

1. What plot **complications** do Sindbad and his companions meet in this story? What is the story's **climax** and **resolution**?

2. Did you feel that Sindbad and his fellow sailors were realistic characters? Why or why not? Did their behavior ever seem unconvincing to you?

3. Some Arab scholars have dismissed *The Thousand and One Nights* as mere popular entertainment. They have argued that the tales are not great literature because the stories have crude and simplistic plots and no depth in characterization or theme. Do you agree with this assessment? Why or why not?

4. Which of Sindbad's qualities enable him to survive? Which of his qualities do not meet the heroic ideal?

Applying Meanings

If the storyteller Scheherazade had been telling this story to you, is there any point at which she would have lost your interest? Does the plot bog down at any point? Give Scheherazade a critique of her storytelling effort.

Creative Writing Response

Creating a Folktale. Imagine that you are a modern-day Scheherazade forced to tell intriguing stories night after night in order to save your life. What story would you tell that first night? Make up a brief folktale of your own about a modern hero who launches on an adventure and encounters many strange creatures. To help structure your tale, design a plot diagram like the one below, showing the different creatures your hero encounters. Be sure to include fantastic and imaginative details.

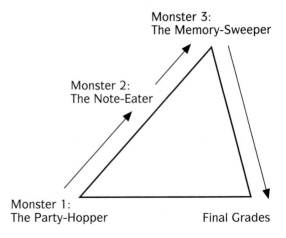

THE JOURNEY THROUGH FINAL EXAM WEEK

Monster 3: The Memory-Sweeper

Monster 2: The Note-Eater

Monster 1: The Party-Hopper

Final Grades

Critical Writing Response

Analyzing the Narrator as a Character. Sindbad's story is written from the **first-person point of view**. The character of a first-person narrator is revealed by what he or she says and does in the story, as well as by the way he or she reveals the actions of the other characters. Write an analysis of Sindbad's character. Cite specific details from the narrative to support your analysis.

BEHIND THE SCENES

A Thousand and One Nights of Inspiration

The stories in *The Thousand and One Nights*—especially the adventures of Sindbad, Ali Baba, Aladdin, and the enchanting storyteller, Scheherazade—have inspired many artists. An example is classical composer Rimsky-Korsakov's symphonic suite *Scheherazade,* which was produced by the noted Russian ballet master, Sergei Diaghilev, in 1910. It also became the score for an animated sequence in the film *Invitation to the Dance.*

The great French artist Henri Matisse (1869–1954) produced "The Thousand and One Nights," a series of charming paper cutouts based on the tales. A number of other artists, including the Russian painter Marc Chagall (1889–1985), have also used the tales as a subject for their work.

Several classic swashbuckler movies of the 1930s and 1940s were loosely based on the adventures of the Arabian Nights heroes. These films include *The Thief of Baghdad* (1940) and *Sinbad the Sailor* (1947). Many more recent films, such as *The Seventh Voyage of Sinbad the Sailor* (1958) and *Sinbad and the Eye of the Tiger* (1977) have brought the fantastic elements of these tales to life with special effects technology.

Look around for examples of the influence of *The Thousand and One Nights* on the arts. You may find examples in advertisements, on the covers of recordings, in art books, and in popular novels. Find out what aspect of the Arabian Nights tales might have inspired the artist, what tales the work refers to, and what fantastic elements the work contains. You may wish to look up the original stories that inspired the modern work. Share your findings with the class. If you like, create your own story, poem, drawing, or other artwork inspired by *The Thousand and One Nights*.

From "The Thousand and One Nights," a collection of cut-paper illustrations by Henri Matisse.

Introduction

The *Shahname:* The Epic of Persia

The *Shahname* (shä·nä·me'), or *Book of Kings*, is an epic poem of more than 60,000 **couplets**, or rhymed pairs of lines. Unlike the *Odyssey* or the *Aeneid*, the *Shahname* does not tell a single story or have a single hero. Instead, it is organized according to a

---

couplet: *a consecutive pair of rhymed lines.*

---

loose chronological sequence of dynasties—some of them mythical, some historical—tracing the line of Persian kings back to the beginning of time.

The Contents of the *Shahname*

The *Shahname* begins with a description of the creation of the world. According to Persian mythology, in the thousand years after creation there arose a line of hero-kings, or *shahs,* who struggled against the forces of darkness to bring civilization to the Persian people.

A large part of the poem centers on the warfare between Iran and nearby Turan, an area of central Asia from which Turkish nomads repeatedly invaded Iran. The mythical hero in this centuries-long battle was Rostám

(rō·stam'), an Iranian warrior of supernatural strength and skill, who reappears periodically over a period of three hundred years to drive back the Turks.

Francis Bartlett Donation of 1912 and Picture Fund, Courtesy Museum of Fine Arts, Boston

Page from a manuscript of the *Shahname.* *Different scripts are used in this ornately calligraphed manuscript, which shows Ferdowsi's text in the center rectangular area, surrounded by commentary in the margins.*
? *What does the ornateness of this manuscript page suggest about the importance of the Shahname to Persian culture?*

The Origin of the *Shahname*

Before the ninth century A.D., there was no lyric or epic poetry written in Persian, the native language of Iran. Only Arabic was used, for Arabs had ruled Iran since the Islamic conquest of A.D. 641. But when new rulers, the Samanids (sə·män·idz'), took over from the previous Arab rulership in Iran in A.D. 875, they encouraged the revival of Persian language and culture.

The Samanid rulers commissioned the court poet Dakiki to compile all the scattered stories of Iran's splendid past into a national epic. Dakiki never finished this monumental undertaking; he died after composing only a thousand lines.

The Poet Ferdowsi (c. 940–1020)

Dakiki's unfinished work was taken up by the poet Abol-Qasem Mansur ebn Ebrahim Hasan, known as Ferdowsi (fer·dō·sē'), meaning "Heavenly One." Ferdowsi labored over the epic for the next thirty-five years. He wrote his epic in the "pure" grammar and vocabulary of spoken Persian, avoiding all Arabic words and phrases that had flooded the Persian language.

By the time Ferdowsi finally finished the *Shahname*, the Samanid dynasty had been overthrown. But the new ruler, Mahmud (mä·mōod'), also encouraged the use of the Persian language and was an enthusiastic supporter of the arts. He offered to pay Ferdowsi fifty thousand gold pieces upon completion of the *Shahname*. But, for unknown reasons, Mahmud paid Ferdowsi less than half what the poet had been promised. Disgrun-

The Granger Collection, New York

Detail of manuscript page depicting the poet Ferdowsi (left).

tled, Ferdowsi supposedly gave his payment away to a bath attendant and a street vendor, thus openly displaying his contempt for Mahmud. Then he left Mahmud's court and made his way to the court of a Persian prince named Shareyar (shä'rē·yär), offering to dedicate the poem to him instead of Mahmud. The tactful prince persuaded Ferdowsi to leave the poem's dedication as it was— to Mahmud—and he paid Ferdowsi five times more than the poet had received from Mahmud.

The Legacy of the *Shahname*

Often considered the greatest of the Persian poets, Ferdowsi is credited with preserving the history of Persia and rescuing the Persian language from possible extinction. From his time to the present, no work of Persian literature has been more widely read and admired than the *Shahname*, and no work has done more to shape the Persians'—now the Iranians'—sense of their national identity.

Reader's Guide

from THE TRAGEDY OF SOHRÁB AND ROSTÁM
from the Shahname

Background

This selection from the *Shahname* tells of the battle between the Iranian hero Rostám (rō·stam') and Sohráb (sō·räb'), a young warrior from Turan. Sohráb is Rostám's son, the result of a single encounter some years before between Rostám and Tamine (ta·mē·ne'), a Turanian princess. Tamine has told Sohráb that the great Iranian hero Rostám is his real father. Under his armor, Sohráb wears the seal that Rostám had given to Tamine to bestow on their child as proof of his paternity. But because Tamine had told Rostám that his child was a daughter, Rostám does not know he has a son.

When the armies of Turan and Iran meet, Sohráb hopes to reveal himself to Rostám as his son by challenging the now aging warrior to hand-to-hand combat. Rostám agrees to fight, but out of pride he chooses to appear in unmarked armor and refuses to reveal his name.

Although Sohráb feels that the man he is to fight in one-on-one combat is Rostám, he cannot be entirely sure. For his part, Rostám suspects that the young Turanian favorite is his son, but he rejects the idea. At last father and son meet on the field of battle. Their first duel takes an entire day and ends in a draw when night falls. At dawn they meet again, and in this second encounter Sohráb is almost victorious, but Rostám tricks Sohráb into letting him go. After Rostám regains his strength, the two heroes meet again for a final encounter.

Writer's Response

What do you predict will be the outcome of this fateful meeting between father and son?

Literary Focus

Irony is the contrast between what is expected and what actually happens. **Dramatic irony** occurs when the audience knows something important about a situation that a character in the story does not know. In "The Tragedy of Sohráb and Rostám," dramatic irony is created when Rostám and Sohráb go into battle not knowing that they are father and son.

648 Persian and Arabic Literatures

from THE TRAGEDY OF SOHRÁB AND ROSTÁM

from the Shahname

Ferdowsi

translated by

JEROME W. CLINTON

> *Pay attention to the animal imagery that is used to describe the two heroes as they battle. What do these comparisons to animals suggest about the Persians' views of their heroes?*

Again they firmly hitched their steeds, as ill-
Intentioned fate revolved above their heads.
Once more they grappled hand to hand. Each seized
The other's belt and sought to throw him down.
5   Whenever evil fortune shows its wrath,
It makes a block of granite soft as wax.
Sohráb had mighty arms, and yet it seemed
The skies above had bound them fast. He paused
In fear; Rostám stretched out his hands and seized
10   That warlike leopard by his chest and arms.
He bent that strong and youthful back, and with
A lion's speed, he threw him to the ground.
Sohráb had not the strength; his time had come.
Rostám knew well he'd not stay down for long.
15   He swiftly drew a dagger from his belt
And tore the breast of that stout-hearted youth.
He writhed upon the ground; groaned once aloud,
Then thought no more of good and ill. He told
Rostám, "This was the fate allotted me.
20   The heavens gave my key into your hand.
It's not your fault. It was this hunchback fate,
Who raised me up then quickly cast me down.
While boys my age still spent their time in games,

Star tile depicting the battle of Sohráb and Rostám. *Because the* Shahname *is vital to Persian culture, key scenes from the epic are often depicted in such decorative pieces as pottery and tiles.*

Walters Art Gallery, Baltimore

My neck and shoulders stretched up to the clouds.
25   My mother told me who my father was.
My love for him has ended in my death.
Whenever you should thirst for someone's blood,
And stain your silver dagger with his gore,
Then Fate may thirst for yours as well, and make
30   Each hair upon your trunk a sharpened blade.
Now should you, fishlike, plunge into the sea,
Or cloak yourself in darkness like the night,
Or like a star take refuge in the sky,
And sever from the earth your shining light,
35   Still when he learns that earth's my pillow now,
My father will avenge my death on you.
A hero from among this noble band
Will take this seal and show it to Rostám.
'Sohráb's been slain, and humbled to the earth,'
40   He'll say, 'This happened while he searched for
          you.' "
     When he heard this, Rostám was near to faint.
The world around grew dark before his eyes.
And when Rostám regained his wits once more,
He asked Sohráb with sighs of grief and pain,
45   "What sign have you from him—Rostám? Oh, may
His name be lost to proud and noble men!"
"If you're Rostám," he said, "you slew me while
Some evil humor had confused your mind.
I tried in every way to draw you forth,
50   But not an atom of your love was stirred.
When first they beat the war drums at my door,
My mother came to me with bloody cheeks.°
Her soul was racked by grief to see me go.
She bound a seal upon my arm, and said,
55   'This is your father's gift, preserve it well.
A day will come when it will be of use.'
Alas, its day has come when mine has passed.
The son's abased before his father's eyes.
My mother with great wisdom thought to send
60   With me a worthy pahlaván° as guide.
The noble warrior's name was Zhende Razm,°
A man both wise in action and in speech.
He was to point my father out to me,
And ask for him among all groups of men.
65   But Zhende Razm, that worthy man, was slain.

Manuscript page from the *Shahname*.

New York Public Library Picture Collection

52. **bloody cheeks:** In Persian
poetry, weeping bloody tears
is the conventional image
used to indicate intense grief.

60. **pahlaván** (pa·la·vän′): hero;
warrior.
61. **Zhende Razm** (jən·də räzm′):
the aged warrior whom Ta-
mine had sent with Sohráb to
identify Rostám. During a
night reconnaissance he was
killed by Rostám.

650   Persian and Arabic Literatures

And at his death my star declined as well.
Now loose the binding of my coat of mail,
And look upon my naked, shining flesh."
When he unloosed his armor's ties and saw
70   That seal, he tore his clothes and wept.
"Oh, brave and noble youth, and praised among
All men, whom I have slain with my own hand!"
He wept a bloody stream and tore his hair;
His brow was dark with dust, tears filled his
          eyes.
75   Sohráb then said, "But this is even worse.
You must not fill your eyes with tears. For now
It does no good to slay yourself with grief.
What's happened here is what was meant to be."
      When the radiant sun had left the sky,
80   And Tahamtán° had not returned to camp,
Some twenty cavaliers rode off to see
How matters stood upon the field of war.
They saw two horses standing on the plain,
Both caked with dirt. Rostám was somewhere
          else.
85   Because they did not see his massive form
Upon the battlefield and mounted on
His steed, the heroes thought that he'd been
          slain.
The nobles all grew fearful and perplexed.
They sent a message swiftly to the shah,
90   "The throne of majesty has lost Rostám."
From end to end the army cried aloud,
And suddenly confusion filled the air.
Kavús° commanded that the horns and drums
Be sounded, and his marshal, Tus, approached.
95   Then Kavús spoke, "Be quick, and send a scout
From here to view the battlefield
And see how matters stand with bold Sohráb.
Must we lament the passing of Irán?
If by his hand the brave Rostám's been slain,
100   Who from Irán will dare approach this foe?
We now must strike a wide and general blow;
We dare not tarry long upon this field."
      And while a tumult rose within their camp,
Sohráb was speaking thus with Tahamtán,
105   "The situation of the Turks has changed

80. **Tahamtán** (ta·ham·tan'): an epithet for Rostám, meaning "huge body." Rostám was so large at birth that he had to be delivered by magic.

93. **Kavús** (ka·vōōs'): the shah of Iran.

In every way, now that my days are done.
Be kind to them, and do not let the shah
Pursue this war or urge his army on.
It was for me the Turkish troops rose up,
110   And mounted this campaign against Irán.
I it was who promised victory, and I
Who strove in every way to give them hope.
They should not suffer now as they retreat.
Be generous with them, and let them go."
115   Rostám then mounted Rakhsh,° as swift as
            dust.
He eyes bled tears, his lips were chilled with
    sighs.
He wept as he approached the army's camp,
His heart was filled with pain at what he'd done.
When they first spied his face, the army of Irán
120   Fell prostrate to the earth in gratitude,
And loudly praised the Maker of the World,
That he'd returned alive and well from war.
But when they saw him thus, his chest and
            clothes
All torn, his body heavy and his face
125   Begrimed by dust, they asked him all at once,
"What does this mean? Why are you sad at
            heart?"
He told them of his strange and baffling deed,
Of how he'd slain the one he held most dear.
They all began to weep and mourn with him,
130   And filled the earth and sky with loud lament.

At last he told the nobles gathered there,
"It seems my heart is gone, my body too.
Do not pursue this battle with the Turks.
The evil I have done is quite enough."

115. **Rakhsh** (raksh): Rostám's horse. He is the only horse large and strong enough to carry Rostám. He is described in the epic as an elephant to indicate both his size and his warlike qualities.

Seventeenth-century Iranian helmet with chain mail.
This ornate steel helmet is inscribed with both hunting scenes and the names of heroes from the Shahname.
? *What lessons might Persian warriors have learned from the story of Sohráb and Rostám? Do you think they would have found the story inspiring, cautionary, or both?*

Courtesy of The Arthur M. Sackler Museum, Harvard University, Cambridge, Massachusetts, Gift of John Goelet

First Thoughts

Would you change the outcome of this story if you could? How?

Identifying Facts

1. How does Rostám learn Sohráb's identity?
2. How does Rostám react to the discovery that he has killed his son?
3. Why doesn't Sohráb blame Rostám for his death?
4. What is Sohráb's dying wish? How does Rostám honor it?

Interpreting Meanings

1. Sohráb declares that what happens to him is the work of fate—in other words, it was meant to be and could not be avoided. Do you agree? What factors besides fate might have led to the outcome?
2. Readers are aware, as Rostám is not, that Sohráb is Rostám's son. How does this **dramatic irony** heighten the tragic aspect of this episode?
3. For which of the characters do you feel a greater sympathy—Sohráb or Rostám? Why?
4. How might the final outcome of the battle between Sohráb and Rostám make Sohráb's death seem less pointless?

Applying Meanings

Sometimes we reconsider a first reaction to a situation after we have looked at it more carefully. Look back at your response to "First Thoughts." Would you still change the outcome of the story? Why or why not?

Creative Writing Response

Writing a Diary Entry. How do you think Rostám's life changes after the death of his son? Does he enter into a depression from which he never recovers, gain wisdom and compassion from his experience, or become old and embittered? Does he approach life differently? Imagine that you are Rostám in old age, recording the events of your life in a diary. How did you feel after you learned that you had killed your own son? Did you feel that the entire tragic episode was senseless? Did you find any comfort as time went on? Write several paragraphs of Rostám's diary entry, using the **first-person point of view**.

Speaking and Listening

Creating a News Report. Imagine that you are a television war correspondent reporting on the duel between Sohráb and Rostám. Write a report to be delivered on the evening news after the death of Sohráb. Be sure to identify yourself and include background information about the war and the two heroes, along with a description of their final battle. Remember also to report on the peace that resulted from the duel. End with a brief comment offering perspective on the whole situation. Deliver your report to the class.

Omar Khayyám
C. A.D. 1048–1131

TWO LOVERS LANDING ON THE ISLAND OF TERRESTRIAL BLISS, **Persian, 1556–1565.**

The poet Ghiyasoddin Abolfat'h Omar ebn Ebrahim is known as "Omar Khayyám" (kī·yäm′), which means "Omar, the tentmaker." Khayyám, however, was not a tentmaker, but a scholar whose knowledge extended to an amazing variety of disciplines. Not only was he thoroughly familiar with the works of Greek philosophers, but he also understood the sciences of his day, including medicine and astronomy. He was also an excellent mathematician.

While still in his twenties, he wrote a scholarly paper on algebra in which he showed how to solve a kind of problem no one had ever been able to solve before. Another paper, on elementary geometry, helped advance the knowledge of numbers. He was also one of a group of astronomers who revised the Islamic calendar. The calendar Khayyám and his colleagues produced was unmatched in accuracy until the Gregorian calendar was developed in the West almost five hundred years later.

Impressive as these achievements were, Westerners know of Omar Khayyám today not because of his work in science, but because he wrote a number of four-line verses of poetry, called *rubá'i* (r$\overline{oo}$·bä·ī′), a Persian poetic form. The poet behind the verses is a somewhat mysterious figure. It was not until the 1940s that researchers determined the dates of his birth and death. None of his poetry came to light until well after his death. And although hundreds of these four-line verses have been attributed to Omar Khayyám, scholars have so far been able to confirm his authorship of only a few of them.

In Persia, Omar Khayyám's verses enjoyed only modest popularity. But in the 1850s, an English poet and translator named Edward FitzGerald (1809–1883) was struck by the poetic beauty of the rubáiyát (the plural form of rubá'i) and began translating them into English. It was FitzGerald's translation that brought Khayyám worldwide fame as a poet over seven hundred years after he died.

Reader's Guide

from the RUBÁIYÁT

Background

Omar Khayyám's birthplace, the region of Khorasan, or "the land of the sun," is now divided between Iran and Afghanistan. In the poet's day it lay at the crossroads of trade and travel between Asia and Europe and therefore was a bustling and cosmopolitan area. Merchants and travelers from all over the world passed through the region, enriching the native Persian culture with artistic and philosophical influences from China, India, and classical Greece.

But during Khayyám's lifetime, Khorasan was repeatedly attacked and then ruled by a Turkic people called the Seljuks (sel'jooks'). The Seljuk Turks brought with them an authoritarian and religiously orthodox rule. Muslim orthodoxy prohibited wine and other sensual pleasures that Khayyám so clearly enjoyed. His verse, with its focus on the sweetness and pleasure of life, gently challenged the repression of the times.

Writer's Response

Omar Khayyám's *Rubáiyát* expresses that earthly life is good and to be enjoyed fully. The poet argues that it is foolish to postpone pleasure until another day because the opportunity may never repeat itself. You have met this *carpe diem* motif previously in the *Epic of Gilgamesh* and in the poems of Horace. Do you agree with this view of life? Jot down your reasons for agreeing or disagreeing.

Literary Focus

Rubá'i—rubáiyát (roo'bī·yät') in the plural—is the Persian word for **quatrain**, or four-line verse. In English translation, the standard form for rubáiyát is that the first, second, and last lines rhyme. The third line usually does not rhyme with the other three. The rubá'i is an ancient literary form that Persian poets have used to express their thoughts on diverse subjects. Because a rubá'i is so short and its rhyme scheme so restrictive, it often makes use of metaphor or imagery to express its meaning.

from the RUBÁIYÁT

Omar Khayyám

translated by

EDWARD FITZGERALD

Rubáiyát are often epigrams—*short, witty comments in verse form. Omar Khayyám wrote each rubá'i as a separate poem, but he repeats his major ideas. As you read, note the thoughts that are expressed most frequently in these poems.*

1

Wake! For the Sun, who scattered into flight
The Stars before him from the Field of Night,
   Drives Night along with them from Heav'n
     and strikes
The Sultán's Turret with a Shaft of Light.

7

Come, fill the Cup, and in the fire of Spring
Your Winter-garment of Repentance fling:
   The Bird of Time has but a little way
To flutter—and the Bird is on the Wing.

12

A Book of Verses underneath the Bough,
A Jug of Wine, a Loaf of Bread—and Thou
   Beside me singing in the Wilderness—
Oh, Wilderness were Paradise enow![1]

1. **enow** (ē·nou′): enough (archaic).

13

Some for the Glories of This World; and some
Sigh for the Prophet's[2] Paradise to come;
   Ah, take the Cash, and let the Credit go,
Nor heed the rumble of a distant Drum!

2. **Prophet's:** Mohammed's.

17

Think, in this battered Caravanserai[3]
Whose Portals are alternate Night and Day,
    How Sultán after Sultán with his Pomp
Abode his destined Hour, and went his way.

3. **Caravanserai** (kar'ə·van'sə·rī'): inns providing services for caravans.

19

I sometimes think that never blows so red
The Rose as where some buried Caesar bled;
    That every Hyacinth[4] the Garden wears
Dropped in her Lap from some once lovely Head.

4. **Hyacinth** (hī'ə·sinth'): In classical mythology, the hyacinth sprang up from the blood of Hyacinthus after he was accidentally killed by Apollo. In the *Odyssey*, locks of hair are compared to clusters of hyacinth.

24

Ah, make the most of what we yet may spend,
Before we too into the Dust descend;
    Dust into Dust, and under Dust to lie
Sans[5] Wine, sans Song, sans Singer, and—sans End!

5. **Sans** (sanz): without (French).

27

Myself when young did eagerly frequent
Doctor and Saint, and heard great argument
    About it and about: but evermore
Came out by the same door where in I went.

28

With them the seed of Wisdom did I sow,
And with mine own hand wrought to make it grow;
    And this was all the Harvest that I reaped—
"I came like Water, and like Wind I go."

71

The Moving Finger writes; and, having writ,
Moves on: nor all your Piety nor Wit
    Shall lure it back to cancel half a Line,
Nor all your Tears wash out a Word of it.

Giraudon/Art Resource, New York

Persian manuscript page. *Persian miniatures, or illuminated manuscript pages, are known for their ornate detail, jewel-like colors, and fantastic details of court and battle scenes, people in nature, and plants and animals.*

72

And that inverted Bowl they call the Sky,
Whereunder crawling cooped we live and die,
    Lift not your hands to *It* for help—for It
As impotently moves as you or I.

96

Yet Ah, that Spring should vanish with the Rose!
That Youth's sweet-scented manuscript should close!
    The Nightingale that in the branches sang,
Ah whence, and whither flown again, who knows!

99

Ah Love! could you and I with Him conspire
To grasp this sorry Scheme of Things entire,
    Would not we shatter it to bits—and then
Remold it nearer to the Heart's Desire!

100

Yon rising Moon that looks for us again—
How oft hereafter will she wax and wane;
    How oft hereafter rising look for us
Through this same Garden—and for *one* in vain!

101

And when like her, O Sákí,[6] you shall pass
Among the Guests Star-scattered on the Grass,
    And in your joyous errand reach the spot
Where I made One—turn down an empty Glass!

TAMÁM[7]

6. **Sákí** (sä′kē): wine-bearer (Persian).

7. **Tamám:** finished, complete (Persian).

First Thoughts

What were your first reactions to Omar Khayyám's rubáiyát? Did any of them make a particular impression on you? If so, which ones?

Identifying Facts

1. In verse 12, what does the speaker say would be "Paradise enow" for him?

2. In verse 99, what does the speaker say that he and his love would do if they could?

Interpreting Meanings

1. Paraphrase verse 99. What ironic twist does the speaker give his thoughts? What other verses seem to you to express a similar idea?

2. The theme of *carpe diem* (seize the day) also appears in the Gilgamesh epic and in the poems of Horace. Does Omar Khayyám express the *carpe diem* idea in the same way as the *Epic of Gilgamesh* and the works of Horace, or do their attitudes differ?

3. Verse 24 is a particularly good example of a **rubá'i,** a four-line poem that expresses an idea in a brief, witty style, often with a twist at the end. What is the speaker in verse 24 saying about life and death? How does the ending of the poem provide a clever twist?

4. In verse 71, what is the "Moving Finger"? State the meaning of the verse in your own words. What does it imply about how one should live life?

Applying Meanings

Khayyám's *Rubáiyát* has been consistently in print since FitzGerald's translation in the 1850s. If you were a bookseller, would you order copies of the book to sell to your customers? Do you think there is an audience for the book today? Why or why not?

Creative Writing Response

Writing a Rubá'i. Imagine that you are a new Omar Khayyám, celebrating life in your own hometown in the 1990s. Using some of your favorite images and simple metaphors, write a four-line poem in praise of living each day fully. Try to follow the pattern of Omar Khayyám's rubáiyát, in which the first, second, and fourth lines rhyme.

Critical Writing Response

Interpreting a Poet's Philosophy. A hedonist makes pleasure-seeking a way of life. A pessimist expects the worst to happen. Omar Khayyám has been called both a hedonist and a pessimist. Do you think it is possible to be both at the same time? In an essay of three to four paragraphs, cite passages from the *Rubáiyát* that support your point of view. Organize your ideas by jotting down evidence on a chart like the following one.

Hedonist		Pessimist	
rubá'i #	ideas/ phrases	rubá'i #	ideas/ phrases

THE ART OF TRANSLATION

Two Translations of the Rubáiyát

Edward FitzGerald's translation of the *Rubáiyát of Omar Khayyám* has been called the most famous translation of a literary work into English. Other translations of Omar Khayyám's work have been made, but none has gained the popularity or fame of FitzGerald's, although most scholars agree that the other versions are more literally true to the original. The selections you have just read were taken from FitzGerald's fifth and final version of the *Rubáiyát*.

FitzGerald considered himself a "free translator" who focused on what he felt to be the meaning and spirit of the poetry,

Illustration by Edmund Dulac from the *Rubáiyát of Omar Khayyám. In the late nineteenth and early twentieth centuries, the popularity of the* Rubáiyát *in English-speaking countries led publishers to create many beautifully illustrated versions of the work.*

rather than on the literal meaning of the words. He wanted English readers to respond to the rubáiyát as he imagined the readers of the originals might have responded. Therefore, he used contemporary images that were more familiar to British readers to illustrate Omar Khayyám's ideas whenever the original imagery struck him as obscure.

Here is a translation by FitzGerald of a rubá'i:

> But helpless Pieces of the Game He
> plays
> Upon this Checker-board of Nights and
> Days;
> Hither and thither moves, and
> checks, and slays,
> And one by one back in the Closet lays.

This is a literal translation by A. J. Arberry of the same rubá'i:

> We are playthings, and heaven is the
> player—
> in very truth, not metaphorically: we play
> (our) little game on the board of exis-
> tence,
> (then) we fall back one by one into the
> box of non-existence.

1. What images does FitzGerald use instead of Arberry's "playthings," "heaven," "little game on the board of existence," and "the box of non-existence"?
2. Do you prefer FitzGerald's verse translation or Arberry's literal translation? Explain your choice.

Rumi
A.D. 1207–1273

New York Public Library

Jalāl ad-Dīn Mohammed ebn Moham-med, known as Rumi (rōō′mē), was born in Balkh, in the province of Khorasan, now divided between modern Afghanistan and Iran. His father was a famous teacher and mys-tic—one who believes that God's truth comes not through learning or through the senses, but through flashes of enlightenment.

Rumi grew up to practice Sufism (sōō′fiz′ əm), a mystical form of Islam. Sufis stress the importance of understanding God through personal intuition. By 1240, Rumi's fame as a Sufi teacher had spread throughout the region, and he had gathered about him a group of followers, or disciples.

The turning point in Rumi's life, however, was his relationship with the wandering holy man Shams ad-Dīn ("Sun of Religion"), whom he met in 1244. To Rumi, Shams seemed a nearly perfect example of beauty and truth, and the two mystics became in-separable. However, one night in 1247 Shams mysteriously disappeared. Research-ers have recently established that the holy man was murdered and hurriedly buried close to a well that still exists in Konya. It is believed that followers of Rumi—perhaps with the consent of Rumi's own sons—com-mitted the murder because they were jealous of Shams' relationship with their master. As-suming Shams had abandoned him, Rumi turned to poetry for consolation and wrote a collection of lyrics and odes, the *Divan-i-Shams-i-Tabrizi.* Rumi signed Shams' name to the poems in honor of his beloved friend and in keeping with the Sufi belief that he and Shams were one in spirit.

Rumi's prose work fills three volumes, but he is most famous for a volume of poetry entitled the *Masnavi.* This didactic epic of 26,000 couplets—pairs of rhyming lines—written in informal, colloquial language, de-fines Sufi teachings. Interspersed with the teachings are quotations from the Koran, stories of the life and teachings of Mo-hammed, legends of pre-Islamic poets and prophets, Arabic versions of Sanskrit beast fables, and Near Eastern folktales. It has been said that Rumi's *Masnavi* is for Persians "second in importance only to the Koran."

Reader's Guide

UNMARKED BOXES

Background

The poet Rumi belonged to the branch of Islamic mysticism known as Sufism. Like mystics of other faiths, Sufis believe that knowledge and understanding of God come through personal experience of God, not through the senses or through study. The Sufis believe in the doctrine of *Vahdat-ol-Vojood,* or "the unity of all things." To Sufis, this means that all things profane (that is, impure or not holy) are, in fact, holy. Although this may sound contradictory, it is simply a way of saying that God is present in everything. For example, a rose, a profane object, may embody God's perfect beauty and therefore be sacred for what it represents. Sufi belief also suggests that all things and beings in the visible world are different only in form, for they are essentially one in God. Finally, the doctrine implies that God is at once present and absent—present because God resides in all beings, but absent because we do not directly perceive God through our five senses.

Oral Response

This poem begins with a statement of a comforting belief: "Don't grieve. Anything you lose comes round/ in another form." In other words, the things we think we lose—the carefree pleasures of early childhood, for example—are replaced by other pleasures, such as the privilege of getting a driver's license at age sixteen. What do you think of Rumi's idea? What things have you lost and gained throughout life?

Literary Focus

An **analogy** is a kind of comparison that explains something unfamiliar by describing it in terms of something familiar. For example, someone might draw an analogy between riding in a helicopter and an exciting fairground ride, such as a roller coaster. You might then understand that a helicopter lurches and dips, and you would know the feeling in your stomach that accompanies such a ride. Analogies can help to explain ideas and objects as well as experiences.

UNMARKED BOXES
Rumi
translated by
JOHN MOYNE AND COLEMAN BARKS

As you read Rumi's poem, note how he interprets the Sufi belief that all things are essentially one. According to this poem, what things and beings are manifestations, or physical evidence, of God?

Don't grieve. Anything you lose comes round
in another form. The child weaned from mother's milk
now drinks wine and honey mixed.

God's joy moves from unmarked box to unmarked box,
5   from cell to cell. As rainwater, down into
      flowerbed.
As roses, up from ground.
Now it looks like a plate of rice and fish,
now a cliff covered with vines,
now a horse being saddled.
10 It hides within these,
till one day it cracks them open.

Part of the self leaves the body when we sleep
and changes shape. You might say, "Last night
I was a cypress tree, a small bed of tulips,
15 a field of grapevines." Then the phantasm goes away.
You're back in the room.
I don't want to make anyone fearful.
Hear what's behind what I say.

Fa'ilatun fa'ilatun fa'ilatun fa'ilat.°
20 There's the light gold of wheat in the sun
and the gold of bread made from that wheat.
I have neither. I'm only talking about them,

as a town in the desert looks up
at stars on a clear night.

MYSTICAL JOURNEY. *How do the swirling, dreamlike shapes in this drawing suggest the theme of Rumi's poem?*

19. **Fa'ilatun . . . fa'ilat:** This line is composed of phrases used to indicate various types of poetic "feet." It is the equivalent of "iamb, iamb, iamb, trochee."

First Thoughts

Do you find Rumi's words comforting? Why or why not?

Identifying Facts

1. Why does the speaker say the reader should not grieve?
2. What, according to the speaker, does God's joy look like?

Interpreting Meanings

1. What does Rumi mean by "unmarked boxes"? Explain in your own words what the line "God's joy moves from unmarked box to unmarked box" means.
2. The first stanza suggests that nothing is ever lost; rather, things only change form. Which of the images in stanza 2 best express this idea? Can you think of other examples that illustrate the same idea?
3. In stanza 3, to what kind of sleep is Rumi referring? Explain your answer.
4. How has the poet used **analogy** to explain the idea that "anything you lose comes round in another form"? List the analogies the poet makes.

Applying Meanings

How does the idea that all things are in essence one relate to such modern-day concerns as ecology or recycling?

Creative Writing Response

Writing a Poem. Rumi points out the joy that can come from such everyday sights as a plate of rice and fish, a vine-covered cliff, or a horse being saddled. List some joyous moments that you have experienced. What **images** best capture your moments of joy? Use the images you've chosen and write a poem on the theme of recapturing the experience of joy. If you prefer, collect some favorite images from magazines and other sources and create a collage of "joyous moments."

Critical Writing Response

Analyzing the Poem's Meaning. In lines 17–18, the speaker says, "I don't want to make anyone fearful./Hear what's behind what I say." Why might the poet's words in this stanza make someone fearful? What comforting thought underlies the poet's words? Write a paragraph in which you explain the meaning of the third stanza.

Saadi
c. A.D. 1213–1292

New York Public Library

The poet Musharrif Oddin Muslih Oddin, known as Saadi (sä'dē), which means "fortunate" in Persian, spent much of his life as a wandering dervish, or holy man, moving from place to place, studying and practicing Sufi doctrine (see page 662). He had neither a home nor personal belongings, yet he somehow produced two of the great classics of Persian literature—the _Bustan (The Orchard)_ and the _Gulistan (The Rose Garden)_.

Scholars know only a few facts about Saadi's life. He was born in Shiraz, and his father died at an early age. He attended college at the Nizamiya Academy in Baghdad, where he received a classical Islamic education. A devout Sufi, he chose poverty and rootlessness as a way of life, wandering great distances. His books mention journeys to Central Asia and India, and it is believed that he made several religious pilgrimages to Mecca. On these journeys, he may have studied under the famous mystic Suhrawardi and met the poet Jalal al-Din Rumi, author of the _Masnavi_ (see page 661).

During Saadi's lifetime, the Middle East was in almost constant turmoil. Mongol armies swept down from the plains to the east, and crusaders from Western Europe, intent on claiming the lands around Jerusalem for Christianity, made war on the Islamic peoples. On a journey to North Africa, Saadi was captured by crusaders and held in Tripoli (now part of Libya) where he was forced to labor as a ditch digger. According to one story, he married the daughter of the man who paid his ransom, but the marriage was unhappy. Eventually, Saadi abandoned his wife and made his way back to Shiraz, where he enjoyed the patronage of the royal ruler Sa'd bin Zangi (sä'd bēn zän·jē'), whose first name he adopted as his own.

Saadi's work is greatly beloved by the Iranian people, and his place in Persian literature is firmly established. His stories and sayings seem simple and use plain language, but they express Sufi wisdom in a way that has won admiration from scholars and general readers alike. Because his work had such wide appeal, Saadi ensured the continuation of Sufi beliefs.

Reader's Guide

ANECDOTES AND SAYINGS OF SAADI

Background

Saadi's writings are notable for two reasons: First, their simple, direct language has made them an ideal textbook for beginning students of Persian. Second, although they consist primarily of only simple sayings and stories, they are considered some of the finest expressions of Sufi beliefs.

For Sufis, Sufism is not only a religion or a philosophy, but a way of life. Sufis are not attached to belongings and places, and they are not driven by concerns of time, money, or achievement. They concentrate instead on the development of the human mind and on reaching a higher plane of understanding than can be achieved through the senses. The achievement of Sufi understanding may be likened to the process of a child growing to adulthood—just as a child attains the wisdom of adulthood slowly, a person attains Sufi knowledge through a gradual process of thought and practice. Thus, Sufi mystics withdrew from the material world and devoted themselves to living a stark, homeless existence. As they wandered, they begged for a living and meditated on God's love. It is in their writing that mystics such as Saadi reached out to share their thoughts with the world at large.

Oral Response

What familiar sayings do you know and use? Do you ever say "If the shoe fits, wear it" or "No pain, no gain"? Have you ever considered what these sayings really mean? Brainstorm a list of such sayings with your classmates and discuss their meanings.

Literary Focus

Much of literature can be understood on more than one level. On the surface a story or saying may convey its meaning directly. However, many "simple" pieces of literature have an underlying meaning, or subtext. An **anecdote**, for example, may serve to illustrate an idea about human behavior in general. In the same way, an **aphorism**, or saying, may have wider meaning than is at first apparent. "Don't cry over spilt milk" is about more than milk: it is about not regretting something from the past that cannot be changed.

ANECDOTES AND SAYINGS OF SAADI

Saadi

translated by

IDRIES SHAH

Saadi uses brief anecdotes and aphorisms, or sayings, to convey Sufi thinking on many subjects. As you read the anecdotes and sayings that follow, think about the underlying meanings that each might have.

The Pearl

A raindrop, dripping from a cloud,
Was ashamed when it saw the sea.
"Who am I where there is a sea?" it said.
When it saw itself with the eye of humility,
A shell nurtured it in its embrace.

Learning

None learned the art of archery from me
Who did not make me, in the end, the target.

Conceit

He who has self-conceit in his head—
Do not imagine that he will ever hear the truth.

To Know One's Faults

In the eyes of the wise, the seeker of combat with an
elephant is not really brave.
Brave is he who says nothing unbecoming in wrath.
A lout abused a man who patiently said:
"O you of bright prospects: I am worse even than you say.
I know all my faults, while you do not know them."

Pearls.

What point is Saadi making in his poetic anecdote, "The Pearl"?

A Dervish. Dervishes are holy men who live by begging, often wandering from place to place. By denying themselves earthly comforts, they believe they can come closer to a spiritual reality.
? What does Saadi's anecdote "The Thief and the Blanket" reveal about the dervishes' approach to life?

Relative

A Lamp has no rays at all in the face of the sun;
And a high minaret[1] even in the foothills of a mountain
  looks low.

Information and Knowledge

However much you study, you cannot know without
  action.
A donkey laden with books is neither an intellectual
  nor a wise man.
Empty of essence, what learning has he—
  Whether upon him is firewood or book?

The Sick Man

Throughout the long night a man wept
At the bedside of a sick man.
When day dawned the visitor was dead—
And the patient was alive.

The Thief and the Blanket

A thief entered the house of a Sufi, and found nothing there. As he was leaving, the dervish[2] perceived his disappointment and threw him the blanket in which he was sleeping, so that he should not go away empty-handed.

The Destiny of a Wolf-cub

The destiny of a wolf-cub is to become a wolf, even if it is reared among the sons of men.

The Straight Path

I have never seen a man lost who was on a straight path.

---

1. **minaret** (min′ə·ret′): a tower attached to a mosque from which worshipers are called to prayer.
2. **dervish:** a member of any Muslim sect who lives a life of poverty and chastity. Some dervishes practice a whirling dance as a form of worship.

A Tree Freshly Rooted

A tree, freshly rooted, may be pulled up by one man on his own. Give it time, and it will not be moved, even with a crane.

The Dervish Under a Vow of Solitude

A dervish under a vow of solitude sat in a desert as a king passed with his retinue. Being in a special state of mind he took no notice, not even raising his head as the procession passed.

The king, emotionally overcome by his regal pretensions, was angry and said: "These wearers of the patchwork robe are as impassive as animals, possessing neither politeness nor due humility."

His vizier[3] approached the dervish, saying: "O dervish! The Sultan of the whole of the Earth has just passed by you. Why did you not pay the required homage?"

The dervish answered: "Let the Sultan look for homage from those who seek to benefit from his goodwill. Tell him, too, that kings are created for the protection of their subjects. Subjects are not created for the service of kings."

If You Cannot Stand a Sting

If you cannot stand a sting, do not put your finger in a scorpion's nest.

Ambition

Ten dervishes can sleep beneath one blanket; but two kings cannot reign in one land. A devoted man will eat half his bread, and give the other half to dervishes. A ruler may have a realm, but yet plot to overcome the world.

---

3. **vizier** (vi·zir'): a minister of state in the Ottoman Empire.

WHIRLING DERVISHES. As part of their worship, one order of dervishes, known as whirling dervishes, dance until they reach a state of ecstasy in which they experience a direct communion with Allah.

The Metropolitan Museum of Art, Rogers Fund, 1918 (17.81.4)

The Dervish in Hell

One night a king dreamt that he saw a king in paradise and a dervish in hell.

The dreamer exclaimed: "What is the meaning of this? I should have thought that the positions would be reversed."

A voice answered: "The king is in heaven because he respected dervishes. The dervish is in hell because he compromised with kings."

Heedless Man

Whoever gives advice to a heedless man is himself in need of advice.

The Fool and the Donkey

A foolish man was raving at a donkey. It took no notice. A wiser man who was watching said: "Idiot! The donkey will never learn *your* language—better that you should observe silence and instead master the tongue of the donkey."

Saadi's Visit to an Indian Temple, **seventeenth-century Persian miniature.**
Courtesy of The Arthur M. Sackler Museum, Harvard University, Cambridge, Massachusetts, Gift of Philip Hofer in honor of Stuart Cary Welch

First Thoughts

Which of these sayings had the most meaning for you? Why?

Identifying Facts

1. According to ''To Know One's Faults,'' who is brave in the eyes of the wise?

2. What is ironic, or unexpected, about the outcome of ''The Sick Man''?

3. In ''Heedless Man,'' what does a person need who gives advice to someone who does not listen?

Interpreting Meanings

1. Bearing in mind that a simple saying may have more than one level of interpretation, what do you think is the underlying meaning of ''The Straight Path''?

2. What does ''A Tree Freshly Rooted'' imply about the advantages of allowing something to ''take root''? When might pulling up something freshly rooted be advantageous?

3. In ''Learning,'' what does the speaker suggest about the wisdom of teaching the art of archery? To what might this **aphorism**, or saying, apply besides archery?

4. In ''Conceit,'' why will a person who is conceited ''never hear the truth''? What advice does this **aphorism** imply?

5. In ''Information and Knowledge,'' what does the speaker mean by ''you cannot know without action''? How would you sum up the difference between ''information'' and ''knowledge''?

6. What appears to be the **moral** of the **anecdote** ''The Dervish in Hell''?

Applying Meanings

The Sufis use the sayings and anecdotes of Saadi and others as teaching tools, urging people to meditate upon the deeper meanings contained in them. Do you think that such sayings and anecdotes are effective teaching devices? What did you learn from them?

Creative Writing Response

Writing a Saying. Saadi's saying ''If you cannot stand a sting, do not put your finger in a scorpion's nest'' is analogous to the English expression, ''If you can't stand the heat, stay out of the kitchen.'' Try creating two or three sayings of your own. Use Saadi's sayings, as well as sayings that you already know, as models.

Critical Writing Response

Comparing a Sufi Saying and a Zen Parable. Like Sufism, Zen (see page 589) is a system of belief that expresses complex ideas in simple ways. Read the Zen **parable** ''The Thief Who Became a Disciple'' (see page 593). Then compare and contrast that parable with ''The Thief and the Blanket.'' Discuss how the two tales are alike and different on the surface as well as how they are alike and different in underlying meaning.

WHERE THE MULLA GOES, LAUGHTER FOLLOWS

Heads up, everyone—here comes the Mulla Nasrudin (mul'ə näs·rä·dēn'), master philosopher and adviser to kings, wrapped in his patched cloak, plodding along on his small, gray donkey. As Nasrudin fans the world over know, wherever this unlikely wisdom figure goes, laughter is sure to follow.

> *Mulla made a business of riding his donkey across the border to the neighboring country daily, loading the panniers with straw. The border inspector, suspecting Mulla to be a smuggler, examined his panniers thoroughly every time but failed to find anything. Years later when Mulla retired, he happened to meet the old inspector.*
>
> *"Now that you have retired, Mulla, tell me whatever it was you smuggled so successfully."*
>
> *"Donkeys," answered Mulla.*

In one sense, no one yet has been able to catch Nasrudin. No one even knows whether he really lived, much less when or where. The tales of his exploits apparently originated in Persia. They may have been devised by the Sufis, who saw humor as a useful tool for bringing about enlightenment. Persian stories about the Mulla (the "Master") Nasrudin date from at least the thirteenth century, and, having traveled like Nasrudin himself, they are told today throughout the Near East. In Saudi Arabia, Nasrudin stories sometimes merge with jokes about an Arab prankster called Joha. In Turkey, Nasrudin has become the Hodja Nasr-ed-din, and the town of Eskishehir (Ak Shehir) is considered his birthplace. There, an annual Nasr-ed-din festival is held, while on a nearby hill the Hodja's "tomb" is shown off to tourists.

Stories originally told about Nasrudin appear, in altered form, in Europe as well. From Turkish folklore they slipped into Greek folklore, and from Greek into Italian. The tales also crop up in the written literature of several Western countries.

Nasrudin has crossed even the most rigid political boundaries at the most tension-filled times. During the 1960s, the Coral Gables High-Energy Physics Conference, in Florida, issued a report using Nasrudin tales to explain scientific concepts that would have been cumbersome, if not unintelligible, in ordinary prose. Around the same period, on the other side of the then-impenetrable Iron Curtain, the Soviet Union produced a film called *The Adventures of Nasrudin,* in which the Mulla repeatedly made fools of

Caricature portrait of a Mulla on a donkey.

wealthy capitalists. And almost simultaneously, in Communist China, a book of Nasrudin tales was published as part of a series of folklore studies.

Mulla's watch stopped working. He opened it and found a dead fly inside the springs.

"No wonder it stopped working," said Mulla. "The poor operator is dead!"

Perhaps Nasrudin has remained so popular, and has cut across so many cultural boundaries, precisely because he is, beneath his turban, that most universal of human figures: a clown. Clowns have always been great teachers, because humor is an ideal vehicle for conveying knowledge and insights painlessly and pleasurably—a fact Sufis know well.

A friend visiting Mulla from another town brought him a duck for a gift. Mulla broiled the duck and shared it with his friend. For a time Mulla kept having visitors who claimed they were friends of the friends of the friend who brought him the duck and asked him for a duck meal.

The last stranger who showed up claimed, "I am the friend of the friend of the friend of the friend of the friend who brought you the duck."

Inviting the stranger in, Mulla offered him a bowl of hot water.

"And what is this?" the guest inquired.

"This is the soup of the soup of the soup of the soup of the duck which my friend brought me as a gift," said Mulla.

Considering his seven centuries of popularity, his adaptability, and his continuing power to amuse, the odds are good that old Mulla Nasrudin will continue to amuse audiences the world over for a long time to come.

Translations of Mulla tales by Mehdi Nakosteen

MAINTAINING VERB TENSE CONSISTENCY

By writing, you can project your thoughts into the future; you can map out potential processes and make plans. The tenses of the verbs you use reflect the directions in which your thoughts move. Not only do verb tenses show whether you are dealing with the past, the present, or the future, they also show whether you are dealing with conjecture or fact. Unnecessary tense shifts, then, can distort your meaning.

Change verb tenses only to show changes in actual or relative time. In general, when you begin a passage using one tense, keep all verbs in that tense.

INCONSISTENT

Soon Sindbad *will grow* tired of idleness. Then he *sets* out to roam the world again.

CONSISTENT

Soon Sindbad *will grow* tired of idleness. Then he *will set* out to roam the world again.

In the corrected example, both verbs are in the future tense.

Using Correct Tense Sequences

Sometimes, of course, writers must change tenses to show changes in time. **Tense sequence**—the pattern of verb tenses in a sentence or a passage—usually follows common sense.

INCORRECT

Muslim scholars *consider The Thousand and One Nights* inferior literature, but the tales *delight* readers for centuries.

CORRECT

Muslim scholars *consider The Thousand and One Nights* inferior literature, but the tales *have delighted* readers for centuries.

The present perfect tense is used in the second part of the sentence to show that an action began in the past and continues into the present.

Exercise 1: Correcting Verb Tense Shifts

Correct the tense shift in each sentence.

1. At birth, Rostám was already so big that he has to be delivered by magic.

2. The *Shahname* recounts the life stories of several dynasties of kings; it was much more than a single story about a single hero.

3. When the giant thunders into the palace, he planned to roast and eat Sindbad and his companions.

4. Edward FitzGerald's translation of the *Rubáiyát* is not literally accurate; however, it preserved the spirit of Khayyám's poems.

5. FitzGerald's translation won great popularity within a few years after he has published it.

Special Problems with Tense Shifts

Some constructions create special verb tense problems. Study the examples below.

INCORRECT

Sohráb *would have escaped* death if he *would have recognized* Rostám sooner.

CORRECT

Sohráb *would have escaped* death if he *had recognized* Rostám sooner.

If the main clause in a sentence uses "would have," the dependent clause need only use "had."

Sentences expressing wishes that past events had turned out differently need not use "would" at all.

INCORRECT

Rostám *wished* that he *would have spared* his son's life.

CORRECT

Rostám *wished* that he *had spared* his son's life.

Exercise 2: Correcting Verb Tense Problems

Correct the tense shift, incorrect tense sequence, or other verb tense problem in each sentence.

1. Rostám repents his actions in killing Sohráb. He therefore ordered his army not to pursue war with the Turks.

2. The narrator in the *Rubáiyát* celebrated each moment and cautions readers not to waste time in useless regrets.

3. In his arrogance, the king wished that the dervish would have paid him homage.

4. Muslims believe that the Koran represents truths that the angel Gabriel revealed to Mohammed, and for centuries they consider it the word of God.

5. Al-Khansa would not be famous today if her brother would not have suffered an early and tragic death.

6. Saadi, who lived during the thirteenth century, writes, "The Destiny of a Wolf Cub," exploring the problem of nature versus nurture.

7. The work of Rumi is rich in mystical themes and images. It reflected the traditional Sufi way of viewing life.

8. The customs agents wished that they would have caught the Mulla.

9. Tales of the Mulla's exploits originated in the thirteenth century, and they continued to amuse readers ever since.

10. Mohammed founds Islam, and it remained a major religion today.

OBSERVING AND ANALYZING A PROCESS

Whose way of living appeals to you most? Poets and philosophers, religious leaders and everyday people have always tried to define "the good life." Omar Khayyám focuses on seizing the moment; Saadi and Rumi stress enlightenment; the Koran advocates charity and personal responsibility; and the tale of Sindbad shows the allure of a life of adventure. What approach represents your ideal life? How might you attain such a life?

Writing Assignment

In an informative essay, show what you think a good life is. Then trace the process by which you might achieve it. You may consider the general hallmarks of a fulfilling life, or you may concentrate on one aspect, perhaps an appealing location or a satisfying career. Describe your ideal lifestyle or an aspect of it, and detail the steps you imagine taking in order to reach it. In this essay you will use both description and process analysis.

Background

Much of the literature in this unit reflects a serious inquiry into the significance of life and the meaningful ways in which it can be led.

Review the selections and decide which works relate to your own concept of the good life. You may want to refer to these works as you plan and write your essay.

Prewriting

Focused Questioning. Write at least two sentences to answer each of the following questions as you reflect on your ideal life.

1. Whose lifestyle is especially appealing to you? What makes it so?
2. Which area would you most like to live in? Do you prefer the city or the country?
3. How do you define success? How could you achieve it? How important is it to you?
4. What is the difference between a job and a career? Which would you prefer?
5. How important are love and friendship? What kinds of friends make you happy? Do you foresee marriage and children?
6. What kind of old age will you have? How do you want to be remembered?

Now, choose the one or two questions that intrigue you most. Use them as the basis of a longer, focused freewriting.

Organizing Your Ideas. Review your freewriting and your answers to the preceding questions. Then, in a sentence, sum up your idea of a good life. Next, plan the chronology of your ideal life, constructing a time line like the one on page 677. Along

AGE	18 years old	25 years old	30 years old	40 years old	55 years old	68 years old	80 years old
EVENTS							

the timeline, write each relevant event that you foresee, using an arrow to specify the event's place in a time period.

Writing

Use these guidelines to draft your essay.

1. **Introductory Paragraph.** You might open with song lyrics, a brief anecdote, or several lines of dialogue that reflect your main idea about a good life. Perhaps a line from a work in this unit would be relevant. Lead into a description of one day, or even one hour, in the life you consider good, using specifics from your freewriting and from your observations of others who lead lives you admire. Use concrete, sensory details to show actions, places, objects, and emotions. End the paragraph with a thesis statement summing up your ideal life and the direction that will lead you to it.

2. **Body Paragraphs.** Explain in detail the main steps for achieving your ideal lifestyle. Use chronological order to organize, referring to your timeline for sequence. Your freewriting, and the thoughts and images it inspires, can be a source of specifics as you detail each step. Choose appropriate transitions (see page 56) to clarify the order of the events you foresee and the results you hope they will have.

3. **Concluding Paragraph.** You might conclude by offering a comment on the process you have traced, perhaps assessing its difficulties and its merits. Or you might project your thoughts even further into the future, reflecting on how you will feel, or what changes might occur, once you have attained the kind of life you hope for.

Evaluating and Revising

Use these questions to evaluate and revise your essay.

1. Does your first paragraph vividly describe the life you consider good?
2. Do your body paragraphs detail the steps that could lead to your ideal lifestyle?
3. Do transitions and chronological order make the process easy for readers to follow?
4. Does your conclusion reflect on the process you have traced or project your ideas further into the future?
5. Are your sentences varied in structure and grammatically correct?

Proofreading and Publishing

Proofread carefully, eliminating errors in mechanics, and make a final copy. Compile class essays into a *Book of the Future,* and devise a way to save it for class reunions after graduation.

EUROPE IN THE MIDDLE AGES

Fourteenth Century

NORWAY

SCOTLAND

IRELAND

Origins of Arthurian Legend

DENMARK

WALES

ENGLAND

(GERMANY

Salisbury
Canterbury

Origins of Nibelungen

Rhine River

Origins of Chanson de Geste

BRITTANY

Rheims
Paris

Holy Roman Empire

Seine River

Chartres

Danube

FRANCE

Atlantic Ocean

Troubadors

Avignon

PORTUGAL

SPAIN

(ITA

Barcelona

Mediterranean Sea

Muslim States

THE MIDDLE AGES

▼ **Time** ▼

A.D. 500–1500

▼ **Place** ▼

Europe

▼ **Literary Significance** ▼

The European Middle Ages lie between the classical era and the Renaissance. After the downfall of the Roman Empire, the Frankish king Charlemagne encouraged learning and innovation. Still, most people could not read, and most literature was oral. The oral literature of pre-Christian Europe during this period includes the epics *Beowulf* and the *Nibelungenlied,* as well as the Icelandic sagas, all of which were eventually written down. Christian Europe produced its own heroic tales in the form of saints' lives and *chansons de geste*—tales of heroic deeds that were sung by traveling minstrels. Romances such as Chrétien de Troyes's *Perceval* expressed the ideals of chivalry and courtly love that developed during the Middle Ages. By the late Middle Ages, the authority of feudalism and the Church began to decay. More and more people, not only the clergy, could read and had access to written materials. Writers like Geoffrey Chaucer and Dante Alighieri, writing in vernacular, or native, languages, reflected the new spirit of the age.

TIME LINE

The Middle Ages

LITERARY EVENTS

▼

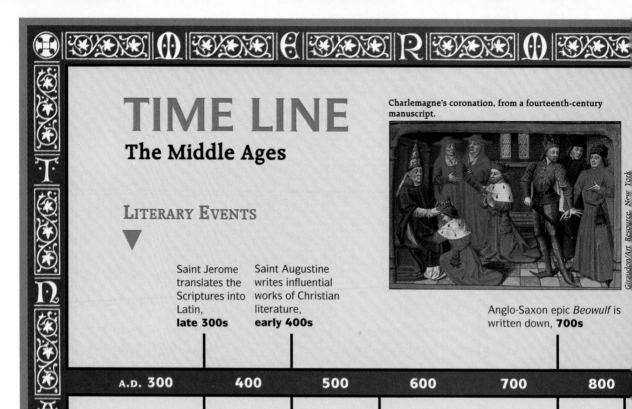

Charlemagne's coronation, from a fourteenth-century manuscript.

Giraudon/Art Resource, New York

Saint Jerome translates the Scriptures into Latin, **late 300s**

Saint Augustine writes influential works of Christian literature, **early 400s**

Anglo-Saxon epic *Beowulf* is written down, **700s**

A.D. 300	400	500	600	700	800

Christianity is proclaimed the official religion of the Roman Empire, **330**

Roman Empire splits into Eastern (or Byzantine) and Western Empires, **395**

Papacy is set up in Rome, **451**

Western Roman Empire falls to Germanic invaders, **476**

Foundations for modern European languages are laid, **late 400s**

Early Middle Ages; feudalism develops; the Christian church becomes the dominant power in Europe, **c. 500–c. 1000**

Moors invade and conquer Spain, **711–718**

Charlemag reigns as fi emperor o Holy Roma Empire, **800–814**

▲

CULTURAL AND HISTORICAL EVENTS

PEASANTS' DANCE, PIETER BRUEGHEL THE ELDER.

Scala/Art Resource, New York

vo knights joust in a tournament.
ench manuscript illumination, 1499.

Song of Roland, French epic, **c. 1100s**

Geoffrey of Monmouth **(c. 1100–1154)**, *History of the Kings of Britain*

Marie de France perfects Breton *lai*, a French poetic form, **c. 1160–c. 1215**

French poet Chretien de Troyes **(c. 1135– c. 1190)**, *Perceval*

Poem of My Cid, Spanish epic, **c. 1140**

Beginnings of medieval drama, **900s**

Snorri Sturluson **(1179– 1241)**, *Prose Edda*

Romance of the Rose, French allegory of courtly love, **c. 1200**

Nibelungenlied, national epic of Germany, **c. 1200**

Notre Dame in Paris, one of the most famous Gothic cathedrals.

The Granger Collection, New York.

Dante Alighieri, *Divine Comedy,* **1308–1320**

Geoffrey Chaucer, *The Canterbury Tales,* **1387– 1400**

Everyman, morality play, **c. 1400s**

Sir Thomas Malory, *Morte d'Arthur* completed **1470**; published **1485**

00	**1000**	**1100**	**1200**	**1300**	**1400**

High Middle Ages; feudalism is the main system of economy and authority; classical Greek and Roman texts are rediscovered; cathedrals are built as cities grow, **c. 1000–c. 1300**

Norman conquest of England, **1066**

Crusades, **1096–1270**

Work of Roger Bacon **(c. 1214– 1292)** lays foundations for modern scientific method

Thomas Aquinas **(c. 1225–1274)**, theologian and philosopher, revolutionizes medieval thought

Late Middle Ages; feudal system begins to weaken; Church has internal divisions, **c. 1300–c. 1500**

Popes live in Avignon, France, during the Babylonian Captivity, **1305–1376**

John Wycliffe **(c. 1330– 1384)** urges Church reforms in England

Black Death begins to ravage Europe, **1374**

Rival popes feud over the papacy during the Great Schism, **1378– 1417**

Moors are driven out of Spain, **1492**

The Granger Collection, New York

Teacher and students at the University of Paris. Fourteenth-century manuscript illumination.

This border contains patterns and letters derived from illuminated manuscripts, which were created by Christian monks in monasteries throughout Europe.

Time Line   **681**

THE MIDDLE AGES

The period between A.D. 500 and A.D. 1500 in Europe is called the "Middle Ages," or the *medieval* (mē′ dē·ē′vəl) period. In one way, the term is useful, for the Middle Ages lie between the era of classical Greek and Roman culture and the later rebirth of classical values in the Renaissance. Although the medieval period has been perceived as a static, or unchanging, interval in history, it was in fact a dynamic time in which new political, economic, and cultural institutions emerged.

Chaos and Collapse: The End of Roman Culture

At the height of its glory in the second century A.D., the Roman Empire commanded all of the territory around the Mediterranean, as far east as modern-day Iran and as far north as Britain. But the size of Rome's territory had a great deal to do with its collapse. The central government could not defend its frontiers or maintain contact with isolated

> When the Roman Empire collapsed under its own weight, it broke into two parts: the Byzantine Empire in the East and the fragmented Western Empire in Europe.

outposts. The Roman Empire thus broke into two large pieces, the Eastern, or Byzantine (biz′ən·tēn′), and the Western. The **Byzantine Empire**, with its seat of government at Constantinople (now Istanbul), ruled Egypt, the eastern Mediterranean, Asia Minor, and the Balkans. Throughout

Illumination of the *Book of Kells*, a ninth-century manuscript created by Irish monks.

the Middle Ages, classical knowledge and culture lost in the West were preserved by the Byzantine Empire.

The **Western Empire** did not fare as well. It fell to invading Germanic tribes who gradually conquered the Roman Empire in the early fifth century A.D. The Lombards controlled Italy, and the Anglo-Saxons dominated Britain. The Franks established a kingdom in northern France and became strong supporters of Christianity. All of these Germanic tribes contributed to the later development of the mainstays of medieval European culture: knighthood, the feudal system, and the code of chivalry.

The Rise of Charlemagne

In 768, **Charlemagne** (shär′lə·mān′) became king of the Franks, and in 800 he became the first emperor of the new Holy Roman Empire. Although he could not read or write, Charlemagne encouraged scholarship, education, innovation in architecture, and expansion into new territories. Charlemagne's reign opened a new era of learning, for he ordered

> In A.D. **800**, Pope Leo III crowned Charlemagne as Holy Roman Emperor, and a new era of learning and expansion began in Europe.

classical Greek and Roman manuscripts to be collected, encouraged the development of a new system for writing Latin, and invited scholars to open schools. Charlemagne's splendid court was copied in other parts of Europe. The arts and architecture began to flourish, and many great cathedrals were raised to glorify God. Over the course of the next three hundred years, Charlemagne's heroic deeds became legendary. The story of his expedition against Muslims in Spain was written down as the *Song of Roland* (see page 692).

With Charlemagne's death in 814, his kingdom, which covered all of France and much of what is now Italy and eastern Europe, was split up among his three sons and invaded by Vikings. The legends and fierce deeds of the Vikings were chronicled in myths and sagas by the Icelandic poet **Snorri Sturluson** (see page 704), in the early eleventh century.

❝People of the Middle Ages existed under mental, moral, and physical circumstances so different from our own as to constitute almost a foreign civilization. **❞**

—A Distant Mirror,
Barbara Tuchman

Art Carolingien IX-X, Statue Equestre de Charlemagne, Louvre. © Photo R.M.N.

Statue of Charlemagne on horseback, ninth century. *As both a warrior king and supporter of the arts and education, Charlemagne transformed medieval Europe.*

Introduction **683**

> **❝** [Charlemagne] made attempts at writing, too, and was accustomed to surround his pillows on his bed with tablets and notebooks for this purpose, so that when he had any spare time he would train his hand to form letters. But he met with little success in these efforts because he had started too late in life. **❞**
>
> —*from* Vita Karoli, *Einhard*

OCTOBER, **an illuminated detail from the Grimani Breviary, 16th century.**

The Age of Faith: The Christian Church as Undisputed Authority

In A.D. 330, the emperor **Constantine** proclaimed Christianity the official religion of the Roman Empire, and in 451, the Pope became the undisputed religious authority of the Church. When the Roman Empire fell apart, the Christian Church maintained and enlarged its authority. The key to its success was a strong organization that enabled it to assert its independence from princes and kings and to build a government of its own.

One way the Church exerted its authority was through its monopoly over knowledge. Because Latin was the language in which knowledge was preserved and transmitted, and because only the clergy could read and write Latin, the Church maintained a firm control over education.

The Church maintained strict control over knowledge and education throughout the Middle Ages.

Although the writings of the Church focused on religion and philosophy, monasteries—communities of monks and other clerics—often maintained **chronicles**, or records of events. Many chronicles were local, recording weather conditions, the state of crops, and day-to-day happenings. Other chronicles mingled legends and local fairy tales with reported facts. As time went on, the chronicles became more factual and detailed. Indeed, the best chroniclers of the later Middle Ages were the forerunners of modern-day historians and journalists. Their records are an invaluable aid to understanding the life of the era.

Feudalism: A System of Allegiance

After Charlemagne's death in 814, rule in Europe fell into the hands of numerous nobles. Powerful and independent, these aristocrats ruled local areas by a system called **feudalism** (fyo͞od′l·iz′əm). Feudalism was an economic, social, and military system in which **vassals** (vas′əlz), or tenants, pledged their loyalty to a lord, exchanging work on his land

TOLL BEING PAID ON BARRELS OF WINE, medieval painting, artist unknown.

or service in his military in return for his protection. Usually, the lord himself was vassal to a more powerful overlord, who in turn served as a vassal to a prince or king. Thus, the feudal system was like a pyramid. At the bottom were

---

Feudalism and the Church were the two great pillars of medieval society.

---

the **serfs**, or peasants, who worked their lord's land, had few rights, and were totally subject to the lord's will. At the top was the king, who recognized only God as his sovereign. Loyalty to one's lord and to one's peers was the vital element that held the feudal system together.

Epic Deeds of Heroes and Heroines

Warfare between feudal lords was commonplace, and medieval literature simultaneously reflected both ideals of valor and the desire for order and peace. Throughout the early Middle Ages, a rich tradition of stories was passed on by minstrels, who sang or chanted the fabulous deeds of earlier heroes. Many of these stories became **epics** that are still enjoyed today. The eighth-century Anglo-Saxon poem *Beowulf*, for example, tells the story of Beowulf, a warrior who

SIEGE OF JERUSALEM, SEBASTIAN MAMEROT. *This illuminated manuscript depicts a battle scene from the Crusades.*

braves the ferocious monster Grendel and kills a terrible dragon. The ***Nibelungenlied***, the national epic of Germany (see page 730), was composed in the early 1200s out of much older tales. It relates the heroic exploits of Siegfried, who has great magical powers. The Norse-Icelandic **sagas**

> Heroism was an important theme of much of the literature of the early Middle Ages. Both the epic hero and the Christian saint opposed evil and stood for what was right.

of Snorri Sturluson and others originated about this time as well. These were tales about historical kings, pre-Christian Norse deities, and legendary heroes. In general, the medieval epics glorify physical strength, courage, and loyalty, celebrating warriors who defeat evil and restore order.

> ❝ On February 16 there were great claps of thunder and the intense heat of the sun scorched the earth, and in certain districts of the land an earthquake occurred, and the fiery shape of a dragon was seen in the air. In the same year, a wicked heresy arose. ❞
>
> —*from the chronicle of the German town of Xanten, 838*

Andrew Mellon Collection, National Gallery of Art, Washington, D.C.

SAINT GEORGE AND THE DRAGON, 1504-06. RAPHAEL. *St. George, the patron saint of England, was one of the Middle Ages' most popular saints. According to legend, he saved a king's daughter from being sacrificed to a dragon.*

686 The Middle Ages

A different approach to heroism evolved in the **saints' lives**, tales of the lives of the Christian saints, many of whom were women. The typical saint's life contained supernatural elements, showing saints miraculously healing people and animals, resisting evil (usually to the point of martyrdom), and being revived after death. In a sense, these stories were the Church's answer to pagan epics like the *Nibelungenlied.* The saints' miraculous deeds glorified the Christian virtues of piety and humble submission to God's will, just as the epics glorified the often militaristic values held dear by the Germanic groups such as the Anglo-Saxons and the Franks.

Medieval Oral Literature

It was not only the church that provided Christian Europe with entertainment during the Middle Ages. From the eleventh to the fourteenth centuries, French poets called **trouvères** (trōō·verz′) composed the popular *chansons de geste* ("songs of heroic deeds"). The Christian epic *Song of Roland* (see page 692) survives as a fine example of this form.

It is important for us today to realize that, as most people during the Middle Ages were illiterate, most literature was presented orally, and sometimes visually, as in the case of drama. Common people in particular entertained themselves with folktales, beast fables, and ballads. **Ballads**, or narrative songs, have endured because they tell the kind of sensational stories that make the headlines in today's tabloids—stories about murder, love, and revenge.

The Romance and Courtly Love

In time, the rough realities of feudalism were refined by the code of chivalry. **Chivalry**, a term derived from the French word for knight, *chevalier,* was basically a military code of behavior. A knight was supposed to be fair to his opponents, loyal to his lord, and honorable in all things. He was also supposed to show Christian humility to his peers, kindness to those beneath him, and generosity to all. Of course, not all knights could live up to this code, or even tried to. Many were, after all, mercenary soldiers available to the highest bidder. But unquestionably, chivalry helped to civilize the competitive, often brutal world of the Middle Ages.

JULY: WHEAT HARVEST AND SHEEPSHEARING, an illuminated detail from the Grimani Breviary, 16th century Italy.

❝ The only pests of London are the immoderate drinking of fools and the frequency of fires. ❞
—*William FitzStephen*

The **romances** were the literary expression of chivalric ideals. These were long poems about knightly adventures that were recited by traveling poets. The stories were later written down, both in verse and in prose.

The **Arthurian romances** were among the most popular of the medieval romances. The stories of Arthur, a legendary Celtic king, and his knights of the Round Table spread first throughout England and Wales and then migrated to the Continent. **Chrétien de Troyes** (see page 720), who wrote in French in the late twelfth century, was one of the most famous of the medieval romance poets. His stories, especially those of Perceval and Lancelot, influenced later versions of the Arthurian legend.

The romance theme of courtly love made the heroic epics seem out of date.

Like epic heroes, the knights who served as heroes of the medieval romance were strong, courageous, and loyal. But they were also courtly lovers who were devoted to one special lady. This new element of **courtly love** served to distinguish the romances from the earlier epics. The knight's glorious deeds were not performed in the service of king or country, but on behalf of a beautiful, fair, and noble lady,

Giraudon/Art Resource, New York

WEDDING DANCE, PIETER BREUGHEL, THE ELDER.
❓ What kind of world does Breughel depict here? Does it seem very different from a modern family or community gathering?

TILTING KNIGHTS: KING RICHARD AND SALADIN.
? *What place did knights hold in the system of feudalism? How did they figure in the literature of the time?*

who was above him in status and usually married—and therefore unattainable. Sometimes she was a person the knight had only glimpsed from a distance or heard about.

Praise for an unattainable courtly lady was already a popular theme in medieval poetry. During the eleventh century in southern France, poet-musicians called **troubadours** (trō͞o′bə·dôrz′)—from a French word meaning "to compose" or "to invent"—had begun to write light, graceful lyrics based on the theme of courtly love.

Also in France, the Breton *lais* (*lai* means "song") were influenced by the ideals of courtly love. The *lais* were short stories with supernatural or fairy-tale elements, written in verse and sung to the accompaniment of the lyre or the lute. A number of *lais* were collected in French by **Marie de France** (see page 715), who lived in the English court not long after the Normans of France had conquered England.

66 Woe to our day, since the pursuit of letters has perished from among us. 99

—History of the Franks,
Gregory of Tours

THE FIRST KISS OF LANCELOT, illumination from a medieval manuscript. *Lancelot was one of King Arthur's knights.*

The Crusades, 1096–1204

Muslim Territory, 1097
Christian Territory, 1097

•••• First Crusade, 1096–1099
—— Second Crusade, 1147–1148
—— Third Crusade, 1189–1192
•••• Fourth Crusade, 1202–1204

The Late Middle Ages

The late Middle Ages, from about 1300 to about 1500, was a time of enormous upheaval that dealt severe blows to the two great medieval institutions, the feudal system and the Church. The **Crusades** (1096–1270), which were Christian attempts to forcefully regain the Holy Land from the Muslims, had cost many European lives but had also opened up trade routes to the East. These routes allowed an influx of new goods and ideas that enhanced the financial status of the merchant class and accelerated the development of towns and cities. Some cities founded universities, new centers of learning that opened doors for the middle class.

A dramatic climate change in the 1300s, later called the Little Ice Age, brought bitterly cold weather and reduced crop yields. Soon after, the Black Death, or bubonic plague, wiped out entire European villages. As a result, there were few serfs to work the fields, and the serfs who remained demanded more freedoms. Technology created change, too, for the development of gunpowder meant that a cannon could decide the outcome of a feudal battle in a matter of hours. Thus the system of feudalism was gradually undermined as the Middle Ages came to a close.

The power of the Church was also being challenged. Charges of corruption and internal arguments, or **schisms** (siz′əmz), weakened the Church at its foundations. The Church's role as biblical interpreter was undermined, too, for another development of the late Middle Ages was that more people learned to read. With the growth of literacy came a new intellectual independence. And with the development of the printing press, critics and reformers were able to write, print, and circulate literary **satires** that ridiculed the Church's corrupt practices.

The most significant development in literature during the late Middle Ages, however, was the rise of the use of the **vernacular**, or regional, languages instead of Latin, the language of the educated elite throughout medieval times. This development signaled that great changes were taking place all over Europe: an emerging sense of nationalism, the increase of educated readers, the availability of printed material, and the recognition and acceptance of the value of

First Lindan book cover, late eighth century.

The late Middle Ages was marked by the building of the great cathedrals, the opening of trade routes, and an increase in the number of people who could read and write in the vernacular languages.

---

such local oral literatures as stories and songs. The use of vernacular in works such as Wycliffe's translation of the Bible into English, Chaucer's *Canterbury Tales*, and Dante's *Divine Comedy* established the vernacular as acceptable in literature. The world was becoming more secular, and this change was more fittingly expressed in literature that used the languages of everyday people.

The Song of Roland
c. 1100

Stories of the Emperor: The Coronation of Charlemagne.

Generally considered the national epic of France, the *Song of Roland* is based on a historical event. The story dates back to the time of Charlemagne, the King of the Franks from A.D. 768 to 814.

In Charlemagne's time, Spain was ruled by Arab Muslims. Charlemagne agreed to help one of two Muslim rivals who were battling each other for control of Spain. But Charlemagne's campaign in Spain was a complete disaster, and in 778 his army was forced to retreat. As they crossed back into France, the rear guard of his army was overrun by the Basques (bäskz), a people who live in the Pyrenees Mountains that divide France and Spain. One of the commanders of Charlemagne's rear guard during this battle at Roncesvalles was a man named Roland.

By the eleventh century, Europe was in the midst of the Crusades, the "holy wars" in which Christians tried to reconquer Jerusalem and wrest it from the Muslims. Anti-Muslim feelings ran high in Europe. As the world had changed, so, too, did the story of Roland and the battle of Roncesvalles. From an account of a power struggle between two Arab Muslims in the eighth century, the story had evolved into a national epic about the religious conflict between Christians and Muslims in the eleventh century. The Basques were transformed into Arabs—referred to in the poem as "Saracens," "pagans," and "idol worshipers." Meanwhile, Roland, who had played only a minor role in history, became a legendary hero, a nephew of Charlemagne, and a model Christian knight.

Reader's Guide

from the SONG OF ROLAND

Background

The *Song of Roland* is the earliest surviving example of the Old French *chansons de geste* (shän·sōnz' də zhest'), or "songs of deeds," composed in the eleventh and twelfth centuries. These epic poems focus on the heroic deeds of Charlemagne and other feudal lords. The *Song of Roland* shares many characteristics with classical epic poems such as the *Iliad* and the *Aeneid:* long speeches, descriptions of battles, dreams, supernatural elements, and the repetition of key phrases.

As the selection begins, Roland, his noble friend Oliver, and their small force are trapped in a mountain pass in the Pyrenees Mountains. Their dire situation is a result of the treachery of Ganelon, Roland's stepfather, who is envious of Roland's reputation as a warrior and furious because Roland has recommended him for dangerous duty as Charlemagne's ambassador to the Saracen king Marsilion. Ganelon has encouraged King Marsilion to attack the rear guard of Charlemagne's army with an overwhelming force—400,000 Saracens against 20,000 Franks. He has also persuaded Charlemagne to place Roland in command of the rear guard, the portion of the army in greatest danger. In this translation of the *Song of Roland,* Charlemagne, which means "Charles the Great," is referred to simply as Charles.

Writer's Response

Roland, the hero of the *Song of Roland,* acts according to his concept of honor. What does *honor* mean to you? List three decisions you or people you know have made that you consider honorable.

Literary Focus

An **epic** is a long narrative poem that relates the great deeds of a larger-than-life figure. The **epic hero**, the main character of an epic, embodies the values of the particular society he represents. For example, a hero of the Indian epic *Mahabharata* (see page 458) exhibits the qualities of intelligence and thoughtfulness, while the Persian epic heroes Sohráb and Rostám (see page 646) are courageous and physically powerful. Roland, on the other hand, is the ultimate medieval European knight: a heroic fighter, a loyal follower of his king, a trusted friend, and a devout Christian.

from the SONG OF ROLAND

translated by

FREDERICK GOLDIN

As you read, pay attention to clues to Roland's character: what he says, what others say to him and about him, and what he does. In what ways is he a hero? Which of his character traits are most responsible for his downfall?

Olifant, carved ivory, c. A.D. 1100. *Roland does not sound his horn, olifant, until it is too late to save the French troops.* **What would you have done in his position?**

Roland's companion Oliver has seen the advancing Saracen army and knows that the small French rear guard is outnumbered. He begs Roland to blow on his horn, the olifant, in order to summon more troops from Charles's (Charlemagne's) army, but Roland refuses, saying that he will lose his reputation and bring shame on the French if he calls for help. He believes that he and the other French fighters are more than equal to the Saracens. Oliver continues to urge Roland to call for help, to no avail. Finally Roland, Oliver, Archbishop Turpin, and the other French fighters clash with the Saracens in the mountain pass. For a time, the French hold their own.

110

The battle is fearful and full of grief.
Oliver and Roland strike like good men,
the Archbishop, more than a thousand blows,
and the Twelve Peers° do not hang back, they
    strike!
5 the French fight side by side, all as one man.
The pagans die by hundreds, by thousands:
whoever does not flee finds no refuge from death,
like it or not, there he ends all his days.
And there the men of France lose their greatest
    arms;

4. **Twelve Peers:** noblemen chosen as Charles's select band of leaders.

10 they will not see their fathers, their kin again,
or Charlemagne, who looks for them in the
    passes.
Tremendous torment now comes forth in France,
a mighty whirlwind, tempests of wind and
    thunder,
rains and hailstones, great and immeasurable,
15 bolts of lightning hurtling and hurtling down:
it is, in truth, a trembling of the earth.
From Saint Michael-in-Peril° to the Saints,
from Besançon° to the port of Wissant,
there is no house whose veil of walls does not
    crumble.
20 A great darkness at noon falls on the land,
there is no light but when the heavens crack.
No man sees this who is not terrified,
and many say: "The Last Day! Judgment Day!
The end! The end of the world is upon us!"
25 They do not know, they do not speak the truth:
it is the worldwide grief for the death of Roland.

17. **Saint Michael-in-Peril**: a sanctuary on the coast of Normandy.
18. **Besançon** (bə·zän·sōn′): a city in east central France, part of the original kingdom of Burgundy.

Roland and the Twelve Peers fight fiercely against the Saracens, but they are greatly outnumbered. At last it becomes apparent even to Roland that the battle cannot be won, and he finally decides to use his magical horn, the olifant, to call Charlemagne's army for relief. But Oliver, angered that Roland's pride had prevented him from blowing the horn earlier, when it could have done some good, stops Roland with harsh words, pointing out that it truly would be a disgrace to sound the horn now, when all hope has been lost.

130

And Roland says: "We are in a rough battle.
I'll sound the olifant, Charles will hear it."
Said Oliver: "No good vassal would do it.
30 When I urged it, friend, you did not think it right.
If Charles were here, we'd come out with no
    losses.
Those men down there—no blame can fall on
    them."
Oliver said: "Now by this beard of mine,
If I can see my noble sister, Aude,°
35 once more, you will never lie in her arms!"

34. **Aude** (ō′dā): Roland's betrothed.

131

And Roland said: "Why are you angry at me?"
Oliver answers: "Companion, it is your doing.
I will tell you what makes a vassal good:
    it is judgment, it is never madness;
    restraint is worth more than the raw nerve of
    a fool.
40 Frenchmen are dead because of your wildness.
And what service will Charles ever have from us?
If you had trusted me, my lord would be here,
we would have fought this battle through to the end,
Marsilion would be dead, or our prisoner.
45 Roland, your prowess—had we never seen it!
    And now, dear friend, we've seen the last of it.
No more aid from us now for Charlemagne,
a man without equal till Judgment Day,
you will die here, and your death will shame
    France.
We kept faith, you and I, we were companions;
    and everything we were will end today.
50 We part before evening, and it will be hard."

132

Turpin the Archbishop hears their bitter words,
digs hard into his horse with golden spurs
and rides to them; begins to set them right:
"You, Lord Roland, and you, Lord Oliver,
55 I beg you in God's name do not quarrel.
To sound the horn could not help us now, true,
but still it is far better that you do it:
let the King come, he can avenge us then—
these men of Spain must not go home exulting!
60 Our French will come, they'll get down on their
        feet,
and find us here—we'll be dead, cut to pieces.
They will lift us into coffins on the backs of
        mules,
and weep for us, in rage and pain and grief,
and bury us in the courts of churches;
65 and we will not be eaten by wolves or pigs or dogs."
Roland replies, "Lord, you have spoken well."

**CHARLEMAGNE, ALBRECHT DÜRER, early
16th century.**
? *What role does Charlemagne—
Charles the Great—play in
this epic?*

133

Roland has put the olifant to his mouth,
he sets it well, sounds it with all his strength.
The hills are high, and that voice ranges far,
70 they heard it echo thirty great leagues away.
King Charles heard it, and all his faithful men.
And the King says: "Our men are in a battle."
And Ganelon disputed him and said:
"Had someone else said that, I'd call him liar!"

134

75 And now the mighty effort of Roland the Count:
he sounds his olifant; his pain is great,
and from his mouth the bright blood comes
      leaping out,
and the temple bursts in his forehead.
That horn, in Roland's hands, has a mighty voice:
80 King Charles hears it drawing through the passes.
Naimon° heard it, the Franks listen to it.
And the King said: "I hear Count Roland's horn;
he'd never sound it unless he had a battle."
Says Ganelon: "Now no more talk of battles!
85 You are old now, your hair is white as snow,
the things you say make you sound like a child.
You know Roland and that wild pride of his—
what a wonder God has suffered it so long!
Remember? he took Noples° without your
      command:
90 the Saracens rode out, to break the siege;
they fought with him, the great vassal Roland.
Afterwards he used the streams to wash the blood
from the meadows: so that nothing would show.
He blasts his horn all day to catch a rabbit,
95 he's strutting now before his peers and bragging—
who under heaven would dare meet him on the
      field?
So now: ride on! Why do you keep on stopping?
The Land of Fathers lies far ahead of us."

81. **Naimon:** a duke and adviser
to Charlemagne.

89. **Noples:** in Spain.

Roland sounds his horn again. Charles commands his army to ride to Roland's aid, but it is too late to save Roland and his peers, who have been defeated by the Saracens. Before he dies, Oliver asks forgiveness of Roland.

168

Now Roland feels that death is very near.
100 His brain comes spilling out through his two ears;
prays to God for his peers: let them be called;
and for himself, to the angel Gabriel;
took the olifant: there must be no reproach!
took Durendal° his sword in his other hand,
105 and farther than a crossbow's farthest shot
he walks toward Spain, into a fallow land,
and climbs a hill: there beneath two fine trees
stand four great blocks of stone, all are of marble;
and he fell back, to earth, on the green grass,
110 has fainted there, for death is very near.

104. **Durendal** (dü'ren·däl): Roland's unbreakable sword; said to be the sword that had belonged to the Trojan hero Hector.

169

High are the hills, and high, high are the trees;
there stand four blocks of stone, gleaming of
    marble.
Count Roland falls fainting on the green grass,
and is watched, all this time, by a Saracen:
115 who has feigned death and lies now with the
    others,
has smeared blood on his face and on his body;
and quickly now gets to his feet and runs—
a handsome man, strong, brave, and so crazed
    with pride
that he does something mad and dies for it:
120 laid hands on Roland, and on the arms of Roland,
and cried: "Conquered! Charles's nephew
    conquered!
I'll carry this sword home to Arabia!"
As he draws it, the Count begins to come round.

170

Now Roland feels *someone taking his sword!*
125 opened his eyes, and had one word for him:
"I don't know you, you aren't one of ours";
grasps that olifant that he will never lose,
strikes on the helm beset with gems in gold,
shatters the steel, and the head, and the bones,
130 sent his two eyes flying out of his head,
dumped him over stretched out at his feet dead;
and said: "You nobody! how could you dare
lay hands on me—rightly or wrongly: how?
Who'll hear of this and not call you a fool?
135 Ah! the bell-mouth of the olifant is smashed,
the crystal and the gold fallen away."

171

Now Roland the Count feels his sight is gone;
gets on his feet, draws on his final strength,
the color on his face lost now for good.
140 Before him stands a rock; and on that dark rock
in rage and bitterness he strikes ten blows:
the steel blade grates, it will not break, it stands unmarked.
"Ah!" said the Count, "Blessed Mary, your help!

French reliquary shrine, mid-fourteenth century. *A reliquary was an ornate case designed to contain religious relics, or physical remains of saints.*

from the Song of Roland **699**

Ah Durendal, good sword, your unlucky day,
145 for I am lost and cannot keep you in my care.
The battles I have won, fighting with you,
the mighty lands that holding you I conquered,
that Charles rules now, our King, whose beard
    is white!
Now you fall to another: it must not be
a man who'd run before another man!
150 For a long while a good vassal held you:
there'll never be the like in France's holy land."

173

Roland the Count strikes down on a dark rock,
and the rock breaks, breaks more than I can tell,
and the blade grates, but Durendal will not break,
155 the sword leaped up, rebounded toward the sky.
The Count, when he sees that sword will not be
    broken,
softly, in his own presence, speaks the lament:
"Ah Durendal, beautiful, and most sacred,
the holy relics in this golden pommel!
160 Saint Peter's tooth and blood of Saint Basile,°
a lock of hair of my lord Saint Denis,°
and a fragment of blessed Mary's robe:
your power must not fall to the pagans,
you must be served by Christian warriors.
165 May no coward ever come to hold you!
It was with you I conquered those great lands
that Charles has in his keeping, whose beard is
    white,
the Emperor's lands, that make him rich and
    strong."

160. **Saint Basile** (ba·sēl′): fourth-century religious writer and monastery administrator; fought for orthodoxy within the Catholic Church.
161. **Saint Denis** (den′is): third-century apostle to the Gauls, who was martyred; patron saint of France.

174

Now Roland feels death coming over him,
170 death descending from his temples to his heart.
He came running underneath a pine tree
and there stretched out, face down, on the green
    grass,
lays beneath him his sword and the olifant.
He turned his head toward the Saracen hosts,

175 and this is why: with all his heart he wants
King Charles the Great and all his men to say,
he died, that noble Count, a conqueror;
makes confession, beats his breast often, so feebly,
offers his glove, for all his sins, to God.

176

180 Count Roland lay stretched out beneath a pine;
he turned his face toward the land of Spain,
began to remember many things now:
how many lands, brave man, he had conquered;
and he remembered: sweet France, the men of
his line,
185 remembered Charles, his lord, who fostered him:
cannot keep, remembering, from weeping, sighing;
but would not be unmindful of himself:
he confesses his sins, prays God for mercy:
"Loyal Father, you who never failed us,
190 who resurrected Saint Lazarus° from the dead,
and saved your servant Daniel° from the lions:
now save the soul of me from every peril
for the sins I committed while I still lived."
Then he held out his right glove to his Lord:
195 Saint Gabriel° took the glove from his hand.
He held his head bowed down upon his arm,
he is gone, his two hands joined, to his end.
Then God sent him his angel Cherubim°
and Saint Michael,° angel of the sea's Peril;
200 and with these two there came Saint Gabriel:
they bear Count Roland's soul to Paradise.

190. **Saint Lazarus:** The story of this miracle appears in John 11:1–44.
191. **Daniel:** The story is told in Daniel 6:16–27.

195. **Saint Gabriel:** one of the seven archangels; messenger of good news.

198. **Cherubim** (cher'yōo·bim): one of the heavenly beings at God's throne.
199. **Saint Michael:** one of the archangels.

First Thoughts

Did Roland fit your idea of a hero? What did you admire about him? Which of his qualities did you *not* admire?

Identifying Facts

1. As the battle proceeds, it becomes clear that the Franks will be defeated. What does Roland want to do? How does Oliver respond?
2. What does Charles think the sound of Roland's horn means?
3. What finally happens to Roland?

Interpreting Meanings

1. The code of chivalry that Roland follows puts great emphasis on personal honor. How does the concern for honor influence the behavior of Roland? Of Oliver? How are the two men's responses similar and different?
2. What does Roland and Oliver's disagreement reveal about their characters?
3. **Repetition** is an important feature of the *chansons de geste*. Give at least two examples of repetition in this poem. In each case, why do you think repetition is used?
4. As an **epic hero**, Roland represents the values of his society. Based on your understanding of his character, list at least three of the values that this epic seems to celebrate.
5. In the **climax** of the selection, Roland dies not from a battle wound but from the bursting of his blood vessels when he blows the horn. Do you think Roland would have preferred this death to one from a Saracen sword? Why or why not?

Applying Meanings

Do you think that in this epic death is a defeat for the hero? Why or why not? If Roland were a contemporary war hero, do you think that his death would be mourned as a defeat or celebrated as a victory?

Critical Writing Response

Comparing Epic Heroes. Write a short essay comparing Roland and Achilles (see page 224) as epic heroes. In your discussion, consider the qualities each figure represents. What faults do they share? Consider, too, how the codes of honor of the two heroes differ. A chart like the following can help you to organize your ideas.

	Roland	Achilles
Codes of honor		
Positive character traits		
Negative character traits		
Conclusion		

Speaking and Listening

Conducting an Interview. Imagine that you are a television newscaster reporting on the Battle of Roncesvalles. Pair yourself with a classmate who will play the part of one of the main characters in the *Song of Roland*—Roland, Oliver, or Charles (Charlemagne). Together, decide what issues your interview will cover. Be sure to deal with the most important aspects of the battle, and be sure that the interviewer asks probing questions that reveal the character's motives and judgment. Then conduct your interview for the rest of the class.

SEEING CONNECTIONS

Poem of the Cid: *Spain's National Epic*

Glory, gore, and God provide the foundations for two of Europe's medieval epics: France's *Song of Roland* and Spain's *Poem of the Cid.* Christianity, in whose name countless Arabs' blood is shed, is a key element in both epics. But while *Song of Roland* is filled with mythic elements—Roland's ancestry is traced to the Trojan hero Hector and the Germanic god Wotan (Odin)—Spain's twelfth-century epic is remarkably free of mythic and supernatural elements and is instead characterized by gritty realism.

The Spanish epic's hero, Ruy Diaz de Bivar, better known as the Cid (thēd), begins his career as one of King Alfonso VI's tribute collectors—a sort of medieval collection agent. His humble origins make him vulnerable to the whims of the King and the counts from whom he collects tribute. When the Cid is unjustly exiled by the king for pressing one of the monarch's own vassals too hard for tribute, the hero sets out to gain the king's pardon. But the Cid is clever enough to realize that the only way to gain King Alfonso's forgiveness is to leave him with no choice: he sets out to become as powerful as the king himself. The Cid and his followers set out to conquer the Moorish strongholds in Seville and Valencia. ("Moors" are the Spanish

equivalent of the Saracens in *Song of Roland*—that is, Arabs.) Only when the king can no longer ignore the now fabulously wealthy Cid does he grant his "pardon."

The climactic moments of *Poem of the Cid* take place not in the battlefield but in the courtroom. The Cid petitions the king for justice after the hero's sons-in-law, the royal princes of Carrión, have dishonored his daughters, beating and abandoning them in the wilderness. Here we see the central issues of the epic—the tension between the aristocracy and the commoner—brought into focus. For the Cid, despite his heroism and enormous wealth, is still for all practical purposes a commoner. His triumph in court reinforces the ideals of medieval Spain, where honor is measured not by bloodlines but by heroism and by wealth *earned* in hard labor.

Poem of the Cid gives its audience a hero not from the classical tradition or even from a nation's royalty, but from the common folk—a hero not unlike themselves. Unlike Roland, who dies at the height of his glory, penitent for his overreaching pride, the Cid dies a wealthy old man, thankful to God for his good fortune but apologizing to no one—for the medieval audience, a deeply satisfying dream come true.

Snorri Sturluson
1179–1241

One-eyed Norse god Odin astride Sleipnir, illumination from *Poetic Edda*, a 13th-century Icelandic manuscript.

The Granger Collection, New York

Snorri Sturluson (snô′rē stur′lə·sən), whose name means "sharp-witted one," was a great poet and historian as well as a rich landowner, a learned lawyer, and the head of Iceland's most important clan. His books are classics of Icelandic literature and are important sources of mythological lore as well as historical information.

As a youth, Snorri developed a fine sense of the beauty of the Icelandic language. However, by the age of twenty, he also displayed an interest in acquiring property and political power. In 1199, he married an heiress and bought an estate near Reykjaholt, then the capital of Iceland. He was twice elected president of the legislative assembly and supreme court of Iceland, first serving

between 1215 and 1218. Snorri lived in harsh times and was constantly shifting his political position in order to hold on to his power. Eventually, his political intrigues aroused ill will, even within his own family, and led to his murder.

Despite his active and controversial political life, Snorri still found time to devote to literature, and it is the grandeur of his writing that makes him one of Iceland's national heroes. Around 1200, Snorri grew concerned with preserving the myths of his ancient Viking heritage. The result was the *Prose Edda*, which is both a handbook for the writing of Icelandic verse and a collection of Scandinavian myths.

The *Prose Edda* includes (in spite of its title) both poetry and mythology, the two most important elements of the Norse heritage. The work was designed to teach poets of Snorri's time the style of the ancient Viking poets, or *skalds.* As examples it presents ancient myths from both written and oral sources. The stories in the *Prose Edda* are among the best accounts we have of the pre-Christian mythology shared by many Norse peoples.

Interestingly enough, no one knows what the word *edda* means. It may possibly signify "great-grandmother" and appear in the title to show the ancient origin of the tales. Or, it may be derived either from *Oddi*, Snorri's birthplace, or from the original Norse word for "poetry."

Reader's Guide

THOR AND LOKI IN GIANTLAND
from the Prose Edda

Background

The tales in Snorri Sturluson's masterpiece, the *Prose Edda,* relate the adventures of the Norse gods, called the Aesir (a'sir'), along with the actions of heroes, giants, and demons. Frequently, no clear line separates the natural and supernatural. Magic and charms work as much for humans and other mortal creatures as they do for the gods, and humans sometimes triumph over the Aesir and other superhuman beings.

The following selection is from ''The Deluding of Gylfi'' in the first part of the *Prose Edda.* In this part, we are told that Gylfi was a king of the lands now called Sweden. As the narrative begins, Gylfi goes among the Aesir to find out about them and their heritage. The Aesir tell him a number of stories about life and death, the origins of the world, and the various gods. After being told that Thor was the greatest of all gods, Gylfi asks the Aesir whether Thor ever met a being with powers greater than his own. In answer to this question, the Aesir tell Gylfi the story that follows.

Writer's Response

In this myth, both Thor and the king of the giants use trickery to achieve their ends. Under what circumstances, if any, is it admirable to use trickery or deception in order to achieve a goal? Think of some characters from television, film, or books who use trickery, or underhanded means, to get what they want. Do these characters succeed? What do you think of these characters? Freewrite your ideas.

Literary Focus

Understatement is a figure of speech that consists of saying less than what is really meant, or saying something with less force than is appropriate. It is a form of **verbal irony**, in which a writer or speaker says one thing but really means the opposite, as when someone comes inside from sub-zero weather and says, ''It's a bit chilly out there.'' Understatement often adds a light, comic flavor to writing.

THOR AND LOKI IN GIANTLAND

from the Prose Edda

Snorri Sturluson

translated by

JEAN I. YOUNG

This myth humorously describes a contest of strength between Thor, the mightiest of gods, and Utgarð-Loki, king of the giants. As you read, decide whom you think deserves to win.

Gods	**Thor:** god of thunder and lightning; the mightiest god. **Loki** (lō′kē): mischief-maker.	
Giants	**Skrymir** (skrē′mər): giant dwelling in the woods. **Utgarð-Loki** (o͞ot′gär*th*′ lō′kē): king of the giants.	
	Logi **Hugi** **Elli**	members of Utgarð-Loki's household.
Humans	**Thjalfi** (thē·al′fē′) and **Roskva** (rœsk′vä′): son and daughter of a farmer.	

"The beginning of the story is that Thor-the-charioteer was on a journey with his goats and in his chariot and with him the god Loki, when they came one evening to a farmer's where they got lodgings for the night. During the evening Thor took the goats and slaughtered them, then had them skinned and put into a caldron. When they were cooked, Thor and his companion sat down to supper and Thor invited the farmer and his wife and children to the meal. The farmer's son was called Thjalfi and his daughter, Roskva. Thor spread the skins out away from the fire, and told the farmer and his household to throw the bones onto the skins. Thjalfi, the farmer's son, took firm hold of a thighbone of one of the goats and split it with his knife, breaking it for the marrow. Thor stayed there that night, and just before daybreak got up and dressed, took the hammer Mjollnir,[1] raised it and consecrated the goatskins. Then the goats stood up. One of them was lame of a hind leg; Thor noticed that and declared that the farmer and his household had done something silly with the bones; he knew that a thighbone was broken. There is no need to make a long story about it; everyone can guess how terrified the farmer would be when he saw Thor letting his eyebrows sink down over his eyes—but when he saw what he did of the eyes he thought he would drop

---

1. **Mjollnir** (myəl′nər)

down dead for the look in them alone. Thor gripped the handle of his hammer so that his knuckles went white. Then the farmer and his whole household did what you might expect, screamed out and begged for mercy for themselves, offering in compensation everything they possessed. But when Thor saw their terror, his anger left him and he calmed down and took from them in reconciliation their children Thjalfi and Roskva. They became his bondservants and accompanied him ever afterwards.

"He left his goats behind him there and set off on an expedition eastwards to Giantland, traveling all the way to the sea and then away over the deep ocean. When he came to land he went ashore and with him Loki and Thjalfi and Roskva. They had not walked very long before they came upon a big wood, and they walked the whole day till dark. Thjalfi, who could run faster than anyone else, was carrying Thor's knapsack, but they were not very well off for food.

"When it got dark they made a search for somewhere to stay the night, and came across an enormous hall with a door opening at the end as broad as the hall was wide. There they sought night quarters for themselves. But at midnight there was a great earthquake; the ground went rocking under them and the building shook. Thor stood up and called to his companions, and they made a search and discovered in the middle of the hall a side-room to the right, and went up to it. Thor sat down in the doorway, but the others went further in from him; they were terrified, but Thor gripped the handle of his hammer and determined to defend himself. Then they heard a great din of muffled roaring. When day came, Thor went outside and saw a man lying a short way off in the wood and he was no pygmy. He was asleep and snoring loudly. Thor thought he understood

then what sort of noises they had been hearing in the night. He put on his belt of strength and his divine power increased, but at that moment the man woke up and sprang to his feet. And they saw that for once Thor was too startled to hit him with the hammer, and asked him what his name was. The man replied it was Skrymir; 'and there's no need for me to ask you yours,' he said, 'I know you are Asa-Thor.[2] Have you moved my glove?' He stretched out his hand and picked up the glove. Then Thor realized that that was what he had had as a sleeping-hall in the night, and the side-room was the thumb.

"Skrymir asked Thor if he would like to have his company and Thor said he would. Then Skrymir undid his provision bag and got ready to eat breakfast, but Thor and his companions had theirs in another place. Skrymir suggested that they should pool their provisions; Thor agreed to that, and Skrymir tied up all their provisions in one bag and put it on his own back. He went on ahead during the day, taking immense strides, and late in the evening found them a lodging for the night under a large oak. Then Skrymir told Thor he wished to lie down and go to sleep, 'but you take the provision bag and get your supper ready.' The next minute Skrymir was asleep and snoring loudly. Thor took the provision bag intending to undo it, but, however incredible it may seem, it must be related that he was unable to get a single knot undone or strap-end moved so that it was tied less tightly than before. When he saw he was wasting his time he grew angry, gripped the hammer Mjollnir with both hands, stepped a pace forward to where Skrymir was lying and struck him on the head. Skrymir woke up

---

2. **Asa-Thor** (a'sä thôr)

and asked if a leaf had fallen on his head or if they had had supper and were ready for bed. Thor said they were just going to sleep, and they went under another oak tree. To tell you the truth they were much too frightened to sleep. At midnight Thor heard Skrymir snoring so that the wood resounded. Then Thor got up, went to him, lifted his hammer quickly and fiercely and struck him in the middle of his crown; he knew that the face of the hammer sank deep into his head. At that instant Skrymir woke up and asked: 'What's the matter now? Did an acorn fall on my head? What's happened to you, Thor?' Thor, however, retreated hastily, saying he had just woken up and that it was the middle of the night and still time to sleep. He reflected, however, that if he got an opportunity of hitting him a third blow Skrymir would never survive it, and he lay still, waiting for Skrymir to fall asleep [again].

"A little before daybreak he knew from what he was hearing that Skrymir had fallen asleep. He stood up and made for him, lifting the hammer with all his might and striking him on the temple that was turned up; the hammer sank in up to the handle. Skrymir, however, sat up rubbing his cheek and asking: 'Are there any birds up in the tree above me? When I was waking up I fancied that some droppings from the twigs fell onto my head. Are you awake, Thor? It's time to get up and dress. You haven't far to go now, however, to reach the stronghold called Utgarð.[3] I've heard you whispering amongst yourselves that I'm no small man, but if you get to Utgarð you'll see bigger men there. Now I'm going to give you some good advice. Don't behave in an arrogant manner; Utgarð-

Loki's retainers won't put up with the bragging of such whippersnappers as you are. Your other course would be to go back and in my opinion it would be better for you to do that, but if you will go on, travel eastwards; my way lies north to those mountains you will be able to see now.'

"Skrymir took the provision bag and throwing it over his back turned abruptly away from them into the wood. It is not related that the Aesir expressed any desire to meet him again.

"Thor and his companions continued their way and walked on till midday. Then they saw a stronghold on a plain. They had to bend their necks right back before they could see over the top of it. They went up to the stronghold and there was a gate in the entrance and it was shut. Thor went up to the gate but could not get it opened. Then they tried their hardest to get inside the stronghold and [finally] did so by squeezing between the bars of the gate. After that they saw a huge hall and went up to it. The door was open and, entering, they saw a large number of men and most of them pretty big, sitting on two benches. Next they came before the king, Utgarð-Loki, and greeted him, but it was some time before he took any notice of them. He smiled contemptuously at them and remarked: 'News travels slowly from distant parts, or am I mistaken in thinking that this urchin is Thor-the-charioteer? You must be stronger than you look to me. At what arts do you and your companions think you excel? We don't allow anyone to stay with us who is not a past master of some craft or accomplishment.'

"Then the one who brought up the rear, Loki, said: 'I have an accomplishment which I am ready to try; there's no one here will eat faster than I can.' Utgarð-Loki replied: 'That's a feat if you can perform it and we'll

---

3. **Utgarð** (o͞ot'gärth): The letter ð ("edh" or "eth") represents a consonant sound like the *th* in *the*.

Thor's Fight with the Giants, Marten Winge 1872.

? *How does this romanticized depiction of Thor compare
to the way he is described in the selection?*

put it to the test.' He called over to the very end of the bench that the man called Logi[4] should take the floor in front of the company and pit himself against Loki. Then a trencher was fetched and brought into the hall and filled with chopped-up meat. Loki sat down at one end and Logi at the other, and each of them ate as fast as he could. They met in the middle of the trencher and by then Loki had left only the bones of his meat, but Logi had eaten all his meat, bones, and trencher into the bargain, so everyone thought that Loki had lost the contest.

"Then Utgarð-Loki asked what the youngster there could do. Thjalfi said he would run a race against anyone Utgarð-Loki produced. Utgarð-Loki said that that was a good accomplishment; he reckoned he must be very good at running to perform this feat,

---

4. **Logi** (lōg'ē)

yet he agreed it should be tried forthwith. Utgarð-Loki got up and went outside then, and there along a level bit of ground was a good running track. Utgarð-Loki called to him a lad whose name was Hugi[5] and told him to run a race with Thjalfi. They ran the first race and Hugi was so far ahead that he turned back to meet Thjalfi at the end of it.

"Then Utgarð-Loki said: 'You will have to exert yourself a bit more, Thjalfi, if you are to win this contest and yet it's true that no men have [ever] come here who have struck me as being quicker on their feet than this.' Then they ran the second race, and this time when Hugi came to the end and turned round, Thjalfi was a long crossbow shot behind. Utgarð-Loki said: 'I think Thjalfi is a good runner, but I don't believe he will win the contest now; we'll prove it, however, when they run the third race.' Then they ran yet another race. Hugi had reached the end and turned back, however, before Thjalfi had come halfway and everyone said that this sport had been put to the test.

"Then Utgarð-Loki asked Thor what accomplishment it would be he was going to display to them—and men after telling such great tales of his mighty deeds. Thor answered that he would like best to pit himself against someone in drinking. Utgarð-Loki said that that might well be and went into

BRONZE STATUETTE OF THOR HOLDING HIS HAMMER, Iceland, C. A.D. 1000.

Werner Forman Archive/National Museum, Iceland

the hall and calling his cupbearer bade him fetch the sconce-horn the retainers were accustomed to drink from. The cupbearer at once came forward with the horn and placed it in Thor's hands. Utgarð-Loki remarked: 'We consider it good drinking if this horn is drained at one drink, some men take two to empty it, but no one is such a wretched drinker that he can't finish it in three.' Thor looked at the horn. It did not strike him as being very big, although it was a bit on the long side, and he was very thirsty. He began drinking in great gulps and thought he would not need to bend to the horn more than once. When, however, his breath failed and he raised his head from it to see what progress had been made in the drinking, it seemed to him that it was only a little lower in the horn than before.

"Then Utgarð-Loki said: 'You drank well but not too much; I would never have believed it if I had been told that Asa-Thor couldn't take a bigger drink. However, I know you will empty it at the second draft.' Thor made no reply, put the horn to his mouth intending to take a bigger drink and strove at the drinking until he was out of breath; yet he saw that the end of the horn would not tilt up as much as he would have liked. When he took the horn from his mouth and looked into it, it seemed to him that he had made still less impression than before, although there was now enough space between the rim and the liquor to carry the horn without spilling.

---

5. **Hugi** (yōō′gē)

"Then Utgarð-Loki said: 'What about it, Thor? Aren't you leaving more for the one drink left over than will be quite convenient for you? It seems to me, if you are going to empty the horn at the third draft, that this will have to be the biggest. You won't be considered so great a man here amongst us as you are with the Aesir, you know, unless you can give a better account of yourself in other contests than it seems to me you will in this.' At that Thor grew angry, put the horn to his mouth and took a tremendously long drink as hard as he could; and when he looked at the horn, he had at any rate made a slight difference. He then gave up the horn and would drink no more.

"Utgarð-Loki remarked: 'It is evident that your strength is not as great as we had imagined. But do you want to make trial of any other feats? It is clear that you don't show to advantage in this one.' Thor answered: 'I can make trial of some feats yet; when I was at home with the Aesir, however, I'd have thought it strange for drinks like these to be called little—what sport are you proposing for me now?'

"Then Utgarð-Loki said: 'Youngsters here perform the feat—it's not thought much of—of lifting my cat up from the ground; I would never have suggested such a thing to Asa-Thor if I'd not seen that you aren't nearly as strong as I thought you were.' Thereupon a gray cat jumped forward onto the hall floor. It was rather a big one, but Thor went up to it, put his arm round under the middle of its belly, and lifted up. The cat arched its back as Thor raised his arm, and when he was stretching up as high as he could, the cat had to lift one of its paws [from the floor]; that was all Thor could do in that trial of skill.

"Then Utgarð-Loki said: 'This contest has gone as I expected; it's rather a big cat and Thor is a short little fellow compared with such big men as we have here.' At that Thor said: 'Call me little if you like, but let someone come and wrestle with me now; now I am angry!' Utgarð-Loki looked along the bench and said: 'I don't see anyone here who wouldn't feel it beneath him to wrestle with you.' He added, however, 'Wait a bit, call my foster mother, the old woman Elli,[6] here, and let Thor wrestle with her if he wants to. She has brought down men who have struck me as being stronger-looking than Thor.'

"Thereupon an aged crone came into the hall and Utgarð-Loki said she was to come to grips with Asa-Thor. There is no need to make a long story of it. The wrestling went so that the harder Thor exerted himself the firmer she stood her ground. Then the old woman began trying holds and Thor lost his balance; there was a tremendous tussle, but it was not long before Thor fell onto one knee. Utgarð-Loki went up to them then and told them to stop wrestling, saying there was no need for Thor to offer to wrestle with any more of his retainers. By that time it was late in the evening. Utgarð-Loki showed Thor and his companions where to sit down and they stayed there the night and were shown great hospitality.

"As soon as dawn broke the next day Thor and his companions got up, dressed, and were ready to go away. Then Utgarð-Loki came to where they were and had a table set up for them. There was no lack of good cheer in the way of food and drink. When they had finished the meal, they set out on their journey and Utgarð-Loki accompanied them, going out of the stronghold with them. At their parting he addressed Thor, asking him how he thought his journey had turned out and whether he had ever met a man mightier than he [Utgarð-Loki] was.

---

6. **Elli** (el'ē)

Thor replied that he would not deny that he had been put to shame in their dealings with each other. 'I know besides that you'll dub me a nobody and I don't like that.'

"Then Utgarð-Loki said: 'I'm going to tell you the truth now that you've come out of the stronghold—if I live and have any say in the matter, you are never going to come inside it again; upon my word you'd never have got in if I'd known you had so much strength; you nearly landed us in disaster. But I have deceived you with spells. The first time when I came across you in the wood I'd come to meet you, and when you were to undo the provision bag, I'd tied it up with iron wire and you didn't discover where to undo it. After that you hit me three blows with the hammer, the first of these was the least and yet if it had reached me it would have been my death. Where you saw a saddle-backed hill close to my stronghold and in it three square-shaped valleys and one very deep—they were the marks left by your hammer. I put the saddle-backed hill in front of your blows, but you didn't see that. The same thing goes for the contests in which you strove against my retainers. The first was what Loki did. He was very hungry and ate fast, but the man called Logi was "wild-fire" and he burned the trencher as quickly as he did the chopped meat. And when Thjalfi was running against the one called Hugi, that was my thought, and Thjalfi couldn't be expected to compete in speed with that. And when you were drinking from the horn and thought you were being slow, upon my word, I never would have believed such a miracle possible; the other end of the horn was in the sea but you didn't perceive that, and now when you come to the ocean you'll see how much you have made it shrink.' That is called the ebb tide now. He continued: 'I thought it no less wonderful when you lifted up the cat and, to tell you the truth, everyone who saw it was terrified when you lifted one of its paws from the ground. That cat was not what it appeared to be; it was the Miðgarð[7] Serpent that lies curled round the world and is scarcely long enough head to tail to encircle the earth. You stretched up so high that it wasn't far to the sky. It was a marvelous thing, too, that you held out so long in the wrestling match and only fell down onto one knee when you were struggling with Elli, because there never has been, nor ever will be anyone (if he grows old enough to become aged), who is not tripped up by old age. And now, as a matter of fact, we are going to part and it will be better for us both for you not to come to see me again. I shall go on defending my stronghold with some such magic or other so that you will not win any power over me.'

"When Thor heard this speech he gripped his hammer and swung it aloft but, when he was going to strike, he saw no Utgarð-Loki. Then he turned round to the stronghold with the idea of destroying it. He saw no stronghold there—[only] spacious and beautiful plains. He turned away and went on his journey until he came back to Thruðvangar.[8] To tell you the truth, however, it was then he resolved to see if he could contrive an encounter with the Miðgarð Serpent, as he afterwards did. Now I don't think that anyone could tell you a better tale about this expedition of Thor's."

---

7. **Miðgarð** (mith'gärth): the middle level of the Norse universe, inhabited by human beings, dwarfs, and giants.
8. **Thruðvangar** (thruth'vän·gər): Thor's realm in Asgard, world of the gods.

First Thoughts

How do you feel about the giant's use of trickery? Would you react the way Thor does when he learns about it?

Identifying Facts

1. Why does Thor become angry with the farmer and his family? How does he punish them?

2. Why does Thor become angry with Skrymir? What happens when, in his anger, Thor strikes Skrymir with his hammer?

3. What contests do the visitors engage in? What are the results?

4. What does Utgarð-Loki admit to Thor as Thor is about to depart?

Interpreting Meanings

1. How is **understatement** used in the description of Skrymir and in Skrymir's reaction to Thor's hammering on his head? What impact does this understatement have on the mood of the story? What other examples of understatement can you find in this story?

2. A **motif** is a word, character, object, image, metaphor, or idea that recurs in a work or in several works. The contest motif is central to this story. What is the importance of the contests here?

3. How is Thor **characterized** here? What do his actions and their results reveal about the Norse system of values?

4. A **myth** is a story about superhuman beings that may be used to explain events and actions in the real world. Myths are usually stories with much action but little description or character development. In what ways does the myth about Thor in Giantland reflect these characteristics?

Applying Meanings

This myth might be interpreted as a depiction of a contest between cleverness and physical strength. In any contest between cleverness and strength, which quality would you expect to win? Why?

Creative Writing Response

Writing a Humorous Episode. This myth presents a god, Thor, from an unusual perspective. Think of a god or goddess, hero or heroine, that you have read about. Imagine that character in a humorous situation that seems beneath his or her dignity. For example, imagine the Egyptian goddess Isis having trouble with her laundry, or the Roman hero Aeneas having difficulty explaining what he does for a living to his young son. Try to use **understatement** and other examples of **verbal irony** in your humorous episode.

Language and Vocabulary

Norse Contributions to English

In the fifth century, England was invaded by Anglo-Saxon tribes who spoke a Germanic language. Their language developed into Old English. Basic words such as *the, you, to,* and *be* date back to the original Anglo-Saxon language.

Centuries later, the Vikings invaded England. The language of these invaders was close enough to Old English to make communication possible, and Old English was soon enriched by words from Old Norse.

Norse contributions to English include many important, everyday terms. Use a dictionary with etymologies to find out the origins of these common words.

1. they
2. sky
3. egg
4. scare
5. wrong
6. dirt

Behind the Scenes

Norse Mythology and Modern Fantasy Writers

The British writers J.R.R. Tolkien (1892–1973) and C. S. Lewis (1898–1963) both developed an early interest in Norse mythology. As adults, both writers continued to pursue their fascination with the Norse myths, and both became famous for writing fantasies that featured mythical worlds.

As a boy, Tolkien was captivated by the old Icelandic tales. His favorite was the story of the Germanic hero Sigurd (Siegfried), who slays the dragon Fafnir. Tolkien became obsessed with dragons and other mythical creatures. This boyhood interest was reflected in his first novel, *The Hobbit,* which features the villainous dragon Smaug.

C. S. Lewis was a young boy when he came across these lines in a book of poems by Henry Wadsworth Longfellow:

> I heard a voice, that cried,
> "Balder the beautiful
>   Is dead, is dead!"

At the time, Lewis did not know that Balder was the Norse god of goodness and harmony. Nevertheless, the words gave him an extraordinary feeling: a vision of great cold expanses of northern sky filled his mind. Later, when he was fifteen, Lewis came across an illustration for a story about Siegfried, and he was hooked. He began reading everything he could about Norse mythology.

Much later, Tolkien and Lewis met at Oxford University in 1926. Tolkien, already a professor, decided to organize a club to read Icelandic sagas and myths. The club was called the Coalbiters, after the humorous Icelandic word *Kolbitar,* which means "those who sit close enough to the fire they could bite the hot coals." Lewis was invited to join.

The Coalbiters began by reading Snorri Sturluson's *Prose Edda* in the original Icelandic. The group then moved on to the *Elder Edda,* an ancient collection of Norse mythology. Out of their shared love for Norse mythology, Tolkien and Lewis developed a strong and lasting friendship.

For a while, Lewis wrote his own versions of existing Norse myths. Then he moved on to other writings, including his classic Narnia tales for children, as well as science-fiction tales focusing on moral problems.

Tolkien, too, decided to invent his own mythical universe. He created a complex realm of legends and heroes, complete with detailed maps and imaginary languages based on the old Norse and Anglo-Saxon languages. His book *The Hobbit* (1937) and his three-volume work *The Lord of the Rings* (1954–1956) chronicle the adventures of hobbits, small, humanlike creatures with furry feet. Elves, dwarfs, and goblins inhabit this magical world. Tolkien gave his characters names from the Norse myths: Gandalf, Thorin, Bombur, and Durin. In Tolkien's works, the grand heroics of the Norse myths are transformed to appeal to new generations of adults and children.

Marie de France
Twelfth Century

Illumination of Tristan and Iseult.

An atmosphere of mystery will probably always surround Marie de France. She is considered one of the greatest writers of the Middle Ages, and yet all we know for certain about her is that her name appears in three separate works written in French between 1160 and 1215. The first, the *Lais*, is a group of narratives written in verse. The second is the *Fables*, a collection of fables translated from English into Old French. The third, *St. Patrick's Purgatory*, is a translation from Latin into French of the life of a saint.

The name "Marie de France" comes from a reference toward the end of the *Fables*. The writer of the *Fables* refers to herself by saying: "Marie is my name, I am of France." Scholars have concluded that Marie was of noble birth, since she was very well educated. In addition to her native French, she knew Latin and English and was familiar with the Greek and Roman classics as well as with contemporary French works.

Marie's *Lais* differed from much of the romantic literature of her day. First, she drew her inspiration from tales of Celtic origin—tales told by the peoples of Brittany, Ireland, Scotland, and Wales. Second, in an age dominated by lengthy romances, Marie's *lais* were brief, presenting an involved story about romantic passion in relatively few lines. Third, the typical literature of the Middle Ages, such as the *Song of Roland* (see page 692) and *Perceval* (see page 720), was dominated by masculine ideas about war, love, and chivalry and focused on the knight's responsibility to society. Although Marie's *lais* are set in chivalric society, she was primarily concerned with presenting the personal lives of both knights and their ladies.

Marie wrote during what is sometimes called the "Renaissance of the Twelfth Century." The educated classes, bored with the larger-than-life portraits of heroes and military events in the epics, wanted stories that were more personal. Marie de France provided for their needs with her stories about human misfortune, unhappy and restricting marriages, and heroes and heroines trapped by life's circumstances.

Osterreichische NationalBibliothek

Reader's Guide

CHEVREFOIL

Background

"Chevrefoil" (shev′rə·fwäl′), which means "honeysuckle," concerns the forbidden love of Tristan and Iseult (i·so̅o̅lt′). According to this famous Celtic story, Tristan goes to Ireland to bring Iseult, a beautiful princess, to Cornwall. There she is supposed to wed Tristan's uncle, King Mark. However, on the way to Cornwall, the pair accidentally drink a magic potion that makes them fall eternally in love. King Mark marries Iseult, but later, he discovers the love between Tristan and Iseult. Mark sends Tristan into exile. Many adventures befall the lovers from that time on, and eventually they die on the same day.

In "Chevrefoil," Marie de France focuses on a single moment in the story of Tristan and Iseult. Because the details of the entire narrative would have been familiar to her readers, Marie is free to concentrate on a scene that summarizes the sorrow and fatefulness of this famous love story.

Because medieval marriages were arranged by parents, romantic love was not a part of marriage. As a result, an elaborate system known as courtly love evolved in upper-class society. Typically, a young lover idealized a married woman of aristocratic background, suffering lovesickness when they were apart and longing to be united with her.

Oral Response

Think of all the love stories that you have read, seen on television or at the movies, or heard about. Discuss the features of these love stories. Are they happy or tragic? Do the lovers die or do they live "happily ever after"?

Literary Focus

A **metaphor** is a figure of speech that makes a direct comparison between two apparently unlike things without using such connective words as *like, as, than,* or *resembles*. An **extended metaphor** is a metaphor that is developed over several lines of writing or throughout an entire work. As you read the narrative verse, you will see that the union of the honeysuckle and the hazel tree is used as an extended metaphor for the love of Tristan and Iseult.

CHEVREFOIL
Marie de France
translated by
ROBERT HANNING AND JOAN FERRANTE

As you read the verse, try to decide what view of love Marie de France is expressing. What do you think her attitude is toward the lovers?

II.
Periclȳmenon perfoliatum.

Honeysuckle (detail), engraving for Basilius Besler's *Florilegium*, Nuremberg, 1613.

I should like very much
to tell you the truth
about the *lai* men call *Chevrefoil*—
why it was composed and where it
    came from.
5 Many have told and recited it to me
and I have found it in writing,
about Tristan and the queen
and their love that was so true,
that brought them much suffering
10 and caused them to die the same day.
King Mark was annoyed,
angry at his nephew Tristan;
he exiled Tristan from his land
because of the queen whom he loved.
15 Tristan returned to his own country,
South Wales, where he was born,
he stayed a whole year;
he couldn't come back.
Afterward he began to expose himself
20 to death and destruction.
Don't be surprised at this:
for one who loves very faithfully
is sad and troubled
when he cannot satisfy his desires.
25 Tristan was sad and worried,
so he set out from his land.
He traveled straight to Cornwall,
where the queen lived,

and entered the forest all alone—
30 he didn't want anyone to see him;
he came out only in the evening
when it was time to find shelter.
He took lodging that night,
with peasants, poor people.
35 He asked them for news
of the king—what he was doing.
They told him they had heard
that the barons had been summoned
      by ban.[1]
They were to come to Tintagel[2]
40 where the king wanted to hold his court;
at Pentecost[3] they would all be there,
there'd be much joy and pleasure,
and the queen would be there too.
Tristan heard and was very happy;
45 she would not be able to go there
without his seeing her pass.
The day the king set out,
Tristan also came to the woods
by the road he knew
50 their assembly must take.
He cut a hazel tree in half,
then he squared[4] it.
When he had prepared the wood,
he wrote his name on it with his knife.
55 If the queen noticed it—
and she should be on the watch for it,
for it had happened before
and she had noticed it then—
she'd know when she saw it,
60 that the piece of wood had come
      from her love.
This was the message of the writing
that he had sent to her:
he had been there a long time,

had waited and remained
65 to find out and to discover
how he could see her,
for he could not live without her.
With the two of them it was just
as it is with the honeysuckle
70 that attaches itself to the hazel tree:
when it has wound and attached
and worked itself around the trunk,
the two can survive together;
but if someone tries to separate them,
75 the hazel dies quickly
and the honeysuckle with it.
"Sweet love, so it is with us:
You cannot live without me, nor I
      without you."
The queen rode along;
80 she looked at the hillside
and saw the piece of wood; she knew
      what it was,
she recognized all the letters.
The knights who were accompanying her,
who were riding with her,
85 she ordered to stop:
she wanted to dismount and rest.
They obeyed her command.
She went far away from her people
and called her girl
90 Brenguein, who was loyal to her.
She went a short distance from the road;
and in the woods she found him
whom she loved more than any living thing.
They took great joy in each other.
95 He spoke to her as much as he desired,
she told him whatever she liked.
Then she assured him
that he would be reconciled with the king—
for it weighed on him
100 that he had sent Tristan away;
he'd done it because of the accusation.
Then she departed, she left her love,
but when it came to the separation,
they began to weep.

---

1. **ban:** official proclamation.
2. **Tintagel** (tin·ta′jəl): cape in northwest Cornwall
   where, according to legend, King Arthur was born.
3. **Pentecost** (pen′ti·kôst′): the seventh Sunday after
   Easter; Whitsunday.
4. **squared:** to cut to a square or rectangular shape.

105 Tristan went to Wales,
to wait until his uncle sent for him.
For the joy that he'd felt
from his love when he saw her,
by means of the stick he inscribed
110 as the queen had instructed,
and in order to remember the words,

Tristan, who played the harp well,
composed a new *lai* about it.
I shall name it briefly:
115 in English they call it *Goat's Leaf*
the French call it *Chevrefoil.*
I have given you the truth
about the *lai* that I have told here.

First Thoughts

What do you think Tristan and Iseult ought to do? Should they renounce their love, or should they follow their hearts? Why?

Identifying Facts

1. What do we learn about Tristan and Iseult in the first twenty-four lines of the poem?

2. How does Tristan discover that the queen will be traveling through the forest?

3. How does Tristan let Iseult know that he wants to meet her?

4. What happens during the meeting between Tristan and Iseult?

Interpreting Meanings

1. In the forest, the lovers meet and speak briefly. What specific details does the poet include to convey their feelings for each other? How would you describe the quality of their relationship?

2. An **extended metaphor** creates a comparison over several lines of a poem or even throughout an entire poem. What is the meaning of the extended metaphor that compares Tristan and Iseult to the honeysuckle and the hazel tree?

3. A **conflict** is a struggle or clash between opposing characters, forces, or emotions. What is the main conflict in "Chevrefoil"?

Applying Meanings

In what ways might Tristan and Iseult behave differently in the modern world? In what ways have the constraints of society changed? Do similar constraints still exist?

Creative Writing Response

Writing a Scene from a Larger Story. "Chevrefoil" focuses on a single event in a much larger story. Think of a well-known story from a book, television, or film and write a brief scene that focuses tightly on the characters and a particular event from the story. You could, for example, write a scene featuring Beauty and the Beast from the fairy tale, or Robin Hood and Maid Marian from *Robin Hood*. The story need not be romantic, but it should, like "Chevrefoil," represent the story as a whole.

Critical Writing Response

Analyzing a Story's Appeal. Many writers throughout the centuries have retold or alluded to the story of the unhappy lovers Tristan and Iseult. Write a three-paragraph essay exploring why this tale of forbidden love has had such a lasting appeal. You might want to consider the comment by a character in Shakespeare's *A Midsummer Night's Dream* who says, "The course of true love never did run smooth." In your essay, mention other tragic love stories that you are familiar with.

Chrétien de Troyes
c. 1135–c. 1190

Bibliotheque Nationale, Paris

King Arthur draws the sword from the stone, from a medieval French illumination.

Chrétien de Troyes (krā·tyan də trwä´) was one of the most famous French medieval court poets. We have little definite knowledge of Chrétien's life, but he probably was born at Troyes, a city in northeastern France, and trained for a position in the Church. His education most likely included study of the classics, since early in his career he wrote verse adaptations of works by the Roman poet Ovid (see page 420). However, he soon became so fascinated by Celtic stories of King Arthur and his knights that he created a new type of poetic narrative called the **Arthurian romance**.

Most of the Arthurian romances focus not on King Arthur but on particular knights of the Round Table and their loves and adventures. Chrétien's most influential work, *Perceval, or the Story of the Grail,* focuses on a new kind of medieval hero, a knight who is less interested in worldly glory than in such Christian values as penitence and charity. Rather than seeking the love of a lady, this hero's quest is for spiritual perfection, and he performs his great deeds for the love of God.

Chrétien's *Perceval* is the earliest known version of the legend of the Holy Grail, a cup or platter regarded as a holy object. The Grail is used to carry communion wafers, which are an important element in Christian ritual. In later Arthurian romances, the Grail is described as the cup from which Christ drank at the Last Supper, the same cup that is later used to collect drops of Christ's blood at the Crucifixion. Many knights of Arthur's Round Table try and fail to find this holy object, which can only be obtained by a person who is absolutely pure.

Chrétien de Troyes died before completing *Perceval,* so no one knows precisely how he intended to resolve the story. What we do know, however, is that Chrétien de Troyes, by uniting Celtic myth and legend with the Christian legend of the Grail, created a story filled with adventure, love, danger, humor, and spirituality that has lasted through the centuries.

Reader's Guide

THE GRAIL
from Perceval

Background

Although Perceval is the son of a great knight, his mother has kept him from knowing anything about knighthood because she does not want her son to die young as her husband and two other sons have done. However, as soon as Perceval meets five wandering knights, he gets a taste of adventure and instantly decides to desert his mother and become a knight himself.

Perceval reaches King Arthur's court, where his worth is immediately recognized. There he receives the armor and weapons of a knight. However, he is also ridiculed at the court because his manners are so crude. An older knight, Gornemant of Gohort, takes Perceval aside and advises him how to behave. Among other things, he advises Perceval not to talk too much, since his speech may reveal his lack of education. Perceval later defends a besieged castle and falls in love with its lady, Blancheflor. As the selection you are about to read opens, Perceval, overcome with regret for abandoning his mother, has just left Blancheflor's castle to find his mother. Along the way, Perceval meets a fisherman who invites him to another castle. There Perceval meets a mysterious, unidentified nobleman known as the Fisher King.

Writer's Response

Have you ever failed to do something and later regretted that you had not taken action? For example, have you ever wished that you had spoken up for something you believed in, or tried to talk to someone you wanted to get to know better? Freewrite about your experience.

Literary Focus

A **description** is a written passage that is intended to create, or re-create, a person, place, thing, event, or experience. Description shows us how something looks, sounds, smells, tastes, or feels. The sentence *It was a fancy room* does not offer much by way of description, but the sentence *The light of hundreds of candles reflected from the golden shields hanging on the walls* appeals to the reader's sense of sight. In the following selection, memorable descriptions help the reader recognize the special importance of two objects: a lance and a grail.

Chrétien de Troyes   **721**

THE GRAIL
from Perceval
Chrétien de Troyes
translated by
RUTH HARWOOD CLINE

> *In this section of the romance, Perceval is referred to only as "the youth" or "the young man," because he does not yet know his true name, Perceval. When you reach line 73, stop and jot down a few words and phrases that describe what kind of person Perceval seems to be.*

The youth began his journey from
the castle, and the daytime whole
he did not meet one living soul:
no creature from the wide earth's span,
5   no Christian woman, Christian man
who could direct him on his way.
The young man did not cease to pray
the sovereign father, God, Our Lord,
if He were willing, to accord
10   that he would find his mother still
alive and well. He reached a hill
and saw a river at its base.
So rapid was the current's pace,
so deep the water, that he dared
15   not enter it, and he declared,
"Oh God Almighty! It would seem,
if I could get across this stream,
I'd find my mother, if she's living."
He rode the bank with some misgiving
20   and reached a cliff, but at that place
the water met the cliff's sheer face
and kept the youth from going through.
A little boat came into view;
it headed down the river, floating
25   and carrying two men out boating.

The Antioch Chalice, fourth century A.D. *This is probably the oldest existing Christian chalice*

The Metropolitan Museum of Art, Cloisters Collection Purchase 1950

The young knight halted there and waited.
He watched the way they navigated
and thought that they would pass the place
he waited by the cliff's sheer face.
30   They stayed in mid-stream, where they stopped
and took the anchor, which they dropped.
The man afore, a fisher, took
a fish to bait his line and hook;
in size the little fish he chose

35   was larger than a minnow grows.
The knight, completely at a loss,
not knowing how to get across,
first greeted them, then asked the pair,
"Please, gentlemen, nearby is there
40   a bridge to reach the other side?"
To which the fisherman replied,
"No, brother, for besides this boat,
the one in which we are afloat,
which can't bear five men's weight
    as charge,
45   there is no other boat as large
for twenty miles each way and more,
and you can't cross on horseback, for
there is no ferry, bridge, nor ford."
"Tell me," he answered, "by Our Lord,
50   where I may find a place to stay."
The fisherman said, "I should say
you'll need a roof tonight and more,
so I will lodge you at my door.
First find the place this rock is breached[1]
55   and ride uphill, until you've reached
the summit of the cliff," he said.
"Between the wood and river bed
you'll see, down in the valley wide,
the manor house where I reside."
60   The knight rode up the cliff until
he reached the summit of the hill.
He looked around him from that stand
but saw no more than sky and land.
He cried, "What have I come to see?
65   Stupidity and trickery!
May God dishonor and disgrace
the man who sent me to this place!
He had the long way round in mind,
when he told me that I would find
70   a manor when I reached the peak.
Oh, fisherman, why did you speak?
For if you said it out of spite,
you tricked me badly!" He caught sight

of a tower starting to appear
75   down in a valley he was near,
and as the tower came into view,
if people were to search, he knew,
as far as Beirut,[2] they would not
find any finer tower or spot.
80   The tower was dark gray stone, and square,
and flanked by lesser towers, a pair.
Before the tower the hall was laid;
before the hall was the arcade.[3]
On toward the tower the young man rode
85   in haste and called the man who showed
the way to him a worthy guide.
No longer saying he had lied,
he praised the fisherman, elated
to find his lodgings as he stated.
90   The youth went toward the gate and found
the drawbridge lowered to the ground.
He rode across the drawbridge span.
Four squires awaited the young man.
Two squires came up to help him doff
95   his arms and took his armor off.
The third squire led his horse away
to give him fodder, oats, and hay.
The fourth brought a silk cloak, new-made,
and led him to the hall's arcade,
100   which was so fine, you may be sure
you'd not find, even if you were
to search as far as Limoges,[4] one
as splendid in comparison.
The young man paused in the arcade,
105   until the castle's master made
two squires escort him to the hall.
The young man entered with them all
and found the hall was square inside:
it was as long as it was wide;
110   and in the center of its span

---

1. **the place this rock is breached:** an opening in the cliff wall.

2. **Beirut** (bā·rōōt'): capital of Lebanon; seaport on the Mediterranean.

3. **arcade** (är·kād'): passage with arched roof or line of arches.

4. **Limoges** (lē·mōzh'): city in west-central France.

he saw a handsome nobleman[5]
with grayed hair, sitting on a bed.
The nobleman wore on his head
a mulberry-black sable cap

115 and wore a dark silk robe and wrap.
He leaned back in his weakened state
and let his elbow take his weight.
Between four columns, burning bright,
a fire of dry logs cast its light.

120 In order to enjoy its heat,
four hundred men could find a seat
around the outsized fire, and not
one man would take a chilly spot.
The solid fireplace columns could

125 support the massive chimney hood,
which was of bronze, built high
      and wide.
The squires, one squire on either side,
appeared before their lord foremost
and brought the youth before his host.

130 He saw the young man, whom he
      greeted.
"My friend," the nobleman entreated,
"don't think me rude not to arise;
I hope that you will realize
that I cannot do so with ease."

135 "Don't even mention it, sir, please,
I do not mind," replied the boy,
"may Heaven give me health and joy."
The lord rose higher on the bed,
as best he could, with pain, and said,

140 "My friend, come nearer, do not be
embarrassed or disturbed by me,
for I command you to come near.
Come to my side and sit down here."
The nobleman began to say,

145 "From where, sir, did you come today?"
He said, "This morning, sir, I came

from Belrepeire,[6] for that's its name."
"So help me God," the lord replied,
"you must have had a long day's ride:

150 to start before the light of morn
before the watchman blew his horn."
"Sir, I assure you, by that time
the morning bells had rung for prime,"[7]
the young man made the observation.

155 While they were still in conversation,
a squire entered through the door
and carried in a sword he wore
hung from his neck and which thereto
he gave the rich man, who withdrew

160 the sword halfway and checked the blade
to see where it was forged and made,
which had been written on the sword.
The blade was wrought, observed the lord
of such fine steel, it would not break

165 save with its bearer's life at stake
on one occasion, one alone,
a peril that was only known
to him who forged and tempered it.
The squire said, "Sir, if you permit,

170 your lovely blonde niece sent this gift,
and you will never see or lift
a sword that's lighter for its strength,
considering its breadth and length.
Please give the sword to whom you
      choose,

175 but if it goes to one who'll use
the sword that he is given well,
you'll greatly please the demoiselle.[8]
The forger of the sword you see
has never made more swords than
      three,

180 and he is going to die before

---

5. **a handsome nobleman:** The lord of the castle is generally known as the Fisher King, who suffers from a mysterious malady.

6. **Belrepeire** (bel·rə·pār'): the castle of Perceval's lady, Blancheflor; before meeting the Fisher King, Perceval defended Belrepeire, which was under seige.

7. **prime:** in the Catholic liturgy, the first hour of daylight.

8. **demoiselle** (dem'wä·zel'): damsel; young lady.

QUEST FOR THE HOLY GRAIL, **tapestry from design by Edward Burne-Jones, woven by Morris and Co., 19th century.**

he ever forges any more.
No sword will be quite like this sword."
Immediately the noble lord
bestowed it on the newcomer,

185 who realized that its hangings were
a treasure and of worth untold.
The pommel[9] of the sword was gold,
the best Arabian or Grecian;
the sheath's embroidery gold Venetian.

190 Upon the youth the castle's lord
bestowed the richly mounted sword
and said to him, "This sword, dear brother,
was destined for you and none other.
I wish it to be yours henceforth.

195 Gird on the sword and draw it forth."
He thanked the lord, and then the knight
made sure the belt was not too tight,
and girded on the sword, and took
the bare blade out for a brief look.

200 Then in the sheath it was replaced:
it looked well hanging at his waist

and even better in his fist.
It seemed as if it would assist
the youth in any time of need

205 to do a brave and knightly deed.
Beside the brightly burning fire
the youth turned round and saw a squire,
who had his armor in his care,
among the squires standing there.

210 He told this squire to hold the sword
and took his seat beside the lord,
who honored him as best he might.
The candles cast as bright a light
as could be found in any manor.

215 They chatted in a casual manner.
Out of a room a squire came, clasping
a lance of purest white: while grasping
the center of the lance, the squire
walked through the hall between the fire

220 and two men sitting on the bed.
All saw him bear, with measured tread,
the pure white lance. From its white tip
a drop of crimson blood would drip
and run along the white shaft and

225 drip down upon the squire's hand,
and then another drop would flow.
The knight who came not long ago

---

9. **pommel** (pum'əl): knob on the hilt of a sword or dagger.

Chrétien de Troyes **725**

beheld this marvel, but preferred
not to inquire why it occurred,
230 for he recalled the admonition
the lord made part of his tuition,[10]
since he had taken pains to stress
the dangers of loquaciousness.[11]
The young man thought his questions might
235 make people think him impolite.
and that's why he did not inquire.
Two more squires entered, and each squire
held candelabra, wrought of fine
pure gold with niello[12] work design.
240 The squires with candelabra fair
were an extremely handsome pair.
At least ten lighted candles blazed
in every holder that they raised.
The squires were followed by a maiden
245 who bore a grail, with both hands laden.
The bearer was of noble mien,[13]
well dressed, and lovely, and serene,
and when she entered with the grail,
the candles suddenly grew pale,
250 the grail cast such a brilliant light,
as stars grow dimmer in the night
when sun or moonrise makes them fade.
A maiden after her conveyed
a silver platter past the bed.
255 The grail, which had been borne ahead,
was made of purest, finest gold
and set with gems; a manifold
display of jewels of every kind,
the costliest that one could find

260 in any place on land or sea,
the rarest jewels there could be,
let not the slightest doubt be cast.
The jewels in the grail surpassed
all other gems in radiance.
265 They went the same way as the lance:
they passed before the lord's bedside
to another room and went inside.
The young man saw the maids' procession
and did not dare to ask a question
270 about the grail or whom they served;
the wise lord's warning he observed,
for he had taken it to heart.
I fear he was not very smart;
I have heard warnings people give:
275 that one can be too talkative,
but also one can be too still.
But whether it was good or ill,
I do not know, he did not ask.
The squires who were assigned the task
280 of bringing in the water and
the cloths obeyed the lord's command.
The men who usually were assigned
performed these tasks before they dined.
They washed their hands in water, warmed,
285 and then two squires, so I'm informed,
brought in the ivory tabletop,
made of one piece: they had to stop
and hold it for a while before
the lord and youth, until two more
290 squires entered, each one with a trestle.[14]
The trestles had two very special,
rare properties, which they contained
since they were built, and which remained
in them forever: they were wrought
295 of ebony, a wood that's thought
to have two virtues: it will not
ignite and burn and will not rot;

---

10. **the lord made part of his tuition:** Perceval had been instructed by the knight Gornemant not to talk too much so that people will not realize how uneducated he is.

11. **loquaciousness** (lō·kwā'shəs·nis): talkativeness.

12. **niello** (nē·el'ō): a method of decorating with inlaid metals.

13. **mien** (mēn): appearance.

14. **trestle** (tres'əl): a frame used to support a tabletop.

King Arthur and his knights at the Round Table, from a medieval French illumination.

315 Again the grail passed by the bed,
and still the youth remained reserved
about the grail and whom they served.
He did not ask, because he had
been told so kindly it was bad
320 to talk too much, and he had taken
these words to heart. He was mistaken;
though he remembered, he was still
much longer than was suitable.
At every course, and in plain sight,
325 the grail was carried past the knight,
who did not ask whom they were
    serving,
although he wished to know, observing
in silence that he ought to learn
about it prior to his return.
330 So he would ask: before he spoke
he'd wait until the morning broke,
and he would ask a squire to tell,
once he had told the lord farewell
and all the others in his train.
335 He put the matter off again
and turned his thoughts toward drink
    and food.
They brought, and in no stingy mood,
the foods and different types of wine,
which were delicious, rich and fine.
340 The squires were able to provide
the lord and young knight at his side
with every course a count, king, queen,
and emperor eat by routine.
At dinner's end, the two men stayed
345 awake and talked, while squires made
the beds and brought them fruit:
    they ate
the rarest fruits: the nutmeg, date,
fig, clove, and pomegranate red.
With Alexandrian gingerbread,
350 electuaries[16] at the end,
restoratives, a tonic blend,

these dangers cause no harm nor loss.
They laid the tabletop across
300 the trestles, and the cloth above.
What shall I say? To tell you of
the cloth is far beyond my scope.
No legate,[15] cardinal, or pope
has eaten from a whiter one.
305 The first course was of venison,
a peppered haunch, cooked in its fat,
accompanied by a clear wine that
was served in golden cups, a pleasant,
delicious drink. While they were present
310 a squire carved up the venison.
He set the peppered haunch upon
a silver platter, carved the meat,
and served the slices they would eat
by placing them on hunks of bread.

---

15. **legate** (leg'it): ambassador.

16. **electuaries** (ē·lek′chōō·er′ēz): medicinal pastes formed by combining honey or syrup with a drug.

and pliris archonticum[17]
for settling his stomachum.
Then various liqueurs were poured
355 for them to sample afterward:
straight piment,[18] which did not contain
sweet honey or a single grain
of pepper, wine of mulberries,
clear syrups, other delicacies.
360 The youth's astonishment persisted;
he did not know such things existed.
"Now, my dear friend," the great lord said,
"the time has come to go to bed.
I'll seek my room—don't think it queer—
365 and you will have your bed out here
and may lie down at any hour.
I do not have the slightest power
over my body anymore
and must be carried to my door."
370 Four nimble servants, strongly set,
came in and seized the coverlet
by its four corners (it was spread
beneath the lord, who lay in bed)
and carried him away to rest.
375 The others helped the youthful guest.
As he required, and when he chose,
they took his clothing off, and hose,[19]
and put him in a bed with white,
smooth linen sheets; he slept all night
380 at peace until the morning broke.
But when the youthful knight awoke,
he was the last to rise and found
that there was no one else around.
Exasperated and alone,
385 he had to get up on his own.
He made the best of it, arose,
and awkwardly drew on his hose

390 without a bit of help or aid.
He saw his armor had been laid
at night against the dais'[20] head
a little distance from his bed.
When he had armed himself at last,
he walked around the great hall past
395 the rooms and knocked at every door
which opened wide the night before,
but it was useless: juxtaposed,
the doors were tightly locked and closed.
He shouted, called, and knocked outside,
but no one opened or replied.
400 At last the young man ceased to call,
walked to the doorway of the hall,
which opened up, and passed through
   there,
and went on down the castle stair.
His horse was saddled in advance.
405 The young man saw his shield and lance
were leaned against the castle wall
upon the side that faced the hall.
He mounted, searched the castle whole,
but did not find one living soul,
410 one servant, or one squire around.
He hurried toward the gate and found
the men had let the drawbridge down,
so that the knight could leave the town
at any hour he wished to go.
415 His hosts had dropped the drawbridge so
the youth could cross it undeterred.
The squires were sent, the youth inferred,
out to the wood, where they were set
to checking every trap and net.
420 The drawbridge lay across the stream.
He would not wait and formed a scheme
of searching through the woods as well
to see if anyone could tell
about the lance, why it was bleeding,
425 about the grail, whom they were feeding,
and where they carried it in state.
The youth rode through the castle gate

---

17. **pliris archonticum** (plē'ris är·kon'tē·kəm): a kind of electuary.
18. **piment:** a drink usually made of wine flavored with honey and spices.
19. **hose:** tight-fitting, stockinglike outer garments worn by men during medieval times.

---

20. **dais** (dā'is): a raised platform.

and out upon the drawbridge plank.
Before he reached the other bank,
430 the young man started realizing
the forefeet of his horse were rising.
His horse made one great leap indeed.
Had he not jumped well, man and steed
would have been hurt. His rider swerved
435 to see what happened and observed
the drawbridge had been lifted high.
He shouted, hearing no reply.

"Whoever raised the bridge," said he,
"where are you? Come and talk to me!
440 Say something to me; come in view.
There's something I would ask of you,
some things I wanted to inquire,
some information I desire."
His words were wasted, vain and fond;[21]
445 no one was willing to respond.

---

21. **fond:** foolish.

First Thoughts

If you were Perceval, what would you have
done to find out what you wanted to know?

Identifying Facts

1. What object does the Fisher King give
   Perceval at his castle? What special
   qualities does this object have?
2. At the feast, why does Perceval fail to
   ask about the unusual objects he has
   seen? Why is he unable to ask about
   them the next morning?

Interpreting Meanings

1. Why does the Fisher King give Perceval
   the sword? What does the gift suggest
   about Perceval's future?
2. What details of **description** let you
   know that the lance and the grail have
   special importance? What do you think
   the lance and grail symbolize?
3. In medieval tales, heroes often have to
   pass various kinds of tests on the path
   to knighthood. Does Perceval undergo a
   test in this episode? If so, what is the
   test, and do you think he passes it?
   Why or why not?

Applying Meanings

Like any youth venturing out into the
world, Perceval is introduced to aspects of
life that are strange to him. What new aspects of life have *you* encountered as you
have matured? How would you advise
someone like Perceval?

Creative Writing Response

Continuing the Narrative. After leaving
the castle, Perceval learns that had he
asked about the lance and grail, the Fisher
King would have been healed. Perceval
vows to find the lance and grail. Chrétien
de Troyes died before he could describe
Perceval's return to the castle. What do
you think might have happened if Perceval
had returned? Write your own ending to
the story of Perceval's quest for the grail.
Try to create an **atmosphere**—that is,
overall mood or feeling—of mystery.

Speaking and Listening

Dramatizing a Scene. Turn the episode
describing Perceval's evening in the Fisher
King's castle into a short play. Prepare a
brief script including the speeches of the
various characters in the poem. You may
want to rewrite the dialogue in your own
words. Also include stage directions that
describe the characters' actions and their
surroundings. With other students, perform the scene for the class, using as
many or as few props as you wish.

Chrétien de Troyes **729**

Introduction

The Nibelungenlied

SIEGFRIED SLAYING THE DRAGON, nineteenth-century colored engraving.

Archiv Für Kunst Und Geschichte, Berlin

The *Nibelungenlied* (nē′bə·lŏŏng′ ən·lēt′), the national epic of Germany, is a gripping tale of love, revenge, and murder. The title literally means "song of the Nibelungs." In German myth and literature, the Nibelungs were an evil family that possessed an accursed treasure, which included a hoard of gold and a magic ring.

A Treasure and a Curse

The hero of the *Nibelungenlied* is Siegfried (sig′frēd), a prince who lives on the lower Rhine River in western Europe. As the epic opens, Siegfried has taken possession of the treasure of the Nibelungs. As a result, he is placed under a curse. Thus, from the start of the story, we know that although Siegfried will accomplish great things, he is ultimately doomed.

The treasure of the Nibelungs bestows magical powers as well as a curse, however. Along with the treasure, Siegfried also comes into possession of a cloak that makes its wearer invisible. Armed with these new powers, Siegfried kills a dragon and bathes in its blood. The blood hardens his skin, thereafter protecting him from all wounds. As he bathes, however, a linden leaf falls between his shoulders, so that the dragon's blood fails to touch one small spot. Thus, Siegfried is forever vulnerable in that one spot—just as the Greek hero Achilles was vulnerable in his heel.

The Epic's Structure

The *Nibelungenlied* was originally written as a long narrative poem divided into two parts. In the first half of the epic, Siegfried woos and weds the beautiful Princess Kriemhild (krēm'hilt'), the sister of King Gunther (gōōn'tər), king of Burgundy, an area of what is now southeast France. Gunther, in turn, woos a warrior princess of Iceland, Brunhild (brōōn'hilt'). However, he cannot win her without Siegfried's secret help.

By helping Gunther win Brunhild, Siegfried sows the seeds of his own downfall, for Brunhild later discovers that she has been tricked and has Siegfried killed. Kriemhild later takes her own revenge for Siegfried's death, but ultimately she, too, is killed.

Origins of the *Nibelungenlied*

The *Nibelungenlied* resembles the *Song of Roland*, the national epic of France (see page 692), in many ways. Like the *Song of Roland*, the *Nibelungenlied* consists of materials pieced together from many oral and written sources that were familiar to medieval audiences. The unknown author of the German epic transformed these materials into a single work. This anonymous author is thought to have lived somewhere near the Danube River in what is now Austria. Scholars generally agree that he composed the poem sometime between the years 1195 and 1205.

As with the plot of the *Song of Roland*, the story of the *Nibelungenlied* is based on real historical events. Again, however, the details of these events are sketchy. As the story unfolds, realism combines with elements of the supernatural. Indeed, the *Nibelungenlied* often has the feel of a German fairy tale, with all the elements of fantasy and horror associated with the tales collected much later by the Grimm brothers.

The Style of the Original Epic

The original *Nibelungenlied* was written in stanzas. Each stanza consists of four lines containing two pairs of rhymed couplets, a form that lends itself to oral presentation. The rhythmic verse of the *Nibelungenlied*, combined with the poem's simple and direct narrative style, produced an epic that has gripped the German artistic imagination for centuries.

Reader's Guide

HOW SIEGFRIED WAS SLAIN
from the Nibelungenlied

Background

Before the events of the selection you are about to read, Siegfried had fallen in love with the famous beauty Kriemhild. He won her hand in marriage by doing "service" for her. As part of this service, he helped her brother, King Gunther, marry the powerful Queen Brunhild.

Brunhild had vowed that she would marry only the man who could beat her at hurling a spear, throwing a stone, and jumping. Using his cloak of invisibility, Siegfried stood beside Gunther and accomplished these feats for him. Years later, however, during an argument, Kriemhild reveals to Brunhild how Siegfried had tricked her. Brunhild vows revenge, and Gunther and his servant Hagen (Hä′gən) become her accomplices in a plot to kill Siegfried during a hunt.

As the selection begins, Siegfried is leaving the worried Kriemhild to take part in the hunt. Hagen, who deeply resents Siegfried's superiority over Gunther, has just tricked Kriemhild into revealing the secret of Siegfried's vulnerable spot.

Oral Response

The theme of betrayal runs through the *Nibelungenlied* and, in fact, through much of the literature of the medieval period. During the Middle Ages, loyalty was one of the supreme virtues and disloyalty one of the greatest wrongs. Discuss the issues of loyalty and betrayal for a few minutes. What do they mean to you? Do you think that most people today value loyalty and think that betrayal is a great wrong?

Literary Focus

A **conflict** is a struggle or clash between opposing characters, forces, or emotions. Usually conflicts are resolved by the end of a story. In an epic such as the *Nibelungenlied*, the plot is usually built around **external conflicts** between characters or forces, rather than an **internal conflict** taking place within a single individual.

How Siegfried Was Slain
from the Nibelungenlied
translated by
A. T. Hatto

 Much of the action of the **Nibelungenlied** *is based on trickery. As you read, note the ways that various characters deceive each other.*

Characters

Siegfried (sig'frēd): a prince of the lower Rhine.

Kriemhild (krēm'hilt'): Siegfried's wife and the sister of King Gunther.

Gunther (gōōn'tər): king of Burgundy.

Hagen (hä'gən): Gunther's chief vassal or subject.

The fearless warriors Gunther and Hagen treacherously proclaimed a hunt in the forest where they wished to chase the boar, the bear, and the bison—and what could be more daring? Siegfried rode with their party in magnificent style. They took all manner of food with them; and it was while drinking from a cool stream that the hero was to lose his life at the instigation of Brunhild, King Gunther's queen.

Bold Siegfried went to Kriemhild while his and his companions' hunting gear was being loaded onto the sumpters[1] in readiness to cross the Rhine, and she could not have been more afflicted. "God grant that I may see you well again, my lady," he said, kissing his dear

---

1. **sumpters:** pack horses.

wife, "and that your eyes may see me, too. Pass the time pleasantly with your relations who are so kind to you, since I cannot stay with you at home."

Kriemhild thought of what she had told Hagen, but she dared not mention it and began to lament that she had ever been born. "I dreamt last night—and an ill-omened dream it was—" said lord Siegfried's noble queen, weeping with unrestrained passion, "that two boars chased you over the heath and the flowers were dyed with blood! How can I help weeping so? I stand in great dread of some attempt against your life.— What if we have offended any men who have the power to vent their malice on us? Stay away, my lord, I urge you."

"I shall return in a few days time, my darling. I know of no people here who bear me any hatred. Your kinsmen without exception wish me well, nor have I deserved otherwise of them."

"It is not so, lord Siegfried. I fear you will come to grief. Last night I had a sinister dream of how two mountains fell upon you and hid you from my sight! I shall suffer cruelly if you go away and leave me." But he clasped the noble woman in his arms and after kissing and caressing her fair person

King Conrad IV, from the Manness Scroll, a fourteenth-century German manuscript.

very tenderly, took his leave and went forthwith. Alas, she was never to see him alive again.

They rode away deep into the forest in pursuit of their sport. Gunther and his men were accompanied by numbers of brave knights, but Gernot and Giselher stayed at home. Ahead of the hunt many horses had crossed the Rhine laden with their bread, wine, meat, fish, and various other provisions such as a King of Gunther's wealth is bound to have with him.

The proud and intrepid hunters were told to set up their lodges on a spacious isle in the river on which they were to hunt, at the skirt of the greenwood over towards the spot where the game would have to break cover. Siegfried, too, had arrived there, and

this was reported to the King. Thereupon the sportsmen everywhere manned their relays.

"Who is going to guide us through the forest to our quarry, brave warriors?" asked mighty Siegfried.

"Shall we split up before we start hunting here?" asked Hagen. "Then my lords and I could tell who are the best hunters on this foray into the woods. Let us share the huntsmen and hounds between us and each take the direction he likes—and then all honor to him that hunts best!" At this, the hunters quickly dispersed.

"I do not need any hounds," said lord Siegfried, "except for one tracker so well fleshed that he recognizes the tracks which the game leave through the wood: then we shall not fail to find our quarry."

An old huntsman took a good sleuthhound and quickly led the lord to where there was game in abundance. The party chased everything that was roused from its lair, as good hunting men still do today. Bold Siegfried of the Netherlands killed every beast that his hound started, for his hunter was so swift that nothing could elude him. Thus, versatile as he was, Siegfried outshone all the others in that hunt.

The very first kill was when he brought down a strong young tusker,[2] after which he soon chanced on an enormous lion. When his hound had roused it he laid a keen arrow to his bow and shot it so that it dropped in its tracks at the third bound. Siegfried's fellow huntsmen acclaimed him for this shot. Next, in swift succession, he killed a wisent, an elk, four mighty aurochs,[3] and a fierce and monstrous buck—so well mounted was

---

2. **tusker:** wild boar.
3. **wisent** (vē′zənt) . . . **aurochs** (ô′räks′): European terms for bison and wild oxen.

he that nothing, be it hart or hind, could evade him. His hound then came upon a great boar, and, as this turned to flee, the champion hunter at once blocked his path, bringing him to bay; and when in a trice the beast sprang at the hero in a fury, Siegfried slew him with his sword, a feat no other hunter could have performed with such ease. After the felling of this boar, the tracker was returned to his leash and Siegfried's splendid bag was made known to the Burgundians.

"If it is not asking too much, lord Siegfried," said his companions of the chase, "do leave some of the game alive for us. You are emptying the hills and woods for us today." At this the brave knight had to smile.

There now arose a great shouting of men and clamor of hounds on all sides, and the tumult grew so great that the hills and the forest re-echoed with it—the huntsmen had unleashed no fewer than four and twenty packs! Thus, many beasts had to lose their lives there, since each of these hunters was hoping to bring it about that *he* should be given the high honors of the chase. But when mighty Siegfried appeared beside the campfire there was no chance of that.

The hunt was over, yet not entirely so. Those who wished to go to the fire brought the hides of innumerable beasts, and game in plenty—what loads of it they carried back to the kitchen to the royal retainers! And now the noble King had it announced to those fine hunters that he wished to take his repast, and there was one great blast of the horn to tell them that he was back in camp.

At this, one of Siegfried's huntsmen said: "Sir, I have heard a horn blast telling us to return to our lodges.—I shall answer it." There was much blowing to summon the companions.

"Let us quit the forest, too," said lord Siegfried. His mount carried him at an even pace, and the others hastened away with him but with the noise of their going they started a savage bear, a very fierce beast.

"I shall give our party some good entertainment," he said over his shoulder. "Loose the hound, for I can see a bear which will have to come back to our lodges with us. It will not be able to save itself unless it runs very fast." The hound was unleashed, and the bear made off at speed. Siegfried meant to ride it down but soon found that his way was blocked and his intention thwarted, while the mighty beast fancied it would escape from its pursuer. But the proud knight leapt from his horse and started to chase it on foot, and the animal, quite off its guard, failed to elude him. And so he quickly caught and bound it, without having wounded it at all—nor could the beast use either claws or teeth on the man. Siegfried tied it to his saddle, mounted his horse, and in his high-spirited fashion led it to the campfire in order to amuse the good knights.

And in what magnificent style Siegfried rode! He bore a great spear, stout of shaft and broad of head; his handsome sword reached down to his spurs; and the fine horn which this lord carried was of the reddest gold. Nor have I ever heard tell of a better hunting outfit: he wore a surcoat of costly black silk and a splendid hat of sable, and you should have seen the gorgeous silken tassels on his quiver, which was covered in panther skin for the sake of its fragrant odor![4] He also bore a bow so strong that apart from Siegfried any who wished to span it would have had to use a rack. His hunting suit was all of otter skin, varied throughout its length with furs of other kinds from

---

4. **odor:** It was believed that the panther's hide gave off a pleasant scent that attracted other animals.

whose shining hair clasps of gold gleamed out on either side of this daring lord of the hunt. The handsome sword that he wore was Balmung,[5] a weapon so keen and with such excellent edges that it never failed to bite when swung against a helmet. No wonder this splendid hunter was proud and gay. And (since I am bound to tell you all) know that his quiver was full of good arrows with gold mountings and heads a span in width, so that any beast they pierced must inevitably soon die.

Thus the noble knight rode along, the very image of a hunting man. Gunther's attendants saw him coming and ran to meet him to take his horse—tied to whose saddle he led a mighty bear! On dismounting, he loosed the bonds from its muzzle and paws, whereupon all the hounds that saw it instantly gave tongue. The beast made for the forest and the people were seized with panic. Affrighted by the tumult, the bear strayed into the kitchen—and how the cooks scuttled from their fire at its approach! Many caldrons were sent flying and many fires were scattered, while heaps of good food lay among the ashes. Lords and retainers leapt from their seats, the bear became infuriated, and the King ordered all the hounds on their leashes to be loosed—and if all had ended well they would have had a jolly day! Bows and spears were no longer left idle, for the brave ones ran towards the bear, yet there were so many hounds in the way that none dared shoot. With the whole mountain thundering with peoples' cries the bear took to flight before the hounds and none could keep up with it but Siegfried, who ran it down and then dispatched it with his sword. The bear was later carried to the campfire, and all who had witnessed this feat declared that Siegfried was a very powerful man.

The proud companions were then summoned to table. There were a great many seated in that meadow. Piles of sumptuous dishes were set before the noble huntsmen, but the butlers who were to pour their wine were very slow to appear. Yet knights could not be better cared for than they and if only no treachery had been lurking in their minds those warriors would have been above reproach.

"Seeing that we are being treated to such a variety of dishes from the kitchen," said lord Siegfried, "I fail to understand why the butlers bring us no wine. Unless we hunters are better looked after, I'll not be a companion of the hunt. I thought I had deserved better attention."

"We shall be very glad to make amends to you for our present lack," answered the perfidious King from his table. "This is Hagen's fault—he wants us to die of thirst."

"My very dear lord," replied Hagen of Troneck, "I thought the day's hunting would be away in the Spessart[6] and so I sent the wine there. If we go without drink today I shall take good care that it does not happen again."

"Damn those fellows!" said lord Siegfried. "It was arranged that they were to bring along seven panniers[7] of spiced wine and mead[8] for me. Since that proved impossible, we should have been placed nearer the Rhine."

---

5. **Balmung** (bäl´mung): In medieval epics, weapons often have names.

6. **Spessart** (spes´ərt): a mountain range in southern Germany.

7. **panniers** (pan´yərz): a large basket for carrying loads on the back.

8. **mead** (mēd): an alcoholic drink made from honey and water, sometimes mixed with spices, fruit, or malt.

Knight receives ring from one of his ladies, from the Manness Scroll.

"You brave and noble knights," said Hagen of Troneck, "I know a cool spring nearby—do not be offended!—let us go there."—A proposal which (as it turned out) was to bring many knights into jeopardy.

Siegfried was tormented by thirst and ordered the board to be removed all the sooner in his eagerness to go to that spring at the foot of the hills. And now the knights put their treacherous plot into execution.

Word was given for the game which Siegfried had killed to be conveyed back to Worms[9] on wagons, and all who saw it gave him great credit for it.

Hagen of Troneck broke his faith with Siegfried most grievously, for as they were leaving to go to the spreading lime tree he said: "I have often been told that no one can keep up with Lady Kriemhild's lord when he cares to show his speed. I wish he would show it us now."

"You can easily put it to the test by racing me to the brook," replied gallant Siegfried of the Netherlands. "Then those who see it shall declare the winner."

"I accept your challenge," said Hagen.

"Then I will lie down in the grass at your feet, as a handicap," replied brave Siegfried, much to Gunther's satisfaction. "And I will tell you what more I shall do. I will carry all my equipment with me, my spear and my shield and all my hunting clothes." And he quickly strapped on his quiver and sword. The two men took off their outer clothing and stood there in their white vests. Then they ran through the clover like a pair of wild panthers. Siegfried appeared first at the brook.

Gunther's magnificent guest who excelled so many men in all things quickly unstrapped his sword, took off his quiver, and after leaning his great spear against a branch of the lime, stood beside the rushing brook. Then he laid down his shield near the flowing water, and although he was very thirsty he most courteously refrained from drinking until the King had drunk. Gunther thanked him very ill for this.

The stream was cool, sweet, and clear. Gunther stooped to its running waters and after drinking stood up and stepped aside. Siegfried in turn would have liked to do the same, but he paid for his good manners. For now Hagen carried Siegfried's sword and bow beyond his reach, ran back for the spear, and searched for the sign[10] on the

---

9. **Worms** (vôrmz): a city on the Rhine.

10. **sign:** Kriemhild had unwittingly told Hagen that Siegfried was vulnerable in only one spot, between his shoulder blades. Hagen suggested that she sew a cross on Siegfried's clothing so that Hagen would know where to shield him in battle.

brave man's tunic. Then, as Siegfried bent over the brook and drank, Hagen hurled the spear at the cross, so that the hero's heart's blood leapt from the wound and splashed against Hagen's clothes. No warrior will ever do a darker deed. Leaving the spear fixed in Siegfried's heart, he fled in wild desperation, as he had never fled before from any man.

When lord Siegfried felt the great wound, maddened with rage he bounded back from the stream with the long shaft jutting from his heart. He was hoping to find either his bow or his sword, and, had he succeeded in doing so, Hagen would have had his pay. But finding no sword, the gravely wounded man had nothing but his shield. Snatching this from the bank he ran at Hagen, and King Gunther's vassal was unable to elude him. Siegfried was wounded to death, yet he struck so powerfully that he sent many precious stones whirling from the shield as it smashed to pieces. Gunther's noble guest would dearly have loved to avenge himself. Hagen fell reeling under the weight of the blow and the riverside echoed loudly. Had Siegfried had his sword in his hand it would have been the end of Hagen, so enraged was the wounded man, as indeed he had good cause to be.

The hero's face had lost its color and he was no longer able to stand. His strength had ebbed away, for in the field of his bright countenance he now displayed Death's token. Soon many fair ladies would be weeping for him.

The lady Kriemhild's lord fell among the flowers, where you could see the blood surging from his wound. Then—and he had cause—he rebuked those who had plotted his foul murder. "You vile cowards," he said as he lay dying. "What good has my service done me now that you have slain me? I was always loyal to you, but now I have paid for

it. Alas, you have wronged your kinsmen so that all who are born in days to come will be dishonored by your deed. You have cooled your anger on me beyond all measure. You will be held in contempt and stand apart from all good warriors."

The knights all ran to where he lay wounded to death. It was a sad day for many of them. Those who were at all loyal-hearted mourned for him, and this, as a gay and valiant knight, he had well deserved.

The King of Burgundy too lamented Siegfried's death.

"There is no need for the doer of the deed to weep when the damage is done," said the dying man. "He should be held up to scorn. It would have been better left undone."

"I do not know what you are grieving for," said Hagen fiercely. "All our cares and sorrows are over and done with. We shall not find many who will dare oppose us now. I am glad I have put an end to his supremacy."

"You may well exult," said Siegfried. "But had I known your murderous bent I should easily have guarded my life from you. I am sorry for none so much as my wife, the lady Kriemhild. May God have mercy on me for ever having got a son who in years to come will suffer the reproach that his kinsmen were murderers. If I had the strength I would have good reason to complain. But if you feel at all inclined to do a loyal deed for anyone, noble King," continued the mortally wounded man, "let me commend my dear sweetheart to your mercy. Let her profit from being your sister. By the virtue of all princes, stand by her loyally! No lady was ever more greatly wronged through her dear friend. As to my father and his vassals, they will have long to wait for me."

The flowers everywhere were drenched with blood. Siegfried was at grips with Death, yet not for long, since Death's sword ever was too sharp. And now the warrior who had been so brave and gay could speak no more.

When those lords saw that the hero was dead they laid him on a shield that shone red with gold, and they plotted ways and means of concealing the fact that Hagen had done the deed. "A disaster has befallen us," many of them said. "You must all hush it up and declare with one voice that Siegfried rode off hunting alone and was killed by robbers as he was passing through the forest."

"I shall take him home," said Hagen of Troneck. "It is all one to me if the woman who made Brunhild so unhappy should come to know of it. It will trouble me very little, however much she weeps."

THE DEATH OF SIEGFRIED, mural.

Earlier in the epic, Siegfried had used his powers to trick Brunhild into marrying Gunther. Do you think he deserved to die for his earlier trickery? Why or why not?

Identifying Facts

1. Why is Kriemhild so concerned for Siegfried as he leaves for the hunt?
2. How does Siegfried show his skill as a hunter?
3. How do Hagen and Gunther manage to lure Siegfried alone to the stream?
4. How does Hagen kill Siegfried?

Interpreting Meanings

1. What is the main **conflict** in this section of the *Nibelungenlied*? Which characters are in opposition to each other, and what is the basis for their conflict?
2. **Foreshadowing** is the use of clues to hint at what is going to happen later in the plot. What clues are given at the beginning of the selection to suggest what will happen to Siegfried? How did these clues affect your reading of the story?
3. Why is the hunt described in such detail? What does it reveal about Siegfried?
4. What is the author's attitude toward Hagen and Gunther's murder of Siegfried? How can you tell?
5. Find two examples of details and language that make Siegfried seem especially heroic.

Applying Meanings

This selection describes Brunhild's dramatic and cruel revenge on Siegfried. What motivates people to seek revenge? Name some other stories you know that deal with the concept of revenge. Is revenge ever an appropriate response to injustice? Explain your answers.

Creative Writing Response

Writing a Persuasive Letter. Imagine that you have found out that Brunhild is plotting to have Siegfried killed. What arguments might you use to persuade her to change her plans? Write a three-paragraph persuasive letter to Brunhild. Tell her that you think she should change her mind, and give her three strong reasons for doing so. Conclude your letter with a strong, convincing appeal.

Critical Writing Response

Analyzing a Foil. A **foil** is a literary character who provides a contrast to another character. Authors often use foils to emphasize certain traits in their heroes, just as shadows make contrasting highlights all the more prominent. In this selection, Hagen provides a foil for Siegfried. Write an essay analyzing the contrast between the two characters. In particular, which of Siegfried's qualities are emphasized by the contrast to Hagen? Before writing, you might want to use a chart like the following to help you organize your thoughts.

	Siegfried	Hagen
Appearance		
Physical strength		
Courage		
Moral sense		
Personality		

Dante Alighieri
1265–1321

Samuel H. Kress Collection, National Gallery of Art, Washington, D.C.

Dante Alighieri (dän′tä ä′lē·gyä′rē), was born in Florence to an old and moderately distinguished family. Little is known about his early life, but one event from his youth stands out. At the age of nine, Dante attended a May Day party at the home of a gentleman named Folco Portinari. There he met and fell in love with Portinari's daughter Beatrice, who was a year younger than he. He met Beatrice again nine years later, and it was at this meeting that she first spoke to him. Unfortunately, a misunderstanding developed between them, and before it could be mended, Beatrice died. Dante was heartbroken. Although he eventually married and had children, Beatrice's spirit dominated his emotional and religious life, as well as his literary work, for as long as he lived.

From an early age, Dante wrote poetry and associated himself with the literary people of Florence, but his life was not limited to the pursuit of the arts. His was a time of political turbulence, and Florence was torn by civil war three times during his residence there. He may have participated in the fighting at least once himself. Certainly he became deeply involved in the political life of the city and, as an elected official, sought to end Florence's civil strife, going so far on one occasion as to exile his best friend and some of his wife's relatives because of their part in the conflict. Dante was strongly opposed to the involvement of the Pope and the Church in political conflicts. He favored the renewal of a Roman empire to take care of worldly concerns so that the Church could focus solely on spiritual matters.

In 1301, while Dante was out of Florence on an official mission, the city was seized by his political enemies, and in his absence he was sentenced to die. He never returned to his beloved city but lived the rest of his life in exile. Where he lived and whether he saw his wife and children again after leaving Florence are not known. What is known is that he died in Ravenna, where he is buried, and that during his exile he completed his great poetic achievement, the *Divine Comedy*, which shows the influence of his political beliefs and experiences.

The Divine Comedy

DANTE'S WORLD, DOMENICO DI MICHELINO, 1465. Notice the artist's rendering of Dante's Hell, in the left foreground. Purgatory is in the background, and Heaven is to the right of Dante.

? *Does this depiction match your image of what Hell would be?*

The *Divine Comedy*, written between 1308 and 1321, tells of an imaginary journey that takes Dante through Hell, Purgatory, and Paradise. This journey is symbolic of the spiritual quest for salvation. It involves recognizing sin (the journey through Hell, or the Inferno), rejecting sin and awaiting redemption (the time in Purgatory), and finally achieving salvation through faith in divine revelation (seeing the light of God in Paradise).

During his journey, especially through Hell, Dante encounters historical figures from ancient Rome, characters from classical Greek mythology, and political enemies from his own era. Because of the range of people and experiences on which Dante reflects in the *Divine Comedy*, the work provides a portrait of almost every aspect of medieval human life.

Form, Number, and Symbol

Dante carefully constructed his epic poem in accord with a special scheme of numbers. The poem contains one hundred **cantos**, or "chapters," because the number one hundred was regarded in the Middle Ages as the perfect number. The work begins with an introductory canto, and it is then divided equally into three sections of thirty-three cantos each. The whole poem is composed in **tercets** (tur′ sits), three-line stanzas, and uses a rhyme scheme called **terza rima** (tert′sə rē′mə). In this rhyme scheme, the middle line of one tercet rhymes with the first and third lines of the next tercet, giving the poem a strong sense of unity.

The number three is important in the *Divine Comedy* because of its relation to the Christian Trinity, which is the union of three divine figures—Father, Son, and Holy Spirit—in one God. The poem is divided into three parts, with the first part, the *Inferno*, focusing on the power of God the Father, as evidenced in the punishments of the damned. The second part, *Purgatorio*, focuses on the wisdom of Christ the Son, and the hope for salvation that he offers to those awaiting final judgment. The third part, *Paradiso*, focuses on the love of the Holy Spirit. In addition, Dante's spiritual journey takes place over three days, beginning in Hell on Good Friday, the day of Christ's crucifixion, and ending symbolically in Paradise on Easter Sunday. Finally, the entire action of the poem takes place under the guidance of three ladies: the Virgin Mary, the mother of Christ who mediates between God and man; Saint Lucia, the patron saint of Dante and of all those without spiritual sight; and Beatrice, Dante's love, who appears to him toward the end of his journey through Purgatory and leads him into Paradise.

The Role of Virgil

For much of his journey through the *Inferno* and *Purgatorio*, Dante is guided not by a saint or an angel but by Virgil, the Roman poet who died nineteen years before the birth of Christ (see page 379). Virgil explains and instructs, and the clarity of his mind is constantly contrasted with Dante's own confusion.

Dante speaks of Virgil with reverence, as if he were talking about a divine figure, calling him "my true master and first author" and "the sole maker from

Tate Gallery, London/Art Resource, New York

INSCRIPTION OVER HELL'S GATE, WILLIAM BLAKE, early 19th century. Blake (1757–1827) is best known to modern readers as an early Romantic poet, though he made his living as an engraver and artist. His poetry and his art both display his vivid imagination and unorthodox vision of the world.

What do you think is the warning of the inscription?

humanism of the Renaissance. The classical poets Homer, Horace, and Ovid, as well as the great philosophers and scientists of the pre-Christian age, are all in Hell, yet Dante feels honored when they call him one of their own. "I glory in the glory I have seen," he exults.

Virgil is the perfect guide for the early part of the journey because, for Dante, he is the ultimate symbol of what human reason can achieve without faith. Reason uses logic and fact to arrive at the truth. However, Dante saw reason as limited; it is only through faith that Dante can grasp the truth of Paradise.

Beatrice—Dante's Spiritual Guide

Beatrice is Dante's symbol of love and faith. She sends Virgil to guide Dante through Hell and Purgatory. It is she alone who can guide Dante toward salvation and Paradise.

The entire journey, blessed throughout by the love of Beatrice, is expected to turn Dante forever from error. It is a journey toward truth and grace, made possible by the love of the woman who first gave Dante a glimpse of spiritual perfection.

Style and Language

Dante's epic poem avoids the lofty language generally used in important works, especially literary epics and trag-

whom I drew the breath." Yet Dante's Christian beliefs require that Virgil, who had never been baptized, be consigned to the first circle of Hell, along with other "virtuous pagans" from the classical eras of Greece and Rome.

Dante's attitude toward Virgil reflects the split between his strict Christian beliefs and his sympathy for the emerging edies. This, along with the fact that the epic has a happy ending, was one of the reasons Dante called his poem a divine "comedy." Dante's language is sparse, direct, and idiomatic, much like the ordinary speech of his time. But the style of the *Divine Comedy* is so perfectly modulated that it is regarded as the finest poetry ever written in Italian. It was a stroke of genius to use everyday language, or the **vernacular**, in a poem of such encyclopedic proportions. The work ranges widely across all levels of imagination and reality. It deals with the mythological, the legendary, the historical, the political, the religious, and the intensely personal. Indeed, the *Divine Comedy* encompasses Dante's vision of God's judgment on every significant aspect of human life.

Eugène Delacroix, Dante et Virgile aux enfers, Louvre. © Photo R.M.N.

DANTE AND VIRGIL IN HELL, EUGÈNE DELACROIX, 1822.
How does the artist convey the tortures of Hell?
How would you describe Dante's reaction to the horrors he sees?

Reader's Guide

from the INFERNO
from the Divine Comedy

Background

The first section of the *Divine Comedy,* the *Inferno,* is the best known and most dramatic of the poem's three parts. The first canto finds Dante lost in the "dark wood" of worldliness and sin. In the following thirty-three cantos, Dante travels through the nine levels of Hell, or the Inferno, descending slowly away from God and into the bowels of the earth. At each level, Dante meets suffering souls tormented for eternity in ways that befit their sins. The condemned sinners include people from the ancient world as well as people from Dante's own time. Many of these sinners are Dante's bitter enemies, the clerics and politicians who banished him from his beloved Florence.

The "Dante" of the poem represents suffering humanity as well as the real-life Florentine poet, Dante Alighieri, who is trying to recover from a spiritual crisis. Dante's plight has been observed in heaven. Through the intercession of the Virgin Mary, Saint Lucia, and Beatrice, the spirit of Virgil has been summoned to help Dante begin the journey that can save him.

Translator John Ciardi precedes each canto with prose summaries and notes and follows the **terza rima** rhyme scheme used by Dante.

Oral Response

In your opinion, what are the greatest wrongs that people can commit? Murder? Betrayal? Revenge? Theft? Cheating? If punishments could be made to fit crimes, what would be the appropriate punishment for each of these wrongdoings? Discuss.

Literary Focus

A **symbol** is a person, place, thing, or event that stands both for itself and for something beyond itself. In the *Inferno,* for example, the structure of Hell is symbolic, since the worst sinners are placed at the lowest levels, farthest from God. As you read, look for other symbols. Note, for example, how people represent different kinds of sin, and how the punishments in the *Inferno* are symbolically appropriate to the sins being punished.

from the INFERNO
from the Divine Comedy
Dante Alighieri
translated by

JOHN CIARDI

As you read, try making a map of where the different types of sinners have been placed in Hell. What does this arrangement of Hell reveal about Dante's system of morality?

THE FOREST, GUSTAVE DORÉ. *The journey into a "dark wood" is a common motif in literature, symbolizing a confrontation with the unknown.*

CANTO 1

The Dark Wood of Error

Midway in his allotted threescore years and ten, Dante comes to himself with a start and realizes that he has strayed from the True Way into the Dark Wood of Error (Worldliness). As soon as he has realized his loss, Dante lifts his eyes and sees the first light of the sunrise (the Sun is the Symbol of Divine Illumination) lighting the shoulders of a little hill (The Mount of Joy). It is the Easter Season, the time of resurrection, and the sun is in its equinoctial rebirth. This juxtaposition of joyous symbols fills Dante with hope and he sets out at once to climb directly up the Mount of Joy, but almost immediately his way is blocked by the Three Beasts of Worldliness: *The Leopard of Malice and Fraud, The Lion of Violence and Ambition,* and *The She-Wolf of Incontinence.* These beasts, and especially the She-Wolf, drive him back despairing into the darkness of error.

But just as all seems lost, a figure appears to him. It is the shade of *Virgil,* Dante's symbol of *Human Reason.*

Virgil explains that he has been sent to lead Dante from error. There can, however, be no direct ascent past the beasts: the man who would escape them must go a longer and harder way. First he must descend through Hell (The Recognition of Sin), then he must ascend through Purgatory (The Renunciation of Sin), and only then may he reach the pinnacle of joy and come to the Light of God. Virgil offers to guide Dante, but only as far as Human Reason can go. Another guide (*Beatrice,* symbol of *Divine Love*) must take over for the final ascent, for Human Reason is self-limited. Dante submits himself joyously to Virgil's guidance and they move off.

Midway in our life's journey,[1] I went astray
  from the straight road and woke to find myself
3 alone in a dark wood. How shall I say

what wood that was! I never saw so drear,
  so rank, so arduous a wilderness!
6 Its very memory gives a shape to fear.

Death could scarce be more bitter than that place!
  But since it came to good, I will recount
9 all that I found revealed there by God's grace.

How I came to it I cannot rightly say,
  so drugged and loose with sleep had I become
12 when I first wandered there from the True Way.

But at the far end of that valley of evil
  whose maze had sapped my very heart with fear
15 I found myself before a little hill

and lifted up my eyes. Its shoulders glowed
  already with the sweet rays of that planet[2]
18 whose virtue leads men straight on every road,

and the shining strengthened me against the
    fright
  whose agony had wracked the lake of my heart
21 through all the terrors of that piteous night.

Just as a swimmer, who with his last breath
  flounders ashore from perilous seas, might turn
24 to memorize the wide water of his death—

---

1. **Midway . . . journey:** Dante sets the action in 1300, when he was thirty-five.

2. **planet:** the sun, which was thought to be a planet by Ptolemaic astronomers in ancient Greece.

so did I turn, my soul still fugitive
from death's surviving image, to stare down
27 that pass that none had ever left alive.

And there I lay to rest from my heart's race
till calm and breath returned to me. Then rose
30 and pushed up that dead slope at such a pace

each footfall rose above the last. And lo!
almost at the beginning of the rise
33 I faced a spotted Leopard, all tremor and flow

and gaudy pelt. And it would not pass, but stood
so blocking my every turn that time and again
36 I was on the verge of turning back to the wood.

This fell at the first widening of the dawn
as the sun was climbing Aries with those stars
39 that rode with him to light the new creation.[3]

Thus the holy hour and the sweet season
of commemoration did much to arm my fear
42 of that bright murderous beast with their good
omen.

Yet not so much but what I shook with dread
at sight of a great Lion that broke upon me
45 raging with hunger, its enormous head

held high as if to strike a mortal terror
into the very air. And down his track,
48 a She-Wolf drove upon me, a starved horror

ravening and wasted beyond all belief.
She seemed a rack for avarice, gaunt and
craving.
51 Oh many the souls she has brought to endless
grief!

She brought such heaviness upon my spirit
at sight of her savagery and desperation,
54 I died from every hope of that high summit.

And like a miser—eager in acquisition
but desperate in self-reproach when Fortune's
wheel
57 turns to the hour of his loss—all tears and
attrition

I wavered back; and still the beast pursued,
forcing herself against me bit by bit
60 till I slid back into the sunless wood.

And as I fell to my soul's ruin, a presence
gathered before me on the discolored air,
63 the figure of one who seemed hoarse from long
silence.

At sight of him in that friendless waste I cried:
"Have pity on me, whatever thing you are,
66 whether shade or living man." And it replied:

"Not man, though man I once was, and my blood
was Lombard, both my parents Mantuan.
69 I was born, though late, *sub Julio*,[4] and bred

in Rome under Augustus in the noon
of the false and lying gods. I was a poet
72 and sang of old Anchises' noble son[5]

who came to Rome after the burning of Troy.
But you—why do *you* return to these distresses
75 instead of climbing that shining Mount of Joy

which is the seat and first cause of man's bliss?"
"And are you then that Virgil and that fountain
78 of purest speech?" My voice grew tremulous:

---

3. **This fell . . . creation:** Dante awakens in the Dark
Wood just before dawn of Good Friday. His spiritual
rebirth begins in the Easter season, the time of the
Resurrection of Christ.

4. *sub Julio:* in the reign of Julius Caesar.
5. **Anchises'** (an·kī'sēz') **noble son:** Aeneas, hero of
the *Aeneid;* according to legend he was the founder
of Rome.

"Glory and light of poets! now may that zeal
and love's apprenticeship that I poured out
81 on your heroic verses serve me well!

For you are my true master and first author,
the sole maker from whom I drew the breath
84 of that sweet style whose measures have
    brought me honor.

See there, immortal sage, the beast I flee.
For my soul's salvation, I beg you, guard me
from her,
87 for she has struck a mortal tremor through me."

And he replied, seeing my soul in tears:
"He must go by another way who would escape
90 this wilderness, for that mad beast that fleers

before you there, suffers no man to pass.
She tracks down all, kills all, and knows no glut,
93 but, feeding, she grows hungrier than she was.

She mates with any beast, and will mate with
    more
before the Greyhound comes to hunt her down.
96 He will not feed on lands nor loot, but honor

and love and wisdom will make straight his way.
He will rise between Feltro and Feltro,[6] and
in him
99 shall be the resurrection and new day

of that sad Italy for which Nisus died,
and Turnus, and Euryalus, and the maid
Camilla.[7]

102 He shall hunt her through every nation of sick
    pride

till she is driven back forever to Hell
whence Envy first released her on the world.
105 Therefore, for your own good, I think it well

you follow me and I will be your guide
and lead you forth through an eternal place.
108 There you shall see the ancient spirits tried

in endless pain, and hear their lamentation
as each bemoans the second death of souls.[8]
111 Next you shall see upon a burning mountain[9]

souls in fire and yet content in fire,
knowing that whensoever it may be
114 they yet will mount into the blessed choir.

To which, if it is still your wish to climb,
a worthier spirit shall be sent to guide you.
117 With her shall I leave you, for the King of Time,

who reigns on high, forbids me to come there
since, living, I rebelled against his law.
120 He rules the waters and the land and air

and there holds court, his city and his throne.
Oh blessed are they he chooses!" And I to him:
123 "Poet, by that God to you unknown,

lead me this way. Beyond this present ill
and worse to dread, lead me to Peter's gate
126 and be my guide through the sad halls of Hell."

And he then: "Follow." And he moved ahead
in silence, and I followed where he led.

---

6. **Feltro and Feltro:** Can Grande della Scala (1290–
1329) was an Italian leader born in Verona, which is
situated between Feltre and Montefeltro.

7. **Nisus . . . Turnus . . . Euryalus . . . Camilla:** When
Aeneas led the Trojans into Italy, these figures were
killed in a war between the Trojans and the Latians.

---

8. **second death of souls:** damnation.
9. **burning mountain:** the mountain Purgatory.

CANTO 3

The Vestibule of Hell

The Opportunists

The Poets pass the Gate of Hell and are immediately assailed by cries of anguish. Dante sees the first of the souls in torment. They are *The Opportunists*, those souls who in life were neither for good nor evil but only for themselves. Mixed with them are those outcasts who took no sides in the Rebellion of the Angels. They are neither in Hell nor out of it. Eternally unclassified, they race round and round pursuing a wavering banner that runs forever before them through the dirty air; and as they run they are pursued by swarms of wasps and hornets, who sting them and produce a constant flow of blood and putrid matter which trickles down the bodies of the sinners and is feasted upon by loathsome worms and maggots who coat the ground.

The law of Dante's Hell is the law of symbolic retribution. As they sinned so are they punished. They took no sides, therefore they are given no place. As they pursued the ever-shifting illusion of their own advantage, changing their courses with every changing wind, so they pursue eternally an elusive, ever-shifting banner. As their sin was a darkness, so they move in darkness. As their own guilty conscience pursued them, so they are pursued by swarms of wasps and hornets. And as their actions were a moral filth, so they run eternally through the filth of worms and maggots which they themselves feed.

Dante recognizes several, among them *Pope Celestine V*, but without delaying to speak to any of these souls, the Poets move on to *Acheron*, the first of the rivers of Hell. Here the newly-arrived souls of the damned gather and wait for monstrous *Charon* to ferry them over to punishment. Charon recognizes Dante as a living man and angrily refuses him passage. Virgil forces Charon to serve them, but Dante swoons with terror, and does not reawaken until he is on the other side.

I AM THE WAY INTO THE CITY OF WOE.
I AM THE WAY TO A FORSAKEN PEOPLE.
3 I AM THE WAY INTO ETERNAL SORROW.

SACRED JUSTICE MOVED MY ARCHITECT.
I WAS RAISED HERE BY DIVINE OMNIPOTENCE,
6 PRIMORDIAL LOVE AND ULTIMATE INTELLECT.

ONLY THOSE ELEMENTS TIME CANNOT WEAR
WERE MADE BEFORE ME, AND BEYOND TIME I
STAND.[10]
9 ABANDON ALL HOPE YE WHO ENTER HERE.[11]

These mysteries I read cut into stone
    above a gate. And turning I said: "Master,
12 what is the meaning of this harsh inscription?"

And he then as initiate to novice:[12]
    "Here must you put by all division of spirit
15 and gather your soul against all cowardice.

This is the place I told you to expect.
    Here you shall pass among the fallen people,
18 souls who have lost the good of intellect."

So saying, he put forth his hand to me,
    and with a gentle and encouraging smile
21 he led me through the gate of mystery.

---

10. **BEYOND TIME I STAND:** The punishment of sin is endless.
11. **YE WHO ENTER HERE:** the damned.

12. **as initiate to novice:** as one who has been instructed to one who has not.

Dante Alighieri **751**

THE EMBARKATION OF THE SOULS, GUSTAVE DORÉ.
❓ *Who are the first souls that Dante sees? How does their punishment fit their crime?*

Here sighs and cries and wails coiled and recoiled
on the starless air, spilling my soul to tears.
24 A confusion of tongues and monstrous accents toiled

in pain and anger. Voices hoarse and shrill
and sounds of blows, all intermingled, raised
27 tumult and pandemonium that still

whirls on the air forever dirty with it
as if a whirlwind sucked at sand. And I,
30 holding my head in horror, cried: "Sweet Spirit,

what souls are these who run through this black
haze?"
And he to me: "These are the nearly soulless
33 whose lives concluded neither blame nor praise.

They are mixed here with that despicable corps
of angels who were neither for God nor Satan,
36 but only for themselves. The High Creator

scourged them from Heaven for its perfect beauty,
and Hell will not receive them since the wicked
39 might feel some glory over them." And I:

"Master, what gnaws at them so hideously
their lamentation stuns the very air?"

42   "They have no hope of death," he answered me,

"and in their blind and unattaining state
their miserable lives have sunk so low

45   that they must envy every other fate.

No word of them survives their living season.
Mercy and Justice deny them even a name.

48   Let us not speak of them: look, and pass on."

I saw a banner there upon the mist.
Circling and circling, it seemed to scorn all
pause.

51   So it ran on, and still behind it pressed

a never-ending rout of souls in pain.
I had not thought death had undone so many

54   as passed before me in that mournful train.

And some I knew among them; last of all
I recognized the shadow of that soul

57   who, in his cowardice, made the Great Denial.[13]

At once I understood for certain: these
were of that retrograde and faithless crew

60   hateful to God and to His enemies.

These wretches never born and never dead
ran naked in a swarm of wasps and hornets

63   that goaded them the more the more they fled,

and made their faces stream with bloody gouts
of pus and tears that dribbled to their feet

66   to be swallowed there by loathsome worms and
maggots.

Then looking onward I made out a throng
assembled on the beach of a wide river,

69   whereupon I turned to him: "Master, I long

to know what souls these are, and what strange
usage
makes them as eager to cross as they seem
to be

72   in this infected light." At which the Sage:

"All this shall be made known to you when we
stand
on the joyless beach of Acheron."[14] And I

75   cast down my eyes, sensing a reprimand

in what he said, and so walked at his side
in silence and ashamed until we came

78   through the dead cavern to that sunless tide.

There, steering toward us in an ancient ferry
came an old man[15] with a white bush of hair,

81   bellowing: "Woe to you depraved souls! Bury

here and forever all hope of Paradise:
I come to lead you to the other shore,

84   into eternal dark, into fire and ice.

And you who are living yet, I say begone
from these who are dead." But when he saw
me stand

87   against his violence he began again:

"By other windings and by other steerage
shall you cross to that other shore. Not here!
Not here!

90   A lighter craft than mine must give you passage."

---

13. I . . . Great Denial: This reference is generally believed to be to Pope Celestine V. Fearing that his
own soul would be corrupted by worldliness, he
abdicated in favor of Pope Boniface VIII, who became a political enemy of Dante's and represented
the worst sort of evil secularization of the Church.

14. Acheron (ak'ər·än'): in Greek mythology, the river
of woe in the underworld; dead souls were ferried
across the river to Hades.

15. an old man: Charon (ker'ən); in Greek mythology,
the ferryman who carried the dead to Hades.

Dante Alighieri   **753**

And my Guide to him: "Charon, bite back your
    spleen:
  this has been willed where what is willed must
  be,
93 and is not yours to ask what it may mean."

The steersman of that marsh of ruined souls,
  who wore a wheel of flame around each eye,
96 stifled the rage that shook his woolly jowls.

But those unmanned and naked spirits there
  turned pale with fear and their teeth began to
  chatter
99 at sound of his crude bellow. In despair

they blasphemed God, their parents, their time on
    earth,
  the race of Adam, and the day and the hour
102 and the place and the seed the womb that gave
    them birth.

But all together they drew to that grim shore
  where all must come who lose the fear of God.
105 Weeping and cursing they come for evermore,

and demon Charon with eyes like burning coals
  herds them in, and with a whistling oar
108 flails on the stragglers to his wake of souls.

As leaves in autumn loosen and stream down
  until the branch stands bare above its tatters
111 spread on the rustling ground, so one by one

the evil seed of Adam in its Fall
  cast themselves, at his signal, from the shore

114 and streamed away like birds who hear their
    call.

So they are gone over that shadowy water,
  and always before they reach the other shore
117 a new noise stirs on this, and new throngs
    gather.

"My son," the courteous Master said to me,
  "all who die in the shadow of God's wrath
120 converge to this from every clime and country.

And all pass over eagerly, for here
  Divine Justice transforms and spurs them so
123 their dread turns wish: they yearn for what they
    fear.[16]

No soul in Grace comes ever to this crossing;
  therefore if Charon rages at your presence
126 you will understand the reason for his cursing."

When he had spoken, all the twilight country
  shook so violently, the terror of it
129 bathes me with sweat even in memory:

the tear-soaked ground gave out a sigh of wind
  that spewed itself in flame on a red sky,
132 and all my shattered senses left me. Blind,

like one whom sleep comes over in a swoon,
  I stumbled into darkness and went down.

---

16. **Divine Justice . . . fear:** The damned have actually
chosen Hell. They have free will and the power to
sin or not to sin.

PAOLO AND FRANCESCA, GUSTAVE DORÉ. *In this canto, Dante meets two lovers whose passions have condemned them to eternal suffering.*
? *Do you think anyone deserves to suffer for loving too much?*

CANTO 5

Circle Two

The Carnal

The Poets leave Limbo and enter the *Second Circle.* Here begin the torments of Hell proper, and here, blocking the way, sits *Minos,* the dread and semi-bestial judge of the damned who assigns to each soul its eternal torment. He orders the Poets back; but Virgil silences him as he earlier silenced Charon, and the Poets move on.

They find themselves on a dark ledge swept by a great whirlwind, which spins within it the souls of the *Carnal,* those who betrayed reason to their appetites. Their sin was to abandon themselves to the tempest of their passions: so they are swept forever in the tempest of Hell, forever denied the light of reason and of God. Virgil identifies many among them. *Semiramis* is there, and *Dido, Cleopatra, Helen, Achilles, Paris,* and *Tristan.* Dante sees *Paolo* and *Francesca* swept together, and in the name of love he calls to them to tell their sad story. They pause from their eternal flight to come to him, and Francesca tells their history while Paolo weeps at her side. Dante is so stricken by compassion at their tragic tale that he swoons once again.

Dante Alighieri   **755**

So we went down to the second ledge[17] alone;
   a smaller circle of so much greater pain
3 the voice of the damned rose in a bestial
     moan.

There Minos[18] sits, grinning, grotesque, and hale.
   He examines each lost soul as it arrives
6 and delivers his verdict with his coiling tail.

That is to say, when the ill-fated soul
   appears before him it confesses all,
9 and that grim sorter of the dark and foul

decides which place in Hell shall be its end,
   then wraps his twitching tail about himself
12 one coil for each degree it must descend.

The soul descends and others take its place:
   each crowds in its turn to judgment, each
     confesses,
15 each hears its doom and falls away through
     space.

"O you who come into this camp of woe,"
   cried Minos when he saw me turn away
18 without awaiting his judgment, "watch where
     you go

once you have entered here, and to whom you
     turn!
   Do not be misled by that wide and easy
     passage!"
21 And my Guide to him: "That is not your
     concern;

it is his fate to enter every door.
   This has been willed where what is willed must be,
24 and is not yours to question. Say no more."

Now the choir of anguish, like a wound,
   strikes through the tortured air. Now I have
     come
27 to Hell's full lamentation, sound beyond sound.

I came to a place stripped bare of every light
   and roaring on the naked dark like seas
30 wracked by a war of winds. Their hellish flight

of storm and counterstorm through time
     foregone,
   sweeps the souls of the damned before its
     charge.
33 Whirling and battering it drives them on,

and when they pass the ruined gap of Hell
   through which we had come, their shrieks begin
     anew.
36 There they blaspheme the power of God eternal.

And this, I learned, was the never ending flight
   of those who sinned in the flesh, the carnal and
     lusty
39 who betrayed reason to their appetite.

As the wings of wintering starlings bear them on
   in their great wheeling flights, just so the blast
42 wherries these evil souls through time foregone.

Here, there, up, down, they whirl and, whirling,
     strain
   with never a hope of hope to comfort them,
45 not of release, but even of less pain.

As cranes go over sounding their harsh cry,
   leaving the long streak of their flight in air,
48 so come these spirits, wailing as they fly.

And watching their shadows lashed by wind,

---

17. **second ledge:** In keeping with a concept borrowed
from Aristotle, Dante places the sins of the flesh
on the upper circles of Hell, where punishment is
mildest; the sins of anger in the middle circles; and
the sins resulting from an abuse of reason at the
lowest circles, where the torment is greatest.

18. **Minos** (mī'näs'): the semibestial judge of the
damned; Minos, the son of Europa and Zeus, is
also one of the judges of Hades in classical Greek
mythology.

I cried:
"Master, what souls are these the very air
51 lashes with its black whips from side to side?"

"The first of these whose history you would know,"
he answered me, "was Empress of many tongues.
54 Mad sensuality corrupted her so

that to hide the guilt of her debauchery
she licensed all depravity alike,
57 and lust and law were one in her decree.

She is Semiramis[19] of whom the tale is told
how she married Ninus and succeeded him
60 to the throne of that wide land the Sultans hold.

The other is Dido;[20] faithless to the ashes
of Sichaeus, she killed herself for love.
63 The next whom the eternal tempest lashes

is sense-drugged Cleopatra. See Helen there,
from whom such ill arose. And great Achilles,[21]
66 who fought at last with love in the house of
   prayer.

And Paris. And Tristan."[22] As they whirled above
he pointed out more than a thousand shades
69 of those torn from the mortal life by love.

I stood there while my Teacher one by one
named the great knights and ladies of dim time;
72 and I was swept by pity and confusion.

At last I spoke: "Poet, I should be glad
to speak a word with those two[23] swept
   together
75 so lightly on the wind and still so sad."

And he to me: "Watch them. When next they
   pass,
call to them in the name of love that drives
78 and damns them here. In that name they will
   pause."

Thus, as soon as the wind in its wild course
brought them around, I called: "O wearied souls!
81 if none forbid it, pause and speak to us."

As mating doves that love calls to their nest
glide through the air with motionless raised
   wings,
84 borne by the sweet desire that fills each breast—

Just so those spirits turned on the torn sky
from the band where Dido whirls across the air;
87 such was the power of pity in my cry.

"O living creature, gracious, kind, and good,
going this pilgrimage through the sick night,
90 visiting us who stained the earth with blood,

were the King of Time our friend, we would pray
   His peace
on you who have pitied us. As long as the wind
93 will let us pause, ask of us what you please.

---

19. **Semiramis** (si·mir'ə·mis): a legendary queen of
   Assyria.
20. **Dido** (dī'dō): a legendary queen of Carthage who
   vowed to be true to her dead husband, Sichaeus,
   but broke her vow when she fell in love with
   Aeneas; after Aeneas abandoned her, Dido threw
   herself on a funeral pyre.
21. **Achilles:** the great Greek warrior who deserted his
   army in order to marry Polyxena (pō·lik'sē·nə), a
   Trojan princess; Achilles was killed by Paris, a Trojan warrior, when he went to the temple for the
   wedding.
22. **Tristan:** In medieval legend, Tristan fell in love
   with Iseult (i·sōolt'), a young princess betrothed to
   his uncle, King Mark of Cornwall. Eventually, both
   lovers died on the same day (see page 716).

---

23. **those two:** Paolo (pä'ô·lô) and Francesca (frän·
   ches'kä); Francesca da Rimini, a niece of Dante's
   patron, had been murdered with her lover, Paolo
   Malatesta, by her husband, Giovanni (who was
   also Paolo's brother), when he found the lovers
   together.

The town where I was born lies by the shore
where the Po descends into its ocean rest
96   with its attendant streams in one long murmur.

Love, which in gentlest hearts will soonest bloom
seized my lover with passion for that sweet
body
99   from which I was torn unshriven to my doom.

Love, which permits no loved one not to love,
took me so strongly with delight in him
102   that we are one in Hell, as we were above.

Love led us to one death. In the depths of Hell
Caina[24] waits for him who took our lives."
105   This was the piteous tale they stopped to tell.

And when I had heard those world-offended
lovers
I bowed my head. At last the Poet spoke:
108   "What painful thoughts are these your lowered
brow covers?"

When at length I answered, I began: "Alas!
What sweetest thoughts, what green and young
desire
111   led these two lovers to this sorry pass."

Then turning to those spirits once again,
I said: "Francesca, what you suffer here
114   melts me to tears of pity and of pain.

But tell me: in the time of your sweet sighs
by what appearances found love the way
117   to lure you to his perilous paradise?"

And she: "The double grief of a lost bliss
is to recall its happy hour in pain.
120   Your Guide and Teacher knows the truth of this.

But if there is indeed a soul in Hell
to ask of the beginning of our love
123   out of his pity, I will weep and tell:

On a day for dalliance we read the rhyme
of Lancelot,[25] how love had mastered him.
126   We were alone with innocence and dim time.

Pause after pause that high old story drew
our eyes together while we blushed and paled;
129   but it was one soft passage overthrew

our caution and our hearts. For when we read
how her fond smile was kissed by such a lover,
132   he who is one with me alive and dead

breathed on my lips the tremor of his kiss.
That book, and he who wrote it,[26] was a
pander.
135   That day we read no further." As she said this,

the other spirit, who stood by her, wept
so piteously, I felt my senses reel
138   and faint away with anguish. I was swept

by such a swoon as death is, and I fell,
as a corpse might fall, to the dead floor of Hell.

---

24. **Caina:** the level of Hell reserved for murderers of kin; named for Cain, the son of Adam and Eve, who slew his brother Abel.

25. **Lancelot:** In the medieval legends of King Arthur, Lancelot fell in love with Guinevere, Arthur's queen, and their love led to the downfall of the Knights of the Round Table.

26. **he who wrote it:** In an old French version of the romance of Lancelot, the character who urges on the secret lovers Lancelot and Guinevere is called Gallehaut. The Italian for *Gallehaut* is *Galeotto*, which is also the word for ''pander,'' that is, a go-between for lovers, one who urges on the passions between secret lovers. The book was thus a kind of ''pander'' between Paolo and Francesca.

First Thoughts

Describe Dante's emotional responses at several key points in the narrative thus far. Do you think your reactions would be similar to his? Explain.

Identifying Facts

1. What is Dante's state of mind at the beginning of the poem?

2. How does Virgil offer to help Dante? Why is Virgil himself unable to take Dante directly to the Light of God?

3. What is the sin of the first group of condemned souls that Dante meets?

4. Who is Charon? According to Virgil, why does Charon refuse to allow Dante to cross Acheron?

5. What is Minos's role in the second circle of Hell? How does he perform this duty?

6. What types of sinners does Dante see in the second circle? What is their eternal punishment?

Interpreting Meanings

1. In line 12 of the first canto, Dante says that he has wandered from the "True Way." If the Dark Wood of Error is a **symbol** of worldliness, what does the "True Way" represent? What might the three animals that try to force Dante back into the Dark Wood symbolize?

2. Dante is the author of the *Divine Comedy* as well as a character in it. How does Dante feel when he learns Virgil's identity in Canto 1? Why is Virgil important to Dante as a poet?

3. As Dante's guide, Virgil often explains things to him. In line 18 of Canto 3, Virgil tells Dante that the fallen people are those " 'who have lost the good of intellect.' " What does he mean?

4. The inscription on the gate of Hell tells the damned to abandon all hope. In what ways does hopelessness torment the spirits of the damned in Canto 3? Comment on lines 42–45 and 100–102.

5. In Canto 5, lines 82–87, Dante compares Paolo and Francesca to doves. Why do you suppose Dante uses such a sympathetic image for the lovers?

6. By including details about Paolo and Francesca's reading, what attitude do you think Dante is expressing toward courtly love poetry?

Applying Meanings

Dante believed that faith was the most important value in life. Next to faith, however, he saw reason as the highest human value. How do you define faith and reason? Which is more valued in today's world? Which do you think *should* be more highly valued? Explain your response.

UGOLINO AND THE ARCHBISHOP RUGGIERI, GUSTAVE DORÉ.
What purpose does Dante serve by telling the tales of various sinners to the world?

Dante and Virgil continue to descend deeper and deeper into Hell, encountering increasingly horrible sins and their corresponding punishments. Near the end of Canto 32, Dante, having reached the frigid ninth circle of Hell, encounters two souls squeezed into the same icy hole. One sinner is chewing on the head of the other. Dante asks the first soul why he is devouring the other, offering to tell the sinner's story to the world. In the following canto, Canto 33, Dante will learn the gruesome history of Count Ugolino and Bishop Ruggieri, both Dante's contemporaries in thirteenth-century Italy.

CANTO 33

Circle Nine: Cocytus
Round Two: Antenora
Round Three: Ptolomea

Compound Fraud
The Treacherous to Country
The Treacherous to Guests and Hosts

In reply to Dante's exhortation, the sinner who is gnawing his companion's head looks up, wipes his bloody mouth on his victim's hair, and tells his harrowing story. He is *Count Ugolino* and the wretch he gnaws is *Archbishop Ruggieri*. Both are in Antenora[1] for treason. In life they had once plotted together. Then Ruggieri betrayed his fellow-plotter and caused his death, by starvation, along with his four "sons." In the most pathetic and dramatic passage of the *Inferno*, Ugolino details how their prison was sealed and how his "sons"[2] dropped dead before him one by one, weeping for food. His terrible tale serves only to renew his grief and hatred, and he has hardly finished it before he begins to gnaw Ruggieri again with renewed fury. In the immutable

Law of Hell, the killer-by-starvation becomes the food of his victim.

The Poets leave Ugolino and enter *Ptolomea*, so named for the Ptolomaeus of *Maccabees*, who murdered his father-in-law at a banquet. Here are punished those who were *Treacherous Against the Ties of Hospitality*. They lie with only half their faces above the ice and their tears freeze in their eye sockets, sealing them with little crystal visors. Thus even the comfort of tears is denied them. Here Dante finds *Friar Alberigo* and *Branca d'Oria*, and discovers the terrible power of Ptolomea: so great is its sin that the souls of the guilty fall to its torments even before they die, leaving their bodies still on earth, inhabited by Demons.

The sinner raised his mouth from his grim repast
   and wiped it on the hair of the bloody head
3 whose nape he had all but eaten away. At last

he began to speak: "You ask me to renew
   a grief so desperate that the very thought
6 of speaking of it tears my heart in two.

But if my words may be a seed that bears
   the fruit of infamy for him I gnaw,
9 I shall weep, but tell my story through my tears.

Who you may be, and by what powers you reach
   into this underworld, I cannot guess,
12 but you seem to me a Florentine by your speech.

I was Count Ugolino, I must explain;
   this reverend grace is the Archbishop Ruggieri:[3]
15 now I will tell you why I gnaw his brain.

That I, who trusted him, had to undergo
   imprisonment and death through his treachery,
18 you will know already. What you cannot know—

---

1. **Antenora:** part of the ninth circle set aside for traitors; named for Antenor, who, in some versions of the story of the Trojan War, betrayed Troy to the Greeks.
2. **"sons":** Actually, two of the four men bricked up with Ugolino were his grandsons; the younger one was fifteen.

3. **Ugolino . . . Ruggieri:** Count Ugolino and Archbishop Ruggieri were originally allies in political factions jockeying for power in the city of Pisa. In 1288, Ruggieri betrayed Ugolino and imprisoned him and his sons. The next year Ruggieri had the dungeon sealed and starved the prisoners to death.

that is, the lingering inhumanity
 of the death I suffered—you shall hear in full:[4]
21 then judge for yourself if he has injured me.

A narrow window in that coop of stone
 now called the Tower of Hunger for my sake
24 (within which others yet must pace alone)

had shown me several waning moons already
 between its bars, when I slept the evil sleep
27 in which the veil of the future parted for me.

This beast[5] appeared as master of a hunt
 chasing the wolf and his whelps across the
 mountain
30 that hides Lucca from Pisa.[6] Out in front

of the starved and shrewd and avid pack he had
 placed
 Gualandi and Sismondi and Lanfranchi[7]
33 to point his prey. The father and sons had raced

a brief course only when they failed of breath
 and seemed to weaken; then I thought I saw
36 their flanks ripped open by the hounds' fierce
 teeth.

Before the dawn, the dream still in my head,
 I woke and heard my sons, who were there
 with me,
39 cry from their troubled sleep, asking for bread.

You are cruelty itself if you can keep
 your tears back at the thought of what
 foreboding
42 stirred in my heart; and if you do not weep,

at what are you used to weeping?—The hour
 when food
 used to be brought, drew near. They were now
 awake,
45 and each was anxious from his dream's dark
 mood.

And from the base of that horrible tower I heard
 the sound of hammers nailing up the gates:
48 I stared at my sons' faces without a word.

I did not weep: I had turned stone inside.
 They wept. 'What ails you, Father, you look so
 strange,'
51 my little Anselm,[8] youngest of them, cried.

But I did not speak a word nor shed a tear:
 not all that day nor all that endless night,
54 until I saw another sun appear.

When a tiny ray leaked into that dark prison
 and I saw staring back from their four faces
57 the terror and the wasting of my own,

I bit my hands in helpless grief. And they,
 thinking I chewed myself for hunger, rose
60 suddenly together. I heard them say:

'Father, it would give us much less pain
 if you ate us: it was you who put upon us
63 this sorry flesh; now strip it off again.'

I calmed myself to spare them. Ah! hard earth,
 why did you not yawn open? All that day

---

4. **you shall hear in full:** By 1300, supposedly the
 date when Dante began the *Divine Comedy,* everyone in adjacent cities would have known that Ruggieri had imprisoned his former ally. But because the
 dungeon was sealed, no one would have known exactly how he and the others met their deaths.

5. **This beast:** i.e., Ruggieri.

6. **the mountain that hides Lucca from Pisa:** Mount
 San Giuliano stands between the two cities.

7. **Gualandi . . . Lanfranchi:** Like Ugolino, these three
 were nobles of Pisa and friends of Archbishop
 Ruggieri.

8. **my little Anselm:** Anselm, Gaddo (line 67), Brigata,
 and Uguccione (line 89) were the sons and grandsons entombed with Ugolino.

66 and the next we sat in silence. On the fourth,

Gaddo, the eldest, fell before me and cried,
stretched at my feet upon that prison floor:
69 'Father, why don't you help me?' There he died.

And just as you see me, I saw them fall
one by one on the fifth day and the sixth.
72 Then, already blind, I began to crawl

from body to body shaking them frantically.
Two days I called their names, and they were
dead.
75 Then fasting overcame my grief and me."

His eyes narrowed to slits when he was done,
and he seized the skull again between his teeth
78 grinding it as a mastiff grinds a bone.

Ah, Pisa! foulest blemish on the land
where "si" sounds sweet and clear,[9] since those
nearby you
81 are slow to blast the ground on which you stand,

may Caprara and Gorgona[10] drift from place
and dam the flooding Arno[11] at its mouth
84 until it drowns the last of your foul race!

For if to Ugolino falls the censure
for having betrayed your castles, you for your
part
87 should not have put his sons to such a torture:

you modern Thebes![12] those tender lives you spilt—
Brigata, Uguccione, and the others

90 I mentioned earlier—were too young for guilt!

We passed on further,[13] where the frozen mine
entombs another crew in greater pain;
93 these wraiths are not bent over, but lie supine.

Their very weeping closes up their eyes;
and the grief that finds no outlet for its tears
96 turns inward to increase their agonies:

for the first tears that they shed knot instantly
in their eye-sockets, and as they freeze they
form
99 a crystal visor above the cavity.

And despite the fact that standing in that place
I had become as numb as any callus,
102 and all sensation had faded from my face,

somehow I felt a wind begin to blow,
whereat I said: "Master, what stirs this wind?
105 Is not all heat extinguished here below?"

And the Master said to me: "Soon you will be
where your own eyes will see the source and
cause
108 and give you their own answer to the
mystery."[14]

And one of those locked in that icy mall
cried out to us as we passed: "O souls so cruel
111 that you are sent to the last post of all,[15]

---

9. **the land . . . sweet and clear:** Italy; *si* is the Italian word for "yes."
10. **Caprara and Gorgona:** two islands near the mouth of the Arno River, possessions of Pisa.
11. **Arno:** river in Italy; Florence and Arezzo are located on its banks, and Pisa is located at its mouth.
12. **you modern Thebes:** Ancient Thebes was the scene of much violence and bloodshed.

13. **We passed on further:** Here Dante and Virgil pass into Ptolomea, the place of punishment for traitors against hospitality; named for Ptolomeus, who invited Simon Maccabaeus, king of Judea, and his two sons to a banquet and then assassinated them in 135 B.C.
14. **their own answer to the mystery:** The answer to Dante's question about the source of the wind will be given in Canto 34.
15. **the last post of all:** This sinner thinks Virgil and Dante are condemned souls who are being sent to the very lowest part of the ninth circle because their crimes were worse than his.

relieve me for a little from the pain
  of this hard veil; let my heart weep a while
114 before the weeping freeze my eyes again."

And I to him: "If you would have my service,
  tell me your name; then if I do not help you
117 may I descend to the last rim of the ice."

"I am Friar Alberigo," he answered therefore,
  "the same who called for the fruits from the bad
  garden.[16]
120 Here I am given dates for figs full store."

"What! Are you dead already?" I said to him.
  And he then: "How my body stands in the
  world
123 I do not know. So privileged is this rim

of Ptolomea, that often souls fall to it
  before dark Atropos has cut their thread.[17]
126 And that you may more willingly free my spirit

of this glaze of frozen tears that shrouds my face,
  I will tell you this: when a soul betrays as I did,
129 it falls from flesh, and a demon takes its place,

ruling the body till its time is spent.[18]
  The ruined soul rains down into this cistern.
132 So, I believe, there is still evident

In the world above, all that is fair and mortal
  of this black shade who winters here behind me.
135 If you have only recently crossed the portal

from that sweet world, you surely must have known
  his body: Branca D'Oria[19] is its name,
138 and many years have passed since he rained down."

"I think you are trying to take me in," I said,
  "Ser Branca D'Oria is a living man;
141 he eats, he drinks, he fills his clothes and his bed."

"Michel Zanche had not yet reached the ditch
  of the Black Talons," the frozen wraith replied,
144 "there where the sinners thicken in hot pitch,

when this one left his body to a devil,
  as did his nephew and second in treachery,
147 and plumbed like lead through space to this
  dead level.

But now reach out your hand, and let me cry."
  And I did not keep the promise I had made,
150 for to be rude to him was courtesy.

Ah, men of Genoa![20] souls of little worth,
  corrupted from all custom of righteousness,
153 why have you not been driven from the earth?

For there beside the blackest soul of all
  Romagna's evil plain,[21] lies one of yours
156 bathing his filthy soul in the eternal

glacier of Cocytus for his foul crime,
  while he seems yet alive in world and time!

---

16. **the fruits from the bad garden:** To avenge an insult, Friar Alberigo invited his brother Manfred and
   Manfred's son to dinner. At the signal, ''Bring in
   the fruit,'' hired murderers killed them.

17. **before . . . thread:** According to Greek mythology,
   there were three Fates: Clotho spun the web of a
   person's life; Lachesis measured out its length;
   Atropos cut it at the moment of death.

18. **a demon . . . its time is spent:** Dante includes in
   Hell the souls of some who were still alive at the
   time of writing. He explains this by suggesting that
   certain sins are so grave that the sinners' spirits
   are immediately damned, while their bodies, animated by demons, live out a natural span of life.

19. **Branca D'Oria:** he invited his father-in-law, Michel
   Zanche, to a feast and then murdered him.

20. **men of Genoa:** Branca D'Oria was a Genoan.

21. **Romagna's evil plain:** a region of northeast Italy,
   formerly part of the Papal States.

THE JUDECCA, LUCIFER, GUSTAVE DORÉ.

? *How does this image of Satan compare with modern conceptions of the Devil?*
Do you find it surprising that the center of Hell is icy rather than fiery?

CANTO 34

Ninth Circle: Cocytus	*Compound Fraud*
Round Four: Judecca	*The Treacherous to Their Masters*
The Center	*Satan*

"On march the banners of the King," Virgil begins as the Poets face the last depth. He is quoting a medieval hymn, and to it he adds the distortion and perversion of all that lies about him. "On march the banners of the King—of Hell." And there before them, in an infernal parody of God-head, they see Satan in the distance, his great wings beating like a windmill. It is their beating that is the source of the icy wind of Cocytus, the exhalation of all evil.

All about him in the ice are strewn the sinners of the last round, *Judecca,* named for Judas Is-

cariot. These are the *Treacherous to Their Masters.* They lie completely sealed in the ice, twisted and distorted into every conceivable posture. It is impossible to speak to them, and the Poets move on to observe Satan.

He is fixed into the ice at the center to which flow all the rivers of guilt; and as he beats his great wings as if to escape, their icy wind only freezes him more surely into the polluted ice. In a grotesque parody of the Trinity, he has three faces, each a different color, and in each mouth he clamps a sinner whom he rips eternally with

Dante Alighieri **765**

his teeth. *Judas Iscariot* is in the central mouth: *Brutus* and *Cassius* in the mouths on either side.

Having seen all, the Poets now climb through the center, grappling hand over hand down the hairy flank of Satan himself—a last supremely symbolic action—and at last, when they have passed the center of all gravity, they emerge from Hell. A long climb from the earth's center to the Mount of Purgatory awaits them, and they push on without rest, ascending along the sides of the river Lethe, till they emerge once more to see the stars of Heaven, just before dawn on Easter Sunday.

———————

"On march the banners of the King of Hell,"[22]
  my Master said. "Toward us. Look straight
    ahead:
3 can you make him[23] out at the core of the
    frozen shell?"

Like a whirling windmill seen afar at twilight,
  or when a mist has risen from the ground—
6 just such an engine rose upon my sight

stirring up such a wild and bitter wind
  I cowered for shelter at my Master's back,
9 there being no other windbreak I could find.

I stood now where the souls of the last class
  (with fear my verses tell it) were covered
    wholly;
12 they shone below the ice like straws in glass.

Some lie stretched out; others are fixed in place
  upright, some on their heads, some on their
    soles;
15 another, like a bow, bends foot to face.

When we had gone so far across the ice
  that it pleased my Guide to show me the foul
    creature
18 that once had worn the grace of Paradise,

he made me stop, and, stepping aside, he said:
  "Now see the face of Dis![24] This is the place
21 where you must arm your soul against all dread."

Do not ask, Reader, how my blood ran cold
  and my voice choked up with fear. I cannot
    write it:
24 this is a terror that cannot be told.

I did not die, and yet I lost life's breath:
  imagine for yourself what I became,
27 deprived at once of both my life and death.

The Emperor of the Universe of Pain
  jutted his upper chest above the ice;
30 and I am closer in size to the great mountain

the Titans[25] make around the central pit,
  than they to his arms. Now, starting from this
    part,
33 imagine the whole that corresponds to it!

If he was once as beautiful as now
  he is hideous, and still turned on his Maker,
36 well may he be the source of every woe!

---

22. **On march . . . Hell:** Virgil is deliberately distorting the words of a medieval hymn that was written to celebrate the Holy Cross.
23. **him:** Satan.

24. **Dis** (dis): Satan; in Greek mythology, the god of the underworld; also the realm of the dead.
25. **Titans** (tīt''nz): in Greek mythology, a family of gods that was overthrown by Zeus and the Olympians and confined to Tartarus, the region below Hades.

With what a sense of awe I saw his head
 towering above me! for it had three faces:
39 one was in front, and it was fiery red;

the other two, as weirdly wonderful,
 merged with it from the middle of each
 shoulder
42 to the point where all converged at the top of
 the skull;

the right was something between white and bile;
 the left was about the color one observes
45 on those who live along the banks of the Nile.

Under each head two wings rose terribly,
 their span proportioned to so gross a bird:
48 I never saw such sails upon the sea.

They were not feathers—their texture and their
 form
 were like a bat's wings—and he beat them so
51 that three winds blew from him in one great
 storm:

it is these winds that freeze all Cocytus.²⁶
 He wept from his six eyes, and down three
 chins
54 the tears ran mixed with bloody froth and
 pus.²⁷

In every mouth he worked a broken sinner
 between his rake-like teeth. Thus he kept three
57 in eternal pain at his eternal dinner.

For the one in front the biting seemed to play
 no part at all compared to the ripping: at times
60 the whole skin of his back was flayed away.

"That soul that suffers most," explained my Guide,
 "is Judas Iscariot,²⁸ he who kicks his legs
63 on the fiery chin and has his head inside.

Of the other two, who have their heads thrust
 forward,
 the one who dangles down from the black face
66 is Brutus:²⁹ note how he writhes without a
 word.

And there, with the huge and sinewy arms, is the
 soul
 of Cassius.³⁰—But the night is coming on
69 and we must go, for we have seen the whole."

Then, as he bade, I clasped his neck, and he,
 watching for a moment when the wings
72 were opened wide, reached over dexterously

and seized the shaggy coat of the king demon;
 then grappling matted hair and frozen crusts
75 from one tuft to another, clambered down.

When we had reached the joint where the great
 thigh
 merges into the swelling of the haunch,
78 my Guide and Master, straining terribly,

turned his head to where his feet had been
 and began to grip the hair as if he were
 climbing;
81 so that I thought we moved toward Hell again.

"Hold fast!" my Guide said, and his breath came
 shrill
 with labor and exhaustion. "There is no way
84 but by such stairs to rise above such evil."

---

26. **Cocytus** (kō·sīt′əs): one of the six rivers of the
 underworld.
27. **bloody . . . pus:** the grisly result of chewing
 sinners.

28. **Judas Iscariot** (jōō′dəs is·ker′ē·ət): the disciple
 who betrayed Jesus Christ.
29. **Brutus:** one of the Roman conspirators who assassinated Julius Caesar.
30. **Cassius** (kas′ē·əs): Brutus's coconspirator.

Dante Alighieri   **767**

At last he climbed out through an opening
   in the central rock, and he seated me on the
   rim;
87 then joined me with a nimble backward spring.

I looked up, thinking to see Lucifer[31]
   as I had left him, and I saw instead
90 his legs projecting high into the air.

Now let all those whose dull minds are still
   vexed
   by failure to understand what point it was
93 I had passed through, judge if I was perplexed.

"Get up. Up on your feet," my Master said.
   "The sun already mounts to middle tierce,[32]
96 and a long road and hard climbing lie ahead."

It was no hall of state we had found there,
   but a natural animal pit hollowed from rock
99 with a broken floor and a close and sunless air.

"Before I tear myself from the Abyss,"
   I said when I had risen, "O my Master,
102 explain to me my error in all this:

where is the ice? and Lucifer—how has he
   been turned from top to bottom: and how can
   the sun
105 have gone from night to day so suddenly?"

And he to me: "You imagine you are still
   on the other side of the center where I grasped
108 the shaggy flank of the Great Worm of Evil

which bores through the world—you _were_ while I
   climbed down,
   but when I turned myself about, you passed
111 the point to which all gravities are drawn.

You are under the other hemisphere where you
   stand;
   the sky above us is the half opposed
114 to that which canopies the great dry land.

Under the midpoint of that other sky
   the Man[33] who was born sinless and who lived
117 beyond all blemish, came to suffer and die.

You have your feet upon a little sphere
   which forms the other face of the Judecca.[34]
120 There it is evening when it is morning here.

And this gross Fiend and Image of all Evil
   who made a stairway for us with his hide
123 is pinched and prisoned in the ice-pack still.

On this side he plunged down from heaven's
   height,
   and the land that spread here once hid in the
   sea
126 and fled North to our hemisphere for fright;

and it may be that moved by that same fear,
   the one peak[35] that still rises on this side
129 fled upward leaving this great cavern here."

Down there, beginning at the further bound
   of Beelzebub's[36] dim tomb, there is a space
132 not known by sight, but only by the sound

of a little stream[37] descending through the hollow
   it has eroded from the massive stone
135 in its endlessly entwining lazy flow."

---

31. **Lucifer** (lōō′sə·fər): Satan.
32. **middle tierce:** seven-thirty A.M.

33. **the Man:** Christ.
34. **Judecca:** the level of Hell named for Judas Iscar-
    iot, who betrayed Christ.
35. **one peak:** the Mount of Purgatory.
36. **Beelzebub's** (bē·el′zə·bub′): here, another name
    for Satan.
37. **a little stream:** Lethe (lē′thē); in classical mythol-
    ogy, the river of forgetfulness.

The Poets Emerge from Hell, Gustave Doré.

? *In feeling and atmosphere, how does this engraving by Doré differ from the others you have seen in this selection?*

My Guide and I crossed over and began
  to mount that little known and lightless road
138 to ascend into the shining world again.

He first, I second, without thought of rest
  we climbed the dark until we reached the point
141 where a round opening brought in sight the
  blest

and beauteous shining of the Heavenly cars.
And we walked out once more beneath the
  Stars.[38]

---

38. **Stars:** Each of the three divisions of Dante's poem ends with the symbolism of heavenly stars. The time—just before dawn on Easter Sunday—is also symbolic of hope.

New York Public Library Picture Collection

First Thoughts

Which images do you find the most striking in Cantos 33 and 34? Why?

Identifying Facts

1. According to Canto 33, what souls are punished in the ninth circle? What sins have they committed?

2. How does Ugolino's grim story make Ugolino himself feel? What does he then do to express his feelings?

3. According to Canto 34, what sinners are punished in the lowest, last circle? How are they punished?

4. According to Dante, what does Satan look like? What is Satan doing?

Interpreting Meanings

1. Describe Ugolino's evil dream (Canto 33, lines 28–36) and explain how it parts "the veil of the future" (line 27)— that is, forecasts coming events.

2. Why does Dante not keep his promise to Friar Alberigo?

3. Why does Dante regard Judas, Brutus, and Cassius as the worst sinners of all? How does Judas's sin differ from that of Brutus and Cassius?

4. In what way could Satan's three faces be explained as **symbols**?

Applying Meanings

By his placement of different sinners in Hell, Dante ranks human sins from the least to the most serious. What sins do people today regard as the least serious? As the most serious? Why do you think so?

Creative Writing Response

Inventing a Board Game. Imagine that you work for a company that manufactures board games. You want to convince the president of your company to manufacture an exciting board game that you have invented based on Dante's *Inferno*. The object of your board game is to journey successfully through Hell without getting caught there forever. Along the way there are helpers, such as Virgil and Beatrice, but there are also those who will try to prevent you from successfully completing your journey, such as Charon the ferryman, the monster Minos, and the various sinners who inhabit the Inferno. Decide on the rules of your game and what pieces it will consist of: figures, playing cards, and so on. Then write a detailed memo describing the game in terms that will convince the president of the company to manufacture it. If you wish, illustrate the various components of your board game.

Critical Writing Response

Making a Literary Judgment. Many readers are surprised to find that Dante describes the center of Hell as a frozen rather than fiery place. English Puritan writer John Milton in *Paradise Lost* pictures Hell as a gigantic furnace, as shown in the following lines from Book I:

A dungeon horrible, on all sides round
As one great furnace flamed, yet from those flames
No light, but rather darkness visible
Served only to discover sights of woe,
Regions of sorrow, doleful shades, where peace
And rest can never dwell, hope never comes
That comes to all; but torture without end
Still urges, and a fiery deluge, fed
With everburning sulphur unconsumed. . . .

Think of the qualities of both fire and ice. In your opinion, which is better suited to symbolically describe the place farthest from God, the center of Hell? Write an essay of three paragraphs defending your position. Be sure to support your choice with at least three strong reasons.

ELEMENTS OF LITERATURE

Allegory

Dante wrote the *Divine Comedy* as an **allegory**, a narrative that takes place on both a literal and a figurative, or symbolic, level. Dante begins the poem with an age-old metaphor that is so common it has become a cliché: the description of life as a journey. When Dante says, "Midway in our life's journey," we can readily understand that he has reached middle age. From "I went astray," we understand that he is no longer acting as he thinks he should. A "dark wood" could be a state of mental confusion. In thinking further about the poem, we may even decide that the *I* in this passage has an allegorical, or symbolic, meaning, since the character of Dante could also be any one of us.

In an allegory, concrete details from the external world are used to represent inner mental states or spiritual truths. By choosing this form of expression, an author may be able to communicate ideas that would otherwise be difficult to explain. An author may also be able to make these truths highly dramatic. It would be one thing for Dante to say that he overcame the evil in his own heart. It is quite another thing for him to describe himself "grappling matted hair and frozen crusts" as he climbs on Satan's flank.

On a literal level in the *Divine Comedy,* the character of Dante travels through Hell, Purgatory, and Paradise before reaching God. On a symbolic level, however, his journey represents the progress of every individual soul toward God as well as the progress of people in their political and social lives toward peace on earth. Throughout the *Divine Comedy,* Dante mentions people, places, ideas, and events that are firmly rooted in his own time. But far from being an outdated work that makes sense only in the context of the Middle Ages, the *Divine Comedy* has great relevance to us today. By writing an allegory, Dante gives his narrative significance that goes far beyond the specifics of particular people and events.

Drawing by Weber © 1991, The New Yorker Magazine, Inc.

"*Hon, what's an allegory?*"

Geoffrey Chaucer
c. 1342–1400

The National Portrait Gallery, London

Generally considered the "Father of English poetry," Chaucer was a well-educated man who knew French and Latin and was familiar with contemporary as well as classical literature. But just as important as his reading was Chaucer's remarkably broad experience of life. In his teens he served as a page, or messenger boy, to royalty, and later he went on to hold important positions in the king's service as a customs officer, a justice of the peace, a clerk of the king's works in charge of maintenance and repairs, and a member of Parliament. These posts brought Chaucer into close contact with people from all walks of life and gave him a rich understanding of human beings and all their follies and frailties.

Chaucer began his most famous work, *The Canterbury Tales*, in 1387. His plan in writing the story was to present a group of men and women representing nearly every level of medieval English society as they traveled on a pilgrimage to Canterbury, a city in southeastern England that is the site of a shrine to the martyred twelfth-century archbishop, St. Thomas à Becket. Each pilgrim was to tell two stories on the way to Canterbury and two on the way home. Chaucer died before completing the whole plan, but he left behind an unforgettable collection of stories and characters.

Chaucer wrote in Middle English, an ancestor of the English spoken today. In choosing to write in English, the vernacular, Chaucer was taking a bold step. French was still the language of the English court, and most serious literature of Chaucer's time was written in either French or Latin. But Chaucer, like Dante, decided to use the everyday language of his countrymen rather than the language of the elite. He thus lent respectability to the English language.

Reader's Guide

THE WIFE OF BATH'S TALE
from The Canterbury Tales

Background

"The Wife of Bath's Tale" is part of a section of *The Canterbury Tales* frequently called the "marriage group." Responding to each other's stories, a number of the pilgrims tell tales about marriages, both good and bad. Through their stories, they conduct a kind of debate about what roles men and women should (and do) play in marriage. The Wife of Bath, who has already outlived five husbands and may have joined the pilgrimage to look for a sixth, has strong opinions on this subject.

In the prologue to her tale, the Wife of Bath (Bath is a city in southwestern England) delivers a very candid autobiography. The unmarried life may be fine for other people, she contends, but not for her. She goes on to assert that marriage is happiest when the wife holds sway over the husband—at least in private. She offers as proof the story of her five marriages, and particularly the fifth, to a younger man named Johnny. Johnny made her miserable until they had a fight in which she pretended he had killed her. After that, he submitted to her, and the couple never quarreled again but lived happily as equals.

Having told the pilgrims her own life story, the Wife of Bath then proceeds to tell them the following tale, which supports her own conclusions about relationships between men and women.

Oral Response

The knight in "The Wife of Bath's Tale" must find the answer to the question "What is the thing that women most desire?" What do you think is the answer to this question? Discuss your ideas with your classmates.

Literary Focus

Some characters in fiction are **dynamic characters**—people who undergo real changes in the course of a story. The decisions these characters make, the things that they say, or simply their inner thoughts reflect these inner changes. **Static characters**, on the other hand, remain unchanged from the beginning of a story to the end. Most works of fiction contain characters of both kinds, but the central characters in lengthier works tend to be dynamic.

THE WIFE OF BATH'S TALE
from The Canterbury Tales
Geoffrey Chaucer
translated by
NEVILL COGHILL

*When you reach line 44 of "The Wife of Bath's Tale," make a
prediction about what will happen to the knight. What fate do
you think he deserves?*

When good King Arthur ruled in ancient days
(A king that every Briton loves to praise)
This was a land brim-full of fairy folk.
The Elf-Queen and her courtiers joined and broke
5   Their elfin dance on many a green mead,
Or so was the opinion once, I read,
Hundreds of years ago, in days of yore.
But no one now sees fairies any more.
For now the saintly charity and prayer
10   Of holy friars seem to have purged the air;
They search the countryside through field and
        stream
As thick as motes that speckle a sunbeam,
Blessing the halls, the chambers, kitchens, bowers,
Cities and boroughs, castles, courts and towers,
15   Thorpes,° barns and stables, outhouses and dairies,
And that's the reason why there are no fairies.
Wherever there was wont to walk an elf
Today there walks the holy friar himself
As evening falls or when the daylight springs,
20   Saying his matins° and his holy things,
Walking his limit round from town to town.
Women can now go safely up and down
By every bush or under every tree;
There is no other incubus° but he,
25   So there is really no one else to hurt you
And he will do no more than take your virtue.

Poverty, carrying a sack of wheat to
the mill, arrives at a dangerous
bridge; from a French manuscript,
c. 1455–1460.

15. **Thorpes:** villages; hamlets.

20. **matins** (mat''nz): morning
prayers.

24. **incubus** (in'kyoo·bəs): an evil
spirit or demon that people
believed descended on a
sleeping woman and made
her pregnant.

Now it so happened, I began to say,
Long, long ago in good King Arthur's day,
There was a knight who was a lusty liver.°
30 One day as he came riding from the river
He saw a maiden walking all forlorn
Ahead of him, alone as she was born.
And of that maiden, spite of all she said,
By very force he took her maidenhead.°
35   This act of violence made such a stir,
So much petitioning to the king for her,
That he condemned the knight to lose his head
By course of law. He was as good as dead
(It seems that then the statutes took that view)
40 But that the queen, and other ladies too,
Implored the king to exercise his grace
So ceaselessly, he gave the queen the case
And granted her his life, and she could choose
whether to show him mercy or refuse.
45   The queen returned him thanks with all her
          might,
And then she sent a summons to the knight
At her convenience, and expressed her will:
"You stand, for such is the position still,
In no way certain of your life," said she,
50 "Yet you shall live if you can answer me:
What is the thing that women most desire?
Beware the axe and say as I require,
     "If you can't answer on the moment, though,
I will concede you this: you are to go
55 A twelvemonth and a day to seek and learn
Sufficient answer, then you shall return.
I shall take gages° from you to extort
Surrender of your body to the court."
     Sad was the knight and sorrowfully sighed,
60 But there! All other choices were denied,
And in the end he chose to go away
And to return after a year and day
Armed with such answer as there might be sent
To him by God. He took his leave and went.
65   He knocked at every house, searched every
          place,
Yes, anywhere that offered hope of grace.
What could it be that women wanted most?

29. **liver:** In medieval times, the liver, and not the heart, was believed to be the source of desires and emotions.

34. **maidenhead:** virginity.

The Knight, detail from the Ellesmere manuscript.

The Huntington Library, San Marino, California

57. **gages:** things pledged to ensure that an obligation will be fulfilled.

But all the same he never touched a coast,
Country or town in which there seemed to be
70 Any two people willing to agree.
    Some said that women wanted wealth and
        treasure,
"Honor," said some, some "Jollity and pleasure,"
Some "Gorgeous clothes" and others "Fun in bed,"
"To be oft widowed and remarried," said
75 Others again, and some that what most mattered
Was that we should be cossetted° and flattered.
That's very near the truth, it seems to me;
A man can win us best with flattery.
To dance attendance on us, make a fuss,
80 Ensnares us all, the best and worst of us.
    Some say the things we most desire are these:
Freedom to do exactly as we please,
With no one to reprove our faults and lies,
Rather to have one call us good and wise.
85 Truly there's not a woman in ten score°
Who has a fault, and someone rubs the sore,
But she will kick if what he says is true;
You try it out and you will find so too.
However vicious we may be within
90 We like to be thought wise and void of sin.
Others assert we women find it sweet
When we are thought dependable, discreet
And secret, firm of purpose and controlled,
Never betraying things that we are told.
95 But that's not worth the handle of a rake;
Women conceal a thing? For Heaven's sake!
Remember Midas?° Will you hear the tale?
    Among some other little things, now stale,
Ovid° relates that under his long hair
100 The unhappy Midas grew a splendid pair
Of ass's ears; as subtly as he might,
He kept his foul deformity from sight;
Save for his wife, there was not one that knew.
He loved her best, and trusted in her too.
105 He begged her not to tell a living creature
That he possessed so horrible a feature.
And she—she swore, were all the world to win,
She would not do such villainy and sin
As saddle her husband with so foul a name;

76. **cossetted** (käs′it·id): pampered; fondled.

85. **score:** twenty; "ten score" is two hundred.

97. **Midas** (mī′dəs): a mythical king who was given the power to turn everything he touched into gold.

99. **Ovid** (äv′id): the Roman poet (43 B.C.—C. A.D. 17); Ovid's *Metamorphoses*, a compilation of mythical tales, includes one version of the story of King Midas.

110 Besides to speak would be to share the shame.
Nevertheless she thought she would have died
Keeping this secret bottled up inside;
It seemed to swell her heart and she, no doubt,
Thought it was on the point of bursting out.

115   Fearing to speak of it to woman or man,
Down to a reedy marsh she quickly ran
And reached the sedge. Her heart was all on fire
And, as a bittern° bumbles in the mire,
She whispered to the water, near the ground,

118. **bittern** (bit'ərn): a kind of wading bird.

120 "Betray me not, O water, with thy sound!
To thee alone I tell it: it appears
My husband has a pair of ass's ears!
Ah! My heart's well again, the secret's out!
I could no longer keep it, not a doubt."

125 And so you see, although we may hold fast
A little while, it must come out at last,
We can't keep secrets; as for Midas, well,
Read Ovid for his story;° he will tell.

128. **Ovid for his story:** In the original story of King Midas, it is Midas's barber, not his wife, who tells the secret of the ears to a hole in the ground. Reeds grow up in the hole and whisper the story whenever they are rustled by a breeze.

    This knight that I am telling you about
130 Perceived at last he never would find out
What it could be that women loved the best.
Faint was the soul within his sorrowful breast,
As home he went, he dared no longer stay;
His year was up and now it was the day.

135   As he rode home in a dejected mood
Suddenly, at the margin of a wood,
He saw a dance upon the leafy floor
Of four and twenty ladies, nay, and more.
Eagerly he approached, in hope to learn
140 Some words of wisdom ere he should return;
But lo! Before he came to where they were,
Dancers and dance all vanished into air!
There wasn't a living creature to be seen
Save one old woman crouched upon the green.
145 A fouler-looking creature I suppose
Could scarcely be imagined. She arose
And said, "Sir knight, there's no way on from
    here.
Tell me what you are looking for, my dear,
For peradventure that were best for you;
150 We old, old women know a thing or two."
    "Dear Mother," said the knight, "alack the day!

Pages from the *Kelmscott Chaucer*, a nineteenth-century masterpiece of bookmaking created by British artist and designer William Morris.

I am as good as dead if I can't say
What thing it is that women most desire;
If you could tell me I would pay your hire."

155 "Give me your hand," she said, "and swear to do
Whatever I shall next require of you
—If so to do should lie within your might—
And you shall know the answer before night."
"Upon my honor," he answered, "I agree."

160 "Then," said the crone, "I dare to guarantee
Your life is safe; I shall make good my claim.
Upon my life the queen will say the same.
Show me the very proudest of them all
In costly coverchief or jeweled caul°

165 That dare say no to what I have to teach.
Let us go forward without further speech."
And then she crooned her gospel in his ear
And told him to be glad and not to fear.
    They came to court. This knight, in full array,

170 Stood forth and said, "O Queen, I've kept my day
And kept my word and have my answer ready."
    There sat the noble matrons and the heady
Young girls, and widows too, that have the grace
Of wisdom, all assembled in that place,

175 And there the queen herself was throned to hear
And judge his answer. Then the knight drew near
And silence was commanded through the hall.

164. **coverchief or jeweled caul** (kôl): articles of headgear for women; the coverchief covered the head entirely. The caul was a small, netted cap, sometimes ornamented.

The queen gave order he should tell them all
What thing it was that women wanted most.
180 He stood not silent like a beast or post,
But gave his answer with the ringing word
Of a man's voice and the assembly heard:
"My liege and lady, in general," said he,
"A woman wants the self-same sovereignty
185 Over her husband as over her lover,
And master him; he must not be above her.
That is your greatest wish, whether you kill
Or spare me; please yourself. I wait your will."
In all the court not one that shook her head
190 Or contradicted what the knight had said;
Maid, wife, and widow cried, "He's saved his life!"
And on the word up started the old wife,
The one the knight saw sitting on the green,
And cried, "Your mercy, sovereign lady queen!
195 Before the court disperses, do me right!
'Twas I who taught this answer to the knight,
For which he swore, and pledged his honor to it,
That the first thing I asked of him he'd do it,
So far as it should lie within his might.
200 Before this court I ask you then, sir knight,
To keep your word and take me for your wife;
For well you know that I have saved your life.
If this be false, deny it on your sword!"
"Alas," he said, "Old Lady, by the Lord
205 I know indeed that such was my behest,
But for God's love think of a new request,
Take all my goods, but leave my body free."
"A curse on us," she said, "If I agree!
I may be foul, I may be poor and old,
210 Yet will not choose to be, for all the gold
That's bedded in the earth or lies above,
Less than your wife, nay, than your very love!"
"My love?" said he. "By heaven, my damnation!
Alas that any of my race and station
215 Should ever make so foul a misalliance!"
Yet in the end his pleading and defiance
All went for nothing, he was forced to wed.
He takes his ancient wife and goes to bed.
Now peradventure some may well suspect
220 A lack of care in me since I neglect

**The Wife of Bath, detail from the
Ellesmere manuscript.**

*The Huntington Library,
San Marino, California*

To tell of the rejoicings and display
Made at the feast upon their wedding-day.
I have but a short answer to let fall;
I say there was no joy or feast at all,
225 Nothing but heaviness of heart and sorrow.
He married her in private on the morrow
And all day long stayed hidden like an owl,
It was such torture that his wife looked foul.
    Great was the anguish churning in his head
230 When he and she were piloted to bed;
He wallowed back and forth in desperate style.
His ancient wife lay smiling all the while;
At last she said "Bless us! Is this, my dear,
How knights and wives get on together here?
235 Are these the laws of good King Arthur's house?
Are knights of his all so contemptuous?
I am your own beloved and your wife,
And I am she, indeed, that saved your life;
And certainly I never did you wrong.
240 Then why, this first of nights, so sad a song?
You're carrying on as if you were half-witted
Say, for God's love, what sin have I committed?
I'll put things right if you will tell me how."
    "Put right?" he cried. "That never can be now!
245 Nothing can ever be put right again!
You're old, and so abominably plain,
So poor to start with, so low-bred to follow;
It's little wonder if I twist and wallow!
God, that my heart would burst within my breast!"
250   "Is that," she said, "the cause of your unrest?"
    "Yes, certainly," he said, "and can you wonder?"
    "I could set right what you suppose a blunder,
That's if I cared to, in a day or two,
If I were shown more courtesy by you.
255 Just now," she said, "you spoke of gentle birth,
Such as descends from ancient wealth and worth.
If that's the claim you make for gentlemen
Such arrogance is hardly worth a hen.
Whoever loves to work for virtuous ends,
260 Public and private, and who most intends
To do what deeds of gentleness he can,
Take him to be the greatest gentleman.
Christ wills we take our gentleness from Him,

A page from the Ellesmere manuscript of Chaucer's *Canterbury Tales*.

Henry E. Huntington Library, San Marino, CA

Not from a wealth of ancestry long dim,
265 Though they bequeath their whole establishment
By which we claim to be of high descent.
Our fathers cannot make us a bequest
Of all those virtues that became them best
And earned for them the name of gentlemen,
270 But bade us follow them as best we can.

"Thus the wise poet of the Florentines,
Dante by name, has written in these lines,
For such is the opinion Dante launches:
'Seldom arises by these slender branches
275 Prowess of men, for it is God, no less,
Wills us to claim of Him our gentleness.'
For of our parents nothing can we claim
Save temporal things, and these may hurt and
    maim.

"But everyone knows this as well as I;
280 For if gentility were implanted by
The natural course of lineage down the line,
Public or private, could it cease to shine
In doing the fair work of gentle deed?
No vice or villainy could then bear seed.

285 "Take fire and carry it to the darkest house
Between this kingdom and the Caucasus,°
And shut the doors on it and leave it there,
It will burn on, and it will burn as fair
As if ten thousand men were there to see,
290 For fire will keep its nature and degree,
I can assure you, sir, until it dies.

"But gentleness, as you will recognize,
Is not annexed in nature to possessions.
Men fail in living up to their professions;°
295 But fire never ceases to be fire.
God knows you'll often find, if you enquire,
Some lording full of villainy and shame.
If you would be esteemed for the mere name
Of having been by birth a gentleman
300 And stemming from some virtuous, noble clan,
And do not live yourself by gentle deed
Or take your father's noble code and creed,
You are no gentleman, though duke or earl.
Vice and bad manners are what make a churl.°
305 "Gentility is only the renown

286. **Caucasus** (kô′kə·səs): a mountain range between the Black Sea and the Caspian Sea; Chaucer uses the name simply to suggest somewhere far away.

294. **professions:** declarations of beliefs.

304. **churl** (chʉrl): a rude, boorish person.

Geoffrey Chaucer **781**

For bounty that your fathers handed down,
Quite foreign to your person, not your own;
Gentility must come from God alone.
That we are gentle comes to us by grace
310 And by no means is it bequeathed with place.
    "Reflect how noble (says Valerius°)
Was Tullius surnamed Hostilius,°
Who rose from poverty to nobleness.
And read Boethius, Seneca° no less,
315 Thus they express themselves and are agreed:
'Gentle is he that does a gentle deed.'
And therefore, my dear husband, I conclude
That even if my ancestors were rude,
Yet God on high—and so I hope He will—
320 Can grant me grace to live in virtue still,
A gentlewoman only when beginning
To live in virtue and to shrink from sinning.
    "As for my poverty which you reprove,
Almighty God Himself in whom we move,
325 Believe and have our being, chose a life
Of poverty, and every man or wife
Nay, every child can see our Heavenly King
Would never stoop to choose a shameful thing.
No shame in poverty if the heart is gay,
330 As Seneca and all the learned say.
He who accepts his poverty unhurt
I'd say is rich although he lacked a shirt.
But truly poor are they who whine and fret
And covet what they cannot hope to get.
335 And he that, having nothing, covets not,
Is rich, though you may think he is a sot.°
    "True poverty can find a song to sing.
Juvenal° says a pleasant little thing:
'The poor can dance and sing in the relief
340 Of having nothing that will tempt a thief.'
Though it be hateful, poverty is good,
A great incentive to a livelihood,
And a great help to our capacity
For wisdom, if accepted patiently.
345 Poverty is, though wanting in estate,
A kind of wealth that none calumniate.°
Poverty often, when the heart is lowly,
Brings one to God and teaches what is holy,

311. **Valerius** (və·lir′ē·əs): a first-century Roman writer who compiled anecdotes for the use of orators.

312. **Tullius** (tul′ē·əs) **surnamed Hostilius** (hos·til′ē·əs): a legendary king of Rome who was said to have risen from humble rustic origins to become ruler of his nation.

314. **Boethius** (bō·ē′thē·əs): a philosopher (c. 480–525); in his *Consolation of Philosophy*, Boethius argues that rank is no guarantee of honorable conduct from those whom society elevates. **Seneca** (sen′i·kə): a first-century philosopher and dramatist whose works were popular in the Middle Ages; Seneca was born in Spain and educated in Rome.

336. **sot**: fool.

338. **Juvenal** (jōō′və·n′l): a Roman satirist who wrote between A.D. 98 and 128.

346. **calumniate** (kə·lum′nē·āt′): make false statements about.

Gives knowledge of oneself and even lends
350 A glass by which to see one's truest friends.
And since it's no offense, let me be plain;
Do not rebuke my poverty again.

   "Lastly you taxed me, sir, with being old.
Yet even if you never had been told
355 By ancient books, you gentlemen engage
Yourselves in honor to respect old age.
To call an old man 'father' shows good breeding,
And this could be supported from my reading.
   "You say I'm old and fouler than a fen.°
360 You need not fear to be a cuckold,° then.
Filth and old age, I'm sure you will agree,
Are powerful wardens over chastity.
Nevertheless, well knowing your delights,
I shall fulfill your worldly appetites.

365   "You have two choices; which one will you try?
To have me old and ugly till I die,
But still a loyal, true, and humble wife
That never will displease you all her life,
Or would you rather I were young and pretty
370 And chance your arm what happens in a city
Where friends will visit you because of me,
Yes, and in other places too, maybe.
Which would you have? The choice is all your
     own."

   The knight thought long, and with a piteous
     groan
375 At last he said, with all the care in life,
"My lady and my love, my dearest wife,
I leave the matter to your wise decision.
You make the choice yourself, for the provision
Of what may be agreeable and rich
380 In honor to us both, I don't care which;
Whatever pleases you suffices me."

   "And have I won the mastery?" said she,
"Since I'm to choose and rule as I think fit?"
"Certainly, wife," he answered her, "that's it."
385 "Kiss me," she cried. "No quarrels! On my oath
And word of honor, you shall find me both,
That is, both fair and faithful as a wife;
May I go howling mad and take my life
Unless I prove to be as good and true

359. **fen:** a swamp.

360. **cuckold** (kuk′əld): a man whose wife has committed adultery.

The Pierpont Morgan Library, New York, M. 399, f.12v

NOVEMBER, detail from the *Book of Hours* of Jean, Duc de Berry, French illuminated manuscript.

Geoffrey Chaucer   **783**

390 As ever wife was since the world was new!
And if tomorrow when the sun's above
I seem less fair than any ladylove,
Than any queen or empress east or west,
Do with my life and death as you think best.
395 Cast up the curtain, husband. Look at me!"
    And when indeed the knight had looked to see,
Lo, she was young and lovely, rich in charms.
In ecstasy he caught her in his arms,
His heart went bathing in a bath of blisses
400 And melted in a hundred thousand kisses,
And she responded in the fullest measure
With all that could delight or give him pleasure.
    So they lived ever after to the end
In perfect bliss; and may Christ Jesus send
405 Us husbands meek and young and fresh in bed,
And grace to overbid them when we wed.
And—Jesu hear my prayer!—cut short the lives
Of those who won't be governed by their wives;
And all old, angry niggards of their pence,
410 God send them soon a very pestilence!

Pilgrims to Canterbury; detail of an English
illuminated manuscript, c. 1400.

First Thoughts

Do you agree that married men should be "governed by their wives"? Why or why not?

Identifying Facts

1. Why does the knight need to find out what women most desire?

2. Where does the knight find the answer to the question? What is the answer he finds?

3. What objection does the knight make to the old woman as a wife? How does she respond?

4. How is the conflict between the knight and his wife resolved?

Interpreting Meanings

1. Reread lines 1–8 in the opening of the tale and lines 135–144 in the section just before the knight meets the old lady. Who do you think the lady *really* is?

2. Do you consider the knight and the lady to be **dynamic** or **static characters**? Explain your answer.

3. A **moral** is a lesson about life that a story teaches. What moral does the Wife of Bath want us to draw from her tale? How does she make this moral clear?

4. What examples of humor do you find in "The Wife of Bath's Tale"? What is the effect of the humor in this story?

Applying Meanings

Based on what you know about her views on marriage, do you believe the Wife of Bath would be happy in contemporary American society? Why or why not?

Speaking and Listening

Interviewing to Find an Answer. Interview at least ten classmates to find the answer to *this* question: "What is the thing that *men* most desire?" Be sure to explain that your question relates to what men want in marriage. Try to interview an equal number of males and females. Keep a record of the answers you get. Then write a one- or two-paragraph summary of what people say. Conclude by giving your own response.

Language and Vocabulary

Comparing Middle English and Modern English. Read the lines below from Chaucer's original Middle English version of *The Canterbury Tales*. (These lines are translated in lines 180–192 on page 799.) Then read the words in the list that follows. Write the Middle English words that were the ancestors of these modern English words. You may find it useful to read the lines aloud. Let context help you figure out which Middle English words preceded our modern English words.

This knyght ne stood nat stille, as dooth a
    best,
But to his questioun anon answerde,
With manly voys, that al the court it herde.
   "My lige lady, generally," quod he,
"Wommen desiren to have sovereyntee
As wel over hir housband as hir love
And for to been in maistrie hym above.
This is youre mooste desir, thogh ye me
    kille.
Dooth as yow list. I am here at youre
    wille."
   In al the court ne was ther wyf, ne
    mayde,
Ne wydwe that contraried that he sayde;
But seyden he was worthy han his lyf.

1. beast
2. desire
3. husband
4. most
5. said
6. widow
7. you
8. wife
9. voice
10. life

LANGUAGE
—AND—
CULTURE

DRAMA IN THE MIDDLE AGES

S hortly before Christmas of 1991, television viewers could
have seen an American production of a medieval Spanish
miracle play, *La Pastorela* (known in English as "The Shepherd's
Play"). Visitors to Salzburg, Austria, are treated to an annual performance of *Everyman*, a morality play popular in Europe in the
1500s. These dramas belong to a centuries-old tradition, yet performances of these and other medieval plays are still well-
attended by modern audiences.

The Roots of Medieval Drama

Medieval drama in France, England, and Germany, and to some
extent in Italy and the Netherlands, developed from Catholic
church services. Starting around the tenth century, priests and
other clergy would act out short plays based on stories from the
Bible, as well as stories about the lives of the saints.

As they grew in popularity, these religious plays caused some
problems within the Church: church buildings became uncomfortably crowded as members of the congregation fought each other
for space, and the audience's loud and sometimes rowdy approval of the plays shocked the clergy and disrupted church services. In 1210, upon the orders of the Pope, the plays moved out
of the churches and into the streets and marketplaces.

The medieval religious plays were typically performed on
carts or wagons called "pageants." In small towns, several separate stands arranged in a circle would be set up in the town
square or another public place. The audience would watch the
scene performed at one stand, and then move on to the next. In
larger towns, whose public squares were too small to hold everyone who wanted to see the shows, the plays were moved around
the town in a procession, from one public square to another. Often there were several levels to the makeshift stage. For instance,
a rickety platform or balcony might indicate heaven. From a lower
level or a trapdoor representing Hell, devils would dramatically
spring out and dash into the frightened audience. Even in medieval times, producers knew the value of special effects.

Mysteries, Miracles, and Morality

Three kinds of religious plays were popular in the Middle Ages.
The **miracle plays**, which dramatized the lives of the saints and
the Virgin Mary, were performed on saints' days, while the **mystery plays**, whose subject was the mystery of Christ's redemption

New York Public Library Picture Collection

Engraving by David Jee of one stage in a mystery play. In towns too large to hold many people in a single square, the stages were moved in a pageant throughout the town.

the religious sermons that were so familiar to medieval audiences.

Medieval Humor

Although religion was a serious affair to the people of the Middle Ages, it was rarely taken *too* seriously in medieval drama. In a play about the Flood, for example, Noah's shrill and stubborn wife refuses to board the ark, and is finally carried aboard, kicking and screaming. In a play about the birth of Jesus, the theft of a sheep leads to a rowdy, comic scene. Even the Devil is often portrayed as a comic character in the miracle plays.

of sinners, were performed on the same days as church festivals. Popular miracle plays in France included the stories of St. Nicholas and the Virgin Mary. In England, long cycles of mystery plays, usually beginning with the Creation, were produced.

Morality plays were a third popular form of medieval drama. *Everyman* is the most famous of the morality plays, which dealt with themes of right and wrong and the struggle between good and evil for man's soul. Other morality plays were produced in France, the Netherlands, and occasionally in Germany. The characters in morality plays are allegorical, abstract personifications such as Truth, Mercy, Good Deeds, and Everyman. These characters dramatized the content of

In England, different guilds—that is, unions of tradesmen or artisans—took over from the Church the task of staging and performing the miracle and mystery plays. Each guild was assigned a play based on the expertise of its craftsmen. For example, the water carrier's guild usually performed the story of Noah and the Flood. In Europe, on the other hand, the plays were usually performed by troupes of trained actors.

The miracle, mystery, and morality plays of the Middle Ages continued to be popular in Europe until the Reformation, when Catholic church leaders began to clamp down on non-official interpretations of biblical events. Meanwhile, the great playwrights of the Renaissance—among them Italy's Ariosto, Spain's Lope de Vega, and England's Shakespeare—ushered in a new age of drama.

CHOOSING EFFECTIVE DICTION

You can probably think of a string of adjectives to describe a medieval hero. But experienced writers know that too many modifiers weaken a sentence. In strong writing, nouns and verbs do most of the work. Two guidelines will help you choose nouns and verbs that invigorate your writing.

Concrete Nouns and Verbs

First, keep nouns and verbs as concrete as possible. **Concrete** nouns and verbs name physical things and show physical actions. **Abstract** nouns and verbs name intangible things and refer to intangible actions.

ABSTRACT

       N   V   N

The *hero observed* the *situation*.

CONCRETE

        N   V   N

Roland's *gaze swept* the *battlefield*.

To write the first sentence above is to create a gap; readers grope to connect the words with their meanings. To write the second is to create action and substance; readers can see Roland's eyes scanning the battlefield.

When you discuss abstractions, you may need abstract nouns or verbs. But concrete nouns and verbs can also express abstract meanings.

Exercise 1: Choosing Concrete Nouns and Verbs

Choose the more concrete words from each set in parentheses.

1. At the shore, Charon waits to (row/convey) Dante into a realm of (extremes/fire and ice).
2. (The youth/Perceval) watches as the Fisher King (baits his hook/proceeds with his task).
3. Blood (reddens/discolors) even the (vegetation/flowers) in the field where Siegfried dies.
4. The Wife of Bath tells of a (character/knight) who (gets involved with/begs for advice from) a hag.
5. Because he waits too long to (call/sound his horn) for (Charlemagne and his troops/help), Roland is killed.
6. Tristan (leaves a sign/carves his name) in (the trunk of a hazel tree/a secret place).

Exact Nouns and Verbs

Second, to avoid overusing modifiers, choose exact nouns and verbs. **Exact** nouns and verbs specify meaning. Vague nouns and verbs do not.

VAGUE

Thor's defiant *words* to the giant *were* loud and angry.

EXACT

Thor *thundered* his *challenge* to the giant.

Notice how replacing *were* with *thundered* wakes up the sentence. *Were*, along with the other forms of "to be," is among the least exact verbs in English. Notice, too, that choosing a more exact verb eliminates two modifiers; *thundered* implies loudness and anger. Similarly, choosing the more exact noun, *challenge,* eliminates the need for the adjective *defiant.* Study the lists of vague verbs and nouns.

Vague Verbs		Vague Nouns	
make	do	thing	situation
have	get	factor	aspect
move	be	type	phase
go	come	kind	area

Vague verbs and nouns are general; strong ones are specific. Sometimes, of course, you need the general words listed above. But in most cases, try to replace general words with specific ones.

VAGUE

Siegfried *goes* from *doing* a dangerous *thing* to *being* in a *situation* that *is* even worse.

EXACT

Siegfried courts danger when he lays aside his sword and shield; he risks even more when he bends to drink at the brook.

The italicized words empty the first sentence of meaning. Try to avoid all forms of vague verbs; *doing* and *being* do not act as verbs here, but they still dilute meaning. In the second sentence, exact nouns and verbs clarify meaning.

Exercise 2: Using Effective Diction

Review a piece of your own writing, underlining each noun and verb. Draw an arrow from each modifier to the noun or verb it modifies. Then follow these steps:

1. Circle all abstract nouns and verbs. Wherever possible, replace them with more concrete ones.
2. Circle all nouns and verbs listed above as weak. Wherever possible, replace them with more exact ones. Reword sentences as necessary.
3. Examine each modifier. Now that your nouns and verbs are more concrete and exact, delete unnecessary modifiers.

Critical Thinking and Writing

WRITING A CHARACTER SKETCH

How would a medieval character fare in modern America? What might Roland, Thor, or the Wife of Bath make of a visit to a mall? In this unit, you have met memorable characters from another time. Now you can use observation and reasoning to bring them into your own world.

Writing Assignment

Write a description of a character from this unit, speculating about how the character might react in a modern setting. Assume that classmates are your audience. In this assignment, you will identify observations on which to base a reliable prediction.

Background

Choose a vivid character and scan the work in which the character appears, noting details about the character. Vivid characterization is often indirect. Look for the following means of indirect characterization:

▪ **Dialogue.** A character's speech patterns and word choices reveal background and motivations.

▪ **Actions.** A character's actions demonstrate likes and dislikes, strengths and weaknesses.

▪ **Other Characters.** The responses and comments of those who associate with a character shed light on his or her looks and personality.

▪ **Setting.** A character's surroundings illustrate his or her tastes and place in society.

▪ **Changes.** Changes in personality indicate the character's depth and potential.

Prewriting

Focused Questioning. To generate descriptive details, freewrite answers to these questions.

1. How does the character look and sound? How does he or she act?
2. What are the character's inner qualities? How would you feel around him or her? What are his or her strengths and weaknesses?
3. How have events or people in the character's life shaped him or her?
4. Which parts of your daily life would you most like to show to the character?

Read over your freewriting and list three or four of your character's most prominent traits. Then sum up the essence of your character in a single sentence. This dominant impression can guide your writing as a thesis would.

Observing and Predicting. Reliable predictions are based on careful observation. Formulate predictions about your character by using a chart like the one below. List prominent character traits. Cite observations—examples from the work that illustrate each trait. Then predict how each trait would cause the character to respond to the things that make up your daily life.

Traits	
Observations	
Predictions	

Writing

Use these guidelines as you draft your essay.

1. **Introductory Paragraph.** Set your character sketch in the present. Begin with an image of your character in action, in a setting from your daily life. You may choose a dramatic action that illustrates a prominent trait, or you may choose a subtle action that reveals general personality. Consulting your prewriting notes, state the relationship between this action and your dominant impression.

2. **Body Paragraphs.** Focus on two or more of your character's main traits, devoting a paragraph to each. Let your character's further reactions to the modern world reveal these traits. Experiment with dialogue and other indirect methods of characterization. Your prewriting notes can provide specifics. Arrange your paragraphs in spatial order or time order.

3. **Concluding Paragraph.** You might conclude by summarizing the ways your character changes in the modern world. Or you might speculate about how the modern world will be changed by your character. In either case, tie your description once more to the dominant impression.

Evaluating and Revising

Use the following questions to revise your draft.

1. Does the introduction show the character in action? Does it state the dominant impression?

2. Is the character sketch set in the present? Does it use specific sensory details to show, rather than tell, what the character is like?

3. Do you tell enough about the character's past actions to justify your ideas of his or her reactions to a modern setting?

4. Does your conclusion leave readers with one clear impression?

5. Are your sentences varied and grammatically correct?

Proofreading and Publishing

Proofread your character sketch to eliminate errors in mechanics, and make a final copy. Work with classmates to dramatize your sketch. Act it out for your class or other classes.

Renaissance Europe
c. 1560

- NORWAY
- SWEDEN
- North Sea
- SCOTLAND
- DENMARK
- Ba... Se...
- IRELAND
- ENGLAND
- NETHERLANDS
- (GERMANY)
- Po...
- WALES
- London
- Antwerp
- Rhine River
- Wittenberg
- Atlantic Ocean
- HOLY ROMAN EMPI...
- Seine River
- Paris
- Danube River
- FRANCE
- SWITZERLAND
- HUNGA...
- Milan
- Florence
- PORTUGAL
- SPAIN
- Madrid
- Rome
- (ITAL...
- Mediterranean Sea
- SICILY
- MUSLIM STATES

FROM THE RENAISSANCE TO THE ENLIGHTENMENT

▼ **Time** ▼

1300–1800

▼ **Place** ▼

Europe

▼ **Literary Significance** ▼

The Renaissance (1300–1650): The literature of the Renaissance reflected a renewed interest in human, rather than religious, affairs as well as a ''rediscovery'' of the Western classical tradition. During the Renaissance, new literary forms, among them the sonnet and short prose fiction, were created to give expression to timeless themes for an ever-growing audience.

The Enlightenment (1650–1800): The Enlightenment was an age that celebrated human reason and scorned human behavior and excess. Literature of the time, mostly poetry, drama, and essays, was valued for its formal qualities: a regular meter, polished images, and verbal wit. Writers like Voltaire and La Fontaine turned to satire to comment on the hypocrisy and immorality of the overindulged upper classes of this period.

TIME LINE

Europe from the Renaissance to the Enlightenment

LITERARY EVENTS ▼

Scala/Art Resource, New York

Fifteenth-century Florence, the center of the Italian Renaissance.

Francesco Petrarca (Petrarch), *Canzionere*, **c. 1325–1374**

Giovanni Boccaccio, *Decameron*, **1353**

Gutenberg Bible is printed, **c. 1455**

Erasmus, leader of the humanist school of philosophy, satirizes the Church in *In Praise of Folly*, **1509**

Niccolo Machiavelli, *The Prince*, **1513**

Teresa of Avila, **(1515–1582)**, religious poet

François Rabelais, *Gargantua and Pantagruel*, **1532**

| 1300 | 1350 | 1400 | 1450 | 1500 |

Rise of city-states in Italy leads to the Italian Renaissance, **c. 1300**

Gunpowder probably first used in Europe during the Battle of Crécy between England and France, **1346**

Great Schism divides the Roman Catholic Church as two Italians and a Frenchman vie for the papacy, **1378–1417**

Joan of Arc defeats the English at Orleans, **1429**

Leonardo da Vinci **(1452–1519)**

Turkish conquest of Constantinople ends Byzantine Empire, **1453**

Johann Gutenberg develops printing by movable type, **c. 1454**

Columbus reaches the Americas, **1492**

Vasco da Gama rounds the Cape of Good Hope, **1497**

Rise of absolute monarchs and modern science in Europe; flowering of English Renaissance, **c. 1500s–1600s**

Martin Luther posts Ninety-Five Theses, **1517**; beginning of Protestant Reformation

Henry VIII breaks with Rome and becomes head of the Church of England, **1534**

Nicholas Copernicus demonstrates that the earth revolves around the sun, **1543**

Scala/Art Resource, New York

MONA LISA. LEONARDO DA VINCI, 1503–1506.

▲ **CULTURAL AND HISTORICAL EVENTS**

World map. c. 1545.

The Granger Collection, New York

Pierre de Ronsard, *Sonnets pour Hélène*, **1578**

Michel de Montaigne, *Essays*, **1580–1588**

Edmund Spenser, *The Faerie Queen*, **1590**

Miguel de Cervantes, *Don Quixote*, **1605, 1615**

Ben Jonson, *Volpone*, **c. 1605**

William Shakespeare, *The Tempest*, **1611**

Blaise Pascal, *Pensées (Thoughts)*, **1662**

Theaters reopen in England; Restoration comedies become popular, **1660**

John Milton, *Paradise Lost*, **1665**

Molière, *The Misanthrope*, **1666**

Jean de la Fontaine, *Fables*, **1668–1694**

The novel becomes popular in England, **1700s**

Jonathan Swift, *Gulliver's Travels*, **1726**

Alexander Pope, *An Essay on Man*, **1733**

Samuel Richardson, *Clarissa*, **1747–1748**

Portrait of Napoleon Bonaparte. JACQUES LOUIS DAVID, 1810.

National Gallery of Art, Washington D.C., Samuel H. Kress Collection

Voltaire, *Candide*, **1759**

Richard Sheridan, *The Rivals* **(1775)**

| 1550 | 1600 | 1650 | 1700 | 1750 | 1800 |

England defeats the Spanish Armada, signaling England's rising power, **1588**

Portrait of the French Monarch Louis XIV. HYACINTHE RIGAUD, 1701.

Age of Absolute Monarchs; baroque style in visual arts, architecture, and music, **c. 1600–1750**

Thirty Years' War between German Catholics and Protestants, **1618–1648**

Italian physicist Galileo is tried by the Inquisition for supporting Copernicus's view of the universe, **1633**

René Descartes, *Discourse on Method* **(1637)**, founds Cartesian school of rational philosophy

English Civil wars, **1642–1649**

Age of Enlightenment; science makes rapid advances; England, France, and Spain become world powers, **c. 1650–1800**

Sir Isaac Newton describes the universe as a machine governed by absolute laws in *The Mathematical Principle of Natural Philosophy* **(1687)**

Restoration in England, **1660–1688**

David Hume shapes modern metaphysics in *A Treatise of Human Nature*, **1739–1740**

Neoclassicism in the arts and architecture, **c. 1750–1850**

Jean Jacques Rousseau influences late eighteenth-century political developments with *The Social Contract*, **1762**

American Revolution, **1775–1783**

U. S. Constitution is written, **1787**; Bill of Rights is added, **1791**

French Revolution, **1789–1795**

Napoleon comes to power, **1799**

This border is composed of family insignia. During the Renaissance, these insignia appeared on flags, coats of arms, and badges and played an important role in marriages and other public festivities.

RENAISSANCE LITERATURE

T he word *renaissance* means "rebirth." Historians use it to describe a period of change and growth, from roughly 1300–1650, during which Europeans began to discover anew the riches of the Greek and Roman classics. During this time, which marks the beginning of the modern world in Europe, people began to be stirred by the imagination, to thirst for knowledge, and to explore the scope of human potential as never before.

66 The entire structure of feudal society, which had been under stress for many years, was undermined by the plague. The upheaval . . . set the stage for the new world of Renaissance Europe and the Reformation. 99

—*Charles L. Mee*

The Renaissance Begins in Italy

The Crusades had introduced new products into the economy of eleventh- and twelfth-century Europe. The rapidly increasing demand for exotic Eastern spices, cloth, and wood created new wealth for traders and merchants. Commercial centers prospered, especially the Italian city-states which were trade links to the Near East and Africa. Wealthy Italian merchant families used the riches they earned from trade to support the exploration of human thought and imagination. They became patrons of the arts, financing the work of writers, musicians, philosophers, and other artists and thinkers.

The Italian poet **Francesco Petrarch** (1304–1374), who was perhaps the first person to use the term "Renaissance" to describe the time in which he lived, was a key figure in the Italian Renaissance. Petrarch's deep interest in human individuality led him to become known as the first **humanist**. He and his contemporary, **Giovanni Boccaccio** (1313–1375), were among the first writers to use the **vernacular**, that is, the language spoken by the people (in this case, Italian), rather than the traditional language of literature, Latin. Boccaccio is best known for the **Decameron**, a collection of stories that shows his lively interest in men and women as unique individuals. The stories are told by people trying to escape the outbreak of bubonic plague that struck Europe in the late 1340s, killing one third of Europe's population and undermining the stability of feudalism.

An Emphasis on the Individual

The humanists' interest in *human* values distinguishes them from medieval philosophers, whose thought was fundamentally centered around God and questions of religion. Humanists believed that people as individuals were the most important subject of study. Their intense curiosity led to the revival of the study of classical Greek and Roman art, literature, history, and philosophy. In doing so, the humanists broke away from the narrow emphasis on Christian theology that characterized medieval learning.

> Unlike medieval thinkers, who took a God-centered view of the universe, the humanists adopted a human-centered view.

The works of Renaissance artists clearly expressed the humanist belief that humankind is the measure of all things. In the 1300s, the Italian painter **Giotto** (jōt′tō) developed a new style of painting that emphasized natural-looking forms instead of flat, stylized figures. The paintings and sculptures of **Michelangelo** demonstrate a fascination with the shape, substance, and power of the human body.

Perhaps the most imaginative and gifted humanist was **Leonardo da Vinci** (1452–1519), who embodied the qualities of the ultimate "Renaissance person"—someone with skills and interests in many areas. Almost everyone knows his famous paintings *Mona Lisa* and *The Last Supper*. In addition to being a great artist, however, Leonardo was also an inventor, an architect, a musician, and a scientist, with interests in meteorology and geology. He studied the moon's effect on the tides, theorized about the formation of fossils, initiated the science of hydraulics, and studied human anatomy. He also believed that humans were capable of flight and designed several flying devices.

> ❝ The Renaissance's primary concern with the world of here and now stimulated experimentation rather than logic, observation rather than inherited precepts. ❞
>
> —Renaissance Culture
> *Julian Mates and*
> *Eugene Cantelupe*

Detail of a fifteenth-century map of Florence. *Florence was the seat of the Italian Renaissance.*

A New Spirit of Inquiry

MAN IN ORNITHOPTER, LEONARDO DA VINCI.

> ❝ In taking a state the conqueror must arrange to commit all his cruelties at once, so as not to have to recur to them every day, and so as to be able to reassure people and win them over by benefiting them. Whoever acts otherwise . . . is always obliged to stand with knife in hand, and can never depend on his subjects . . . ❞
>
> —The Prince, *Machiavelli*

Leonardo da Vinci's meticulous habits of observation—all carefully recorded in his "mirror writings," notebooks which read backwards unless held to a mirror—were fundamental to his work. This method of inquiry was different from the medieval method of relying on outside authorities, especially those authorities approved by the Church. As scientists developed their skills of observation, they also questioned accepted authorities. **Nicolaus Copernicus** (1473–1543), a Polish astronomer who taught in Italy, challenged Ptolemy's second-century idea that the sun revolved around the earth. Copernicus argued that the earth rotated on an axis and revolved around the sun. His ideas frightened many religious people because they contradicted the Church's teaching that the earth was the hub of the universe and that humans

The new science challenged traditional authority by insisting on the power of observation.

were the focus of God's attention. A century later, the Italian astronomer **Galileo** (1564–1642) used the newly-invented telescope to scan the skies. In 1630, Galileo wrote a book defending Copernicus's theory that the earth moved around the sun. The Church's Inquisitors—officials who examined supposed heretics—forced him to recant. But legend has it that as Galileo rose from his knees after his recantation, he whispered "But it does move!"

Like his counterparts in the sciences, one Italian statesman, **Niccolo Machiavelli** (1469–1527), embraced the new humanist spirit of inquiry and observation and turned it toward the political landscape of the Italian city-states. In *The Prince*, Machiavelli gave unusual advice. Whereas most writers advised rulers to be kind and generous, Machiavelli advised them to be calculating and coldblooded. He had observed the way power was actually gained and lost. Because he saw that conflict among the various city-states kept Italy in chaos, he argued that the state needed a powerful central authority to keep order. Machiavelli's name has come to be associated with the philosophy of **pragmatism**: the idea that the ends justify the means.

Later events proved Machiavelli right in his argument for a strong central government. In 1527, Rome was sacked by a mercenary army led by the Duke of Bourbon. This event signaled the end of the Italian Renaissance. The further expansion of the Renaissance imagination occurred in northern Europe and England.

Voyages to New Worlds

The Turkish conquest of Constantinople in 1453 temporarily blocked the overland route to the East. The need for new trade routes led to great voyages of discovery and exploration. In 1492, the Italian explorer **Christopher Columbus**

Portrait of Nicolaus Copernicus, the father of modern astronomy.

QUEEN ISABELLA AND COLUMBUS, HENRY NELSON O'NEIL (1817–1880).
What historical event precipitated the Age of Exploration?

Plate with the figure of a gentleman. Florentine, late sixteenth century.

Nimatallah/Art Resource, New York

persuaded Ferdinand and Isabella, the rulers of Spain, that he could reach the East by sailing west across the Atlantic. Columbus failed to reach Asia; instead, he landed in the Americas. Spain's rapid conquest of the New World brought fabulous wealth and power. In 1497, Portugal commissioned **Vasco da Gama** to open an eastern route to Asia. Da Gama reached India in 1498, and within five years Indian merchandise was flowing into Portugal. In 1519, the Portuguese navigator **Ferdinand Magellan**—in search of a western trade route for Spain—sailed around South America and into a vast ocean that he called "Pacific."

The Rise of Printing: Fuel for New Thought

The imaginative fervor that had begun in Italy and spread throughout Europe was fueled by the technology of printing. Around 1455, **Johann Gutenberg** (c. 1400–c. 1468) produced Europe's first printed book, the Bible. But the new print technology met strong resistance from the Church. Through-

> **Humanism attempted to reform the Church and encourage people to make religious choices for themselves.**

out Europe, Church leaders imposed strong restrictions on the printing and sales of books, and more than one printer was burned at the stake as a heretic.

The Church had good reason to try to control printing technology. In northern Europe, humanism had taken the form of a widespread effort to reform the corrupt Church and to loosen its hold on people's minds. Humanist critics questioned the sale of indulgences—the practice of "forgiving" sins in exchange for money—and demanded that the wealthy Church practice the poverty it preached. Other humanists directly undermined the authority of the Church. **John Wycliffe** (c. 1329–1384), for example, translated the Bible into English and sent teachers, called "Poor Preachers," to read it in the churches. Wycliffe taught that people had a direct relationship to God and did not need priests to act as go-betweens. The Bible, he said, was the sole source of divine authority. The Church had Wycliffe executed in 1384 and—to drive its point home—removed his body from its grave and had it burned in 1415.

But reform could not be stopped. Humanists like **Desiderius Erasmus** (c. 1466–1536), a Dutch priest and scholar, exerted an enormous intellectual influence. Erasmus was a sharp critic of the Church and an effective advocate of reform. His scholarly study, and that of humanists such as **Sir Thomas More** in England, paved the way for the radical reforms of Martin Luther and John Calvin.

The Reformation: The Church Loses Power

The **Reformation** officially began in 1517 when the German monk **Martin Luther** (1483–1546) made public a list of complaints against Church practices. These complaints, called the **Ninety-five Theses**, brought Pope Leo's condemnation. The Pope ordered Luther to recant, but Luther refused, and the reform movement, called **Protestantism**, gathered force. Reformers appeared in Scandinavia, Scotland, Switzerland, and the Netherlands. The ideas of the

MARTIN LUTHER, LUCAS CRANACH THE ELDER (1472–1553). *Luther's Ninety-five Theses sparked the Reformation and led to the development of Protestantism.*

> The Reformation was fired by the idea that people did not need the Church to mediate between them and God.

most famous reformer, the French theologian **John Calvin** (1509–1564), were accepted in Switzerland and Scotland. In France, however, Protestant reforms were resisted, and the Church maintained its spiritual authority.

The active individualism that fired the Reformation in northern Europe energized art and literature as well. The Flemish brothers Jan and Hubert Van Eyck, the two Breughels, and the German artist Albrecht Dürer created paintings rich with realistic detail based on close observation of their settings and subjects. Artists were interested in movement—in people *doing* things.

Writers were also interested in showing people as active and dynamic. Authors increasingly wrote stories held together by carefully crafted plots, which in turn were determined by the actions and motivations of characters. In Spain, **Miguel de Cervantes** (1547–1616) wrote what many consider to be the first novel, about a would-be knight named Don Quixote.

To the poets, particularly French poets, the humanist spirit demanded the imitation of classical Greek and Roman forms. This imitation is called **neoclassicism**. **Pierre de Ronsard** (1524–1585) is famous for the French poems he modeled after classical poets, as well as for his sonnets.

England: From Reformation to Renaissance

In England, the Renaissance of culture would have to wait until the turmoil created by the English Reformation subsided. England's Reformation was very different from Europe's; it sprang largely from the political and personal motivations of one person, **King Henry VIII** (1491–1547). In 1533, Henry broke with the Roman Catholic Church when the Pope refused to recognize Henry's divorce and remarriage to Anne Boleyn, the mother of Elizabeth I. Henry had Parliament appoint him and his successors Supreme Head of the newly created Anglican Church, or the Church of England. After Henry died in 1547, his son Edward VI

PORTRAIT OF A GENTLEMAN, Holland, 1611.

Giraudon/Art Resource, New York

THE FAERIE QUEENE, WILLIAM BLAKE (1757–1827). *Blake's illustration was inspired by* The Faerie Queene, *a narrative poem by Edmund Spenser that was popular during the English Renaissance.*

opened England to the Protestants. Edward was followed in 1553 by his sister Mary, a Catholic. Her persecution of non-Catholics earned her the name Bloody Mary. When Mary's Anglican sister Elizabeth became queen five years later, England welcomed the peace she brought.

With Elizabeth's reign came an exuberant swelling of English pride. England defeated Spain's previously indomitable navy, the Armada, in 1588, and England emerged as a naval power. Trade and industry grew, and the economy expanded. In this atmosphere of buoyant optimism, the arts flourished. Nowhere was the spirit of the English Renaissance better expressed than in drama, and in particular in the plays of **William Shakespeare**. His comedies, such as *As You Like It* and *Twelfth Night* (1600), show both the endearing and the silly sides of human nature. His tragedies, such as *Hamlet* (1601) and *King Lear* (1605), triumphantly affirm the courage of the human spirit. *The Tempest* (1611), one of his last plays, celebrates the power of the imagination. Shakespeare's skill in language and characterization earned him a place with the greatest playwrights of all time.

The exuberance of the English Renaissance was muted after Elizabeth I died in 1603. The satiric plays of Ben Jonson (such as *Volpone* in 1605 and *The Alchemist* in 1610) were more sober than those of the Elizabethan period. With the works of **metaphysical poets** such as John Donne, poetry became less musical and more complex and intellectual. *Paradise Lost*, John Milton's epic poem which sets the biblical story of the Fall of Adam and Eve against the backdrop of the cosmic conflict between God and Satan, may be considered the last poem of the English Renaissance.

JOHN MILTON, artist unknown. *One of England's most celebrated poets, Milton marked the turning point in literature between the Renaissance and the Enlightenment.*

Introduction

The Sonnet in the Renaissance

The word *sonnet* is derived from the Italian word *sonetto*, meaning "little sound" or "song." A **sonnet** is a fourteen-line lyric poem. It is one of the most difficult forms for a poet to master because it must conform to strict patterns of rhythm and rhyme.

The Petrarchan Sonnet

In Italy, the sonnet form was perfected by Francesco Petrarca, known in English as Petrarch. The form he popularized is called the **Italian**, or **Petrarchan**, **sonnet**.

The Petrarchan sonnet has two parts: an eight-line section, called the **octave**, followed by a six-line section, called the **sestet**. The octave rhymes *abbaabba*, and the sestet rhymes *cdecde*, *cdcdcd*, *ccdeed*, or *cdcdee*. This form makes the Italian sonnet perfectly suited for a two-part statement: question/answer, problem/solution, or theme/comment. The transition between the two parts, called the **volta**, or turn, is usually found in the ninth line—the beginning of the sestet—as in Petrarch's Sonnet 42, below.

Sonnet 42
Petrarch
translated by Joseph Auslander

The spring returns, the spring wind softly blowing	a
Sprinkles the grass with gleam and glitter of showers,	b
Powdering pearl and diamond, dripping with flowers,	b
Dropping wet flowers, dancing the winters going;	a
The swallow twitters, the groves of midnight are glowing	a
With nightingale music and madness; the sweet fierce powers	b
Of love flame up through the earth; the seed-soul towers	b
And trembles; nature is filled to overflowing . . .	a
The spring returns, but there is no returning	c
Of spring for me. O heart with anguish burning!	c
She that unlocked all April in a breath	d
Returns not . . . And these meadows, blossoms, birds	e
These lovely gentle girls—words, empty words	e
As bitter as the black estates of death!	d

octave (lines 1–8)
volta (line 9)
sestet (lines 9–14)

The Shakespearean Sonnet

Petrarchan sonnets are difficult to write in English because of the demanding rhyme scheme. English poets, limited by their "rhyme-poor" language, soon created their own version, called the **English**, or **Shakespearean**, **sonnet**. Like the Petrarchan sonnet, the Shakespearean sonnet is fourteen lines long. However, instead of the octave-sestet arrangement, this sonnet form uses three four-line units, called **quatrains**, followed by a final **couplet**. The Shakespearean sonnet is written in a particular **meter**, or rhythmic pattern, called **iambic pentameter**, with each line consisting of five unstressed (‿) syllables alternating with five stressed (′) syllables. The typical rhyme scheme of the Shakespearean sonnet is *abab cdcd efef gg*. William Shakespeare's Sonnet 73, which describes old age, is an example:

THE MONTH OF APRIL, SIMON BENNICK (1483–1561). *Flemish, watercolor on parchment.*

Victoria & Albert Museum, London/Art Resource, New York

Sonnet 73
William Shakespeare

That time of year thou mayst in me behold	a
When yellow leaves, or none, or few, do hang	b
Upon those boughs which shake against the cold,	a quatrain
Bare ruined choirs where late the sweet birds sang.	b
In me thou see'st the twilight of such day	c
As after sunset fadeth in the west;	d
Which by and by black night doth take away,	c quatrain
Death's second self that seals up all in rest.	d
In me thou see'st the glowing of such fire	e
That on the ashes of his youth doth lie,	f
As the deathbed whereon it must expire,	e quatrain
Consumed with that which it was nourished by.	f
This thou perceiv'st, which makes thy love more strong,	g couplet
To love that well which thou must leave ere long.	g

Renaissance Sonnet Writers

FRANCESCO PETRARCH, artist unknown.

Giraudon/Art Resource, New York

Francesco Petrarch, 1304–1374

The Italian poet Petrarch was a man of two worlds: the dying Middle Ages and the emerging Renaissance. Although Petrarch achieved great fame as a poet and scholar, he suffered considerably as he tried to balance his own worldly ambitions and desires with the religious values of medieval life.

Although Petrarch's love for a woman named Laura is legendary, a personal relationship never developed between them. He managed to see her only occasionally from a distance. She died of the plague in 1348. Laura's idealized image inspired the 317 sonnets contained in Petrarch's *Canzoniere* ("Song Book"). This first series of sonnets, written in Italian, set the fashion throughout the Renaissance for bittersweet love lyrics in various European languages.

Pierre de Ronsard, 1524–1585

With six other poets, Pierre de Ronsard (rōn·sàr′) founded an influential group known as the *Pléiade*—a name derived from the seven stars of the constellation of the *Pléiades.* The *Pléiade* maintained that vernacular French was worthy of more than just popular *lais* and *ballades.* The group used the vernacular in their odes, elegies, and satires based on the works of classical Greek and Roman poets. Ronsard's four books of *Odes* (1550–1552), written in French and dedicated to the classical poets Pindar and Horace, were so successful that his own generation called him "the Prince of Poets."

William Shakespeare, 1564–1616

During the Renaissance, sonnets were frequently written in the form of a **sequence**, a collection of poems linked by a common theme. Shakespeare's sonnet sequence consists of 154 poems, probably written during his middle years. The entire sequence provides a rough outline of a mysterious story that has intrigued scholars for centuries. Most of the poems are addressed to a young nobleman whom the speaker admires. Some are concerned with a rival poet who has also written poems to this young man. The final sonnets in the series are addressed to a "dark lady" with whom both the speaker and the young man are in love. (For more information about Shakespeare's life and works, see page 839.)

Reader's Guide

RENAISSANCE SONNETS

Background

The sonnet became popular during the Renaissance because people were writing more about worldly things: science, politics, geographic exploration, and romantic love. During the Middle Ages, most lyric poems had been written to praise God. But the sonnet of the Renaissance is secular, or nonreligious. The sonnet serves as an expression of a poet's intense personal feelings, whether they be feelings of romantic love or regret in old age. Sometimes both emotions manage to make their way into the sonnets. A major theme in Renaissance poetry was *carpe diem* (kär′pē dī′em), a Latin phrase meaning "seize the day"—that is, make the most of the present moment because life is short. *Carpe diem* implies that the best things in life, such as youth, love, and beauty, are only fleeting pleasures and need to be enjoyed while they can. The sonnets presented here reveal a bittersweet mixture of love and sadness typical of much Renaissance poetry.

Oral Response

Love has probably been the most written-about emotion of all. As a class, discuss contemporary views of love relationships. Do we tend to idealize love as many writers of the past did? Or is our view of love more "practical"? Consider what our culture conveys about love relationships (all types: romantic, familial, patriotic) through movies, television programs, popular songs, and romance novels.

Literary Focus

The sonnets of the Renaissance followed not only strict formal conventions of **meter** and **rhyme scheme**, but they used many stylistic conventions as well. For instance, the poet could not simply express his feelings outright, but had to disguise or camouflage them in **figures of speech**. Petrarchan and Shakespearean sonnets are characterized by certain recurring **similes**, used to describe the idealized beauty of a lady: "cheeks like roses," "eyes like stars," "teeth like pearls." The poets also use **metaphors** to draw comparisons of themselves to captive birds, wounded stags, or moths drawn to a flame. **Personification** occurs frequently, too. Love, for example, is often personified as Cupid.

SONNET 61
Francesco Petrarch
translated by
JOSEPH AUSLANDER

◆ *In Sonnet 61 the poet blesses, or expresses grateful thanks
for, all things connected with his first encounter with Laura.
What is the most important word in this sonnet?*

APRIL: GATHERING
FLOWERS, from
the *Playfair
Book of Hours*,
French, late 1400s.

Blest be the day, and blest the month and year,
Season and hour and very moment blest,
The lovely land and place where first possessed
By two pure eyes I found me prisoner;
5   And blest the first sweet pain, the first most dear,
Which burned my heart when Love° came in as guest;
And blest the bow, the shafts which shook my breast,
And even the wounds which Love delivered there.
Blest be the words and voices which filled grove
10 And glen with echoes of my lady's name;
The sighs, the tears, the fierce despair of love;
And blest the sonnet-sources of my fame;
And blest that thought of thoughts which is her own,
Of her, her only, of herself alone!

6. **Love:** Cupid, the god of love,
often depicted as a winged
child with bow and arrow.

TO HÉLÈNE
Pierre de Ronsard
translated by
ROBERT HOLLANDER

One of Ronsard's most famous sonnets, "To Hélène" is part of a collection of love poems dedicated to a court lady who may have rejected the then-aging poet. What argument does Ronsard develop? How do you think the real Hélène would have responded to this argument?

When you are very old, in evening candlelight,
Moved closer to the coals and carding out your
    wool,[1]
You'll sing my songs and marvel that you were
    such a fool:
"O Ronsard did praise me when I was young and
    bright."

5   Then you'll have no handmaid to help you pass
      the night,
Spinning while your gossip leads her into lull,
Until you say my name and her rousèd eyes grow
    full
In wonder of your glory in what Ronsard did
    write.

When I am in the earth, poor ghost without his
    bones,
10   A sleeper in the shade of myrtle trees and stones,
Then you, beside the hearth, old and crouched
    and gray,
Will yearn for all that's lost, repenting your
    disdain.
Live it well, I pray you, today won't come again:
Gather up the roses before they fall away.

ARACHNE, **an illumination from a sixteenth-century French manuscript,** *The Lives of Famous Women.*

Giraudon/Art Resource, New York

---

1. **carding out your wool:** combing strands of wool
   to untangle them before spinning threads.

SONNETS
William Shakespeare

What does the speaker complain about in each poem? Does the thought of love add to or relieve the complaint?

Sonnet 29

When in disgrace with fortune and men's eyes
I all alone beweep my outcast state,°
And trouble deaf Heaven with my bootless° cries,
And look upon myself and curse my fate,
5   Wishing me like to one more rich in hope,
Featured like him,° like him with friends possessed,
Desiring this man's art and that man's scope,°
With what I most enjoy contented least—
Yet in these thoughts myself almost despising,
10   Haply I think on thee, and then my state,
Like to the lark at break of day arising
From sullen earth, sings hymns at Heaven's gate.
    For thy sweet love remembered such wealth brings
    That then I scorn to change my state with kings.

2. **state:** condition.
3. **bootless:** useless; futile.
6. **like him:** like another.
7. **scope:** breadth of knowledge.

Sonnet 64

When I have seen by Time's fell° hand defaced
The rich proud cost of outworn buried age;
When sometime lofty towers I see down-razed,
And brass eternal slave to mortal rage;°
5   When I have seen the hungry ocean gain
Advantage on the kingdom of the shore,
And the firm soil win of the watery main,
Increasing store with loss, and loss with store;
When I have seen such interchange of state,
10   Or state itself confounded to decay;
Ruin hath taught me thus to ruminate—
That Time will come and take my love away.
    This thought is as a death, which cannot choose
    But weep to have that which it fears to lose.

1. **fell:** cruel; deadly.
4. **And brass eternal slave to mortal rage:** Several interpretations are possible; brass is "a slave to mortal rage" because it can be melted into many forms, including weapons; it also becomes dented when thrown.

First Thoughts

Was one poem more "realistic" to you than any other? Which one? Explain why.

Interpreting Meanings

1. What **metaphors**, or direct comparisons, does the speaker in Petrarch's Sonnet 61 use to describe his state of mind? Find two examples.

2. **Oxymoron** (äks'i·mō'rän') is a figure of speech that states an apparent contradiction, such as "deafening silence" or "hateful love." Identify two oxymorons in Petrarch's Sonnet 61. What is the effect of these figures of speech?

3. In your own words, tell what advice Ronsard is giving to Hélène in the last two lines of "To Hélène." What can we conclude overall about the poet's feelings for her?

4. Find at least two **similes**, or comparisons, that Shakespeare uses in Sonnet 29 to describe the speaker's feelings about love.

5. What situation is the speaker in Shakespeare's Sonnet 64 contemplating? How would you summarize the speaker's views?

Applying Meanings

Suppose you were the recipient of any one of these sonnets. How would you respond? Would you be touched or would you laugh? Explain your reaction.

Creative Writing Response

Writing a Poem. In Sonnet 29, Shakespeare describes how he overcomes feelings of despair and failure by remembering his love. People today also experience temporary periods of depression when they feel their looks, possessions, friends, or accomplishments don't measure up. Write a modern version of Shakespeare's Sonnet 29, but instead of following the sonnet form write the poem entirely in couplets. To get ideas for your poem, consider these questions: What might people today envy in their neighbors? What might help a modern person feel more satisfied? You may wish to pattern your poem after the model below.

When I am feeling low and sad and blue
I sit alone and sigh and think of you.
And _____
And _____
Wanting _____
Wishing _____
Desiring _____
Contented least with _____
Yet _____
Suddenly _____
Then _____
Like _____
For remembering _____
That then I _____

Critical Writing Response

Comparing and Contrasting Love Poems. Read "When You Are Old," by the Irish poet W. B. Yeats (1865–1939), written in imitation of Ronsard's sonnet "To Hélène":

When you are old and gray and full of sleep,
And nodding by the fire, take down this book,
And slowly read, and dream of the soft look
Your eyes had once, and of their shadows deep;

How many loved your moments of glad grace,
And loved your beauty with love false or true;
But one man loved the pilgrim soul in you,
And loved the sorrows of your changing face.

And bending down beside the glowing bars,
Murmur, a little sadly, how Love fled
And paced upon the mountains overhead
And hid his face amid a crowd of stars.

Write four paragraphs comparing and contrasting Yeats's poem, "When You Are Old," with Ronsard's "To Hélène." Your essay should include answers to the following questions:

1. To whom is each poem addressed? In what way are these persons similar?

2. How does the speaker in each poem want the person addressed to think of him in the future?

3. What does each speaker want the person he is addressing to do?

4. In what ways are the speakers' intentions similar and different?

ELEMENTS OF LITERATURE

Enjambment

Enjambment, or run-on lines, refers to the spilling over of a thought from one line of verse to the next. The term is from a French word meaning "to straddle"—that is, the sentence or idea "straddles" two or more lines. Inexperienced readers tend to stop at the end of each line in a poem, usually at a rhyme, regardless of the punctuation. As a result, many poems when read aloud sound like nursery rhymes, and the rhyme interferes with the meaning of the lines. Readers with more experience know that if a thought continues for more than one line they should read through to the end of the thought and not stop simply because there is a rhyme.

Often enjambment is used to create suspense: the first part of the thought may lead up to something that the second part in the next line may or may not carry through. Also, enjambment takes the emphasis off the rhyme scheme. Otherwise the poem would become boring and singsong, a mere repetition of sounds and a strict reproduction of form rather than the expression of a poet's complex thoughts and feelings.

Try to get a sense of the flow of the lines by reading aloud the sonnets of Petrarch, Ronsard, and Shakespeare. Pay attention to the punctuation and the enjambment. Enjambment works to make a poem more meaningful or more like a real person speaking his or her thoughts. Read a sonnet for a classmate and then have that person read the same sonnet to you. How are your readings different? Which interpretation sounds more natural? Why?

Giovanni Boccaccio
1313–1375

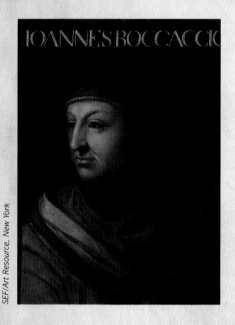

SEF/Art Resource, New York

Giovanni Boccaccio (bō·kä′chō) was born in the summer of 1313, perhaps in Florence or possibly in Certaldo, a small Tuscan town twenty miles outside the city. The illegitimate son of an unknown French-woman and a Florentine merchant banker, Boccaccio spent his boyhood with his father. At the age of fourteen, however, he was sent to Naples, where his father had arranged for him to be a clerk in one of his banks.

After finishing his apprenticeship at the bank, Boccaccio entered the University of Naples and earned a degree in law. But in 1340, Boccaccio's father suffered a financial setback, and he asked his son to return to Florence. There Boccaccio met Francesco Petrarch, the great Italian poet (see page 806),

who became a lifelong friend and literary advisor. And there, too, he experienced the most catastrophic event of his lifetime: in 1348, the Black Death struck Florence. During this plague three out of four people in Florence died a gruesome death, their bodies covered with black spots.

Boccaccio used the plague as the backdrop for his masterpiece, the *Decameron.* Written in Italian, instead of Latin, the *Decameron* is a collection of one hundred tales told by ten wealthy young Florentines, seven women and three men, who have retreated to a villa in the hills of Fiesole to escape the Black Death. Here, safe from the pestilence, they pass the time by telling each other stories. They stay ten days—the word *decameron* comes from the Greek words for "ten" and "day"—and on each day the group hears ten stories.

Completed about 1353, the *Decameron* established Boccaccio's literary reputation. Boccaccio, however, did not consider the *Decameron* to be his best work. In fact, he considered it trifling and, in later life, shifted his attention to writing scholarly works in Latin. He made great strides in the humanistic study of the ancient Greek and Roman classics. Nevertheless, it is the *Decameron* that has survived the test of time. William Shakespeare, John Milton, and many other writers in English and other languages have used Boccaccio's work as both a model and a source.

Reader's Guide

THE TALE OF THE FALCON
from the Decameron

Background

The *Decameron,* a masterpiece of Italian prose, presents the comic exploits and tragic foibles of a world of people. Many of these tales were adaptations of folktales, fables, and anecdotes that Boccaccio learned as a youth. Boccaccio places these tales in a **frame story**, a story that serves to bind together several different narratives. In Boccaccio's frame story, ten young Florentines entertain one another by telling tales while waiting out the plague. Each day one young Florentine youth is chosen king or queen for that day and is allowed to select a certain theme for the tales. As a result, there are many different types of stories: tales of adventure, tales of romantic exploits, tales of trickery, and stories of unhappy love affairs and courtly romance.

"The Tale of the Falcon," the ninth tale of the fifth day, features some of the stock themes of the medieval tale of courtly love: the handsome young man who loves a beautiful married lady; his despair over being refused; his gallant sacrifice; and his process of learning courtesy and, above all, humility before he can hope for success. However, Boccaccio's characters do not come from the chivalric order, and this otherwise formulaic story is invested with a surprising ironic twist.

Writer's Response

Have you ever had a prized possession, something you felt you could never give up? Write briefly about your reasons for valuing the possession, and what it would take to make you sacrifice it.

Literary Focus

Situational irony occurs when what actually happens in a story, novel, or drama is the opposite of what is expected or appropriate. For example, in Greek mythology, the story of greedy King Midas, whose touch turned everything to gold, is filled with situational irony. Midas soon discovers to his dismay that he turns food, drink, and even his beloved daughter to gold. Thus, far from making him happy as he expected, Midas's golden touch ironically makes him miserable. Situational irony always produces an unexpected turn of events.

THE TALE OF THE FALCON

from the Decameron

Giovanni Boccaccio

translated by

MARK MUSA AND PETER BONDANELLA

> *Read to the fourth paragraph, when Monna Giovanna's son asks for Federigo's falcon, believing that it will make him well. What do you predict will happen? Will the boy get his wish? Will Federigo part with his falcon? Read on to find out.*

There was once in Florence a young man named Federigo,[1] the son of Messer Filippo Alberighi,[2] renowned above all other men in Tuscany for his prowess in arms and for his courtliness. As often happens to most gentlemen, he fell in love with a lady named Monna Giovanna, in her day considered to be one of the most beautiful and one of the most charming women that ever there was in Florence; and in order to win her love, he participated in jousts and tournaments, organized and gave feasts, and spent his money without restraint; but she, no less virtuous than beautiful, cared little for these things done on her behalf, nor did she care for the one who did them. Now, as Federigo was spending far beyond his means and was taking nothing in, as easily happens he lost his wealth and became poor, with nothing but his little farm to his name (from whose revenues he lived very meagerly) and one falcon which was among the best in the world.

Giraudon/Art Resource, New York

AUGUST, from *Tres Riches Heures du Duc du Berry*, a fifteenth-century French Book of Hours, or prayer book.

---

1. **Federigo** (fed·ər·ē′gō)
2. **Messer Filippo Alberighi** (mes′ər fə·lē′pō al·bər·ē′gē): Messer is a title of address, similar to *sir*.

More in love than ever, but knowing that he would never be able to live the way he wished to in the city, he went to live at Campi, where his farm was. There he passed his time hawking whenever he could, asked nothing of anyone, and endured his poverty patiently. Now, during the time that Federigo was reduced to dire need, it happened that the husband of Monna Giovanna fell ill, and realizing death was near, he made his last will: he was very rich, and he made his son, who was growing up, his heir, and, since he had loved Monna Giovanna very much, he made her his heir should his son die without a legitimate heir; and then he died.

Monna Giovanna was now a widow, and as is the custom among our women, she went to the country with her son to spend a year on one of her possessions very close by to Federigo's farm, and it happened that this young boy became friends with Federigo and began to enjoy birds and hunting dogs; and after he had seen Federigo's falcon fly many times, it pleased him so much that he very much wished it were his own, but he did not dare to ask for it, for he could see how dear it was to Federigo. And during this time, it happened that the young boy took ill, and his mother was much grieved, for he was her only child and she loved him enormously; she would spend the entire day by his side, never ceasing to comfort him, and often asking him if there was anything he desired, begging him to tell her what it might be, for if it were possible to obtain it, she would certainly do everything possible to get it. After the young boy had heard her make this offer many times, he said:

"Mother, if you can arrange for me to have Federigo's falcon, I think I would be well very soon."

When the lady heard this, she was taken aback for a moment, and she began to think what she should do. She knew that Federigo had loved her for a long while, in spite of the fact that he never received a single glance from her, and so, she said to herself:

"How can I send or go and ask for this falcon of his which is, as I have heard tell, the best that ever flew, and besides this, his only means of support? And how can I be so insensitive as to wish to take away from this gentleman the only pleasure which is left to him?"

And involved in these thoughts, knowing that she was certain to have the bird if she asked for it, but not knowing what to say to her son, she stood there without answering him. Finally the love she bore her son persuaded her that she should make him happy, and no matter what the consequences might be, she would not send for the bird, but rather go herself for it and bring it back to him; so she answered her son:

"My son, take comfort and think only of getting well, for I promise you that the first thing I shall do tomorrow morning is to go for it and bring it back to you."

The child was so happy that he showed some improvement that very day. The following morning, the lady, accompanied by another woman, as if going for a stroll, went to Federigo's modest house and asked for him. Since it was not the season for it, Federigo had not been hawking for some days and was in his orchard, attending to certain tasks; when he heard that Monna Giovanna was asking for him at the door, he was very surprised and happy to run there; as she saw him coming, she greeted him with feminine charm, and once Federigo had welcomed her courteously, she said:

"Greetings, Federigo!" Then she continued: "I have come to compensate you for the harm you have suffered on my account by loving me more than you needed to; and the

THE SEVENTH DAY OF THE DECAMERON, PAUL FALCONER POOLES (1807–1879).

compensation is this: I, along with this companion of mine, intend to dine with you—a simple meal—this very day."

To this Federigo humbly replied: "Madonna,[3] I never remember having suffered any harm because of you; on the contrary: so much good have I received from you that if ever I have been worth anything, it has been because of your merit and the love I bore for you; and your generous visit is certainly so dear to me that I would spend all over again that which I spent in the past; but you have come to a poor host."

And having said this, he received her into his home humbly, and from there he led her into his garden, and since he had no one there to keep her company, he said:

"My lady, since there is no one else, this good woman here, the wife of this workman, will keep you company while I go to set the table."

Though he was very poor, Federigo, until now, had never before realized to what extent he had wasted his wealth; but this morning, the fact that he found nothing with which he could honor the lady for the love of whom he had once entertained countless men in the past gave him cause to reflect: in great anguish, he cursed himself and his fortune and, like a man beside himself, he started running here and there, but could find neither money nor a pawnable object. The hour was late and his desire to honor the gracious lady was great, but not wishing to turn for help to others (not even to his own workman), he set his eyes upon his good falcon, perched in a small room; and since he had nowhere else to turn, he took the bird, and finding it plump, he decided that it would be a worthy food for such a lady. So, without further thought, he wrung its neck and quickly gave it to his servant girl to pluck, prepare, and place on a spit to

---

3. **Madonna** (mə·dän′ə): a title for a woman, similar to *madam*.

Giovanni Boccaccio **817**

be roasted with care; and when he had set the table with the whitest of tablecloths (a few of which he still had left), he returned, with a cheerful face, to the lady in his garden, saying that the meal he was able to prepare for her was ready.

The lady and her companion rose, went to the table together with Federigo, who waited upon them with the greatest devotion, and they ate the good falcon without knowing what it was they were eating. And having left the table and spent some time in pleasant conversation, the lady thought it time now to say what she had come to say, and so she spoke these kind words to Federigo:

"Federigo, if you recall your past life and my virtue, which you perhaps mistook for harshness and cruelty, I do not doubt at all that you will be amazed by my presumption when you hear what my main reason for coming here is; but if you had children, through whom you might have experienced the power of parental love, it seems certain to me that you would, at least in part, forgive me. But, just as you have no child, I do have one, and I cannot escape the common laws of other mothers; the force of such laws compels me to follow them, against my own will and against good manners and duty, and to ask of you a gift which I know is most precious to you; and it is naturally so, since your extreme condition has left you no other delight, no other pleasure, no other consolation; and this gift is your falcon, which my son is so taken by that if I do not bring it to him, I fear his sickness will grow so much worse that I may lose him. And therefore I

THE CONCERT, French tapestry, late 1400s.
Which of Monna Giovanna's qualities make her a "lady" according to the chivalric ideal?

beg you, not because of the love that you bear for me, which does not oblige you in the least, but because of your own nobleness, which you have shown to be greater than that of all others in practicing courtliness, that you be pleased to give it to me, so that I may say that I have saved the life of my son by means of this gift, and because of it I have placed him in your debt forever."

When he heard what the lady requested and knew that he could not oblige her since he had given her the falcon to eat, Federigo began to weep in her presence, for he could not utter a word in reply. The lady, at first, thought his tears were caused more by the sorrow of having to part with the good falcon than by anything else, and she was on the verge of telling him she no longer wished it, but she held back and waited for Federigo's reply after he stopped weeping. And he said:

"My lady, ever since it pleased God for me to place my love in you, I have felt that Fortune has been hostile to me in many things, and I have complained of her, but all this is nothing compared to what she has just done to me, and I must never be at peace with her again, thinking about how you have come here to my poor home where, while it was rich, you never deigned to come, and you requested a small gift, and Fortune worked to make it impossible for me to give it to you; and why this is so I shall tell you briefly. When I heard that you, out of your kindness, wished to dine with me, I considered it fitting and right, taking into account your excellence and your worthiness, that I should honor you, according to my possibilities, with a more precious food than that which I usually serve to other people; therefore, remembering the falcon that you requested and its value, I judged it a food worthy of you, and this very day you

had it roasted and served to you as best I could; but seeing now that you desired it in another way, my sorrow in not being able to serve you is so great that I shall never be able to console myself again."

And after he had said this, he laid the feathers, the feet, and the beak of the bird before her as proof. When the lady heard and saw this, she first reproached him for having killed such a falcon to serve as a meal to a woman; but then to herself she commended the greatness of his spirit, which no poverty was able or would be able to diminish; then, having lost all hope of getting the falcon and, perhaps because of this, of improving the health of her son as well, she thanked Federigo both for the honor paid to her and for his good will, and she left in grief, and returned to her son. To his mother's extreme sorrow, either because of his disappointment that he could not have the falcon, or because his illness must have necessarily led to it, the boy passed from this life only a few days later.

After the period of her mourning and bitterness had passed, the lady was repeatedly urged by her brothers to remarry, since she was very rich and was still young; and although she did not wish to do so, they became so insistent that she remembered the merits of Federigo and his last act of generosity—that is, to have killed such a falcon to do her honor—and she said to her brothers:

"I would prefer to remain a widow, if that would please you; but if you wish me to take a husband, you may rest assured that I shall take no man but Federigo degli Alberighi."

In answer to this, making fun of her, her brothers replied:

"You foolish woman, what are you saying? How can you want him; he hasn't a penny to his name?"

To this she replied: "My brothers, I am well aware of what you say, but I would rather have a man who needs money than money that needs a man."

Her brothers, seeing that she was determined and knowing Federigo to be of noble birth, no matter how poor he was, accepted her wishes and gave her in marriage to him with all her riches; when he found himself the husband of such a great lady, whom he had loved so much and who was so wealthy besides, he managed his financial affairs with more prudence than in the past and lived with her happily the rest of his days.

First Thoughts

Do you think that Federigo was wise or foolish in making his sacrifice?

Identifying Facts

1. At first, what does Federigo do to win Monna Giovanna's love?
2. What does Monna Giovanna do when she learns what Federigo has made for supper?
3. When her brothers urge her to remarry, what does Monna Giovanna remember?

Interpreting Meanings

1. The unexpected visit of Monna Giovanna to Federigo after he has lost all his money is an example of **situational irony**, which occurs when what actually happens is the opposite of what is expected. Cite two other examples of situational irony in the story. How is the falcon central to these ironic events?
2. How does Federigo's sacrifice change Monna Giovanna's opinion of him? Why will she "take no man but Federigo"?
3. This story is a mixture of the romantic and the realistic. Which aspects of the story are romantic? Which are realistic?

Applying Meanings

"The Tale of the Falcon" focuses on a chivalric sacrifice to suggest that spiritual values are more important than money or possessions. Can you think of a modern work of film or literature that features a chivalric sacrifice? Do you think that such stories teach positive values, or are they "fairy tales" that promote unrealistic expectations?

Creative Writing Response

Exchanging Letters. Imagine that Monna Giovanna and Federigo exchange letters after Monna Giovanna's period of mourning is over. With a partner, write a letter from Monna Giovanna to Federigo, accepting his love and offering to marry him. Make sure that this letter explains why she "'would rather have a man who needs money than money that needs a man.'" What does she mean by "a man"? Then write Federigo's reply, keeping in mind his courtliness and longtime love for his lady.

Speaking and Listening

A Storytelling Session. The seven women and three men in the frame story of Boccaccio's *Decameron* tell stories while the Black Death rages around them. The stories they tell include folktales, fables, and anecdotes. Imagine that you and your classmates are isolated along with Boccaccio's storytellers. What story will you tell to entertain your companions and pass the time? Tell your story to the class. It can be a story you have made up yourself, a story you have read or heard, or even a lengthy joke. If you wish, record your storytelling session and critique one another's oral performance.

Miguel de Cervantes
1547–1616

The Granger Collection, New York

Miguel de Cervantes (sər·vän′täz′), son of a wandering apothecary, or druggist, was born near Madrid, Spain, in 1547. In 1569, Cervantes, seeing no prospects at home, enlisted in the army, fought valiantly, and was wounded at the Battle of Lepanto in 1571. His left hand was crippled, earning him the nickname, "el manco de Lepanto"— "the one-handed man of Lepanto."

Cervantes hoped to be promoted to an army captain after the war, but his plans were later thwarted when he was captured by Barbary pirates and held as a slave for five years in Algeria. He returned to Spain in 1580, jobless, in debt, and without any hope of regaining his army career. Over the years he worked as a playwright, bureaucrat, and tax collector before finally landing in jail for failure to pay his debts, many of which had accrued as a result of his family scraping together the ransom money to buy his freedom from the pirates.

According to legend, it was while he was in jail that the idea for *Don Quixote* came to Cervantes. His hero, Don Quixote, is a poor, aging landowner who reads nothing but romantic tales of chivalry. As he teeters on the edge of insanity, the old man becomes convinced that he is a knight-errant, even though the age of knights is long past.

The Ingenious Gentleman Don Quixote of La Mancha was published in January of 1605, and immediately caused a sensation. Once the first edition sold out, pirated—illegally printed—copies began to appear. Six editions were issued in the first year, and translations into French and English appeared within ten years. It seemed that everyone in Spain, and soon everyone in Europe, was laughing at the droll adventures of the ridiculous knight, Don Quixote.

Cervantes, at the age of fifty-eight, was now a famous author, but he was still poor. As was common until the nineteenth century, authors were at the mercy of publishers and were seldom able to retain the copyrights on their books. Thus, *Don Quixote*'s publisher, not Cervantes, reaped the lion's share of the book's profits. Spain's greatest writer died in poverty on April 22, 1616. To his family Cervantes left only a little money and many debts. To the world he left a comic masterpiece that earned him the title of "father of the modern novel."

Reader's Guide

from DON QUIXOTE

Background

Initially, Cervantes intended *Don Quixote* to lampoon tales of **chivalry** and **courtly romances**, stories from the medieval period about romantic love and knightly adventure, which were still eagerly devoured by the audience of Cervantes' time. In these stories, idealized knights fought villains, dragons, and monsters, and embarked on quests in honor of ladies to whom they had sworn their love. Such heroes stood for military values such as honor, courage, and loyalty, combined with Christian virtues such as piety, courtesy, and chastity.

Cervantes used the conventions of chivalric romances and satirized them at the same time. Don Quixote wears a cardboard visor on his helmet and mistakes windmills for giants. These actions, and others like them, suggest the discrepancy between the real world and the idealism portrayed in chivalric romances. Yet *Don Quixote* is much more than a parody of the romances of Cervantes' day. It touchingly develops two of literature's most enduring themes: the struggle of the idealist in a materialistic world and the interplay of fantasy and reality.

Writer's Response

Cervantes' novel resulted in a new word used to describe a person who is a well-intentioned, impractical, foolishly idealistic dreamer: *quixotic* (kwiks·ät′ik). What quixotic heroes in popular culture—films, comic strips, television, and books—can you think of? What traits do these heroes share? Do they succeed in their adventures?

Literary Focus

A literary **parody** is an imitation of another work of literature for amusement or instruction. A parody uses exaggeration or inappropriate subject matter to make something serious seem laughable. For example, in a serious chivalric romance a hero would be dubbed a knight by his lord, usually a king, and he would prepare for the ceremony during an all-night vigil in which he watched over his armor in a chapel. In *Don Quixote,* Don Quixote arranges to be dubbed a knight by the fat innkeeper of a rural inn that he mistakes for a castle, and he places his rusty armor in a horse-trough rather than on an altar. In the novel, many other uproarious scenes parody chivalric romances.

from DON QUIXOTE
Miguel de Cervantes
translated by
SAMUEL PUTNAM

 As you read, note how often Don Quixote refers to chivalric romances he has read to explain or justify what he does or what happens to him.

Chapter 1

Which treats of the station in life and the pursuits of the famous gentleman, Don Quixote de la Mancha.

In a village of La Mancha,[1] the name of which I have no desire to recall, there lived not so long ago one of those gentlemen who always have a lance in the rack, an ancient buckler, a skinny nag, and a greyhound for the chase. A stew with more beef than mutton in it, chopped meat for his evening meal, scraps for a Saturday, lentils on Friday, and a young pigeon as a special delicacy for Sunday went to account for three quarters of his income. The rest of it he laid out on a broadcloth greatcoat and velvet stockings for feast days, with slippers to match, while the other days of the week he cut a figure in a suit of the finest homespun. Living with him were a housekeeper in her forties, a niece who was not yet twenty, and a lad of the field and marketplace who saddled his horse for him and wielded the pruning knife.

This gentleman of ours was close on to fifty, of a robust constitution but with little flesh on his bones and a face that was lean and gaunt. He was noted for his early rising, being very fond of the hunt. They will try to tell you that his surname was Quijada or Quesada[2]—there is some difference of opinion among those who have written on the subject—but according to the most likely conjectures we are to understand that it was really Quejana. But all this means very little so far as our story is concerned, providing that in the telling of it we do not depart one iota from the truth.

You may know, then, that the aforesaid gentleman, on those occasions when he was at leisure, which was most of the year around, was in the habit of reading books of chivalry with such pleasure and devotion as to lead him almost wholly to forget the life of a hunter and even the administration of his estate. So great was his curiosity and infatuation in this regard that he even sold many acres of tillable land in order to be able to buy and read the books that he loved,

---

1. **La Mancha:** a province of south-central Spain, a poor plateau land lying alongside the mountains called Sierra Morena; to Cervantes, La Mancha represented a poor, backward area in the middle of nowhere.

2. **Quijada** (kē·hä′dä) **or Quesada** (kä·sä′dä): distinguished Spanish family names.

DON QUIXOTE IN HIS STUDY, GEORGE CATTERMOLE (1800–1868).
? *What tone does the narrator adopt to report Don Quixote's obsession with romances?*

and he would carry home with him as many of them as he could obtain.

Of all those that he thus devoured, none pleased him so well as the ones that had been composed by the famous Feliciano de Silva,[3] whose lucid prose style and involved conceits were as precious to him as pearls; especially when he came to read those tales of love and amorous challenges that are to be met with in many places, such a passage as the following, for example: "The reason of the unreason that afflicts my reason, in such a manner weakens my reason that I with reason lament me of your comeliness." And he was similarly affected when his eyes fell upon such lines as these: ". . . the high heaven of your divinity divinely fortifies you with the stars and renders you deserving of that desert your greatness doth deserve."

The poor fellow used to lie awake nights in an effort to disentangle the meaning and make sense out of passages such as these, although Aristotle himself would not have been able to understand them, even if he had been resurrected for that sole purpose. He was not at ease in his mind over those wounds that Don Belianís gave and received;

---

3. **Feliciano de Silva:** a sixteenth-century writer of romances, including *Don Florisel de Niquea,* from which the following quotation is taken.

for no matter how great the surgeons who treated him, the poor fellow must have been left with his face and his entire body covered with marks and scars. Nevertheless, he was grateful to the author for closing the book with the promise of an interminable adventure to come; many a time he was tempted to take up his pen and literally finish the tale as had been promised, and he undoubtedly would have done so, and would have succeeded at it very well, if his thoughts had not been constantly occupied with other things of greater moment.

He often talked it over with the village curate, who was a learned man, a graduate of Sigüenza,[4] and they would hold long discussions as to who had been the better knight, Palmerin of England or Amadis of Gaul;[5] but Master Nicholas, the barber of the same village, was in the habit of saying that no one could come up to the Knight of Phoebus,[6] and that if anyone *could* compare with him it was Don Galaor, brother of Amadis of Gaul, for Galaor was ready for anything— he was none of your finical knights who went around whimpering as his brother did, and in point of valor he did not lag behind him.

In short, our gentleman became so immersed in his reading that he spent whole nights from sundown to sunup and his days from dawn to dusk in poring over his books, until, finally, from so little sleeping and so much reading, his brain dried up and he went completely out of his mind. He had filled his imagination with everything that he had read, with enchantments, knightly encounters, battles, challenges, wounds, with tales of love and its torments, and all sorts of impossible things, and as a result had come to believe that all these fictitious happenings were true; they were more real to him than anything else in the world. He would remark that the Cid[7] Ruy Díaz had been a very good knight, but there was no comparison between him and the Knight of the Flaming Sword, who with a single backward stroke had cut in half two fierce and monstrous giants. He preferred Bernardo del Carpio, who at Roncesvalles had slain Roland despite the charm[8] the latter bore, availing himself of the stratagem which Hercules employed when he strangled Antaeus,[9] the son of Earth, in his arms.

He had much good to say for Morgante[10] who, though he belonged to the haughty, overbearing race of giants, was of an affable disposition and well brought up. But, above all, he cherished an admiration for Rinaldo of Montalbán,[11] especially as he beheld him sallying forth from his castle to rob all those that crossed his path, or when he thought of him overseas stealing the image of Mohammed which, so the story has it, was all of gold. And he would have liked very well to have had his fill of kicking that traitor Galalón,[12] a privilege for which he would have given his housekeeper with his niece thrown into the bargain.

---

4. **Sigüenza:** a minor Spanish university with a poor reputation, hence an ironic reference.
5. **Palmerin of England or Amadis of Gaul:** famous heroes of chivalric romances.
6. **Phoebus:** Apollo, the sun god in Greek mythology; here used as a symbolic name.
7. **Cid** (thēd): the subject of Spain's national epic.
8. **charm:** magic that made him invulnerable.
9. **Antaeus** (an·tē′əs): In Greek mythology, Antaeus could not be killed as long as he remained in contact with the earth. Hercules lifted him and then strangled him.
10. **Morgante:** a character in an Italian epic.
11. **Rinaldo of Montalbán:** one of Charlemagne's knights.
12. **Galalón:** Ganelon, who in the *Song of Roland* betrayed the French at the pass of Roncesvalles.

At last, when his wits were gone beyond repair, he came to conceive the strangest idea that ever occurred to any madman in this world. It now appeared to him fitting and necessary, in order to win a greater amount of honor for himself and serve his country at the same time, to become a knight-errant and roam the world on horseback, in a suit of armor; he would go in quest of adventures, by way of putting into practice all that he had read in his books; he would right every manner of wrong, placing himself in situations of the greatest peril such as would redound to the eternal glory of his name. As a reward for his valor and the might of his arm, the poor fellow could already see himself crowned Emperor of Trebizond[13] at the very least; and so, carried away by the strange pleasure that he found in such thoughts as these, he at once set about putting his plan into effect.

The first thing he did was to burnish up some old pieces of armor, left him by his great-grandfather, which for ages had lain in a corner, moldering and forgotten. He polished and adjusted them as best he could, and then he noticed that one very important thing was lacking: there was no closed helmet, but only a morion,[14] or visorless headpiece, with turned-up brim of the kind foot soldiers wore. His ingenuity, however, enabled him to remedy this, and he proceeded to fashion out of cardboard a kind of halfhelmet, which, when attached to the morion, gave the appearance of a whole one. True, when he went to see if it was strong enough to withstand a good slashing blow, he was somewhat disappointed; for when he drew his sword and gave it a couple of

Equestrian Portrait, Albrecht Dürer (1471–1528).
Art Resource, New York

thrusts, he succeeded only in undoing a whole week's labor. The ease with which he had hewed it to bits disturbed him no little, and he decided to make it over. This time he placed a few strips of iron on the inside, and then, convinced that it was strong enough, refrained from putting it to any further test; instead, he adopted it then and there as the finest helmet ever made.

After this, he went out to have a look at his nag; and although the animal had more *cuartos*, or cracks, in its hoof than there are quarters in a real,[15] and more blemishes than

---

13. **Trebizond** (treb′i·zänd′): Greek empire that was an offshoot of the Byzantine Empire.
14. **morion** (mōr′ē·än′): a helmet with a curved peak, used in the sixteenth and seventeenth centuries.

15. **real** (rä·äl′): an old Spanish coin, something like a nickel; there were eight *cuartos* (meaning both "quarter" and "crack") in a real.

Gonela's steed[16] which *tantum pellis et ossa fuit*,[17] it nonetheless looked to its master like a far better horse than Alexander's Bucephalus or the Babieca[18] of the Cid. He spent all of four days in trying to think up a name for his mount; for—so he told himself—seeing that it belonged to so famous and worthy a knight, there was no reason why it should not have a name of equal renown. The kind of name he wanted was one that would at once indicate what the nag had been before it came to belong to a knight-errant and what its present status was; for it stood to reason that, when the master's worldly condition changed, his horse also ought to have a famous, high-sounding appellation, one suited to the new order of things and the new profession that it was to follow.

After he in his memory and imagination had made up, struck out, and discarded many names, now adding to and now subtracting from the list, he finally hit upon "Rocinante,"[19] a name that impressed him as being sonorous and at the same time indicative of what the steed had been when it was but a hack, whereas now it was nothing other than the first and foremost of all the hacks in the world.

Having found a name for his horse that pleased his fancy, he then desired to do as much for himself, and this required another week, and by the end of that period he had made up his mind that he was henceforth to be known as Don Quixote,[20] which, as has been stated, has led the authors of this veracious history to assume that his real name must undoubtedly have been Quijada, and not Quesada as others would have it. But remembering that the valiant Amadis was not content to call himself that and nothing more, but added the name of his kingdom and fatherland that he might make it famous also, and thus came to take the name Amadis of Gaul, so our good knight chose to add his place of origin and become "Don Quixote de la Mancha"; for by this means, as he saw it, he was making very plain his lineage and was conferring honor upon his country by taking its name as his own.[21]

And so, having polished up his armor and made the morion over into a closed helmet, and having given himself and his horse a name, he naturally found but one thing lacking still: he must seek out a lady of whom he could become enamored; for a knight-errant without a ladylove was like a tree without leaves or fruit, a body without a soul.

"If," he said to himself, "as a punishment for my sins or by a stroke of fortune I should come upon some giant hereabouts, a thing that very commonly happens to knights-errant, and if I should slay him in a hand-to-hand encounter or perhaps cut him in two, or, finally, if I should vanquish and subdue him, would it not be well to have someone to whom I may send him as a present, in order that he, if he is living, may

---

16. **Gonela's steed:** Gonela, the jester of the Duke of Ferrara, had a horse that was the butt of many jokes.
17. *tantum . . . fuit:* "was nothing but skin and bones" (Latin).
18. **Bucephalus** (byo͞o·sef′ə·ləs): war horse of Alexander the Great . . . **Babieca** (bä·bye′kə); Cid's champion horse.
19. **Rocinante** (rō′sē·nän′tā): coined from the word *rocin*, meaning "a nag" or "hack" and the word *ante*, meaning "before"; *Rocinante* therefore means "formerly a nag" and implies a grand new status.

20. **Quixote** (kē·hōt′ē): the name for a piece of armor that covers the thigh.
21. **name as his own:** If a man named Smith from Wichita called himself Lord Smythe of Kansas, the effect might be something like this.

Don Quixote, Honoré Daumier (1808–1879).

🔵 *Do you think that this and the following painting (page 831) succeed at capturing the atmosphere of the selection? Why or why not?*

come in, fall upon his knees in front of my sweet lady, and say in a humble and submissive tone of voice, 'I, lady, am the giant Caraculiambro, lord of the island Malindrania, who has been overcome in single combat by that knight who never can be praised enough, Don Quixote de la Mancha, the same who sent me to present myself before your Grace that your Highness may dispose of me as you see fit'?"

Oh, how our good knight reveled in this speech, and more than ever when he came to think of the name that he should give his lady! As the story goes, there was a very good-looking farm girl who lived nearby, with whom he had once been smitten, although it is generally believed that she never knew or suspected it. Her name was Aldonza Lorenzo, and it seemed to him that she was the one upon whom he should bestow the title of mistress of his thoughts. For her he wished a name that should not be incongruous with his own and that would convey the suggestion of a princess or a great lady; and accordingly, he resolved to call her "Dulcinea[22] del Toboso," she being a native of that place. A musical name to his ears, out of the ordinary and significant, like the others he had chosen for himself and his appurtenances.

from Chapter 2

Which treats of the first sally that the ingenious Don Quixote made from his native heath.

Having, then, made all these preparations, he did not wish to lose any time in putting his plan into effect, for he could not but blame himself for what the world was losing by his delay, so many were the wrongs that were to be righted, the grievances to be redressed, the abuses to be done away with, and the duties to be performed. Accordingly, without informing anyone of his intention and without letting anyone see him, he set out one morning before daybreak on one of those very hot days in July. Donning all his armor, mounting Rocinante, adjusting his ill-contrived helmet, bracing his shield on his arm, and taking up his lance, he sallied forth by the back gate of his stable yard into the open countryside. It was with great contentment and joy that he saw how easily he had made a beginning towards the fulfillment of his desire.

No sooner was he out on the plain, however, than a terrible thought assailed him, one that all but caused him to abandon the enterprise he had undertaken. This occurred when he suddenly remembered that he had never formally been dubbed a knight, and so, in accordance with the law of knighthood, was not permitted to bear arms against one who had a right to that title. And even if he had been, as a novice knight he would have had to wear white armor,[23] without any device on his shield, until he should have earned one by his exploits. These thoughts led him to waver in his purpose, but, madness prevailing over reason, he resolved to have himself knighted by the first person he met, as many others had done if what he had read in those books that he had at home was true. And so far as white armor was concerned, he would scour his own the first chance that offered until it shone whiter than any ermine. With this he became more tranquil and continued on his

---

22. **Dulcinea** (dul′sə·nē′ə) derived from the Spanish word *dulce,* meaning "sweet."

23. **white armor:** that is, armor without any insignia or signs of use. Here Don Quixote is taking the term literally.

way, letting his horse take whatever path it chose, for he believed that therein lay the very essence of adventures. . . .

Don Quixote gets himself "knighted" by a bewildered innkeeper, who marvels at such an extraordinary variety of madness, but he is finally tricked by his friends and brought home, where he is treated as a lunatic. His family deprives him of the dangerous books, and they hope that the madness will pass.

from Chapter 7

Of the second sally of our good knight, Don Quixote de la Mancha.

. . . He remained at home very tranquilly for a couple of weeks, without giving sign of any desire to repeat his former madness. During that time he had the most pleasant conversations with his two old friends, the curate and the barber, on the point he had raised to the effect that what the world needed most was knights-errant and a revival of chivalry. The curate would occasionally contradict him and again would give in, for it was only by means of this artifice that he could carry on a conversation with him at all.

In the meanwhile Don Quixote was bringing his powers of persuasion to bear upon a farmer who lived nearby, a good man—if this title may be applied to one who is poor—but with very few wits in his head. The short of it is, by pleas and promises, he got the hapless rustic to agree to ride forth with him and serve him as his squire. Among other things, Don Quixote told him that he ought to be more than willing to go, because no telling what adventure might occur which would win them an island, and then he (the farmer) would be left to be the governor of it. As a result of these and other similar assurances, Sancho Panza forsook his wife and children and consented to take upon himself the duties of squire to his neighbor.

Next, Don Quixote set out to raise some money, and by selling this thing and pawning that and getting the worst of the bargain always, he finally scraped together a reasonable amount. He also asked a friend of his for the loan of a buckler[24] and patched up his broken helmet as well as he could. He advised his squire, Sancho, of the day and hour when they were to take the road and told him to see to laying in a supply of those things that were most necessary, and, above all, not to forget the saddlebags. Sancho replied that he would see to all this and added that he was also thinking of taking along with him a very good ass that he had, as he was not much used to going on foot.

With regard to the ass, Don Quixote had to do a little thinking, trying to recall if any knight-errant had ever had a squire thus asininely mounted. He could not think of any, but nevertheless he decided to take Sancho with the intention of providing him with a nobler steed as soon as occasion offered; he had but to appropriate the horse of the first discourteous knight he met. Having furnished himself with shirts and all the other things that the innkeeper had recommended, he and Panza rode forth one night unseen by anyone and without taking leave of wife and children, housekeeper or niece. They went so far that by the time morning came they were safe from discovery had a hunt been started for them.

Mounted on his ass, Sancho Panza rode along like a patriarch, with saddlebags and flask, his mind set upon becoming governor

---

24. **buckler:** a small shield.

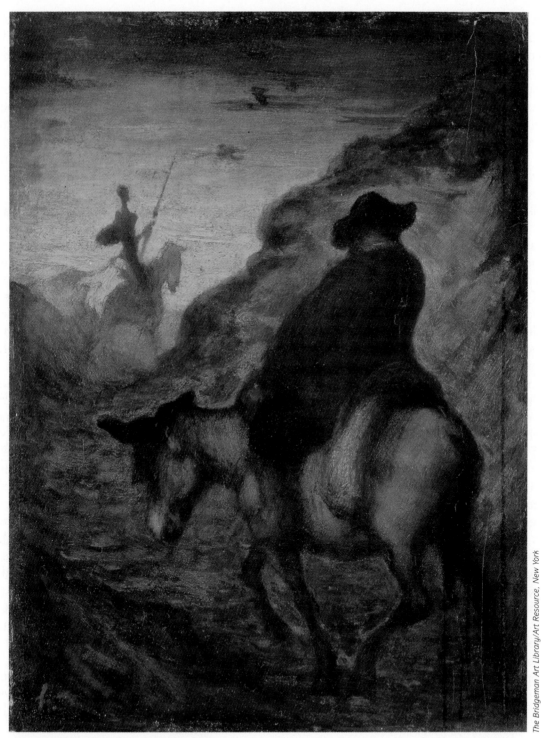

SANCHO AND DON QUIXOTE, HONORÉ DAUMIER.

Miguel de Cervantes **831**

of that island that his master had promised him. Don Quixote determined to take the same route and road over the Campo de Montiel[25] that he had followed on his first journey; but he was not so uncomfortable this time, for it was early morning and the sun's rays fell upon them slantingly and accordingly did not tire them too much.

"Look, Sir Knight-errant," said Sancho, "your Grace should not forget that island you promised me; for no matter how big it is, I'll be able to govern it right enough."

"I would have you know, friend Sancho Panza," replied Don Quixote, "that among the knights-errant of old it was a very common custom to make their squires governors of the islands or the kingdoms that they won, and I am resolved that in my case so pleasing a usage shall not fall into desuetude.[26] I even mean to go them one better; for they very often, perhaps most of the time, waited until their squires were old men who had had their fill of serving their masters during bad days and worse nights, whereupon they would give them the title of count, or marquis at most, of some valley or province more or less. But if you live and I live, it well may be that within a week I shall win some kingdom with others dependent upon it, and it will be the easiest thing in the world to crown you king of one of them. You need not marvel at this, for all sorts of unforeseen things happen to knights like me, and I may readily be able to give you even more than I have promised."

"In that case," said Sancho Panza, "if by one of those miracles of which your Grace was speaking I should become king, I would certainly send for Juana Gutiérrez, my old

lady, to come and be my queen, and the young ones could be infantes."[27]

"There is no doubt about it," Don Quixote assured him.

"Well, I doubt it," said Sancho, "for I think that even if God were to rain kingdoms upon the earth, no crown would sit well on the head of Mari Gutiérrez,[28] for I am telling you, sir, as a queen she is not worth two maravedis.[29] She would do better as a countess, God help her."

"Leave everything to God, Sancho," said Don Quixote, "and he will give you whatever is most fitting; but I trust you will not be so pusillanimous[30] as to be content with anything less than the title of viceroy."

"That I will not," said Sancho Panza, "especially seeing that I have in your Grace so illustrious a master who can give me all that is suitable to me and all that I can manage."

from Chapter 8

Of the good fortune which the valorous Don Quixote had in the terrifying and never-before-imagined adventure of the windmills, along with other events that deserve to be suitably recorded.

At this point they caught sight of thirty or forty windmills which were standing on the plain there, and no sooner had Don Quixote laid eyes upon them than he turned to his squire and said, "Fortune is guiding our affairs better than we could have wished; for you see there before you, friend Sancho

---

25. **Campo de Montiel** (käm′pō dā mōn·tyēl′): the site of a famous battle in 1369.
26. **desuetude** (des′wi·tōod′): disuse.

27. **infantes** (in·fan′tāz′): a term used to designate the children of a Spanish king.
28. **Mari Gutiérrez:** Sancho's wife, who appears under several names during the course of the story.
29. **maravedis** (mar′ə·vä′dēz): old Spanish coins of trifling value.
30. **pusillanimous** (pyōo′si·lan′ə·məs): timid.

Panza, some thirty or more lawless giants with whom I mean to do battle. I shall deprive them of their lives, and with the spoils from this encounter we shall begin to enrich ourselves; for this is righteous warfare, and it is a great service to God to remove so accursed a breed from the face of the earth."

"What giants?" said Sancho Panza.

"Those that you see there," replied his master, "those with the long arms, some of which are as much as two leagues in length."

"But look, your Grace, those are not giants but windmills, and what appear to be arms are their wings which, when whirled in the breeze, cause the millstone to go."

"It is plain to be seen," said Don Quixote, "that you have had little experience in this matter of adventures. If you are afraid, go off to one side and say your prayers while I am engaging them in fierce, unequal combat."

Saying this, he gave spurs to his steed Rocinante, without paying any heed to Sancho's warning that these were truly windmills and not giants that he was riding forth to attack. Nor even when he was close upon them did he perceive what they really were, but shouted at the top of his lungs, "Do not seek to flee, cowards and vile creatures that you are, for it is but a single knight with whom you have to deal!"

At that moment a little wind came up and the big wings began turning.

"Though you flourish as many arms as did

DON QUIXOTE AND THE WINDMILL, FRANCISCO J. TORROME, C. 1900.

the giant Briareus,"[31] said Don Quixote when he perceived this, "you still shall have to answer to me."

He thereupon commended himself with all his heart to his lady Dulcinea, beseeching her to succor him in this peril; and, being well covered with his shield and with his lance at rest, he bore down upon them at a full gallop and fell upon the first mill that stood in his way, giving a thrust at the wing, which was whirling at such a speed that his lance was broken into bits and both horse and horseman went rolling over the plain, very much battered indeed. Sancho upon his donkey came hurrying to his master's assistance as fast as he could, but when he reached the spot, the knight was unable to move, so great was the shock with which he and Rocinante had hit the ground.

"God help us!" exclaimed Sancho, "did I not tell your Grace to look well, that those were nothing but windmills, a fact which no one could fail to see unless he had other mills of the same sort in his head?"

"Be quiet, friend Sancho," said Don Quixote. "Such are the fortunes of war, which more than any other are subject to constant change. What is more, when I come to think of it, I am sure that this must be the work of that magician Frestón, the one who robbed me of my study and my books, and who has thus changed the giants into windmills in order to deprive me of the glory of overcoming them, so great is the enmity that he bears me; but in the end his evil arts shall not prevail against this trusty sword of mine."

"May God's will be done," was Sancho Panza's response. And with the aid of his squire the knight was once more mounted on Rocinante, who stood there with one shoulder half out of joint. And so, speaking of the adventure that had just befallen them, they continued along the Puerto Lápice highway; for there, Don Quixote said, they could not fail to find many and varied adventures, this being a much-traveled thoroughfare. The only thing was, the knight was exceedingly downcast over the loss of his lance.

"I remember," he said to his squire, "having read of a Spanish knight by the name of Diego Pérez de Vargas, who, having broken his sword in battle, tore from an oak a heavy bough or branch and with it did such feats of valor that day, and pounded so many Moors, that he came to be known as Machuca,[32] and he and his descendants from that day forth have been called Vargas y Machuca. I tell you this because I, too, intend to provide myself with just such a bough as the one he wielded, and with it I propose to do such exploits that you shall deem yourself fortunate to have been found worthy to come with me and behold and witness things that are almost beyond belief."

"God's will be done," said Sancho. "I believe everything that your Grace says; but straighten yourself up in the saddle a little, for you seem to be slipping down on one side, owing, no doubt, to the shaking up that you received in your fall."

"Ah, that is the truth," replied Don Quixote, "and if I do not speak of my sufferings, it is for the reason that it is not permitted knights-errant to complain of any wound whatsoever, even though their bowels may be dropping out."

"If that is the way it is," said Sancho, "I have nothing more to say; but, God knows,

---

31. **Briareus** (brī·är'ē·əs): in Greek mythology, a giant with a hundred arms, who helped Zeus overthrow the Titans.

32. **Machuca** (mä·chōō′kä): literally, ''the pounder,'' the hero of an old ballad.

Knights Jousting, Albrecht Dürer.

it would suit me better if your Grace did complain when something hurts him. I can assure you that I mean to do so, over the least little thing that ails me—that is, unless the same rule applies to squires as well."

Don Quixote laughed long and heartily over Sancho's simplicity, telling him that he might complain as much as he liked and where and when he liked, whether he had good cause or not; for he had read nothing to the contrary in the ordinances[33] of chivalry. Sancho then called his master's attention to the fact that it was time to eat. The knight replied that he himself had no need of food at the moment, but his squire might

eat whenever he chose. Having been granted this permission, Sancho seated himself as best he could upon his beast, and, taking out from his saddlebags the provisions that he had stored there, he rode along leisurely behind his master, munching his victuals and taking a good, hearty swig now and then at the leather flask in a manner that might well have caused the biggest-bellied tavernkeeper of Málaga to envy him. Between drafts he gave not so much as a thought to any promise that his master might have made him, nor did he look upon it as any hardship, but rather as good sport, to go in quest of adventures however hazardous they might be.

The short of the matter is, they spent the night under some trees, from one of which Don Quixote tore off a withered bough to

---

33. **ordinances** (ôrd′′n·əns·əz): authoritative commands.

Miguel de Cervantes **835**

serve him as a lance, placing it in the lance head from which he had removed the broken one. He did not sleep all night long for thinking of his lady Dulcinea; for this was in accordance with what he had read in his books, of men of arms in the forest or desert places who kept a wakeful vigil, sustained by the memory of their ladies fair. Not so with Sancho, whose stomach was full, and not with chicory water.[34] He fell into a dreamless slumber, and had not his master called him, he would not have been awakened either by the rays of the sun in his face or by the many birds who greeted the coming of the new day with their merry song.

Upon arising, he had another go at the flask, finding it somewhat more flaccid than it had been the night before, a circumstance which grieved his heart, for he could not see that they were on the way to remedying the deficiency within any very short space of time. Don Quixote did not wish any breakfast; for, as has been said, he was in the habit of nourishing himself on savorous memories. They then set out once more along the road to Puerto Lápice, and around three in the afternoon they came in sight of the pass that bears that name.

---

34. **chicory water:** an inexpensive coffee substitute.

"There," said Don Quixote as his eyes fell upon it, "we may plunge our arms up to the elbow in what are known as adventures. But I must warn you that even though you see me in the greatest peril in the world, you are not to lay hand upon your sword to defend me, unless it be that those who attack me are rabble and men of low degree, in which case you may very well come to my aid; but if they be gentlemen, it is in no wise permitted by the laws of chivalry that you should assist me until you yourself shall have been dubbed a knight."

"Most certainly, sir," replied Sancho, "your Grace shall be very well obeyed in this; all the more so for the reason that I myself am of a peaceful disposition and not fond of meddling in the quarrels and feuds of others. However, when it comes to protecting my own person, I shall not take account of those laws of which you speak, seeing that all laws, human and divine, permit each one to defend himself whenever he is attacked."

"I am willing to grant you that," assented Don Quixote, "but in this matter of defending me against gentlemen you must restrain your natural impulses."

"I promise you I shall do so," said Sancho. "I will observe this precept as I would the Sabbath day." ...

> **First Thoughts**

Do you like Don Quixote? Did your attitudes toward him change as you read? Explain your answer.

Identifying Facts

1. What sorts of books does Don Quixote like to read, and what effect do these books have on his life?

2. What preparations does Don Quixote make before setting out on his quest?

3. Why does Sancho Panza become a squire to Don Quixote?

4. After being knocked down by the windmill, how does Don Quixote explain the fact that he has not killed a giant?

5. What natural human needs, which Don Quixote ignores, does Sancho Panza insist on satisfying for himself?

Interpreting Meanings

1. How are Don Quixote's helmet, horse, and mistress examples of **parody**?

2. A **foil** is a character who is used as a contrast to another character. Sancho Panza functions as a foil to Don Quixote. How does the behavior of the two men suggest that they are opposites? What traits in Don Quixote become more prominent because of the contrast between Quixote and Sancho?

3. What are Don Quixote's reasons for going on his quest? How are his reasons similar to those of **epic heroes**? How are they different?

4. An idealist, or romantic, views the world as he or she thinks it ought to be. A realist views the world as it is. Is Don Quixote an idealist or a realist? Which role does Sancho Panza fit?

Applying Meanings

Don Quixote's exploits have given us the term *quixotic* to describe any idealistically impractical project, whether great or small. The phrase "going off to fight windmills" suggests the same idea. Do you know anybody whose behavior could be described as "quixotic"? Have you ever "gone off to fight windmills"?

Creative Writing Response

Writing a Parody. Don Quixote is inspired to become a knight-errant by reading stories about heroic knights in shining armor. Imagine a modern character like Quixote fascinated by twentieth-century romances about heroes, perhaps in movies, comic books, or TV shows. Write a parody in which your character takes on the role of a modern hero and goes to places such as the supermarket or the video rental store in search of adventure.

Critical Writing Response

Interpreting a Poem. The following poem refers to the sentence in Chapter 2 which describes Quixote continuing on his way, "letting his horse take whatever path it chose, for he believed that therein lay the very essence of adventures."

> Parable
> Richard Wilbur
>
> I read how Quixote in his random ride
>   Came to a crossing once, and lest he lose
> The purity of chance, would not decide
> Whither to fare, but wished his horse to
>   choose.
> For glory lay wherever he might turn.
> His head was light with pride, his horse's
>   shoes
> Were heavy, and he headed for the barn.

In the novel, Rocinante does not head for the barn. The fact that the nag *does* in the poem suggests a certain attitude toward Don Quixote and his quest. Explain that attitude in a short essay. Do you agree or disagree with the poet's view of Don Quixote's quest?

ELEMENTS OF LITERATURE

Satire

A **satire** is any work that ridicules human weakness, vice, or folly. Cervantes' original purpose in writing *Don Quixote* was to satirize romantic tales of chivalry that were popular in his day. Cervantes found these stories absurd because they portrayed a world that no longer existed and indeed never had existed in the falsely glowing colors in which it had been painted by storytellers. Eventually, Cervantes widened his satire to include the institutions of his day as well as all kinds of timeless human follies. In writing *Don Quixote*, Cervantes used many satiric techniques that are familiar to us today, such as **exaggeration**, **verbal irony** (saying one thing and meaning another), **incongruity** (deliberately pairing things that don't belong together), and **parody** (a humorous imitation of a work).

Throughout the novel, Cervantes parodies the chivalric romance, imitating it in an exaggerated way. Quixote tries to set himself up like the knights of old, but his armor is rusty, his horse is a nag, and his noble squire is a chubby peasant who does not particularly respect his master, much less feel like laying down his life for him.

Cervantes frequently uses exaggeration to ridicule the chivalric romance. The narrator tells us that Quixote read so many romances that "his brain dried up." Many passages from such tales are seen as so tangled and confusing that "Aristotle himself would not have been able to understand them, even if he had been resurrected for that sole purpose." Wickedly, Cervantes quotes literally from a tale by a sixteenth-century writer whose language is so exaggerated that Cervantes does not need to embellish it further: "The reason of the unreason that afflicts my reason, in such a manner weakens my reason that I with reason lament me of your comeliness."

Cervantes' voice is often ironic—that is, he says one thing and means another. For example, the village curate is described as a "learned man, a graduate of Sigüenza," which was, in fact, a minor institution with a poor reputation. The comment pokes fun at people who show off their academic degrees. But underneath it all, Cervantes' satire is rooted in incongruity that arises from the clash between the romantic and the real. In this sense, the novel goes beyond its specific targets to universal human qualities. We can laugh at Quixote, but there is something of him in all of us. Like Quixote, who wished to live before his time, and like Cervantes himself, who wished to be a great military hero, we all have dreams that cannot come true. Yet we cannot relinquish these dreams without giving up an important part of ourselves.

William Shakespeare
1564–1616

AP/Wide World Photos

William Shakespeare, often called "the immortal bard," was, of course, as mortal as the rest of us. During his lifetime, he was known simply as a successful playwright. Because few people of his day considered him extraordinary, no one took pains to record the details of his life.

We know for certain that Shakespeare was born in Stratford-on-Avon, a market town on the river Avon about one hundred miles northwest of London. Shakespeare's father was a shopkeeper who was also active in town government. His mother, Mary Arden, was from one of the most prominent families of the area. Shakespeare probably attended the Stratford Grammar School. There he studied Latin, some Greek, the Bible, and the great Roman dramatists. Most scholars believe that Shakespeare went to London sometime between 1586 and 1588 to begin his apprenticeship as an actor. We do know that by 1592 he had become a successful actor and playwright.

Although Shakespeare spent most of his life in London, he also had a family in Stratford. In 1582, he married Anne Hathaway, who was 27. Together, they had a daughter, Susanna, and two years later, twins: Hamnet, who died in childhood, and Judith.

In 1594, Shakespeare joined the Lord Chamberlain's Men, a company of actors that became the King's Men in 1603. The company performed in a playhouse called simply "The Theater." Shakespeare wrote about two plays a year for this company, and by 1596, he was a moderately wealthy man, earning money as an actor, a playwright, and a shareholder in The Theater. In 1599, he financed a new theater on the south side of the Thames, the Globe. In 1612, Shakespeare retired to his comfortable home in Stratford. He had written 37 plays—comedies, histories, tragedies, and romances—and more than 150 poems. He died on April 23, 1616. The epitaph over his grave inside the church at Stratford warns those who may be tempted to move him to the graveyard outdoors:

> Good friend, for Jesus' sake forbear
> To dig the bones enclosèd here!
> Blest be the man that spares these stones,
> And curst be he that moves my bones.

The Elizabethan Theater

During the Elizabethan (ē·liz′ ə·bē′thən) period in England (1558–1603, the years of Elizabeth I's reign), drama underwent a renaissance of its own. The Globe is the most famous of the Elizabethan theaters not only because it was owned by the company that Shakespeare belonged to but also because it is where Shakespeare's greatest plays were first performed. The Globe consisted of three parts: the building proper, the stage, and the backstage area. In *Henry V*, Shakespeare refers to

The Globe theater, London. Drawing, c. 1600.

The Granger Collection, New York

the theater building as "this wooden O." It was, in fact, a sixteen-sided polygon surrounding an open space about sixty-five feet in diameter. The building was three stories high and had tiers of seats built into the walls (or galleries). Most of the spectators, however, stood in the open courtyard area in the center. These "groundlings" paid a penny admission while those in the gallery paid another penny or so. The richest members of the audience could buy seats on the stage itself. The stage and the gallery seats were protected by a roof or awning, but the groundlings were subject to the whims of the unpredictable English weather. The theater could hold about three thousand people altogether.

The stage was a large platform about five feet off the ground. It projected about halfway into the open circle. Below the stage was an area used by musicians and sound effects men. At the back of the stage were dressing rooms, places for machinery, and a curtained inner stage with a second floor used for balcony scenes like that in *Romeo and Juliet* or to suggest the walls of a castle or the bridge of a ship. The front part of the stage had a trap door that was especially useful for burial scenes or for the entrances and exits of ghosts and other supernatural creatures.

Reconstruction of the second Globe theater in London. *On stage, one actor arises through a trap door. Elizabethan theaters were often equipped with pulleys and trap doors to allow the dramatic entrances and exits of ghosts, faeries, and the like.*

Stagecraft: Sets, Costumes, Lighting

Much of what is accomplished in the modern theater through the technology of stagecraft was achieved in the Elizabethan theater almost entirely with language. Shakespeare's audiences needed to listen closely and use their imaginations to fill out what the actors' lines suggested. In *As You Like It,* for example, the character Rosalind creates a forest scene by announcing, "Well, this is the forest of Arden." In *Hamlet,* Shakespeare indicates that the night is over by having Horatio say, "But look, the morn in russet mantle clad/Walks o'er the dew of yon high eastward hill."

Because the audience could imagine such scenes, there was no need for elaborate scenery. And because there were no scene changes, the scenes flowed with no interruption—just as they flow today in movies or on television.

The stage itself was very lively. Characters were lowered from the heavens by cranes, and there were often elaborate processions, music and dancing, and sound effects, including gunpowder explosions. There were also beautiful banners or tapestries at the back of the stage. Because the plays were performed in the afternoons, there was no need for lighting. Characters carried torches or lanterns to indicate that certain scenes were occurring at night.

The audience wanted excitement, humor, passion, and action—even gore. (*Titus Andronicus* is as gory as any *Friday the Thirteenth* horror movie.) They also appreciated puns and word games. *The Tempest* provides vigorous action, boisterous humor, and splendid poetry. All of Shakespeare's plays provide subtle poetry, deep philosophy, and scenes of both sensational violence and quiet, psychological conflict.

Kings and other rich or royal characters were often spectacularly costumed. Some costumes conveyed agreed-upon meanings: one theater manager's inventory included "a robe for to go invisible in." The manager-producer Philip Henslowe lists properties of the Globe theater that include chariots, fountains, dragons, beds, tents, thrones, and other fanciful props.

Drawing of the Swan theater, London, by Johannes De Witt, c. 1596.

The Granger Collection, New York

Actors in Shakespeare's Time

Elizabethan actors *had* to be good, or the audience would quickly get out of hand. Today we go to the theater and sit quietly in darkness. The Elizabethan theater was a much livelier occasion— more like a rowdy party. The audience came early, talked with friends, met new people, walked about, and ate and drank before and during the performance. All sorts of shady characters mingled with the crowd—most notably, pimps and pickpockets. Because of all the distractions, the Elizabethan playwright had to write lively scenes, and the actors had to perform them with energy and verve— and sometimes, outright overblown acting—to hold the attention of some three thousand restless people, many of whom would just as soon go back to their talking, eating, and drinking.

In Shakespeare's time, the theater was considered a rather disreputable profession—certainly not a profession for women. Thus, all actors were men. All female parts were played by young boys who still had high-pitched voices. Because women's fashions consisted of long dresses, wigs, and heavy makeup, it was not difficult to transform a young boy into a beautiful woman.

The Tempest

The Tempest, the last of Shakespeare's romances or tragicomedies, is a far-fetched fantasy with love as a central concern. As with other romances of its

Detail from Cornelius Visscher's View of London, 1616.
The Globe theater is visible on the south bank of the Thames.

time, the surface action is a simple fairy tale, complete with good and bad characters, a pure, uncomplicated love, and many miraculous incidents, such as magic storms, charms that paralyze the evil characters and protect the good, and a play within a play featuring mythological deities. The play is rich in atmosphere and poetry, featuring characters that are somewhat symbolic and abstract.

Although the events and situations in *The Tempest* are improbable, the characters' emotions and responses to events are real. As a tragicomedy, it contains tragic elements in the form of malevolent characters and actions. Caliban plots to murder Prospero. Antonio and Sebastian plot against Alonso and Gonzalo. The play constantly reminds us that the world contains evil. Prospero's victory is won only by constant vigilance and an understanding of the evil within humanity. The malevolence is overcome and the play ends happily.

The Tempest has often been called a "summing up" play in which Shakespeare expresses "farewell to his art." Prospero, like Shakespeare, is the supreme creator of a unique universe, which he rules through the enormous power of his intellect and his imagination. At the end of the play, Prospero clears the stage—just as a tired Shakespeare might have done in the days of the Globe theater—and makes one last request of the audience: that they pause and think about the meaning of the drama.

Reader's Guide

THE TEMPEST

Background

William Shakespeare's earliest plays—among them *Romeo and Juliet, Henry IV, Hamlet,* and *As You Like It*—were either tragedies, comedies, or historical dramas. In the last few years of his career, Shakespeare began to write romantic, lyrical plays with elements of both tragedy and comedy: **tragicomedies**. Critics suggest different reasons for this shift in Shakespeare's later works, but it is most likely that he had said all he wanted to say with the tragedies and comedies and simply wanted to explore a different kind of expression. Audiences' preferences were changing as well; the utopian themes presented in romances and tragicomedies became increasingly popular during the Renaissance. *The Tempest* fit the bill. With its exotic portrayal of a distant land, it created an optimistic picture of human society.

There has been much speculation about the source of *The Tempest*. It is reasonable to assume that Shakespeare had access to a translation of French writer Montaigne's essay "Of Cannibals" when he was writing the play. In this essay, Montaigne argued that "primitive" societies may possess greater harmony and justice than "civilized" groups. A shipwreck on Bermuda in 1609, which caused much excitement in England, may also have sparked Shakespeare's imagination.

Writer's Response

The Tempest is often called a fantasy—a work that takes place in an unreal world and features incredible characters. How prevalent is fantasy in popular entertainment today—in movies, comics, television, and books? Do you prefer fantasy to other kinds of entertainment? Why or why not? Write a paragraph exploring these questions.

Literary Focus

Shakespeare's plays demonstrate a fairly consistent **dramatic structure**, or method of development. The five acts of *The Tempest* can be broken down, respectively, into **exposition**, where relevant background information is presented; **rising action**, where the plot accelerates and complications are introduced; the **climax**, or **turning point**, which is the point of greatest emotional intensity or suspense; **falling action**; and the **resolution**, where the play's conflicts are resolved.

THE TEMPEST
Act 1
William Shakespeare

❦ *Act 1 presents the exposition, or basic situation, of the play.*
Who are the major characters, and what are their conflicts?

CHARACTERS

Alonso, King of Naples

Sebastian, brother to Alonso

Prospero, the rightful Duke of
Milan

Antonio, brother to Prospero,
the usurping Duke of
Milan

Ferdinand, son to the King of
Naples

Gonzalo, an honest old
counselor

Adrian ⎫
Francisco ⎭ lords

Caliban, a savage and
deformed slave

Trinculo, a jester

Stephano, a drunken butler

Master of a ship

Boatswain

Mariners

Miranda, daughter to
Prospero

Ariel, an airy spirit

Iris ⎫
Ceres ⎬ spirits
Juno ⎭

Nymphs

Reapers

Other Spirits, attendants to
Prospero

Scene: a ship at sea; an
uninhabited island

Summary of Act 1, Scene 1. *Alonso, King of Naples, is returning from his daughter's wedding to a foreign prince with his brother Sebastian and Antonio, the Duke of Milan.*

Their ship is overcome by a tremendous storm. As the scene ends, it seems certain that the ship will sink and that all lives will be lost.

ACT 1

Scene 1. *A ship at sea.*

[*A tempestuous noise of thunder and lightning heard.
Enter a* SHIPMASTER *and a* BOATSWAIN.]

Master.

Boatswain!

Boatswain.

Here, master. What cheer?

Master.

Good, speak to the mariners; fall to't yarely,° or we run
ourselves aground! Bestir, bestir!   [*Exit.*]

[*Enter* MARINERS.]

Boatswain.

5   Heigh, my hearts! Cheerly, cheerly, my hearts! Yare,
yare! Take in the topsail! Tend to the master's whistle!
Blow till thou burst thy wind, if room enough!

[*Enter* ALONSO, SEBASTIAN, ANTONIO, FERDINAND,
GONZALO, *and others.*]

Alonso.

Good boatswain, have care. Where's the master?
Play the men.°

Boatswain.

10   I pray now, keep below.

Antonio.

Where is the master, bos'n?

Boatswain.

Do you not hear him? You mar our labor. Keep your
cabins: you do assist the storm!

Gonzalo.

Nay, good, be patient.

Boatswain.

15   When the sea is. Hence! What cares these roarers for
the name of king? To cabin! Silence! Trouble us not!

Gonzalo.

Good, yet remember whom thou hast aboard.

Boatswain.

None that I more love than myself. You are a counselor:
if you can command these elements to silence and work
20   the peace of the present,° we will not hand a rope
more; use your authority. If you cannot, give thanks
you have lived so long, and make yourself ready in your

3. **Good:** my good fellow;
yarely: immediately, briskly.

9. **Play the men:** behave like
men.

? How would you describe the
boatswain's attitude toward
the king?

19–20. **work the peace of the
present:** calm the storm.

cabin for the mischance of the hour, if it so hap.—
Cheerly, good hearts!—Out of our way, I say.   [*Exit.*]

Gonzalo.

I have great comfort from this fellow. Methinks he
hath no drowning mark upon him; his complexion is
perfect gallows.° Stand fast, good Fate, to his hanging!
Make the rope of his destiny our cable, for our own
doth little advantage. If he be not born to be hanged,
our case is miserable.   [*Exeunt.*]

25–27. **Methinks . . . perfect gallows:** an old proverb stated, "He that is born to be hanged shall never be drowned."

[*Reenter* BOATSWAIN.]

Boatswain.

Down with the topmast! Yare! Lower, lower! Bring her
to try with the main course!° (*a cry within*) A plague
upon this howling! They are louder than the weather
or our office.°

32. **main course:** mainsail; leaving only the mainsail set will, the boatswain hopes, keep the ship stable enough that it neither founders nor runs aground.
34. **office:** duty, which is, at this moment, yelling orders to the sailors.

[*Enter* SEBASTIAN, ANTONIO, *and* GONZALO.]

Yet again? What do you here? Shall we give o'er and
drown? Have you a mind to sink?

Sebastian.

A pox o' your throat, you bawling, blasphemous, in-
charitable dog!

What impression are you forming of Sebastian and Gonzalo?

Boatswain.

Work you then.

Antonio.

Hang, cur, hang, you whoreson, insolent noisemaker!
We are less afraid to be drowned than thou art.

Gonzalo.

I'll warrant him for drowning,° though the ship were
no stronger than a nutshell and as leaky as an un-
stanched wench.

42. **I'll warrant him for drowning:** I will guarantee that he will not drown. Gonzalo still has the proverb in mind.

Boatswain.

Lay her ahold, ahold! Set her two courses!° Off to sea
again! Lay her off!°

45. **Set her two courses:** Raise another sail.
46. **Lay her off:** turn away from shore; the ship is getting too close to shore.

[*Enter* MARINERS, *wet.*]

Mariners.

All lost! To prayers, to prayers! All lost!   [*Exeunt.*]

Boatswain.

What, must our mouths be cold?°

48. **cold:** full of prayers; as opposed to warm and full of liquor, as the boatswain's mouth is.

Gonzalo.

The King and Prince at prayers! Let's assist them,
For our case is as theirs.

Sebastian.   I am out of patience.

Antonio.

We are merely° cheated of our lives by drunkards.
This wide-chopped° rascal—would thou mightst lie drowning
The washing of ten tides!°

Gonzalo.   He'll be hanged yet,
Though every drop of water swear against it
55   And gape at wid'st to glut° him.

[*A confused noise within*]

"Mercy on us—
We split, we split!—Farewell, my wife and children!—
Farewell, brother!—We split, we split, we split!"
[*Exit* BOATSWAIN.]

Antonio.

Let's all sink with the King.

Sebastian.   Let's take leave of him.
[*Exeunt* ANTONIO *and* SEBASTIAN.]

Gonzalo.

Now would I give a thousand furlongs of sea for an
60   acre of barren ground—long heath, brown furze, anything. The wills above be done, but I would fain die a
dry death.   [*Exit.*]

The storm has gotten so violent that even Gonzalo is ready to admit defeat. How would you indicate the increasing force of the tempest throughout Scene 1?

A SEASTORM, PIETER BRUEGHEL THE ELDER (c. 1525–1569).

Saskia/Art Resource, New York

Summary of Act 1, Scene 2. *Miranda questions her father Prospero about his motives for causing the tempest. Reassuring Miranda that all aboard the ship are safe, Prospero tells her that he is the former Duke of Milan, whose throne was taken from him by his scheming brother Antonio with the support of Alonso, King of Naples. He explains that they had been cast into the sea, where they floated until they reached this enchanted island. A wise old counselor, Gonzalo, had aided them with food, clothing, and books.*

Prospero puts Miranda to sleep, then questions Ariel, a spirit who is in bondage to him, about the storm. When Ariel begs for his freedom, Prospero reminds Ariel that he had released him from a cruel punishment imposed by Sycorax, the witch who had once ruled the island, and that Ariel's debt to Prospero for his deliverance has not been fully repaid. Prospero summons his slave Caliban, Sycorax's son. Caliban curses Prospero, whom he despises and fears.

Ariel brings Ferdinand, Prince of Naples, forth from the shipwreck. It is Prospero's wish that Miranda and Ferdinand will fall in love, but he first intends to test him to see if he is worthy of Miranda's love.

Scene 2. *The island. Before* PROSPERO's *cell.*

[*Enter* PROSPERO *and* MIRANDA.]

Miranda.
    If by your art, my dearest father, you have
    Put the wild waters in this roar, allay them.
    The sky, it seems, would pour down stinking pitch
    But that the sea, mounting to the welkin's° cheek,
5   Dashes the fire out. O, I have suffered
    With those that I saw suffer! A brave vessel
    (Who had no doubt some noble creature in her)
    Dashed all to pieces! O, the cry did knock
    Against my very heart! Poor souls, they perished!
10   Had I been any god of power, I would
    Have sunk the sea within the earth or ere
    It should the good ship so have swallowed and
    The fraughting souls° within her.

Prospero.   Be collected.
    No more amazement. Tell your piteous heart
15   There's no harm done.

Miranda.   O, woe the day!

Prospero.   No harm.
    I have done nothing but in care of thee,
    Of thee, my dear one, thee my daughter, who
    Art ignorant of what thou art, naught knowing
20   Of whence I am; nor that I am more better
    Than Prospero, master of a full poor cell,
    And thy no greater father.

4. **welkin's:** sky's.

? In what specific ways does Miranda show her compassionate nature in lines 1–13?

13. **fraughting souls:** the human beings the ship carried as freight.

? In this scene, Prospero appears in several of his different roles: magician, father, and duke. As the scene progresses, try to determine which role is dominant. What makes you say so?

Miranda.   More to know
Did never meddle with my thoughts.

Prospero.   'Tis time
I should inform thee farther. Lend thy hand
25   And pluck my magic garment from me. So,

[*Takes off his magic robe.*]

Lie there, my art.° Wipe thou thine eyes; have
    comfort.
The direful spectacle of the wrack,° which touched
The very virtue of compassion in thee,
I have with such provision° in mine art
30   So safely ordered that there is no soul—
No, not so much perdition° as an hair
Betid° to any creature in the vessel
Which thou heardst cry, which thou sawst sink. Sit
    down;
For thou must now know farther.

Miranda.   You have often
35   Begun to tell me what I am, but stopped
And left me to a bootless° inquisition,
Concluding, "Stay! Not yet."

Prospero.   The hour's now come;
The very minute bids thee ope thine ear.
Obey, and be attentive. Canst thou remember
40   A time before we came unto this cell?
I do not think thou canst, for then thou wast not
Out° three years old.

Miranda.   Certainly, sir, I can.

Prospero.
By what? By any other house or person?
Of anything the image tell me that
45   Hath kept with thy remembrance.

Miranda.   'Tis far off,
And rather like a dream than an assurance
That my remembrance warrants. Had I not
Four or five women once that tended me?

Prospero.
Thou hadst, and more, Miranda. But how is it
50   That this lives in thy mind? What seest thou else
In the dark backward and abysm of time?
If thou remem'brest aught ere thou camest here,
How thou camest here thou mayst.

Miranda.   But that I do not.

26. **my art:** Prospero's cloak is the source of his powerful magic.
27. **wrack:** wreck.

29. **provision:** foreknowledge; foresight.

31. **perdition:** loss.
32. **Betid:** befallen; occurred.

36. **bootless:** useless; futile.

? Shakespeare never describes Prospero's "cell" (line 40) for us. What do you imagine it looks like?

42. **Out:** beyond.

Prospero.
Twelve year since, Miranda, twelve year since,
55 Thy father was the Duke of Milan and
A prince of power.

Miranda.   Sir, are not you my father?

Prospero.
Thy mother was a piece of virtue, and
She said thou wast my daughter; and thy father
Was Duke of Milan; and his only heir
60 A princess—no worse issued.

Miranda.   O the heavens!
What foul play had we that we came from thence?
Or blessed was't we did?

Prospero.   Both, both, my girl!
By foul play, as thou sayst, were we heaved thence,
But blessedly holp° hither.

Miranda.   O, my heart bleeds
65 To think o' the teen° that I have turned you to,
Which is from my remembrance! Please you, farther.

Prospero.
My brother, and thy uncle, called Antonio—
I pray thee mark me—that a brother should
Be so perfidious!—he whom next thyself
70 Of all the world I loved, and to him put
The manage of my state, as at that time
Through all the seignories° it was the first,
And Prospero the prime duke, being so reputed
In dignity, and for the liberal arts
75 Without a parallel; those being all my study,
The government I cast upon my brother
And to my state grew stranger, being transported
And rapt in secret studies—thy false uncle—
Dost thou attend me?

Miranda.   Sir, most heedfully.

Prospero.
80 Being once perfected° how to grant suits,
How to deny them, who t' advance, and who
To trash for overtopping,° new-created
The creatures that were mine, I say, or changed 'em,
Or else new-formed 'em; having both the key
85 Of officer and office, set all hearts i' the state
To what tune pleased his ear, that now he was
The ivy which had hid my princely trunk
And sucked my verdure out on't.° Thou attendst
not!

64. **holp:** helped.

65. **teen:** sorrow.

72. **seignories:** states; dukedoms.

❓ Why did Prospero give over the management of the state to his brother, according to his speech in lines 67–79?

80. **Being once perfected:** once understanding.

82. **trash for overtopping:** inhibit the speed of one that is able to run ahead of the others (e.g., a dog in a pack).

88. **verdure:** power; **on't:** of it.

Miranda.
O, good sir, I do.

Prospero.   I pray thee mark me.
90   I thus neglecting worldly ends, all dedicated
To closeness, and the bettering of my mind
With that which, but by being so retired,
O'erprized all popular rate,° in my false brother
Awaked an evil nature, and my trust,
95   Like a good parent, did beget of him
A falsehood in its contrary as great
As my trust was, which had indeed no limit,
A confidence sans° bound. He being thus lorded,
Not only with what my revenue yielded
100   But what my power might else exact, like one
Who having unto truth, by telling of it,
Made such a sinner of his memory
To credit his own lie, he did believe
He was indeed the Duke, out o' the substitution
105   And executing the outward face of royalty
With all prerogative. Hence his ambition growing—
Dost thou hear?

Miranda.   Your tale, sir, would cure deafness.

Prospero.
To have no screen between this part he played
And him he played it for, he needs will be
110   Absolute Milan.° Me (poor man) my library
Was dukedom large enough! Of temporal royalties°
He thinks me now incapable; confederates°
(So dry he was for sway°) with the King of Naples
To give him annual tribute, do him homage,
115   Subject his coronet to his° crown, and bend
The dukedom yet unbowed (alas, poor Milan!)
To most ignoble stooping.

Miranda.   O the heavens!

Prospero.
Mark his condition, and the event; then tell me
If this might be a brother.

Miranda.   I should sin
120   To think but nobly of my grandmother.
Good wombs have borne bad sons.

Prospero.   Now the condition.
This King of Naples, being an enemy
To me inveterate, hearkens my brother's suit;
Which was, that he, in lieu o' the premises,°
125   Of homage and I know not how much tribute,

92–93. **but by being so retired,/ O'erprized all popular rate:** It (the topic of Prospero's studies) would have been valued above all else if it had been widely known.

98. **sans:** without.

? Prospero's speech in lines 89–107 touches upon one of the key themes in Shakespeare's work: appearance vs. reality. How were appearances—and Antonio's beliefs—different from the reality of the situation, according to Prospero?

110. **Absolute Milan:** sole and legal Duke of Milan.
111. **temporal royalties:** worldly power (to rule).
112. **confederates:** unites in conspiracy.
113. **So dry he was for sway:** so thirsty was he for power.
115. **his coronet:** the Duke of Milan's crown; a coronet was worn by rulers of lower rank than a king. **his:** the King of Naples'.

124. **in lieu o' the premises:** in return for payments of money, according to an agreement.

Should presently extirpate me and mine
Out of the dukedom and confer fair Milan,
With all the honors, on my brother. Whereon,
A treacherous army levied, one midnight
130 Fated to the purpose, did Antonio open
The gates of Milan; and, i' the dead of darkness,
The ministers for the purpose hurried thence
Me and thy crying self.

Miranda.   Alack, for pity!
I, not rememb'ring how I cried out then,
135 Will cry it o'er again. It is a hint°
That wrings mine eyes to't.

135. **hint:** opportunity; occasion.

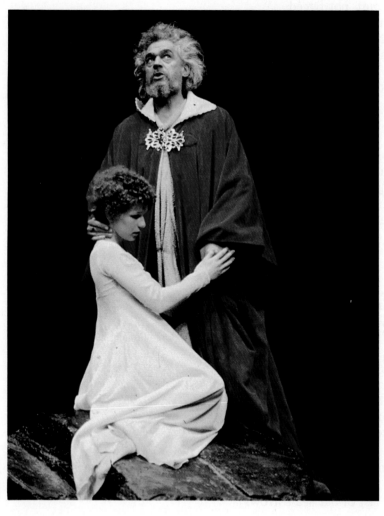

Zoe Dominic

Still from a 1975 production of
***The Tempest* at the Wyndham**
Theater, London.

Prospero. Hear a little further,
And then I'll bring thee to the present business
Which now's upon's; without the which this story
Were most impertinent.

Miranda. Wherefore did they not
140 That hour destroy us?

Prospero. Well demanded, wench.
My tale provokes that question. Dear, they durst
not,
So dear the love my people bore me; nor set
A mark so bloody on the business; but
With colors fairer painted their foul ends.
145 In few, they hurried us aboard a bark,
Bore us some leagues to sea; where they prepared
A rotten carcass of a butt, not rigged,
Nor tackle, sail, nor mast; the very rats
Instinctively have quit it. There they hoist us,
150 To cry to the sea, that roared to us; to sigh
To the winds, whose pity, sighing back again,
Did us but loving wrong.

Miranda. Alack, what trouble
Was I then to you!

Prospero. O, a cherubin
Thou wast that did preserve me! Thou didst smile,
155 Infused with a fortitude from heaven,
When I have decked the sea with drops full salt,
Under my burden groaned; which raised in me
An undergoing stomach,° to bear up
Against what should ensue.

Miranda. How came we ashore?

Prospero.
160 By providence divine.
Some food we had, and some fresh water, that
A noble Neapolitan, Gonzalo,
Out of his charity, who being then appointed
Master of this design, did give us, with
165 Rich garments, linens, stuffs, and necessaries
Which since have steaded much. So, of his gentleness,
Knowing I loved my books, he furnished me
From mine own library with volumes that
I prize above my dukedom.

Miranda. Would I might
170 But ever see that man!

Prospero. Now I arise.
Sit still, and hear the last of our sea-sorrow.

158. **undergoing stomach:** courage to continue; the stomach was thought to be the seat of courage.

? The forces that control human action are dramatized again and again in *The Tempest*. According to Prospero in line 160, what force brought him to the island?

? Explain the irony of Miranda's lines (169–170). What type of irony is it?

Here in this island we arrived; and here
Have I, thy schoolmaster, made thee more profit
Than other princess can, that have more time
175 For vainer hours, and tutors not so careful.

Miranda.
Heavens thank you for't! And now I pray you,
    sir,—
For still 'tis beating in my mind,—your reason
For raising this sea-storm?

Prospero.   Know thus far forth.°
By accident most strange, bountiful Fortune
180 (Now my dear lady)° hath mine enemies
Brought to this shore; and by my prescience°
I find my zenith doth depend upon
A most auspicious star, whose influence
If now I court not, but omit, my fortunes
185 Will ever after droop.° Here cease more questions.
Thou art inclined to sleep. 'Tis a good dullness,
And give it away. I know thou canst not choose.

[MIRANDA *sleeps.*]

Come away, servant, come! I am ready now.
Approach, my Ariel. Come!

[*Enter* ARIEL.]

Ariel.
190 All hail, great master! Grave sir, hail! I come
To answer thy best pleasure; be't to fly,
To swim, to dive into the fire, to ride
On the curled clouds. To thy strong bidding task°
Ariel and all his quality.°

Prospero.   Hast thou, spirit,
195 Performed to point the tempest that I bade thee?

Ariel.
To every article.
I boarded the King's ship. Now on the beak,
Now in the waist, the deck, in every cabin,
I flamed amazement.° Sometime I'ld divide
200 And burn in many places; on the topmast,
The yards, and bowsprit would I flame distinctly,°
Then meet and join. Jove's lightnings, the precursors
O' the dreadful thunderclaps, more momentary
And sight-outrunning were not. The fire and cracks
205 Of sulphurous roaring the most mighty Neptune
Seem to besiege and make his bold waves tremble;
Yea, his dread trident shake.

178. **thus far forth:** this much further.
179–180. **Fortune (Now my dear lady):** Fortune, now being kind to me. Fortune is personified here as a woman.
181. **prescience:** foreknowledge.
182–185. **I find . . . will ever after droop:** I foresee that if I do not act now, while the stars of my horoscope are favorable, I will never have another chance to regain my rightful place.

How would you stage Miranda's falling asleep and Prospero's summoning of Ariel?

Elizabethans believed that all matter was composed of water, fire, air, and earth. How does Ariel's entrance speech (lines 190–194) relate to three of these elements?

193. **task:** give a task to.
194. **quality:** band of fellow spirits.

199. **flamed amazement:** frightened and amazed the men by appearing on the ship in the form of fire.
201. **distinctly:** simultaneously.

How would you have Ariel perform lines 196–207?

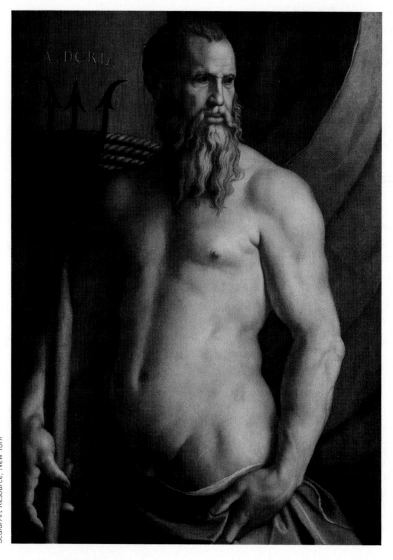

PORTRAIT OF ANDREA DORIA AS NEPTUNE, AGNOLO BRONZINO (1503–1572). *Andrea Doria was a celebrated sixteenth-century Italian admiral and statesman.*

Prospero.   My brave spirit!
Who was so firm, so constant, that this coil°
Would not infect his reason?

Ariel.   Not a soul
210   But felt a fever of the mad° and played
Some tricks of desperation. All but mariners
Plunged in the foaming brine and quit the vessel,
Then all afire with me. The King's son Ferdinand,
With hair up-staring (then like reeds, not hair),
215   Was the first man that leapt; cried "Hell is empty,
And all the devils are here!"

208. **coil:** commotion; confusion.

210. **of the mad:** of madness.

Prospero.   Why, that's my spirit!
But was not this nigh shore?

Ariel.   Close by, my master.

Prospero.
But are they, Ariel, safe?

Ariel.   Not a hair perished.
On their sustaining garments° not a blemish,
220 But fresher than before; and as thou badest me,
In troops I have dispersed them 'bout the isle.
The King's son have I landed by himself,
Whom I left cooling of the air with sighs
In an odd angle of the isle, and sitting,
225 His arms in this sad knot.

Prospero.   Of the King's ship
The mariners say° how thou hast disposed,
And all the rest o' the fleet.

Ariel.   Safely in harbor
Is the King's ship; in the deep nook where once
Thou calledst me up at midnight to fetch dew
230 From the still-vexed Bermoothes,° there she's hid;
The mariners all under hatches stowed,
Who, with a charm joined to their suff'red labor,
I have left asleep; and for the rest o' the fleet,
Which I dispersed, they all have met again,
235 And are upon the Mediterranean float°
Bound sadly home for Naples,
Supposing that they saw the King's ship wracked
And his great person perish.

Prospero.   Ariel, thy charge
Exactly is performed; but there's more work.
240 What is the time o' the day?

Ariel.   Past the mid season.

Prospero.
At least two glasses.° The time 'twixt six and now
Must by us both be spent most preciously.

Ariel.
Is there more toil? Since thou dost give me pains,
Let me remember thee what thou hast promised,
245 Which is not yet performed me.

Prospero.   How now? moody?
What is't thou canst demand?

Ariel.   My liberty.

Prospero.
Before the time be out? No more!

219. **sustaining garments:** their clothing, which kept them afloat.

225–226. **Of the King's ship/ The mariners say:** Of the King's ship and the mariners, say.

230. **still-vexed Bermoothes:** ever-stormy Bermudas.

235. **float:** sea.

241. **glasses:** turns of the hour-glass; i.e., hours.

Ariel.   I prithee,
      Remember I have done thee worthy service,
      Told thee no lies, made no mistakings, served
250   Without or grudge or grumblings. Thou didst promise
      To bate° me a full year.

251. **bate:** abate; shorten (the length of Ariel's service).

Prospero.   Dost thou forget
      From what a torment I did free thee?

Ariel.   No.

Prospero.
      Thou dost; and thinkst it much to tread the ooze
      Of the salt deep,
255   To run upon the sharp wind of the North,
      To do me business in the veins o' the earth
      When it is baked with frost.

Ariel.   I do not, sir.

Prospero.
      Thou liest, malignant thing! Hast thou forgot
      The foul witch Sycorax, who with age and envy
260   Was grown into a hoop? Hast thou forgot her?

Ariel.
      No, sir.

Prospero. Thou hast. Where was she born?
      Speak! Tell me!

Ariel.
      Sir, in Argier.°

264. **Argier:** Algiers.

Prospero.   O, was she so? I must
265   Once in a month recount what thou hast been,
      Which thou forgetst. This damned witch Sycorax,
      For mischiefs manifold, and sorceries terrible
      To enter human hearing, from Argier
      Thou knowst was banished. For one thing she did
270   They would not take her life. Is not this true?

? "Once in a month," according to Prospero (line 265), Ariel must be reminded of his past suffering. What important information does this speech of Prospero's convey to the audience?

Ariel.
      Ay, sir.

Prospero.
      This blue-eyed° hag was hither brought with child
      And here was left by the sailors. Thou, my slave,
      As thou reportst thyself, wast then her servant;
275   And, for thou wast a spirit too delicate
      To act her earthy and abhorred commands,
      Refusing her grand hests, she did confine thee,
      By help of her more potent ministers,
      And in her most unmitigable rage,
280   Into a cloven pine; within which rift

272. **blue-eyed:** eyes discolored blue, by circles or shadows.

Imprisoned thou didst painfully remain
A dozen years; within which space she died
And left thee there; where thou didst vent thy
    groans
As fast as mill wheels strike. Then was this island
285 (Save for the son that she did litter here,
A freckled whelp, hag-born) not honored with
A human shape.

Ariel.   Yes, Caliban, her son.

Prospero.
Dull thing, I say so! he, that Caliban
Whom now I keep in service. Thou best knowst
290 What torment I did find thee in. Thy groans
Did make wolves howl and penetrate the breasts
Of ever-angry bears. It was a torment
To lay upon the damned, which Sycorax
Could not again undo. It was mine art,
295 When I arrived and heard thee, that made gape
The pine, and let thee out.

Ariel.   I thank thee, master.

Prospero.
If thou more murmurst, I will rend an oak
And peg thee in his knotty entrails till
Thou hast howled away twelve winters.

Ariel.   Pardon, master.
300 I will be correspondent to command°
And do my spriting gently.

Prospero.   Do so; and after two days
I will discharge thee.

Ariel.   That's my noble master!
What shall I do? Say what! What shall I do?

Prospero.
Go make thyself like a nymph o' the sea. Be subject
305 To no sight but thine and mine; invisible
To every eyeball else. Go take this shape
And hither come in't. Go! Hence with diligence!
                              [*Exit* ARIEL.]
Awake, dear heart, awake! Thou hast slept well.
Awake!

Miranda.
310 The strangeness of your story put
Heaviness in me.

Prospero.   Shake it off. Come on.
We'll visit Caliban, my slave, who never

The way that Ariel says the
name "Caliban" in line 287
may betray fear; the two characters are completely alien to each
other—Caliban is of the earth, and
Ariel is of the air. What famous
actors would you choose to play
each role?

300. **I will be correspondent to
    command:** I will obey your
    commands.

How would you dramatize
Ariel's shift in mood in lines
302–303?

What have his interactions with
Ariel revealed about Prospero's
character? Do you like or dislike
Prospero at this point in the play?

Yields us kind answer.

Miranda.   'Tis a villain, sir,
I do not love to look on.

Prospero.   But as 'tis,
We cannot miss° him. He does make our fire,
315 Fetch in our wood, and serves in offices
That profit us. What, ho! slave! Caliban!
Thou earth,° thou! Speak!

Caliban.
(*within*)   There's wood enough within.

Prospero.
Come forth, I say! There's other business for thee.
Come, thou tortoise! When?

[*Enter* ARIEL *like a water nymph.*]

320 Fine apparition! My quaint Ariel,
Hark in thine ear.

Ariel.   My lord, it shall be done.   [*Exit.*]

Prospero.
Thou poisonous slave, got by the Devil himself
Upon thy wicked dam, come forth!

[*Enter* CALIBAN.]

Caliban.
As wicked dew as e'er my mother brushed
325 With raven's feather from unwholesome fen°
Drop on you both! A southwest blow on ye
And blister you all o'er!

Prospero.
For this, be sure, tonight thou shalt have cramps,
Side-stitches that shall pen thy breath up; urchins°
330 Shall, for that vast of night that they may work,
All exercise on thee; thou shalt be pinched
As thick as honeycomb, each pinch more stinging
Than bees that made 'em.

Caliban.   I must eat my dinner.
This island's mine by Sycorax my mother,
335 Which thou takest from me. When thou camest first,
Thou strokedst me and made much of me; wouldst
    give me
Water with berries in't; and teach me how
To name the bigger light, and how the less,
That burn by day, and night; and then I loved thee
340 And showed thee all the qualities o' the isle,
The fresh springs, brine-pits, barren place and fertile.

314. **miss:** get by without.

317. **earth:** piece of the earth; i.e., dirt.

An Elizabethan theater might have featured entrances through trapdoors in the floor of the stage or by pulleys suspended from the ceiling. Which entrance would be most appropriate for Ariel? for Caliban? Why?

325. **fen:** marshland; swamp.

329. **urchins:** goblins that assumed the form of hedgehogs.

How is Prospero's treatment of Caliban similar to his treatment of Ariel? How is it different?

Zoe Dominic

Cursed be I that did so! All the charms
Of Sycorax—toads, beetles, bats light on you!
For I am all the subjects that you have,
Which first was mine own king; and here you sty° me
In this hard rock, whiles you do keep from me
The rest o' the island.

345. **sty:** to lodge, as in a pigpen.

Prospero.   Thou most lying slave,
Whom stripes may move, not kindness! I have used thee
(Filth as thou art) with humane care, and lodged thee
In mine own cell till thou didst seek to violate
The honor of my child.

Caliban.
O ho, O ho! Would't had been done!
Thou didst prevent me; I had peopled else
This isle with Calibans.

What is Caliban's reaction to Prospero's fatherly concern for Miranda (lines 352–354)?

Miranda.   Abhorred slave,
Which any print of goodness wilt not take,
Being capable of all ill! I pitied thee,
Took pains to make thee speak, taught thee each hour
One thing or other. When thou didst not, savage,
Know thine own meaning, but wouldst gabble like
A thing most brutish, I endowed thy purposes

345

350

355

360

With words that made them known. But thy vile
    race,
Though thou didst learn, had that in't which
    good natures
Could not abide to be with. Therefore wast thou
Deservedly confined into this rock, who hadst
365   Deserved more than a prison.

Caliban.
    You taught me language, and my profit on't
    Is, I know how to curse. The red plague rid you
    For learning me your language!

Prospero.   Hag-seed, hence!
    Fetch us in fuel; and be quick, thou'rt best,
370   To answer other business. Shrugst thou, malice?
    If thou neglectst or dost unwillingly
    What I command, I'll rack thee with old° cramps,
    Fill all thy bones with aches, make thee roar
    That beasts shall tremble at thy din.

Caliban.   No, pray thee.
375   (*aside*) I must obey. His art is of such pow'r
    It would control my dam's god, Setebos,°
    And make a vassal of him.

Prospero.   So, slave; hence!

                            [*Exit* CALIBAN.]

[*Enter* FERDINAND; *and* ARIEL, *invisible, playing
and singing.*]

                [ARIEL's *song.*]
        Come unto these yellow sands,
            And then take hands.
380   Curtsied when you have° and kissed,
            The wild waves whist,°
        Foot it featly° here and there;
        And, sweet sprites, the burden bear.
            Hark, hark!

385   [*Burden dispersedly.*°]   Bow, wow!
            The watchdogs bark.

[*Burden dispersedly.*]   Bow, wow!

Ariel.   Hark, hark! I hear
        The strain of strutting chanticleer
390   Cry, cock-a-diddle-dowe.
Ferdinand.
    Where should this music be? I' the air, or the earth?

Some directors and editors give this speech (lines 354–365) to Prospero, arguing that it is too strong for Miranda. Others argue that if she does not speak occasionally, she would not need to be included in this scene. Which position would you side with?

372. **old:** terrible.

376. **Setebos:** a god of the natives of South America, known to Europeans through travelogues.

380. **Curtsied when you have:** when you have curtsied.
381. **whist:** quiet.
382. **featly:** skillfully; gracefully.

385. **dispersedly:** from several different directions.

FERDINAND LURED BY ARIEL, SIR JOHN EVERETT MILLAIS (1826–1896).

The Bridgeman Art Library/Art Resource, New York

It sounds no more; and sure it waits upon
Some god o' the island. Sitting on a bank,
Weeping again the King my father's wrack,
395   This music crept by me upon the waters,
Allaying both their fury and my passion
With its sweet air. Thence I have followed it,
Or it hath drawn me rather; but 'tis gone.
No, it begins again.

             [ARIEL's *song*.]
400   Full fathom five thy father lies;
              Of his bones are coral made;
           Those are pearls that were his eyes;
              Nothing of him that doth fade
           But doth suffer a sea-change
405   Into something rich and strange.
           Sea nymphs hourly ring his knell:

[*Burden.*]   Ding-dong.
          Hark! now I hear them—Ding-dong bell.

Would this song have the same mood and tempo as Ariel's previous one (lines 378–384)? How would you perform each song?

Ferdinand.
The ditty does remember my drowned father.

410 This is no mortal business, nor no sound
That the earth owes.° I hear it now above me.

411. **owes:** owns; possesses.

Prospero.
The fringed curtains of thine eye advance°
And say what thou seest yond.

412. **advance:** draw back.

Miranda.   What is't? a spirit?
Lord, how it looks about! Believe me, sir,

415 It carries a brave form. But 'tis a spirit.

Prospero.
No, wench. It eats, and sleeps, and hath such
    senses
As we have, such. This gallant which thou seest
Was in the wrack; and, but he's something stained
With grief (that's beauty's canker), thou mightst call
    him

420 A goodly person. He hath lost his fellows
And strays about to find 'em.

Miranda.   I might call him
A thing divine, for nothing natural
I ever saw so noble.

How would Miranda deliver lines 421–423? What can you gather about her emotional state at this moment?

423. **It goes on:** My plan progresses.

Prospero (*aside*).   It goes on,° I see,
As my soul prompts it. Spirit, fine spirit! I'll free
    thee

425 Within two days for this.

Ferdinand.   Most sure, the goddess
On whom these airs attend! Vouchsafe my pray'r
May know if you remain upon this island,
And that you will some good instruction give
How I may bear° me here. My prime request,

430 Which I do last pronounce, is (O you wonder!)
If you be maid or no?

429. **bear:** behave; conduct.

Miranda.   No wonder, sir,
But certainly a maid.

Ferdinand.   My language? Heavens!
I am the best° of them that speak this speech,
Were I but where 'tis spoken.

Prospero.   How? the best?

435 What wert thou if the King of Naples heard thee?

433. **the best:** the highest ranking; believing that his father is dead, Ferdinand considers himself to be king.

Ferdinand.
A single thing, as I am now, that wonders
To hear thee speak of Naples. He does hear me;
And that he does I weep. Myself am Naples,

440　Who with mine eyes, never since at ebb, beheld
　　　The King, my father, wracked.

Miranda.　　　　　　　　　　　Alack, for mercy!

Ferdinand.
　　　Yes, faith, and all his lords, the Duke of Milan
　　　And his brave son being twain.

Prospero (*aside*).　　　　　　　The Duke of Milan
　　　And his more braver daughter could control thee,°
　　　If now 'twere fit to do't. At the first sight
445　They have changed eyes.° Delicate Ariel,
　　　I'll set thee free for this!—A word, good sir.
　　　I fear you have done yourself some wrong. A word!

Miranda.
　　　Why speaks my father so ungently? This
　　　Is the third man that e'er I saw; the first
450　That e'er I sighed for. Pity move my father
　　　To be inclined my way!

Ferdinand.　　　　　　　　O, if a virgin,
　　　And your affection not gone forth, I'll make you
　　　The Queen of Naples.

Prospero.　　　　　　　Soft, sir! one word more.
　　　(*aside*) They are both in either's pow'rs. But this
　　　　swift business
455　I must uneasy make, lest too light winning
　　　Make the prize light.—One word more! I charge
　　　　thee
　　　That thou attend me. Thou dost here usurp
　　　The name thou owest not, and hast put thyself
　　　Upon this island as a spy, to win it
460　From me, the lord on't.

Ferdinand.　　　　　　　No, as I am a man!

Miranda.
　　　There's nothing ill can dwell in such a temple.
　　　If the ill spirit have so fair a house,
　　　Good things will strive to dwell with't.

Prospero.　　　　　　　　　　Follow me.—
　　　Speak not you for him; he's a traitor.—Come!
465　I'll manacle thy neck and feet together;
　　　Sea water shalt thou drink; thy food shall be
　　　The fresh brook mussels, withered roots, and husks
　　　Wherein the acorn cradled. Follow.

Ferdinand.　　　　　　　　　　　No.
　　　I will resist such entertainment till
470　Mine enemy has more power.

443. **control thee:** inform you correctly; Prospero knows that all these men are alive and on the island.
445. **changed eyes:** exchanged loving glances.

Why is Prospero accusing Ferdinand of being a spy in lines 457–460, knowing full well that he is not?

[*He draws, and is charmed from moving.*]

Miranda.   O dear father,
Make not too rash a trial of him, for
He's gentle, and not fearful.°

Prospero.   What, I say,
My foot my tutor?°—Put thy sword up, traitor!
Who makest a show but darest not strike, thy con-
    science
475   Is so possessed with guilt. Come, from thy ward!°
For I can here disarm thee with this stick
And make thy weapon drop.

Miranda.   Beseech you, father!

Prospero.
Hence! Hang not on my garments.

Miranda.   Sir, have pity.
I'll be his surety.

Prospero.   Silence! One word more
480   Shall make me chide thee, if not hate thee. What,
An advocate for an impostor? Hush!
Thou thinkst there is no more such shapes as he,
Having seen but him and Caliban. Foolish wench!
To the most of men this is a Caliban,
485   And they to him are angels.

Miranda.   My affections
Are then most humble. I have no ambition
To see a goodlier man.

Prospero.   Come on, obey!
Thy nerves° are in their infancy again
And have no vigor in them.

Ferdinand.   So they are.
490   My spirits, as in a dream, are all bound up.
My father's loss, the weakness which I feel,
The wrack of all my friends, nor this man's threats
To whom I am subdued, are but light to me,
Might I but through my prison once a day
495   Behold this maid. All corners else o' the earth
Let liberty make use of; space enough
Have I in such a prison.

Prospero (*aside*).   It works. (*to* FERDINAND)
Come on.—
Thou hast done well, fine Ariel! (*to* FERDINAND)
Follow me.—
500   (*to* ARIEL) Hark what thou else shalt do me.

472. **He's gentle, and not fearful:** He is a gentleman, not a coward.
473. **My foot my tutor:** My daughter presumes to tell me what to do.

475. **ward:** defensive stance.

Is Prospero really angry in lines 479–485, or is he "acting"? How do you feel about his behavior toward Miranda?

488. **nerves:** muscles.

In lines 497–499, Prospero is delighted that the "magic" of love has bloomed. Has he *caused* Miranda and Ferdinand to fall in love, or merely helped their romance along by throwing them together?

Miranda.   Be of comfort.
My father's of a better nature, sir,
Than he appears by speech. This is unwonted
Which now came from him.

Prospero.   Thou shalt be as free
As mountain winds; but then exactly do
505   All points of my command.

Ariel.   To the syllable.

Prospero.
Come, follow —Speak not for him.   [*Exeunt.*]

First Thoughts

What kind of person is Prospero? In your opinion, what is Prospero's primary ambition—Miranda's happiness, or revenge upon his enemies?

Identifying Facts

1. What is the **setting** of the play's first scene? What is the purpose of the voyage made by the king and his party?

2. Gonzalo believes that the ship's passengers will be saved. What reason does he give?

3. Who were Caliban's parents?

4. Who is Prospero's brother? What has he done to Prospero?

5. What does Prospero reveal to Miranda about his past and about how they came to the island?

6. Where and for how long had Ariel been imprisoned?

7. What happens when Miranda and Ferdinand meet?

Interpreting Meanings

1. Scene 1 presents the **exposition**, or **basic situation**, of the play, giving us a first glimpse of the **characters** of Gonzalo, Antonio, Sebastian, and Alonso. Compare and contrast these characters, listing everything you have learned about them thus far.

2. One critic has suggested that the play's dominant **image** is sound. Give examples of the use of sound **imagery** in Act 1. What effect does this imagery have?

3. What has been unique about Miranda's upbringing? How is she different from other young women?

4. What does Prospero's treatment of Ariel, Caliban, and Miranda reveal about his **character**?

5. Why does Prospero want Miranda and Ferdinand to fall in love?

6. **Theme** is the central idea or insight of a work of literature. One of the major themes of *The Tempest* is that of change or transformation. Give examples from Act 1 of this theme.

Applying Meanings

Important elements of fantasy are introduced in Act 1 of *The Tempest*. Refer to the paragraph you wrote in the Writer's Response (see page 844). Is Prospero's island like another world of fantasy you have seen in a movie or read or heard about? Do the characters of Ariel and Caliban remind you of other fantasy characters? Why do you think this fantasy world—invented nearly four hundred years ago—still appeals to modern readers and audiences?

THE TEMPEST
Act 2

❦ *As you read the second act, notice how the events that make up the* **rising action** *complicate the story. How do the plots against Alonso and Prospero and the comic scene with Caliban help to create suspense?*

Summary of Act 2, Scene 1. *Gonzalo, King Alonso's counselor, tries to console the king for the loss of his son Ferdinand. Sebastian and Antonio are sarcastic about Gonzalo's compassion. Alonso regrets having married his daughter to the King of Tunis, because their ship was destroyed returning home from the wedding. An invisible Ariel casts a spell on all of Alonso's party except* Antonio and Sebastian. Antonio convinces Sebastian that if they assassinate Alonso, Sebastian will become the King of Naples. As they draw their weapons to murder the king, Ariel awakens Gonzalo. Sebastian and Antonio claim that they drew their weapons to fight off wild beasts who were threatening to attack them. The king's party leaves to continue the search for Ferdinand.

═ ACT 2 ═

Scene 1. *Another part of the island.*

[*Enter* ALONSO, SEBASTIAN, ANTONIO, GONZALO, ADRIAN, FRANCISCO, *and others.*]

Gonzalo.
Beseech you, sir, be merry. You have cause
(So have we all) of joy; for our escape
Is much beyond our loss. Our hint° of woe
Is common. Every day some sailor's wife,
5   The master of some merchant, and the merchant,°
Have just our theme of woe; but for the miracle,
I mean our preservation, few in millions
Can speak like us. Then wisely, good sir, weigh
Our sorrow with our comfort.

Alonso.   Prithee peace.

Sebastian.
10   He receives comfort like cold porridge.

Antonio.
The visitor° will not give him o'er so.

3. **hint:** occasion.

5. **merchant:** merchant ship; **the merchant:** the ship's owner.

11. **visitor:** comforter; consoler (Gonzalo).

Sebastian.
    Look, he's winding up the watch of his wit;
    by-and-by it will strike.
Gonzalo.
    Sir—
Sebastian.
15 One. Tell.
Gonzalo.
    When every grief is entertained that's offered,
    Comes to the entertainer—
Sebastian.
    A dollar.
Gonzalo.
    Dolor comes to him, indeed. You have spoken
20 truer than you purposed.
Sebastian.
    You have taken it wiselier than I meant you
    should.
Gonzalo.
    Therefore, my lord—
Antonio.
    Fie, what a spendthrift is he of his tongue!
Alonso.
    I prithee spare.
Gonzalo.
25 Well, I have done. But yet—
Sebastian.
    He will be talking.
Antonio.
    Which, of he or Adrian, for a good wager, first
    begins to crow?
Sebastian.
    The old cock.
Antonio.
30 The cock'rel.°
Sebastian.
    Done! The wager?
Antonio.
    A laughter.°
Sebastian.
    A match!
Adrian.
    Though this island seem to be desert—

? Notice how Gonzalo will not be
  intimidated by the cynical
Antonio and Sebastian and uses
the word *dolor*, which means
sorrow, as a pun on *dollar* (line
19). How does this incident affect
your perception of Gonzalo?

? The mood in this scene is
  tense. What do you imagine is
the tone of each character's
speech? How is Gonzalo's tone
different from Sebastian's and
Antonio's?

30. **cock'rel:** young rooster.

32. **laughter:** the winner gets a
good laugh.

Antonio.

35 Ha, ha, ha!

Sebastian.

So, you're paid.

Adrian.

Uninhabitable and almost inaccessible—

Sebastian.

Yet—

Adrian.

Yet—

Antonio.

40 He could not miss't.

Adrian.

It must needs be of subtle, tender, and delicate
temperance.

Antonio.

Temperance was a delicate wench.

Sebastian.

Ay, and a subtle, as he most learnedly delivered.°

Adrian.

45 The air breathes upon us here most sweetly.

Sebastian.

As if it had lungs, and rotten ones.

Antonio.

Or as 'twere perfumed by a fen.

Gonzalo.

Here is everything advantageous to life.

In what way is Adrian like
Gonzalo? How do Sebastian
and Antonio treat Adrian?

44. **delivered:** proclaimed;
stated.

Antonio.

True; save means to live.

Sebastian.

50 Of that there's none, or little.

Gonzalo.

How lush and lusty the grass looks! how green!

Antonio.

The ground indeed is tawny.

Sebastian.

With an eye of green in't.

Antonio.

He misses not much.

Sebastian.

55 No; he doth but mistake the truth totally.

Gonzalo.

But the rarity of it is—which is indeed almost beyond credit—

Sebastian.

As many vouched° rarities are.

Gonzalo.

That our garments, being, as they were, drenched in
60 the sea, hold, notwithstanding, their freshness and
gloss, being rather new-dyed than stained with salt
water.

Antonio.

If but one of his pockets could speak, would it not
say he lies?

Sebastian.

65 Ay, or very falsely pocket up his report.

Gonzalo.

Methinks our garments are now as fresh as when we
put them on first in Afric, at the marriage of the King's
fair daughter Claribel to the King of Tunis.

Sebastian.

'Twas a sweet marriage, and we prosper well in our
70 return.

Adrian.

Tunis was never graced before with such a paragon to
their queen.

Gonzalo.

Not since widow Dido's° time.

Antonio.

Widow? A pox o' that! How came that "widow" in?
75 Widow Dido!

> How would you direct Antonio
> and Sebastian in this scene?
> Should they deliver their lines as
> playful banter or with heavy
> cynicism?

58. **vouched:** avowed; sworn.

73. **widow Dido's:** In the *Aeneid,*
Dido was the widowed queen
of Carthage (now Tunis) who
fell in love with and was
abandoned by Aeneas.

Sebastian.

What if he had said "widower Aeneas" too?
Good Lord, how you take it!

Adrian.

"Widow Dido," said you? You make me study of that.
She was of Carthage, not of Tunis.

Gonzalo.

80 This Tunis, sir, was Carthage.

Adrian.

Carthage?

Gonzalo.

I assure you, Carthage.

Antonio.

His word is more than the miraculous harp.°

Sebastian.

He hath raised the wall, and houses too.

Antonio.

85 What impossible matter will he make easy next?

Sebastian.

I think he will carry this island home in his pocket
and give it his son for an apple.

Antonio.

And, sowing the kernels of it in the sea, bring forth
more islands.

Gonzalo.

90 Ay!

Antonio.

Why, in good time!

Gonzalo.

Sir, we were talking that our garments seem now as
fresh as when we were at Tunis at the marriage of
your daughter, who is now Queen.

Antonio.

95 And the rarest that e'er came there.

Sebastian.

Bate,° I beseech you, widow Dido.

Antonio.

O, widow Dido? Ay, widow Dido!

Gonzalo.

Is not, sir, my doublet as fresh as the first day I
wore it? I mean, in a sort.

Antonio.

100 That "sort" was well fished for.

83. **the miraculous harp:** According to Ovid, Amphion created the walls of Thebes by playing on his harp; Gonzalo has just "recreated" the ancient city of Carthage out of modern Tunis; therefore, his word is more powerful than the "miraculous harp."

96. **Bate:** except.

? Why do Sebastian and Antonio keep repeating "widow Dido"?

Gonzalo.

    When I wore it at your daughter's marriage.

Alonso.

    You cram these words into mine ears against
    The stomach of my sense. Would I had never
    Married my daughter there! for, coming thence,
105   My son is lost; and, in my rate,° she too,
    Who is so far from Italy removed
    I ne'er again shall see her. O thou mine heir
    Of Naples and of Milan, what strange fish
    Hath made his meal on thee!

Francisco.   Sir, he may live.

110   I saw him beat the surges under him
    And ride upon their backs. He trod the water,
    Whose enmity he flung aside, and breasted
    The surge most swol'n that met him. His bold head
    'Bove the contentious waves he kept, and oared
115   Himself with his good arms in lusty stroke
    To the shore, that o'er his wave-worn basis° bowed,
    As stooping to relieve him. I not doubt
    He came alive to land.

Alonso.   No, no, he's gone.

Sebastian.

    Sir, you may thank yourself for this great loss,
120   That would not bless our Europe with your daugh-
       ter,
    But rather lose her to an African,
    Where she, at least, is banished from your eye
    Who hath cause to wet the grief° on't.

Alonso.   Prithee peace.

Sebastian.

    You were kneeled to and importuned otherwise
125   By all of us; and the fair soul herself
    Weighed, between loathness° and obedience, at
    Which end o' the beam should bow. We have lost
      your son,
    I fear, forever. Milan and Naples have
    Mo° widows in them of this business' making
130   Than we bring men to comfort them.
    The fault's your own.

Alonso.   So is the dear'st o' the loss.

Gonzalo.

    My Lord Sebastian,
    The truth you speak doth lack some gentleness,

105. **rate:** view; opinion.

How does the mood of the scene change when the king speaks in lines 102–109?

116. **his:** the island's; **basis:** beach.

How do you think Sebastian would deliver lines 119–123?

123. **wet the grief:** cry for sadness.

126. **Weighed:** poised; balanced; **loathness:** reluctance.

129. **Mo:** More.

And time° to speak it in. You rub the sore
135   When you should bring the plaster.
Sebastian.   Very well.
Antonio.
        And most chirurgeonly.°
Gonzalo.
        It is foul weather in us all, good sir,
        When you are cloudy.
Sebastian.   Foul weather?
Antonio.   Very foul.
Gonzalo.
        Had I plantation° of this isle, my lord—
Antonio.
140   He'd sow't with nettle seed.
Sebastian.   Or docks, or mallows.
Gonzalo.
        And were the king on't, what would I do?
Sebastian.
        'Scape being drunk, for want of wine.
Gonzalo.
        I' the commonwealth I would by contraries°
        Execute all things; for no kind of traffic°
145   Would I admit; no name of magistrate;
        Letters should not be known; riches, poverty,
        And use of service,° none; contract, succession,
        Bourn, bound of land, tilth,° vineyard, none;
        No use of metal,° corn, or wine, or oil;
150   No occupation; all men idle, all;
        And women too, but innocent and pure;
        No sovereignty.
Sebastian.   Yet he would be king on't.
Antonio.
        The latter end of his commonwealth forgets the be-
        ginning.
Gonzalo.
155   All things in common nature should produce
        Without sweat or endeavor. Treason, felony,
        Sword, pike, knife, gun, or need of any engine°
        Would I not have; but nature should bring forth,
        Of it own kind, all foison,° all abundance,
160   To feed my innocent people.
Sebastian.
        No marrying 'mong his subjects?

134. **time:** appropriate time.

136. **chirurgeonly:** like an accomplished surgeon.

139. **plantation:** authority to colonize.

143. **by contraries:** contrary to the usual manner.
144. **traffic:** trade.

147. **service:** servants.
148. **Bourn:** boundary; **tilth:** agriculture.
149. **metal:** currency; money.

157. **engine:** destructive weapon.

159. **foison:** plentifulness.

Antonio.

None, man! All idle—whores and knaves.

Gonzalo.

I would with such perfection govern, sir,
T'excel the golden age.

Sebastian.   Save his Majesty!

Antonio.

165   Long live Gonzalo!

Gonzalo.   And—do you mark me, sir?

Alonso.

Prithee no more. Thou dost talk nothing to me.

Gonzalo.

I do well believe your Highness; and did it to minister
occasion° to these gentlemen, who are of such sensi-
ble° and nimble lungs that they always use to laugh
170   at nothing.

Antonio.

'Twas you we laughed at.

Gonzalo.

Who in this kind of merry fooling am nothing to you.
So you may continue, and laugh at nothing still.

Antonio.

What a blow was there given!

Sebastian.

175   An it had not fall'n flatlong.°

Gonzalo.

You are gentlemen of brave metal. You would lift the
moon out of her sphere if she would continue in it
five weeks without changing.

[*Enter ARIEL, invisible, playing solemn music.*]

Sebastian.

We would so, and then go a-batfowling.°

Antonio.

180   Nay, good my lord, be not angry.

Gonzalo.

No, I warrant you. I will not adventure my discretion
so weakly.° Will you laugh me asleep, for I am very
heavy?

Antonio.

Go sleep, and hear us.

[*All sleep except* ALONSO, SEBASTIAN, *and*
ANTONIO.]

? What are the characteristics of
Gonzalo's "golden age" (line
164)? What is his purpose in
describing it?

167–168. **minister occasion:** provide occasion for laughter.
168–169. **sensible:** responsive.

175. **An:** if; **flatlong:** on the flat
rather than the edge of a
sword.

179. **a-batfowling:** a technique of
hunting birds at night that
used a bright light (here, the
moon).

181–182. **adventure my discretion so weakly:** risk my reputation as a reasonable man
over such a small matter.

? Ariel is supposed to be
invisible as he moves among
the courtiers, putting them to
sleep. How would you convey his
invisibility to the audience?

Alonso.

185   What, all so soon asleep? I wish mine eyes
    Would, with themselves, shut up my thoughts. I find
    They are inclined to do so.

Sebastian.   Please you, sir
    Do not omit the heavy offer of it.°
    It seldom visits sorrow; when it doth,
190   It is a comforter.

Antonio.   We two, my lord,
    Will guard your person while you take your rest,
    And watch your safety.

Alonso.   Thank you. Wondrous heavy.

[ALONSO *sleeps.*]   [*Exit* ARIEL.]

Sebastian.
    What a strange drowsiness possesses them!

Antonio.
    It is the quality o' the climate.

Sebastian.   Why
195   Doth it not then our eyelids sink? I find not
    Myself disposed to sleep.

Antonio.   Nor I. My spirits are nimble.
    They fell together all, as by consent.
    They dropped as by a thunderstroke. What might,
    Worthy Sebastian—O, what might?—No more!
200   And yet methinks I see it in thy face,
    What thou shouldst be. The occasion speaks thee,°
        and
    My strong imagination sees a crown
    Dropping upon thy head.

Sebastian.   What? Art thou waking?

Antonio.
    Do you not hear me speak?

Sebastian.   I do; and surely
205   It is a sleepy language, and thou speakst
    Out of thy sleep. What is it thou didst say?
    This is a strange repose, to be asleep
    With eyes wide open; standing, speaking, moving—
    And yet so fast asleep.

Antonio.   Noble Sebastian,
210   Thou letst thy fortune sleep—die, rather; winkst
    Whiles thou art waking.

Sebastian.   Thou dost snore distinctly;
    There's meaning in thy snores.

188. **omit the heavy offer of it:** miss the opportunity to sleep.

201. **occasion speaks thee:** opportunity names you.

? What is Antonio getting at in lines 197–203? What is the tone of the following exchange between Sebastian and Antonio?

Antonio.
I am more serious than my custom. You
Must be so too, if heed me; which to do
215   Trebles thee o'er.

Sebastian.   Well, I am standing water.°

Antonio.
I'll teach you how to flow.°

Sebastian.   Do so. To ebb
Hereditary sloth instructs me.

Antonio.   O,
If you but knew how you the purpose cherish
Whiles thus you mock it! how, in stripping it,
220   You more invest it! Ebbing men indeed
(Most often) do so near the bottom run
By their own fear or sloth.

Sebastian.   Prithee say on.
The setting° of thine eye and cheek proclaim
A matter° from thee; and a birth, indeed,
225   Which throes° thee much to yield.

215. **Trebles thee o'er:** triples your wealth and power; **standing water:** quiet, in order to listen carefully.
216. **flow:** move forward (toward wealth and power).

223. **setting:** look; expression.
224. **matter:** significant concern.
225. **throes:** pains.

Still from a 1989 production of *The Tempest* by the Roundabout Theater Company.

Martha Swope

Antonio.   Thus, sir:
    Although this lord of weak remembrance,° this
    Who shall be of as little memory
    When he is earthed, hath here almost persuaded
    (For he's a spirit of persuasion, only
230 Professes to persuade) the King his son's alive,
    'Tis as impossible that he's undrowned
    As he that sleeps here swims.

Sebastian.   I have no hope
    That he's undrowned.

Antonio.   O, out of that no hope
    What great hope have you! No hope that way is
235 Another way so high a hope that even
    Ambition cannot pierce a wink beyond,
    But doubts discovery° there. Will you grant with me
    That Ferdinand is drowned?

Sebastian.   He's gone.

Antonio.   Then tell me,
    Who's the next heir of Naples?

Sebastian.   Claribel.

Antonio.
240 She that is Queen of Tunis; she that dwells
    Ten leagues beyond man's life;° she that from Naples
    Can have no note, unless the sun were post°—
    The man i' the moon's too slow—till newborn chins
    Be rough and razorable; she that from whom
245 We all were sea-swallowed, though some cast° again,
    And, by that destiny, to perform an act
    Whereof what's past is prologue, what to come,
    In yours and my discharge.

Sebastian.   What stuff is this? How say you?
    'Tis true my brother's daughter's Queen of Tunis;
250 So is she heir of Naples; 'twixt which regions
    There is some space.

Antonio.   A space whose ev'ry cubit
    Seems to cry out "How shall that Claribel
    Measure us° back to Naples? Keep in Tunis,
    And let Sebastian wake!" Say this were death
255 That now hath seized them, why, they were no
        worse
    Than now they are. There be that can rule Naples
    As well as he that sleeps; lords that can prate
    As amply and unnecessarily
    As this Gonzalo. I myself could make

226. **this lord of weak remembrance:** Francisco; Antonio does not believe Francisco's story of Ferdinand swimming to safety.

❓ Does Sebastian in lines 232–233 yet fully comprehend Antonio's meaning?

237. **doubts discovery:** does not believe what he (Ambition) sees.

241. **Ten leagues beyond man's life:** i.e., too far away to be of concern.
242. **post:** messenger.

245. **though some cast:** were somehow cast upon the shore.

❓ Lines 247–248 are often quoted. What do they mean? Paraphrase them in your own words.

253. **Measure us:** journey the long distance that the cubits measure. (The cubits are ''speaking'' here.)

A chough of as deep chat.° O, that you bore
The mind that I do! What a sleep were this
For your advancement! Do you understand me?

Sebastian.
Methinks I do.

Antonio.   And how does your content
Tender your own good fortune?

Sebastian.   I remember
265   You did supplant your brother Prospero.

Antonio.   True.
And lock how well my garments sit upon me,
Much feater° than before! My brother's servants
Were then my fellows; now they are my men.

Sebastian.
But, for your conscience—

Antonio.
270   Ay, sir! Where lies that? If 'twere a kibe,°
'Twould put me to° my slipper; but I feel not
This deity in my bosom. Twenty consciences
That stand 'twixt me and Milan, candied be they
And melt, ere they molest!° Here lies your brother,
275   No better than the earth he lies upon
If he were that which now he's like—that's dead;
Whom I with this obedient steel (three inches of it)
Can lay to bed forever; whiles you, doing thus,
To the perpetual wink° for aye might put
280   This ancient morsel, this Sir Prudence, who
Should not upbraid our course. For all the rest,
They'll take suggestion as a cat laps milk;
They'll tell the clock to° any business that
We say befits the hour.

Sebastian.   Thy case, dear friend,
285   Shall be my precedent. As thou gotst Milan,
I'll come by Naples. Draw thy sword. One stroke
Shall free thee from the tribute which thou payest,
And I the King shall love thee.

Antonio.   Draw together;
And when I rear my hand, do you the like,
290   To fall it on Gonzalo.

[*They draw.*]

Sebastian.   O, but one word!

[*They converse apart.*]

[*Enter* ARIEL, *invisible, with music and song.*]

259–260. **make/A chough of as deep chat:** teach a jackdaw to speak as profoundly.

267. **feater:** more neatly or appropriately.

270. **kibe:** a sore or ulcerated spot on the heel.
271. **'Twould put me to:** it would lead me to wear.

274. **melt:** eaten; **molest:** bother me.

What do you imagine Antonio is doing as he speaks lines 270–284?

279. **wink:** sleep.

283. **tell the clock to:** agree it is time for.

Sebastian is finally drawn into the conspiracy in lines 284–288. Has he struggled with his conscience, or readily decided to plot against his brother? How would you dramatize either possibility?

Ariel.
My master through his art foresees the danger
That you, his friend, are in, and sends me forth
(For else his project dies) to keep them living.

[*Sings in* GONZALO's *ear.*]

> While you here do snoring lie,
295   Open-eyed conspiracy
>   His time° doth take.
> If of life you keep a care,
> Shake off slumber and beware.
>   Awake, awake!

296. **time:** chance; opportunity.

Antonio.
300   Then let us both be sudden.

Gonzalo.
[*Wakes.*] Now good angels preserve the King!

Alonso.
[*Wakes.*] Why, how now? Ho, awake! Why are you
    drawn?
Wherefore this ghastly looking?

Gonzalo.   What's the matter?

Sebastian.
Whiles we stood here securing your repose,
305   Even now, we heard a hollow burst of bellowing
Like bulls, or rather lions. Did't not wake you?
It struck mine ear most terribly.

Alonso.   I heard nothing.

If you were directing this play, how would you instruct the actor playing Sebastian to deliver lines 304–307?

Antonio.
O, 'twas a din to fright a monster's ear,
To make an earthquake! Sure it was the roar
310   Of a whole herd of lions.

Alonso.   Heard you this, Gonzalo?

Gonzalo.
Upon mine honor, sir, I heard a humming,
And that a strange one too, which did awake me.
I shaked you, sir, and cried. As mine eyes opened,
I saw their weapons drawn. There was a noise;
315   That's verily.° 'Tis best we stand upon our guard,
Or that we quit this place. Let's draw our weapons.

315. **verily:** true.

Alonso.
Lead off this ground, and let's make further search
For my poor son.

Gonzalo.   Heavens keep him from these beasts!
For he is sure i' the island.

Alonso.   Lead away.

Ariel.
320   Prospero my lord shall know what I have done.
      So, King, go safely on to seek thy son.

                              [*Exeunt.*]

The entire party prepares to leave. How might the exit be handled? How would Sebastian and Antonio act, considering their narrow escape?

Summary of Act 2, Scene 2.   *On another part of the island, Caliban is gathering wood for Prospero and cursing his master. When Trinculo appears, Caliban, thinking that he might be one of Prospero's spirits sent to plague him, lies down to hide. A storm has just passed and another is about to begin. Trinculo, thinking there is no other shelter, hides under Caliban's cloak, though he is disgusted by the monster's smell and appearance. Stephano, another victim of the shipwreck, enters drunkenly and sees the strange combination of Caliban and Trinculo. In his drunken stupor, he thinks he has discovered a rare monster with two heads and four legs. He gives each of the "heads" some wine. Trinculo and Stephano renew their acquaintance, and Caliban, quite drunk, pledges allegiance to Stephano as his new master. They then go off to explore the island which is to be Stephano's new kingdom, believing that the rest of the ship's party were killed in the storm.*

Scene 2. *Another part of the island.*

[*Enter* CALIBAN *with a burden of wood. A noise of thunder heard.*]

Caliban.
      All the infections that the sun sucks up
      From bogs, fens, flats, on Prosper fall and make him
      By inchmeal° a disease! His spirits hear me,
      And yet I needs must curse. But they'll nor pinch,
5   Fright me with urchin-shows, pitch me i' the mire,
      Nor lead me, like a firebrand,° in the dark
      Out of my way, unless he bid 'em; but
      For every trifle are they set upon me;
      Sometime like apes that mow° and chatter at me,
10   And after bite me; then like hedgehogs which
      Lie tumbling in my barefoot way and mount
      Their pricks at my footfall; sometime am I
      All wound with adders, who with cloven tongues
      Do hiss me into madness.

[*Enter* TRINCULO.]

3. **By inchmeal:** inch by inch.

6. **firebrand:** will-o'-the-wisp.

9. **mow:** grimace; make faces.

How would you have Caliban deliver this soliloquy (lines 1–14): coldly and matter-of-factly, or with heated anger?

Lo, now, lo!

15 Here comes a spirit of his, and to torment me
For bringing wood in slowly. I'll fall flat;
Perchance he will not mind° me.

17. **mind:** see.

[*Lies down.*]
Trinculo.
Here's neither bush nor shrub to bear off any weather
at all, and another storm brewing. I hear it sing i' the
20 wind. Yond same black cloud, yond huge one, looks
like a foul bombard° that would shed his liquor. If it
should thunder as it did before, I know not where to
hide my head. Yond same cloud cannot choose but
fall by pailfuls. What have we here? a man or a fish?
25 dead or alive? A fish: he smells like a fish; a very
ancient and fishlike smell; a kind of, not of the newest,
poor John.° A strange fish! Were I in England now, as
once I was, and had but this fish painted,° not a
holiday fool there but would give a piece of silver.
30 There would this monster make a man.° Any strange
beast there makes a man. When they will not give a
doit° to relieve a lame beggar, they will lay out ten to
see a dead Indian. Legged like a man! and his fins like
arms! Warm, o' my troth! I do now let loose my
35 opinion, hold it no longer: this is no fish, but an
islander, that hath lately suffered by a thunderbolt.
[*Thunder.*] Alas, the storm is come again! My best way
is to creep under his gaberdine. There is no other
shelter hereabout. Misery acquaints a man with
40 strange bedfellows. I will here shroud° till the dregs
of the storm be past.

21. **bombard:** a jug made of leather.

What do you imagine Trinculo is doing as he speaks these lines?

27. **poor John:** a type of fish that has been dried and salted.
28. **painted:** painted on a sign for a sideshow.
30. **make a man:** make one a rich man.

32. **doit:** a coin that was worth very little.

40. **shroud:** take cover.

[*Creeps under* CALIBAN's *garment.*]

[*Enter* STEPHANO, *singing; a bottle in his hand.*]
Stephano.
I shall no more to sea, to sea;
Here shall I die ashore.

This is a very scurvy tune to sing at a man's funeral.°
45 Well, here's my comfort.

[*Drinks.*]
The master, the swabber, the boatswain, and I,
The gunner, and his mate,
Loved Mall, Meg, and Marian, and Margery,
But none of us cared for Kate.

What do you imagine Caliban's costume looks like?

44. **scurvy:** low; vile; **funeral:** Stephano thinks Trinculo is dead.

The three characters of Scene 2—Stephano, Trinculo, and Caliban— are now assembled. What is the general tone of this scene?

THE TEMPEST (detail), WILLIAM HOGARTH (1697–1764).
Does this painting match your image of Caliban? Why or why not?

50 For she had a tongue with a tang,
       Would cry to a sailor "Go hang!"
    She loved not the savor of tar nor of pitch;
    Yet a tailor might scratch her where'er she
          did itch.
    Then to sea, boys, and let her go hang!

55 This is a scurvy tune too; but here's my comfort.

[*Drinks.*]

Caliban.
    Do not torment me! O!

Stephano.
    What's the matter? Have we devils here? Do you put
    tricks upon's with savages and men of Inde,° ha? I
    have not 'scaped drowning to be afeard now of your
60 four legs; for it hath been said, "As proper a man as
    ever went on four legs cannot make him give ground";
    and it shall be said so again, while Stephano breathes
    at nostrils.

Caliban.
    The spirit torments me. O!

58. **Inde:** India.

How would you stage this scene? Remember, Trinculo is still hidden under Caliban.

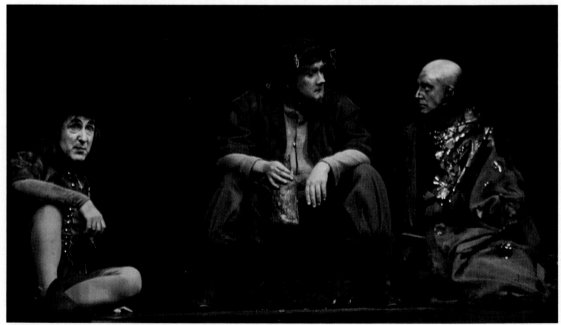

Zoe Dominic

Stephano.

65   This is some monster of the isle, with four legs, who
hath got, as I take it, an ague.° Where the devil should
he learn our language? I will give him some relief, if
it be but for that. If I can recover him, and keep him
tame, and get to Naples with him, he's a present for
70   any emperor that ever trod on neat's° leather.

Caliban.

    Do not torment me prithee! I'll bring my wood home
faster.

Stephano.

    He's in his fit now and does not talk after the wisest.
He shall taste of my bottle. If he have never drunk
75   wine afore, it will go near to remove his fit. If I can
recover him and keep him tame, I will not take° too
much for him; he shall pay for him that hath him, and
that soundly.

Caliban.

    Thou dost me yet but little hurt. Thou wilt anon; I
80   know it by thy° trembling. Now Prosper works upon
thee.

Stephano.

    Come on your ways. Open your mouth. Here is that
which will give language to you, cat.° Open your
mouth. This will shake your shaking, I can tell you,
85   and that soundly. [*Gives* CALIBAN *drink.*] You cannot
tell who's your friend. Open your chaps again.

Trinculo.

    I should know that voice. It should be—but he is
drowned; and these are devils. O, defend me!

Stephano.

    Four legs and two voices—a most delicate monster!
90   His forward voice now is to speak well of his friend;
his backward voice is to utter foul speeches and to
detract. If all the wine in my bottle will recover him,
I will help his ague. Come!

[*Gives drink.*]

    Amen! I will pour some in thy other mouth.

Trinculo.

95   Stephano!

Stephano.

    Doth thy other mouth call me? Mercy, mercy! This is
a devil, and no monster. I will leave him; I have no
long spoon.°

---

66. **ague** (āˈgyo͞oˈ): a fit of shivering.

70. **neat's:** cow's.

? Who or what does Caliban think is tormenting him in line 71?

76. **will not take:** cannot ask.

? According to lines 73–78, what is Stephano's scheme?

80. **thy:** Trinculo's, who is under Caliban's cloak.

83. **cat:** a reference to a proverb that says a drink of liquor can make a cat speak.

98. **long spoon:** alludes to an old proverb that says, "He must have a long spoon that eats with the Devil."

Trinculo.

100 Stephano! If thou beest Stephano, touch me and speak to me; for I am Trinculo—be not afeard—thy good friend Trinculo.

Stephano.

If thou beest Trinculo, come forth. I'll pull thee by the lesser legs. If any be Trinculo's legs, these are they. [*Pulls him out.*] Thou art very Trinculo indeed! How 105 camest thou to be the siege of this mooncalf?° Can he vent Trinculos?

105. **siege:** excrement; **mooncalf:** monstrous creature.

Trinculo.

I took him to be killed with a thunderstroke. But art thou not drowned, Stephano? I hope now thou art not drowned. Is the storm overblown? I hid me under the 110 dead mooncalf's gaberdine for fear of the storm. And art thou living, Stephano? O Stephano, two Neapolitans 'scaped?

What actions do you imagine accompany Trinculo's speech in lines 107–112?

Stephano.

Prithee do not turn me about. My stomach is not constant.

Caliban (*aside*).

115 These be fine things, an if° they be not sprites. That's a brave god and bears celestial liquor. I will kneel to him.

115. **an if:** if.

Stephano.

How didst thou 'scape? How camest thou hither? Swear by this bottle how thou camest hither. I escaped 120 upon a butt of sack° which the sailors heaved o'erboard, by this bottle, which I made of the bark of a tree with mine own hands since I was cast ashore.

120. **butt of sack:** cask of wine.

Caliban.

I'll swear upon that bottle to be thy true subject, for the liquor is not earthly.

Stephano.

125 Here! Swear then how thou escapedst.

Trinculo.

Swum ashore, man, like a duck. I can swim like a duck, I'll be sworn.

Stephano.

Here, kiss the book.° [*Gives him drink.*] Though thou canst swim like a duck, thou art made like a goose.°

128. **the book:** the bottle.
129. **like a goose:** foolish.

Trinculo.

130 O Stephano, hast any more of this?

Stephano.

The whole butt, man. My cellar is in a rock by the seaside, where my wine is hid. How now, mooncalf? How does thine ague?

Caliban.

Hast thou not dropped from heaven?

Stephano.

135   Out o' the moon, I do assure thee. I was the Man i' the Moon when time was.°

Caliban.

I have seen thee in her, and I do adore thee. My mistress showed me thee, and thy dog, and thy bush.°

Stephano.

Come, swear to that; kiss the book. I will furnish it
140   anon with new contents. Swear.

[CALIBAN *drinks.*]

Trinculo.

By this good light, this is a very shallow monster! I afeard of him? A very weak monster! The Man i' the Moon? A most poor credulous monster! Well drawn,° monster, in good sooth.°

Caliban.

145   I'll show thee every fertile inch o' the island; and I will kiss thy foot. I prithee be my god.

Trinculo.

By this light, a most perfidious and drunken monster! When's god's asleep he'll rob his bottle.

Caliban.

I'll kiss thy foot. I'll swear myself thy subject.

Stephano.

150   Come on then. Down, and swear!

Trinculo.

I shall laugh myself to death at this puppyheaded monster. A most scurvy monster! I could find in my heart to beat him—

Stephano.

Come, kiss.

Trinculo.

155   But that the poor monster's in drink. An abominable monster!

Caliban.

I'll show thee the best springs; I'll pluck thee berries;

136. **when time was:** at one time.

138. **thy dog, and thy bush:** those things that the Man in the Moon was said to have with him.

143. **Well drawn:** drawn from the bottle; Caliban took a long drink.
144. **in good sooth:** to be sure; truly.

❓ What about Stephano impresses Caliban? What does he want from Stephano?

❓ How would you describe Stephano's attitude toward Caliban? How would you describe Trinculo's?

Martha Swope

I'll fish for thee, and get thee wood enough.
A plague upon the tyrant that I serve!
160   I'll bear him no more sticks, but follow thee,
Thou wondrous man.

Trinculo.
    A most ridiculous monster, to make a wonder of a
poor drunkard!

Caliban.
    I prithee let me bring thee where crabs° grow;
165   And I with my long nails will dig thee pignuts,
Show thee a jay's nest, and instruct thee how
To snare the nimble marmoset; I'll bring thee
To clust'ring filberts, and sometimes I'll get thee
Young scamels° from the rock. Wilt thou go with me?

Stephano.
170   I prithee now lead the way without any more talking.
Trinculo, the King and all our company else being
drowned, we will inherit here. Here, bear my bottle.
Fellow Trinculo, we'll fill him by-and-by again.

[CALIBAN *sings drunkenly.*]

> In what tone would you have
> Caliban deliver his pledge to
> Stephano (lines 157–161)?

164. **crabs:** crab apples.

169. **scamels:** meaning uncertain;
perhaps a type of seabird.

Caliban.
Farewell, master; farewell, farewell!

Trinculo.
175   A howling monster! a drunken monster!

Caliban.
No more dams I'll make for fish,
      Nor fetch in firing
      At requiring,
Nor scrape trenchering,° nor wash dish.
180   'Ban, 'Ban, Ca—Caliban
      Has a new master. Get a new man.

Freedom, highday! highday, freedom! freedom, highday, freedom!

Stephano.
O brave monster! lead the way.   [*Exeunt.*]

> To what master is Caliban
> bidding farewell in line 174?

179. **trenchering:** A trencher is a
wooden platter on which
food is served.

First Thoughts

Do you find Caliban to be a terrifying or a
pathetic creature? Why?

Identifying Facts

1. At the beginning of Act 2, why is Alonso
   unhappy? What does he regret?
2. What do Antonio and Sebastian plan to
   do to Alonso?
3. What does Ariel do before and after the
   conversation between Sebastian and
   Antonio?
4. What does Stephano think when he
   finds Trinculo and Caliban together?
5. What does Caliban swear to Stephano?
   What does he hope to achieve?

Interpreting Meanings

1. What does Gonzalo's speech in Scene 1
   reveal about his view of human nature?
2. What do we learn about the characters
   of Sebastian and Antonio from their
   treatment of Gonzalo?
3. Using Ariel, Prospero encourages Sebastian and Antonio to plot against the
   king but then frustrates their plans.

Why do you think Shakespeare introduced this twist in the plot?
4. How is Stephano's treatment of Caliban
   similar to Prospero's? How is it different?
5. Note the concrete details in Caliban's
   speech. How does his language show
   that he is a creature of ''earth,'' unlike
   Ariel, who is an ''airy spirit''?
6. Act 2 presents the **rising action** of the
   play. What **complications** are introduced in this act? How do these complications propel the **plot** forward? What
   do you predict will happen next?

Applying Meanings

Although they need him, Stephano and
Trinculo treat Caliban with scorn and contempt. In a similar way, European settlers
in North America considered the Native
Americans to be ''savage,'' since they did
not conform to European values and behavior. Think of your own behavior and
feelings when meeting someone exotic,
frightening, or just ''different.'' How have
you treated that person?

The Tempest, Act 2   **889**

THE TEMPEST
Act 3

❚❙ *The plot reaches a* climax *in the third act. As you read the following scenes, identify the* turning point(s) *of the plot.*

Summary of Act 3, Scene 1. *Prospero has decided to test Ferdinand's love for Miranda by requiring him to collect wood. Miranda takes pity on Ferdinand and offers to help* *him. They pledge their love for one another. Prospero, who has been secretly watching, is pleased that his plan is progressing so well.*

═ ACT 3 ═══════════

Scene 1. *Before* PROSPERO's *cell.*

[*Enter* FERDINAND, *bearing a log.*]
Ferdinand.
　　There be some sports are painful, and their labor
　　Delight in them sets off; some kinds of baseness
　　Are nobly undergone, and most poor matters
　　Point to rich ends. This my mean task
5　　Would be as heavy to me as odious, but
　　The mistress which I serve quickens° what's dead
　　And makes my labors pleasures. O, she is
　　Ten times more gentle than her father's crabbed;
　　And he's composed of harshness! I must remove
10　　Some thousands of these logs and pile them up,
　　Upon a sore injunction.° My sweet mistress
　　Weeps when she sees me work, and says such base-
　　　　ness
　　Had never like executor. I forget;
　　But these sweet thoughts do even refresh my labors.
15　　Most busy least when I do it.°

[*Enter* MIRANDA; *and* PROSPERO, *behind, unseen.*]
Miranda.　　　　　　　　　　　　Alas, now pray you
　　Work not so hard! I would the lightning had
　　Burnt up those logs that you are enjoined to pile!
　　Pray set it down and rest you. When this burns,
　　'Twill weep° for having wearied you. My father

❓ Consider how Ferdinand delivers lines 1–15 as he alternates between comments about Miranda and her father, Prospero. What changes in tone would you expect?

6. **quickens:** enlivens.

11. **sore injunction:** harsh command.

15. **Most busy least when I do it:** At my busiest moments, thoughts of Miranda make my work seem like nothing.

19. **weep:** The log will drip sap as it burns.

20 Is hard at study; pray now rest yourself;
He's safe for these three hours.

Ferdinand.   O most dear mistress,
The sun will set before I shall discharge
What I must strive to do.

Miranda.   If you'll sit down,
I'll bear your logs the while. Pray give me that.
25 I'll carry it to the pile.

Ferdinand.   No, precious creature.
I had rather crack my sinews, break my back,
Than you should such dishonor undergo
While I sit lazy by.

Miranda.   It would become me
As well as it does you; and I should do it
30 With much more ease; for my good will is to it,
And yours it is against.

Prospero (*aside*).   Poor worm, thou art infected!
This visitation shows it.

Miranda.   You look wearily.

Ferdinand.
No, noble mistress. 'Tis fresh morning with me
When you are by at night. I do beseech you,
35 Chiefly that I might set it in my prayers,
What is your name?

Miranda.   Miranda. O my father,
I have broke your hest° to say so!

Ferdinand.   Admired° Miranda!
Indeed the top of admiration, worth
What's dearest to the world! Full many a lady
40 I have eyed with best regard, and many a time
The harmony of their tongues hath into bondage
Brought my too diligent ear; for several virtues
Have I liked several women; never any
With so full soul but some defect in her
45 Did quarrel with the noblest grace she owed,°
And put it to the foil;° but you, O you,
So perfect and so peerless, are created
Of every creature's best!

Miranda.   I do not know
One of my sex; no woman's face remember,
50 Save, from my glass, mine own; nor have I seen
More that I may call men than you, good friend,
And my dear father. How features are abroad
I am skill-less of;° but, by my modesty

❓ Remembering that Prospero has planned for Miranda to fall in love with Ferdinand, how do you imagine Prospero would say line 31?

37. **hest:** injunction; command; **Admired:** *Miranda* means "wonderful," "admirable" in Latin.

❓ How do you think Ferdinand would pronounce the name of his new love in line 37? How should Miranda react to having her name pronounced?

45. **owed:** possessed.
46. **put it to the foil:** ruined or destroyed it.

53. **am skill-less of:** have no knowledge of.

The Tempest, Act 3, Scene 1   **891**

(The jewel in my dower), I would not wish
55 Any companion in the world but you;
Nor can imagination form a shape,
Besides yourself, to like of.° But I prattle
Something too wildly, and my father's precepts
I therein do forget.

Ferdinand.   I am, in my condition,
60 A prince, Miranda; I do think, a king
(I would not so!), and would no more endure
This wooden slavery° than to suffer
The flesh fly blow° my mouth. Hear my soul speak!
The very instant that I saw you, did
65 My heart fly to your service, there resides,

57. **like of:** liken to.

62. **wooden slavery:** enslavement as a wood hauler.
63. **blow:** lay its eggs in.

❓ Why would Ferdinand wish he
were not a king?

Martha Swope

To make me slave to it; and for your sake
Am I this patient log-man.

Miranda. Do you love me?

Ferdinand.
O heaven, O earth, bear witness to this sound,
And crown what I profess with kind event°
70 If I speak true! if hollowly, invert
What best is boded° me to mischief! I,
Beyond all limit of what else i' the world,
Do love, prize, honor you.

Miranda. I am a fool
To weep at what I am glad of.

Prospero (aside). Fair encounter
75 Of two most rare affections! Heavens rain grace
On that which breeds between 'em!

Ferdinand. Wherefore weep you?

Miranda.
At mine unworthiness, that dare not offer
What I desire to give, and much less take
What I shall die to want.° But this is trifling;
80 And all the more it seeks to hide itself,
The bigger bulk it shows. Hence, bashful cunning!
And prompt me plain and holy innocence!
I am your wife, if you will marry me;
If not, I'll die your maid. To be your fellow°
85 You may deny me; but I'll be your servant,
Whether you will or no.

Ferdinand. My mistress, dearest!
And I thus humble ever.

Miranda. My husband then?

Ferdinand.
Ay, with a heart as willing
As bondage e'er of freedom. Here's my hand.

Miranda.
90 And mine, with my heart in't; and now farewell
Till half an hour hence.

Ferdinand. A thousand thousand!°

[*Exeunt* FERDINAND *and* MIRANDA *severally.*°]

Prospero.
So glad of this as they I cannot be,
Who are surprised withal; but my rejoicing
At nothing can be more. I'll to my book;
95 For yet ere suppertime must I perform
Much business appertaining. [*Exit.*]

69. **kind event:** positive outcome.

71. **boded:** destined.

79. **to want:** for lack of.

84. **fellow:** partner; wife.

? Do you find it surprising that Miranda is the one to propose to Ferdinand? How do you think she would deliver this speech (lines 77–86)? Bashfully? Confidently?

91. **A thousand thousand:** a thousand farewells. **severally:** in different directions.

? Why is Prospero not as "glad of this" (line 92) as Miranda and Ferdinand are?

Summary of Act 3, Scene 2. *Caliban, Trinculo, and Stephano have become quite drunk. Caliban begins to think of Stephano as a "god," and urges him to murder Prospero so that he, Caliban, can be set free, and that Stephano can then rule the island, with Miranda as his queen. Stephano agrees to the plan. Ariel, invisible, has overheard the plot, and with beautiful music diverts them from their plans.*

Scene 2. *Another part of the island.*

[*Enter* CALIBAN, STEPHANO, *and* TRINCULO.]

Stephano.
Tell not me! What the butt is out we will drink water; not a drop before. Therefore bear up and board 'em!° Servant monster, drink to me.

Trinculo.
5 Servant monster? The folly° of this island! They say there's but five upon this isle. We are three of them. If the other two be brained like us, the state totters.

Stephano.
Drink, servant monster, when I bid thee. Thy eyes are almost set° in thy head.

Trinculo.
10 Where should they be set else? He were a brave monster indeed if they were set in his tail.

Stephano.
My man-monster hath drowned his tongue in sack. For my part, the sea cannot drown me. I swam, ere I could recover the shore, five-and-thirty leagues off and on, by this light. Thou shalt be my lieutenant, monster,
15 or my standard.°

Trinculo.
Your lieutenant, if you list; he's no standard.°

Stephano.
We'll not run, Monsieur Monster.

Trinculo.
Nor go neither; but you'll lie like dogs, and yet say nothing neither.

Stephano.
20 Mooncalf, speak once in thy life, if thou beest a good mooncalf.

Caliban.
How does thy honor? Let me lick thy shoe. I'll not serve him; he is not valiant.

Trinculo.
Thou liest, most ignorant monster! I am in case° to

2. **bear up and board 'em:** keep drinking!

4. **folly:** fool.

Caliban, Stephano, and Trinculo have been sharing a cask of wine since they met and, by now, they are quite drunk. Explain the joke about the state of the island's affairs (lines 4–6).

8. **set:** glazed over (from drink).

15. **standard:** standard-bearer.

16. **list:** please; **standard:** one who can stand up.

Another, more common, meaning of the word *list* is "to tilt or incline to one side." How does this double meaning give line 16 a comic twist?

What is the irony of Caliban pledging to serve the drunken Stephano in lines 22–23? Do you think Stephano will make a better master for him than Prospero?

24. **in case:** in condition.

25 justle a constable. Why, thou deboshed fish thou, was
there ever man a coward that hath drunk so much
sack as I today? Wilt thou tell a monstrous lie, being
but half a fish and half a monster?

Caliban.

Lo, how he mocks me! Wilt thou let him, my lord?

Trinculo.

30 "Lord" quoth he? That a monster should be such a
natural!°

31. **natural:** idiot.

Caliban.

Lo, lo, again! Bite him to death I prithee.

Stephano.

Trinculo, keep a good tongue in your head. If you
prove a mutineer—the next tree! The poor monster's
35 my subject, and he shall not suffer indignity.

Stephano, now emboldened by drink and Caliban's attentions, threatens Trinculo with hanging from "the next tree" (line 34). What is ironic about Stephano's treatment of his friend, Trinculo, and of Caliban?

Caliban.

I thank my noble lord. Wilt thou be pleased
To hearken once again to the suit I made to thee?

Stephano.

Marry, will I. Kneel and repeat it; I will stand, and so
shall Trinculo.

[*Enter* ARIEL, *invisible.*]

Caliban.

40 As I told thee before, I am subject to a tyrant,
A sorcerer, that by his cunning hath
Cheated me of the island.

Do you think Caliban's lines 40–42 are a fair description of Prospero?

Ariel.

Thou liest.

Caliban.   Thou liest, thou jesting monkey thou!
I would my valiant master would destroy thee.
45 I do not lie.

Ariel has been carefully watching this exchange under the cover of invisibility. What happens when he speaks out in line 43? Who does Caliban think has spoken?

Stephano.

Trinculo, if you trouble him any more in's tale, by this
hand, I will supplant some of your teeth.

Trinculo.

Why, I said nothing.

Stephano.

Mum then, and no more.—Proceed.

Caliban.

50 I say by sorcery he got this isle;
From me he got it. If thy greatness will
Revenge it on him—for I know thou darest,
But this thing dare not—

Stephano.

That's most certain.

Caliban.

55   Thou shalt be lord of it, and I'll serve thee.

Stephano.

How now shall this be compassed?
Canst thou bring me to the party?

Caliban.

Yea, yea, my lord! I'll yield him thee asleep,
Where thou mayst knock a nail into his head.

Ariel.

60   Thou liest; thou canst not.

Caliban.

What a pied ninny's this! Thou scurvy patch!°
I do beseech thy greatness give him blows
And take his bottle from him. When that's gone,
He shall drink naught but brine, for I'll not show
    him

65   Where the quick freshes° are.

Stephano.

Trinculo, run into no further danger. Interrupt the
monster one word further and, by this hand, I'll turn
my mercy out o' doors and make a stockfish° of
thee.

Trinculo.

70   Why, what did I? I did nothing. I'll go farther off.

Stephano.

Didst thou not say he lied?

Ariel.

Thou liest.

Stephano.

Do I so? Take thou that!

[*Strikes* TRINCULO.]

As you like this, give me the lie° another time.

Trinculo.

75   I did not give thee the lie. Out o' your wits, and hearing
too? A pox o' your bottle! This can sack and drinking
do. A murrain° on your monster, and the Devil take
your fingers!

Caliban.

Ha, ha, ha!

Stephano.

80   Now forward with your tale.—Prithee stand further off.

> **?** What does Caliban think he stands to gain from his new lord (line 55)?

61. **pied:** multicolored (refers to a jester's colorful costume); **patch:** fool; jester.

65. **quick freshes:** fresh-water springs.

68. **stockfish:** dried fish that is beaten to make it more tender.

74. **give me the lie:** call me a liar.

77. **murrain:** disease; plague.

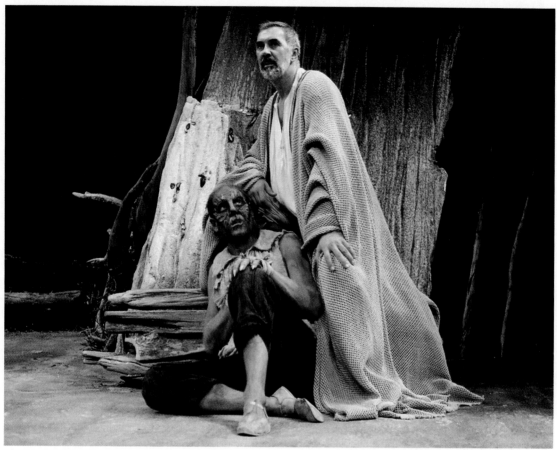

Martha Swope

Caliban.
 Beat him enough. After a little time
 I'll beat him too.

Stephano.   Stand farther.—Come, proceed.

Caliban.
 Why, as I told thee, 'tis a custom with him
85 I' the afternoon to sleep. There thou mayst
   brain him,
 Having first seized his books, or with a log
 Batter his skull, or paunch° him with a stake,
 Or cut his weasand° with thy knife. Remember
 First to possess his books; for without them
90 He's but a sot, as I am, nor hath not

87. **paunch:** stab in the stomach.
88. **weasand:** windpipe.

One spirit to command. They all do hate him
As rootedly as I. Burn but his books.
He has brave utensils° (for so he calls them)
Which, when he has a house, he'll deck withal.
95 And that most deeply to consider is
The beauty of his daughter. He himself
Calls her a nonpareil.° I never saw a woman
But only Sycorax my dam and she;
But she as far surpasseth Sycorax
100 As great'st does least.

Stephano.   Is it so brave a lass?

Caliban.
Ay, lord. She will become thy bed, I warrant, And
bring thee forth brave brood.

Stephano.
Monster, I will kill this man. His daughter and I will
be king and queen, save our Graces! and Trinculo and
105 thyself shall be viceroys. Dost thou like the plot,
Trinculo?

Trinculo.
Excellent.

Stephano.
Give me thy hand. I am sorry I beat thee; but while
thou livest, keep a good tongue in thy head.

Caliban.
110 Within this half hour will he be asleep.
Wilt thou destroy him then?

Stephano.   Ay, on mine honor.

Ariel.
This will I tell my master.

Caliban.
Thou makest me merry; I am full of pleasure.
Let us be jocund. Will you troll the catch°
115 You taught me but whilere?°

Stephano.
At thy request, monster, I will do reason,° any reason.
Come on, Trinculo, let us sing.

[*Sings.*]
          Flout 'em and scout 'em
          And scout 'em and flout 'em!
120   Thought is free.

Caliban.
That's not the tune.

? Why are Prospero's books (line 92) so important to Caliban?

93. **utensils:** furnishings.

97. **nonpareil:** being unparalleled; unequaled.

? Where do you think Ariel is during this entire scene? Does he move around much? How do you imagine he reacts to Caliban's plan of action and persuasive speeches?

? What finally persuades Stephano to act (lines 103–106)? How do you think Trinculo states his agreement to join Caliban and Stephano? Heartily? Moodily? What does Trinculo stand to gain from this plot?

114. **troll the catch:** sing the round.
115. **whilere:** a short time ago.
116. **do reason:** perform any reasonable request.

? Why might the song sung by Stephano and Trinculo (lines 118–120) be a source of pleasure to Caliban?

[ARIEL *plays the tune on a tabor° and pipe.*]

Stephano.

    What is this same?

Trinculo.

    This is the tune of our catch, played by the picture of
    Nobody.°

Stephano.

125   If thou beest a man, show thyself in thy likeness. If
    thou beest a devil, take 't° as thou list.

Trinculo.

    O, forgive me my sins!

Stephano.

    He that dies pays all debts. I defy thee.
    Mercy upon us!

Caliban.

130   Art thou afeard?

Stephano.

    No, monster, not I.

Caliban.

    Be not afeard. The isle is full of noises,
    Sounds, and sweet airs that give delight and hurt
      not.
    Sometimes a thousand twangling instruments
135   Will hum about mine ears; and sometime voices
    That, if I then had waked after long sleep,
    Will make me sleep again; and then, in dreaming,
    The clouds methought would open and show riches
    Ready to drop upon me, that, when I waked,
140   I cried to dream again.

Stephano.

    This will prove a brave kingdom to me, where
    I shall have my music for nothing.

Caliban.

    When Prospero is destroyed.

Stephano.

    That shall be by-and-by. I remember the story.

Trinculo.

145   The sound is going away. Let's follow it, and after do
    our work.

Stephano.

    Lead, monster; we'll follow. I would I could see this
    taborer! He lays it on.

Trinculo.

    Wilt come? I'll follow Stephano.   [*Exeunt.*]

---

tabor: small drum.

? What is the reaction of the characters to the music? Wonder? Fear? Interest?

123–124. **picture of Nobody:** a traditional picture of a man with head, arms, and legs, but no body. Trinculo means an invisible person.

126. **take 't:** do.

? What does Caliban's description of the island voices (lines 132–140) reveal about his character? Does he seem to be entirely a monster here?

Summary of Act 3, Scene 3. *Wearied by their efforts to find Ferdinand, the king and his party sit down to rest. As Antonio and Sebastian renew their assassination plot, an unusual spectacle is presented to the party. Ariel, disguised as a harpy (part woman, part bird), presents the illusion of a banquet to the king's party. He chastises them for their wrongdoings, and warns them to repent and change their lives. Alonso, filled with grief, runs from the others and vows to find Ferdinand. The faithful old Gonzalo follows him, afraid that Alonso may do something foolish.*

Scene 3. *Another part of the island.*

[*Enter* ALONSO, SEBASTIAN, ANTONIO, GONZALO, ADRIAN, FRANCISCO, *etc.*]

Gonzalo.
By'r Lakin,° I can go no further, sir!
My old bones ache. Here's a maze trod indeed
Through forthrights and meanders. By your patience,
I needs must rest me.

Alonso. Old lord, I cannot blame thee,
5   Who am myself attached with weariness
To the dulling of my spirits. Sit down and rest.
Even here I will put off my hope, and keep it
No longer for my flatterer. He is drowned
Whom thus we stray to find; and the sea mocks
10   Our frustrate search on land. Well, let him go.

Antonio.
(*aside to* SEBASTIAN) I am right glad that he's so out
   of hope.
Do not for one repulse forego the purpose
That you resolved t' effect.

Sebastian. (*aside to* ANTONIO) The next advantage
15   Will we take throughly.

Antonio.
(*aside to* SEBASTIAN) Let it be tonight;
For, now they are oppressed with travel, they
Will not nor cannot use such vigilance
As when they are fresh.

Sebastian.
20   (*aside to* ANTONIO) I say tonight. No more.

[*Solemn and strange music; and* PROSPERO *on the top, invisible.*]

Alonso.
What harmony is this? My good friends, hark!

1. **By'r Lakin:** by our Ladykin (an oath invoking the Virgin Mary).

❓ Of what "advantage" is Sebastian speaking in lines 14–15? How do you feel about these two characters when they speak in whispered asides?

Gonzalo.
Marvelous sweet music!

[*Enter several strange* SHAPES, *bringing in a banquet; and dance about it with gentle actions of salutations; and, inviting the King, etc., to eat, they depart.*]

Alonso.
Give us kind keepers, heavens! What were these?

Sebastian.
A living drollery.° Now I will believe
25   That there are unicorns; that in Arabia
There is one tree, the phoenix' throne, one phoenix
At this hour reigning there.

Antonio.   I'll believe both;
And what does else want credit, come to me,
And I'll be sworn 'tis true. Travelers ne'er did lie,
30   Though fools at home condemn 'em.

Gonzalo.   If in Naples
I should report this now, would they believe me?
If I should say, I saw such islanders
(For certes° these are people of the island),
Who, though they are of monstrous shape, yet, note,
35   Their manners are more gentle, kind, than of
Our human generation you shall find
Many—nay, almost any.

Prospero (*aside*).   Honest lord,
Thou hast said well; for some of you there present
Are worse than devils.

Alonso.   I cannot too much muse°
40   Such shapes, such gesture, and such sound, expressing
(Although they want the use of tongue) a kind
Of excellent dumb discourse.

Prospero (*aside*).   Praise in departing.°

Francisco.
They vanished strangely.

Sebastian.   No matter, since
They have left their viands behind; for we have
stomachs.
45   Will't please you taste of what is here?

Alonso.   Not I.

Gonzalo.
Faith, sir, you need not fear. When we were boys,
Who would believe that there were mountaineers

What do you imagine these Shapes look like? Are they ghostly or animal-like? Knowing the characters' personalities as you do, how do you think they will each react to the appearance of the Shapes and the sound of their music?

24. **drollery:** puppet show.

33. **certes:** certainly.

Of whom is Prospero speaking in this aside (lines 37–39)? Why does he need to say this as an aside?

39. **muse:** wonder at.

42. **Praise in departing:** refers to an old proverb that says it is wise to withhold judgment until a matter is concluded.

Dewlapped° like bulls, whose throats had hanging at
    'em
.Wallets of flesh? or that there were such men
50   Whose heads stood in their breasts?° which now
        we find
Each putter-out of five for one° will bring us
Good warrant° of.

Alonso.   I will stand to, and feed;
    Although my last, no matter, since I feel
    The best is past. Brother, my lord the Duke,
55   Stand to, and do as we.

[*Thunder and lightning. Enter* ARIEL, *like a harpy;°
claps his wings upon the table; and with a quaint°
device the banquet vanishes.*]

Ariel.
    You are three men of sin, whom destiny—
    That hath to instrument° this lower world
    And what is in't—the never-surfeited sea
    Hath caused to belch up you, and on this island,
60   Where man doth not inhabit—you 'mongst men
    Being most unfit to live. I have made you mad;
    And even with suchlike valor men hang and drown
    Their proper selves.

[ALONSO, SEBASTIAN, *etc., draw their swords.*]
                    You fools! I and my fellows
    Are ministers of Fate. The elements,
65   Of whom your swords are tempered, may as well
    Wound the loud winds, or with bemocked-at stabs
    Kill the still-closing waters, as diminish
    One dowle° that's in my plume. My fellow ministers
    Are like invulnerable. If you could hurt,
70   Your swords are now too massy° for your strengths
    And will not be uplifted. But remember
    (For that's my business to you) that you three
    From Milan did supplant good Prospero;
    Exposed unto the sea, which hath requit it,°
75   Him and his innocent child; for which foul deed
    The powers, delaying (not forgetting), have
    Incensed the seas and shores, yea, all the creatures,
    Against your peace. Thee of thy son, Alonso,
    They have bereft; and do pronounce by me
80   Ling'ring perdition° (worse than any death
    Can be at once) shall step by step attend
    You and your ways; whose wraths to guard you
        from,

48. **Dewlapped:** A dewlap is a loose fold of flesh that hangs from the throat.

50. **Whose heads stood in their breasts:** a sight often reported in travel books.

51. **putter-out of five for one:** Before leaving, voyagers would deposit a sum of money with the merchant they worked for, and would receive five times that amount on their return.

52. **Good warrant:** affirmation.

harpy: a hideous creature of mythology with the head and trunk of a woman and the wings and talons of a bird.
quaint: clever.

57. **hath to instrument:** controls.

? How do you think this speech (lines 56–63) should be delivered by Ariel? Forcefully? Arrogantly? Angrily? How do you think his harpy costume will make his speech more effective?

68. **dowle:** small feather.

70. **massy:** massive; heavy.

74. **requit it:** revenged the deed.

? What do you think is the purpose of Ariel's speech in lines 56–85? What are some of the key words? What do these words suggest to you?

80. **perdition:** ruin.

Which here, in this most desolate isle, else falls
Upon your heads, is nothing but heart's sorrow
85   And a clear life ensuing.°

[*He vanishes in thunder; then, to soft music, enter the*
SHAPES *again, and dance, with mocks and mows,° and*
carrying out the table.]

Prospero.
(*aside*) Bravely the figure of this harpy hast thou
Performed, my Ariel; a grace it had, devouring.°
Of my instruction hast thou nothing bated°
In what thou hadst to say. So, with good life°
90   And observation strange, my meaner° ministers
Their several kinds° have done. My high charms
        work,
And these, mine enemies, are all knit up
In their distractions.° They now are in my pow'r;
And in these fits I leave them, while I visit
95   Young Ferdinand, whom they suppose is drowned,
And his and mine loved darling.   [*Exit above.*]

Gonzalo.
I' the name of something holy, sir, why stand you
In this strange stare?

Alonso.   O, it is monstrous, monstrous!
Methought the billows spoke and told me of it;
100 The winds did sing it to me; and the thunder,
That deep and dreadful organ pipe, pronounced
The name of Prosper. It did bass my trespass.°
Therefore my son i' the ooze is bedded; and
I'll seek him deeper than e'er plummet sounded
105 And with him there lie mudded.   [*Exit.*]

Sebastian.   But one fiend at a time,
I'll fight their legions o'er!

Antonio.   I'll be thy second.

[*Exeunt* SEBASTIAN *and* ANTONIO.]

Gonzalo.
All three of them are desperate. Their great guilt,
Like poison given to work a great time after,
Now 'gins to bite the spirits. I do beseech you,
110 That are of suppler joints, follow them swiftly
And hinder them from what this ecstasy°
May now provoke them to.

Adrian.   Follow, I pray you.
                [*Exeunt omnes.°*]

84–85. **nothing but heart's sor-
row/And a clear life ensuing:**
only sincere repentance and
living moral lives (can save
you from destruction).
mocks and mows: move-
ments and faces expressing
derision and disgust.

87. **a grace it had, devouring:**
Ariel, as the harpy, per-
formed gracefully, especially
when causing the banquet to
vanish.
88. **bated:** omitted.
89. **life:** realism.
90. **observation strange:** remarkable; **meaner:** inferior;
of lower rank.
91. **several kinds:** individual as-
signments.
92–93. **knit up/In their distractions:** ensnared in madness.

102. **bass my trespass:** speak of
my sin (in a deep voice).

❓ What did Alonso hear in the
thunder (lines 98–105)? What
is his intention as he runs in
madness from the stage? Do
Sebastian and Antonio rush from
the stage with the same intentions?

❓ Why are Gonzalo and Adrian
not affected by the madness of
Ariel's spell?

111. **ecstasy:** madness.

omnes: all.

The Tempest, Act 3, Scene 3   **903**

First Thoughts

Did you find either of the conspiracies in this act suspenseful? Why or why not?

Identifying Facts

1. What task does Prospero set for Ferdinand? Why?

2. What happens when Ferdinand and Miranda meet in the forest?

3. What does Caliban convince Stephano to do? Why does Stephano agree to act on Caliban's plan?

4. How does Ariel use a magical banquet to confuse the conspirators? What does he say when the banquet disappears?

Interpreting Meanings

1. Do you think Caliban's complaints about Prospero are justified? Is Caliban a sympathetic character? Explain.

2. In what ways is Prospero a godlike figure?

3. In Act 3, Scene 2, how does Shakespeare keep the comedy from turning serious as the characters discuss murder and abduction?

4. How is Scene 3 parallel to Scene 2? What is the effect of a "serious" scene following a comic scene?

5. How is the magic banquet **symbolic**?

6. *The Tempest* really contains three related plots: one romantic, one comic, and one political. Summarize these three plots in the play thus far. How does each plot reach a **climax**, or **turning point**, in Act 3?

Applying Meanings

Prospero's learning gives him his power and sets him above Caliban and the rest of the characters in the drama. Caliban tells his companions to destroy Prospero's books. Bookburning and censorship have occurred at different times in different societies. Does Caliban have a point in wanting to destroy Prospero's books? Is too much learning a dangerous thing? Or do you think that learning is necessary for society to function well?

THE TEMPEST
Act 4

▌ *Notice what happens after the climax, during the* **falling**
▌ **action** *of the play. How are the various subplots each*
▌ *approaching a resolution?*

Summary of Act 4, Scene 1. *Prospero, pleased with Ferdinand, promises him Miranda's hand in marriage. Ariel is ordered to prepare a masque, a special kind of entertainment. Spirit figures representing the goddesses Iris, Ceres, and Juno bless the young lovers and promise them a happy marriage. Suddenly, Prospero interrupts the festivities when he remembers Caliban's conspiracy against him. Ariel reports that the three conspirators were last seen dancing by a pond, and he is told to lure them to Prospero's cell with showy garments. Caliban is impatient with Stephano and Trinculo, who are delighted by the finery, and pushes them to go through with the murder of Prospero. Prospero and Ariel call forth spirits and goblins to pursue and torment the conspirators.*

═ ACT 4 ═══════════

Scene 1. *Before* PROSPERO's *cell.*

[*Enter* PROSPERO, FERDINAND, *and* MIRANDA.]

Prospero.
   If I have too austerely punished you,
   Your compensation makes amends; for I
   Have given you here a third° of mine own life,
   Or that for which I live; who once again
5 I tender° to thy hand. All thy vexations
   Were but my trials of thy love, and thou
   Hast strangely° stood the test. Here, afore heaven,
   I ratify this my rich gift. O Ferdinand,
   Do not smile at me that I boast her off,°
10 For thou shalt find she will outstrip all praise
   And make it halt behind her.

Ferdinand.   I do believe it
   Against an oracle.°

Prospero.
   Then, as my gift, and thine own acquisition
   Worthily purchased, take my daughter. But

❓ How is the mood now immediately different from that of the preceding scene?

3. **a third:** i.e., his daughter Miranda.

5. **tender:** present.

7. **strangely:** surpassingly.

9. **boast her off:** speak so highly of her.

12. **Against an oracle:** even if an oracle should proclaim against it.

The Tempest, Act 4, Scene 1   **905**

15   If thou dost break her virgin-knot before
       All sanctimonious° ceremonies may
       With full and holy rite be minist'red,
       No sweet aspersion° shall the heavens let fall
       To make this contract grow;° but barren hate,
20   Sour-eyed disdain, and discord shall bestrew
       The union of your bed with weeds so loathly
       That you shall hate it both. Therefore take heed,
       As Hymen's° lamp shall light you!

Ferdinand.   As I hope
       For quiet days, fair issue, and long life,
25   With such love as 'tis now, the murkiest den,
       The most opportune place, the strong'st suggestion°
       Our worser genius can,° shall never melt
       Mine honor into lust, to take away
       The edge of that day's celebration
30   When I shall think or Phoebus'° steeds are foundered
       Or Night kept chained below.

Prospero.   Fairly spoke.
       Sit then and talk with her; she is thine own.
       What, Ariel! my industrious servant, Ariel!

[*Enter* ARIEL.]

Ariel.
       What would my potent master? Here I am.

Prospero.
35   Thou and thy meaner fellows your last service
       Did worthily perform; and I must use you
       In such another trick. Go bring the rabble,
       O'er whom I give thee pow'r, here to this place.
       Incite them to quick motion; for I must
40   Bestow upon the eyes of this young couple
       Some vanity° of mine art. It is my promise,
       And they expect it from me.

Ariel.   Presently?

Prospero.
       Ay, with a twink.

Ariel.
       Before you can say "Come" and "Go,"
45   And breathe twice and cry, "So, so,"
       Each one, tripping on his toe,
       Will be here with mop and mow.°
       Do you love me master? No?

Prospero.
       Dearly, my delicate Ariel. Do not approach

16. **sanctimonious:** blessed; holy.

18. **aspersion:** blessing (literally, a sprinkling).
19. **grow:** be fruitful.

23. **Hymen's:** Hymen, the Greek god of marriage.

26. **suggestion:** temptation.
27. **Our worser genius can:** our evil angel can offer.

30. **or:** either; **Phoebus:** the Greek god who carried the sun across the sky in his horse-drawn chariot.

How would you describe the tone of this exchange between Prospero and Ferdinand (lines 23–33)? Stern? Friendly? Respectful?

41. **vanity:** demonstration.

47. **mop and mow:** gesture and grimace.

50 Till thou dost hear me call.

Ariel.   Well! I conceive.°   [*Exit.*]

Prospero.
Look thou be true. Do not give dalliance°
Too much the rein. The strongest oaths are straw
To the fire i' the blood. Be more abstemious,
Or else good night your vow!

Ferdinand.   I warrant you, sir.
55 The white cold virgin snow upon my heart
Abates the ardor of my liver.°

Prospero.   Well.
Now come, my Ariel! Bring a corollary°
Rather than want a spirit. Appear, and pertly!
No tongue! All eyes! Be silent.

[*Soft music.*]

[*Enter* IRIS.°]

Iris.
60 Ceres, most bounteous lady, thy rich leas°
Of wheat, rye, barley, fetches, oats, and pease;
Thy turfy mountains, where live nibbling sheep,
And flat meads thatched with stover,° them to keep;
Thy banks with pioned and twilled° brims,
65 Which spongy April at thy hest betrims
To make cold nymphs chaste crowns; and thy
    broom° groves,
Whose shadow the dismissed bachelor loves,
Being lasslorn; thy pole-clipt vineyard;
And thy sea-marge,° sterile and rocky-hard,
70 Where thou thyself dost air—the queen o' the sky,°
Whose wat'ry arch° and messenger am I,
Bids thee leave these, and with her sovereign Grace,

[JUNO *descends.*]

Here on this grass-plot, in this very place,
To come and sport. Her peacocks fly amain;°
75 Approach, rich Ceres, her to entertain.

[*Enter* CERES.]

Ceres.
Hail, many-colored messenger, that ne'er
Dost disobey the wife of Jupiter,
Who, with thy saffron wings, upon my flow'rs
Diffusest honey drops, refreshing show'rs,
80 And with each end of thy blue bow dost crown

50. **conceive:** understand.

51. **dalliance:** caressing;
fondling.

56. **liver:** thought to be the seat
of passion.

57. **corollary:** extra (spirit).

Iris: Greek goddess of the
rainbow.

60. **Ceres:** Roman goddess of agriculture; **leas:** fields.

63. **stover:** hay or grass.

64. **pioned and twilled:** undercut
banks held in place by
branches woven together.

66. **broom:** a shrub bearing yellow flowers.

69. **sea-marge:** seashore.

70. **queen o' the sky:** the Roman
goddess Juno, whose hus-
band Jupiter ruled the skies.

71. **wat'ry arch:** rainbow.

74. **amain:** speedily.

? Juno is able to literally
descend through a trap door in
the floor of the stage, a common
device in Elizabethan theater. Her
descent would be slow, to suggest
both the dignity of her rank and a
sense of movement in a rather
static scene. What differences do
you notice in the language and
tone of each goddess' speech?

French tapestry illustrating the musical arts. *Songs were an important device in Shakespeare's drama, serving both to entertain the audience and to create a particular mood.*

My bosky acres and my unshrubbed down,°
Rich scarf to my proud earth—why hath thy queen
Summoned me hither to this short-grassed green?

Iris.
A contract of true love to celebrate
85   And some donation freely to estate
On° the blest lovers.

Ceres.   Tell me, heavenly bow,
If Venus or her son, as thou dost know,
Do now attend the queen. Since they did plot
The means that dusky Dis° my daughter got,
90   Her and her blind boy's° scandaled company
I have forsworn.

Iris.   Of her society
Be not afraid. I met her Deity
Cutting the clouds towards Paphos,° and her son
Dove-drawn with her. Here thought they to have
    done

95   Some wanton charm upon this man and maid,
Whose vows are, that no bed-right shall be paid
Till Hymen's torch be lighted; but in vain.
Mars's hot minion° is returned again;
Her waspish-headed° son has broke his arrows,
100   Swears he will shoot no more, but play with spar-
    rows
And be a boy right out.

[*Enter* JUNO.]

Ceres.   Highest queen of state,
Great Juno, comes; I know her by her gait.

Juno.
How does my bounteous sister? Go with me
To bless this twain, that they may prosperous be
105   And honored in their issue.

[*They sing.*]

Juno.
Honor, riches, marriage blessing,
Long continuance, and increasing,
Hourly joys be still° upon you!
Juno sings her blessings on you.

Ceres.
110   Earth's increase, foison° plenty,

Barns and garners never empty,
Vines with clust'ring bunches growing,
Plants with goodly burden bowing;
Spring come to you at the farthest
115   In the very end of harvest!°
Scarcity and want shall shun you,
Ceres' blessing so is on you.

Ferdinand.
This is a most majestic vision, and
Harmonious charmingly. May I be bold
120   To think these spirits?

Prospero.   Spirits, which by mine art
I have from their confines called to enact
My present fancies.

Ferdinand.   Let me live here ever!
So rare a wond'red father and a wise
Makes this place Paradise.

[JUNO *and* CERES *whisper, and send* IRIS *on employment.*]

Prospero.   Sweet now, silence!
125   Juno and Ceres whisper seriously.
There's something else to do. Hush and be mute,
Or else our spell is marred.

Iris.
You nymphs, called Naiads, of the wind'ring°
    brooks,
With your sedged crowns and ever-harmless looks,
130   Leave your crisp channels, and on this green land
Answer your summons. Juno does command.
Come, temperate nymphs, and help to celebrate
A contract of true love. Be not too late.

[*Enter certain* NYMPHS.]
You sunburned sicklemen, of August weary,
135   Come hither from the furrow and be merry.
Make holiday. Your rye-straw hats put on,
And these fresh nymphs encounter every one
In country footing.

[*Enter certain* REAPERS, *properly habited.*° *They join
with the* NYMPHS *in a graceful dance; towards the end
whereof* PROSPERO *starts suddenly and speaks; after
which, to a strange, hollow, and confused noise, they
heavily*° *vanish.*]

114–115. **Spring come . . .
harvest:** May spring come
for you immediately after
autumn.

How do you think Prospero
reacts to Ferdinand's expression of wonder in lines 122–124?
Is he flattered? Annoyed?
Indifferent?

128. **wind'ring:** winding, or perhaps wandering.

habited: dressed.

heavily: unwillingly.

Prospero.

(*aside*) I had forgot that foul conspiracy

140 Of the beast Caliban and his confederates

Against my life. The minute of their plot

Is almost come.—(*to the* SPIRITS) Well done!

Avoid!° No more!

Ferdinand.

This is strange. Your father's in some passion

145 That works him strongly.

Miranda. Never till this day

Saw I him touched with anger so distempered.

Prospero.

You do look, my son, in a moved sort,

As if you were dismayed. Be cheerful, sir.

Our revels now are ended. These our actors,

? What has made Prospero so upset in lines 139–143?

143. **Avoid:** Away with you.

? Lines 145–146 are the first time Miranda has spoken in this scene. Why do you think she has been silent up till now?

Giraudon/Art Resource, New York

JUNO ASCENDING TO HEAVEN IN HER CHARIOT, CHRÉTIEN LEGOUAIS, fourteenth century.

150	As I foretold you, were all spirits and
	Are melted into air, into thin air;
	And, like the baseless fabric of this vision,
	The cloud-capped towers, the gorgeous palaces,
	The solemn temples, the great globe itself,
155	Yea, all which it inherit, shall dissolve,
	And, like this insubstantial pageant faded,
	Leave not a rack° behind. We are such stuff
	As dreams are made on, and our little life
	Is rounded with a sleep. Sir, I am vexed.
160	Bear with my weakness. My old brain is troubled.
	Be not disturbed with my infirmity.
	If you be pleased, retire into my cell
	And there repose. A turn or two I'll walk
	To still my beating mind.

157. **rack:** cloud.

> Some critics consider this speech (lines 147–164) Shakespeare's "farewell to the stage." What in this speech, in terms of tone and language, suggests this interpretation?

165 **Ferdinand.** ⎫
 Miranda. ⎭ We wish your peace.　　　　 [*Exeunt.*]

[*Enter* ARIEL.]

Prospero.
　Come with a thought! I thank thee, Ariel.
　　Come.

Ariel.
　Thy thoughts I cleave to. What's thy pleasure?

Prospero.
　Spirit, we must prepare to meet with Caliban.

Ariel.
　Ay, my commander. When I presented Ceres,
170　I thought to have told thee of it, but I feared
　Lest I might anger thee.

Prospero.
　Say again, where didst thou leave these varlets?°

172. **varlets:** rascals.

Ariel.
　I told you, sir, they were redhot with drinking;
　So full of valor that they smote the air
175　For breathing in their faces, beat the ground
　For kissing of their feet; yet always bending
　Towards their project. Then I beat my tabor;
　At which like unbacked° colts they pricked their
　　ears,
　Advanced their eyelids, lifted up their noses
180　As they smelt music. So I charmed their ears
　That calf-like they my lowing followed through
　Toothed briers, sharp furzes, pricking goss,° and
　　thorns,

178. **unbacked:** unbroken; never ridden.

182. **goss:** gorse, a prickly shrub.

Which ent'red their frail shins. At last I left them
I' the filthy mantled pool° beyond your cell,
There dancing up to the chins, that the foul lake
O'erstunk their feet.

Prospero.   This was well done, my bird.
Thy shape invisible retain thou still.
The trumpery° in my house, go bring it hither
For stale° to catch these thieves.

Ariel.   I go, I go.   [*Exit.*]

Prospero.
A devil, a born devil, on whose nature
Nurture° can never stick! on whom my pains,
Humanely taken, all, all lost, quite lost!
And as with age his body uglier grows,
So his mind cankers.° I will plague them all,
Even to roaring.

[*Enter ARIEL, loaden with glistening apparel, etc.*]
                    Come, hang them on this line.°

[PROSPERO *and* ARIEL *remain, invisible.*]

[Enter CALIBAN, STEPHANO, *and* TRINCULO, *all wet.*]
Caliban.
Pray you tread softly, that the blind mole may not
Hear a foot fall. We now are near his cell.

Stephano.
Monster, your fairy, which you say is a harmless fairy,
has done little better than played the Jack° with us.

Trinculo.
Monster, I do smell all horse-piss, at which my nose
is in great indignation.

Stephano.
So is mine. Do you hear, monster? If I should take a
displeasure against you, look you—

Trinculo.
Thou wert but a lost monster.

Caliban.
Good my lord, give me thy favor still.
Be patient, for the prize I'll bring thee to
Shall hoodwink this mischance.° Therefore speak
    softly.
All's hushed as midnight yet.

Trinculo.
Ay, but to lose our bottles in the pool—

184. **filthy mantled pool:** scum-covered pond.

188. **trumpery:** showy, yet worthless, things.
189. **stale:** bait.

191. **Nurture:** training; education.

194. **cankers:** becomes infested with hate and ugliness.

195. **line:** linden or lime tree.

A scene leading up to the murder of a king should be one of suspense, but this scene is very comical. What strikes you as comical in this scene?

199. **Jack:** trickster.

207. **hoodwink this mischance:** erase this misfortune.

Stephano.

210   There is not only disgrace and dishonor in that, monster, but an infinite loss.

Trinculo.

    That's more to me than my wetting. Yet this is your harmless fairy, monster.

Stephano.

215   I will fetch off my bottle, though be o'er ears° for my labor.

Caliban.

    Prithee, my king, be quiet. Seest thou here?
    This is the mouth o' the cell. No noise, and enter.
    Do that good mischief which may make this island
    Thine own forever, and I, thy Caliban,
220   For aye thy foot-licker.

Stephano.

    Give me thy hand. I do begin to have bloody
      thoughts.

Trinculo.

    O King Stephano! O peer! O worthy Stephano, look
    what a wardrobe here is for thee!

Caliban.

    Let it alone, thou fool! It is but trash.

Trinculo.

225   O ho, monster! we know what belongs to a frippery.°
    O King Stephano!

Stephano.

    Put off that gown, Trinculo. By this hand, I'll have that
    gown!

Trinculo.

    Thy Grace shall have it.

Caliban.

230   The dropsy drown this fool! What do you mean
    To dote thus on such luggage? Let't alone,
    And do the murder first. If he awake,
    From toe to crown he'll fill our skins with pinches,
    Make us strange stuff.

Stephano.

235   Be you quiet, monster. Mistress line, is not this my
    jerkin? [*Takes it down.*] Now is the jerkin under the
    line. Now, jerkin, you are like to lose your hair and
    prove a bald jerkin.°

Trinculo.

    Do, do! We steal by line and level, an't like your Grace.

214. **fetch off:** get back; **o'er ears:** over my ears (in pond water).

? Why are Stephano and Trinculo so distressed? What do their complaints suggest about their dedication to murdering Prospero?

? The phrase "good mischief" (line 218) is an example of an oxymoron, or contradiction. What does Caliban mean by "good mischief"? Who will benefit from it?

? Line 221 may be an allusion to Shakespeare's tragedy *Macbeth*, in which Macbeth also has bloody thoughts before murdering King Duncan. What is ironic about this allusion here?

? Line 222 is where Caliban's plans go wrong. What happens? What distracts Stephano and Trinculo from their goal of killing Prospero?

225. **frippery:** used-clothes shop.

? How do you imagine Stephano and Trinculo reacting to the discovery of the "frippery" in lines 225–229? How would you stage their discovery to its full comic effect?

236–238. **jerkin:** jacket; **under the line . . . bald jerkin:** under the linden tree, with a pun; "under the line" also meant "south of the equator." Sailors on such voyages sometimes contracted diseases that resulted in hair loss.

Stephano.

240   I thank thee for that jest. Here's a garment for't. Wit
    shall not go unrewarded while I am king of this coun-
    try. "Steal by line and level" is an excellent pass of
    pate.° There's another garment for't.

Trinculo.

    Monster, come put some lime° upon your fingers, and
245   away with the rest!

Caliban.

    I will have none on't. We shall lose our time
    And all be turned to barnacles,° or to apes
    With foreheads villainous low.

Stephano.

    Monster, lay-to your fingers. Help to bear this away
250   where my hogshead of wine is, or I'll turn you out of
    my kingdom. Go to, carry this.

Trinculo.

    And this.

Stephano.

    Ay, and this.

[*A noise of hunters heard. Enter divers* SPIRITS *in
shape of dogs and hounds, hunting them about,*
PROSPERO *and* ARIEL *setting them on.*]

Prospero.

    Hey, Mountain, hey!

Ariel.

255   Silver! there it goes, Silver!

Prospero.

    Fury, Fury! There, Tyrant, there! Hark, hark!

[CALIBAN, STEPHANO, *and* TRINCULO *are driven out.*]

    Go, charge my goblins that they grind their joints
    With dry convulsions, shorten up their sinews
    With aged cramps,° and more pinch-spotted make
      them
260   Than pard or cat o' mountain.°

Ariel.   Hark, they roar.

Prospero.

    Let them be hunted soundly. At this hour
    Lie at my mercy all mine enemies.
    Shortly shall all my labors end, and thou
    Shalt have the air at freedom. For a little
265   Follow, and do me service.

[*Exeunt.*]

243. **pate:** wit; cleverness.

244. **lime:** a sticky substance, often said to be on thieves'
hands.

247. **barnacles:** geese that were
believed to grow from the
shellfish.

? How do you imagine the staging of the trapping of Caliban,
Stephano, and Trinculo? Is it
chaotically or skillfully done?
How do you imagine the Spirits
could be made to appear like
dogs?

? Do you think Caliban, Trinculo,
and Stephano deserve such
pain as punishment (lines 257–
260)?

259. **aged cramps:** the pains and
discomforts that accompany
old age.
260. **pard:** leopard; **cat o' mountain:** wildcat.

First Thoughts

Do you think Prospero has succeeded in revenging himself against all of the conspirators—both those who exiled him and those who planned to kill him and Alonso?

Identifying Facts

1. What entertainment do Ariel and his spirits provide? Who is honored by the entertainment?

2. Why does Prospero stop the festivities?

3. How are Trinculo and Stephano baited by Prospero and Ariel? What does Prospero do at the end of the act? What does he promise to Ariel?

Interpreting Meanings

1. Some critics have said that the masque in Act 4 is merely a transitional device that does little to further the plot. Do you agree? Why or why not?

2. What are the **tone** and **mood** of the masque?

3. Compare Caliban's behavior in Act 4 with his earlier behavior in the presence of Trinculo and Stephano.

4. By the end of Act 4, it is clear that Prospero has succeeded in all of his aims but one. His daughter is betrothed, and the two murder plots have been thwarted. What is there still left for him to do?

5. **Falling action** occurs in the fourth act of a Shakespearean play, after the **turning point**. Some critics refer to "fourth-act fatigue," in which the fourth act is seen mainly as a "catching-up" act which simply explores the effects of the climax on the various characters and marks time while the characters figure out what to do next. Do you think that Act 4 of *The Tempest* simply "marks time"? Why or why not?

Applying Meanings

The masque is presented to honor Ferdinand and Miranda, and to celebrate their betrothal. It also honored King James's daughter and her bridegroom, who witnessed a performance of *The Tempest* in 1613. Can you think of a modern equivalent of the masque, or of a special entertainment meant to celebrate a wedding, engagement, graduation, or other festive occasion?

THE TEMPEST
Act 5

> In the final act of the play, the political, comic, and romantic aspects of the plot are resolved as the play reaches its conclusion. Pay attention to the events in the **resolution** of the play, and note the order in which they occur. Are all loose ends tied up?

Summary of Act 5, Scene 1. *Prospero asks Ariel about the king's party, all of whom are still spellbound. Ariel reports that even he, who is not human, is deeply moved, and states that he believes even Prospero would be affected by their pitiable condition. Releasing them from the spell and then casting off his magical powers, Prospero explains everything to Alonso and his followers and forgives them. Prospero reunites Alonso with Ferdinand, and Alonso gives permission for the coming wedding. Next, Caliban and his co-conspirators, Stephano and Trinculo, are forgiven for their plot against Prospero. Prospero assures the others that all will sail in the morning. Ariel is at long last granted his freedom.*

ACT 5

Scene 1. *Before the cell of* PROSPERO.

[*Enter* PROSPERO *in his magic robes, and* ARIEL.]

Prospero.
Now does my project gather to a head.
My charms crack not,° my spirits obey, and Time
Goes upright with his carriage.° How's the day?

Ariel.
On the sixth hour, at which time, my lord
5   You said our work should cease.

Prospero.   I did say so
When first I raised the tempest. Say, my spirit,
How fares the King and 's followers?

Ariel.   Confined together
In the same fashion as you gave in charge,
Just as you left them—all prisoners, sir,
10 In the line grove which weather-fends° your cell.

2. **crack not:** do not fail.

3. **Goes upright with his carriage:** walks upright, despite the load (of events) he carries; i.e., time carries Prospero's plans forward smoothly.

❓ How do you think Ariel might say line 5? Cautiously? Excitedly? Why is it important?

10. **weather-fends:** defends from weather.

They cannot budge till your release. The King,
His brother, and yours abide all three distracted,
And the remainder mourning over them,
Brimful of sorrow and dismay; but chiefly

15 Him that you termed, sir, the good old Lord Gon-
zalo.
His tears run down his beard like winter's drops
From eaves of reeds.° Your charm so strongly works
'em,
That if you now beheld them, your affections
Would become tender.

Prospero.   Dost thou think so, spirit?
Ariel.

20 Mine would, sir, were I human.

Prospero.   And mine shall.
Hast thou, which art but air, a touch, a feeling
Of their afflictions, and shall not myself,
One of their kind, that relish all as sharply
Passion° as they, be kindlier moved than thou art?

25 Though with their high wrongs I am struck to
the quick,
Yet with my nobler reason 'gainst my fury
Do I take part. The rarer° action is
In virtue than in vengeance. They being penitent,
The sole drift of my purpose doth extend

30 Not a frown further. Go, release them, Ariel.
My charms I'll break, their senses I'll restore,
And they shall be themselves.

Ariel.   I'll fetch them, sir. [*Exit.*]
Prospero.

[*Makes a magic circle with his staff.*]
Ye elves of hills, brooks, standing lakes, and
groves,
And ye that on the sands with printless foot

35 Do chase the ebbing Neptune, and do fly him
When he comes back; you demipuppets° that
By moonshine do the green sour ringlets° make,
Whereof the ewe not bites; and you, whose pastime
Is to make midnight mushrumps,° that rejoice

40 To hear the solemn curfew;° by whose aid
(Weak masters though ye be) I have bedimmed
The noontide sun, called forth the mutinous winds,
And 'twixt the green sea and the azured vault
Set roaring war; to the dread rattling thunder

17. **eaves of reeds:** thatched roofs.

Of what is Prospero convinced by Ariel in line 20? How does Ariel persuade him?

24. **Passion:** feel strong emotion.

27. **rarer:** nobler; higher.

36. **demipuppets:** small creatures.
37. **green sour ringlets:** bitter grass generally avoided by sheep and thought to grow where a fairy had danced.
39. **mushrumps:** mushrooms; because they grow so quickly, mushrooms were said to be made by fairies.
40. **curfew:** After curfew (approximately 9:00 P.M.), humans stayed indoors and fairies were free to move about.

45 Have I given fire and rifted° Jove's stout oak
    With his own bolt; the strong-based promontory
    Have I made shake and by the spurs° plucked up
    The pine and cedar; graves at my command
    Have waked their sleepers, oped, and let 'em forth
50 By my so potent art. But this rough magic
    I here abjure; and when I have required
    Some heavenly music (which even now I do)
    To work mine end upon their senses that
    This airy charm is for, I'll break my staff,
55 Bury it certain fathoms in the earth,
    And deeper than did ever plummet sound
    I'll drown my book.

[*Solemn music.*]

[*Here enters* ARIEL *before; then* ALONSO, *with a
frantic gesture, attended by* GONZALO; SEBASTIAN
and ANTONIO *in like manner, attended by* ADRIAN
and FRANCISCO. *They all enter the circle which*
PROSPERO *had made, and there stand charmed;
which* PROSPERO *observing, speaks.*]

    A solemn air, and the best comforter
    To an unsettled fancy, cure thy brains,
60 Now useless, boiled within thy skull! There stand,
    For you are spell-stopped.
    Holy Gonzalo, honorable man,
    Mine eyes, ev'n sociable to° the show of thine,
    Fall fellowly drops. The charm dissolves apace;°
65 And as the morning steals upon the night,
    Melting the darkness, so their rising senses
    Begin to chase the ignorant fumes that mantle
    Their clearer reason. O good Gonzalo,
    My true preserver, and a loyal sir
70 To him thou followst! I will pay thy graces
    Home° both in word and deed. Most cruelly
    Didst thou, Alonso, use me and my daughter.
    Thy brother was a furtherer in the act.
    Thou art pinched for't now, Sebastian. Flesh and
        blood,
75 You, brother mine, that entertained ambition,
    Expelled remorse and nature; who, with Sebastian
    (Whose inward pinches therefore are most strong),
    Would here have killed your king, I do forgive thee,
    Unnatural though thou art. Their understanding
80 Begins to swell, and the approaching tide
    Will shortly fill the reasonable shore,°

45. **rifted:** split.

47. **spurs:** roots.

? This speech (lines 33–57) is crucial as Prospero renounces his powers. What is striking to you about the language in this speech?

? Why is Prospero willing to give up his powers? Would you have done the same in his place?

? This is the first time the ship-wreck survivors all see Prospero. Considering their personalities and their ties to him, how do you predict they will react to him?

63. **ev'n sociable to:** in sympathetic fellowship with.
64. **apace:** rapidly.

70–71. **pay thy graces/Home:** reward you generously for your loyal services.

? Do you think Alonso, Sebastian, and Antonio deserve or have earned Prospero's forgiveness? How do you imagine Prospero delivers lines 71–79?

81. **the reasonable shore:** i.e., their minds, which are again filling with comprehension.

That now lies foul and muddy. Not one of them
That yet looks on me or would know me. Ariel,
Fetch me the hat and rapier in my cell.

85 I will discase me,° and myself present
As I was sometime Milan.° Quickly, spirit!
Thou shalt ere long be free.

85. **discase me:** take off my
magic robe.
86. **As I was sometime Milan:**
dressed as I used to be when
Duke of Milan.

[*Exit* ARIEL *and returns immediately.*]

[ARIEL *sings and helps to attire him.*]

Where the bee sucks, there suck I;
In a cowslip's bell I lie;
90 There I couch when owls do cry.
    On the bat's back I do fly
    After summer merrily.
Merrily, merrily shall I live now
Under the blossom that hangs on the bough.

This is a famous song of
Shakespeare's. What is its
tone? Of what does Ariel sing?

Prospero.
95 Why, that's my dainty Ariel! I shall miss thee,
But yet thou shalt have freedom. So, so, so.
To the King's ship, invisible as thou art!
There shalt thou find the mariners asleep
Under the hatches. The master and the boatswain
100 Being awake, enforce them to this place,
And presently,° I prithee.

101. **presently:** immediately.

Ariel.
I drink the air before me, and return
Or ere your pulse twice beat.   [*Exit.*]

Gonzalo.
All torment, trouble, wonder, and amazement
105 Inhabits here. Some heavenly power guide us
Out of this fearful country!

What is Gonzalo's reaction to
seeing Prospero in lines 104–
106?

Prospero.   Behold, sir King,
The wronged Duke of Milan, Prospero.
For more assurance that a living prince
Does now speak to thee, I embrace thy body,
110 And to thee and thy company I bid
A hearty welcome.

Alonso.   Whe'r° thou beest he or no,
Or some enchanted trifle to abuse° me,
As late I have been, I not know. Thy pulse
Beats, as of flesh and blood; and, since I saw thee,
115 The affliction of my mind amends, with which,
I fear, a madness held me. This must crave
(An if this be at all°) a most strange story.

111. **Whe'r:** whether.
112. **abuse:** fool.

117. **An if this be at all:** if this is
at all real.

Thy dukedom I resign and do entreat
Thou pardon me my wrongs. But how should Prospero
120   Be living and be here?

Prospero.   First, noble friend,
Let me embrace thine age, whose honor cannot
Be measured or confined.

Gonzalo.   Whether this be
Or be not, I'll not swear.

Prospero.   You do yet taste
Some subtleties o' the isle, that will not let you
125   Believe things certain. Welcome, my friends all.
(*aside to* SEBASTIAN *and* ANTONIO) But you, my
      brace of lords, were I so minded,
I here could pluck his Highness' frown upon you,
And justify you traitors. At this time
I will tell no tales.

Sebastian (*aside*).   The Devil speaks in him.

Prospero.   No.
130   For you, most wicked sir, whom to call brother
Would even infect my mouth, I do forgive
Thy rankest fault—all of them; and require
My dukedom of thee, which perforce I know
Thou must restore.

Alonso.   If thou beest Prospero,
135   Give us particulars of thy preservation;
How thou hast met us here, who three hours since
Were wracked upon this shore; where I have lost
(How sharp the point of this remembrance is!)
My dear son Ferdinand.

Prospero.   I am woe° for't, sir.

Alonso.
140   Irreparable is the loss, and patience
Says it is past her cure.

Prospero.   I rather think
You have not sought her help, of whose soft grace
For the like loss I have her sovereign aid
And rest myself content.

Alonso.   You the like loss?

Prospero.
145   As great to me as late;° and, supportable
To make the dear loss, have I means much weaker
Than you may call to comfort you; for I
Have lost my daughter.

> What is happening in this exchange between Prospero and Antonio and Sebastian in lines 126–134? Why does Prospero not reveal the plot of Antonio and Sebastian to King Alonso?

139. **woe:** filled with sorrow.

> Patience is personified, or treated like a character, in lines 140–141. How would (or will) Alonso have benefited from having patience?

145. **as late:** just as recent.

> What is Prospero doing in lines 145–148 by telling Alonso of his own loss?

Martha Swope

Alonso.   A daughter?
O heavens, that they were living both in Naples,
The King and Queen there! That they were, I wish
Myself were mudded in that oozy bed
Where my son lies. When did you lose your
          daughter?

Prospero.
In this last tempest. I perceive these lords
At this encounter do so much admire°
That they devour their reason, and scarce think
Their eyes do offices of truth,° their words
Are natural breath. But, howsoev'r you have
Been justled from your senses, know for certain
That I am Prospero, and that very duke
Which was thrust forth of Milan, who most
          strangely
Upon this shore, where you were wracked, was
          landed.
To be the lord on't. No more yet of this;
For 'tis a chronicle of day by day,
Not a relation for a breakfast, nor
Befitting this first meeting. Welcome, sir.
This cell's my court. Here have I few attendants,
And subjects none abroad. Pray you look in.
My dukedom since you have given me again,
I will requite° you with as good a thing,
At least bring forth a wonder to content ye
As much as me my dukedom.

*Line numbers in left margin:* 150, 155, 160, 165, 170

? What is the irony of Alonso's speech (lines 148–152)?

154. **admire:** marvel.

156. **offices of truth:** see correctly.

169. **requite:** repay.

[Here PROSPERO *discovers°* FERDINAND *and* MIRANDA *playing at chess.*]

Miranda.
Sweet lord, you play me false.

Ferdinand.   No, my dearest love,
I would not for the world.

Miranda.
Yes, for a score of kingdoms you should wrangle,
175   And I would call it fair play.

Alonso.   If this prove
A vision of the island, one dear son
Shall I twice lose.

Sebastian.   A most high miracle!

Ferdinand.
Though the seas threaten, they are merciful.
I have cursed them without cause.

[*Kneels.*]

Alonso.   Now all the blessings
180   Of a glad father compass thee about!
Arise, and say how thou camest here.

Miranda.   O, wonder!
How many goodly creatures are there here!
How beauteous mankind is! O brave new world
That has such people in't!

Prospero.   'Tis new to thee.

Alonso.
185   What is this maid with whom thou wast at play?
Your eld'st° acquaintance cannot be three hours.
Is she the goddess that hath severed us
And brought us thus together?

Ferdinand.   Sir, she is mortal;
But by immortal providence she's mine.
190   I chose her when I could not ask my father
For his advice, nor thought I had one. She
Is daughter to this famous Duke of Milan,
Of whom so often I have heard renown
But never saw before; of whom I have
195   Received a second life; and second father
This lady makes him to me.

Alonso.   I am hers.°
But, O, how oddly will it sound that I
Must ask my child° forgiveness!

Prospero.   There, sir, stop.

discovers: reveals.

? Remembering that Miranda has seen only two human beings in her life, how do you imagine she reacts when she sees the crowd of shipwreck survivors? How should she deliver lines 183–184?

186. **eld'st:** longest possible.

196. **hers:** her father; Alonso accepts her as a daughter-in-law.
198. **my child:** Miranda.

The Tempest, Act 5, Scene 1   **923**

Let us not burden our remembrance with

200 A heaviness that's gone.

Gonzalo.   I have inly wept,
Or should have spoke ere this. Look down, you
gods,
And on this couple drop a blessed crown!
For it is you that have chalked forth the way
Which brought us hither.

Alonso.   I say amen, Gonzalo.

Gonzalo.

205 Was Milan thrust from Milan that his issue
Should become kings of Naples? O, rejoice
Beyond a common joy, and set it down
With gold on lasting pillars: In one voyage
Did Claribel her husband find at Tunis,

210 And Ferdinand her brother found a wife
Where he himself was lost; Prospero his dukedom
In a poor isle; and all of us ourselves
When no man was his own.

Alonso.

(*to* FERDINAND *and* MIRANDA) Give me your
hands.

215 Let grief and sorrow still° embrace his heart
That doth not wish you joy.

Gonzalo.   Be it so! Amen!

[*Enter* ARIEL, *with the* MASTER *and* BOATSWAIN
amazedly following.]

O, look, sir; look, sir! Here is more of us!
I prophesied, if a gallows were on land,
This fellow could not drown. Now, blasphemy,°

220 That swearst grace o'erboard,° not an oath on shore?
Hast thou no mouth by land? What is the news?

Boatswain.

The best news is that we have safely found
Our king and company; the next, our ship,
Which, but three glasses° since, we gave out split,

225 Is tight and yare and bravely rigged as when
We first put out to sea.

Ariel.

(*aside to* PROSPERO) Sir, all this service
Have I done since I went.

Prospero.

(*aside to* ARIEL) My tricksy spirit!

> **?** Gonzalo points out several examples of people finding or discovering things during the course of the play. What other discoveries were made that he does not mention or know about? What does he mean by the last line of his speech: "and all of us ourselves/ When no man was his own" (lines 212–213)?

215. **still:** always; forever.

219. **blasphemy:** blasphemer.
220. **swearst grace o'erboard:** drive heavenly grace from the ship with your profanity.

224. **glasses:** hours.

Alonso.

230 These are not natural events; they strengthen
From strange to stranger. Say, how came you hither?

Boatswain.

If I did think, sir, I were well awake,
I'ld strive to tell you. We were dead of sleep
And (how we know not) all clapped under hatches,
235 Where, but even now, with strange and several
noises
Of roaring, shrieking, howling, jingling chains,
And mo diversity of sounds, all horrible,
We were awaked; straightway at liberty;
Where we, in all her trim, freshly beheld
240 Our royal, good and gallant ship, our master
Cap'ring to eye her. On a trice, so please you,
Even in a dream, were we divided from them
And were brought moping hither.

Ariel (*aside to* PROSPERO).   Was't well done?

Prospero.

(*aside to* ARIEL) Bravely, my diligence.
245 Thou shalt be free.

Alonso.

This is as strange a maze as e'er men trod,
And there is in this business more than nature
Was ever conduct° of. Some oracle
Must rectify our° knowledge.

248. **conduct:** conductor.
249. **rectify our:** correct our lack of.

Prospero.   Sir, my liege,
250 Do not infest your mind with beating on
The strangeness of this business. At picked leisure,
Which shall be shortly, single I'll resolve° you
(Which to you shall seem probable) of every
These happened accidents; till when, be cheerful
255 And think of each thing well. (*aside to* ARIEL) Come
hither, spirit.
Set Caliban and his companions free.
Untie the spell. [*Exit* ARIEL.] How fares my
gracious sir?
There are yet missing of your company
Some few odd lads that you remember not.

252. **resolve:** end your ignorance.

[*Enter* ARIEL, *driving in* CALIBAN, STEPHANO, *and*
TRINCULO, *in their stol'n apparel.*]

Stephano.

260 Every man shift for all the rest, and let no man take
care for himself; for all is but fortune. Coragio,° bully-
monster, coragio!

261. **Coragio:** courage.

Trinculo.

If these be true spies which I wear in my head, here's
a goodly sight.

Caliban.

265   O Setebos, these be brave spirits indeed!
How fine my master is! I am afraid
He will chastise me.

Sebastian.   Ha, ha!
What things are these, my Lord Antonio?
Will money buy 'em?

Antonio.   Very like. One of them
270   Is a plain fish and no doubt marketable.

Prospero.

Mark but the badges° of these men, my lords,
Then say if they be true. This misshapen knave,
His mother was a witch, and one so strong
That could control the moon, make flows and ebbs,
275   And deal in her command° without her power.
These three have robbed me, and this demidevil
(For he's a bastard one) had plotted with them
To take my life. Two of these fellows you
Must know and own; this thing of darkness I
280   Acknowledge mine.

Caliban.   I shall be pinched to death.

Alonso.

Is not this Stephano, my drunken butler?

Sebastian.

He is drunk now. Where had he wine?

Alonso.

And Trinculo is reeling ripe. Where should they
Find this grand liquor that hath gilded 'em?
285   How camest thou in this pickle?

Trinculo.

I have been in such a pickle, since I saw you last, that
I fear me will never out of my bones. I shall not fear
fly-blowing.°

Sebastian.

Why, how now, Stephano?

Stephano.

290   O, touch me not! I am not Stephano, but a cramp.

Prospero.

You'ld be king o' the isle, sirrah?

Stephano.

I should have been a sore one then.

Alonso.

This is as strange a thing as e'er I looked on.

Prospero.

He is as disproportioned in his manners

295   As in his shape. Go, sirrah, to my cell;

Take with you your companions. As you look

To have my pardon, trim° it handsomely.

Caliban.

Ay, that I will! and I'll be wise hereafter,

And seek for grace. What a thrice-double ass

300   Was I to take this drunkard for a god

And worship this dull fool!

Prospero.   Go to! Away!

Alonso.

Hence, and bestow your luggage where you found it.

Sebastian.

Or stole it rather.

      [*Exeunt* CALIBAN, STEPHANO, *and* TRINCULO.]

Prospero.

Sir, I invite your Highness and your train

305   To my poor cell, where you shall take your rest

For this one night; which, part of it, I'll waste

297 **trim:** clean.

? Do you think Caliban really repents in lines 298–301? Why or why not?

Martha Swope

With such discourse as, I not doubt, shall make it
Go quick away—the story of my life,
And the particular accidents° gone by

309. **accidents:** happenings.

310 Since I came to this isle; and in the morn
I'll bring you to your ship, and so to Naples,
Where I have hope to see the nuptial
Of these our dear-beloved solemnized;
And thence retire me to my Milan, where
315 Every third thought shall be my grave.

Alonso.   I long
To hear the story of your life, which must
Take° the ear strangely.

317. **Take:** delight.

Prospero.   I'll deliver all;
And promise you calm seas, auspicious gales,
And sail so expeditious that shall catch
320 Your royal fleet far off.—My Ariel, chick,
That is thy charge. Then to the elements
Be free, and fare thou well.—Please you draw near.

How do you imagine Ariel reacts to his new freedom? With exuberance? With disbelief?

[*Exeunt omnes.*]

EPILOGUE

[*Spoken by* PROSPERO.]
Now my charms are all o'erthrown,
And what strength I have's mine own,
Which is most faint. Now 'tis true
I must be here confined by you,
5 Or sent to Naples. Let me not,
Since I have my dukedom got
And pardoned the deceiver, dwell
In this bare island by your spell;
But release me from my bands
10 With the help of your good hands.°
Gentle breath° of yours my sails
Must fill, or else my project fails,
Which was to please. Now I want°
Spirits to enforce, art to enchant;
15 And my ending is despair
Unless I be relieved by prayer,
Which pierces so that it assaults
Mercy itself and frees all faults.
As you from crimes would pardoned be,
20 Let your indulgence set me free.

One of the themes of *The Tempest* is harmonious reconciliation. Do you think everyone enjoys reconciliation at the conclusion of the play? Do you think everyone deserves it?

10. **good hands:** applause.
11. **Gentle breath:** good breeze (caused by the applause).

13. **want:** lack.

How do "you," the audience (or reader) "confine" Prospero? How will your applause and his prayer release him?

[*Exit.*]

A CRITICAL COMMENT

The Tempest *and Shakespeare's Vision of the World*

In *The Tempest,* critics have seen Shakespeare acting out his own career as a playwright and saying farewell to it. The idea is an attractive one. Prospero/Shakespeare, the magician/artist, manipulates his characters through the mazes of terror and joy created by life and their own natures. Finally, he brings them through to reconciliation and bids farewell to his special powers, which could not last forever, in a mixed spirit of regret and satisfaction.

The Tempest is the last of Shakespeare's own plays (he later collaborated on a few plays) and Prospero's final words are too appropriate a valedictory to be denied. Nevertheless, this idea that Prospero represents Shakespeare is at most only one element—and probably the most incidental one—in a play of such richness that all attempts to interpret it allegorically are more or less misleading.

The Tempest is set on an island that is obviously off-course from the route between Naples and Tunis. This island is its own world; Prospero's enchantment has imposed its rule on the island and on the island creatures. By his magic, Prospero brings into this enchanted world a group of people from the world of Naples and Milan, which had formerly been his domain. His purpose is not merely to restore this corrupt world to its former state (Prospero admits that he had been less than perfect as a ruler of Milan) but to bring about the condition of harmony that his magic has achieved on the island. By

bitter experience Prospero has gained knowledge of the world; by study and contemplation he has gained the wisdom to control it. The island has benefited, but he has yet to use his power in the real world.

Prospero has to contend with greed and violence and lust. These vices are manifest in the monstrous figure of Caliban, the "natural" man unimproved by knowledge and discipline. The same vices are embodied more realistically in Alonso and Antonio and Sebastian. Prospero must also contend with the naiveté of Gonzalo and Ferdinand, since innocence is not sturdy enough to prevail in a corrupt world. Tests and ordeals serve to bring both the corrupt and the naive into the light. But there are those who will remain forever in the dark, who, in a harmonious world, must be subjected to rigid control. Caliban is the most notable example, but controls must also be placed on Antonio, who never admits the error of his ways, but recognizes only his failure this time to get what he wanted. Finally we behold Prospero's vision of a restored world, which is presumably Shakespeare's own, when Prospero sets all to rights.

Above all, Prospero brings together Ferdinand and Miranda. Their meeting is the principal purpose of the magic shipwreck at the beginning of the play; their declaration of love is the pivotal scene; and Prospero's revelation of the pair to the rest of the characters is the climactic point of the play. Love; the continuity of life; a wise, instructed innocence; youth and beauty—these make up the world's harmony.

The Tempest is full of the English Renaissance. Its setting on an "uninhabited island" calls up the excitement associated in the 1500s with discoveries of new lands across remote and dangerous seas. The figure of Caliban reflects contemporary interest in the "savages" which the explorers were telling about. The strange ways of these savages—as reported in accounts that were often highly romanticized—invited critical comparison with European civilization. Some Europeans, like the French essayist Montaigne, tended to view the New World natives as "noble savages" unspoiled by the false values of civilized society. Shakespeare, however, shows Caliban, the "natural man," as a near-brute who needs the restraints and the ideals that reason and the accumulated wisdom of civilization show to human beings.

Like the famous *Utopia* (1516) of Sir Thomas More, *The Tempest* creates in an exotic and untouched land an image of ideal human society. In the play's story greedy men bring ugliness and unhappiness into a world made for man's sustenance and delight, but forces of love and benevolent authority overcome and reform them. This optimistic estimate of human potentialities is characteristic of the Renaissance, and the inquiry into how the principles of universal order can be used to achieve perfect harmony among men was a concern central to many humanistic philosophers of the Renaissance.

Shakespeare presents these serious ideas in *The Tempest* in the exuberant and colorful manner that we associate with Renaissance "style." The speeches show the soaring lyricism and verbal richness typical of the best Renaissance poetry, and the heroine presents an ideal of beauty and purity such as was imagined by sonnet composers from Petrarch on (see page 806). The earthy comedy of Stephano and Trinculo, the pageantry, and the whole atmosphere of gaiety reflect the popular side of Renaissance vitality in Elizabethan London.

First Thoughts

Do you think that Prospero dealt fairly with all the conspirators? How do you think a modern court would have treated them?

Identifying Facts

1. What does Prospero say to Alonso, Sebastian, Antonio, and Gonzalo when they are brought before him?

2. What does Alonso see that brings him joy? Whom does he meet for the first time?

3. What happens to Caliban and his co-conspirators?

4. What has Prospero lost by the end of the play?

Interpreting Meanings

1. Early in this act, how does Ariel's song illustrate his feeling of release? Why does he prefer freedom to Prospero's benevolent rule?

2. Alonso and Antonio have very different reactions to the disclosures made by Prospero in the final act. What do these reactions reveal about their characters? How do Antonio's reactions affect the **resolution** of the play?

3. At one point in Act 5, Prospero, speaking of Caliban, says: "This thing of darkness I acknowledge mine." Does he mean that Caliban is merely his servant, or do you think that Prospero means something deeper—that he recognizes some flaw within himself? Explain.

4. Discuss the play's **epilogue**. What, if anything, does it contribute to your understanding of Prospero's character?

Applying Meanings

Much has been written about the "forgiveness" theme in many of Shakespeare's plays. Do you think that Prospero was merely practicing self-interest by forgiving those who had plotted against him? Think of a time in your life when you forgave someone for a wrong. Was the forgiveness unconditional, or did you hope to gain something from the person you were forgiving?

The Play as a Whole
Interpreting Meanings

1. What evidence is given in the play that, if Prospero had been a better leader, he might have retained his power in Milan? Are his learning and intellect in some ways detrimental to his being a leader in the "real world," or does he possess some other flaw? In your response, consider Antonio's opinions of Prospero and Prospero's failure to see the obvious problems with Caliban.

2. *The Tempest* is sometimes called a "tragicomedy." Look up the definition of this word—as well as the separate definitions of the words *tragedy* and *comedy*—in a dictionary or a book of literary terms. Using evidence from the play, explain whether or not you believe *The Tempest* should be considered a tragicomedy.

3. Trace the plot lines that involve the three distinct groups of characters in the play: Prospero, Ferdinand, and Miranda; Alonso and his party; and Caliban, Trinculo, and Stephano. In what order are the separate plots presented? How is each plot resolved? What direct connections are there among these plot lines?

4. Michel de Montaigne's (1533–1592) essay "Of Cannibals" was almost certainly one of Shakespeare's sources for *The Tempest*. In this essay, Montaigne presents the idea that primitive societies may actually possess greater justice and harmony than so-called civilized society; they do not need courts, laws, or other confining social institutions. How does Shakespeare explore these ideas in *The Tempest*? Do you think that he agreed with Montaigne's idealized views of "primitive" societies, or was he trying to punch holes in Montaigne's theory?

Creative Writing Response

Writing a Synopsis. Like all of Shakespeare's best works, *The Tempest* can be set in different times and places and still not lose its appeal. Imagine that you are the director of a theater company, and that you have been assigned to create a new version of *The Tempest,* set in a different time and place. Write a synopsis—a brief overview or summary—of how you would change the play and yet keep the basic plot and theme. You could, for example, set the story in a Native American community in the eighteenth century, with Prospero cast as a shaman or medicine man. Be sure to include the major elements of exposition, climax, and resolution in your synopsis.

Critical Writing Response

1. **Contrasting Characters.** Caliban and Ariel are both supernatural beings, but they are very different. In a brief essay, contrast their characters. A chart like

the following may help you organize the material for your essay.

	Caliban	Ariel
Relationship to Prospero		
Appearance		
Speech		
Ambitions		

2. **Editing Shakespeare.** Imagine that Shakespeare is alive today and that you are his editor. You want to publish *The Tempest*, but you feel that there are certain scenes and characters that don't quite work. You need to write Shakespeare a brief letter in which you outline the changes you want to see him make to *The Tempest*. Perhaps, for example, the masque scene left you cold and you feel it should be removed or shortened. Or perhaps you think that readers will be turned off by the lengthy references to the "widow Dido" in Act 2, Scene 1. Make at least two suggestions for revision in your letter.

Speaking and Listening

Staging an Episode of the Play. Shakespeare is known for his verbal humor, but many of his plays also include scenes that rely on physical comedy. Choose a scene from *The Tempest* that relies on some physical humor. You might, for example, try presenting the episode in Act 2, Scene 2 in which Caliban is mistaken for a fish with four legs. Stage the scene for the class.

Language and Vocabulary

Blank Verse

All of Shakespeare's plays, including *The Tempest*, are written in **blank verse**. Blank verse is unrhymed poetry that is written in

iambic pentameter, which means that there are five ("penta") iambs in each line of poetry. An **iamb** is a poetic foot, or group of syllables, that is made up of an unaccented syllable followed by an accented one (⌣ ′). The words *because* and *Christine* are both iambs, as is the phrase *on time*. Study the following two lines from *The Tempest*, which are written in blank verse:

> How many goodly creatures are there here!
> How beauteous mankind is! Oh, brave new world,

Much of English is naturally spoken in iambic rhythm. Of course, if the whole play were written in this pattern, it would soon become quite dull. Shakespeare, in order to add variety and emphasis to certain lines, sometimes reversed the pattern of accented and unaccented syllables or used fewer than five feet per line, as in the following example:

> Where the bee sucks there suck I.
> In a cowslip's bell I lie,

It is important to follow the punctuation marks at the ends of lines, and not to assume that each line is complete in itself. Lines that end with a punctuation mark, such as a period or a comma, are called **end-stopped** lines. Other lines, which do not end with a punctuation mark, are called **run-on** lines, also known as **enjambment** (see page 812). In order to understand the meaning of these run-on lines, it is necessary to read on to the next line.

Go back through the play and find at least five examples of blank verse—unrhymed iambic pentameter. How many variations of this pattern can you find? Also, look for examples of end-stopped and run-on lines. Why do you think Shakespeare used both of these forms? What do they add to the play?

BEHIND THE SCENES

Shakespeare Around the World

Shakespeare is very much alive today—on the stage, in films, and on television. Continent by continent, Shakespeare draws audiences of eager theatergoers. In India, the celebrated producing-directing team of Ismail Merchant and James Ivory produced a popular comedy entitled *Shakespeare Wallah (Shakespeare Seller)*, about a group of touring actors bringing Shakespeare to India's remote provinces. In Japan, the great director Akira Kurosawa created two magnificent films based on Shakespearean masterpieces: *Throne of Blood*, adapted from *Macbeth*, and *Ran*, adapted from *King Lear*.

In North America, Mayan Indians from the Yucatan Peninsula in Mexico presented a colorful production of *Romeo and Juliet* that attained international success. The New York Shakespeare Festival productions have featured some of Hollywood's biggest names—Denzel Washington, Kevin Kline, Meryl Streep, and Tracey Ullman. *Kiss Me Kate*—Cole Porter's musical version of *The Taming of the Shrew*—is always in production somewhere in the U.S., as is *West Side Story*—Leonard Bernstein's musical based loosely on *Romeo and Juliet*. Many people consider the Stratford Festival in Ontario, Canada—which frequently stars Dame Maggie Smith and Christopher Plummer—to be the best Shakespearean company in North America.

In South America, the Teatro do Onitorrinco of Brazil reset *A Midsummer Night's Dream* (in Portuguese, *Sonho de Uma Noite de Verao*) in the Amazon rain forest. The Compania Rajatabla of Venezuela presented *The Tempest* (in Spanish, *La Tempestad*) with Prospero's refuge symbolized by an enormous pre-Columbian idol's head buried in the island's surface.

In England, Stratford-on-Avon is one of the two homes of the Royal Shakespeare Company; the other is at the Barbican Centre in London. Nearby is the home of the Royal National Theatre on the Thames—within walking distance of the site of the former Globe theater. There are also many repertory companies dotted throughout the British Isles. One of these theaters produced the internationally famous rock musical, *Return to the Forbidden Planet*, based on the science fiction film *Forbidden Planet*, which was in turn based on Shakespeare's *The Tempest*.

Shakespeare is very much alive in continental Europe as well. Italian filmmaker Franco Zeffirelli has directed productions of *The Taming of the Shrew, Romeo and Juliet*, and *Hamlet*. Denmark's Kronborg Castle, the historic site of *Hamlet*, has been the location of several film productions of the tragedy. Finnish filmmakers have produced an updated version of *Hamlet* with the unlikely title of *Hamlet Goes Business*.

Whether in Texas or Tokyo, Broadway or Brazil, Shakespeare's immortal works are very much a part of the modern world and are likely to remain so for centuries—perhaps millenia—to come.

LITERATURE OF THE ENLIGHTENMENT

D uring the **Age of Enlightenment**, or, as it is sometimes called, the **Age of Reason**, thinkers continued the Renaissance humanist tradition of challenging authority. Between the seventeenth and eighteenth centuries, people came to believe that human reason was the only reliable authority. Through reason, human beings could probe the secrets of the universe and understand the true relationship between themselves and God.

> **❝** The first precept was never to accept a thing as true until I knew it as such without a single doubt. **❞**
>
> —René Descartes

The Fruits of Discovery

In the seventeenth and eighteenth centuries, Europe and England enjoyed the rewards of exploration. Exotic goods from the East and immense quantities of gold and silver from the Americas enriched the absolute monarchs of Europe—monarchs like France's **Louis XIV**, who dubbed himself the "Sun King" and built the Palace of Versailles.

Aristocrats led elegant lives. In every European capital, ladies and gentlemen wearing silks and powdered wigs were carried through the muddy streets in elegant sedan chairs. Fashionable buildings with lavishly decorated interiors were surrounded by vast formal gardens and parks. The wealthy enhanced their reputations by becoming patrons of the arts, particularly of music, which filled their leisure hours. During this period, the great Austrian composers **Wolfgang Amadeus Mozart** and **Joseph Haydn** and the German composer **Johann Sebastian Bach** were favorites of Europe's royal courts. These musicians and others developed the opera, the sonata, and the concerto—all new musical forms.

A Time of Contrasts

In the midst of the affluence enjoyed by a few, many lived in great poverty. The poor flocked to the cities in search of

MINERVA SUMMONING LOUIS XIV TO ARMS, late seventeenth-century French tapestry. *Louis XIV's opulent lifestyle typified the monarchies of seventeenth-century Europe.*

work, living in slums and suffering from malnutrition. Inflation was rampant and even basic food was costly. There was no sanitation or safe water supplies, and epidemic illnesses ravaged the cities. In 1665, the plague struck again,

> **In the eighteenth century, the contrast between aristocratic affluence and lower-class poverty foreshadowed social upheaval.**

killing thousands. The crime rate was high, and the wooden thatch-roofed houses in which common people lived were especially vulnerable to fire. In cities like Paris, the contrast between the rich and the poor was inescapable. The restlessness of the poor during this time foreshadowed social upheavals to come.

Science: A Clockwork Universe

The search for knowledge expanded in a climate of inquiry. The Royal Society of London for Improving Natural Knowledge began meeting in 1645 to support scientific research. In France, the Academy of Sciences was created in 1666 to promote mathematics, astronomy, and the physical sciences. The fruits of new scientific research were soon evident in the introduction of the pendulum clock (1656), the steam engine (1705), and the cotton gin (1793).

The most influential scientific developments occurred in mathematics. **René Descartes** believed that human beings, by reason alone, could discover universal truths. **Sir Isaac Newton** developed this idea in *The Mathematical Principles of Natural Philosophy* (1687). This work describes a clockwork universe governed by mechanical laws that can be discovered by reason alone, using the principles of deduction.

WOLF AND FOX HUNT, PETER PAUL RUBENS (1577–1640). *The aristocrats of Enlightenment Europe sought out often extravagant leisure time activities to lend excitement and variety to their lives.*

The Rise of Rationalism

The ideas propounded by Descartes, Newton, and others came to be called **rationalism**. Rationalism's influence reached beyond science. It supported the idea that unchanging laws govern politics and morality. In the work of philosophers like **Thomas Hobbes**, rationalism led to the social theory that people choose what is in their best interest. Hobbes argued that people's common interests lead them to make a "social contract." They accept their sovereign's power over them in exchange for protection against their own greedy, evil nature.

Social Theory: The Spark of Revolution

The British philosopher **John Locke** (1632–1704) disagreed with Hobbes and the rationalists. He was an **empiricist**—one who believes that experience, rather than logic, is the only source of knowledge. Locke proposed that at birth, the mind is a blank slate (a *tabula rasa*) on which experience is recorded. His social ideas—that people are born equal and independent—followed from this premise. In Locke's view, revolution was not only a right but often an obligation. His political theories sparked the American Revolution and inspired its leaders—Thomas Paine, Thomas Jefferson, and Benjamin Franklin.

In France, **Jean Jacques Rousseau** (1712–1778) wrote that humanity is naturally good but is corrupted by the

> **❝** Every body continues in its state of rest, or of uniform motion in a right line, unless it is compelled to change that state by forces impressed upon it. **❞**
>
> —*Sir Isaac Newton,*
> Laws of Motion, I

> **"** Satire is a sort of glass, wherein beholders do generally discover everybody's face but their own. **"**
>
> —*Jonathan Swift, Preface to The Battle of the Books*

environment, by education, and by government. He believed that governments must be subject to the will of the people. His writings influenced the architects of the United States Constitution and those of the French government following the French Revolution in 1798.

Literature: The Impact of New Ideas

More than in almost any other age, the literature of the seventeenth and eighteenth centuries reflected the enormous impact of new social and scientific ideas. Many writers used **satire** as a weapon against the corrupt social world. **Jean de La Fontaine** (1621–1695) wrote the shrewdly satiric *Fables.* **Moliére** (1622–1673) wrote satiric dramas aimed at outmoded social conventions that disguised the worst in human nature. Perhaps the most scathing satire was written by Irish-born writer **Jonathan Swift** (1667–1745). His works, such as *Gulliver's Travels* and "A Modest Proposal," reflect Swift's bitter outrage at the corruption he saw.

> The literature of the seventeenth and eighteenth centuries was strongly influenced by new social and scientific ideas. Satire was a popular literary form.

Table talk with Voltaire and his fellow intellectual friends. *Eighteenth-century engraving.*

The French philosopher and rational skeptic **Voltaire** (1694–1778) used satire to mock the ideas of his contemporary, Rousseau. Voltaire's ***Candide*** continually challenges Rousseau's assertion that humans are "naturally" good. Voltaire maintained that art should be used to change society, and his satires were directed at people who abused privilege and power.

Government: Revolutions Ignited

The new ideas of the Enlightenment took on concrete form as masses of people, desiring a better life, challenged the power of the monarchies. In England, the civil war that began in 1642 climaxed with the beheading of Charles I.

The **American Revolution** a century later echoed the same themes in its insistence on the rights of individuals. The **French Revolution** (1789–1795) was also based on the desire for personal freedom. This was somewhat obscured, however, when the lower classes, who had long endured poverty and deprivation, savagely retaliated against the French aristocracy.

> The ideas of the Renaissance and the Enlightenment challenged people to free themselves from the oppressions of government.

In the short run, the French Revolution failed to establish the ideal government that the philosophers envisioned. The American Revolution, however, succeeded in establishing a stable, representative government with a Constitution and Bill of Rights created by people whose ideas were shaped by the science, the philosophy, and the art of the Age of Enlightenment.

WASHINGTON CROSSING THE DELAWARE, EMANUEL GOTTLIEB LEUTZE (1816–1868). *The American Revolution was a culmination of the political ideas of the Enlightenment.*

The Metropolitan Museum of Art, Gift of John Stewart Kennedy, 1897

Jean de La Fontaine
1621–1695

Jean de La Fontaine (zhän de la fōn·ten′) was said to be an impractical dreamer who was awkward in social situations. One story illustrates his lack of social graces at a boring dinner party. After making excuses that he needed to leave an hour early for another engagement, his hostess noted that it would only take him twenty minutes to reach his destination. He replied: "But you see, I prefer the longest way."

La Fontaine seems also to have chosen the longest route to a literary career. He was born in 1621 at Château-Thierry (sha′tō′ tē·er′ē) where his father supervised forest areas and water management for the region.

While in school, La Fontaine was first introduced to Greek and Latin, the languages of the classical writers he later came to admire. Rather than pursue classical scholarship, however, La Fontaine entered a seminary in Paris to study theology. But seminary discipline did not suit his dreamy absent-mindedness, and at age twenty-two he returned to Château-Thierry to dabble in legal studies. Four years later, according to his father's wishes, he married Marie Hericart, who was only fourteen years old at the time. La Fontaine had little interest in his marriage, however, and some time later he embarked on his literary career.

When he was thirty-three, La Fontaine published his first work, *The Eunuch*, an adaptation of a comedy by the Roman writer Terence. The play was a failure, but La Fontaine kept writing, and eventually his writing and his charm won him generous sums of money from powerful patrons, including ministers in the king's court. Thanks to this patronage, La Fontaine produced other, more popular works, the most successful being the *Fables*. Based in part on the animal fables of classical writers like Aesop and Phaedrus, the *Fables* appeared in a series of twelve books between the years 1668 and 1694. They were very popular at the time of their publication and continue to be memorized by French students today. They have long been regarded by the French as tiny masterpieces, as models of perfect style.

Reader's Guide

from FABLES

Background

The fables of La Fontaine seem lighthearted at first. They have a playful rhyme scheme and regular rhythm, and their characters are animals that often appear in children's books. But these animals are not those of Disney films—they demonstrate human characteristics in a way that is less than flattering to humans. As a result, La Fontaine's fables reveal a world of deceit and cowardice. One reason beast fables are effective is that particular qualities commonly associated with certain animals (pigs are greedy, donkeys are stubborn, for example) are understandable even to unsophisticated readers.

La Fontaine's fables were not written specifically for children. They contain messages or morals that reflect a harsh reality that only adult readers can fully appreciate. And yet, the didactic, or educational, nature of the fables makes them good teaching tools. In fact, La Fontaine wrote in his preface to the *Fables* about the need for children to learn early the messages of his writings. He believed that children ''should not be left in ignorance if we can help it. We should teach them what a lion is, a fox, and so on and why a person is sometimes compared to a fox or a lion.''

Writer's Response

As a class, make a list of animals and the human traits we assign to them. For each animal, explain why we associate a certain characteristic with it. Why do you think we enjoy reading about animals who are ''like'' us?

Literary Focus

The **beast fable** is a brief story in which animals take on the traits of people in order to teach a practical lesson about human life. Animal fables are usually very practical and are often used for satirical purposes—usually to mock corrupt or thoughtless people. The morals or lessons of La Fontaine's fables are expressed in **epigrams**, or clever sayings, that sum up a theme in very compact rhyme like the refrains of songs.

from FABLES
Jean de La Fontaine
translated by
ELIZUR WRIGHT, JR.

> *"So the fables are a panorama in which we see ourselves,"* wrote La Fontaine in the preface to his book. As you read these fables, consider how these stories about animals with human characteristics cast light on human behavior.

The Council Held by the Rats

Old Rodilard, a certain cat,
　　Such havoc of the rats had made,
'Twas difficult to find a rat
　　With nature's debt unpaid.[1]
The few that did remain,
　　To leave their holes afraid,
From usual food abstain,
　　Not eating half their fill.
　　And wonder no one will,
That one who made on rats his revel,
With rats passed not for cat, but devil.
Now, on a day, this dread rat eater,
Who had a wife, went out to meet her;
And while he held his caterwauling,[2]
The unkilled rats, their chapter calling,
Discussed the point, in grave debate,
How they might shun impending fate.
　　Their dean, a prudent rat,
Thought best, and better soon than late,
　　To bell the fatal cat;
That, when he took his hunting round,
The rats, well cautioned by the sound,

Might hide in safety underground;
　　Indeed he knew no other means.
　　　　And all the rest
　　　　At once confessed
　　Their minds were with the dean's.
No better plan, they all believed,
Could possibly have been conceived.
No doubt the thing would work right well,
If any one would hang the bell.
　　But, one by one, said every rat,
　　I'm not so big a fool as that.
The plan, knocked up in this respect,
The council closed without effect.
And many a council I have seen,
Or reverend chapter with its dean,
　　That, thus resolving wisely,
　　Fell through like this precisely.

　　　To argue or refute
　　　　Wise counselors abound;
　　　The man to execute
　　　　Is harder to be found.

---

1. **With nature's debt unpaid:** remaining alive.
2. **caterwauling:** the shrill howl characteristic of cats during mating.

FOX IN A CHICKEN YARD, JEAN-BAPTISTE HUET (1745–1811).

The Cock and the Fox

Upon a tree there mounted guard
  A veteran cock, adroit and cunning,
  When to the roots a fox up running,
Spoke thus, in tones of kind regard:—
  Our quarrel, brother, is at an end;
  Henceforth I hope to live your friend;
    For peace now reigns
    Throughout the animal domains.
I bear the news:—come down, I pray,
  And give me the embrace fraternal;
And please, my brother, don't delay.
  So much the tidings do concern all,
That I must spread them far today.
Now you and yours can take your walks
Without a fear or thought of hawks.
And should you clash with them or others,
In us you'll find the best of brothers;—
For which you may, this joyful night,
  Your merry bonfires light.
    But, first, let's seal the bliss
    With one fraternal kiss.

"Good friend," the cock replied, "upon my word,
A better thing I never heard;
    And doubly I rejoice
    To hear it from your voice:
And really, there must be something in it,
  For yonder come two greyhounds, which, I
  flatter
  Myself, are couriers on this very matter:
They come so fast, they'll be here in a minute.
  I'll down, and all of us will seal the blessing
  With general kissing and caressing."
    "Adieu,"[1] said Fox, "my errand's pressing:
    I'll hurry on my way,
      And we'll rejoice some other day."
So off the fellow scampered, quick and light,
To gain the foxholes of a neighboring height—
Less happy in his stratagem than flight.
  The cock laughed sweetly in his sleeve—
  'Tis doubly sweet deceiver to deceive.

---

1. **Adieu** (ə·dyo͞o'): French for goodbye.

Jean de La Fontaine **943**

First Thoughts

La Fontaine's fables have been criticized for their cynical tone. How would you describe the tone of these two fables?

Identifying Facts

1. What plan does the "dean rat" devise to protect the rats from the cat?
2. Why are the rats unable to put this plan into effect?
3. What does the fox say to trick the cock? What is his real intention?
4. How does the cock get the better of the fox in the end?

Interpreting Meanings

1. In the final **quatrain**, or four lines, of "The Council Held by the Rats," La Fontaine explicitly gives the **moral** of the story in the form of an **epigram**. What is the moral in "The Cock and the Fox"?
2. How could the expression "my enemy's enemy is my friend" apply to the story of the cock and the fox?

3. Consider the characters of the animals in the fables. What qualities do we typically associate with the fox and the rat? How are they apparent in these stories?
4. What human traits are ridiculed in these two **beast fables**?

Applying Meanings

How do you feel about the morals of La Fontaine's fables, and the tone in which they are delivered? Do you think they are too bitter or jaded, or do they confirm any of your own experiences? Explain.

Creative Writing Response

Writing a Fable. Consider a lesson you have learned lately, whether it be the virtue of being on time or the wisdom of not speaking in anger. "Translate" your experience into a fable with its own moral. (You might want to write the moral first.) Your characters should be animals who demonstrate human qualities, like those in the fables of La Fontaine.

Voltaire
1694–1778

Archiv Für Kunst Und Geschichte, Berlin

Voltaire was a writer who believed in writing the truth. He criticized the wastefulness of war, religious intolerance, and the unnecessary poverty and powerlessness of the average citizen. As a result of his frankness, he was twice imprisoned, once exiled from Paris, had his books and pamphlets banned by the French government, and was denied burial by the Parisian clergy when he died. Yet the spirit of his writing prevailed, and thirteen years after his death, the new postrevolutionary government brought Voltaire's remains back to Paris with great ceremony. Thousands of people lined the streets to see the funeral procession.

Voltaire was one of the main founders of modern historical science. He debunked traditional approaches to writing history, preferring to write philosophical treatises on morals. These essays were not abstract, but focused on how people actually lived and worked according to their moral principles. His efforts were not well-received, however, by the people in power. The publication of his most formidable work, *Essay on the Morals and the Spirit of the Nations from Charlemagne to Louis XIII*, caused the book to be banned and Voltaire to be exiled.

Aside from his voluminous correspondence and hundreds of pamphlets on every issue that arose in his time, Voltaire wrote in every literary genre. *La Henriade*, an epic poem about Henry IV, which he wrote during his first imprisonment, was regarded by some of his contemporaries as equal to the works of Homer and Virgil. Between *Oedipe*, written when he was eighteen, and *Irene*, written at age eighty-three, Voltaire wrote numerous plays, most of them great successes. His *Philosophic Dictionary* was perhaps the most widely read nonfiction book of his time. He wrote numerous romances and tales, of which *Candide* has proved to be the most enduring. Voltaire had little patience for purely metaphysical speculation. This emphasis on modest but practical achievement is reflected in the last page of *Candide:* "Let us work without arguing . . . it's the only way to make life endurable."

Reader's Guide

from CANDIDE

Background

Candide is subtitled "Optimism" and tells a tale of the woes that befall a naive simpleton who is brought up to believe that this world is the best of all possible worlds. The point of Voltaire's story is to show how Candide's optimism is foolish in a world in which people's lives are shaped for the most part by cruel and incomprehensible forces.

The plot of *Candide* takes the form of a quest: the young man's quest for union with his beloved, Cunegonde. They go through a series of separations and reunions, as Cunegonde is taken as booty by the Bulgarians, held prisoner by the Grand Inquisitor, and forcibly kept as a mistress by the Governor of Buenos Aires—in this, the best of all possible worlds. What happens to Candide himself is no better, but the two lovers somehow survive. The tale is told with great verve and hilarity, and, like all quests of this kind, the journey involves much suffering but ends in wisdom.

Writer's Response

If it were possible for you to live in the "best of all possible worlds" right here on earth, what would such a place be like? What kinds of things would you *not* find there? Write a paragraph describing your ideal world.

Literary Focus

Satire is writing that ridicules human weakness, vice, or folly in order to bring about social reform. An expert satirist like Voltaire uses a variety of tools to expose his subject to ridicule—from witty barbs to heavy bludgeons that flatten his opponent's sacred cows. As Voltaire exposes one absurdity after another, readers become convinced that they would be fools not to agree with his point of view. As you read *Candide,* look for Voltaire's outrageous exaggerations and deadpan understatements, for illogic dressed up as common sense, and for situations that are simply silly.

from CANDIDE
François-Marie Arouet de Voltaire
translated by
RICHARD ALDINGTON

 Note the first few places where Voltaire's writing makes you chuckle. Then, as you continue reading, think of possible reasons why Voltaire might have wanted to keep you laughing.

Chapter 1

How Candide was brought up in a noble castle, and how he was expelled from the same

In the castle of Baron Thunder-ten-tronckh in Westphalia[1] there lived a youth, endowed by Nature with the most gentle character. His face was the expression of his soul. His judgment was quite honest and he was extremely simple-minded; and this was the reason, I think, that he was named Candide. Old servants in the house suspected that he was the son of the Baron's sister and a decent honest gentleman of the neighborhood, whom this young lady would never marry because he could only prove seventy-one quarterings,[2] and the rest of his genealogical tree was lost, owing to the injuries of time.

The Baron was one of the most powerful lords in Westphalia, for his castle possessed a door and windows. His Great Hall was even decorated with a piece of tapestry. The dogs in his stable yards formed a pack of hounds when necessary; his grooms were his huntsmen; the village curate was his Grand Almoner.[3] They all called him "My Lord," and laughed heartily at his stories.

The Baroness weighed about three hundred and fifty pounds, was therefore greatly respected, and did the honors of the house with a dignity which rendered her still more respectable. Her daughter Cunegonde, aged seventeen, was rosy-cheeked, fresh, plump and tempting. The Baron's son appeared in every respect worthy of his father. The tutor Pangloss was the oracle of the house, and little Candide followed his lessons with all the candor of his age and character.

Pangloss taught metaphysico-theologo-cosmoloonigology.[4] He proved admirably that there is no effect without a cause and that in this best of all possible worlds, My Lord the Baron's castle was the best of castles and his wife the best of all possible Baronesses.

---

1. **Westphalia:** region in western Germany, noted for its hams. Voltaire considered it "vast, sad, sterile, detestable."
2. **quarterings:** divisions on a coat of arms or family tree. Seventy-one quarterings would trace a person's genealogy back over 2,000 years.
3. **Grand Almoner:** member of a noble household responsible for distributing charity to the poor.
4. **metaphysico-theologo-cosmoloonigology:** Voltaire is satirizing the philosopher Leibniz and his followers by embedding the word "loony" in this made-up term.

THE SWING, JEAN-HONORÉ FRAGONARD (1732–1806).
*Fragonard was a master of Rococo, the highly
ornamental style that dominated eighteenth-
century European art.*

"'Tis demonstrated," said he, "that things cannot be otherwise; for, since everything is made for an end, everything is necessarily for the best end. Observe that noses were made to wear spectacles; and so we have spectacles. Legs were visibly instituted to be breeched, and we have breeches. Stones were formed to be quarried and to build castles; and My Lord has a very noble castle; the greatest Baron in the province should have the best house; and as pigs were made to be eaten, we eat pork all the year round; consequently, those who have asserted that all is well talk nonsense; they ought to have said that all is for the best."

Candide listened attentively and believed innocently; for he thought Miss Cunegonde extremely beautiful, although he was never bold enough to tell her so. He decided that after the happiness of being born Baron of Thunder-ten-tronckh, the second degree of happiness was to be Miss Cunegonde; the third, to see her every day; and the fourth, to listen to Doctor Pangloss, the greatest philosopher of the province and therefore of the whole world.

One day when Cunegonde was walking near the castle, in a little wood which was called The Park, she observed Doctor Pangloss in the bushes, giving a lesson in experimental physics to her mother's waiting-maid, a very pretty and docile brunette. Miss Cunegonde had a great inclination for science and watched breathlessly the reiterated experiments she witnessed; she observed clearly the Doctor's sufficient reason, the effects and the causes, and returned home very much excited, pensive, filled with the desire of learning; reflecting that she might be the sufficient reason of young Candide and that he might be hers.

On her way back to the castle she met Candide and blushed; Candide also blushed. She bade him good-morning in a hesitating voice; Candide replied without knowing what he was saying. Next day, when they left the table after dinner, Cunegonde and Candide found themselves behind a screen; Cunegonde dropped her handkerchief, Candide picked it up; she innocently held his hand; the young man innocently kissed the young lady's hand with remarkable vivacity, tenderness and grace; their lips met, their eyes sparkled, their knees trembled, their hands wandered. Baron Thunder-ten-tronckh passed near the screen, and, observing this cause and effect, expelled Candide from the castle by kicking him in the backside frequently and hard. Cunegonde swooned; when she recovered her senses, the Baroness slapped her in the face; and all was in consternation in the noblest and most agreeable of all possible castles.

Chapter 2

What happened to Candide among the Bulgarians

Candide, expelled from the earthly paradise, wandered for a long time without knowing where he was going, weeping, turning up his eyes to Heaven, gazing back frequently at the noblest of castles which held the most beautiful of young Baronesses; he lay down to sleep supperless between two furrows in the open fields; it snowed heavily in large flakes. The next morning the shivering Candide, penniless, dying of cold and exhaustion, dragged himself towards the neighboring town, which was called Wald-berghoff-trarbk-dikdorff. He halted sadly at the door of an inn. Two men dressed in blue noticed him.

"Comrade," said one, "there's a well-built young man of the right height."

They went up to Candide and very civilly invited him to dinner.

"Gentlemen," said Candide with charming modesty, "you do me a great honor, but I have no money to pay my share."

"Ah, sir," said one of the men in blue, "persons of your figure and merit never pay anything; are you not five feet five tall?"

"Yes, gentlemen," said he, bowing, "that is my height."

"Ah, sir, come to table; we will not only pay your expenses, we will never allow a man like you to be short of money; men were only made to help each other."

"You are in the right," said Candide, "that is what Doctor Pangloss was always telling me, and I see that everything is for the best."

They begged him to accept a few crowns,[5] he took them and wished to give them an I.O.U.; they refused to take it and all sat down to table.

"Do you not love tenderly. . . ."

"Oh, yes," said he. "I love Miss Cunegonde tenderly."

"No," said one of the gentlemen. "We were asking if you do not tenderly love the King of the Bulgarians."[6]

"Not a bit," said he, "for I have never seen him."

"What! He is the most charming of Kings, and you must drink his health."

"Oh, gladly, gentlemen."

And he drank.

"That is sufficient," he was told. "You are now the support, the aid, the defender, the hero of the Bulgarians; your fortune is made and your glory assured."

They immediately put irons on his legs and took him to a regiment. He was made to turn to right and left, to raise the ramrod and return the ramrod, to take aim, to fire, to double up, and he was given thirty strokes with a stick; the next day he drilled not quite so badly, and received only twenty strokes; the day after, he only had ten and was looked on as a prodigy by his comrades.

Candide was completely mystified and could not make out how he was a hero. One fine spring day he thought he would take a walk, going straight ahead, in the belief that to use his legs as he pleased was a privilege of the human species as well as of animals.

---

5. **crowns:** units of money.
6. **King of the Bulgarians:** Voltaire is satirizing the recruiting practices of King Frederick the Great of Prussia, in whose household he once served.

He had not gone two leagues[7] when four other heroes, each six feet tall, fell upon him, bound him and dragged him back to a cell. He was asked by his judges whether he would rather be thrashed thirty-six times by the whole regiment or receive a dozen lead bullets at once in his brain. Although he protested that men's wills are free and that he wanted neither one nor the other, he had to make a choice; by virtue of that gift of God which is called *liberty*, he determined to run the gauntlet[8] thirty-six times and actually did so twice. There were two thousand men in the regiment. That made four thousand strokes which laid bare the muscles and nerves from his neck to his backside. As they were about to proceed to a third turn, Candide, utterly exhausted, begged as a favor that they would be so kind as to smash his head; he obtained this favor; they bound his eyes and he was made to kneel down. At that moment the King of the Bulgarians came by and inquired the victim's crime; and as this King was possessed of a vast genius, he perceived from what he learned about Candide that he was a young metaphysician[9] very ignorant in worldly matters, and therefore pardoned him with a clemency which will be praised in all newspapers and all ages. An honest surgeon healed Candide in three weeks with the ointments recommended by Dioscorides.[10] He

had already regained a little skin and could walk when the King of the Bulgarians went to war with the King of the Abares.[11]

After escaping the slaughter of the Seven Years' War, Candide encounters Pangloss in Holland. He informs Candide that his beloved Cunegonde has been disemboweled by the Bulgarians and that the Baron's castle and everyone in it is destroyed. While en route to Portugal, the two survive a shipwreck and arrive in Lisbon just in time for the great earthquake. There the Inquisition arrests them as heretics responsible for the devastation and Candide is publicly flogged; Pangloss, however, is hanged and presumed dead. A "good old woman" then reunites Candide with Cunegonde, who describes how she survived the Bulgarians and came to be held by the Grand Inquisitor. Candide kills the Inquisitor and sails with Cunegonde for South America, where they hope to find the best of all possible worlds and lasting happiness. But Candide loses Cunegonde for the sake of the immediate happiness of the governor of Buenos Aires, and again the sweet-natured youth is forced to run, along with his new footman Cacambo. In their flight, they are nearly skewered and boiled by cannibals, the Oreillons, but Cacambo exhibits his clearheadedness by talking the savages out of their dinner plans.

Chapter 17

Arrival of Candide and his valet in the country of Eldorado and what they saw there

When they reached the frontiers of the Oreillons,[12] Cacambo said to Candide:

---

7. **leagues:** units of distance, each one equal to about three miles.
8. **run the gauntlet:** to run between two rows of soldiers who would strike the victim with clubs or other weapons.
9. **metaphysician:** philosopher who studies the nature of being and reality and the origin and structure of the world.
10. **Dioscorides:** Greek army physician of the first century A.D. who wrote medical treatises. Even in Voltaire's day Dioscorides' works were out of date.

11. **Abares:** that is, the French, who fought against the "Bulgarians," or Prussians, in the Seven Years' War (1756–1763).
12. **Oreillons:** *French,* roughly meaning "Big Ears."

THE STORY OF THE SOLDIER, KAREL DUJARDIN
(1622–1678).

? *From this story, what can you gather about Voltaire's attitude toward the military?*

"You see this hemisphere is no better than the other; take my advice, let us go back to Europe by the shortest road."

"How can we go back," said Candide, "and where can we go? If I go to my own country, the Bulgarians and the Abares are murdering everybody; if I return to Portugal[13] I shall be burned; if we stay here, we run the risk of being spitted at any moment. But how can I make up my mind to leave that part of the world where Miss Cunegonde is living?"

"Let us go to Cayenne,"[14] said Cacambo, "we shall find Frenchmen there, for they go all over the world; they might help us. Perhaps God will have pity on us."

It was not easy to go to Cayenne. They knew roughly the direction to take, but mountains, rivers, precipices, brigands and savages were everywhere terrible obstacles. Their horses died of fatigue; their provisions were exhausted; for a whole month they lived on wild fruits and at last found themselves near a little river fringed with coconut-trees which supported their lives and their hopes.

Cacambo, who always gave advice as prudent as the old woman's,[15] said to Candide:

"We can go no further, we have walked far enough; I can see an empty canoe in the bank, let us fill it with coconuts, get into the little boat and drift with the current; a river always leads to some inhabited place. If we do not find anything pleasant, we shall at least find something new."

"Come on then," said Candide, "and let us trust to Providence."

They drifted for some leagues between banks which were sometimes flowery, sometimes bare, sometimes flat, sometimes steep. The river continually became wider; finally it disappeared under an arch of frightful rocks which towered up to the very sky. The two travelers were bold enough to trust themselves to the current under this arch. The stream, narrowed between walls, carried them with horrible rapidity and noise. After twenty-four hours they saw daylight again; but their canoe was wrecked on reefs; they had to crawl from rock to rock for a whole league and at last they discovered an immense horizon, bordered by inaccessible mountains. The country was cultivated for pleasure as well as for necessity; everywhere the useful was agreeable. The roads were

---

13. **Portugal:** Following the earthquake in Lisbon, Candide had been persecuted by the Inquisition. He fears being burned as a heretic if he returns.

14. **Cayenne** (kī·en′): seaport in French Guiana in South America.

15. **the old woman:** The old woman had traveled with Candide and Cunegonde to the New World. She knew everything of life, having survived kidnapping by pirates, enslavement in Morocco, catching the plague in Algiers, and being disfigured by the Turks.

SOUTH AMERICAN JUNGLE, from the series *Geographische Charakterbilder* by Adolf Lehmanns, 1911. *Many Europeans of Voltaire's day actually did believe that a utopian land called Eldorado existed in the New World.*

covered or rather ornamented with carriages of brilliant material and shape, carrying men and women of singular beauty, who were rapidly drawn along by large red sheep whose swiftness surpassed that of the finest horses of Andalusia, Tetuan and Mequinez.

"This country," said Candide, "is better than Westphalia."

He landed with Cacambo near the first village he came to. Several children of the village, dressed in torn gold brocade, were playing coits[16] outside the village. Our two men from the other world amused themselves by looking on; their coits were large round pieces, yellow, red, and green, which

shone with peculiar luster. The travelers were curious enough to pick up some of them; they were of gold, emeralds, and rubies, the least of which would have been the greatest ornament in the Mogul's throne.

"No doubt," said Cacambo, "these children are the sons of the King of this country playing at coits."

At that moment the village schoolmaster appeared to call them into school.

"This," said Candide, "is the tutor of the Royal Family."

The little beggars immediately left their game, abandoning their coits and everything with which they had been playing. Candide picked them up, ran to the tutor, and presented them to him humbly, giving him to

---

16. **coits:** quoits, a game resembling horseshoes.

understand by signs that their Royal Highnesses had forgotten their gold and their precious stones. The village schoolmaster smiled, threw them on the ground, gazed for a moment at Candide's face with much surprise, and continued on his way.

The travelers did not fail to pick up the gold, the rubies, and the emeralds.

"Where are we?" cried Candide. "The children of the Kings must be well brought up, since they are taught to despise gold and precious stones."

Cacambo was as much surprised as Candide. At last they reached the first house in the village, which was built like a European palace. There were crowds of people round the door and still more inside; very pleasant music could be heard and there was a delicious smell of cooking. Cacambo went up to the door and heard them speaking Peruvian; it was his maternal tongue, for everyone knows that Cacambo was born in a village of Tucuman where nothing else is spoken.

"I will act as your interpreter," he said to Candide, "this is an inn, let us enter."

Immediately two boys and two girls of the inn, dressed in cloth of gold, whose hair was bound up with ribbons, invited them to sit down to the table d'hôte.[17] They served four soups each garnished with two parrots, a boiled condor which weighed two hundred pounds, two roast monkeys of excellent flavor, three hundred colibris[18] in one dish and six hundred hummingbirds in another, exquisite ragouts and delicious pastries, all in dishes of a sort of rock-crystal. The boys and girls brought several sorts of drinks made of sugar-cane. Most of the guests were merchants and coachmen, all extremely polite,

who asked Cacambo a few questions with the most delicate discretion and answered his in a satisfactory manner.

When the meal was over, Cacambo, like Candide, thought he could pay the reckoning by throwing on the table two of the large pieces of gold he had picked up; the host and hostess laughed until they had to hold their sides. At last they recovered themselves.

"Gentlemen," said the host, "we perceive you are strangers; we are not accustomed to seeing them. Forgive us if we began to laugh when you offered us in payment the stones from our highways. No doubt you have none of the money of this country, but you do not need any to dine here. All the hotels established for the utility of commerce are paid for by the government. You have been ill-entertained here because this is a poor village; but everywhere else you will be received as you deserve to be."

Cacambo explained to Candide all that the host had said, and Candide listened in the same admiration and disorder with which his friend Cacambo interpreted.

"What can this country be," they said to each other, "which is unknown to the rest of the world and where all nature is so different from ours? Probably it is the country where everything is for the best; for there must be one country of that sort. And, in spite of what Dr. Pangloss said, I often noticed that everything went very ill in Westphalia."

Chapter 18

What they saw in the land of Eldorado

Cacambo informed the host of his curiosity, and the host said:

"I am a very ignorant man and am all the better for it; but we have here an old man

---

17. **table d'hôte** (tä′bəl dōt′): a complete meal served at a fixed price.
18. **colibris:** hummingbirds with curved bills, once classified as a separate species.

who has retired from the court and who is the most learned and most communicative man in the kingdom."

And he at once took Cacambo to the old man. Candide now played only the second part and accompanied his valet.

They entered a very simple house, for the door was only of silver and the paneling of the apartments in gold, but so tastefully carved that the richest decorations did not surpass it. The antechamber indeed was only encrusted with rubies and emeralds; but the order with which everything was arranged atoned for this extreme simplicity.

The old man received the two strangers on a sofa padded with colibri feathers, and presented them with drinks in diamond cups; after which he satisfied their curiosity in these words:

"I am a hundred and seventy-two years old and I heard from my late father, the King's equerry,[19] the astonishing revolutions of Peru of which he had been an eyewitness. The kingdom where we now are is the ancient country of the Incas, who most imprudently left it to conquer part of the world and were at last destroyed by the Spaniards.

"The princes of their family who remained in their native country had more wisdom; with the consent of the nation, they ordered that no inhabitants should ever leave our little kingdom, and this it is that has preserved our innocence and our felicity. The Spaniards had some vague knowledge of this country, which they called Eldorado,[20] and about a hundred years ago an Englishman named Raleigh[21] came very near to it; but, since we are surrounded by inaccessible rocks and precipices, we have hitherto been exempt from the rapacity[22] of the nations of Europe who have an inconceivable lust for the pebbles and mud of our land and would kill us to the last man to get possession of them."

The conversation was long; it touched upon the form of the government, manners, women, public spectacles, and the arts. Finally Candide, who was always interested in metaphysics, asked through Cacambo whether the country had a religion. The old man blushed a little.

"How can you doubt it?" said he. "Do you think we are ingrates?"

Cacambo humbly asked what was the religion of Eldorado. The old man blushed again.

"Can there be two religions?" said he. "We have, I think, the religion of everyone else; we adore God from evening until morning."

"Do you adore only one god?" said Cacambo, who continued to act as the interpreter of Candide's doubts.

"Manifestly," said the old man, "there are not two or three or four. I must confess that the people of your world ask very extraordinary questions."

Candide continued to press the old man with questions; he wished to know how they prayed to God in Eldorado.

"We do not pray," said the good and respectable sage, "we have nothing to ask from him; he has given us everything necessary and we continually give him thanks."

Candide was curious to see the priests; and asked where they were. The good old man smiled.

---

19. **equerry** (ek'wər·ē): officer in charge of horses.

20. **Eldorado** (el'də·rä'dō): Spanish for "the Golden Man," after the practice of certain Colombian natives of coating their new kings in gold dust. The name eventually came to refer to any legendary place of spectacular riches.

21. **Raleigh:** Sir Walter Raleigh's *Discovery of Guiana* (1595) helped spread the legend of Eldorado.

22. **rapacity:** greed.

"My friends," said he, "we are all priests; the King and all the heads of families solemnly sing praises every morning, accompanied by five or six thousand musicians."

"What! Have you no monks to teach, to dispute, to govern, to intrigue and to burn people who do not agree with them?"

"For that, we should have to become fools," said the old man; "here we are all of the same opinion and do not understand what you mean with your monks."

At all this Candide was in an ecstasy and said to himself:

"This is very different from Westphalia and the castle of His Lordship the Baron; if our friend Pangloss had seen Eldorado, he would not have said that the castle of Thunder-ten-tronckh was the best of all that exists on the earth; certainly, a man should travel."

After this long conversation the good old man ordered a carriage to be harnessed with six sheep and gave the two travelers twelve of his servants to take them to court.

"You will excuse me," he said, "if my age deprives me of the honor of accompanying you. The King will receive you in a manner which will not displease you and doubtless you will pardon the customs of the country if any of them disconcert you."

Candide and Cacambo entered the carriage; the six sheep galloped off and in less than four hours they reached the King's palace, which was situated at one end of the capital. The portal was two hundred and twenty feet high and a hundred feet wide; it is impossible to describe its material. Anyone can see the prodigious superiority it must have over the pebbles and sand we call *gold* and *gems*.

Twenty beautiful maidens of the guard received Candide and Cacambo as they alighted from the carriage, conducted them to the baths and dressed them in robes woven from the down of colibris; after which the principal male and female officers of the Crown led them to his Majesty's apartment through two files of a thousand musicians each, according to the usual custom. As they approached the throne room, Cacambo asked one of the chief officers how they should behave in his Majesty's presence; whether they should fall on their knees or flat on their faces, whether they should put their hands on their heads or on their backsides; whether they should lick the dust of the throne room; in a word, what was the ceremony?

"The custom," said the chief officer, "is to embrace the King and to kiss him on either cheek."

Candide and Cacambo threw their arms round his Majesty's neck; he received them with all imaginable favor and politely asked them to supper.

Meanwhile they were carried to see the town, the public buildings rising to the very skies, the marketplaces ornamented with thousands of columns, the fountains of pure water, the fountains of rose-water and of liquors distilled from sugar-cane, which played continually in the public squares paved with precious stones which emitted a perfume like that of cloves and cinnamon.

Candide asked to see the law courts; he was told there were none, and that nobody ever went to law. He asked if there were prisons and was told there were none. He was still more surprised and pleased by the palace of sciences, where he saw a gallery two thousand feet long, filled with instruments of mathematics and physics.

After they had explored all the afternoon about a thousandth part of the town, they were taken back to the King. Candide sat down to table with his Majesty, his valet

Cacambo and several ladies. Never was better cheer, and never was anyone wittier at supper than his Majesty. Cacambo explained the King's witty remarks to Candide and even when translated they still appeared witty. Among all the things which amazed Candide, this did not amaze him the least.

They enjoyed this hospitality for a month. Candide repeatedly said to Cacambo:

"Once again, my friend, it is quite true that the castle where I was born cannot be compared with this country; but then Miss Cunegonde is not here and you probably have a mistress in Europe. If we remain here, we shall only be like everyone else; but if we return to our own world with only twelve sheep laden with Eldorado pebbles, we shall be richer than all the kings put together; we shall have no more Inquisitors[23] to fear and we can easily regain Miss Cunegonde."

Cacambo agreed with this; it is so pleasant to be on the move, to show off before friends, to make a parade of the things seen on one's travels, that these two happy men resolved to be so no longer and to ask his Majesty's permission to depart.

"You are doing a very silly thing," said the King. "I know my country is small; but when we are comfortable anywhere we should stay there; I certainly have not the right to detain foreigners, that is a tyranny which does not exist either in our manners or our laws; all men are free, leave when you please, but the way out is very difficult. It is impossible to ascend the rapid river by which you miraculously came here and which flows under arches of rock. The mountains which surround the whole of my kingdom are ten thousand feet high and as perpendicular as rocks; they are more than ten leagues broad and you can only get down from them by way of precipices. However, since you must go, I will give orders to the directors of machinery to make a machine which will carry you comfortably. When you have been taken to the other side of the mountains, nobody can proceed any farther with you; for my subjects have sworn never to pass this boundary and they are too wise to break their oath. Ask anything else of me you wish."

"We ask nothing of your Majesty," said Cacambo, "except a few sheep laden with provisions, pebbles, and the mud of this country."

The King laughed.

"I cannot understand," said he, "the taste you people of Europe have for our yellow mud; but take as much as you wish, and much good may it do you."

He immediately ordered his engineers to make a machine to hoist these two extraordinary men out of his kingdom.

Three thousand learned scientists worked at it; it was ready in a fortnight and only cost about twenty million pounds sterling in the money of that country. Candide and Cacambo were placed on the machine; there were two large red sheep saddled and bridled for them to ride on when they had passed the mountains, twenty sumpter[24] sheep laden with provisions, thirty carrying presents of the most curious productions of the country and fifty laden with gold, precious stones and diamonds. The King embraced the two vagabonds tenderly.

Their departure was a splendid sight and so was the ingenious manner in which they and their sheep were hoisted on to the top of the mountains.

---

23. **Inquisitors:** members of the Roman Catholic tribunal charged with combating heresy.

24. **sumpter:** used for carrying packs and other loads.

The scientists took leave of them after having landed them safely, and Candide's only desire and object was to go and present Miss Cunegonde with his sheep.

"We have sufficient to pay the governor of Buenos Aires," said he, "if Miss Cunegonde can be bought. Let us go to Cayenne, and take ship, and then we will see what kingdom we will buy."

Chapter 19

What happened to them at Surinam, and how Candide made the acquaintance of Martin

Our two travelers' first day was quite pleasant. They were encouraged by the idea of possessing more treasures than all Asia, Europe and Africa could collect. Candide in transport carved the name of Cunegonde on the trees.

On the second day two of the sheep stuck in a marsh and were swallowed up with their loads; two other sheep died of fatigue a few days later; then seven or eight died of hunger in a desert; several days afterwards others fell off precipices. Finally, after they had traveled for a hundred days, they had only two sheep left. Candide said to Cacambo:

"My friend, you see how perishable are the riches of this world; nothing is steadfast but virtue and the happiness of seeing Miss Cunegonde again."

The Cleveland Museum of Art, John L. Severance Fund, 71.102

THE KISS OF PEACE AND JUSTICE, LAURENT DE LA HYRE (1606–1656).
Does justice exist in Voltaire's world?

"I admit it," said Cacambo, "but we still have two sheep with more treasures than ever the King of Spain will have, and in the distance I see a town I suspect is Surinam,[25] which belongs to the Dutch. We are at the end of our troubles and the beginning of our happiness."

As they drew near the town they met a Negro lying on the ground wearing only half his clothes, that is to say, a pair of blue cotton drawers; this poor man had no left leg and no right hand.

"Good Heavens!" said Candide to him in Dutch, "what are you doing there, my friend, in this horrible state?"

"I am waiting for my master, the famous merchant Mr. Vanderdendur."

"Was it Mr. Vanderdendur," said Candide, "who treated you in this way?"

"Yes, sir," said the Negro, "it is the custom. We are given a pair of cotton drawers twice a year as clothing. When we work in the sugar-mills and the grindstone catches our fingers, they cut off the hand; when we try to run away, they cut off a leg. Both these things happened to me. This is the price paid for the sugar you eat in Europe. But when my mother sold me for ten patagons[26] on the coast of Guinea, she said to me: 'My dear child, give thanks to our fetishes,[27] always worship them, and they will make you happy; you have the honor to be a slave of our lords the white men and thereby you have made the fortune of your father and mother.' Alas! I do not know whether I made their fortune, but they certainly did not make mine. Dogs, monkeys, and parrots are a thousand times less miserable than we are; the Dutch fetishes who converted me tell me every Sunday that we are all of us, whites and blacks, the children of Adam. I am not a genealogist, but if these preachers tell the truth, we are all second cousins. Now, you will admit that no one could treat his relatives in a more horrible way."

"O Pangloss!" cried Candide. "This is an abomination you had not guessed; this is too much, in the end I shall have to renounce optimism."

"What is optimism?" said Cacambo.

"Alas!" said Candide, "it is the mania of maintaining that everything is well when we are wretched."

PORTRAIT OF JEAN-GABRIEL LA PORTE DU THEIL, JACQUES AVED, 1740.

---

25. **Surinam** (so͞or′i·näm′): former Dutch colony in South America.

26. **patagons:** units of money used in Patagonia, in southern South America.

27. **fetishes:** sacred objects believed to possess magical powers.

And he shed tears as he looked at his Negro; and he entered Surinam weeping.

The first thing they inquired was whether there was any ship in the port which could be sent to Buenos Aires. The person they addressed happened to be a Spanish captain, who offered to strike an honest bargain with them. He arranged to meet them at an inn. Candide and the faithful Cacambo went and waited for him with their two sheep.

Candide, who blurted everything out, told the Spaniard all his adventures and confessed that he wanted to elope with Miss Cunegonde.

"I shall certainly not take you to Buenos Aires," said the captain. "I should be hanged and you would too. The fair Cunegonde is his Lordship's favorite mistress."

Candide was thunderstruck; he sobbed for a long time; then he took Cacambo aside.

"My dear friend," said he, "this is what you must do. We each have in our pockets five or six million pounds' worth of diamonds; you are more skillful than I am; go to Buenos Aires and get Miss Cunegonde. If the governor makes any difficulties give him a million; if he is still obstinate give him two; you have not killed an Inquisitor, so they will not suspect you. I will fit out another ship, I will go and wait for you at Venice; it is a free country where there is nothing to fear from Bulgarians, Abares, Jews, or Inquisitors."

Cacambo applauded this wise resolution; he was in despair at leaving a good master who had become his intimate friend; but the pleasure of being useful to him overcame the grief of leaving him. They embraced with tears. Candide urged him not to forget the good old woman. Cacambo set off that very same day; he was a very good man, this Cacambo.

Candide remained some time longer at Surinam waiting for another captain to take him to Italy with the two sheep he had left. He engaged servants and bought everything necessary for a long voyage. At last Mr. Vanderdendur, the owner of a large ship, came to see him.

"How much do you want," he asked this man, "to take me straight to Venice with my servants, my baggage, and these two sheep?"

The captain asked for ten thousand piasters.[28] Candide did not hesitate.

"Oh! Ho!" said the prudent Vanderdendur to himself, "this foreigner gives ten thousand piasters immediately! He must be very rich."

He returned a moment afterwards and said he could not sail for less than twenty thousand.

"Very well, you shall have them," said Candide.

"Whew!" said the merchant to himself, "this man gives twenty thousand piasters as easily as ten thousand."

He came back again, and said he could not take him to Venice for less than thirty thousand piasters.

"Then you shall have thirty thousand," replied Candide.

"Oho!" said the Dutch merchant to himself again, "thirty thousand piasters is nothing to this man; obviously the two sheep are laden with immense treasures; I will not insist any further; first let me make him pay the thirty thousand piasters, and then we will see."

Candide sold two little diamonds, the smaller of which was worth more than all the money the captain asked. He paid him in advance. The two sheep were taken on board. Candide followed in a little boat to join the ship which rode at anchor; the captain watched his time, set his sails and weighed anchor; the wind was favorable.

---

28. **piasters:** units of money.

Dutch Men-of-War in the West Indies, Bonaventura Peeters (1614–1652).

Candide, bewildered and stupefied, soon lost sight of him.

"Alas!" he cried, "this is a trick worthy of the old world."

He returned to shore, in grief; for he had lost enough to make the fortune of twenty kings.

He went to the Dutch judge; and, as he was rather disturbed, he knocked loudly at the door; he went in, related what had happened and talked a little louder than he ought to have done. The judge began by fining him ten thousand piasters for the noise he had made; he then listened patiently to him, promised to look into his affair as soon as the merchant returned, and charged him another ten thousand piasters for the expenses of the audience.

This behavior reduced Candide to despair; he had indeed endured misfortunes a thousand times more painful; but the calmness of the judge and of the captain who had robbed him, stirred up his bile[29] and plunged him into a black melancholy. The malevolence of men revealed itself to his mind in all its ugliness; he entertained only gloomy ideas. At last a French ship was about to leave for Bordeaux[30] and, since he no longer had any sheep laden with diamonds to put on board, he hired a cabin at a reasonable price and announced throughout the town that he would give the passage, food and

---

29. **bile:** bodily fluid once believed to cause bitterness of spirit or melancholy.

30. **Bordeaux** (bôr·do′): a port city in southwest France, located in the region of the same name.

two thousand piasters to an honest man who would make the journey with him, on condition that this man was the most unfortunate and the most disgusted with his condition in the whole province.

Such a crowd of applicants arrived that a fleet would not have contained them. Candide, wishing to choose among the most likely, picked out twenty persons who seemed reasonably sociable and who all claimed to deserve his preference. He collected them in a tavern and gave them supper, on condition that each took an oath to relate truthfully the story of his life, promising that he would choose the man who seemed to him the most deserving of pity and to have the most cause for being discontented with his condition, and that he would give the others a little money.

The sitting lasted until four o'clock in the morning. As Candide listened to their adventures he remembered what the old woman had said on the voyage to Buenos Aires and how she had wagered that there was nobody on the boat who had not experienced very great misfortunes. At each story which was told him, he thought of Pangloss.

"This Pangloss," said he, "would have some difficulty in supporting his system. I wish he were here. Certainly, if everything is well, it is only in Eldorado and not in the rest of the world."

He finally determined in favor of a poor man of letters who had worked ten years for the booksellers at Amsterdam. He judged that there was no occupation in the world which could more disgust a man.

This man of letters,[31] who was also a good man, had been robbed by his wife, beaten by his son, and abandoned by his daughter, who had eloped with a Portuguese. He had just been deprived of a small post on which he depended and the preachers of Surinam were persecuting him because they thought he was a Socinian.[32]

It must be admitted that the others were at least as unfortunate as he was; but Candide hoped that this learned man would help to pass the time during the voyage. All his other rivals considered that Candide was doing them a great injustice; but he soothed them down by giving each of them a hundred piasters.

With Martin to counsel him, Candide finds his way back to Europe, where little by little he loses the rest of his fortune from Eldorado. Eventually, he is reunited with Cunegonde as well as Cacambo, Pangloss, and the old woman. Candide marries Cunegonde, even though she has by now grown horribly ugly. With their companions, they retire to a little farm, where they learn to work together to cultivate a garden in the hope of making life bearable.

---

31. **man of letters:** a term used to refer to a writer or scholar; here, Martin.
32. **Socinian:** a heretic, follower of the sixteenth-century Polish theologian Socinus, whose ''rational'' Christianity, among other things, denied the divinity of Christ.

First Thoughts

Do you feel sympathy for Candide, or do you think he deserves everything he gets?

Identifying Facts

1. What does Candide do to get himself expelled from the Baron's castle?

2. What happens to Candide among the Bulgarians?

3. Briefly describe the main characteristics of Eldorado. What value do the inhabitants place on gold and gems?

4. What reasons does Candide give for wanting to leave Eldorado and return to his own world?

5. Explain how "the prudent Vanderdendur" and the Dutch judge trick Candide.

6. Why does Candide ultimately select Martin—"a poor man of letters"—to be his traveling companion?

Interpreting Meanings

1. **Satire**, or writing that ridicules human shortcomings in order to improve society, relies on many elements usually associated with comedy—exaggeration, understatement, warped logic, and improbable situations. Using these four elements as headings, list as many examples of each as you can find in the selection.

2. As Chapter 2 illustrates, Candide suffers every time he exercises what he believes to be his free will. What forces does Voltaire suggest get in the way of a person's exercise of free will?

3. From Voltaire's description of Eldorado, what can you infer are his views on organized religion, on the proper role of government, and on wealth?

4. From the contrast he draws between Eldorado and Surinam, what does Voltaire imply are the causes of evil in the world?

5. The character of Candide is used to reflect Voltaire's attitudes both directly and by contrast. Which of Candide's statements do you think most closely expresses Voltaire's personal definition of optimism? Do you agree with Voltaire's view? Explain.

Applying Meanings

Voltaire wrote *Candide* more than 230 years ago. In your opinion, how well has its satire aged? What value, if any, does *Candide* hold for someone growing up in today's world?

Critical Writing Response

Analyzing an Author's Use of Humor. Few readers would deny that Voltaire's writing in *Candide* is savagely witty. But is his humor intended merely to amuse, or does it have a more serious purpose? (Why, for example, do you suppose we find ourselves laughing *at* Voltaire's characters and never *with* them?) Write an essay in which you explain how Voltaire uses humor in *Candide* and how it enables him to fulfill his purpose.

Creative Writing Response

Writing a Satire. Working alone or with a partner, write a short skit in which you satirize a public folly. First, choose a well-known subject and identify the folly that you feel needs to be reformed. Next, devise an improbable situation that will expose the folly. Use exaggeration, understatement, and warped logic to create satiric humor. Remember, your purpose is to promote social reform.

ELEMENTS OF LITERATURE

The Utopia as a Literary Genre

The word *utopia* (yo͞o·tō′pē·ə) is derived from Greek and means "no place." Sir Thomas More was the first to employ this word for a literary genre when he wrote his famous book *Utopia* (1516), an account of an imaginary republic. He fully intended a pun on the Greek word *eutopia,* which means "place (where all is) well."

The idea of an imaginary earthly paradise goes back to antiquity. Elements of it can be found in the Mesopotamian classic *Gilgamesh* (see page 136), as well as in Homer's descriptions of the Elysian Fields in the *Odyssey.* Plato's *Republic* was the first full-fledged description of a utopia, though of a distinctly Spartan and authoritarian type. Within medieval Christianity itself, and especially after St. Augustine, the attainment of a heavenly city was considered a perfectly reasonable objective.

The main impulse in utopian literature is to imagine a social and political order free of the cruelties and corruptions of the existing order. More's *Utopia,* for example, retains some of Plato's authoritarianism and incorporates the harsh moral codes of More's own time, but its welfare state is socialistic in character, with its abolition of private property and its free universal education, medicine, food, and the like. Voltaire's Eldorado, the city of gold where gold has no monetary value, is essentially in More's tradition.

Countless literary utopias were explored in the seventeenth and eighteenth centuries. Much later, H. G. Wells, the author of *A Modern Utopia,* among many other books of this type, became perhaps the most interesting writer of this genre in the present century. The popularity of utopian literature has produced its opposite as well, the **dystopia**, or anti-utopia, which portrays an imaginary world of pure horror. Aldous Huxley's *Brave New World* and George Orwell's *Animal Farm* and *Nineteen Eighty-four* are examples of this countergenre. Much of science fiction, we might note, hovers between the utopian and the anti-utopian.

If, as Candide concludes, everything is well "only in Eldorado," why do you suppose he does not try to return there? In other words, what ironic point is Voltaire making by having his hero end up with an ugly wife on a little farm where he does nothing more earth-shattering than cultivate a garden?

BEHIND THE SCENES

Drama in the Enlightenment

Although Renaissance playwrights such as Shakespeare produced a variety of types of plays—comedies, histories, tragedies, and romances—comedy was the form that flourished in the Enlightenment. During this period, writers were concerned with style, wit, and, above all, a rational approach to life. Comedy, by its very nature, tests the rationality of society's norms. Many comic plots dramatize a leading character's temporary departure from such norms, eventually followed by a "return" to society.

In France, the leading comic dramatist was Molière (mōl·yer') (1622–1673). Molière brilliantly succeeded at combining the grace, wit, and elegance of **high comedy**—derived from the ancient Roman tradition of Plautus and Terence—with the slapstick of the commedia dell'arte (kôm·me'dyä del lär'te), a form that was highly popular in seventeenth-century France. After a long period of apprenticeship in the provinces, Molière returned to Paris in 1658 to perform for King Louis XIV, who became his chief patron.

The central characters in Molière's plays suffer from obsessions such as greed in *The Miser,* social status in *The Would-Be Gentleman,* religious hypocrisy in *Tartuffe,* or relentless honesty in *The Misanthrope.* Molière satirizes the extreme natures of these characters, exploiting their comic potential.

Molière and the Comedy of Manners

Because of Molière's keen psychological insight into the manners and mannerisms of his characters, his plays are often said to be the first examples of the **comedy of manners**. The focus of this kind of comedy is on the customs, social class, costume, speech, and gestures of the characters, who are usually drawn from society's middle or upper classes. Comedies of manners usually feature a love plot in which two young people conquer all obstacles to their union—often posed by their curmudgeonly elders—and marry at the end of the play. Some comedies of manners, like Molière's, satirize the behavior of their leading characters, but many rely on the wit and sophistication of their subjects to entertain and amuse the audience.

At about the same time Molière was transforming theater in France, political forces were shaping a new theater in England. In 1642, a civil war between the Puritans, led by Oliver Cromwell, and the supporters of King Charles I rocked England. The Puritans, who eventually defeated the King's forces and beheaded Charles, closed all theaters in England. In 1660, Parliament invited Charles II to return from his exile in France, and the monarchy was restored. The new king, who was especially fond of plays, lost no time in ordering the reopening of the theaters. Thus was born the Restoration Period.

Restoration Drama in England

Several playwrights led the development of **Restoration drama**, which produced mainly witty—and often satirical—comedies of manners. George Etherege (eth'ər·ij) (c. 1635?–1692?) produced only

Molière in the role of Arnolphe in *École des femmes (School for Wives).* Lithograph by Delpech.

three plays, but these satirical comedies had an important role in setting the tone for drama of the age. Etherege's best play was *The Man of Mode* (1676), which made fun of the affected manners of upper-class courtiers.

William Wycherley (wich'ər·lē) (1640–1716) also satirized phoniness and hypocrisy in comedies such as *The Country Wife* (1675) and *The Plain Dealer* (1676). But it was only in the plays of William Congreve (1670–1729) that the barbed satire of Restoration comedy was tempered by a strain of tolerance and good humor. Critics have often praised Congreve's *The Way of the World* (1700) as the masterpiece of this period.

In the eighteenth century, two playwrights, Oliver Goldsmith (1730–1774) and Richard B. Sheridan (1750–1816), had outstanding success in combining elements of the comedy of manners with satire. Goldsmith triumphed with *She Stoops to Conquer* (1773). The best known of Sheridan's plays is probably *The School for Scandal,* which delighted London audiences even as British troops were attempting to stifle the rebellion of the American colonies.

Innovations in Staging

Drama of the Enlightenment developed a number of theatrical innovations that we now take for granted. In Restoration England, for example, plays were performed in enclosed theaters, as opposed to the semi-open-air playhouses of Elizabethan times. This meant that artificial lighting became an important aspect of stage production for the first time. Restoration playhouses also featured the proscenium (prō·sē′nē·əm) arch stage, consisting of a raised platform enclosed above by an arch behind which a curtain could be drawn. Modern departures from the conventional proscenium stage—such as the theater-in-the-round—still tend to be regarded as rather daring, experimental stagings.

Finally, English Restoration drama gave birth to the career of actresses. For the first time, women could play female parts (these had been taken by boys in Shakespeare's era). King Charles II himself, who acquired the nickname of the "Merry Monarch," was pleased by this shift, making no attempt to disguise his fondness for one of the leading actresses of the Restoration theater, Nell Gwyn.

LANGUAGE
—AND—
CULTURE

THE PRINT REVOLUTION

Who Really *Invented* Printing?

Many people at many different times contributed to the invention of printing. Four thousand years before Christ, the Babylonians stamped soft clay with engraved seals. About 175 B.C., the Chinese engraved stone blocks and made paper copies by rubbing. In A.D. 868, the Chinese produced the oldest existing printed book, made by pressing blank paper to carved wooden blocks. About the same time, Arabic block printing was coming into use in Egypt. In 1405, printing technology in Asia took a giant leap forward in Korea, where artisans cast a bronze movable type. Movable type revolutionized printing. Now, instead of carving a new block for each page of text, printers could rearrange individual characters to create different pages of type.

Europeans got the idea of movable type at the same time, around 1440, but without knowing about the Korean invention. Credit for the invention of movable type in Europe is usually given to Johann Gutenberg, a German. Before Gutenberg's invention, European books were made almost exclusively in monasteries. Many monks, called scribes, would simultaneously hand copy what another monk read aloud. Gutenberg's innovation would make this painstaking process obsolete. Between 1450 and 1455, using a press modeled after a wine press, lead type cast in bronze molds, and traditional pen and ink combined with linseed oil,

Pages from the Gutenberg Bible.

Harry Ransom Humanities Research Center, The University of Texas at Austin

he produced a two-volume Bible. He worked slowly, printing only about twenty impressions an hour. Gutenberg's venture was financed by a wealthy goldsmith named Johann Fust. Unfortunately, Gutenberg could not repay his debt, and Fust seized his equipment.

Printing in the Renaissance

Over the next few decades, many developments occurred in the new printing technology. Since Germans at the time were using Gothic script, which resembles a series of heavy vertical lines, distinguished by dots, dashes, and lighter connecting lines, the first type was cut to look like Gothic handwriting. Unfortunately, Gothic type was almost as much work to read as it was to print. In 1470, Nicholas Jenson designed a much more readable ''roman'' type that is still used today. The first printed newspaper, called the *Gazetta* after the coin paid for one copy, appeared in 1536 in Venice. By the 1570s, printers were able to produce five hundred sheets a day, and apprentice printers in France were complaining that their working days (from 2 A.M. to 8 P.M.) were too long.

One of the first effects of the new technology was increased censorship, for printing threatened the Church's traditional monopoly over knowledge. A printer had to obtain a license from the government authorities for each printed item. But there were many secret presses, and the Reformation kept them humming, producing a constant flow of documents that were not Church-approved. Another change caused by printing was the standardization of European languages. People

New York Public Library Picture Collection

English print office.

from the same country often used many different words to mean the same thing. In fifteenth-century England, for instance, people could not agree whether to use the word *egg* or *eyren*. Variations like these caused inconsistencies in the printers' texts and slowed the printing process. The need for dictionaries showing standardized spellings became urgent. In 1604, Robert Cawdrey, a schoolmaster, compiled the first English dictionary, *The Table Alphabeticall of Hard Words*.

Perhaps the most important outcome of the new technology was the spread of literacy among ordinary people. During the Middle Ages, books belonged to the privileged few and most people could not read. But during the sixteenth century printed books became cheap and plentiful. More and more people learned to read. Books on such subjects as arithmetic, anatomy, and history were read and discussed, and information that once might have belonged only to a few now was available to anyone who could read. In the few short decades since Gutenberg's invention, printing had transformed Europe.

USING ACTIVE AND PASSIVE VOICES EFFECTIVELY

"English," observes author Roger Garrison, "is a cause-and-effect language." With its noun-verb format, English focuses on who did what. To ensure that your writing is direct and clear, keep verbs in the active voice.

Active and Passive Voices

Voice, like tense, is a characteristic of verbs. Verbs can be in the **active** or the **passive** voice. Verbs in the passive voice can blur the focus. Sentences with verbs in the passive tell what happened, but not who did it. For this reason, overusing the passive makes your writing seem vague or evasive.

PASSIVE VOICE

Voltaire *was exiled* for his writings.

ACTIVE VOICE

The kings of France and Prussia *exiled* Voltaire for his writings.

The passive consists of a form of "to be" and a past participle.

Notice that, in the examples above, the first sentence does not tell who exiled Voltaire. From the Renaissance through modern times, writers have used the passive to conceal responsibility for unpopular actions.

Some sentences using the passive have extra phrases to show who or what performs the action.

PASSIVE

Laura *is admired* from afar by Petrarch.

ACTIVE

Petrarch *admires* Laura from afar.

Though the first sentence does specify who admires Laura, it is unnecessarily wordy and indirect.

Exercise 1: Choosing the Active Voice

Underline the verb in each sentence. Then, for each set, circle the sentence whose verb is in the active voice.

1. a. Petrarch was appointed poet laureate of Italy.
   b. The king of Italy appointed Petrarch poet laureate.
2. a. Barbary pirates captured Cervantes.
   b. Cervantes was captured by Barbary pirates.
3. a. In his sonnets, Shakespeare praises love.
   b. In Shakespeare's sonhets, love is praised.
4. a. Don Quixote has read the medieval epics of the Cid and Roland.
   b. The medieval epics of the Cid and Roland have been read by Don Quixote.
5. a. In *The Tempest*, a "sea change" is mentioned in Ariel's song.

b. Ariel's song in *The Tempest* mentions a "sea change."

6. a. The rats make a decision to bell the cat.
   b. The decision to bell the cat is made by the rats.

7. a. Pangloss advises Candide that everything happens for the best.
   b. Candide is advised that everything happens for the best.

8. a. La Fontaine retells several fables attributed to Aesop.
   b. Several fables attributed to Aesop are retold by La Fontaine.

9. a. The *Mona Lisa* was painted by Leonardo da Vinci.
   b. Leonardo da Vinci painted the *Mona Lisa*.

10. a. Boccaccio's literary reputation was established by the *Decameron*.
    b. The *Decameron* established Boccaccio's literary reputation.

Uses of the Active and Passive Voices

In a few situations, you may use the passive voice. Writers sometimes choose the passive when they do not know who or what performs an action.

PASSIVE   Candide *had been robbed*.
ACTIVE   The captain *had robbed* Candide.

You might write the first sentence if you did not know who had robbed Candide. Writers can also use the passive to create emphasis. In the examples above, the first sentence emphasizes the word *robbed* by placing it last. In most situations, however, choose the active voice. It will keep your writing concise and straightforward.

Exercise 2: Using Active and Passive Voices

Write an original sentence for each situation outlined below. After your sentence, write *A* or *P* to indicate whether you have used the active or the passive voice. Be prepared to give reasons for your choices.

1. You want to summarize Ronsard's message to Hélène: One day, she will be overtaken by old age. She will then be filled with regret for spurning Ronsard.

2. You want to convey the fact that, although Cervantes was plagued by debt throughout his life, his writing was not hindered by his financial difficulties.

3. You want readers to understand that, near the beginning of *The Tempest,* a shipwreck occurs. You do not remember what wrecks the ship.

4. You want to communicate two ideas: 1) that *The Tempest* is filled with fantasy and romance, and 2) that several serious purposes are served by the fantasy and romance.

5. You want to define **satire** and give an example of satire from *Candide.*

RESOLVING A CONTROVERSY

The Renaissance and the Enlightenment were not vastly different from our own time. Breakthroughs in science and thinking had changed the world, just as they have today. As a result, people strove for social and political reforms, just as we do today. Think of modern reforms you and your friends would like to see. In your school, your community, the nation, or the world, which things are most in need of change?

Writing Assignment

Write an informative essay in which you analyze a controversial problem and propose a solution to it. Assume that your audience has not explored the problem in detail. For this assignment, you will examine two sides of an issue, taking both into account to devise a solution.

Background

Sometimes pointing out a problem is the first step toward resolving it. Cervantes' humor exposes the public's shallow tastes. Voltaire and La Fontaine use satire to spotlight hypocrisy and corruption. Reflect on the issues these writers deal with. Then think of modern problems, large or small, that are important to you personally. Choose one that is creating significant controversy.

Prewriting

Defining the Problem. Once you have selected a controversial problem, you need to establish its boundaries. Answering the following questions in depth will help.

1. What is the problem?
2. Why should people care about it? What could happen if it remains unsolved?
3. What is the controversy over the problem? Explain the views and concerns of each side.
4. What is the history of the problem?

Look over your answers, and decide which questions cannot be answered fully without more facts. Conduct a survey, interview experts, or carry out other research to get the facts you need. Then compose a statement summarizing the problem and the controversy that surrounds it.

Developing the Solution. Brainstorm a list of as many solutions as you can come up with. Then go over your list, circling the solutions that represent a compromise in the controversy. Use a chart like the following one to evaluate the solutions you have circled.

Solutions	Merits	Drawbacks
1.		
2.		
3.		
4.		

Choose the solution that best addresses the concerns of both sides in the controversy and that has the fewest drawbacks. Then freewrite to plan in detail how the solution could be implemented.

Writing

Use these guidelines to draft your essay.

1. **Introductory Paragraph.** Begin with either a quote or an anecdote that dramatizes the problem or the controversy. Follow with the statement you composed to summarize the issue. Then supply any brief background information that is basic to an understanding of the issue.

2. **Body Paragraphs.** Though all your body paragraphs should offer more details about the problem you have chosen, each paragraph can also serve a separate purpose. For example, in one paragraph you can show why readers should care about the problem; in another you can explore each side of the controversy; and in yet another you can put forth your solution, noting how it addresses both sides of the issue. You can write an additional paragraph about the way to implement the solution. Use your prewriting notes as sources of facts and details for each paragraph. Be sure that transitions in each paragraph are appropriate to the paragraph's purpose (see page 56).

3. **Concluding Paragraph.** Summarize both the controversial issue and the solution you have proposed. Then, referring to your chart, evaluate your solution, noting its weaknesses but ending with emphasis on its strengths.

Evaluating and Revising

Use these questions to evaluate and revise your essay.

1. Does your introductory paragraph capture readers' attention and define the problem?

2. Do you provide facts and examples to show why readers should care about the problem?

3. Do you explain the controversy in adequate detail, exploring the history of the issue and specifying the concerns of each side?

4. Have you explained your solution clearly?

5. Does your analysis proceed logically from problem to solution? Have you used appropriate transitions to reveal your line of reasoning?

6. Are your sentences grammatically correct and varied in structure?

Proofreading and Publishing

Proofread to eliminate errors in mechanics, and make a final copy of your essay. Submit it to the editorial department of your local newspaper.

EUROPE
IN 1815

----- Boundary of
German States, 1815

KINGDOM OF NORWAY AND SWEDEN

SCOTLAND

DENMARK

UNITED KINGDOM OF
GREAT BRITAIN AND IRELAND

NETHERLANDS

IRELAND

ENGLAND

• Berlin PRUSSIA

London •

PRUSSIA

Rhine River

GERMAN
STATES

AUSTR

Paris •

Seine River

Danube Vie
River

SWITZERLAND

FRANCE

ITALIAN
STATES

Rome •

PORTUGAL

• Madrid

SPAIN

Mediterranean Sea

SICI

Atlantic Ocean

NORTH AFRICA

THE NINETEENTH CENTURY: ROMANTICISM TO REALISM

▼ **Time** ▼
the 1800s

▼ **Place** ▼
Europe

▼ **Literary Significance** ▼

The early nineteenth-century Romantics broke away from the restrained styles and ideas favored by the leaders of the eighteenth-century Enlightenment. The Romantics exalted values that are still important today: a love of nature and the simple life, individual daring, innovation, and the free expression of feelings. Later in the nineteenth century, Realists rebelled against Romanticism. The Realists felt that Romantic emotionalism was no longer an effective tool to describe—or to reform—industrial society. Realistic values, such as the emphasis on factual observation of ordinary people's lives, still exert a powerful influence on today's literature and thought.

973

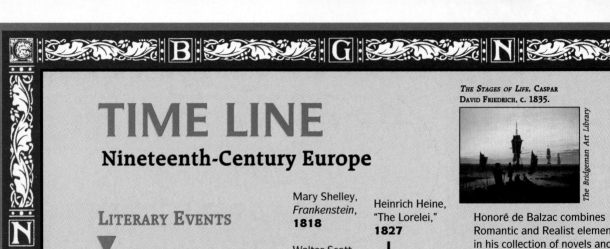

TIME LINE
Nineteenth-Century Europe

THE STAGES OF LIFE, CASPAR DAVID FRIEDRICH, c. 1835.

The Bridgeman Art Library

LITERARY EVENTS

▼

Romantic movement begins, **c. 1800**

William Wordsworth, *The Prelude,* **1805**

Johann Wolfgang von Goethe, *Faust,* **1808**

George Gordon, Lord Byron, *Childe Harold's Pilgrimage,* **1812**

Mary Shelley, *Frankenstein,* **1818**

Walter Scott, Romantic novelist, *Ivanhoe,* **1819**

John Keats, "La Belle Dame sans Merci," **1819**

Heinrich Heine, "The Lorelei," **1827**

Alexander Pushkin, Russian poet and novelist, publishes *Yevgeny Onegin,* **1833**

Honoré de Balzac combines Romantic and Realist element in his collection of novels and short stories *The Human Comedy,* **1842**

Charles Dickens, *David Copperfie* **1849–1850**

1800 **1810** **1820** **1830** **1840**

Age of Progress and the Industrial Revolution, **1800s**

Napoleon becomes emperor of France and much of continental Europe, **1804–1815**

Ludwig von Beethoven composes the *Third Symphony (Eroica)* in honor of Napoleon, **c. 1804**

Napoleon's army invades Russia and is routed, **1812**

Napoleon is defeated and sent into exile; European monarchies are restored at the Congress of Vienna, **1815**

Russian military officers attempt to establish a constitutional government in the failed Decembrist uprising of **1825**

Darwin voyages aboard the *Beagle,* **1831–1836**

Victorian era in England begins as Victoria is crowned, **1837**

Karl Marx and Friedrich Engels develop theory of scientific socialism in *The Communist Manifesto,* 1

Louis Napoleon Bonapar becomes president of Fr in the Revolution of 184

CULTURAL AND HISTORICAL EVENTS

The Industrial Revolution started with the textile industry. Engraving, 1834.

The Granger Collection, New York

QUEEN VICTORIA, THOMAS SULLY, 1835.

The Granger Collection, New York

Charles Baudelaire, *Fleurs du Mal (Flowers of Evil)*, **1857**

Alfred, Lord Tennyson combines Romanticism with Victorian standards in *Idylls of the King* **(1859–1885)**

Victor Hugo, *Les Misérables*, **1862**

Leo Tolstoy and Fyodor Dostoevsky create the age of the Russian novel with *War and Peace* **(1865)** and *Crime and Punishment* **(1866)**

French poets Paul Verlaine and Arthur Rimbaud help found the Symbolist movement, **c. 1870s**

French writer Émile Zola and his followers found the Naturalist movement, **c. 1880s**

Guy de Maupassant perfects a brief form of the short story, **1880–1893**

Henrik Ibsen ushers in Realism in drama with *A Doll's House*, **1879**

Anton Chekhov's play *The Sea Gull* is the first production of the Moscow Arts Theater, **1898**

1850   1860   1870   1880   1890

Louis Napoleon Bonaparte becomes Emperor Louis Napoleon III; Second French Empire begins, **1852**

Charles Darwin develops a theory of biological evolution in *On the Origin of Species*, **1859**

The Granger Collection, New York

H.M.S. *Beagle*, on which Charles Darwin sailed. Engraving.

Italy is unified, **1861**

Emancipation Edict frees Russian serfs from enslavement, **1861**

Franco-Prussian War, **1870–1871**

Germany is unified, **1871**

Otto von Bismarck becomes German imperial chancellor and virtual dictator, **1871–1890**

Third French Republic is established, **1875**

Social unrest grows in Russia; Czar Alexander II is assassinated by terrorists; succeeding czar steps up repression of liberalism, **1881**

Spanish-American War, **1898**

Marie and Pierre Curie discover first radioactive element, **1898**

Giraudon/Art Resource, New York

DANCE AT THE MOULIN DE LA GALETTE MONTMARTE, AUGUSTE RENOIR, 1876.

This time line border is derived from the pattern-work of William Morris, the Victorian artist, poet, and designer who criticized the deadening effect of industrialism on nineteenth-century art.

THE NINETEENTH CENTURY

> **"** Bliss was it in that dawn to be alive,/but to be young was very heaven. **"**
>
> —*William Wordsworth*

Some people think of literature as a quiet, peaceful pursuit. However, literature seems tame only in societies where freedom of speech is taken for granted. In our time, writers helped to prepare the way for the anti-Communist revolution in Eastern Europe. Two hundred years ago, the writings of the philosophers Voltaire and Jean Jacques Rousseau in France and John Locke in England created a new awareness of social injustice and lit the fuse for the revolutionary explosion in America and Europe.

A Revolt Against Reason?

As the eighteenth century had billed itself as the Age of Reason, the Romantic era is sometimes thought of as a revolt against reason. But it is doubtful whether the average eighteenth-century citizen was more rational than citizens and intellectuals before or since. The Romantic era produced such powerful thinkers as Germany's Arthur Schopenhauer, America's Ralph Waldo Emerson, Denmark's Søren Kierkegaard, and England's Samuel Taylor Coleridge. The Romantics did not reject reason. They did, however, elevate emotion and imagination to a new status.

Shock Waves of Revolution

News of revolt in the American colonies reached Europe in 1775, arousing both fears and hopes. Monarchs and aristocrats were alarmed by the American Revolution, but the discontented middle class and peasantry of Europe were inspired by the Americans' struggle for liberty. When the **French Revolution** broke out in 1789, Europe changed overnight. On July 14, 1789, an angry mob stormed the Bastille

The Storming of the Bastille on July 14, 1789, artist unknown.

prison in Paris. That date, now called Bastille Day, which the French celebrate just as Americans celebrate July 4, 1776, marked the beginning of a new era.

Revolutionary fever spread throughout Europe, horrifying most aristocrats and thrilling democratic idealists. During its early years, the French Revolution became a kind of tourist attraction. Intellectuals and artists from across Europe and America visited France to see the new regime firsthand. Thomas Paine, the most powerful propagandist of the American Revolution, emigrated to France to participate in the uprising against the aristocracy. At the beginning of the new century, the French Revolution inspired Simon Bolivar's revolt against the Spanish empire in Latin America.

The Reign of Terror and the Reign of Napoleon

William Wordsworth (see page 1002) was one of many British liberals who was at first thrilled by the French Revolution. But soon intoxication turned to despair. For in 1793, the revolutionaries executed King Louis XVI, and the French Revolution became the **Reign of Terror**. The guillotines (gil′ə·tēnz′) worked overtime as the extremists of the Revo-

Early nineteenth-century British cartoon showing Ned Ludd, the namesake of the Luddites. *Luddites were English laborers who destroyed machinery, which they viewed as a threat to their livelihood. The Luddites' cause captured the imaginations of several Romantic writers. Today,* Luddite *refers to anyone who opposes technological advances.*

THE LAST ROLL CALL OF THE VICTIM OF THE TERROR, CHARLES-LOUIS MÜLLER (1815–1892). *The idealism that surrounded the French Revolution exploded with the political chaos and mass executions that followed, known as the Reign of Terror.*

lution beheaded not only their opponents, but also former allies with whom they now disagreed. In 1794 the radical leader of the Reign of Terror, Robespierre, was himself executed. The French Republic was in a state of confusion that did not ease until a young Corsican military officer, **Napoleon Bonaparte** (1769–1821), staged a *coup,* or forceful overthrow, in 1799.

Using aggressive military tactics, Napoleon soon became dictator of continental Europe. The devastation of the Napoleonic wars is one of the themes of the great Russian novel *War and Peace* by **Leo Tolstoy** (see page 1043). Napoleon's ill-fated invasion and subsequent retreat from Russia are described in Victor Hugo's "Russia 1812" (see page 1017). In 1815, Napoleon was finally defeated by a coalition of English, Prussian, and Russian forces at the Battle of Waterloo and spent the rest of his life in exile.

The writers, artists, and thinkers who reached maturity in the 1790s reacted to these events in different ways. Some, like **Heinrich Heine** in Germany (see page 1011), retained their liberal ideals, while others, like Wordsworth, became increasingly disillusioned and ultimately conservative in their political views. Nevertheless, most of the members of that generation, and the generation that followed it, had enough ideals and views in common to be called by a single label: the **Romantics**.

What Is Romanticism?

Romanticism was a revolt against the restrictions imposed by the classical, aristocratic ideals of the eighteenth century. It was a liberation of the artist's imagination and style. Poets such as Wordsworth declared themselves free to write in the language of everyday speech about everyday people and events. The Romantics idealized nature and the lifestyles of people who lived close to nature, such as farmers and shepherds. This reverence for nature was in part a reaction to the increasingly urban and industrial character of Europe. For some Romantics, disillusionment with nineteenth-century life led to an interest in settings more exotic than the countryside. These writers and artists found inspiration in medieval ballads and courtly tales, as well as in tales of the supernatural.

Another important characteristic of Romanticism is the belief in the importance of the individual. The Romantic individual was daring, rebellious, and free to express previously taboo emotions—to express, in Wordsworth's phrase, "the spontaneous overflow of powerful feelings."

> Romanticism prizes the free expression of the individual's thoughts and feelings. Love of nature, respect for ordinary people, and an interest in fantasy are typical Romantic values.

Poets such as **Victor Hugo** (see page 1015), **Paul Verlaine** and **Arthur Rimbaud** (see page 1027), and **Charles Baudelaire** (see page 1021), experimented with rhyme, meter, and subject matter, breaking rules that had been obeyed for generations. In music, the German composer Beethoven turned the highly structured classical sonata into an expansive form for the expression of powerful internal struggles.

> 66 Classicism is . . . stability within known limits; Romanticism is expansion within limits known and unknown. 99
> —*Jacques Barzun*

Kunsthalle, Hamburg, Germany/Bridgeman Art Library, London/SuperStock, Inc.

THE WANDERER, CASPAR DAVID FRIEDRICH (1774–1840). *Friedrich, with his emphasis on the isolation of the individual, was a leader in the German Romantic school of painting.*

Spring, Jean-François Millet (1814–1875). *In painting, as in literature, the Romantics presented an idealized view of nature and the peasant life.*

The Granger Collection, New York

The New Age Falters

As a new generation of Romantics grew up in the first half of the nineteenth century, it became clear that Europe was in turmoil. In France, the monarchy was restored after Napoleon's downfall. The new monarchy, in turn, was replaced by the Second Republic in 1848. Unsuccessful popular revolts occurred in Italy, Austria, Poland, Hungary, and Belgium.

The most famous of these unsuccessful revolts was the **Decembrist** uprising of 1825 in Russia, in which many intellectuals and writers, including **Alexander Pushkin** (see page 1006), were implicated. The czar executed the military officers who had tried to establish a constitutional government, and a century of botched reforms and revolutions followed. The Russian serfs were freed in 1861, but the nation continued to be plagued by censorship, ignorance, poverty, and tyranny. Russian literature in the nineteenth century became a forum for reformist ideas, in which educated Russians were intensely interested.

Progress, Pollution, and Poverty

The political events of the early and mid-nineteenth century—an era often labeled the Age of Progress—went hand in hand with the **Industrial Revolution**. The explosion of scientific knowledge led to many technological achievements, such as the steam engine, the electric dynamo, and the processes for producing aluminum and steel. New inventions—the telegraph, the electric light, and the repeating rifle—were changing the world in exciting, sometimes frightening, ways. Factories were built, and steamboats and railroads, with their attendant noise and smoke, became part of the rural and urban landscape. Farm workers moved to cities to work in factories, but these cities, unprepared for the rapid population growth, offered them only slums to live in. In addition, during this great age of scientific progress and rapid change, **Charles Darwin** (1809–1882) developed a theory of evolution that upset people's ideas about who they were and where they had come from.

Many people prospered during the Industrial Revolution. A new middle class of manufacturers, bankers, and lawyers became the most significant force in European society. This dominant class was optimistic that material progress would improve life for all humanity. Few poor people shared this optimism, however. The economic theorist **Karl Marx** (1818–1883), whose ideas influenced Tolstoy and later, in the twentieth century, led to the establishment of communist systems around the world, was a persuasive critic of the new social order. Most peasants lived in abject poverty. In the cities, people lived in slums, crowding into unsafe and unsanitary buildings. City streets were filthy, and working conditions in factories and mines were inhumane. Children and adults worked twelve-hour days, six days a week,

KARL MARX, painting c. 1880, artist unknown. *Marx's economic theories, based on his observations of nineteenth-century European society, led to the Communist revolutions that transformed half the world in the twentieth century.*

Archiv Für Kunst Und Geschichte, Berlin

> The Industrial Revolution gave rise to a prosperous middle class, but poverty raged amid the growing lower class.

with no safety standards or compensation for accidents. British children working in the mines were used as draft animals, pulling carts full of coal. They rarely saw daylight. Furthermore, European nations had escalated their policies of imperialism, increasing their domination of smaller, less powerful countries.

Many writers were troubled by these conditions. The liberal reforms begun during the revolutions of the late eighteenth century had not brought about an era of justice—in fact, the gap between rich and poor was wider than ever.

The Realist Creed

A reaction against Romanticism, which called itself **Realism**, flourished during the last half of the nineteenth century. Like most labels, "Realism" is a bit misleading. The Realists were not the first writers to describe the world as it is. The Romantics were also careful observers of the lives of ordinary people. In fact, some writers, such as Hugo and Pushkin, can be identified with both Romanticism and Realism.

> 66 The Realist, if he is an artist, will try not to show us a commonplace photograph of life, but to give us a more complete view of it, more striking, more convincing than reality itself. 99
>
> —*Guy de Maupassant*

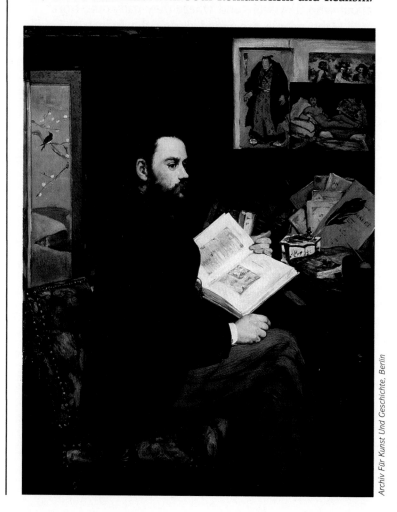

ÉMILE ZOLA, EDOUARD MANET, 1868. Zola was a leader of the Naturalist movement in literature.

Archiv Für Kunst Und Geschichte, Berlin

In France, under the leadership of the novelist **Gustave Flaubert**, the Realists tried to make a science of their art by eliminating sentimentality from their tone and excessive decoration from their descriptions. Their aim was to observe and record the daily lives of ordinary people without distorting the truth. Unlike writers who emphasized the noble, uplifting aspects of human life, Realists simply tried to mirror life, whether noble or ignoble, without making judgments. Of course, no artist can ever completely withhold judgment or feeling from his or her work, and good writing does much more than mirror reality. Flaubert's *Madame Bovary* is admired today not so much for its objectivity as for its perfect prose and its satire of the middle class.

> **Realism was a reaction against Romanticism in the second half of the nineteenth century. Some Realist writers aimed for scientific objectivity; others inclined toward social satire; and some hoped for social reform.**

Naturalism, a radical offshoot of Realism, arose in France in the 1870s. Members of this movement, led by **Émile Zola**, considered free will an illusion, and often showed their characters as helpless victims of heredity, fate, and environment. Writers were no longer to be subjective in their choice of details; in fact, the Naturalists attempted to abolish the boundary between scientist and artist. The most talented Naturalists, however, could not stay within the narrow ideology of their school. French author **Guy de Maupassant** (see page 1032) is sometimes called a Naturalist, but his work is sharpened by irony and an unsurpassed gift for choosing the right detail.

In poetry, **Symbolism** became the major literary movement. Symbolist poets avoided direct statements of meaning and instead used symbols to suggest meaning or mood. Charles Baudelaire is widely acknowledged to be the forerunner of this movement, and Arthur Rimbaud and Paul Verlaine are considered its most prominent poets.

Fyodor Dostoevsky, V. Perov, 1872. *Russian authors such as Dostoevsky created their own brand of Realist literature in the second half of the nineteenth century.*

Tass/SOVFOTO

IRONWORKS, ADOLPH VON MENZEL, 1875.

Realism in Russia

Several of the most important Realists emerged from the fringes of Europe: Russia and Norway. When Realism reached Russia, it acquired a softer tone and a grander vision. **Ivan Turgenev**, a Russian writer who had lived in Paris and had been influenced by Flaubert, Zola, and other French writers, examined the lives of serfs and nobles in *A Sportsman's Sketches* (1852), helping to create a clamor for emancipation. He wrote in ornate, lyrical prose brimming with sympathy and warmth. Later Russian novelists, including Leo Tolstoy and **Fyodor Dostoevsky**, learned a great deal from Turgenev. Realism flourished in Russia, fostering a powerful movement that called for the liberation of the serfs and, later, the entire society. Yet the primary aim of the Russian Realists was not social reform, but a desire to answer the ultimate questions of human life. In very different ways, Tolstoy and Dostoevsky repeatedly asked, "How should people live?" and "What are good and evil?"

Both Tolstoy and Dostoevsky wrote gigantic, sprawling novels filled with violence, love, and family crises and peopled with characters from a wide cross section of society. Unlike these two giants, the playwright and short-story writer **Anton Chekhov** (see page 1060) "painted" on a much smaller canvas. He found his subjects and themes in the common illusions and daily sufferings of unremarkable people. Like Tolstoy and Dostoevsky, however, Chekhov dealt with meanings of life and death. His stories and plays are about people's attempts—usually frustrated—to find meaning and purpose in their lives.

Drama: The Stage as Living Room

In the Romantic era, the dominant literary form was poetry. Perhaps this is because poetry seems naturally to lean toward the expression of feelings rather than facts. In the Realist era, the dominant form was prose fiction. Except for some great German Romantic plays (including Goethe's *Faust*, see page 988), Hugo's *Hernani*, and one Russian comedy, Nikolai Gogol's *Inspector General*, drama lagged behind poetry and prose during the nineteenth century. The Realist whose work helped to transform drama was the Norwegian playwright **Henrik Ibsen** (see page 1069).

Nowadays, playgoers are used to seeing plays that reveal the secret scandals, griefs, and pretenses of people who might be their neighbors. We go to a theater and see a living room on the stage, with one of its walls removed so that we can peek in. We eavesdrop upon families in the midst of crisis. But before Ibsen, most plays were not like that. Even Ibsen's early plays were historical tragedies or romantic comedies in verse. In middle age, however, Ibsen began writing about ordinary Norwegians, their families and communities, and the things they didn't want said out loud. He invented the "problem play"—a label that does not do justice to his achievement, because his plays live through their characters rather than their messages about social problems.

The Legacy of the Nineteenth Century

The literary styles of the nineteenth century—from effusive Romantic poetry to terse Realist prose—still influence modern writing. Realistic descriptions of life and powerful expressions of feeling now seem like hallmarks of literary excellence. The great ideas of the nineteenth century—progress, social reform, evolution, psychology—have become the foundations of twentieth-century thought.

> **❝** The thing that caused the new social plays of Ibsen to take hold of people with such amazing power was his remarkable ability to translate ethical conflicts into human life, so that we seem always to see people of flesh and blood engaged in breathless struggles about the greatest problems in life. **❞**
>
> —The Life of Ibsen,
> *Halvdan Koht*

A MASKED BALL IN A THEATER, ALOIS SCHONN (1826–1897).

Johann Wolfgang von Goethe
1749–1832

The Granger Collection, New York

G oethe (gö′tə) is one of the greatest writers in German literature. A versatile and prolific writer, he was also a universal genius who made important contributions to the fields of science, philosophy, and government. In addition, Goethe was a skilled musician, painter, and athlete.

Goethe was born in Frankfurt. After a false start as a law student, Goethe began studying the arts at Strasbourg, where he met Johann Gottfried Herder, a leader of the Sturm und Drang (Storm and Stress) movement that heralded the beginning of German Romanticism. Members of this movement rebelled against the rationalism of the Enlightenment; they emphasized the power of the imagination and spontaneous expression. Goethe's most notable contribution to the Sturm und Drang movement was the novel *The Sorrows of Young Werther* (1774), which made him internationally famous. Werther, the young hero who kills himself out of hopeless love, became a symbol of the Romantic hero.

In 1775, the young duke of Saxe-Weimar, Karl August, invited Goethe to stay at his court, and, within a few years, Weimar blossomed into the cultural center of Germany. During his first ten years at Weimar, Goethe served as chief minister of state, instituting important political reforms; in addition, he studied music, biology, and painting. In 1786, Goethe left to travel in Italy. This trip marked an important shift in his artistic development, as he became influenced by classical art and architecture.

Goethe's life after his return from Italy was especially productive. He wrote several masterpieces during this period: love poems, prose plays, travel books, novels, narrative poems, and several poetic dramas, most notably *Faust* (Part I, 1808; Part II, 1833), generally considered his greatest work.

Goethe did not advertise himself as a mystic, a hermit, or an adventurer, unlike many other Romantic artists. In many ways, he thought of himself as an ordinary man—a public servant, a husband, and a father. But in his old age, Goethe became a living monument, receiving pilgrims who visited him from around the world. No wonder Napoleon, after meeting Goethe, said, *"Voilà un homme!"* ("There is a man!")

Reader's Guide

from FAUST, PART I

Background

There really was a Dr. Faust. In Germany, in the early sixteenth century, a man named Johannes Faustus gained a wide reputation as a skillful magician. People said that this man, who became a legend in his own time, had sold his soul to the Devil in exchange for knowledge of the magical arts. An English translation of the Faust legend found its way into the hands of Christopher Marlowe (1564–1593), who wrote a popular play called *The Tragical History of Doctor Faustus* (c. 1588).

Goethe's *Faust* follows the traditional plot of the Dr. Faustus legend, but it also expands and enriches the basic elements of the story. In Marlowe's play, Faust, who desires limitless knowledge, makes a pact with the Devil and loses his soul. Goethe's Faust, on the other hand, seeks unlimited experience and at the end of his quest achieves salvation. Later writers and musicians continued to amplify the Faust legend. Most notably, in the German novelist Thomas Mann's *Doktor Faustus* (1947), a modern composer sells his soul in exchange for musical greatness.

Writer's Response

Do you believe that some people are entitled to be "above the law," pushing beyond all limitations, even if in so doing they injure themselves or others? Write a paragraph or two exploring these ideas.

Literary Focus

The **genre** of a literary work is the category or type in which it belongs. Some examples of genre include **drama**, the **epic**, the **novel**, the **short story**, and **lyric poetry**. Goethe's *Faust* is work that transcends genres. The work includes the dialogue and stage directions common to **drama**, but it is so long, with so many changes of scene, that it is difficult to perform onstage in its entirety. Goethe called it a **tragedy**, but Goethe's version of the story ends with Faust's salvation. In its vast scope, and in the way its hero embodies the values of German society, it resembles an **epic**—but epics are narratives, rather than dramas. Furthermore, the individual scenes in Faust vary in style and verse forms, encompassing virtually all the types of poetry known in Goethe's day.

from FAUST, PART I

Johann Wolfgang von Goethe

translated by

LOUIS MACNEICE

> As you read the Prologue, think about how Goethe uses the conversation between the Lord and Mephistopheles to characterize Faust.

Prologue in Heaven

[*Enter the* LORD *and the* HEAVENLY HOSTS, *with* MEPHISTOPHELES° *following. The* THREE ARCHANGELS *step forward.*]

Raphael.

The chanting sun, as ever, rivals
The chanting of his brother spheres
And marches round his destined circuit—
A march that thunders in our ears.

5   His aspect cheers the Hosts of Heaven
Though what his essence none can say;
These inconceivable creations
Keep the high state of their first day.°

Gabriel.

And swift, with inconceivable swiftness,

10   The earth's full splendor rolls around,
Celestial radiance alternating
With a dread night too deep to sound;
The sea against the rocks' deep bases
Comes foaming up in far-flung force,

15   And rock and sea go whirling onward
In the swift spheres' eternal course.

Michael.

And storms in rivalry are raging
From sea to land, from land to sea,
In frenzy forge the world a girdle

20   From which no inmost part is free.
The blight of lightning flaming yonder

Mephistopheles (mef′ə·stäf′ə·lēz′): the Devil.

8. **the high state of their first day:** Although human beings have fallen from the innocent state in which they were created, the rest of creation—the sun, planets, and other "inconceivable creations"—remains "unfallen."

Marks where the thunderbolt will play;
And yet Thine envoys, Lord, revere
The gentle movement of Thy day.

Choir of Angels.

25 Thine aspect cheers the Hosts of Heaven
Though what Thine essence none can say,
And all Thy loftiest creations
Keep the high state of their first day.

[MEPHISTOPHELES *steps forward.*]

Mephistopheles.

Since you, O Lord, once more approach and ask
30 If business down with us be light or heavy—
And in the past you've usually welcomed me—
That's why you see me also at your levee.°

Excuse me, I can't manage lofty words—
Not though your whole court jeer and find
    me low;
35 My pathos certainly would make you laugh
Had you not left off laughing long ago.
Your suns and worlds mean nothing much to me;
How men torment themselves, that's all I see.
The little god of the world, one can't reshape,
    reshade him;

Archiv Für Kunst Und Geschichte, Berlin

40 He is as strange today as that first day you
    made him.
His life would be not so bad, not quite,
Had you not granted him a gleam of Heaven's
    light;
He calls it Reason, uses it not the least
Except to be more beastly than any beast.
45 He seems to me—if your Honor does not
    mind—
Like a grasshopper—the long-legged kind—
That's always in flight and leaps as it flies along
And then in the grass strikes up its same old song.
I could only wish he confined himself to the grass!
50 He thrusts his nose into every filth, alas.

Lord.

Mephistopheles, have you no other news?
Do you always come here to accuse?
Is nothing ever right in your eyes on earth?

Painting by August von Kreling, 1872, depicting Faust and Mephistopheles.

Johann Wolfgang von Goethe **989**

Mephistopheles.

No, Lord! I find things there as downright bad
    as ever.

55   I am sorry for men's days of dread and dearth;
Poor things, *my* wish to plague 'em isn't fervent.

Lord.

Do you know Faust?

Mephistopheles.

       The Doctor?°

Lord.

            Aye, my servant.

Mephistopheles.

Indeed! He serves you oddly enough, I think.
The fool has no earthly habits in meat and
    drink.

60   The ferment in him drives him wide and far,
That he is mad he too has almost guessed;
He demands of heaven each fairest star
And of earth each highest joy and best,
And all that is new and all that is far

65   Can bring no calm to the deep-sea swell of his
    breast.

Lord.

Now he may serve me only gropingly,
Soon I shall lead him into the light.
The gardener knows when the sapling first
    turns green
That flowers and fruit will make the future
    bright.

Mephistopheles.

70   What do you wager? You will lose him yet,
Provided *you* give *me* permission
To steer him gently the course I set.

Lord.

So long as he walks the earth alive,
So long you may try what enters your head;

75   Men make mistakes as long as they strive.

Mephistopheles.

I thank you for that; as regards the dead,
The dead have never taken my fancy.
I favor cheeks that are full and rosy-red;

57. **The Doctor:** Doctor of Philosophy; Ph.D.

GRETCHEN IN PRISON, JOSEF FAY (1813–1875). *Gretchen features prominently later in the poem as the "pure maid" with whom Mephistopheles hopes to tempt Faust.*

No corpse is welcome to my house;
80 I work as the cat does with the mouse.

Lord.

Very well; you have my full permission.
Divert this soul from its primal source
And carry it, if you can seize it,
Down with you upon your course—
85 And stand ashamed when you must needs admit:
A good man with his groping intuitions
Still knows the path that is true and fit.

Mephistopheles.

All right—but it won't last for long.
I'm not afraid my bet will turn out wrong.
90 And, if my aim prove true and strong,
Allow me to triumph wholeheartedly.
Dust shall he eat—and greedily—
Like my cousin the Snake° renowned in tale
    and song.

93. **my cousin the Snake:** In the Garden of Eden, the Devil took on the shape of a serpent and tempted Eve to eat an apple from the Tree of Knowledge.

Johann Wolfgang von Goethe **991**

Lord.
>That too you are free to give a trial;
>95 I have never hated the likes of you.
>Of all the spirits of denial
>The joker is the last that I eschew.
>Man finds relaxation too attractive—
>Too fond too soon of unconditional rest;
>100 Which is why I am pleased to give him a
>>companion
>Who lures and thrusts and must, as devil, be
>>active.
>But ye, true sons of Heaven, it is your duty
>To take your joy in the living wealth of beauty.
>The changing Essence which ever works and
>>lives
>105 Wall you around with love, serene, secure!
>And that which floats in flickering appearance
>Fix ye it firm in thoughts that must endure.

Choir of Angels.
>Thine aspect cheers the Hosts of Heaven
>Though what Thine essence none can say,
>110 And all Thy loftiest creations
>Keep the high state of their first day.

[*Heaven closes.*]

Mephistopheles (*alone*).
>I like to see the Old One now and then
>And try to keep relations on the level.
>It's really decent of so great a person
>115 To talk so humanely even to the Devil.

Scene from Auerbach's Cellar, **lithograph, nineteenth century.**

The Granger Collection, New York

Dr. Faust has become disappointed with the extent of human knowledge. Although as a doctor of philosophy he has explored many areas of learning, he still has not learned the meaning of life. He has even dabbled in the art of "white magic," but he has found that it yields him no more knowledge than his own reason. Despairing, Faust considers suicide, but, when he hears the bells ringing in celebration of Easter, he is brought back to the world of simple enjoyment. He goes for a walk in the countryside, thinking that he, like other people, might be satisfied with an acceptance of his limitations. Returning to his study, he struggles with Mephistopheles, who tries to persuade him to try the Devil's way, the way of sensual pleasures, without thought of the why's or the consequences. Faust is in despair again! He cries a curse on love, on hope, on faith, and on patience.

Mephistopheles.

    Stop playing with your grief which battens
    Like a vulture on your life, your mind!
    The worst of company would make you feel
    That you are a man among mankind.
5   Not that it's really my proposition
    To shove you among the common men;
    Though I'm not one of the Upper Ten,°
    If you would like a coalition
    With me for your career through life,
10   I am quite ready to fit in,
    I'm yours before you can say knife.
    I am your comrade;
    If you so crave,
    I am your servant, I am your slave.

Faust.

15   And what have I to undertake in return?

Mephistopheles.

    Oh it's early days to discuss what that is.

Faust.

    No, no, the devil is an egoist
    And ready to do nothing gratis°
    Which is to benefit a stranger.
20   Tell me your terms and don't prevaricate!
    A servant like you in the house is a danger.

Mephistopheles.

    I will bind myself to your service in this world,
    To be at your beck and never rest nor slack;
    When we meet again on the other side,
25   In the same coin you shall pay me back.

7. **the Upper Ten:** In medieval theology, the Upper Ten referred to a hierarchy of devils, in which Mephistopheles does not rank.

18. **gratis** (grāt′is): for free.

Mephistopheles Appears Before Faust, Eugène Delacroix (1798–1863).

? *Why do you think the Faust legend has been a popular theme in literature for centuries? Why do you think it appealed to the Romantics?*

Faust.
> The other side gives me little trouble;
> First batter this present world to rubble,
> Then the other may rise—if that's the plan.
> This earth is where my springs of joy have
>   started,
> 30   And this sun shines on me when brokenhearted;
> If I can first from them be parted,
> *Then* let happen what will and can!
> I wish to hear no more about it—
> Whether there too men hate and love
> 35   Or whether in those spheres too, in the future,
> There is a Below or an Above.

Mephistopheles.
> With such an outlook you can risk it.
> Sign on the line! In these next days you will get
> Ravishing samples of my arts;
> 40   I am giving you what never man saw yet.

Faust.

> Poor devil, can *you* give anything ever?
> Was a human spirit in its high endeavor
> Even once understood by one of your breed?
> Have you got food which fails to feed?
45 > Or red gold which, never at rest,
> Like mercury runs away through the hand?
> A game at which one never wins?
> A girl who, even when on my breast,
> Pledges herself to my neighbor with her eyes?
50 > The divine and lovely delight of honor
> Which falls like a falling star and dies?
> Show me the fruits which, before they are
> plucked, decay
> And the trees which day after day renew their
> green!

Mephistopheles.

> Such a commission doesn't alarm me,
55 > I have such treasures to purvey.
> But, my good friend, the time draws on when we
> Should be glad to feast at our ease on some-
> thing good.

Faust.

> If ever I stretch myself on a bed of ease,
> Then I am finished! Is that understood?
60 > If ever your flatteries can coax me
> To be pleased with myself, if ever you cast
> A spell of pleasure that can hoax me—
> Then let *that* day be my last!
> That's my wager!

Mephistopheles.

> Done!

Faust.

> Let's shake!
65 > If ever I say to the passing moment
> "Linger a while! Thou art so fair!"
> Then you may cast me into fetters,
> I will gladly perish then and there!
> Then you may set the death bell tolling,
70 > Then from my service you are free,
> The clock may stop, its hand may fall,
> And that be the end of time for me!

Mephistopheles.
    Think what you're saying, we shall not forget it.

Faust.
    And you are fully within your rights;
75   I have made no mad or outrageous claim.
    If I stay as I am, I am a slave—
    Whether yours or another's, it's all the same.

Mephistopheles.
    I shall this very day at the College Banquet
    Enter your service with no more ado,
80   But just one point—As a life-and-death
        insurance
    I must trouble you for a line or two.

Faust.
    So you, you pedant, you too like things in
        writing?
    Have you never known a man? Or a man's
        word? Never?
    Is it not enough that my word of mouth
85   Puts all my days in bond forever?
    Does not the world rage on in all its streams
    And shall a promise hamper *me?*
    Yet this illusion reigns within our hearts
    And from it who would be gladly free?
90   Happy the man who can inwardly keep his
        word;
    Whatever the cost, he will not be loath to pay!
    But a parchment, duly inscribed and sealed,
    Is a bogey from which all wince away.
    The word dies on the tip of the pen
95   And wax and leather lord it then.
    What do you, evil spirit, require?
    Bronze, marble, parchment, paper?
    Quill or chisel or pencil of slate?
    You may choose whichever you desire.

Mephistopheles.
100   How can you so exaggerate
    With such a hectic rhetoric?
    Any little snippet is quite good—
    And you sign it with one little drop of blood.

Faust.
    If that is enough and is some use,

A scene from *Faust,* in which Mephistopheles tempts Faust with enchanting visions. *Lithograph by Theodor Hosemann, after Peter Cornelius, 1835.*

105   One may as well pander to your fad.

Mephistopheles.

Blood is a very special juice.

Faust.

Only do not fear that I shall break this contract.
What I promise is nothing more
Than what all my powers are striving for.
110   I have puffed myself up too much, it is only
Your sort that really fits my case.
The great Earth Spirit has despised me
And Nature shuts the door in my face.
The thread of thought is snapped asunder,
115   I have long loathed knowledge in all its
        fashions.

In the depths of sensuality
Let us now quench our glowing passions!
And at once make ready every wonder
Of unpenetrated sorcery!
120 Let us cast ourselves into the torrent of time,
Into the whirl of eventfulness,
Where disappointment and success,
Pleasure and pain may chop and change
As chop and change they will and can;
125 It is restless action makes the man.

Mephistopheles.

No limit is fixed for you, no bound;
If you'd like to nibble at everything
Or to seize upon something flying round—
Well, may you have a run for your money!
130 But seize your chance and don't be funny!

Faust.

I've told you, it is no question of happiness.
The most painful joy, enamored hate, enlivening
Disgust—I devote myself to all excess.
My breast, now cured of its appetite for knowledge,
135 From now is open to all and every smart,
And what is allotted to the whole of mankind
That will I sample in my inmost heart,
Grasping the highest and lowest with my spirit,
Piling men's weal and woe upon my neck,
140 To extend myself to embrace all human selves
And to founder in the end, like them, a wreck.

Mephistopheles.

O believe *me*, who have been chewing
These iron rations many a thousand year,
No human being can digest
145 This stuff, from the cradle to the bier.°
This universe—believe a devil—
Was made for no one but a god!
He exists in eternal light
But *us* he has brought into the darkness
150 While *your* sole portion is day and night.

Faust.

I will all the same!

FAUST AND GRETCHEN, ADOLPHE MONTICELLI (1824–1886).

Archiv Für Kunst Und Geschichte, Berlin

145. **bier** (bir): a platform on which a coffin or corpse is placed.

Mephistopheles.
> That's very nice.
> There's only one thing I find wrong;
> Time is short, art is long.
> You could do with a little artistic advice.
155 Confederate with one of the poets
> And let him flog his imagination
> To heap all virtues on your head,
> A head with such a reputation:
> Lion's bravery,
160 Stag's velocity,
> Fire of Italy,
> Northern tenacity.
> Let *him* find out the secret art
> Of combining craft with a noble heart
165 And of being in love like a young man,
> Hotly, but working to a plan.
> Such a person—*I'd* like to meet him;
> "Mr. Microcosm"° is how I'd greet him.

168. **Mr. Microcosm:** i.e., man as the microcosm, or essence, of the world.

Faust.
> What am I then if fate must bar
170 My efforts to reach that crown of humanity
> After which all my senses strive?

Mephistopheles.
> You are in the end ... what you are.
> You can put on full-bottomed wigs with a
>   million locks,
> You can put on stilts instead of your socks,
175 You remain forever what you are.

Faust.
> I feel my endeavors have not been worth a pin
> When I raked together the treasures of the
>   human mind,
> If at the end I but sit down to find
> No new force welling up within.
180 I have not a hair's breadth more of height,
> I am no nearer the Infinite.

Mephistopheles.
> My very good sir, you look at things
> Just in the way that people do;
> We must be cleverer than that
185 Or the joys of life will escape from you.

Hell! You have surely hands and feet,
Also a head and you-know-what;
The pleasures I gather on the wing,
Are they less mine? Of course they're not!
190 Suppose I can afford six stallions,
I can add that horsepower to my score
And dash along and be a proper man
As if my legs were twenty-four.
So goodbye to thinking! On your toes!
195 The world's before us. Quick! Here goes!
I tell you, a chap who's intellectual
Is like a beast on a blasted heath
Driven in circles by a demon
While a fine green meadow lies round beneath.

Faust.
200 How do we start?

Mephistopheles.
                    We just say go—and skip.
But please get ready for this pleasure trip.

                    [*Exit* FAUST.]

Only look down on knowledge and reason,
The highest gifts that men can prize,
Only allow the spirit of lies
205 To confirm you in magic and illusion,
And then I have you body and soul.
Fate has given this man a spirit
Which is always pressing onwards, beyond
    control,
And whose mad striving overleaps
210 All joys of the earth between pole and pole.
Him shall I drag through the wilds of life
And through the flats of meaninglessness,
I shall make him flounder and gape and stick
And to tease his insatiableness
215 Hang meat and drink in the air before his
    watering lips;
In vain he will pray to slake his inner thirst,
And even had he not sold himself to the devil
He would be equally accursed.

First Thoughts

Do you think that Faust is foolish to make a pact with the Devil?

Identifying Facts

1. Why has the Lord asked Mephistopheles to visit Heaven?
2. What does Mephistopheles criticize about the world the Lord has made?
3. What agreement do Mephistopheles and the Lord make about Faust?
4. What agreement does Mephistopheles make with Faust?
5. Faust tells Mephistopheles that he is not seeking happiness. What *does* Faust claim to be seeking?

Interpreting Meanings

1. In the Prologue, Mephistopheles refers to "the little god of the world" and "the Old One." To whom is he referring? What does Mephistopheles' choice of words reveal about his **tone**, or attitude, toward these characters?
2. What is "Romantic" about Goethe's portrayal of the Lord allowing Faust to be tested by Mephistopheles? How is Goethe's Romanticism shown in Faust's unwillingness to rest and be quiet?
3. What is Faust's attitude toward Mephistopheles? What are his reasons for this attitude?
4. Compare and contrast the **characters** of Faust and Mephistopheles. What do their styles of speech reveal about their characters?

Applying Meanings

The world today is very different from the way it was when Goethe wrote *Faust*. Modern scientists, unlocking many of nature's secrets, have gone far beyond what Dr. Faust could have imagined. What are the present dangers of the search for scientific knowledge and the human mastery of nature? How do you think Faust would have responded to the modern world? Do you think he would have been satisfied by the knowledge he could gain in the twentieth century, or would he still want more?

Creative Writing Response

1. **Writing a Speech for a Character.** Choose one of the following characters: Faust, Mephistopheles, the Lord, or one of the Archangels. Write a speech of about ten lines, either in prose or verse, in which the character says something that was on his mind but that he did not say aloud during the sections of *Faust* you have just read.

2. **Writing a Skit.** We sometimes say that a person has sold his or her soul even though that person hasn't actually made a pact with the Devil. For example, a music fan might say, "I'd sell my soul for a ticket to tonight's concert." The expression "I'd sell my soul for . . ." simply means that the speaker is willing to go to great lengths to get what he or she wants. Write a brief skit about a person who wants something so badly that he or she says "I'll sell my soul for . . ." —and is taken literally when the Devil appears. Explore the situation thoroughly in your skit. If possible, perform the skit for the class.

Critical Writing Response

Evaluating a Character's Actions. Refer to the paragraph you wrote in the Writer's Response (see page 987). Have any of your ideas changed since reading *Faust*? Do you think that Faust was justified in pursuing knowledge at the risk of his own soul? Or do you think he should be punished for making such a dangerous bargain with the Devil? What decision would you have made if you were in Faust's shoes? Write a brief essay in which you evaluate Faust's decision.

William Wordsworth
1770–1850

The Granger Collection, New York

Wordsworth was the most influential of the early English Romantic poets. His life paralleled the intellectual and political movements of his time. Rebellious and daring in his youth, he grew increasingly conservative as he got older.

He was born in the Lake District in northwest England, a beautiful area that inspired his poetry all through his life. He lost both of his parents by the time he was thirteen. For many years he was separated from his sister Dorothy, to whom he was very close. Wordsworth consoled himself for these losses by wandering alone in the country, collecting impressions that would inspire some of his greatest poetry.

Wordsworth graduated from Cambridge in 1791, but he had little interest in the careers open to a young man who was educated but without prospects. Then, in 1795, Wordsworth inherited some money from a friend. He set up housekeeping in southwest England with his sister, who became his closest friend and advisor. Like her brother, Dorothy Wordsworth was an accomplished writer. In her diary, she recorded simple, everyday experiences, many of which Wordsworth later transformed into verse by using her notes to jog his memory.

Equally important for Wordsworth's development was his friendship with the poet and critic Samuel Taylor Coleridge. They collaborated on *Lyrical Ballads,* the 1798 volume that ushered in English Romanticism.

Wordsworth's abilities declined as he grew older, although he continued to publish a great deal. Contributing to this decline was a series of tragedies, including the drowning of his beloved brother John in 1805, the deaths of two of his children around the same time, a bitter break with Coleridge that was never healed, and a chronic illness that made Dorothy an invalid.

As he grew older, Wordsworth was regarded as the foremost living English poet. In 1843 he was named Poet Laureate of Great Britain. His masterpiece, *The Prelude,* considered one of the finest long poems in English, appeared immediately after his death in 1850.

Reader's Guide

THE WORLD IS TOO MUCH WITH US

Background

Wordsworth marked the beginning of his life as a poet from a moment when he was fourteen years old and marveled at the sight of tree branches silhouetted against the evening sky. From that time on, Wordsworth's poetry expressed an enthusiasm for childhood memories and revealed deep insights about nature and the poetic imagination.

Wordsworth wrote some of the greatest sonnets in the English language. During the eighteenth century, the sonnet had fallen out of favor. Wordsworth and other Romantic poets gave it new life. Wordsworth chose the **Petrarchan sonnet** form (see page 804). Wordsworth uses the sonnet to express political and social themes; in particular, the sonnet becomes a vehicle for statements against tyranny and the urban world of commerce and industry. As in his other poetry, Wordsworth followed the creed set forth in his famous Preface to *Lyrical Ballads:* that poets should use a style of language similar to that spoken by everyday people, rather than the lofty, elevated diction that was currently fashionable. He did not intend, however, to imitate ordinary speech. Rather, he hoped to poetically transform the language that people really spoke.

Wordsworth believed that by developing a close sympathy with nature, human beings could tap their innate and indestructible sense of harmony and joy. "The World Is Too Much with Us" expresses his belief that modern people lack a feeling of identification with nature.

Writer's Response

What does it mean to be "out of tune" with nature? Write a few sentences exploring this issue.

Literary Focus

The **sonnet** is a fourteen-line poem written in **iambic pentameter**. Each line contains ten syllables, five of which are stressed. The **Petrarchan** or **Italian sonnet** has two parts, an **octave** (eight lines) and a **sestet** (six lines). The usual rhyme scheme is *abbaabbacdecde*. In some sonnets the first eight lines raise a question or problem that is answered in the last six lines, or the sestet opposes what is said in the octave. This shift or turn from octave to sestet is often dramatic.

THE WORLD IS TOO MUCH WITH US

William Wordsworth

THE HORSES OF NEPTUNE, WALTER CRANE, 1892.

> *Notice the restless, choppy rhythm of the first several lines of the poem and the reflective and melancholy tone of the last four lines. How do the rhythm and tone affect your mood as you read the poem?*

The world is too much with us; late and soon,
Getting and spending, we lay waste our powers:
Little we see in Nature that is ours;
We have given our hearts away, a sordid boon!
5   This Sea that bares her bosom to the moon;
The winds that will be howling at all hours,
And are up-gathered now like sleeping flowers;
For this, for everything, we are out of tune;
It moves us not.—Great God! I'd rather be
10 A Pagan suckled in a creed outworn;
So might I, standing on this pleasant lea,°
Have glimpses that would make me less forlorn;
Have sight of Proteus rising from the sea;
Or hear old Triton° blow his wreathèd horn.

11. **lea** (lē): meadow.

13–14. **Proteus** (prō′tē·əs) . . . **Triton** (trīt′′n): in Greek mythology, sons of Neptune, god of the sea.

First Thoughts

Do you agree with Wordsworth that "we lay waste our powers" in the world?

Identifying Facts

1. What does Wordsworth say we have given away?
2. Where is the speaker of the poem standing?
3. What references to ancient Greek mythology does Wordsworth make in this poem?
4. What examples of nature's beauty does Wordsworth describe in the poem?

Interpreting Meanings

1. In your own words, restate the first two lines of the poem.
2. What do you think is the central meaning, or **theme**, of the poem? Does Wordsworth state this theme directly, or is it implied? Explain the dramatic shift in line 9.
3. How does the personification of the sea and the winds contribute to Wordsworth's theme?
4. What is Wordsworth's purpose in alluding to mythology in the last lines of the poem? What do these allusions signify?
5. What advantage does Wordsworth see in being "a Pagan suckled in a creed outworn"? What relationships to nature are represented in the Greek myths?

Applying Meanings

Think about the concerns for saving the environment and for protecting endangered species. Do you see the relevance of Wordsworth's poem to our own time?

Creative Writing Response

Writing a Dialogue. Imagine that you have built a time machine and transported William Wordsworth into the twentieth century. Write a one-page dialogue between Wordsworth and yourself in which Wordsworth expresses his reaction to nature and industry in modern America.

Critical Writing Response

Analyzing the Sonnet Form. Write a brief essay analyzing the **sonnet** form of "The World Is Too Much with Us." Identify the **volta,** or turn, and consider the effect created by the rhyming words before and after the turn. Note the progression of the argument. Finally, explain how an understanding of these elements contributes to your appreciation of the poem. (To review the **Petrarchan sonnet** form, see page 804.)

Alexander Pushkin
1799–1837

Tass/SOVFOTO

Alexander Pushkin is considered by many critics to be the father of modern Russian literature. He was born in Moscow to an aristocratic family that had lost most of its fortune. His great-grandfather, of whom he was very proud, was Abram Hannibal, an African who had been brought to the Russian court by Czar Peter the Great. Pushkin's father gave him access to a good library and spurred his interest in literature. Pushkin developed an interest in radical politics and began writing poetry. When he was fifteen, he published his first poem.

Pushkin's early narrative poems made him famous in Russian literary circles. Although the settings and plots of his narrative works were highly Romantic, their portrayals of Russian characters and customs struck a new, realistic note. Later prose works such as *Tales of The Late I. P. Belkin* (1830), *The Queen of Spades* (1834), and *The Negro of Peter the Great* (1837), showed great mastery of character and style.

Pushkin's highest achievement was in poetry, particularly the historical play *Boris Godunov* (1825), and the long narratives *Eugene Onegin* (1833) and *The Bronze Horseman* (1833). His shorter poems reveal his gift for finding beauty in everyday things. And all his work, like his life, exhibits a high-spirited, dashing casualness that reveals powerful feelings underneath. Peter Ilyich Tchaikovsky, one of several composers who adapted Pushkin's works to music, said that his poems "sang themselves."

In 1831, Pushkin married a flirtatious beauty, Natalya Goncharova. She became involved with a French nobleman at the Russian court, Baron Georges d'Anthes, who pursued her so feverishly that he married her sister in order to be closer to her. Finally Pushkin's patience came to an end and, in January 1837, he provoked d'Anthes into a duel. D'Anthes fired first, and Pushkin was fatally wounded. At his death he was mourned as a national hero. Today he is viewed as a founder of Russian culture, equivalent in stature to Dante in Italy, Shakespeare in England, and Goethe in Germany.

Reader's Guide

I HAVE VISITED AGAIN

Background

Exile has been a major theme for Russian writers throughout the nine-teenth and twentieth centuries, for the simple and painful reason that many Russian writers have been exiled for their political views, Push-kin included. Pushkin's first job, when he was eighteen, was at the foreign office in Russia's capital, St. Petersburg. While there, Pushkin wrote verses that were critical of the czar. Disturbed by the popularity of these politically liberal verses, the government transferred Pushkin to southern Russia. For the rest of his life, Pushkin's every move was observed and reported on by the secret police. He was finally dis-missed from the foreign service in 1824 and exiled to his mother's estate. In "I Have Visited Again," a poem written late in his career, Pushkin tells of returning to the estate ten years after his two-year exile there. Notice the several layers of memory in the poem. The speaker remembers his years of exile; but during those years, he re-membered other years still further back. He anticipates the future and also imagines that he will be remembered by his descendants.

Writer's Response

Imagine that you have returned to a place—a natural setting, your ele-mentary school, a relative's house, or your childhood home—that you have not visited for several years. Jot down a few sentences describing the mixture of emotions you might feel upon your return.

Literary Focus

The **setting** of a work is the place and time where it occurs. "I Have Visited Again" is a poem about the setting of Pushkin's ancestral es-tate. It was the scene of some of his most intense memories, both painful and sweet. Pushkin knew every corner of the estate so well, during so many different phases of his life and seasons of the year, that his descriptions of it are quite varied. The estate during his exile, the estate during his return, and the estate as he imagines it in the future are the same location at three different times—in effect they are three different settings.

I Have Visited Again

Alexander Pushkin

translated by

D. M. Thomas

Autumn Landscape, **Constantin Kryzhitski.**

As you read, visualize both the speaker of the poem and the place he is visiting. What kind of person do you imagine the speaker is, and what does this place mean for him?

> ... I have visited again
> That corner of the earth where I spent two
> Unnoticed, exiled years. Ten years have passed
> Since then, and many things have changed for me,
> 5 And I have changed too, obedient to life's law—
> But now that I am here again, the past
> Has flown out eagerly to embrace me, claim me,
> And it seems that only yesterday I wandered
> Within these groves.
>
> Here is the cottage, sadly
> 10 Declined now, where I lived with my poor old nurse.
> She is no more. No more behind the wall

Do I hear her heavy footsteps as she moved
Slowly, painstakingly about her tasks.

Here are the wooded slopes where often I
15 Sat motionless, and looked down at the lake,
Recalling other shores and other waves . . .
It gleams between golden cornfields and green meadows,
A wide expanse; across its fathomless waters
A fisherman passes, dragging an ancient net.
20 Along the shelving banks, hamlets are scattered
—Behind them the mill, so crooked it can scarcely
Make its sails turn in the wind . . .

On the bounds
Of my ancestral acres, at the spot
Where a road, scarred by many rainfalls, climbs
25 The hill, three pine trees stand—one by itself,
The others close together. When I rode
On horseback past them in the moonlit night,
The friendly rustling murmur of their crowns
Would welcome me. Now, I have ridden out
30 Upon that road, and seen those trees again.

They have remained the same, make the same murmur—
But round their aging roots, where all before
Was barren, naked, a thicket of young pines
Has sprouted; like green children round the shadows
35 Of the two neighboring pines. But in the distance
Their solitary comrade stands, morose,
Like some old bachelor, and round its roots
All is barren as before.

I greet you, young
And unknown tribe of pine trees! I'll not see
40 Your mighty upward thrust of years to come
When you will overtop these friends of mine
And shield their ancient summits from the gaze
Of passers-by. But may my grandson hear
Your welcome murmur when, returning home
45 From lively company, and filled with gay
And pleasant thoughts, he passes you in the night,
And thinks perhaps of me . . .

First Thoughts

What feelings did the poem arouse in you? How do you think Pushkin feels about the **setting** he describes?

Identifying Facts

1. Describe the **setting** of the poem in your own words.
2. In which building did the speaker live during his exile? With whom did he live, and what happened to that person?
3. What about the speaker's favorite grove of pine trees has remained the same? What has changed?

Interpreting Meanings

1. Briefly describe the **mood**, or atmosphere, of this poem as a whole. Cite the lines and passages that, in your opinion, most strongly express that mood. What elements of the **setting** are described in those passages?
2. **Personification** is a form of figurative language in which an author describes a nonhuman thing or quality in human terms. What objects does Pushkin **personify** in this poem? What comparison does he make between these objects and human beings?
3. In the first stanza, the speaker says that change is "life's law." State two examples from the later stanzas that demonstrate the law of change at work on the speaker's estate.

Applying Meanings

Based on your personal experience and knowledge, do you agree that change often brings its own compensations, and that the new makes up for the loss of the old? Write a paragraph or more explaining your answer.

Creative Writing Response

Writing a Poem. Write either a short poem or a long prose paragraph about returning to an important place—for instance, your home or school—twenty years from now. What do you think will have changed about the place? What do you think will be the same? How do you think *you* will be different? When writing your poem, you might want to choose one object or person to use as a focus of comparison between the past and the present.

Critical Writing Response

Comparing Two Poems. In a brief essay, compare Pushkin's "I Have Visited Again" with the English Romantic poet Percy Bysshe Shelley's "Mutability." Consider what each poet says about the inevitability of change in nature and human lives, and compare the moods evoked by the imagery in both poems.

Mutability
by Percy Bysshe Shelley

1

The flower that smiles today
    Tomorrow dies;
All that we wish to stay
    Tempts and then flies.
5 What is this world's delight?
Lightning that mocks the night,
  Brief even as bright.

2

Virtue, how frail it is!
    Friendship how rare!
10 Love, how it sells poor bliss
    For proud despair!
But we, though soon they fall,
Survive their joy and all
  Which ours we call.

3

15 Whilst skies are blue and bright,
    Whilst flowers are gay,
Whilst eyes that change ere night
    Make glad the day,
Whilst yet the calm hours creep,
20 Dream thou—and from thy sleep
  Then wake to weep.

Heinrich Heine
1797–1856

The Bettmann Archive

Heinrich Heine (hīn′riH hī′nə) was born to German parents in Düsseldorf, which was at that time occupied by France. It later became part of Prussia, the chief state in the German empire. Because they were Jews, the members of Heine's family were subject to severe restrictions. The prejudice he experienced in his youth made Heine a lifelong lover of freedom.

In 1819, Heine, supported by his rich uncle Salomon, enrolled in the University of Bonn, where he studied literature and history, and the next year he transferred to Gottingen to study law. Expelled from school for fighting a duel, Heine moved to Berlin, where he met the great German philosopher Hegel (hā′gəl). He continued his studies until he received his degree in 1825. Meanwhile, he fell in love with and wrote many passionate poems to his uncle's beautiful but vain daughter Amalie, who eventually spurned him and married a wealthier suitor. The rejection provided Heine with fresh inspiration for dozens of beautiful poems, among them "The Lorelei" (lôr′ə·lī) and other *lieder,* or "songs."

In 1831 Heine, weary of being criticized by German authorities for his liberal views, moved to Paris, where he lived for the rest of his life. He quickly made friends with several important French writers, including Victor Hugo (see page 1015). His relationship with his wife—called "Mathilde" in his poetry—was a devoted one even though she was uneducated and, according to Heine, had no idea her husband was a famous poet.

Heine suffered from an incurable disease of the spine. His last eight years were spent in bed—in "my mattress grave," as he called it. Unable to write and in great pain, he dictated poems to a patient young woman he called "La Mouche"—French for "the fly." Some of his greatest poems were written during these years of agony.

For his epitaph, Heine had suggested the modest "Here lies a German poet." Not surprisingly, his last words, gasped out in a coughing fit, were "Paper! Pencil!"

Reader's Guide

THE LORELEI

Background

The Lorelei is the name of a steep, rocky cliff on the Rhine River in Germany. According to legend, the spirit of a woman sits on this rock on full moon nights, combing her hair, singing, and luring boatmen to their deaths. The story of the Lorelei echoes the Greek myth of the Sirens, who tempted Odysseus and his sailors with their sweet singing.

In German, "The Lorelei" has a haunting, melancholy rhythm that cannot be fully captured in an English translation. But in English we can appreciate the visual imagery, the speaker's emotion, and much of the figurative language. The translator also has succeeded in capturing the songlike quality of the poem.

"The Lorelei" first appeared in 1827 in Heine's collection *The Book of Songs,* which has been called the most famous book of poetry in German literature. Composers such as Franz Schubert and Felix Mendelssohn set many of its poems to music. "The Lorelei" became such a beloved song among the German people that when the Nazis banned the works of Jewish writers, including Heine, they kept this lyric in their songbooks with the notation "Author Unknown."

Writer's Response

What classical myth, fairy tale, ghost story, or modern urban legend can you think of that is similar to the myth of the Lorelei? In other words, what story comes to mind that involves a conflict or a relationship between a human being and an alluring but dangerous supernatural being? Briefly sketch the story's basic plot. If you are not familiar with such a tale, feel free to make one up.

Literary Focus

Imagery is language that appeals to the senses of sight, hearing, touch, taste, and smell. "The Lorelei" is brilliant in its use of imagery, especially imagery that appeals to our senses of sight and hearing. Notice the simple language of "The Lorelei" in this translation. The German version is equally straightforward. Yet the pictures Heine creates are surprisingly complex.

THE LORELEI

Heinrich Heine

translated by

LOUIS UNTERMEYER

Have you ever been so captivated by a real event or a fantasy that you became mesmerized, unable to move? As you read, think of yourself as the boatman in the river, spellbound by the beautiful woman combing her hair.

I cannot tell why this imagined
    Despair has fallen on me;
The ghost of an ancient legend
    That will not let me be:

5   The air is cool, and twilight
        Flows down the quiet Rhine;
A mountain alone in the high light
        Still holds the faltering shine.

The last peak rosily gleaming
10   Reveals, enthroned in air,
A maiden, lost in dreaming,
        Who combs her golden hair.

Combing her hair with a golden
        Comb in her rocky bower,°
15   She sings the tune of an olden
        Song that has magical power.

The boatman has heard; it has bound him
        In throes of a strange, wild love;
Blind to the reefs that surround him,
20   He sees but the vision above.

And lo, hungry waters are springing—
        Boat and boatman are gone. . . .
Then silence. And this, with her singing,
        The Lorelei has done.

German picture postcard illustrating lines from "The Lorelei," 1905.

14. **bower:** an enclosed place or retreat; a lady's bedroom or private room. Can also refer to any natural enclosure.

What kind of melody do you imagine would accompany the lyrics of "The Lorelei"?

Interpreting Meanings

1. What attitude toward love is reflected in this poem?
2. The lines, "Blind to the reefs that surround him/ He sees but the vision above" refer to the boatman. What broader meaning about human life might they also have?
3. Write down three **images** that appeal to the sense of sight and three images that appeal to the sense of hearing in "The Lorelei." What **mood**, or emotional atmosphere, do these images create?

Applying Meanings

Although the Lorelei is beautiful, she is very dangerous. Why are people sometimes attracted to things that are harmful? Have you ever had this experience? What did you learn from the experience that you wish you had known beforehand?

Creative Writing Response

Writing About a Legend. Refer to the notes you made in the Writer's Response (see page 1012) about a myth, fairy tale, ghost story, or modern legend involving a human being and a supernatural being. Cast yourself as an observer of the scene, and relate an important episode from the tale. You may write your tale in prose or verse. Be sure to use striking **imagery** that appeals to the senses in order to convey the **tone**—cheerful, ironic, gloomy, etc.— that you are striving for.

Critical Writing Response

Comparing Two Poems. The following poem is by Edgar Allan Poe, an American poet who, like Heine, wrote during the Romantic period of the early nineteenth century. In "Eldorado," Poe also wrote about a popular legend—the search for the imaginary land of gold. Write a two- to three-paragraph essay in which you compare "The Lorelei" with "Eldorado." Consider the following elements: **tone,** supernatural agents, **imagery,** the treasure that is sought, and the fates of the boatman and the knight.

Eldorado
by Edgar Allan Poe

Gaily bedight,°   1. **bedight:** dressed.
A gallant knight,
In sunshine and in shadow,
Had journeyed long,
5   Singing a song,
In search of Eldorado.

But he grew old—
This knight so bold—
And o'er his heart a shadow
10   Fell as he found
No spot of ground
That looked like Eldorado.

And, as his strength
Failed him at length,
15   He met a pilgrim shadow—
"Shadow," said he,
"Where can it be—
This land of Eldorado?"

"Over the Mountains
20   Of the Moon,
Down the Valley of the Shadow,
Ride, boldly ride,"
The shade replied,—
"If you seek for Eldorado!"

Victor Hugo
1802–1885

Topham/The Image Works

Even people who knew nothing of Victor Hugo's work were awed by his physical presence. He was a man of legendary strength, energy, and appetite. He was also a man of enormous vanity, who said at one point that Paris should be renamed "Hugo."

The son of one of Napoleon's officers, Hugo spent his childhood in Madrid, Naples, and Paris. In his schoolwork and in his personal writing, he soon revealed his talent, his perfectionism, and his amazing stamina. Within two years, between the ages of seventeen and nineteen, he wrote 272 articles for a journal he edited with his brother. He published his first collection of poetry in 1822, the year he married his childhood sweetheart, Adèle Foucher. By the time he

was thirty-eight, he had published eight plays, seven volumes of poetry, and the novels *Han d'islande* (1823) and *The Hunchback of Notre Dame* (1831). At forty, as the most popular and respected author in France, Hugo was elected to the French Academy.

In 1843, Hugo's first failure—a play called *Les Burgraves*—led directly to the collapse of Romanticism in the French theater. The same year also brought a personal tragedy. His favorite daughter and her husband were drowned in a boating accident. Hugo's grief, like everything else about him, was colossal. For the next ten years he published nothing. He wrote only for himself, to ease his grief.

As a distraction from his pain during these years, Hugo entered political life. He was formally exiled as a political rebel in 1852, but he was not forgotten. His banishment contributed to his already enormous popularity. In exile, Hugo wrote many of his greatest poems and the protest novel *Les Misérables* (1862). When Napoleon III fell from power in 1870, Hugo returned to France.

Hugo's funeral—attended by more than a million people—was a tremendous spectacle. The funeral parade was miles long, led by entire regiments of cavalry. Behind them followed carriages filled with the greatest dignitaries of Europe. The French people felt they were burying not just a writer, but a national hero.

Reader's Guide

RUSSIA 1812
from The Expiation

Background

"Russia 1812," which shows the influence of both Romanticism and Realism, is excerpted from Hugo's poem *The Expiation* (1852). The subject of this excerpt is Napoleon Bonaparte's retreat from Moscow in 1812. The French army, known also as the Grand Army, had invaded Russia and reached Moscow on September 15 of that year. Expecting to find food and shelter in the city, Napoleon and his soldiers discovered instead that the Russians had evacuated Moscow, set it on fire, and taken all its supplies with them. On October 19, after a brief occupation, Napoleon ordered the Grand Army to retreat. The retreat across the frozen plains of Russia was devastating for the French. It has been said that the Russian winter, not the Russian army, defeated Napoleon. Of the 600,000 men who left for Russia, no more than one third returned.

Oral Response

On a map or globe, find the distance from Moscow to Paris. Then, in an encyclopedia or geographical dictionary, find out as much as you can about the terrain and climate of the territory between Moscow and Paris. With your classmates, discuss the hardships that an army retreating along this route in wintertime might face.

Literary Focus

Imagery is descriptive writing that appeals to our senses of sight, hearing, smell, touch, or taste. "Russia 1812" presents a vivid picture of the retreat from Moscow. As you read, notice the sensory images Hugo uses. Consider how the details in Hugo's poem compare with the details you might find in a nonfiction account of the same event. How does the use of imagery contribute to this realism?

RUSSIA 1812

from The Expiation

Victor Hugo

translated by

ROBERT LOWELL

▌ *As you read, notice what emotions are stirred in you by the*
▌ *imagery of the poem.*

The snow fell, and its power was multiplied.
For the first time the Eagle° bowed its head—
dark days! Slowly the Emperor returned—
behind him Moscow! Its onion domes still burned.
5 The snow rained down in blizzards—rained and
     froze.
Past each white waste a further white waste rose.
None recognized the captains or the flags.
Yesterday the Grand Army, today its dregs!
No one could tell the vanguard from the flanks.
10 The snow! The hurt men struggled from the
      ranks,
hid in the bellies of dead horses, in stacks
of shattered caissons.° By the bivouacs,
one saw the picket° dying at his post,
still standing in his saddle, white with frost,
15 the stone lips frozen to the bugle's mouth!
Bullets and grapeshot° mingled with the snow,
that hailed ... The Guard, surprised at shivering,
      march
in a dream now; ice rimes° the gray mustache.
The snow falls, always snow! The driving mire
20 submerges; men, trapped in that white empire,
have no more bread and march on barefoot—
      gaps!
They were no longer living men and troops,
but a dream drifting in a fog, a mystery,
mourners parading under the black sky.

2. **Eagle:** Napoleon's nickname;
    also the standard for Napo-
    leon's armies.

12. **caissons** (kā'sənz): wagons
     used for transporting ammunition.
13. **picket:** a soldier stationed to
     guard a body of troops against
     a surprise attack.

16. **grapeshot:** a cluster of small
     iron balls fired from a cannon.

18. **rimes:** frosts.

NAPOLEON'S CAMPAIGN IN FRANCE, ERNEST MEISSONIER, 1864.

Archiv Für Kunst Und Geschichte, Berlin

25 The solitude, vast, terrible to the eye,
    was like a mute avenger everywhere,
    as snowfall, floating through the quiet air,
    buried the huge army in a huge shroud.
    Could anyone leave this kingdom? A crowd—
30 each man, obsessed with dying, was alone.
    Men slept—and died! The beaten mob sludged on,
    ditching the guns to burn their carriages.
    Two foes. The North, the Czar.° The North was
        worse.
    In hollows where the snow was piling up,
35 one saw whole regiments fallen asleep.
    Attila's dawn, Cannaes of Hannibal!°
    The army marching to its funeral!
    Litters, wounded, the dead, deserters—swarms,

33. **Czar** (zär): the ruler of Russia.

36. **Attila's** (at''l·ə) . . . **Hannibal**
    (han'ə·b'l): Attila, leader of the
    barbaric Huns, was finally de-
    feated when he attacked Gaul
    in A.D. 451. Hannibal, a Car-
    thaginian general, destroyed
    the Roman army at Cannae,
    but it was his final victory.

crushing the bridges down to cross a stream.
40 They went to sleep ten thousand, woke up four.
Ney,° bringing up the former army's rear,
hacked his horse loose from three disputing
    Cossacks . . .
All night, the *qui vive?*° The alert! Attacks;
retreats! White ghosts would wrench away our
    guns,
45 or we would see dim, terrible squadrons,
circles of steel, whirlpools of savages,
rush sabering through the camp like dervishes.°
And in this way, whole armies died at night.

The Emperor was there, standing—he saw.
50 This oak already trembling from the axe,
watched his glories drop from him branch by
    branch:
chiefs, soldiers. Each one had his turn and
    chance—
they died! Some lived. These still believed his star,
and kept their watch. They loved the man of war,
55 this small man with his hands behind his back,
whose shadow, moving to and fro, was black
behind the lighted tent. Still believing, they
accused their destiny of *lèse-majesté.*°
His misfortune had mounted on their back.
60 The man of glory shook. Cold stupefied
him, then suddenly he felt terrified.
Being without belief, he turned to God:
"God of armies, is this the end?" he cried.
And then at last the expiation° came,
65 as he heard someone call him by his name,
someone half-lost in shadow, who said, "No,
Napoleon." Napoleon understood,
restless, bareheaded, leaden, as he stood
before his butchered legions in the snow.

41. **Ney** (nā): marshal in charge of the defense of the rear in the French army's retreat from Moscow.
43. *qui vive?* (kē vēv'): a sentry's challenge; literally, "who lives?"

47. **dervishes:** Muslims dedicated to a life of poverty and chastity.

58. **lèse-majesté** (lez' ma'zhes·tā'): treason; literally, "injured majesty."

64. **expiation:** reparation; atonement.

Did this poem make you sympathize with the French army? What specific words and phrases helped form your response?

Identifying Facts

1. What two foes of Napoleon does the speaker mention? Which foe was more powerful?

2. What did the French soldiers do to stay alive?

3. Observing the destruction of his army, how did Napoleon feel?

Interpreting Meanings

1. Why do you think Hugo repeats the word *snow* so many times in the opening lines? What effect does this repetition have? What other **imagery** is repeated in the poem?

2. A **metaphor** is a comparison between two unlike things that does not use the words *like* or *as*. In lines 50–52, what metaphor does the poet use in his description of the French army? Explain the comparison in your own words.

3. According to lines 53–58, what was the attitude of the surviving soldiers toward Napoleon?

4. Explain the **irony** of the sentry's question, *"qui vive?"* ("who lives?").

5. Explain how the choice of words reveals the poet's attitude toward Napoleon.

6. Reread lines 67–69. What do you think Napoleon "understood"?

7. Consider the connotations of the word *expiation*. Why do you think Hugo

called the long poem from which "Russia 1812" was taken *The Expiation*? In what sense is the fate of the French army an "expiation"? Of what crime or error have the French been guilty?

Applying Meanings

"Russia 1812" contains many disturbing, graphic images of suffering. Think of a book, magazine article, movie, or television program that contains similar images. What purpose do such graphic portrayals serve today? Do you think people have become insensitive to suffering in literature and the media? Could most people still be affected by the imagery in Hugo's poem? Why or why not?

Creative Writing Response

Writing a Newspaper Account. Imagine that you are a reporter for either a French or a Russian newspaper in 1812. Write a news story—with a catchy headline—describing the French retreat from Moscow. Include specific details from the poem. Remember to "slant" your story according to your chosen nationality. If you like, accompany your story with an illustration.

Critical Writing Response

Comparing Poets' Views. Compare and contrast Pushkin's and Hugo's views about nature, providing examples from "I Have Visited Again" and "Russia 1812." What role does nature play in each poem? Does the poet view nature as benevolent or malevolent?

Charles Baudelaire
1821–1867

The Bettmann Archive

One short book, *Flowers of Evil,* made Charles Baudelaire (shȧrl bōd·ler′) the most influential French poet of the nineteenth century. Baudelaire was the first "decadent"—an artist who rejected middle-class society and experienced firsthand the poverty and sordidness of Paris street life. Most of his poems are melancholy and deal with vice, poverty, drunkenness, or something Baudelaire considered worse—boredom.

Baudelaire was born into a well-to-do family, and from the beginning he was a sensitive boy. His father died when he was six, and his mother married someone the boy hated. His stepfather sent him to military school, but Baudelaire rebelled against the school's authorities. When he was eighteen, he moved to Paris, where he lived as a Bohemian in the Paris art community, struggling to write. Disturbed and embarrassed by his decadent lifestyle, his family sent him on a sea voyage to India, but, seasick, he left the ship and spent three weeks on a tropical island.

Back in Paris, young Baudelaire inherited some money from his father's estate; living extravagantly, he managed to squander half of the money in two years. He then launched into an intense period of dissipation, physical illness, and mental disturbance. He lived on the small allowance his mother gave him and devoted himself to art, vowing that writing was the only thing worth doing.

A perfectionist, Baudelaire struggled for many years writing and rewriting the poems in his only published work, *Flowers of Evil.* The title of this collection reflects the quality of its poems, whose morbid, melancholy, and occasionally horrifying images are expressed with delicate skill and exquisite phrases. When the book was published in 1857, the author was fined for offending public morals, and six poems had to be cut out with scissors before the already-printed edition could be offered for sale. This censorship may have contributed to the long downslide that marked Baudelaire's last ten years. During that time he wrote some important prose poems and some fragments, but no poetic masterpieces to match his earlier success. At the age of forty-six, insane and paralyzed, he died in his mother's arms.

Reader's Guide

INVITATION TO THE VOYAGE

Background

Like the Romantic poets, Baudelaire wrote subjectively, casting the light of his own moods over his entire world. He was attracted to gloomy subjects and bizarre experiences. Baudelaire, however, saw himself as an anti-Romantic, for he prized precise language and form and considered most Romantic poetry vague and formless. Unlike most Romantics, Baudelaire found inspiration in alleys, sidewalks, and gutters, rather than in hills, brooks, and rainbows. In French literature, Baudelaire's poetry is a bridge between the work of the Romantics and that of the Symbolists, poets who used symbols to suggest, rather than directly state, meaning or mood.

"Invitation to the Voyage" is a rarity among Baudelaire's poems—its tone is mostly light and happy. Much of the poem was inspired by his interrupted sea voyage to India; the final stanza describes Holland as Baudelaire imagined it to be from looking at Dutch landscape paintings. The speaker of the poem invites a woman to accompany him to this imaginary land of bliss. The real-life model for the woman was Marie Daubrun, an actress with whom Baudelaire was infatuated.

The two lines repeated at the end of each stanza—the **refrain**—have been quoted often. The great modern painter Henri Matisse used the second repeated line as the title for a major painting; in French, it is *Luxe, Calme, et Volupté.*

Writer's Response

What is your imaginary land of bliss? In a few sentences, describe what it looks like, what you would do there, and who would accompany you on the voyage.

Literary Focus

A word, phrase, line, or group of lines that is repeated in a literary work is called a **refrain**. Refrains are most often used in songs or in poems that have a songlike quality. "Invitation to the Voyage" has a famous refrain: the two lines that appear as lines 13–14, 27–28, and 41–42. When writers use a refrain, they are usually trying to create some specific emotional effect or **mood**. As you read "Invitation to the Voyage," ask what the refrain contributes to the mood of the poem.

INVITATION TO THE VOYAGE

Charles Baudelaire

translated by

RICHARD WILBUR

SEASCAPE AT SAINT-MARIE (VIEW OF MEDITERRANEAN), VINCENT VAN GOGH (1853–1890). *Van Gogh is noted for the striking mood of his paintings.*
What do you feel is the mood of this painting? Is it an appropriate illustration for the poem? Why or why not?

As you read, see if you can visualize the places to which the poem's speaker would like to journey. Which images are the most striking?

My child, my sister,
                          dream
How sweet all things would seem
Were we in that kind land to live together,
      And there love slow and long,

5   There love and die among
Those scenes that image you, that sumptuous
     weather.
          Drowned suns that glimmer there
          Through cloud-disheveled air
Move me with such a mystery as appears
10   Within those other skies
          Of your treacherous eyes
When I behold them shining through their tears.

There, there is nothing else but grace and measure,
Richness, quietness, and pleasure.

15   Furniture that wears
          The luster of the years
Softly would glow within our glowing chamber,
          Flowers of rarest bloom
          Proffering their perfume
20 Mixed with the vague fragrances of amber;
          Gold ceilings would there be,
          Mirrors deep as the sea,
The walls all in an Eastern splendor hung—
          Nothing but should address
25   The soul's loneliness,
Speaking her sweet and secret native tongue.

There, there is nothing else but grace and measure,
Richness, quietness, and pleasure.

          See, sheltered from the swells
30   There in the still canals
Those drowsy ships that dream of sailing forth;
          It is to satisfy
          Your least desire, they ply
Hither through all the waters of the earth.
35   The sun at close of day
          Clothes the fields of hay,
Then the canals, at last the town entire
          In hyacinth and gold;
          Slowly the land is rolled
40 Sleepward under a sea of gentle fire.

There, there is nothing else but grace and measure,
Richness, quietness, and pleasure.

First Thoughts

Would you like to accompany Baudelaire on his voyage? Why or why not?

Interpreting Meanings

1. In line 1, the speaker addresses his lover as "My child, my sister." How does this sentiment contrast with that of "treacherous eyes" in line 11?

2. Find at least two lines or phrases in the poem that hint that the speaker's real life is not happy.

3. What does the first stanza reveal about Baudelaire's concept of love?

4. Lines 13–14 are repeated as a **refrain**. List as many other examples of repetition as you can find in the poem, including repetition of words, sounds, and images. How do these repetitions affect the **mood**, or atmosphere, of the poem?

5. The three stanzas of "Invitation to the Voyage" support the idea presented in the **refrain**. The first stanza represents "pleasure," the second "richness," and the third "quietness." How does the **imagery** of each stanza contribute to this interpretation?

Applying Meanings

"People who lead troubled lives dream of peace; people who lead peaceful lives dream of excitement." Do you agree or disagree with this statement? Apply your opinion to "Invitation to the Voyage."

Creative Writing Response

Describing an Imaginary Land. Drawing on the notes you took for the Writer's Response (see page 1022), describe your imaginary land of bliss. Use **images** that appeal to the senses of sight, hearing, touch, taste, or smell. Feel free to write your description in either poetry or prose. If you use poetry, you might want to experiment with using a refrain.

Critical Writing Response

Comparing Translations. In reading "Invitation to the Voyage," you are not just reading Baudelaire. You are also reading a translation from nineteenth-century French into twentieth-century English. In this case, the translator is one of America's leading poets, Richard Wilbur (b. 1921). Wilbur's book of poems, *Things of This World,* which includes his version of "Invitation to the Voyage," won both the Pulitzer Prize and the National Book Award in 1957.

Here is a different translation of the first stanza and the refrain of Baudelaire's poem, by Francis Duke.

> *from* Invitation to Travel
> by Charles Baudelaire
> translated by
> Francis Duke
>
> My sister, my child,
> How life would have smiled
> At us two, together, down there,
> In love at each breath,
> 5   In love until death,
> In that land whose nature you share!
> Whose suns, in their shrouds
> Of scudding wet clouds
> Arouse in my heart the same cheer,
> 10 The same charmed surprise,
> As your fickle eyes
> When sparkles dart forth through a tear!
>
> There, beauty and harmony dwell
> Where springs of voluptuousness well.

In a two- or three-paragraph essay, compare and contrast Duke's and Wilbur's translations. Consider the meaning and mood of each version; the diction, or word choice; the use of rhythm, rhyme, and other sound effects; and the naturalness of the language. Which title do you prefer? Overall, which version of the poem do you prefer? Why?

SEEING CONNECTIONS

The French Connection: Charles Baudelaire and Edgar Allan Poe

In America, Edgar Allan Poe was long regarded as a minor writer, an author of melodramatic poems such as ''The Raven'' and ''Annabel Lee'' and thrilling tales of mystery and suspense like ''The Fall of the House of Usher'' and ''The Tell-Tale Heart.'' However, largely because of the efforts of the French poet Charles Baudelaire, Poe is considered in France to be one of the greatest writers of the nineteenth century.

When Baudelaire was twenty-five, he discovered Poe. Immediately, he felt that he had found his spiritual twin and alter ego. In a letter to a friend, Baudelaire wrote: ''The first time I opened a book of his I saw, with horror and delight, not just subjects I had dreamt of, but *sentences* I had thought of, and written by him twenty years before.'' Baudelaire not only identified with Poe the writer, but also with Poe the man. He saw himself and Poe as tormented artists whose troubled lives drove them to write poems and stories of passion and spiritual and emotional pain. Both men spent most of their professional years in poverty and illness, their work being the driving force of their lives. Identifying with Poe so thoroughly, Baudelaire proceeded to build an elaborate mythology about Poe's life.

The French poet became increasingly obsessed with Poe. Some sources claim that Baudelaire even prayed to the spirit of Edgar Allan Poe. He spent much time and energy studying English and asking any American he met to clarify his understanding of a certain line or passage of Poe's. According to one story, Baudelaire once questioned an American tourist who was buying shoes, but he was so disgusted by the man's ignorance of Poe that he insulted the man in anger. Twenty years of Baudelaire's life were devoted to translating Poe's fiction and championing his genius. These translations are today considered some of the finest translations in the world.

The publication of Baudelaire's translations and his aggressive promotion of Poe's works and ideas brought Poe a notoriety in France and Europe that he would not experience in America until more than a century after his death. The Symbolist poets, including Valéry, Verlaine, and Mallarmé, were fascinated by Poe and considered him their literary master.

Edgar Allan Poe was either ignored or disparaged by nineteenth-century American critics. He was, however, voraciously read and discussed in France and other European countries. The first and most exhaustive critical work on Poe was published not in America, but in France, in 1933. Poe began to be the subject of literary study in America in the mid-twentieth century, mainly because of the effect of these French critical works. The French, it seems, have taught Americans to appreciate one of their own greatest writers.

Paul Verlaine (1844–1896)
Arthur Rimbaud (1854–1891)

The Granger Collection, New York

The lives of Paul Verlaine (pōl ver·len′) and Arthur Rimbaud (år·tür′ ram·bō′) were closely linked. These two Symbolist poets shared a turbulent friendship. Both men rebelled against conventional society, sought out experiences of squalor and degradation, died relatively young, and became legendary for their poetry.

Verlaine was one of France's leading poets during the second half of the nineteenth century, though he began his career as an insurance clerk. He hoped that his marriage to sixteen-year-old Mathilde would help cure him of alcoholism, and indeed, he wrote a number of moving poems to her. Soon, however, he discovered Rimbaud and came under his influence. Verlaine abandoned Mathilde for a year-long spree that ended when he shot and wounded Rimbaud in a quarrel and was subsequently sent to prison. When he was released from prison, he found that he had lost his wife and his relationship with Rimbaud forever. From this point on, his life went downhill.

Like Verlaine, Rimbaud was a self-destructive genius. His father abandoned the family when Rimbaud was six, and he was raised in poverty by a strict mother. At the age of fourteen, Rimbaud was already writing first-rate poetry, experimenting with syntax and unusual imagery. In 1871, Rimbaud wrote to Verlaine and sent him a couple of poems, asking for his financial help and patronage. Verlaine responded enthusiastically. Before long Rimbaud began to dominate Verlaine psychologically.

After his stormy relationship with Verlaine, Rimbaud gave up poetry forever and began a career of full-time wandering during which he served with and later deserted the Dutch army, toured with a circus in Scandinavia, and worked in Africa as a gunrunner and possibly a slave trader. Ironically, while he was living in a palm-leaf hut in Africa, Rimbaud became a celebrity in Paris: Verlaine, who thought that his former friend was dead, had published Rimbaud's earlier work, *Illuminations*, with great success, though Rimbaud seemed unaware of it. After a decade of wandering and suffering, Rimbaud returned to France, where he died of cancer.

Reader's Guide

THE SKY IS JUST BEYOND THE ROOF
THE SLEEPER OF THE VALLEY

Background

"The Sky Is Just Beyond the Roof" is one of the poems Verlaine wrote while he was in prison for the shooting of Arthur Rimbaud. As you read the poem, imagine that the speaker is looking out the barred window of his cell, over the roof of the prison, at a clear blue sky that represents freedom.

"The Sleeper of the Valley" is one of Rimbaud's more accessible and straightforward poems. Its descriptions present a landscape with one human figure. The poem is built upon a surprising twist.

Writer's Response

People usually associate sunny weather and peaceful landscapes with happiness, but their feelings are often not in tune with their surroundings. In words, briefly sketch a scene—from your own experience, the experience of someone you know, or from your imagination—in which you contrast a person's surroundings with his or her feelings.

Literary Focus

The **Symbolist** poets felt that Romantic poetry was full of overly rich language and **imagery,** and they criticized Romanticism for its sometimes stereotyped imagery and empty wordiness. The Symbolists avoided making direct statements in poetry and instead strove to suggest meaning through the use of precise and evocative images, as well as through the sound of language. In this way, **Symbolism** was akin to music in its ability to suggest an impression or **mood.**

Both Verlaine and Rimbaud were Symbolists who mastered the use of sensory imagery. Their visual images are compact and suggestive, like those of a painter who creates a broad landscape in a few brushstrokes. In addition, both poets have the knack of appealing to more than one sense with a single image or figure of speech. How many distinct images can you find in "The Sky Is Just Beyond the Roof" and "The Sleeper of the Valley"? In what ways are the sounds, imagery, and suggestive language of these poems representative of Symbolism?

THE SKY IS JUST BEYOND THE ROOF

Paul Verlaine

translated by
BERGEN APPLEGATE

As you read, compare and contrast the views and emotions expressed by Verlaine and Rimbaud. What similarities can you find in the two poets' outlooks on nature and human life? What differences can you find?

The sky is just beyond the roof
  So blue, so calm;
A treetop just beyond the roof
  Rocks its slow palm.

5 The chime in the sky that I see
    Distantly rings:
A bird on the tree that I see
  Plaintively[1] sings.

My God, my God, but life is there,
10   Tranquil and sweet:
This peaceful murmur that I hear
  Comes from the street!

What have you done, you who stand here,
  In tears and ruth?[2]
15 Say, what have you done, you who are here,
  With your lost youth?

THE ROAD TO VERSAILLES, ALFRED SISLEY, 1873.

Archiv Für Kunst Und Geschichte, Berlin

---

1. **Plaintively:** mournfully.
2. **ruth:** remorse; sorrow.

THE SLEEPER OF THE VALLEY

Arthur Rimbaud

translated by

LUDWIG LEWISOHN

WATERLILIES IN A POND, ISAAC ILYITAH LEVIATAN (1860–1900).

There's a green hollow where a river sings
Silvering the torn grass in its glittering flight,
And where the sun from the proud mountain flings
Fire—and the little valley brims with light.

5   A soldier young, with open mouth, bare head,
Sleeps with his neck in dewy watercress,°
Under the sky and on the grass his bed,
Pale in the deep green and the light's excess.

He sleeps amid the iris and his smile
10 Is like a sick child's slumbering for a while.
Nature, in thy warm lap his chilled limbs hide!

The perfume does not thrill him from his rest.
He sleeps in sunshine, hand upon his breast,
Tranquil—with two red holes in his right side.

6. **watercress:** a white-flowered plant, growing generally in running water.

First Thoughts

Which poem did you prefer, and why?

Identifying Facts

1. What is the vantage point of the speaker in "The Sky Is Just Beyond the Roof"? What does he see?
2. Who is the young man in "The Sleeper of the Valley," and what has happened to him?

Interpreting Meanings

1. What emotion does line 9 in "The Sky Is Just Beyond the Roof" express?
2. The first three stanzas of "The Sky Is Just Beyond the Roof" are narrated from the **first-person point of view**. In your opinion, who is the "you" in the fourth stanza? Why is this person in tears?
3. What is the effect of **imagery** that appeals to more than one sense in Rimbaud's "The Sleeper of the Valley"?
4. **Irony** occurs when one thing is said and another thing is meant. Explain how irony is created by the language and imagery of "The Sleeper of the Valley."
5. In what sense do both poems use imagery to suggest the loss of youth?
6. What features of **Symbolism** do you see in these poems? How do these poems differ from the earlier Romantic poetry you have read, such as Wordsworth's "The World Is Too Much with Us" and Pushkin's "I Have Visited Again"?

Applying Meanings

The beautiful imagery of both poems and the irony of "The Sleeper of the Valley" serve to enhance the impact of each situation that the poet is describing. Think of how something you have recently read, seen on television, or seen in a movie dealt with a serious, even depressing, subject, such as imprisonment or the carnage of war. How did the treatment of the subject affect your reaction to it?

Creative Writing Response

Writing a Poem. Refer to the sketch you made in the Writer's Response (see page 1028). Use this sketch as the basis for a poem. In your poem, use imagery to describe the contrast between the person's surroundings and his or her feelings.

Critical Writing Response

Analyzing Diction. In "The Sky Is Just Beyond the Roof" we find words such as *sky, roof, bird,* and *street*. In "The Sleeper of the Valley" we find words and phrases such as *silvering, dewy watercress, iris,* and *chilled limbs*. Write a brief essay comparing and contrasting the **diction**, or word choice, of Verlaine and Rimbaud. Which poet uses simpler, plainer words? Which poet uses more adjectives and adverbs? For each poem, analyze how the poet's diction affects the way we see the objects in the poem and the way we feel about them. Then state why you think each poet might have chosen the kinds of descriptive words he did. Assume that the translations accurately reflect the differences in diction in the original French. You might want to use a chart like the one below to organize your ideas.

	"The Sky Is Just Beyond the Roof"	"The Sleeper of the Valley"
Use of simple, direct language (nouns/verbs)		
Adjectives and adverbs		
Effect of diction		

Guy de Maupassant
1850–1893

Guy de Maupassant (gē də mō·pä·sän′) gave new shape and direction to the short story. His many works have set the standard of excellence for many writers of short fiction.

Maupassant was born into a family of merchants in rural Normandy. Among the friends of his family were many artists and writers, including the great Realist novelist Gustave Flaubert (1821–1880). Maupassant was encouraged to write from an early age, especially by his mother and Flaubert.

After serving in the French army during the Franco-Prussian War, Maupassant studied law and then took a government post in Paris. There he got in touch with Flaubert, who became his mentor. Every week, several great Realist writers met at Flaubert's house to discuss literature. They included Émile

Zola (1840–1902), and the Russian novelist Ivan Turgenev (1818–1883). Flaubert invited the young Maupassant to join the group. At that time, Maupassant was writing poems, historical dramas in verse, and horror stories. Under the influence of his new friends, he turned to realistic prose fiction.

Flaubert's influence was also helpful in getting Maupassant a better job and introductions to literary salons. Later, Maupassant joined a spinoff group of younger Realists, or Naturalists, who met at Zola's house. The Naturalists treated the older Realists with respect, but they were less interested in stylistic beauty and more intent on describing social conditions objectively.

Maupassant's twenties were a period of literary apprenticeship. He did not publish his first Realist story until 1879. But by his thirties, Maupassant had become one of the best-known artists in France, earning enough to quit his government job and support himself as a writer. In 1883 alone, he turned out two novels and seventy short stories. His novels of this time are examples of Realism at its most observant.

Few of his friends suspected that the strong young writer was in constant pain, nearly blind from overwork and disease. Painkilling drugs made his health worse. The end of 1891 brought a complete mental breakdown from which Maupassant never recovered. He died in an asylum before his forty-third birthday.

Reader's Guide

THE JEWELS

Background

The realistic short story as a distinct literary form came into its own in the second half of the nineteenth century. Earlier Romantic writers—especially Americans such as Washington Irving, Edgar Allan Poe, and Nathaniel Hawthorne—had created marvelous short tales of fantasy. In contrast, later Realist writers perfected the use of the short story to illuminate the problems of real people. Maupassant is considered to be the most accomplished and influential of these writers. His stories are known for their realistic details, brisk pacing, concentration on essentials, and the unexpected plot twists with which they end. By deftly selecting a detail or two, Maupassant gives individuality to characters who also represent distinct social types.

One of the chief lessons Maupassant learned from the discussion groups at Flaubert's and Zola's homes and from his own writing practice was the importance of being concise. As you read "The Jewels," notice that Maupassant uses only a few sentences to describe major events and characters. The terse style found in this story, as in many others, is partly the result of the fact that Maupassant's stories were originally published in newspapers, which severely restricted the length of his material.

Writer's Response

Imagine that you have inherited a large sum of money, but that it has come from the questionable actions of someone you loved. Would you be ashamed to keep the money, or would you gladly enjoy your good fortune? Write a few sentences on this topic.

Literary Focus

As you read "The Jewels," notice how Maupassant compresses the entire adult lives of the Lantins into a handful of pages. This tightly constructed **plot**, or series of related events, consists of the following elements: **exposition**, or the description of the characters, setting, and conflict; **complications**, which occur when characters attempt to resolve the conflict; the **climax**, when the outcome is determined; and finally, the **resolution**, when all of the story's conflicts are resolved, one way or another.

THE JEWELS

Guy de Maupassant

translated by

ROGER COLET

> *As you read, pay attention to what is not said as well as what is said. What crucial aspects of the story are implied "between the lines"?*

THE THEATER BOX, PIERRE-AUGUSTE RENOIR (1841–1919). *Renoir, an Impressionist painter, moved in the same social circles as Maupassant and fellow Naturalist Émile Zola.*

The Granger Collection, New York

Monsieur Lantin had met the girl at a party given one evening by his office superior and love had caught him in its net.

She was the daughter of a country tax collector who had died a few years before. She had come to Paris then with her mother, who struck up acquaintance with a few middle-class families in her district in the hope of marrying her off. They were poor and decent, quiet and gentle. The girl seemed the perfect example of the virtuous woman to whom every sensible young man dreams of entrusting his life. Her simple beauty had a modest, angelic charm and the imperceptible smile which always hovered about her lips seemed to be a reflection of her heart.

Everybody sang her praises and people who knew her never tired of saying: "Happy the man who marries her. Nobody could find a better wife."

Monsieur Lantin, who was then a senior clerk at the Ministry of the Interior with a salary of three thousand five hundred francs[1] a year, proposed to her and married her.

He was incredibly happy with her. She ran his household so skillfully and economically that they gave the impression of living in luxury. She lavished attention on her husband, spoiling and coddling him, and the charm of her person was so great that six

---

1. **francs:** The franc is the basic monetary unit of France.

years after their first meeting he loved her even more than in the early days.

He found fault with only two of her tastes: her love for the theater and her passion for imitation jewelry.

Her friends (she knew the wives of a few petty officials) often obtained a box at the theater for her for popular plays, and even for first nights; and she dragged her husband along willy-nilly to these entertainments, which he found terribly tiring after a day's work at the office. He therefore begged her to go to the theater with some lady of her acquaintance who would bring her home afterwards. It was a long time before she gave in, as she thought that this arrangement was not quite respectable. But finally, just to please him, she agreed, and he was terribly grateful to her.

Now this love for the theater soon aroused in her a desire to adorn her person. True, her dresses remained very simple, always in good taste, but unpretentious; and her gentle grace, her irresistible, humble, smiling charm seemed to be enhanced by the simplicity of her gowns. But she took to wearing two big rhinestone earrings which sparkled like diamonds, and she also wore necklaces of fake pearls, bracelets of imitation gold, and combs set with colored glass cut to look like real stones.

Her husband, who was rather shocked by this love of show, often used to say: "My dear, when a woman can't afford to buy real jewels, she ought to appear adorned with her beauty and grace alone: those are still the rarest of gems."

But she would smile sweetly and reply: "I can't help it. I like imitation jewelry. It's my only vice. I know you're right, but people can't change their natures. I would have loved to own some real jewels."

Then she would run the pearl necklaces through her fingers and make the cut-glass gems flash in the light, saying: "Look! Aren't they beautifully made? Anyone would swear they were real."

He would smile and say: "You have the taste of a gypsy."

Sometimes, in the evening, when they were sitting together by the fireside, she would place on the tea table the leather box in which she kept her "trash," as Monsieur Lantin called it. Then she would start examining these imitation jewels with passionate attention, as if she were enjoying some deep and secret pleasure; and she would insist on hanging a necklace around her husband's neck, laughing uproariously and crying: "How funny you look!" And then she would throw herself into his arms and kiss him passionately.

One night in winter when she had been to the Opera, she came home shivering with cold. The next morning she had a cough, and a week later she died of pneumonia.

Lantin very nearly followed her to the grave. His despair was so terrible that his hair turned white within a month. He wept from morning to night, his heart ravaged by unbearable grief, haunted by the memory, the smile, the voice, the every charm of his dead wife.

Time did nothing to assuage his grief. Often during office hours, when his colleagues came along to chat about the topics of the day, his cheeks would suddenly puff out, his nose wrinkle up, his eyes fill with tears, and with a terrible grimace he would burst out sobbing.

He had left his wife's room untouched, and every day would shut himself in it and think about her. All the furniture and even her clothes remained exactly where they had been on the day she had died.

But life soon became a struggle for him.

His income, which in his wife's hands had covered all their expenses, was now no longer sufficient for him on his own; and he wondered in amazement how she had managed to provide him with excellent wines and rare delicacies which he could no longer afford on his modest salary.

He incurred a few debts and ran after money in the way people do when they are reduced to desperate shifts. Finally, one morning, finding himself without a sou[2] a whole week before the end of the month, he decided to sell something; and immediately the idea occurred to him of disposing of his wife's "trash." He still harbored a sort of secret grudge against those false gems which had irritated him in the past, and indeed the sight of them every day somewhat spoiled the memory of his beloved.

He rummaged for a long time among the heap of gaudy trinkets she had left behind, for she had stubbornly gone on buying jewelry until the last days of her life, bringing home a new piece almost every evening. At last he decided on the large necklace which she had seemed to like best, and which, he thought, might well be worth six or seven francs, for it was beautifully made for a piece of paste.[3]

He put it in his pocket and set off for his Ministry, following the boulevards and looking for a jeweler's shop which inspired confidence.

At last he spotted one and went in, feeling a little ashamed of exposing his poverty in this way, and of trying to sell such a worthless article.

"Monsieur," he said to the jeweler, "I would like to know what you think this piece is worth."

The man took the necklace, examined it, turned it over, weighed it, inspected it with a magnifying glass, called his assistant, made a few remarks to him in an undertone, placed the necklace on the counter and looked at it from a distance to gauge the effect.

Monsieur Lantin, embarrassed by all this ritual, was opening his mouth to say: "Oh, I know perfectly well that it isn't worth anything," when the jeweler said: "Monsieur, this necklace is worth between twelve and fifteen thousand francs; but I couldn't buy it unless you told me where it came from."

The widower opened his eyes wide and stood there gaping, unable to understand what the jeweler had said. Finally he stammered: "What was that you said? . . . Are you sure?"

The other misunderstood his astonishment and said curtly: "You can go somewhere else and see if they'll offer you more. In my opinion it's worth fifteen thousand at the most. Come back and see me if you can't find a better price."

Completely dumbfounded, Monsieur Lantin took back his necklace and left the shop, in obedience to a vague desire to be alone and to think.

Once outside, however, he felt an impulse to laugh, and he thought: "The fool! Oh, the fool! But what if I'd taken him at his word? There's a jeweler who can't tell real diamonds from paste!"

And he went into another jeweler's shop at the beginning of the Rue de la Paix. As soon as he saw the necklace, the jeweler exclaimed: "Why, I know that necklace well: it was bought here."

Monsieur Lantin asked in amazement: "How much is it worth?"

"Monsieur, I sold it for twenty-five thousand. I am prepared to buy it back for

---

2. **sou** (sōō): a former French coin.
3. **paste**: fake gem.

BOULEVARD DES CAPUCINES, CLAUDE MONET (1840–1926).
Why have Monsieur Lantin's finances suffered since his wife's death?

The Nelson-Atkins Museum, Kansas City, Missouri

eighteen thousand once you have told me, in accordance with the legal requirements, how you came to be in possession of it."

This time Monsieur Lantin was dumbfounded. He sat down and said: "But ... but ... examine it carefully, Monsieur. Until now I thought it was paste."

"Will you give me your name, Monsieur?" said the jeweler.

"Certainly. My name's Lantin. I'm an official at the Ministry of the Interior, and I live at No. 16, Rue des Martyrs."

The jeweler opened his books, looked for the entry, and said: "Yes, this necklace was sent to Madame Lantin's address, No. 16, Rue des Martyrs, on the 20th of July 1876."

The two men looked into each other's eyes, the clerk speechless with astonishment, the jeweler scenting a thief. Finally the latter said: "Will you leave the necklace with me for twenty-four hours? I'll give you a receipt."

"Why, certainly," stammered Monsieur Lantin. And he went out folding the piece of paper, which he put in his pocket.

Then he crossed the street, walked up it again, noticed that he was going the wrong way, went back as far as the Tuileries, crossed the Seine, realized that he had gone wrong again, and returned to the Champs-Élysées,[4] his mind a complete blank. He tried to think it out, to understand. His wife couldn't have afforded to buy something so valuable—that was certain. But in that case it was a present! A present! But a present from whom? And why was it given her?

He halted in his tracks and remained standing in the middle of the avenue. A horrible doubt crossed his mind. Her? But in that case all the other jewels were presents,

too! The earth seemed to be trembling under his feet and a tree in front of him to be falling; he threw up his arms and fell to the ground unconscious.

He came to his senses in a chemist's shop into which the passersby had carried him. He took a cab home and shut himself up.

He wept bitterly until nightfall, biting on a handkerchief so as not to cry out. Then he went to bed worn out with grief and fatigue and slept like a log.

A ray of sunlight awoke him and he slowly got up to go to his Ministry. It was hard to think of working after such a series of shocks. It occurred to him that he could ask to be excused and he wrote a letter to his superior. Then he remembered that he had to go back to the jeweler's and he blushed with shame. He spent a long time thinking it over, but decided that he could not leave the necklace with that man. So he dressed and went out.

It was a fine day and the city seemed to be smiling under the clear blue sky. People were strolling about the streets with their hands in their pockets.

Watching them, Lantin said to himself: "How lucky rich people are! With money you can forget even the deepest of sorrows. You can go where you like, travel, enjoy yourself. Oh, if only I were rich!"

He began to feel hungry, for he had eaten nothing for two days, but his pocket was empty. Then he remembered the necklace. Eighteen thousand francs! Eighteen thousand francs! That was a tidy sum, and no mistake!

When he reached the Rue de la Paix he started walking up and down the pavement opposite the jeweler's shop. Eighteen thousand francs! A score of times he almost went in, but every time shame held him back.

He was hungry, though, very hungry, and

---

4. **Champs-Élysées** (shänz·ā·lē·zā'): an elegant boulevard in Paris.

he had no money at all. He quickly made up his mind, ran across the street so as not to have any time to think, and rushed into the shop.

As soon as he saw him the jeweler came forward and offered him a chair with smiling politeness. His assistants came into the shop, too, and glanced surreptitiously at Lantin with laughter in their eyes and on their lips.

"I have made inquiries, Monsieur," said the jeweler, "and if you still wish to sell the necklace, I am prepared to pay you the price I offered you."

"Why, certainly," stammered the clerk.

The jeweler took eighteen large bank notes out of a drawer, counted them and handed them to Lantin, who signed a little receipt and with a trembling hand put the money in his pocket.

Then, as he was about to leave the shop, he turned towards the jeweler, who was still smiling, and lowering his eyes said: "I have ... I have some other jewels which have come to me from ... from the same legacy. Would you care to buy them from me, too?"

The jeweler bowed.

"Certainly, Monsieur."

One of the assistants went out, unable to contain his laughter; another blew his nose loudly.

Lantin, red faced and solemn, remained unmoved.

"I will bring them to you," he said.

And he took a cab to go and fetch the jewels.

When he returned to the shop an hour

OUTSIDE THE THEATRE DU VAUDEVILLE, JEAN BERAUD (1849–1936).

later he still had had nothing to eat. The jeweler and his assistants began examining the jewels one by one, estimating the value of each piece. Almost all of them had been bought at that shop.

Lantin now began arguing about the valuations, lost his temper, insisted on seeing the sales registers, and spoke more and more loudly as the sum increased.

The large diamond earrings were worth twenty thousand francs, the bracelets thirty-five thousand, the brooches, rings, and lockets sixteen thousand, a set of emeralds and sapphires fourteen thousand, and a solitaire pendant on a gold chain forty thousand—making a total sum of one hundred and ninety-six thousand francs.

The jeweler remarked jokingly: "These obviously belonged to a lady who invested all her savings in jewelry."

Lantin replied seriously: "It's as good a way as any of investing one's money."

And he went off after arranging with the jeweler to have a second expert valuation the next day.

Out in the street he looked at the Vendôme column[5] and felt tempted to climb up it as if it were a greasy pole. He felt light enough to play leapfrog with the statue of the Emperor perched up there in the sky.

He went to Voisin's for lunch and ordered wine with his meal at twenty francs a bottle.

Then he took a cab and went for a drive in the Bois. He looked at the other carriages with a slightly contemptuous air, longing to call out to the passersby: "I'm a rich man, too! I'm worth two hundred thousand francs!"

Suddenly he remembered his Ministry. He drove there at once, strode into his superior's office, and said: "Monsieur, I have come to resign my post. I have just been left three hundred thousand francs."

He shook hands with his former colleagues and told them some of his plans for the future; then he went off to dine at the Café Anglais.

Finding himself next to a distinguished-looking gentleman, he was unable to refrain from informing him, with a certain coyness, that he had just inherited four hundred thousand francs.

For the first time in his life he was not bored at the theater, and he spent the night with some prostitutes.

Six months later he married again. His second wife was a very virtuous woman, but extremely bad-tempered. She made him very unhappy.

---

5. **Vendôme** (vän·dōm′) **column:** monument to a French marshal in Paris.

First Thoughts

Did you find this story realistic, or unbelievable? Why?

Identifying Facts

1. In two or three sentences, describe the Lantins' married life, including the way they met, their feelings about one another, and their economic circumstances.
2. What two tastes of Madame Lantin's does Monsieur Lantin object to?
3. How does the death of his wife affect Monsieur Lantin's standard of living?

Interpreting Meanings

1. Summarize the **plot** of "The Jewels." Identify the **exposition**, **complications**, **climax**, and **resolution**. How is the story unified by the plot device of Madame Lantin's jewelry?
2. People who know Madame Lantin say, "Happy the man who marries her. Nobody could find a better wife." Evaluate these statements based on what you have learned about Madame Lantin during the course of the story.
3. Monsieur Lantin suffers a **conflict** about whether or not to accept the eighteen thousand francs the jeweler offers for the necklace. Why do you think he hesitates? Why do you think he ultimately decides to take the money?
4. Describe Lantin's behavior at the end of the story, after he has decided to take money for the jewels. Why do you think he resigns his post and brags about his plans for the future? Why does he keep inflating the amount of money he is actually worth?

5. Reread the last paragraph of the story. What is **ironic** about the fact that Monsieur Lantin is unhappy with his second wife? What might this seemingly offhand detail add to the meaning of the story?

Applying Meanings

Would you forgive someone who had disappointed or betrayed you, if you ultimately benefited from his or her behavior?

Creative Writing Response

Writing a Character Sketch. Madame Lantin is the key character in "The Jewels," yet we are told scarcely anything about her—not even her first name. However, from the few details that Maupassant does provide, we are given some clues that help us to understand her personality. Write a brief sketch of Madame Lantin's character as you imagine her. You may create a narrative, a letter, a diary entry, or any other form. Feel free to experiment with **point of view**. For example, you might choose to write from the point of view of Monsieur Lantin or from the perspective of an omniscient narrator.

Critical Writing Response

Supporting an Opinion. Using the notes you made in the Writer's Response (see page 1033), write a brief essay stating and then supporting your opinion about whether or not Monsieur Lantin should have profited from his wife's "legacy." Begin your essay with a thesis statement, in which you concisely state your opinion. Next, cite at least three details from the story or your own experience that support the conclusion you have drawn. Finally, conclude your essay with a restatement of your thesis statement.

A CRITICAL COMMENT

The Short Story in the Nineteenth Century

The short story as a distinct genre of literature is a development of the nineteenth century. There are many earlier examples of short prose fiction, but the "tale" was usually a piece of didactic folk literature or a light literary diversion, and it was seldom undertaken by an important writer. When the tale was taken seriously, as, for example, by Boccaccio and Chaucer (see pages 813 and 772), it was usually used for satire or for moralizing. For the most part, short stories before the nineteenth century were told purely for the sake of entertainment.

By the nineteenth century, Guy de Maupassant in France, Anton Chekhov in Russia, and Edgar Allan Poe (1809–1849) in America were turning the story into a more complex literary form. The compactness of the story form gives it a suspenseful intensity and focus of emotional effect that is not found in the novel form. It is significant, in fact, that the first of the modern short stories were suspense tales of mystery and terror, among them Edgar Allan Poe's "Murders in the Rue Morgue," now regarded as the first detective story. Poe and Maupassant developed a technique that for a long time was a hallmark of the short story: the sharp and unexpected twist at the end, which makes a dramatic and usually ironic climax.

In the nineteenth century, the short story, like the novel, was a vehicle for making critical observations about society. As with novelists, and later dramatists such as Ibsen (see page 1069), short story writers were concerned with depicting realistic characters and situations in their works. Yet, writers like Maupassant, Émile Zola, and their followers created a style of writing that moved beyond **Realism**. They called themselves **Naturalists**, a term which they felt was an appropriate way to describe a literature that not only showed the gritty details of everyday life but also exposed various social ills and factors that affected the human condition. The Naturalists used their writings to show how the various factors in a person's life—social class, economic conditions, education, upbringing, environment—all determine or affect his or her behavior and ultimately his or her fate.

The Naturalists were often accused of dwelling on the sordid side of life and ignoring the spiritual qualities of human existence. Despite these criticisms, however, important influences came from the Naturalist movement. Writers ever since have been concerned with facing the truth about the sufferings of people, especially of the poor and exploited, and they have insisted on the freedom to express themselves in realistic language—even if it seems shocking. But the Naturalists did not want merely to shock; they wanted to expose the unpleasant and ugly facts of life with the thought that, by their revelations, something could be done to improve the world in which they lived.

Leo Tolstoy
1828–1910

W hen Count Leo Nikolayevich Tolstoy (lē′ō nē′kô·lä′ye·vich′ tôl′stoi′) died in an obscure railroad station at the age of eighty-two, he may have been the most famous man in the world. His death from pneumonia was front-page news in England and America. For, in addition to being the greatest living Russian novelist, Tolstoy was also a social and religious reformer and a symbol of Russia's yearning for freedom.

Tolstoy was born to wealthy aristocratic parents, but he became an orphan when he was nine. He, his three older brothers, and his younger sister were raised by aunts on the family estate. As Tolstoy grew older, he, like many young men of the Russian nobility, led an aimless life.

At nineteen, Tolstoy split his inheritance with his brothers and became the master of his family's estate and its three hundred serfs. Within three years, he managed to gamble away about one fourth of his inher-itance. Looking for adventure, he joined the Russian army and fought bravely during the Crimean War. The sufferings that he witnessed during the war helped bring out his serious, morally questioning nature.

In 1859, Tolstoy opened a school on his estate for his serfs' children. Soon after, he married Sonya Andreyevna Bers. In addition to bearing him thirteen children, Sonya re-copied her husband's illegible manuscripts and took over the management of his estate, enabling Tolstoy to write his greatest works, *War and Peace* and *Anna Karenina.*

After years of moral questioning, Tolstoy underwent a spiritual conversion. During the last thirty years of his life, he condemned ownership, capitalism, the Orthodox Church, and Russia's czarist government. He also repudiated much of his earlier writing—including *Anna Karenina* (1877) and *War and Peace* (1869)—for their "bourgeois" preoccupation with the Russian aristocracy. He became the leader of a utopian movement that championed the poor and was based on principles of community and social justice. His ideas inspired later pacifist reformers such as Mahatma Gandhi and Martin Luther King, Jr.

Although Tolstoy was a pacifist, a Christian, and an aristocrat, the Communist leaders of Russia never dared to ban his books. His rural grave is a major Soviet tourist attraction, and his house in Moscow is now the Tolstoy Museum.

Reader's Guide

HOW MUCH LAND DOES A MAN NEED?

Background

Until 1861, when they were emancipated by Czar Alexander II, the millions of serfs working on Russian farms were the property of land-owners. As property, they were frequently sold, flogged, transferred to other estates, or sent to serve in the army. After 1861, serfs were free to acquire land and money of their own. A few of these serfs, who bought the farms of other peasants or debt-ridden aristocrats, became wealthy. Pahom, the main character of "How Much Land Does a Man Need?", becomes one of these rich, landowning peasants during the course of the story.

As you read, notice how realistically Tolstoy describes several distinct Russian lifestyles. One of these is the lifestyle of the Bashkir (bash·kir') nomads, who live on the steppes, or great, treeless plains. Tolstoy owned a 6,700-acre horse-breeding farm, including a private racetrack at which he held races and wrestling contests with nomads of several tribes.

"How Much Land Does a Man Need?" is one of the best moral tales that Tolstoy wrote after becoming disillusioned with his earlier writings. In this story Tolstoy blends realism and allegory. Written in 1886, the story tells about a peasant who is corrupted and eventually destroyed by the illusion of private ownership.

Writer's Response

If you had the opportunity to become rich, how much land, money, or other possessions would satisfy you? Write a few sentences explaining how much you would need in order to feel completely satisfied.

Literary Focus

Tolstoy's story is often called a **parable**. A parable is a short, simple tale that has a moral lesson. A parable is related to **allegory**, which is a narrative with a double meaning: An allegory can be read at two or more levels. As you follow Pahom's adventures in "How Much Land Does a Man Need?" ask yourself what **theme** Tolstoy is expressing through the actions of his main character. One important clue is the way the character develops in the course of the story. Another clue is the way in which the major **conflict** in the story is resolved.

How Much Land Does a Man Need?

Leo Tolstoy

translated by

Louise and Aylmer Maude

> *As you read this story, think about how its ideas might apply not only to nineteenth-century Russian peasants but also to modern Americans. What prices do people sometimes pay for their ambitions?*

An elder sister came to visit her younger sister in the country. The elder was married to a shopkeeper in town, the younger to a peasant in the village. As the sisters sat over their tea talking, the elder began to boast of the advantages of town life, saying how comfortably they lived there, how well they dressed, what fine clothes her children wore, what good things they ate and drank, and how she went to the theater, promenades, and entertainments.

The younger sister was piqued, and in turn disparaged the life of a shopkeeper, and stood up for that of a peasant.

"I wouldn't change my way of life for yours," said she. "We may live roughly, but at least we're free from worry. You live in better style than we do, but though you often earn more than you need, you're very likely to lose all you have. You know the proverb, 'Loss and gain are brothers twain.' It often happens that people who're wealthy one day are begging their bread the next. Our way is safer. Though a peasant's life is not a rich one, it's long. We'll never grow rich, but we'll always have enough to eat."

The elder sister said sneeringly:

"Enough? Yes, if you like to share with the pigs and the calves! What do you know of elegance or manners! However much your good man may slave, you'll die as you live— in a dung heap—and your children the same."

"Well, what of that?" replied the younger sister. "Of course our work is rough and hard. But on the other hand, it's sure, and we need not bow to anyone. But you, in your towns, are surrounded by temptations; today all may be right, but tomorrow the Evil One may tempt your husband with cards, wine, or women, and all will go to ruin. Don't such things happen often enough?"

Pahom, the master of the house, was lying on the top of the stove[1] and he listened to the women's chatter.

---

1. **lying on the top of the stove:** lying on a brick or tile oven; the oven's use as a principal item of furniture indicates that the house is both poor and cold.

THE PEASANT WOMAN, KASMIR MALEWITSCH (1878–1935).

Archiv Für Kunst Und Geschichte, Berlin

"It is perfectly true," thought he. "Busy as we are from childhood tilling mother earth, we peasants have no time to let any nonsense settle in our heads. Our only trouble is that we haven't land enough. If I had plenty of land, I shouldn't fear the Devil himself!"

The women finished their tea, chatted a while about dress, and then cleared away the tea things and lay down to sleep.

But the Devil had been sitting behind the stove and had heard all that had been said. He was pleased that the peasant's wife had led her husband into boasting and that he had said that if he had plenty of land he would not fear the Devil himself.

"All right," thought the Devil. "We'll have a tussle. I'll give you land enough; and by means of the land I'll get you into my power."

2

Close to the village there lived a lady, a small landowner who had an estate of about three hundred acres. She had always lived on good terms with the peasants until she engaged as her manager an old soldier, who took to burdening the people with fines. However careful Pahom tried to be, it happened again and again that now a horse of his got among the lady's oats, now a cow strayed into her garden, now his calves found their way into her meadows—and he always had to pay a fine.

Pahom paid up, but grumbled, and, going home in a temper, was rough with his family. All through that summer Pahom had much trouble because of this manager, and he was actually glad when winter came and the cattle had to be stabled. Though he grudged the fodder when they could no longer graze on the pasture land, at least he was free from anxiety about them.

In the winter the news got about that the lady was going to sell her land and that the keeper of the inn on the high road was bargaining for it. When the peasants heard this they were very much alarmed.

"Well," thought they, "if the innkeeper gets the land, he'll worry us with fines worse than the lady's manager. We all depend on that estate."

So the peasants went on behalf of their village council and asked the lady not to sell the land to the innkeeper, offering her a better price for it themselves. The lady agreed to let them have it. Then the peasants tried to arrange for the village council to buy the whole estate, so that it might be held by them all in common. They met twice to discuss it, but could not settle the matter; the Evil One sowed discord among them and they could not agree. So they decided to buy the land individually, each according to his means; and the lady agreed to this plan as she had to the other.

Presently Pahom heard that a neighbor of his was buying fifty acres, and that the lady had consented to accept one half in cash and to wait a year for the other half. Pahom felt envious.

"Look at that," thought he, "the land is all being sold, and I'll get none of it." So he spoke to his wife.

"Other people are buying," said he, "and we must also buy twenty acres or so. Life is becoming impossible. That manager is sim-ply crushing us with his fines."

So they put their heads together and considered how they could manage to buy it. They had one hundred rubles laid by. They sold a colt and one half of their bees, hired out one of their sons as a farm hand and took his wages in advance, borrowed the rest from a brother-in-law, and so scraped together half the purchase money.

Having done this, Pahom chose a farm of forty acres, some of it wooded, and went to the lady to bargain for it. They came to an agreement and he shook hands with her upon it and paid her a deposit in advance. Then they went to town and signed the deeds, he paying half the price down, and undertaking to pay the remainder within two years.

So now Pahom had land of his own. He borrowed seed and sowed it on the land he had bought. The harvest was a good one, and within a year he had managed to pay off his debts both to the lady and to his brother-in-law. So he became a landowner, plowing and sowing his own land, making hay on his own land, cutting his own trees, and feeding his cattle on his own pasture. When he went out to plow his fields, or to look at his growing corn, or at his grass meadows, his heart would fill with joy. The grass that grew and the flowers that bloomed there seemed to him unlike any that grew elsewhere. Formerly, when he had passed by that land, it had appeared the same as any other land, but now it seemed quite different.

3

So Pahom was well contented, and everything would have been right if the neighboring peasants would only not have trespassed on his wheatfields and meadows. He appealed to them most civilly, but they still went on: now the herdsmen would let the village cows stray into his meadows, then horses from the night pasture would get among his corn. Pahom turned them out again and again, and forgave their owners, and for a long time he forbore to prosecute anyone. But at last he lost patience and complained to the District Court. He knew it was the peasants' want of land, and no evil intent on their part, that caused the trouble, but he thought:

"I can't go on overlooking it, or they'll destroy all I have. They must be taught a lesson."

So he had them up, gave them one lesson, and then another, and two or three of the peasants were fined. After a time Pahom's neighbors began to bear him a grudge for this, and would now and then let their cattle onto his land on purpose. One peasant even got into Pahom's wood at night and cut down five young lime trees for their bark. Pahom, passing through the wood one day, noticed something white. He came nearer and saw the stripped trunks lying on the ground, and close by stood the stumps where the trees had been. Pahom was furious.

"If he'd only cut one here and there it would have been bad enough," thought Pahom, "but the rascal has actually cut down a whole clump. If I could only find out who did this, I'd get even with him."

He racked his brains as to who it could be. Finally he decided: "It must be Simon—no one else could have done it." So he went to Simon's homestead to have a look around, but he found nothing and only had an angry scene. However, he now felt more certain than ever that Simon had done it, and he lodged a complaint. Simon was summoned. The case was tried, and retried, and at the end of it all Simon was acquitted, there being no evidence against him. Pahom felt still

MAN IN THE FIELD, WLADIMIR JEGOROWITSCH MAKOWSKI (1846–1920).

more aggrieved, and let his anger loose upon the Elders and the Judges.

"You let thieves grease your palms," said he. "If you were honest folk yourselves you wouldn't let a thief go free."

So Pahom quarreled with the judges and with his neighbors. Threats to burn his hut began to be uttered. So though Pahom had more land, his place in the community was much worse than before.

About this time a rumor got about that many people were moving to new parts.

"There's no need for me to leave my land," thought Pahom. "But some of the others may leave our village and then there'd be more room for us. I'd take over their land myself and make my estates somewhat bigger. I could then live more at ease. As it is, I'm still too cramped to be comfortable."

One day Pahom was sitting at home when a peasant, passing through the village, happened to drop in. He was allowed to stay the night, and supper was given him. Pahom had a talk with this peasant and asked him where he came from. The stranger answered that he came from beyond the Volga,[2] where he had been working. One word led to another, and the man went on to say that many people were settling in those parts. He told how some people from his village had settled there. They had joined the community there and had had twenty-five acres per man granted them. The land was so good, he said, that the rye sown on it grew as high as a horse, and so thick that five cuts of a sickle made a sheaf. One peasant, he said, had brought nothing with him but his bare hands, and now he had six horses and two cows of his own.

Pahom's heart kindled with desire.

"Why should I suffer in this narrow hole, if one can live so well elsewhere?" he thought. "I'll sell my land and my homestead here, and with the money I'll start afresh over there and get everything new. In this crowded place one is always having trouble. But I must first go and find out all about it myself."

Toward summer he got ready and started out. He went down the Volga on a steamer to Samara, then walked another three hundred miles on foot, and at last reached the place. It was just as the stranger had said. The peasants had plenty of land: every man had twenty-five acres of communal land given him for his use, and anyone who had

money could buy, besides, at a ruble and a half an acre, as much good freehold land as he wanted.

Having found out all he wished to know, Pahom returned home as autumn came on, and began selling off his belongings. He sold his land at a profit, sold his homestead and all his cattle, and withdrew from membership in the village. He only waited till the spring, and then started with his family for the new settlement.

4

As soon as Pahom and his family reached their new abode, he applied for admission into the council of a large village. He stood treat to the Elders[3] and obtained the necessary documents. Five shares of communal land were given him for his own and his sons' use: that is to say—125 acres (not all together, but in different fields) besides the use of the communal pasture. Pahom put up the buildings he needed and bought cattle. Of the communal land alone he had three times as much as at his former home, and the land was good wheat land. He was ten times better off than he had been. He had plenty of arable land and pasturage, and could keep as many head of cattle as he liked.

At first, in the bustle of building and settling down, Pahom was pleased with it all, but when he got used to it he began to think that even here he hadn't enough land. The first year he sowed wheat on his share of the communal land and had a good crop. He wanted to go on sowing wheat, but had not enough communal land for the purpose, and what he had already used was not available, for in those parts wheat is sown only on

---

2. **the Volga:** the Volga River of western Russia.

3. **stood treat to the Elders:** treated the Elders of the council to food and drink.

virgin soil or on fallow land. It is sown for one or two years, and then the land lies fallow till it is again overgrown with steppe grass. There were many who wanted such land, and there was not enough for all, so that people quarreled about it. Those who were better off wanted it for growing wheat, and those who were poor wanted it to let to dealers, so that they might raise money to pay their taxes. Pahom wanted to sow more wheat, so he rented land from a dealer for a year. He sowed much wheat and had a fine crop, but the land was too far from the village—the wheat had to be carted more than ten miles. After a time Pahom noticed that some peasant dealers were living on separate farms and were growing wealthy, and he thought:

"If I were to buy some freehold land and have a homestead on it, it would be a different thing altogether. Then it would all be fine and close together."

The question of buying freehold land recurred to him again and again.

He went on in the same way for three years, renting land and sowing wheat. The seasons turned out well and the crops were good, so that he began to lay by money. He might have gone on living contentedly, but he grew tired of having to rent other people's land every year and having to scramble for it. Wherever there was good land to be had, the peasants would rush for it and it was taken up at once, so that unless you were sharp about it, you got none. It happened in the third year that he and a dealer together rented a piece of pasture land from some peasants, and they had already plowed it up, when there was some dispute and the peasants went to law about it, and things fell out so that the labor was all lost.

"If it were my own land," thought Pahom, "I should be independent, and there

wouldn't be all this unpleasantness."

So Pahom began looking out for land which he could buy, and he came across a peasant who had bought thirteen hundred acres, but having got into difficulties was willing to sell again cheap. Pahom bargained and haggled with him, and at last they settled the price at fifteen hundred rubles, part in cash and part to be paid later. They had all but clinched the matter when a passing dealer happened to stop at Pahom's one day to get feed for his horses. He drank tea with Pahom, and they had a talk. The dealer said that he was just returning from the land of the Bashkirs,[4] far away, where he had bought thirteen thousand acres of land, all for a thousand rubles. Pahom questioned him further, and the dealer said:

"All one has to do is to make friends with the chiefs. I gave away about one hundred rubles' worth of silk robes and carpets, besides a case of tea, and I gave wine to those who would drink it; and I got the land for less than three kopecks[5] an acre." And he showed Pahom the title deed, saying:

"The land lies near a river, and the whole steppe is virgin soil."

Pahom plied him with questions, and the dealer said:

"There's more land there than you could cover if you walked a year, and it all belongs to the Bashkirs. They're as simple as sheep, and land can be got almost for nothing."

"There, now," thought Pahom, "with my one thousand rubles, why should I get only thirteen hundred acres, and saddle myself with a debt besides? If I take it out there, I can get more than ten times as much for my money."

---

4. **the Bashkirs** (bash·kirz′): nomads who live on the vast Russian steppes, or plains.
5. **kopecks:** Russian monetary units.

A House for the Nieces and Nephews, Konjew.

Archiv Für Kunst Und Geschichte, Berlin

5

Pahom inquired how to get to the place, and as soon as the grain dealer had left him, he prepared to go there himself. He left his wife to look after the homestead, and started on his journey, taking his hired man with him. They stopped at a town on their way and bought a case of tea, some wine, and other presents, as the grain dealer had advised.

On and on they went until they had gone more than three hundred miles, and on the seventh day they came to a place where the Bashkirs had pitched their round tents. It was all just as the dealer had said. The people lived on the steppe, by a river, in felt-covered tents. They neither tilled the ground nor ate bread. Their cattle and horses grazed in herds on the steppe. The colts were tethered behind the tents, and the mares were driven to them twice a day. The mares were milked, and from the milk kumiss[6] was made. It was the women who prepared the kumiss, and they also made cheese. As far as the men were concerned, drinking kumiss and tea, eating mutton, and playing on their pipes was all they cared about. They were all stout and merry, and all the summer long they never thought of doing any work. They were quite ignorant, and knew no Russian, but were good-natured enough.

As soon as they saw Pahom, they came out of their tents and gathered around the visitor. An interpreter was found, and Pahom told them he had come about some land. The Bashkirs seemed very glad; they took Pahom and led him into one of the best tents, where they made him sit on some down cushions placed on a carpet, while they sat around him. They gave him some

tea and kumiss, and had a sheep killed, and gave him mutton to eat. Pahom took presents out of his cart and distributed them among the Bashkirs, and divided the tea amongst them. The Bashkirs were delighted. They talked a great deal among themselves and then told the interpreter what to say.

"They wish to tell you," said the interpreter, "that they like you and that it's our custom to do all we can to please a guest and to repay him for his gifts. You have given us presents, now tell us which of the things we possess please you best, that we may present them to you."

"What pleases me best here," answered Pahom, "is your land. Our land is crowded and the soil is worn out, but you have plenty of land, and it is good land. I never saw the likes of it."

The interpreter told the Bashkirs what Pahom had said. They talked among themselves for a while. Pahom could not understand what they were saying, but saw they were much amused and heard them shout and laugh. Then they were silent and looked at Pahom while the interpreter said:

"They wish me to tell you that in return for your presents they will gladly give you as much land as you want. You have only to point it out with your hand and it is yours."

The Bashkirs talked again for a while and began to dispute. Pahom asked what they were disputing about, and the interpreter told him that some of them thought they ought to ask their chief about the land and not act in his absence, while others thought there was no need to wait for his return.

6

While the Bashkirs were disputing, a man in a large fox-fur cap appeared on the scene. They all became silent and rose to their feet.

---

6. **kumiss** (ko͞o′mis): a fermented drink made from horse's milk; highly esteemed in Russia as a tonic.

The interpreter said: "This is our chief himself."

Pahom immediately fetched the best dressing gown and five pounds of tea, and offered these to the chief. The chief accepted them and seated himself in the place of honor. The Bashkirs at once began telling him something. The chief listened for a while, then made a sign with his head for them to be silent, and addressing himself to Pahom, said in Russian:

"Well, so be it. Choose whatever piece of land you like; we have plenty of it."

"How can I take as much as I like?" thought Pahom. "I must get a deed to make it secure, or else they may say: 'It is yours,' and afterward may take it away again."

"Thank you for your kind words," he said aloud. "You have much land, and I only want a little. But I should like to be sure which portion is mine. Could it not be measured and made over to me? Life and death are in God's hands. You good people give it to me, but your children might wish to take it back again."

"You are quite right," said the chief. "We will make it over to you."

"I heard that a dealer had been here," continued Pahom, "and that you gave him a little land, too, and signed title deeds to that effect. I should like to have it done in the same way."

The chief understood.

"Yes," replied he, "that can be done quite easily. We have a scribe, and we will go to town with you and have the deed properly sealed."

"And what will be the price?" asked Pahom.

"Our price is always the same: one thousand rubles a day."

Pahom did not understand.

"A day? What measure is that? How many acres would that be?"

"We do not know how to reckon it out," said the chief. "We sell it by the day. As much as you can go around on your feet in a day is yours, and the price is one thousand rubles a day."

Pahom was surprised.

"But in a day you can get around a large tract of land," he said.

The chief laughed.

"It will all be yours!" said he. "But there is one condition: If you don't return on the same day to the spot whence you started, your money is lost."

"But how am I to mark the way that I have gone?"

"Why, we shall go to any spot you like and stay there. You must start from that spot and make your round, taking a spade with you. Wherever you think necessary, make a mark. At every turning, dig a hole and pile up the turf; then afterward we will go around with a plow from hole to hole. You may make as large a circuit as you please, but before the sun sets you must return to the place you started from. All the land you cover will be yours."

Pahom was delighted. It was decided to start early next morning. They talked a while, and after drinking some more kumiss and eating some more mutton, they had tea again, and then the night came on. They gave Pahom a feather bed to sleep on, and the Bashkirs dispersed for the night, promising to assemble the next morning at daybreak and ride out before sunrise to the appointed spot.

7

Pahom lay on the feather bed, but could not sleep. He kept thinking about the land.

"What a large tract I'll mark off!" thought he, "I can easily do thirty-five miles in a day.

The days are long now, and within a circuit of thirty-five miles what a lot of land there will be! I'll sell the poorer land or let it to peasants, but I'll pick out the best and farm it myself. I'll buy two ox teams and hire two more laborers. About a hundred and fifty acres shall be plowland, and I'll pasture cattle on the rest."

Pahom lay awake all night and dozed off only just before dawn. Hardly were his eyes closed when he had a dream. He thought he was lying in that same tent and heard somebody chuckling outside. He wondered who it could be, and rose and went out, and he saw the Bashkir chief sitting in front of the tent holding his sides and rolling about with laughter. Going nearer to the chief, Pahom asked: "What are you laughing at?" But he saw that it was no longer the chief but the grain dealer who had recently stopped at his house and had told him about the land. Just as Pahom was going to ask: "Have you been here long?" he saw that it was not the dealer, but the peasant who had come up from the Volga long ago, to Pahom's old home. Then he saw that it was not the peasant either, but the Devil himself with hoofs and horns, sitting there and chuckling, and before him lay a man, prostrate on the ground, barefooted, with only trousers and a shirt on. And Pahom dreamed that he looked more attentively to see what sort of man it was

HAYING, KONSTANTINE RODKO (b. 1908).

SuperStock, Inc.

lying there, and he saw that the man was dead, and that it was himself. Horror-struck, he awoke.

"What things one dreams about!" thought he.

Looking around he saw through the open door that the dawn was breaking.

"It's time to wake them up," thought he. "We ought to be starting."

He got up, roused his man (who was sleeping in his cart), bade him harness, and went to call the Bashkirs.

"It's time to go to the steppe to measure the land," he said.

The Bashkirs rose and assembled, and the chief came, too. Then they began drinking kumiss again, and offered Pahom some tea, but he would not wait.

"If we are to go, let's go. It's high time," said he.

8

The Bashkirs got ready and they all started; some mounted on horses and some in carts. Pahom drove in his own small cart with his servant and took a spade with him. When they reached the steppe, the red dawn was beginning to kindle. They ascended a hillock (called by the Bashkirs a *shikhan*) and, dismounting from their carts and their horses, gathered in one spot. The chief came up to Pahom and, stretching out his arm toward the plain:

"See," said he, "all this, as far as your eye can reach, is ours. You may have any part of it you like."

Pahom's eyes glistened: it was all virgin soil, as flat as the palm of your hand, as black as the seed of a poppy, and in the hollows different kinds of grasses grew breast-high.

The chief took off his fox-fur cap, placed it on the ground, and said:

"This will be the mark. Start from here, and return here again. All the land you go around shall be yours."

Pahom took out his money and put it on the cap. Then he took off his outer coat, remaining in his sleeveless undercoat. He unfastened his girdle and tied it tight below his stomach, put a little bag of bread into the breast of his coat, and, tying a flask of water to his girdle, he drew up the tops of his boots, took the spade from his man, and stood ready to start. He considered for some moments which way he had better go—it was tempting everywhere.

"No matter," he concluded, "I'll go toward the rising sun."

He turned his face to the east, stretched himself, and waited for the sun to appear above the rim.

"I must lose no time," he thought, "and it's easier walking while it's still cool."

The sun's rays had hardly flashed above the horizon when Pahom, carrying the spade over his shoulder, went down into the steppe.

Pahom started walking neither slowly nor quickly. After having gone a thousand yards he stopped, dug a hole, and placed pieces of turf one on another to make it more visible. Then he went on; and now that he had walked off his stiffness he quickened his pace. After a while he dug another hole.

Pahom looked back. The hillock could be distinctly seen in the sunlight, with the people on it, and the glittering iron rims of the cartwheels. At a rough guess Pahom concluded that he had walked three miles. It was growing warmer; he took off his undercoat, slung it across his shoulder, and went on again. It had grown quite warm now; he looked at the sun—it was time to think of breakfast.

"The first shift is done, but there are four

in a day, and it's too soon yet to turn. But I'll just take off my boots," said he to himself.

He sat down, took off his boots, stuck them into his girdle, and went on. It was easy walking now.

"I'll go on for another three miles," thought he, "and then turn to the left. This spot is so fine that it would be a pity to lose it. The further one goes, the better the land seems."

He went straight on for a while, and when he looked around, the hillock was scarcely visible and the people on it looked like black ants, and he could just see something glistening there in the sun.

"Ah," thought Pahom, "I have gone far enough in this direction; it's time to turn. Besides, I'm in a regular sweat, and very thirsty."

He stopped, dug a large hole, and heaped up pieces of turf. Next he untied his flask, had a drink, and then turned sharply to the left. He went on and on; the grass was high, and it was very hot.

Pahom began to grow tired: he looked at the sun and saw that it was noon.

"Well," he thought, "I must have a rest."

He sat down, and ate some bread and drank some water; but he did not lie down, thinking that if he did he might fall asleep. After sitting a little while, he went on again. At first he walked easily; the food had strengthened him; but it had become terribly hot and he felt sleepy. Still he went on, thinking: "An hour to suffer, a lifetime to live."

He went a long way in this direction also, and was about to turn to the left again, when he perceived a damp hollow: "It would be a pity to leave that out," he thought. "Flax would do well there." So he went on past the hollow and dug a hole on the other side of it before he made a sharp turn. Pahom

looked toward the hillock. The heat made the air hazy: it seemed to be quivering, and through the haze the people on the hillock could scarcely be seen.

"Ah," thought Pahom, "I have made the sides too long; I must make this one shorter." And he went along the third side, stepping faster. He looked at the sun: it was nearly halfway to the horizon, and he had not yet done two miles of the third side of the square. He was still ten miles from the goal.

"No," he thought, "though it will make my land lopsided, I must hurry back in a straight line now. I might go too far, and as it is I have a great deal of land."

So Pahom hurriedly dug a hole and turned straight toward the hillock.

9

Pahom went straight toward the hillock, but he now walked with difficulty. He was exhausted from the heat, his bare feet were cut and bruised, and his legs began to fail. He longed to rest, but it was impossible if he meant to get back before sunset. The sun waits for no man, and it was sinking lower and lower.

"Oh, Lord," he thought, "if only I have not blundered trying for too much! What if I am too late?"

He looked toward the hillock and at the sun. He was still far from his goal, and the sun was already near the rim of the sky.

Pahom walked on and on; it was very hard walking, but he went quicker and quicker. He pressed on, but was still far from the place. He began running, threw away his coat, his boots, his flask, and his cap, and kept only the spade which he used as a support.

"What am I to do?" he thought again. I've

THE BIRCH GROVE, A. I. KUIDZHI, 1879.

? *Do you see Pahom as a canny businessman, a greedy opportunist, or something in between?*

grasped too much and ruined the whole affair. I can't get there before the sun sets."

And this fear made him still more breathless. Pahom kept on running; his soaking shirt and trousers stuck to him, and his mouth was parched. His breast was working like a blacksmith's bellows, his heart was beating like a hammer, and his legs were giving way as if they did not belong to him. Pahom was seized with terror lest he should die of the strain.

Though afraid of death, he could not stop. "After having run all that way they will call me a fool if I stop now," thought he.

And he ran on and on, and drew near and heard the Bashkirs yelling and shouting to him, and their cries inflamed his heart still more. He gathered his last strength and ran on.

The sun was close to the rim of the sky and, cloaked in mist, looked large, and red as blood. Now, yes, now, it was about to set!

The sun was quite low, but he was also quite near his goal. Pahom could already see the people on the hillock waving their arms to make him hurry. He could see the fox-fur cap on the ground and the money in it, and the chief sitting on the ground holding his sides. And Pahom remembered his dream.

"There's plenty of land," thought he, "but will God let me live on it? I have lost my life, I have lost my life! Never will I reach that spot!"

Pahom looked at the sun, which had reached the earth: one side of it had already disappeared. With all his remaining strength he rushed on, bending his body forward so that his legs could hardly follow fast enough to keep him from falling. Just as he reached the hillock it suddenly grew dark. He looked up—the sun had already set!

He gave a cry: "All my labor has been in vain," thought he, and was about to stop, but he heard the Bashkirs still shouting and

Leo Tolstoy **1057**

remembered that though to him, from below, the sun seemed to have set, they on the hillock could still see it. He took a long breath and ran up the hillock. It was still light there. He reached the top and saw the cap. Before it sat the chief, laughing and holding his sides. Again Pahom remembered his dream, and he uttered a cry: his legs gave way beneath him, he fell forward and reached the cap with his hands.

"Ah, that's a fine fellow!" exclaimed the chief. "He has gained much land!"

Pahom's servant came running up and tried to raise him, but he saw that blood was flowing from his mouth. Pahom was dead.

The Bashkirs clicked their tongues to show their pity.

His servant picked up the spade and dug a grave long enough for Pahom to lie in, and buried him in it.

Six feet from his head to his heels was all he needed.

First Thoughts

What do you think about the conclusion of the story? Do you think Pahom met a fitting end? Why or why not?

Identifying Facts

1. Pahom buys his first forty acres of land from an aristocrat. How does he raise the money?
2. After buying his first farm, why does Pahom quarrel with the neighboring peasants?
3. What happens when Pahom attempts to purchase land from the Bashkirs?
4. According to Tolstoy, how much land does a man really need? How is the question in the story's title answered?

Interpreting Meanings

1. What is the central idea, or **theme**, of this story? State it in a sentence or two. How does the **resolution** of the story's **conflict** support the story's theme?

2. Think about the discussion between the two sisters at the beginning of the story. How does their conversation **foreshadow** Pahom's end? What other events foreshadow the ending of the story?

3. Contrast Pahom's attitude toward land with the attitude of the Bashkir chief. What do you think accounts for the difference in their values?

4. A story's **tone** is the attitude the author takes toward its subject or characters. What tone does Tolstoy use when describing Pahom? Cite examples from the story that best reflect the author's attitude toward his main character.

5. How does this story serve as a **parable** that reflects Tolstoy's beliefs about private ownership of property?

Applying Meanings

Have you ever ''grasped too much and ruined the whole affair''—that is, lost something because you were too ambitious? Can you think of examples of people from current events, history, or other fictional stories who have failed by being greedy or attempting too much? Describe one such example, applying to it the message of Tolstoy's story.

Creative Writing Response

Writing an Allegory. An **allegory** is a story with characters, settings, and events that symbolize, or stand for, other people or events, or abstract qualities or ideas. As such, an allegory can be read on one level for its literal meaning and on another level for its symbolic meaning. Try writing a brief allegory of your own that illustrates Tolstoy's theme of losing everything by grasping too much. Your allegory may be written as a skit or as a short parable. It should, like Tolstoy's story, blend symbolism and realism.

Critical Writing Response

Comparing and Contrasting Characters in Two Works. Both Goethe's *Faust* (see page 988) and Tolstoy's ''How Much Land Does a Man Need?'' have characters who are tempted by the Devil. Write an essay in which you compare and contrast the protagonists, Pahom and Faust, and the characters of the Devil as drawn by Goethe and Tolstoy. What do these characters have in common? What characteristics do they *not* share? Consider the motivation, background, and ambition of each character when deciding on your response. You might want to use a chart such as the following to organize your ideas.

	''How Much Land Does a Man Need?''	*Faust*
Devil		
Protagonist		

Anton Chekhov
1860–1904

The Bettmann Archive

Anton Pavlovich Chekhov (än·tōn′ pä· vlô′vich che′kôf′), the grandson of a serf who had bought his own and his family's freedom, was born in the seaport town of Taganrog in the south of Russia. As a child, Anton spent long hours working in his father's grocery store.

When Chekhov was sixteen, his father went bankrupt and fled with his family to Moscow to avoid a prison sentence. Chekhov stayed behind to finish his schooling and supported himself by tutoring. He moved to Moscow after graduation and entered medical school on a scholarship. In order to support himself and his family, who were living in a Moscow slum, Chekhov began writing comic stories for sale to periodicals.

Medicine was good training for his career as a writer. Through his practice as a doctor,

Chekhov came to know hundreds of ordinary people. He continued to write while practicing medicine; eventually, however, he gave up his full-time practice because it took too much of his time away from writing.

Chekhov's fiction was noticed by the influential novelist Dmitri Grigorovich, who advised him to take his writing more seriously. Chekhov also became acquainted with a publisher who supported his efforts as his talent continued to mature. But it was not until the last years of his life that Chekhov achieved some affluence and fame. At this time, he settled with his family on a large country estate. Here he organized famine relief, fought cholera epidemics, and continued to examine poor patients without charge. Although the theme of many of his works is the individual's alienation from others, Chekhov's real-life activities demonstrate that humanity, reason, and generosity were his highest values.

His life was cut short by tuberculosis. Chekhov's finest stories—those of the 1890s—and his four great plays, *The Sea Gull* (1896), *Uncle Vanya* (1897), *The Three Sisters* (1901), and *The Cherry Orchard* (1904), were written while he was fatally ill. In 1901, he married the actress who played the lead role in *The Sea Gull*, but the couple spent their honeymoon in a sanitarium, or health resort. He died in Germany three years later, at the age of forty-four, during the height of his creativity.

Reader's Guide

A PROBLEM

Background

What does the term *Chekhovian* mean? It refers to a quiet, wry understanding of the melancholy of everyday life. Chekhov's style is understated, muted, and gloomily comic. His major stories and plays were
innovative because they emphasized character and mood rather than
plot. The typical Chekhov character is sensitive and intelligent but also
idle, foolish, self-deceiving, and alienated—yearning for a fulfillment
that never arrives.

Chekhov is famous for communicating **mood**, or atmosphere. Traditional **plot** structure, which relies on action, complications, and a
climax, is rarely found in Chekhov's works. His stories and plays—of
which "A Problem" is a good example—are primarily concerned with
portraying a group of characters and the moods they project. This
exploration of mood and the inner world of fictional characters, at the
expense of traditional plot structure, has strongly influenced modern
fiction writers such as Katherine Mansfield, James Joyce, and Ernest
Hemingway.

Writer's Response

Imagine that you are a parent whose son or daughter has been arrested for shoplifting. Would you insist that he or she be brought to
justice and punished, or would you pay for the stolen items quietly if
possible? What, if anything, do your ideas about family honor have to
do with your response? Write a few sentences on these questions.

Literary Focus

Tone is the attitude a writer takes toward a character, a subject, or
the reader. In "A Problem," Chekhov's tone is **ironic**—that is, there is
a contrast between what is said and what is meant, between what
appears to be true and what is really true, and between what is expected and what really happens. In Chekhov's works, characters are
often foolish and pathetically touching at the same time. As you read,
ask yourself how an ironic tone is used to sketch the various characters of the Uskov family.

A PROBLEM

Anton Chekhov

translated by

CONSTANCE GARNETT

> As you read the story, notice the argument each character makes for or against helping Sasha. Notice, too, how each character's position or argument contributes to our image of his or her personality.

INTERIOR WITH THE ARTIST'S BROTHERS, WILHELM BENDZ, C. 1830.

The Granger Collection, New York

The strictest measures were taken that the Uskovs' family secret might not leak out and become generally known. Half of the servants were sent off to the theater or the circus; the other half were sitting in the kitchen and not allowed to leave it. Orders were given that no one was to be admitted. The wife of the Colonel, her sister, and the governess, though they had been initiated into the secret, kept up a pretense of knowing nothing; they sat in the dining room and did not show themselves in the drawing room or the hall.

Sasha Uskov, the young man of twenty-five who was the cause of all the commotion, had arrived some time before, and by the advice of kind-hearted Ivan Markovitch, his uncle, who was taking his part, he sat meekly in the hall by the door leading to the study, and prepared himself to make an open, candid explanation.

The other side of the door, in the study, a family council was being held. The subject under discussion was an exceedingly disagreeable and delicate one. Sasha Uskov had cashed at one of the banks a false promissory note,[1] and it had become due for payment three days before, and now his two paternal uncles and Ivan Markovitch, the brother of his dead mother, were deciding the question whether they should pay the money and save the family honor, or wash their hands of it and leave the case to go for trial.

To outsiders who have no personal interest in the matter such questions seem simple; for those who are so unfortunate as to have to decide them in earnest they are extremely difficult. The uncles had been talking for a long time, but the problem seemed no nearer decision.

"My friends!" said the uncle who was a colonel, and there was a note of exhaustion and bitterness in his voice. "Who says that family honor is a mere convention? I don't say that at all. I am only warning you against a false view; I am pointing out the possibility of an unpardonable mistake. How can you fail to see it? I am not speaking Chinese; I am speaking Russian!"

"My dear fellow, we do understand," Ivan Markovitch protested mildly.

"How can you understand if you say that I don't believe in family honor? I repeat once more; fa-mil-y ho-nor false-ly un-der-stood is a prejudice! Falsely understood! That's

what I say: whatever may be the motives for screening a scoundrel, whoever he may be, and helping him to escape punishment, it is contrary to law and unworthy of a gentleman. It's not saving the family honor; it's civic cowardice! Take the army, for instance.... The honor of the army is more precious to us than any other honor, yet we don't screen our guilty members, but condemn them. And does the honor of the army suffer in consequence? Quite the opposite!"

The other paternal uncle, an official in the Treasury, a taciturn,[2] dull-witted, and rheumatic man, sat silent, or spoke only of the fact that the Uskovs' name would get into the newspapers if the case went for trial. His opinion was that the case ought to be hushed up from the first and not become public property; but, apart from publicity in the newspapers, he advanced no other argument in support of this opinion.

The maternal uncle, kind-hearted Ivan Markovitch, spoke smoothly, softly, and with a tremor in his voice. He began with saying that youth has its rights and its peculiar temptations. Which of us has not been young, and who has not been led astray? To say nothing of ordinary mortals, even great men have not escaped errors and mistakes in their youth. Take, for instance, the biography of great writers. Did not every one of them gamble, drink, and draw down upon himself the anger of right-thinking people in his young days? If Sasha's error bordered upon crime, they must remember that Sasha had received practically no education; he had been expelled from the high school in the fifth class; he had lost his parents in early childhood, and so had been left at the tenderest age without guidance and good, benevolent influences. He was nervous,

---

1. **promissory note:** a written promise to pay a certain sum of money on demand; an IOU.

2. **taciturn** (tas′ə·tʉrn′): silent.

excitable, had no firm ground under his feet, and, above all, he had been unlucky. Even if he were guilty, anyway he deserved indulgence and the sympathy of all compassionate souls. He ought, of course, to be punished, but he was punished as it was by his conscience and the agonies he was enduring now while awaiting the sentence of his relations. The comparison with the army made by the Colonel was delightful, and did credit to his lofty intelligence; his appeal to their feeling of public duty spoke for the chivalry of his soul, but they must not forget that in each individual the citizen is closely linked with the Christian. . . .

"Shall we be false to civic duty," Ivan Markovitch exclaimed passionately, "if instead of punishing an erring boy we hold out to him a helping hand?"

Ivan Markovitch talked further of family honor. He had not the honor to belong to the Uskov family himself, but he knew their distinguished family went back to the thirteenth century; he did not forget for a minute, either, that his precious, beloved sister had been the wife of one of the representatives of that name. In short, the family was dear to him for many reasons, and he refused to admit the idea that, for the sake of a paltry fifteen hundred rubles,[3] a blot should be cast on the escutcheon[4] that was beyond all price. If all the motives he had brought forward were not sufficiently convincing, he, Ivan Markovitch, in conclusion, begged his listeners to ask themselves what was meant by crime? Crime is an immoral act founded upon ill-will. But is the will of man free? Philosophy has not yet given a positive answer to that question. Different

views were held by the learned. The latest school of Lombroso,[5] for instance, denies the freedom of the will, and considers every crime as the product of the purely anatomical peculiarities of the individual.

"Ivan Markovitch," said the Colonel, in a voice of entreaty, "we are talking seriously about an important matter, and you bring in Lombroso, you clever fellow. Think a little, what are you saying all this for? Can you imagine that all your thunderings and rhetoric will furnish an answer to the question?"

Sasha Uskov sat at the door and listened. He felt neither terror, shame, nor depression, but only weariness and inward emptiness. It seemed to him that it made absolutely no difference to him whether they forgave him or not; he had come here to hear his sentence and to explain himself simply because kind-hearted Ivan Markovitch had begged him to do so. He was not afraid of the future. It made no difference to him where he was: here in the hall, in prison, or in Siberia.

"If Siberia, then let it be Siberia, damn it all!"

He was sick of life and found it insufferably hard. He was inextricably involved in debt; he had not a farthing[6] in his pocket; his family had become detestable to him; he would have to part from his friends and his women sooner or later, as they had begun to be too contemptuous of his sponging on them. The future looked black.

Sasha was indifferent, and was only disturbed by one circumstance; the other side of the door they were calling him a scoun-

---

3. **rubles:** The ruble is the basic monetary unit of Russia.
4. **escutcheon** (e·skuch'ən): a shield or area on which a coat of arms is displayed.

5. **Lombroso:** Cesare Lombroso (1836–1909) was an Italian physician and criminologist. He believed that a criminal was a distinct human type with specific physical and mental deviations, and that criminals were the result of such factors as heredity.
6. **farthing:** a coin of little value.

Coin de Table (Corner of the Table), Henri Fantin-Latour (1836–1904).

drel and a criminal. Every minute he was on the point of jumping up, bursting into the study and shouting in answer to the detestable metallic voice of the Colonel:

"You are lying!"

"Criminal" is a dreadful word—that is what murderers, thieves, robbers are; in fact, wicked and morally hopeless people. And Sasha was very far from being all that.... It was true he owed a great deal and did not pay his debts. But debt is not a crime, and it is unusual for a man not to be in debt. The Colonel and Ivan Markovitch were both in debt....

"What have I done wrong besides?" Sasha wondered.

He had discounted a forged note. But all the young men he knew did the same. Handrikov and Von Burst always forged IOU's

from their parents or friends when their allowances were not paid at the regular time, and then when they got their money from home they redeemed them before they became due. Sasha had done the same, but had not redeemed the IOU because he had not got the money which Handrikov had promised to lend him. He was not to blame; it was the fault of circumstances. It was true that the use of another person's signature was considered reprehensible; but, still, it was not a crime but a generally accepted dodge, an ugly formality which injured no one and was quite harmless, for in forging the Colonel's signature Sasha had had no intention of causing anybody damage or loss.

"No, it doesn't mean that I am a criminal ..." thought Sasha. "And it's not in my character to bring myself to commit a crime. I am soft, emotional.... When I have the money I help the poor...."

Sasha was musing after this fashion while they went on talking the other side of the door.

"But, my friends, this is endless," the Colonel declared, getting excited. "Suppose we were to forgive him and pay the money. You know he would not give up leading a dissipated life, squandering money, making debts, going to our tailors and ordering suits in our names! Can you guarantee that this will be his last prank? As far as I am concerned, I have no faith whatever in his reforming!"

The official of the Treasury muttered something in reply; after him Ivan Markovitch began talking blandly and suavely again. The Colonel moved his chair impatiently and drowned the other's words with his detestable metallic voice. At last the door opened and Ivan Markovitch came out of the study; there were patches of red on his cleanshaven face.

"Come along," he said, taking Sasha by the hand. "Come and speak frankly from your heart. Without pride, my dear boy, humbly and from your heart."

Sasha went into the study. The official of the Treasury was sitting down; the Colonel was standing before the table with one hand in his pocket and one knee on a chair. It was smoky and stifling in the study. Sasha did not look at the official or the Colonel; he felt suddenly ashamed and uncomfortable. He looked uneasily at Ivan Markovitch and muttered:

"I'll pay it ... I'll give it back...."

"What did you expect when you discounted the IOU?" he heard a metallic voice.

"I ... Handrikov promised to lend me the money before now."

Sasha could say no more. He went out of

ROULETTE, WLADIMIR MAJAKOWSKI *(1893–1930).*

the study and sat down again on the chair near the door. He would have been glad to go away altogether at once, but he was choking with hatred and he awfully wanted to remain, to tear the Colonel to pieces, to say something rude to him. He sat trying to think of something violent and effective to say to his hated uncle, and at that moment a woman's figure, shrouded in the twilight, appeared at the drawing room door. It was the Colonel's wife. She beckoned Sasha to her, and, wringing her hands, said, weeping:

"*Alexandre*, I know you don't like me, but ... listen to me; listen, I beg you.... But, my dear, how can this have happened? Why, it's awful, awful! For goodness' sake, beg them, defend yourself, entreat them."

Sasha looked at her quivering shoulders, at the big tears that were rolling down her cheeks, heard behind his back the hollow, nervous voices of worried and exhausted people, and shrugged his shoulders. He had not in the least expected that his aristocratic relations would raise such a tempest over a paltry fifteen hundred rubles! He could not understand her tears nor the quiver of their voices.

An hour later he heard that the Colonel was getting the best of it; the uncles were finally inclining to let the case go for trial.

"The matter's settled," said the Colonel, sighing. "Enough."

After this decision all the uncles, even the emphatic Colonel, became noticeably depressed. A silence followed.

"Merciful Heavens!" sighed Ivan Markovitch. "My poor sister!"

And he began saying in a subdued voice that most likely his sister, Sasha's mother, was present unseen in the study at that moment. He felt in his soul how the unhappy, saintly woman was weeping, grieving, and begging for her boy. For the sake of her peace beyond the grave, they ought to spare Sasha.

The sound of a muffled sob was heard. Ivan Markovitch was weeping and muttering something which it was impossible to catch through the door. The Colonel got up and paced from corner to corner. The long conversation began over again.

But then the clock in the drawing room struck two. The family council was over. To avoid seeing the person who had moved him to such wrath, the Colonel went from the study, not into the hall, but into the vestibule.[7] . . . Ivan Markovitch came out into the hall. . . . He was agitated and rubbing his hands joyfully. His tear-stained eyes looked good-humored and his mouth was twisted into a smile.

_____

7. **vestibule:** a small entrance hall or room.

"Capital," he said to Sasha. "Thank God! You can go home, my dear, and sleep tranquilly. We have decided to pay the sum, but on condition that you repent and come with me tomorrow into the country and set to work."

A minute later Ivan Markovitch and Sasha in their greatcoats and caps were going down the stairs. The uncle was muttering something edifying. Sasha did not listen, but felt as though some uneasy weight were gradually slipping off his shoulders. They had forgiven him; he was free! A gust of joy sprang up within him and sent a sweet chill to his heart. He longed to breathe, to move swiftly, to live! Glancing at the street lamps and the black sky, he remembered that Von Burst was celebrating his name day that evening at the "Bear," and again a rush of joy flooded his soul. . . .

"I am going!" he decided.

But then he remembered he had not a farthing, that the companions he was going to would despise him at once for his empty pockets. He must get hold of some money, come what may!

"Uncle, lend me a hundred rubles," he said to Ivan Markovitch.

His uncle, surprised, looked into his face and backed against a lamppost.

"Give it to me," said Sasha, shifting impatiently from one foot to the other and beginning to pant. "Uncle, I entreat you, give me a hundred rubles."

His face worked; he trembled, and seemed on the point of attacking his uncle. . . .

"Won't you?" he kept asking, seeing that his uncle was still amazed and did not understand. "Listen. If you don't, I'll give myself up tomorrow! I won't let you pay the IOU! I'll present another false note tomorrow!"

Petrified, muttering something incoherent in his horror, Ivan Markovitch took a hundred-ruble note out of his pocketbook and gave it to Sasha. The young man took it and walked rapidly away from him. . . .

Taking a sledge,[8] Sasha grew calmer, and felt a rush of joy within him again. The "rights of youth" of which kind-hearted Ivan

---

8. **sledge:** a horse-drawn sled or sleigh used for transportation over snow or ice.

Markovitch had spoken at the family council woke up and asserted themselves. Sasha pictured the drinking party before him, and, among the bottles, the women, and his friends, the thought flashed through his mind:

"Now I see that I am a criminal; yes, I am a criminal."

First Thoughts

Does Sasha remind you of anyone you know or have heard about? Discuss.

Identifying Facts

1. What "problem" does the story's title refer to? What solutions are proposed by the characters in the story?
2. What decision does the family council finally make?
3. What request does Sasha make of Ivan Markovitch at the end of the story?

Interpreting Meanings

1. Ivan Markovitch pleads with the family on Sasha's behalf. What argument does he make? Considering what we learn about Sasha during the course of the story, how is his argument **ironic**?
2. What do you think Chekhov's attitude is toward Sasha? Is his **tone** judgmental, compassionate, or sarcastic? Explain your answer by providing examples from the story.
3. In the first part of ''A Problem,'' how does Sasha manage to justify his behavior, concluding that he is not a criminal? Explain why his opinion of himself changes at the end of the story.
4. Chekhov's description of each character is brief and concise. In a sentence or two, describe each of the following characters in your own words:

a. Ivan Markovitch; b. the Colonel; c. Sasha.

Applying Meanings

In nineteenth-century Russia, debtors could be thrown into prison for failing to meet their obligations. In twentieth-century America, ''having good credit'' is generally assumed to be an advantage, and many people carry credit cards—the modern-day promissory note—with pride. Think about how you, your family, and your friends perceive debt. Is it dishonorable to owe money today, or is being in debt a sign of status?

Creative Writing Response

1. **Entering the Story.** Imagine that you are a judge, another relative of Sasha's. Delayed by a court case, you arrive late to the Uskov family council. Your relatives present Sasha's problem to you and say they will abide by whatever decision you make. What is your decision, and why?
2. **Imagining a Character's Future.** What kind of person do you think Sasha will be ten years after the events in the story, when he is thirty-five years old? Do you think he will have changed, or will he still look to his family to bail him out of tight situations? Compose a brief sketch in which members of Sasha's family meet and discuss his character.

Henrik Ibsen
1828–1906

Henrik Ibsen was born in Skien, Norway, the oldest child in a large, well-to-do family. When he was seven, his father suddenly went bankrupt and the family had to move to a farm, where they lived in much-reduced circumstances. A loner, he read avidly and lived mostly in the world of his imagination.

Unable to go to medical school, Ibsen worked for a time as a pharmacist's apprentice. Then, as his interests shifted from science to literature, Ibsen began to read widely and write verse plays until, at twenty-three, with some university theatrical experience behind him, he became stage manager and resident playwright for a new theater at Bergen. There, and later at Christiania (now Oslo), Ibsen became expert in all aspects of stage technique.

Ibsen got married, drifted from job to job, and wrote verse comedies. During this period, Ibsen was extremely poor, and he was discouraged by the negative reception given to most of his plays.

In his late thirties Ibsen finally achieved commercial success with the verse plays *Brand* (1866) and *Peer Gynt* (1867). But, dissatisfied with the quality of his work, Ibsen gave up verse and began to write realistic dramas in prose. Finally, in 1879, came *A Doll's House.* This portrayal of a woman who frees herself from a confining marriage created a scandal throughout northern Europe. Ibsen's next play, *Ghosts* (1881) dealt with the even more controversial subject of syphilis; the play was violently attacked by critics and rejected by all theaters and bookstores. Ibsen's response to his critics was his next masterpiece, *An Enemy of the People* (1882), in which an honest doctor is vilified by his townspeople for speaking the truth about the polluted water of the town.

The great plays that streamed from Ibsen's imagination in his fifties and sixties became the foundation of modern realistic drama. *The Wild Duck* (1884), *Hedda Gabler* (1890), *The Master Builder* (1892), and others were unlike any plays that had been written before. Ibsen's plays are charged with social criticism. The great Realist playwrights who followed Ibsen—George Bernard Shaw, Eugene O'Neill, and Tennessee Williams—continued to develop the techniques that Ibsen had brought to the modern stage.

Reader's Guide

A DOLL'S HOUSE

Background

During the nineteenth century, most middle-class European and American women were economically and legally dependent on their husbands. Realistic writers such as Leo Tolstoy, Guy de Maupassant, and Thomas Hardy wrote works sympathizing with defiant, unconventional women, but their rebellious female characters usually came to ruin. In *A Doll's House,* Ibsen creates a modern tragic heroine and allows her to achieve independence.

Upon its publication in 1879, *A Doll's House* was widely translated, read, discussed, attacked, and performed. The portrayal of marital conflict in the play was considered so scandalous that the producers of the German version changed the last act. Ibsen himself, under considerable pressure, wrote an alternate ending. He later regretted this, stating that the entire play was written for the sake of the final scene and its famous "slamming door."

In *A Doll's House,* Ibsen imitates the technique of analysis and retrospection first developed by Sophocles in ancient Greece (see page 301). The major events affecting the characters have already occurred before the curtain is raised; the action of the play serves to expose these events. Ibsen's contemporaries were startled by the detailed set descriptions, the natural dialogue, and the use of real-life situations. In fact, modern drama is often said to date from the appearance of *A Doll's House.*

Writer's Response

How would you define a good marriage? Write a few sentences expressing your views. Do your ideas about marriage come from observing married couples, from television, from books, or elsewhere?

Literary Focus

Characterization is the process by which an author reveals the personality of the characters. In drama, characterization occurs mostly through dialogue, a form of **indirect characterization**. We make up our minds about the characters by listening to the things they say and how they say them, what they look like, and how they act.

A Doll's House

Henrik Ibsen

translated by
Michael Meyer

◆ *When you read a play, you have the chance to "direct" a performance in your own head. As you read, visualize the set, and imagine the tone of voice and the gestures the actors might use. If you like, "rehearse" several voices for the same line of dialogue until you find the one that best reveals the character.*

IN THE WINTER GARDEN, EDOUARD MANET, 1879.

The action takes place in the Helmers' apartment.

═ ACT 1 ═

A comfortably and tastefully, but not expensively furnished room. Backstage right a door leads to the hall; backstage left, another door to HELMER's study. Between these two doors stands a piano. In the middle of the left-hand wall is a door, with a window downstage of it. Near the window, a round table with armchairs and a small sofa. In the right-hand wall, slightly upstage, is a door; downstage of this, against the same wall, a stove lined with porcelain tiles, with a couple of armchairs and a rocking chair in front of it. Between the stove and the side door is a small table. Engravings on the wall. A whatnot with china and other bric-a-brac; a small bookcase with leather-bound books. A carpet on the floor; a fire in the stove. A winter day.

[*A bell rings in the hall outside. After a moment we hear the front door being opened. NORA enters the room, humming contentedly to herself. She is wearing outdoor clothes and carrying a lot of parcels, which she puts down on the table right. She leaves the door to the hall open; through it, we can see a PORTER carrying a Christmas tree and a basket. He gives these to the MAID, who has opened the door for them.*]

Nora. Hide that Christmas tree away, Helen. The children mustn't see it before I've decorated it this evening. (*to the POR-TER, taking out her purse*) How much?

Porter. A shilling.[1]

Nora. Here's ten shillings. No, keep it.

[*The PORTER touches his cap and goes. NORA closes the door. She continues to laugh happily to herself as she removes her coat, etc. She takes from her pocket a bag containing macaroons and eats a couple. Then she tiptoes across and listens at her husband's door.*]

Nora. Yes, he's here. (*starts humming again as she goes over to the table, right.*)

Helmer (*from his room*). Is that my skylark twittering out there?

Nora (*opening some of the parcels*). It is!

Helmer. Is that my squirrel rustling?

Nora. Yes!

Helmer. When did my squirrel come home?

Nora. Just now. (*pops the bag of macaroons in her pocket and wipes her mouth*) Come out here, Torvald, and see what I've bought.

Helmer. You mustn't disturb me!

[*Short pause; then he opens the door and looks in, his pen in his hand.*]

---

1. **shilling:** a coin of little value.

Helmer. Bought, did you say? All that? Has my little squanderbird been overspending again?

Nora. Oh, Torvald, surely we can let ourselves go a little this year! It's the first Christmas we don't have to scrape.

Helmer. Well, you know, we can't afford to be extravagant.

Nora. Oh yes, Torvald, we can be a little extravagant now. Can't we? Just a tiny bit? You've got a big salary now, and you're going to make lots and lots of money.

Helmer. Next year, yes. But my new salary doesn't start till April.

Nora. Pooh; we can borrow till then.

Helmer. Nora! (*goes over to her and takes her playfully by the ear*) What a little spendthrift[2] you are! Suppose I were to borrow fifty pounds today, and you spent it all over Christmas, and then on New Year's Eve a tile fell off a roof onto my head—

Nora (*puts her hand over his mouth*). Oh, Torvald! Don't say such dreadful things!

Helmer. Yes, but suppose something like that did happen? What then?

Nora. If anything as frightful as that happened, it wouldn't make much difference whether I was in debt or not.

Helmer. But what about the people I'd borrowed from?

Nora. Them? Who cares about them? They're strangers.

Helmer. Oh, Nora, Nora, how like a woman! No, but seriously, Nora, you know how I feel about this. No debts! Never borrow! A home that is founded on debts and borrowing can never be a place of freedom and beauty. We two have stuck it out bravely up to now; and we shall continue to do so for the few weeks that remain.

Nora (*goes over towards the stove*). Very

---

2. **spendthrift:** someone who spends money carelessly or wastefully.

well, Torvald. As you say.

Helmer (*follows her*). Now, now! My little songbird mustn't droop her wings. What's this? Is little squirrel sulking? (*takes out his purse*) Nora; guess what I've got here!

Nora (*turns quickly*). Money!

Helmer. Look. (*hands her some bank notes*) I know how these small expenses crop up at Christmas.

Nora (*counts them*). One—two—three—four. Oh, thank you, Torvald, thank you! I should be able to manage with this.

Helmer. You'll have to.

Nora. Yes, yes, of course I will. But come over here, I want to show you everything I've bought. And so cheap! Look, here are new clothes for Ivar—and a sword. And a horse and a trumpet for Bob. And a doll and a cradle for Emmy—they're nothing much, but she'll pull them apart in a few days. And some bits of material and handkerchiefs for the maids. Old Annie-Marie ought to have had something better, really.

Helmer. And what's in that parcel?

Nora (*cries*). No, Torvald, you mustn't see that before this evening!

Helmer. Very well. But now, tell me, my little spendthrift, what do you want for Christmas?

Nora. Me? Oh, pooh, I don't want anything.

Helmer. Oh yes, you do. Now tell me, what within reason would you most like?

Nora. No, I really don't know. Oh, yes—Torvald—!

Helmer. Well?

Nora (*plays with his coat buttons; not looking at him*). If you really want to give me something, you could—you could—

Helmer. Come on, out with it.

Nora (*quickly*). You could give me money, Torvald. Only as much as you feel you can afford; then later I'll buy something with it.

Helmer. But, Nora—

Nora. Oh yes, Torvald dear, please! Please! Then I'll wrap up the notes in pretty gold paper and hang them on the Christmas tree. Wouldn't that be fun?

Helmer. What's the name of that little bird that can never keep any money?

Nora. Yes, yes, squanderbird; I know. But let's do as I say, Torvald; then I'll have time to think about what I need most. Isn't that the best way? Mm?

Helmer (*smiles*). To be sure it would be, if you could keep what I give you and really buy yourself something with it. But you'll spend it on all sorts of useless things for the house, and then I'll have to put my hand in my pocket again.

Nora. Oh, but Torvald—

Helmer. You can't deny it, Nora dear. (*puts his arm around her waist*) The squanderbird's a pretty little creature, but she gets through an awful lot of money. It's incredible what an expensive pet she is for a man to keep.

Nora. For shame! How can you say such a thing? I save every penny I can.

Helmer (*laughs*). That's quite true. Every penny you can. But you can't.

Nora (*hums and smiles, quietly gleeful*). Hm. If you only knew how many expenses we larks and squirrels have, Torvald.

Helmer. You're a funny little creature. Just like your father used to be. Always on the lookout for some way to get money, but as soon as you have any it just runs through your fingers and you never know where it's gone. Well, I suppose I must take you as you are. It's in your blood. Yes, yes, yes, these things are hereditary, Nora.

Nora. Oh, I wish I'd inherited more of Papa's qualities.

Helmer. And I wouldn't wish my darling little songbird to be any different from what she is. By the way, that reminds me. You look awfully—how shall I put it?—

awfully guilty today.

Nora. Do I?

Helmer. Yes, you do. Look me in the eyes.

Nora (*looks at him*). Well?

Helmer (*wags his finger*). Has my little sweet tooth been indulging herself in town today, by any chance?

Nora. No, how can you think such a thing?

Helmer. Not a tiny little digression into a pastry shop?

Nora. No, Torvald, I promise—

Helmer. Not just a wee jam tart?

Nora. Certainly not.

Helmer. Not a little nibble at a macaroon?

Nora. No, Torvald—I promise you, honestly—!

Helmer. There, there. I was only joking.

Nora (*goes over to the table, right*). You know I could never act against your wishes.

Helmer. Of course not. And you've given me your word—(*goes over to her*) Well, my beloved Nora, you keep your little Christmas secrets to yourself. They'll be revealed this evening, I've no doubt, once the Christmas tree has been lit.

Nora. Have you remembered to invite Dr. Rank?

Helmer. No. But there's no need; he knows he'll be dining with us. Anyway, I'll ask him when he comes this morning. I've ordered some good wine. Oh, Nora, you can't imagine how I'm looking forward to this evening.

Nora. So am I. And, Torvald, how the children will love it!

Helmer. Yes, it's a wonderful thing to know that one's position is assured and that one has an ample income. Don't you agree? It's good to know that, isn't it?

Nora. Yes, it's almost like a miracle.

Helmer. Do you remember last Christmas? For three whole weeks you shut yourself away every evening to make flowers for the

Christmas tree, and all those other things you were going to surprise us with. Ugh, it was the most boring time I've ever had in my life.

Nora. I didn't find it boring.

Helmer (*smiles*). But it all came to nothing in the end, didn't it?

Nora. Oh, are you going to bring that up again? How could I help the cat getting in and tearing everything to bits?

Helmer. No, my poor little Nora, of course you couldn't. You simply wanted to make us happy, and that's all that matters. But it's good that those hard times are past.

Nora. Yes, it's wonderful.

Helmer. I don't have to sit by myself and be bored. And you don't have to tire your pretty eyes and your delicate little hands—

Nora (*claps her hands*). No, Torvald, that's true, isn't it? I don't have to any longer! Oh, it's really all just like a miracle. (*takes his arm*) Now I'm going to tell you what I thought we might do, Torvald. As soon as Christmas is over—

[*A bell rings in the hall.*]

Oh, there's the doorbell. (*tidies up one or two things in the room*) Someone's coming. What a bore.

Helmer. I'm not at home to any visitors. Remember!

Maid (*in the doorway*). A lady's called, madam. A stranger.

Nora. Well, ask her to come in.

Maid. And the doctor's here too, sir.

Helmer. Has he gone to my room?

Maid. Yes, sir.

[HELMER *goes into his room. The* MAID *shows in* MRS. LINDE, *who is dressed in traveling clothes; then closes the door.*]

Mrs. Linde (*shyly and a little hesitantly*). Good morning, Nora.

Nora (*uncertainly*). Good morning—

Still from a production of *A Doll's House* by the Midland Community Theatre, Midland, Texas.

Mrs. Linde. I don't suppose you recognize me.

Nora. No, I'm afraid I—Yes, wait a minute—surely—I—(*exclaims*) Why, Christine! Is it really you?

Mrs. Linde. Yes, it's me.

Nora. Christine! And I didn't recognize you! But how could I—? (*more quietly*) How you've changed, Christine!

Mrs. Linde. Yes, I know. It's been nine years—nearly ten—

Nora. Is it so long? Yes, it must be. Oh, these last eight years have been such a happy time for me! So you've come to town? All that way in winter! How brave of you!

Mrs. Linde. I arrived by the steamer this morning.

Nora. Yes, of course, to enjoy yourself over Christmas. Oh, how splendid! We'll have to celebrate! But take off your coat. You're not cold, are you? (*helps her off with it*) There! Now let's sit down here by the stove and be comfortable. No, you take the armchair. I'll sit here in the rocking chair. (*clasps MRS. LINDE's hands*) Yes, now you look like your old self. Just at first I—you've got a little paler, though, Christine. And perhaps a bit thinner.

Mrs. Linde. And older, Nora. Much, much older.

Nora. Yes, perhaps a little older. Just a tiny bit. Not much (*checks herself suddenly and says earnestly*) Oh, but how thoughtless of me to sit here and chatter away like this! Dear, sweet Christine, can you forgive me?

Mrs. Linde. What do you mean, Nora?

Nora (*quietly*). Poor Christine, you've become a widow.

Mrs. Linde. Yes. Three years ago.

Nora. I know, I know—I read it in the papers. Oh, Christine, I meant to write to you so often, honestly. But I always put it off, and something else always cropped up.

Mrs. Linde. I understand, Nora dear.

Nora. No, Christine, it was beastly of me. Oh, my poor darling, what you've gone through! And he didn't leave you anything?

Mrs. Linde. No.

Nora. No children, either?

Mrs. Linde. No.

Nora. Nothing at all, then?

Mrs. Linde. Not even a feeling of loss or sorrow.

Nora (*looks incredulously at her*). But, Christine, how is that possible?

Mrs. Linde (*smiles sadly and strokes NORA's hair*). Oh, these things happen, Nora.

Nora. All alone. How dreadful that must be for you. I've three lovely children. I'm afraid you can't see them now, because they're out with Nanny. But you must tell me everything—

Mrs. Linde. No, no, no. I want to hear about you.

Nora. No, you start. I'm not going to be selfish today, I'm just going to think about you. Oh, but there's one thing I *must* tell you. Have you heard of the wonderful luck we've just had?

Mrs. Linde. No. What?

Nora. Would you believe it—my husband's just been made vice-president of the bank!

Mrs. Linde. Your husband? Oh, how lucky—!

Nora. Yes, isn't it? Being a lawyer is so uncertain, you know, especially if one isn't prepared to touch any case that isn't—well—quite nice. And of course Torvald's been very firm about that—and I'm absolutely with him. Oh, you can imagine how happy we are! He's joining the bank in the new year, and he'll be getting a big salary, and lots of percentages too. From now on we'll be able to live quite differently—we'll be able to do whatever we want. Oh, Christine, it's such a relief! I feel so happy! Well, I mean, it's lovely to have heaps of money and not to have to worry about anything. Don't you think?

Mrs. Linde. It must be lovely to have enough to cover one's needs, anyway.

Nora. Not just our needs! We're going to have heaps and heaps of money!

Mrs. Linde (*smiles*). Nora, Nora, haven't you grown up yet? When we were at school you were a terrible little spendthrift.

Nora (*laughs quietly*). Yes, Torvald still says that. (*wags her finger*) But "Nora, Nora" isn't as silly as you think. Oh, we've been in no position for me to waste money. We've both had to work.

Mrs. Linde. You too?

Nora. Yes, little things—fancywork, crocheting, embroidery and so forth. (*casually*) And other things, too. I suppose you know Torvald left the Ministry when we got married? There were no prospects of promotion in his department, and of course he needed more money. But the first year he overworked himself dreadfully. He had to take on all sorts of extra jobs, and worked day and night. But it was too much for him, and he became frightfully ill. The doctors said he'd have to go to a warmer climate.

Mrs. Linde. Yes, you spent a whole year in Italy, didn't you?

Nora. Yes. It wasn't easy for me to get away, you know. I'd just had Ivar. But, of course, we had to do it. Oh, it was a marvelous trip! And it saved Torvald's life. But it cost an awful lot of money, Christine.

Mrs. Linde. I can imagine.

Nora. Two hundred and fifty pounds. That's a lot of money, you know.

Mrs. Linde. How lucky you had it.

Nora. Well, actually, we got it from my father.

Mrs. Linde. Oh, I see. Didn't he die just about that time?

Nora. Yes, Christine, just about then. Wasn't it dreadful, I couldn't go and look after him. I was expecting little Ivar any day. And then I had my poor Torvald to care for—we really didn't think he'd live. Dear, kind Papa! I never saw him again, Christine. Oh, it's the saddest thing that's happened to me since I got married.

Mrs. Linde. I know you were very fond of him. But you went to Italy—?

Nora. Yes. Well, we had the money, you see, and the doctors said we mustn't delay. So we went the month after Papa died.

Mrs. Linde. And your husband came back completely cured?

Nora. Fit as a fiddle!

Mrs. Linde. But—the doctor?

Nora. How do you mean?

Mrs. Linde. I thought the maid said that the gentleman who arrived with me was the doctor.

Nora. Oh yes, that's Dr. Rank, but he doesn't come because anyone's ill. He's our best friend, and he looks us up at least once every day. No, Torvald hasn't had a moment's illness since we went away. And the children are fit and healthy and so am I. (*jumps up and claps her hands*) Oh, God, oh God, Christine, isn't it a wonderful thing to be alive and happy! Oh, but how beastly of me! I'm only talking about myself. (*sits on a footstool and rests her arms on* MRS. LINDE's *knee*) Oh, please don't be angry with me! Tell me, is it really true you didn't love your husband? Why did you marry him, then?

Mrs. Linde. Well, my mother was still alive; and she was helpless and bedridden. And I had my two little brothers to take care of. I didn't feel I could say no.

Nora. Yes, well, perhaps you're right. He was rich then, was he?

Mrs. Linde. Quite comfortably off, I believe. But his business was unsound, you see, Nora. When he died it went bankrupt and there was nothing left.

Nora. What did you do?

Mrs. Linde. Well, I had to try to make ends meet somehow, so I started a little shop, and a little school, and anything else I could turn my hand to. These last three years have been just one endless slog for me, without a moment's rest. But now it's over, Nora. My poor dead mother doesn't need me any more; she's passed away. And the boys don't need me either; they've got jobs now and can look after themselves.

Nora. How relieved you must feel—

Mrs. Linde. No, Nora. Just unspeakably empty. No one to live for any more. (*gets up restlessly*) That's why I couldn't bear to stay out there any longer, cut off from the world. I thought it'd be easier to find some work here that will exercise and occupy my mind. If only I could get a regular job—office work of some kind—

Nora. Oh but, Christine, that's dreadfully exhausting; and you look practically fin-

Grandmother's House, Wassili Dmitrijewitsch Polenow (1844–1927).

ished already. It'd be much better for you if you could go away somewhere.

Mrs. Linde (*goes over to the window*). I have no papa to pay for my holidays, Nora.

Nora (*gets up*). Oh, please don't be angry with me.

Mrs. Linde. My dear Nora, it's I who should ask you not to be angry. That's the worst thing about this kind of situation—it makes one so bitter. One has no one to work for; and yet one has to be continually sponging for jobs. One has to live; and so one becomes completely egocentric. When

you told me about this luck you've just had with Torvald's new job—can you imagine?—I was happy not so much on your account, as on my own.

Nora. How do you mean? Oh, I understand. You mean Torvald might be able to do something for you?

Mrs. Linde. Yes, I was thinking that.

Nora. He will too, Christine. Just you leave it to me. I'll lead up to it so delicately, so delicately; I'll get him in the right mood. Oh, Christine, I do so want to help you.

Mrs. Linde. It's sweet of you to bother so much about me, Nora. Especially since you know so little of the worries and hardships of life.

Nora. I? You say *I* know little of—?

Mrs. Linde (*smiles*). Well, good heavens—those bits of fancywork of yours—well, really! You're a child, Nora.

Nora (*tosses her head and walks across the room*). You shouldn't say that so patronizingly.

Mrs. Linde. Oh?

Nora. You're like the rest. You all think I'm incapable of getting down to anything serious—

Mrs. Linde. My dear—

Nora. You think I've never had any worries like the rest of you.

Mrs. Linde. Nora dear, you've just told me about all your difficulties—

Nora. Pooh—that! (*quietly*) I haven't told you about the big thing.

Mrs. Linde. What big thing? What do you mean?

Nora. You patronize me, Christine; but you shouldn't. You're proud that you've worked so long and so hard for your mother.

Mrs. Linde. I don't patronize anyone, Nora. But you're right—I am both proud and happy that I was able to make my mother's last months on earth comparatively easy.

Nora. And you're also proud at what you've done for your brothers.

Mrs. Linde. I think I have a right to be.

Nora. I think so, too. But let me tell you something, Christine. I, too, have done something to be proud and happy about.

Mrs. Linde. I don't doubt it. But—how do you mean?

Nora. Speak quietly! Suppose Torvald should hear! He mustn't, at any price—no one must know, Christine—no one but you.

Mrs. Linde. But what is this?

Nora. Come over here. (*pulls her down onto the sofa beside her*) Yes, Christine—I, too, have done something to be happy and proud about. It was I who saved Torvald's life.

Mrs. Linde. Saved his—? How did you save it?

Nora. I told you about our trip to Italy. Torvald couldn't have lived if he hadn't managed to get down there—

Mrs. Linde. Yes, well—your father provided the money—

Nora (*smiles*). So Torvald and everyone else thinks. But—

Mrs. Linde. Yes?

Nora. Papa didn't give us a penny. It was I who found the money.

Mrs. Linde. You? All of it?

Nora. Two hundred and fifty pounds. What do you say to that?

Mrs. Linde. But, Nora, how could you? Did you win a lottery or something?

Nora (*scornfully*). Lottery? (*sniffs*) What would there be to be proud of in that?

Mrs. Linde. But where did you get it from, then?

Nora (*hums and smiles secretively*). Hm; tra-la-la-la!

Mrs. Linde. You couldn't have borrowed it.

Nora. Oh? Why not?

Mrs. Linde. Well, a wife can't borrow money without her husband's consent.

Nora (*tosses her head*). Ah, but when a wife has a little business sense, and knows how to be clever—

Mrs. Linde. But Nora, I simply don't understand—

Nora. You don't have to. No one has said I borrowed the money. I could have got it in some other way. (*throws herself back on the sofa*) I could have got it from an admirer. When a girl's as pretty as I am—

Mrs. Linde. Nora, you're crazy!

Nora. You're dying of curiosity now, aren't you, Christine?

Mrs. Linde. Nora dear, you haven't done anything foolish?

Nora (*sits up again*). Is it foolish to save one's husband's life?

Mrs. Linde. I think it's foolish if without his knowledge you—

Nora. But the whole point was that he mustn't know! Great heavens, don't you see? He hadn't to know how dangerously ill he was. It was me they told that his life was in danger and that only going to a warm climate could save him. Do you suppose I didn't try to think of other ways of getting him down there? I told him how wonderful it would be for me to go abroad like other young wives; I cried and prayed; I asked him to remember my condition, and said he ought to be nice and tender to me; and then I suggested he might quite easily borrow the money. But then he got almost angry with me, Christine. He said I was frivolous, and that it was his duty as a husband not to pander to my moods and caprices—I think that's what he called them. Well, well, I thought, you've got to be saved somehow. And then I thought of a way—

Mrs. Linde. But didn't your husband find out from your father that the money hadn't come from him?

Nora. No, never. Papa died just then. I'd thought of letting him into the plot and asking him not to tell. But since he was so ill—! And as things turned out, it didn't become necessary.

Mrs. Linde. And you've never told your husband about this?

Nora. For heaven's sake, no! What an idea! He's frightfully strict about such matters. And besides—he's so proud of being a man—it'd be so painful and humiliating for him to know that he owed anything to me. It'd completely wreck our relationship. This life we have built together would no longer exist.

Mrs. Linde. Will you never tell him?

Nora (*thoughtfully, half-smiling*). Yes—sometime, perhaps. Years from now, when I'm no longer pretty. You mustn't laugh! I mean, of course, when Torvald no longer loves me as he does now; when it no longer amuses him to see me dance and dress up and play the fool for him. Then it might be useful to have something up my sleeve. (*breaks off*) Stupid, stupid, stupid! That time will never come. Well, what do you think of my big secret, Christine? I'm not completely useless, am I? Mind you, all this has caused me a frightful lot of worry. It hasn't been easy for me to meet my obligations punctually. In case you don't know, in the world of business there are things called quarterly installments and interest, and they're a terrible problem to cope with. So I've had to scrape a little here and save a little there, as best I can. I haven't been able to save much on the housekeeping money, because Torvald likes to live well; and I couldn't let the children go short of clothes—I couldn't take anything out of what he gives me for them. The poor little angels!

Mrs. Linde. So you've had to stint yourself, my poor Nora?

Nora. Of course. Well, after all, it was my problem. Whenever Torvald gave me money to buy myself new clothes, I never used more than half of it; and I always bought what was cheapest and plainest. Thank heaven anything suits me, so that Torvald's never noticed. But it made me a bit sad sometimes, because it's lovely to wear pretty clothes. Don't you think?

Mrs. Linde. Indeed it is.

Nora. And then I've found one or two other sources of income. Last winter I managed to get a lot of copying to do. So I shut myself away and wrote every evening, late into the night. Oh, I often got so tired, so tired. But it was great fun, though, sitting there working and earning money. It was almost like being a man.

Mrs. Linde. But how much have you managed to pay off like this?

Nora. Well, I can't say exactly. It's awfully difficult to keep an exact check on these kind of transactions. I only know I've paid everything I've managed to scrape together. Sometimes I really didn't know where to turn. (*smiles*) Then I'd sit here and imagine some rich old gentleman had fallen in love with me—

Mrs. Linde. What! What gentleman?

Nora. Silly! And that now he'd died and when they opened his will it said in big letters: "Everything I possess is to be paid forthwith to my beloved Mrs. Nora Helmer in cash."

Mrs. Linde. But, Nora dear, who was this gentleman?

Nora. Great heavens, don't you understand? There wasn't any old gentleman; he was just something I used to dream up as I sat here evening after evening wondering how on earth I could raise some money. But what does it matter? The old bore can stay imaginary as far as I'm concerned, because now I don't have to worry any longer! (*jumps up*) Oh, Christine, isn't it wonderful? I don't have to worry any more! No more troubles! I can play all day with the children, I can fill the house with pretty things, just the way Torvald likes. And, Christine, it'll soon be spring, and the air'll be fresh and the skies blue—and then perhaps we'll be able to take a little trip somewhere. I shall be able to see the sea again. Oh, yes, yes, it's a wonderful thing to be alive and happy!

[*The bell rings in the hall.*]

Mrs. Linde (*gets up*). You've a visitor. Perhaps I'd better go.

Nora. No, stay. It won't be for me. It's someone for Torvald—

Maid (*in the doorway*). Excuse me, madam, a gentleman's called who says he wants to speak to the master. But I didn't know—seeing as the doctor's with him—

Nora. Who is this gentleman?

Krogstad (*in the doorway*). It's me, Mrs. Helmer.

[MRS. LINDE *starts, composes herself and turns away to the window.*]

Nora (*takes a step towards him and whispers tensely*). You? What is it? What do you want to talk to my husband about?

Krogstad. Business—you might call it. I hold a minor post in the bank, and I hear your husband is to become our new chief—

Nora. Oh—then it isn't—?

Krogstad. Pure business, Mrs. Helmer. Nothing more.

Nora. Well, you'll find him in his study.

[*Nods indifferently as she closes the hall door behind him. Then she walks across the room and sees to the stove.*]

Mrs. Linde. Nora, who was that man?

Nora. A lawyer called Krogstad.

Mrs. Linde. It was him, then.

Nora. Do you know that man?

Mrs. Linde. I used to know him—some years ago. He was a solicitor's[3] clerk in our town, for a while.

Nora. Yes, of course, so he was.

Mrs. Linde. How he's changed!

Nora. He was very unhappily married, I believe.

Mrs. Linde. Is he a widower now?

Nora. Yes, with a lot of children. Ah, now it's alight.

[*She closes the door of the stove and moves the rocking chair a little to one side.*]

Mrs. Linde. He does—various things now, I hear?

---

3. **solicitor:** lawyer.

Nora. Does he? It's quite possible—I really don't know. But don't let's talk about business. It's so boring.

[DR. RANK *enters from* HELMER's *study.*]

Dr. Rank (*still in the doorway*). No, no, my dear chap, don't see me out. I'll go and have a word with your wife. (*closes the door and notices* MRS. LINDE) Oh, I beg your pardon. I seem to be *de trop*[4] here, too.

Nora. Not in the least. (*introduces them*) Dr. Rank. Mrs. Linde.

Rank. Ah! A name I have often heard in this house. I believe I passed you on the stairs as I came up.

Mrs. Linde. Yes. Stairs tire me. I have to take them slowly.

Rank. Oh, have you hurt yourself?

Mrs. Linde. No, I'm just a little run down.

Rank. Ah, is that all? Then I take it you've come to town to cure yourself by a round of parties?

Mrs. Linde. I have come here to find work.

Rank. Is that an approved remedy for being run down?

Mrs. Linde. One has to live, Doctor.

Rank. Yes, people do seem to regard it as a necessity.

Nora. Oh, really, Dr. Rank. I bet you want to stay alive.

Rank. You bet I do. However wretched I sometimes feel, I still want to go on being tortured for as long as possible. It's the same with all my patients; and with people who are morally sick, too. There's a moral cripple in with Helmer at this very moment—

Mrs. Linde (*softly*). Oh!

Nora. Whom do you mean?

Rank. Oh, a lawyer fellow called Krogstad—you wouldn't know him. He's crippled all

right, morally twisted. But even he started off by announcing, as though it were a matter of enormous importance, that he had to live.

Nora. Oh? What did he want to talk to Torvald about?

Rank. I haven't the faintest idea. All I heard was something about the bank.

Nora. I didn't know that Krog—that this man Krogstad had any connection with the bank.

Rank. Yes, he's got some kind of job down there. (*to* MRS. LINDE) I wonder if in your part of the world you too have a species of creature that spends its time fussing around trying to smell out moral corruption? And when they find a case they give him some nice, comfortable position so that they can keep a good watch on him. The healthy ones just have to lump it.

Mrs. Linde. But surely it's the sick who need care most?

Rank (*shrugs his shoulders*). Well, there we have it. It's that attitude that's turning human society into a hospital.

[NORA, *lost in her own thoughts, laughs half to herself and claps her hands.*]

Rank. Why are you laughing? Do you really know what society is?

Nora. What do I care about society? I think it's a bore. I was laughing at something else—something frightfully funny. Tell me, Dr. Rank—will everyone who works at the bank come under Torvald now?

Rank. Do you find that particularly funny?

Nora (*smiles and hums*). Never you mind! Never you mind! (*walks around the room*) Yes, I find it very amusing to think that we—I mean, Torvald—has obtained so much influence over so many people. (*takes the paper bag from her pocket*) Dr. Rank, would you like a small macaroon?

Rank. Macaroons! I say! I thought they were forbidden here.

---

4. *de trop* (də trō′): French for "in the way."

Nora. Yes, well, these are some Christine gave me.

Mrs. Linde. What? I—?

Nora. All right, all right, don't get frightened. You weren't to know Torvald had forbidden them. He's afraid they'll ruin my teeth. But, dash it—for once—! Don't you agree, Dr. Rank? Here! (*pops a macaroon into his mouth*) You, too, Christine. And I'll have one, too. Just a little one. Two at the most. (*begins to walk round again*) Yes, now I feel really, really happy. Now there's just one thing in the world I'd really love to do.

Rank. Oh? And what is that?

Nora. Just something I'd love to say to Torvald.

Rank. Well, why don't you say it?

Nora. No, I daren't. It's too dreadful.

Mrs. Linde. Dreadful?

Rank. Well then, you'd better not. But you can say it to us. What is it you'd so love to say to Torvald?

Nora. I've the most extraordinary longing to say: "Bloody hell!"

Rank. Are you mad?

Mrs. Linde. My dear Nora—!

Rank. Say it. Here he is.

Nora (*hiding the bag of macaroons*). Ssh! Ssh!

[HELMER, *with his overcoat on his arm and his hat in his hand, enters from his study.*]

Nora (*goes to meet him*). Well, Torvald dear, did you get rid of him?

Helmer. Yes, he's just gone.

Nora. May I introduce you—? This is Christine. She's just arrived in town.

Helmer. Christine—? Forgive me, but I don't think—

Nora. Mrs. Linde, Torvald dear. Christine Linde.

Helmer. Ah. A childhood friend of my wife's, I presume?

Mrs. Linde. Yes, we knew each other in earlier days.

Nora. And imagine, now she's traveled all this way to talk to you.

Helmer. Oh?

Mrs. Linde. Well, I didn't really—

Nora. You see, Christine's frightfully good at office work, and she's mad to come under some really clever man who can teach her even more than she knows already—

Helmer. Very sensible, madam.

Nora. So when she heard you'd become head of the bank—it was in her local paper—she came here as quickly as she could and—Torvald, you will, won't you? Do a little something to help Christine? For my sake?

Helmer. Well, that shouldn't be impossible. You are a widow, I take it, Mrs. Linde?

Mrs. Linde. Yes.

Helmer. And you have experience of office work?

Mrs. Linde. Yes, quite a bit.

Helmer. Well, then, it's quite likely I may be able to find some job for you—

Nora (*claps her hands*). You see, you see!

Helmer. You've come at a lucky moment, Mrs. Linde.

Mrs. Linde. Oh, how can I ever thank you—?

Helmer. There's absolutely no need. (*puts on his overcoat*) But now I'm afraid I must ask you to excuse me—

Rank. Wait. I'll come with you.

[*He gets his fur coat from the hall and warms it at the stove.*]

Nora. Don't be long, Torvald dear.

Helmer. I'll only be an hour.

Nora. Are you going, too, Christine?

Mrs. Linde (*puts on her outdoor clothes*). Yes, I must start to look round for a room.

Helmer. Then perhaps we can walk part of the way together.

Nora (*helps her*). It's such a nuisance we're so cramped here—I'm afraid we can't offer to—

Mrs. Linde. Oh, I wouldn't dream of it. Goodbye, Nora dear, and thanks for everything.

Nora. Au revoir.[5] You'll be coming back this evening, of course. And you too, Dr. Rank. What? If you're well enough? Of course you'll be well enough. Wrap up warmly, though.

[*They go out, talking, into the hall.* CHILDREN's *voices are heard from the stairs.*]

Nora. Here they are! Here they are!

[*She runs out and opens the door. The* NURSE, ANNE-MARIE, *enters with the* CHILDREN.]

Nora. Come in, come in! (*stoops down and kisses them*) Oh, my sweet darlings—! Look at them, Christine! Aren't they beautiful?

Rank. Don't stand here chattering in this draft!

---

5. *Au revoir* (ō′ rə·vwär′): French for "goodbye."

Helmer. Come, Mrs. Linde. This is for mothers only.

[DR. RANK, HELMER, *and* MRS. LINDE *go down the stairs. The* NURSE *brings the* CHILDREN *into the room.* NORA *follows, and closes the door to the hall.*]

Nora. How well you look! What red cheeks you've got! Like apples and roses!

[*The* CHILDREN *answer her inaudibly as she talks to them.*]

Nora. Have you had fun? That's splendid. You gave Emmy and Bob a ride on the sledge? What, both together? I say! What a clever boy you are, Ivar! Oh, let me hold her for a moment, Anne-Marie! My sweet little baby doll! (*takes the* SMALLEST CHILD *from the* NURSE *and dances with her*) Yes, yes, mummy will dance with Bob, too. What? Have you been throwing snowballs? Oh, I wish I'd been there! No, don't—I'll undress them myself, Anne-Marie. No, please let me; it's such fun. Go inside and warm yourself; you look frozen. There's some hot coffee on the stove.

[*The* NURSE *goes into the room on the left.* NORA *takes off the* CHILDREN's *outdoor clothes and throws them anywhere while they all chatter simultaneously.*]

Nora. What? A big dog ran after you? But he didn't bite you? No, dogs don't bite lovely little baby dolls. Leave those parcels alone, Ivar. What's in them? Ah, wouldn't you like to know! No, no; it's nothing nice. Come on, let's play a game. What shall we play? Hide-and-seek? Yes, let's play hide-and-seek. Bob shall hide first. You want me to? All right, let me hide first.

[NORA *and the* CHILDREN *play around the room, and in the adjacent room to the right, laughing and shouting. At length* NORA *hides under the table. The* CHILDREN *rush in, look, but cannot find her. Then they hear her half-stifled laughter, run*

to the table, lift up the cloth and see her. Great excitement. She crawls out as though to frighten them. Further excitement. Meanwhile, there has been a knock on the door leading from the hall, but no one has noticed it. Now the door is half opened and* KROGSTAD *enters. He waits for a moment; the game continues.*]

Krogstad. Excuse me, Mrs. Helmer—

Nora (*turns with a stifled cry and half jumps up*). Oh! What do you want?

Krogstad. I beg your pardon—the front door was ajar. Someone must have forgotten to close it.

Nora (*gets up*). My husband is not at home, Mr. Krogstad.

Krogstad. I know.

Nora. Well, what do you want here, then?

Krogstad. A word with you.

Nora. With—? (*to the* CHILDREN, *quietly*) Go inside to Anne-Marie. What? No, the strange gentleman won't do anything to hurt mummy. When he's gone we'll start playing again.

[*She takes the* CHILDREN *into the room on the left and closes the door behind them.*]

Nora (*uneasy, tense*). You want to speak to me?

Krogstad. Yes.

Nora. Today? But it's not the first of the month yet.

Krogstad. No, it is Christmas Eve. Whether or not you have a merry Christmas depends on you.

Nora. What do you want? I can't give you anything today—

Krogstad. We won't talk about that for the present. There's something else. You have a moment to spare?

Nora. Oh, yes. Yes, I suppose so—though—

Krogstad. Good. I was sitting in the café down below and I saw your husband cross the street—

Nora. Yes.

Krogstad. With a lady.

Nora. Well?

Krogstad. Might I be so bold as to ask; was not that lady a Mrs. Linde?

Nora. Yes.

Krogstad. Recently arrived in town?

Nora. Yes, today.

Krogstad. She is a good friend of yours, is she not?

Nora. Yes, she is. But I don't see—

Krogstad. I used to know her, too, once.

Nora. I know.

Krogstad. Oh? You've discovered that. Yes, I thought you would. Well then, may I ask you a straight question: is Mrs. Linde to be employed at the bank?

Nora. How dare you presume to cross-examine me, Mr. Krogstad? You, one of my husband's employees? But since you ask, you shall have an answer. Yes, Mrs. Linde is to be employed by the bank. And I arranged it, Mr. Krogstad. Now you know.

Krogstad. I guessed right, then.

Nora (*walks up and down the room*). Oh, one has a little influence, you know. Just because one's a woman it doesn't necessarily mean that—When one is in a humble position, Mr. Krogstad, one should think twice before offending someone who—hm—!

Krogstad. —who has influence?

Nora. Precisely.

Krogstad (*changes his tone*). Mrs. Helmer, will you have the kindness to use your influence on my behalf?

Nora. What? What do you mean?

Krogstad. Will you be so good as to see that I keep my humble position at the bank?

Nora. What do you mean? Who is thinking of removing you from your position?

Krogstad. Oh, you don't need to play the innocent with me. I realize it can't be very pleasant for your friend to risk bumping into me. And now I also realize whom I have to thank for being hounded out like this.

Nora. But I assure you—

Krogstad. Look, let's not beat about the bush. There's still time, and I'd advise you to use your influence to stop it.

Nora. But, Mr. Krogstad, I have no influence!

Krogstad. Oh? I thought you just said—

Nora. But I didn't mean it like that! I? How on earth could you imagine that I would have any influence over my husband?

Krogstad. Oh, I've known your husband since we were students together. I imagine he has his weaknesses like other married men.

Nora. If you speak impertinently[6] of my husband, I shall show you the door.

Krogstad. You're a bold woman, Mrs. Helmer.

Nora. I'm not afraid of you any longer. Once the new year is in, I'll soon be rid of you.

Krogstad (*more controlled*). Now listen to me, Mrs. Helmer. If I'm forced to, I shall fight for my little job at the bank as I would fight for my life.

Nora. So it sounds.

Krogstad. It isn't just the money—that's the last thing I care about. There's something else. Well, you might as well know. It's like this, you see. You know of course, as everyone else does, that some years ago I committed an indiscretion.

Nora. I think I did hear something—

Krogstad. It never came into court; but from that day, every opening was barred to me. So I turned my hand to the kind of

---

6. **impertinently:** insolently; without the proper respect or manners.

business you know about. I had to do something; and I don't think I was one of the worst. But now I want to give up all that. My sons are growing up; for their sake, I must try to regain what respectability I can. This job in the bank was the first step on the ladder. And now your husband wants to kick me off that ladder back into the dirt.

Nora. But, my dear Mr. Krogstad, it simply isn't in my power to help you.

Krogstad. You say that because you don't want to help me. But I have the means to make you.

Nora. You don't mean you'd tell my husband that I owe you money?

Krogstad. And if I did?

Nora. That'd be a filthy trick! (*almost in tears*) This secret that is my pride and my joy—that he should hear about it in such a filthy, beastly way—hear about it from you! It'd involve me in the most dreadful unpleasantness—

Krogstad. Only—unpleasantness?

Nora (*vehemently*). All right, do it! You'll be the one who'll suffer. It'll show my husband the kind of man you are, and then you'll never keep your job.

Krogstad. I asked you whether it was merely domestic unpleasantness you were afraid of.

Nora. If my husband hears about it, he will of course immediately pay you whatever is owing. And then we shall have nothing more to do with you.

Krogstad (*takes a step closer*). Listen, Mrs. Helmer. Either you've a bad memory or else you know very little about financial transactions. I had better enlighten you.

Nora. What do you mean?

Krogstad. When your husband was ill, you came to me to borrow two hundred and fifty pounds.

Nora. I didn't know anyone else.

Krogstad. I promised to find that sum for you—

Nora. And you did find it.

Krogstad. I promised to find that sum for you on certain conditions. You were so worried about your husband's illness and so keen to get the money to take him abroad that I don't think you bothered much about the details. So it won't be out of place if I refresh your memory. Well—I promised to get you the money in exchange for an I.O.U., which I drew up.

Nora. Yes, and which I signed.

Krogstad. Exactly. But then I added a few lines naming your father as security for the debt. This paragraph was to be signed by your father.

Nora. Was to be? He did sign it.

Krogstad. I left the date blank for your father to fill in when he signed this paper. You remember, Mrs. Helmer?

Nora. Yes, I think so—

Krogstad. Then I gave you back this I.O.U. for you to post to your father. Is that not correct?

Nora. Yes.

Krogstad. And of course you posted it at once; for within five or six days you brought it along to me with your father's signature on it. Whereupon I handed you the money.

Nora. Yes, well. Haven't I repaid the installments as agreed?

Krogstad. Mm—yes, more or less. But to return to what we are speaking about—that was a difficult time for you just then, wasn't it, Mrs. Helmer?

Nora. Yes, it was.

Krogstad. Your father was very ill, if I am not mistaken.

Nora. He was dying.

Krogstad. He did in fact die shortly afterwards?

Nora. Yes.

Krogstad. Tell me, Mrs. Helmer, do you by any chance remember the date of your father's death? The day of the month, I mean.

Nora. Papa died on the twenty-ninth of September.

Krogstad. Quite correct; I took the trouble to confirm it. And that leaves me with a curious little problem—(*takes out a paper*)—which I simply cannot solve.

Nora. Problem? I don't see—

Krogstad. The problem, Mrs. Helmer, is that your father signed this paper three days after his death.

Nora. What? I don't understand—

Krogstad. Your father died on the twenty-ninth of September. But look at this. Here your father has dated his signature the second of October. Isn't that a curious little problem, Mrs. Helmer?

[NORA *is silent.*]

Krogstad. Can you suggest any explanation?

[*She remains silent.*]

Krogstad. And there's another curious thing. The words "second of October" and the year are written in a hand which is not your father's, but which I seem to know. Well, there's a simple explanation to that. Your father could have forgotten to write in the date when he signed, and someone else could have added it before the news came of his death. There's nothing criminal about that. It's the signature itself I'm wondering about. It *is* genuine, I suppose, Mrs. Helmer? It was your father who wrote his name here?

Nora (*after a short silence, throws back her head and looks defiantly at him*). No, it was not. It was I who wrote Papa's name there.

Krogstad. Look, Mrs. Helmer, do you realize this is a dangerous admission?

Nora. Why? You'll get your money.

Krogstad. May I ask you a question? Why didn't you send this paper to your father?

Nora. I couldn't. Papa was very ill. If I'd asked him to sign this, I'd have had to tell him what the money was for. But I couldn't have told him in his condition that my husband's life was in danger. I couldn't have done that!

Krogstad. Then you would have been wiser to have given up your idea of a holiday.

Nora. But I couldn't! It was to save my husband's life. I couldn't put it off.

Krogstad. But didn't it occur to you that you were being dishonest towards me?

Nora. I couldn't bother about that. I didn't care about you. I hated you because of all the beastly difficulties you'd put in my way when you knew how dangerously ill my husband was.

Krogstad. Mrs. Helmer, you evidently don't appreciate exactly what you have done. But I can assure you that it is no bigger nor worse a crime than the one I once committed and thereby ruined my whole social position.

Nora. You? Do you expect me to believe that you would have taken a risk like that to save your wife's life?

Krogstad. The law does not concern itself with motives.

Nora. Then the law must be very stupid.

Krogstad. Stupid or not, if I show this paper to the police, you will be judged according to it.

Nora. I don't believe that. Hasn't a daughter the right to shield her father from worry and anxiety when he's old and dying? Hasn't a wife the right to save her husband's life? I don't know much about the law, but there must be something somewhere that says that such things are allowed. You ought to know that, you're meant to be a lawyer, aren't you? You can't be a very good lawyer, Mr. Krogstad.

Krogstad. Possibly not. But business, the

kind of business we two have been trans-
acting—I think you'll admit I understand
something about that? Good. Do as you
please. But I tell you this. If I get thrown
into the gutter for a second time, I shall
take you with me.

[*He bows and goes out through the hall.*]

Nora (*stands for a moment in thought, then
tosses her head*). What nonsense! He's
trying to frighten me! I'm not that stupid.
(*busies herself gathering together the children's clothes; then she suddenly stops.*)
But—? No, it's impossible. I did it for love,
didn't I?

Children (*in the doorway, left*). Mummy,
the strange gentleman has gone out into
the street.

Nora. Yes, yes, I know. But don't talk to
anyone about the strange gentleman. You
hear? Not even to Daddy.

Children. No, Mummy. Will you play with
us again now?

Nora. No, no. Not now.

Children. Oh but, Mummy, you promised!

Nora. I know, but I can't just now. Go back
to the nursery. I've a lot to do. Go away,
my darlings, go away.

[*She pushes them gently into the other
room, and closes the door behind them.
She sits on the sofa, takes up her embroidery, stitches for a few moments, but soon
stops.*]

Nora. No! (*throws the embroidery aside,
gets up, goes to the door leading to the hall
and calls*) Helen! Bring in the Christmas
tree! (*She goes to the table on the left and
opens the drawer in it; then pauses again.*)
No, but it's utterly impossible!

Maid (*enters with the tree*). Where shall I
put it, madam?

Nora. There, in the middle of the room.

Maid. Will you be wanting anything else?

Nora. No, thank you. I have everything I need.

[*The* MAID *puts down the tree and goes
out.*]

Nora (*busy decorating the tree*). Now—
candles here—and flowers here. That loathsome man! Nonsense, nonsense, there's
nothing to be frightened about. The Christmas tree must be beautiful. I'll do everything that you like, Torvald. I'll sing for
you, dance for you—

[HELMER, *with a bundle of papers under
his arm, enters.*]

Nora. Oh—are you back already?

Helmer. Yes. Has anyone been here?

Nora. Here? No.

Helmer. That's strange. I saw Krogstad
come out of the front door.

Nora. Did you? Oh yes, that's quite right—
Krogstad was here for a few minutes.

Helmer. Nora, I can tell from your face, he
has been here and asked you to put in a
good word for him.

Nora. Yes.

Helmer. And you were to pretend you
were doing it of your own accord? You
weren't going to tell me he'd been here?
He asked you to do that too, didn't he?

Nora. Yes, Torvald. But—

Helmer. Nora, Nora! And you were ready
to enter into such a conspiracy? Talking to
a man like that, and making him promises—and then, on top of it all, to tell me
an untruth!

Nora. An untruth?

Helmer. Didn't you say no one had been
here? (*wags his finger*) My little songbird
must never do that again. A songbird must
have a clean beak to sing with. Otherwise
she'll start twittering out of tune. (*puts his
arm around her waist*) Isn't that the way
we want things? Yes, of course it is. (*lets go
of her*) So let's hear no more about that.
(*sits down in front of the stove*) Ah, how
cosy and peaceful it is here! (*glances for a
few moments at his papers*)

Nora (*busy with the tree; after a short silence*). Torvald.

Helmer. Yes.

Nora. I'm terribly looking forward to that fancy-dress ball at the Stenborgs on Boxing Day.[7]

Helmer. And I'm terribly curious to see what you're going to surprise me with.

Nora. Oh, it's so maddening.

Helmer. What is?

Nora. I can't think of anything to wear. It all seems so stupid and meaningless.

Helmer. So my little Nora has come to that conclusion, has she?

Nora (*behind his chair, resting her arms on its back*). Are you very busy, Torvald?

Helmer. Oh—

Nora. What are those papers?

Helmer. Just something to do with the bank.

Nora. Already?

Helmer. I persuaded the trustees to give me authority to make certain immediate changes in the staff and organization. I want to have everything straight by the new year.

Nora. Then that's why this poor man Krogstad—

Helmer. Hm.

Nora (*still leaning over his chair, slowly strokes the back of his head*). If you hadn't been so busy, I was going to ask you an enormous favor. Torvald.

Helmer. Well, tell me. What was it to be?

Nora. You know I trust your taste more than anyone's. I'm so anxious to look really beautiful at the fancy-dress ball. Torvald, couldn't you help me to decide what I shall go as, and what kind of costume I ought to wear?

Helmer. Aha! So little Miss Independent's

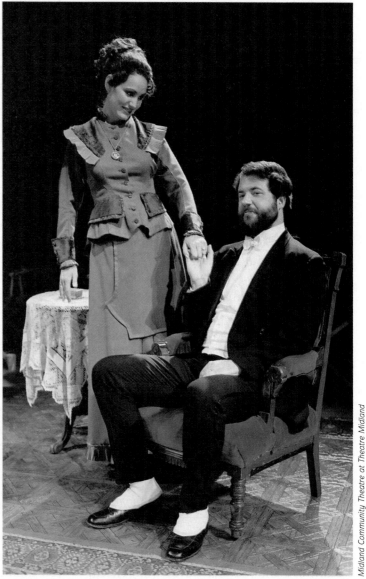

---

7. **Boxing Day:** the first weekday after Christmas.

in trouble and needs a man to rescue her, does she?

Nora. Yes, Torvald. I can't get anywhere without your help.

Helmer. Well, well, I'll give the matter thought. We'll find something.

Nora. Oh, how kind of you! (*goes back to the tree; pauses*) How pretty these red flowers look! But, tell me, is it so dreadful, this thing that Krogstad's done?

Helmer. He forged someone else's name. Have you any idea what that means?

Nora. Mightn't he have been forced to do it by some emergency?

Helmer. He probably just didn't think— that's what usually happens. I'm not so heartless as to condemn a man for an isolated action.

Nora. No, Torvald, of course not!

Helmer. Men often succeed in reestablishing themselves if they admit their crime and take their punishment.

Nora. Punishment?

Helmer. But Krogstad didn't do that. He chose to try and trick his way out of it. And that's what has morally destroyed him.

Nora. You think that would—?

Helmer. Just think how a man with that load on his conscience must always be lying and cheating and dissembling—how he must wear a mask even in the presence of those who are dearest to him, even his own wife and children! Yes, the children. That's the worst danger, Nora.

Nora. Why?

Helmer. Because an atmosphere of lies contaminates and poisons every corner of the home. Every breath that the children draw in such a house contains the germs of evil.

Nora (*comes closer behind him*). Do you really believe that?

Helmer. Oh, my dear, I've come across it so often in my work at the bar. Nearly all young criminals are the children of mothers who are constitutional liars.

Nora. Why do you say mothers?

Helmer. It's usually the mother—though of course the father can have the same influence. Every lawyer knows that only too well. And yet this fellow Krogstad has been sitting at home all these years poisoning his children with his lies and pretenses. That's why I say that, morally speaking, he is dead. (*stretches out his hand towards her*) So my pretty little Nora must promise me not to plead his case. Your hand on it. Come, come, what's this? Give me your hand. There. That's settled, now. I assure you it'd be quite impossible for me to work in the same building as him. I literally feel physically ill in the presence of a man like that.

Nora (*draws her hand from his and goes over to the other side of the Christmas tree*). How hot it is in here! And I've so much to do.

Helmer (*gets up and gathers his papers*). Yes, and I must try to get some of this read before dinner. I'll think about your costume, too. And I may even have something up my sleeve to hang in gold paper on the Christmas tree. (*lays his hand on her head*) My precious little songbird!

[*He goes into his study and closes the door.*]

Nora (*softly, after a pause*). It's nonsense. It must be. It's impossible. It *must* be impossible!

Nurse (*in the doorway, left*). The children are asking if they can come in to Mummy.

Nora. No, no, no—don't let them in. You stay with them, Anne-Marie.

Nurse. Very good, madam. (*closes the door*)

Nora (*pale with fear*). Corrupt my little children—! Poison my home! (*short pause; she throws back her head*) It isn't true! It *couldn't* be true!

First Thoughts

Do you believe that Nora is as happy as she claims to be? Why or why not?

Identifying Facts

1. Why do Nora and Torvald feel Christmas is going to be especially happy this year?

2. Who is Mrs. Linde, and why does she visit Nora? How is her life different from Nora's?

3. Why did Nora borrow money? From whom did she borrow it? What was illegal about the way she borrowed the money?

4. What does Krogstad want Nora to do for him? How does he try to persuade her?

5. How does Torvald respond to Nora's request to help Mrs. Linde? To help Krogstad?

Interpreting Meanings

1. What do Torvald's nicknames for Nora, such as "skylark," "squirrel," and "squanderbird" tell you about their relationship? How does Nora react to these nicknames? How do Torvald's nicknames and Nora's reactions to them help to **characterize** them and reveal the nature of their marriage?

2. On page 1091, Torvald describes Krogstad as a man who "must wear a mask even in the presence of those who are dearest to him." Because of this, Torvald says, "an atmosphere of lies contaminates and poisons" Krogstad's home. How do you know that this statement applies to the Helmers' home as well?

3. Compare and contrast the way Nora interacts with Dr. Rank and with Torvald. What does this behavior tell you about her **character**?

4. Based on what she says about Krogstad and how she reacts to the mention of his name, how do you think Mrs. Linde feels about Krogstad?

Applying Meanings

Do you think the marriage of Nora and Torvald Helmer could be used as the basis of a play about a modern American couple? What aspects of their relationship would you change in order to update it? What aspects of their relationship could be kept unchanged?

Creative Writing Response

Adopting a Character's Point of View. Write a one-page narrative from the point of view of Torvald, Mrs. Linde, Krogstad, or Dr. Rank, in which you discuss Nora's personality and behavior. Your narrative might take the form of a journal entry, a letter, or any other first-person narrative form. In your narrative, have the character whose point of view you have adopted predict what will happen to Nora. Remember that not every character knows everything about Nora at this point in the play.

Midland Community Theatre at Theatre Midland

ACT 2

The same room. In the corner by the piano the Christmas tree stands, stripped and disheveled, its candles burned to their sockets. NORA's outdoor clothes lie on the sofa. She is alone in the room, walking restlessly to-and-fro. At length she stops by the sofa and picks up her coat.

Nora (*drops the coat again*). There's someone coming! (*goes to the door and listens*) No, it's no one. Of course—no one'll come today, it's Christmas Day. Nor tomorrow. But perhaps—! (*opens the door and looks out*) No. Nothing in the letter box. Quite empty. (*walks across the room*) Silly, silly. Of course he won't do anything. It couldn't happen. It isn't possible. Why, I've three small children.

[*The* NURSE, *carrying a large cardboard box, enters from the room on the left.*]

Nurse. I found those fancy dress clothes at last, madam.

Nora. Thank you. Put them on the table.

Nurse (*does so*). They're all rumpled up.

Nora. Oh, I wish I could tear them into a million pieces!

Nurse. Why, madam! They'll be all right. Just a little patience.

Nora. Yes, of course. I'll go and get Mrs. Linde to help me.

Nurse. What, out again? In this dreadful weather? You'll catch a chill, madam.

Nora. Well, that wouldn't be the worst. How are the children?

Nurse. Playing with their Christmas presents, poor little dears. But—

Nora. Are they still asking to see me?

Nurse. They're so used to having their mummy with them.

Nora. Yes, but, Anne-Marie, from now on I shan't be able to spend so much time with them.

Nurse. Well, children get used to anything in time.

Nora. Do you think so? Do you think they'd forget their mother if she went away from them—forever?

Nurse. Mercy's sake, madam! Forever!

Nora. Tell me, Anne-Marie—I've so often wondered. How could you bear to give your child away—to strangers?

Nurse. But I had to when I came to nurse my little Miss Nora.

Nora. Do you mean you wanted to?

Nurse. When I had the chance of such a good job? A poor girl what's got into trouble can't afford to pick and choose. That good-for-nothing didn't lift a finger.

Nora. But your daughter must have completely forgotten you.

Nurse. Oh no, indeed she hasn't. She's written to me twice, once when she got confirmed and then again when she got married.

Nora (*hugs her*). Dear old Anne-Marie, you were a good mother to me.

Nurse. Poor little Miss Nora, you never had any mother but me.

Nora. And if my little ones had no one else, I know you would—no, silly, silly, silly! (*opens the cardboard box*) Go back to them, Anne-Marie. Now I must—! Tomorrow you'll see how pretty I shall look.

Nurse. Why, there'll be no one at the ball as beautiful as my Miss Nora.

[*She goes into the room, left.*]

Nora (*begins to unpack the clothes from the box, but soon throws them down again*). Oh, if only I dared go out! If I could be sure no one would come and nothing would happen while I was away! Stupid, stupid! No one will come. I just mustn't think about it. Brush this muff. Pretty gloves, pretty gloves! Don't think about it, don't think about it! One, two, three, four, five, six—(*cries*) Ah—they're coming—!

[*She begins to run towards the door, but stops uncertainly.* MRS. LINDE *enters from*

the hall, where she has been taking off her outdoor clothes.]

Nora. Oh, it's you, Christine. There's no one else outside, is there? Oh, I'm so glad you've come.

Mrs. Linde. I hear you were at my room asking for me.

Nora. Yes, I just happened to be passing. I want to ask you to help me with something. Let's sit down here on the sofa. Look at this. There's going to be a fancy-dress ball tomorrow night upstairs at Consul Stenborg's, and Torvald wants me to go as a Neapolitan fisher-girl and dance the tarantella. I learned it in Capri.

Mrs. Linde. I say, are you going to give a performance?

Nora. Yes, Torvald says I should. Look, here's the dress. Torvald had it made for me in Italy—but now it's all so torn, I don't know—

Mrs. Linde. Oh, we'll soon put that right— the stitching's just come away. Needle and thread? Ah, here we are.

Nora. You're being awfully sweet.

Mrs. Linde (*sews*). So you're going to dress up tomorrow, Nora? I must pop over for a moment to see how you look. Oh, but I've completely forgotten to thank you for that nice evening yesterday.

Nora (*gets up and walks across the room*). Oh, I didn't think it was as nice as usual. You ought to have come to town a little earlier, Christine. . . . Yes, Torvald understands how to make a home look attractive.

Mrs. Linde. I'm sure you do, too. You're not your father's daughter for nothing. But, tell me—is Dr. Rank always in such low spirits as he was yesterday?

Nora. No, last night it was very noticeable. But he's got a terrible disease—he's got spinal tuberculosis, poor man. His father was a frightful creature who kept mistresses and so on. As a result Dr. Rank has been sickly ever since he was a child—you understand—

Mrs. Linde (*puts down her sewing*). But, my dear Nora, how on earth did you get to know about such things?

Nora (*walks about the room*). Oh, don't be silly, Christine—when one has three children, one comes into contact with women who—well, who know about medical matters, and they tell one a thing or two.

Mrs. Linde (*sews again; a short silence*). Does Dr. Rank visit you every day?

Nora. Yes, every day. He's Torvald's oldest friend, and a good friend to me too. Dr. Rank's almost one of the family.

Mrs. Linde. But, tell me—is he quite sincere? I mean, doesn't he rather say the sort of thing he thinks people want to hear?

Nora. No, quite the contrary. What gave you that idea?

Mrs. Linde. When you introduced me to him yesterday, he said he'd often heard my name mentioned here. But later I noticed your husband had no idea who I was. So how could Dr. Rank—

Nora. Yes, that's quite right, Christine. You see, Torvald's so hopelessly in love with me that he wants to have me all to himself—those were his very words. When we were first married, he got quite jealous if I as much as mentioned any of my old friends back home. So naturally, I stopped talking about them. But I often chat with Dr. Rank about that kind of thing. He enjoys it, you see.

Mrs. Linde. Now listen, Nora. In many ways you're still a child; I'm a bit older than you and have a little more experience of the world. There's something I want to say to you. You ought to give up this business with Dr. Rank.

Nora. What business?

Mrs. Linde. Well, everything. Last night you were speaking about this rich admirer of yours who was going to give you money—

Nora. Yes, and who doesn't exist—unfortunately. But what's that got to do with—?

Mrs. Linde. Is Dr. Rank rich?

Nora. Yes.

Mrs. Linde. And he has no dependants?

Nora. No, no one. But—

Mrs. Linde. And he comes here to see you every day?

Nora. Yes, I've told you.

Mrs. Linde. But how dare a man of his education be so forward?

Nora. What on earth are you talking about?

Mrs. Linde. Oh, stop pretending, Nora. Do you think I haven't guessed who it was who lent you that two hundred pounds?

Nora. Are you out of your mind? How could you imagine such a thing? A friend, someone who comes here every day! Why, that'd be an impossible situation!

Mrs. Linde. Then it really wasn't him?

Nora. No, of course not. I've never for a moment dreamed of—anyway, he hadn't any money to lend then. He didn't come into that till later.

Mrs. Linde. Well, I think that was a lucky thing for you, Nora dear.

Nora. No, I could never have dreamed of asking Dr. Rank— Though I'm sure that if ever I did ask him—

Mrs. Linde. But of course you won't.

Nora. Of course not. I can't imagine that it should ever become necessary. But I'm perfectly sure that if I did speak to Dr. Rank—

Mrs. Linde. Behind your husband's back?

Nora. I've got to get out of this other business—and *that's* been going on behind his back. I've *got* to get out of it.

Mrs. Linde. Yes, well, that's what I told you yesterday. But—

Nora (*walking up and down*). It's much

easier for a man to arrange these things than a woman—

Mrs. Linde. One's own husband, yes.

Nora. Oh, bosh. (*stops walking*) When you've completely repaid a debt, you get your I.O.U. back, don't you?

Mrs. Linde. Yes, of course.

Nora. And you can tear it into a thousand pieces and burn the filthy, beastly thing!

Mrs. Linde (*looks hard at her, puts down her sewing and gets up slowly*). Nora, you're hiding something from me.

Nora. Can you see that?

Mrs. Linde. Something has happened since yesterday morning. Nora, what is it?

Nora (*goes towards her*). Christine! (*listens*) Ssh! There's Torvald. Would you mind going into the nursery for a few minutes? Torvald can't bear to see sewing around. Anne-Marie'll help you.

Mrs. Linde (*gathers some of her things together*). Very well. But I shan't leave this house until we've talked this matter out.

[*She goes into the nursery, left. As she does so,* HELMER *enters from the hall.*]

Nora (*runs to meet him*). Oh, Torvald dear, I've been so longing for you to come back!

Helmer. Was that the dressmaker?

Nora. No, it was Christine. She's helping me mend my costume. I'm going to look rather splendid in that.

Helmer. Yes, that was quite a bright idea of mine, wasn't it?

Nora. Wonderful! But wasn't it nice of me to give in to you?

Helmer (*takes her chin in his hand*). Nice— to give in to your husband? All right, little silly, I know you didn't mean it like that. But I won't disturb you. I expect you'll be wanting to try it on.

Nora. Are you going to work now?

Helmer. Yes. (*shows her a bundle of papers*) Look at these. I've been down to the bank—(*turns to go into his study*)

Nora. Torvald.

Helmer (*stops*). Yes.

Nora. If little squirrel asked you really prettily to grant her a wish—

Helmer. Well?

Nora. Would you grant it to her?

Helmer. First I should naturally have to know what it was.

Nora. Squirrel would do lots of pretty tricks for you if you granted her wish.

Helmer. Out with it, then.

Nora. Your little skylark would sing in every room—

Helmer. My little skylark does that already.

Nora. I'd turn myself into a little fairy and dance for you in the moonlight, Torvald.

Helmer. Nora, it isn't that business you were talking about this morning?

Nora (*comes closer*). Yes, Torvald—oh, please! I beg of you!

Helmer. Have you really the nerve to bring that up again?

Nora. Yes, Torvald, yes, you must do as I ask! You must let Krogstad keep his place at the bank!

Helmer. My dear Nora, his is the job I'm giving to Mrs. Linde.

Nora. Yes, that's terribly sweet of you. But you can get rid of one of the other clerks instead of Krogstad.

Helmer. Really, you're being incredibly obstinate. Just because you thoughtlessly promised to put in a word for him, you expect me to—

Nora. No, it isn't that, Helmer. It's for your own sake. That man writes for the most beastly newspapers—you said so yourself. He could do you tremendous harm. I'm so dreadfully frightened of him—

Helmer. Oh, I understand. Memories of the past. That's what's frightening you.

Nora. What do you mean?

Helmer. You're thinking of your father, aren't you?

Nora. Yes, yes. Of course. Just think what those dreadful men wrote in the papers about Papa! The most frightful slanders. I really believe it would have lost him his job if the Ministry hadn't sent you down to investigate, and you hadn't been so kind and helpful to him.

Helmer. But, my dear little Nora, there's a considerable difference between your father and me. Your father was not a man of unassailable reputation. But I am. And I hope to remain so all my life.

Nora. But no one knows what spiteful people may not dig up. We could be so peaceful and happy now, Torvald—we could be free from every worry—you and I and the children. Oh, please, Torvald, please—!

Helmer. The very fact of your pleading his cause makes it impossible for me to keep him. Everyone at the bank already knows that I intend to dismiss Krogstad. If the rumor got about that the new vice-president had allowed his wife to persuade him to change his mind—

Nora. Well, what then?

Helmer. Oh, nothing, nothing. As long as my little Miss Obstinate gets her way—! Do you expect me to make a laughingstock of myself before my entire staff—give people the idea that I am open to outside influence? Believe me, I'd soon feel the consequences! Besides—there's something else that makes it impossible for Krogstad to remain in the bank while I am its manager.

Nora. What is that?

Helmer. I might conceivably have allowed myself to ignore his moral obloquies[1]—

Nora. Yes, Torvald, surely?

Helmer. And I hear he's quite efficient at his job. But we—well, we were school

Stratford Festival

friends. It was one of those friendships that one enters into overhastily and so often comes to regret later in life. I might as well confess the truth. We—well, we're on Christian name terms. And the tactless idiot makes no attempt to conceal it when other people are present. On the contrary, he thinks it gives him the right to be familiar with me. He shows off the whole time, with "Torvald this" and "Torvald that." I can tell you, I find it damned annoying. If he stayed, he'd make my position intolerable.

Nora. Torvald, you can't mean this seriously.

Helmer. Oh? And why not?

Nora. But it's so petty.

Helmer. What did you say? Petty? You think *I* am petty?

Nora. No, Torvald dear, of course you're not. That's just why—

Helmer. Don't quibble! You call my motives petty. Then I must be petty too. Petty!

---

1. **obloquies** (äb′lə·kwēz): verbal abuse; censure.

I see. Well, I've had enough of this. (*goes to the door and calls into the hall*) Helen!

Nora. What are you going to do?

Helmer (*searching among his papers*). I'm going to settle this matter once and for all.

[*The* MAID *enters.*]

Helmer. Take this letter downstairs at once. Find a messenger and see that he delivers it. Immediately! The address is on the envelope. Here's the money.

Maid. Very good, sir. (*goes out with the letter*)

Helmer (*putting his papers in order*). There now, little Miss Obstinate.

Nora (*tensely*). Torvald—what was in that letter?

Helmer. Krogstad's dismissal.

Nora. Call her back, Torvald! There's still time. Oh, Torvald, call her back! Do it for my sake—for your own sake—for the children! Do you hear me, Torvald? Please do it! You don't realize what this may do to us all!

Helmer. Too late.

Nora. Yes. Too late.

Helmer. My dear Nora, I forgive you this anxiety. Though it is a bit of an insult to me. Oh, but it is! Isn't it an insult to imply that I should be frightened by the vindictiveness of a depraved hack journalist? But I forgive you, because it so charmingly testifies to the love you bear me. (*takes her in his arms*) Which is as it should be, my own dearest Nora. Let what will happen, happen. When the real crisis comes, you will not find me lacking in strength or courage. I am man enough to bear the burden for us both.

Nora (*fearfully*). What do you mean?

Helmer. The whole burden, I say—

Nora (*calmly*). I shall never let you do that.

Helmer. Very well. We shall share it, Nora—as man and wife. And that's as it should be. (*caresses her*) Are you happy now? There, there, there; don't look at me with those frightened little eyes. You're simply imagining things. You go ahead now and do your tarantella, and get some practice on that tambourine. I'll sit in my study and close the door. Then I won't hear anything, and you can make all the noise you want. (*turns in the doorway*) When Dr. Rank comes, tell him where to find me. (*He nods to her, goes into his room with his papers and closes the door.*)

Nora (*desperate with anxiety, stands as though transfixed, and whispers*). He said he'd do it. He will do it. He will do it, and nothing'll stop him. No, never that. I'd rather anything. There must be some escape—Some way out—!

[*The bell rings in the hall.*]

Nora. Dr. Rank—! Anything but that! Anything, I don't care—!

[*She passes her hand across her face, composes herself, walks across and opens the door to the hall.* DR. RANK *is standing there, hanging up his fur coat. During the following scene it begins to grow dark.*]

Nora. Good evening, Dr. Rank. I recognized your ring. But you mustn't go in to Torvald yet. I think he's busy.

Rank. And—you?

Nora (*as he enters the room and she closes the door behind him*). Oh, you know very well I've always time to talk to you.

Rank. Thank you. I shall avail myself of that privilege as long as I can.

Nora. What do you mean by that? As long as you *can*?

Rank. Yes. Does that frighten you?

Nora. Well, it's rather a curious expression. Is something going to happen?

Rank. Something I've been expecting to happen for a long time. But I didn't think it would happen quite so soon.

Nora (*seizes his arm*). What is it? Dr. Rank, you must tell me!

Rank (*sits down by the stove*). I'm on the way out. And there's nothing to be done about it.

Nora (*sighs with relief*). Oh, it's you—?

Rank. Who else? No, it's no good lying to oneself. I am the most wretched of all my patients, Mrs. Helmer. These last few days I've been going through the books of this poor body of mine, and I find I am bankrupt. Within a month I may be rotting up there in the churchyard.

Nora. Ugh, what a nasty way to talk!

Rank. The facts aren't exactly nice. But the worst is that there's so much else that's nasty that's got to come first. I've only one more test to make. When that's done I'll have a pretty accurate idea of when the final disintegration is likely to begin. I want to ask you a favor. Helmer's a sensitive chap, and I know how he hates anything ugly. I don't want him to visit me when I'm in hospital—

Nora. Oh but, Dr. Rank—

Rank. I don't want him there. On any pretext. I shan't have him allowed in. As soon as I know the worst, I'll send you my visiting card with a black cross on it, and then you'll know that the final filthy process has begun.

Nora. Really, you're being quite impossible this evening. And I did hope you'd be in a good mood.

Rank. With death on my hands? And all this to atone for someone else's sin? Is there justice in that? And in every single family, in one way or another, the same merciless law of retribution is at work—

Nora (*holds her hands to her ears*). Nonsense! Cheer up! Laugh!

Rank. Yes, you're right. Laughter's all the damned thing's fit for. My poor innocent spine must pay for the fun my father had as a gay young lieutenant.

Nora (*at the table, left*). You mean he was too fond of asparagus and *foie gras?*[2]

Rank. Yes; and truffles too.

Nora. Yes, of course, truffles, yes. And oysters too, I suppose?

Rank. Yes, oysters, oysters. Of course.

Nora. And all that port and champagne to wash them down. It's too sad that all those lovely things should affect one's spine.

Rank. Especially a poor spine that never got any pleasure out of them.

Nora. Oh yes, that's the saddest thing of all.

Rank (*looks searchingly at her*). Hm—

Nora (*after a moment*). Why did you smile?

Rank. No, it was you who laughed.

Nora. No, it was you who smiled, Dr. Rank!

Rank (*gets up*). You're a worse little rogue than I thought.

Nora. Oh, I'm full of stupid tricks today.

Rank. So it seems.

Nora (*puts both her hands on his shoulders*). Dear, dear Dr. Rank, you mustn't die and leave Torvald and me.

Rank. Oh, you'll soon get over it. Once one is gone, one is soon forgotten.

Nora (*looks at him anxiously*). Do you believe that?

Rank. One finds replacements, and then—

Nora. Who will find a replacement?

Rank. You and Helmer both will, when I am gone. You seem to have made a start already, haven't you? What was this Mrs. Linde doing here yesterday evening?

Nora. Aha! But surely you can't be jealous of poor Christine?

Rank. Indeed I am. She will be my successor in this house. When I have moved on, this lady will—

Nora. Ssh—don't speak so loud! She's in there!

---

2. *foie gras* (fwä grä): a pâté, or spread, made from goose liver.

Rank. Today again? You see!

Nora. She's only come to mend my dress. Good heavens, how unreasonable you are! (*sits on the sofa*) Be nice now, Dr. Rank. Tomorrow you'll see how beautifully I shall dance; and you must imagine that I'm doing it just for you. And for Torvald, of course; obviously. (*takes some things out of the box*) Dr. Rank, sit down here and I'll show you something.

Rank (*sits*). What's this?

Nora. Look here! Look!

Rank. Silk stockings!

Nora. Flesh-colored. Aren't they beautiful? It's very dark in here now, of course, but tomorrow—! No, no, no; only the soles. Oh well, I suppose you can look a bit higher if you want to.

Rank. Hm—

Nora. Why are you looking so critical? Don't you think they'll fit me?

Rank. I can't really give you a qualified opinion on that.

Nora (*looks at him for a moment*). Shame on you! (*flicks him on the ear with the stockings*) Take that. (*puts them back in the box*)

Rank. What other wonders are to be revealed to me?

Nora. I shan't show you anything else. You're being naughty.

[*She hums a little and looks among the things in the box.*]

Rank (*after a short silence*). When I sit here like this being so intimate with you, I can't think—I cannot imagine what would have become of me if I had never entered this house.

Nora (*smiles*). Yes, I think you enjoy being with us, don't you?

Rank (*more quietly, looking into the middle distance*). And now to have to leave it all—

Nora. Nonsense. You're not leaving us.

Rank (*as before*). And not to be able to leave even the most wretched token of gratitude behind; hardly even a passing sense of loss; only an empty place, to be filled by the next comer.

Nora. Suppose I were to ask you to—? No—

Rank. To do what?

Nora. To give me proof of your friendship—

Rank. Yes, yes?

Nora. No, I mean—to do me a very great service—

Rank. Would you really for once grant me that happiness?

Nora. But you've no idea what it is.

Rank. Very well, tell me, then.

Nora. No, but, Dr. Rank, I can't. It's far too much—I want your help and advice, and I want you to do something for me.

Rank. The more the better. I've no idea what it can be. But tell me. You do trust me, don't you?

Nora. Oh, yes, more than anyone. You're my best and truest friend. Otherwise I couldn't tell you. Well then, Dr. Rank—there's something you must help me to prevent. You know how much Torvald loves me—he'd never hesitate for an instant to lay down his life for me—

Rank (*leans over towards her*). Nora—do you think he is the only one—?

Nora (*with a slight start*). What do you mean?

Rank. Who would gladly lay down his life for you?

Nora (*sadly*). Oh, I see.

Rank. I swore to myself I would let you know that before I go. I shall never have a better opportunity. . . . Well, Nora, now you know that. And now you also know that you can trust me as you can trust nobody else.

Nora (*rises; calmly and quietly*). Let me pass, please.

Rank (*makes room for her but remains seated*). Nora—

Nora (*in the doorway to the hall*). Helen, bring the lamp. (*goes over to the stove*) Oh, dear Dr. Rank, this was really horrid of you.

Rank (*gets up*). That I have loved you as deeply as anyone else has? Was that horrid of me?

Nora. No—but that you should go and tell me. That was quite unnecessary—

Rank. What do you mean? Did you know, then—?

[*The* MAID *enters with the lamp, puts it on the table and goes out.*]

Rank. Nora—Mrs. Helmer—I am asking you, did you know this?

Nora. Oh, what do I know, what did I know, what didn't I know—I really can't say. How could you be so stupid, Dr. Rank? Everything was so nice.

Rank. Well, at any rate now you know that I am ready to serve you, body and soul. So—please continue.

Nora (*looks at him*). After this?

Rank. Please tell me what it is.

Nora. I can't possibly tell you now.

Rank. Yes, yes! You mustn't punish me like this. Let me be allowed to do what I can for you.

Nora. You can't do anything for me now. Anyway, I don't need any help. It was only my imagination—you'll see. Yes, really. Honestly. (*sits in the rocking chair, looks at him and smiles*) Well, upon my word you *are* a fine gentleman, Dr. Rank. Aren't you ashamed of yourself, now that the lamp's been lit?

Rank. Frankly, no. But perhaps I ought to say—*adieu?*

Nora. Of course not. You will naturally continue to visit us as before. You know quite well how Torvald depends on your company.

Rank. Yes, but you?

Nora. Oh, I always think it's enormous fun having you here.

Rank. That was what misled me. You're a riddle to me, you know. I'd often felt you'd just as soon be with me as with Helmer.

Nora. Well, you see, there are some people whom one loves, and others whom it's almost more fun to be with.

Rank. Oh yes, there's some truth in that.

Nora. When I was at home, of course I loved Papa best. But I always used to think it was terribly amusing to go down and talk to the servants; because they never told me what I ought to do; and they were such fun to listen to.

Rank. I see. So I've taken their place?

Nora (*jumps up and runs over to him*). Oh, dear, sweet Dr. Rank, I didn't mean that at all. But I'm sure you understand—I feel the same about Torvald as I did about Papa.

Maid (*enters from the hall*). Excuse me, madam. (*whispers to her and hands her a visiting card*)

Nora (*glances at the card*). Oh! (*puts it quickly in her pocket*)

Rank. Anything wrong?

Nora. No, no, nothing at all. It's just something that—it's my new dress.

Rank. What? But your costume is lying over there.

Nora. Oh—that, yes—but there's another— I ordered it specially—Torvald mustn't know—

Rank. Ah, so that's your big secret?

Nora. Yes, yes. Go in and talk to him—he's in his study—keep him talking for a bit—

Rank. Don't worry. He won't get away from me. (*goes into* HELMER's *study*)

Nora (*to the* MAID). Is he waiting in the kitchen?

Maid. Yes, madam, he came up the back way—

Nora. But didn't you tell him I had a visitor?

Maid. Yes, but he wouldn't go.

Nora. Wouldn't go?

Maid. No, madam, not until he'd spoken with you.

Nora. Very well, show him in; but quietly. Helen, you mustn't tell anyone about this. It's a surprise for my husband.

Maid. Very good, madam. I understand. (*goes*)

Nora. It's happening. It's happening after all. No, no, no, it can't happen, it mustn't happen.

[*She walks across and bolts the door of* HELMER's *study. The* MAID *opens the door from the hall to admit* KROGSTAD, *and closes it behind him. He is wearing an overcoat, heavy boots and a fur cap.*]

Nora (*goes towards him*). Speak quietly. My husband's at home.

Krogstad. Let him hear.

Nora. What do you want from me?

Krogstad. Information.

Nora. Hurry up, then. What is it?

Krogstad. I suppose you know I've been given the sack.

Nora. I couldn't stop it, Mr. Krogstad. I did my best for you, but it didn't help.

Krogstad. Does your husband love you so little? He knows what I can do to you, and yet he dares to—

Nora. Surely you don't imagine I told him?

Krogstad. No, I didn't really think you had. It wouldn't have been like my old friend Torvald Helmer to show that much courage—

Nora. Mr. Krogstad, I'll trouble you to speak respectfully of my husband.

Krogstad. Don't worry, I'll show him all the respect he deserves. But since you're so anxious to keep this matter hushed up, I presume you're better informed than you were yesterday of the gravity of what you've done?

Nora. I've learned more than you could ever teach me.

Krogstad. Yes, a bad lawyer like me—

Nora. What do you want from me?

Krogstad. I just wanted to see how things were with you, Mrs. Helmer. I've been thinking about you all day. Even duns and hack journalists have hearts, you know.

Nora. Show some heart, then. Think of my little children.

Krogstad. Have you and your husband thought of mine? Well, let's forget that. I just wanted to tell you, you don't need to take this business too seriously. I'm not going to take any action, for the present.

Nora. Oh, no—you won't, will you? I knew it.

Krogstad. It can all be settled quite amicably. There's no need for it to become public. We'll keep it among the three of us.

Nora. My husband must never know about this.

Krogstad. How can you stop him? Can you pay the balance of what you owe me?

Nora. Not immediately.

Krogstad. Have you any means of raising the money during the next few days?

Nora. None that I would care to use.

Krogstad. Well, it wouldn't have helped anyway. However much money you offered me now I wouldn't give you back that paper.

Nora. What are you going to do with it?

Krogstad. Just keep it. No one else need ever hear about it. So in case you were thinking of doing anything desperate—

Nora. I am.

Krogstad. Such as running away—

Nora. I am.

Krostad. Or anything more desperate—

Nora. How did you know?

Krogstad. —just give up the idea.

Nora. How did you know?

ISABELLA STEWART GARDNER, JOHN SINGER SARGENT (1856–1925).

Krogstad. Most of us think of that at first. I did. But I hadn't the courage—

Nora (*dully*). Neither have I.

Krogstad (*relieved*). It's true, isn't it? You haven't the courage, either?

Nora. No. I haven't. I haven't.

Krogstad. It'd be a stupid thing to do anyway. Once the first little domestic explosion is over . . . I've got a letter in my pocket here addressed to your husband—

Nora. Telling him everything?

Krogstad. As delicately as possible.

Nora (*quickly*). He must never see that letter. Tear it up. I'll find the money somehow—

Krogstad. I'm sorry, Mrs. Helmer. I thought I'd explained—

Nora. Oh, I don't mean the money I owe you. Let me know how much you want from my husband, and I'll find it for you.

Krogstad. I'm not asking your husband for money.

Nora. What do you want, then?

Krogstad. I'll tell you. I want to get on my feet again, Mrs. Helmer. I want to get to the top. And your husband's going to help me. For eighteen months now my record's been clean. I've been in hard straits all that time: I was content to fight my way back inch by inch. Now I've been chucked back into the mud, and I'm not going to be satisfied with just getting back my job. I'm going to get to the top, I tell you. I'm going to get back into the bank, and it's going to be higher up. Your husband's going to create a new job for me—

Nora. He'll never do that!

Krogstad. Oh yes, he will. I know him. He won't dare to risk a scandal. And once I'm in there with him, you'll see! Within a year I'll be his right-hand man. It'll be Nils Krogstad who'll be running that bank, not Torvald Helmer!

Nora. That will never happen.

Krogstad. Are you thinking of—?

Nora. Now I *have* the courage.

Krogstad. Oh, you can't frighten me. A pampered little pretty like you—

Nora. You'll see! You'll see!

Krogstad. Under the ice? Down in the cold, black water? And then, in the spring, to float up again, ugly, unrecognizable, hairless—?

Nora. You can't frighten me.

Krogstad. And you can't frighten me. People don't do such things, Mrs. Helmer. And anyway, what'd be the use? I've got him in my pocket.

Nora. But afterwards? When I'm no longer—?

Krogstad. Have you forgotten that then your reputation will be in my hands?

[*She looks at him speechlessly.*]

Krogstad. Well, I've warned you. Don't do anything silly. When Helmer's read my letter, he'll get in touch with me. And remember, it's your husband who has forced me to act like this. And for that I'll never forgive him. Goodbye, Mrs. Helmer. (*He goes out through the hall.*)

Nora (*runs to the hall door, opens it a few inches and listens*). He's going. He's not going to give him the letter. Oh, no, no, it couldn't possibly happen. (*opens the door, a little wider*) What's he doing? Standing outside the front door. He's not going downstairs. Is he changing his mind? Yes, he—!

[*A letter falls into the letter box. KROG-STAD's footsteps die away down the stairs.*]

Nora (*with a stifled cry, runs across the room towards the table by the sofa; a pause*). In the letter box. (*steals timidly over towards the hall door*) There it is! Oh, Torvald, Torvald! Now we're lost!

Mrs. Linde (*enters from the nursery with NORA's costume*). Well, I've done the best I can. Shall we see how it looks—?

Nora (*whispers hoarsely*). Christine, come here.

Mrs. Linde (*throws the dress on the sofa*). What's wrong with you? You look as though you'd seen a ghost!

Nora. Come here. Do you see that letter? There—look—through the glass of the letter box.

Mrs. Linde. Yes, yes, I see it.

Nora. That letter's from Krogstad—

Mrs. Linde. Nora! It was Krogstad who lent you the money!

Nora. Yes. And now Torvald's going to discover everything.

Mrs. Linde. Oh, believe me, Nora, it'll be best for you both.

Nora. You don't know what's happened. I've committed a forgery—

Mrs. Linde. But, for heaven's sake—!

Nora. Christine, all I want is for you to be my witness.

Mrs. Linde. What do you mean? Witness what?

Nora. If I should go out of my mind—and it might easily happen—

Mrs. Linde. Nora!

Nora. Or if anything else should happen to me—so that I wasn't here any longer—

Mrs. Linde. Nora, Nora, you don't know what you're saying!

Nora. If anyone should try to take the blame, and say it was all his fault—you understand—?

Mrs. Linde. Yes, yes—but how can you think—?

Nora. Then you must testify that it isn't true, Christine. I'm not mad—I know exactly what I'm saying—and I'm telling you, no one else knows anything about this. I did it entirely on my own. Remember that.

Mrs. Linde. All right. But I simply don't understand—

Nora. Oh, how could you understand? A—miracle—is about to happen.

Mrs. Linde. Miracle?

Nora. Yes. A miracle. But it's so frightening, Christine. It mustn't happen, not for anything in the world.

Mrs. Linde. I'll go over and talk to Krogstad.

Nora. Don't go near him. He'll only do something to hurt you.

Mrs. Linde. Once upon a time he'd have done anything for my sake.

Nora. He?

Mrs. Linde. Where does he live?

Nora. Oh, how should I know—? Oh yes, wait a moment—! (*feels in her pocket*) Here's his card. But the letter, the letter—!

Helmer (*from his study, knocks on the door*). Nora!

Nora (*cries in alarm*). What is it?

Helmer. Now, now, don't get alarmed. We're not coming in—you've closed the door. Are you trying on your costume?

Nora. Yes, yes—I'm trying on my costume. I'm going to look so pretty for you, Torvald.

Mrs. Linde (*who has been reading the card*). Why, he lives just round the corner.

Nora. Yes; but it's no use. There's nothing to be done now. The letter's lying there in the box.

Mrs. Linde. And your husband has the key?

Nora. Yes, he always keeps it.

Mrs. Linde. Krogstad must ask him to send the letter back unread. He must find some excuse—

Nora. But Torvald always opens the box at just about this time—

Mrs. Linde. You must stop him. Go in and keep him talking. I'll be back as quickly as I can.

[*She hurries out through the hall.*]

Nora (*goes over to* HELMER's *door, opens it and peeps in*). Torvald!

Helmer (*offstage*). Well, may a man enter his own drawing room again? Come on, Rank, now we'll see what—(*in the doorway*) But what's this?

Nora. What, Torvald dear?

Helmer. Rank's been preparing me for some great transformation scene.

Rank (*in the doorway*). So I understood. But I seem to have been mistaken.

Nora. Yes, no one's to be allowed to see me before tomorrow night.

Helmer. But, my dear Nora, you look quite worn out. Have you been practicing too hard?

Nora. No, I haven't practiced at all yet.

Helmer. Well, you must.

Nora. Yes, Torvald, I must, I know. But I can't get anywhere without your help. I've completely forgotten everything.

Helmer. Oh, we'll soon put that to rights.

Nora. Yes, help me, Torvald. Promise me you will? Oh, I'm so nervous. All those people—! You must forget everything except me this evening. You mustn't think of business—I won't even let you touch a pen. Promise me, Torvald?

Helmer. I promise. This evening I shall think of nothing but you—my poor, helpless little darling. Oh, there's just one thing I must see to—(*goes towards the hall door*)

Nora. What do you want out there?

Helmer. I'm only going to see if any letters have come.

Nora. No, Torvald, no!

Helmer. Why what's the matter?

Nora. Torvald, I beg you. There's nothing there.

Helmer. Well, I'll just make sure.

[*He moves towards the door.* NORA *runs to the piano and plays the first bars of the Tarantella.*]

Helmer (*at the door, turns*). Aha!

Nora. I can't dance tomorrow if I don't practice with you now.

Helmer (*goes over to her*). Are you really so frightened, Nora dear?

Nora. Yes, terribly frightened. Let me start

practicing now, at once—we've still time before dinner. Oh, do sit down and play for me, Torvald dear. Correct me, lead me, the way you always do.

Helmer. Very well, my dear, if you wish it.

[*He sits down at the piano.* NORA *seizes the tambourine and a long multicolored shawl from the cardboard box, wraps the shawl hastily around her, then takes a quick leap into the center of the room and cries:*]

Nora. Play for me! I want to dance!

[HELMER *plays and* NORA *dances.* DR. RANK *stands behind* HELMER *at the piano and watches her.*]

Helmer (*as he plays*). Slower, slower!

Nora. I can't!

Helmer. Not so violently, Nora.

Nora. I must!

Helmer (*stops playing*). No, no, this won't do at all.

Nora (*laughs and swings her tambourine*). Isn't that what I told you?

Rank. Let me play for her.

Helmer (*gets up*). Yes, would you? Then it'll be easier for me to show her.

[RANK *sits down at the piano and plays.* NORA *dances more and more wildly.* HELMER *has stationed himself by the stove and tries repeatedly to correct her, but she seems not to hear him. Her hair works loose and falls over her shoulders; she ignores it and continues to dance.* MRS. LINDE *enters.*]

Mrs. Linde (*stands in the doorway as though tongue-tied*). Ah—!

Nora (*as she dances*). Oh, Christine, we're having such fun!

Helmer. But, Nora darling, you're dancing as if your life depended on it.

Nora. It does.

Helmer. Rank, stop it! This is sheer lunacy. Stop it, I say!

[RANK *ceases playing.* NORA *suddenly stops dancing.*]

Helmer (*goes over to her*). I'd never have believed it. You've forgotten everything I taught you.

Nora (*throws away the tambourine*). You see!

Helmer. I'll have to show you every step.

Nora. You see how much I need you! You must show me every step of the way. Right to the end of the dance. Promise me you will, Torvald?

Helmer. Never fear. I will.

Nora. You mustn't think about anything but me—today or tomorrow. Don't open any letters—don't even open the letter box—

Helmer. Aha, you're still worried about that fellow—

Nora. Oh, yes, yes, him too.

Helmer. Nora, I can tell from the way you're behaving, there's a letter from him already lying there.

Nora. I don't know. I think so. But you mustn't read it now. I don't want anything ugly to come between us till it's all over.

Rank (*quietly to* HELMER). Better give her her way.

Helmer (*puts his arm round her*). My child shall have her way. But tomorrow night, when your dance is over—

Nora. Then you will be free.

Maid (*appears in the doorway, right*). Dinner is served, madam.

Nora. Put out some champagne, Helen.

Maid. Very good, madam. (*goes*)

Helmer. I say! What's this, a banquet?

Nora. We'll drink champagne until dawn! (*calls*) And, Helen! Put out some macaroons! Lots of macaroons—for once!

Helmer (*takes her hands in his*). Now, now, now. Don't get so excited. Where's my little songbird, the one I know?

Nora. All right. Go and sit down—and you, too, Dr. Rank. I'll be with you in a minute. Christine, you must help me put my hair up.

Rank (*quietly, as they go*). There's nothing wrong, is there? I mean, she isn't—er—expecting—?

Helmer. Good heavens no, my dear chap. She just gets scared like a child sometimes—I told you before—

[*They go out, right.*]

Nora. Well?

Mrs. Linde. He's left town.

Nora. I saw it from your face.

Mrs. Linde. He'll be back tomorrow evening. I left a note for him.

Nora. You needn't have bothered. You can't

stop anything now. Anyway, it's wonderful really, in a way—sitting here and waiting for the miracle to happen.

Mrs. Linde. Waiting for what?

Nora. Oh, you wouldn't understand. Go in and join them. I'll be with you in a moment.

[MRS. LINDE *goes into the dining room.*]

Nora (*stands for a moment as though collecting herself. Then she looks at her*

watch). Five o'clock. Seven hours till midnight. Then another twenty-four hours till midnight tomorrow. And then the tarantella will be finished. Twenty-four and seven? Thirty-one hours to live.

Helmer (*appears in the doorway, right*). What's happened to my little songbird?

Nora (*runs to him with her arms wide*). Your songbird is here!

First Thoughts

How do you think Torvald will respond when he reads the letter from Krogstad?

Identifying Facts

1. What does Nora learn from Dr. Rank that changes her mind about asking him for help?

2. When Krogstad visits Nora, he reveals that he does not want more money. What does he want?

3. What offer does Mrs. Linde make that encourages Nora? What makes Mrs. Linde think she has the power to help?

Interpreting Meanings

1. Do you agree with Nora that Torvald's reasons for firing Krogstad are ''petty''? Why or why not?

2. Dr. Rank has inherited a fatal illness from his father. Bitterly, he tells Nora that ''in every single family, in one way or another, the same merciless law of retribution is at work.'' In what way is retribution for past deeds at work in the Helmer family?

3. Near the end of Act 2, Nora believes that a ''miracle'' will happen. What is the miracle that she hopes for?

4. **Foreshadowing** is the use of clues to hint at what is going to happen later in the plot. What do you anticipate will happen?

Applying Meanings

Nora desperately thinks of ways to postpone the time when her husband will read the letter from Krogstad. Think of a time when you, or someone you know, tried to avoid accepting consequences for something unpleasant. Do you believe that the truth should always come out?

Critical Writing Response

Interpreting Symbolism. Letters and letter boxes play an important part in *A Doll's House*. State three or more ways in which letters or messages help build **suspense** in *A Doll's House*. How does Ibsen use letters as a **symbol**—a physical representation of something abstract—of the fact that Nora and Torvald have not communicated honestly over the years? Think about the way Nora repeatedly tries to keep messages from being sent or received.

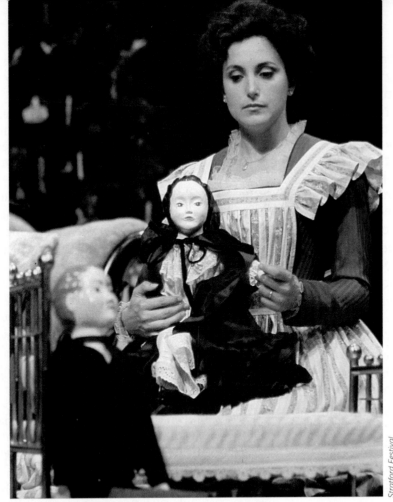

Act 3 opens with a sense of tension and anticipation.

❓ *Do you think Nora's "miracle" will occur? Do you think she will be saved from the consequences of her actions?*

ACT 3

The same room. The table which was formerly by the sofa has been moved into the center of the room; the chairs surround it as before. A lamp is burning on the table. The door to the hall stands open. Dance music can be heard from the floor above. MRS. LINDE is seated at the table, absentmindedly glancing through a book. She is trying to read, but seems unable to keep her mind on it. More than once she turns and listens anxiously towards the front door.

Mrs. Linde (*looks at her watch*). Not here yet. There's not much time left. Please God he hasn't—! (*listens again*) Ah, here he is.

[*Goes out into the hall and cautiously opens the front door. Footsteps can be heard softly ascending the stairs.*]

Mrs. Linde (*whispers*). Come in. There's no one here.

Krogstad (*in the doorway*). I found a note from you at my lodgings. What does this mean?

A Doll's House, Act 3 **1109**

Mrs. Linde. I must speak with you.

Krogstad. Oh? And must our conversation take place in this house?

Mrs. Linde. We couldn't meet at my place; my room has no separate entrance. Come in. We're quite alone. The maid's asleep, and the Helmers are at the dance upstairs.

Krogstad (*comes into the room*). Well, well! So the Helmers are dancing this evening? Are they indeed?

Mrs. Linde. Yes, why not?

Krogstad. True enough. Why not?

Mrs. Linde. Well, Krogstad. You and I must have a talk together.

Krogstad. Have we two anything further to discuss?

Mrs. Linde. We have a great deal to discuss.

Krogstad. I wasn't aware of it.

Mrs. Linde. That's because you've never really understood me.

Krogstad. Was there anything to understand? It's the old story, isn't it—a woman chucking a man because something better turns up?

Mrs. Linde. Do you really think I'm so utterly heartless? You think it was easy for me to give you up?

Krogstad. Wasn't it?

Mrs. Linde. Oh, Nils, did you really believe that?

Krogstad. Then why did you write to me the way you did?

Mrs. Linde. I had to. Since I had to break with you, I thought it my duty to destroy all the feelings you had for me.

Krogstad (*clenches his fists*). So that was it. And you did this for money!

Mrs. Linde. You mustn't forget I had a helpless mother to take care of, and two little brothers. We couldn't wait for you, Nils. It would have been so long before you'd have had enough to support us.

Krogstad. Maybe. But you had no right to

cast me off for someone else.

Mrs. Linde. Perhaps not. I've often asked myself that.

Krogstad (*more quietly*). When I lost you, it was just as though all solid ground had been swept from under my feet. Look at me. Now I'm a shipwrecked man, clinging to a spar.[1]

Mrs. Linde. Help may be near at hand.

Krogstad. It was near. But then you came, and stood between it and me.

Mrs. Linde. I didn't know, Nils. No one told me till today that this job I'd found was yours.

Krogstad. I believe you, since you say so. But now you know, won't you give it up?

Mrs. Linde. No—because it wouldn't help you even if I did.

Krogstad. Wouldn't it? I'd do it all the same.

Mrs. Linde. I've learned to look at things practically. Life and poverty have taught me that.

Krogstad. And life has taught me to distrust fine words.

Mrs. Linde. Then it has taught you a useful lesson. But surely you still believe in actions?

Krogstad. What do you mean?

Mrs. Linde. You said you were like a shipwrecked man clinging to a spar.

Krogstad. I have good reason to say it.

Mrs. Linde. I'm in the same position as you. No one to care about, no one to care for.

Krogstad. You made your own choice.

Mrs. Linde. I had no choice—then.

Krogstad. Well?

Mrs. Linde. Nils, suppose we two shipwrecked souls could join hands?

Krogstad. What are you saying?

---

1. **spar:** a pole or mast that supports or extends the sail of a ship.

Mrs. Linde. Castaways have a better chance of survival together than on their own.

Krogstad. Christine!

Mrs. Linde. Why do you suppose I came to this town?

Krogstad. You mean—you came because of me?

Mrs. Linde. I must work if I'm to find life worth living. I've always worked, for as long as I can remember. It's been the greatest joy of my life—my only joy. But now I'm alone in the world, and I feel so dreadfully lost and empty. There's no joy in working just for oneself. Oh, Nils, give me something—someone—to work for.

Krogstad. I don't believe all that. You're just being hysterical and romantic. You want to find an excuse for self-sacrifice.

Mrs. Linde. Have you ever known me to be hysterical?

Krogstad. You mean you really—? Is it possible? Tell me—you know all about my past?

Mrs. Linde. Yes.

Krogstad. And you know what people think of me here?

Mrs. Linde. You said just now that with me you might have become a different person.

Krogstad. I know I could have.

Mrs. Linde. Couldn't it still happen?

Krogstad. Christine—do you really mean this? Yes—you do—I see it in your face. Have you really the courage—?

Mrs. Linde. I need someone to be a mother to; and your children need a mother. And you and I need each other. I believe in you, Nils. I am afraid of nothing—with you.

Krogstad (*clasps her hands*). Thank you, Christine—thank you! Now I shall make the world believe in me as you do! Oh—but I'd forgotten—

Mrs. Linde (*listens*). Ssh! The tarantella! Go quickly, go!

Krogstad. Why? What is it?

Mrs. Linde. You hear that dance? As soon as it's finished, they'll be coming down.

Krogstad. All right, I'll go. It's no good, Christine. I'd forgotten—you don't know what I've just done to the Helmers.

Mrs. Linde. Yes, Nils. I know.

Krogstad. And yet you'd still have the courage to—?

Mrs. Linde. I know what despair can drive a man like you to.

Krogstad. Oh, if only I could undo this!

Mrs. Linde. You can. Your letter is still lying in the box.

Krogstad. Are you sure?

Mrs. Linde. Quite sure. But—

Krogstad (*looks searchingly at her*). Is that why you're doing this? You want to save your friend at any price? Tell me the truth. Is that the reason?

Mrs. Linde. Nils, a woman who has sold herself once for the sake of others doesn't make the same mistake again.

Krogstad. I shall demand my letter back.

Mrs. Linde. No, no.

Krogstad. Of course I shall. I shall stay here till Helmer comes down. I'll tell him he must give me back my letter—I'll say it was only to do with my dismissal, and that I don't want him to read it—

Mrs. Linde. No, Nils, you mustn't ask for that letter back.

Krogstad. But—tell me—wasn't that the real reason you asked me to come here?

Mrs. Linde. Yes—at first, when I was frightened. But a day has passed since then, and in that time I've seen incredible things happen in this house. Helmer must know the truth. This unhappy secret of Nora's must be revealed. They must come to a full understanding. There must be an end of all these shiftings and evasions.

Krogstad. Very well. If you're prepared to risk it. But one thing I can do—and at once—

Mrs. Linde (*listens*). Hurry! Go, go! The dance is over. We aren't safe here another moment.

Krogstad. I'll wait for you downstairs.

Mrs. Linde. Yes, do. You can see me home.

Krogstad. I've never been so happy in my life before!

[*He goes out through the front door. The door leading from the room into the hall remains open.*]

Mrs. Linde (*tidies the room a little and gets her hat and coat*). What a change! Oh, what a change! Someone to work for—to live for! A home to bring joy into! I won't let this chance of happiness slip through my fingers. Oh, why don't they come? (*listens*) Ah, here they are. I must get my coat on.

[*She takes her hat and coat.* HELMER's *and* NORA's *voices become audible outside. A key is turned in the lock and* HELMER *leads* NORA *almost forcibly into the hall. She is dressed in an Italian costume with a large black shawl. He is in evening dress, with a black coat.*]

Nora (*still in the doorway, resisting him*). No, no, no—not in here! I want to go back upstairs. I don't want to leave so early.

Helmer. But my dearest Nora—

Nora. Oh, please, Torvald, please! Just another hour!

Helmer. Not another minute, Nora, my sweet. You know what we agreed. Come along, now. Into the drawing room. You'll catch cold if you stay out here.

[*He leads her, despite her efforts to resist him, gently into the room.*]

Mrs. Linde. Good evening.

Nora. Christine!

Midland Community Theatre at Theatre Midland

Helmer. Oh, hullo, Mrs. Linde. You still here?

Mrs. Linde. Please forgive me. I did so want to see Nora in her costume.

Nora. Have you been sitting here waiting for me?

Mrs. Linde. Yes. I got here too late, I'm afraid. You'd already gone up. And I felt I really couldn't go home without seeing you.

Helmer (*takes off* NORA's *shawl*). Well, take a good look at her. She's worth looking at, don't you think? Isn't she beautiful, Mrs. Linde?

Mrs. Linde. Oh, yes, indeed—

Helmer. Isn't she unbelievably beautiful? Everyone at the party said so. But dreadfully stubborn she is, bless her pretty little heart. What's to be done about that? Would you believe it, I practically had to use force to get her away!

Nora. Oh, Torvald, you're going to regret not letting me stay—just half an hour longer.

Helmer. Hear that, Mrs. Linde? She dances her tarantella—makes a roaring success—and very well deserved—though possibly a trifle too realistic—more so than was aesthetically necessary, strictly speaking. But never mind that. Main thing is—she had a success—roaring success. Was I going to let her stay on after that and spoil the impression? No, thank you! I took my beautiful little Capri² signorina—my capricious little Capricienne, what?—under my arm—a swift round of the ballroom, a curtsy to the company, and, as they say in novels, the beautiful apparition disappeared! An exit should always be dramatic, Mrs. Linde. But unfortunately that's just what I can't get Nora to realize. I say, it's hot in here. (*throws his cloak on a chair and opens the door to his study*) What's this? It's dark in here. Ah, yes, of course—excuse me. (*goes in and lights a couple of candles*)

Nora (*whispers softly, breathlessly*). Well?

Mrs. Linde (*quietly*). I've spoken to him.

Nora. Yes?

Mrs. Linde. Nora—you must tell your husband everything.

Nora (*dully*). I knew it.

Mrs. Linde. You have nothing to fear from Krogstad. But you must tell him.

Nora. I shan't tell him anything.

Mrs. Linde. Then the letter will.

Nora. Thank you, Christine. Now I know what I must do. Ssh!

Helmer (*returns*). Well, Mrs. Linde, finished admiring her?

Mrs. Linde. Yes. Now I must say good night.

2. **Capri . . . Capricienne:** "Capri signorina" and "Capricienne" both refer to a lady from Capri, a small island off the coat of Italy. Helmer is playing on the similarities in the words *capricious* and *Capricienne.*

Helmer. Oh, already? Does this knitting belong to you?

Mrs. Linde (*takes it*). Thank you, yes. I nearly forgot it.

Helmer. You knit, then?

Mrs. Linde. Why, yes.

Helmer. Know what? You ought to take up embroidery.

Mrs. Linde. Oh? Why?

Helmer. It's much prettier. Watch me, now. You hold the embroidery in your left hand, like this, and then you take the needle in your right hand and go in and out in a slow, easy movement—like this. I am right, aren't I?

Mrs. Linde. Yes, I'm sure—

Helmer. But knitting, now—that's an ugly business—can't help it. Look—arms all huddled up—great clumsy needles going up and down—I say that really was a magnificent champagne they served us.

Mrs. Linde. Well, good night, Nora. And stop being stubborn! Remember!

Helmer. Quite right, Mrs. Linde!

Mrs. Linde. Good night, Mr. Helmer.

Helmer (*accompanies her to the door*). Good night, good night! I hope you'll manage to get home all right? I'd gladly—but you haven't far to go, have you? Good night, good night.

[*She goes. He closes the door behind her and returns.*]

Helmer. Well, we've got rid of her at last. Dreadful bore that woman is!

Nora. Aren't you very tired, Torvald?

Helmer. No, not in the least.

Nora. Aren't you sleepy?

Helmer. Not a bit. On the contrary, I feel extraordinarily exhilarated. But what about you? Yes, you look very sleepy and tired.

Nora. Yes, I am very tired. Soon I shall sleep.

Helmer. You see, you see! How right I was not to let you stay longer!

Nora. Oh, you're always right, whatever you do.

Helmer (*kisses her on the forehead*). Now my little songbird's talking just like a real big human being. I say, did you notice how cheerful Rank was this evening?

Nora. Oh? Was he? I didn't have a chance to speak with him.

Helmer. I hardly did. But I haven't seen him in such a jolly mood for ages. (*looks at her for a moment, then comes closer*) I say, it's nice to get back to one's home again, and be all alone with you. Upon my word, you're a distractingly beautiful young woman.

Nora. Don't look at me like that, Torvald!

Helmer. What, not look at my most treasured possession? At all this wonderful beauty that's mine, mine alone, all mine.

Nora (*goes round to the other side of the table*). You mustn't talk to me like that tonight.

Helmer (*follows her*). You've still the tarantella in your blood, I see. And that makes you even more desirable. Listen! Now the other guests are beginning to go. (*more quietly*) Nora—soon the whole house will be absolutely quiet.

Nora. Yes, I hope so.

Helmer. Yes, my beloved Nora, of course you do! You know—when I'm out with you among other people like we were tonight, do you know why I say so little to you, why I keep so aloof from you, and just throw you an occasional glance? Do you know why I do that? It's because I pretend to myself that you're my secret mistress, my clandestine little sweetheart, and that nobody knows there's anything at all between us.

Nora. Oh, yes, yes, yes—I know you never think of anything but me.

Helmer. And then when we're about to go, and I wrap the shawl round your lovely young shoulders, over this wonderful curve of your neck—then I pretend to myself that you are my young bride, that we've just come from the wedding, that I'm taking you to my house for the first time—that, for the first time, I am alone with you—quite alone with you, as you stand there young and trembling and beautiful. All evening I've had no eyes for anyone but you. When I saw you dance the tarantella, like a huntress, a temptress, my blood grew hot, I couldn't stand it any longer! That was why I seized you and dragged you down here with me—

Nora. Leave me, Torvald! Get away from me! I don't want all this.

Helmer. What? Now, Nora, you're joking with me. Don't want, don't want—? Aren't I your husband?

[*There is a knock on the front door.*]

Nora (*starts*). What was that?

Helmer (*goes towards the hall*). Who is it?

Dr. Rank (*outside*). It's me. May I come in for a moment?

Helmer (*quietly, annoyed*). Oh, what does he want now? (*calls*) Wait a moment. (*walks over and opens the door*) Well! Nice of you not to go by without looking in.

Rank. I thought I heard your voice, so I felt I had to say goodbye. (*His eyes travel swiftly around the room.*) Ah, yes—these dear rooms, how well I know them. What a happy, peaceful home you two have.

Helmer. You seemed to be having a pretty happy time yourself upstairs.

Rank. Indeed I did. Why not? Why shouldn't one make the most of this world? As much as one can, and for as long as one can. The wine was excellent—

Helmer. Especially the champagne.

Rank. You noticed that, too? It's almost incredible how much I managed to get down.

Nora. Torvald drank a lot of champagne, too, this evening.

Rank. Oh?

Nora. Yes. It always makes him merry afterwards.

Rank. Well, why shouldn't a man have a merry evening after a well-spent day?

Helmer. Well-spent? Oh, I don't know that I can claim that.

Rank (*slaps him across the back*). I can, though, my dear fellow!

Nora. Yes, of course, Dr. Rank—you've been carrying out a scientific experiment today, haven't you?

Rank. Exactly.

Helmer. Scientific experiment! Those are big words for my little Nora to use!

Nora. And may I congratulate you on the finding?

Rank. You may indeed.

Nora. It was good then?

Rank. The best possible finding—both for the doctor and the patient. Certainty.

Nora (*quickly*). Certainty?

Rank. Absolute certainty. So aren't I entitled to have a merry evening after that?

Nora. Yes, Dr. Rank. You were quite right to.

Helmer. I agree. Provided you don't have to regret it tomorrow.

Rank. Well, you never get anything in this life without paying for it.

Nora. Dr. Rank—you like masquerades, don't you?

Rank. Yes, if the disguises are sufficiently amusing.

Nora. Tell me. What shall we two wear at the next masquerade?

Helmer. You little gadabout! Are you thinking about the next one already?

Rank. We two? Yes, I'll tell you. You must go as the Spirit of Happiness—

Helmer. You try to think of a costume that'll convey that.

Rank. Your wife need only appear as her normal, everyday self—

Helmer. Quite right! Well said! But what are you going to be? Have you decided that?

Rank. Yes, my dear friend. I have decided that.

Helmer. Well?

Rank. At the next masquerade, I shall be invisible.

Helmer. Well, that's a funny idea.

Rank. There's a big, black hat—haven't you heard of the invisible hat? Once it's over your head, no one can see you any more.

Helmer (*represses a smile*). Ah yes, of course.

Rank. But I'm forgetting what I came for. Helmer, give me a cigar. One of your black Havanas.

Helmer. With the greatest pleasure. (*offers him the box*)

Rank (*takes one and cuts off the tip*). Thank you.

Nora (*strikes a match*). Let me give you a light.

Rank. Thank you. (*She holds out the match for him. He lights his cigar.*) And now—goodbye.

Helmer. Goodbye, my dear chap, goodbye.

Nora. Sleep well, Dr. Rank.

Rank. Thank you for that kind wish.

Nora. Wish me the same.

Rank. You? Very well—since you ask. Sleep well. And thank you for the light. (*He nods to them both and goes.*)

Helmer (*quietly*). He's been drinking too much.

Nora (*abstractedly*). Perhaps.

[HELMER *takes his bunch of keys from his pocket and goes out into the hall.*]

Nora. Torvald, what do you want out there?

Helmer. I must empty the letter box. It's absolutely full. There'll be no room for the newspapers in the morning.

Nora. Are you going to work tonight?

Helmer. You know very well I'm not. Hullo, what's this? Someone's been at the lock.

Nora. At the lock—

Helmer. Yes, I'm sure of it. Who on earth—? Surely not one of the maids? Here's a broken hairpin. Nora, it's yours—

Nora (*quickly*). Then it must have been the children.

Helmer. Well, you'll have to break them of that habit. Hm, hm. Ah, that's done it. (*takes out the contents of the box and calls into the kitchen*) Helen! Helen! Put out the light on the staircase. (*comes back into the drawing room and closes the door to the hall*)

Helmer (*with the letters in his hand*). Look at this! You see how they've piled up? (*glances through them*) What on earth's this?

Nora (*at the window*). The letter! Oh no, Torvald, no!

Helmer. Two visiting cards—from Rank.

Nora. From Dr. Rank?

Helmer (*looks at them*). Peter Rank, M.D. They were on top. He must have dropped them in as he left.

Nora. Has he written anything on them?

Helmer. There's a black cross above his name. Rather gruesome, isn't it? It looks just as though he was announcing his death.

Nora. He is.

Helmer. What? Do you know something? Has he told you anything?

Nora. Yes. When these cards come, it means he's said goodbye to us. He wants to shut himself up in his house and die.

Helmer. Ah, poor fellow. I knew I wouldn't be seeing him for much longer. But so soon—! And now he's going to slink away and hide like a wounded beast.

Nora. When the time comes, it's best to go silently. Don't you think so, Torvald?

Helmer (*walks up and down*). He was so much a part of our life. I can't realize that he's gone. His suffering and loneliness seemed to provide a kind of dark background to the happy sunlight of our marriage. Well, perhaps it's best this way. For him, anyway. (*stops walking*) And perhaps for us too, Nora. Now we have only each other. (*embraces her*) Oh, my beloved wife—I feel as though I could never hold you close enough. Do you know, Nora, often I wish some terrible danger might threaten you, so that I could offer my life and my blood, everything, for your sake.

Nora (*tears herself loose and says in a clear, firm voice*). Read your letters now, Torvald.

Helmer. No, no. Not tonight. Tonight I want to be with you, my darling wife—

Nora. When your friend is about to die—?

Helmer. You're right. This news has upset us both. An ugliness has come between us; thoughts of death and dissolution. We must try to forget them. Until then—you go to your room; I shall go to mine.

Nora (*throws her arms round his neck*). Good night, Torvald! Good night!

Helmer (*kisses her on the forehead*). Good night, my darling little songbird. Sleep well, Nora. I'll go and read my letters.

[*He goes into the study with the letters in his hand, and closes the door.*]

Nora (*wild-eyed, fumbles around, seizes HELMER's cloak, throws it round herself and whispers quickly, hoarsely*). Never see him again. Never. Never. Never. (*throws the shawl over her head*) Never see the children again. Them, too. Never. Never. Oh— the icy black water! Oh—that bottomless— that—! Oh, if only it were all over! Now he's got it—he's reading it. Oh no, no! Not yet! Goodbye, Torvald! Goodbye, my darlings!

[*She turns to run into the hall. As she does so,* HELMER *throws open his door and stands there with an open letter in his hand.*]

Helmer. Nora!

Nora (*shrieks*). Ah—!

Helmer. What is this? Do you know what is in this letter?

Nora. Yes, I know. Let me go! Let me go!

Helmer (*holding her back*). Go? Where?

Nora (*tries to tear herself loose*). You mustn't try to save me, Torvald!

Helmer (*staggers back*). Is it true? Is it true, what he writes? Oh, my God! No, no—it's impossible, it can't be true!

EDOUARD MANET, HENRI FANTIN-LATOUR (1836–1904).

Nora. It *is* true. I've loved you more than anything else in the world.

Helmer. Oh, don't try to make silly excuses.

Nora (*takes a step towards him*). Torvald—

Helmer. Wretched woman! What have you done?

Nora. Let me go! You're not going to suffer for my sake. I won't let you!

Helmer. Stop being theatrical. (*locks the front door*) You're going to stay here and explain yourself. Do you understand what you've done? Answer me! Do you understand?

Nora (*looks unflinchingly at him and, her expression growing colder, says*). Yes. Now I am beginning to understand.

Helmer (*walking round the room*). Oh, what a dreadful awakening! For eight whole years—she who was my joy and pride—a hypocrite, a liar—worse, worse—a criminal! Oh, the hideousness of it! Shame on you, shame!

[NORA *is silent and stares unblinkingly at him.*]

Helmer (*stops in front of her*). I ought to have guessed that something of this sort would happen. I should have foreseen it. All your father's recklessness and instability—be quiet!—I repeat, all your father's recklessness and instability he has handed on to you! No religion, no morals, no sense of duty! Oh, how I have been punished for closing my eyes to his faults! I did it for your sake. And now you reward me like this.

Nora. Yes. Like this.

Helmer. Now you have destroyed all my happiness. You have ruined my whole future. Oh, it's too dreadful to contemplate! I am in the power of a man who is completely without scruples. He can do what he likes with me, demand what he pleases, order me to do anything—I dare not disobey him. I am condemned to humiliation and ruin simply for the weakness of a woman.

Nora. When I am gone from this world, you will be free.

Helmer. Oh, don't be melodramatic. Your father was always ready with that kind of remark. How would it help me if you were "gone from this world," as you put it? It wouldn't assist me in the slightest. He can still make all the facts public; and if he does, I may quite easily be suspected of having been an accomplice in your crime. People may think that I was behind it— that it was I who encouraged you! And for all this I have to thank you, you whom I have carried on my hands through all the years of our marriage! Now do you realize what you've done to me?

Nora (*coldly calm*). Yes.

Helmer. It's so unbelievable I can hardly credit it. But we must try to find some way out. Take off that shawl. Take it off, I say! I must try to buy him off somehow. This thing must be hushed up at any price. As regards our relationship—we must appear to be living together just as before. Only *appear,* of course. You will therefore continue to reside here. That is understood. But the children shall be taken out of your hands. I dare no longer entrust them to you. Oh, to have to say this to the woman I once loved so dearly—and whom I still—! Well, all that must be finished. Henceforth there can be no question of happiness, we must merely strive to save what shreds and tatters—

[*The front door bell rings.* HELMER *starts.*]

Helmer. What can that be? At this hour? Surely not—? He wouldn't—? Hide yourself, Nora. Say you're ill.

[NORA *does not move.* HELMER *goes to the door of the room and opens it. The* MAID *is standing half-dressed in the hall.*]

Maid. A letter for madam.

Helmer. Give it me. (*seizes the letter and shuts the door*) Yes, it's from him. You're not having it. I'll read this myself.

Nora. Read it.

Helmer (*by the lamp*). I hardly dare to. This may mean the end for us both. No. I must know. (*tears open the letter hastily; reads a few lines; looks at a piece of paper which is enclosed with it; utters a cry of joy*) Nora! (*She looks at him questioningly.*) Nora! No—I must read it once more. Yes, yes, it's true! I am saved! Nora, I am saved!

Nora. What about me?

Helmer. You too, of course. We're both saved, you and I. Look! He's returning your I.O.U. He writes that he is sorry for what has happened—a happy accident has changed his life—oh, what does it matter what he writes? We are saved, Nora! No one can harm you now. Oh, Nora, Nora— no, first let me destroy this filthy thing. Let me see—! (*glances at the I.O.U.*) No, I don't want to look at it. I shall merely regard the whole business as a dream. (*He tears the I.O.U. and both letters into pieces, throws them into the stove and watches them burn.*) There. Now they're destroyed. He wrote that ever since Christmas Eve you've been—oh, these must have been three dreadful days for you, Nora.

Nora. Yes. It's been a hard fight.

Helmer. It must have been terrible—seeing no way out except—no, we'll forget the whole sordid business. We'll just be happy and go on telling ourselves over and over again: "It's over! It's over!" Listen to me, Nora. You don't seem to realize. It's over! Why are you looking so pale? Ah, my poor little Nora, I understand. You can't believe that I have forgiven you. But I have, Nora. I swear it to you. I have forgiven you everything. I know that what you did you did for your love of me.

Nora. That is true.

Helmer. You have loved me as a wife

seemed to be tumbling about my ears. I have forgiven you, Nora. I swear it to you; I have forgiven you.

Nora. Thank you for your forgiveness. (*She goes out through the door, right.*)

Helmer. No, don't go—(*looks in*) What are you doing there?

Nora (*offstage*). Taking off my fancy dress.

Helmer (*by the open door*). Yes, do that. Try to calm yourself and get your balance again, my frightened little songbird. Don't be afraid. I have broad wings to shield you. (*begins to walk around near the door*) How lovely and peaceful this little home of ours is, Nora. You are safe here; I shall watch over you like a hunted dove which I have snatched unharmed from the claws of the falcon. Your wildly beating little heart shall find peace with me. It will happen, Nora; it will take time; but it will happen, believe me. Tomorrow all this will seem quite different. Soon everything will be as it was before. I shall no longer need to remind you that I have forgiven you; your own heart will tell you that it is true. Do you really think I could ever bring myself to disown you, or even to reproach you? Ah, Nora, you don't understand what goes on in a husband's heart. There is something indescribably wonderful and satisfying for a husband in knowing that he has forgiven his wife—forgiven her unreservedly, from the bottom of his heart. It means that she has become his property in a double sense; he has, as it were, brought her into the world anew; she is now not only his wife but also his child. From now on that is what you shall be to me, my poor, helpless, bewildered little creature. Never be frightened of anything again, Nora. Just open your heart to me. I shall be both your will and your conscience. What's this? Not in bed? Have you changed?

Nora (*in her everyday dress*). Yes, Torvald. I've changed.

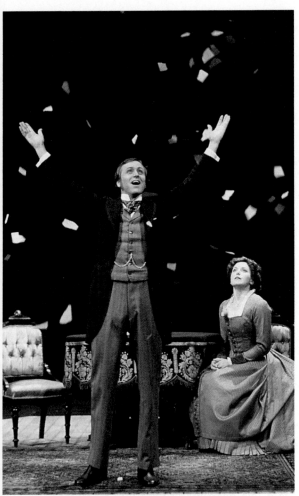

Do you think Nora deserves Torvald's forgiveness? How would you describe Torvald's feelings for his wife?

Stratford Festival

should love her husband. It was simply that in your inexperience you chose the wrong means. But do you think I love you any the less because you don't know how to act on your own initiative? No, no. Just lean on me. I shall counsel you. I shall guide you. I would not be a true man if your feminine helplessness did not make you doubly attractive in my eyes. You mustn't mind the hard words I said to you in those first dreadful moments when my whole world

Helmer. But why now—so late—?

Nora. I shall not sleep tonight.

Helmer. But, my dear Nora—

Nora (*looks at her watch*). It isn't that late. Sit down there, Torvald. You and I have a lot to talk about.

[*She sits down on one side of the table.*]

Helmer. Nora, what does this mean? You look quite drawn—

Nora. Sit down. It's going to take a long time. I've a lot to say to you.

Helmer (*sits down on the other side of the table*). You alarm me, Nora. I don't understand you.

Nora. No, that's just it. You don't understand me. And I've never understood you—until this evening. No, don't interrupt me. Just listen to what I have to say. You and I have got to face facts, Torvald.

Helmer. What do you mean by that?

Nora (*after a short silence*). Doesn't anything strike you about the way we're sitting here?

Helmer. What?

Nora. We've been married for eight years. Does it occur to you that this is the first time we two, you and I, man and wife, have ever had a serious talk together?

Helmer. Serious? What do you mean, serious?

Nora. In eight whole years—no, longer—ever since we first met—we have never exchanged a serious word on a serious subject.

Helmer. Did you expect me to drag you into all my worries—worries you couldn't possibly have helped me with?

Nora. I'm not talking about worries. I'm simply saying that we have never sat down seriously to try to get to the bottom of anything.

Helmer. But, my dear Nora, what on earth has that got to do with you?

Nora. That's just the point. You have never understood me. A great wrong has been done to me, Torvald. First by Papa, and then by you.

Helmer. What? But we two have loved you more than anyone in the world!

Nora (*shakes her head*). You have never loved me. You just thought it was fun to be in love with me.

Helmer. Nora, what kind of a way is this to talk?

Nora. It's the truth, Torvald. When I lived with Papa, he used to tell me what he thought about everything, so that I never had any opinions but his. And if I did have any of my own, I kept them quiet, because he wouldn't have liked them. He called me his little doll, and he played with me just the way I played with my dolls. Then I came here to live in your house—

Helmer. What kind of a way is that to describe our marriage?

Nora (*undisturbed*). I mean, then I passed from Papa's hands into yours. You arranged everything the way you wanted it, so that I simply took over your taste in everything—or pretended I did—I don't really know—I think it was a little of both—first one and then the other. Now I look back on it, it's as if I've been living here like a pauper, from hand to mouth. I performed tricks for you, and you gave me food and drink. But that was how you wanted it. You and Papa have done me a great wrong. It's your fault that I have done nothing with my life.

Helmer. Nora, how can you be so unreasonable and ungrateful? Haven't you been happy here?

Nora. No; never. I used to think I was. But I haven't ever been happy.

Helmer. Not—not happy?

Nora. No. I've just had fun. You've always been very kind to me. But our home has never been anything but a playroom. I've been your doll-wife, just as I used to be

Papa's doll-child. And the children have been my dolls. I used to think it was fun when you came in and played with me, just as they think it's fun when I go in and play games with them. That's all our marriage has been, Torvald.

Helmer. There may be a little truth in what you say, though you exaggerate and romanticize. But from now on it'll be different. Playtime is over. Now the time has come for education.

Nora. Whose education? Mine or the children's?

Helmer. Both yours and the children's, my dearest Nora.

Nora. Oh, Torvald, you're not the man to educate me into being the right wife for you.

Helmer. How can you say that?

Nora. And what about me? Am I fit to educate the children?

Helmer. Nora!

Nora. Didn't you say yourself a few minutes ago that you dare not leave them in my charge?

Helmer. In a moment of excitement. Surely you don't think I meant it seriously?

Nora. Yes. You were perfectly right. I'm not fitted to educate them. There's something else I must do first. I must educate myself. And you can't help me with that. It's something I must do by myself. That's why I'm leaving you.

Helmer (*jumps up*). What did you say?

Nora. I must stand on my own feet if I am to find out the truth about myself and about life. So I can't go on living here with you any longer.

Helmer. Nora, Nora!

Nora. I'm leaving you now, at once. Christine will put me up for tonight—

Helmer. You're out of your mind! You can't do this! I forbid you!

Nora. It's no use your trying to forbid me any more. I shall take with me nothing but what is mine. I don't want anything from you, now or ever.

Helmer. What kind of madness is this?

Nora. Tomorrow I shall go home—I mean, to where I was born. It'll be easiest for me to find some kind of a job there.

Helmer. But you're blind! You've no experience of the world—

Nora. I must try to get some, Torvald.

Helmer. But to leave your home, your husband, your children! Have you thought what people will say?

Nora. I can't help that. I only know that I must do this.

Helmer. But this is monstrous! Can you neglect your most sacred duties?

Nora. What do you call my most sacred duties?

Helmer. Do I have to tell you? Your duties towards your husband, and your children.

Nora. I have another duty which is equally sacred.

Helmer. You have not. What on earth could that be?

Nora. My duty towards myself.

Helmer. First and foremost you are a wife and mother.

Nora. I don't believe that any longer. I believe that I am first and foremost a human being, like you—or anyway, that I must try to become one. I know most people think as you do, Torvald, and I know there's something of the sort to be found in books. But I'm no longer prepared to accept what people say and what's written in books. I must think things out for myself, and try to find my own answer.

Helmer. Do you need to ask where your duty lies in your own home? Haven't you an infallible guide in such matters—your religion?

Nora. Oh, Torvald, I don't really know what religion means.

Helmer. What are you saying?

Nora. I only know what Pastor Hansen told me when I went to confirmation. He explained that religion meant this and that. When I get away from all this and can think things out on my own, that's one of the questions I want to look into. I want to find out whether what Pastor Hansen said was right—or anyway, whether it is right for me.

Helmer. But it's unheard of for so young a woman to behave like this! If religion cannot guide you, let me at least appeal to your conscience. I presume you have some moral feelings left? Or—perhaps you haven't? Well, answer me.

Nora. Oh, Torvald, that isn't an easy question to answer. I simply don't know. I don't know where I am in these matters. I only know that these things mean something quite different to me from what they do to you. I've learned now that certain laws are different from what I'd imagined them to be; but I can't accept that such laws can be right. Has a woman really not the right to spare her dying father pain, or save her husband's life? I can't believe that.

Helmer. You're talking like a child. You don't understand how society works.

Nora. No, I don't. But now I intend to learn. I must try to satisfy myself which is right, society or I.

Helmer. Nora, you're ill. You're feverish. I almost believe you're out of your mind.

Nora. I've never felt so sane and sure in my life.

Helmer. You feel sure that it is right to leave your husband and your children?

Nora. Yes. I do.

Helmer. Then there is only one possible explanation.

Nora. What?

Helmer. That you don't love me any longer.

Nora. No, that's exactly it.

Helmer. Nora! How can you say this to me?

Nora. Oh, Torvald, it hurts me terribly to have to say it, because you've always been so kind to me. But I can't help it. I don't love you any longer.

Helmer (*controlling his emotions with difficulty*). And you feel quite sure about this, too?

Nora. Yes, absolutely sure. That's why I can't go on living here any longer.

Helmer. Can you also explain why I have lost your love?

Nora. Yes, I can. It happened this evening, when the miracle failed to happen. It was then that I realized you weren't the man I'd thought you to be.

Helmer. Explain more clearly. I don't understand you.

Nora. I've waited so patiently, for eight whole years—well, good heavens, I'm not such a fool as to suppose that miracles occur every day. Then this dreadful thing happened to me, and then I *knew:* "Now the miracle will take place!" When Krogstad's letter was lying out there, it never occurred to me for a moment that you would let that man trample over you. I *knew* that you would say to him: "Publish the facts to the world!" And when he had done this—

Helmer. Yes, what then? When I'd exposed my wife's name to shame and scandal—

Nora. Then I was certain that you would step forward and take all the blame on yourself, and say: "I am the one who is guilty!"

Helmer. Nora!

Nora. You're thinking I wouldn't have accepted such a sacrifice from you? No, of course I wouldn't! But what would my word have counted for against yours? That was the miracle I was hoping for, and dreading. And it was to prevent it happening that I wanted to end my life.

Helmer. Nora, I would gladly work for you

night and day, and endure sorrow and hardship for your sake. But no man can be expected to sacrifice his honor, even for the person he loves.

Nora. Millions of women have done it.

Helmer. Oh, you think and talk like a stupid child.

Nora. That may be. But you neither think nor talk like the man I could share my life with. Once you'd got over your fright—and you weren't frightened of what might threaten me, but only of what threatened you—once the danger was past, then as far as you were concerned it was exactly as though nothing had happened. I was your little songbird just as before—your doll whom henceforth you would take particular care to protect from the world because she was so weak and fragile. (*gets up*) Torvald, in that moment I realized that for eight years I had been living here with a complete stranger, and had borne him three children—! Oh, I can't bear to think of it! I could tear myself to pieces!

Summer Night's Dream, (The Voice), Edvard Munch, 1893.

❓ *Do you think that Nora has succeeded in finding her voice, that is, her independence?*

Helmer (*sadly*). I see it, I see it. A gulf has indeed opened between us. Oh, but Nora—couldn't it be bridged?

Nora. As I am now, I am no wife for you.

Helmer. I have the strength to change.

Nora. Perhaps—if your doll is taken from you.

Helmer. But to be parted—to be parted from you! No, no, Nora. I can't conceive of it happening!

Nora (*goes into the room, right*). All the more necessary that it should happen.

[*She comes back with her outdoor things and a small traveling bag, which she puts down on a chair by the table.*]

Helmer. Nora, Nora, not now! Wait till tomorrow!

Nora (*puts on her coat*). I can't spend the night in a strange man's house.

Helmer. But can't we live here as brother and sister, then—?

Nora (*fastens her hat*). You know quite well it wouldn't last. (*puts on her shawl*) Goodbye, Torvald. I don't want to see the children. I know they're in better hands than mine. As I am now, I can be nothing to them.

Helmer. But some time, Nora—some time—?

Nora. How can I tell? I've no idea what will happen to me.

Helmer. But you are my wife, both as you are and as you will be.

Nora. Listen, Torvald. When a wife leaves her husband's house, as I'm doing now, I'm told that according to the law he is freed of any obligations towards her. In any case, I release you from any such obligations. You mustn't feel bound to me in any way however small, just as I shall not feel bound to you. We must both be quite free. Here is your ring back. Give me mine.

Helmer. That too?

Nora. That too.

Helmer. Here it is.

Nora. Good. Well, now it's over. I'll leave the keys here. The servants know about everything to do with the house—much better than I do. Tomorrow, when I have left town, Christine will come to pack the things I brought here from home. I'll have them sent on after me.

Helmer. This is the end, then! Nora, will you never think of me any more?

Nora. Yes, of course. I shall often think of you and the children and this house.

Helmer. May I write to you, Nora?

Nora. No. Never. You mustn't do that.

Helmer. But at least you must let me send you—

Nora. Nothing. Nothing.

Helmer. But if you should need help—?

Nora. I tell you, no. I don't accept things from strangers.

Helmer. Nora—can I never be anything but a stranger to you?

Nora (*picks up her bag*). Oh, Torvald! Then the miracle of miracles would have to happen.

Helmer. The miracle of miracles!

Nora. You and I would both have to change so much that—oh, Torvald, I don't believe in miracles any longer.

Helmer. But I want to believe in them. Tell me. We should have to change so much that—!

Nora. That life together between us two could become a marriage. Goodbye.

[*She goes out through the hall.*]

Helmer (*sinks down on a chair by the door and buries his face in his hands*). Nora! Nora! (*looks round and gets up*) Empty! She's gone! (*a hope strikes him*) The miracle of miracles—?

[*The street door is slammed shut downstairs.*]

First Thoughts

Do you think that Nora made the right decision? Will a reconciliation between Nora and Torvald be possible in the future?

Identifying Facts

1. What agreement do Mrs. Linde and Krogstad come to that makes them both happy? How does their agreement affect the Helmers?
2. What message does Dr. Rank convey by leaving a calling card with a black cross written on it?
3. What do the first and second letters from Krogstad say? How does Torvald react to each letter?
4. What major action does Nora take at the end of Act 3? What are her plans as the play closes? What violent alternative had she been considering while Torvald was reading the first letter?

Interpreting Meanings

1. Mrs. Linde could stop Krogstad's letter from reaching Torvald, but she decides that Torvald should know the truth about Nora's actions. What is her motive? Do you approve or disapprove of her decision?
2. A **metaphor** is a figure of speech that compares one thing to another without using the words *like* or *as*. When a metaphor is developed over several lines, it is called an **extended metaphor**. Ibsen creates an extended metaphor in Act 3—the "doll's house"—which gives the play its title. What does this metaphor suggest about Nora's relationships with her father, husband, and children?
3. Torvald and Nora have very different ideas about what is moral and just. What do their opinions about the forged note reveal about their attitudes toward law and society?

4. Why does Nora call her husband "a strange man"? Do you think she is justified in using that term? Why or why not?
5. In Act 2, Nora hopes that a "miracle" will take place. Near the end of Act 3, she tells Torvald that in order for their marriage to be restored, "the miracle of miracles" will have to take place. What does Nora mean by "the miracle of miracles?" How does it differ from the miracle she hoped for earlier?
6. Briefly summarize Nora's reasons for leaving Torvald. What has Nora gained that might make up for the loss of her marriage and her children?

Applying Meanings

Act 3 ends with the sound of the front door slamming as Nora leaves her husband. Some critics have said that the echo of that slamming door is still sounding in our world today. Explain the comment, and state whether you agree or disagree, and why.

Creative Writing Response

1. **Writing a Fourth Act.** Write a brief Act 4 for *A Doll's House*, showing what happens to Nora and Torvald after the breakup of their marriage. In order to explain what is happening to Torvald in his household and what is happening to Nora elsewhere, you may need to convey some information through dialogue about absent characters. You may use the same set used for the first three acts, or create an entirely different one. Use any characters from Ibsen's play, or, if you wish, create new characters.
2. **Analyzing a Character.** You are an actress preparing to play the role of Nora. Write a page of notes about her character to help you portray Nora effectively. Consider some or all of the following points: What are Nora's thoughts and

feelings at the beginning of the play? How do they change by the end? How are the things she says sometimes different from her inner thoughts and feelings? When other characters are speaking and Nora is onstage, how does she react? Include specific lines of dialogue, and describe what tone of voice, gestures, or bits of stage business you would use in order to bring out the characterization in each passage.

Critical Writing Response

1. **Interpreting a Passage.** In Act 3, we find the following exchange between Torvald and Nora:

Helmer. Nora, I would gladly work for you night and day, and endure sorrow and hardship for your sake. But no man can be expected to sacrifice his honor, even for the person he loves.

Nora. Millions of women have done it.

In two or more paragraphs, give your interpretation of this passage. Begin by **paraphrasing** it—restating its meaning in your own words. Then, to focus your interpretation, consider some or all of the following questions: What are Torvald and Nora saying about the differences between men and women? What does Torvald mean by "honor"? What does Nora mean by it? How, in Nora's view, have millions of women sacrificed their honor for love?

To what extent do you agree or disagree with the statements in the passage? What is your view of honor, and of whether people should sacrifice it for love? Do you feel that men and women today have essentially different views of love and honor?

2. **Identifying Theme.** **Theme** is the central idea or insight in a work of literature. A statement of theme is not a plot summary; nor does it mention specific events or characters. In one sentence, state the theme of *A Doll's House*. In a two- to three-paragraph essay, provide evidence from the play that supports your theme statement. Finally, state whether or not you agree with the theme, and explain the reason for your opinion.

A CRITICAL COMMENT

The Realistic Stage

Although the literature of the nineteenth century held up a mirror to society as it really was, it was not until Ibsen that theater began to reflect the world in a similar way. Before Ibsen, nineteenth-century audiences went to the theater to see spectacle and romance. Theatergoers expected sensational and contrived stories of lost heirs and love affairs, not realistic or truthful depictions of everyday life. Ibsen, and later playwrights such as Anton Chekhov, George Bernard Shaw, and August Strindberg, dramatically altered the theater experience by making the stage an extension of real life. In their plays, these playwrights concentrated on the kinds of conflicts experienced by people in real life.

Ibsen was one of the first playwrights to make an audience forget that what it was watching was imaginary, not real. He treated the stage as if it were a room in which real events were actually taking place. For the audience, it was as though the "fourth wall" of the room had been removed. In order to create a realistic "room," the whole look of the stage changed. Suddenly every detail was important: the set had to look like an actual place, such as a sitting room or a front porch; lighting was used to indicate different times of day both to suggest mood and to create special effects. The way actors moved on stage was intended to look real, not affected or posed.

Finally, the language of the stage had to change to accommodate Realism. A master of dramatic technique, Ibsen developed a style that revealed the inner conflicts of his characters. His dialogue sounds like colloquial speech spoken by real, believable people. Depths of characterization are frequently revealed in an offhand statement or gesture, such as when Torvald pats Nora on the head, calling her his "precious little songbird" at the end of Act 1 of *A Doll's House*. Ibsen was also one of the first playwrights to incorporate elaborate stage directions that would help the actors convey a certain feeling to the audience. He wrote detailed descriptions of the settings and added directions to the script ("a little embarrassed," "laughing," and so on) to indicate how lines should be delivered. Stage directions of this kind were virtually nonexistent in earlier drama, but they have become standard in contemporary Western plays.

THE GOTHIC NOVEL

Imagine a woman in white fleeing from a shadowy castle on the mist-ridden moors on a moonless night. . . . If this image is familiar, you have likely seen or read a popular kind of historical/supernatural novel available in most bookstores. These works belong to a genre called the **Gothic novel**. Though Gothic fiction is very much a part of contemporary literature, its history is a long one. The Gothic novel first became popular during the mid-eighteenth century in England. Unlike people of previous times, members of eighteenth-century English society, especially women, had new-found leisure time and literacy skills to read fiction.

Gothic novels were an unusual literary form because, unlike other novels of this time, their emphasis was on the arousal of terror of both the heroine and the reader—perhaps an unexpectedly lowbrow form of entertainment in a society that considered itself educated and sophisticated. Yet for all their entertainment value, Gothic novels addressed important social concerns, especially those pertaining to women. It is not surprising, then, that Gothic fiction became a special province of women readers and writers.

Nevertheless, the first Gothic novel was written by a man, Horace Walpole, whose *Castle of Otranto* was published in 1764. This work introduced the components that were to become standard in the Gothic genre: a haunted castle; an innocent woman

The Granger Collection, New York

THE VALE OF REST, SIR JOHN EVERETT MILLAIS, 1858–1859. *This painting reflects the Gothic atmosphere that was popular in English art and literature in the nineteenth century.*

whose virtue is powerless against a lecherous villain; and a daughter who must rebel against the authority of her father.

Many early Gothic novels, such as Ann Radcliffe's *The Mysteries of Udolpho* (1794), are set in a different historical time, usually in a medieval, southern European, Roman Catholic country. Some critics think that this sense of distance from the writers' own time allowed them to use the novels to make subtle comments on certain social concerns, particularly women's issues. For example, by describing the threats made against a virtuous woman by the villain, writers may have been highlighting the moral, psychological, and legal dependence and vulnerability of women. Also, by representing a woman who acts on her own will in defiance of her father, Gothic writers may have been commenting on the need for women to have a way to voice their concerns.

Gothic novels often employed lurid and sensational plots and narrative styles, and were therefore not always taken seriously by critics and other writers. Even critics who found elements of Gothics praiseworthy easily dismissed the genre in general as light reading. Jane Austen, an important English woman writer of the late eighteenth century, used Gothic devices in her novel *Northanger Abbey* to show the foolishness of interpreting Gothic situations too literally. Yet this did not prevent other important writers from incorporating Gothic images and scenarios into their novels: Mary Shelley's *Frankenstein,* Charlotte Brontë's *Jane Eyre,* and Emily Brontë's *Wuthering Heights* are all examples of the strong influence of the Gothic on the nineteenth-century imagination.

Illustration by Lady Edna Clark Hall (1879–1979) for *Wuthering Heights*.

By the mid-nineteenth century, the Gothic form had been thoroughly exhausted. Despite this, the legacy of the Gothic novel is discernible in popular entertainment today. For example, elements of Gothic terror, such as the haunted house, have been modified in television programs such as *Dark Shadows* and countless horror films. The Gothic novel also introduced the notion of writing for the sake of arousing terror in the reader. Thus, the Gothic novel is a precursor to modern novels such as Daphne du Maurier's *Rebecca* and *The House on the Strand* and Shirley Jackson's *The Haunting of Hill House,* and to the more graphically violent suspense fiction of Stephen King and horror films such as *Halloween* and *A Nightmare on Elm Street.* Ultimately, the kind of Gothic influences that survive today demonstrate perhaps just how much readers and audiences enjoy entertainments that terrify them.

KEEPING PRONOUN REFERENCE CLEAR

You've probably heard someone, after a long argument, say, "But *that's* the whole point!" If you weren't sure exactly what *that* meant, you were experiencing the effects of unclear pronoun reference. Avoiding reference problems helps you to maintain coherence in your writing and your thinking.

Clear Pronoun Reference

Make each pronoun refer unmistakably to its antecedent. A **pronoun**—a word that stands for a noun or another pronoun— can refer to a word, a phrase, or a whole clause. The words referred to are the **antecedents.** Sometimes a pronoun seems to refer to more than one antecedent. To repair this ambiguous reference, reword your sentence.

AMBIGUOUS

Faust sells his soul to the devil in exchange for knowledge of magical arts. *This* is the start of Faust's undoing.

CLEAR

Faust sells his soul to the devil in exchange for knowledge of magical arts. *This exchange* is the start of Faust's undoing.

In the first example, *this* could refer either to Faust's selling of his soul or to the knowledge of magical arts. In the second example, rewording has made the idea clear.

Exercise 1: Correcting Ambiguous Pronoun Reference

Number a paper from 1 to 10 and reword any of the following sentences in which pronoun reference is ambiguous. Mark a *C* by the number of any sentence with no pronoun reference problems.

1. The friendship between Verlaine and Rimbaud caused him trouble for much of his life.
2. Noticing three towering old pine trees and several younger ones, Pushkin realizes that he will not live to see them grow tall.
3. Pushkin knows that his grandson may someday see the pines. Then will he think of him?
4. Because he took him under his wing, Heine's mother was fond of his rich uncle Salomon.
5. The speaker in "The Lorelei" sees an alluring river goddess and falls in love with her. She enchants him and he drowns.
6. Baudelaire had great talents offset by crippling mental problems. He wrote about them beautifully.
7. Ibsen's plays dealt with controversial topics. They are less controversial today.
8. In a short story about jewels, Maupassant demonstrates his mastery of sus-

pense and irony. They bring pleasure but not happiness.

9. Tolstoy was a reformer who embraced pacifist ideas. These later influenced Mahatma Gandhi and Martin Luther King, Jr.

10. In *A Doll's House,* Ibsen explores the effects of possessiveness and immaturity in human relationships. He illustrates them in the interplay between Nora and her husband.

Vague Pronoun Reference

In some sentences, pronouns do not refer clearly to anything. To correct vague pronoun reference in your writing, first clarify your ideas. Then reword your sentences.

VAGUE
Verlaine gazes at a palm against the sky, listens to tranquil sounds coming from outdoors, and laments his lost youth. *This* creates the poem's impact.

CLEAR
Verlaine gazes at a palm against the sky, listens to tranquil sounds coming from outdoors, and laments his lost youth.

The contrast between low-key imagery and devastating regret creates the poem's impact.

In the first example, the italicized pronoun does not refer to anything specific. In the second example, the writer has thought the idea through more completely. The clearer thought permits clearer writing.

Exercise 2: Revising for Clear Pronoun Reference

Reread a composition you have written, underlining each pronoun you have used. Then do the following:

1. Locate the antecedent of each pronoun. Remember that an antecedent can be a word, a phrase, or a clause. Draw an arrow from the pronoun to the antecedent.

2. If you find an ambiguous pronoun reference, decide what the pronoun was meant to refer to. Then reword the sentence for coherence and clarity.

3. If you find a vague pronoun reference, think your ideas through more carefully. Then rewrite the passage, explaining in more detail what you mean.

WRITING A LITERARY REVIEW

If the selections in this unit were dramatized on TV, which might you watch? Which would you avoid? On what would you base your decisions? Nineteenth-century European poetry, drama, and prose, so varied in style and rich in scope, call forth a wide range of responses. Your reasons for liking or disliking one of these works can form the basis of an objective judgment.

Writing Assignment

Write a review of one selection from this unit, explaining why you think—or do not think—that the selection is worth reading. Your audience is people your age who share your general interests. In this assignment, you will base your review on a variety of **criteria**, that is, standards or tests by which something can be judged.

Background

To form an evaluation or judgment, you need criteria. Your responses to questions about a given work will reveal what your personal standards, or criteria, for literature are. Choose a work you feel strongly about, and use the questions below to clarify your responses and to pinpoint the elements that evoke them.

1. What **action** takes place in the work? Why does (or doesn't) it interest you?

2. How does the **diction** of the work affect you? Which wording is particularly appealing (or unappealing)?

3. What thoughts and feelings underlie the work, or form its **themes**? How do you respond to them?

4. Which **figurative language** and **images** add to (or detract from) the overall effect?

5. If your work is poetry, which **sound devices**—rhyme, meter, alliteration, assonance—stand out? How do they enhance (or diminish) the appeal of the work? If your work is prose, consider **style**—sentence length and complexity, parallel structure, and repetition.

6. How can you discern the **tone**—the author's attitude? What is your response to it?

Prewriting

Selecting Criteria. To select criteria for your evaluation, review your answers to the questions above. Then make a chart like the following one. Rate each class of criterion from 1 to 10. In the right column, jot down the line or page numbers of the passage on which you based your evaluation of the work.

Criterion	Rating	Examples
Effectiveness of action		
Effectiveness of diction		
Effectiveness of themes		
Effectiveness of figurative language/imagery		
Effectiveness of sound devices/style		
Effectiveness of tone		

If your overall response to the work is positive, focus your review on the elements you rate highest. If your response is negative, focus on the elements you rate lowest.

Examining Background. Freewrite answers to the following questions. If you are unsure of the answers, review the unit introduction as well as the selection introduction.

1. How is the work representative of its time period?
2. How do the events of the author's life contribute to the work?

Writing

Use the following guidelines as you draft your essay.

1. **Introductory Paragraph.** Begin with a clear statement of your opinion of the work's merit. Cite the author and title of the work. Go on to summarize your criteria.

2. **Body Paragraphs.** Devote at least one paragraph to each criterion, using quotes and examples from the work to show the author's treatment of the element in question. Your rating chart will provide a starting point. Include explanations of your own responses. Also, use your freewriting material to speculate on why the author treated each element as he or she did.

3. **Concluding Paragraph.** Here you might reflect on your reasons for choosing your criteria. End with a recommendation to your audience.

Evaluating and Revising

Use these questions to evaluate and revise your draft.

1. Does the introductory paragraph state your opinion and summarize your criteria?
2. Do body paragraphs detail your criteria and show how the work addresses them?
3. Do you include enough examples and quotations?
4. Do you include speculation on why the author wrote as he or she did?
5. Does your conclusion show the worth of your criteria and give a recommendation?
6. Are your sentences varied in structure and grammatically correct?

Proofreading and Publishing

Proofread to eliminate errors, and make a final copy of your review. Submit it to your school magazine or newspaper.

THE
WORLD
IN THE
TWENTIETH
CENTURY

THE TWENTIETH CENTURY

▼ **Time** ▼

1900s

▼ **Place** ▼

The World

▼ **Literary Significance** ▼

In an age of stunning technological advances, widespread warfare, and global communication, humans have gained an increased awareness of the impact they have on their world. Twentieth-century writers have taken on the age-old challenge of finding new ways to express themselves, to understand their places in a constantly—often volatilely—changing world, and to understand the workings of their own minds. The result has been a vibrant array of literary movements ranging from modernism to existentialism, from absurdism to magical realism.

The literature of the twentieth century spans many forms: poetry, fiction, drama, autobiography, and journalism. It has raised new questions and presented new responses to eternal problems such as war, the limitation of personal, political, and intellectual freedoms, and the expression of personal experience. The writings of the twentieth century represent a mosaic of experiences at once bizarre and familiar, at once global and personal.

TIME LINE
The Twentieth Century

LITERARY EVENTS

▼

Modernism, **c. 1890–1940**

Selma Lagerlöf is awarded the Nobel Prize, **1909**

James Joyce, *Dubliners*, **1914**

Franz Kafka, *The Metamorphosis*, **1915**

Anna Akhmatova, "Lot's Wife," **early 20s**

T.S. Eliot, *The Waste Land*, **1922**

Isak Dinesen, *Out of Africa*, **1937**

Aimé Césaire coins the term *négritude* and becomes one of the founders of the Negritude movement, **1939**

Gabriela Mistral is awarded t Nobel Priz **1945**

1900	1910	1920	1930	1940

Great Britain defeats Boers of South Africa in Boer War, **1902**

Wright brothers develop the first aircraft, **1903**

Russo-Japanese War, **1904–1905**

Albert Einstein proposes the theory of relativity, **1905**

Chinese Revolution forces led by Sun Yat-sen overthrow the Manchu dynasty, **1911**

World War I, **1914–1918**

Russian Revolution; V.I. Lenin comes to power in Russia, **1917**

Nineteenth Amendment to U.S. Constitution gives women the vote, **1920**

Rise of Adolf Hitler in Germany and Benito Mussolini in Italy, **1920s**

Josef Stalin replaces Lenin as leader of the USSR, **1924**

Worldwide economic depression begins, **1929**

Adolf Hitler becomes chancellor of Germany, **1933**

The Holocaust—Nazis murder over twelve million Jews, Gypsies, and other "undesirables," **1938—1945**

Spanish Civil War, **1936–1939**

Japan invades China, **1937**

World War II begins in Europe; Germany invades Poland, **1939**

Japanese bomb Pearl Harbor, **1941**

U.S. drops atom bombs on Japar World War II ends; United Nations founded Cold War begins **1945**

European decolonization **1945–1970s**

State of Israel is proclaimed, **1948**

People's Republ of China is established, **1949**

▲

CULTURAL AND HISTORICAL EVENTS

Library of Congress

The Wright brothers and their aircraft, 1903.

...ohandas K. Gandhi.

...antha Rama Rau, *Gifts
* Passage*, **1951**

...bert Camus is awarded
...e Nobel Prize, **1957**

...ie Wiesel, *Night,* **1958**

Postmodernism
movement; magical
realism develops in
Latin America,
1960s

Léopold Sédar
Senghor is elected
first president of
Senegal, **1960**

Barbara Kimenye,
Kalasanda, **1965**

Margaret Atwood,
*The Animals in That
Country*, **1968**

Pablo Neruda is
awarded the
Nobel Prize,
1971

Yehuda Amichai,
*Laments on the
War Dead,* **1974**

Chinese students
protested for
democratic reforms
at Tiananmen
Square, Beijing,
1989.

Gabriel García Márquez
is awarded the Nobel
Prize, **1982**

Jamaica Kincaid, *Annie
John,* **1983**

Wole Soyinka is awarded
the Nobel Prize, **1986**

Octavio Paz
is awarded
the Nobel
Prize, **1990**

Naguib
Mahfouz, *The
Time and the
Place,* **1991**

1950 1960 1970 1980 1990

...orean War, **1950–1953**

...oviets launch the first
...atellite into outer space,
957

.. American astronaut on a
..acewalk above the earth.

Berlin Wall is built, **1961**

Cuban missile crisis; U.S.
troops go to South
Vietnam, **1962**

President John F. Kennedy
is assassinated, **1963**

Cultural Revolution in
People's Republic of China,
1966–1969

Six-Day War between Israel
and Arab nations, **1967**

Assassination of Martin
Luther King, Jr.; USSR
invades Czechoslovakia,
1968

U.S. astronauts land on
the moon, **1969**

OPEC oil
embargo leads
to energy crisis,
1973

Watergate
scandal causes
President Nixon
to resign, **1974**

Vietnam War
ends, **1975**

Shah deposed in
Iran; Ayatollah
Khomeini comes
to power, **1979**

Solidarity trade union
is founded in Poland,
1980

Mikhail Gorbachev
becomes premier of
USSR and estab-
lishes policy of
glasnost (openness),
1985

Berlin Wall is
dismantled; Commu-
nist regimes are
replaced by demo-
cratic ones in Poland,
Czechoslovakia, etc.;
Chinese hardliners
crack down on pro-
democracy students
in Tiananmen Square,
1989

East and West
Germany are
reunited, **1990**

U.S. and allies
wage war
against Iraq and
liberate Kuwait;
USSR dissolves,
1991

This time line border contains international symbols and contemporary letter forms
from a variety of alphabets worldwide.

THE TWENTIETH CENTURY

A t the beginning of the twentieth century, the colonies of the European empires covered most of the earth. But Europe's long period of exploration, conquest, and colonization was coming to an end. Much of the twentieth century would be marked by periods of widespread warfare with interim periods of uneasy peace. Colonies' demands for independence become increasingly intense, and many European countries that began the century as world powers found their once seemingly limitless resources dwindling. Throughout the world, artists, writers, and poets sought new forms to express the monumental changes they witnessed during this turbulent century.

World War I

Intense competition among the European powers for overseas colonies and markets was a major cause of **World War I** (1914–1918). Germany, Turkey, and Bulgaria joined Austria-Hungary to fight the Allies, who included Great Britain, France, Russia, Italy, and the United States. The conflict was a brutal exercise in trench warfare.

The peace that followed World War I was short-lived. In 1929, an economic downturn known as the **Great Depression** devastated economies throughout the world. The legacy of war and dire economic circumstances was great change and continued aggression in some parts of the world. The **Russian Revolution**, for example, caused the downfall of the monarchy and established Communist rule in Russia. In the Far East, Japan began invading China and other neighboring countries. In Europe, dictators such as Hitler, Mussolini, and Franco came into power, thus planting the seeds for further destruction in World War II.

American troops in France, 1918. *The use of poisoned gas in World War I added a devastating new dimension to warfare.*

World War II

World War II began in 1939, when Nazi Germany invaded Poland. The main participants in the war were the **Axis powers**—Germany, Italy, and Japan—and the **Allies**—Great Britain, France, the U.S.S.R., China, the United States, and others.

In May 1945, Germany surrendered to the Allies, but it wasn't until August, when President Harry Truman ordered the atomic bombings of the Japanese cities of Hiroshima and Nagasaki, that the war finally ended. The jubilation of the victorious allies was tempered as the world became aware of two horrors: the destructive power of the atomic bomb, and the Nazi attempt to exterminate all European Jews and others they considered "undesirable." In Hiroshima and Nagasaki, over 300,000 people, mostly civilians,

> ❝ The people, and the people alone, are the motive force in the making of world history. ❞
>
> —Quotations of Chairman Mao,
> *Mao Tse Tung*

World War II in Europe, 1939–1945

Axis Powers
Allied Nations
Neutral Nations
Area of Axis Control
Area of Allied Control

were burned or irradiated to death by the two bombs. In the German death camps of Auschwitz, Dachau, and elsewhere, the Nazis killed over twelve million people. Altogether, over twelve million soldiers and twenty million civilians were killed during World War II.

The Cold War

The end of World War II marked the beginning of the nuclear age. The United States and the Soviet Union emerged as antagonistic superpowers, and the **Cold War** began. From the end of World War II until the period of *glasnost* ("openness" in Russian) ushered in by Mikhail Gorbachev in the mid-1980s, the U.S. and U.S.S.R. were involved in a stupendous arms race. At the height of the Cold War, both sides had stockpiled enough nuclear weapons to kill every man, woman, and child on the planet twelve times.

New Nations Emerge

More significant in the long run than the Cold War was the decline of the Western imperial powers and its result—the emergence of dozens of newly independent states in Africa and Asia, as well as the political redefinition of older nations

> The end of World War II ushered in a new era of politics with new players: the U.S. and Soviet superpowers and newly independent nations in Africa, Asia, and Latin America.

there and in Latin America. These nations and others began to assert their own identities and reclaim territories. This process of self-determination, however, was seldom achieved without conflict. For example, war has broken out several times in the Middle East over the establishment of Jewish and Arab states in former British Palestine. Despite much mediation, many Arabs have opposed the creation of a Jewish homeland by the United Nations. Countries like Korea and Vietnam, once freed from foreign rule, were torn apart

Poster for Hitler's National Student Organization during World War II; the caption reads, "The German student fights for leader and land." *Nazi propaganda helped rally the support Hitler needed to carry out his diabolical objectives.*

66 Nonviolence is the first article of my faith. It is also the last article of my creed. 99

—*Speech, March 23, 1922, Mohandas K. Gandhi*

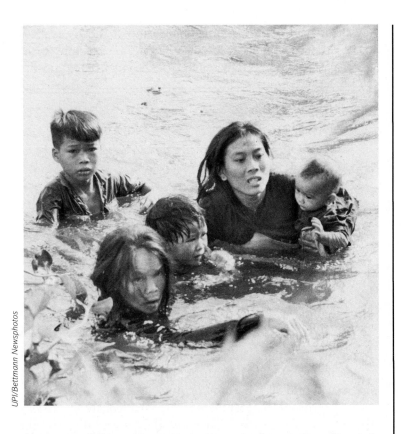

Victims of the war in Vietnam, 1965.

by internal factions trying to impose their own rule. Both the Korean and Vietnam wars were, in simplest terms, conflicts between supporters of Communist and democratic governments. South Africa, Northern Ireland, and Central America are some other regions of the globe where violence is a common experience due to the conflicts of race, religion, and political beliefs.

Science and Technology ■

The twentieth century has seen amazing developments in science and technology—telephones, phonographs, televisions, automobiles, airplanes, computers, space technology, and medical advances such as antibiotics. Particularly important advances have been made in communication and transportation. Not everyone has enjoyed the benefits of these advances, however. The majority of the world's less-industrialized nations still suffers from the effects of poverty and disease. Nor have technological advances in themselves

❝ Perfection of means and confusion of goals seem, in my opinion, to characterize our age. ❞

—Out of My Later Years,
Albert Einstein

always been a boon to humanity—many of these advances have produced dangerous side effects. For example, technological progress contributed to the massacres in the

Mushroom cloud resulting from the atomic bombing of Nagasaki, Japan, by the U.S. in World War II.

> ❝ He: You saw nothing in Hiroshima. Nothing.
> She: I saw everything. Everything. ❞
>
> —Hiroshima, Mon Amour,
> *Marguerite Duras*

The twentieth century has seen remarkable advances in science and technology. But accompanying these advances have been large-scale disasters.

---

trenches of World War I, the Holocaust in World War II, nuclear weapons, and ecological disasters such as the nuclear accident at the Chernobyl power plant in the Soviet Union.

Artistic Responses to the Twentieth Century

For many, the nineteenth-century belief that human history was a record of slow but certain progress died in the aftermath of World War I. Traditional values came under attack, and art forms of the past were seen as inadequate to express the experiences of the modern world. By rejecting the old forms, writers, painters, musicians, and other creative artists were free to experiment with new themes and styles.

Film, Art, and Music

Most twentieth-century painters rejected the styles of previous centuries. For example, Pablo Picasso and Georges Braque, who were influenced by African sculpture and by concepts of geometry, developed a style called *cubism*, which reduced objects and figures to their basic geometric forms. In 1937 Picasso painted *Guernica* in reaction to the brutal German bombing of the village of Guernica during the Spanish Civil War. Shortly after he painted this large mural, the German secret police began harassing him at his studio in Nazi-occupied Paris. One officer, noticing a photograph of *Guernica* lying on a table, asked "Did you do that?" "No," Picasso replied, "you did."

After the invention of the motion picture around the turn of the century, films quickly became a new popular art

GUERNICA, PABLO PICASSO
(1881–1973).

form. Most films were escapist—adventures, comedies, or romantic dramas—but others reflected the pessimism of the postwar era. Charlie Chaplin, an early cinematic master, wrote, directed, and acted in many films that took an ironic look at war, industry, and other important issues of the day.

A determination to break new ground was also apparent in popular music. Two of the most innovative popular musical forms of the century were developed by African Americans: jazz and the blues. During the 1950s, rock-and-roll burst on the scene, causing fans to scream and swoon over their new heroes—Buddy Holly, Chuck Berry, Elvis Presley, and Little Richard. Then, in the 1960s, superstar groups such as the Beatles and the Rolling Stones gained adulation. Since then, hard rock, punk rock, new wave, reggae, and rap music have evolved.

Literature in the Twentieth Century

In literature, a broad movement called **modernism** flourished between 1890 and 1940. In general, modernists were concerned with the loss of traditional values brought on by the major advances and disasters of the early twentieth century. Modernist literature usually reflects the fragmentation and uncertainty that writers and poets perceived all around them. Many modernists emphasized psychological exploration over direct social commentary. Some, like **James**

Jazz great Dizzy Gillespie has helped revolutionize the sound of music in the U.S. and abroad.

Joyce (see page 1207), turned to experimental techniques such as **stream of consciousness**. In *Ulysses*, Joyce used this technique to describe everything that happens to a man in a single day—including all his thoughts, both conscious and unconscious. Other writers, such as **Franz Kafka** (see page 1154) and **Akutagawa Ryunosuke** (see page 1393), used nightmarish settings and situations to express the alienation of the individual in modern society.

Poets such as T. S. Eliot and **Rainer Maria Rilke** (see page 1148) broke with traditional forms to express their own personal visions. In his most famous poem, *The Waste Land,* Eliot describes a world without faith, incapable of restoring its spiritual and moral values. Many other poets of this time abandoned traditional rhyme and meter. Their free-verse poems also experimented with punctuation and the physical appearance of the poem on the page.

Historia/Photo

Sigmund Freud (1856–1939), the founder of modern psychology. *Freud's psychoanalytic theories greatly influenced the works of many twentieth-century artists.*

THE KEY OF THE COUNTRY, RENÉ MAGRITTE, 1948. Surrealism is a literary and artistic movement that rejects the division between rational and irrational thought and instead expresses the play of the unconscious mind. The movement had a profound effect on the development of post-World War II artistic movements, such as abstract expressionism in painting and absurdism in literature.

Art Resource, New York

Responses to War

While many modernists wrote elaborate, inward-looking "studies" of human consciousness, other twentieth-century authors turned their pens to direct and blistering accounts of the wars that raged on nearly every continent of the world. Erich Maria Remarque's *All Quiet on the Western Front* and Ernest Hemingway's *A Farewell to Arms* are two novels, written from opposite sides of the battle line, that reveal the tragedy of World War I. **Elie Wiesel** wrote an autobiography of his own imprisonment in a Nazi concentration camp during World War II in *Night* (see page 1232).

In the period of general disenchantment following the world wars, literature increasingly focused on themes of alienation, uncertainty, and despair.

Absurdism and Existentialism

To reflect a world in which human existence is seemingly unreasonable and incoherent, playwrights such as Eugène Ionesco, Samuel Beckett, and Harold Pinter created dramas with characters that speak only in banalities and with plots that go nowhere. At the end of Beckett's *Waiting for Godot,* one tramp says, "Well? Shall we go?" and the other responds, "Yes, let's go." The final stage direction, however, is "*They do not move.*"

While the **theater of the absurd** tried to dramatize the "facts" of human existence, some writers began searching for a philosophy that would allow them to understand and accept the apparent senselessness of existence. Simone de Beauvoir, Jean-Paul Sartre, **Albert Camus** (see page 1244), and others developed one such philosophy, which they called **existentialism**. Existentialism takes its name from the idea that a person's physical existence precedes his or her "essence," or meaning. This means that there are no preexisting meanings, values, or guidelines for human beings. But since we want and need clarity and rationality in our lives, the existentialists concluded that each person must create his or her own meaning, or essence, in life. Existentialism had a deep impact on Christian and Jewish thought, and theologians of both faiths developed their own brands of existentialism, which emphasized a reexamination of humanity's relationship with God.

> **"** I, a stranger and afraid
> In a world I never made. **"**
>
> —Last Poems,
> A. E. Housman

Simone de Beauvoir and Jean-Paul Sartre, two founders of the literary and philosophical movement existentialism.

AP/Wide World Photos

The Fantastic

Some writers responded to the increasingly hostile and confusing world by creating fantasy or **science-fiction** stories. Although the earliest examples of science fiction in literature can be traced back to the 1600s, the genre did not reach its present form until the late 1800s. In the twentieth century, science fiction has developed in two basic directions: an infatuation with technology (Isaac Asimov and others), or an exploration of humanity's precarious place in the universe (H. G. Wells and others). The novels of William Burroughs, Kurt Vonnegut, and **Stanislaw Lem** (see page 1271) often use the conventions of science fiction to make serious comments about our world.

Cultural Identity and Literature

Twentieth-century writers from less-industrialized nations often address the problems of cultural identity. They have seen their local cultures uprooted by colonialism or foreign influence, and they have had to ask themselves whether they are to celebrate their native traditions, imitate foreign models, or create new modes of expression.

In Latin America, artists have responded in different ways. The Argentinian author **Jorge Luis Borges** (see page 1298), one of the central figures in the Latin American literary "Boom" that followed World War II, devoured nearly everything European libraries had to offer, yet his brand of fiction, which blends fantastic events and philosophical inquiry, is strikingly unique and much imitated today by writers around the world. Chilean poet **Pablo Neruda** (see page 1294) was greatly influenced by the modernist movement, but his epic work, *Las Alturas de Machu Picchu* (*The Heights of Machu Picchu*), reconciles the poet with his country's ancient Indian heritage.

The 1960s saw the development of **magical realism**, which contains elements of both the real world and the world of fantasy. Magical realists such as Colombia's **Gabriel García Márquez** (see page 1307) were influenced by **surrealism**, which encouraged the free association of ideas as a means of exploring the unconscious mind. But they were just as much influenced by the rich folklore traditions of Latin America.

NASA

American astronaut
on the moon.

HBJ Photo

Buenos Aires, Argentina, the center of Latin America's literary "Boom."

In Africa, there was much controversy over the literary movement known as **négritude**, which asserted the value of African traditions. Some writers believed that négritude was a necessary response to years of imperialism, while others, like **Chinua Achebe** (see page 1343) and **Wole Soyinka** (see page 1351), felt that négritude tended to idealize Africa's precolonial past and that African literature must instead examine that past more critically.

African writers have also debated the question of which language they should write in: that of the colonizers, which in many cases has become the only common language for the descendants of different tribes, or their native tongues. Kenyan author **Ngũgĩ wa Thiong'o** (see page 1429) has taken the latter position, turning to his native language Kikuyu after much success writing in English. Achebe, Soyinka, and others feel that by writing in English they reach a wider audience.

Twentieth-century women writers also struggled to establish a cultural identity, for until the early twentieth century, most women had virtually no political voice and little representation in literature. As the twentieth century unfolded, more and more women writers addressed the plight of their sex in a world controlled by men. In her work *The Second Sex*, Simone de Beauvoir analyzed women's secondary status in society and denounced the male middle class for perceiving women as objects. Colette, **Margaret Atwood** (see page 1316), and **Jamaica Kincaid** (see page 1320), among many others, have also helped define the politics and culture of the women's movement of the twentieth century.

Diversity of World Literatures

In literature, as in history, many different stories are proceeding at once. As we approach the year 2000, both the end of a century and the end of a millennium, we look back on cataclysmic changes that cannot be easily reduced to some clear shape or significance. Very few people could have predicted the reunification of East and West Germany or the dissolution of the Soviet Union. We know only that challenges to our understanding and imagination remain. "The only certain thing about the future," historian Eric Hobsbawm writes in *The Age of Empire*, "is that it will surprise even those who have seen furthest into it."

> **"A great writer is, so to speak, a second government in his country. And for that reason no regime has ever loved great writers, only minor ones."**
> —The First Circle,
> *Aleksandr Solzhenitsyn*

Reuters/Bettmann Newsphotos

In November of 1989, the Berlin Wall, which divided Communist East Berlin and democratic West Berlin, came down, heralding the end of Communism in Eastern Europe.

Rainer Maria Rilke
1875–1926, Austria/Czechoslovakia

The Granger Collection, New York

The German-language poet Rainer Maria Rilke (rī′nər mä·rē′ä ril′kə) thought that the monotonous routines of everyday life functioned as a husk that prevented new ideas from entering people's minds and souls. To prevent the husk from forming, Rilke spent his life on the road—wandering from nation to nation, stopping briefly wherever admirers provided food and shelter.

Rilke was born to a German-speaking family in Prague, now the capital of Czechoslovakia, when the area was still part of the Austrian empire. During childhood, he was torn between his mother, who dressed him as a girl, and his father, who sent him to military academies. In 1892, Rilke's wealthy

uncle came to the rescue by offering to pay for his nephew's studies in philosophy, art, and German literature. Rilke liked these subjects and continued to study them in Munich, Germany. In 1901, Rilke married the German sculptor Clara Westhoff. But he soon discovered that married life did not suit him, and he abandoned his wife and baby daughter so that he could travel and write.

One of the greatest influences on Rilke and his work was the French sculptor Auguste Rodin (rô·dan′), with whom Rilke worked. Rodin showed the young poet that art was hard work, not merely an outpouring of emotion.

After leaving Rodin, Rilke revised much of his earlier verse and composed some of his finest poetry. Soon after this burst of creativity, however, Rilke entered a dry period. Seeking inspiration, he visited northern Africa and then lived in the Italian city of Trieste. Here he began a series of philosophical poems, the *Duino Elegies* (1923). The project was interrupted by World War I, in which he served briefly in the Austrian military. After the war, Rilke settled in Switzerland, completed the *Duino Elegies*, and wrote his complex *Sonnets to Orpheus* (1923). Plagued by ill health since the war, Rilke died of a blood disease when he was only fifty-one. By this time his poems, with their meticulously chiseled images, had already established him as one of the most original poets of the twentieth century.

Reader's Guide

BLACK CAT
THE SWAN

Background

When Rilke was working for Auguste Rodin, he confided to the sculptor that he was suffering from writer's block. Rodin advised him to go to the zoo and look at an animal until he could "see" it, adding that it might take as long as two or three weeks, possibly more. Rilke took this strange advice. He went to the zoo, concentrated on a panther, and then wrote the first of his *Dinggedichte* (ding′gə·dikh′t), or "thing poems." What Rilke most admired about Rodin's sculptures was their ability to capture not only the outward appearance of a person, animal, or object, but also its inner vitality and spirit. Each of Rilke's "thing poems," like Rodin's sculptures, seeks to communicate both external reality and the "inward nature of things."

Writer's Response

Choose a person, animal, or thing that you can observe closely. In your journal, write a paragraph describing it in as much detail as you can. Try to also describe what it makes you think of and how it makes you feel. Does it make you feel happy or sad, calm or excited, or something else?

Literary Focus

Figurative language describes one thing in terms of another, usually very different, thing. Figurative language, which includes similes and metaphors, is not meant to be understood on a literal level. A **simile** compares two seemingly unlike things by using a connective word such as *like* or *as* ("My feet are as cold as two chunks of ice"). A **metaphor** compares two seemingly unlike things without the connective ("My feet are chunks of ice"). When the comparison is developed over several lines, it is called an **extended metaphor**. Many writers, for example, have compared life to a journey through a maze: We often make wrong turns or run into dead ends, and we can never know exactly how things will turn out.

BLACK CAT

Rainer Maria Rilke

translated by

STEPHEN MITCHELL

*In describing the cat, Rilke avoids such clichés as "black as coal" or "black as night." Keep track of the unusual **similes** and **metaphors** he uses to describe the cat, and decide which you find the most effective.*

Elaine Tin Nyo

A ghost, though invisible, still is like a place
your sight can knock on, echoing; but here
within this thick black pelt, your strongest gaze
will be absorbed and utterly disappear:

5   just as a raving madman, when nothing else
can ease him, charges into his dark night
howling, pounds on the padded wall, and feels
the rage being taken in and pacified.

She seems to hide all looks that have ever fallen
10   into her, so that, like an audience,
she can look them over, menacing and sullen,
and curl to sleep with them. But all at once

as if awakened, she turns her face to yours;
and with a shock, you see yourself, tiny,
15   inside the golden amber of her eyeballs
suspended, like a prehistoric fly.°

15–16. **amber . . . prehistoric fly:** Small, prehistoric creatures such as flies are sometimes perfectly preserved for millions of years in amber, or fossilized tree sap. The color amber takes its name from the translucent yellow or brownish yellow color of this sap.

THE SWAN

Rainer Maria Rilke

translated by

ROBERT BLY

 There is an extended comparison in this poem. What things are being compared?

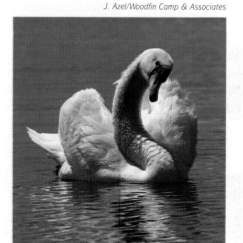

This clumsy living that moves lumbering
as if in ropes through what is not done
reminds us of the awkward way the swan walks.

And to die, which is a letting go
5 of the ground we stand on and cling to every day,
is like the swan when he nervously lets himself down

into the water, which receives him gaily
and which flows joyfully under
and after him, wave after wave,
10 while the swan, unmoving and marvelously calm,
is pleased to be carried, each minute more fully grown,
more like a king, composed, farther and farther on.

First Thoughts

Which of these poems best expresses the "inward nature" of its subject? Why do you say so?

Identifying Facts

1. According to the first stanza of "Black Cat," why is it easier to "see" a ghost than the black cat?

2. What does the first stanza of "The Swan" compare the swan's walk to? What does the rest of the poem compare the swan's swimming to?

Interpreting Meanings

1. Do you think the **simile** in the second stanza of "Black Cat" is effective? How does it help you to understand the cat's inner nature? Find three other **similes** in the poem, and explain how they contribute to the meaning of the poem.

2. In the last stanza of "Black Cat," the speaker is shocked to see himself reflected in the cat's eyes as if he were a fly suspended in amber. How does this **simile** reveal how the speaker views himself or humanity in general?

3. Explain the **extended metaphor** in "The Swan." How might it refer to a religious or spiritual concept of death and the afterlife?

Applying Meanings

In "The Swan," Rilke says that death is one kind of "letting go / of the ground we stand on and cling to every day." What are other things we "cling to"? Have you ever "let go" of any of these things? Were you nervous at first, like the swan? Think of examples of "letting go" from your own life.

Creative Writing Response

1. **Writing a "Thing Poem" About an Animal.** Choose an animal that you are familiar with or one that you feel strongly about. You may even choose a mythical animal if you like. Then, like Rilke, try to capture the essential spirit of the creature by describing its outward appearance. Use **imagery** and **figurative language** to describe the animal and to convey your feelings about it. If you wrote about an animal in the Writer's Response (see page 1149), you may use this paragraph as the starting point for your poem.

2. **Writing from Another Point of View.** Imagine yourself being seen from the **point of view** of another person, or even an animal. Think of a characteristic action that reveals your inner nature. For example, imagine someone (or something) observing you as you perform some task that you do well and enjoy—or a task that you do poorly and hate. How would the onlooker see you?

Write a brief prose passage or poem describing yourself as seen from this other point of view.

Language and Vocabulary
German and English

German, like English, belongs to the **Germanic branch** of the Indo-European family of languages. German and English went their separate ways long ago, but in modern times, English has borrowed many words from German. Some of these words entered English in Europe; others were introduced to American English by German-speaking immigrants in the New World. On a separate piece of paper, match each English word listed in the left-hand column with the right-hand column's information about the word's origin. Check your answers in a dictionary.

1. blitz | a. from a German term going back to medieval Latin for "small biscuit with crossed arms"

2. delicatessen | b. from the German compound of "bell" + "play"

3. glockenspiel | c. from the German words for "garden of children"

4. kindergarten | d. shortened from the German words for "lightning war"

5. pretzel | e. from the German words for "choice foods"

Rilke's Letters to a Young Poet

Early in the twentieth century, an aspiring young poet named Franz Xaver Kappus wrote to Rilke for advice. The two corresponded for several years. After Rilke died, Kappus published Rilke's letters in Letters to a Young Poet *(1929). The following excerpt is from Rilke's first letter to Kappus.*

You ask whether your verses are any good. You ask me. You have asked others before this. You send them to magazines. You compare them with other poems, and you are upset when certain editors reject your work. Now (since you have said you want my advice) I beg you to stop doing that sort of thing. You are looking outside, and that is what you should most avoid right now. No one can advise or help you— no one. There is only one thing you should do. Go into yourself. Find out the reason that commands you to write; see whether it has spread its roots into the very depths of your heart; confess to yourself whether you would have to die if you were forbidden to write. This most of all: ask yourself in the most silent hour of your night: *must* I write? Dig into yourself for a deep answer. And if this answer rings out in assent, if you meet this solemn question with a strong, simple ''*I must*,'' then build your life in accordance with this necessity; your whole life, even into its humblest and most indifferent hour, must become a sign and witness to this impulse. Then come close to Nature. Then, as if no one had ever tried before, try to say what you see and feel and love and lose. Don't write love poems; avoid those forms that are too facile and ordinary: they are the hardest to work with, and it takes a great, fully ripened power to create something individual where good, even glorious, traditions exist in abundance. So rescue yourself from these general themes and write about what your everyday life offers you; describe your sorrows and desires, the thoughts that pass through your mind and your belief in some kind of beauty—describe all these with heartfelt, silent, humble sincerity and, when you express yourself, use the Things around you, the images from your dreams, and the objects that you remember. If your everyday life seems poor, don't blame *it*; blame yourself; admit to yourself that you are not enough of a poet to call forth its riches; because for the creator there is no poverty and no poor, indifferent place. And even if you found yourself in some prison, whose walls let in none of the world's sounds— wouldn't you still have your childhood, that jewel beyond all price, that treasure house of memories? Turn your attention to it. Try to raise up the sunken feelings of this enormous past; your personality will grow stronger, your solitude will expand and become a place where you can live in the twilight, where the noise of other people passes by, far in the distance.—And if out of this turning-within, out of this immersion in your own world, *poems* come, then you will not think of asking anyone whether they are good or not.

Franz Kafka
1883–1924, Austria/Czechoslovakia

Franz Kafka once wrote that literature should be an axe that smashes through the "frozen sea" inside every person. The "frozen sea" is, in part, the alienation and despair that Kafka and many others felt in the unstable years of the early twentieth century. Kafka's grotesque tales often do strike the reader with the force of an axe. In *The Metamorphosis* (1915), for instance, a man transforms into a giant insect and is treated as a vermin by his family. In *The Trial* (1925), a man is arrested, convicted, tried by a mysterious court, and executed without ever knowing his crime. In *The Castle* (1926), the hero is not allowed to communicate with his employer in a castle.

Like many of his characters, Kafka was lonely and insecure. His insecurities stemmed in part from social frictions in his native Prague, now the capital of Czechoslovakia, which for most of Kafka's life was under Austrian control. Although Kafka was educated in Prague's elite German-language academy and became part of a group of German-speaking Jewish intellectuals known as the Prague Circle, he was keenly aware of his status as an outsider in the Czech population. In fact, as a Czech Jew, Kafka was doubly an outsider: He was distrusted by the Czechs because he spoke German and despised by the Germans because he was a Jew.

Kafka had a distant relationship with his father, a stern man who treated his son with indifference and even contempt. Kafka expressed his feelings of dislike and fear, as well as his continued search for approval, in *Letter to His Father*, a one-hundred-page document that was never actually sent to his father.

Kafka was rarely satisfied with his literary efforts, and before his death from tuberculosis he asked his friend and editor Max Brod (1884–1968) to burn his manuscripts. Fortunately for future readers, Brod ignored the request and published the manuscripts. Kafka's works have had an enormous impact on modern literature. They are so famous that they have given rise to the English word *Kafkaesque*, which is used to describe any situation or setting that is characterized by spiritual anxiety, isolation, surreal distortion, or senselessness.

Reader's Guide

THE METAMORPHOSIS

Background

Nearly every culture has myths and folktales about people, animals, or objects that undergo startling transformations. Fairy tales often include such metamorphoses: A frog turns into a prince; a pumpkin turns into Cinderella's coach. One of the world's first story collections, *Metamorphoses* by the Roman poet Ovid (see page 420), retells famous transformation stories from Greek and Roman mythology. While Kafka's story draws on traditions from mythology and folklore, it belongs not to the wonderful, magical world of myth, but to the bizarre world of **surrealism**—art or literature that goes beyond realism to portray the irrational events of dreams or nightmares. *The Metamorphosis* begins with a transformation that plunges us immediately into Kafka's world, where extraordinary events are commonplace.

Although it would be a mistake to reduce Kafka's fiction to its autobiographical elements, tensions in his life can be seen in all of his works, perhaps especially in *The Metamorphosis*. Some scholars have pointed out that *Samsa,* the family name of the characters in the story, is a cryptogram (code version) of *Kafka.* Gregor Samsa, the main character, is like Kafka himself in that he has a boring job, wants to spend more time in artistic pursuits, and has mixed feelings toward his family. Sometimes called a novella, *The Metamorphosis* was the longest work that Kafka published in his lifetime.

Writer's Response

Recall a dream you have had that involved bizarre events that could never happen in real life. In a paragraph or two, describe those events and your reaction to them.

Literary Focus

A **symbol** is a person, place, thing, or event that stands both for itself and something beyond itself. Some symbols are widely recognized: a heart is a symbol for love; a snake is a symbol for evil. Sometimes writers create less obvious symbols. For example, a shark may function as the animal itself while it also stands for something else—cruelty or power or nature. A symbol usually represents an abstract idea or a range of related ideas.

THE METAMORPHOSIS

Franz Kafka

translated by

STANLEY CORNGOLD

Some readers view the transformation that occurs at the beginning of this story as a literalization of the hostile expression "You vermin!" which Kafka's father had once used to deride one of Kafka's friends. As you read **The Metamorphosis,** *decide whether the transformation could be a* **symbol.** *If so, what does it symbolize?*

Treat Davidson/Photo Researchers, Inc.

1

When Gregor Samsa woke up one morning from unsettling dreams, he found himself changed in his bed into a monstrous vermin. He was lying on his back as hard as armor plate, and when he lifted his head a little, he saw his vaulted brown belly, sectioned by arch-shaped ribs, to whose dome the cover, about to slide off completely, could barely cling. His many legs, pitifully thin compared with the size of the rest of him, were waving helplessly before his eyes.

"What's happened to me?" he thought. It was no dream. His room, a regular human room, only a little on the small side, lay quiet between the four familiar walls. Over the table, on which an unpacked line of fabric samples was all spread out—Samsa was a traveling salesman—hung the picture which he had recently cut out of a glossy magazine and lodged in a pretty gilt frame. It showed a lady done up in a fur hat and a fur boa,[1] sitting upright and raising up against the viewer a heavy fur muff in which her whole forearm had disappeared.

Gregor's eyes then turned to the window, and the overcast weather—he could hear raindrops hitting against the metal window ledge—completely depressed him. "How about going back to sleep for a few minutes and forgetting all this nonsense," he thought, but that was completely impracticable, since he was used to sleeping on his right side and in his present state could not get into that position. No matter how hard he threw himself onto his right side, he always rocked onto his back again. He must have tried it a hundred times, closing his eyes so as not to have to see his squirming legs, and stopped only when he began to feel a slight, dull pain in his side, which he had never felt before.

"Oh God," he thought, "what a grueling job I've picked! Day in, day out—on the road. The upset of doing business is much worse than the actual business in the home office, and, besides, I've got the torture of traveling, worrying about changing trains, eating miserable food at all hours, constantly seeing new faces, no relationships that last or get more intimate. To the devil with it all!" He felt a slight itching up on top of his belly; shoved himself slowly on his back closer to the bedpost, so as to be able to lift his head better; found the itchy spot, studded with small white dots which he had no idea what to make of; and wanted to touch the spot with one of his legs but immediately pulled it back, for the contact sent a cold shiver through him.

He slid back again into his original position. "This getting up so early," he thought, "makes anyone a complete idiot. Human beings have to have their sleep. Other traveling salesmen live like harem women.[2] For instance, when I go back to the hotel before lunch to write up the business I've done, these gentlemen are just having breakfast. That's all I'd have to try with my boss; I'd be fired on the spot. Anyway, who knows if that wouldn't be a very good thing for me. If I didn't hold back for my parents' sake, I would have quit long ago, I would have marched up to the boss and spoken my piece from the bottom of my heart. He would have fallen off the desk! It is funny, too, the way he sits on the desk and talks down from the heights to the employees, especially when they have to come right up close on account of the boss's being hard of hearing. Well, I haven't given up hope completely; once I've gotten the money together to pay off my parents' debt to him—that will probably take another five or six years—I'm going to do it without fail. Then I'm going to make the big break. But for the time being I'd better get up, since my train leaves at five."

And he looked over at the alarm clock, which was ticking on the chest of drawers. "God Almighty!" he thought. It was six-thirty, the hands were quietly moving forward, it was actually past the half-hour, it was already nearly a quarter to. Could it be that the alarm hadn't gone off? You could

---

1. **boa** (bō′ə): long scarf worn around the neck.

2. **live like harem women:** that is, lead pampered, leisurely lives.

see from the bed that it was set correctly for four o'clock; it certainly had gone off, too. Yes, but was it possible to sleep quietly through a ringing that made the furniture shake? Well, he certainly hadn't slept quietly, but probably all the more soundly for that. But what should he do now? The next train left at seven o'clock; to make it, he would have to hurry like a madman, and the line of samples wasn't packed yet, and he himself didn't feel especially fresh and ready to march around. And even if he did make the train, he could not avoid getting it from the boss, because the messenger boy had been waiting at the five-o'clock train and would have long ago reported his not showing up. He was a tool of the boss, without brains or backbone. What if he were to say he was sick? But that would be extremely embarrassing and suspicious because during his five years with the firm Gregor had not been sick even once. The boss would be sure to come with the health-insurance doctor, blame his parents for their lazy son, and cut off all excuses by quoting the health-insurance doctor, for whom the world consisted of people who were completely healthy but afraid to work. And, besides, in this case would he be so very wrong? In fact, Gregor felt fine, with the exception of his drowsiness, which was really unnecessary after sleeping so late, and he even had a ravenous appetite.

Just as he was thinking all this over at top speed, without being able to decide to get out of bed—the alarm clock had just struck a quarter to seven—he heard a cautious knocking at the door next to the head of his bed. "Gregor," someone called—it was his mother—"it's a quarter to seven. Didn't you want to catch the train?" What a soft voice! Gregor was shocked to hear his own voice answering, unmistakably his own voice, true, but in which, as if from below, an insistent distressed chirping intruded, which left the clarity of his words intact only for a moment really, before so badly garbling them as they carried that no one could be sure if he had heard right. Gregor had wanted to answer in detail and to explain everything, but, given the circumstances, confined himself to saying, "Yes, yes, thanks, Mother, I'm just getting up." The wooden door must have prevented the change in Gregor's voice from being noticed outside, because his mother was satisfied with this explanation and shuffled off. But their little exchange had made the rest of the family aware that, contrary to expectations, Gregor was still in the house, and already his father was knocking on one of the side doors, feebly but with his fist. "Gregor, Gregor," he called, "what's going on?" And after a little while he called again in a deeper, warning voice, "Gregor! Gregor!" At the other side door, however, his sister moaned gently, "Gregor? Is something the matter with you? Do you want anything?" Toward both sides Gregor answered: "I'm all ready," and made an effort, by meticulous pronunciation and by inserting long pauses between individual words, to eliminate everything from his voice that might betray him. His father went back to his breakfast, but his sister whispered, "Gregor, open up, I'm pleading with you." But Gregor had absolutely no intention of opening the door and complimented himself instead on the precaution he had adopted from his business trips, of locking all the doors during the night even at home.

First of all he wanted to get up quietly, without any excitement; get dressed; and, the main thing, have breakfast, and only then think about what to do next, for he saw clearly that in bed he would never think things through to a rational conclusion. He remembered how even in the past he had often felt some kind of slight pain, possibly caused by lying in an uncomfortable position, which, when he got up, turned out to be purely imaginary, and he was eager to see how today's fantasy would gradually fade away. That the change in his voice was nothing more than the first sign of a bad cold, an occupational ailment of the traveling salesman, he had no doubt in the least.

It was very easy to throw off the cover; all he had to do was puff himself up a little, and it fell off by itself. But after this, things got difficult, especially since he was so unusually broad. He would have needed hands and arms to lift himself up, but instead of that he had only his numerous little legs, which were in every different kind of perpetual motion and which, besides, he could not control. If he wanted to bend one, the first thing that happened was that it stretched itself out; and if he finally succeeded in getting this leg to do what he wanted, all the others in the meantime, as if set free, began to work in the most intensely painful agitation. "Just don't stay in bed being useless," Gregor said to himself.

First he tried to get out of bed with the lower part of his body, but this lower part—which by the way he had not seen yet and which he could not form a clear picture of—proved too difficult to budge; it was taking so long; and when finally, almost out of his mind, he lunged forward with all his force, without caring, he had picked the wrong direction and slammed himself violently against the lower bedpost, and the searing pain he felt taught him that exactly the lower part of his body was, for the moment anyway, the most sensitive.

He therefore tried to get the upper part of his body out of bed first and warily turned his head toward the edge of the bed. This worked easily, and in spite of its width and weight, the mass of his body finally followed, slowly, the movement of his head. But when at last he stuck his head over the edge of the bed into the air, he got too scared to continue any further, since if he finally let himself fall in this position, it would be a miracle if he didn't injure his head. And just now he had better not for the life of him lose consciousness; he would rather stay in bed.

But when, once again, after the same exertion, he lay in his original position, sighing, and again watched his little legs struggling, if possible more fiercely, with each other and saw no way of bringing peace and order into this mindless motion, he again told himself that it was impossible for him to stay in bed and that the most rational thing was to make any sacrifice for even the smallest hope of freeing himself from the bed. But at the same time he did not forget to remind himself occasionally that thinking things over calmly—indeed, as calmly as possible—was much better than jumping to desperate decisions. At such moments he fixed his eyes as sharply as possible on the window, but unfortunately there was little confidence and cheer to be gotten from the view of the morning fog, which shrouded even the other side of the narrow street. "Seven o'clock already," he said to himself as the alarm clock struck again, "seven o'clock already and still such a fog." And for a little while he lay quietly, breathing shallowly, as if expecting, perhaps, from the complete silence the return of things to the way they really and naturally were.

But then he said to himself, "Before it strikes a quarter past seven, I must be completely out of bed without fail. Anyway, by that time someone from the firm will be here to find out where I am, since the office opens before seven." And now he started rocking the complete length of his body out of the bed with a smooth rhythm. If he let himself topple out of bed in this way, his head, which on falling he planned to lift up sharply, would presumably remain unharmed. His back seemed to be hard; nothing was likely to happen to it when it fell onto the carpet. His biggest misgiving came from his concern about the loud crash that was bound to occur and would probably create, if not terror, at least anxiety behind all the doors. But that would have to be risked.

When Gregor's body already projected halfway out of bed—the new method was more of a game than a struggle, he only had to keep on rocking and jerking himself along—he thought how simple everything would be if he could get some help. Two strong persons—he thought of his father and the maid—would have been completely sufficient; they would only have had to shove their arms under his arched back, in this way scoop him off the bed, bend down with their burden, and then just be careful and patient while he managed to swing himself down onto the floor, where his little legs would hopefully acquire some purpose. Well, leaving out the fact that the doors were locked, should he really call for help? In spite of all his miseries, he could not repress a smile at this thought.

He was already so far along that when he rocked more strongly he could hardly keep his balance, and very soon he would have to commit himself, because in five minutes it would be a quarter past seven—when the doorbell rang. "It's someone from the firm," he said to himself and almost froze, while his little legs only danced more quickly. For a moment everything remained quiet. "They're not going to answer," Gregor said to himself, captivated by some senseless

hope. But then, of course, the maid went to the door as usual with her firm stride and opened up. Gregor only had to hear the visitor's first word of greeting to know who it was—the office manager himself. Why was only Gregor condemned to work for a firm where at the slightest omission they immediately suspected the worst? Were all employees louts without exception, wasn't there a single loyal, dedicated worker among them who, when he had not fully utilized a few hours of the morning for the firm, was driven half-mad by pangs of conscience and was actually unable to get out of bed? Really, wouldn't it have been enough to send one of the apprentices to find out—if this prying were absolutely necessary—did the manager himself have to come, and did the whole innocent family have to be shown in this way that the investigation of this suspicious affair could be entrusted only to the intellect of the manager? And more as a result of the excitement produced in Gregor by these thoughts than as a result of any real decision, he swung himself out of bed with all his might. There was a loud thump, but it was not a real crash. The fall was broken a little by the carpet, and Gregor's back was more elastic than he had thought, which explained the not very noticeable muffled sound. Only he had not held his head carefully enough and hit it; he turned it and rubbed it on the carpet in anger and pain.

"Something fell in there," said the manager in the room on the left. Gregor tried to imagine whether something like what had happened to him today could one day happen even to the manager; you really had to grant the possibility. But, as if in rude reply to this question, the manager took a few decisive steps in the next room and made his patent leather boots creak. From the room on the right his sister whispered, to inform Gregor, "Gregor, the manager is here." "I know," Gregor said to himself; but he did not dare raise his voice enough for his sister to hear.

"Gregor," his father now said from the room on the left, "the manager has come and wants to be informed why you didn't catch the early train. We don't know what we should say to him. Besides, he wants to speak to you personally. So please open the door. He will certainly be so kind as to excuse the disorder of the room." "Good morning, Mr. Samsa," the manager called in a friendly voice. "There's something the matter with him," his mother said to the manager while his father was still at the door, talking. "Believe me, sir, there's something the matter with him. Otherwise how would Gregor have missed a train? That boy has nothing on his mind but the business. It's almost begun to rile me that he never goes out nights. He's been back in the city for eight days now, but every night he's been home. He sits there with us at the table, quietly reading the paper or studying timetables. It's already a distraction for him when he's busy working with his fret saw.[3] For instance, in the span of two or three evenings he carved a little frame. You'll be amazed how pretty it is; it's hanging inside his room. You'll see it right away when Gregor opens the door. You know, I'm glad that you've come, sir. We would never have gotten Gregor to open the door by ourselves; he's so stubborn. And there's certainly something wrong with him, even though he said this morning there wasn't." "I'm coming right away," said Gregor slowly and deliberately, not moving in order not to miss a word of the conversation. "I haven't any other explanation myself," said the manager. "I hope it's nothing serious. On the other hand, I must say that we businessmen—fortunately or unfortunately, whichever you prefer—very often simply have to overcome a slight indisposition for business reasons." "So can the manager come in now?" asked his father, impatient, and knocked on the door again. "No," said Gregor. In the room on the left there was an embarrassing silence; in the room on the right his sister began to sob.

Why didn't his sister go in to the others? She had probably just got out of bed and not even started to get dressed. Then what was she crying about? Because he didn't get up and didn't let the manager in, because he was in danger of losing his job, and because then the boss would start hounding his parents about the old debts? For the time being, certainly, her worries were unnecessary. Gregor was still here and hadn't the slightest intention of letting the family down. True, at the moment he was lying on the carpet, and no one knowing his condition could seriously have expected him to let the manager in. But just because of this slight discourtesy, for which an appropriate excuse would easily be found later on, Gregor could not simply be dismissed. And to Gregor it seemed much more sensible to leave him alone now than to bother him with crying and persuasion. But it was just the uncertainty that was tormenting the others and excused their behavior.

"Mr. Samsa," the manager now called, raising his voice, "what's the matter? You barricade yourself in your room, answer only 'yes' and 'no,' cause your parents serious, unnecessary worry, and you neglect—I mention this only in passing—your duties to the firm in a really shocking manner. I am speaking here in the name of your parents and of

---

3. **fret saw:** saw with a long narrow blade and fine teeth, used to cut scrolls and other curved patterns in boards or metal plates.

your employer and ask you in all seriousness for an immediate, clear explanation. I'm amazed, amazed. I thought I knew you to be a quiet, reasonable person, and now you suddenly seem to want to start strutting about, flaunting strange whims. The head of the firm did suggest to me this morning a possible explanation for your tardiness—it concerned the cash payments recently entrusted to you—but really, I practically gave my word of honor that this explanation could not be right. But now, seeing your incomprehensible obstinacy, I am about to lose even the slightest desire to stick up for you in any way at all. And your job is not the most secure. Originally I intended to tell you all this in private, but since you make me waste my time here for nothing, I don't see why your parents shouldn't hear, too. Your performance of late has been very unsatisfactory; I know it is not the best season for doing business, we all recognize that; but a season for not doing any business, there is no such thing. Mr. Samsa, such a thing cannot be tolerated."

"But sir," cried Gregor, beside himself, in his excitement forgetting everything else, "I'm just opening up, in a minute. A slight indisposition, a dizzy spell, prevented me from getting up. I'm still in bed. But I already feel fine again. I'm just getting out of bed. Just be patient for a minute! I'm not as well as I thought yet. But really I'm fine. How something like this could just take a person by surprise! Only last night I was fine, my parents can tell you, or wait, last night I already had a slight premonition. They must have been able to tell by looking at me. Why didn't I report it to the office! But you always think that you'll get over a sickness without staying home. Sir! Spare my parents! There's no basis for any of the accusations that you're making against me now; no one has ever said a word to me about them. Perhaps you haven't seen the last orders I sent in. Anyway, I'm still going on the road with the eight o'clock train; these few hours of rest have done me good. Don't let me keep you, sir. I'll be at the office myself right away, and be so kind as to tell them this, and give my respects to the head of the firm."

And while Gregor hastily blurted all this out, hardly knowing what he was saying, he had easily approached the chest of drawers, probably as a result of the practice he had already gotten in bed, and now he tried to raise himself up against it. He actually intended to open the door, actually present himself and speak to the manager; he was eager to find out what the others, who were now so anxious to see him, would say at the sight of him. If they were shocked, then Gregor had no further responsibility and could be calm. But if they took everything calmly, then he, too, had no reason to get excited and could, if he hurried, actually be at the station by eight o'clock. At first he slid off the polished chest of drawers a few times, but at last, giving himself a final push, he stood upright; he no longer paid any attention to the pains in his abdomen, no matter how much they were burning. Now he let himself fall against the back of a nearby chair, clinging to its slats with his little legs. But by doing this he had gotten control of himself and fell silent, since he could now listen to what the manager was saying.

"Did you understand a word?" the manager was asking his parents. "He isn't trying to make fools of us, is he?" "My God," cried his mother, already in tears, "maybe he's seriously ill, and here we are, torturing him. Grete![4] Grete!" she then cried. "Mother?" called his sister from the other side. They

---

4. **Grete** (grē'tə)

communicated by way of Gregor's room. "Go to the doctor's immediately. Gregor is sick. Hurry, get the doctor. Did you just hear Gregor talking?" "That was the voice of an animal," said the manager, in a tone conspicuously soft compared with the mother's yelling. "Anna!" "Anna!" the father called through the foyer into the kitchen, clapping his hands, "get a locksmith right away!" And already the two girls were running with rustling skirts through the foyer—how could his sister have gotten dressed so quickly?—and tearing open the door to the apartment. The door could not be heard slamming; they had probably left it open, as is the custom in homes where a great misfortune has occurred.

But Gregor had become much calmer. It was true that they no longer understood his words, though they had seemed clear enough to him, clearer than before, probably because his ear had grown accustomed to them. But still, the others now believed that there was something the matter with him and were ready to help him. The assurance and confidence with which the first measures had been taken did him good. He felt integrated into human society once again and hoped for marvelous, amazing feats from both the doctor and the locksmith, without really distinguishing sharply between them. In order to make his voice as clear as possible for the crucial discussions that were approaching, he cleared his throat a little—taking pains, of course, to do so in a very muffled manner, since this noise, too, might sound different from human coughing, a thing he no longer trusted himself to decide. In the next room, meanwhile, everything had become completely still. Perhaps his parents were sitting at the table with the manager, whispering; perhaps they were all leaning against the door and listening.

Gregor slowly lugged himself toward the door, pushing the chair in front of him, then let go of it, threw himself against the door, held himself upright against it—the pads on the bottom of his little legs exuded a little sticky substance—and for a moment rested there from the exertion. But then he got started turning the key in the lock with his mouth. Unfortunately it seemed that he had no real teeth—what was he supposed to grip the key with?—but in compensation his jaws, of course, were very strong; with their help he actually got the key moving and paid no attention to the fact that he was undoubtedly hurting himself in some way, for a brown liquid came out of his mouth, flowed over the key, and dripped onto the floor. "Listen," said the manager in the next room, "he's turning the key." This was great encouragement to Gregor; but everyone should have cheered him on, his father and mother, too. "Go, Gregor," they should have called, "keep going, at that lock, harder, harder!" And in the delusion that they were all following his efforts with suspense, he clamped his jaws madly on the key with all the strength he could muster. Depending on the progress of the key, he danced around the lock; holding himself upright only by his mouth, he clung to the key, as the situation demanded, or pressed it down again with the whole weight of his body. The clearer click of the lock as it finally snapped back literally woke Gregor up. With a sigh of relief he said to himself, "So I didn't need the locksmith after all," and laid his head down on the handle in order to open wide one wing of the double doors.

Since he had to use this method of opening the door, it was really opened very wide while he himself was still invisible. He first had to edge slowly around the one wing of the door, and do so very carefully if he was not to fall flat on his back just before entering. He was still busy with this difficult maneuver and had no time to pay attention to anything else when he heard the manager burst out with a loud "Oh!"—it sounded like a rush of wind—and now he could see him, standing closest to the door, his hand pressed over his open mouth, slowly backing away, as if repulsed by an invisible, unrelenting force. His mother—in spite of the manager's presence she stood with her hair still unbraided from the night, sticking out in all directions—first looked at his father with her hands clasped, then took two steps toward Gregor, and sank down in the midst of her skirts spreading out around her, her face completely hidden on her breast. With a hostile expression his father clenched his fist, as if to drive Gregor back into his room, then looked uncertainly around the living room, shielded his eyes with his hands, and sobbed with heaves of his powerful chest.

Now Gregor did not enter the room after all but leaned against the inside of the firmly bolted wing of the door, so that only half his body was visible and his head above it, cocked to one side and peeping out at the others. In the meantime it had grown much lighter; across the street one could see clearly a section of the endless, grayish black building opposite—it was a hospital—with its regular windows starkly piercing the façade; the rain was still coming down, but only in large, separately visible drops that were also pelting the ground literally one at a time. The breakfast dishes were laid out lavishly on the table, since for his father breakfast was the most important meal of the day, which he would prolong for hours while reading various newspapers. On the wall directly opposite hung a photograph of Gregor from his army days, in a lieutenant's uniform, his hand on his sword, a carefree

smile on his lips, demanding respect for his bearing and his rank. The door to the foyer was open, and since the front door was open, too, it was possible to see out onto the landing and the top of the stairs going down.

"Well," said Gregor—and he was thoroughly aware of being the only one who had kept calm—"I'll get dressed right away, pack up my samples, and go. Will you, will you please let me go? Now, sir, you see, I'm not stubborn and I'm willing to work; traveling is a hardship, but without it I couldn't live. Where are you going, sir? To the office? Yes? Will you give an honest report of everything? A man might find for a moment that he was unable to work, but that's exactly the right time to remember his past accomplishments and to consider that later on, when the obstacle has been removed, he's bound to work all the harder and more efficiently. I'm under so many obligations to the head of the firm, as you know very well. Besides, I also have my parents and my sister to worry about. I'm in a tight spot, but I'll also work my way out again. Don't make things harder for me than they already are. Stick up for me in the office, please. Traveling salesmen aren't well liked there, I know. People think they make a fortune leading the gay life. No one has any particular reason to rectify this prejudice. But you, sir, you have a better perspective on things than the rest of the office, an even better perspective, just between the two of us, than the head of the firm himself, who in his capacity as owner easily lets his judgment be swayed against an employee. And you also know very well that the traveling salesman, who is out of the office practically the whole year round, can so easily become the victim of gossip, coincidences, and unfounded accusations, against which he's completely unable to defend himself,

PAROIS D'OREINES, JEAN DUBUFFET (1901–1985)
? *What is Gregor's initial reaction to his transformation? Does his reaction surprise you?*

since in most cases he knows nothing at all about them except when he returns exhausted from a trip, and back home gets to suffer on his own person the grim consequences, which can no longer be traced back to their causes. Sir, don't go away without a word to tell me you think I'm at least partly right!"

But at Gregor's first words the manager had already turned away and with curled lips looked back at Gregor only over his twitching shoulder. And during Gregor's speech he did not stand still for a minute but, without letting Gregor out of his sight, backed toward the door, yet very gradually, as if there were some secret prohibition against leaving the room. He was already in the foyer, and from the sudden movement with which he took his last step from the living room, one might have thought he had just burned the sole of his foot. In the foyer, however, he stretched his right hand far out toward the staircase, as if nothing less than an unearthly deliverance were awaiting him there.

Gregor realized that he must on no account let the manager go away in this mood if his position in the firm were not to be jeopardized in the extreme. His parents did not understand this too well; in the course of the years they had formed the conviction that Gregor was set for life in this firm; and furthermore, they were so preoccupied with their immediate troubles that they had lost all consideration for the future. But Gregor had this forethought. The manager must be detained, calmed down, convinced, and finally won over; Gregor's and the family's future depended on it! If only his sister had been there! She was perceptive; she had already begun to cry when Gregor was still lying calmly on his back. And certainly the manager, this ladies' man, would have listened to her; she would have shut the front door and in the foyer talked him out of his scare. But his sister was not there, Gregor had to handle the situation himself. And without stopping to realize that he had no idea what his new faculties of movement were, and without stopping to realize either that his speech had possibly—indeed, probably—not been understood again, he let go of the wing of the door; he shoved himself through the opening, intending to go to the manager, who was already on the landing, ridiculously holding onto the banisters with both hands; but groping for support, Gregor immediately fell down with a little cry onto his numerous little legs. This had hardly happened when for the first time that morning he had a feeling of physical well-being; his little legs were on firm ground; they obeyed him completely, as he noted to his joy; they even strained to carry him away wherever he wanted to go; and he already believed that final recovery from all his sufferings was imminent. But at that very moment, as he lay on the floor rocking with repressed motion, not far from his mother and just opposite her, she, who had seemed so completely self-absorbed, all at once jumped up, her arms stretched wide, her fingers spread, and cried, "Help, for God's sake, help!" held her head bent as if to see Gregor better, but inconsistently darted madly backward instead; had forgotten that the table laden with the breakfast dishes stood behind her; sat down on it hastily, as if her thoughts were elsewhere, when she reached it; and did not seem to notice at all that near her the big coffeepot had been knocked over and coffee was pouring in a steady stream onto the rug.

"Mother, Mother," said Gregor softly and looked up at her. For a minute the manager had completely slipped his mind; on the other hand at the sight of the spilling coffee he could not resist snapping his jaws several times in the air. At this his mother screamed once more, fled from the table, and fell into the arms of his father, who came rushing up to her. But Gregor had no time now for his parents; the manager was already on the stairs; with his chin on the banister, he was taking a last look back. Gregor was off to a running start, to be as sure as possible of catching up with him; the manager must have suspected something like this, for he leaped down several steps and disappeared; but still he shouted "Agh," and the sound carried through the whole staircase. Unfortunately the manager's flight now seemed to confuse his father completely, who had been relatively calm until now, for instead of running after the manager himself, or at least not hindering Gregor in his pursuit, he

seized in his right hand the manager's cane, which had been left behind on a chair with his hat and overcoat, picked up in his left hand a heavy newspaper from the table, and stamping his feet, started brandishing the cane and the newspaper to drive Gregor back into his room. No plea of Gregor's helped, no plea was even understood; however humbly he might turn his head, his father merely stamped his feet more forcefully. Across the room his mother had thrown open a window in spite of the cool weather, and leaning out, she buried her face, far outside the window, in her hands. Between the alley and the staircase a strong draft was created, the window curtains blew in, the newspapers on the table rustled, single sheets fluttered across the floor. Pitilessly his father came on, hissing like a wild man. Now Gregor had not had any practice at all walking in reverse, it was really very slow going. If Gregor had only been allowed to turn around, he could have gotten into his room right away, but he was afraid to make his father impatient by this time-consuming gyration, and at any minute the cane in his father's hand threatened to come down on his back or his head with a deadly blow. Finally, however, Gregor had no choice, for he noticed with horror that in reverse he could not even keep going in one direction; and so, incessantly throwing uneasy side glances at his father, he began to turn around as quickly as possible, in reality turning only very slowly. Perhaps his father realized his good intentions, for he did not interfere with him; instead, he even now and then directed the maneuver from afar with the tip of his cane. If only his father did not keep making this intolerable hissing sound! It made Gregor lose his head completely. He had almost finished the turn when—his mind continually on this hissing—he made a mistake and even started turning back around to his original position. But when he had at last successfully managed to get his head in front of the opened door, it turned out that his body was too broad to get through as it was. Of course in his father's present state of mind it did not even remotely occur to him to open the other wing of the door in order to give Gregor enough room to pass through. He had only the fixed idea that Gregor must return to his room as quickly as possible. He would never have allowed the complicated preliminaries Gregor needed to go through in order to stand up on one end and perhaps in this way fit through the door. Instead, he drove Gregor on, as if there were no obstacle, with exceptional loudness; the voice behind Gregor did not sound like that of only a single father; now this was really no joke anymore, and Gregor forced himself—come what may—into the doorway. One side of his body rose up, he lay lopsided in the opening, one of his flanks was scraped raw, ugly blotches marred the white door, soon he got stuck and could not have budged any more by himself, his little legs on one side dangled tremblingly in midair, those on the other were painfully crushed against the floor—when from behind his father gave him a hard shove, which was truly his salvation, and bleeding profusely, he flew far into his room. The door was slammed shut with the cane, then at last everything was quiet.

2

It was already dusk when Gregor awoke from his deep, comalike sleep. Even if he had not been disturbed, he would certainly not have woken up much later, for he felt that he had rested and slept long enough, but it seemed to him that a hurried step and a cautious shutting of the door leading to the foyer had awakened him. The light of the electric streetlamps lay in pallid streaks on the ceiling and on the upper parts of the furniture, but underneath, where Gregor was, it was dark. Groping clumsily with his antennae, which he was only now beginning to appreciate, he slowly dragged himself toward the door to see what had been happening there. His left side felt like one single long, unpleasantly tautening scar, and he actually had to limp on his two rows of legs. Besides, one little leg had been seriously injured in the course of the morning's events—it was almost a miracle that only one had been injured—and dragged along lifelessly.

Only after he got to the door did he notice what had really attracted him—the smell of something to eat. For there stood a bowl filled with fresh milk, in which small slices of white bread were floating. He could almost have laughed for joy, since he was even hungrier than he had been in the morning, and he immediately dipped his head into the milk, almost to over his eyes. But he soon drew it back again in disappointment; not only because he had difficulty eating on account of the soreness in his left side—and he could eat only if his whole panting body cooperated—but because he didn't like the milk at all, although it used to be his favorite drink, and that was certainly why his sister had put it in the room; in fact, he turned away from the bowl almost with repulsion and crawled back to the middle of the room.

In the living room, as Gregor saw through the crack in the door, the gas had been lit, but while at this hour of the day his father was in the habit of reading the afternoon newspaper in a loud voice to his mother and sometimes to his sister, too, now there wasn't a sound. Well, perhaps this custom of reading aloud, which his sister was always telling him and writing him about, had recently been discontinued altogether. But in all the other rooms, too, it was just as still, although the apartment certainly was not empty. "What a quiet life the family has been leading," Gregor said to himself, and while he stared rigidly in front of him into the darkness, he felt very proud that he had been able to provide such a life in so nice an apartment for his parents and his sister. But what now if all the peace, the comfort, the contentment, were to come to a horrible end? In order not to get involved in such thoughts, Gregor decided to keep moving, and he crawled up and down the room.

During the long evening first one of the side doors and then the other was opened a small crack and quickly shut again; someone had probably had the urge to come in and then had had second thoughts. Gregor now settled into position right by the living-room door, determined somehow to get the hesitating visitor to come in, or at least to find out who it might be; but the door was not opened again, and Gregor waited in vain. In the morning, when the doors had been locked, everyone had wanted to come in; now that he had opened one of the doors and the others had evidently been opened during the day, no one came in, and now the keys were even inserted on the outside.

It was late at night when the light finally went out in the living room, and now it was easy for Gregor to tell that his parents and his sister had stayed up so long, since, as he could distinctly hear, all three were now retiring on tiptoe. Certainly no one would come in to Gregor until the morning; and so he had ample time to consider undisturbed how best to rearrange his life. But the empty high-ceilinged room in which he was forced to lie flat on the floor made him nervous,

without his being able to tell why—since it was, after all, the room in which he had lived for the past five years—and turning half unconsciously and not without a slight feeling of shame, he scuttled under the couch where, although his back was a little crushed and he could not raise his head any more, he immediately felt very comfortable and was only sorry that his body was too wide to go completely under the couch.

There he stayed the whole night, which he spent partly in a sleepy trance, from which hunger pangs kept waking him with a start, partly in worries and vague hopes, all of which, however, led to the conclusion that for the time being he would have to lie low and, by being patient and showing his family every possible consideration, help them bear the inconvenience which he simply had to cause them in his present condition.

Early in the morning—it was still almost night—Gregor had the opportunity of testing the strength of the resolutions he had just made, for his sister, almost fully dressed, opened the door from the foyer and looked in eagerly. She did not see him right away, but when she caught sight of him under the couch—God, he had to be somewhere, he couldn't just fly away—she became so frightened that she lost control of herself and slammed the door shut again. But, as if she felt sorry for her behavior, she immediately opened the door again and came in on tiptoe, as if she were visiting someone seriously ill or perhaps even a stranger. Gregor had pushed his head forward just to the edge of the couch and was watching her. Would she notice that he had left the milk standing, and not because he hadn't been hungry, and would she bring in a dish of something he'd like better? If she were not going to do it of her own free will, he would rather starve than call it to her attention, although, really, he felt an enormous urge to shoot out from under the couch, throw himself at his sister's feet, and beg her for something good to eat. But his sister noticed at once, to her astonishment, that the bowl was still full, only a little milk was spilled around it; she picked it up immediately—not with her bare hands, of course, but with a rag—and carried it out. Gregor was extremely curious to know what she would bring him instead, and he racked his brains on the subject. But he would never have been able to guess what his sister, in the goodness of her heart, actually did. To find out his likes and dislikes, she brought him a wide assortment of things, all spread out on an old newspaper: old, half-rotten vegetables; bones left over from the evening meal, caked with congealed white sauce; some raisins and almonds; a piece of cheese, which two days before Gregor had declared inedible; a plain slice of bread, a slice of bread and butter, and one with butter and salt. In addition to all this she put down some water in the bowl apparently permanently earmarked for Gregor's use. And out of a sense of delicacy, since she knew that Gregor would not eat in front of her, she left hurriedly and even turned the key, just so that Gregor should know that he might make himself as comfortable as he wanted. Gregor's legs began whirring now that he was going to eat. Besides, his bruises must have completely healed, since he no longer felt any handicap, and marveling at this he thought how, over a month ago, he had cut his finger very slightly with a knife and how this wound was still hurting him only the day before yesterday. "Have I become less sensitive?" he thought, already sucking greedily at the cheese, which had immediately and forcibly attracted him ahead of all the other dishes. One right after the other, and with

eyes streaming with tears of contentment, he devoured the cheese, the vegetables, and the sauce; the fresh foods, on the other hand, he did not care for; he couldn't even stand their smell and even dragged the things he wanted to eat a bit farther away. He had finished with everything long since and was just lying lazily at the same spot when his sister slowly turned the key as a sign for him to withdraw. That immediately startled him, although he was almost asleep, and he scuttled under the couch again. But it took great self-control for him to stay under the couch even for the short time his sister was in the room, since his body had become a little bloated from the heavy meal, and in his cramped position he could hardly breathe. In between slight attacks of suffocation he watched with bulging eyes as his unsuspecting sister took a broom and swept up, not only his leavings, but even the foods which Gregor had left completely untouched—as if they too were no longer usable—and dumping everything hastily into a pail, which she covered with a wooden lid, she carried everything out. She had hardly turned her back when Gregor came out from under the couch, stretching and puffing himself up.

This, then, was the way Gregor was fed each day, once in the morning, when his parents and the maid were still asleep, and a second time in the afternoon after everyone had had dinner, for then his parents took a short nap again, and the maid could be sent out by his sister on some errand. Certainly they did not want him to starve either, but perhaps they would not have been able to stand knowing any more about his meals than from hearsay, or perhaps his sister wanted to spare them even what was possibly only a minor torment, for really, they were suffering enough as it was.

Gregor could not find out what excuses had been made to get rid of the doctor and the locksmith on that first morning, for since the others could not understand what he said, it did not occur to any of them, not even to his sister, that he could understand what they said, and so he had to be satisfied, when his sister was in the room, with only occasionally hearing her sighs and appeals to the saints. It was only later, when she had begun to get used to everything—there could never, of course, be any question of a complete adjustment—that Gregor sometimes caught a remark which was meant to be friendly or could be interpreted as such. "Oh, he liked what he had today," she would say when Gregor had tucked away a good helping, and in the opposite case, which gradually occurred more and more frequently, she used to say, almost sadly, "He's left everything again."

But if Gregor could not get any news directly, he overheard a great deal from the neighboring rooms, and as soon as he heard voices, he would immediately run to the door concerned and press his whole body against it. Especially in the early days, there was no conversation that was not somehow about him, if only implicitly. For two whole days there were family consultations at every mealtime about how they should cope; this was also the topic of discussion between meals, for at least two members of the family were always at home, since no one probably wanted to stay home alone and it was impossible to leave the apartment completely empty. Besides, on the very first day the maid—it was not completely clear what and how much she knew of what had happened—had begged his mother on bended knees to dismiss her immediately; and when she said goodbye a quarter of an hour later, she thanked them in tears for the dismissal,

as if for the greatest favor that had ever been done to her in this house, and made a solemn vow, without anyone asking her for it, not to give anything away to anyone.

Now his sister, working with her mother, had to do the cooking, too; of course, that did not cause her much trouble, since they hardly ate anything. Gregor was always hearing one of them pleading in vain with one of the others to eat and getting no answer except, "Thanks, I've had enough," or something similar. They did not seem to drink anything either. His sister often asked her father if he wanted any beer and gladly offered to go out for it herself; and when he did not answer, she said, in order to remove any hesitation on his part, that she could also send the janitor's wife to get it, but then his father finally answered with a definite "No," and that was the end of that.

In the course of the very first day his father explained the family's financial situation and prospects to both the mother and the sister. From time to time he got up from the table to get some kind of receipt or notebook out of the little strongbox he had rescued from the collapse of his business five years before. Gregor heard him open the complicated lock and secure it again after taking out what he had been looking for. These explanations by his father were to some extent the first pleasant news Gregor had heard since his imprisonment. He had always believed that his father had not been able to save a penny from the business, at least his father had never told him anything to the contrary, and Gregor, for his part, had never asked him any questions. In those days Gregor's sole concern had been to do everything in his power to make the family forget as quickly as possible the business disaster which had plunged everyone into a state of total despair. And so he had begun to work with special ardor and had risen almost overnight from stock clerk to traveling salesman, which of course had opened up very different moneymaking possibilities, and in no time his successes on the job were transformed, by means of commissions, into hard cash that could be plunked down on the table at home in front of his astonished and delighted family. Those had been wonderful times, and they had never returned, at least not with the same glory, although later on Gregor earned enough money to meet the expenses of the entire family and actually did so. They had just gotten used to it, the family as well as Gregor, the money was received with thanks and given with pleasure, but no special feeling of warmth went with it any more. Only his sister had remained close to Gregor, and it was his secret plan that she, who, unlike him, loved music and could play the violin movingly, should be sent next year to the Conservatory,[5] regardless of the great expense involved, which could surely be made up for in some other way. Often during Gregor's short stays in the city the Conservatory would come up in his conversations with his sister, but always merely as a beautiful dream which was not supposed to come true, and his parents were not happy to hear even these innocent allusions; but Gregor had very concrete ideas on the subject and he intended solemnly to announce his plan on Christmas Eve.

Thoughts like these, completely useless in his present state, went through his head as he stood glued to the door, listening. Sometimes out of general exhaustion he could not listen any more and let his head bump carelessly against the door, but immediately pulled it back again, for even the slight noise he made by doing this had been heard in the next room and made them all lapse into silence. "What's he carrying on about in there now?" said his father after a while, obviously turning toward the door, and only then would the interrupted conversation gradually be resumed.

Gregor now learned in a thorough way—for his father was in the habit of often repeating himself in his explanations, partly because he himself had not dealt with these matters for a long time, partly, too, because his mother did not understand everything the first time around—that in spite of all their misfortunes, a bit of capital, a very little bit, certainly, was still intact from the old days, which in the meantime had increased a little through the untouched interest. But besides that, the money Gregor had brought home every month—he had kept only a few dollars for himself—had never been completely used up and had accumulated into a tidy principal. Behind his door Gregor nodded emphatically, delighted at this unexpected foresight and thrift. Of course he actually could have paid off more of his father's debt to the boss with this extra money, and the day on which he could have gotten rid of his job would have been much closer, but now things were undoubtedly better the way his father had arranged them.

Now this money was by no means enough to let the family live off the interest; the principal was perhaps enough to support the family for one year, or at the most two, but that was all there was. So it was just a sum that really should not be touched and that had to be put away for a rainy day; but the money to live on would have to be earned. Now his father was still healthy, certainly, but he was an old man who had not worked for the past five years and who in any case

5. **Conservatory:** school of music.

could not be expected to undertake too much; during these five years, which were the first vacation of his hard-working yet unsuccessful life, he had gained a lot of weight and as a result had become fairly sluggish. And was his old mother now supposed to go out and earn money, when she suffered from asthma, when a walk through the apartment was already an ordeal for her, and when she spent every other day lying on the sofa under the open window, gasping for breath? And was his sister now supposed to work—who for all her seventeen years was still a child and whom it would be such a pity to deprive of the life she had led until now, which had consisted of wearing pretty clothes, sleeping late, helping in the house, enjoying a few modest amusements, and above all, playing the violin? At first, whenever the conversation turned to the necessity of earning money, Gregor would let go of the door and throw himself down on the cool leather sofa which stood beside it, for he felt hot with shame and grief.

Often he lay there the whole long night through, not sleeping a wink and only scrabbling on the leather for hours on end. Or, not balking at the huge effort of pushing an armchair to the window, he would crawl up to the window sill and, propped up in the chair, lean against the window, evidently in some sort of remembrance of the feeling of freedom he used to have from looking out the window. For, in fact, from day to day he saw things even a short distance away less and less distinctly; the hospital opposite, which he used to curse because he saw so much of it, was now completely beyond his range of vision, and if he had not been positive that he was living in Charlotte Street—a quiet but still very much a city street—he might have believed that he was looking out of his window into a desert where the gray

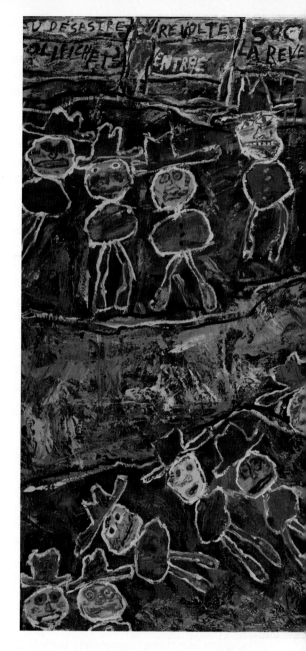

sky and the gray earth were indistinguishably fused. It took his observant sister only twice to notice that his armchair was standing by the window for her to push the chair back to the same place by the window each time she had finished cleaning the room, and from then on she even left the inside casement of the window open.

How would you describe the tone of Kafka's novella thus far? Comic? Ironic? Tragic? Explain your answer.

If Gregor had only been able to speak to his sister and thank her for everything she had to do for him, he could have accepted her services more easily; as it was, they caused him pain. Of course his sister tried to ease the embarrassment of the whole situation as much as possible, and as time went on, she naturally managed it better and better, but in time Gregor, too, saw things much more clearly. Even the way she came in was terrible for him. Hardly had she entered the room than she would run straight to the window without taking time to close the door—though she was usually so careful to spare everyone the sight of Gregor's room—then tear open the casements with eager hands, almost as if she were suffocating, and remain for a little while at the window even in the coldest weather, breathing deeply. With this racing and crashing she frightened Gregor twice a day; the whole time he cowered under the couch, and yet he knew very well that she would certainly have spared him this if only she had found it possible to stand being in a room with him with the window closed.

One time—it must have been a month since Gregor's metamorphosis, and there was certainly no particular reason any more for his sister to be astonished at Gregor's appearance—she came a little earlier than usual and caught Gregor still looking out the window, immobile and so in an excellent position to be terrifying. It would not have surprised Gregor if she had not come in, because his position prevented her from immediately opening the window, but not only did she not come in, she even sprang back and locked the door; a stranger might easily have thought that Gregor had been lying in wait for her, wanting to bite her. Of course Gregor immediately hid under the couch, but he had to wait until noon before his sister came again, and she seemed much more uneasy than usual. He realized from this that the sight of him was still repulsive to her and was bound to remain repulsive to her in the future, and that she probably had to overcome a lot of resistance not to run away at the sight of even the small part of his body that jutted out from under the couch. So, to spare her even this sight, one day he carried the sheet on his back to the couch—the job took four hours—and arranged it in such a way that he was now completely covered up and his sister could not see him even when she stooped. If she had considered this sheet unnecessary, then of course she could have removed it, for it was

clear enough that it could not be for his own pleasure that Gregor shut himself off altogether, but she left the sheet the way it was, and Gregor thought that he had even caught a grateful look when one time he cautiously lifted the sheet a little with his head in order to see how his sister was taking the new arrangement.

During the first two weeks, his parents could not bring themselves to come in to him, and often he heard them say how much they appreciated his sister's work, whereas until now they had frequently been annoyed with her because she had struck them as being a little useless. But now both of them, his father and his mother, often waited outside Gregor's room while his sister straightened it up, and as soon as she came out she had to tell them in great detail how the room looked, what Gregor had eaten, how he had behaved this time, and whether he had perhaps shown a little improvement. His mother, incidentally, began relatively soon to want to visit Gregor, but his father and his sister at first held her back with reasonable arguments to which Gregor listened very attentively and of which he wholeheartedly approved. But later she had to be restrained by force, and then when she cried out, "Let me go to Gregor, he is my unfortunate boy! Don't you understand that I have to go to him?" Gregor thought that it might be a good idea after all if his mother did come in, not every day of course, but perhaps once a week; she could still do everything much better than his sister, who, for all her courage, was still only a child and in the final analysis had perhaps taken on such a difficult assignment only out of childish flightiness.

Gregor's desire to see his mother was soon fulfilled. During the day Gregor did not want to show himself at the window, if only out of consideration for his parents, but he couldn't crawl very far on his few square yards of floor space, either; he could hardly put up with just lying still even at night; eating soon stopped giving him the slightest pleasure, so, as a distraction, he adopted the habit of crawling crisscross over the walls and the ceiling. He especially liked hanging from the ceiling; it was completely different from lying on the floor; one could breathe more freely; a faint swinging sensation went through the body; and in the almost happy absent-mindedness which Gregor felt up there, it could happen to his own surprise that he let go and plopped onto the floor. But now, of course, he had much better control of his body than before and did not hurt himself even from such a big drop. His sister immediately noticed the new entertainment Gregor had discovered for himself—after all, he left behind traces of his sticky substance wherever he crawled—and so she got it into her head to make it possible for Gregor to crawl on an altogether wider scale by taking out the furniture which stood in his way— mainly the chest of drawers and the desk. But she was not able to do this by herself; she did not dare ask her father for help; the maid would certainly not have helped her, for although this girl, who was about sixteen, was bravely sticking it out after the previous cook had left, she had asked for the favor of locking herself in the kitchen at all times and of only opening the door on special request. So there was nothing left for his sister to do except to get her mother one day when her father was out. And his mother did come, with exclamations of excited joy, but she grew silent at the door of Gregor's room. First his sister looked to see, of course, that everything in the room was in order; only then did she let her mother come in. Hurrying as fast as he could, Gregor had pulled the sheet down lower still and pleated it more tightly—it really looked just like a sheet accidently thrown over the couch. This time Gregor also refrained from spying from under the sheet; he renounced seeing his mother for the time being and was simply happy that she had come after all. "Come on, you can't see him," his sister said, evidently leading her mother in by the hand. Now Gregor could hear the two frail women moving the old chest of drawers— heavy for anyone—from its place and his sister insisting on doing the harder part of the job herself, ignoring the warnings of her mother, who was afraid that she would over- exert herself. It went on for a long time. After struggling for a good quarter of an hour, his mother said that they had better leave the chest where it was, because, in the first place, it was too heavy, they would not finish before his father came, and with the chest in the middle of the room, Gregor would be completely barricaded; and, in the second place, it was not at all certain that they were doing Gregor a favor by removing his furniture. To her the opposite seemed to be the case; the sight of the bare wall was heartbreaking; and why shouldn't Gregor also have the same feeling, since he had been used to his furniture for so long and would feel abandoned in the empty room. "And doesn't it look," his mother concluded very softly—in fact she had been almost whis- pering the whole time, as if she wanted to avoid letting Gregor, whose exact where- abouts she did not know, hear even the sound of her voice, for she was convinced that he did not understand the words—"and doesn't it look as if by removing his furniture we were showing him that we have given up all hope of his getting better and are leaving him to his own devices without any consideration? I think the best thing would be to try to keep the room exactly the way it was before, so that when Gregor comes back to us again, he'll find everything unchanged and can forget all the more easily what's happened in the meantime."

When he heard his mother's words, Gregor realized that the monotony of family life, combined with the fact that not a soul had addressed a word directly to him, must have addled his brain in the course of the past two months, for he could not explain to himself in any other way how in all seriousness he could have been anxious to have his room cleared out. Had he really wanted to have his warm room, comfortably fitted with furniture that had always been in the family, changed into a cave, in which, of course, he would be able to crawl around unhampered in all directions but at the cost of simultaneously, rapidly, and totally forgetting his human past? Even now he had been on the verge of forgetting, and only his mother's voice, which he had not heard for so long, had shaken him up. Nothing should be removed; everything had to stay; he could not do without the beneficial influence of the furniture on his state of mind; and if the furniture prevented him from carrying on this senseless crawling around, then that was no loss but rather a great advantage.

But his sister unfortunately had a different opinion; she had become accustomed, certainly not entirely without justification, to adopt with her parents the role of the particularly well-qualified expert whenever Gregor's affairs were being discussed; and so her mother's advice was now sufficient reason for her to insist, not only on the removal of the chest of drawers and the desk, which was all she had been planning at first, but also on the removal of all the furniture with the exception of the indispensable couch. Of course it was not only childish defiance and

the self-confidence she had recently acquired so unexpectedly and at such a cost that led her to make this demand; she had in fact noticed that Gregor needed plenty of room to crawl around in; and on the other hand, as best she could tell, he never used the furniture at all. Perhaps, however, the romantic enthusiasm of girls her age, which seeks to indulge itself at every opportunity, played a part, by tempting her to make Gregor's situation even more terrifying in order that she might do even more for him. Into a room in which Gregor ruled the bare walls all alone, no human being beside Grete was ever likely to set foot.

And so she did not let herself be swerved from her decision by her mother, who, besides, from the sheer anxiety of being in Gregor's room, seemed unsure of herself, soon grew silent, and helped her daughter as best she could to get the chest of drawers out of the room. Well, in a pinch Gregor could do without the chest, but the desk had to stay. And hardly had the women left the room with the chest, squeezing against it and groaning, than Gregor stuck his head out from under the couch to see how he could feel his way into the situation as considerately as possible. But unfortunately it had to be his mother who came back first, while in the next room Grete was clasping the chest and rocking it back and forth by herself, without of course budging it from the spot. His mother, however, was not used to the sight of Gregor, he could have made her ill, and so Gregor, frightened, scuttled in reverse to the far end of the couch but could not stop the sheet from shifting a little at the front. That was enough to put his mother on the alert. She stopped, stood still for a moment, and then went back to Grete.

Although Gregor told himself over and over again that nothing special was happening, only a few pieces of furniture were being moved, he soon had to admit that this coming and going of the women, their little calls to each other, the scraping of the furniture along the floor had the effect on him of a great turmoil swelling on all sides, and as much as he tucked in his head and his legs and shrank until his belly touched the floor, he was forced to admit that he would not be able to stand it much longer. They were clearing out his room; depriving him of everything that he loved; they had already carried away the chest of drawers, in which he kept the fret saw and other tools; were now budging the desk firmly embedded in the floor, the desk he had done his homework on when he was a student at business college, in high school, yes, even in public school—now he really had no more time to examine the good intentions of the two women, whose existence, besides, he had almost forgotten, for they were so exhausted that they were working in silence, and one could hear only the heavy shuffling of their feet.

And so he broke out—the women were just leaning against the desk in the next room to catch their breath for a minute—changed his course four times, he really didn't know what to salvage first, then he saw hanging conspicuously on the wall, which was otherwise bare already, the picture of the lady all dressed in furs, hurriedly crawled up on it and pressed himself against the glass, which gave a good surface to stick to and soothed his hot belly. At least no one would take away this picture, while Gregor completely covered it up. He turned his head toward the living-room door to watch the women when they returned.

They had not given themselves much of a rest and were already coming back; Grete had put her arm around her mother and was practically carrying her. "So what should we take now?" said Grete and looked around. At that her eyes met Gregor's as he clung to the wall. Probably only because of her mother's presence she kept her self-control, bent her head down to her mother to keep her from looking around, and said, though in a quavering and thoughtless voice: "Come, we'd better go back into the living room for a minute." Grete's intent was clear to Gregor; she wanted to bring his mother into safety and then chase him down from the wall. Well, just let her try! He squatted on his picture and would not give it up. He would rather fly in Grete's face.

But Grete's words had now made her mother really anxious; she stepped to one side, caught sight of the gigantic brown blotch on the flowered wallpaper, and, before it really dawned on her that what she saw was Gregor, cried in a hoarse, bawling voice: "Oh, God, Oh, God!"; and, as if giving up completely, she fell with outstretched arms across the couch and did not stir. "You, Gregor!" cried his sister with raised fist and piercing eyes. These were the first words she had addressed directly to him since his metamorphosis. She ran into the next room to get some kind of spirits to revive her mother; Gregor wanted to help, too—there was time to rescue the picture—but he was stuck to the glass and had to tear himself loose by force; then he, too, ran into the next room, as if he could give his sister some sort of advice, as in the old days; but then had to stand behind her doing nothing while she rummaged among various little bottles; moreover, when she turned around she was startled, a bottle fell on the floor and broke, a splinter of glass wounded Gregor in the face, some kind of corrosive medicine flowed around him; now without waiting any longer, Grete grabbed as many little bottles as she could carry and ran with them inside to her mother; she slammed the door behind her with her foot. Now Gregor was cut off from his mother, who was perhaps near death through his fault; he could not dare open the door if he did not want to chase away his sister, who had to stay with his mother; now there was nothing for him to do except wait; and tormented by self-reproaches and worry, he began to crawl, crawled over everything, walls, furniture and ceiling, and finally in desperation, as the whole room was beginning to spin, fell down onto the middle of the big table.

A short time passed; Gregor lay there prostrate; all around, things were quiet, perhaps that was a good sign. Then the doorbell rang. The maid, of course, was locked up in her kitchen and so Grete had to answer the door. His father had come home. "What's happened?" were his first words; Grete's appearance must have told him everything. Grete answered in a muffled voice, her face was obviously pressed against her father's chest; "Mother fainted, but she's better now. Gregor's broken out." "I knew it," his father said. "I kept telling you, but you women don't want to listen." It was clear to Gregor that his father had put the worst interpretation on Grete's all-too-brief announcement and assumed that Gregor was guilty of some outrage. Therefore, Gregor now had to try to calm his father down, since he had neither the time nor the ability to enlighten him. And so he fled to the door of his room and pressed himself against it for his father to see, as soon as he came into the foyer, that Gregor had the best intentions of returning to his room immediately and that it was not necessary to drive him back; if only the door were opened for him, he would disappear at once.

But his father was in no mood to notice

such subtleties; "Ah!" he cried as he entered, in a tone that sounded as if he were at once furious and glad. Gregor turned his head away from the door and lifted it toward his father. He had not really imagined his father looking like this, as he stood in front of him now; admittedly Gregor had been too absorbed recently in his newfangled crawling to bother as much as before about events in the rest of the house and should really have been prepared to find some changes. And yet, and yet—was this still his father? Was this the same man who in the old days used to lie wearily buried in bed when Gregor left on a business trip; who greeted him on his return in the evening, sitting in his bathrobe in the armchair, who actually had difficulty getting to his feet but as a sign of joy only lifted up his arms; and who, on the rare occasions when the whole family went out for a walk, on a few Sundays in June and on the major holidays, used to shuffle along with great effort between Gregor and his mother, who were slow walkers themselves, always a little more slowly than they, wrapped in his old overcoat, always carefully planting down his crutch-handled cane, and, when he wanted to say something, nearly always stood still and assembled his escort around him? Now, however, he was holding himself very erect, dressed in a tight-fitting blue uniform with gold buttons, the kind worn by messengers at banking concerns; above the high stiff collar of the jacket his heavy chin protruded; under his bushy eyebrows his black eyes darted bright, piercing glances; his usually rumpled white hair was combed flat, with a scrupulously exact, gleaming part. He threw his cap—which was adorned with a gold monogram, probably that of a bank—in an arc across the entire room onto the couch, and with the tails of his long uniform jacket slapped back, his hands in his pants pockets, went for Gregor with a sullen look on his face. He probably did not know himself what he had in mind; still he lifted his feet unusually high off the floor, and Gregor staggered at the gigantic size of the soles of his boots. But he did not linger over this, he had known right from the first day of his new life that his father considered only the strictest treatment called for in dealing with him. And so he ran ahead of his father, stopped when his father stood still, and scooted ahead again when his father made even the slightest movement. In this way they made more than one tour of the room, without anything decisive happening; in fact, the whole movement did not even have the appearance of a chase because of its slow tempo. So Gregor kept to the floor for the time being, especially since he was afraid that his father might interpret a flight onto the walls or the ceiling as a piece of particular nastiness. Of course, Gregor had to admit that he would not be able to keep up even this running for long, for whenever his father took one step, Gregor had to execute countless movements. He was already beginning to feel winded, just as in the old days he had not had very reliable lungs. As he now staggered around, hardly keeping his eyes open in order to gather all his strength for the running; in his obtuseness not thinking of any escape other than by running; and having almost forgotten that the walls were at his disposal, though here of course they were blocked up with elaborately carved furniture full of notches and points—at that moment a lightly flung object hit the floor right near him and rolled in front of him. It was an apple; a second one came flying right after it; Gregor stopped dead with fear; further running was useless, for his father was determined to bombard him. He had filled his pockets from the fruit bowl on the buffet and was now pitching one apple after another, for the time being without taking good aim. These little red apples rolled around on the floor as if electrified, clicking into each another. One apple, thrown weakly, grazed Gregor's back and slid off harmlessly. But the very next one that came flying after it literally forced its way into Gregor's back; Gregor tried to drag himself away, as if the startling, unbelievable pain might disappear with a change of place; but he felt nailed to the spot and stretched out his body in a complete confusion of all his senses. With his last glance he saw the door of his room burst open as his mother rushed out ahead of his screaming sister, in her chemise,[6] for his sister had partly undressed her while she was unconscious in order to let her breathe more freely; saw his mother run up to his father and on the way her unfastened petticoats slid to the floor one by one; and saw as, stumbling over the skirts, she forced herself onto his father, and embracing him, in complete union with him—but now Gregor's sight went dim—her hands clasping his father's neck, begged for Gregor's life.

3

Gregor's serious wound, from which he suffered for over a month—the apple remained imbedded in his flesh as a visible souvenir since no one dared to remove it—seemed to have reminded even his father that Gregor was a member of the family, in spite of his present pathetic and repulsive shape, who could not be treated as an enemy; that, on the contrary, it was the commandment of family duty to swallow their disgust and endure him, endure him and nothing more.

---

6. **chemise** (shə·mēz′): loose, sliplike undergarment.

And now, although Gregor had lost some of his mobility probably for good because of his wound, and although for the time being he needed long, long minutes to get across his room, like an old war veteran—crawling above ground was out of the question—for this deterioration of his situation he was granted compensation which in his view was entirely satisfactory: every day around dusk the living-room door—which he was in the habit of watching closely for an hour or two beforehand—was opened, so that, lying in the darkness of his room, invisible from the living room, he could see the whole family sitting at the table under the lamp and could listen to their conversation, as it were with general permission; and so it was completely different from before.

Of course, these were no longer the animated conversations of the old days, which Gregor used to remember with a certain nostalgia in small hotel rooms when he'd had

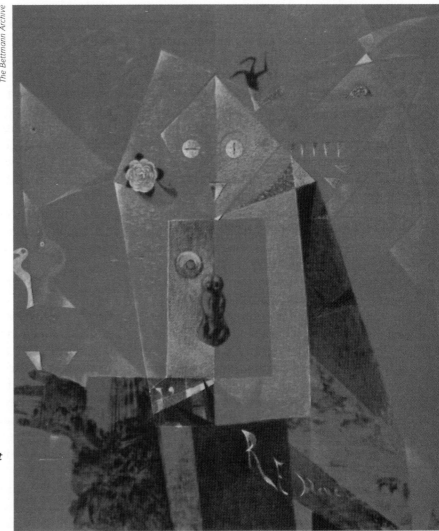

THE BLUE HOUR, MAX ERNST (1891–1976).

? **Do you think Gregor might have done anything to deserve—or to make him a likely victim for—his strange transformation; or was it a chance misfortune? Explain your answer.**

to throw himself wearily into the damp bedding. Now things were mostly very quiet. Soon after supper his father would fall asleep in his armchair; his mother and sister would caution each other to be quiet; his mother, bent low under the light, sewed delicate lingerie for a clothing store; his sister, who had taken a job as a salesgirl, was learning shorthand and French in the evenings in order to attain a better position some time in the future. Sometimes his father woke up, and as if he had absolutely no idea that he had been asleep, said to his mother, "Look how long you're sewing again today!" and went right back to sleep, while mother and sister smiled wearily at each other.

With a kind of perverse obstinacy his father refused to take off his official uniform even in the house; and while his robe hung uselessly on the clothes hook, his father dozed, completely dressed, in his chair, as if he were always ready for duty and were waiting even here for the voice of his superior. As a result, his uniform, which had not been new to start with, began to get dirty in spite of all the mother's and sister's care, and Gregor would often stare all evening long at this garment, covered with stains and gleaming with its constantly polished gold buttons, in which the old man slept most uncomfortably and yet peacefully.

As soon as the clock struck ten, his mother tried to awaken his father with soft encouraging words and then persuade him to go to bed, for this was no place to sleep properly, and his father badly needed his sleep, since he had to be at work at six o'clock. But with the obstinacy that had possessed him ever since he had become a messenger, he always insisted on staying at the table a little longer, although he invariably fell asleep and then could be persuaded only with the greatest effort to exchange his armchair for bed. However much mother and sister might pounce on him with little admonitions, he would slowly shake his head for a quarter of an hour at a time, keeping his eyes closed, and would not get up. Gregor's mother plucked him by the sleeves, whispered blandishments into his ear, his sister dropped her homework in order to help her mother, but all this was of no use. He only sank deeper into his armchair. Not until the women lifted him up under his arms did he open his eyes, look alternately at mother and sister, and usually say, "What a life. So this is the peace of my old age." And leaning on the two women, he would get up laboriously, as if he were the greatest weight on himself, and let the women lead him to the door, where, shrugging them off, he would proceed independently, while Gregor's mother threw down her sewing and his sister her pen as quickly as possible so as to run after his father and be of further assistance.

Who in this overworked and exhausted family had time to worry about Gregor any more than was absolutely necessary? The household was stinted more and more; now the maid was let go after all; a gigantic bony cleaning woman with white hair fluttering about her head came mornings and evenings to do the heaviest work; his mother took care of everything else, along with all her sewing. It even happened that various pieces of family jewelry, which in the old days his mother and sister had been overjoyed to wear at parties and celebrations, were sold, as Gregor found out one evening from the general discussion of the prices they had fetched. But the biggest complaint was always that they could not give up the apartment, which was much too big for their present needs, since no one could figure out how Gregor was supposed to be moved. But Gregor understood easily that it was not only consideration for him which prevented their moving, for he could easily have been transported in a suitable crate with a few air holes; what mainly prevented the family from moving was their complete hopelessness and the thought that they had been struck by a misfortune as none of their relatives and acquaintances had ever been hit. What the world demands of poor people they did to the utmost of their ability; his father brought breakfast for the minor officials at the bank, his mother sacrificed herself to the underwear of strangers, his sister ran back and forth behind the counter at the request of the customers; but for anything more than this they did not have the strength. And the wound in Gregor's back began to hurt anew when mother and sister, after getting his father to bed, now came back, dropped their work, pulled their chairs close to each other and sat cheek to cheek; when his mother, pointing to Gregor's room, said, "Close that door, Grete"; and when Gregor was back in darkness, while in the other room the women mingled their tears or stared dry-eyed at the table.

Gregor spent the days and nights almost entirely without sleep. Sometimes he thought that the next time the door opened he would take charge of the family's affairs again, just as he had done in the old days; after this long while there again appeared in his thoughts the boss and the manager, the salesmen and the trainees, the handyman who was so dense, two or three friends from other firms, a chambermaid in a provincial hotel—a happy fleeting memory—a cashier in a millinery store,[7] whom he had courted

earnestly but too slowly—they all appeared, intermingled with strangers or people he had already forgotten; but instead of helping him and his family, they were all inaccessible, and he was glad when they faded away. At other times he was in no mood to worry about his family, he was completely filled with rage at his miserable treatment, and although he could not imagine anything that would pique his appetite, he still made plans for getting into the pantry to take what was coming to him, even if he wasn't hungry. No longer considering what she could do to give Gregor a special treat, his sister, before running to business every morning and afternoon, hurriedly shoved any old food into Gregor's room with her foot; and in the evening, regardless of whether the food had only been toyed with or—the most usual case—had been left completely untouched, she swept it out with a swish of the broom. The cleaning up of Gregor's room, which she now always did in the evenings, could not be done more hastily. Streaks of dirt ran along the walls, fluffs of dust and filth lay here and there on the floor. At first, whenever his sister came in, Gregor would place himself in those corners which were particularly offending, meaning by his position in a sense to reproach her. But he could probably have stayed there for weeks without his sister's showing any improvement; she must have seen the dirt as clearly as he did, but she had just decided to leave it. At the same time she made sure—with an irritableness that was completely new to her and which had in fact infected the whole family—that the cleaning of Gregor's room remain her province. One time his mother had submitted Gregor's room to a major housecleaning, which she managed only after employing a couple of pails of water—all this dampness, of course, irritated Gregor,

---

7. **millinery store:** store that sells women's hats.

too, and he lay prostrate, sour and immobile, on the couch—but his mother's punishment was not long in coming. For hardly had his sister noticed the difference in Gregor's room that evening than, deeply insulted, she ran into the living room and, in spite of her mother's imploringly uplifted hands, burst out in a fit of crying, which his parents—his father had naturally been startled out of his armchair—at first watched in helpless amazement; until they too got going; turning to the right, his father blamed his mother for not letting his sister clean Gregor's room; but turning to the left, he screamed at his sister that she would never again be allowed to clean Gregor's room; while his mother tried to drag his father, who was out of his mind with excitement, into the bedroom; his sister, shaken with sobs, hammered the table with her small fists; and Gregor hissed loudly with rage because it did not occur to any of them to close the door and spare him such a scene and a row.[8]

But even if his sister, exhausted from her work at the store, had gotten fed up with taking care of Gregor as she used to, it was not necessary at all for his mother to take her place and still Gregor did not have to be neglected. For now the cleaning woman was there. This old widow, who thanks to her strong bony frame had probably survived the worst in a long life, was not really repelled by Gregor. Without being in the least inquisitive, she had once accidentally opened the door of Gregor's room, and at the sight of Gregor—who, completely taken by surprise, began to race back and forth although no one was chasing him—she had remained standing, with her hands folded on her stomach, marveling. From that time on she never failed to open the door a crack every morning and every evening and peek in hurriedly at Gregor. In the beginning she also used to call him over to her with words she probably considered friendly, like, "Come over here for a minute, you old dung beetle!" or "Look at that old dung beetle!" To forms of address like these Gregor would not respond but remained immobile where he was, as if the door had not been opened. If only they had given this cleaning woman orders to clean up his room every day, instead of letting her disturb him uselessly whenever the mood took her. Once, early in the morning—heavy rain, perhaps already a sign of approaching spring, was beating on the window panes—Gregor was so exasperated when the cleaning woman started in again with her phrases that he turned on her, of course slowly and decrepitly, as if to attack. But the cleaning woman, instead of getting frightened, simply lifted up high a chair near the door, and as she stood there with her mouth wide open, her intention was clearly to shut her mouth only when the chair in her hand came crashing down on Gregor's back. "So, is that all there is?" she asked when Gregor turned around again, and she quietly put the chair back in the corner.

Gregor now hardly ate anything anymore. Only when he accidentally passed the food laid out for him would he take a bite into his mouth just for fun, hold it in for hours, and then mostly spit it out again. At first he thought that his grief at the state of his room kept him off food, but it was the very changes in his room to which he quickly became adjusted. His family had gotten into the habit of putting in this room things for which they could not find any other place, and now there were plenty of these, since one of the rooms in the apartment had been

---

8. **row** (rou): quarrel.

rented to three boarders. These serious gentlemen—all three had long beards, as Gregor was able to register once through a crack in the door—were obsessed with neatness, not only in their room, but since they had, after all, moved in here, throughout the entire household and especially in the kitchen. They could not stand useless, let alone dirty, junk. Besides, they had brought along most of their own household goods. For this reason many things had become superfluous, and though they certainly weren't salable, on the other hand they could not just be thrown out. All these things migrated into Gregor's room. Likewise the ash can and the garbage can from the kitchen. Whatever was not being used at the moment was just flung into Gregor's room by the cleaning woman, who was always in a big hurry; fortunately, Gregor generally saw only the object involved and the hand that held it. Maybe the cleaning woman intended to reclaim the things as soon as she had a chance or else to throw out everything together in one fell swoop, but, in fact, they would have remained lying wherever they had been thrown in the first place if Gregor had not squeezed through the junk and set it in motion, at first from necessity, because otherwise there would have been no room to crawl in, but later with growing pleasure, although after such excursions, tired to death and sad, he did not budge again for hours.

Since the roomers sometimes also had their supper at home in the common living room, the living-room door remained closed on certain evenings, but Gregor found it very easy to give up the open door, for on many evenings when it was opened he had not taken advantage of it, but instead, without the family's noticing, had lain in the darkest corner of his room. But once the cleaning woman had left the living-room door slightly open, and it also remained opened a little when the roomers came in in the evening and the lamp was lit. They sat down at the head of the table where in the old days his father, his mother, and Gregor had eaten, unfolded their napkins, and picked up their knives and forks. At once his mother appeared in the doorway with a platter of meat, and just behind her came his sister with a platter piled high with potatoes. A thick vapor steamed up from the food. The roomers bent over the platters set in front of them as if to examine them before eating, and, in fact, the one who sat in the middle, and who seemed to be regarded by the other two as an authority, cut into a piece of meat while it was still on the platter, evidently to find out whether it was tender enough or whether it should perhaps be sent back to the kitchen. He was satisfied, and mother and sister, who had been watching anxiously, sighed with relief and began to smile.

The family itself ate in the kitchen. Nevertheless, before going into the kitchen, his father came into this room and, bowing once, cap in hand, made a turn around the table. The roomers rose as one man and mumbled something into their beards. When they were alone again, they ate in almost complete silence. It seemed strange to Gregor that among all the different noises of eating he kept picking up the sound of their chewing teeth, as if this were a sign to Gregor that you needed teeth to eat with and that even with the best make of toothless jaws you couldn't do a thing. "I'm hungry enough," Gregor said to himself, full of grief, "but not for these things. Look how these roomers are gorging themselves, and I'm dying!"

On this same evening—Gregor could not remember having heard the violin during the whole time—the sound of violin playing came from the kitchen. The roomers had already finished their evening meal, the one in the middle had taken out a newspaper, given each of the two others a page, and now, leaning back, they read and smoked. When the violin began to play, they became attentive, got up, and went on tiptoe to the door leading to the foyer, where they stood in a huddle. They must have been heard in the kitchen, for his father called, "Perhaps the playing bothers you, gentlemen? It can be stopped right away." "On the contrary," said the middle roomer. "Wouldn't the young lady like to come in to us and play in here where it's much roomier and more comfortable?" "Oh, certainly," called Gregor's father, as if he were the violinist. The boarders went back into the room and waited. Soon Gregor's father came in with the music stand, his mother with the sheet music, and his sister with the violin. Calmly his sister got everything ready for playing; his parents—who had never rented out rooms before and therefore behaved toward the roomers with excessive politeness—did not even dare sit down on their own chairs; his father leaned against the door, his right hand inserted between two buttons of his uniform coat, which he kept closed; but his mother was offered a chair by one of the roomers, and since she left the chair where the roomer just happened to put it, she sat in a corner to one side.

His sister began to play. Father and mother, from either side, attentively followed the movements of her hands. Attracted by the playing, Gregor had dared to come out a little further and already had his head in the living room. It hardly surprised him that lately he was showing so little consideration for the others; once such consideration had been his greatest pride. And yet he would never have had better reason to keep hidden; for now, because of the dust which lay all over his room and blew around at the slightest movement, he, too, was completely covered with dust; he dragged around with him on his back and along his sides fluff and hairs and scraps of food; his indifference to everything was much too deep for him to have gotten on his back and scrubbed himself clean against the carpet, as once he had done several times a day. And in spite of his state, he was not ashamed to inch out a little farther on the immaculate living-room floor.

Admittedly no one paid any attention to him. The family was completely absorbed by the violin-playing; the roomers, on the other hand, who at first had stationed themselves, hands in pockets, much too close behind his sister's music stand, so that they could all have followed the score, which certainly must have upset his sister, soon withdrew to the window, talking to each other in an undertone, their heads lowered, where they remained, anxiously watched by his father. It now seemed only too obvious that they were disappointed in their expectation of hearing beautiful or entertaining violin-playing, had had enough of the whole performance, and continued to let their peace be disturbed only out of politeness. Especially the way they all blew the cigar smoke out of their nose and mouth toward the ceiling suggested great nervousness. And yet his sister was playing so beautifully. Her face was inclined to one side, sadly and probingly her eyes followed the lines of music. Gregor crawled forward a little farther, holding his head close to the floor, so that it might be possible to catch her eye. Was he an animal, that music could move him so? He felt as if the way to the unknown nourishment he longed for were coming to light. He was determined to force himself on until he reached his sister, to pluck at her skirt, and to let her know in this way that she should bring her violin into his room, for no one here appreciated her playing the way he would appreciate it. He would never again let her out of his room—at least not for as long as he lived; for once, his nightmarish looks would be of use to him; he would be at all the doors of his room at the same time and hiss and spit at the aggressors; his sister, however, should not be forced to stay with him, but would do so of her own free will; she should sit next to him on the couch, bending her ear down to him, and then he would confide to her that he had had the firm intention of sending her to the Conservatory, and that, if the catastrophe had not intervened, he would have announced this to everyone last Christmas—certainly Christmas had come and gone?—without taking notice of any objections. After this declaration his sister would burst into tears of emotion, and Gregor would raise himself up to her shoulder and kiss her on the neck which, ever since she started going out to work, she kept bare, without a ribbon or collar.

"Mr. Samsa!" the middle roomer called to Gregor's father and without wasting another word pointed his index finger at Gregor, who was slowly moving forward. The violin stopped, the middle roomer smiled first at his friends, shaking his head, and then looked at Gregor again. Rather than driving Gregor out, his father seemed to consider it more urgent to start by soothing the roomers although they were not at all upset, and Gregor seemed to be entertaining them more than the violin-playing. He rushed over to them and tried with outstretched arms to drive them into their room and at the same time with his body to block their view of Gregor. Now they actually did get a little angry—it was not clear whether because of his father's behavior or because of their dawning realization of having had without knowing it such a next-door neighbor as Gregor. They demanded explanations from his father; in their turn they raised their arms, plucked excitedly at their beards, and, dragging their feet, backed off toward their room. In the meantime his sister had overcome the abstracted mood into which she had fallen after her playing had been so suddenly interrupted; and all at once, after holding violin and bow for a while in her slackly hanging hands and continuing to follow the score as if she were still playing, she pulled herself together, laid the instrument on the lap of her mother—who was still sitting in her chair, fighting for breath, her lungs violently heaving—and ran into the next room, which the roomers, under pressure from her father, were nearing more quickly than before. One could see the covers and bolsters on the beds, obeying his sister's practiced hands, fly up and arrange themselves. Before the boarders had reached the room, she had finished turning down the beds and had slipped out. Her father seemed once again to be gripped by his perverse obstinacy to such a degree that he completely forgot any respect still due his tenants. He drove them on and kept on driving until, already at the bedroom door, the middle boarder stamped his foot thunderingly and thus brought him to a standstill. "I herewith declare," he said, raising his hand and casting his eyes around for Gregor's mother and sister, too, "that in view of the disgusting conditions prevailing in this apartment and family"—here he spat curtly and decisively on the floor—"I give notice as of now. Of course, I won't pay a cent for the days I have been living here, either; on the contrary, I shall consider taking some sort of action against you with claims that—believe me—will be easy to substantiate." He stopped and looked straight in front of him, as if he were expecting something. And, in fact, his two friends at once chimed in with the words, "We, too, give notice as of now." Thereupon he grabbed the doorknob and slammed the door with a bang.

Gregor's father, his hands groping, staggered to his armchair and collapsed into it; it looked as if he were stretching himself out for his usual evening nap, but the heavy drooping of his head, as if it had lost all support, showed that he was certainly not asleep. All this time Gregor had lain quietly at the spot where the roomers had surprised him. His disappointment at the failure of his plan—but perhaps also the weakness caused by so much fasting—made it impossible for him to move. He was afraid with some certainty that in the very next moment a general debacle would burst over him, and he waited. He was not even startled by the violin as it slipped from under his mother's trembling fingers and fell off her lap with a reverberating clang.

"My dear parents," said his sister and by way of an introduction pounded her hand on the table, "things can't go on like this. Maybe you don't realize it, but I do. I won't pronounce the name of my brother in front of this monster, and so all I say is: we have to try to get rid of it. We've done everything humanly possible to take care of it and to put up with it; I don't think anyone can blame us in the least."

"She's absolutely right," said his father to himself. His mother, who still could not catch her breath, began to cough dully behind her hand, a wild look in her eyes.

His sister rushed over to his mother and held her forehead. His father seemed to have been led by Grete's words to more definite thoughts, had sat up, was playing with the cap of his uniform among the plates which were still lying on the table from the roomers' supper, and from time to time looked at Gregor's motionless form.

"We must try to get rid of it," his sister now said exclusively to her father, since her mother was coughing too hard to hear anything. "It will be the death of you two, I can see it coming. People who already have to work as hard as we do can't put up with this constant torture at home, too. I can't stand it anymore either." And she broke out crying so bitterly that her tears poured down onto her mother's face, which she wiped off with mechanical movements of her hand.

"Child," said her father kindly and with unusual understanding, "but what can we do?"

Gregor's sister only shrugged her shoulders as a sign of the bewildered mood that had now gripped her as she cried, in contrast with her earlier confidence.

"If he could understand us," said her father, half questioning; in the midst of her crying Gregor's sister waved her hand violently as a sign that that was out of the question.

"If he could understand us," his father repeated and by closing his eyes, absorbed his daughter's conviction of the impossibility of the idea, "then maybe we could come to an agreement with him. But the way things are——"

"It has to go," cried his sister. "That's the only answer, Father. You just have to try to get rid of the idea that it's Gregor. Believing it for so long, that is our real misfortune. But how can it be Gregor? If it were Gregor, he would have realized long ago that it isn't possible for human beings to live with such a creature, and he would have gone away of his own free will. Then we wouldn't have a brother, but we'd be able to go on living and honor his memory. But as things are, this animal persecutes us, drives the roomers away, obviously wants to occupy the whole apartment and for us to sleep in the gutter. Look, Father," she suddenly shrieked, "he's starting in again!" And in a fit of terror that was completely incomprehensible to Gregor, his sister abandoned even her mother, literally shoved herself off from her chair, as if she would rather sacrifice her mother than stay near Gregor, and rushed behind her father, who, upset only by her behavior, also stood up and half-lifted his arms in front of her as if to protect her.

But Gregor had absolutely no intention of frightening anyone, let alone his sister. He had only begun to turn around in order to trek back to his room; certainly his movements did look peculiar, since his ailing condition made him help the complicated turning maneuver along with his head, which he lifted up many times and knocked against the floor. He stopped and looked around. His good intention seemed to have been recognized; it had only been a momentary scare. Now they all watched him, silent and sad. His mother lay in her armchair, her legs stretched out and pressed together, her eyes almost closing from exhaustion; his father and his sister sat side by side, his sister had put her arm around her father's neck.

Now maybe they'll let me turn around, Gregor thought and began his labors again. He could not repress his panting from the exertion, and from time to time he had to rest. Otherwise no one harassed him, he was left completely on his own. When he had completed the turn, he immediately began to crawl back in a straight line. He was astonished at the great distance separating him from his room and could not understand at all how, given his weakness, he had covered the same distance a little while ago almost without realizing it. Constantly intent only on rapid crawling, he hardly noticed that not a word, not an exclamation from his family, interrupted him. Only when he was already in the doorway did he turn his head—not completely, for he felt his neck stiffening; nevertheless, he still saw that behind him nothing had changed except that his sister had gotten up. His last glance ranged over his mother, who was now fast asleep.

He was hardly inside his room when the door was hurriedly slammed shut, firmly bolted, and locked. Gregor was so frightened at the sudden noise behind him that his little legs gave way under him. It was his sister who had been in such a hurry. She had been standing up straight, ready and waiting, then she had leaped forward nimbly, Gregor had not even heard her coming, and she cried "Finally!" to her parents as she turned the key in the lock.

"And now?" Gregor asked himself, looking around in the darkness. He soon made the discovery that he could no longer move at all. It did not surprise him; rather, it seemed unnatural that until now he had actually been able to propel himself on these thin little legs. Otherwise he felt relatively comfortable. He had pains, of course, throughout his whole body, but it seemed to him that they were gradually getting fainter and fainter and would finally go away altogether. The rotten apple in his back and the inflamed area around it, which were completely covered with fluffy dust, already hardly bothered him. He thought back on his family with deep emotion and love. His conviction that he would have to disappear was, if possible, even firmer than his sister's. He remained in this state of empty and peaceful reflection until the tower clock struck three in the morning. He still saw that outside the window everything was beginning to grow light. Then, without his consent, his head sank down to the floor, and from his nostrils streamed his last weak breath.

When early in the morning the cleaning woman came—in sheer energy and impatience she would slam all the doors so hard although she had often been asked not to, that once she had arrived, quiet sleep was no longer possible anywhere in the apartment—she did not at first find anything out of the ordinary on paying Gregor her usual short visit. She thought that he was deliberately lying motionless, pretending that his feelings were hurt; she credited him with unlimited intelligence. Because she happened to be holding the long broom, she

Toad (Le Crapaud), Pablo Picasso, 1949.

tried from the doorway to tickle Gregor with it. When this too produced no results, she became annoyed and jabbed Gregor a little, and only when she had shoved him without any resistance to another spot did she begin to take notice. When she quickly became aware of the true state of things, she opened her eyes wide, whistled softly, but did not dawdle; instead, she tore open the door of the bedroom and shouted at the top of her voice into the darkness: "Come and have a look, it's croaked; it's lying there, dead as a doornail!"

The couple Mr. and Mrs. Samsa sat up in their marriage bed and had a struggle overcoming their shock at the cleaning woman before they could finally grasp her message. But then Mr. and Mrs. Samsa hastily scrambled out of bed, each on his side, Mr. Samsa threw the blanket around his shoulders, Mrs. Samsa came out in nothing but her nightgown; dressed this way, they entered Gregor's room. In the meantime, the door of the living room had also opened, where Grete had been sleeping since the roomers had moved in; she was fully dressed, as if she had not been asleep at all; and her pale face seemed to confirm this. "Dead?" said Mrs. Samsa and looked inquiringly at the cleaning woman, although she could scrutinize everything for herself and could recognize the truth even without scrutiny. "I'll say," said the cleaning woman, and to prove it she pushed Gregor's corpse with her broom a good distance sideways. Mrs. Samsa made a movement as if to hold the broom back but did not do it. "Well," said Mr. Samsa, "now we can thank God!" He crossed himself, and the three women followed his example. Grete, who never took her eyes off the corpse, said, "Just look how thin he was. Of course he didn't eat anything for such a long time. The food came out again just the

way it went in." As a matter of fact, Gregor's body was completely flat and dry; this was obvious now for the first time, really, since the body was no longer raised up by his little legs and nothing else distracted the eye.

"Come in with us for a little while, Grete," said Mrs. Samsa with a melancholy smile, and Grete, not without looking back at the corpse, followed her parents into their bedroom. The cleaning woman shut the door and opened the window wide. Although it was early in the morning, there was already some mildness mixed in with the fresh air. After all, it was already the end of March.

The three boarders came out of their room and looked around in astonishment for their breakfast; they had been forgotten. "Where's breakfast?" the middle roomer grumpily asked the cleaning woman. But she put her finger to her lips and then hastily and silently beckoned the boarders to follow her into Gregor's room. They came willingly and then stood, their hands in the pockets of their somewhat shabby jackets, in the now already very bright room, surrounding Gregor's corpse.

At that point the bedroom door opened, and Mr. Samsa appeared in his uniform, his wife on one arm, his daughter on the other. They all looked as if they had been crying; from time to time Grete pressed her face against her father's sleeve.

"Leave my house immediately," said Mr. Samsa and pointed to the door, without letting go of the women. "What do you mean by that?" said the middle roomer, somewhat nonplussed, and smiled with a sugary smile. The two others held their hands behind their back and incessantly rubbed them together, as if in joyful anticipation of a big argument, which could only turn out in their favor. "I mean just what I say," answered Mr. Samsa, and with his two companions marched in a straight line toward the roomer. At first the roomer stood still and looked at the floor, as if the thoughts inside his head were fitting themselves together in a new order. "So, we'll go, then," he said and looked up at Mr. Samsa as if, suddenly overcome by a fit of humility, he were asking for further permission even for this decision. Mr. Samsa merely nodded briefly several times, his eyes wide open. Thereupon the roomer actually went immediately into the foyer, taking long strides; his two friends had already been listening for a while, their hands completely still, and now they went hopping right after him, as if afraid that Mr. Samsa might get into the foyer ahead of them and interrupt the contact with their leader. In the foyer all three took their hats from the coat rack, pulled their canes from the umbrella stand, bowed silently, and left the apartment. In a suspicious mood which proved completely unfounded, Mr. Samsa led the two women out onto the landing; leaning over the banister, they watched the three roomers slowly but steadily going down the long flight of stairs, disappearing on each landing at a particular turn of the stairway and a few moments later emerging again; the farther down they got, the more the Samsa family's interest in them wore off, and when a butcher's boy with a carrier on his head came climbing up the stairs with a proud bearing, toward them and then up on past them, Mr. Samsa and the women quickly left the banister and all went back, as if relieved, into their apartment.

They decided to spend this day resting and going for a walk; they not only deserved a break in their work, they absolutely needed one. And so they sat down at the table and wrote three letters of excuse, Mr. Samsa to the management of the bank, Mrs. Samsa to her employer, and Grete to the store owner. While they were writing, the cleaning woman came in to say that she was going, since her morning's work was done. The three letter writers at first simply nodded without looking up, but as the cleaning woman still kept lingering, they looked up, annoyed. "Well?" asked Mr. Samsa. The cleaning woman stood smiling in the doorway, as if she had some great good news to announce to the family but would do so only if she were thoroughly questioned. The little ostrich feather which stood almost upright on her hat and which had irritated Mr. Samsa the whole time she had been with them swayed lightly in all directions. "What do you want?" asked Mrs. Samsa, who inspired the most respect in the cleaning woman. "Well," the cleaning woman answered, and for good-natured laughter could not immediately go on, "look, you don't have to worry about getting rid of the stuff next door. It's already been taken care of." Mrs. Samsa and Grete bent down over their letters, as if to continue writing; Mr. Samsa, who noticed that the cleaning woman was now about to start describing everything in detail, stopped her with a firmly outstretched hand. But since she was not going to be permitted to tell her story, she remembered that she was in a great hurry, cried, obviously insulted, "So long, everyone," whirled around wildly, and left the apartment with a terrible slamming of doors.

"We'll fire her tonight," said Mr. Samsa, but did not get an answer from either his wife or his daughter, for the cleaning woman seemed to have ruined their barely regained peace of mind. They got up, went to the window, and stayed there, holding each other tight. Mr. Samsa turned around in his chair toward them and watched them quietly for a while. Then he called, "Come on now, come over here. Stop brooding over the past. And have a little consideration for me, too." The women obeyed him at once, hurried over to him, fondled him, and quickly finished their letters.

Then all three of them left the apartment together, something they had not done in months, and took the trolley into the open country on the outskirts of the city. The car, in which they were the only passengers, was completely filled with warm sunshine. Leaning back comfortably in their seats, they discussed their prospects for the time to come, and it seemed on closer examination that these weren't bad at all, for all three positions—about which they had never really asked one another in any detail—were exceedingly advantageous and especially promising for the future. The greatest immediate improvement in their situation would come easily, of course, from a change in apartments; they would now take a smaller and cheaper apartment, but one better situated and in every way simpler to manage than the old one, which Gregor had picked for them. While they were talking in this vein, it occurred almost simultaneously to Mr. and Mrs. Samsa, as they watched their daughter getting livelier and livelier, that lately, in spite of all the troubles which had turned her cheeks pale, she had blossomed into a good-looking, shapely girl. Growing quieter and communicating almost unconsciously through glances, they thought that it would soon be time, too, to find her a good husband. And it was like a confirmation of their new dreams and good intentions when at the end of the ride their daughter got up first and stretched her young body.

First Thoughts

Kafka explicitly forbade his publishers to include any illustration of Gregor as an insect. He felt that any literal representation would be meaningless. Do you agree with his view? Did you form a mental image of the metamorphosed Gregor? Draw your image of Gregor after his transformation, then discuss your drawing with the class.

Identifying Facts

1. After discovering that he has changed into a "monstrous vermin," what is Gregor's chief concern?

2. What does Gregor do for a living? What does he dislike about his job? Explain why he feels he cannot resign.

3. Who is Gregor's primary caretaker? In the course of the story, what change takes place in this person's attitude toward Gregor?

4. How does the family's treatment of Gregor deteriorate? What does Gregor's father do that permanently injures Gregor?

5. After Gregor dies, what do his parents plan? What is "like a confirmation of their new dreams"?

Interpreting Meanings

1. **Irony** is the difference between what one expects to happen and what actually happens. What is ironic about Gregor's family's reaction to his change in form? Identify another example of irony in the story.

2. Gregor's reaction to Grete's violin playing leads to the **climax** of the novel.

How is his entrance into the living room the "final straw"?

3. In your opinion, what does the "monstrous vermin" **symbolize**? In symbolic terms, what is significant about the kind of creature Gregor transforms into—as opposed, say, to a dog or a cat?

4. The word *samsja* in Czech means "being alone." Do you think it was Gregor's change in form or his inability to communicate that contributed more to his isolation? How might things have been different if he had been able to express himself?

5. As Gregor's condition deteriorates, his family's condition improves. Some critics have said that the title of the novel refers not only to Gregor's metamorphosis, but also to his family's. Do you agree? Explain your response.

Applying Meanings

Although Kafka's story takes place more than seventy years ago, we still read about Gregor with fascination and curiosity. Do you think that this story is relevant to life today? You may not wake up tomorrow and find yourself changed into a bug, but do you ever suffer the same feelings and frustrations as Gregor did? Might there be other ways in which people "transform" because of their problems? Discuss your opinions with the class.

Creative Writing Response

1. **Writing from a Different Point of View.** Except for the last part, after Gregor's death, this novella is told from the **limited third-person point of view**: We are limited to Gregor's view of events. Gregor gives a very matter-of-fact account of his metamorphosis, but we can imagine how the other members of the family are reacting. In a few paragraphs, tell about Gregor's metamorphosis from Grete's point of view. You might start

with, "One morning, as I whispered through the wall to Gregor, I heard strange chirping noises coming out of his room. . . ."

2. **Describing Another Metamorphosis.** Since ancient times, the **motif** of a metamorphosis has been used in stories. Describe a story in which a metamorphosis takes place—it can be from a myth, a book, or a movie. (Think of all those weird shape changes that take place in science-fiction movies.) You can make up your own metamorphosis story if you like. Does the metamorphosed form reflect any traits of the original being?

Critical Writing Response

1. **Analyzing a Character.** One of the central conflicts in the story is the relationship between Gregor and his father, which some critics see as reflecting Kafka's view of his relationship with his own father. Write a paragraph in which you analyze Mr. Samsa's character. Before you write, consider the following questions:

   a. How does Mr. Samsa view Gregor's metamorphosis? (Is he sympathetic? indifferent?) How does he treat Gregor?

   b. How does Mr. Samsa change after he gets a job and begins to support the family again?

   c. How do you think Gregor views his father? As a symbol of authority? Or does he think his father is weak? Does Gregor like his father?

2. **Responding to a Critic.** Critic Paul L. Landsburg believes that *The Metamorphosis* is an **allegory**, or a story in which each character and event stands for something else. In an allegory, the writer is trying to teach some moral meaning about life. As you read the

quotation below, think about any individuals or groups in society that could suffer the same kind of alienation and treatment that Gregor suffered.

> "To be an exception or in the minority is the original social sin. When in society any group of men characterized by anomalous tastes or racial or social heredity is denounced as 'vermin,' there will always be one group that from then on will see nothing but the other's rottenness, and another fraction within the scorned group that will think and act as if they had truly been transformed into vermin."
> —Paul L. Landsburg

Write two paragraphs in which you discuss how individuals or groups of people can actually begin to act the way they are treated.

Language and Vocabulary

Adjectives from People's Names

The adjective *Kafkaesque* is just one of many English words that come from the names of real people or fictional characters. Such adjectives usually develop when a person's or character's behavior or achievements are so well known that similar behavior or achievements are compared to them.

Choose the correct meaning of each italicized adjective in the phrases below. Check your answers in a dictionary and identify the person or character whose name gave rise to the adjective.

1. a *Herculean* task
   a) arduous   b) tedious
   c) short   d) easy

2. a *Machiavellian* politician
   a) weak   b) idealistic
   c) up-to-date   d) crafty

3. a *platonic* friendship
   a) spiritual or intellectual   b) passionate
   c) deceitful   d) long-standing

4. *quixotic* behavior
   a) mature   b) mysterious
   c) romantic and idealistic   d) fickle

5. *Shakespearean* language
   a) vulgar   b) poetic
   c) redundant   d) puzzling

THE ART OF TRANSLATION

Two Translations of The Metamorphosis

In reading *The Metamorphosis*, you are not simply reading a story by Kafka. You are also reading the work of a skilled translator who has tried to convey the meaning and spirit of Kafka's German in lively, natural English prose.

Whether a translator is faced with a text in French, Russian, Spanish, or Japanese, he or she takes on a difficult task. First of all, a word-for-word translation from the original language into English would probably not make sense. In addition, many foreign words have several possible English equivalents, and some words may have no English equivalents. Furthermore, **idioms**, or expressions specific to a particular language, cannot be translated literally. For example, the idiomatic expression, "He's a wet blanket'' doesn't make much sense when translated to another language, but most languages probably *do* have an equivalent, figurative expression that conveys the same meaning: ''He always manages to bring out the negative aspect of things.'' Translators must find these approximations. Just look at the many ways Gregor's metamorphosed form (*ungeheueres Ungeziefer* in German) has been translated: ''monstrous vermin,'' ''gigantic insect,'' ''enormous bug,'' ''a giant kind of vermin,'' and ''monstrous bug.''

Here are several passages from *The Metamorphosis*. The first passage in each example is from the translation you have just read, by Stanley Corngold. The second passage is from a translation by Willa and Edwin Muir. Read each pair of passages aloud, and discuss how they differ in diction (word choice), naturalness of language, rhythm, and ultimate meaning. Which version do you prefer, and why?

1. **a.** ''Traveling salesmen aren't well liked there, I know. People think they make a fortune leading the gay life. No one has any particular reason to rectify this prejudice.''

   b. ''Travelers are not popular there, I know. People think they earn sacks of money and have a good time. A preju-dice there's no particular reason for revising.''

2. **a.** ''In fact, Gregor felt fine, with the exception of his drowsiness, which was really unnecessary after sleeping so late, and he even had a ravenous appetite.''

   b. ''Gregor really felt quite well, apart from a drowsiness that was utterly superfluous after such a long sleep and he was even unusually hungry.''

3. **a.** '' 'That was the voice of an animal,' said the manager, in a tone conspicuously soft compared with the mother's yelling.''

   b. '' 'That was no human voice,' said the chief clerk in a voice noticeably low beside the shrillness of the mother's.''

4. **a.** ''Then, without his consent, his head sank down to the floor, and from his nostrils streamed his last weak breath.''

   b. ''Then his head sank to the floor of its own accord and from his nostrils came the last faint flicker of his breath.''

5. **a.** '' 'Come and have a look, it's croaked; it's lying there, dead as a doornail.' ''

   b. '' 'Just look at this, it's dead; it's lying here dead and done for.' ''

Selma Lagerlöf
1858–1940, Sweden

When Selma Lagerlöf (lä′gər·lŭf′) was studying to become a schoolteacher, she attended a lecture that was to change her life. The subject of the lecture was Swedish folk ballads. These narrative songs reminded her of the folklore she had learned as a child in Sweden's Värmland district, and of the happy days in the house that her family was forced to sell when her father died. Lagerlöf's bittersweet memories inspired her to begin writing about the legends and folktales of her childhood. The books she wrote became so popular that she was soon able to repurchase her beloved family home with the money she made.

As a child, Lagerlöf listened to her grandmother tell Swedish folktales, and she never tired of reading books from the family library.

Her first novel, *The Story of Gösta Berling* (1891), was set in her childhood home, Värmland. To her surprise, the novel won first prize in a competition. Success followed success as *Invisible Links* (1894), a collection of Swedish legends and other tales, earned her a Swedish Academy writing scholarship and praise from Sweden's king. By now a household name in her homeland, Lagerlöf retired from her teaching career to devote herself to writing. A trip to the Middle East prompted *Jerusalem* (1901–1902), a two-volume novel about Swedes who immigrated to Jerusalem in quest for spiritual fulfillment. Four years later came the children's book, *The Wonderful Adventures of Nils*, which recounts a young boy's adventures as he travels across Sweden on the back of a goose.

In 1909, Lagerlöf became the first woman writer to win the Nobel Prize for literature. By the time she reached seventy, she was so famous that her birthday was celebrated in Sweden and in several neighboring nations. Although she was a committed pacifist and feminist, her social concerns rarely found their way into her novels. In her final years, however, Lagerlöf was outraged to find herself hailed as a "Nordic princess" in Nazi Germany, and began defiantly arranging for German intellectuals to escape Nazi persecution by coming to Sweden—an activity she continued even after World War II broke out and Sweden declared itself neutral.

Reader's Guide

THE RAT TRAP

Background

This story takes place in the Värmland area of Sweden where Selma Lagerlöf spent her childhood. Because the region had many iron ore deposits, it became a center of Sweden's iron industry during the second half of the nineteenth century. Iron ore mined in the district was brought to furnaces called ironworks, where it was smelted to remove impurities and then shaped into bars or sheets. The ironmasters who owned the ironworks became very wealthy and bought vast tracts of land, some of which they leased to tenant farmers and retired ironworkers. While the Industrial Revolution brought prosperity to some, it brought poverty to many others. Many farm laborers lost their jobs and became wandering peddlers or beggars. This story includes such a peddler, as well as an ironmaster, his daughter, and an elderly tenant farmer.

Writer's Response

There is a vast difference between the wealthiest and poorest people in our country today. Write a few sentences contrasting the lifestyles of the wealthiest and poorest people in your community.

Literary Focus

Point of view is the vantage point from which a writer tells a story. The traditional vantage point for storytelling is the **omniscient** (or all-knowing) **point of view**. The omniscient narrator is not a character in the story, but a godlike observer who knows everything that is going on in each character's heart and mind. This narrator can also provide us with information that no character knows. ("Thomas was sailing along effortlessly on his roller blades, unaware that the getaway car would soon burst out of the quiet side street.") Selma Lagerlöf uses the omniscient point of view in "The Rat Trap."

THE RAT TRAP

Selma Lagerlöf

translated by

FLORENCE AND NABOTH HEDIN

Read the first three paragraphs of "The Rat Trap" and think about the peddler's "rat trap theory" of the world. Does this theory make sense to you? What does the theory reveal about the peddler's view of life?

EVENING IN THE KARL JOHAN STREET, EDVARD MUNCH (1863–1944).

Once upon a time there was a man who went around selling small rat traps of wire. He made them himself at odd moments, from material he got by begging in the stores or at the big farms. But even so, the business was not especially profitable, so he had to resort to both begging and petty thievery to keep body and soul together. Even so, his clothes were in rags, his cheeks were sunken, and hunger gleamed in his eyes.

No one can imagine how sad and monotonous life can appear to such a vagabond, who plods along the road, left to his own meditations. But one day this man had fallen into a line of thought which really seemed to him entertaining. He had naturally been thinking of his rat traps when suddenly he was struck by the idea that the whole world about him—the whole world with its lands and seas, its cities and villages—was nothing but a big rat trap. It had never existed for any other purpose than to set baits for people. It offered riches and joys, shelter and food, heat and clothing, exactly as the rat trap offered cheese and pork, and as soon as anyone let himself be tempted to touch the bait, it closed in on him, and then everything came to an end.

The world had, of course, never been very kind to him, so it gave him unwonted[1] joy to think ill of it in this way. It became a cherished pastime of his, during many dreary ploddings, to think of people he knew who had let themselves be caught in the dangerous snare, and of others who were still circling around the bait.

One dark evening as he was trudging along the road he caught sight of a little gray cottage by the roadside, and he knocked on the door to ask shelter for the night. Nor was he refused. Instead of the sour faces which ordinarily met him, the owner, who was an old man without wife or child, was happy to get someone to talk to in his loneliness. Immediately he put the porridge pot on the fire and gave him supper; then he carved off such a big slice from his tobacco roll that it was enough both for the stranger's pipe and his own. Finally he got out an old pack of cards and played *mjölis*[2] with his guest until bedtime.

The old man was just as generous with his confidences as with his porridge and tobacco. The guest was informed at once that in his days of prosperity his host had been a crofter at Ramsjö Ironworks[3] and had worked on the land. Now that he was no longer able to do day labor, it was his cow which supported him. Yes, that bossy[4] was extraordinary. She could give milk for the creamery every day, and last month he had received all of thirty kronor[5] in payment.

The stranger must have seemed incredulous, for the old man got up and went to the window, took down a leather pouch which hung on a nail in the very window frame, and picked out three wrinkled ten-kronor bills. These he held up before the eyes of his guest, nodding knowingly, and then stuffed them back into the pouch.

The next day both men got up in good season. The crofter was in a hurry to milk his cow, and the other man probably thought he should not stay in bed when the head of the house had gotten up. They left the cottage at the same time. The crofter locked the door and put the key in his pocket. The man with the rat traps said goodbye and thank you, and thereupon each went his own way.

But half an hour later the rat-trap peddler stood again before the door. He did not try to get in, however. He only went up to the window, smashed a pane, stuck in his hand, and got hold of the pouch with the thirty kronor. He took the money and thrust it into his own pocket. Then he hung the leather pouch very carefully back in its place and went away.

As he walked along with the money in his pocket he felt quite pleased with his smartness. He realized, of course, that at first he dared not continue on the public highway, but must turn off the road, into the woods. During the first few hours this caused him no difficulty. Later in the day it

---

1. **unwonted** (un·wän'tid): unaccustomed.
2. *mjölis* (myŏ'lis): Swedish card game.
3. **crofter at Ramsjö** (räm'shyŏ) **Ironworks:** tenant farmer on land owned by the Ramsjö Ironworks.
4. **bossy:** colloquial term for a cow.
5. **thirty kronor** (krŏ'nôr'): about six dollars when the story takes place; the krona is the monetary unit of Sweden; *kronor* is the plural form.

became worse, for it was a big and confusing forest which he had gotten into. He tried, to be sure, to walk in a definite direction, but the paths twisted back and forth so strangely! He walked and walked, without coming to the end of the wood, and finally he realized that he had only been walking around in the same part of the forest. All at once he recalled his thoughts about the world and the rat trap. Now his own turn had come. He had let himself be fooled by a bait and had been caught. The whole forest, with its trunks and branches, its thickets and fallen logs, closed in upon him like an impenetrable prison from which he could never escape.

It was late in December. Darkness was already descending over the forest. This increased the danger, and increased also his gloom and despair. Finally he saw no way out, and he sank down on the ground, tired to death, thinking that his last moment had come. But just as he laid his head on the ground, he heard a sound—a hard, regular thumping. There was no doubt as to what that was. He raised himself. "Those are the hammer strokes from an iron mill," he thought. "There must be people nearby." He summoned all his strength, got up, and staggered in the direction of the sound.

The Ramsjö Ironworks, which is now closed down, was, not so long ago, a large plant, with smelter,[6] rolling mill,[7] and forge.[8] In the summertime, long lines of heavily-loaded barges and scows slid down the canal which led to a large inland lake, and in the wintertime the roads near the mill were black from all the coal dust which sifted down from the big charcoal crates.

During one of the long dark evenings just before Christmas, the master smith and his helper sat in the dark forge near the furnace waiting for the pig iron, which had been put in the fire, to be ready to put on the anvil.[9] Every now and then one of them got up to stir the glowing mass with a long iron bar, returning in a few moments, dripping with perspiration, though, as was the custom, he wore nothing but a long shirt and a pair of wooden shoes.

All the time there were many sounds to be heard in the forge. The big bellows groaned and the burning coal cracked. The fire boy shoveled charcoal into the maw of the furnace with a great deal of clatter. Outside roared the waterfall, and a sharp north wind whipped the rain against the brick-tiled roof.

It was probably on account of all this noise that the blacksmith did not notice that a man had opened the gate and entered the forge, until he stood close up to the furnace.

Surely it was nothing unusual for poor vagabonds without any better shelter for the night to be attracted to the forge by the glow of light which escaped through the sooty panes, and to come in to warm themselves in front of the fire. The blacksmiths glanced only casually and indifferently at the intruder. He looked the way people of his type usually did, with a long beard, dirty, ragged, and with a bunch of rat traps dangling on his chest.

He asked permission to stay, and the master blacksmith nodded a haughty consent without honoring him with a single word.

The tramp did not say anything, either.

---

6. **smelter:** place where iron ore is fused or melted in order to separate out the impurities.
7. **rolling mill:** machine used to roll out metal bars or sheets.
8. **forge:** here, place where metal is heated in a furnace and then hammered or molded into shape.

---

9. **anvil:** metal block on which objects are hammered into shape.

THE FOUNDRY, EYRE CROWE (1824–1910).

He had not come there to talk but only to warm himself and sleep.

In those days the Ramsjö iron mill was owned by a very prominent ironmaster whose greatest ambition was to ship out good iron to the market. He watched both night and day to see that the work was done as well as possible, and at this very moment he came into the forge on one of his nightly rounds of inspection.

Naturally the first thing he saw was the tall ragamuffin who had eased his way so close to the furnace that steam rose from his wet rags. The ironmaster did not follow the example of the blacksmiths, who had hardly deigned to look at the stranger. He walked close up to him, looked him over very carefully, then tore off his slouch hat[10]

---

10. **slouch hat:** style of hat with a drooping brim.

to get a better view of his face.

"But of course it is you, Nils Olof!" he said. "How you do look!"

The man with the rat traps had never before seen the ironmaster of Ramsjö and did not even know what his name was. But it occurred to him that if the fine gentleman thought he was an old acquaintance, he might perhaps throw him a couple of kronor. Therefore he did not want to undeceive him all at once.

"Yes, God knows things have gone downhill with me," he said.

"You should not have resigned from the regiment," said the ironmaster. "That was the mistake. If only I had still been in the service at the time, it never would have happened. Well, now, of course, you will come home with me."

To go along up to the manor house and be received by the owner like an old

Selma Lagerlöf **1201**

regimental comrade—that, however, did not please the tramp.

"No, I couldn't think of it!" he said, looking quite alarmed.

He thought of the thirty kronor. To go up to the manor house would be like throwing himself voluntarily into the lions' den. He only wanted a chance to sleep here in the forge and then sneak away as inconspicuously as possible.

The ironmaster assumed that he felt embarrassed because of his miserable clothing.

"Please don't think that I have such a fine home that you cannot show yourself there," he said. "Elizabeth is dead, as you may already have heard. My boys are abroad, and there is no one at home except my oldest daughter and myself. We were just saying that it was too bad we didn't have any company for Christmas. Now come along with me and help us make the Christmas food disappear a little faster."

But the stranger said no, and no, and again no, and the ironmaster saw that he must give in.

"It looks as though Captain von Ståhle[11] preferred to stay with you tonight, Stjernström,"[12] he said to the master blacksmith, and turned on his heel.

But he laughed to himself as he went away, and the blacksmith, who knew him, understood very well that he had not said his last word.

It was not more than half an hour before they heard the sound of carriage wheels outside the forge, and a new guest came in, but this time it was not the ironmaster. He had sent his daughter, apparently hoping that she would have better powers of persuasion than he himself.

She entered, followed by a valet,[13] carrying on his arm a big fur coat. She was not at all pretty, but seemed modest and quite shy. In the forge everything was just as it had been earlier in the evening. The master blacksmith and his apprentice still sat on their bench, and iron and charcoal still glowed in the furnace. The stranger had stretched himself out on the floor and lay with a piece of pig iron under his head and his hat pulled down over his eyes. As soon as the young girl caught sight of him she went up and lifted his hat. The man was evidently used to sleeping with one eye open. He jumped up abruptly and seemed to be quite frightened.

"My name is Edla Willmansson," said the young girl. "My father came home and said that you wanted to sleep here in the forge tonight, and then I asked permission to come and bring you home to us. I am so sorry, Captain, that you are having such a hard time."

She looked at him compassionately, with her heavy eyes, and then she noticed that the man was afraid. "Either he has stolen something or else he has escaped from jail," she thought, and added quickly, "You may be sure, Captain, that you will be allowed to leave us just as freely as you came. Only please stay with us over Christmas Eve."

She said this in such a friendly manner that the rat-trap peddler must have felt confidence in her.

"It would never have occurred to me that you would bother with me yourself, miss," he said. "I will come at once."

He accepted the fur coat, which the valet handed him with a deep bow, threw it over his rags, and followed the young lady out to the carriage, without granting the astonished

---

11. **von Ståhle** (fon stô′lə)
12. **Stjernström** (styern′strôm)

13. **valet** (val′it): personal manservant.

blacksmiths so much as a glance.

But while he was riding up to the manor house he had evil forebodings.

"Why the devil did I take that fellow's money?" he thought. "Now I am sitting in the trap and will never get out of it."

The next day was Christmas Eve, and when the ironmaster came into the dining room for breakfast he probably thought with satisfaction of his old regimental comrade whom he had run across so unexpectedly.

"First of all we must see to it that he gets a little flesh on his bones," he said to his daughter, who was busy at the table. "And then we must see that he gets something else to do than to run around the country selling rat traps."

"It is queer that things have gone downhill with him as badly as that," said the daughter. "Last night I did not think there was anything about him to show that he had once been an educated man."

"You must have patience, my little girl," said the father. "As soon as he gets clean and dressed up, you will see something different. Last night he was naturally embarrassed. The tramp manners will fall away from him with the tramp clothes."

Just as he said this the door opened and the stranger entered. Yes, now he was truly clean and well dressed. The valet had bathed him, cut his hair, and shaved him. Moreover, he was dressed in a good-looking suit of clothes which belonged to the ironmaster. He wore a white shirt and a starched collar and whole shoes.

But although his guest was now so well groomed, the ironmaster did not seem pleased. He looked at him with puckered brow, and it was easy enough to understand that when he had seen the strange fellow in the uncertain reflection from the furnace he

might have made a mistake, but that now, when he stood there in broad daylight, it was impossible to mistake him for an old acquaintance.

"What does this mean?" he thundered.

The stranger made no attempt to dissimulate. He saw at once that all the splendor had come to an end.

"It is not my fault, sir," he said. "I never pretended to be anything but a poor trader, and I pleaded and begged to be allowed to stay in the forge. But no harm has been done. At worst I can put on my rags again and go away."

"Well," said the ironmaster, hesitating a little, "it was not quite honest, either. You must admit that, and I should not be surprised if the sheriff would like to have something to say in the matter."

The tramp took a step forward and struck the table with his fist.

"Now I am going to tell you, Mr. Ironmaster, how things are," he said. "This whole world is nothing but a big rat trap. All the good things that are offered you are nothing but cheese rinds and bits of pork, set out to drag a poor fellow into trouble. And if the sheriff comes now and locks me up for this, then you, Mr. Ironmaster, must remember that a day may come when you yourself may want to get a big piece of pork, and then you will get caught in the trap."

The ironmaster began to laugh.

"That was not so badly said, my good fellow. Perhaps we should let the sheriff alone on Christmas Eve. But now get out of here as fast as you can."

But just as the man was opening the door, the daughter said, "I think he ought to stay with us today. I don't want him to go." And with that she went and closed the door.

"What in the world are you doing?" said the father.

The daughter stood there quite embarrassed and hardly knew what to answer. That morning she had felt so happy when she thought how homelike and Christmassy she was going to make things for the poor hungry wretch. She could not get away from the idea all at once, and that was why she had interceded for the vagabond.

"I am thinking of this stranger here," said the young girl. "He walks and walks the whole year long, and there is probably not a single place in the whole country where he is welcome and can feel at home. Wherever he turns he is chased away. Always he is afraid of being arrested and cross-examined. I should like to have him enjoy a day of peace with us here—just one in the whole year."

The ironmaster mumbled something in his beard. He could not bring himself to oppose her.

"It was all a mistake, of course," she continued. "But anyway I don't think we ought to chase away a human being whom we have asked to come here, and to whom we have promised Christmas cheer."

"You do preach worse than a parson," said the ironmaster. "I only hope you won't have to regret this."

The young girl took the stranger by the hand and led him up to the table.

"Now sit down and eat," she said, for she could see that her father had given in.

The man with the rat traps said not a word; he only sat down and helped himself to the food. Time after time he looked at

Early landscape by Wassily Kandinsky (1866–1944).
❓ *Do you think that the rat-trap seller has indeed fallen into a trap? What do you predict will happen to him?*

the young girl who had interceded for him. Why had she done it? What could the crazy idea be?

After that, Christmas Eve at Ramsjö passed just as it always had. The stranger did not cause any trouble because he did nothing but sleep. The whole forenoon he lay on the sofa in one of the guest rooms and slept at one stretch. At noon they woke him up so that he could have his share of the good Christmas fare, but after that he slept again. It seemed as though for many years he had not been able to sleep as quietly and safely as here at Ramsjö.

In the evening, when the Christmas tree was lighted, they woke him up again, and he stood for a while in the drawing room, blinking as though the candlelight hurt him, but after that he disappeared again. Two hours later he was aroused once more. He then had to go down into the dining room and eat the Christmas fish and porridge.

As soon as they got up from the table he went around to each one present and said thank you and good night, but when he came to the young girl she gave him to understand that it was her father's intention that the suit which he wore was to be a Christmas present—he did not have to return it; and if he wanted to spend next Christmas Eve in a place where he could rest in peace, and be sure that no evil would befall him, he would be welcomed back again.

The man with the rat traps did not answer anything to this. He only stared at the young girl in boundless amazement.

The next morning the ironmaster and his daughter got up in good season to go to the early Christmas service. Their guest was still asleep, and they did not disturb him.

When, at about ten o'clock, they drove back from church, the young girl sat and hung her head even more dejectedly than usual. At church she had learned that one of the old crofters of the ironworks had been robbed by a man who went around selling rat traps.

"Yes, that was a fine fellow you let into the house," said her father. "I only wonder how many silver spoons are left in the cupboard by this time."

The wagon had hardly stopped at the front steps when the ironmaster asked the valet whether the stranger was still there. He added that he had heard at church that the man was a thief. The valet answered that the fellow had gone and that he had not taken anything with him at all. On the contrary, he had left behind a little package which Miss Willmansson was to be kind enough to accept as a Christmas present.

The young girl opened the package, which was so badly done up that the contents came into view at once. She gave a little cry of joy. She found a small rat trap, and in it lay three wrinkled ten-kronor notes. But that was not all. In the rat trap lay also a letter written in large, jagged characters:

Honored and noble Miss:

Since you have been so nice to me all day long, as if I was a captain, I want to be nice to you, in return, as if I was a real captain: for I do not want you to be embarrassed at this Christmas season by a thief; but you can give back the money to the old man on the roadside, who has the money pouch hanging on the window frame as a bait for poor wanderers.

The rat trap is a Christmas present from a rat who would have been caught in this world's rat trap if he had not been raised to captain, because in that way he got power to clear himself.

Written with friendship and high regard,
Captain von Ståhle

First Thoughts

Did you think the peddler would return the thirty kronor in the end? Did you find his action believable? Why or why not?

Identifying Facts

1. In the rat-trap peddler's theory of the world, what is the bait? What happens after someone takes the bait?
2. Why does the peddler return to the crofter's cottage? Why does he later feel like a rat in a trap?
3. Why does the ironmaster invite the peddler into his home? What kindnesses does Edla show the peddler?
4. What do Edla and her father learn at church on Christmas morning? What do they discover when they return home?

Interpreting Meanings

1. What effect does Lagerlöf achieve with the opening words of the story? What **point of view** is associated with stories that open with these words?
2. After the peddler steals the thirty kronor, he becomes lost in a forest. The forest is clearly real, but it may also be a **symbol**—something that represents a larger idea or concept. What do you think the forest might **symbolize**? Cite details from the story to support your answer.
3. How does Lagerlöf's use of the **omniscient point of view** help us understand the peddler better than if he were telling the story himself?
4. In the peddler's note to Edla, how does he say he managed to avoid "this world's rat trap"? Why do you think the peddler signed his note "Captain von Ståhle"?

Applying Meanings

This story seems to suggest that if someone, even a criminal, is treated with honor and respect, he or she will become honorable and respectable. Do you think this is generally true, or do you think this theory is too simplistic? Discuss your opinion, giving examples from your own experiences.

Creative Writing Response

Writing a Different Conclusion. This story is about a man who was treated honorably and who then acted honorably. If the ironmaster and his daughter had not been kind to the peddler after they discovered he was not who they thought he was, how do you think the peddler would have reacted? How would the story have ended? Write a different ending to the story, beginning with the ironmaster's words on page 1203, "What does this mean?"

Critical Writing Response

Comparing and Contrasting Characters. In a brief essay, compare and contrast Lagerlöf's character of the peddler in "The Rat Trap" with Tolstoy's character Pahom in "How Much Land Does a Man Need?" (see page 1045). Name at least one way in which the characters are alike and at least one way in which they are different. In your final paragraph, state whether you think Lagerlöf or Tolstoy has the more positive view of human nature. You may also state whose view you agree with. Be sure to support general statements with details from the stories. As a prewriting exercise, fill in a chart like the one below.

	Peddler	Pahom
General intelligence		
Effects of poverty		
Effects of greed		

James Joyce
1882–1941, Ireland

The Bettmann Archive

James Joyce was the oldest of ten children born to a poor Roman Catholic family in "dear, dirty Dublin." He was an enthusiastic student and eventually enrolled at Dublin's University College. When he was twenty, however, he left Dublin and repressive Irish Catholic society for the cosmopolitan cities of Paris, Trieste, Rome, and Zurich. At the time of his death he had not set foot in his homeland for nearly thirty years. Yet, ironically, all of his writings deal with his childhood home.

In his first major work, a collection of short stories called *Dubliners* (1914), Joyce provides snapshots of the paralyzing world from which he fled. His simple style here contrasts sharply with his later, more revolutionary, works. Joyce's poetic, autobio-graphical novel *A Portrait of the Artist as a Young Man* (1916) followed. The novel is full of experimental wordplay and was praised in literary circles on both sides of the Atlantic, though it had met with several rejections before an American company agreed to publish it. Joyce had even greater difficulty publishing his next book, *Ulysses* (1922). This novel vividly illustrates Joyce's blend of realism and symbolism, his groundbreaking use of inventive language, and his ability to capture characters' thoughts with the stream-of-consciousness technique. Loosely paralleling Homer's *Odyssey*, it takes place in Dublin on a single day—June 16, 1904—which, not coincidentally, was the day Joyce fell in love with his future wife, Nora Barnacle.

Joyce's last major work was *Finnegans Wake* (1939). This highly experimental novel is so filled with allusions, foreign expressions, and word coinages that no one can read it without guidance. For example, this passage describes Finnegan's fall off a wall and his subsequent death: "The great fall of the offwall entailed at such short notice the pftjschute of Finnegan, erse solid man, that the humptyhillhead of himself prumptly sends an unquiring one well to the west in quest of his tumptytumtoes. . . ."

Although Joyce's books were banned, pirated, and often misunderstood, he is now regarded as one of the greatest literary talents of the twentieth century.

Reader's Guide

EVELINE

Background

"Eveline" is the fourth of the fifteen stories in *Dubliners*. Although it is one of the first stories Joyce ever wrote, his characteristic focus on the inner workings of characters' minds is already evident. In all the stories in *Dubliners,* Joyce uses a device he called an **epiphany**. Joyce borrowed the term from theology and used it to mean a sudden remark, symbol, or moment that sums up and clarifies the meaning of a complex experience. Joyce's epiphanies usually occur at or near the end of each story. Sometimes a character achieves a new insight; at other times, only the reader becomes aware of the character's true nature. In either case, the new awareness is not stated directly. Instead, Joyce provides details from which readers must make their own inferences.

Writer's Response

Think of a time when you suddenly changed your opinion, attitude, or behavior. Freewrite about the change and explain what caused it.

Literary Focus

Joyce was one of the first modernists to use **stream of consciousness** as a narrative technique. Early in the century, writers interested in psychology began to recognize that the human mind does not usually operate in a linear fashion; instead, it leaps around from thought to thought and feeling to feeling in what seems to be a random way. For example, eating a cinnamon roll for breakfast may remind a woman of the smell that often filled her grandmother's kitchen. She may then recall a childhood trip to her grandmother's in which the family car broke down, and that may remind her that her own car needs repairs, and so on. Joyce brought stream of consciousness to its highest form in his novels *Ulysses* and *Finnegans Wake,* and we see the beginnings of this technique in "Eveline."

EVELINE

James Joyce

Joyce once wrote that he chose to set his stories in Dublin "because that city seemed to me the center of paralysis." As you read, think about how this famous phrase, "center of paralysis," applies to the character of Eveline.

She sat at the window watching the evening invade the avenue. Her head was leaned against the window curtains and in her nostrils was the odor of dusty cretonne.[1] She was tired.

Few people passed. The man out of the last house passed on his way home; she heard his footsteps clacking along the concrete pavement and afterwards crunching on the cinder path before the new red houses. One time there used to be a field there in which they used to play every evening with other people's children. Then a man from Belfast bought the field and built houses in it—not like their little brown houses but bright brick houses with shining roofs. The children of the avenue used to play together in that field—the Devines, the Waters, the Dunns, little Keogh the cripple, she and her brothers and sisters. Ernest, however, never played: he was too grown up. Her father used often to hunt them in out of the field with his blackthorn stick; but usually little Keogh used to keep *nix*[2] and call out when he saw her father coming. Still they seemed to have been rather happy then. Her father was not so bad then; and besides, her mother was alive. That was a long time ago; she and her brothers and sisters were all grown up; her mother was dead. Tizzie Dunn was dead, too, and the Waters had gone back to England. Everything changes. Now she was going to go away like the others, to leave her home.

Home! She looked round the room, reviewing all its familiar objects which she had dusted once a week for so many years, wondering where on earth all the dust came from. Perhaps she would never see again those familiar objects from which she had never dreamed of being divided. And yet during all those years she had never found out the name of the priest whose yellowing photograph hung on the wall above the broken harmonium[3] beside the colored print of the promises made to Blessed Margaret Mary Alacoque.[4] He had been a school friend of her father. Whenever he showed the photograph to a visitor her father used to pass it with a casual word:

---

1. **cretonne** (krē·tän′): heavy printed cloth used for curtains.
2. **keep *nix***: serve as a lookout.
3. **harmonium:** small organ.
4. **promises . . . Alacoque** (à·là·kôk′): the Lord's promises to Margaret Mary Alacoque (1647–1690), French nun who as a child suffered from self-inflicted paralysis but was miraculously cured when she dedicated herself to a holy life.

DUBLIN FROM THE LIFFEY, engraving.

The Granger Collection, New York

? *How does Eveline feel about leaving home?*

"He is in Melbourne now."

She had consented to go away, to leave her home. Was that wise? She tried to weigh each side of the question. In her home anyway she had shelter and food; she had those whom she had known all her life about her. Of course she had to work hard both in the house and at business. What would they say of her in the Stores when they found out that she had run away with a fellow? Say she was a fool, perhaps; and her place would be filled up by advertisement. Miss Gavan would be glad. She had always had an edge on her, especially whenever there were people listening.

"Miss Hill, don't you see these ladies are waiting?"

"Look lively, Miss Hill, please."

She would not cry many tears at leaving the Stores.

But in her new home, in a distant unknown country, it would not be like that. Then she would be married—she, Eveline. People would treat her with respect then. She would not be treated as her mother had been. Even now, though she was over nineteen, she sometimes felt herself in danger of her father's violence. She knew it was that that had given her the palpitations. When they were growing up he had never gone for her, like he used to go for Harry and Ernest, because she was a girl; but latterly he had begun to threaten her and say what he would do to her only for her dead mother's sake. And now she had nobody to protect her. Ernest was dead and Harry, who was in the church decorating business, was nearly always down somewhere in the country. Besides, the invariable squabble for money on Saturday nights had begun to weary her unspeakably. She always gave her entire wages—seven shillings[5]—and Harry always sent up what he could but the trouble was to get any money from her father. He said she used to squander the money, that she had no head, that he wasn't going to give her his hard-earned money to throw about the streets, and much more, for he was usually fairly bad of a Saturday night. In the end he would give her the money and ask her had she any intention of buying Sunday's dinner. Then she had to rush out as quickly as she could and do her marketing, holding her black leather purse tightly in her hand as she elbowed her way through the crowds and returning home late under her load of provisions. She had hard work to keep the house together and to see that the two young children who had been left to her charge went to school regularly and got their meals regularly. It was hard work—a hard life—but now that she was about to leave it she did not find it a wholly undesirable life.

She was about to explore another life with Frank. Frank was very kind, manly, open-hearted. She was to go away with him by the night boat to be his wife and to live with him in Buenos Aires where he had a home waiting for her. How well she remembered the first time she had seen him; he was lodging in a house on the main road where she used to visit. It seemed a few weeks ago. He was standing at the gate, his peaked cap pushed back on his head and his hair tumbled forward over a face of bronze. Then they had come to know each other. He used to meet her outside the Stores every evening and see her home. He took her to see *The Bohemian Girl* and she felt elated as she sat in an unaccustomed part of the theater with him. He was awfully fond of music and sang a little. People knew that they were courting and, when he sang about the lass that loves a sailor, she always felt pleasantly confused. He used to call her Poppens out of fun. First of all it had been an excitement for her to have a fellow and then she had begun to like him. He had tales of distant countries. He had started as a deck boy at a pound a month on a ship of the Allan Line going out to Canada. He told her the names of the ships he had been on and the names of the different services. He had sailed through the Strait of Magellan and he told her stories of the terrible Patagonians.[6] He had fallen on his feet in Buenos Aires, he said, and had come over to the old country just for a holiday. Of course, her father had found out the affair and had forbidden her to have anything to say to him.

"I know these sailor chaps,"[7] he said.

One day he had quarreled with Frank and after that she had to meet her lover secretly.

The evening deepened in the avenue. The white of two letters in her lap grew indistinct. One was to Harry; the other was to her father. Ernest had been her favorite but she liked Harry, too. Her father was becoming old lately, she noticed; he would miss her. Sometimes he could be very nice. Not long before, when she had been laid up for

---

5. **seven shillings:** A shilling is a former British coin worth five pennies, or one-twentieth of a pound. Seven shillings would have been a low salary.

6. **Patagonians** (pat′ə·gō′nē·ənz): inhabitants of the southern part of Argentina; at the time of the story, Patagonia was still a frontier area, similar to the American West of the last century.

7. **chaps:** fellows.

a day, he had read her out a ghost story and made toast for her at the fire. Another day, when their mother was alive, they had all gone for a picnic to the Hill of Howth. She remembered her father putting on her mother's bonnet to make the children laugh.

Her time was running out but she continued to sit by the window, leaning her head against the window curtain, inhaling the odor of dusty cretonne. Down far in the avenue she could hear a street organ playing. She knew the air. Strange that it should come that very night to remind her of the promise to her mother, her promise to keep the home together as long as she could. She remembered the last night of her mother's illness; she was again in the close dark room at the other side of the hall and outside she heard a melancholy air of Italy. The organ player had been ordered to go away and given sixpence. She remembered her father strutting back into the sickroom saying:

"Damned Italians! coming over here!"

As she mused the pitiful vision of her mother's life laid its spell on the very quick of her being—that life of commonplace sacrifices closing in final craziness. She trembled as she heard again her mother's voice saying constantly with foolish insistence:

"Derevaun Seraun![8] Derevaun Seraun!"

She stood up in a sudden impulse of terror. Escape! She must escape! Frank would save her. He would give her life, perhaps love, too. But she wanted to live. Why should she be unhappy? She had a right to happiness. Frank would take her in his arms, fold her in his arms. He would save her.

She stood among the swaying crowd in the station at the North Wall.[9] He held her hand and she knew that he was speaking to her, saying something about the passage over and over again. The station was full of soldiers with brown baggages. Through the wide doors of the sheds she caught a glimpse of the black mass of the boat, lying in beside the quay wall, with illumined portholes. She anwered nothing. She felt her cheek pale and cold and, out of a maze of distress, she prayed to God to direct her, to show her what was her duty. The boat blew a long mournful whistle into the mist. If she went, tomorrow she would be on the sea with Frank, steaming towards Buenos Aires. Their passage had been booked. Could she still draw back after all he had done for her? Her distress awoke a nausea in her body and she kept moving her lips in silent fervent prayer.

A bell clanged upon her heart. She felt him seize her hand:

"Come!"

All the seas of the world tumbled about her heart. He was drawing her into them: he would drown her. She gripped with both hands at the iron railing.

"Come!"

No! No! No! It was impossible. Her hands clutched the iron in frenzy. Amid the seas she sent a cry of anguish!

"Eveline! Evvy!"

He rushed beyond the barrier and called to her to follow. He was shouted at to go on but he still called to her. She set her white face to him, passive, like a helpless animal. Her eyes gave him no sign of love or farewell or recognition.

---

8. **Derevaun Seraun:** Some scholars suggest that the phrase is corrupt Irish Gaelic for "the end of song is raving madness" or "the end of pleasure is pain." Although it does appear to be based on Irish Gaelic, the phrase as it stands is gibberish.

---

9. **North Wall:** wharf that is part of Dublin Harbor.

First Thoughts

Why do you think Eveline decides to stay in Ireland rather than escape to Buenos Aires with Frank? Do you think she made the right decision?

Identifying Facts

1. What are Eveline's responsibilities in the Hill household?
2. What was Mr. Hill's reaction to the relationship between Frank and his daughter?
3. Summarize the final scene at the quay.

Interpreting Meanings

1. Find an example of loosely associated thoughts or memories that illustrate Joyce's use of the **stream-of-consciousness** narrative technique. What do Eveline's thoughts and memories reveal about her character and the kind of life she led before meeting Frank?
2. Around what **internal conflict** do Eveline's thoughts center? In what way is this also an **external conflict** between her and her society?
3. What finally causes Eveline to refuse to leave with Frank? What events or thoughts earlier in the story **foreshadowed**, or hinted at, this decision?

Applying Meanings

Do you think that the desire to assert our independence must always conflict with our responsibilities to others? Discuss this in relation to a time you felt a conflict between your duties to others and your own need for independence.

Creative Writing Response

Capturing Your Own Stream of Consciousness. In a freewriting exercise, try to capture your own **stream of consciousness**. Remember that stream of consciousness attempts to portray the thinking mind directly, without organizing the thoughts. Start with something you are seeing or thinking or feeling right now. Then jot down the flow of thoughts, emotions, memories, and associations that run through your mind. Don't worry about sentence structure or punctuation or even making sense. Just write down whatever enters your mind. If you wish, you may then edit these jottings and organize them so that you can use them later in a sketch or short story.

Critical Writing Response

Writing About an Epiphany. Write a brief essay about the **epiphany** in "Eveline." In your essay, answer these questions:

1. What is the story's epiphany, or moment of awareness, about Eveline's true nature and desires?
2. What do we learn about Eveline at this point? How does this new awareness differ from our earlier impressions and the impressions she had of herself?
3. Would you say that *she* experiences a new awareness? Or is the awareness merely on the reader's part?

Before writing, you may find it helpful to jot down general answers to these questions and then find details in the story that will help you support and explain your answers.

Isak Dinesen
1885–1962, Denmark

The Granger Collection, New York

When the American author Ernest Hemingway accepted the 1954 Nobel Prize for literature, he remarked that the award should instead have gone to Danish writer Isak Dinesen. Hemingway, who loved Africa and set several works there, was especially impressed with Dinesen's *Out of Africa*, an autobiographical account of her years in British East Africa, now Kenya. Although Dinesen is often recognized as the European author who best captured the beauty of the African landscape, she wrote equally well of northern Europe and the Danish upper class.

Born into a family of wealthy aristocrats in coastal Denmark, Dinesen's spirit of adventure was often at odds with her sheltered upbringing. After her father died and the cousin she loved refused to marry her, she defiantly set sail for Africa to marry the cousin's twin brother, Bror Blixen-Finecke. In 1914, the couple established a coffee plantation in what is now Kenya. Blixen's wayward lifestyle, however, left his wife often on her own. After the couple divorced in 1921, Dinesen ran the six-thousand-acre farm by herself for ten years.

Many of Dinesen's stories celebrate the power of women. In *Out of Africa*, Dinesen says that she often visited the Somali women on her property to listen to their stories. "It was a trait common to all these tales," Dinesen wrote, "that the heroine, chaste or not, would get the better of the male characters and come out of the tale triumphant. . . . Within this enclosed women's world . . . I felt the presence . . . of a Millennium when women were to reign supreme in the world."

In 1931, the price of coffee plummeted and Dinesen's plantation went bankrupt. In the same year her lover, the British pilot Denys Finch-Hatton, was killed in a plane crash. These events led Dinesen to return to Denmark and to devote herself to writing. Three years later she published *Seven Gothic Tales*, stories about mysterious events and persecuted heroines in Europe hundreds of years ago. Dinesen's international reputation was cemented with *Out of Africa*, which was published simultaneously in Denmark and Britain in 1937.

Reader's Guide

THE RING

Background

Denmark, Dinesen's homeland and the setting of "The Ring," is a democratic constitutional monarchy. At the time this story takes place, however, the nation was not democratic. The nobility lived in a grand style, while the rest of the population was very poor and sometimes had to turn to crimes such as poaching—trespassing on a landowner's property to hunt game or catch fish—in order to feed themselves and their families. Such crimes were harshly punished; a livestock thief often faced death if he were caught. Upper-class attitudes toward the plight of the poor varied widely. Some members of the upper class—like Sigismund in "The Ring"—held humanitarian views and advocated social, political, and economic reforms. Many others found such ideas dangerous.

As the story opens, we learn that Lise, the main character, has been determined since childhood to marry Sigismund, a landowner who nevertheless comes from a family of lower rank than hers. Lise's parents have finally agreed to the marriage, and the newlyweds are blissfully happy.

Writer's Response

What kind of person do you think that Lise, a newly married young woman from the upper class, will be? Write your predictions in a few sentences.

Literary Focus

Characters are often classified as static or dynamic. A **static character** is one who changes little or not at all in the course of the story. A **dynamic character**, on the other hand, changes in an important way as a result of the action of the story. The **protagonist**, or main character, of a story is almost always a dynamic character. How the protagonist changes or what he or she learns is usually our best clue as to a story's **theme**, or larger meaning.

THE RING

Isak Dinesen

Read until you come to the paragraph on page 1219 that begins, "This meeting in the wood from beginning to end passed without a word. . . ." Stop and write down what you think will happen during this encounter. When you finish the story, see if your prediction was correct.

On a summer morning a hundred and fifty years ago a young Danish squire and his wife went out for a walk on their land. They had been married a week. It had not been easy for them to get married, for the wife's family was higher in rank and wealthier than the husband's. But the two young people, now twenty-four and nineteen years old, had been set on their purpose for ten years; in the end her haughty parents had had to give in to them.

They were wonderfully happy. The stolen meetings and secret, tearful love letters were now things of the past. To God and man they were one; they could walk arm in arm in broad daylight and drive in the same carriage, and they would walk and drive so till the end of their days. Their distant paradise had descended to earth and had proved, surprisingly, to be filled with the things of everyday life: with jesting and railleries, with breakfasts and suppers, with dogs, haymaking, and sheep. Sigismund, the young husband, had promised himself that from now there should be no stone in his bride's path, nor should any shadow fall across it. Lovisa,[1] the wife, felt that now, every day and for

the first time in her young life, she moved and breathed in perfect freedom because she could never have any secret from her husband.

To Lovisa—whom her husband called Lise[2]—the rustic atmosphere of her new life was a matter of wonder and delight. Her husband's fear that the existence he could offer her might not be good enough for her filled her heart with laughter. It was not a long time since she had played with dolls; as now she dressed her own hair, looked over her linen press and arranged her flowers, she again lived through an enchanting and cherished experience: one was doing everything gravely and solicitously, and all the time one knew one was playing.

It was a lovely July morning. Little woolly clouds drifted high up in the sky, the air was full of sweet scents. Lise had on a white muslin frock and a large Italian straw hat. She and her husband took a path through the park; it wound on across the meadows, between small groves and groups of trees, to the sheep field. Sigismund was going to show his wife his sheep. For this reason she

---

1. **Lovisa** (lō·vē′sə)

2. **Lise** (lē′sə)

A Mountain Path at Capel Curig, Wales, Ebenezer Downard, 1860.

had not brought her small white dog, Bijou,[3] with her, for he would yap at the lambs and frighten them, or he would annoy the sheep dogs. Sigismund prided himself on his sheep; he had studied sheep breeding in Mecklenburg[4] and England, and had brought back with him Cotswold rams[5] by which to improve his Danish stock. While they

---

3. **Bijou** (bē′zhoo′): "jewel" (French).
4. **Mecklenburg:** agricultural region in northern Germany.
5. **Cotswold rams:** the males of a kind of sheep originally bred in the Cotswold Hills of southwestern England.

walked he explained to Lise the great possibilities and difficulties of the plan.

She thought: "How clever he is, what a lot of things he knows!" and at the same time: "What an absurd person he is, with his sheep! What a baby he is! I am a hundred years older than he."

But when they arrived at the sheepfold the old sheepmaster Mathias met them with the sad news that one of the English lambs was dead and two were sick. Lise saw that her husband was grieved by the tidings; while he questioned Mathias on the matter she kept silent and only gently pressed his arm. A couple of boys were sent off to fetch the sick lambs, while the master and servant went into the details of the case. It took some time.

Lise began to gaze about her and to think of other things. Twice her own thoughts made her blush deeply and happily, like a red rose, then slowly her blush died away, and the two men were still talking about sheep. A little while after, their conversation caught her attention. It had turned to a sheep thief.

This thief during the last months had broken into the sheepfolds of the neighborhood like a wolf, had killed and dragged away his prey like a wolf, and like a wolf had left no trace after him. Three nights ago the shepherd and his son on an estate ten miles away had caught him in the act. The thief had killed the man and knocked the boy senseless, and had managed to escape. There were men sent out to all sides to catch him, but nobody had seen him.

Lise wanted to hear more about the horrible event, and for her benefit old Mathias went through it once more. There had been a long fight in the sheep house, in many places the earthen floor was soaked with blood. In the fight the thief's left arm was broken; all the same, he had climbed a tall fence with a lamb on his back. Mathias added that he would like to string up the murderer with these two hands of his, and Lise nodded her head at him gravely in approval. She remembered Red Riding Hood's wolf, and felt a pleasant little thrill running down her spine.

Sigismund had his own lambs in his mind, but he was too happy in himself to wish anything in the universe ill. After a minute he said: "Poor devil."

Lise said: "How can you pity such a terrible man? Indeed Grandmamma was right when she said that you were a revolutionary and a danger to society!" The thought of Grandmamma, and of the tears of past days, again turned her mind away from the gruesome tale she had just heard.

The boys brought the sick lambs and the men began to examine them carefully, lifting them up and trying to set them on their legs; they squeezed them here and there and made the little creatures whimper. Lise shrank from the show and her husband noticed her distress.

"You go home, my darling," he said, "this will take some time. But just walk ahead slowly, and I shall catch up with you."

So she was turned away by an impatient husband to whom his sheep meant more than his wife. If any experience could be sweeter than to be dragged out by him to look at those same sheep, it would be this. She dropped her large summer hat with its blue ribbons on the grass and told him to carry it back for her, for she wanted to feel the summer air on her forehead and in her hair. She walked on very slowly, as he had told her to do, for she wished to obey him in everything. As she walked she felt a great new happiness in being altogether alone, even without Bijou. She could not remember that she had ever before in all her life been altogether alone. The landscape around her was still, as if full of promise, and it was hers. Even the swallows cruising in the air were hers, for they belonged to him,[6] and he was hers.

She followed the curving edge of the grove and after a minute or two found that she was out of sight to the men by the sheep

---

6. **him:** that is, Sigismund; in Denmark at the time of the story, birds and other wild animals on an estate were the owner's property and anyone who hunted or caught them without permission would be prosecuted.

house. What could now, she wondered, be sweeter than to walk along the path in the long flowering meadow grass, slowly, slowly, and to let her husband overtake her there? It would be sweeter still, she reflected, to steal into the grove and to be gone, to have vanished from the surface of the earth from him when, tired of the sheep and longing for her company, he should turn the bend of the path to catch up with her.

An idea struck her; she stood still to think it over.

A few days ago her husband had gone for a ride and she had not wanted to go with him, but had strolled about with Bijou in order to explore her domain. Bijou then, gamboling, had led her straight into the grove. As she had followed him, gently forcing her way into the shrubbery, she had suddenly come upon a glade in the midst of it, a narrow space like a small alcove with hangings of thick green and golden brocade, big enough to hold two or three people in it. She had felt at that moment that she had come into the very heart of her new home. If today she could find the spot again she would stand perfectly still there, hidden from all the world. Sigismund would look for her in all directions; he would be unable to understand what had become of her and for a minute, for a short minute—or, perhaps, if she was firm and cruel enough, for five—he would realize what a void, what an unendurably sad and horrible place the universe would be when she was no longer in it. She gravely scrutinized the grove to find the right entrance to her hiding place, then went in.

She took great care to make no noise at all, therefore advanced exceedingly slowly. When a twig caught the flounces of her ample skirt she loosened it softly from the muslin, so as not to crack it. Once a branch

took hold of one of her long golden curls; she stood still, with her arms lifted, to free it. A little way into the grove the soil became moist; her light steps no longer made any sound upon it. With one hand she held her small handkerchief to her lips, as if to emphasize the secretness of her course. She found the spot she sought and bent down to divide the foliage and make a door to her sylvan closet. At this, the hem of her dress caught her foot and she stopped to loosen it. As she rose she looked into the face of a man who was already in the shelter.

He stood up erect, two steps off. He must have watched her as she made her way straight toward him.

She took him in in one single glance. His face was bruised and scratched, his hands and wrists stained with dark filth. He was dressed in rags, barefooted, with tatters wound round his naked ankles. His arms hung down to his sides, his right hand clasped the hilt of a knife. He was about her own age. The man and the woman looked at each other.

This meeting in the wood from beginning to end passed without a word; what happened could only be rendered by pantomime. To the two actors in the pantomime it was timeless; according to a clock it lasted four minutes.

She had never in her life been exposed to danger. It did not occur to her to sum up her position, or to work out the length of time it would take to call her husband or Mathias, whom at this moment she could hear shouting to his dogs. She beheld the man before her as she would have beheld a forest ghost: the apparition itself, not the sequels of it, changes the world to the human who faces it.

Although she did not take her eyes off the face before her, she sensed that the alcove had been turned into a covert. On the ground a couple of sacks formed a couch; there were some gnawed bones by it. A fire must have been made here in the night, for there were cinders strewn on the forest floor.

After a while she realized that he was observing her just as she was observing him. He was no longer just run to earth and crouching for a spring, but he was wondering, trying to know. At that she seemed to see herself with the eyes of the wild animal at bay in his dark hiding place: her silently approaching white figure, which might mean death.

He moved his right arm till it hung down straight before him between his legs. Without lifting the hand he bent the wrist and slowly raised the point of the knife till it pointed at her throat. The gesture was mad, unbelievable. He did not smile as he made it, but his nostrils distended, the corners of his mouth quivered a little. Then slowly he put the knife back in the sheath by his belt.

She had no object of value about her, only the wedding ring which her husband had set on her finger in church, a week ago. She drew it off, and in this movement dropped her handkerchief. She reached out her hand with the ring toward him. She did not bargain for her life. She was fearless by nature, and the horror with which he inspired her was not fear of what he might do to her. She commanded him, she besought him to vanish as he had come, to take a dreadful figure out of her life, so that it should never have been there. In the dumb movement her young form had the grave authoritativeness of a priestess conjuring down some monstrous being by a sacred sign.

He slowly reached out his hand to hers, his finger touched hers, and her hand was steady at the touch. But he did not take the ring. As she let it go it dropped to the ground as her handkerchief had done.

For a second the eyes of both followed it. It rolled a few inches toward him and stopped before his bare foot. In a hardly perceivable movement he kicked it away and again looked into her face. They remained like that, she knew not how long, but she felt that during that time something happened, things were changed.

He bent down and picked up her handkerchief. All the time gazing at her, he again drew his knife and wrapped the tiny bit of cambric round the blade. This was difficult for him to do because his left arm was broken. While he did it his face under the dirt

PORTRAIT OF THE ARTIST'S SISTER, HANS THOMA (1839–1924).

Describe Lise's feelings toward her husband: are they wholly loving, or ambivalent?

and suntan slowly grew whiter till it was almost phosphorescent. Fumbling with both hands, he once more stuck the knife into the sheath. Either the sheath was too big and had never fitted the knife, or the blade was much worn—it went in. For two or three more seconds his gaze rested on her face; then he lifted his own face a little, the strange radiance still upon it, and closed his eyes.

The movement was definitive and unconditional. In this one motion he did what she had begged him to do: he vanished and was gone. She was free.

She took a step backward, the immovable, blind face before her, then bent as she had done to enter the hiding place, and glided away as noiselessly as she had come. Once outside the grove she stood still and looked round for the meadow path, found it and began to walk home.

Her husband had not yet rounded the edge of the grove. Now he saw her and helloed to her gaily; he came up quickly and joined her.

The path here was so narrow that he kept half behind her and did not touch her. He began to explain to her what had been the matter with the lambs. She walked a step before him and thought: All is over.

After a while he noticed her silence, came up beside her to look at her face and asked, "What is the matter?"

She searched her mind for something to say, and at last said: "I have lost my ring."

"What ring?" he asked her.

She answered, "My wedding ring."

As she heard her own voice pronounce the words she conceived their meaning.

Her wedding ring. "With this ring"—dropped by one and kicked away by another—"with this ring I thee wed."[7] With this lost ring she had wedded herself to something. To what? To poverty, persecution, total loneliness. To the sorrows and the sinfulness of this earth. "And what therefore God had joined together let man not put asunder."

"I will find you another ring," her husband said. "You and I are the same as we were on our wedding day; it will do as well. We are husband and wife today, too, as much as yesterday, I suppose."

Her face was so still that he did not know if she had heard what he said. It touched him that she should take the loss of his ring so to heart. He took her hand and kissed it. It was cold, not quite the same hand as he had last kissed. He stopped to make her stop with him.

"Do you remember where you had the ring on last?" he asked.

"No," she answered.

"Have you any idea," he asked, "where you may have lost it?"

"No," she answered. "I have no idea at all."

---

7. **With this ring . . . I thee wed:** quotation from the vows exchanged at a wedding ceremony.

Did you find any character or event in this story confusing or unsettling? If so, describe your thoughts and feelings about it.

Identifying Facts

1. How old is Lise when the story opens? What recent event has made her "wonderfully happy"?

2. What prompts Lise to hide in the clearing in the shrubbery? Summarize the events that take place there.

3. When Sigismund asks if she has any idea where she lost the ring, what does Lise say?

Interpreting Meanings

1. Why do you think Lise says at the beginning of the story that never having secrets from her husband allows her to move and breathe "in perfect freedom"?

2. Why do you think Lise keeps the incident in the glade a secret from her husband?

3. Which of the three main characters are **static**, or unchanging, and which are **dynamic**, or changing? Cite details from the story to support your answer.

4. What might the ring **symbolize**, or represent, in Lise's life? What change in Lise does the loss of the ring represent?

5. What is the **irony** in Sigismund being touched that his wife "should take the loss of his ring so to heart"?

6. Consider the biblical story of the fall of Adam and Eve (see page 166). Explain how "The Ring" could be seen as a modern version of this story.

Applying Meanings

Do you think married people should never have secrets from each other? Or do you think secrets are inevitable? Discuss.

Creative Writing Response

Writing a Dialogue. If Lise and the stranger had spoken, what do you think they would have said to each other? Write the conversation that you imagine taking place between them. Be sure to punctuate their dialogue correctly.

Critical Writing Response

Analyzing a Dynamic Character. Write an essay analyzing Lise, concentrating on the change that occurred when she encountered the man in the glade. In describing her character before and after this incident, remember to consider **(a)** her appearance, **(b)** her actions, **(c)** what she says, **(d)** the response of other characters, and **(e)** the writer's direct comments about her. Include answers to these questions in your essay: Why did Lise decide to enter the glade? Why did she not speak with the man? Why did she offer him her wedding ring? Why did she not tell her husband about the man in the glade?

Language and Vocabulary

Words from Place Names

Many English words come from the names of cities and other places around the world. For example, the strong sheer cotton fabric known as *muslin* was first made in the city of Mosul in northern Iraq, and the fine thin linen known as *cambric* was first made in the northern French town of Cambrai.

All of the following English words also come from the names of places. Use a dictionary to help you explain the origin of each word and the meanings of any unfamiliar words.

1. chihuahua
2. denim
3. dollar
4. madras
5. mausoleum
6. mecca
7. sardine
8. shanghai
9. tangerine
10. tuxedo

Anna Akhmatova
1889–1966, Russia

The Granger Collection, New York

When writers express political views in their writing, they often run into problems with government authorities. Anna Akhmatova (uk·mät′ə·və), however, was persecuted for many years because she did *not* write on political themes. In the years following the Russian Revolution in 1917, only "socially useful" art was tolerated. Akhmatova was viciously attacked and her poems suppressed because they were too "personal."

Akhmatova grew up just outside St. Petersburg in the suburb that had been for centuries the summer palace of the czars. Here she became part of the thriving artistic community of prerevolutionary St. Petersburg. The poetry that Akhmatova began publishing in 1912 illustrates ideas of **acmeism**,

a movement she and her husband, the poet Nikolai Gumilev, helped found. A reaction to French Symbolism (see page 983), which was then fashionable in Russia, acmeism rejected ambiguous symbols and the Symbolists' view of the artist as a mystic. For Akhmatova, the poet was not a visionary but a craftsperson, patiently building poems from words.

Akhmatova's early successes came to an abrupt end with the Russian Revolution in 1917. Five years later, her ex-husband was shot for allegedly plotting against the new Soviet government. Although he and Akhmatova were divorced at this time, she was deemed guilty by association and her poetry suppressed. She was not allowed to publish at all from 1922 to 1940, and in 1946 she was expelled from the Soviet Writers' Union.

In the years of Stalinist terror that followed, Akhmatova watched as friends and colleagues were arrested and sent to prison camps, many never to return. Her own son was imprisoned until Stalin's death in 1953. Akhmatova's long poem "Requiem" captures those dark days in the image of an anonymous woman standing month after month outside a St. Petersburg prison waiting for news of a loved one.

Akhmatova's home became the refuge and meeting place of a younger generation of Russian poets. In her final years, she was recognized officially again and was even allowed to travel to the West.

Reader's Guide

LOT'S WIFE

Background

"Lot's Wife" is based on the biblical incident recounted in Genesis 19 in which God sends angels to punish the city of Sodom for its wickedness. When the angels arrive disguised as men, only a man named Lot treats them justly. As a result, the angels warn him that God will destroy the city. They tell him to flee with his family and not look back. Lot's wife, however, disobeys the command and glances back. She is immediately turned into a pillar of salt. Akhmatova wrote "Lot's Wife," which was originally published in the *Paris Review,* in the early 1920s, shortly after her former husband was executed, but before the worst years of the Stalin era. At that time, many Russian intellectuals had begun to flee the country, but Akhmatova chose to stay.

Writer's Response

In a paragraph or two, describe how you might feel if you lived in a country that you were compelled to leave because of an intolerable situation—politics, war, or famine. Would you need to "look back" on your life there, or would you leave without a backward glance and concentrate on starting anew?

Literary Focus

Akhmatova was a founder of a movement called **acmeism**. Acmeists strove to eliminate ambiguous symbols from their work and instead emphasized the clear communication of ideas through richly textured language. As they saw it, part of the craft of poetry involved organizing thoughts into **stanzas**—line groupings that followed a **rhyme scheme**, or pattern of end-of-line rhymes. In the original Russian, "Lot's Wife" is arranged in **quatrains**, or four-line stanzas, in which the first and third lines always rhyme, as do the second and fourth lines. In this English translation by poet Richard Wilbur, the stanza structure and rhyme scheme match those of the original Russian.

LOT'S WIFE
Anna Akhmatova
translated by
RICHARD WILBUR

Read to the end of the second stanza. From the images of the city that the speaker recalls, how do you think she feels about leaving?

THE STORY OF ABRAHAM AND LOT: THE FLIGHT FROM SODOM, RAPHAEL (1483–1520).

Scala/Art Resource, New York

The just man followed then his angel guide
Where he strode on the black highway, hulking
   and bright;
But a wild grief in his wife's bosom cried,
Look back, it is not too late for a last sight

5   *Of the red towers of your native Sodom, the square*
Where once you sang, the gardens you shall mourn,

And the tall house with empty windows where
You loved your husband and your babes were born.

She turned, and looking on the bitter view
10 Her eyes were welded shut by mortal pain;
Into transparent salt her body grew,
And her quick feet were rooted in the plain.

Who would waste tears upon her? Is she not
The least of our losses, this unhappy wife?
15 Yet in my heart she will not be forgot
Who, for a single glance, gave up her life.

First Thoughts

How do you think the speaker feels about Lot's wife? Is she seen as foolish and dis-obedient, or as passionate and coura-geous? Do you agree with the speaker's views?

Identifying Facts

1. Whom does Lot follow?
2. What particular places in Sodom does Lot's wife want to see one last time? When she looks back and sees Sodom's destruction, what happens to her eyes and body?
3. According to the last stanza, where will Lot's wife not be forgotten?

Interpreting Meanings

1. What, in general, makes Lot's wife care about Sodom, despite its evils? What does the phrase "mortal pain" (line 10) suggest about how we should view her attitude?
2. Often a **stanza** expresses one unit of thought. Which of these stanzas contain one thought? Which express more than one thought?

3. Do you think that Akhmatova is simply retelling a biblical incident in verse? Re-read the biography and background sections and explain how the poem might also relate to Akhmatova's life and to the political situation in Russia at the time she wrote the poem.

Applying Meanings

What events in your past do you look back on with affection or nostalgia? Do you think this is usually a negative or a positive thing to do? Explain, providing examples to illustrate your opinion.

Creative Writing Response

Writing a Rhymed Stanza. Write a four-line stanza imitating the *abab* rhyme scheme of Akhmatova's poem. On a sepa-rate sheet of paper, you may write two lines to complete the stanza below, or you may write one or more stanzas that are entirely your own.

(a) I came upon a secret place
(b) Where all the world was far away
(a) _____
(b) _____

Pasternak's Tribute to Akhmatova

Russian poet and novelist Boris Pasternak
(1890–1960).

One of Anna Akhmatova's friends and colleagues was Boris Pasternak, a famous poet and novelist (his most famous novel is *Doctor Zhivago*). In this tribute poem, Pasternak compares Akhmatova's composition of poetry to the work of a seamstress. What does Pasternak's final line suggest about the value he found in all of Akhmatova's poetry?

To Anna Akhmatova
Boris Pasternak
translated by
Eugene M. Kayden

It seems I'm choosing the essential words
That I can liken to your pristine power.
And if I err, it's all the same to me,

For I shall cling to all my errors still.

I hear the constant patter on wet roofs,
The smothered eclogue[1] of the wooden pavements.
A certain city[2] comes clear in every line,
And springs to life in every syllable.

The roads are blocked, despite the tide of spring
All round. Your clients are a stingy, cruel lot.
Bent over piles of work, the sunset burns;
Eyes blear and moist from sewing by a lamp.

You long for the boundless space of Ladoga,[3]
And hasten, weary, to the lake for change
And rest. It's little in the end you gain.
The canals smell rank like musty closet-chests.

And like an empty nut the hot wind frets
Across their waves, across the blinking eyelids
Of stars and branches, posts and lamps, and one
Lone seamstress gazing far above the bridge.

I know that eyes and objects vary greatly
In singleness and sharpness, yet the essence
Of greatest strength, dissolving fear, is the sky
At night beneath the gaze of polar light.

That's how I call to mind your face and glance.
No, not the image of that pillar of salt
Exalts me now, in which five years ago
You set in rhymes our fear of looking back.

But as it springs in all your early work,
Where crumbs of unremitting prose grew strong,
In all affairs, like wires conducting sparks,
Your work throbs high with our remembered past.

---

1. **eclogue:** here, dialogue; used figuratively.
2. **A certain city:** St. Petersburg.
3. **Ladoga** (lä'dô·gä'): a large Russian lake.

Federico García Lorca
1898–1936, Spain

Art Resource, New York

On the evening of July 19, 1936, Chilean poet Pablo Neruda (ne·rōō'də) (see page 1294), then living in Spain, went to meet his friend Federico García Lorca (fe'de·rē'kô gär·sē'ä lôr'kä). Neruda waited and waited, but García Lorca never appeared because he had been kidnapped by Fascist supporters of Spanish dictator Francisco Franco. The kidnappers took García Lorca to a Granada cemetery, forced him to dig his own grave, and then shot him. The murder shocked the world, especially since the thirty-eight-year-old writer had never taken an active role in politics. Viewed as a martyr, he became

known as the "Poet of the Blood," and many of his poems about sorrow and death took on additional significance.

Granada, the site of his brutal murder, was also the city near which García Lorca grew up. Born to a well-to-do farm family, García Lorca valued the simple pleasures of rural life and also learned to love music, poetry, and all the arts. In 1919 García Lorca went to Madrid to study at the city's university. Among the talented artists he met there were Juan Ramón Jiménez, already a distinguished poet, and Salvador Dalí, the experimental painter whose surrealism would influence García Lorca's poetry and plays.

His most famous plays are tragedies dealing with thwarted womanhood. *Blood Wedding* (1933) is the story of a bride who runs away with a previous lover and is then murdered by her husband. This play, together with *Yerma* (1934) and *The House of Bernarda Alba* (1936), are considered to be García Lorca's finest dramatic works.

Shortly before his death, García Lorca published *Lament for the Death of a Bullfighter* (1935), considered to be the greatest elegy in modern Spanish poetry and a moving premonition of his own death. García Lorca was at the height of his celebrity when he was murdered by the Fascists. As Pablo Neruda later mourned, "Who could have believed there were monsters on this earth, in his own Granada, capable of such an inconceivable crime?"

Reader's Guide

THE GUITAR

Background

García Lorca often drew inspiration from the Andalusian (an'də·lōo'zhən) area of southern Spain where he grew up. Here there is a rich tradition of Gypsy folk music that includes *cante jondo* (kän'te hōn'dō), literally "deep song." Highly emotional and rhythmic, *cante jondo* is usually performed by colorfully dressed dancers in the passionate style known as flamenco. Many of García Lorca's poems, including "The Guitar," use modernist images to evoke the passionate feelings associated with *cante jondo*.

The guitar, on which *cante jondo* is traditionally played, is a musical instrument long associated with Spain. It arose, probably in sixteenth-century Spain, from the *vihuela* (ve·wā'la), a guitar-shaped instrument that medieval Spanish minstrels played in place of a lute. Later modifications resulted in what is known as the classical or Spanish guitar, whose reputation as a concert instrument was much enhanced by the great Spanish guitarist Andrés Segovia (si·gō'vē·ə).

Writer's Response

Different sounds bring different feelings and emotions to mind. Write a few sentences describing your feelings when you hear a guitar (electric or acoustic) or some other musical instrument.

Literary Focus

Free verse is poetry that is free of traditional rules of meter and form. While it does not have a regular **meter** or **rhyme scheme**, free verse does have a conversational rhythm. It also uses poetic devices such as **imagery**, **alliteration**, **repetition**, **assonance** (repeated vowel sounds), and **onomatopoeia**. Because there is no fixed meter to determine where each line should end, the free-verse poet must carefully decide how to break the poem into lines. In making such decisions, he or she considers both the emphasis in meaning and the sound or rhythm that a particular line break helps create. Translators of free-verse poetry must keep the same considerations in mind. "The Guitar," both in the original Spanish and in the English translation, uses free verse.

GUITAR, PABLO PICASSO, 1920.

The Bettmann Archive

THE GUITAR

Federico García Lorca
translated by
RACHEL BENSON AND ROBERT O'BRIEN

 As you read "The Guitar," note the images that convey emotion. What overriding emotion does García Lorca associate with the guitar?

The cry of the guitar
begins.
The crystals of dawn are
breaking.
5 The cry of the guitar
begins.
It's useless to stop it.
It's impossible to
stop it.
10 Its cry monotonous
as the weeping of water,
as the weeping of wind
over the snowfall.
It's impossible to

15 stop it.
It cries for
distant things.
Sand of the scalding South
seeking white camellias.[1]
20 It mourns the arrow without target,
evening without morning, and the first
bird dead upon the branch.
Oh, guitar!
25 Heart wounded by five swords.

---

1. **camellias** (kə·mēl'yəz): the blooms of an evergreen shrub that grows in mild climates; camellia bushes would not thrive in a hot, sandy place.

First Thoughts

What is the main emotion you felt while reading the poem? What is the poem's **tone**? Identify the words or phrases that contributed to this tone.

Identifying Facts

1. What word names the sound of the guitar in lines 1 and 5? What is its sound compared to in lines 11–13?
2. According to lines 20–23, what three things does the guitar mourn?
3. What is the guitar compared to in the last line?

Interpreting Meanings

1. In saying that it is "impossible to stop" the guitar, what might García Lorca be suggesting?
2. What aspects of human experience might the **image** in lines 18–19 represent? Explain your answer.
3. What do the **images** in lines 20–23 suggest about the causes of human sorrow?
4. What do you think the "five swords" represent?

Applying Meanings

Music is often used as a symbol for life itself. What instrument or type of music symbolizes life for you? Compare your answer with those of your classmates.

Critical Writing Response

Comparing Translations. In a brief essay, compare the translation by poet Robert Bly (below) with the translation by Benson and O'Brien that you have just read. Focus on differences in **diction**, or word choice, **imagery**, and the way wording in specific lines contributes to the overall sound or **rhythm**. In your topic sentence, state which translation you prefer. In the body of your paper, give examples to explain your preference. Conclude by restating which translation you like better and why.

The Guitar
Federico García Lorca
translated by
Robert Bly

The crying of the guitar
starts.
The goblets
of the dawn break.
5 The crying of the guitar
starts.
No use to stop it.
It is impossible
to stop it.
10 It cries repeating itself
as the water cries,
as the wind cries
over the snow.
It is impossible
15 to stop it.
It is crying for things
far off.
The warm sand of the South
that asks for white camellias.
20 For the arrow with nothing to hit,
the evening with no dawn coming,
and the first bird of all dead
on the branch.
Guitar!
25 Heart wounded, gravely,
by five swords.

Elie Wiesel
b. 1928, Romania

AP/Wide World Photos

Elie Wiesel (el'ē vē·zel'), a survivor of the Nazi concentration camps, turned to writing as a way to keep alive the memory of the atrocities committed during World War II. Seeking to avert new holocausts, Wiesel has also drawn attention to the plight of Cambodians, Soviet Jews, South African blacks, and other victims of persecution throughout the world.

Wiesel grew up among the devout Hasidic Jews of Sighet, a village in Romania's Carpathian Mountains. News from the outside world rarely filtered into this remote community. When the Nazis arrived in 1944 and rounded up all of the Jews, Wiesel and his family had no idea that they were being sent to Nazi death camps. They ended up in Auschwitz (oush'vits), the most infamous of these camps. Here Elie's mother and youngest sister were among the many Jews who were gassed to death. Meanwhile, Elie and his father were made slave laborers and sent to Buchenwald (bo͞o'k'n·wôld'), another concentration camp, where Elie's father died of starvation and disease.

Finally, on April 11, 1945, the surviving prisoners of Buchenwald were liberated by the United States Third Army. As one of Europe's millions of displaced persons, Wiesel at first settled in France. Always interested in writing, Wiesel began working for a French newspaper while still a student at the Sorbonne in Paris. His friend, the writer François Mariac, encouraged Wiesel to record for humanity the horrors he had endured. But Wiesel waited ten years before writing about his wartime ordeal. "I was afraid that words might betray it," he later explained. What Wiesel finally wrote was his autobiography *Night* (1958), one of the most significant and powerful accounts of Nazi atrocities ever written.

Since then, Wiesel has written many works about the Holocaust—the term he first used for the Nazi policy of systematic mass murder of European Jews. He has also described prewar Hasidic life and published several collections of Jewish folktales.

Reader's Guide

from NIGHT

Background

In the wake of Germany's defeat in World War I, an obscure war veteran named Adolf Hitler wrote a book called *Mein Kampf* that outlined his plan to restore German military might. According to Hitler, Germans were the "master race" and everyone else was inferior. The Jews in particular were made the scapegoat for all the world's evils.

Throughout the 1930s, Hitler's followers, the Nazis, made strong political advances in Germany. After their power was consolidated, they began invading neighboring nations. As more and more Jews fell into Nazi hands with each new German conquest, the Nazis secretly began transporting them to concentration camps like Auschwitz in Poland and Buchenwald in Germany. In these camps, Jews were shot by firing squads, executed in gas chambers, tortured in medical experiments, worked to death as slave laborers, or killed by starvation and disease. The dead were then burned in ditches or ovenlike structures called *crematoria*.

Jews were not the only victims of the Nazi mass murders. A similar fate awaited Gypsies, political opponents, homosexuals, captured Resistance fighters in conquered lands, and others. In all, about twelve million people were killed, nearly six million of them Jews. In Auschwitz alone, about two and a half million people were executed and another half million died of starvation and neglect.

Writer's Response

The horrors of World War II have been recorded in many books, movies, and television programs. Write a paragraph describing what you remember most clearly about such depictions of World War II events. What feelings did these depictions evoke in you?

Literary Focus

An **autobiography** is a written account of a person's own life. People write their autobiographies for a variety of reasons. Some simply want to recapture the events and emotions of their lives, while others want to make some political or philosophical point. Wiesel has said that his purpose in writing *Night* was to "bear witness" to what happened to Jews and other victims of the Nazis.

from NIGHT

Elie Wiesel

translated by

STELLA RODWAY

> *As you read this excerpt from* **Night**, *focus on the events that Wiesel witnesses and his growing awareness of what is happening to him. Which details show that Wiesel, for all his emotional involvement, is nevertheless giving a fairly objective portrait of events?*

The train stopped at Kaschau, a little town on the Czechoslovak frontier. We realized then that we were not going to stay in Hungary. Our eyes were opened, but too late.

The door of the car slid open. A German officer, accompanied by a Hungarian lieutenant-interpreter, came up and introduced himself.

"From this moment, you come under the authority of the German army. Those of you who still have gold, silver, or watches in your possession must give them up now. Anyone who is later found to have kept anything will be shot on the spot. Secondly, anyone who feels ill may go to the hospital car. That's all."

The Hungarian lieutenant went among us with a basket and collected the last possessions from those who no longer wished to taste the bitterness of terror.

"There are eighty of you in this wagon," added the German officer. "If anyone is missing, you'll all be shot, like dogs. . . ."

They disappeared. The doors were closed. We were caught in a trap, right up to our necks. The doors were nailed up; the way back was finally cut off. The world was a cattle wagon hermetically sealed.[1]

We had a woman with us named Madame Schächter.[2] She was about fifty; her ten-year-old son was with her, crouched in a corner. Her husband and two eldest sons had been deported with the first transport by mistake. The separation had completely broken her.

I knew her well. A quiet woman with tense, burning eyes, she had often been to our house. Her husband, who was a pious man, spent his days and nights in study, and it was she who worked to support the family.

Madame Schächter had gone out of her mind. On the first day of the journey she had already begun to moan and to keep asking why she had been separated from her family. As time went on, her cries grew hysterical.

On the third night, while we slept, some of us sitting one against the other and some standing, a piercing cry split the silence:

"Fire! I can see a fire! I can see a fire!"

---

1. **hermetically sealed:** airtight; used figuratively here to mean completely sealed off.
2. **Schächter** (shäkh'tər)

Arriving at Auschwitz train station. *Immediately upon arrival at the concentration camp at Auschwitz, prisoners were divided into those who would go directly to the gas chambers and those who would be sent into slave labor.*

There was a moment's panic. Who was it who had cried out? It was Madame Schächter. Standing in the middle of the wagon, in the pale light from the windows, she looked like a withered tree in a cornfield. She pointed her arm toward the window, screaming:

"Look! Look at it! Fire! A terrible fire! Mercy! *Oh, that fire!*"

Some of the men pressed up against the bars. There was nothing there; only the darkness.

The shock of this terrible awakening stayed with us for a long time. We still trembled from it. With every groan of the wheels on the rail, we felt that an abyss was about

Elie Wiesel **1235**

to open beneath our bodies. Powerless to still our own anguish, we tried to console ourselves:

"She's mad, poor soul. . . ."

Someone had put a damp cloth on her brow, to calm her, but still her screams went on:

"Fire! Fire!"

Her little boy was crying, hanging onto her skirt, trying to take hold of her hands. "It's all right, Mummy! There's nothing there. . . . Sit down. . . ." This shook me even more than his mother's screams had done.

Some women tried to calm her. "You'll find your husband and your sons again . . . in a few days. . . ."

She continued to scream, breathless, her voice broken by sobs. "Jews, listen to me! I can see a fire! There are huge flames! It is a furnace!"

It was as though she were possessed by an evil spirit which spoke from the depths of her being.

We tried to explain it away, more to calm ourselves and to recover our own breath than to comfort her. "She must be very thirsty, poor thing! That's why she keeps talking about a fire devouring her."

But it was in vain. Our terror was about to burst the sides of the train. Our nerves were at breaking point. Our flesh was creeping. It was as though madness were taking possession of us all. We could stand it no longer. Some of the young men forced her to sit down, tied her up, and put a gag in her mouth.

Silence again. The little boy sat down by his mother, crying. I had begun to breathe normally again. We could hear the wheels churning out that monotonous rhythm of a train traveling through the night. We could begin to doze, to rest, to dream. . . .

An hour or two went by like this. Then another scream took our breath away. The woman had broken loose from her bonds and was crying out more loudly than ever:

"Look at the fire! Flames, flames everywhere. . . ."

Once more the young men tied her up and gagged her. They even struck her. People encouraged them:

"Make her be quiet! She's mad! Shut her up! She's not the only one. She can keep her mouth shut. . . ."

They struck her several times on the head—blows that might have killed her. Her little boy clung to her; he did not cry out; he did not say a word. He was not even weeping now.

An endless night. Toward dawn, Madame Schächter calmed down. Crouched in her corner, her bewildered gaze scouring the emptiness, she could no longer see us.

She stayed like that all through the day, dumb, absent, isolated among us. As soon as night fell, she began to scream: "There's a fire over there!" She would point at a spot in space, always the same one. They were tired of hitting her. The heat, the thirst, the pestilential stench, the suffocating lack of air—these were as nothing compared with these screams which tore us to shreds. A few days more and we should all have started to scream, too.

But we had reached a station. Those who were next to the windows told us its name:

"Auschwitz."

No one had ever heard that name.

The train did not start up again. The afternoon passed slowly. Then the wagon doors slid open. Two men were allowed to get down to fetch water.

When they came back, they told us that, in exchange for a gold watch, they had discovered that this was the last stop. We would be getting out here. There was a labor camp. Conditions were good. Families would not be split up. Only the young people would go to work in the factories. The old men and invalids would be kept occupied in the fields.

The barometer of confidence soared. Here was a sudden release from the terrors of the previous nights. We gave thanks to God.

Madame Schächter stayed in her corner, wilted, dumb, indifferent to the general confidence. Her little boy stroked her hand.

As dusk fell, darkness gathered inside the wagon. We started to eat our last provisions. At ten in the evening, everyone was looking for a convenient position in which to sleep for a while, and soon we were all asleep. Suddenly:

"The fire! The furnace! Look, over there! . . ."

Waking with a start, we rushed to the window. Yet again we had believed her, even if only for a moment. But there was nothing outside save the darkness of night. With shame in our souls, we went back to our places, gnawed by fear, in spite of ourselves. As she continued to scream, they began to hit her again, and it was with the greatest difficulty that they silenced her.

The man in charge of our wagon called a German officer who was walking about on the platform, and asked him if Madame Schächter could be taken to the hospital car.

"You must be patient," the German replied. "She'll be taken there soon."

Toward eleven o'clock, the train began to move. We pressed against the windows. The convoy was moving slowly. A quarter of an hour later, it slowed down again. Through the windows we could see barbed wire; we realized that this must be the camp.

We had forgotten the existence of Madame Schächter. Suddenly, we heard terrible screams:

"Jews, look! Look through the window! Flames! Look!"

And as the train stopped, we saw this time that flames were gushing out of a tall chimney into the black sky.

Madame Schächter was silent herself. Once more she had become dumb, indifferent, absent, and had gone back to her corner.

We looked at the flames in the darkness. There was an abominable odor floating in the air. Suddenly, our doors opened. Some odd-looking characters, dressed in striped shirts and black trousers, leapt into the wagon. They held electric torches[3] and truncheons. They began to strike out to right and left, shouting:

"Everybody get out! Everyone out of the wagon! Quickly!"

We jumped out. I threw a last glance toward Madame Schächter. Her little boy was holding her hand.

In front of us flames. In the air that smell of burning flesh. It must have been about midnight. We had arrived—at Birkenau, reception center for Auschwitz.

The cherished objects we had brought with us thus far were left behind in the train, and with them, at last, our illusions.

Every two yards or so an SS man held his Tommy gun[4] trained on us. Hand in hand we followed the crowd.

An SS noncommissioned officer came to meet us, a truncheon in his hand. He gave the order:

"Men to the left! Women to the right!"

Eight words spoken quietly, indifferently, without emotion. Eight short, simple words. Yet that was the moment when I parted

---

3. **electric torches:** flashlights.
4. **Tommy gun:** submachine gun.

from my mother. I had not had time to think, but already I felt the pressure of my father's hand: we were alone. For a part of a second I glimpsed my mother and my sisters moving away to the right. Tzipora held Mother's hand. I saw them disappear into the distance; my mother was stroking my sister's fair hair, as though to protect her, while I walked on with my father and the other men. And I did not know that in that place, at that moment, I was parting from my mother and Tzipora forever. I went on walking. My father held onto my hand.

Behind me, an old man fell to the ground. Near him was an SS man, putting his revolver back in its holster.

My hand shifted on my father's arm. I had one thought—not to lose him. Not to be left alone.

The SS officers gave the order:

"Form fives!"

Commotion. At all costs we must keep together.

"Here, kid, how old are you?"

It was one of the prisoners who asked me this. I could not see his face, but his voice was tense and weary.

"I'm not quite fifteen yet."

"No. Eighteen."

"But I'm not," I said, "Fifteen."

"Fool. Listen to what *I* say."

Then he questioned my father, who replied:

"Fifty."

Victims of the Holocaust.

In what way were Madame Schächter's visions prophetic?

The other grew more furious than ever.

"No, not fifty. Forty. Do you understand? Eighteen and forty."

He disappeared into the night shadows. A second man came up, spitting oaths at us.

"What have you come here for, you sons of bitches? What are you doing here, eh?"

Someone dared to answer him.

"What do you think? Do you suppose we've come here for our own pleasure? Do you think we asked to come?"

A little more, and the man would have killed him.

"You shut your trap, you filthy swine, or I'll squash you right now! You'd have done better to have hanged yourselves where you were than come here. Didn't you know what was in store for you at Auschwitz? Haven't you heard about it? In 1944?"

No, we had not heard. No one had told us. He could not believe his ears. His tone of voice became increasingly brutal.

"Do you see that chimney over there? See it? Do you see those flames? (Yes, we did see the flames.) Over there—that's where you're going to be taken. That's your grave, over there. Haven't you realized it yet? You dumb bastards, don't you understand anything? You're going to be burned. Frizzled away. Turned into ashes."

He was growing hysterical in his fury. We stayed motionless, petrified. Surely it was all a nightmare? An unimaginable nightmare?

I heard murmurs around me.

"We've got to do something. We can't let ourselves be killed. We can't go like beasts to the slaughter. We've got to revolt."

There were a few sturdy young fellows among us. They had knives on them, and they tried to incite the others to throw themselves on the armed guards.

One of the young men cried:

"Let the world learn of the existence of Auschwitz. Let everybody hear about it, while they can still escape...."

But the older ones begged their children not to do anything foolish:

"You must never lose faith, even when the sword hangs over your head. That's the teaching of our sages...."

The wind of revolt died down. We continued our march toward the square. In the middle stood the notorious Dr. Mengele (a typical SS officer: a cruel face, but not devoid of intelligence, and wearing a monocle); a conductor's baton in his hand, he was standing among the other officers. The baton moved unremittingly, sometimes to the right, sometimes to the left.

I was already in front of him:

"How old are you?" he asked, in an attempt at a paternal tone of voice.

"Eighteen." My voice was shaking.

"Are you in good health?"

"Yes."

"What's your occupation?"

Should I say that I was a student?

"Farmer," I heard myself say.

This conversation cannot have lasted more than a few seconds. It had seemed like an eternity to me.

The baton moved to the left. I took half a step forward. I wanted to see first where they were sending my father. If he went to the right, I would go after him.

The baton once again pointed to the left for him, too. A weight was lifted from my heart.

We did not yet know which was the better side, right or left; which road led to prison and which to the crematory. But for the moment I was happy; I was near my father. Our procession continued to move slowly forward.

Another prisoner came up to us:

"Satisfied?"

"Yes," someone replied.

"Poor devils, you're going to the crematory."

He seemed to be telling the truth. Not far from us, flames were leaping up from a ditch, gigantic flames. They were burning something. A lorry[5] drew up at the pit and delivered its load—little children. Babies! Yes, I saw it—saw it with my own eyes . . . those children in the flames. (Is it surprising that I could not sleep after that? Sleep had fled from my eyes.)

So this was where we were going. A little farther on was another and larger ditch for adults.

I pinched my face. Was I still alive? Was I awake? I could not believe it. How could it be possible for them to burn people, children, and for the world to keep silent? No, none of this could be true. It was a nightmare. . . . Soon I should wake with a start, my heart pounding, and find myself back in the bedroom of my childhood, among my books. . . .

My father's voice drew me from my thoughts:

"It's a shame . . . a shame that you couldn't have gone with your mother. . . . I saw several boys of your age going with their mothers. . . ."

His voice was terribly sad. I realized that he did not want to see what they were going to do to me. He did not want to see the burning of his only son.

My forehead was bathed in cold sweat. But I told him that I did not believe that they could burn people in our age, that humanity would never tolerate it. . . .

"Humanity? Humanity is not concerned with us. Today anything is allowed. Anything is possible, even these crematories. . . ."

His voice was choking.

"Father," I said, "if that is so, I don't want to wait here. I'm going to run to the electric wire. That would be better than slow agony in the flames."

He did not answer. He was weeping. His body was shaken convulsively. Around us, everyone was weeping. Someone began to recite the Kaddish, the prayer for the dead. I do not know if it has ever happened before, in the long history of the Jews, that people have ever recited the prayer for the dead for themselves.

"*Yitgadal veyitkadach shmé raba.* . . . May His Name be blessed and magnified . . . ," whispered my father.

For the first time, I felt revolt rise up in me. Why should I bless His name? The Eternal, Lord of the Universe, the All-Powerful and Terrible, was silent. What had I to thank Him for?

We continued our march. We were gradually drawing closer to the ditch, from which an infernal heat was rising. Still twenty steps to go. If I wanted to bring about my own death, this was the moment. Our line had now only fifteen paces to cover. I bit my lips so that my father would not hear my teeth chattering. Ten steps still. Eight. Seven. We marched slowly on, as though following a hearse at our own funeral. Four steps more. Three steps. There it was now, right in front of us, the pit and its flames. I gathered all that was left of my strength, so that I could break from the ranks and throw myself upon the barbed wire. In the depths of my heart, I bade farewell to my father, to the whole universe; and, in spite of myself, the words formed themselves and issued in a whisper from my lips: *Yitgadal veyitkadach shmé raba.* . . . May His name be blessed and magnified. . . . My heart was bursting. The moment had come. I was face to face with

5. **lorry** (lôr′ē): truck.

the Angel of Death. . . .

No. Two steps from the pit we were ordered to turn to the left and made to go into a barracks.

I pressed my father's hand. He said:

"Do you remember Madame Schächter, in the train?"

Never shall I forget that night, the first night in camp, which has turned my life into one long night, seven times cursed and seven times sealed. Never shall I forget that smoke. Never shall I forget the little faces of the children, whose bodies I saw turned into wreaths of smoke beneath a silent blue sky.

Never shall I forget those flames which consumed my faith forever.

Never shall I forget that nocturnal silence which deprived me, for all eternity, of the desire to live. Never shall I forget those moments which murdered my God and my soul and turned my dreams to dust. Never shall I forget these things, even if I am condemned to live as long as God Himself. Never.

First Thoughts

What psychological effects do the events that Wiesel relates have on the prisoners? How do you think you would have acted in their place?

Identifying Facts

1. Throughout the journey, what does Madame Schächter say she sees? How do her fellow passengers respond?

2. What causes the soaring "barometer of confidence" among the prisoners? What do they smell when they arrive at Auschwitz?

3. What significance does Wiesel later attach to the SS officer's eight-word order? What does one prisoner tell Wiesel and his father to say about their ages?

4. As they move toward the flaming pit, what does Wiesel say he does not believe could happen "in our age"? How does his father respond?

Interpreting Meanings

1. Why do you think Madame Schächter sees what she does? Why do several prisoners treat her harshly?

2. Why do you think Wiesel and his father were told to lie about their ages?

3. Which details about the prisoners show that Wiesel has not allowed sentiment to overshadow accurate reporting of events in this **autobiography**?

4. What feeling overwhelms Wiesel's father shortly after they enter Auschwitz? What prompts his final remark?

5. Read the last three paragraphs aloud. What is the effect of Wiesel's use of **repetition**?

Applying Meanings

For years Wiesel was torn by two opposing feelings: that he should "bear witness" to what happened in the Nazi death camps, and that any attempt to put his concentration camp experiences into words would show disrespect for the dead. Which of these two concerns do you think is more important? Do you think that he ultimately resolved this problem or not?

Creative Writing Response

1. **Narrating a Dramatic Event.** Think of a dramatic incident in your recent past. It may have been a sports event, an accident, or a special time with a friend.

Let the reader know, as Wiesel does, exactly what happened and exactly how you felt every step of the way.

2. **Writing a Script.** Wiesel's *Night* is a powerful, unforgettable, dramatic narrative. Take a portion of this excerpt from *Night*—or find a copy of the book and choose another scene—and convert it to a dramatic script, complete with dialogue and stage directions. If you wish, perform the scene for the class, or tape it as a radio play.

Critical Writing Response

Writing About a Title. Wiesel chose one word as the title of his autobiography. This word carries more weight and more meanings than you might at first suppose. Think about the **connotations** and **denotations** of the word *night*. Are there both positive and negative connotations? Is Wiesel speaking of a literal or a figurative night? Use your thoughts about these questions to write a brief essay in which you explain why you think Wiesel chose to title his autobiography *Night*.

PRIMARY SOURCES

Elie Wiesel Accepts the Nobel Peace Prize

The Nobel Prize is awarded each year for achievements in the sciences and humanities. Generally considered the world's most prestigious award for a number of fields, the prize is named for Swedish chemist and industrialist Alfred Nobel, who instructed that, after his death, the interest on the considerable fortune he left behind be awarded annually to people who made outstanding achievements in the areas of chemistry, physics, medicine, economics, literature, and peace. The prize is awarded for a life's work, rather than a single achievement.

The following passage is from the speech Elie Wiesel gave on accepting the 1986 Nobel Peace Prize. To what does Wiesel's phrase "kingdom of night" refer? What light does the passage throw on Wiesel's past experiences and their effects on his future values and behavior?

It is with a profound sense of humility that I accept the honor you have chosen to bestow upon me. I know: your choice transcends me. This both frightens and pleases me.

It frightens me because I wonder: do I have the right to represent the multitudes who have perished? Do I have the right to accept this great honor on their behalf? I do not. That would be presumptuous. No one may speak for the dead; no one may interpret their mutilated dreams and visions.

It pleases me because I may say that this honor belongs to all the survivors and their children and, through us, to the Jewish people with whose destiny I have always identified.

I remember: it happened yesterday or eternities ago. A young Jewish boy discovered the kingdom of night. I remember his bewilderment; I remember his anguish. It all happened so fast. The ghetto. The deportation. The sealed cattle car. The fiery altar upon which the history of our people and the future of mankind were meant to be sacrificed.

I remember: he asked his father, "Can this be true? This is the twentieth century, not the Middle Ages. Who would allow such crimes to be committed? How could the world remain silent?"

And now the boy is turning to me: "Tell me," he asks. "What have you done with my future? What have you done with your life?"

And I tell him that I have tried. That I have tried to keep memory alive, that I have tried to fight those who would forget. Because if we forget, we are guilty, we are accomplices.

And then I explain to him how naive we were, that the world did know and remain silent. And that is why I swore never to be silent whenever and wherever human beings endure suffering and humiliation. We must always take sides. Neutrality helps the oppressor, never the victim. Silence encourages the tormentor, never the tormented.

The concentration camp at Buchenwald, where Wiesel and his father were eventually taken. *Wiesel lies in the second berth from the bottom, the center cubicle, on the right.*

Albert Camus
1913–1960, Algeria/France

Cartier-Bresson/Magnum Photos, Inc.

Albert Camus (ka·mōō′) believed that the question "Why" is asked at some point in every person's life. We wonder why we are here, what we are doing, and what life itself means. **Existentialism**, a philosophy that arose in response to the confusion many people felt in the early decades of the twentieth century, answered these questions by saying that neither the universe nor human life has any intrinsic, or already present, meaning. Camus reacted to this nihilistic attitude by formulating his own brand of humanistic existentialism. He believed that although existence probably has no ultimate meaning, human beings have the capacity— and the need—to create meaningful lives for themselves. Camus suggested that instead of giving up, each person must try to create his or her own meaning in life by making choices and acting upon them.

Of French and Spanish descent, Camus grew up in Algeria when it was still a French colony. After studying philosophy at the University of Algiers, Camus became active in Algeria's French-language theater. He also worked for a French-language newspaper and published two essay collections. In these essays and in his later work, Camus articulated his philosophy of moral commitment that later earned him the title of *le Juste*, "the just man."

In 1942, Camus published *The Stranger* and *The Myth of Sisyphus*, which illustrate the human quest for moral purpose in a meaningless world. The protagonist of *The Stranger* refuses to "play the game" by telling the white lies of polite society. He also refuses to believe in any religion or in human love. He nevertheless discovers, while in prison awaiting execution, a passion for the simple fact of life itself. In *The Myth of Sisyphus*, Camus reinterprets a classical myth to show that no matter how futile life may seem to be, a person can find value in the struggle to reach an impossible moral goal. Camus sees Sisyphus, whom the gods have condemned to endlessly roll a boulder uphill, as being happy because he has found meaning in rolling the rock. By extension, Camus believes that life is our rock—what matters most is that we do something with it.

Reader's Guide

THE GUEST

Background

Algeria was a colony of France for over a hundred years. During this time, native Arabs and Berbers were treated as second-class citizens. After a long and bloody struggle, the nation achieved independence in 1962 and most Algerians of European background left the country.

"The Guest" takes place when rebellion was brewing before Algerian independence. The protagonist, Daru, was born and raised in Algeria but is of European descent. As an Algerian and a Frenchman, he finds it impossible to take sides in the revolt. His feelings and experiences in many ways duplicate those of Camus, who was uncomfortable with his position as a European colonial in Africa. Much of Camus's fiction, like "The Guest," explores the topics of human freedom and isolation in mid-twentieth-century Algeria.

Writer's Response

In a few paragraphs, describe your feelings about the country, town, or neighborhood where you grew up. What aspects of your cultural or physical environment made you feel especially at home? Did you ever feel like an outsider? If so, why?

Literary Focus

Existentialism is a modern European philosophy that emphasizes the meaninglessness of the outer world. Some existentialists respond to this meaninglessness by recognizing that each person is free to make moral choices that define and give meaning to his or her life. Through their choices and actions, human beings are responsible for what they make of themselves and their lives. As you read "The Guest," consider how Daru's experiences reflect existentialist thinking.

THE GUEST

Albert Camus

translated by

JUSTIN O'BRIEN

Both Daru and the Arab are faced with existential choices in this story. What are their choices, and what decisions do they make?

The schoolmaster was watching the two men climb toward him. One was on horseback, the other on foot. They had not yet tackled the abrupt rise leading to the schoolhouse built on the hillside. They were toiling onward, making slow progress in the snow, among the stones, on the vast expanse of the high, deserted plateau. From time to time the horse stumbled. Without hearing anything yet, he could see the breath issuing from the horse's nostrils. One of the men, at least, knew the region. They were following the trail although it had disappeared days ago under a layer of dirty white snow. The schoolmaster calculated that it would take them half an hour to get onto the hill. It was cold; he went back into the school to get a sweater.

He crossed the empty, frigid classroom. On the blackboard the four rivers of France,[1] drawn with four different colored chalks, had been flowing toward their estuaries for the past three days. Snow had suddenly fallen in mid-October after eight months of drought without the transition of rain, and the twenty pupils, more or less, who lived in the villages scattered over the plateau had stopped coming. With fair weather they would return. Daru now heated only the single room that was his lodging, adjoining the classroom and giving also onto the plateau to the east. Like the class windows, his window looked to the south, too. On that side the school was a few kilometers from the point where the plateau began to slope toward the south. In clear weather could be seen the purple mass of the mountain range where the gap opened onto the desert.

Somewhat warmed, Daru returned to the window from which he had first seen the two men. They were no longer visible. Hence they must have tackled the rise. The sky was not so dark, for the snow had stopped falling during the night. The morning had opened with a dirty light which had scarcely become brighter as the ceiling of clouds lifted. At two in the afternoon it seemed as if the day were merely beginning. But still this was better than those three days when the thick snow was falling amidst unbroken darkness with little gusts of wind that rattled the double door of the classroom. Then Daru had spent long hours in his room, leaving it only to go to the shed and feed the chickens or get some coal.

---

1. **the four rivers of France:** that is, four main rivers—the Seine, Loire, Garônne, and Rhône—that divide France geographically.

Arab City, Wassily Kandinsky, 1905.

? **Why is Daru alone in the school?**

Fortunately the delivery truck from Tadjid,[2] the nearest village to the north, had brought his supplies two days before the blizzard. It would return in forty-eight hours.

Besides, he had enough to resist a siege, for the little room was cluttered with bags of wheat that the administration left as a stock to distribute to those of his pupils whose families had suffered from the drought. Actually they had all been victims because they were all poor. Everyday Daru would distribute a ration to the children. They had missed it, he knew, during these bad days. Possibly one of the fathers or big brothers would come this afternoon and he could supply them with grain. It was just a matter of carrying them over to the next harvest. Now shiploads of wheat were arriving from France and the worst was over. But it would be hard to forget that poverty, that army of ragged ghosts wandering in the sunlight, the plateaus burned to a cinder month after month, the earth shriveled up little by little, literally scorched, every stone bursting into dust under one's foot. The sheep had died then by thousands and even a few men, here and there, sometimes without anyone's knowing.

In contrast with such poverty, he who lived almost like a monk in his remote schoolhouse, nonetheless satisfied with the little he had and with the rough life, had felt like a lord with his white-washed walls, his narrow couch, his unpainted shelves, his

---

2. **Tadjid** (tä·jēd′)

well, and his weekly provision of water and food. And suddenly this snow, without warning, without the foretaste of rain. This is the way the region was, cruel to live in, even without men—who didn't help matters either. But Daru had been born here. Everywhere else, he felt exiled.

He stepped out onto the terrace in front of the schoolhouse. The two men were now halfway up the slope. He recognized the horseman as Balducci,[3] the old gendarme[4] he had known for a long time. Balducci was holding on the end of a rope an Arab who was walking behind him with hands bound and head lowered. The gendarme waved a greeting to which Daru did not reply, lost as he was in contemplation of the Arab dressed in a faded blue djellaba,[5] his feet in sandals but covered with socks of heavy raw wool, his head surmounted by a narrow, short *chèche.*[6] They were approaching. Balducci was holding back his horse in order not to hurt the Arab, and the group was advancing slowly.

Within earshot, Balducci shouted: "One hour to do the three kilometers from El Ameur!"[7] Daru did not answer. Short and square in his thick sweater, he watched them climb. Not once had the Arab raised his head. "Hello," said Daru when they got up onto the terrace. "Come in and warm up." Balducci painfully got down from his horse without letting go the rope. From under his bristling mustache he smiled at the schoolmaster. His little dark eyes, deep set under a tanned forehead, and his mouth surrounded with wrinkles made him look attentive and studious. Daru took the bridle, led the horse to the shed, and came back to the two men, who were now waiting for him in the school. He led them into his room. "I am going to heat up the classroom," he said. "We'll be more comfortable there." When he entered the room again, Balducci was on the couch. He had undone the rope tying him to the Arab, who had squatted near the stove. His hands still bound, the *chèche* pushed back on his head, he was looking toward the window. At first Daru noticed only his huge lips, fat, smooth, almost Negroid; yet his nose was straight, his eyes were dark and full of fever. The *chèche* revealed an obstinate forehead and, under the weathered skin now rather discolored by the cold, the whole face had a restless and rebellious look that struck Daru when the Arab, turning his face toward him, looked him straight in the eyes. "Go into the other room," said the schoolmaster, "and I'll make you some mint tea." "Thanks," Balducci said. "What a chore! How I long for retirement." And addressing his prisoner in Arabic: "Come on, you." The Arab got up and, slowly, holding his bound wrists in front of him, went into the classroom.

With the tea, Daru brought a chair. But Balducci was already enthroned on the nearest pupil's desk and the Arab had squatted against the teacher's platform facing the stove, which stood between the desk and the window. When he held out the glass of tea to the prisoner, Daru hesitated at the sight of his bound hands. "He might perhaps be untied." "Sure," said Balducci. "That was for the trip." He started to get to his feet. But Daru, setting the glass on the floor, had knelt beside the Arab. Without saying anything, the Arab watched him with his feverish eyes. Once his hands were free, he

3. **Balducci** (bäl·dōō′chē)
4. **gendarme** (zhän·därm′): French police officer.
5. **djellaba** (jə·lä′bə): long robe worn by males in North Africa.
6. ***chèche*** (shā′shə): tall round cap worn by males in North Africa.
7. **El Ameur** (el äm·yōōr′)

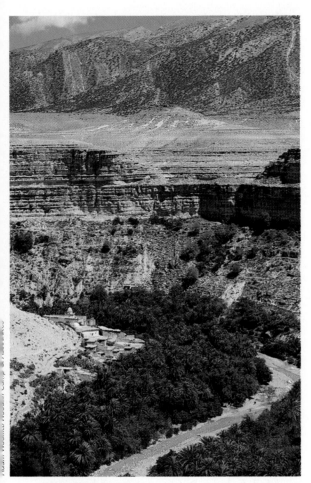

Algerian landscape.

rubbed his swollen wrists against each other, took the glass of tea, and sucked up the burning liquid in swift little sips.

"Good," said Daru. "And where are you headed?"

Balducci withdrew his mustache from the tea. "Here, son."

"Odd pupils! And you're spending the night?"

"No. I'm going back to El Ameur. And you will deliver this fellow to Tinguit.[8] He is expected at police headquarters."

Balducci was looking at Daru with a friendly little smile.

"What's this story?" asked the schoolmaster. "Are you pulling my leg?"

"No, son. Those are the orders."

"The orders? I'm not . . ." Daru hesitated, not wanting to hurt the old Corsican.[9] "I mean, that's not my job."

"What! What's the meaning of that? In wartime people do all kinds of jobs."

"Then I'll wait for the declaration of war." Balducci nodded.

"O.K. But the orders exist and they concern you, too. Things are brewing, it appears. There is talk of a forthcoming revolt. We are mobilized, in a way."

Daru still had his obstinate look.

"Listen, son," Balducci said. "I like you and you must understand. There's only a dozen of us at El Ameur to patrol throughout the whole territory of a small department[10] and I must get back in a hurry. I was told to hand this guy over to you and return without delay. He couldn't be kept there. His village was beginning to stir; they wanted to take him back. You must take him to Tinguit tomorrow before the day is over. Twenty kilometers shouldn't faze a husky fellow like you. After that, all will be over. You'll come back to your pupils and your comfortable life."

Behind the wall the horse could be heard snorting and pawing the earth. Daru was looking out the window. Decidedly, the weather was clearing and the light was increasing over the snowy plateau. When all the snow was melted, the sun would take over again and once more would burn the

8. **Tinguit** (ting'wēt)

9. **Corsican** (kôr'si·kən): native of the Mediterranean island of Corsica, governed by France but populated by many people of Italian descent.

10. **department:** here, administrative district.

fields of stone. For days, still, the unchanging sky would shed its dry light on the solitary expanse where nothing had any connection with man.

"After all," he said, turning around toward Balducci, "what did he do?" And, before the gendarme had opened his mouth, he asked: "Does he speak French?"

"No, not a word. We had been looking for him for a month, but they were hiding him. He killed his cousin."

"Is he against us?"

"I don't think so. But you can never be sure."

"Why did he kill?"

"A family squabble, I think. One owed the other grain, it seems. It's not at all clear. In short, he killed his cousin with a billhook.[11] You know, like a sheep, *kreezk!*"

Balducci made the gesture of drawing a blade across his throat and the Arab, his attention attracted, watched him with a sort of anxiety. Daru felt a sudden wrath against the man, against all men with their rotten spite, their tireless hates, their blood lust.

But the kettle was singing on the stove. He served Balducci more tea, hesitated, then served the Arab again, who, a second time, drank avidly. His raised arms made the djellaba fall open and the schoolmaster saw his thin, muscular chest.

"Thanks, kid," Balducci said. "And now, I'm off."

He got up and went toward the Arab, taking a small rope from his pocket.

"What are you doing?" Daru asked dryly.

Balducci, disconcerted, showed him the rope.

"Don't bother."

The old gendarme hesitated. "It's up to you. Of course, you are armed?"

"I have my shotgun."

"Where?"

"In the trunk."

"You ought to have it near your bed."

"Why? I have nothing to fear."

"You're crazy, son. If there's an uprising, no one is safe, we're all in the same boat."

"I'll defend myself. I'll have time to see them coming."

Balducci began to laugh, then suddenly the mustache covered the white teeth.

"You'll have time? O.K. That's just what I was saying. You have always been a little cracked. That's why I like you, my son was like that."

At the same time he took out his revolver and put it on the desk.

"Keep it; I don't need two weapons from here to El Ameur."

The revolver shone against the black paint of the table. When the gendarme turned toward him, the schoolmaster caught the smell of leather and horseflesh.

"Listen, Balducci," Daru said suddenly, "every bit of this disgusts me, and first of all your fellow here. But I won't hand him over. Fight, yes, if I have to. But not that."

The old gendarme stood in front of him and looked at him severely.

"You're being a fool," he said slowly. "I don't like it either. You don't get used to putting a rope on a man even after years of it, and you're even ashamed—yes, ashamed. But you can't let them have their way."

"I won't hand him over," Daru said again.

"It's an order, son, and I repeat it."

"That's right. Repeat to them what I've said to you: I won't hand him over."

Balducci made a visible effort to reflect. He looked at the Arab and at Daru. At last he decided.

---

11. **billhook:** sharp hand tool usually used for cutting or trimming trees and bushes.

"No, I won't tell them anything. If you want to drop us, go ahead; I'll not denounce you. I have an order to deliver the prisoner and I'm doing so. And now you'll just sign this paper for me."

"There's no need. I'll not deny that you left him with me."

"Don't be mean with me. I know you'll tell the truth. You're from hereabouts and you are a man. But you must sign, that's the rule."

Daru opened his drawer, took out a little square bottle of purple ink, the red wooden penholder with the "sergeant-major" pen[12] he used for making models of penmanship, and signed. The gendarme carefully folded the paper and put it into his wallet. Then he moved toward the door.

"I'll see you off," Daru said.

"No," said Balducci. "There's no use being polite. You insulted me."

He looked at the Arab, motionless in the same spot, sniffed peevishly, and turned away toward the door. "Goodbye, son," he

---

12. **"sergeant-major" pen:** type of fountain pen.

The village of In Salah, Algeria.

George Rodger/Magnum Photos, Inc.

said. The door shut behind him. Balducci appeared suddenly outside the window and then disappeared. His footsteps were muffled by the snow. The horse stirred on the other side of the wall and several chickens fluttered in fright. A moment later Balducci reappeared outside the window leading the horse by the bridle. He walked toward the little rise without turning around and disappeared from sight with the horse following him. A big stone could be heard bouncing down. Daru walked back toward the prisoner, who, without stirring, never took his eyes off him. "Wait," the schoolmaster said in Arabic and went toward the bedroom. As he was going through the door, he had a second thought, went to the desk, took the revolver, and stuck it in his pocket. Then, without looking back, he went into his room.

For some time he lay on his couch watching the sky gradually close over, listening to the silence. It was this silence that had seemed painful to him during the first days here, after the war. He had requested a post in the little town at the base of the foothills separating the upper plateaus from the desert. There, rocky walls, green and black to the north, pink and lavender to the south, marked the frontier of eternal summer. He had been named to a post farther north, on the plateau itself. In the beginning, the solitude and the silence had been hard for him on these wastelands peopled only by stones. Occasionally, furrows suggested cultivation, but they had been dug to uncover a certain kind of stone good for building. The only plowing here was to harvest rocks. Elsewhere a thin layer of soil accumulated in the hollows would be scraped out to enrich paltry village gardens. This is the way it was: bare rock covered three quarters of the region. Towns sprang up, flourished, then dis-

appeared; men came by, loved one another or fought bitterly, then died. No one in this desert, neither he nor his guest, mattered. And yet, outside this desert neither of them, Daru knew, could have really lived.

When he got up, no noise came from the classroom. He was amazed at the unmixed joy he derived from the mere thought that the Arab might have fled and that he would be alone with no decision to make. But the prisoner was there. He had merely stretched out between the stove and the desk. With eyes open, he was staring at the ceiling. In that position, his thick lips were particularly noticeable, giving him a pouting look. "Come," said Daru. The Arab got up and followed him. In the bedroom, the schoolmaster pointed to a chair near the table under the window. The Arab sat down without taking his eyes off Daru.

"Are you hungry?"

"Yes," the prisoner said.

Daru set the table for two. He took flour and oil, shaped a cake in a frying pan, and lighted the little stove that functioned on bottled gas. While the cake was cooking, he went out to the shed to get cheese, eggs, dates, and condensed milk. When the cake was done he set it on the window sill to cool, heated some condensed milk diluted with water, and beat up the eggs into an omelette. In one of his motions he knocked against the revolver stuck in his right pocket. He set the bowl down, went into the classroom, and put the revolver in his desk drawer. When he came back to the room, night was falling. He put on the light and served the Arab. "Eat," he said. The Arab took a piece of the cake, lifted it eagerly to his mouth, and stopped short.

"And you?" he asked.

"After you. I'll eat, too."

The thick lips opened slightly. The Arab

hesitated, then bit into the cake determinedly.

The meal over, the Arab looked at the schoolmaster. "Are you the judge?"

"No, I'm simply keeping you until tomorrow."

"Why do you eat with me?"

"I'm hungry."

The Arab fell silent. Daru got up and went out. He brought back a folding bed from the shed, set it up between the table and the stove, perpendicular to his own bed. From a large suitcase which, upright in a corner, served as a shelf for papers, he took two blankets and arranged them on the camp bed. Then he stopped, felt useless, and sat down on his bed. There was nothing more to do or to get ready. He had to look at this man. He looked at him, therefore, trying to imagine his face bursting with rage. He couldn't do so. He could see nothing but the dark yet shining eyes and the animal mouth.

"Why did you kill him?" he asked in a voice whose hostile tone surprised him.

The Arab looked away.

"He ran away. I ran after him."

He raised his eyes to Daru again and they were full of a sort of woeful interrogation. "Now what will they do to me?"

"Are you afraid?"

He stiffened, turning his eyes away.

"Are you sorry?"

The Arab stared at him openmouthed. Obviously he did not understand. Daru's annoyance was growing. At the same time he felt awkward and self-conscious with his big body wedged between the two beds.

"Lie down there," he said impatiently. "That's your bed."

The Arab didn't move. He called to Daru: "Tell me!"

The schoolmaster looked at him.

"Is the gendarme coming back tomorrow?"

"I don't know."

"Are you coming with us?"

"I don't know. Why?"

The prisoner got up and stretched out on top of the blankets, his feet toward the window. The light from the electric bulb shone straight into his eyes and he closed them at once.

"Why?" Daru repeated, standing beside the bed.

The Arab opened his eyes under the blinding light and looked at him, trying not to blink.

"Come with us," he said.

In the middle of the night, Daru was still not asleep. He had gone to bed after undressing completely; he generally slept naked. But when he suddenly realized that he had nothing on, he hesitated. He felt vulnerable and the temptation came to him to put his clothes back on. Then he shrugged his shoulders; after all, he wasn't a child and, if need be, he could break his adversary in two. From his bed he could observe him, lying on his back, still motionless with his eyes closed under the harsh light. When Daru turned out the light, the darkness seemed to coagulate all of a sudden. Little by little, the night came back to life in the window where the starless sky was stirring gently. The schoolmaster soon made out the body lying at his feet. The Arab still did not move, but his eyes seemed open. A faint wind was prowling around the schoolhouse. Perhaps it would drive away the clouds and the sun would reappear.

During the night the wind increased. The hens fluttered a little and then were silent. The Arab turned over on his side with his back to Daru, who thought he heard him moan. Then he listened for his guest's breathing become heavier and more regular.

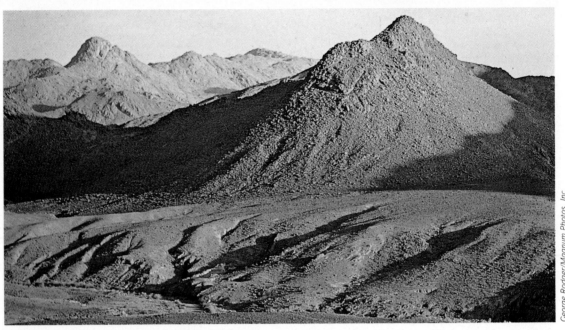

The Hoggar Mountains near Tamanrasset, Algeria.

? *Does the Arab prisoner make Daru feel uncomfortable? Why?*

He listened to that breath so close to him and mused without being able to go to sleep. In this room where he had been sleeping alone for a year, this presence bothered him. But it bothered him also by imposing on him a sort of brotherhood he knew well but refused to accept in the present circumstances. Men who share the same rooms, soldiers or prisoners, develop a strange alliance as if, having cast off their armor with their clothing, they fraternized every evening, over and above their differences, in the ancient community of dream and fatigue. But Daru shook himself; he didn't like such musings, and it was essential to sleep.

A little later, however, when the Arab stirred slightly, the schoolmaster was still not asleep. When the prisoner made a second move, he stiffened, on the alert. The Arab was lifting himself slowly on his arms with almost the motion of a sleepwalker. Seated upright in bed, he waited motionless without turning his head toward Daru, as if he were listening attentively. Daru did not stir; it had just occurred to him that the revolver was still in the drawer of his desk. It was better to act at once. Yet he continued to observe the prisoner, who, with the same slithery motion, put his feet on the ground, waited again, then began to stand up slowly. Daru was about to call out to him when the Arab began to walk, in a quite natural but extraordinarily silent way. He was heading toward the door at the end of the room that opened into the shed. He lifted the latch with precaution and went out, pushing the door behind him but without shutting it. Daru had not stirred. "He is running away," he merely thought. "Good riddance!" Yet he listened attentively. The hens were not fluttering; the guest must be on the plateau. A faint sound of water reached him, and he didn't know what it was until the Arab again stood framed in the doorway, closed the door carefully, and came back to bed without a sound. Then Daru turned his back on him and fell asleep. Still later he seemed, from the depths of his sleep, to hear furtive steps around the schoolhouse. "I'm dreaming! I'm dreaming!" he repeated to himself. And he went on sleeping.

When he awoke the sky was clear; the loose window let in a cold, pure air. The Arab was asleep, hunched up under the blankets now, his mouth open, utterly relaxed. But when Daru shook him, he started dreadfully, staring at Daru with wild eyes as if he had never seen him and such a frightened expression that the schoolmaster stepped back. "Don't be afraid. It's me. You must eat." The Arab nodded his head and said yes. Calm had returned to his face, but his expression was vacant and listless.

The coffee was ready. They drank it seated together on the folding bed as they munched their pieces of the cake. Then Daru led the Arab under the shed and showed him the faucet where he washed. He went back into the room, folded the blankets and the bed, made his own bed and put the room in order. Then he went through the classroom and out onto the terrace. The sun was already rising in the blue sky; a soft, bright light was bathing the deserted plateau. On the ridge the snow was melting in spots. The stones were about to reappear. Crouched on the edge of the plateau, the schoolmaster looked at the deserted expanse. He thought of Balducci. He had hurt him, for he had sent him off in a way as if he didn't want to be associated with him. He could still hear the gendarme's farewell and, without knowing why, he felt strangely empty and vulnerable. At that moment, from the other side of the schoolhouse, the prisoner coughed. Daru listened to him almost despite himself and then, furious, threw a pebble that whistled through the air before sinking into the snow. That man's stupid crime revolted him, but to hand him over was contrary to honor. Merely thinking

of it made him smart with humiliation. And he cursed at one and the same time his own people who had sent him this Arab and the Arab, too, who had dared to kill and not managed to get away. Daru got up, walked in a circle on the terrace, waited motionless, and then went back into the schoolhouse.

The Arab, leaning over the cement floor of the shed, was washing his teeth with two fingers. Daru looked at him and said: "Come." He went back into the room ahead of the prisoner. He slipped a hunting jacket on over his sweater and put on walking shoes. Standing, he waited until the Arab had put on his *chèche* and sandals. They went into the classroom and the schoolmaster pointed to the exit, saying: "Go ahead." The fellow didn't budge. "I'm coming," said Daru. The Arab went out. Daru went back into the room and made a package of pieces of rusk,[13] dates, and sugar. In the classroom, before going out, he hesitated a second in front of his desk, then crossed the threshold and locked the door. "That's the way," he said. He started toward the east, followed by the prisoner. But, a short distance from the schoolhouse, he thought he heard a slight sound behind them. He retraced his steps and examined the surroundings of the house; there was no one there. The Arab watched him without seeming to understand, "Come on," said Daru.

They walked for an hour and rested beside a sharp peak of limestone. The snow was melting faster and faster and the sun was drinking up the puddles at once, rapidly cleaning the plateau, which gradually dried and vibrated like the air itself. When they resumed walking, the ground rang under their feet. From time to time a bird rent the

---

13. **rusk:** dried bread.

space in front of them with a joyful cry. Daru breathed in deeply the fresh morning light. He felt a sort of rapture before the vast familiar expanse, now almost entirely yellow under its dome of blue sky. They walked an hour more, descending toward the south. They reached a level height made up of crumbly rocks. From there on the plateau sloped down, eastward, toward a low plain where there were a few spindly trees and, to the south, toward outcroppings of rock that gave the landscape a chaotic look.

Daru surveyed the two directions. There was nothing but the sky on the horizon. Not a man could be seen. He turned toward the Arab, who was looking at him blankly. Daru held out the package to him. "Take it," he said. "There are dates, bread, and sugar. You can hold out for two days. Here are a thousand francs,[14] too." The Arab took the package and the money but kept his full hands at chest level as if he didn't know what to do with what was being given him. "Now look," the schoolmaster said as he pointed in the direction of the east, "there's the way to Tinguit. You have a two-hour walk. At Tinguit you'll find the administration and the police. They are expecting you." The Arab looked toward the east, still holding the package and the money against his chest. Daru took his elbow and turned him rather roughly toward the south. At the foot of the height on which they stood could be seen a faint path. "That's the trail across the plateau. In a day's walk from here you'll find pasturelands and the first nomads. They'll take you in and shelter you according to their law." The Arab had now turned toward Daru

and a sort of panic was visible in his expression. "Listen," he said. Daru shook his head: "No, be quiet. Now I'm leaving you." He turned his back on him, took two long steps in the direction of the school, looked hesitantly at the motionless Arab, and started off again. For a few minutes he heard nothing but his own step resounding on the cold ground and did not turn his head. A moment later, however, he turned around. The Arab was still there on the edge of the hill, his arms hanging now, and he was looking at the schoolmaster. Daru felt something rise in his throat. But he swore with impatience, waved vaguely, and started off again. He had already gone some distance when he again stopped and looked. There was no longer anyone on the hill.

Daru hesitated. The sun was now rather high in the sky and was beginning to beat down on his head. The schoolmaster retraced his steps, at first somewhat uncertainly, then with decision. When he reached the little hill, he was bathed in sweat. He climbed it as fast as he could and stopped, out of breath, at the top. The rock fields to the south stood out sharply against the blue sky, but on the plain to the east a steamy heat was already rising. And in that slight haze, Daru, with heavy heart, made out the Arab walking slowly on the road to prison.

A little later, standing before the window of the classroom, the schoolmaster was watching the clear light bathing the whole surface of the plateau, but he hardly saw it. Behind him on the blackboard, among the winding French rivers, sprawled the clumsily chalked-up words he had just read: "You handed over our brother. You will pay for this." Daru looked at the sky, the plateau, and, beyond, the invisible lands stretching all the way to the sea. In this vast landscape he had loved so much, he was alone.

---

14. **a thousand francs:** about eighty dollars at the time of the story; the franc, chief monetary unit of France, was used in Algeria while it was a French colony.

First Thoughts

"The Guest" has a quiet but troubling ending. Do you think Daru made the right decision? What do you think happens after the end of the story?

Identifying Facts

1. What crime has the Arab committed? What is Daru's attitude toward that crime and toward the colonial government's action in relation to it?

2. What two routes does Daru point out to the Arab? Which route does the Arab take?

3. On returning to his schoolhouse, what message does Daru find on the black-board?

Interpreting Meanings

1. What does Balducci mean when he says that Daru has "always been a little cracked"? Why does Balducci feel that Daru has insulted him?

2. Why doesn't Daru want to admit the existence of a bond between himself and the Arab? Do Daru's actions acknowledge such a brotherhood? Cite details from the story to support your answer.

3. Why do you think Daru feels "empty and vulnerable"? Do you think his vulnerability is heroic? Do you agree that handing over the Arab is "contrary to honor"? Explain your opinions.

4. Why do you think the Arab chooses the route he does? Based on his choice, in what way is he different from Daru? How do both men's choices reflect Camus's view of **existentialism**?

5. Who wrote the message on Daru's blackboard? What does the appearance of the message suggest about Daru's refusal to take sides in his society's political conflicts?

Applying Meanings

Can freedom be frightening? Do you think it can cause a feeling of isolation? Explain your answers.

Creative Writing Response

Continuing the Story. Imagine what happens between Daru and the Arab after the story ends. Does Daru defend his decision and actions? If so, how? Write the conversation or action that might occur.

Critical Writing Response

Writing About Existentialism. Unlike earlier philosophies that attempted to define objective moral truths and then apply them to the specifics of human existence, **existentialism** suggests that existence comes first and can never be completely defined or understood in objective, scientific terms. Instead, each person gives a *subjective* meaning or purpose to his or her own life through his or her actions and decisions. Existentialism thus places great emphasis on individual freedom. Such freedom, however, can be either liberating or isolating, since each person must journey alone down his or her own moral road.

In a three-paragraph essay, write about how Daru's behavior, attitudes, and experiences reflect Camus's ideas of existentialism. Be sure to address the following three questions. Include a thesis statement at the beginning of your essay.

1. How does Daru's disgust with both the Arab's crime and the colonial government's punishment reflect ideas of existentialism?

2. How does existential thinking help explain Daru's refusal to take the Arab any farther after showing him the two routes?

3. What does the story's outcome suggest about the existentialist's relationship to society?

Italo Calvino
1923–1985, Italy

AP/Wide World Photos

When asked who he considered the greatest Italian writer, Italo Calvino (ē·tal′ō kal·vē′nō) did not choose a poet, playwright, or novelist. Instead he named the Renaissance astronomer, physicist, and philosopher Galileo Galilei. Among Galileo's many accomplishments was the invention of an early telescope. Calvino found Galileo's prose surprisingly poetic and imaginative, especially his descriptions of the moon, which deftly combined objective scientific details with a unique lyrical vision. Calvino's own background in science and in literature led to a similar ability to combine poetic vision and scientific details.

The son of two scientists, Calvino was born in Cuba while his parents were studying tropical plant life there. Soon after Calvino's birth, the family returned to Italy and Calvino's father took a job running a botanical garden in San Remo, on the Italian Riviera. It was here that Calvino fell in love with nature. He intended to study agricultural science at the University of Turin, but World War II interrupted his plans.

Calvino was only nineteen when he joined the Italian Resistance to fight the Germans. After the war Calvino returned to college but decided to study literature rather than science. Upon graduating, he joined the staff of a newly formed publishing house in Turin. He soon published his first book, *The Path to the Nest of Spiders* (1947), a realistic novel based on his experiences as a Resistance fighter. Calvino also began collecting folktales from all over Italy. These were published in *Italian Folktales* (1956).

Calvino's first English anthology, *Adam, One Afternoon* (1957), contains some stories that blend elements of fantasy and realism, and others that are purely realistic. His later works, however, are more fanciful. *Baron in the Trees* (1957) is a story about a boy who moves to the treetops when his family annoys him, and then decides to spend the rest of his life there. The hero of *The Nonexistent Knight* (1962) is an empty suit of armor named Agilulf. The stories are often allegorical, with symbolic meanings that apply to today's world.

THE ENCHANTED GARDEN

Italo Calvino

translated by

ARCHIBALD COLQUHOUN AND PEGGY WRIGHT

Reader's Guide

Background Many of the stories in *Adam, One Afternoon* (1957) are set on the Italian Riviera, the fashionable seaside resort where Calvino spent his youth. Like the French Riviera, the Italian Riviera has over the years attracted many wealthy summer residents who built elegant mansions along the coast. Such mansions—or villas, as they are called in Italy—are usually hidden away behind enclosed private gardens like the one described in the following story.

Writer's Response Think of a place that seemed magical or "enchanted" to you—either during your childhood or more recently. In a few sentences, describe the place and how it made you feel.

Literary Focus **Atmosphere** is the emotional effect, the mood or feeling, created by the **setting** of a work of literature. The **atmosphere** may be mild or harsh, gloomy or cheery, beautiful or ugly. It is usually created through evocative imagery and **descriptive details**. The adjective in the title of this story gives us an idea of the atmosphere that Calvino is trying to create.

THE ENCHANTED GARDEN

 In whose eyes is the garden in this story "enchanted"?

Giovannino and Serenella were strolling along the railroad tracks. Below was a scaly sea of somber, clear blue; above, a sky lightly streaked with white clouds. The railroad tracks were shimmering and burning hot. It was fun going along the tracks, there were so many games to play—he balancing on one rail and holding her hand while she walked along on the other, or else both jumping from one sleeper[1] to the next without ever letting their feet touch the stones in between. Giovannino and Serenella had been out looking for crabs, and now they had decided to explore the raiload tracks as far as the tunnel. He liked playing with Serenella, for she did not behave as all the other

---

1. **sleeper:** tie or crossbar supporting a railroad track.

GARDEN IN MAY, MARIA OAKEY DEWING, 1895.

little girls did, forever getting frightened or bursting into tears at every joke. Whenever Giovannino said, "Let's go there," or "Let's do this," Serenella followed without a word.

Ping! They both gave a start and looked up. A telephone wire had snapped off the top of the pole. It sounded like an iron stork shutting its beak in a hurry. They stood with their noses in the air and watched. What a pity not to have seen it! Now it would never happen again.

"There's a train coming," said Giovannino.

Serenella did not move from the rail. "Where from?" she asked.

Giovannino looked around in a knowledgeable way. He pointed at the black hole of the tunnel, which showed clear one moment, then misty the next, through the invisible heat haze rising from the stony track.

"From there," he said. It was as though they already heard a snort from the darkness of the tunnel, and saw the train suddenly appear, belching out fire and smoke, the wheels mercilessly eating up the rails as it hurtled toward them.

"Where shall we go, Giovannino?"

There were big gray aloes down by the sea, surrounded by dense, impenetrable nettles, while up the hillside ran a rambling hedge with thick leaves but no flowers. There was still no sign of the train; perhaps it was coasting, with the engine cut off, and would jump out at them all of a sudden. But Giovannino had now found an opening in the hedge. "This way," he called.

The fence under the rambling hedge was an old bent rail. At one point it twisted about on the ground like the corner of a sheet of paper. Giovannino had slipped into the hole and already half vanished.

"Give me a hand, Giovannino."

They found themselves in the corner of a garden, on all fours in a flower bed, with their hair full of dry leaves and moss. Everything was quiet; not a leaf was stirring.

"Come on," said Giovannino, and Serenella nodded in reply.

There were big old flesh-colored eucalyptus trees and winding gravel paths. Giovannino and Serenella tiptoed along the paths, taking care not to crunch the gravel. Suppose the owners appeared now?

Everything was so beautiful: sharp bends in the path and high, curling eucalyptus leaves and patches of sky. But there was always the worrying thought that it was not their garden, and that they might be chased away any moment. Yet not a sound could be heard. A flight of chattering sparrows rose from a clump of arbutus[2] at a turn in the path. Then all was silent again. Perhaps it was an abandoned garden?

But the shade of the big trees came to an end, and they found themselves under the open sky facing flower beds filled with neat rows of petunias and convolvulus,[3] and paths and balustrades and rows of box trees.[4] And up at the end of the garden was a large villa with flashing windowpanes and yellow-and-orange curtains.

And it was all quite deserted. The two children crept forward, treading carefully over the gravel: perhaps the windows would suddenly be flung open, and angry ladies and gentlemen appear on the terraces to unleash great dogs down the paths. Now they found a wheelbarrow standing near a ditch. Giovannino picked it up by the handles and began pushing it along: it creaked like a whistle at every turn. Serenella seated herself in it and they moved slowly forward, Giovannino pushing the barrow with her on top, along the flower beds and fountains.

Every now and then Serenella would point to a flower and say in a low voice, "That one," and Giovannino would put the barrow down, pluck it, and give it to her. Soon she had a lovely bouquet.

Eventually the gravel ended and they reached an open space paved in bricks and mortar. In the middle of this space was a big empty rectangle: a swimming pool. They crept up to the edge; it was lined with blue tiles and filled to the brim with clear water. How lovely it would be to swim in!

"Shall we go for a dip?" Giovannino asked Serenella. The idea must have been quite dangerous if he asked her instead of just saying, "In we go!" But the water was so clear and blue, and Serenella was never afraid. She jumped off the barrow and put her bunch of flowers in it. They were already in bathing suits, since they'd been out for crabs before. Giovannino plunged in—not from the diving board, because the splash would have made too much noise, but from the edge of the pool. Down and down he went with his eyes wide open, seeing only the blue from the tiles and his pink hands like goldfish; it was not the same as under the sea, full of shapeless green-black shadows.

---

2. **arbutus** (är·byōōt′əs): flowering shrubs or trailing plants with strawberrylike fruit.
3. **convolvulus** (kən·väl′vyōō·ləs): compact, bushy morning glories.
4. **box trees**: small trees that are often clipped and used as hedges; also called boxwood.

A pink form appeared above him: Serenella! He took her hand and they swam up to the surface, a bit anxiously. No, there was no one watching them at all. But it was not so nice as they'd thought it would be; they always had that uncomfortable feeling that they had no right to any of this, and might be chased out at any moment.

They scrambled out of the water, and there beside the swimming pool they found a Ping-Pong table. Instantly Giovannino picked up the paddle and hit the ball, and Serenella, on the other side, was quick to return his shot. And so they went on playing, though giving only light taps at the ball, in case someone in the villa heard them. Then Giovannino, in trying to parry a shot that had bounced high, sent the ball sailing away through the air and smack against a gong hanging in a pergola.[5] There was a long, somber boom. The two children crouched down behind a clump of ranunculus.[6] At once two menservants in white coats appeared, carrying big trays; when they had put the trays down on a round table under an orange-and-yellow-striped umbrella, off they went.

Giovannino and Serenella crept up to the table. There was tea, milk, and sponge cake. They had only to sit down and help themselves. They poured out two cups of tea and cut two slices of cake. But somehow they did not feel at all at ease, and sat perched on the edge of their chairs, their knees shaking. And they could not really enjoy the tea and cake, for nothing seemed to have any taste. Everything in the garden was like that: lovely but impossible to enjoy properly, with that worrying feeling inside that they were only there through an odd stroke of luck,

and the fear that they'd soon have to give an account of themselves.

Very quietly they tiptoed up to the villa. Between the slits of a Venetian blind they saw a beautiful shady room, with collections of butterflies hanging on the walls. And in the room was a pale little boy. Lucky boy, he must be the owner of this villa and garden. He was stretched out on a chaise longue, turning the pages of a large book filled with figures. He had big white hands and wore pajamas buttoned up to the neck, though it was summer.

As the two children went on peeping through the slits, the pounding of their hearts gradually subsided. Why, the little rich boy seemed to be sitting there and turning the pages and glancing around with more anxiety and worry than their own. Then he got up and tiptoed around, as if he were afraid that at any moment someone would come and turn him out, as if he felt that that book, that chaise longue, and those butterflies framed on the wall, the garden and games and tea trays, the swimming pool and paths, were only granted to him by some enormous mistake, as if he were incapable of enjoying them and felt the bitterness of the mistake as his own fault.

The pale boy was wandering about his shady room furtively, touching with his white fingers the edges of the cases studded with butterflies; then he stopped to listen. The pounding of Giovannino and Serenella's hearts, which had died down, now got harder than ever. Perhaps it was the fear of a spell that hung over this villa and garden and over all these lovely, comfortable things, the residue of some injustice committed long ago.

Clouds darkened the sun. Very quietly Giovannino and Serenella crept away. They went back along the same paths they had

---

5. **pergola** (pᵿr′gə·lə): arbor; trellis.
6. **ranunculus** (rə·nung′kyo͞o·ləs): buttercups.

come, stepping fast but never at a run. And they went through the hedge again on all fours. Between the aloes they found a path leading down to the small, stony beach, with banks of seaweed along the shore. Then they invented a wonderful new game: a seaweed fight. They threw great handfuls of it in each other's faces till late in the afternoon. And Serenella never once cried.

First Thoughts

What might have made the little rich boy pale, afraid, and unhappy?

Identifying Facts

1. Before entering the garden, what are Giovannino and Serenella doing to amuse themselves?
2. What adjective describes ''everything'' in the garden?
3. After they leave the garden, what new game do Giovannino and Serenella invent?

Interpreting Meanings

1. How would you describe the **atmosphere** of the garden? Which descriptive details contribute to this atmosphere?
2. Consider the ''anxiety and worry'' that Giovannino and Serenella feel as they explore the garden and that the boy in pajamas seems to feel later. What may have caused the uneasiness in each case?
3. In what ways is the boy in the villa different from Giovannino and Serenella? What might the contrast suggest about the lives of the rich?
4. What might the garden **symbolize**?

Applying Meanings

Would you say young children are more or less sensitive to their surroundings than adults? Discuss with your classmates.

Creative Writing Response

Creating an Atmosphere. Write a brief descriptive essay in which you recreate the **atmosphere** of a place you found magical or enchanted. You may expand upon the sentences you wrote for the Writer's Response (see page 1259). Use vivid words and **images** to capture the sights, sounds, smells, and textures of the place. Before you write, fill out a chart like the one below to be sure you have enough specific sensory **details**.

Sights	
Sounds	
Smells	
Textures or temperatures	
Tastes	

Critical Writing Response

Writing about Style. In a brief essay, discuss the descriptive style that Calvino employs in this story. Consider his use of vivid **imagery** and precise, scientific **details**, as well as the more mysterious or fantastic details that he uses. As a prewriting activity, list details on a chart like the one below.

Realistic or Precise Details	Mysterious or Fantastic Details

Aleksandr Solzhenitsyn
b. 1918, Russia

Craig Line/Wide World Photos

Aleksandr Solzhenitsyn (sōl′zhə·nēt′sin) became aware of the shortcomings of the Soviet Union after he had fought bravely for three years in World War II. Then, in a letter to a friend, he referred to premier Josef Stalin as "the boss" in criminals' slang. For this "crime" he was arrested and sent to prisons and labor camps for eight years. He was released after Stalin died in 1953 but still had to spend three years in internal exile in central Asia. There he worked as a teacher and wrote about his experiences.

The result of his efforts was *One Day in the Life of Ivan Denisovich* (1962), a novel about a farmer serving ten years at a Soviet labor camp for a political crime he did not commit. Since Nikita Krushchev, the new Soviet premier, had risen to power by attacking Stalin, books like Solzhenitsyn's were encouraged.

Solzhenitsyn's period of acceptance in his homeland, however, was short-lived. After Krushchev was ousted in 1964, the new, more conservative regime became increasingly uncomfortable with Solzhenitsyn's accounts of Stalinist oppression. The government barred publication of his work and confiscated many of his manuscripts. Solzhenitsyn's relationship with the government deteriorated further after a Paris firm published his famous attack on the Soviet penal system, *The Gulag Archipelago* (1974). Solzhenitsyn was charged with treason, stripped of his Soviet citizenship, and exiled from his homeland. Eventually he settled in the United States, where he became the Soviet Union's best-known writer-in-exile.

When Soviet premier Mikhail Gorbachev (mē′khä·ēl′ gôr′bə·chôf′) instituted his new policy of glasnost, or "openness," in the 1980s, Solzhenitsyn's citizenship was restored and his works were gradually published or reissued in his homeland. In 1990, Solzhenitsyn wrote a long essay entitled "How to Revitalize Russia." More remarkable than his ideas was the fact that he was permitted to express them in Soviet government periodicals that only five years before had denounced him as a traitor.

Reader's Guide

FREEDOM TO BREATHE
A JOURNEY ALONG THE OKA

Background

Rulers of the Soviet Union, like those of the Russian empire, have generally allowed their people very few freedoms. Under the czars, critics of the government were executed or exiled to remote parts of the empire, such as arctic Siberia, where they often died. A few years after the Russian Revolution of 1917, the new Communist regime began following similar practices. Soviet oppression reached its height under dictator Josef Stalin during the Great Purge of the mid-1930s, when the secret police shot or imprisoned millions of citizens. Matters improved only after Soviet premier Mikhail Gorbachev began instituting reforms in the late 1980s.

As a result of the Russian people's long history of suffering under tyrannical regimes, Russian writers since the time of Pushkin (see page 1006) have often spoken out against government oppression. Solzhenitsyn entered this long tradition when he began publishing in the early 1960s. Most of his works, including the prose poems you are about to read, deal with the lack of human rights and freedom in his homeland.

Writer's Response

People fight in different ways to bring about social and political change—some use guns or bombs while others use pens or videotape. Do you think the "pen is mightier than the sword" in exposing abuses? Write a paragraph expressing your opinion. Try to provide some examples from recent current events to support your opinion.

Literary Focus

Prose poetry is written in prose form, but uses poetic devices such as **rhythm**, **imagery**, and **figurative language** to express a single strong emotion or idea. Solzhenitsyn's prose poems are brief nonfiction pieces that combine the features of prose and poetry.

FREEDOM TO BREATHE

Aleksandr Solzhenitsyn

translated by

MICHAEL GLENNY

Stop after you read the first two paragraphs of this prose poem. What kind of a place do you think the speaker is describing? After you finish the poem, see if your impression was correct.

A shower fell in the night and now dark clouds drift across the sky, occasionally sprinkling a fine film of rain.

I stand under an apple tree in blossom and I breathe. Not only the apple tree but the grass round it glistens with moisture; words cannot describe the sweet fragrance that pervades the air. I inhale as deeply as I can, and the aroma invades my whole being; I breathe with my eyes open, I breathe with my eyes closed—I cannot say which gives me the greater pleasure.

This, I believe, is the single most precious freedom that prison takes away from us: the freedom to breathe freely, as I now can. No food on earth, no wine, not even a woman's kiss is sweeter to me than this air steeped in the fragrance of flowers, of moisture and freshness.

No matter that this is only a tiny garden, hemmed in by five-story houses like cages in a zoo. I cease to hear the motorcycles backfiring, radios whining, the burble of loudspeakers. As long as there is fresh air to breathe under an apple tree after a shower, we may survive a little longer.

Saint Sophia Church in Kiev, in the former Soviet Union.

A JOURNEY ALONG THE OKA

Aleksandr Solzhenitsyn

translated by
MICHAEL GLENNY

 Solzhenitsyn uses a description of the Russian countryside to reveal how he feels about an aspect of Soviet life. What are his feelings?

Traveling along country roads in central Russia, you begin to understand why the Russian countryside has such a soothing effect.

It is because of its churches. They rise over ridge and hillside, descending towards wide rivers like red and white princesses, towering above the thatch and wooden huts of everyday life with their slender, carved, and fretted belfries. From far away they greet each other; from distant, unseen villages they rise towards the same sky.

Wherever you may wander, over field or pasture, many miles from any homestead, you are never alone: above the wall of trees, above the hayricks, even above the very curve of the earth itself, the dome of a belfry

Aleksandr Solzhenitsyn   **1267**

? **What poetic features do Solzhenitsyn's prose poems exhibit?**

is always beckoning to you, from Borki Lovetskie, Lyubichi, or Gavrilovskoe.[1]

But as soon as you enter a village you realize that the churches which welcomed you from afar are no longer living. Their crosses have long since been bent or broken off; the dome with its peeling paint reveals its rusty ribcage; weeds grow on the roofs and in the cracks of the walls; the cemetery is hardly ever cared for, its crosses knocked over and its graves ransacked; the ikons[2] behind the altar have faded from a decade of rain and are scrawled with obscene graffiti.

In the porch there are barrels of salt and a tractor is swinging round towards them, or a lorry is backing up to the vestry door to collect some sacks. In one church, machine tools are humming away; another stands silent, simply locked up. Others have been turned into clubs where propaganda meetings are held ("We Will Achieve High Yields of Milk!") or films shown: *Poem About the Sea, The Great Adventure.*

People have always been selfish and often evil. But the Angelus[3] used to toll and its echo would float over village, field, and wood. It reminded man that he must abandon his trivial earthly cares and give up one hour of his thoughts to life eternal. The tolling of the eventide bell, which now survives for us only in a popular song, raised man above the level of a beast.

Our ancestors put their best into these stones and these belfries—all their knowledge and all their faith.

Come on, Vitka,[4] buck up and stop feeling sorry for yourself! The film starts at six, and the dance is at eight....

---

1. **Borki Lovetskie, Lyubichi, Gavrilovskoe:** cities in the former Soviet Union.
2. **ikons** (ī′kän′): religious images or figures, usually of Jesus, Mary, or a saint; also spelled *icon*.

3. **Angelus** (an′jə·ləs): the bell rung to announce the time for the Angelus, a prayer said at morning, noon, and evening.
4. **Vitka** (vēt′kä): a familiar form for Viktor; usually the familiar form would be Vitya. The "ka" ending here shows that the speaker is slightly annoyed at the person being addressed.

Fred Euphrat

Were you surprised by the new information about the speaker's location in the last paragraph in "Freedom to Breathe"? Why do you think Solzhenitsyn provided this information in the last paragraph rather than in the first one?

Identifying Facts

1. What does the speaker in "Freedom to Breathe" say words cannot describe?
2. What does the same speaker say is the single most precious freedom that prison takes away?
3. What does the speaker in "A Journey Along the Oka" find soothing about the Russian countryside?
4. What are the churches used for now?

Interpreting Meanings

1. Solzhenitsyn uses **imagery**—language that appeals to the senses—in both of these **prose poems**. Identify images in "Freedom to Breathe" that relate to at least three different senses.
2. What do the details of **setting** in the last paragraph of "Freedom to Breathe" emphasize about the speaker's view of freedom?
3. Why does the speaker in "A Journey Along the Oka" say the churches are no longer "living"?
4. Prose poems often use **figures of speech**. Find an example of **simile** and **personification** in the second paragraph of "A Journey Along the Oka."

5. The churches in "A Journey Along the Oka" can be taken on both a literal and a symbolic level. What would you say the churches **symbolize**, or represent?

Applying Meanings

Those who have never been in prison probably take the "freedom to breathe" for granted. What are some other freedoms we often take for granted?

Do you think that if we take certain freedoms for granted (the freedom to worship, for example) we risk losing them? Give examples to support your opinion.

Creative Writing Response

Writing a Prose Poem Using Imagery. Think of an experience that is still vivid in your memory. Write a **prose poem** in which you use **images** to communicate what you saw, heard, smelled, tasted, or touched. Try to select images that create the emotions and sensations you associate with the experience: joy, sadness, excitement, peace, or some other feeling.

Critical Writing Response

Analyzing the Poem's Theme.   Theme is the poem's central idea about life. Write a paragraph about the theme of either "Freedom to Breathe" or "A Journey Along the Oka." Your topic sentence should state what the theme is. Then discuss how Solzhenitsyn gets his theme across and provide examples from the poem. End your paragraph with a sentence telling how you feel about poetry with social, political, or religious messages.

PRIMARY SOURCES

Solzhenitsyn Accepts the Nobel Prize

In 1970, less than four years before he was exiled from the Soviet Union, Solzhenitsyn was awarded the Nobel Prize for literature. He did not travel to Sweden to collect the prize because he feared that he would not be allowed to return to his homeland. Instead, he wrote an acceptance, a portion of which appears below. As you read the passage, consider what Solzhenitsyn believes the role of literature to be. What dangers of censorship does he point out?

The only substitute for what we ourselves have not experienced is art and literature. They have the marvelous capacity of transmitting from one nation to another—despite differences in language, customs, and social structure—practical experience, the harsh national experience of many decades never tasted by the other nation. Sometimes this may save a whole nation from what is a dangerous or mistaken or plainly disastrous path, thus lessening the twists and turns of human history.

Today, from this Nobel lecture platform, I should like to emphasize this great, beneficent attribute of art.

Literature transmits condensed and irrefutable human experience in still another priceless way: from generation to generation. It thus becomes the living memory of a nation. What has faded into history it thus keeps warm and preserves in a form that defies distortion and falsehood. Thus literature, together with language, preserves and protects a nation's soul. . . .

But woe to the nation whose literature is cut off by the interposition of force. That is not simply a violation of "freedom of the press"; it is stopping up the nation's heart, carving out the nation's memory. The nation loses its memory; it loses its spiritual unity—and, despite their supposedly common language, fellow countrymen suddenly cease understanding each other. Speechless generations are born and die, having recounted nothing of themselves either to their own times or to their descendants. That such masters as Akhmatova [see page 1223] and [Soviet author Yevgeny] Zamyatin were buried behind four walls for their whole lives and condemned even to the grave to create in silence, without hearing one reverberation of what they wrote, is not only their own personal misfortune but a tragedy for the whole nation—and, too, a real threat to all nationalities.

In certain cases, it is a danger for all mankind as well: when HISTORY as a whole ceases to be understood because of that silence.

Stanislaw Lem
b. 1921, Poland

Michael Lange/Visum Fotoreportagen

As a boy, Stanislaw Lem (stan'is·läf' lem') loved to tinker with broken things—alarm clocks, spark plugs, and anything else that needed repairing. He planned to put his tinkering talents to good use by becoming a doctor or a scientist, but Germany's invasion of Poland at the beginning of World War II interrupted his education. It did not, however, interrupt his tinkering. During the Nazi occupation, Lem sabotaged German vehicles while pretending to repair them.

The war years were a harrowing time for Lem and his family, whose Jewish heritage put them in particular jeopardy. They survived by obtaining false papers certifying them to be Christian. Yet Lem often put himself at risk by smuggling food to Jewish friends and carrying messages for Resistance fighters. His frequent close calls led him to view life as a chancy business. He was keenly aware that the difference between living another day and dying suddenly and unexpectedly could depend upon something as simple and arbitrary as arriving at a destination on time or twenty minutes late.

When Lem resumed his studies after the war, he was appalled by the scientific doctrines he was told to accept without question. Because he refused to bow to the official Communist party views on science, Lem failed to graduate from medical school. Not long afterward, he abandoned science for science fiction.

After his first science-fiction novel *The Astronauts* (1951) became a bestseller in Eastern Europe, he wrote a number of books about distant galaxies and strange life forms. Among the best of these is *Solaris* (1961), about a planet whose only sentient, or conscious, being is a kaleidoscopic sea. Both *Solaris* and *The Invincible* (1964), about a gigantic spaceship defeated by an army of insectlike robots, use satire directed against human attempts to control the universe.

While Lem's science fiction has been popular in Europe for decades, English translations appeared in the United States only in the 1970s, spurred by the 1972 release of the Russian film version of *Solaris.* American critics were quick to add to the praise that Lem's writing had won elsewhere.

Reader's Guide

TRURL'S MACHINE

Background

Most Polish writers who survived World War II quickly grew disillusioned with the Communist government. Some, like Nobel Prize-winning poet Czeslaw Milosz (ches'läf mē'wōsh), immigrated to the West. Others remained and coped as best they could. For Stanislaw Lem, writing science fiction turned out to be a way to write without being censored. Because science fiction is generally set on other planets or on earth in the distant future, Communist government censors rarely scrutinized it closely.

Most of Lem's fiction satirizes Communist government practices, but it does so in a symbolic way, carefully veiled by action-adventure and humor. In his novel *The Invincible,* for example, the enormous, seemingly all-powerful spaceship that falls prey to tiny robots probably represents the huge and inefficient Communist bureaucracy. Similarly, the stories in Lem's collection *The Cyberiad* (1965) contain carefully disguised attacks on Communist government practices. These stories, including the one reprinted here, feature the rival robot constructors Trurl and Klapaucius.

Writer's Response

Think of something in your present life that you find difficult or frustrating (traffic jams, waking up for school, doing homework). Write a paragraph or two about it in a satirical science-fiction style by exaggerating the characteristics of whatever it is that you dislike, and placing it on a distant planet or in the distant future.

Literary Focus

Science fiction is a form of fantasy writing in which scientific facts, assumptions, or hypotheses form the basis of adventures in the future, on other planets, in other dimensions of space or time, or under new variants of scientific laws. Many popular television shows and movies, such as *Star Trek* and *Star Wars,* are part of the science-fiction genre.

Although science fiction is usually set in the future, it often comments on the present. These comments sometimes come in the form of **satire**, a kind of writing that ridicules human weakness, vice, or folly.

TRURL'S MACHINE
Stanislaw Lem
translated by
MICHAEL KANDEL

As you read "Trurl's Machine," identify details that might be satirizing life in a totalitarian state. Also identify details that seem to be poking fun at human nature in general.

Once upon a time Trurl the constructor built an eight-story thinking machine. When it was finished, he gave it a coat of white paint, trimmed the edges in lavender, stepped back, squinted, then added a little curlicue on the front and, where one might imagine the forehead to be, a few pale orange polka dots. Extremely pleased with himself, he whistled an air and, as is always done on such occasions, asked it the ritual question of how much is two plus two.

The machine stirred. Its tubes began to glow, its coils warmed up, current coursed through all its circuits like a waterfall, transformers hummed and throbbed, there was a clanging, and a chugging, and such an ungodly racket that Trurl began to think of adding a special mentation muffler. Meanwhile the machine labored on, as if it had been given the most difficult problem in the Universe to solve; the ground shook, the sand slid underfoot from the vibration, valves popped like champagne corks, the relays nearly gave way under the strain. At last, when Trurl had grown extremely impatient, the machine ground to a halt and said in a voice like thunder: SEVEN!

"Nonsense, my dear," said Trurl. "The answer's four. Now be a good machine and adjust yourself! What's two and two?" "SEVEN!" snapped the machine. Trurl sighed and put his coveralls back on, rolled up his sleeves, opened the bottom trapdoor and crawled in. For the longest time he hammered away inside, tightened, soldered, ran clattering up and down the metal stairs, now on the sixth floor, now on the eighth, then pounded back down to the bottom and threw a switch, but something sizzled in the middle, and the spark plugs grew blue whiskers. After two hours of this he came out, covered with soot but satisfied, put all his tools away, took off his coveralls, wiped his face and hands. As he was leaving, he turned and asked, just so there would be no doubt about it:

"And now what's two and two?"

"SEVEN!" replied the machine.

Trurl uttered a terrible oath, but there was no help for it—again he had to poke around inside the machine, disconnecting, correcting, checking, resetting, and when he learned for the third time that two and two was seven, he collapsed in despair at the foot of the machine, and sat there until Klapaucius found him. Klapaucius inquired what was wrong, for Trurl looked as if he had just returned from a funeral. Trurl explained the problem. Klapaucius crawled into the machine himself a couple of times, tried to fix this and that, then asked it for the sum of one plus two, which turned out to be six. One plus one, according to the machine, equaled zero. Klapaucius scratched his head, cleared his throat, and said:

"My friend, you'll just have to face it. That isn't the machine you wished to make. However, there's a good side to everything, including this."

"What good side?" muttered Trurl, and kicked the base on which he was sitting.

"Stop that," said the machine.

"H'm, it's sensitive too. But where was I? Oh yes ... there's no question but that we have here a stupid machine, and not merely stupid in the usual, normal way, oh no! This is, as far as I can determine—and you know I am something of an expert—this is the stupidest thinking machine in the entire world, and that's nothing to sneeze at! To construct deliberately such a machine would be far from easy; in fact, I would say that no one could manage it. For the thing is not only stupid, but stubborn as a mule, that is, it has a personality common to idiots, for idiots are uncommonly stubborn."

"What earthly use do I have for such a machine?!" said Trurl, and kicked it again.

"I'm warning you, you better stop!" said the machine.

"A warning, if you please," observed Klapaucius dryly. "Not only is it sensitive, dense, and stubborn, but quick to take offense, and believe me, with such an abundance of qualities there are all sorts of things you might do!"

"What, for example?" asked Trurl.

"Well, it's hard to say offhand. You might put it on exhibit and charge admission; people would flock to see the stupidest thinking machine that ever was—what does it have,

eight stories? Really, could anyone imagine a bigger dunce? And the exhibition would not only cover your costs, but—"

"Enough, I'm not holding any exhibition!" Trurl said, stood up, and, unable to restrain himself, kicked the machine once more.

"This is your third warning," said the machine.

"What?" cried Trurl, infuriated by its imperious manner. "You ... you ..." And he kicked it several times, shouting: "You're only good for kicking, you know that?"

"You have insulted me for the fourth, fifth, sixth, and eighth times," said the machine. "Therefore, I refuse to answer all further questions of a mathematical nature."

"It refuses! Do you hear that?" fumed Trurl, thoroughly exasperated. "After six comes eight—did you notice, Klapaucius?—not seven, but eight! And *that's* the kind of mathematics Her Highness refuses to perform! Take that! And that! And that! Or perhaps you'd like some more?"

The machine shuddered, shook, and without another word started to lift itself from its foundations. They were very deep, and the girders began to bend, but at last it scrambled out, leaving behind broken concrete blocks with steel spokes protruding— and it bore down on Trurl and Klapaucius like a moving fortress. Trurl was so dumbfounded that he didn't even try to hide from the machine, which to all appearances intended to crush him to a pulp. But Klapaucius grabbed his arm and yanked him away, and the two of them took to their heels. When finally they looked back, they saw the machine swaying like a high tower, advancing slowly, at every step sinking to its second floor, but stubbornly, doggedly pulling itself out of the sand and heading straight for them.

"Whoever heard of such a thing?" Trurl

gasped in amazement. "Why, this is mutiny! What do we do now?"

"Wait and watch," replied the prudent Klapaucius. "We may learn something."

But there was nothing to be learned just then. The machine had reached firmer ground and was picking up speed. Inside, it whistled, hissed, and sputtered.

"Any minute now the signal box will knock loose," said Trurl under his breath. "That'll jam the program and stop it...."

"No," said Klapaucius, "this is a special case. The thing is so stupid, that even if the whole transmission goes, it won't matter. But—look out!!"

The machine was gathering momentum, clearly bent on running them down, so they fled just as fast as they could, the fearful rhythm of crunching steps in their ears. They ran and ran—what else could they do? They tried to make it back to their native district, but the machine outflanked them, cut them off, forced them deeper and deeper into a wild, uninhabited region. Mountains, dismal and craggy, slowly rose out of the mist. Trurl, panting heavily, shouted to Klapaucius:

"Listen! Let's turn into some narrow canyon ... where it won't be able to follow us ... the cursed thing ... what do you say?"

"No ... better go straight," wheezed Klapaucius. "There's a town up ahead ... can't remember the name ... anyway, we can find—oof!—find shelter there...."

So they ran straight and soon saw houses before them. The streets were practically deserted at this time of day, and the constructors had gone a good distance without meeting a living soul, when suddenly an awful crash, like an avalanche at the edge of the town, indicated that the machine was coming after them.

Trurl looked back and groaned.

"Good heavens! It's tearing down the houses, Klapaucius!!" For the machine, in stubborn pursuit, was plowing through the walls of the buildings like a mountain of steel, and in its wake lay piles of rubble and white clouds of plaster dust. There were dreadful screams, confusion in the streets, and Trurl and Klapaucius, their hearts in their mouths, ran on till they came to a large town hall, darted inside, and raced down endless stairs to a deep cellar.

"It won't get us in here, even if it brings the whole building down on our heads!" panted Klapaucius. "But really, the devil himself had me pay you a visit today.... I was curious to see how your work was going—well, I certainly found out...."

"Quiet," interrupted Trurl. "Someone's coming...."

And indeed, the cellar door opened up and the mayor entered, accompanied by several aldermen. Trurl was too embarrassed to explain how this strange and calamitous situation had come about; Klapaucius had to do it. The mayor listened in silence. Suddenly the walls trembled, the ground heaved, and the sound of cracking stone reached them in the cellar.

"It's here?!" cried Trurl.

"Yes," said the mayor. "And it demands that we give you up, otherwise it says it will level the entire town...."

Just then they heard, far overhead, words that honked as if from a muffled horn:

"Trurl's here ... I smell Trurl...."

"But surely you won't give us up?" asked in a quavering voice the object of the machine's obstinate fury.

"The one of you who calls himself Trurl must leave. The other may remain, since surrendering him does not constitute part of the conditions...."

"Have mercy!"

"We are helpless," said the mayor. "And were you to stay here, Trurl, you would have to answer for all the damage done to this town and its inhabitants, since it was because of you that the machine destroyed sixteen homes and buried beneath their ruins many of our finest citizens. Only the fact that you yourself stand in imminent peril permits me to let you leave unpunished. Go then, and nevermore return."

Trurl looked at the aldermen and, seeing his sentence written on their stern faces, slowly turned and made for the door.

"Wait! I'll go with you!" cried Klapaucius impulsively.

"You?" said Trurl, a faint hope in his voice. "But no . . ." he added after a moment. "Why should you have to perish too? . . ."

"Nonsense!" rejoined Klapaucius with great energy. "What, us perish at the hands of that iron imbecile? Never! It takes more than that, my friend, to wipe two of the most famous constructors off the face of the globe! Come, Trurl! Chin up!"

Encouraged by these words, Trurl ran up the stairs after Klapaucius. There was not a soul outside in the square. Amid clouds of dust and the gaunt skeletons of demolished homes, stood the machine, higher than the town hall tower itself, puffing steam, covered with the blood of powdered brick and smeared with chalk.

"Careful!" whispered Klapaucius. "It doesn't see us. Let's take that first street on the left, then turn right, then straight for those mountains. There we can take refuge and think of how to make the thing give up once and for all its insane . . . *Now!*" he yelled, for the machine had just spotted them and was charging, making the pavement buckle.

Breathless, they ran from the town and galloped along for a mile or so, hearing be-

Chest (La Poitrine), René Magritte, 1961.

hind them the thunderous stride of the colossus that followed relentlessly.

"I know that ravine!" Klapaucius suddenly cried. "That's the bed of a dried-out stream and it leads to cliffs and caves—faster, faster, the thing'll have to stop soon! . . ."

So they raced uphill, stumbling and wavstones that flew from under their feet. The opening in the rock breathed chill and darkness. As quickly as they could, they leaped inside, ran a few extra steps, then stopped.

"Well, here at least we're safe," said Trurl, calm once again. "I'll just take a look, to see where it got stuck. . . ."

"Be careful," cautioned Klapaucius. Trurl inched his way to the edge of the cave, leaned out, and immediately jumped back in fright.

"It's coming up the mountain!!" he cried.

"Don't worry, it'll never be able to get in here," said Klapaucius, not altogether convinced. "But what's that? Is it getting dark? Oh no!"

At that moment a great shadow blotted out the bit of sky visible through the mouth of the cave, and in its place appeared a smooth steel wall with rows of rivets. It was the machine slowly closing with the rock, thereby sealing up the cave as if with a mighty metal lid.

"We're trapped . . ." whispered Trurl, his voice breaking off when the darkness became absolute.

"That was idiotic on our part!" Klapaucius exclaimed, furious. "To jump into a cave that it could barricade! How could we have done such a thing?"

"What do you think it's waiting for now?" asked Trurl after a long pause.

"For us to give up—that doesn't take any great brains."

Again there was silence. Trurl tiptoed in the darkness, hands outstretched, in the direction of the opening, running his fingers along the stone until he touched the smooth steel, which was warm, as if heated from within. . . .

"I feel Trurl . . ." boomed the iron voice. Trurl hastily retreated, took a seat alongside his friend, and for some time they sat there,

ing their arms to keep their balance, but the machine still gained on them. Scrambling up over the gravel of the dried-out riverbed, they reached a crevice in the perpendicular rock and, seeing high above them the murky mouth of a cave, began to climb frantically toward it, no longer caring about the loose

Stanislaw Lem **1277**

motionless. At last Klapaucius whispered:

"There's no sense our just sitting here. I'll try to reason with it. . . ."

"That's hopeless," said Trurl. "But go ahead. Perhaps it will at least let *you* go free. . . ."

"Now, now, none of that!" said Klapaucius, patting him on the back. And he groped his way toward the mouth of the cave and called: "Hello out there, can you hear us?"

"Yes," said the machine.

"Listen, we'd like to apologize. You see . . . well, there was a little misunderstanding, true, but it was nothing, really. Trurl had no intention of. . . ."

"I'll pulverize Trurl!" said the machine. "But first, he'll tell me how much two and two makes."

"Of course he will, of course he will, and you'll be happy with his answer, and make it up with him for sure, isn't that right, Trurl?" said the mediator soothingly.

"Yes, of course . . ." mumbled Trurl.

"Really?" said the machine. "Then how much is two and two?"

"Fo . . . that is, seven . . ." said Trurl in an even lower voice.

"Ha! Not four, but seven, eh?" crowed the machine. "There, I told you so!"

"Seven, yes, seven, we always knew it was seven!" Klapaucius eagerly agreed. "Now will you, uh, let us go?" he added cautiously.

Machine, Turn Quickly (Machine Tournez Vite), Francis Picabia.
Trurl asserts that it is useless to try to reason with the machine.
? **Do you find Trurl's statement ironic? Why or why not?**

Giraudon/Art Resource, New York

"No. Let Trurl say how sorry he is and tell me how much is two times two. . . ."

"And you'll let us go, if I do?" asked Trurl.

"I don't know. I'll think about it. I'm not making any deals. What's two times two?"

"But you probably will let us go, won't you?" said Trurl, while Klapaucius pulled on his arm and hissed in his ear: "The thing's an imbecile, don't argue with it, for heaven's sake!"

"I won't let you go, if I don't want to," said the machine. "You just tell me how much two times two is...."

Suddenly Trurl fell into a rage.

"I'll tell you, I'll tell you all right!" he screamed. "Two and two is four and two times two is four, even if you stand on your head, pound these mountains all to dust, drink the ocean dry, and swallow the sky—do you hear? Two and two is four!!"

"Trurl! What are you saying? Have you taken leave of your senses? Two and two is seven, nice machine! Seven, seven!!" howled Klapaucius, trying to drown out his friend.

"No! It's four! Four and only four, four from the beginning to the end of time—FOUR!!" bellowed Trurl, growing hoarse.

The rock beneath their feet was seized with a feverish tremor.

The machine moved away from the cave, letting in a little pale light, and gave a piercing scream:

"That's not true! It's seven! Say it's seven or I'll hit you!"

"Never!" roared Trurl, as if he no longer cared what happened, and pebbles and dirt rained down on their heads, for the machine had begun to ram its eight-story hulk again and again into the wall of stone, hurling itself against the mountainside until huge boulders broke away and went tumbling down into the valley.

Thunder and sulfurous fumes filled the cave, and sparks flew from the blows of steel on rock, yet through all this pandemonium one could still make out, now and then, the ragged voice of Trurl bawling:

"Two and two is four! Two and two is four!!"

Klapaucius attempted to shut his friend's mouth by force, but, violently thrown off, he gave up, sat and covered his head with his arms. Not for a moment did the machine's mad efforts flag, and it seemed that any minute now the ceiling would collapse, crush the prisoners, and bury them forever. But when they had lost all hope, and the air was thick with acrid smoke and choking dust, there was suddenly a horrible scraping, and a sound like a slow explosion, louder than all the maniacal banging and battering, and the air whooshed, and the black wall that blocked the cave was whisked away, as if by a hurricane, and monstrous chunks of rock came crashing down after it. The echoes of that avalanche still rumbled and reverberated in the valley below when the two friends peered out of their cave. They saw the machine. It lay smashed and flattened, nearly broken in half by an enormous boulder that had landed in the middle of its eight floors. With the greatest care they picked their way down through the smoking rubble. In order to reach the riverbed, it was necessary to pass the remains of the machine, which resembled the wreck of some mighty vessel thrown up upon a beach. Without a word, the two stopped together in the shadow of its twisted hull. The machine still quivered slightly, and one could hear something turning, creaking feebly, within.

"Yes, this is the bad end you've come to, and two and two is—as it always was—" began Trurl, but just then the machine made a faint, barely audible croaking noise and said, for the last time, "SEVEN."

Then something snapped inside, a few stones dribbled down from overhead, and now before them lay nothing but a lifeless mass of scrap. The two constructors exchanged a look and silently, without any further comment or conversation, walked back the way they came.

First Thoughts

Which incident in this story did you find the funniest? What might Lem be **satirizing** by way of this humorous incident?

Identifying Facts

1. What "test question" does Trurl ask his thinking machine? How does the machine respond?

2. What interconnected qualities does Klapaucius recognize in the machine? What does he suggest Trurl might do to recover his costs?

3. Why does the machine lift itself from its foundations and try to destroy Trurl?

4. Where are Trurl and Klapaucius finally trapped? Summarize how the machine is finally destroyed.

Interpreting Meanings

1. What event immediately establishes the futuristic **setting** of this **science-fiction** tale?

2. How does Lem give the thinking machine a personality? Describe this personality.

3. How would you describe the relationship between Trurl and Klapaucius? How does the interplay between them add interest to the story?

4. Reread Lem's biography (see page 1271). How might the machine's behavior **satirize** Lem's own experiences under totalitarian governments? What view of the world does the story suggest such governments try to instill?

5. What does the fate of the machine suggest about its usefulness? What does it suggest about the reasons totalitarian governments eventually fail?

Applying Meanings

What dangers does the story suggest often accompany ignorance? Give an example from your own life about the dangers of ignorance.

Creative Writing Response

Writing a Science-Fiction Story. Take a common story ("Little Red Riding Hood") or television show (an episode of the *Cosby Show*) and set it in the future or on another planet. Retell the story, including as many elements of science fiction as you like (laser weapons, computerized gadgets, and so on). Let your imagination run wild, while keeping the basic plot and character elements the same as in the original story.

Critical Writing Response

Writing About Satire. In a brief essay, show how Lem's story pokes fun at both specific political and economic situations and human nature in general. Discuss story details in more general terms and identify what they suggest or ridicule. Before you begin writing, you may find it helpful to complete a chart like this one.

Detail	What It Says About Politics/ Economics	What It Says About Human Nature

Joaquim Maria Machado de Assis
1838–1908, Brazil

Benson Latin American Collection, The University of Texas at Austin

Why do people do the things they do? What is "real" and what is not? Can we ever completely understand the world around us? These are the kinds of questions that Joaquim Maria Machado de Assis (zhō·ä·kēm′ mä·rē′ə mä·shä′dō dā ä·sēs′) investigates in his novels and more than two hundred short stories. Although Machado de Assis has only recently been recognized in the English-speaking world, he has always enjoyed enormous respect in his native

Brazil. When the Brazilian Academy of Letters was founded in the late 1890s, Machado de Assis was named its president for life.

The son of a poor house painter who was partially of African descent, Machado de Assis faced many obstacles early in his life. As a child he suffered from epilepsy and had a tendency to stutter. His mother died when he was only ten and his father died two years later. Shy and lonely, Joaquim began frequenting a local bookstore whose owner, Paula Brito, became his friend and adviser. By the time he was seventeen, he was working as a proofreader for Brito's publishing company and had begun writing his own poetry and fiction.

Most of Machado de Assis' early writings were in the Romantic tradition. In the 1880s, however, he began writing the innovative fiction for which he is known today. Machado de Assis was far ahead of his time in his interest in psychological motivations. *Dom Casmurro* (1899) (literally "Mr. Stubborn" or "Mr. Pigheaded"), the novel that most critics regard as his masterpiece, is a powerful study of jealousy and its consequences. When the book first appeared in English in 1953, translator Helen Caldwell said that she considered it among the finest novels produced in either North or South America.

Reader's Guide

A CANARY'S IDEAS

Background

Machado de Assis was a pioneer of **psychological realism**. This off-shoot of Realism focuses not on outer realities but on the inner workings of a character's mind. Machado de Assis examined human mental processes years before Marcel Proust and James Joyce (see page 1207) began reproducing in prose the stream of their characters' thoughts, emotions, associations, and memories. Machado de Assis also anticipated twentieth-century trends in fiction by breaking down the barriers between realistic writing and fantasy. In combining the two forms, Machado de Assis was a forerunner of such Latin American **magical realists** as Gabriel García Márquez (see page 1307). In ''A Canary's Ideas,'' notice how the events surrounding the incredible discovery of a talking canary are realistically described.

Writer's Response

How do you think a caged bird might view the world around it and its place in that world? How might a free, wild bird view the world? Jot down a few of your ideas.

Literary Focus

There are different types of irony. In **verbal irony**, a character says one thing but really means something else. (Jill stepped into the downpour and said, ''Nice day.'') In **situational irony**, what happens is different from what we expect to happen. (A firefighter's house burns down.) In **dramatic irony**, the audience knows something that a character in a play does *not* know. (In *Romeo and Juliet,* the audience knows Juliet is only drugged, but Romeo believes she is dead.) The canary in this story says things that we can see as comically ironic.

A CANARY'S IDEAS

Joaquim Maria Machado de Assis

translated by

LORIE ISHIMATSU AND JACK SCHMITT

Pay careful attention to the canary's words. What is the bird's attitude toward human beings? Do you find this amusing?

A man by the name of Macedo,[1] who had a fancy for ornithology,[2] related to some friends an incident so extraordinary that no one took him seriously. Some came to believe he had lost his mind. Here is a summary of his narration.

At the beginning of last month, as I was walking down the street, a carriage darted past me and nearly knocked me to the ground. I escaped by quickly side-stepping into a secondhand shop. Neither the racket of the horse and carriage nor my entrance stirred the proprietor, dozing in a folding chair at the back of the shop. He was a man of shabby appearance: his beard was the color of dirty straw, and his head was covered by a tattered cap which probably had not found a buyer. One could not guess that there was any story behind him, as there could have been behind some of the objects he sold, nor could one sense in him that austere, disillusioned sadness inherent in the objects which were remnants of past lives.

The shop was dark and crowded with the sort of old, bent, broken, tarnished, rusted articles ordinarily found in secondhand shops, and everything was in that state of semidisorder befitting such an establishment. This assortment of articles, though banal, was interesting. Pots without lids, lids without pots, buttons, shoes, locks, a black skirt, straw hats, fur hats, picture frames, binoculars, dress coats, a fencing foil, a stuffed dog, a pair of slippers, gloves,

Hans Reinhard/Bruce Coleman, Inc.

---

1. **Macedo** (mä·sä′dō)
2. **ornithology:** the study of birds.

nondescript vases, epaulets,[3] a velvet satchel, two hatracks, a slingshot, a thermometer, chairs, a lithographed portrait by the late Sisson,[4] a backgammon board, two wire masks for some future Carnival[5]—all this and more, which I either did not see or do not remember, filled the shop in the area around the door, propped up, hung, or displayed in glass cases as old as the objects inside them. Further inside the shop were many objects of similar appearance. Predominant were the large objects—chests of drawers, chairs, and beds—some of which were stacked on top of others which were lost in the darkness.

I was about to leave, when I saw a cage hanging in the doorway. It was as old as everything else in the shop, and I expected it to be empty so it would fit in with the general appearance of desolation. However, it wasn't empty. Inside, a canary was hopping about. The bird's color, liveliness, and charm added a noted of life and youth to that heap of wreckage. It was the last passenger of some wrecked ship, who had arrived in the shop as complete and happy as it had originally been. As soon as I looked at the bird, it began to hop up and down, from perch to perch, as if it meant to tell me that a ray of sunshine was frolicking in the midst of that cemetery. I'm using this image to describe the canary only because I'm speaking to rhetorical[6] people, but the truth is that the canary thought about neither cemetery nor sun, according to what it

THE GREAT FAMILY, RENÉ MAGRITTE (1898–1967).
What details provided thus far give the story an air of realism?

Herscovici/Art Resource, New York

---

3. **epaulets** (ep′ə·lets′): shoulder ornaments worn on military and other uniforms.
4. **lithographed . . . Sisson:** relatively inexpensive print by a minor artist.
5. **Carnival:** period of feasting and merrymaking before the start of Lent; in Brazil, Carnival is a major festival similar to the Mardi Gras in New Orleans.
6. **rhetorical** (ri·tôr′i·kəl): here, able to use and understand effective, eloquent language.

told me later. Along with the pleasure the sight of the bird brought me, I felt indignation regarding its destiny and softly murmured these bitter words:

"What detestable owner had the nerve to rid himself of this bird for a few cents? Or what indifferent soul, not wishing to keep his late master's pet, gave it away to some child, who sold it so he could make a bet on a soccer game?"

The canary, sitting on top of its perch, trilled this reply:

"Whoever you may be, you're certainly not in your right mind. I had no detestable owner, nor was I given to any child to sell. Those are the delusions of a sick person. Go and get yourself cured, my friend . . ."

"What?" I interrupted, not having had time to become astonished. "So your master didn't sell you to this shop? It wasn't misery or laziness that brought you, like a ray of sunshine, to this cemetery?"

"I don't know what you mean by 'sunshine' or 'cemetery.' If the canaries you've seen use the first of those names, so much the better, because it sounds pretty, but really, I'm sure you're confused."

"Excuse me, but you couldn't have come here by chance, all alone. Has your master always been that man sitting over there?"

"What master? That man over there is my servant. He gives me food and water every day, so regularly that if I were to pay him for his services, it would be no small sum, but canaries don't pay their servants. In fact, since the world belongs to canaries, it would be extravagant for them to pay for what is already in the world."

Astonished by these answers, I didn't know what to marvel at more—the language or the ideas. The language, even though it entered my ears as human speech, was uttered by the bird in the form of charming trills. I looked all around me so I could determine if I were awake and saw that the street was the same, and the shop was the same dark, sad, musty place. The canary, moving from side to side, was waiting for me to speak. I then asked if it were lonely for the infinite blue space . . .

"But, my dear man," trilled the canary, "what does 'infinite blue space' mean?"

"But, pardon me, what do you think of this world? What is the world to you?"

"The world," retorted the canary, with a certain professorial air, "is a secondhand shop with a small rectangular bamboo cage hanging from a nail. The canary is lord of the cage it lives in and the shop that surrounds it. Beyond that, everything is illusion and deception."

With this, the old man woke up and approached me, dragging his feet. He asked me if I wanted to buy the canary. I asked if he had acquired it in the same way he had acquired the rest of the objects he sold and learned that he had bought it from a barber, along with a set of razors.

"The razors are in very good condition," he said.

"I only want the canary."

I paid for it, ordered a huge, circular cage of wood and wire, and had it placed on the veranda of my house so the bird could see the garden, the fountain, and a bit of blue sky.

It was my intention to do a lengthy study of this phenomenon, without saying anything to anyone until I could astound the world with my extraordinary discovery. I began by alphabetizing the canary's language in order to study its structure, its relation to music, the bird's appreciation of aesthetics,[7] its ideas and recollections. When this philological[8] and psychological analysis was done, I entered specifically into the study of canaries: their origin, their early history, the geology and flora of the Canary Islands,[9] the

---

7. **aesthetics** (es·thet'iks): the study or theory of beauty, especially as captured in art.
8. **philological** (fil'ō·läj'i·kəl): here, relating to the study of language; linguistic.
9. **flora of the Canary Islands**: plantlife of an island group in the Atlantic Ocean off Africa's northwest coast; the birds known as canaries are native to these islands.

Joaquim Maria Machado de Assis   **1285**

bird's knowledge of navigation, and so forth. We conversed for hours while I took notes, and it waited, hopped about, and trilled.

As I have no family other than two servants, I ordered them not to interrupt me, even to deliver a letter or an urgent telegram or to inform me of an important visitor. Since they both knew about my scientific pursuits, they found my orders perfectly natural and did not suspect that the canary and I understood each other.

Needless to say, I slept little, woke up two or three times each night, wandered about aimlessly, and felt feverish. Finally, I returned to my work in order to reread, add, and emend. I corrected more than one observation, either because I had misunderstood something or because the bird had not expressed it clearly. The definition of the world was one of these. Three weeks after the canary's entrance into my home, I asked it to repeat to me its definition of the world.

"The world," it answered, "is a sufficiently broad garden with a fountain in the middle, flowers, shrubbery, some grass, clear air, and a bit of blue up above. The canary, lord of the world, lives in a spacious cage, white and circular, from which it looks out on the rest of the world. Everything else is illusion and deception."

The language of my treatise also suffered some modifications, and I saw that certain conclusions which had seemed simple were actually presumptuous. I still could not write the paper I was to send to the National Museum, the Historical Institute, and the German universities, not due to a lack of material but because I first had to put together all my observations and test their validity. During the last few days, I neither left the house, answered letters, nor wanted to hear from friends or relatives. The canary was everything to me. One of the servants had the job of cleaning the bird's cage and giving it food and water every morning. The bird said nothing to him, as if it knew the man was completely lacking in scientific background. Besides, the service was no more than cursory, as the servant was not a bird lover.

On Saturday I awoke ill, my head and back aching. The doctor ordered complete rest. I was suffering from an excess of studying and was not to read or even think, nor was I even to know what was going on in the city or the rest of the outside world. I remained in this condition for five days. On the sixth day I got up, and only then did I find out that the canary, while under the servant's care, had flown out of its cage. My first impulse was to strangle the servant—I was choking with indignation and collapsed into my chair, speechless and bewildered. The guilty man defended himself, swearing he had been careful, but the wily bird had nevertheless managed to escape.

"But didn't you search for it?"

"Yes, I did, sir. First it flew up to the roof, and I followed it. It flew to a tree, and then who knows where it hid itself? I've been asking around since yesterday. I asked the neighbors and the local farmers, but no one has seen the bird."

I suffered immensely. Fortunately, the fatigue left me within a few hours, and I was soon able to go out to the veranda and the garden. There was no sign of the canary. I ran everywhere, making inquiries and posting announcements, all to no avail. I had already gathered my notes together to write my paper, even though it would be disjointed and incomplete, when I happened to visit a friend who had one of the largest and most beautiful estates on the outskirts of town. We were taking a stroll before dinner when this question was trilled to me:

"Greetings, Senhor[10] Macedo, where have you been since you disappeared?"

It was the canary, perched on the branch of a tree. You can imagine how I reacted and what I said to the bird. My friend presumed I was mad, but the opinions of friends are of no importance to me. I spoke tenderly to the canary and asked it to come home and continue our conversations in that world of ours, composed of a garden, a fountain, a veranda, and a white circular cage.

---

10. **Senhor** (si·nyôr): "mister" (Portuguese).

"What garden? What fountain?"

"The world, my dear bird."

"What world? I see you haven't lost any of your annoying professorial habits. The world," it solemnly concluded, "is an infinite blue space, with the sun up above."

Indignant, I replied that if I were to believe what it said, the world could be anything—it had even been a secondhand shop . . .

"A secondhand shop?" it trilled to its heart's content. "But is there really such a thing as a secondhand shop?"

First Thoughts

It is easy for us to feel superior to the canary and to laugh at its narrow view of the world and its limited understanding of reality. Do you think Machado de Assis wrote this story to show that human perceptions of the world are superior? Or might he be implying that our perceptions, like the canary's, are faulty and limited?

Identifying Facts

1. A **frame story** is a story which "frames," or contains within it, yet another story. According to the first paragraph, what is the frame for this story?

2. When Macedo finds the canary in the secondhand shop, what does the bird say about "infinite blue space"? How does the canary define the world?

3. After Macedo takes the canary home to study, what new definition of the world does the bird give? How does the canary escape?

4. What is the canary's definition of the world when Macedo encounters it on his friend's estate? What does the bird say about the secondhand shop?

Interpreting Meanings

1. Make a generalization about the canary's view of the world. Support your generalization with details from the story.

2. Why is it **ironic** for the canary to consider itself "lord" of the shop and later "lord of the world"? What might these remarks suggest about our own perceptions of our place in the world?

3. What earlier comment makes the canary's last remarks especially humorous and **ironic**? What might the canary's final question imply about human attitudes toward the past?

Applying Meanings

In past centuries, human perception of the world was very different from what it is today. For example, long ago everyone "knew" that the earth was flat and that the sun moved around it. Today we know that the earth is round and that it revolves around the sun. Do you think that in the future people will laugh at some of our ideas about the world, just as you may have laughed at this canary's ideas? Discuss your responses to this question.

Creative Writing Response

Writing From a Bird's Point of View.
Using the ideas that you jotted down in the Writer's Response activity (see page 1282), write a brief description of the world from a bird's point of view. Let the bird speak as ''I.'' If you prefer, write from another creature's point of view (dog, cat, flea, and so on).

Critical Writing Response

Responding to a Story.   In a brief essay, respond to *one* of these comments:

1. This is a story about a crazy man and it has nothing to do with a person's normal, daily life.
2. This story is about the nature of reality and of perception, and it shows how we are all limited in our interpretations of the world.

In the opening sentence of your essay, state whether you agree or disagree with the comment. Then give two or three reasons to support your response. Your reasons may be drawn both from the story and from your own experiences.

Language and Vocabulary

Portuguese and English

Portuguese, the main language of Portugal and Brazil, is one of the **Romance languages**—that is, like French, Italian, and Spanish, it is derived from Latin.

In the sentences below, words that have entered English from Portuguese have been italicized and defined. On a separate piece of paper, indicate whether the words are defined correctly by writing *True* or *False* beside the corresponding numbers. Check your answers in a dictionary. If the definition is false, write a correction.

1. An *albino* is an amateur musician.
2. A *cobra* is a poisonous insect.
3. *Lacquer* is a varnish that makes wood hard and shiny.
4. *Marmalade* was a popular hair gel.
5. *Molasses* is a kind of sweet syrup.
6. *Pagoda* is a Japanese dessert made with sweet beans and cream.
7. A *piranha* is a twirling dance step.
8. *Tapioca* is granular starch made from the cassava plant.

Gabriela Mistral
1889–1957, Chile

Mural dedicated to Gabriela Mistral, Santiago de Chile.

Gabriela Mistral (mēs·träl′) was the first woman poet and the first Latin American to win the Nobel Prize. When the Chilean poet Pablo Neruda (see page 1294) was a young boy, Mistral, a woman of considerable height, became the principal of a girls' school near his hometown. The story goes that the ladies of the community suggested that she wear a hat—everyone wore one then—and she answered with a smile that a hat would be an unnecessary addition to one so tall. This good-humored directness was characteristic of the person whose poetry captured the simple, strong feelings of the common people.

Mistral was born Lucila Godoy Alcayaga in the village of Vicuna, Chile, high in the Andes Mountains. The first part of her pen name refers to the archangel Gabriel, and the second to the hot, dry wind known as the *mistral* that blows across southern France. Mistral may have also been paying homage to two of her favorite poets: Italy's Gabriele D'Annunzio (1863–1938) and France's Frederic Mistral (1830–1914).

Mistral wrote much of her early poetry in response to the suicide of a man she had been engaged to marry. She received worldwide attention when Federico de Onis, a Spanish professor at Columbia University in New York City, "discovered" her poetry and had it published.

Mistral continued to write poetry while working as a teacher and a principal, and later as an international cultural ambassador. In the 1920s she helped reorganize the rural school systems of Mexico, and in the 1930s she lectured at several American universities and was Chile's cultural representative to the League of Nations. After World War II, Mistral served as the Chilean consul in Los Angeles and Italy and was a delegate to a United Nations subcommittee on women's rights. On her frequent trips back to Chile, Mistral was often greeted by thousands of schoolchildren singing her poems. When she received the Nobel Prize for literature in 1945, she remarked that she must have been voted in by women and children.

Mistral once said that artists are to society what the soul is to the individual. Her life and writing reflected this sentiment. Her simple, strong verse is intimately linked by the use of vernacular, or local, language to the culture and concerns of her people.

I Am Not Lonely

Gabriela Mistral

translated by

Langston Hughes

Reader's Guide

Background Much of Mistral's poetry revolves around the theme of love—either the intimate relationship between lovers or the special relationship shared by a mother and her child. Although Gabriela Mistral never had a child of her own, she wrote many poems for and about children. One of the poems you are about to read, ''I Am Not Lonely,'' is from *Ternura* (''Tenderness''), Mistral's collection of children's songs, poems, and lullabies.

Writer's Response Write a few sentences describing a situation in which you felt lonely. What might have made you feel less lonely at that time?

Literary Focus Poetry is often classified as lyric, narrative, or dramatic. **Lyric poetry** expresses private thoughts or emotions. **Narrative poetry** tells a story. **Dramatic poetry** uses dialogue or monologue to convey one or more characters' personalities. Some poems, like these by Mistral, combine elements of all three types of poetry. But the major purpose of Mistral's poems is lyrical—to reveal intense personal feelings. Notice how close her poems are to song lyrics.

I Am Not Lonely

 In this poem, the speaker is talking to someone. Who might this second person be?

The night is left lonely
from the hills to the sea.
But I, who cradle you,
I am not lonely!

5   The sky is left lonely
should the moon fall in the sea.

But I, who cling to you,
I am not lonely!

The world is left lonely
10 and all know misery.
But I, who hug you close,
I am not lonely!

WOMAN WITH INFANT, PABLO PICASSO (1881–1973).

Scala/Art Resource, New York

THE LITTLE GIRL THAT LOST A FINGER

Gabriela Mistral

translated by

MUNA LEE DE MUÑOZ MARÍN

When you think about it, this lyric has a disturbing title. Is it a serious poem, or does it sound like a fairy tale?

And a clam caught my little finger,
and the clam fell into the sand,
and the sand was swallowed by the sea,
and the whaler caught it in the sea,
5 and the whaler arrived at Gibraltar,°
and in Gibraltar the fishermen sing:

5. **Gibraltar** (ji·brôl′tər): peninsula at the southern tip of Spain, jutting into the Mediterranean Sea.

Gabriela Mistral **1291**

"News of the earth we drag up from the sea,
news of a little girl's finger:
let her who lost it come get it!"

10 Give me a boat to go fetch it,
and for the boat give me a captain,
for the captain give me wages,
and for his wages let him ask for the city:
Marseilles° with towers and squares and boats,
15 in all the wide world the finest city,
which won't be lovely with a little girl
that the sea robbed of her finger,
and that whalers chant for like town criers,°
and that they're waiting for on Gibraltar . . .

14. **Marseilles** (mär·sā′): large French port on the Mediterranean Sea, not far from Gibraltar.

18. **town criers:** in the past, people who made public announcements by crying them out in the streets.

HRW Photo by Helene Kolda

First Thoughts

What dominant emotions did you identify in the two poems?

Identifying Facts

1. What things are lonely in stanzas 1, 2, and 3 of "I Am Not Lonely"? Why isn't the speaker lonely?
2. Why does the speaker in "The Little Girl That Lost a Finger" ask for a boat? What payment does she say the boat's captain should receive?

Interpreting Meanings

1. What does the verb "cradle" suggest about the identities of the speaker and the person being addressed in "I Am Not Lonely"? Do the verbs "cling" and "hug" in the next stanzas suggest other people? Discuss how you interpret the identities of the people in the poem.
2. **Personification** is a figure of speech in which human feelings are attributed to nonhuman things. What is personified in "I Am Not Lonely"? What do the personifications reveal about the speaker's feelings?
3. Do you think young children would enjoy "The Little Girl That Lost a Finger"? In what ways does the poem express a wish that the world were really this caring and loving toward even the little finger of one little girl?
4. Mistral's poems are essentially examples of lyric poetry, but what elements of **narrative poetry** and **dramatic poetry** do they contain? What feelings would you say these poems give voice to?

Applying Meanings

"The Little Girl That Lost a Finger" is structured on a series of causes and effects—one thing happens and this causes something else to happen, and so on. What popular children's stories or rhymes or songs are based on a similar structure? Why is this structure appealing?

Creative Writing Response

1. **Adding a Stanza to a Poem.** Write another four-line stanza for the poem "I Am Not Lonely." Open with two lines that describe some way that nature herself is lonely. Then address two lines to yourself. You may follow Mistral's format:

   The ____ is left lonely
   ____
   But I, who ____
   I am not lonely.

   Or, if your mood is different, **personify** nature as having different feelings (such as joy or tenderness).

2. **Writing About a Chain of Events.** Life is full of causes and effects. Suppose you watch a late-night movie. This has the effect of making you oversleep. This means you will be late for school, so you run out the door. Because you are running you fall down and twist your ankle, and a long chain of other events may follow from this.

   Write a brief chain-of-events poem or story. First, think of a cause. This cause leads to some effect and this effect then becomes the cause for another effect, and so on. You might want to begin by diagramming the chain of events in a series of boxes like this:

Watch late movie	Oversleep	Run out the door	Fall down	etc.

Pablo Neruda
1904–1973, Chile

Sergio Larrain/Magnum Photos, Inc.

When Chilean poet Pablo Neruda (pä′ blô ne·rōō′də) was a young boy looking for "creaturely things" behind his house, he saw a boy's hand poking through a hole in a fence to give him a toy lamb made of real wool. Thrilled, Neruda raced home to return with his most treasured possession, a pine cone—"half-open, balsamic, sweet-smelling." He dropped it through the same hole for the unseen boy on the other side of the fence. Later in life, when people asked him why he became a poet, Neruda often related this incident. He said that poetry was a gift to share with the world because it always brought something in return.

Pablo Neruda began publishing poetry while he was still a teenager in Temuco, a frontier town in Chile's sparsely populated south. Neruda's real name was Neftali Reyes Basoalto. He adopted a pen name to avoid upsetting his father, a railway worker, who frowned on his son's poetic ambitions. Neruda was only twenty years old when he published *Twenty Love Poems and a Song of Despair* (1924), the poetry collection that won him fame throughout his homeland.

Because Chile, like other Latin American nations, often honors writers with diplomatic posts, Neruda was appointed consul to several Asian nations and then to Argentina and Spain. In Spain he became close friends with the great poet Federico García Lorca (see page 1228). When García Lorca was murdered by Fascist forces in the Spanish Civil War (1936–1939), Neruda suddenly became very political. Like many idealists of the time, he joined the Communist party and wrote letters attacking Chile's repressive right-wing government. In 1946 he was accused of treason and was forced to flee his homeland. It was during his exile that he wrote *Canto General (General Poems)*, a politically charged book of poems to which "Discoverers of Chile" belongs.

Neruda returned to Chile in 1952 and began writing his *Odas Elementales*, or *Elementary Odes* (1954). These short poems praise the ordinary things of life. "Poetry is like bread," Neruda wrote, "and it must be shared by everyone, the men of letters and the peasants, by everyone in our vast, incredible, extraordinary family of man."

Reader's Guide

DISCOVERERS OF CHILE

Background

In "Discoverers of Chile," Neruda refers to Chile's climate, terrain, and mineral wealth, and to Diego de Almagro, who in 1531 followed the Spanish conquistador Francisco Pizarro to Peru. The Spaniards, outnumbered by the Incas but heavily armed, captured Atahualpa, the Inca chief. As ransom, they demanded one room filled with gold and another filled with silver. But upon the urgings of Almagro, Pizarro did not release Atahualpa after the rooms were filled with gold and silver. Instead, the Spaniards strangled the Incan emperor to death.

Hungry for more gold, Pizarro sent Almagro to conquer Chile. The journey was a disaster. Hundreds of Spaniards and thousands of Indians died. None of the expected riches were found.

Ironically, Chile was later found to be rich in mineral resources. Today it is the world's leading producer of copper, and it also has deposits of gold, silver, coal, oil, and a gray, rocklike substance called *caliche* (kə·lē′chē), the world's only natural source of sodium nitrate. Caliche is used to make fertilizers and explosives. Scientists think that it was formed from the droppings of ocean birds.

Writer's Response

Do you think it is correct to say that people like Francisco Pizarro and Diego de Almagro "discovered" Peru and Chile, when the land was inhabited for thousands of years before the Europeans came? Write a few sentences supporting your point of view.

Literary Focus

A **figure of speech** is a word or phrase that describes one thing in terms of another, very different thing. A figure of speech is not literally true, but it helps us see the world in a fresh, imaginative way. There are many types of figures of speech, including similes and metaphors. A **simile** makes a comparison between two seemingly unlike things by using a connective word such as *like, as, than,* or *resembles* (*The stars were* like *diamonds*). A **metaphor** makes a comparison between two seemingly unlike things without using a connective word (*The stars were diamonds*). Neruda uses both kinds of figures of speech in the following poem.

Los Cuernos Peaks, Chile.

DISCOVERERS OF CHILE
Pablo Neruda
translated by
ROBERT BLY

How does this speaker feel toward his country? How does he feel toward the Spaniard, Almagro?

Almagro brought his wrinkled lightning down from the north,
and day and night he bent over this country
between gunshots and twilight, as if over a letter.
Shadow of thorn, shadow of thistle and of wax,
5   the Spaniard, alone with his dried-up body,
watching the shadowy tactics of the soil.
My slim nation has a body made up
of night, snow, and sand,
the silence of the world is in its long coast,

10   the foam of the world rises from its seaboard,
      the coal of the world fills it with mysterious kisses.
      Gold burns in its finger like a live coal
      and silver lights up like a green moon
      its petrified shadow that's like a gloomy planet.
15   The Spaniard, sitting one day near a rose,
      near oil, near wine, near the primitive sky,
      could not really grasp how this spot of furious stone
      was born beneath the droppings of the ocean eagle.

First Thoughts

Why do you think Neruda titled this poem "Discoverers of Chile"?

Identifying Facts

1. What did Almagro do with his "wrinkled lightning"?
2. What could Almagro not understand?

Interpreting Meanings

1. What might Almagro's "wrinkled lightning" be? (In the **metaphor** implied by this phrase, what is being compared to lightning?)
2. What specific words in the poem compare Almagro to someone who is brutishly attacking a fragile victim? How does his body contrast with that of his victim's?
3. Reread the Background that precedes the poem (see page 1295). Which of Chile's mineral resources, unrecognized by Almagro, are directly or indirectly mentioned in the poem, and where?
4. Identify four **similes** in the poem. What contrasting qualities about Chile do the similes in lines 12–14 help convey?
5. Do you think the word *discoverers* in the title is used **ironically** when applied to Almagro? Why or why not?

Applying Meanings

The conquistadors and other European explorers seldom showed respect for Native Americans and their cultures. Identify at least one situation in the world today that could be compared to Almagro's failure to understand the country he conquers.

Creative Writing Response

Writing About a Familiar Place. Write a poem in which you describe the physical appearance of a place that you are very familiar with. Like Neruda, use **similes** and other **figures of speech** to convey your emotions and to help readers picture the physical terrain.

You may want to begin by listing specific details about the place and creating similes to go with them. For example:

Place	Detail	Simile
a stream	small fish	dartlike video-game villains
	dragonflies	hover like miniature helicopters

Jorge Luis Borges
1899–1986, Argentina

UPI/Bettmann Newsphotos

When he was six years old, Jorge Luis Borges (hôr′he lōō·ēs′ bôr′hes) announced that he intended to become a writer. He began working at his chosen profession immediately: at the age of nine he translated Oscar Wilde's fairy tale "The Happy Prince" into Spanish. Later in his life, Borges credited his father with inspiring his writing career: He felt that his father had made him aware of poetry—of the idea that words could be powerful and symbolic, not just a means of everyday communication.

Borges learned English at an early age from his English-born grandmother, and he devoured her extensive library. He loved the horror stories of Edgar Allan Poe, the adventures of Robert Louis Stevenson, and the exotic Persian fairy tales in *The Thousand and One Nights* (see page 638). Ironically, Borges first read the great Spanish classics *El Cid* and *Don Quixote* (see pages 703 and 821) in English translations. Later, when he read *Don Quixote* in its original Spanish, he said it sounded like a bad translation!

The Borges family was traveling in Europe when World War I broke out. They took refuge in neutral Switzerland, where Borges attended school and learned to speak three more languages—French, Latin, and German. After the war, the family moved first to Italy, then to Spain, and finally back to Argentina.

Borges began his career as a poet, and he always considered himself a poet first and foremost. In the 1940s, however, Borges turned to experimental prose, writing stories about transparent tigers, wizards who conjure up visions in a bowl of ink, and encyclopedias that do not record events but cause them. The stories in *The Garden of the Forking Paths* (1941) and *El Aleph* (1945) ignore plot and character and most of the usual elements of fiction. They instead blend fact and fantasy in a world of games and riddles, literary mystery, and philosophical inquiry.

It was also during the 1940s that Borges began using one of his most famous images—that of the labyrinth, or maze. Borges used the labyrinth as a metaphor for our journey through life, with all its surprising twists, turns, and dead ends.

Reader's Guide

BORGES AND MYSELF

Background

Borges was interested in philosophical issues, such as the nature of reality and the interplay between the imagined and the real. He was especially interested in how art affects the way we perceive the world. He believed that reality consists not only of what we have actually seen and done, but also of what we have read and what our reading has led us to imagine.

Borges calls the following story "my personal rendering of the old Jekyll-and-Hyde theme, save that in their case the opposition is between good and evil and in my version the opposites are the spectator and the spectacle."

Writer's Response

Writers and artists often feel that they live two very different lives—an imaginative life and a life as a regular person. Think of a writer or artist you have read or heard about. Describe how that person's public image differs from his or her real personality. (For example, Stephen King writes horror stories but lives a peaceful life in the countryside of New England.)

Literary Focus

Borges writes this story from the **first-person point of view**. The **first-person narrator** is the "I" character who tells the story. Generally, when we read a story with a first-person narrator, we feel as if we are listening to a friend, or as if we are reading someone's letters or diary. In this unusual story, the first-person narrator and the "other man" that he is talking about are different aspects of the same person.

BORGES AND MYSELF

Jorge Luis Borges

translated by

N. T. DI GIOVANNI AND JORGE LUIS BORGES

As you read, notice how the speaker and Borges are different.

It's to the other man, to Borges, that things happen. I walk along the streets of Buenos Aires, stopping now and then—perhaps out of habit—to look at the arch of an old entranceway or a grillwork gate; of Borges I get news through the mail and glimpse his name among a committee of professors or in a dictionary of biography. I have a taste for hourglasses, maps, eighteenth-century typography, the roots of words, the smell of coffee, and Stevenson's[1] prose; the other man shares these likes, but in a showy way that turns them into stagy mannerisms. It would be an exaggeration to say that we are on bad terms; I live, I let myself live, so that Borges can weave his tales and poems, and

DRAWING HANDS, M. C. ESCHER, 1948.
Do you think that this drawing aptly reflects Borges' ideas? Why or why not?

those tales and poems are my justification. It is not hard for me to admit that he has managed to write a few worthwhile pages, but these pages cannot save me, perhaps because what is good no longer belongs to anyone—not even the other man—but rather to speech or tradition. In any case, I am

---

1. **Stevenson's:** Robert Louis Stevenson (1850–1894), Scottish writer of adventure novels, poems, and essays.

fated to become lost once and for all, and only some moment of myself will survive in the other man. Little by little, I have been surrendering everything to him, even though I have evidence of his stubborn habit of falsification and exaggerating. Spinoza[2] held that all things try to keep on being themselves; a stone wants to be a stone and the tiger, a tiger. I shall remain in Borges, not in myself (if it is so that I am someone), but I recognize myself less in his books than in those of others or than in the laborious tuning of a guitar. Years ago, I tried ridding myself of him and I went from myths of the outlying slums of the city to games with time and infinity, but those games are now part of Borges and I will have to turn to other things. And so, my life is a running away, and I lose everything and everything is left to oblivion or to the other man.

Which of us is writing this page I don't know.

---

2. **Spinoza:** Baruch Spinoza (1632–1677), Dutch philosopher.

First Thoughts

Who is the speaker in this ''story''? How is he different from ''Borges''?

Identifying Facts

1. According to the speaker, to whom do ''things happen''?
2. According to the speaker, what is the justification for his life?
3. What is the speaker ''fated'' to become?
4. What does the speaker ''have evidence'' of?
5. At the end, what is it that the speaker does not know?

Interpreting Meanings

1. What distinction does the speaker make between ''Borges'' and ''myself''? Why would ''Borges'' seem ''showy'' or ''stagy''?
2. What things does the speaker like? What does he mean when he says that ''Borges'' turns these things into ''stagy mannerisms''?
3. According to the speaker, ''Borges' '' work does not belong to him, but to ''speech or tradition.'' What do you think this means?

Applying Meanings

Do you think most people can feel like two different people? If so, when and why might someone feel like this?

Creative Writing Response

Letting a ''Double'' Speak. Think about the different sides of your personality. What part of your personality comes out more strongly at school? at home? when you are alone? Write a short diary entry following the model of ''Borges and Myself.'' The ''I'' character is your private side that others do not often see. The character with your name is the public part of your personality. You may have the ''I'' character comment on the daily activities of the other character.

Before you begin writing you may want to fill out a chart like this:

Characteristics I Show in Public	How I Really Am

SEEING CONNECTIONS

The Divided Self

Modernism is a twentieth-century literary movement that began in Europe. Influenced by new ideas in psychology, the modernists explored the split between the artist's social and private selves, seeing the artist as a lonely figure struggling in an insensitive world.

The Puerto Rican poet Julia de Burgos (hōōl′ē·ə dā bōōr′gôs) (1914–1953), as both a woman and an artist, was keenly aware of the struggle to remain faithful to her art in the face of society's prejudices and pressures. During her short lifetime, she took part in the fierce controversy over Puerto Rican independence. Because her political views and feminist leanings were not popular, she had difficulty supporting herself through her writing, and she ultimately died in poverty at the age of thirty-nine.

The following poem by de Burgos, like "Borges and Myself," explores the idea that the artist's everyday self is divided from his or her creative self. How is de Burgos's view of this division similar to Borges's? How is it different?

To Julia de Burgos
Julia de Burgos
translated by
Grace Schulman

The people are saying that I am your enemy,
That in poetry I give you to the world.

They lie, Julia de Burgos. They lie, Julia
de Burgos.
The voice that rises in my verses is not your
voice: it is my voice;
5 For you are the clothing and I am the
essence;
Between us lies the deepest abyss.

You are the bloodless doll of social lies
And I the virile spark of human truth;

You are the honey of courtly hypocrisy;
not I—
10 I bare my heart in all my poems.

You, like your world, are selfish; not I—
I gamble everything to be what I am.

You are only the serious lady. Señora.
Doña[1] Julia.
Not I. I am life. I am strength. I am woman.

15 You belong to your husband, your master.
Not I:
I belong to nobody or to all, for to all, to all
I give myself in my pure feelings and
thoughts.

You curl your hair and paint your face.
Not I:
I am curled by the wind, painted by the sun.

20 You are the lady of the house, resigned,
submissive,
Tied to the bigotry of men. Not I:
I am Rocinante,[2] bolting free, wildly
Snuffling the horizons of the justice of God.

---

1. **Doña** (dô′nyä): a Spanish title of respect given to a woman, equivalent to "Lady" or "Madam."
2. **Rocinante** (rō′sē·nän′tā): the horse that carried Don Quixote on his quests (see page 823).

Octavio Paz
b. 1914, Mexico

Octavio Paz and his wife, María José.

Octavio Paz (ôk·tä′vyô päs) was born in Mexico City into a family he calls "typically Mexican"—part Spanish, part Indian, and not very wealthy. Paz grew up in his grandfather's home, which he remembers as an old house that was falling apart, but that had a huge, overgrown garden and one large room full of books. Paz read all the books in his grandfather's library and enjoyed his crumbling surroundings.

Paz's poetic talents were recognized when he was very young. His first volume of poetry, *Forest Moon* (1933), was published just after he graduated from the National University of Mexico. By the time his next volume was published in 1937, he was well on his way to literary celebrity. Diplomatic appointments took Paz to Paris, the Far East, and India. An enthusiastic scholar, Paz studied the literature and history of every nation he visited. In form, Paz's poetry often shows the influence of European modernist or Oriental verse, but his subjects and imagery are usually rooted in the sand, stones, and soil of the Mexican landscape. With these simple images, Paz often explores difficult philosophical concepts, such as the nature of truth and reality. For example, the subject of his longest poem, *Sun Stone* (1957), is the carved stone disc that the ancient Aztecs used as their calendar. The poem deals with the complex ideas of circular time and the interrelatedness of all things. Paz is perhaps best known for his literary essays, such as those collected in *Labyrinth of Solitude*, which deals with the character of the Mexican people.

In accepting the 1990 Nobel Prize for literature, Octavio Paz recalled his early years as a writer. He claimed that he had no idea then why he wrote his poems—he only knew that he felt a deep need to write them. Only later did he come to understand that his poems were his passage to the present, his way of connecting himself to his place and to the modern world. And indeed, as one of the most influential poets and essayists in the world today, Octavio Paz has become a man of his century.

Reader's Guide

WIND AND WATER AND STONE

Background

The cycles of Mexico's social/political history and of its natural history have inspired many of Paz's poems, including the one you are about to read. Much of Mexico is dry, rocky, and sparsely forested. The effects of wind and water are easily visible in this landscape, as certain areas are worn down and other areas are built up. Mexico's great civilizations have followed similar patterns of breaking down and building up. Around the year 900, the Mayans (see page 17) were replaced by the Toltecs, who in turn were conquered by the Aztecs. Centered at Tenochtitlán (now Mexico City), which means ''stone rising in water,'' the Aztec empire fell to the Spanish conquerors early in the sixteenth century. Paz singles out the Spaniards' conquest of the Indians as the moment that the true Mexico became isolated and obscured. Mexico remained a colony of Spain until 1821, when a revolution won the new nation its independence.

Writer's Response

Think about some of the cycles in the world—the changing seasons, the water cycle, the human life cycle. Choose a cycle you have observed and write a paragraph describing it. Can you describe it in terms of birth, growth, maturity, decay, death, and rebirth?

Literary Focus

Personification is a figure of speech in which something nonhuman is given human characteristics. For example, if you say ''The breeze whispered through the trees,'' you are personifying the breeze. A breeze can't really whisper; only a human being can. If you say, ''The night is lonely,'' you are personifying the night, an inanimate or nonliving thing, by giving it feelings which it really doesn't have. Personification is an important element in the following poem by Paz.

WIND AND WATER AND STONE

Octavio Paz

translated by

MARK STRAND

❦ *As you read the poem, make a note of the words Paz uses to* **personify** *the wind, water, and stone.*

for Roger Caillois[1]

The water hollowed the stone,
the wind dispersed the water,
the stone stopped the wind.
Water and wind and stone.

5   The wind sculpted the stone,
the stone is a cup of water,
the water runs off and is wind.
Stone and wind and water.

The wind sings in its turnings,
10 the water murmurs as it goes,
the motionless stone is quiet.
Wind and water and stone.

One is the other, and is neither:
among their empty names
15 they pass and disappear,
water and stone and wind.

Robert Frerck/Woodfin Camp & Associates

Ruins of the Mayan pyramid "el Castillo,"
Mexico.

❓ *Does the* **parallelism** *of this poem remind you of other poems or stories you have read in this book? Explain.*

---

1. **Roger Caillois** (rō·zhä′ kī·wä′): French writer
   (1913–1978) who suggested that people were inspired to begin writing when they saw the natural
   markings on stones.

What deeper meanings can you see in this description of the way wind, water, and stone change and eventually disappear to be transformed into something else?

Identifying Facts

1. What does the water do in stanza 1? What does the wind do? the stone?

2. In stanza 2, what does the stone become when the wind sculpts it? What does the water become after it runs off?

3. In stanza 3, how is the stone different from the wind and water? What eventually happens to the wind and water and stone in stanza 4?

Interpreting Meanings

1. To what three scientific or natural processes do lines 1, 5, and 7 refer?

2. Given what you learned about the ancient meaning of the name *Tenochtitlán* in the Background (see page 1304), do you think the stone in this poem is more than a mere stone? Explain your answer.

3. How are the wind, water, and stone **personified** in stanzas 2 and 3?

4. What does the poem suggest about the relationship of all things in nature? What does the last stanza suggest about the ability of natural things to endure?

5. In what sense might the poem actually be about human beings or human civilizations?

Applying Meanings

Do you see human life and human civilizations as moving in cycles that are constantly repeated? In other words, does everything pass through stages of birth, growth, maturity, decay, death, rebirth, and so on? Discuss your response to Paz's ideas.

Creative Writing Response

Personifying Nature. Write a poem or paragraph in which you **personify** some element of nature, such as a tree, a flower, an animal, or the sun, moon, stars, or sea.

After you have found a subject, fill out a chart like the one below until you are satisfied with your personification. Then use the chart as you write your paragraph or poem.

Subject: Sunset

Detail	Human Quality
Appearance	Dressed in a dusky rose gown
Actions	Lingered like a lover
Feelings	Sadly ducked under the horizon

Gabriel García Márquez
b. 1928, Colombia

AP/Wide World Photos

Gabriel García Márquez (gär·sē'ä mär'kes) recalls that when he was nineteen and reading Franz Kafka's novella *The Metamorphosis* (see page 1154), he suddenly realized that the story's strangeness reminded him of tales his grandmother used to tell him. The surrealistic fiction of Kafka and the imaginative stories told by ordinary Latin Americans were to become major influences on García Márquez's fiction. But it was the second factor, the rich storytelling traditions and the unique imaginative fantasies of Latin America, that he found most valuable.

In his acceptance speech for the Nobel Prize for literature in 1982, García Márquez deplored the way Latin Americans ignore their own heritage and accept the hand-me-downs of European history and culture. He told the audience a story about a statue that stands in the main square of a Central American capital city. The statue is meant to represent the nation's president, but it is in fact a likeness of one of Napoleon's commanders that was purchased from a warehouse of secondhand sculpture in Paris. It is this kind of wholesale borrowing from the traditions of Europe that García Márquez dislikes. He wants Latin Americans to write from their own experience, with its unique blend of rituals and beliefs.

García Márquez spent the first eight years of his life with his grandparents in the small village of Aracataca, just off Colombia's northern Caribbean coast. He re-created this village, calling it Macondo, in his first short novel, *Leaf Storm* (1955), and later in his great novel *One Hundred Years of Solitude* (1967). Although Macondo is little more than a railway station set in a swampy wilderness, it seems that nearly anything that could possibly happen happens there—from the merely strange to the supernatural. With the publication of *One Hundred Years of Solitude* in English in 1970, the technique now called **magical realism** came to international attention. In García Márquez's fiction, as in that of a number of other Latin American authors, the reader is never certain about what is "real" and what is "fantasy."

Gabriel García Márquez   **1307**

Reader's Guide

THE HANDSOMEST DROWNED MAN IN THE WORLD

Background

"The Handsomest Drowned Man in the World" has many characteristics of **myth**: it features a superhuman character, supernatural events, and includes a marvelous **metamorphosis**, or transformation. This so-called "tale for children" is also enriched by **allusions** that connect it with Homer's *Odyssey,* the epic story of another "superman" who also washes ashore from the sea. Like a mythic hero, Esteban arrives mysteriously and, even though he is dead, soon becomes an important part of the villagers' lives. The story is not about Esteban, however—it is about the villagers, whose imaginations are fired by this bizarre gift from the sea.

Writer's Response

Since the village in which this story is set is on the edge of the sea, drownings would not be unusual. Stop after you finish the first two paragraphs of the story. Then freewrite your responses to the scene. Is there any hint in these opening paragraphs that the story won't be a realistic tale about a drowning?

Literary Focus

Magical realism, a literary style that was born in Latin America and has since been imitated by writers the world over, combines incredible events with realistic details and relates them all in a matter-of-fact tone. The term *magical realism* (*lo real maravilloso*) was coined in 1949 by the Cuban novelist, essayist, and musicologist Alejo Carpentier. He used the term to describe a blurring of the lines that usually separate what seems "real" to the reader from what seems imagined or "unreal" to the same reader. Carpentier believed that by incorporating magic, myth, imagination, and religion into literature, we can expand our rigid concept of "reality."

THE HANDSOMEST DROWNED MAN IN THE WORLD

Gabriel García Márquez

translated by

GREGORY RABASSA

García Márquez subtitles this story "A Tale for Children," even though it is more complex than an ordinary children's tale. In what sense must the reader become a child to accept and respond to the magical realism of the story?

Pre-Columbian gold mask. *Archaeologists believe this may have been a funerary mask.*

George Holton/Photo Researchers, Inc.

The first children who saw the dark and slinky bulge approaching through the sea let themselves think it was an enemy ship. Then they saw it had no flags or masts and they thought it was a whale. But when it was washed up on the beach, they removed the clumps of seaweed, the jellyfish tentacles, and the remains of fish and flotsam, and only then did they see that it was a drowned man.

They had been playing with him all afternoon, burying him in the sand and digging him up again, when someone chanced to see them and spread the alarm in the village. The men who carried him to the nearest house noticed that he weighed more than any dead man they had ever known, almost as much as a horse, and they said to each other that maybe he'd been floating too long and the water had got into his bones. When they laid him on the floor they said he'd been taller than all other men because there was barely enough room for him in the house, but they thought that maybe the ability to keep on growing after death was part of the nature of certain drowned men. He had the smell of the sea about him and only his shape gave one to suppose that it was the corpse of a human being, because the skin was covered with a crust of mud and scales.

They did not even have to clean off his face to know that the dead man was a stranger. The village was made up of only twenty-odd wooden houses that had stone courtyards with no flowers and which were spread about on the end of a desertlike cape. There was so little land that mothers always went about with the fear that the wind would carry off their children, and the few dead that the years had caused among them had to be thrown off the cliffs. But the sea was calm and bountiful and all the men fit into seven boats. So when they found the drowned man they simply had to look at one another to see that they were all there.

That night they did not go out to work at sea. While the men went to find out if anyone was missing in neighboring villages, the women stayed behind to care for the drowned man. They took the mud off with grass swabs, they removed the underwater stones entangled in his hair, and they scraped the crust off with tools used for scaling fish. As they were doing that they noticed that the vegetation on him came from faraway oceans and deep water and that his clothes were in tatters, as if he had sailed through labyrinths of coral. They noticed, too, that he bore his death with pride, for he did not have the lonely look of other drowned men who came out of the sea or that haggard, needy look of men who drowned in rivers. But only when they finished cleaning him off did they become aware of the kind of man he was, and it left

Quilt from Cartagena, Colombia.

❓ *Do you find the villagers' reaction to the discovery of the corpse strange? Why or why not?*

Robert Frerck/Woodfin Camp & Associates

them breathless. Not only was he the tallest, strongest, most virile, and best built man they had ever seen, but even though they were looking at him there was no room for him in their imagination.

They could not find a bed in the village large enough to lay him on, nor was there a table solid enough to use for his wake. The tallest men's holiday pants would not fit him, not the fattest ones' Sunday shirts, nor the shoes of the one with the biggest feet. Fascinated by his huge size and his beauty, the women then decided to make him some pants from a large piece of sail and a shirt from some bridal brabant linen[1] so that he could continue through his death with dignity. As they sewed, sitting in a circle and gazing at the corpse between stitches, it seemed to them that the wind had never been so steady nor the sea so restless as on that night, and they supposed that the change had something to do with the dead man. They thought that if that magnificent man had lived in the village, his house would have had the widest doors, the highest ceiling, and the strongest floor, his bedstead would have been made from a midship frame held together by iron bolts, and his wife would have been the happiest woman. They thought that he would have had so much authority that he could have drawn fish out of the sea simply by calling their names and that he would have put so much work into his land that springs would have burst forth from among the rocks so that he would have been able to plant flowers on the cliffs. They secretly compared him to their own men, thinking that for all their lives theirs were incapable of doing what he could do in one night, and they ended up dismissing them deep in their hearts as the weakest, meanest, and most useless creatures on earth. They were wandering through that maze of fantasy when the oldest woman, who as the oldest had looked upon the drowned man with more compassion than passion, sighed:

"He has the face of someone called Esteban."[2]

It was true. Most of them had only to take another look at him to see that he could not have any other name. The more stubborn among them, who were the youngest, still lived for a few hours with the illusion that when they put his clothes on and he lay among the flowers in patent leather shoes his name might be Lautaro.[3] But it was a vain illusion. There had not been enough canvas, the poorly cut and worse sewn pants were too tight, and the hidden strength of his heart popped the buttons on his shirt. After midnight the whistling of the wind died down and the sea fell into its Wednesday drowsiness. The silence put an end to any last doubts: he was Esteban. The women who had dressed him, who had combed his hair, had cut his nails and shaved him, were unable to hold back a shudder of pity when they had to resign themselves to his being dragged along the ground. It was then that they understood how unhappy he must have been with that huge body since it bothered him even after death. They could see him in life, condemned to going through doors sideways, cracking his head on crossbeams, remaining on his feet during visits, not knowing what to do with his soft, pink, sea-lion hands while the lady of the house looked for her most resistant chair and begged him, frightened to death, sit here, Esteban, please, and he, leaning against the wall, smiling, don't bother, ma'am, I'm fine where I am, his heels raw and his back roasted from having done the same thing so

---

1. **brabant** (brə·bant') **linen:** linen from Brabant, an area in Holland and Belgium known for its fine lace and cloth.

2. **Esteban** (es·te'bän): "Stephen" (Spanish); in Christian tradition, Stephen was the first martyr. He was said to have been stoned to death for his beliefs.

3. **Lautaro** (lou·tär'o)

many times whenever he paid a visit, don't bother, ma'am, I'm fine where I am, just to avoid the embarrassment of breaking up the chair, and never knowing perhaps that the ones who said don't go, Esteban, at least wait till the coffee's ready, were the ones who later on would whisper the big boob finally left, how nice, the handsome fool has gone. That was what the women were thinking beside the body a little before dawn. Later, when they covered his face with a handkerchief so that the light would not bother him, he looked so forever dead, so defenseless, so much like their men that the first furrows of tears opened in their hearts. It was one of the younger ones who began the weeping. The others, coming to, went from sighs to wails, and the more they sobbed the more they felt like weeping, because the drowned man was becoming all the more Esteban for them, and so they wept so much, for he was the most destitute, most peaceful, and most obliging man on earth, poor Esteban. So when the men returned with the news that the drowned man was not from the neighboring villages either, the women felt an opening of jubilation in the midst of their tears.

"Praise the Lord," they sighed, "he's ours!"

The men thought the fuss was only womanish frivolity. Fatigued because of the difficult nighttime inquiries, all they wanted was to get rid of the bother of the newcomer once and for all before the sun grew strong on that arid, windless day. They improvised a litter with the remains of foremasts and gaffs,[4] tying it together with rigging so that it would bear the weight of the body until they reached the cliffs. They wanted to tie the anchor from a cargo ship to him so that he would sink easily into the deepest waves, where fish are blind and divers die of nostalgia, and bad currents would not bring him back to shore, as had happened with other bodies. But the more they hurried, the more the women thought of ways to waste time. They walked about like startled hens, pecking with the sea charms[5] on their breasts, some interfering on one side to put a scapular[6] of the good wind on the drowned man, some on the other side to put a wrist compass on him, and after a great deal of *get away from there, woman, stay out of the way, look, you almost made me fall on top of the dead man,* the men began to feel mistrust in their livers and started grumbling about why so many main-altar decorations for a stranger, because no matter how many nails and holy-water jars he had on him, the sharks would chew him all the same, but the women kept piling on their junk relics, running back and forth, stumbling, while they released in sighs what they did not in tears, so that the men finally exploded with *since when has there ever been such a fuss over a drifting corpse, a drowned nobody, a piece of cold Wednesday meat.*[7] One of the women, mortified by so much lack of care, then removed the handkerchief from the dead man's face and the men were left breathless, too.

He was Esteban. It was not necessary to repeat it for them to recognize him. If they had been told Sir Walter Raleigh, even they might have been impressed with his gringo accent, the macaw on his shoulder, his cannibal-killing blunderbuss, but there could

---

4. **gaffs:** poles supporting a sail.

5. **sea charms:** magic charms that supposedly protect the wearer from dangers at sea.

6. **scapular** (skap′yə·lər): holy images on a string, worn under the clothes as a mark of religious devotion.

7. **Wednesday meat:** meat left over from Sunday dinner.

be only one Esteban in the world and there he was, stretched out like a sperm whale, shoeless, wearing the pants of an undersized child, and with those stony nails that had to be cut with a knife. They only had to take the handkerchief off his face to see that he was ashamed, that it was not his fault that he was so big or so heavy or so handsome, and if he had known that this was going to happen, he would have looked for a more discreet place to drown in, seriously, I even would have tied the anchor off a galleon around my neck and staggered off a cliff like someone who doesn't like things in order not to be upsetting people now with this Wednesday dead body, as you people say, in order not to be bothering anyone with this filthy piece of cold meat that doesn't have anything to do with me. There was so much truth in his manner that even the most mistrustful men, the ones who felt the bitterness of endless nights at sea fearing that their women would tire of dreaming about them and begin to dream of drowned men, even they and others who were harder still shuddered in the marrow of their bones at Esteban's sincerity.

That was how they came to hold the most splendid funeral they could conceive of for an abandoned drowned man. Some women who had gone to get flowers in the neighboring villages returned with other women who could not believe what they had been told, and those women went back for more flowers when they saw the dead man, and they brought more and more until there were so many flowers and so many people that it was hard to walk about. At the final moment it pained them to return him to the waters as an orphan and they chose a father and mother from among the best people, and aunts and uncles and cousins, so that through him all the inhabitants of the village became kinsmen. Some sailors who heard the weeping from a distance went off course, and people heard of one who had himself tied to the mainmast, remembering ancient fables about sirens.[8] While they fought for the privilege of carrying him on their shoulders along the steep escarpment by the cliffs, men and women became aware for the first time of the desolation of their streets, the dryness of their courtyards, the narrowness of their dreams as they faced the splendor and beauty of their drowned man. They let him go without an anchor so that he could come back if he wished and whenever he wished, and they all held their breath for the fraction of centuries the body took to fall into the abyss. They did not need to look at one another to realize that they were no longer all present, that they would never be. But they also knew that everything would be different from then on, that their houses would have wider doors, higher ceilings, and stronger floors so that Esteban's memory could go everywhere without bumping into beams and so that no one in the future would dare whisper the big boob finally died, too bad, the handsome fool has finally died, because they were going to paint their house fronts gay colors to make Esteban's memory eternal and they were going to break their backs digging for springs among the stones and planting flowers on the cliffs so that in future years at dawn the passengers on great liners would awaken, suffocated by the smell

---

8. **sirens:** in Greek mythology, beautiful but destructive creatures, half-woman and half-bird, whose seductive songs lured sailors to turn their ships onto the rocky coasts; Odysseus, hero of Homer's *Odyssey,* filled his crew's ears with wax so that they could pass the sirens safely. But Odysseus wanted to hear their songs. He had the crew tie him to the ship's mast so that he could listen to the sirens' songs yet not turn the boat onto the rocks.

Gabriel García Márquez   **1313**

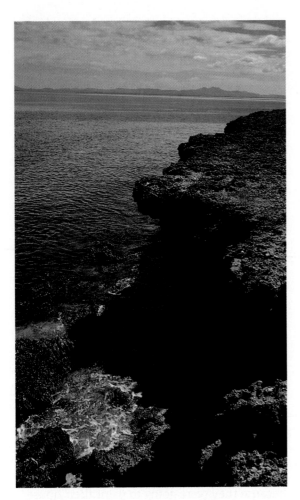

of gardens on the high seas, and the captain would have to come down from the bridge in his dress uniform, with his astrolabe,[9] his pole star,[10] and his row of war medals, and, pointing to the promontory of roses on the horizon, he would say in fourteen languages, look there, where the wind is so peaceful now that it's gone to sleep beneath the beds, over there, where the sun's so bright that the sunflowers don't know which way to turn, yes, over there, that's Esteban's village.

---

9. **astrolabe:** instrument that can find a star's altitude and help navigators determine their position at sea.

10. **pole star:** Polaris, or the North Star; it is used by navigators in the northern hemisphere to determine their location because it remains almost fixed throughout the night.

Medialuna Bay, Colombia.

Loren McIntyre/Woodfin Camp & Associates

First Thoughts

What image of the drowned man is strongest in your mind? How did you feel about some of the realistic passages describing Esteban?

Identifying Facts

1. What do details such as the galleon, the blunderbuss, and the astrolabe suggest about the time period of the story?

2. What is unusual about the drowned man? How do the men explain his unusual characteristics?

3. What name do the villagers give the drowned man? Why?

4. How does the village change after the drowned man washes ashore?

Interpreting Meanings

1. **Setting** is a major element in this story, as it is in all of García Márquez's fiction. Briefly describe this story's setting and

explain how it contributes to the **magical realism** of the story.

2. A strong **theme** is suggested by the fabulous events of this story and the subsequent changes in the village. What does this story reveal about the universal need for heroes and great dreams?

3. This story is told from the **third-person point of view**, but Esteban becomes so real in the minds of the villagers that they imagine him speaking in the **first person**. When Esteban speaks using the pronoun "I" (see pages 1311 and 1312), does he become more real to you?

Applying Meanings

The events of this story make the villagers see "for the first time the desolation of their streets, the dryness of their courtyards," and "the narrowness of their dreams." What experiences in real life might make people look at their lives in a different way and see the shortcomings of how they live?

Creative Writing Response

Changing the Premise. If the man who washed to shore had been alive, do you think the outcome of this story would have been the same? Would the villagers have extended as much love and hospitality toward a live man as they did toward the dead man? Write a story using the same setting, but bring Esteban to life. Be sure to explain who Esteban is and how he happened to wash up on the shore of this village. Feel free to use elements of **magical realism** in your story.

Critical Writing Response

Analyzing Magical Realism. In a brief essay, analyze García Márquez's use of **magical realism** in this story. Before you write, review the story to locate some particularly realistic details. Then locate some of the story's fantastic elements. You might organize your details on a chart like the one below.

Fantastic Events	Realistic Details

At the end of your essay, state your general response to the use of magical realism. Do you like this blurring of fantasy and reality? Or do you prefer either pure fantasy or pure realism?

Margaret Atwood
b. 1939, Canada

Margaret Atwood, one of Canada's most prominent writers, began writing when she was five years old. Except for a "dark period between the ages of eight and sixteen," she has been writing ever since—poetry, novels, children's books, essays, criticism, and television plays. When asked by an interviewer why she writes, Atwood replied, "It's a human activity. I think the real question is 'Why doesn't everyone?'"

Atwood spent a good portion of her childhood in the Canadian wilderness. Her father, an entomologist, or one who studies insects, often spent weeks working in remote areas. Because Margaret was part of these family trips, she did not attend a full year of school until she was in the eighth grade. Yet she graduated from the University of Toronto and received a master's degree in English literature from Radcliffe College.

Atwood is often credited with helping (some say single-handedly) to define Canada's literary identity. For years, Canadian literature had been viewed as indistinguishable from that of Britain or the United States. Atwood corrected this view in her guide to Canadian literature *Survival* (1972), by showing that survival is the central theme in Canadian writing. In Atwood's fiction, animals, women, and Canada itself are all seen as victims as they struggle to survive in a hostile world.

Atwood often uses nature metaphorically in her writing. In her novel *Surfacing* (1972), a woman returns to the Canadian wilderness of her youth to search for her missing father. Here, the natural landscape is a reservoir of mythic meaning, representing childhood innocence as well as an escape from commercialization. In her novel *The Handmaid's Tale* (1986), Atwood reworks the science-fiction genre from a feminist perspective. She envisions a United States run by a puritanical dictatorship that seeks to control women and their reproductive capabilities. Whether she is dealing with love, politics, ecology, or feminism, Atwood says, "I'm interested in edges, undertows, permutations, in taking things that might be viewed as eccentric or marginal and pulling them into the center."

Reader's Guide

ELEGY FOR THE GIANT TORTOISES

Background

The giant tortoises that Atwood writes about in "Elegy for the Giant Tortoises" are magnificent creatures that weigh over five hundred pounds and live over one hundred and fifty years. Millions of these animals used to be found on thousands of islands in the Pacific and Indian oceans. During the seventeenth, eighteenth, and nineteenth centuries, however, the crews of whaling ships and other vessels slaughtered so many tortoises that some species became extinct and others still teeter on the brink of extinction. Today, scientists are working on breeding programs to save the giant tortoises living on the Galápagos Islands off the coast of Ecuador.

The poem that you are about to read is from the collection *The Animals in That Country* (1968), which vividly demonstrates how human civilization can damage and destroy the natural world. In the poem, Atwood mentions three other creatures that became extinct or are threatened with extinction—the dodo, the passenger pigeon, and the whooping crane. Dodo birds had disappeared by 1680, chiefly because Europeans hunted them for sport. In colonial times, the passenger pigeon population in North America numbered in the billions, and flocks passing overhead would block out the sun. But the birds were so widely hunted by America's settlers that in 1914 the last passenger pigeon died in a Cincinnati zoo. The breeding grounds of the whooping crane have been so threatened by development that this bird has joined numerous other animals on the list of endangered species.

Writer's Response

Briefly write down your feelings about extinct or endangered animals like the giant tortoises. Do you think they should be protected? Or is extinction just part of life and something we shouldn't worry about?

Literary Focus

An **elegy** is a poem of mourning, usually over the death of a person. An elegy may also be a lament over the passing of life or beauty, or it may be a meditation on the nature of death. Elegies are usually formal in language and structure, and solemn or even melancholy in tone.

ELEGY FOR THE GIANT TORTOISES

Margaret Atwood

The title says that this is an elegy for giant tortoises. Who or what else might it be an elegy for?

Let others pray for the passenger pigeon,
the dodo, the whooping crane, the Eskimo:
everyone must specialize

I will confine myself to a meditation
5   upon the giant tortoises
withering finally on a remote island.

I concentrate in subway stations,
in parks, I can't quite see them,
they move to the peripheries of my eyes

10 but on the last day they will be there;
already the event
like a wave traveling shapes vision:

on the road where I stand they will materialize,
plodding past me in a straggling line
15 awkward without water

their small heads pondering
from side to side, their useless armor
sadder than tanks and history,

in their closed gaze ocean and sunlight paralyzed,
20 lumbering up the steps, under the archways
toward the square glass altars

where the brittle gods are kept,
the relics of what we have destroyed,
our holy and obsolete symbols.

Giant tortoise.

First Thoughts

Do you think acts of imagination like the speaker's (or like Atwood's in creating this poem) can help save the tortoises or restore "what we have destroyed"?

Identifying Facts

1. In the first stanza, what does the speaker say she will *not* pray for? Why not?

2. Where does the speaker have trouble seeing the tortoises? When is she sure "they will be there"?

3. Where does the speaker say the tortoises will appear? Where will they go?

Interpreting Meanings

1. Why do you think Atwood includes the Eskimo in the first stanza?

2. On one level, what "last day" is the speaker referring to in line 10? The term "last day" might also refer to Judgment Day, when the dead are able to rise and be judged by God. If so, what judgment on humanity does the poem suggest may be made on that day?

3. What do the "tanks and history" in line 18 bring to your mind? What does the speaker mean when she says that the armor of the tortoises is "useless" and "sadder than tanks and history"?

4. Reread the last five lines of the poem carefully. What actual buildings might these lines refer to? What other building is Atwood comparing them to in using words like *archways, altars,* and *gods*?

5. What religious **images** can you find in the poem? What message about our treatment of nature does this imagery suggest?

6. Do you think that this is an **elegy** only for the tortoises, or is it also for humans? Explain.

Applying Meanings

What are some of the environmental concerns that you think we need to address? Make a list of four important environmental concerns and discuss them with the class.

Creative Writing Response

Describing Visual Images. If you were going to illustrate this poem, what **images** would you concentrate on? In a few sentences, cite the lines that contain these images and describe how you would depict them. You might want to draw a picture to accompany your description.

Critical Writing Response

Writing About a Poem's Theme. The **theme** is the central insight about life or the world revealed in a work of literature. A possible theme of this poem is: Human beings must think beyond themselves and imagine the lives of other creatures so that we do not destroy them.

In a brief essay, either support or refute this theme, citing details from the poem to support your choice. If you disagree with this theme, suggest a more accurate one in your essay.

Jamaica Kincaid
b. 1949, Antigua

Sigrid Estrada

Over the kitchen table in the Vermont home that Jamaica Kincaid shares with her American-born husband and children is a map of the island of Antigua (än·tē′gwə). It serves as a constant reminder of the tiny Caribbean island where Kincaid grew up and where she still sets most of her fiction.

Born Elaine Potter Richardson to an Antiguan couple of African descent, Kincaid grew up in St. John's, Antigua's largest city. Antigua was still a British colony during Kin-

caid's childhood, and she came to hate the European colonialism that had exploited her people for so many centuries.

At school Kincaid was a bright but unruly pupil, often punished for her outspokenness. Once, her punishment was to copy long passages from John Milton's epic *Paradise Lost*, a work she can now quote at length.

After attending college in New Hampshire, Kincaid returned to New York City and began writing for a teenage girls' magazine, using her pen name for the first time. Soon Kincaid published her first story, "Girl," in *The New Yorker.* The story consists of a single long sentence of instructions given by a mother to a daughter who is possibly, from the mother's point of view, headed for rebellion and trouble.

One of the central subjects of Kincaid's fiction is the parent-child relationship and the problems her rebellious heroines have with their worried mothers. Kincaid also writes about the anger that West Indians of African descent feel about their colonial past. "As I sit here enjoying myself to a degree," Kincaid told *New York Times* interviewer Leslie Garis, "I never give up thinking about the way I came into the world, how my ancestors came from Africa to the West Indies as slaves. I just could never forget it."

Reader's Guide

A WALK TO THE JETTY
from Annie John

Background

Antigua, the main island of the nation of Antigua and Barbuda, was a British colony for over three hundred years. The British forcibly brought people from Africa to work as slaves on the island's sugar plantations. Today the descendants of these Africans make up most of Antigua's population. Antigua won its independence in 1981, but British influences are still strong on the island. The people speak English and many belong to the Anglican (Episcopalian) Church. The school Jamaica Kincaid attended as a girl was modeled on British schools of the time—boys and girls were educated separately, uniforms were required, and a British curriculum, especially in literature, was stressed.

The selection you are about to read is taken from the last part of the last chapter of Kincaid's coming-of-age novel *Annie John*. In this section of the novel, the young narrator is about to leave Antigua by boat for England.

Writer's Response

When you think back over the years of your childhood, what incidents and images come to your mind? Make a few notes about your strongest memories. Which memories make you happy? Which ones make you sad or angry?

Literary Focus

Much of twentieth-century literature deals with **internal conflicts**, rather than with action-packed **external conflicts**. Annie John, the narrator of this selection, has all kinds of conflicts with other characters throughout the book, but in this excerpt, we see only her internal conflicts.

A WALK TO THE JETTY
from Annie John
Jamaica Kincaid

As you read, think about why the narrator is leaving her home and how she feels about leaving.

My mother had arranged with a stevedore[1] to take my trunk to the jetty ahead of me. At ten o'clock on the dot, I was dressed, and we set off for the jetty. An hour after that, I would board a launch that would take me out to sea, where I then would board the ship. Starting out, as if for old time's sake and without giving it a thought, we lined up in the old way: I walking between my mother and my father. I loomed way above my father and could see the top of his head. We must have made a strange sight: a grown girl all dressed up in the middle of a morning, in the middle of the week, walking in step in the middle between her two parents, for people we didn't know stared at us. It was all of half an hour's walk from our house to the jetty, but I was passing through most of the years of my life. We passed by the house where Miss Dulcie, the seamstress that I had been apprenticed to for a time, lived, and just as I was passing by, a wave of bad feeling for her came over me, because I suddenly remembered that the months I spent with her all she had me do was sweep the floor, which was always full of threads and pins and needles, and I never seemed

Antiguan landscape.
What happens to the narrator as she passes in front of the seamstress's shop? How have her feelings about the seamstress changed?

---

1. **stevedore** (stē′və·dôr′): a person who loads and unloads cargo on a ship.

to sweep it clean enough to please her. Then she would send me to the store to buy buttons or thread, though I was only allowed to do this if I was given a sample of the button or thread, and then she would find fault even though they were an exact match of the samples she had given me. And all the while she said to me, "A girl like you will never learn to sew properly, you know." At the time, I don't suppose I minded it, because it was customary to treat the first-year apprentice with such scorn, but now I

placed on the dustheap of my life Miss Dulcie and everything that I had had to do with her.

We were soon on the road that I had taken to school, to church, to Sunday school, to choir practice, to Brownie meetings, to Girl Guide meetings, to meet a friend. I was five years old when I first walked on this road unaccompanied by someone to hold my hand. My mother had placed three pennies in my little basket, which was a duplicate of her bigger basket, and sent me to the chemist's shop[2] to buy a pennyworth of senna leaves, a pennyworth of eucalyptus leaves, and a pennyworth of camphor. She then instructed me on what side of the road to walk, where to make a turn, where to cross, how to look carefully before I crossed, and if I met anyone that I knew to politely pass greetings and keep on my way. I was wearing a freshly ironed yellow dress that had printed on it scenes of acrobats flying through the air and swinging on a trapeze. I had just had a bath, and after it, instead of powdering me with my baby-smelling talcum powder, my mother had, as a special favor, let me use her own talcum powder, which smelled quite perfumy and came in a can that had painted on it people going out to dinner in nineteenth-century London and was called Mazie. How it pleased me to walk out the door and bend my head down to sniff at myself and see that I smelled just like my mother. I went to the chemist's shop, and he had to come from behind the counter and bend down to hear what it was that I wanted to buy, my voice was so little and timid then. I went back just the way I had come, and when I walked into the yard and presented my basket with its three

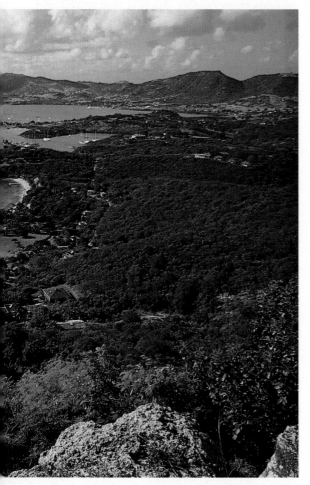

---

2. **chemist's shop:** the British term for a pharmacy or drugstore.

packages to my mother, her eyes filled with tears and she swooped me up and held me high in the air and said that I was wonderful and good and that there would never be anybody better. If I had just conquered Persia, she couldn't have been more proud of me.

We passed by our church—the church in which I had been christened and received and had sung in the junior choir. We passed by a house in which a girl I used to like and was sure I couldn't live without had lived. Once, when she had mumps, I went to visit her against my mother's wishes, and we sat on her bed and ate the cure of roasted, buttered sweet potatoes that had been placed on her swollen jaws, held there by a piece of white cloth. I don't know how, but my mother found out about it, and I don't know how, but she put an end to our friendship. Shortly after, the girl moved with her family across the sea to somewhere else. We passed the doll store, where I would go with my mother when I was little and point out the doll I wanted that year for Christmas. We passed the store where I bought the much-fought-over shoes I wore to church to be received in. We passed the bank. On my sixth birthday, I was given, among other things, the present of a sixpence. My mother and I then went to this bank, and with the sixpence I opened my own savings account. I was given a little gray book with my name in big letters on it, and in the balance column it said "6d." Every Saturday morning after that, I was given a sixpence—later a shilling, and later a two-and-sixpence piece—and I would take it to the bank for deposit. I had never been allowed to withdraw even a farthing[3] from my bank account until just a

few weeks before I was to leave; then the whole account was closed out, and I received from the bank the sum of six pounds ten shillings and two and a half pence.

We passed the office of the doctor who told my mother three times that I did not need glasses, that if my eyes were feeling weak a glass of carrot juice a day would make them strong again. This happened when I was eight. And so every day at recess I would run to my school gate and meet my mother, who was waiting for me with a glass of juice from carrots she had just grated and then squeezed, and I would drink it and then run back to meet my chums. I knew there was nothing at all wrong with my eyes, but I had recently read a story in *The Schoolgirl's Own Annual* in which the heroine, a girl a few years older than I was then, cut such a figure to my mind with the way she was always adjusting her small, round, horn-rimmed glasses that I felt I must have a pair exactly like them. When it became clear that I didn't need glasses, I began to complain about the glare of the sun being too much for my eyes, and I walked around with my hands shielding them—especially in my mother's presence. My mother then bought for me a pair of sunglasses with the exact horn-rimmed frames I wanted, and how I enjoyed the gestures of blowing on the lenses, wiping them with the hem of my uniform, adjusting the glasses when they slipped down my nose, and just removing them from their case and putting them on. In three weeks, I grew tired of them and they found a nice resting place in a drawer, along with some other things that at one time or another I couldn't live without.

We passed the store that sold only grooming aids, all imported from England. This store had in it a large porcelain dog—white, with black spots all over and a red ribbon

---

3. **farthing:** a former small British coin worth a fourth of a penny.

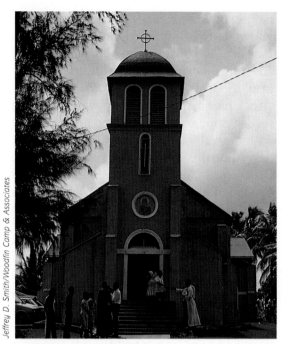

Jeffrey D. Smith/Woodfin Camp & Associates

Sunday at church, Antigua.

of satin tied around its neck. The dog sat in front of a white porcelain bowl that was always filled with fresh water, and it sat in such a way that it looked as if it had just taken a long drink. When I was a small child, I would ask my mother, if ever we were near this store, to please take me to see the dog, and I would stand in front of it, bent over slightly, my hands resting on my knees, and stare at it and stare at it. I thought this dog more beautiful and more real than any actual dog I had ever seen or any actual dog I would ever see. I must have outgrown my interest in the dog, for when it disappeared I never asked what became of it. We passed the library, and if there was anything on this walk that I might have wept over leaving, this most surely would have been the thing. My mother had been a member of the library long before I was born. And since she took me everywhere with her when I was quite little, when she went to the library she

took me along there, too. I would sit in her lap very quietly as she read books that she did not want to take home with her. I could not read the words yet, but just the way they looked on the page was interesting to me. Once, a book she was reading had a large picture of a man in it, and when I asked her who he was she told me that he was Louis Pasteur and that the book was about his life. It stuck in my mind, because she said it was because of him that she boiled my milk to purify it before I was allowed to drink it, that it was his idea, and that that was why the process was called pasteurization. One of the things I had put away in my mother's old trunk in which she kept all my childhood things was my library card. At that moment, I owed sevenpence in overdue fees.

As I passed by all these places, it was as if I were in a dream, for I didn't notice the people coming and going in and out of them, I didn't feel my feet touch ground, I didn't even feel my own body—I just saw these places as if they were hanging in the air, not having top or bottom, and as if I had gone in and out of them all in the same moment. The sun was bright; the sky was blue and just above my head. We then arrived at the jetty.

My heart now beat fast, and no matter how hard I tried, I couldn't keep my mouth from falling open and my nostrils from spreading to the ends of my face. My old fear of slipping between the boards of the jetty and falling into the dark-green water where the dark-green eels lived came over me. When my father's stomach started to go bad, the doctor had recommended a walk every evening right after he ate his dinner. Sometimes he would take me with him. When he took me with him, we usually went to the jetty, and there he would sit and talk to the night watchman about cricket or some other thing that didn't interest me, because it was not personal; they didn't talk about their wives, or their children, or their parents, or about any of their likes and dislikes. They talked about things in such a strange way, and I didn't see what they found funny, but sometimes they made each other laugh so much that their guffaws would bound out to sea and send back an echo. I was always sorry when we got to the jetty and saw that the night watchman on duty was the one he enjoyed speaking to; it was like being locked up in a book filled with numbers and diagrams and what-ifs. For the thing about not being able to understand and enjoy what they were saying was I had nothing to take my mind off my fear of slipping in between the boards of the jetty.

Now, too, I had nothing to take my mind off what was happening to me. My mother and my father—I was leaving them forever. My home on an island—I was leaving it forever. What to make of everything? I felt a familiar hollow space inside. I felt I was being held down against my will. I felt I was burning up from head to toe. I felt that someone was tearing me up into little pieces and soon I would be able to see all the little pieces as they floated out into nothing in the deep blue sea. I didn't know whether to laugh or cry. I could see that it would be better not to think too clearly about any one thing. The launch was being made ready to take me, along with some other passengers, out to the ship that was anchored in the sea. My father paid our fares, and we joined a line of people waiting to board. My mother checked my bag to make sure that I had my passport, the money she had given me, and a sheet of paper placed between some pages in my Bible on which were written the names of the relatives—people I had not known existed—with whom I would live in England. Across from the jetty was a wharf, and some stevedores were loading and unloading barges. I don't know why seeing that struck me so, but suddenly a wave of strong feeling came over me, and my heart swelled with a great gladness as the words "I shall never see this again" spilled out inside me. But then, just as quickly, my heart shriveled up and the words "I shall never see this again" stabbed at me. I don't know what stopped me from falling in a heap at my parents' feet.

When we were all on board, the launch headed out to sea. Away from the jetty, the water became the customary blue, and the launch left a wide path in it that looked like a road. I passed by sounds and smells that were so familiar that I had long ago stopped paying any attention to them. But now here they were, and the ever-present "I shall never see this again" bobbed up and down inside me. There was the sound of the seagull diving down into the water and coming up with something silverish in its mouth. There was the smell of the sea and the sight of small pieces of rubbish floating around in it. There were boats filled with fishermen coming in early. There was the sound of their voices as they shouted greetings to each other. There was the hot sun, there was the blue sea, there was the blue sky. Not very far away, there was the white sand of the shore, with the run-down houses all crowded in next to each other, for in some places only poor people lived near the shore. I was seated in the launch between my parents, and when I realized that I was gripping their hands tightly I glanced quickly to see if they were looking at me with scorn, for I felt sure that they must have known of my never-see-this-again feelings. But instead my father kissed me on the forehead and my mother kissed me on the mouth, and they both gave over their hands to me, so that I could grip them as much as I wanted. I was on the verge of feeling that it had all been a mistake, but I remembered that I wasn't a child anymore, and that now when I made up my mind about something I had to see it through. At that moment, we came to the ship, and that was that.

The goodbyes had to be quick, the captain said. My mother introduced herself to him and then introduced me. She told him to keep an eye on me, for I had never gone this far away from home on my own. She gave him a letter to pass on to the captain of the next ship that I would board in Barbados. They walked me to my cabin, a small space that I would share with someone else—a woman I did not know. I had never before slept in a room with someone I did not know. My father kissed me goodbye and told me to be good and to write home often. After he said this, he looked at me, then looked at the floor and swung his left foot, then looked at me again. I could see that he wanted to say something else, something that he had never said to me before, but then he just turned and walked away. My mother said, "Well," and then she threw her

arms around me. Big tears streamed down her face, and it must have been that—for I could not bear to see my mother cry—which started me crying, too. She then tightened her arms around me and held me to her close, so that I felt that I couldn't breathe. With that, my tears dried up and I was suddenly on my guard. "What does she want now?" I said to myself. Still holding me close to her, she said, in a voice that raked across my skin, "It doesn't matter what you do or where you go, I'll always be your mother and this will always be your home."

I dragged myself away from her and backed off a little, and then I shook myself, as if to wake myself out of a stupor. We looked at each other for a long time with smiles on our faces, but I know the opposite of that was in my heart. As if responding to some invisible cue, we both said, at the very same moment, "Well." Then my mother turned around and walked out the cabin door. I stood there for I don't know how long, and then I remembered that it was customary to stand on deck and wave to your relatives who were returning to shore. From the deck, I could not see my father, but I could see my mother facing the ship, her eyes searching to pick me out. I removed from my bag a red cotton handkerchief that she had earlier given me for this purpose, and I waved it wildly in the air. Recognizing me immediately, she waved back just as wildly, and we continued to do this until she became just a dot in the matchbox-size launch swallowed up in the big blue sea.

I went back to my cabin and lay down on my berth. Everything trembled as if it had a spring at its very center. I could hear the small waves lap-lapping around the ship. They made an unexpected sound, as if a vessel filled with liquid had been placed on its side and now was slowly emptying out.

Jamaica Kincaid **1327**

The narrator has conflicting feelings about her parents and her home. Which of her feelings came through most strongly for you?

Identifying Facts

1. As the narrator walks to the jetty she passes many places that stimulate memories from her childhood. Which places bring back good memories and which evoke bad memories?
2. Which place does the narrator most regret leaving?
3. When the narrator reaches the jetty, what old fear comes over her again?

Interpreting Meanings

1. What does the story about the eyeglasses reveal about the narrator's personality? What do her comments about the library reveal about her own **character**?
2. Why do you think the narrator suddenly notices sounds and smells that she never paid attention to before?
3. What **internal conflict** does the narrator experience about leaving the island? Is it resolved?
4. Reread the passage describing the father's actions after he kisses his daughter goodbye. What **internal conflict** do you think he is feeling? What do you think he wants to say to Annie John?
5. Based on what her daughter tells you, how would you describe the **character** of Annie's mother? What conflicting feelings does Annie seem to have toward this mother who obviously adores her?
6. The last sentence in this selection could be interpreted as a literal description of the ship Annie John is on. But suppose it could also be interpreted **metaphorically**—that is, figuratively. What might the writer really be talking about when she describes a vessel "emptying out"?

Applying Meanings

Do the narrator's feelings about her childhood remind you of any of your own feelings? At what point in her narrative did you most identify with her?

Creative Writing Response

Describing a Place. Suppose you are leaving the place where you live and that you know you will not return for a long time. Write a brief description of the spots you will remember and of the experiences and people you associate with them. You might want to imitate the style of this story and describe this place as if you are taking a last walk, perhaps to a bus or train station. Before you write, collect your details in a word cluster or list.

Critical Writing Response

Analyzing an Internal Conflict. Discrepancies, or differences, between a character's thoughts, words, and actions are good indications of an **internal conflict**. In a brief essay, analyze the narrator's internal conflicts. Discuss her personality, her attitudes, and the differences between her thoughts and actions. Support general statements with specific details from the selection. As a first step, you might find it helpful to list details on a chart like the one below to help you see and understand Annie's internal conflicts.

Annie's Remarks	
Annie's Actions	
Annie's Thoughts	
What Discrepancies Reveal	

SEEING CONNECTIONS

Tales of the Islands *by Derek Walcott*

Few people could have predicted that the tiny Caribbean island of St. Lucia, where the predominant language is French creole, would produce a world-famous English-language poet. Yet Jamaica Kincaid's fellow West Indies writer Derek Walcott (born 1930) has achieved international fame for his poetry. His most recent work, *Omeros* (1990), is a book-length narrative poem loosely based on Homer's epic poem the *Odyssey.* (*Omeros* is Greek for "Homer.")

Walcott makes his permanent home in the West Indies, although he has frequently traveled abroad. The islands' exotic beauty and their tragic colonial history (St. Lucia is a former French colony) are central subjects of his work. Many critics suggest that Walcott is torn between cultures: Caribbean and British, black and white. But Walcott sees his own mixed racial heritage as symbolic of the New World.

In the following poem, the final sonnet from a work entitled *Tales of the Islands,* Walcott describes his mixed feelings upon leaving St. Lucia for the first time. The poem's **epigraph**, or opening quotation— "*Adieu foulard*" (ə·dyo͞o′ fo͞o·lär′)—comes from a Creole folk song traditionally sung when people leave St. Lucia. The song bids *adieu,* or "farewell," to the *foulard,* or neckerchief, that is part of St. Lucia's national costume. As you read the poem, compare Walcott's tone and mood to that expressed by Jamaica Kincaid in "A Walk to the Jetty." How are these farewells alike and different?

Sunset in St. Lucia.

Timothy O'Keefe/Bruce Coleman, Inc.

Chapter X
"Adieu foulard . . ."
from Tales of the Islands
Derek Walcott

I watched the island narrowing the fine
Writing of foam around the precipices then
The roads as small and casual as twine
Thrown on its mountains; I watched till the plane
5 Turned to the final north and turned above
The open channel with the gray sea between
The fishermen's islets until all that I love
Folded in cloud; I watched the shallow green
That broke in places where there would be reef,
10 The silver glinting on the fuselage, each mile
Dividing us and all fidelity strained
Till space would snap it. Then, after a while
I thought of nothing, nothing, I prayed, would change;
When we set down at Seawell it had rained.

Léopold Sédar Senghor
b. 1906, Senegal

Peter Jordan/Time Magazine

Léopold Sédar Senghor (lā·ô·pôld′ sā·dàr′ sä*r*gôr′) has had a remarkable career as a poet, literary critic, political thinker, four-term president of Senegal, and spokesperson for the **négritude** movement. He was also the first black African to join the faculty of a French university and the first black member of the prestigious French Academy. Born and educated at a time when the colonizers of French West Africa were encouraging Africans to think of themselves as French, Senghor truly believed that he was a Frenchman who just happened to be black. When he went to Paris to study, however, he realized that the French would never accept him as one of their countrymen. He also realized that he was proud of his own culture and history and afraid that

both would soon disappear in the wake of European colonialism. He shared these thoughts with other black writers in Paris, such as Aimé Césaire and Birago Diop. From their discussions the ideas of négritude emerged.

Just as many African American leaders urge members of their community to learn about and take pride in their African heritage, so did the proponents of négritude assert the value and beauty of African culture. The négritude writers drew on African history and art to celebrate black civilizations, and sought to bring African accomplishments before the eyes of the world.

After serving in World War II and helping the French Resistance fight the Nazis, Senghor was one of two West Africans elected to represent his homeland in the French National Assembly. Here he helped draft the new constitutions that gradually brought independence to France's West African possessions. During the 1950s, he was a leading spokesperson for African unity and independence achieved through peaceful means.

In 1960, Senghor became the first president of the new nation of Senegal. Displaying as much skill in politics as he did in poetry, he was elected to the presidency four more times. Today Senegal is recognized as one of Africa's most democratic nations, and Senghor is hailed as a great statesperson, poet, and political and literary theorist.

Reader's Guide

AND WE SHALL BE STEEPED

Background

Senghor cofounded the black cultural journal *Presence Africaine,* and stressed an "African presence" in all of his poetry. Although the poems are written in French, their images are drawn from Africa's landscape and history. Their sound—especially when read aloud in the original French—is reminiscent of the powerful, rhythmic chanting of the traditional West African storytellers known as *griots* (grē′ōz). Capturing an "African sound" was so important to Senghor that he specified the traditional African musical instrument that should ideally accompany each poem's recitation. He chose the *khalam* (khä′läm), a four-stringed African guitar, as the instrument to accompany "And We Shall Be Steeped."

Writer's Response

Make a list of reasons why you are proud of your heritage—either as an American or as a member of an ethnic group.

Literary Focus

Imagery is language that appeals to the senses. While most **images** appeal to our sense of sight (*sparkling smile*), some may also appeal to our senses of hearing (*joyous laughter*), smell (*sweaty socks*), touch (*slimy slug*), and taste (*bitter tea*). In the poem you are about to read, Senghor uses a series of vivid images to help "steep" the reader in the "presence of Africa."

AND WE SHALL BE STEEPED

Léopold Sédar Senghor

translated by

JOHN REED AND CLIVE WAKE

As you read this poem, try to recreate in your mind the sights, smells, and sounds of Senghor's imagery.

Sassoonian/Art Resource, New York

For Khalam

And we shall be steeped my dear in the presence
    of Africa.
Furniture from Guinea and Congo,[1] heavy and
    polished, somber and serene.
On the walls, pure primordial masks distant and
    yet present.
Stools of honor for hereditary guests, for the
    Princes of the High Lands.[2]

5   Wild perfumes, thick mats of silence
Cushions of shade and leisure, the noise of a
    wellspring of peace.
Classic words. In a distance, antiphonal singing
    like Sudanese[3] cloths
And then, friendly lamp, your kindness to soothe
    this obsessive presence
White black and red, oh red as the African soil.

---

1. **Guinea (gin′ē) and Congo:** here, not just the present-day nations of Guinea and Congo, but the entire West African coast from Senegal's Cape Verde
   peninsula to southern Angola, and the entire river
   basin of the Congo, West Africa's longest river.
2. **hereditary . . . Lands:** honored ancestors and rulers of great African kingdoms of centuries past.
3. **antiphonal (an·tif′ə·nəl) . . . Sudanese:** alternately
   sung and chanted, like traditional African ritual
   songs or poems; here, Sudanese refers not to the
   present-day nation of Sudan but to the western
   portion of the fertile savanna, or plain, stretching
   across all of Africa just below the Sahara.

**Ceremonial mask from the Ibo people
of West Africa.**

First Thoughts

Which **image** of the "presence of Africa" could you see, smell, or feel most clearly?

Identifying Facts

1. In the first line, what does the speaker say about "the presence of Africa"? What objects illustrate this presence in later lines?

2. What adjectives describe the African presence in the last line?

Interpreting Meanings

1. In what way are the objects in lines 2, 3, and 4 related to one another? Which **images** in later lines appeal to senses other than sight?

2. The colors in the final line refer to Africa's soils, but they may also refer to the white colonists, the black Africans, and the bloodshed between them. In this context, what earlier **image** does the "red" in the last line contrast with? What does the contrast stress about African history?

3. What overall attitude toward African culture and history does the poem convey?

4. The translators of this poem chose English words that are faithful both to the meaning and musical sounds of the original French. Find examples of **alliteration** and **assonance** that help make the poem musical.

Applying Meanings

What are some of the benefits of taking pride in one's racial or ethnic heritage? Are there also drawbacks? If so, what are they?

Creative Writing Response

Writing About Heritage. Write a poem or a paragraph about your racial or ethnic heritage or your heritage as an American. Include concrete **images** like Senghor does, and choose images that will convey your thoughts and feelings about your heritage.

Critical Writing Response

Writing About Négritude. Senghor's poem is an example of the work inspired by the **négritude** movement, which encouraged black writers to turn to African culture and history as a source of inspiration and pride. In a brief essay, show how this poem illustrates the ideas of négritude. Discuss specific **images** and the attitudes toward Africa that they convey. Before you begin writing, you may find it helpful to list the specific images that you plan to discuss and the attitudes that they convey.

Abioseh Nicol
b. 1924, Sierra Leone

Like many other African writers, Abioseh Nicol (äb·ē·ō′se nē′kōl) studied abroad. When he returned to his native Sierra Leone after years in Britain, he wrote "Upcountry," a poem contrasting the rural villages to the new cities sprouting up along the Guinea coast. He felt that the heart and spirit of the "real Africa" still survived only in the countryside. This is why he sets most of his stories in small, rural villages. Best known for his 1965 collection, *The Truly Married Woman and Other Stories*, Nicol is regarded as one of Africa's best short-story writers.

Despite active careers in public service, health, science, and education, Nicol has always found time to write. In the 1950s, when he was a student in Britain, most books about Africa were written by Europeans. While Nicol recognized the skill of some of these authors, he also saw serious flaws in their portraits of native Africans. It was in part to correct these flaws that he took to writing fiction. He felt that African characters were too often portrayed in disparaging ways, and he sought to correct this slanted view.

In addition to his writing, Nicol excelled in a wide range of fields and made outstanding contributions in all of them. The son of a pharmacist in Freetown, Sierra Leone, Davidson Nicol (Abioseh is a pen name) won a scholarship to study medicine at the University of London. He later became the first black African to receive a fellowship at Cambridge University. In medical circles he won fame for his research into the structure of insulin, the hormone used to treat diabetes. After teaching medicine in England and Nigeria, Nicol returned to his homeland to serve as principal of Fourah Bay College and vice-chancellor of the University of Sierra Leone. He was also his country's ambassador to the United Nations and has been affiliated with the Red Cross, the World Health Organization, UNESCO, and just about every important West African conference and committee.

Reader's Guide

LIFE IS SWEET AT KUMANSENU

Background

A small nation on the coast of West Africa, Sierra Leone was a British colony until 1961. Its capital, Freetown, was founded by British abolitionists in 1787 as a haven for freed and runaway slaves. Nicol grew up in Freetown, which is now a large modern city. The rest of his Sierra Leone, however, is largely rural. In the villages, the old tribal religions remain strong, even among villagers who have become Christian or Muslim. Although specific beliefs vary from village to village, most involve faith in spirits and in magic, both good and bad. The story you are about to read focuses on the old West African belief that the spirit of a dead child can creep back into its mother's womb and be born again. To know whether her next child is a manifestation of this restless spirit, the mother marks the body of her dead child and sees if that mark appears on the next child she bears. To break the cycle, the mother must follow special burial customs prescribed by the village spiritual leader.

Writer's Response

One of the **themes** in this story has to do with the clash between an individual and institutional authority. In a few sentences, describe a situation you have witnessed or heard about in which an individual defies the rules or advice of an authority figure. What are the reasons for this challenge to established law or tradition? What are the results of the challenge?

Literary Focus

Foreshadowing is the use of clues to hint at what is going to happen later in a story. Writers use foreshadowing to hook our interest. For example, if a writer mentions (even casually) that a character keeps a gun in her dresser drawer, we instantly wonder why it's there and when she might use it. In "Life Is Sweet at Kumansenu," Nicol drops clues in the very first descriptions of Meji to foreshadow his story's surprise ending.

LIFE IS SWEET AT KUMANSENU

Abioseh Nicol

As you read the story, look for a general statement about life that Meji makes and the widow Bola repeats. How would you expand this statement to express the story's theme?

The sea and the wet sand to one side of it; green tropical forest on the other; above it, the slow, tumbling clouds. The clean round blinding disc of sun and the blue sky covered and surrounded the small African village, Kumansenu.

A few square mud houses with roofs like helmets were here thatched, and there covered with corrugated zinc, where the prosperity of cocoa or trading had touched the head of the family.

The widow Bola stirred her palm-oil stew[1] and thought of nothing in particular. She chewed a kola nut[2] rhythmically with her strong toothless jaws, and soon unconsciously she was chewing in rhythm with the skipping of Asi, her granddaughter. She looked idly at Asi, as the seven-year-old brought the twisted palmleaf rope smartly over her head and jumped over it, counting in English each time the rope struck the ground and churned up a little red dust. Bola herself did not understand English well, but

The village of Karamasi, Sierra Leone.

Jean Gaumy/Magnum Photos, Inc.

she could easily count up to twenty in English, for market purposes. Asi shouted six and then said nine, ten. Bola called out that after six came seven. And I should know, she sighed. Although now she was old and her womb and breasts were withered, there

---

1. **palm-oil stew:** native dish in which various ingredients are cooked in an oil taken from the seeds of palm trees.
2. **kola nut:** fruit of an African tree called the kola; also spelled cola. Kola nuts contain caffeine and are often chewed for their mild stimulating effects.

was a time when she bore children regularly every two years. Six times she had borne a boy child and six times they had died. Some had swollen up and with weak plaintive cries had faded away. Others had shuddered in sudden convulsions, with burning skins, and had rolled up their eyes and died. They had all died; or rather he had died, Bola thought; because she knew it was one child all the time whose spirit had crept up restlessly into her womb to be born and mock her. The sixth time, Musa, the village magician whom time had now transformed into a respectable Muslim, had advised her and her husband to break the bones of the quiet little corpse and mangle it so that it could not come back to torment them alive again. But she had held on to the child and refused to let them mutilate it. Secretly, she had marked it with a sharp pointed stick at the left buttock before it was wrapped in a mat and taken away. When at the seventh time she had borne a son and the purification ceremonies had taken place, she had turned it surreptitiously to see whether the mark was there. It was. She showed it to the old woman who was the midwife and asked her what it was, and she had forced herself to believe that it was an accidental scratch made while the child was being scrubbed with herbs to remove placental blood. But this child had stayed. Meji,[3] he had been called. And he was now thirty years of age and a second-class clerk in government offices in a town ninety miles away. Asi, his daughter, had been left with her to do the things an old woman wanted a small child for: to run and take messages to the neighbors, to fetch a cup of water from the earthenware pot in the kitchen, to sleep with her, and to be fondled.

She threw the washed and squeezed cassava leaves[4] into the red boiling stew, putting in a finger's pinch of salt, and then went indoors, carefully stepping over the threshold to look for the dried red pepper. She found it and then dropped it, leaning against the wall with a little cry. He turned round from the window and looked at her with a twisted half smile of love and sadness. In his short-sleeved, open-necked white shirt and gray gabardine trousers, gold-plated wrist watch and brown suede shoes, he looked like the picture in African magazines of a handsome clerk who would get to the top because he ate the correct food or regularly took the correct laxative, which was being advertised. His skin was grayish brown and he had a large red handkerchief tied round his neck.

"Meji, God be praised," Bola cried. "You gave me quite a turn. My heart is weak and I can no longer take surprises. When did you come? How did you come? By lorry,[5] by fishing boat? And how did you come into the house? The front door was locked. There are so many thieves nowadays. I'm so glad to see you, so glad," she mumbled and wept, leaning against his breast.

Meji's voice was hoarse, and he said, "I'm glad to see you, too, mother," rubbing her back affectionately.

Asi ran in and cried "Papa, Papa," and was rewarded with a lift and a hug.

"Never mind how I came, mother," Meji said, laughing, "I'm here, and that's all that matters."

"We must make a feast, we must have a big feast. I must tell the neighbors at once. Asi, run this very minute to Mr. Addai, the

---

3. **Meji** (mā′jē)

4. **cassava** (kə·sä′və) **leaves:** leaves of a tropical food plant whose roots are something like potatoes.

5. **lorry** (lôr′ē): truck.

catechist,[6] and tell him your papa is home. Then to Mamie Gbera[7] to ask her for extra provisions, and to Pa Babole[8] for drummers and musicians . . ."

"Stop," said Meji, raising his hand. "This is all quite unnecessary. I don't want to see *anyone*, no one at all. I wish to rest quietly and completely. No one is to know I'm here."

Bola looked very crestfallen. She was so proud of Meji and wanted to show him off. The village would never forgive her for concealing such an important visitor. Meji must have sensed this because he held her shoulder comfortingly and said, "They will know soon enough. Let us enjoy one another, all three of us, this time. Life is too short."

Bola turned to Asi, picked up the packet of pepper and told her to go and drop a little into the boiling pot outside, taking care not to go too near the fire or play with it. After the child had gone, Bola said to her son, "Are you in trouble? Is it the police?"

He shook his head, "No," he said, "it's just that I like returning to you. There will always be this bond of love and affection between us, and I don't wish to share it with others. It is our private affair and that is why I've left my daughter with you." He ended up irrelevantly, "Girls somehow seem to stay with relations longer."

"And don't I know it," said Bola. "But you look pale," she continued, "and you keep scraping your throat. Are you ill?" she laid her hand on his brow. "And you're cold, too."

"It's the cold wet wind," he said, a little harshly. "I'll go and rest now if you can open and dust my room for me. I'm feeling very tired. Very tired indeed. I've traveled very far today and it has not been an easy journey."

"Of course, my son, of course," Bola replied, bustling away hurriedly but happily.

Meji slept all afternoon till evening, and his mother brought his food to his room and, later, took the empty basins away. Then he slept again till morning.

The next day, Saturday, was a busy one, and after further promising Meji that she would tell no one he was about, Bola went off to market. Meji took Asi for a long walk through a deserted path and up into the hills. She was delighted. They climbed high until they could see the village below in front of them, and the sea in the distance, and the boats with their wide white sails. Soon the sun had passed its zenith and was half way towards the west. Asi had eaten all the food, the dried fish and the flat tapioca pancakes[9] and the oranges. Her father said he wasn't hungry, and this had made the day perfect for Asi, who had chattered, eaten, and then played with her father's fountain pen and other things from his pocket. They soon left for home because he had promised that they would be back before dark; he had carried her down some steep boulders and she had held on to his shoulders because he had said his neck hurt so and she must not touch it. She had said, "Papa, I can see behind you and you haven't got a shadow. Why?"

He had then turned her round facing the sun. Since she was getting drowsy, she had started asking questions and her father had joked with her and humored her. "Papa, why has your watch stopped at twelve o'clock?"

---

6. **Addai** (ə·dī'), **the catechist** (kat'ə·kist'): someone who teaches the catechism to Christians; a catechism is a book that contains all the fundamentals of the religion, usually in question and answer form.

7. **Gbera** ('g·bā'rə)

8. **Babole** (bä·bō'lä)

9. **tapioca pancakes** (tap'ē·ō'kə): pancakes made from a granular substance obtained from the potatolike roots of the cassava plant.

A West African village.
*Have you noted
anything strange
about Meji's behavior?*

"Because the world ends at noon." Asi had chuckled at that. "Papa, why do you wear a scarf always round your neck?" "Because my head will fall off if I don't." She had laughed out loud at that. But soon she had fallen asleep as he bore her homewards.

Just before nightfall, with his mother dressed in her best, they had all three, at her urgent request, gone to his father's grave, taking a secret route and avoiding the main village. It was a small cemetery, not more than twenty years or so old, started when the Rural Health Department had insisted that no more burials were to take place in the backyard of households. Bola took a bottle of wine and a glass and four split halves of kola, each a half sphere, two red and two white. They reached the graveside and she poured some wine into the glass. Then she spoke to her dead husband softly and caressingly. She had brought his son to see him, she said. This son whom God had given success, to the confusion and discomfiture of their enemies. Here he was, a man with a pensionable clerk's job and not a poor farmer, a fisherman, or a simple mechanic.

All the years of their married life, people had said she was a witch because her children had died young. But this boy of theirs had shown that she was a good woman. Let her husband answer her now, to show that he was listening. She threw the four kola nuts up into the air and they fell on to the grave. Three fell with the flat face upwards and one with its flat face downwards. She picked them up again and conversed with him once more and threw the kola nuts up again. But still there was an odd one or sometimes two.

They did not fall with all four faces up, or with all four faces down, to show that he was listening and was pleased. She spoke endearingly, she cajoled, she spoke severely. But all to no avail. She then asked Meji to perform. He crouched by the graveside and whispered. Then he threw the kola nuts and they rolled a little, Bola following them eagerly with her sharp old eyes. They all ended up face downwards. Meji emptied the glass of wine on the grave and then said that he felt nearer his father at that moment than he had ever done before in his life.

It was sundown, and they all three went back silently home in the short twilight. That night, going outside the house towards her son's window, she had found, to her sick disappointment, that he had been throwing all the cooked food away out there. She did not mention this when she went to say good night, but she did sniff and say that there was a smell of decay in the room. Meji said that he thought there was a dead rat up in the rafters, and he would clear it away after she had gone to bed.

That night it rained heavily, and sheet lightning turned the darkness into brief silver daylight for one or two seconds at a time. Then the darkness again and the rain. Bola woke soon after midnight and thought she could hear knocking. She went to Meji's room to ask him to open the door, but he wasn't there. She thought he had gone out for a while and had been locked out by mistake. She opened the door quickly, holding an oil lamp upwards. He stood on the veranda, curiously unwet, and refused to come in.

"I have to go away," he said hoarsely, coughing.

Ceremonial mask of the Yoruba people of West Africa.

Sassoonian/Art Resource, New York

"Do come in," she said.

"No," he said, "I have to go, but I wanted to thank you for giving me a chance."

"What nonsense is this?" she said. "Come in out of the rain."

"I did not think I should leave without thanking you."

The rain fell hard, the door creaked, and the wind whistled.

"Life is sweet, mother dear, goodbye, and thank you."

He turned round and started running.

There was a sudden diffuse flash of silent lightning and she saw that the yard was empty. She went back heavily and fell into a restless sleep. Before she slept she said to herself that she must see Mr. Addai next morning, Sunday, or better still, Monday, and tell him about all this, in case Meji was in trouble. She hoped Meji would not be annoyed. He was such a good son.

But it was Mr. Addai who came instead, on Sunday afternoon, quiet and grave, and met Bola sitting on an old stool in the veranda, dressing Asi's hair in tight thin plaits.

Mr. Addai sat down and, looking away, he said, "The Lord giveth and the Lord taketh away." Soon half the village were sitting round the veranda and in the yard.

"But I tell you, he was here on Friday and left Sunday morning," Bola said. "He couldn't have died on Friday."

Bola had just recovered from a fainting fit after being told of her son's death in town. His wife, Asi's mother, had come with the news, bringing some of his property. She said Meji had died instantly at noon on Friday and had been buried on Saturday at sundown. They would have brought him to Kumansenu for burial. He had always wished that. But they could not do so in time as bodies did not last more than a day in the hot season, and there were no lorries available for hire.

"He was here, he was here," Bola said, rubbing her forehead and weeping.

Asi sat by quietly. Mr. Addai said comfortingly, "Hush, hush, he couldn't have been, because no one in the village saw him."

"He said we were to tell no one," Bola said.

The crowd smiled above Bola's head and shook their heads. "Poor woman," someone said, "she is beside herself with grief."

"He died on Friday," Mrs. Meji repeated, crying. "He was in the office and he pulled up the window to look out and call the messenger. Then the sash broke. The window fell, broke his neck, and the sharp edge almost cut his head off; they say he died at once."

"My papa had a scarf around his neck." Asi shouted suddenly.

"Hush," said the crowd.

Mrs. Meji dipped her hand into her bosom and produced a small gold locket and put it round Asi's neck, to quiet her.

"Your papa had this made last week for your Christmas present. You may as well have it now."

Asi played with it and pulled it this way and that.

"Be careful, child," Mr. Addai said, "it is your father's last gift."

"I was trying to remember how he showed me yesterday to open it," Asi said.

"You have never seen it before," Mrs. Meji said, sharply, trembling with fear mingled with anger.

She took the locket and tried to open it.

"Let me have it," said the village goldsmith, and he tried whispering magic words of incantation. Then he said, defeated, "It must be poor quality gold; it has rusted. I need tools to open it."

"I remember now," Asi said in the flat complacent voice of childhood.

The crowd gathered round quietly and the setting sun glinted on the soft red African gold of the dangling trinket. The goldsmith handed the locket over to Asi and asked in a loud whisper, "How did he open it?"

"Like so," Asi said and pressed a secret catch. It flew open and she spelled out gravely the word inside, "A-S-I."

The silence continued.

"His neck, poor boy," Bola said a little wildly. "This is why he could not eat the lovely meals I cooked for him."

Mr. Addai announced a service of intercession after vespers[10] that evening. The crowd began to leave quietly.

Musa, the magician, was one of the last to leave. He was now very old and bent. In times of grave calamity, it was known that even Mr. Addai did not raise objection to his being consulted.

He bent over further and whispered in Bola's ear. "You should have had his bones broken and mangled thirty-one years ago when he went for the sixth time and then he would not have come back to mock you all these years by pretending to be alive. I told you so. But you women are naughty and stubborn."

Bola stood up, her black face held high, her eyes terrible with maternal rage and pride.

"I am glad I did not," she said, "and that is why he came back specially to thank me before he went for good."

She clutched Asi to her. "I am glad I gave him the opportunity to come back, for life is sweet. I do not expect you to understand why I did so. After all, you are only a man."

---

10. **vespers:** evening prayers in a Christian church.

Is this tale merely an entertaining ghost story, or is there more to it than that? Discuss.

Identifying Facts

1. Summarize the background information that the opening paragraphs provide about Bola's seven children. Who is Asi?

2. What reasons does Meji give for wanting no feast or company during his visit home? What are his final words to his mother?

3. What does Mr. Addai tell Bola that Bola at first refuses to believe? How does Asi prove that she *had* seen her father?

4. What does Musa, the village magician, tell Bola at the end? How does Bola respond?

Interpreting Meanings

1. What details in this story **foreshadow** the tale's surprise ending? Reread the story to the end of page 1339. Describe how foreshadowing is used to provide suspense.

2. Bola hugs Asi when Musa says that Bola behaved foolishly years ago. Why is Bola's action significant? What does Bola think that Musa cannot understand because he is a man?

3. Despite its eerie details, would you say this story is life-affirming? Why or why not? How do you feel about the values stressed in the story?

4. The **theme** of a story is sometimes revealed in a single significant passage. In this story, where would you say the theme is stated? What do you think of this theme?

Applying Meanings

In his famous poem ''In Memoriam,'' British poet Alfred, Lord Tennyson (1809–1892)

said, '' 'Tis better to have loved and lost/ Than never to have loved at all.'' Do you think that Bola would agree with this sentiment? Do you agree with it? Explain.

Critical Writing Response

Writing About Foreshadowing. In a brief essay, analyze Nicol's use of foreshadowing. Cite all the examples of foreshadowing that you can find and explain what later events they relate to. Before you begin writing, you may find it helpful to list in one column on a separate sheet of paper the examples of foreshadowing that you find. In another column, list the later event each example points to.

Clue	Event It Foreshadows
1. Red handkerchief around Meji's neck	1. His neck was broken.

Language and Vocabulary

African Languages and English

The *kola,* an African tree mentioned several times in the story, takes its English name from a West African word for this tree. From the tree's nutlike seeds comes an extract used to flavor the popular soft drink that we call *cola.* Cola is one of several words that came to English from the native languages of Africa. Some of these words entered English in the Old World; others were brought to the New World by Africans who came here as slaves.

Use a dictionary to find the meanings and origins of these words derived from African languages.

1. banjo
2. chimpanzee
3. gnu
4. gumbo
5. jazz
6. jumbo
7. marimba
8. okra
9. safari
10. tote

Chinua Achebe
b. 1930, Nigeria

AP/Wide World Photos

Chinua Achebe (chin'wä' ä·chā'bä) was born and grew up in the Ibo village of Ogidi when Nigeria was still a British colony. Although Achebe won a scholarship to study medicine, his love of literature and growing involvement with African nationalism changed his career. The nationalist movement after World War II brought with it a new sense of African self-awareness and confidence, and it occurred to Achebe that he and his fellow Africans might have their own stories to tell. Achebe's insight made him question the colonial-era notion that African culture was inferior to the culture

the European colonists had grafted onto Africa, usually by force. As a gesture defining his roots, Achebe dropped his first name, Albert, which his parents had given him in honor of Queen Victoria's husband.

In 1958, while working for the Nigerian Broadcasting Company, Achebe published his first novel, *Things Fall Apart.* The novel tells of an Ibo man whose personal life is ruined as a result of colonial pressures. This was the first of three novels that Achebe wrote to explore the Ibo past and the destructive effects of colonialism on African cultures and on individual Africans.

In 1960, the new nation of Nigeria, with over two hundred ethnic groups, was not a unified country. The four largest ethnic groups, the Ibo, Hausa, Fulani, and Yoruba, were constantly fighting for land and power. Many of the frictions originated in the groups' very different religions, languages, and outlooks on life. Eventually, in 1967, things fell apart. Achebe was one of the many Ibo who unsuccessfully tried to secede from Nigeria and establish a new republic called Biafra. In the worst months of the bloody, three-year civil war, about twelve thousand people, mostly children, starved to death each day. Overall, somewhere between one million and two million people died—many of them from disease and hunger. Several stories in Achebe's story collection *Girls at War* (1973) describe the tragedies and horrors of these years of civil war.

Reader's Guide

MARRIAGE IS A PRIVATE AFFAIR

Background

Nigeria is a West African nation of great ethnic diversity. Two of the largest ethnic groups in the southeast are the Ibo and the Ibibio. Since the end of World War II, many young Nigerians have left their rural villages to attend universities and settle in large cities such as Lagos, Nigeria's capital. As a result of this migration, some young people have abandoned their communities' traditions for more westernized ways. Yet many have found it difficult to break away from their roots, and these young people find themselves caught in the clash between the old and the new. "Marriage Is a Private Affair" is about two young people, an Ibo man and an Ibibio woman. They have moved to Lagos and have broken traditions by marrying each other. In contrast to the young couple is the man's father, a rural villager who rigidly adheres to traditional Ibo ways.

Writer's Response

This story involves a conflict between generations. Do you think that it is inevitable that generations clash? Describe a situation that you have witnessed or heard about that illustrates the problem of conflict between older and younger generations.

Literary Focus

In **verbal irony**, language is used to say one thing but to mean the opposite. For example, a friend is probably being ironic if he tells you, "I just *love* doing five hours of grammar homework every night." As you read "Marriage Is a Private Affair," think about whether Achebe is using verbal irony in the title of his story.

Marriage Is a Private Affair

Chinua Achebe

> *Read the first five paragraphs, stopping after Nene's question,* *" 'Why shouldn't it?' " Write down at least three questions you* *have about the characters and events of this story. When you* *finish reading the story, see if your questions have been answered.*

"Have you written to your dad yet?" asked Nene[1] one afternoon as she sat with Nnaemeka[2] in her room at 16 Kasanga Street, Lagos.[3]

"No. I've been thinking about it. I think it's better to tell him when I get home on leave!"

"But why? Your leave is such a long way off yet—six whole weeks. He should be let into our happiness now."

Nnaemeka was silent for a while, and then began very slowly as if he groped for his words: "I wish I were sure it would be happiness to him."

"Of course it must," replied Nene, a little surprised. "Why shouldn't it?"

Traffic jam on Broad Street in Lagos, Nigeria.

Jackie Phillips/Time Magazine

"You have lived in Lagos all your life, and you know very little about people in remote parts of the country."

"That's what you always say. But I don't believe anybody will be so unlike other people that they will be unhappy when their sons are engaged to marry."

"Yes. They are most unhappy if the engagement is not arranged by them. In our case it's worse—you are not even an Ibo."[4]

This was said so seriously and so bluntly that Nene could not find speech immediately. In the cosmopolitan atmosphere of the city it had

---

1. **Nene** (nā'nā)
2. **Nnaemeka** ('n·nä·ä·mä'kə)
3. **Lagos** (lā'gäs'): former capital of Nigeria.

4. **Ibo** (ē'bō): member of an African ethnic group living mostly in southeastern Nigeria.

Carving on a Nigerian church door depicting a scene from the Bible.

always seemed to her something of a joke that a person's tribe could determine whom he married.

At last she said, "You don't really mean that he will object to your marrying me simply on that account? I had always thought you Ibos were kindly disposed to other people."

"So we are. But when it comes to marriage, well, it's not quite so simple. And this," he added, "is not peculiar to the Ibos. If your father were alive and lived in the heart of Ibibio-land[5] he would be exactly like my father."

"I don't know. But anyway, as your father is so fond of you, I'm sure he will forgive you soon enough. Come on then, be a good boy and send him a nice lovely letter . . ."

"It would not be wise to break the news to him by writing. A letter will bring it upon him with a shock. I'm quite sure about that."

"All right, honey, suit yourself. You know your father."

As Nnaemeka walked home that evening he turned over in his mind different ways of overcoming his father's opposition, especially now that he had gone and found a girl for him. He had thought of showing his letter to Nene but decided on second thoughts not to, at least for the moment. He read it again when he got home, and couldn't help smiling to himself. He remembered Ugoye[6] quite well, an Amazon[7] of a girl who used to beat up all the boys, himself included, on the way to the stream, a complete dunce at school.

> I have found a girl who will suit you admirably—Ugoye Nweke,[8] the eldest daughter of our neighbor, Jacob Nweke. She has a proper Christian upbringing. When she stopped schooling some years ago her father (a man of sound judgment) sent her to live in the house of a

---

5. **Ibibio-land** (ib'ə·bē'ō'-): region of southeastern Nigeria that is the traditional homeland of the Ibibio, another African ethnic group.

6. **Ugoye** (oo·gō'yä)
7. **Amazon:** tall, physically powerful female; from the Amazons, a tribe of strong women warriors in Greek mythology.
8. **Nweke** ('n·wä'kä)

pastor where she has received all the training a wife could need. Her Sunday School teacher has told me that she reads her Bible very fluently. I hope we shall begin negotiations when you come home in December.

On the second evening of his return from Lagos, Nnaemeka sat with his father under a cassia tree. This was the old man's retreat where he went to read his Bible when the parching December sun had set and a fresh, reviving wind blew on the leaves.

"Father," began Nnaemeka suddenly, "I have come to ask for forgiveness."

"Forgiveness? For what, my son?" he asked in amazement.

"It's about this marriage question."

"Which marriage question?"

"I can't—we must—I mean it is impossible for me to marry Nweke's daughter."

"Impossible? Why?" asked his father.

"I don't love her."

"Nobody said you did. Why should you?" he asked.

"Marriage today is different . . ."

"Look here, my son," interrupted his father, "nothing is different. What one looks for in a wife are a good character and a Christian background."

Nnaemeka saw there was no hope along the present line of argument.

"Moreover," he said. "I am engaged to marry another girl who has all of Ugoye's good qualities, and who . . ."

His father did not believe his ears. "What did you say?" he asked slowly and disconcertingly.

"She is a good Christian," his son went on, "and a teacher in a Girls' School in Lagos."

"Teacher, did you say? If you consider that a qualification for a good wife I should like to point out to you, Emeka, that no Christian woman should teach. St. Paul in his letter to

the Corinthians[9] says that women should keep silence." He rose slowly from his seat and paced forwards and backwards. This was his pet subject, and he condemned vehemently those church leaders who encouraged women to teach in their schools. After he had spent his emotion on a long homily he at last came back to his son's engagement, in a seemingly milder tone.

"Whose daughter is she, anyway?"

"She is Nene Atang."

"What!" All the mildness was gone again. "Did you say Neneataga, what does that mean?"

"Nene Atang from Calabar. She is the only girl I can marry." This was a very rash reply and Nnaemeka expected the storm to burst. But it did not. His father merely walked away into his room. This was most unexpected and perplexed Nnaemeka. His father's silence was infinitely more menacing than a flood of threatening speech. That night the old man did not eat.

When he sent for Nnaemeka a day later, he applied all possible ways of dissuasion. But the young man's heart was hardened, and his father eventually gave him up as lost.

"I owe it to you, my son, as a duty to show you what is right and what is wrong. Whoever put this idea into your head might as well have cut your throat. It is Satan's work." He waved his son away.

"You will change your mind, Father, when you know Nene."

"I shall never see her," was the reply. From that night the father scarcely spoke to his son. He did not, however, cease hoping that he would realize how serious was the danger he was heading for. Day and night he put him in his prayers.

---

9. **St. Paul . . . Corinthians:** reference to a book in the Bible's New Testament (I Corinthians 14:34).

Nnaemeka, for his own part, was very deeply affected by his father's grief. But he kept hoping that it would pass away. If it had occurred to him that never in the history of his people had a man married a woman who spoke a different tongue, he might have been less optimistic. "It has never been heard," was the verdict of an old man speaking a few weeks later. In that short sentence he spoke for all of his people. This man had come with others to commiserate with Okeke[10] when news went round about his son's behavior. By that time the son had gone back to Lagos.

"It has never been heard," said the old man again with a sad shake of his head.

"What did Our Lord say?" asked another gentleman. "Sons shall rise against their Fathers; it is there in the Holy Book."

"It is the beginning of the end," said another.

The discussion thus tending to become theological, Madubogwu, a highly practical man, brought it down once more to the ordinary level.

"Have you thought of consulting a native doctor about your son?" he asked Nnaemeka's father.

"He isn't sick," was the reply.

"What is he then? The boy's mind is diseased and only a good herbalist can bring him back to his right senses. The medicine he requires is *Amalile*, the same that women apply with success to recapture their husbands' straying affection."

"Madubogwu is right," said another gentleman. "This thing calls for medicine."

"I shall not call in a native doctor." Nnaemeka's father was known to be obstinately ahead of his more superstitious neighbors in

these matters. "I will not be another Mrs. Ochuba. If my son wants to kill himself, let him do it with his own hands. It is not for me to help him."

"But it was her fault," said Madubogwu. "She ought to have gone to an honest herbalist. She was a clever woman, nevertheless."

"She was a wicked murderess," said Jonathan, who rarely argued with his neighbors because, he often said, they were incapable of reasoning. "The medicine was prepared for her husband, it was his name they called in its preparation and I am sure it would have been perfectly beneficial to him. It was wicked to put it into the herbalist's food, and say you were only trying it out."

Six months later, Nnaemeka was showing his young wife a short letter from his father:

It amazes me that you could be so unfeeling as to send me your wedding picture. I would have sent it back. But on further thought I decided just to cut off your wife and send it back to you because I have nothing to do with her. How I wish that I had nothing to do with you either.

When Nene read through this letter and looked at the mutilated picture, her eyes filled with tears, and she began to sob.

"Don't cry, my darling," said her husband. "He is essentially good-natured and will one day look more kindly on our marriage." But years passed and that one day did not come.

For eight years, Okeke would have nothing to do with his son, Nnaemeka. Only three times (when Nnaemeka asked to come home and spend his leave) did he write to him.

"I can't have you in my house," he replied on one occasion. "It can be of no interest to me where or how you spend your leave—or your life, for that matter."

---

10. **Okeke** (ō·kā′kā)

The prejudice against Nnaemeka's marriage was not confined to his little village. In Lagos, especially among his people who worked there, it showed itself in a different way. Their women, when they met at their village meeting, were not hostile to Nene. Rather, they paid her such excessive deference as to make her feel she was not one of them. But as time went on, Nene gradually broke through some of this prejudice and even began to make friends among them. Slowly and grudgingly they began to admit that she kept her home much better than most of them.

The story eventually got to the little village in the heart of the Ibo country that Nnaemeka and his young wife were a most happy couple. But his father was one of the few people in the village who knew nothing about this. He always displayed so much temper whenever his son's name was mentioned that everyone avoided it in his presence. By a tremendous effort of will he had succeeded in pushing his son to the back of his mind. The strain had nearly killed him but he had persevered, and won.

Then one day he received a letter from Nene, and in spite of himself he began to glance through it perfunctorily until all of a sudden the expression on his face changed and he began to read more carefully.

> . . . *Our two sons, from the day they learnt that they have a grandfather, have insisted on being taken to him. I find it impossible to tell them that you will not see them. I implore you to allow Nnaemeka to bring them home for a short time during his leave next month. I shall remain here in Lagos . . .*

The old man at once felt the resolution he had built up over so many years falling in. He was telling himself that he must not give in. He tried to steel his heart against all

Marc & Evelyne Bernheim/Woodfin Camp & Associates

Ibo ceremonial mask.
Does Nene receive the same treatment from Nnaemeka's friends in Lagos as she does from her father-in-law?

emotional appeals. It was a reenactment of that other struggle. He leaned against a window and looked out. The sky was overcast with heavy black clouds and a high wind began to blow filling the air with dust and dry leaves. It was one of those rare occasions when even Nature takes a hand in a human fight. Very soon it began to rain, the first rain in the year. It came down in large sharp drops and was accompanied by the lightning and thunder which mark a change of season. Okeke was trying hard not to think of his two grandsons. But he knew he was now fighting a losing battle. He tried to hum a favorite hymn but the pattering of large raindrops on the roof broke up the tune. His mind immediately returned to the children. How could he shut his door against them? By a curious mental process he imagined them standing, sad and forsaken, under the harsh angry weather—shut out from his house.

That night he hardly slept, from remorse—and a vague fear that he might die without making it up to them.

Chinua Achebe   **1349**

First Thoughts

Do you think that Okeke will see his grandsons and make peace with his son and daughter-in-law? Or do you think he will continue to stick by his traditional beliefs and die without seeing his grandsons? What makes you say so?

Identifying Facts

1. What ethnic difference separates Nnaemeka and Nene? In predicting that his father will be unhappy with their marriage, what reasons does Nnaemeka give?

2. What does Okeke, Nnaemeka's father, believe a man must look for in a wife? What is his opinion of Nene's job as a teacher?

3. In a sentence, summarize Okeke's treatment of his son and daughter-in-law for the first eight years of their marriage. In contrast, how do Nnaemeka's Ibo friends in Lagos feel about Nene?

4. What request does Nene make in her letter to her father-in-law? After reading the letter, what happens to the resolution Okeke has "built up over so many years," and what feelings disturb his sleep that night?

Interpreting Meanings

1. Explain in your own words the change of heart that Okeke experiences at the story's end. Why do you think learning about his grandchildren has affected him more than seeing his son's wedding photograph?

2. What role does nature seem to play near the end of the story?

3. Do you think Achebe is using **verbal irony** in the title of this story? Does the story reveal that marriage is a private affair or a public affair? Explain.

4. In the **conflict** between Nnaemeka's ways and his father's, does Achebe seem strongly to favor one side or the other?

5. The **subject** of this story is a marriage that occurs in opposition to a father's wishes. The **theme** is the truth about human nature revealed in the story. In your own words, state what you see as the theme of this story. Remember that a change in a main character and the nature of the conflict's resolution often indicate the theme of a story.

Applying Meanings

In your opinion, should marriage be a "private affair," or should social considerations play an important role? Discuss your views with the class.

Creative Writing Response

Writing a Sequel.   Achebe ends his story without resolving the conflict between Okeke and his son. What do you think Okeke will do? Write a brief sequel in which you show Okeke's subsequent behavior. You may incorporate ideas discussed in the First Thoughts question. Be sure your sequel takes into account the characters of Okeke, Nnaemeka, and Nene as Achebe has presented them.

Critical Writing Response

Analyzing a Conflict.   The central **conflict** of this story, as in much of Achebe's fiction, is between the old ways and the new. This conflict takes many forms: rural vs. urban lifestyles, arranged marriages vs. love marriages, and housewives vs. career women. Choose one of these conflicts. In a brief essay, describe the conflict and discuss how it is, or is not, resolved by the story's end. At the end of your essay, describe your own response to the issues raised by this conflict.

Wole Soyinka
b. 1934, Nigeria

In 1986, Nigerian writer Wole Soyinka (wō'lā shô·ying'kə') became the first black African to win the Nobel Prize for literature. He dedicated his acceptance speech to the political activist Nelson Mandela, then still in prison in South Africa. Like Mandela, Soyinka also had spent time in jail, under deplorable conditions, for his political beliefs. Although he was denied writing materials, Soyinka managed to keep a diary by making his own ink and writing on toilet paper, cigarette packages, and in between the lines of the few books he secretly obtained. The results were eventually published as *The Man Died: Prison Notes of Wole Soyinka* (1972).

Akinwande Oluwole (*Wole* for short) Soyinka was born in western Nigeria, where his father was active in local politics. Raised as a Christian, Soyinka was also steeped in the ways of the Yoruba, a West African people with a long tradition of oral poetry and ritual dance, music, and drama. As a child, Soyinka was comfortable in the two cultures, but as he grew older he became aware of a conflict between African traditions and Western ways. He recorded this conflict in his autobiography *Ake: The Years of Childhood* (1981).

After attending Ibadan University, Soyinka traveled to northern England to study drama at the University of Leeds. Soyinka's experiences in England were mixed. On the one hand, he received encouragement from his professors, wrote several well-regarded plays, and even saw some of them produced. On the other hand, he suffered from racial prejudice, which he satirized in poems like "Telephone Conversation," reprinted here.

In his plays, poems, and other writings, Soyinka often uses his satiric wit to attack injustice, political corruption, and racism. He also warns against both a nostalgia for Africa's past and an unequivocal embrace of Western ways. In the play *A Dance of the Forests* (1962), Soyinka ridicules people's tendency to glorify the past. His next play, *The Lion and the Jewel* (1962), combines poetry and prose to provide a comic view of the perils of Western modernizations.

Reader's Guide

TELEPHONE CONVERSATION

Background

Although Soyinka draws on his Yoruba heritage in his writing, he is primarily concerned with Africa today and he has criticized the négritude movement for excessive nostalgia. "A tiger does not shout its tigritude," he once declared. The remark—as linguistically imaginative as it is witty and well observed—is pure Soyinka.

Since World War II, millions of people from British colonies and former colonies have traveled to England. Some, like Wole Soyinka, came to receive an education; others came to stay, hoping to find a better life. Yet for many of these people, life in England was marred by racial and ethnic prejudices. Soyinka had several such experiences when he went to London in the late 1950s to work with the Royal Court Theatre and see his plays produced. "Telephone Conversation" records one of these experiences. The poem takes place in a London telephone booth (they are painted red), where the speaker—an educated black African—is phoning about an apartment he hopes to rent. Older, coin-operated telephones had two buttons, button A and button B, that the caller had to push to switch from a speaking mode to a listening mode.

Writer's Response

Write a few sentences describing how you would feel and how you might react if a landlord refused to let you rent an apartment because of your race or ethnic background.

Literary Focus

Satire is a kind of writing that ridicules human weakness, vice, or folly in order to bring about social reform. Satire often tries to persuade people to do or believe something by showing that their present behavior or attitude is foolish. In "Telephone Conversation," Soyinka never states what he wants readers to think, but his mocking portrayal of the rude and ignorant landlady makes his message clear.

TELEPHONE CONVERSATION
Wole Soyinka

◆ *In this poem, Soyinka reports an incident of racial prejudice with his characteristically satirical eye. Notice examples of wit and humor as you read the poem. How do they contribute to the poem's effectiveness?*

The price seemed reasonable, location
Indifferent. The landlady swore she lived
Off premises. Nothing remained
But self-confession. "Madam," I warned,
5   "I hate a wasted journey—I am African."
Silence. Silenced transmission of
Pressurized good breeding. Voice, when it came,
Lipstick-coated, long gold-rolled
Cigarette-holder pipped. Caught I was, foully.

10   "HOW DARK?" . . . I had not misheard . . . "ARE YOU LIGHT
OR VERY DARK?" Button B. Button A. Stench
Of rancid breath of public hide-and-speak.
Red booth. Red pillar box. Red double-tiered
Omnibus squelching tar. It *was* real! Shamed
15   By ill-mannered silence, surrender
Pushed dumbfoundment to beg simplification.
Considerate she was, varying the emphasis—

"ARE YOU DARK? OR VERY LIGHT?" Revelation came.
"You mean—like plain or milk chocolate?"
20   Her assent was clinical, crushing in its light
Impersonality. Rapidly, wave length adjusted,
I chose, "West African sepia"°—and as an
     afterthought,
"Down in my passport." Silence for spectroscopic°
Flight of fancy, till truthfulness clanged her accent
25   Hard on the mouthpiece "WHAT'S THAT?" conceding,
"DON'T KNOW WHAT THAT IS." "Like brunette."
"THAT'S DARK, ISN'T IT?" "Not altogether.

Steve Benbow/Woodfin Camp & Associates

22. **sepia** (sē'pē·ə): dark reddish brown.

23. **spectroscopic:** here, related to the study of a color spectrum.

Facially, I am brunette, but madam, you should
   see
The rest of me. Palm of my hand, soles of my feet
30   Are a peroxide blonde. Friction, caused—
Foolishly, madam—by sitting down, has turned
My bottom raven black—One moment madam!"—
   sensing
Her receiver rearing on the thunder clap
About my ears—"Madam," I pleaded, "wouldn't
   you rather
35   See for yourself?"

First Thoughts

What message do you think Soyinka wants to get across in this poem?

Identifying Facts

1. Identify the speaker in the poem. What does the speaker want?
2. Once the speaker understands what the woman wants to know, what does *he* ask?

Interpreting Meanings

1. Why does the speaker tell the woman that he is African? By making this remark, what does he reveal about his past experience?
2. Why do you think the prospective landlady asks these questions? What does she reveal about herself in the course of the poem?
3. Explain the humorous double meaning of the speaker's last question.
4. "Telephone Conversation" is a **satire**, a type of writing that attacks and ridicules some social evil or human weakness. What is Soyinka mocking in this poem? One of the tools of the satirist is the absurd comparison. How does the contrast between the speaker and the landlady contribute to the satirical message?

Applying Meanings

Do you think satirical writing can help change people's attitudes? Discuss your own responses to this poem.

Creative Writing Response

Writing a Satiric Dialogue. One of the devices satirists use to make their targets look absurd is **exaggeration**. You can expose the absurdity of any situation or attitude by carrying it to an extreme. For example, imagine that you have found a nice apartment and made arrangements to rent it. When you meet the owner, however, she refuses to give you the keys because she doesn't rent to people with your eye (or hair) color.

Write a brief dialogue between such a landlady or landlord and a prospective tenant. Begin the conversation with this line: "I'd like to rent the apartment you advertised in the paper." You may work with a partner and then present your dialogue to the class.

Barbara Kimenye
b. 1940, Uganda

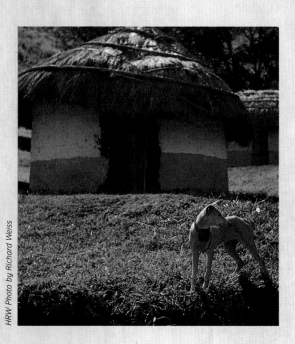

HRW Photo by Richard Weiss

Barbara Kimenye (kə·men′yā) grew up in an extremely small village in Uganda. Many of her popular stories are set in the fictional village of Kalasanda, obviously patterned after her actual home village. Kalasanda Village is in Buganda, the traditional kingdom of the Ganda people in what is today part of the nation of Uganda. After attending local schools, Kimenye worked as secretary to the *kabaka,* or Bugandan king, until his governmental authorities were abolished in 1967. In the ensuing political upheaval, Kimenye fled her homeland and spent several years in England, where for a time she was a social worker.

Kimenye was working for the *kabaka* when she began making a name for herself as a writer. Her best-known stories are collected in *Kalasanda* (1965), published when she was twenty-five years old, and *Kalasanda Revisited* (1966). Kimenye also wrote a regular column for the popular newspaper *Uganda Nation.* In 1967, she published the first of her series of children's books about a boy named Moses. Over the years, Moses, a lovable, mischievous character, has been embroiled in more than ten action-packed adventures such as *Moses and the Kidnappers* (1968) and *Moses and the Ghost* (1971). The Moses books are very popular in East Africa, where excerpts often appear in elementary school textbooks. Kimenye continued to publish children's fiction while she was living in England.

Kimenye brings the charm and humor of her children's stories to her adult fiction. In the adult stories, however, she observes life with a more mature and mildly satirical eye. According to one critic, Kimenye is a powerful writer who demonstrates time and again that supposedly commonplace lives lived in tiny, out-of-the-way places are nevertheless full of meaning and interest.

THE PIG

Barbara Kimenye

Reader's Guide

Background The East African nation of Uganda takes its name from its largest ethnic group, the Ganda people, who called their traditional tribal kingdom (in what is now southern Uganda) Buganda. During the 1950s the traditional ruler of Buganda, the *kabaka,* was in power and Buganda had its own parliament, or *lukiko.* This situation lasted until 1967, when Uganda's government was centralized and Buganda's special status was revoked. Barbara Kimenye's Kalasanda stories, including ''The Pig,'' take place in rural Buganda before 1967.

Writer's Response Create a cast of characters for a story or play about the peo-

ple in your town or neighborhood. List the characters and after their names write a few phrases describing each person's job or role in the community. You may also tell something about his or her personality, talents, and interests.

Literary Focus **Tone** is the attitude a writer takes toward the reader, a subject, or a character. Tone is usually described with an adjective—*amused, angry, playful, sorrowful, ironic, disgusted, mocking, tender,* and so on. Tone is conveyed through the author's diction and descriptions of characters and setting. It is important to correctly identify the tone of a work so that you do not misread it.

THE PIG

As you read, notice Kimenye's diction and her descriptions of characters and the setting. Decide what adjective or adjectives you would use to describe the tone of the story.

Old Kibuka had long believed that retirement was no sort of life for a man like himself, who would, so he modestly believed, pass for not a day over forty-five. He had held a responsible post at the Ggom-

bolola Headquarters,[1] until the Government had sent somebody from the Public Service

---

1. **Ggombolola** ('g·gom'bə·lō'lə) **Headquarters:** local administrative headquarters—something like an American town hall.

Commission to nose around the offices and root out all employees over retirement age. Then the next thing Kibuka knew, despite his youthfully dyed hair, he had a pension, a Certificate of Service, but no longer a job.

He still worried about the state his filing system must be in today, for having once called in at the Headquarters, merely to see if the youngster who had replaced him needed any advice or help, he had been appalled at the lack of order. Papers were scattered everywhere, confidential folders were open for all the world to read, and his successor was flirting madly with some pin-brained girl at the other end of the newly installed telephone.

The visit had not been anything near a success, for not even his former colleagues showed anything but superficial interest in what Kibuka had to say.

So there he was, destined to waste the remainder of his life in the little cottage beside the Kalasanda stream, with plenty indeed to look back on, but not very much to look forward to, and his greatest friend, Yosefu Mukasa, was away in Buddu County on business.

The self-pitying thought "I might as well be dead" kept recurring in his mind as he pumped his pressure stove to boil a kettle of tea. Then the noise of a car, grinding its way along the narrow, uneven track, heading in his direction, sent him eagerly to the door. It was his eldest grandson who climbed out of the battered Landrover.[2] A tall, loose-limbed young man in a khaki shirt and blue jeans. Old Kibuka practically choked with happiness as his frail fingers were squeezed in a sinewy grip, and the bones of his shoulders almost snapped under an affectionate hug.

---

2. **Landrover:** a jeep-like vehicle.

"What a wonderful surprise! Come in, my boy. I was just making a cup of tea."

"Grandfather, this is a very short visit. I'm afraid I can't stay more than a few minutes." The boy's voice was musically deep, very much like his grandfather's once had been, before the tremor of age had changed it. "I just came to see how you are getting on, and I brought you a present."

"That's very kind of you, son!" The unexpected visit and now a present: in a matter of seconds Kibuka had completely reversed his opinion that life was no longer worth living. He was aglow with excitement.

"Yes. It's one of the piglets from the Farm School. The sow doesn't seem able to feed this new litter, so I thought you might like one for eating; it should make an excellent meal."

The boy strode back to the Landrover and returned with a black, squealing bundle under his arm.

Kibuka was more delighted than ever. He had never seen so small a pig before, and he spent a good ten minutes marveling at its tiny twinkling eyes, its minute hoofs, and its wisp of a tail. When his grandson drove away, he waved happily from the doorstep, the piglet clutched tenderly to his chest.

He had told his grandson that he would take the creature up to the Mukasas and ask Miriamu to prepare it as a special "welcome home" supper for Yosefu, but he soon sensed a certain reluctance within himself to do this, because the piglet followed him about the house or squatted trustingly at his feet each time he sat down. Moreover, it obviously understood every word Kibuka said to it, for, whenever he spoke, it listened gravely with its dainty forefeet placed lightly upon his knee.

By nightfall Kibuka was enchanted with his new companion, and would have as much considered eating it as he would consider eating the beloved grandson who had given it to him. He fed the piglet little scraps of food from his own plate, besides providing it with a rich porridge mixture. Nevertheless, within a few days it was clear that the pig's appetite was increasing out of all proportion to its size, and Kibuka had to resort to collecting matoke peelings[3] in an old bucket from his friends and nearest neighbors.

The news that Kibuka was keeping a pig, the first ever actually reared in Kalasanda, caused something of a sensation. In no time at all there was little need for him to cart the bucket from house to house, because the women and children, on their way to draw water from the stream, made a practice of bringing the peelings and food scraps with them as part of the excuse for calling on him, and being allowed to fondle the animal and discuss its progress as if it were a dear relative with a delicate hold on life.

No pig had ever had it so good. Fortunately, it proved to be a fastidiously clean creature, and for this reason Kibuka allowed it to spend its nights at the foot of his bed, although he was careful not to let his neighbors know of this. The pig, naturally enough, positively flourished in this cozy atmosphere of good will and personal attention. From a squealing bundle small enough to be held in one hand, it quickly developed into a handsome, hefty porker with eyes which held the faintest glint of malice even when it was at its most affectionate with Kibuka.

However, as the weeks went by, its rapid growth was accompanied by a variety of problems. For instance, it required more and more food, and, having been reared on the leavings of every kitchen in Kalasanda, was inclined to turn up its enormous snout at the idea of having to root in the shamba[4] whenever it felt like something to eat. Every time it started to kick its empty dish about noisily, pausing now and then to glare balefully at old Kibuka and utter snorts of derision, the old man was driven to taking up his bucket and trudging forth to see if any scraps in the village had been overlooked.

Also, while Kibuka had at first secretly enjoyed the warmth of a cuddly little piglet lying across his feet each night, he found himself at a distinct disadvantage when that same piglet acquired a bulk of some fifty or so pounds, and still insisted upon ponderously hoisting itself onto his bed as of right. Worse still, along with the weight, the piglet also produced a snore which regularly kept poor Kibuka awake until dawn. It was a grave decision he was finally called upon to make, yet one on which he simply dare not waver: in future, the pig would have to stay outside, tethered to a tree.

Who suffered most, Kibuka or his pig, would be hard to tell, for the animal's lamentations, continuing throughout the night, were equal in strength to the black remorse and wealth of recrimination churning in Kibuka's bosom. That pig never knew how often it was near to being brought indoors and pacified with a bowl of warm milk.

During the day it still was free to roam about until, that is, it adopted the irritating habit of falling into the stream. There it would be, placidly ambling after Kibuka as he pottered in his small shamba, or gently napping in the shade of a coffee tree, and

---

3. **matoke** (mə·tō′kā) **peelings:** skins of plantains or bananas. Matoke is a widely eaten food in Buganda.

4. **shamba:** homeowner's vegetable garden or cultivated field, where both vegetables and coffee are usually grown.

then, for no apparent reason, off it would go to the water's edge, and either fall or plunge in before anybody could say "bacon."

The Kalasanda stream had no real depth; many Kalasandans often bathed there or waded in; but sometimes, after a drop or two of rain, the current had more strength, and was quite capable of sweeping a child off its feet. The pig seemed always to choose such times for its immersion, and there wasn't anything anybody could really do as it spluttered and floundered with its hoofs flaying madly, and terror written plainly across its broad, black face.

At first, Kibuka would rush back and forth along the bank, calling frantically in the hope that it would struggle towards him, but what usually happened in the end was that a particularly strong eddy would sweep it round

? *What image of village life does the narrator of this story create?*

the bend into a thicket of weeds and rushes, and then the children playing there would have a good half-hour's fun driving it home.

This happened so often that Kibuka was forced to keep the pig tethered day and night. He visualized the time when no children would be playing in the reeds, and the pig would perhaps become entangled, dragged under and drowned.

By way of compensation he decided upon a regular evening walk for the animal, so by and by Kalasanda became accustomed to the sight of Kibuka, slight yet patriarchal in his kanzu and black waistcoat,[5] sedately traversing the countryside with a huge black pig at the end of a rope, and only strangers saw anything out of the ordinary in it. Without doubt, these walks were a source of great pleasure and exercise to the pig, who found them a wonderful change from the all too familiar view of Kibuka's shamba. Unfortunately, the same could not be said of their effect on old Kibuka. To be frank, Kibuka's corns were killing him, and the excruciating pain of every step sometimes brought tears to his eyes. Still, he tried to bear his discomfort with stoic fortitude, for, as he said to Daudi Kulubya, who showed concern over his limp, it was always the same before the heavy rains; in fact, his corns were as good as a barometer when it came to forecasting the weather. But he was always glad to return home, where he could sit for an hour with his poor feet in a bowl of hot water and try to keep his mind off the small fortune he was spending on corn plasters[6] brought to Kalasanda by the peddlers in the market.

---

5. **kanzu and black waistcoat:** Bugandan male's traditional long cotton garment and black vest.

6. **corn plasters:** small bandages placed on corns to prevent them from rubbing painfully against shoes.

Ugandan village.

F. & H. Schreider/Photo
Researchers, Inc.

How long this state of affairs would have continued is anybody's guess. There were occasions when Kibuka actually entertained the notion of parting with his pet at the first good offer from a reputable farmer or butcher. And yet, one trusting glance or gesture of affection from that waddling hunk of pork was enough for him to feel ashamed of what he regarded as his own treachery.

The end came at last in the most unlikely manner. One minute there was Kibuka contemplating the sunset, and, incidentally, giving his feet a rest by one of the obscure paths leading to the Sacred Tree,[7] while the pig scratched happily at the root of a clump of shrubs, its head hidden by foliage, while its carcass, broadside on, barricaded the path, and then, seconds later, there was the snarl of a motorcycle engine, the horrible grinding of brakes, followed by a whirling kaleidoscope of disaster. Kibuka, pig, bike and rider seemed to explode in all direc-

tions. Each had a momentary vision of the others sailing through the air.

When Kibuka eventually dared to open his eyes and cautiously move each limb, he was relieved to find he was still in one piece, although one shoulder felt painfully bruised and there was blood on both his hands. The rider, whom he now recognized as a certain Nathaniel Kiggundu, did not appear to have fared very badly either. He was staggering out of a tangled mass of weeds, wiping mud off his face, and fingering a long tear in the knee of his trousers.

Somewhere from behind the hedge came the raucous cries of a pig in distress, and it was in this direction that both men headed, once they had regained their bearings. They were only just in time to see the injured animal give up the ghost and join its ancestors in that heavenly piggery which surely must exist somewhere above. There was scarcely a mark on it, but its head lay at a strange and awkward angle, so it can be safely assumed that it died of a broken neck.

Old Kibuka was terribly upset, and the

---

7. **Sacred Tree:** local landmark of former religious significance.

accident had left him in a generally shaky condition. He sat down beside the dead animal and wondered what would happen next. Nathaniel Kiggundu, however, seeing Kibuka was comparatively unhurt, showed more concern over his motorcycle, which lay grotesquely twisted in a ditch. The inevitable crowd collected almost as soon as the pig expired, so there was much coming and going, first to stare at the fatal casualty, and then to stare at the motorbike. Nantondo kept up a running commentary, her version of how the accident happened, although nobody believed she had seen it, and by the time Musisi the Ggombolola Chief arrived on the scene, she had fully adopted the role of Mistress of Ceremonies.

After taking a statement from Kiggundu, Musisi approached Kibuka and insisted upon taking him home in the Landrover. "You don't look at all well, Sir. Come. You can make your statement in the morning, when you have had a rest."

"But I can't leave my pig here." Kibuka refused to budge from the spot.

"Well, I can put it in the back of the Landrover, if you like. Only it would be better to have the butcher cut it up, because I don't think pork will keep for long in this weather."

The idea of eating the pig had never entered Kibuka's mind. While sitting beside the body, he had been seriously considering just whereabouts in the shamba he could bury it. Now he opened his mouth to tell Musisi in no uncertain terms that eating one's good friends was a practice reserved for barbarians: and then, he suddenly had a clear picture of himself struggling to dig a grave. He was sure no Kalasandans would want to help him do it. Then came the realization of the effect a perpetual reminder of his porking friend in his shamba would have on him. He

did not think he could stand it. Far better, indeed, to let the past bury itself and, besides, why deprive his fellow villagers of a tasty treat? They were, after all, the people who had nourished the creature on their leftovers.

"Very well. Get somebody to carve it up and share it out among the people who eat pork,[8] and do be sure to send a whole back leg up to the Mukasas," he said at last, suddenly feeling far too weary to care.

"Musa the butcher won't do it," Nantondo piped. "He's a Muslim."

"Well, I'll take it along to the Ggombolola Headquarters and ask one of the askaris[9] to carve it up. Anybody who wants pork must go there at about seven o'clock tonight," declared Musisi, and ordered two of the onlookers to help him lift the carcass into the back of his vehicle.

Back at his cottage, Kibuka rubbed his injured shoulder with a concoction he used to cure most of his ailments, be they loose bowels or a sore throat, and then sat brooding over a cup of tea. He went to bed very early and awoke next day to find the sun well risen. He decided he had had the best night's sleep he had enjoyed for many a month. Musisi arrived as Kibuka was leaving home to see if the leg of pork had been safely delivered to Yosefu and Miriamu.

"No, I'm taking the meat there now, Sir," Musisi said. "Would you care to come with me?"

Kibuka gladly accepted the lift, although he declined the lump of pork Musisi had brought for him, personally. "You have it, son. I'm not a great lover of pork."

---

8. **people who eat pork:** In accordance with their religious teachings, local Muslims would not eat pork.

9. **askaris:** native African soldiers or police officers.

Miriamu went into raptures over the leg of pork, and Yosefu showed the keenest interest in the details of the accident. They pressed both Kibuka and Musisi to stay to lunch, but Musisi had to leave to attend a committee meeting in Mmengo,[10] so only Kibuka remained. He and Yosefu, who lately had not seen as much of each other as usual, had plenty to discuss, and lunch was an exhilarating meal.

---

10. **Mmengo** ('m·men'gō): larger town nearby.

"I must say, you really are a wonderful cook!" Kibuka told Miriamu, helping himself to more food. Miriamu preened herself, shyly. "Well, that pork was as tender as a chicken, and very tasty, too!"

There was a moment of dismay when Kibuka realized he was eating and thoroughly enjoying the succulence of his late friend, but it quickly passed, and he continued piling his plate with meat, smiling to himself at the knowledge that there would be no need to take a walk in the late afternoon; he could have a good nap instead.

First Thoughts

Did you think that Kibuka would be upset when he discovered he had eaten some of his pet pig? Did you find his reaction believable? Why or why not?

Identifying Facts

1. Why has Kibuka lost his job? Who brings Kibuka the piglet, and how does Kibuka greet this visitor?

2. What stops Kibuka from giving the piglet to Miriamu to serve at her husband's welcome-home dinner? Summarize Kalasanda's reaction to the news that Kibuka is keeping a pet pig.

3. Identify four problems that the pig creates for Kibuka as it grows older. How does the pig die?

4. What does Kibuka finally tell Musisi to do with the dead pig?

Interpreting Meanings

1. Why is Kibuka so delighted with the piglet? How would you describe his overall attitude toward the pet while it is alive?

2. What adjectives would you use to describe the community of Kalasanda?

Find story details that support your choice of adjectives.

3. What adjectives would you use to describe Kimenye's attitude toward the characters in "The Pig"? Find passages that illustrate this **tone**.

4. Explain the **internal conflict** between practical and sentimental considerations that Kibuka experiences once the pig is dead. What do his behavior and thoughts in the last paragraph suggest about human nature in general?

Applying Meanings

The Kalasanda that Kimenye depicts is a typical Bugandan village of its day. Did you find some aspects of the village typical of some American communities or neighborhoods? Why or why not?

Creative Writing Response

Writing About a Pet. Write a brief humorous story about an unusual pet. It may be an animal that people do not usually keep as a pet, or it may be a common pet that displays unusual talents or behavior. Your story may be purely fictional, or it may be based on someone's real-life experiences (including your own).

Mark Mathabane
b. 1960, South Africa

Mark Mathabane and members of his family.

If you were to ask Mark Mathabane (mä·tä′bä·nä) who his role models were as he was growing up, he would probably name Arthur Ashe and Joseph Conrad, among others. Ashe, the black American tennis star who in 1973 was finally allowed to play in South Africa, inspired Mathabane to practice the game that eventually won him a scholarship to an American university. Reading Conrad, the Polish-born English novelist, gave Mathabane the courage to try his hand at writing in English even though it was not his native tongue. The result of Mathabane's efforts was *Kaffir Boy* (1986), one of the first accounts of growing up black in twentieth-century South Africa.

In Mathabane's homeland, however, *Kaffir Boy* was banned. This action came as little surprise to Mathabane, who had faced far greater hardships as a result of his country's apartheid laws. These laws have kept blacks and whites separate and forced nonwhites into inferior jobs, housing, and schools. Raised in a small shack in Alexandra, a black slum just outside Johannesburg, Mathabane's family was extremely poor. There was often no food to eat, and the children slept under the kitchen table.

By law, Mathabane could attend only an all-black "tribal school"—crumbling, understaffed, overcrowded, and inadequately supplied. The school was not free and Mathabane's mother had to scrimp and save to pay his tuition. By law, pupils at the tribal schools studied mainly in their native Bantu languages. Mathabane desperately wanted to improve his English—which he saw as his passport to knowledge and freedom.

Although Mathabane won a tennis scholarship to an American university, he soon realized that he would not become a professional tennis player. He then began to devote more time to his studies and to writing his autobiography. When *Kaffir Boy* was published, one of its early admirers was TV talk-show host Oprah Winfrey, who invited Mathabane to appear on her show and arranged a surprise reunion with family members from South Africa. The reunion made headlines nationwide and helped *Kaffir Boy* to become a bestseller around the world.

Reader's Guide

from KAFFIR BOY

Background

The word *Kaffir* (ka'fər), Arabic for "infidel," was originally applied to certain Bantu-speaking tribes of South Africa. Over the decades it became a derogatory term used by many white South Africans to refer to any black South African. South Africa has long been a nation of great political, economic, and social inequality. This inequality became the law of the land in 1948 when the policy of apartheid (ə·pär'tāt' or -tīt) was instituted. The policy divided the nation along racial lines and protected the interests of the white population (less than a fifth of the population) by ensuring that the nonwhite majority would neither vote nor own valuable land. When Mark Mathabane was growing up—and even when he published *Kaffir Boy* in 1986—South Africa's apartheid laws were very much in place. The South African parliament began to repeal some of these laws in 1991, but political, educational, economic, and social disparities between blacks and whites still divide the nation.

Writer's Response

If you were writing your autobiography, what would you call the book? Choose a title and write it down. Underneath, make a list of the most important events in your life that you would be sure to include in your autobiography.

Literary Focus

An **autobiography** is an account of a person's life as he or she remembers it. The autobiography may be written simply to record an interesting life, or it may have more political or social purposes. Autobiographies are considered **nonfiction**, although some authors are more concerned with accuracy than others. *Kaffir Boy* is viewed as a remarkably honest account, even though Mathabane did change some people's names for their or his own protection.

from KAFFIR BOY

Mark Mathabane

As you read this selection, think about the reasons Mathabane wrote his autobiography. What do you think he wanted to prove or achieve? What political changes do you think he wanted to contribute to?

The seven o'clock bus for blacks to Johannesburg was jampacked with men and women on their way to the white world to work. A huge sign above the driver's booth read:

AUTHORIZED TO CARRY ONLY 65 SEATED PASSENGERS, AND 15 STANDING.

But there must have been close to a hundred perspiring people squeezed into the stuffy bus. People sat on top of one another; some were sandwiched in the narrow aisle between the rows of seats, and some crowded on the steps. I sat on Granny's lap, in the middle of the bus, by a large smudged window. As the bus droned past Alexandra's boundaries, I glued my eyes to the window, anticipating my first look at the white world. What I saw made me think I had just made a quantum leap into another galaxy. I couldn't stop asking questions.

"What are those?"

"Skyscrapers."

"Why do they reach all the way to the sky?"

"Because many white people live and work in them."

Seconds later. "Wow! look at all those nice houses, Granny! They're so big! Do many white people live and work there, too?"

"No, those are mansions. Each is owned by one family."

"By one family!" I cried in disbelief. Each mansion occupied an area about three times that of the yard I lived in, yet the latter was home for over twenty families.

"Yes," Granny said matter-of-factly. "Your grandpa, when he first came to Johannesburg, worked for one such family. The family was so rich they owned an airplane."

"Why are there so many cars in the white people's homes?"

"Because they like to have many cars."

"Those people dressed in white, what game are they playing?"

"The men are playing cricket. Master Smith plays that, too. The women are playing tennis. Mrs. Smith plays it, too, on Tuesday and Thursday."

Suddenly the bus screeched to a halt, and people crashed into each other. I was thrown into the back of the wooden seat in front of me. Smarting, I asked, "Why did the bus suddenly stop? I didn't see any robots."[1]

"Look over there," Granny pointed. "White schoolchildren are crossing the road."

I gazed through the window and for the first time in my life saw white schoolchildren.

---

1. **robots:** traffic lights.

I scrutinized them for any differences from black schoolchildren, aside from color. They were like little mannequins. The boys were neatly dressed in snow-white shirts, blazers with badges, preppy caps with badges, ties matching the badges, shiny black and brown shoes, worsted[2] knee-high socks. The girls wore pleated gymdresses with badges, snow-white shirts, caps with badges, blazers with badges, ties matching badges, shining black and brown shoes. A few of the girls had pigtails. On the back of each boy and girl was slung a schoolbag; and each frail, milky-white arm had a wristwatch on it. It suddenly struck me that we didn't even own a clock; we had to rely on cocks for time.[3]

The white schoolchildren were filing out of a large, red-brick building with many large windows, in front of which were beds of multicolored flowers. A tall black man wearing a traffic uniform, a whistle between his thick lips, stood in the middle of the paved road, one hand raised to stop traffic, the other holding a sign that read in English and Afrikaans:

CHILDREN CROSSING
STOP
KINDERS STAP OOR

None of this orderly and safe crossing of the street ever took place at my school; we had to dash across.

The red-brick building stood on a vast tract of land with immaculate lawns, athletic fields, swings, merry-go-rounds, an Olympic-sized swimming pool, tennis courts, and rows of brightly leafed trees. In the driveway leading to the entrance of the building,

scores of yellow school buses were parked. Not even the best of tribal schools in Alexandra—in the whole of South Africa—came close to having such magnificent facilities. At our school we didn't even have a school bus.

René Burri/Magnum Photos, Inc.

White schoolboy in Capetown, South Africa.
What are the narrator's feelings toward the white schoolchildren that he sees?

---

2. **worsted** (wŏŏs′tĭd): made of a smooth, hard-twisted wool.

3. **rely on cocks for time:** that is, rely on roosters crowing to know what time it is.

Oh, how I envied the white schoolchildren, how I longed to attend schools like theirs.

Minutes after all the white schoolchildren were safely across, traffic moved. At the next bus stop, we got off, and crossed the street when the robot flashed green. As we walked along the pavement, headed for Granny's workplace, I clutched her long dress, afraid of letting go, lest I be swallowed by the tremendous din of cars zooming up and down and honking in the busy streets. I began feeling dizzy as my eyes darted from one wonder to the next.

There were so many new and fantastic things around me that I walked as if in a dream. As we continued down the road, I became increasingly conscious of the curious looks white people gave us, as if we were a pair of escaped monkeys. Occasionally, Granny and I had to jump off the pavement to make way for *madams* and their poodles and English toy spaniels. By constantly throwing my eyes sideways, I accidentally bumped into a parking meter.

We went up a side street. "There is Mrs. Smith's house," Granny remarked as she led me up a long driveway of a beautiful villa-type house surrounded by a well-manicured lawn with several beds of colorful, sweet-smelling flowers and rosebushes. We went to a steel gate in the back of the yard, where Granny rang a bell.

"I'm here, madam," she shouted through the gate. Immediately a dog started barking from within; I trembled.

Granny calmed me. A door creaked open, and a high-pitched woman's voice called out, "I'm coming, Ellen. Quiet, Buster, you naughty dog, it's Ellen." The barking ceased. Presently the gate clicked open, and there appeared a short, slender white woman with silver hair and slightly drooping shoulders. She wore white slacks, a white sweater, white shoes, and a white visor.

"I was just getting ready to leave for tennis," she said to Granny; she had not yet seen me.

"Madam, guess who I have with me today," Granny said with the widest smile.

I appeared like a jack-in-the-box. "Oh, my, you finally brought him with you!" Mrs. Smith exclaimed.

Breaking into a wide smile, revealing gleaming teeth, several of which were made of gold, she continued, "My, what a big lad he is! What small ears!"—touching them playfully—"Is he really your grandson, Ellen?" The warmth in her voice somehow reduced my fears of her; her eyes shone with the same gentleness of the Catholic sisters[4] at the clinic.

"Yes, madam," Granny said proudly; "this is the one I've been telling you about. This is the one who'll some day go to university, like Master Clyde, and take care of me."

"I believe you, Ellen," said Mrs. Smith. "He looks like a very smart pickaninny."[5] Turning to me, she asked, "How old are you?"

"Eleven, madam, eleven," I said, with so wide a smile I thought my jaws would lock.

"He's a year younger than Master Clyde," Granny said, "though the master is much bigger."

"A little chubby, you mean," Mrs. Smith said with a smile. "If you knew how much the little master eats, Ellen; I'm afraid he'll soon turn into a piglet. Sometimes I regret not having had another child. With a sibling, Master Clyde might have turned out differently. As it is, he's so spoiled as an only child."

---

4. **sisters:** here, hospital nurses.
5. **pickaninny:** This term for a small black child, though highly offensive in the United States, is here used more condescendingly than disparagingly.

Black South African youths. *South African children like these, who do not have documents stating their racial group, do not officially exist according to South African policy and cannot attend public schools. Local residents have taken them off the streets to try to teach them the basics in a community center.*

"Pickaninny has one brother and three sisters," Granny said of me, "and the fifth one is on the way."

"My God! What a large family!" Mrs. Smith exclaimed. "What's the pickaninny's name?"

Using pidgin English,[6] I proceeded not only to give my name and surname, but also my grade in school, home address, tribal affiliation, name of school, principal and teacher—all in a feverish attempt to justify Granny's label of me as a "smart one."

Mrs. Smith was astounded. "What a clever, clever pickaninny!" She turned to a tall, lean black man with an expressionless face and slightly stooping shoulders, dressed in housekeeper's livery[7] (khaki shirt and pants), who had just emerged from the

house and who led a poodle on a leash, and said, "Did you hear that, Absalom? Bantu[8] children are smart. Soon they'll be running the country." Absalom simply tortured out a grin and took the poodle for a walk, after receiving instructions to bring brandy, whisky, wine and gin from the bottle store.[9] Granny remarked that I was a "clever pickaninny" because of all the toys, games and comic books I had received from Master Clyde. Mrs. Smith seemed extremely pleased to hear that.

Before Mrs. Smith left for tennis, she said, "Ellen, your breakfast is near the washing machine in the garage. I'll be back sometime this afternoon. Please see to it that the flowers near the pool are watered, and that the

---

6. **pidgin** (pij'in) **English:** here, a form of simplified English that incorporates Bantu vocabulary and syntax.
7. **livery:** uniform.

8. **Bantu** (ban'tōō): here, black South African, because most black South Africans speak one of the Bantu languages as their first language.
9. **bottle store:** liquor store.

rosebushes near the front of the gate are trimmed."

After a breakfast of coffee and peanut butter-and-jam sandwiches, Granny took out her gardening tools from the shed, and we started working. As the two of us went about the large yard, I raked leaves and watered the flowers; Granny weeded the lawn. Mrs. Smith's neighbor's children kept on casting curious glances over the fence. From the way they looked at me, it seemed they were seeing a black child for the first time in their lives.

At midday, despite a scorching sun, Granny, seemingly indefatigable, went about with impressive skill trimming the rosebushes as we talked about trees and flowers and how to best cultivate them.

"Someday I'll build a house as big and beautiful as Mrs. Smith's," I said to Granny. "And a garden just as big and beautiful."

"Then I'll be your gardener," Granny said with a smile.

Toward early afternoon Mrs. Smith returned. She called me to the car to remove several shopping bags from the back seat. She took her tennis rackets, closed the doors, then sighed, "Phew, what a tiring day. Don't ever play tennis," she said to me, "it's a killer."

"What's tennis, madam?" I asked.

"You don't know tennis?" she exclaimed. "What sports do you play?"

"Soccer, madam."

"Ugh, that dangerous sport. Soccer is too rough. You should try tennis someday. It's a gentlemen's sport. Wouldn't you like to be a gentleman?"

"I would like to be a gentleman, madam," I replied, even though I hadn't the faintest idea what constituted a gentleman.

"Do you have tennis courts in Alexandra?"

"Yes, madam." The stadium where I played soccer was adjacent to four ramshackle sand courts, used primarily by kitchen girls and kitchen boys on their day off.

"Then I'll see if I can find an old racket for you," she said.

As we were talking, a busload of white schoolchildren stopped in front of the house, and a young boy, with a mop of rebellious brown hair, alighted and ran up the driveway toward Mrs. Smith. After giving her a kiss, he turned and demanded, "Who is he, Mother?"

"That's Ellen's grandson. The one you've been giving all those comic books and toys to."

"What is he doing here?"

"He's visiting us."

"What for? I don't want him here."

"Why not, Clyde," Mrs. Smith said, "he's a nice pickaninny. Ellen is always nice to you, isn't she?"—the boy nodded with pursed lips—"now be nice to her grandson. Now run along inside and Absalom will show you the things I bought you today."

"Did you get my new bicycle and roller skates?"

"Yes, they'll be delivered Saturday. Now run in and change, and have something to eat. Then maybe you can play with pickaninny."

"I don't play with Kaffirs,"[10] the white boy declared. "At school they say we shouldn't."

"Watch your filthy mouth, Clyde," Mrs. Smith said, flushing crimson. "I thought I told you a million times to leave all that rubbish about Kaffirs in the classroom. Ellen's people are not Kaffirs, you hear! They're Bantus. Now go in and do as I told you." Turning to Granny, pruning a rosebush

---

10. **Kaffirs:** In South Africa, ''Kaffir'' is a disparaging term for any black African.

nearby, Mrs. Smith said, in a voice of someone fighting a losing battle, "You know, Ellen, I simply don't understand why those damn uncivilized Boers from Pretoria[11] teach children such things. What future does this country have if this goes on?"

"I agree *makulu*,[12] madam," Granny said, wiping her sweaty brow with her forearm. "All children, black and white, are God's children, madam. The preacher at my church tells us the Bible says so. 'Suffer little children to come unto me, and forbid them not; for of such is the kingdom of heaven,'[13] the Bible says. Is that not so, madam? Do you believe in the words of the Bible, madam?"

"I'm afraid you're right, Ellen," Mrs. Smith said, somewhat touched. "Yes, I do believe in the Bible. That's why I cannot accept the laws of this country. We white people are hypocrites. We call ourselves Christians, yet our deeds make the Devil look like a saint. I sometimes wish I hadn't left England."

I was struck by the openness of the discussion between Granny and Mrs. Smith.

"You're not like most white people I've worked for, madam," Granny said. "Master and you are kind toward our people. You treat us like human beings."

Mrs. Smith didn't answer; she hurried back indoors. Shortly thereafter, Clyde emerged in a pair of denims and a T-shirt advertising a South African rock group. He called out to me. "Come here, pickaninny. My mother says I should show you around."

South African youth doing homework.

I went.

I followed him around as he showed me all the things his parents regularly bought him: toys, bicycles, go-carts, pinball machines, Ping-Pong tables, electric trains. I only half-listened; my mind was preoccupied with comparing my situation with his. I couldn't understand why he and his people had to have all the luxuries money can buy, while I and my people lived in abject poverty. Was it because they were whites and we were black? Were they better than we? I could not find the answers; yet I felt there

---

11. **Boers** (bōorz) **from Pretoria** (pri·tôr′ē·ə): white South Africans of mainly Dutch descent whose National Party initiated the apartheid (ə·pär′tāt′) laws when it gained control of South Africa's government in 1948. Pretoria, a city northeast of Johannesburg, is the administrative capital of South Africa.

12. *makulu:* very much; in a big way.

13. **'Suffer . . . heaven':** Mark 10:14.

a student population of over two thousand, did not have half as many books. I was dazed.

Sensing that I was in awe of his magnificent library, Clyde said, "Do you have this many books in your playroom?"

"I don't have a playroom."

"You don't have a playroom," he said bug-eyed. "Can you read?" he smiled sinisterly. "Our boy Absalom can't. And he says black children aren't taught much English at school."

"I can read a little English," I said.

"I doubt if you can read any of my books. Here, read," he ordered, pulling one out of the shelves. The book was thick, looked formidable.

I nervously opened a page, toiled through a couple lines, encountering long words I could not pronounce, let alone understand their meaning. Shaking my head in embarrassment, I handed the book back, "I can't read this type of English."

"Then you must be retarded," Clyde laughed. Though he might have meant it in jest, my pride was deeply wounded. "This book is by William Shakespeare," he went on, waving it in my face, "the greatest English writer that ever lived. I could read it from cover to cover when I was half your age. But I don't blame you if you can't. My teachers tell us that Kaffirs can't read, speak, or write English like white people because they have smaller brains, which are already full of tribal things. My teachers say you're not people like us, because you belong to a jungle civilization. That's why you can't live or go to school with us, but can only be our servants."

"Stop saying that rubbish, you naughty boy," Mrs. Smith said angrily as she entered the room just in time to catch the tail end of her son's knowledge of black people's in-

was something wrong about white people having everything, and black people nothing.

We finally came to Clyde's playroom. The room was roughly the size of our house, and was elaborately decorated with posters, pennants of various white soccer and cricket teams, rock stars and photographs of Clyde in various stages of development. But what arrested my attention were the stacks of comic books on the floor, and the shelves and shelves of books. Never had I seen that many books in my life; even our school, with telligence, as postulated by the doctrine of apartheid. "How many times have I told you that what your teachers say about black people is not true?"

"What do you know, Mama?" Clyde retorted impudently, "you're not a teacher. Besides, there are textbooks where it's so written."

"Still it's not true," insisted Mrs. Smith. "Everything that's in your books is not necessarily true, especially your history books about this country." Changing the subject, she said, "Show him your easy books, and then get your things ready so I can drive you over to your friend's birthday party." Clyde quickly ran down his long list of "easy" books: *The Three Musketeers, Treasure Island, David Copperfield*, the Hardy Boys series, the Sherlock Holmes series, *Tom Sawyer, Robinson Crusoe, The Swiss Family Robinson, The Hunchback of Notre Dame, Black Beauty, A Tale of Two Cities*, and so on. Oh, how I envied Clyde's collection of books. I would have given my life to own just a handful of them.

The remark that black people had smaller brains and were thus incapable of reading, speaking, or writing English like white people had so wounded my ego that I vowed that, whatever the cost, I would master English, that I would not rest till I could read, write and speak it just like any white man, if not better. Finally, I had something to aspire to.

Back with Granny, I told her to be on the lookout whenever Mrs. Smith junked any books. At the end of the day, as Granny and I prepared to leave, I was given a small box by Mrs. Smith.

"It's from Clyde," she said. "He's sorry that he treated you badly. He's promised not to do it again. I'll see to it he keeps his promise. Come and help Ellen in the garden whenever you can; that way you'll earn some pocket money."

The box contained a couple shirts, pants, and jerseys.[14] Underneath the articles of clothing was a copy of *Treasure Island*.

To learn to express my thoughts and feelings effectively in English became my main goal in life. I saw command of the English language as the crucial key with which to unlock doors leading into that wonderful world of books revealed to me through the reading of Robert Louis Stevenson's gripping tale of buried treasure, mutiny on the high seas, one-legged seamen, and the old sea song that I could recite even in my dreams:

> *Fifteen men on a dead man's chest*
> *Yo-ho-ho, and a bottle of rum.*

My heart ached to explore more such worlds, to live them in the imagination in much the same way as I lived the folktales of my mother and grandmother. I reasoned that if I somehow kept improving my English and ingratiated Mrs. Smith by the fact, then possibly she would give me more books like *Treasure Island* each time Granny took me along. Alas, such trips were few and far between. I could not afford to skip school regularly; and besides, each trip did not yield a book. But I clung to my dream.

A million times I wondered why the sparse library at my tribal school did not carry books like *Treasure Island*, why most of the books we read had tribal points of view. I would ask teachers and would be told that under the Bantu Education law black children were supposed to acquire a solid foundation in tribal life, which would prepare them for a productive future in their respective homelands. In this way the dream

---

14. **jerseys:** sweaters.

of Dr. Verwoerd,[15] prime minister of South Africa and the architect of Bantu Education, would be realized, for he insisted that "the native child must be taught subjects which will enable him to work with and among his own people; therefore there is no use misleading him by showing him the green pastures of European society, in which he is not allowed to graze. Bantu Education should not be used to create imitation whites."

How I cursed Dr. Verwoerd and his law for prescribing how I should feel and think. I started looking toward the Smiths to provide me with the books about a different reality. Each day Granny came back from work around five in the afternoon, I would be the first to meet her at the gate, always with the same question, "Any books for me today?" Many times there weren't any. Unable to read new English books on a regular basis, I reread the ones I had over and over again, till the pages became dogeared. With each reading each book took on new life, exposed new angles to the story, with the result that I was never bored.

My bleak vocabulary did not diminish my enthusiasm for reading. I constantly borrowed Mr. Brown's[16] pocket-size dictionary to look up meanings of words, and would memorize them like arithmetic tables and write them in a small notebook. Sometimes I would read the dictionary. My pronunciation was appalling, but I had no way of finding out. I was amazed at the number of words in the English language, at the fact that a word could have different shades of meaning, or that certain words looked and sounded alike and yet differed greatly in meaning. Would I ever be able to learn all that?

At the same time I was discovering the richness of the English language I began imitating how white people talked, in the hope of learning proper pronunciation. My efforts were often hilarious, but my determination increased with failure. I set myself the goal of learning at least two new English words a day.

---

15. **Dr. Verwoerd** (fər·voort'): Hendrik Frensch Verwoerd (1901–1966), South African politician and one of the chief architects of apartheid. Verwoerd served as prime minister from 1958 to 1966.

16. **Mr. Brown's:** referring to one of the author's better-educated neighbors, who appears earlier in *Kaffir Boy*.

First Thoughts

What did you most admire about the narrator? Was there anything you did not admire?

Identifying Facts

1. When Mathabane visits white Johannesburg for the first time, what differences does he notice between white South African life and his own life?

2. Summarize Mrs. Smith's reprimand when her son calls Mathabane a "Kaffir." What does she then say about white South Africa?

3. What does Clyde give Mathabane to test his literacy? What easier book comes in the box with Clyde's hand-me-downs?

4. What question does Mathabane ask each time his grandmother returns from work? What goal does he set at the end of the selection?

Interpreting Meanings

1. Contrast conditions on the bus for blacks with conditions in white Johannesburg. What does the contrast suggest about South Africa? Based on contrasts like these, identify one of the author's purposes in writing his **autobiography**.

2. What adjectives would you use to describe the author as a young boy? What proof do you have that he will master English?

3. What positive and negative qualities does Mrs. Smith display? In what ways is Clyde cruel to the author? Where do you think he learned to behave this way?

Do you think Mathabane uses Clyde's behavior to point to a larger problem in white South African society? If so, what is that problem?

4. What does the different behavior of the people here suggest about South Africa's future?

Applying Meanings

What role does peer pressure play in racial or ethnic prejudice and the way we treat outsiders in general? Why do you think people succumb to peer pressure?

Creative Writing Response

Writing an Autobiographical Episode. Look over the list of life events you wrote down in the Writer's Response. Choose one event and write a few paragraphs about it, presenting it as an episode in the **autobiography** that you may someday write.

Critical Writing Response

Writing About an Author's Purpose. In a brief essay, discuss Mathabane's chief purposes in writing his **autobiography**. Based on this selection, state what those purposes seem to be, and then discuss selection details that help him achieve each purpose. Before writing, you may want to list two or three purposes and supporting details on a chart like the one below.

Purpose	Details That Help Achieve This Purpose

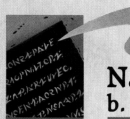

Naguib Mahfouz
b. 1911, Egypt

T. Cambra Pierce/Wide World Photos

As a boy in Cairo's picturesque old quarter, Naguib Mahfouz (nä·jēb′ mä′fōōz) encountered many unusual characters who would influence his life and work. Among them was journalist El-Muwaylili, who was experimenting in new forms of fiction. At the time, the novel form was virtually unknown in Arabic literature, where poetry and nonfiction were stressed. El-Muwaylili's efforts inspired Mahfouz to introduce full-fledged novels to Arabic literature. Eventually Mahfouz would become the best-known fiction writer in the Arabic language and the first Arabic author to win the Nobel Prize for literature.

Interested in both philosophy and literature, Mahfouz attended Cairo University, where classes were conducted in English and French. His growing proficiency in these languages allowed him to read many European classics and to familiarize himself with the novel and short-story forms. Still uncertain of his future, Mahfouz submitted a short story to a Cairo magazine. He considers the day it was accepted the most important day of his life.

The course of Mahfouz's writing career seems to recapitulate two centuries of literary movements. His early historical novels, set in the time of the pharaohs, display the idealistic nationalism of Romantic Age authors like Johann Wolfgang von Goethe (see page 986). In the chaotic period leading up to World War II, Mahfouz turned to social realism in books like *New Cairo* (1946) and *Midaq Alley* (1947), which vividly evoke his boyhood neighborhood and the effects of war on the average Egyptian. Mahfouz continued in this realistic vein with his masterful Cairo trilogy—*Between the Two Palaces* (1956), *The Palace of Desire* (1957), and *The Sugar Bowl* (1957)—about three generations of a Cairo family who symbolize Egyptian experience in modern times. In the 1960s Mahfouz began to experiment with the stream-of-consciousness technique, as well as the more indirect symbolism associated with modernism. His preoccupation with the individual facing spiritual and emotional crises was prompted in part by the growing Arab-Israeli conflict and Egypt's bitter defeat in the 1967 Six-Day War.

Reader's Guide

HALF A DAY

Background

Today, Egypt's chief language is Arabic, and more than ninety percent of all Egyptians are Muslims. Because so much of Egypt is desert, Egyptians have traditionally lived on the fertile banks of the Nile River. Since World War II, more and more people from rural areas along the Nile have moved to Egypt's major cities, also located on the river. The largest of these cities is Cairo (kī′rō), Egypt's capital, where Mahfouz grew up and where the upcoming story is set.

   Cairo's population has increased dramatically since Mahfouz was a boy, and many of the city's fields and gardens have given way to tall modern buildings. As in other urban centers all over the world, overcrowding has created many problems, among them noise pollution, inadequate waste removal, and insufficient public transportation. Cairo is also famous for having some of the world's worst traffic jams.

Writer's Response

Write a paragraph supporting or refuting the following statement: "There are too many human beings living on the earth today." Cite details from your everyday life to back up your opinion.

Literary Focus

Theme is the central idea or insight behind a work of literature. Theme moves beyond the specifics of the work to express a general idea or insight about life or human nature. For instance, a story may be about a father watching his son play a baseball game, but the theme may be about fathers' unfulfilled ambitions. The theme of a story usually reveals something about the writer's personal attitudes toward some aspect of life.

HALF A DAY

Naguib Mahfouz

translated by

DENYS JOHNSON-DAVIES

| *Notice specific details that indicate how Mahfouz feels about the modernization of Egypt.*

I proceeded alongside my father, clutching his right hand, running to keep up with the long strides he was taking. All my clothes were new: the black shoes, the green school uniform, and the red tarboosh.[1] My delight in my new clothes, however, was not altogether unmarred, for this was no feast day[2] but the day on which I was to be cast into school for the first time.

My mother stood at the window watching our progress, and I would turn toward her from time to time, as though appealing for help. We walked along a street lined with gardens; on both sides were extensive fields planted with crops, prickly pears, henna trees, and a few date palms.

"Why school?" I challenged my father openly. "I shall never do anything to annoy you."

"I'm not punishing you," he said, laughing. "School's not a punishment. It's the factory that makes useful men out of boys. Don't you want to be like your father and brothers?"

I was not convinced. I did not believe there was really any good to be had in tearing me away from the intimacy of my home and throwing me into this building that stood at the end of the road like some huge, high-walled fortress, exceedingly stern and grim.

When we arrived at the gate we could see the courtyard, vast and crammed full of boys and girls. "Go in by yourself," said my father, "and join them. Put a smile on your face and be a good example to others."

I hesitated and clung to his hand, but he

---

1. **tarboosh** (tär·bōōsh'): brimless cloth cap worn by Muslim men.
2. **feast day:** holiday.

The Bettmann Archive

El Azhar Mosque in Cairo, Egypt.
? *Does the narrator's reluctance to go to school for the first time strike you as realistic?*

gently pushed me from him. "Be a man," he said. "Today you truly begin life. You will find me waiting for you when it's time to leave."

I took a few steps, then stopped and looked but saw nothing. Then the faces of boys and girls came into view. I did not know a single one of them, and none of them knew me. I felt I was a stranger who had lost his way. But glances of curiosity were directed toward me, and one boy approached and asked, "Who brought you?"

"My father," I whispered.

"My father's dead," he said quite simply.

I did not know what to say. The gate was closed, letting out a pitiable screech. Some of the children burst into tears. The bell rang. A lady came along, followed by a group of men. The men began sorting us into ranks. We were formed into an intricate pattern in the great courtyard surrounded on three sides by high buildings of several floors; from each floor we were overlooked by a long balcony roofed in wood.

"This is your new home," said the woman. "Here, too, there are mothers and fathers. Here there is everything that is enjoyable and beneficial to knowledge and religion. Dry your tears and face life joyfully."

We submitted to the facts, and this submission brought a sort of contentment. Living beings were drawn to other living beings, and from the first moments my heart made friends with such boys as were to be my friends and fell in love with such girls as I was to be in love with, so that it seemed my misgivings had had no basis. I had never imagined school would have this rich variety. We played all sorts of different games: swings, the vaulting horse,[3] ball games. In

A busy street in Cairo.

Thomas Nebbia/Woodfin Camp & Associates

the music room we chanted our first songs. We also had our first introduction to language. We saw a globe of the Earth, which revolved and showed the various continents and countries. We started learning the numbers. The story of the Creator of the universe was read to us, we were told of His present world and of His Hereafter, and we heard examples of what He said. We ate delicious food, took a little nap, and woke up to go on with friendship and love, play and learning.

As our path revealed itself to us, however, we did not find it as totally sweet and

---

3. **vaulting horse**: that is, the horse one leaps over in gymnastics.

unclouded as we had presumed. Dust-laden winds and unexpected accidents came about suddenly, so we had to be watchful, at the ready, and very patient. It was not all a matter of playing and fooling around. Rivalries could bring about pain and hatred or give rise to fighting. And while the lady would sometimes smile, she would often scowl and scold. Even more frequently she would resort to physical punishment.

In addition, the time for changing one's mind was over and gone and there was no question of ever returning to the paradise of home. Nothing lay ahead of us but exertion, struggle, and perseverance. Those who were able took advantage of the opportunities for success and happiness that presented themselves amid the worries.

The bell rang announcing the passing of the day and the end of work. The throngs of children rushed toward the gate, which was opened again. I bade farewell to friends and sweethearts and passed through the gate. I peered around but found no trace of my father, who had promised to be there. I stepped aside to wait. When I had waited for a long time without avail, I decided to return home on my own. After I had taken a few steps, a middle-aged man passed by, and I realized at once that I knew him. He came toward me, smiling, and shook me by the hand, saying, "It's a long time since we last met—how are you?"

With a nod of my head, I agreed with him and in turn asked, "And you, how are you?"

"As you can see, not all that good, the Almighty be praised!"

Again he shook me by the hand and went off. I proceeded a few steps, then came to a startled halt. Good Lord! Where was the street lined with gardens? Where had it disappeared to? When did all these vehicles invade it? And when did all these hordes of humanity come to rest upon its surface? How did these hills of refuse come to cover its sides? And where were the fields that bordered it? High buildings had taken over, the street surged with children, and disturbing noises shook the air. At various points stood conjurers[4] showing off their tricks and making snakes appear from baskets. Then there was a band announcing the opening of a circus, with clowns and weight lifters walking in front. A line of trucks carrying central security troops crawled majestically by. The siren of a fire engine shrieked, and it was not clear how the vehicle would cleave its way to reach the blazing fire. A battle raged between a taxi driver and his passenger, while the passenger's wife called out for help and no one answered. Good God! I was in a daze. My head spun. I almost went crazy. How could all this have happened in half a day, between early morning and sunset? I would find the answer at home with my father. But where was my home? I could see only tall buildings and hordes of people. I hastened on to the crossroads between the gardens and Abu Khoda.[5] I had to cross Abu Khoda to reach my house, but the stream of cars would not let up. The fire engine's siren was shrieking at full pitch as it moved at a snail's pace, and I said to myself, "Let the fire take its pleasure in what it consumes."[6] Extremely irritated, I wondered when I would be able to cross. I stood there a long time, until the young lad employed at the ironing shop on the corner came up to me. He stretched out his arm and said gallantly, "Grandpa, let me take you across."

---

4. **conjurers:** magicians.
5. **Abu Khoda:** (ä·bōō′ kō′dä)
6. **Let the fire . . . consumes:** an Egyptian proverb.

First Thoughts

Were you surprised by the story's ending? Did it add to your enjoyment of the story or did it confuse you? Explain.

Identifying Facts

1. As the story opens, where is the narrator's father taking him for the first time? What explanations and advice does the father give?

2. Identify four things the narrator likes about his new experience and two things he dislikes.

3. After the bell rings, for whom does the narrator wait in vain? As he walks home alone, what does a middle-aged man on the street do?

4. List three questions the narrator asks himself while walking home. As he waits to cross the busy intersection, what does the "young lad" do and say?

Interpreting Meanings

1. What surprise was revealed at the end of the story? Did you have any idea that the story might end in this way?

2. Reread the story and identify three details that **foreshadow** the surprise ending.

3. Perhaps you have heard the expression, "His life flashed before his eyes." Do you think that Mahfouz, in this story, realistically presents the way an older person's mind might work? Why or why not?

4. What **theme** about time does the ending help convey? How is the title of the story relevant to this theme?

5. Does the story also express **themes** on any of these subjects: change, old age, youth, school, and parent-child relationships? If so, what are they?

Applying Meanings

Why is the first day of school such a memorable event in most children's lives?

Creative Writing Response

Writing About a Childhood Memory.
Write a brief story based on your first day of school or another memorable event in your childhood. Like Mahfouz, you might play tricks with time to make a point about time's passage.

Critical Writing Response

Comparing Themes in Two Stories.
"Half a Day" and Santha Rama Rau's essay "By Any Other Name" (see page 1387) deal with a child's experience of school. Write a statement of **theme** for each selection (both should relate to the effects of school on a child's life). Decide whether the two stories share more similarities or differences and write a brief essay comparing and contrasting their themes.

Language and Vocabulary

Arabic and English

Over the centuries, English has borrowed dozens of words from Arabic. Some came to English directly, others came by way of other European languages such as Spanish, French, Italian, and Latin. Use a dictionary to help you find the origins of these English words, some of which appear in the English translation of "Half a Day." Also provide the meanings of any unfamiliar words.

1. admiral
2. algebra
3. caliber
4. tariff
5. carmine
6. cipher
7. ghoul
8. henna
9. saffron
10. sheik

Yehuda Amichai
b. 1924, Israel

Like many Israelis of his generation, Yehuda Amichai (yə·hoō'də ä'mi·khī') has spent much of his life as a soldier. During World War II he served in the Jewish brigade of the British army fighting against German forces in the Middle East. In 1948, after Israel won independence and was attacked by neighboring Arab nations, Amichai fought with the special strike force of the Israeli army. Later, as an army reservist, he was often called upon to fight for his country.

Born to an orthodox Jewish family in southern Germany, Amichai escaped Nazi persecution when he was only twelve. Like many other European Jews lucky enough to escape, Amichai and his family immigrated to the Holy Land, then British-controlled Palestine. There they eventually settled in the city of Jerusalem, where the young Amichai continued his studies of Hebrew literature and the Bible. After serving as a soldier in the 1940s, Amichai completed his studies at Jerusalem's Hebrew University. By then he had already published several Hebrew-language poems in magazines, although his first poetry collection, *Now and in Other Days*, did not appear until 1955.

In addition to writing poems, novels, short stories, and plays, Amichai has taught Hebrew literature both in Israel and abroad. While Hebrew was not his first language, Amichai began learning it during his childhood religious studies in Germany, since ancient Hebrew is the language of Jewish scripture and ritual. Modern spoken Hebrew, however, is very different from ancient Hebrew. Mastering the differences has been a challenge for contemporary Israeli authors, and Amichai is considered one of Israel's first writers to meet that challenge successfully. His style combines the informality of modern spoken Hebrew with the powerful poetic images found in the Old Testament.

At the heart of virtually all of Amichai's poetry is his concern with the effects that frequent warfare and a constant war-ready state have had on the Israeli consciousness.

Reader's Guide

from LAMENTS ON THE WAR DEAD

Background

After the ancient Romans conquered the Holy Land, which they called Palestine, the area's Jews revolted unsuccessfully and most were driven into exile. Many of these exiles settled in Europe, where they were severely persecuted over the centuries. In the late 1800s, European Jews formed the Zionist movement, which sought to reestablish in the Holy Land a nation where Jews could live free of oppression. By now Arabs had become Palestine's chief inhabitants, but soon more and more Jews began returning. In 1947, in the wake of world horror at the Holocaust, the United Nations voted to partition Palestine into a Jewish nation and an Arab nation. The Jews accepted the plan, but the Arabs did not. On May 15, 1948, a day after the new Jewish nation of Israel came into being, neighboring Arab countries attacked in the first of several Arab-Israeli wars. With each war, the Israelis emerged as victors, acquiring more land and working to build modern cities and productive farms.

Yehuda Amichai wrote his poetic sequence *Laments on the War Dead* soon after the war of 1973, when Egypt and Syria attacked Israel on the Jewish high holy day of Yom Kippur. Israel won the war, but at great cost, both economically and in terms of human lives.

Writer's Response

Comment on recent events in the Middle East, researching them in current newspapers if necessary. How do you assess the situation? Do you have more sympathy for one group than another?

Literary Focus

Poets often use **repetition** to create rhythm, build suspense, or emphasize a particular word or idea. In **incremental repetition**, a line or section of a poem or song is repeated with some variation in wording. Usually the variation adds significant new information or expresses a significant change in meaning or attitude.

from LAMENTS ON THE WAR DEAD

Yehuda Amichai

translated by
WARREN BARGAD AND STANLEY F. CHYET

🔖 *Look for the answers the speaker gives to the poem's opening question.*

Modern-day Israel.

6

Is all this sorrow? I don't know.
I stood in the cemetery dressed
in the camouflage clothing of a live man, brown
pants and a shirt yellow as the sun.

5   Graveyards are cheap and unassuming.
Even the wastebaskets are too small to hold
the thin paper that wrapped the store-bought
    flowers.
Graveyards are disciplined, mannered things.
"I'll never forget you," reads
10   a small brick tablet in French.°
I don't know who it is who won't forget,
who's more unknown than the one who's dead.

Is all this sorrow? I think
so. "Be consoled in building the land." How
15   long can we build the land,
to gain in the terrible, three-sided
game of building, consolation, and death?
Yes, all this is sorrow. But
leave a little love always lit,
20   like the nightlight in a sleeping infant's room,
not that he knows what light is
and where it comes from, but it gives him
a bit of security and some silent love.

10. **in French:** Although Hebrew is Israel's chief language, an immigrant from Europe or elsewhere might also continue to use his or her first language, especially on a tombstone.

Would you say the poem ends on a positive or a negative note? Explain your response.

Identifying Facts

1. What is the speaker's first answer to the opening question? What is he wearing as he stands in the cemetery?

2. What two statements does the speaker make about graveyards? What does he not know about the inscription on the small brick tablet?

3. What two answers to the opening question does the speaker give in lines 13–23? What other question does he ask here?

4. In lines 13–23, what does the speaker request? What comparison does he make?

Interpreting Meanings

1. How would you describe the speaker's attitude until line 17? What growing realization on the speaker's part is traced by the **incremental repetition** in lines 1, 13–14, and 18?

2. Identify another example of **incremental repetition** and the contrast it presents. What overall effect does all the repetition have?

3. Who might the speaker be quoting in line 14? What does the question in lines 14–17 reveal about modern Israeli experience?

4. In his request in lines 18–19, whom might the speaker be addressing? What advice might the **extended simile** in lines 18–23 be giving to modern Israelis and other war victims?

Applying Meanings

What positive functions does grieving for the dead provide? When can such grieving become negative?

Creative Writing Response

Writing an Elegy. An **elegy** is a poem of mourning or lament. Write an elegy in which you honor the memory of the victims of a particular war or another human disaster. Your poem may also address the needs and feelings of survivors, as Amichai's does.

Critical Writing Response

Writing About an Extended Simile. In a brief essay, explain how the **extended simile** in lines 18–23 helps express the theme of the poem. Include answers to the following questions in your essay: What two dissimilar things are being compared? What qualities do they share? How does the simile bring an abstract concept down to earth?

Language and Vocabulary

Hebrew and English

Over the centuries English has borrowed words from Hebrew. Some came to English directly; many came from other languages, including Yiddish, the Germanic tongue once used by many European Jews. For the exercise below, use a dictionary to help you match the English words in the left-hand column with the information about their origins in the right-hand column. Also be sure you know the meanings of all the listed words.

1. amen   a. from the Hebrew for "fitting; right; proper"

2. kibbutz   b. from a Hebrew term meaning "anointed (one)"

3. kosher   c. from the Hebrew for "to rest"

4. messiah   d. from a Hebrew exclamation literally meaning "truly; certainly"

5. sabbath   e. from the modern Hebrew for a collective farm in Israel

Santha Rama Rau
b. 1923, India

Wide World Photo

Santha Rama Rau (sän'thä räm'ä rou) was raised by broad-minded parents who had traveled all over the globe. Still, they were upset when she took her first job. "My family didn't mind my *working*," she explained, "but they were worried about the idea of my *earning money*. It wasn't considered entirely respectable for a girl whose family could afford to support her until she got married to be actually picking up a paycheck." Nevertheless, Rama Rau insisted on a writing career, and finally her parents

relented. After all, their daughter had already published her first book, *Home to India* (1945), and the positive reviews of this autobiographical memoir were strong persuasion indeed.

The daughter of an Indian diplomat, Rama Rau was born when India was still a colony of Britain. When she was eleven, Rama Rau went to Europe to stay with her father, who was serving as India's Deputy High Commissioner in London. She attended London's St. Paul's School for Girls and during the summer often vacationed in France. When she was sixteen, she returned to India and found that she was something of an outsider. In an effort to rediscover her native land, she wrote *Home to India* while she was a student at Wellesley College in Massachusetts.

Living in India after World War II, Rama Rau witnessed firsthand all the excitement surrounding her nation's independence in 1947. In that same year she took a sabbatical, or period of leave, from her editing job at Bombay's *Trend* magazine to accompany her father to his new post as India's first ambassador to Japan. She recounted her experiences in the highly regarded travel book *East of Home*, published in 1950.

Two years later Rama Rau married an American and settled in New York City, where she began contributing articles to American magazines. Her essay "By Any Other Name," reprinted here, was published first in *The New Yorker*.

Reader's Guide

By Any Other Name

Background

During the long British presence in India, many British soldiers, settlers, and public officials moved to India to seek their fortunes and aid
in governing and controlling the land. These people became known as
Anglo-Indians. While the British contributed to the modernization of
India, they also often neglected, misinterpreted, or denigrated native
Indian customs. In "By Any Other Name," Santha Rama Rau illumi-
nates this clash of cultures by recalling a childhood incident.

Writer's Response

Recall an incident in your own childhood that first introduced you to
the traditions of a different ethnic, religious, or national group, either
in real life or through a book, movie, or television show. How were
these people different from you, and how did you feel about them? Did
the incident make you see yourself or your own culture differently?

Literary Focus

An **essay** is a short piece of nonfiction prose that usually examines a
single subject. Essays are sometimes classified as formal or informal. A
formal essay is serious and impersonal in tone. Often it carefully and
logically explains a subject or tries to persuade readers to accept a
particular way of thinking. An **informal essay**, also called a **personal
essay**, generally reveals far more about the personality and feelings of
the author. Many informal essays—including Santha Rama Rau's—are
autobiographical in nature, recounting an episode or series of related
episodes from the author's life.

BY ANY OTHER NAME

Santha Rama Rau

The title of this essay comes from Shakespeare's **Romeo and Juliet:**

> *What's in a name? That which we call a rose*
> *By any other name would smell as sweet.*

As you read the essay, think about Rama Rau's reasons for choosing this particular title.

At the Anglo-Indian day school in Zorinabad[1] to which my sister and I were sent when she was eight and I was five and a half, they changed our names. On the first day of school, a hot, windless morning of a north Indian September, we stood in the headmistress's study and she said, "Now you're the *new* girls. What are your names?"

My sister answered for us. "I am Premila, and she"—nodding in my direction—"is Santha."

The headmistress had been in India, I suppose, fifteen years or so, but she still smiled her helpless inability to cope with Indian names. Her rimless half-glasses glittered, and the precarious bun on the top of her head trembled as she shook her head. "Oh, my dears, those are much too hard for me. Suppose we give you pretty English names. Wouldn't that be more jolly? Let's see, now—Pamela for you, I think." She shrugged in a baffled way at my sister. "That's as close as I can get. And for *you*" she said to me, "how about Cynthia? Isn't that nice?"

My sister was always less easily intimi-dated than I was, and while she kept a stubborn silence, I said, "Thank you," in a very tiny voice.

We had been sent to that school because my father, among his responsibilities as an officer of the civil service, had a tour of duty to perform in the villages around that steamy little provincial town, where he had his headquarters at that time. He used to make his shorter inspection tours on horseback, and a week before, in the stale heat of a typically postmonsoon[2] day, we had waved goodbye to him and a little procession—an assistant, a secretary, two bearers, and the man to look after the bedding rolls and luggage. They rode away through our large garden, still bright green from the rains, and we turned back into the twilight of the house and the sound of fans whispering in every room.

Up to then, my mother had refused to send Premila to school in the British-run establishments of that time, because, she

---

1. **Zorinabad:** town in northern India.

2. **postmonsoon:** referring to the dry spell that generally follows the rainy season, when ocean winds called monsoons bring rain to India.

used to say, "you can bury a dog's tail for seven years and it still comes out curly, and you can take a Britisher away from his home for a lifetime and he still remains insular." The examinations and degrees from entirely Indian schools were not, in those days, considered valid. In my case, the question had never come up, and probably never would have come up if Mother's extraordinary good health had not broken down. For the first time in my life, she was not able to continue the lessons she had been giving us every morning. So our Hindi[3] books were put away, the stories of the Lord Krishna[4] as a little boy were left in midair, and we were sent to the Anglo-Indian school.

That first day at school is still, when I think of it, a remarkable one. At that age, if one's name is changed, one develops a curious form of dual personality. I remember having a certain detached and disbelieving concern in the actions of "Cynthia," but certainly no responsibility. Accordingly, I followed the thin, erect back of the headmistress down the veranda to my classroom feeling, at most, a passing interest in what was going to happen to me in this strange, new atmosphere of School.

The building was Indian in design, with wide verandas opening onto a central courtyard, but Indian verandas are usually whitewashed, with stone floors. These, in the tradition of British schools, were painted dark brown and had matting on the floors. It gave a feeling of extra intensity to the heat.

I suppose there were about a dozen Indian children in the school—which contained perhaps forty children in all—and four of them were in my class. They were all sitting at the back of the room, and I went to join them. I sat next to a small, solemn girl who didn't smile at me. She had long, glossy black braids and wore a cotton dress, but she still kept on her Indian jewelry—a gold chain around her neck, thin gold bracelets, and tiny ruby studs in her ears. Like most Indian children, she had a rim of black kohl[5] around her eyes. The cotton dress should have looked strange, but all I could think of was that I should ask my mother if I couldn't wear a dress to school, too, instead of my Indian clothes.

I can't remember too much about the proceedings in class that day, except for the beginning. The teacher pointed to me and asked me to stand up. "Now, dear, tell the class your name."

I said nothing.

"Come along," she said, frowning slightly. "What's your name, dear?"

"I don't know," I said, finally.

The English children in the front of the class—there were about eight or ten of them—giggled and twisted around in their chairs to look at me. I sat down quickly and opened my eyes very wide, hoping in that way to dry them off. The little girl with the braids put out her hand and very lightly touched my arm. She still didn't smile.

Most of that morning I was rather bored. I looked briefly at the children's drawings pinned to the wall, and then concentrated on a lizard clinging to the ledge of the high, barred window behind the teacher's head. Occasionally it would shoot out its long yellow tongue for a fly, and then it would rest, with its eyes closed and its belly palpitating,

---

3. **Hindi** (hin′dē): an Indo-European language that is now considered the official language of India.
4. **Lord Krishna:** in the Hindu religion, human form taken by the god Vishnu; many Hindu stories recount episodes in the life of Lord Krishna.

---

5. **kohl** (kōl): dark powder used as eye makeup.

Schoolgirl in Ahmadabad, India.

as though it were swallowing several times quickly. The lessons were mostly concerned with reading and writing and simple numbers—things that my mother had already taught me—and I paid very little attention. The teacher wrote on the easel blackboard words like "bat" and "cat," which seemed babyish to me; only "apple" was new and incomprehensible.

When it was time for the lunch recess, I followed the girl with braids out onto the veranda. There the children from the other classes were assembled. I saw Premila at once and ran over to her, as she had charge of our lunchbox. The children were all opening packages and sitting down to eat sandwiches. Premila and I were the only ones who had Indian food—thin wheat chapatties,[6] some vegetable curry, and a bottle of buttermilk. Premila thrust half of it into my hand and whispered fiercely that I should go and sit with my class, because that was what the others seemed to be doing.

The enormous black eyes of the little Indian girl from my class looked at my food longingly, so I offered her some. But she only shook her head and plowed her way solemnly through her sandwiches.

I was very sleepy after lunch, because at home we always took a siesta. It was usually a pleasant time of day, with the bedroom darkened against the harsh afternoon sun, the drifting off into sleep with the sound of Mother's voice reading a story in one's mind, and, finally, the shrill, fussy voice of the ayah[7] waking one for tea.

At school, we rested for a short time on low, folding cots on the veranda, and then we were expected to play games. During the hot part of the afternoon we played indoors, and after the shadows had begun to lengthen and the slight breeze of the evening had come up we moved outside to the wide courtyard.

I had never really grasped the system of competitive games. At home, whenever we played tag or guessing games, I was always allowed to "win"—"because," Mother used to tell Premila, "she is the youngest, and we have to allow for that." I had often heard her say it, and it seemed quite reasonable to

---

6. **chapatties** (chə·pä′tēz): thin unleavened fried bread.

7. **ayah** (ä′yə): nanny in India.

me, but the result was that I had no clear idea of what "winning" meant.

When we played twos-and-threes[8] that afternoon at school, in accordance with my training, I let one of the small English boys catch me, but was naturally rather puzzled when the other children did not return the courtesy. I ran about for what seemed like hours without ever catching anyone, until it was time for school to close. Much later I learned that my attitude was called "not being a good sport," and I stopped allowing myself to be caught, but it was not for years that I really learned the spirit of the thing.

When I saw our car come up to the school gate, I broke away from my classmates and rushed toward it yelling, "Ayah! Ayah!" It seemed like an eternity since I had seen her that morning—a wizened, affectionate figure in her white cotton sari,[9] giving me dozens of urgent and useless instructions on how to be a good girl at school. Premila followed more sedately, and she told me on the way home never to do that again in front of the other children.

When we got home we went straight to Mother's high, white room to have tea with her, and I immediately climbed onto the bed and bounced gently up and down on the springs. Mother asked how we had liked our first day in school. I was so pleased to be home and to have left that peculiar Cynthia behind that I had nothing whatever to say about school, except to ask what "apple" meant. But Premila told Mother about the classes, and added that in her class they had weekly tests to see if they had learned their lessons well.

I asked, "What's a test?"

Premila said, "You're too small to have them. You won't have them in your class for donkey's years."[10] She had learned the expression that day and was using it for the first time. We all laughed enormously at her wit. She also told Mother, in an aside, that we should take sandwiches to school the next day. Not, she said, that *she* minded. But they would be simpler for me to handle.

That whole lovely evening I didn't think about school at all. I sprinted barefoot across the lawns with my favorite playmate, the cook's son, to the stream at the end of the garden. We quarreled in our usual way, waded in the tepid water under the lime trees, and waited for the night to bring out the smell of the jasmine.[11] I listened with fascination to his stories of ghosts and demons, until I was too frightened to cross the garden alone in the semidarkness. The ayah found me, shouted at the cook's son, scolded me, hurried me in to supper—it was an entirely usual, wonderful evening.

It was a week later, the day of Premila's first test, that our lives changed rather abruptly. I was sitting at the back of my class, in my usual inattentive way, only half listening to the teacher. I had started a rather guarded friendship with the girl with the braids, whose name turned out to be Nalini (Nancy in school). The three other Indian children were already fast friends. Even at that age it was apparent to all of us that friendship with the English or Anglo-Indian children was out of the question. Occasionally, during the class, my new friend and I

---

8. **twos-and-threes:** game similar to tag.
9. **sari** (sä′rē): a long piece of cloth wrapped around the body to form a skirt and mantle; it is the main form of dress worn by Hindu women.
10. **donkey's years:** English expression meaning "a long time."
11. **jasmine** (jaz′min): tropical shrub with fragrant flowers.

would draw pictures and show them to each other secretly.

The door opened sharply and Premila marched in. At first, the teacher smiled at her in a kindly and encouraging way and said, "Now, you're little Cynthia's sister?"

Premila didn't even look at her. She stood with her feet planted firmly apart and her shoulders rigid, and addressed herself directly to me. "Get up," she said. "We're going home."

I didn't know what had happened, but I was aware that it was a crisis of some sort. I rose obediently and started to walk toward my sister.

"Bring your pencils and your notebook," she said.

I went back for them, and together we left the room. The teacher started to say something just as Premila closed the door, but we didn't wait to hear what it was.

In complete silence we left the school grounds and started to walk home. Then I asked Premila what the matter was. All she would say was "We're going home for good."

It was a very tiring walk for a child of five and a half, and I dragged along behind Premila with my pencils growing sticky in my hand. I can still remember looking at the dusty hedges, and the tangles of thorns in the ditches by the side of the road, smelling the faint fragrance from the eucalyptus trees and wondering whether we would ever reach home. Occasionally a horse-drawn tonga[12] passed us, and the women, in their pink or green silks, stared at Premila and me trudging along on the side of the road. A few coolies[13] and a line of women carrying baskets of vegetables on their heads smiled at us. But it was nearing the hottest time of day, and the road was almost deserted. I walked more and more slowly, and shouted to Premila, from time to time, "Wait for me!" with increasing peevishness. She spoke to me only once, and that was to tell me to carry my notebook on my head, because of the sun.

When we got to our house the ayah was just taking a tray of lunch into Mother's room. She immediately started a long, worried questioning about what are you children doing back here at this hour of the day.

Mother looked very startled and very concerned, and asked Premila what had happened.

Premila said, "We had our test today, and She made me and the other Indians sit at the back of the room, with a desk between each one."

Mother said, "Why was that, darling?"

"She said it was because Indians cheat," Premila added. "So I don't think we should go back to that school."

Mother looked very distant, and was silent a long time. At last she said, "Of course not, darling." She sounded displeased.

We all shared the curry she was having for lunch, and afterward I was sent off to the beautifully familiar bedroom for my siesta. I could hear Mother and Premila talking through the open door.

Mother said, "Do you suppose she understood all that?"

Premila said, "I shouldn't think so. She's a baby."

Mother said, "Well, I hope it won't bother her."

Of course, they were both wrong. I understood it perfectly, and I remember it all very clearly. But I put it happily away, because it had all happened to a girl called Cynthia, and I never was really particularly interested in her.

---

12. **tonga:** two-wheeled carriage.
13. **coolies:** manual laborers.

Do you think that because the author was called Cynthia at school, she would have always felt that what happened there was not significant? Why do you think that Premila's name change did not have a similar effect on her?

Identifying Facts

1. How old are the author and her sister at the time of this incident? Why had the girls' mother not sent them to a British-run school before?
2. For about how long has the headmistress lived in India? What reason does she give for changing Santha's and Premila's names?
3. What causes the English children to laugh at the author on her first day of school? How do her clothes and lunch differ from those of the Indian children who have been there longer?

Interpreting Meanings

1. What is Santha's mother afraid might happen if her daughters attend a British-run school? What do the details about the other Indian students show about her fears?
2. What criticisms of the headmistress does the third paragraph imply? What related criticism of the British in India does the eighth paragraph imply?
3. What prompts Premila to leave school? What does the incident reveal about the British attitude toward and treatment of Indians?
4. How do you know that this is an **informal essay**? How does the author's childhood attitude toward names contrast with the idea implied by the title?
5. Why do you think Rama Rau drew her title from a Shakespearean play instead of a classical Indian work?

Applying Meanings

Have you ever felt differently when people called you a different name (Beth or Lizzy instead of Elizabeth, or Chuck instead of Charles)? Explain, providing examples.

Creative Writing Response

Writing a Personal Essay. Write a brief personal essay describing your first day of school or some other school-related experience from your childhood.

Critical Writing Response

Analyzing an Essay's Purpose. In one paragraph, explain what you see as Rama Rau's main purpose in writing this essay. In a second paragraph, describe your response to the essay and tell whether or not you think Rama Rau accomplishes her purpose.

To help you decide what the essay's purpose is, you may find it helpful to list, on a chart like the one below, the selection details that point to the author's purpose. Remember to consider how the title relates to the essay's message.

Detail or Incident	Message It Helps to Convey

Akutagawa Ryunosuke
1892–1927, Japan

Courtesy of Iwanami Shoten, Publishers

Akutagawa Ryunosuke (ä·kōō·tä·gä·wä ryōō·nō·sōō·kə) was a perfectionist who labored painstakingly over every line he wrote. Although he destroyed many stories that did not measure up to his high standards, his *Complete Works* (1954) fill twenty volumes. Akutagawa wrote poems, essays, and a semiautobiographical novel, *Kappa* (1927), but he is best known for his short stories. In fact, the annual award for Japan's best short story is named the Akutagawa Prize in his honor.

Akutagawa was a sensitive, troubled child who found solace and escape in reading. Because his mother suffered a nervous breakdown a year after he was born, he was reared by his aunt and uncle. While still a child, he devoured the tales of medieval

Japan that filled his uncle's library. At ten he began writing his own stories. At Tokyo Imperial University, Akutagawa studied English and East Asian literature and, with other young writers, revived the literary magazine *New Thought.*

Although Akutagawa wrote and published throughout his youth, he was not recognized until the famous Japanese writer Natsume Soseki read his story "The Nose" in 1916. Natsume recommended "The Nose" to a colleague, who republished it in a magazine with a large circulation. This exposure brought Akutagawa instant celebrity, and he was able to publish stories he had written previously. These appeared in collections such as *Rashomon* (1916), *Tobacco and the Devil* (1916) and *The Puppeteer* (1919). Akutagawa often drew upon medieval Japanese legends or European literature when writing his stories. He particularly liked tales that were bizarre and disturbing.

As a student of human nature, Akutagawa constantly observed the behavior of the people around him. On the whole he did not like what he saw. This displeasure is reflected in the harshly ironic tone of his later stories as he details the devious, petty motivations of human beings. Akutagawa was also plagued by doubts about his own artistic abilities, and by an inability to deal with the practical aspects of life. This all fed into the vague uneasiness that he gave as the reason for his suicide at the age of thirty-five.

Reader's Guide

THE NOSE

Background

The protagonist of "The Nose" is a Buddhist priest. Buddhism was founded in northern India around the sixth century B.C. Its founder, Gautama Buddha, taught that worldly life cannot provide final happiness, and that one must perform good deeds in order to achieve tranquility and enlightenment. The branch of Buddhism that spread to China, Korea, and Japan is called Mahayana Buddhism. It flourished in medieval Japan and is one of modern Japan's main religions. "The Nose" mentions two important Mahayana sutras, or narratives from holy scriptures: the Lotus Sutra and a sutra about the goddess of mercy, known as Kannon (or Kwannon) in Japan.

Writer's Response

A famous proverb says "You can't judge a book by its cover," yet most people *do* judge others at least partially on their appearance. Write a paragraph explaining why you think appearances are important or why you think they are not.

Literary Focus

Theme is the central idea or insight expressed in a work of literature. It moves beyond the specifics of the work to express a general idea or insight about life or human nature. Sometimes the theme is stated directly within the work, but more often it is merely implied, or suggested by certain details. The most important of these details are the change in the protagonist and the resolution of the conflict. In "The Nose," Akutagawa uses humor and irony to suggest a serious theme about human nature.

THE NOSE

Akutagawa Ryunosuke

translated by

TAKASHI KOJIMA

As you read, pay attention to Zenchi's feelings about his extraordinarily long nose. How do his feelings change throughout the story? What causes the changes?

Kamakura Buddha, Japan.

Japan Tourist Association

In the town of Ike-no-O there was no one who had not heard of Zenchi Naigu's nose. Dangling from his upper lip to below his chin, five or six inches long, it was of the same thickness from end to end.

For fifty years he had been tormented at heart by the presence of his nose—from his young days as an acolyte[1] until the time he rose to the respected office of Palace Chaplain. To others he tried to appear unconcerned about his nose, not so much because his preoccupation with such a matter was not worthy of a man whose duty it was to devote himself ardently to prayer for the advent of Paradise as because he wished to keep from the knowledge of others that he was worried over his nose. With him his apparent concern was rather a matter of pride, and his greatest dread in everyday conversation was to hear the word *nose.*

His nose was, of course, an intolerable nuisance. In the first place, he could not take his meals by himself. If he tried, the tip of his nose would reach down into the boiled rice in his bowl. So at meals he had to have one of his disciples sit opposite him and hold

1. **acolyte** (ak'ə·līt): attendant; helper.

up the end of his nose with an oblong piece of wood about two feet long and an inch wide. This manner of taking meals was, of course, no easy matter for the priest whose nose was held up or for his disciple who held it up.

Once a page,[2] who was acting in the place of the disciple, happened to sneeze and dropped the nose into the bowl—this incident was talked about as far as Kyoto.[3] He could accept the practical inconvenience of having a long nose, but the loss of his dignity on account of it was intolerable.

The Ike-no-O townspeople used to say that it was fortunate for the priest that he was not a layman, for surely no woman would care to be the wife of a man who had such a nose. Some went so far as to say that were it not for his nose, he might not have taken holy orders.

He did not consider that his priesthood had been a refuge which offered him any service in lightening the burden of his nose. Moreover his pride was too delicately strung for him to be influenced in the least by such a worldly eventuality as matrimony. His sole concern was to resort to every possible means to heal the wounds his pride had suffered and to repair the losses his dignity had sustained.

He exhausted all possible means to make his nose appear shorter than it really was. When there was no one about, he would examine his nose in the mirror and look at it from various angles, taxing his ingenuity to the utmost. Just changing the reflections of his face in the mirror was not enough: prodding his cheeks, or putting his finger on the tip of his chin, he would patiently study

Kinkakuji Temple, Japan.
What seems to be the narrator's attitude toward Zenchi?

his face in the mirror. But not once could he satisfy himself that his nose was shorter. Indeed, it often happened that the more he studied his nose the longer it seemed to be. On such occasions, he would put his mirror back into its box, sighing heavily, and sadly going back to his lectern would continue chanting the sutra to Kwannon, or the Goddess of Mercy.

He paid close attention to other people's noses. The Temple of Ike-no-O, frequented by a large number of visitors, both priests and laymen, held Buddhist masses, receptions for visiting priests, and sermons for parishioners. The precincts of the Temple were lined with closely built cells, with a bathhouse which had heated water daily. He would closely scrutinize the visitors, patiently trying to find at least one person who might possibly have a nose like his own in

---

2. **page:** boy servant.
3. **Kyoto** (kē′ōt′ō): Japanese city that was the imperial capital at the time of the story.

order that he might ease his troubled mind. He took no notice of the rich silken attire, the ordinary hempen[4] clothes, the priests' saffron[5] hoods nor their dark sacerdotal[6] robes, all of which counted for next to nothing in his eyes. That which arrested his eyes was not the people or their attire but their noses. He could find hooked noses but none like his own. Each additional failure made his thinking darker and gloomier.

While talking with others, unconsciously he would take between his fingers the tip of his dangling nose; then he would blush with shame for an act ill fitting his years and office. His misfortune had driven him to such extremes.

In his desperate attempt to find some consolation by discovering someone with a nose like his own, he delved into the voluminous Buddhist scriptures; but in all the scriptures there was not one reference to a long nose. How comforting it would have been to find, for instance, that either Mu Lien or Sha Lien[7] had a long nose.

He did find that King Liu Hsan-ti[8] of the Kingdom of Chu-han in the third century A.D. had long ears, and thought how reassuring it would have been if it had happened that the King's nose, instead of his ears, had been long.

It need hardly be said that while taking assiduous pains to seek spiritual consolation, he did try most earnestly a variety of elaborate practical measures to shorten his nose.

---

4. **hempen:** made of hemp, a tough, heavy fiber often twisted into rope.
5. **saffron:** here, orange-yellow.
6. **sacerdotal** (sas′ər·dōt′′l): priestly.
7. **Mu Lien** (mōō′ lyen′) and **Sha Lien** (shä′ lyen′): two important disciples of the historic Buddha. Mu Lien was famous for his magic powers; Sha Lien, for his scholarship.
8. **King Liu Hsan-ti** (lyōō′ hsän′tē′): Chinese king described in Buddhist legends.

At one time he took a concoction with a snake-gourd[9] base. At another he bathed his nose in the urine of mice; yet with all his persistent and unremitting efforts, he still had five to six inches of nose dangling down over his lips.

One autumn day a disciple went on a trip to Kyoto, partly on his master's business, and before his returning to Ike-no-O, his physician acquaintance happened to introduce him to the mysteries of shortening noses. The physician, who had come to Japan from China, was at that time a priest attached to the Choraku Temple.

Zenchi, with an assumed nonchalance, avoided calling for an immediate test of the remedy, and could only drop casual hints about his regret that he must cause his disciple so much bother at meals, although he eagerly waited in his heart for his disciple to persuade him to try the remedy. The disciple could not fail to see through his master's design. But his master's innermost feelings, which led him to work out such an elaborate scheme, aroused his disciple's sympathy. As Zenchi had expected, his disciple advised him to try this method with such extraordinary urgency that, according to his premeditated plan, he finally yielded to his earnest counsel.

The formula was a simple one: first to boil the nose in hot water, and then to let another trample on it and torment it.

At the Temple bathhouse water was kept "at the boil" daily, so his disciple brought in an iron ladle, water so hot that no one could have put a finger into it. It was feared that Zenchi's face would be scalded by steam; so they bored a hole in a wooden tray and used the tray as a lid to cover the pot so that his nose could be immersed in the boiling water.

---

9. **snake-gourd:** a type of squash or melon.

As for his nose, no matter how long it was soaked in the scalding water, it was immune from ill effect.

"Your Reverence," the disciple said after a while, "I suppose it must be sufficiently boiled by now."

The Chaplain, with a wry smile, was thinking that no one who overheard this remark could suspect that it concerned a remedy for shortening his nose.

Heated by water and steam, his nose itched as if bitten by mosquitoes.

When the nose was withdrawn from the hole in the lid, the disciple set about trampling on that steaming object, exerting all his strength in pounding it with both his feet. Zenchi, lying on his side, and stretching his nose on the floorboards, watched his disciple's legs move up and down.

"Does it hurt, Your Reverence?" his disciple asked from time to time, looking down sympathetically on the priest's bald head. "The physician told me to trample hard on it. Doesn't it hurt?"

Zenchi tried to shake his head by way of indicating that he was not feeling any pain, but as his nose was being trampled on he could not do this, so rolling his eyes upwards, in a tone that suggested he was offended, and with his gaze fixed on his disciple's chapped feet, he said, "No, it doesn't hurt." Although his itching nose was being trampled on, it was a comfortable rather than a painful sensation.

His nose having undergone this treatment for some time, what seemed to be grains of millet began to appear, at which sight his disciple stopped trampling and said in soliloquy, "I was told to pull them out with tweezers."

The nose looked like a plucked and roasted chicken. With cheeks puffed out, though disgruntled, the priest suffered his disciple to deal with his nose as the man saw fit—although, however aware of his disciple's kindness he might have been, he did not relish his nose being treated as if it were a piece of inert matter. Like a patient undergoing an operation at the hands of a surgeon in whom he does not place implicit trust, Zenchi reluctantly watched his disciple extract, from the pores of his nose, feathers of fat curled to half an inch in diameter. The treatment finished, the disciple looked relieved and said: "Now, your Reverence, we have only to boil it once more, and it'll be all right."

Zenchi, with knit brow, submitted to the treatment meted out to him.

When his nose was taken out of the pot for the second time, it was found, to their great surprise, remarkably shorter than before and was not very different from a normal hooked nose. Stroking his greatly shortened nose, he timidly and nervously peered into the mirror which his disciple held out to him.

The nose, which previously had dangled below his chin, had miraculously dwindled, and, not protruding below his upper lip, was barely a relic of what it had once been. The red blotches which bespeckled it were probably only bruises caused by the trampling.

"No one will laugh at me any more," the priest thought to himself. He saw in the mirror that the face reflected there was looking into the face outside the mirror, blinking its eyes in satisfaction.

But all day long he was uneasy and feared that his nose might grow long; so whenever he had the chance, whether in chanting sutras or in eating meals, he stealthily touched his nose. However, he found his nose installed in good shape above his upper lip, without straying beyond his lower lip.

Early in the morning, at the moment of

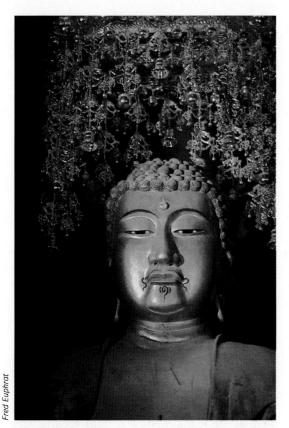

Fred Euphrat

Statue of Buddha.

to laugh, casting down his eyes, he could not for long withhold his burst of laughter. The sextons[10] under Zenchi's supervision would listen respectfully while seated face to face with their master, but on more than one occasion they fell to chuckling as soon as he turned his back.

Zenchi at first attributed the laughter of his page and the sextons to the marked change in his features, but by and by, with his head cocked on one side, interrupting the sutra he was chanting, he would mutter to himself: "The change alone does not give a plausible explanation for their laughter. Zenchi Naigu! their laughter is now different from what it was when your nose was long. If you could say that the unfamiliar nose looks more ridiculous than the familiar one, that would once and for all settle the matter. But there must be some other reason behind it; they didn't laugh heartily or irresistibly as before."

The poor amiable priest on such occasions would look up at Fugen, Goddess of Wisdom,[11] pictured on the scroll hanging close beside him, and calling to mind the long nose he had wielded until four or five days previously, he would lapse into melancholy "like one sunken low recalleth his glory of bygone days."[12] But it was to be regretted that he was deficient in judgment sufficient to find a solution to this quandary.

Man is possessed of two contradictory sentiments. Everyone will sympathize with another's misfortune. But when the other

waking, he stroked the tip of his nose, and he found that it was still as short as ever. After a gap of many years he at that moment recognized the same relief he had felt when he had completed the austerities required for his transcription of the lengthy Lotus Sutra of his sect.

Within the course of several days, however, Zenchi had a most surprising experience. A samurai who, on business, visited the Temple of Ike-no-O, looked amused as never before, and, quite incapable of uttering a word, he could but stare fixedly at the priest's nose. This was not all. The page who once had dropped Zenchi's nose into the bowl of gruel happened to pass by Zenchi in the lecture hall; at first, resisting his impulse

---

10. **sextons:** temple officials in charge of maintaining the grounds.

11. **Fugen, Goddess of Wisdom:** Fugen Bosatsu, the Bodhisattva—or morally and spiritually superior being—who sits at Buddha's side and offers human beings redemption through mercy.

12. **like . . . bygone days:** quotation from Buddhist scripture.

manages to pull through his misfortune, he not only thinks it safe to laugh at him to his face but also comes even to regard him with envy. In extreme cases some may feel like casting him into his former misfortune again and may even harbor some enmity, if negative, toward him.

Zenchi was at a loss to know what precisely made him forlorn, but his unhappiness was caused by nothing more than the wayward caprices of those surrounding him—the priests and laymen of Ike-no-O.

Day after day Zenchi, becoming more and more unhappy and vexed, would not open his mouth without speaking sharply to someone and was ever out-of-sorts until even the disciple who had administered to him the effective remedy began to backbite him, saying, "The master will be punished for his sins."

What especially enraged Zenchi was the mischief played on him by the page. One day, hearing a dog yelping wildly, he casually looked outside and found the page, with a stick about two feet long in his hand, chasing a lean and shaggy dog and shouting: "Watch out there for your *nose!* Watch out or I'll hit your *nose.*" Snatching the wooden stick from the page's hand, the priest struck him sharply across the face; it was the very stick which had been used to hold up Zenchi's nose.

Finally Zenchi came to feel sorry and even resentful for having had his long nose shortened.

One night after sunset it happened that the wind seeming to have arisen suddenly, the noisy tinkling of the pagoda wind bells[13] came to his cell. The cold, moreover, had so noticeably increased in severity that Zenchi could not go to sleep, try as he might; tossing and turning in his bed he became aware of an itching in his nose. Putting his hand to his nose he felt that it had become swollen as if with dropsy;[14] it seemed feverish, too.

"It was so drastically shortened that I might have caught some disease," he muttered to himself, caressing his nose as reverently as he would if he were holding the offerings of incense and flowers to be dedicated at the altar.

On the following morning Zenchi as usual awoke early, and he noticed that the garden was as bright as if it were carpeted with gold, because in the garden the ginkgo trees and horse chestnuts had overnight shed all their leaves; and the crest of the pagoda must have been encrusted with frost, for the nine copper rings of the spire were brightly shining in the still faint glimmer of the rising sun. Sitting on the veranda, the shutters already opened, he drew a deep breath, and at that same moment a certain feeling, the nature of which he had all but forgotten, came back to him.

Instinctively he put his hand to his nose, and what he touched was not the short nose that had been his the night before, but the former long nose that had dangled five or six inches over his lips; in one night, he found, his nose had grown as long as it had been previously, and this, for some reason, made him feel refreshed and as happy as he had felt in the first moments when his nose had been shortened.

"Nobody will laugh at me any more," he whispered to himself.

His long nose dangled in the autumn breeze of early morning.

---

13. **pagoda** (pə·gō′də) **wind bells:** wind chimes hung at the corners of the temple; the use of such chimes is traditional in Japan, where their chiming is said to create a sense of coolness in summer.

14. **dropsy:** accumulation of fluid that causes swelling; now usually called edema (ē·dē′mə).

First Thoughts

Were you surprised that Zenchi was happy to get his long nose back again? If you were Zenchi, would your response have been similar or different? Explain.

Identifying Facts

1. According to the opening paragraphs, how does Zenchi try to appear to others? Why?

2. After his nose is shortened, what change does Zenchi discover in others' behavior? How does his own behavior change?

3. When Zenchi awakens to find his nose has grown back to its original length, what does he whisper to himself?

Interpreting Meanings

1. Do you think Zenchi's unhappiness at the beginning of the story is caused solely by his ungainly nose? If not, what else might be causing it?

2. Why do you think people begin laughing at Zenchi after his nose is shortened? How does the narrator explain their reactions?

3. What **theme** or central insight about human nature do Zenchi and the story's events suggest to you?

4. Which story details do you find especially humorous or ironic? How does the use of **humor** and **irony** help make the story effective?

Applying Meanings

Some people go to great lengths to improve or change their appearances through face lifts, liposuction, and other surgical and nonsurgical means. Do you think such changes in appearance generally make people happier? Why or why not?

Creative Writing Response

Imagining a Bizarre Change. Suppose that you woke up one morning with a bizarre change in personal appearance: bright purple hair, huge pointed ears, snakelike scaly skin, or wings sprouting from your shoulder blades. Imagine the practical difficulties this change would create in your everyday life, and the emotional and psychological trauma it might cause. Write a few paragraphs detailing your reactions and the reactions of others to your bizarre appearance. You might begin with a sentence like this: ''This morning I woke up to find that two lobster claws had sprouted where my hands used to be.'' You might want to insert moments of humor and irony in your story.

Critical Writing Response

Writing About Psychological Insights. Akutagawa is famous for his keen understanding of human psychology. In a brief essay, show how ''The Nose'' illustrates his insight into human behavior and motivation. Discuss Zenchi's behavior and motivation throughout the story. Why does he want to shorten his nose? Why does his shortened nose make him even more miserable? Why is he relieved when his nose returns to its original length? Before you begin writing, list on a separate sheet the story details that you will cite in answering the questions above.

Language and Vocabulary

East Asian and Pacific Languages

English has borrowed a number of words from Chinese, Japanese, and other Asian and Pacific languages. Use a dictionary to find the origins of each of the following words. Write down the meaning of any unfamiliar words.

1. boomerang
2. karate
3. kiwi
4. taboo
5. yak
6. boondocks
7. ketchup
8. rickshaw
9. tycoon
10. yo-yo

Hwang Sun-won
b. 1915, Korea

Courtesy of Mercury House Books

Hwang Sun-won has lived through many tragic times in his homeland. Born when Korea was a colony of Japan, Hwang saw the Japanese imprison his father for supporting the unsuccessful Korean rebellion of 1919. He went to Japanese-language schools in Korea and then attended a university in Tokyo. Hwang returned home just as Japanese expansionist policies escalated into World War II. Although he was able to publish his first story collection, *The Marsh*, in 1940, Japanese authorities banned Korean writing soon afterward and Hwang had to continue his work in secret.

With the Japanese surrender in 1945, Korea was free of Japanese oppression, but Hwang and others who lived in the north were now subject to Soviet oppression. As communism spread in the north, Hwang and his family fled to the south, then occupied by American forces. They settled for a time in the capital city of Seoul (sōl), but became refugees again when the Communists invaded Seoul at the beginning of the Korean War. The end of the war in 1953 brought only limited happiness to most Koreans, for their nation remained divided and many people found themselves separated from friends and relatives.

Throughout these turbulent times, Hwang continued to produce fiction, even though its publication was often delayed. "Cranes," reprinted here, and many of Hwang's other works suggest that the political divisions between North Korea and South Korea are arbitrary and cruel.

Hwang has enjoyed widespread acclaim in South Korea since the mid-1950s, when his short novel *Descendents of Cain* (1954) won the Free Literature Prize. Although his work, like that of other Korean writers, has been slow to draw the attention of the West, Hwang recently became one of the first Koreans to have his tales appear in English translations in two full-length volumes, *The Book of Masks* (1989) and *Shadows of a Sound* (1990).

Reader's Guide

CRANES

Background

After Japan's defeat in World War II, Korea was liberated by Russian forces in the North and American forces in the South. The two groups then helped establish governments with very different ideologies. The dividing line between North and South Korea became the Thirty-eighth Parallel—a line representing a latitude of 38° North. However, in June of 1950—just a year after the Americans had withdrawn most of their troops—Communist forces from the North crossed that parallel in an invasion that marked the beginning of the Korean War. With the support of the United Nations, American and other Western forces helped the South Koreans defend their territory. In 1953 a truce was finally arranged, although skirmishes at the Thirty-eighth Parallel continued to erupt periodically.

During the Korean War, many villages along the Thirty-eighth Parallel changed hands several times. "Cranes" is set in one such village and the countryside around it.

Writer's Response

A title often provides clues to a story's theme. From Southeast Asia to parts of the Mediterranean, the crane is a symbol of justice, longevity, and goodness. Given this information, what are your expectations of a story that is titled "Cranes"?

Literary Focus

The plots of many stories revolve around a **conflict**, a struggle or clash between opposing characters, forces, or emotions. In an **external conflict**, the struggle is against an outside force, such as another character, society as a whole, or an aspect of nature. In an **internal conflict**, the struggle is between opposing desires, choices, or emotions within a single character. Sometimes a story features an internal conflict that is prompted by an external one. For example, a character who must face a deadly lion may also experience an internal struggle between courage and cowardice.

CRANES

Hwang Sun-won

translated by

PETER H. LEE

> *As you read this story, pay special attention to the conflicting emotions felt by the main character, Song-sam. How is his* **internal conflict** *related to the* **external conflict** *in which he is involved? Can you sympathize with his feelings?*

The northern village at the border of the Thirty-eighth Parallel was snugly settled under the high, bright autumn sky.

One white gourd lay against another on the dirt floor of an empty farmhouse. The occasional village elders first put out their bamboo pipes before passing by, and the children, too, turned aside some distance off. Their faces were ridden with fear.

The village as a whole showed few traces of destruction from the war, but it did not seem like the same village Song-sam[1] had known as a boy.

At the foot of a chestnut grove on the hill behind the village he stopped and climbed a chestnut tree. Somewhere far back in his mind he heard the old man with a wen[2] shout, "You bad boy, you're climbing up my chestnut tree again!"

The old man must have passed away, for among the few village elders Song-sam had met, the old man was not to be found. Holding the trunk of the tree, Song-sam gazed at the blue sky for a while. Some chestnuts fell to the ground as the dry clusters opened of their own accord.

In front of the farmhouse that had been turned into a public peace-police office, a young man stood, tied up. He seemed to be a stranger, so Song-sam approached him to have a close look. He was taken aback; it was none other than his boyhood playmate, Tok-chae.[3]

Song-sam asked the police officer who had come with him from Chontae[4] what it was all about. The prisoner was vice-chairman of the Farmers' Communist League and had just been flushed out of his hideout in his own house, Song-sam learned.

Song-sam sat down on the dirt floor and lit a cigarette.

Tok-chae was to be escorted to Chongdan[5] by one of the peace policemen.

After a time, Song-sam lit a new cigarette from the first and stood up.

"I'll take the fellow with me."

---

1. **Song-sam** (sung'säm')
2. **wen:** benign fatty tumor, often on the scalp or face.

3. **Tok-chae** (tuk'chā')
4. **Chontae** (chun'tā')
5. **Chongdan** (chung'dän')

Tok-chae, his face averted, refused to look at Song-sam. They left the village.

Song-sam kept on smoking, but the tobacco had no taste. He just kept drawing in the smoke and blowing it out. Then suddenly he thought that Tok-chae, too, must want a puff. He thought of the days when they used to share dried gourd leaves behind walls, hidden from the adults. But today, how could he offer a cigarette to a fellow like this?

Once, when they were small, he went with Tok-chae to steal some chestnuts from the grandpa[6] with the wen. It was Song-sam's turn to go up the tree. Suddenly there came shouts from the old man. He slipped and fell to the ground. Song-sam got chestnut needles all over his bottom, but he kept on running. It was only when they reached a safe place where the old man could not overtake them that he turned his bottom to Tok-chae. Plucking out those needles hurt so much that he could not keep tears from welling up in his eyes. Tok-chae produced a fistful of chestnuts from his pocket and thrust them into Song-sam's . . . Song-sam threw away the cigarette he had just lit. Then he made up his mind not to light another while he was escorting Tok-chae.

They reached the hill pass, the hill where he and Tok-chae used to cut fodder for the cows until Song-sam had had to move near Chontae, south of the Thirty-eighth Parallel, two years before the liberation.

Song-sam felt a sudden surge of anger in spite of himself and shouted, "So how many have you killed?"

For the first time, Tok-chae cast a quick glance at him and then turned away.

"How many did you kill, you?" he asked again.

Tok-chae turned toward him once again and glared. The glare grew intense and his mouth twitched.

"So you managed to kill many, eh?" Song-sam felt his heart becoming clear from within, as if an obstruction had been removed. "If you were vice-chairman of the Communist League, why didn't you run? You must have been lying low with a secret mission."

Tok-chae did not answer.

"Speak up, what was your mission?"

Tok-chae kept walking. Tok-chae is hiding

Mt. Sorak, Korea.

Brent Bear/Westlight

---

6. **grandpa:** here, not a relative, but a colloquial term for any elderly man.

something, Song-sam thought. He wanted to take a good look at him, but Tok-chae would not turn his averted face.

Fingering the revolver at his side, Song-sam went on: "No excuse is necessary. You are sure to be shot anyway. Why don't you tell the truth, here and now?"

"I'm not going to make any excuses. They made me vice-chairman of the league because I was one of the poorest and I was a hard-working farmer. If that constitutes a crime worthy of death, so be it. I am still what I used to be—the only thing I'm good at is digging in the soil." After a short pause, he added, "My old man is bedridden at home. He's been ill almost half a year." Tok-chae's father was a widower, a hard-working poor farmer who lived only for his son. Seven years ago his back had given out and his skin had become diseased.

"You married?"

"Yes," replied Tok-chae after a while.

"To whom?"

"Shorty."

"To Shorty?" How interesting! A woman so small and plump that she knew the earth's vastness but not the sky's altitude. Such a cold fish! He and Tok-chae used to tease her and make her cry. And Tok-chae had married that girl.

"How many kids?"

"The first is arriving this fall, she says."

Song-sam had difficulty swallowing a laugh about to explode in spite of himself. Although he had asked how many kids Tok-chae had, he could not help wanting to burst into laughter at the image of her sitting down, with a large stomach, one span around. But he realized this was no time to laugh or joke over such matters.

"Anyway, it's strange you did not run away."

"I tried to escape. They said that once the

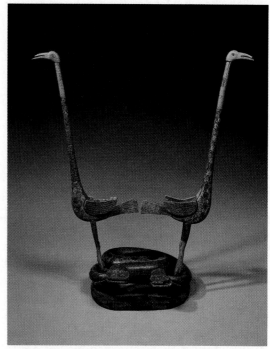

Cranes, highly symbolic in all parts of Asia, adorn this Chinese drum stand, 481–221 B.C.

The Cleveland Museum of Art, Purchase from the J. H. Wade Fund, 38.9

South invaded, no man would be spared. So men between seventeen and forty were forcibly taken to the North. I thought of evacuating, even if I had to carry my father on my back. But father said no. How could the farmers leave the land behind when the crops were ready for harvest? He grew old on that farm depending on me as the prop and mainstay of the family. I wanted to be with him in his last moments so that I could close his eyes with my own hand. Besides, where can farmers like us go, who know only living on the land?"

Last June Song-sam had had to take refuge. At night he had broken the news privately to his father. But his father had said the same thing! Where can a farmer go, leaving all the chores behind? So Song-sam left alone. Roaming about the strange streets and villages in the South, Song-sam had been haunted by thoughts of his old parents and the young children, left with all the chores. Fortunately, his family was safe then, as now.

They crossed the ridge of a hill. This time Song-sam walked with his face averted. The autumn sun was hot on his forehead. This was an ideal day for the harvest, he thought.

When they reached the foot of the hill, Song-sam hesitatingly stopped. In the middle of a field he spied a group of cranes that looked like men in white clothes bending over. This used to be the neutralized zone[7] along the Thirty-eighth Parallel. The cranes were still living here, as before, while the people were all gone.

Once, when Song-sam and Tok-chae were about twelve, they had set a trap here, without the knowledge of the adults, and had caught a crane, a Tanjong crane.[8] They had roped the crane, even its wings, and had paid daily visits, patting its neck and riding on its back. Then one day they overheard the neighbors whispering. Someone had come from Seoul with a permit from the governor-general's office[9] to catch cranes as specimens or something. Then and there the two boys dashed off to the field. That they would be found out and punished was no longer a weighty concern; all they worried about was the fate of their crane. Without a moment's delay, still out of breath from running, they untied the crane's feet and wings. But the bird could hardly walk. It must have been worn out from being bound.

The two held it up in the air. Then, all of a sudden, a shot was fired. The crane fluttered its wings a couple of times and came down again.

It was shot, they thought. But the next moment, as another crane from a nearby bush fluttered its wings, the boys' crane stretched its long neck with a whoop and disappeared into the sky. For a long time the two boys could not take their eyes away from the blue sky into which their crane had soared.

"Hey, why don't we stop here for a crane hunt?" Song-sam spoke up suddenly.

Tok-chae was puzzled, struck dumb.

"I'll make a trap with this rope; you flush[10] a crane over here."

Having untied Tok-chae's hands, Song-sam had already started crawling among the weeds.

Tok-chae's face turned white. "You are sure to be shot anyway"—these words flashed through his mind. Pretty soon a bullet would fly from where Song-sam has gone, he thought.

Some paces away, Song-sam quickly turned toward him.

"Hey, how come you're standing there like you're dumb? Go flush the crane!"

Only then did Tok-chae catch on. He started crawling among the weeds.

A couple of Tanjong cranes soared high into the clear blue autumn sky, fluttering their huge wings.

---

7. **neutralized zone:** demilitarized zone, or strip of no man's land, separating North and South Korea at the Thirty-eighth Parallel.

8. **Tanjong** (tän′jung′) **crane:** large, long-legged bird that breeds in North Korea.

9. **governor-general's office:** headquarters of Korea's chief executive appointed by the Japanese government when Korea was a colony of Japan (during Song-sam's boyhood).

---

10. **flush:** to drive a bird from cover.

Do you think Song-sam did the right thing in allowing Tok-chae to go free? Would you have acted similarly if you were in Song-sam's position? Explain.

Identifying Facts

1. Where is the village located? What was Song-sam's relationship with Tok-chae when they were children?
2. For which side in the Korean War is Song-sam fighting? Why is Tok-chae a prisoner?
3. What reasons does Tok-chae give for becoming vice-chairman of the Communist League and for remaining in the village after the Communists abandoned it?
4. When he unties Tok-chae's hands, in what childhood activity does Song-sam suggest the two engage?

Interpreting Meanings

1. In his **internal conflict**, Song-sam must decide between which two courses of action? What is the connection between this conflict and the larger **external conflict** of the story?
2. As Song-sam escorts Tok-chae, he remembers incidents from their childhoods. How do these **flashbacks** contribute to the resolution of the **conflict**?
3. What do the characters' experiences suggest about civil wars in general and the Korean War in particular? What does the story suggest about ties of kinship and friendship?
4. In many Asian cultures, the crane symbolizes long life. Birds often symbolize the soul or spirit, and flight often symbolizes rising to a higher moral plane. Reread the last sentence of the story. What **symbolic** meanings might it have?

Applying Meanings

Do you think individual ties should carry more weight than political or national affiliations? Explain.

Creative Writing Response

Writing About a Moment of Decision. Write a brief personal essay or short story about an important decision in your life. The decision may involve a moral choice, as Song-sam's does. Before you write, ask yourself what events led up to your decision, and how your life, or your outlook on life, has changed since you made the decision.

Critical Writing Response

Writing About Conflict. Write a brief essay about Song-sam's **internal conflict** and the way he eventually resolves it. First, identify the reasons for and against releasing Tok-chae that constitute Song-sam's internal conflict. You may organize your thoughts by listing these factors on a chart like the one below. Conclude your essay by evaluating Song-sam's decision. Explain why you think it was a good or bad resolution to his dilemma.

Taking Tok-chae to Face Execution	Letting Tok-chae Go

Nguyen Thi Vinh
b. 1924, Vietnam

South Vietnamese refugees.

N guyen Thi Vinh (nōō′yin tī vin′) bears a family name with a long history. From the sixteenth century to the eighteenth century, the house of Nguyen was one of two ruling families in Vietnam. In 1773 a member of the Nguyen family became Vietnam's emperor, and his descendants ruled the country until its conquest by French forces in the late nineteenth century.

Nguyen Thi Vinh writes about Vietnam's more recent history—especially its decades of warfare during her lifetime. In the early 1950s, she was among the many northerners who fled south to escape the Communists.

She settled in Saigon, capital of the newly created government of South Vietnam, and soon became part of that city's thriving intellectual community.

Best known in Vietnam for her fiction, Nguyen first won fame with *Two Sisters* (1953). She also published a highly regarded book of poetry and served as editor of the South Vietnamese literary journal *New Wind* and the magazine *The East.* Although she was proud of her literary accomplishments, Nguyen did not find peace and contentment in Vietnam. The North-South conflict soon escalated into the Vietnam War, and the violence was underscored by the heartbreaking knowledge that people she had loved in childhood were now fighting as bitter enemies. Those feelings are powerfully expressed in her poem "Thoughts of Hanoi," reprinted here.

After the fall of Saigon to North Vietnamese forces and the subsequent reunification of Vietnam under a Communist government in 1975, Nguyen remained in her homeland as millions of other South Vietnamese fled in fear. She managed to survive those trying times, and in 1983 she emigrated to Norway, where other members of her family had settled.

Reader's Guide

THOUGHTS OF HANOI

Background

For centuries, Vietnam has been the site of conflicts between local kingdoms. In the nineteenth century, foreign imperial powers became interested in the region. The French gained control of the country in the late nineteenth century, but they were forced from power by the Japanese, who occupied the area from 1940 to 1945. French attempts to regain control after Japan's defeat in World War II were countered by Communists in the North led by Ho Chi Minh. The two groups fought from 1946 until 1954, when France agreed to withdraw. The country was then temporarily divided into Communist North Vietnam with its capital at Hanoi, and non-Communist South Vietnam with its capital at Saigon. In 1957, Communists in the South began rebelling and Western democracies came to the aid of South Vietnam. The conflict soon escalated into the Vietnam War, in which the United States was a leading player. At a 1973 peace conference, the combatants agreed to a cease-fire and the United States withdrew its troops. Not long afterward, the North Vietnamese government invaded the South and made Vietnam a single nation. The country's decades of warfare sparked massive migrations among the Vietnamese people.

Writer's Response

Write a few sentences about a place you remember fondly. It might be a lake, a neighborhood, a basketball court, or some other place. Include specific details that will make the place come alive to a reader.

Literary Focus

A **lyric poem** is one that expresses personal emotions or thoughts instead of telling a story or portraying characters in action. The voice that talks to us in a lyric poem is called the **speaker**. Sometimes the speaker is the poet, but often the poet assumes a different voice. In "Thoughts of Hanoi," Nguyen Thi Vinh assumes the voice of a Vietnamese male to express her own thoughts and emotions.

THOUGHTS OF HANOI
Nguyen Thi Vinh
translated by
NGUYEN NGOC BICH

> As you read the poem, notice how the speaker's childhood
> memories contrast with his present situation.

The night is deep and chill
as in early autumn. Pitchblack,
it thickens after each lightning flash.
I dream of Hanoi:
5   Co-ngu° Road
ten years of separation
the way back sliced by a frontier of hatred.
I want to bury the past
to burn the future
10 still I yearn
still I fear
those endless nights
waiting for dawn.

Brother,
15 how is Hang Dao° now?
How is Ngoc Son° temple?
Do the trains still run
each day from Hanoi
to the neighboring towns?
20 To Bac-ninh,° Cam-giang,° Yen-bai,°
the small villages, islands
of brown thatch in a lush green sea?

The girls
   bright eyes
25   ruddy cheeks
   four-piece dresses
      raven-bill scarves°
   sowing harvesting
      spinning weaving
30   all year round,
the boys

5. **Co-ngu** (kō′nōo′)

15. **Hang Dao** (häng′ dou′)
16. **Ngoc Son** (nōk′ sōn′)

20. **Bac-ninh** (bäk′nin′), **Cam-giang** (käm′gyäng′), **Yen-bai** (yen′bī′): towns near Hanoi.

27. **raven-bill scarves:** head-scarves folded into straight-edged triangular forms, like the bill or beak of a raven.

plowing
    transplanting
in the fields
35   in their shops
running across
    the meadow at evening
to fly kites
    and sing alternating songs.°

40   Stainless blue sky,
    jubilant voices of children
stumbling through the alphabet,
    village graybeards strolling to the temple,
grandmothers basking in twilight sun,
45   chewing betel leaves°
while the children run—

Brother,
how is all that now?
Or is it obsolete?
50   Are you like me,
reliving the past,
imagining the future?
Do you count me as a friend
or am I the enemy in your eyes?
55   Brother, I am afraid
that one day I'll be with the March-North Army°
meeting you on your way to the South.
I might be the one to shoot you then
or you me
60   but please
not with hatred.

For don't you remember how it was,
you and I in school together,
plotting our lives together?
65   Those roots go deep!

Brother, we are men,
conscious of more
than material needs.
How can this happen to us
70   my friend
my foe?

39. **alternating songs:** songs in which different singers take different parts; rounds.

45. **betel** (bēt′l) **leaves:** leaves of the betel palm, a tree found in southeastern Asia; both the leaves and nuts are often chewed like chewing gum.

56. **March-North Army:** that is, the South Vietnamese army marching into North Vietnam.

Larry Downing/Woodfin Camp & Associates

Vietnamese child in Hanoi.

First Thoughts

Did the **paradox**, or apparent contradiction, of the last two lines make sense to you? Think of another circumstance in which someone might be both your friend *and* your foe.

Identifying Facts

1. How many years ago did the speaker leave Hanoi, and by what is the way back now "sliced"?

2. List three specific questions about Hanoi that the speaker asks. What does the speaker ask about the past and future?

3. What kinds of **images** does the speaker describe in lines 23–46?

4. What is the speaker afraid may happen one day? What final question does he ask?

Interpreting Meanings

1. What might "each lightning flash" (line 3) be, and why might the speaker "fear/those endless nights"? What is the "frontier of hatred"?

2. Where does the **speaker** come from, and where is he living now? Which details suggest that the speaker is not the poet?

3. Why do you think the poet wrote so many lines describing the boys and girls of the Hanoi area? What is the "lush green sea"?

4. What is the apparent relationship between the speaker and the person addressed as "Brother"?

5. What overall attitude does this **lyric poem** convey toward warfare, especially civil warfare?

Applying Meanings

The United States was heavily involved in the Vietnam War. What are your feelings about the war, based on your studies and your conversations with older Americans or with Vietnamese refugees in the U.S.?

Creative Writing Response

Writing a Poem. Write a short, free-verse poem called "Thoughts of *X*," in which *X* is some time or place that you miss. You may use the place you wrote about in the Writer's Response (see page 1410) or choose another place or time.

Critical Writing Response

Comparing Viewpoints. Like "Thoughts of Hanoi," Hwang Sun-won's "Cranes" (see page 1404) was written at a time of civil warfare in the author's homeland. In a brief essay, compare and contrast the thoughts, feelings, and actions of the speaker in "Thoughts of Hanoi" and the protagonist in "Cranes." Focus on the physical and emotional effects of warfare in general and civil warfare in particular. Before you begin, you may find it helpful to list your ideas on a chart like the one below.

	"Thoughts of Hanoi"	"Cranes"
Feeling toward the "enemy"		
Thoughts about war		
Actions		
Writer's tone		

Nguyen Thi Vinh   **1413**

Zhang Jie
b. 1937, People's Republic of China

Isolde Ohlbaum

■n the early 1980s, the American writer Annie Dillard documented in her book *Encounters with Chinese Writers* a heated exchange between Zhang Jie (jan′ jyē′) and the American beat poet Allen Ginsberg. Although Zhang is a small, seemingly fragile woman, and Ginsberg is a large, imposing man, Zhang was not afraid to speak her mind. "Mr. Ginsberg! you should not think only of yourself!" she exclaimed. "You must live and work so as to fulfill your obligations! Have your goals firmly in your mind. You should not take drugs! Think of your responsibility to society!" Such outspokenness and conviction are characteristic of Zhang's novels and short stories, which have caused controversy in China and won praise abroad.

Zhang's concern with social responsibility stems in part from the circumstances of her childhood. Raised in the Chinese capital of Beijing (bā′jing′) (formerly Peking), Zhang grew up in dire poverty after her father abandoned the family a few months after her birth. She observed that in China at that time, her father had no binding or legal responsibility to his family.

Feeling that women had more rights under China's new Communist government, Zhang joined the Communist Party as a young woman and supported government policy even when it meant compromising her own desires. She had hoped, for example, to study literature in college. Instead, she studied economics, which the new government felt was of more use to society. Later she was among the many men and women who left their homes to work in factories or on farms in the hopes of improving China's shaky economy.

Speaking of her early life, Zhang recalls that she was "like a darting dragonfly, with no goals in life and no substantial pursuits. Only through literature did I discover myself." Zhang was not able to begin her writing career, however, until the Cultural Revolution ended and more moderate leaders came to power. In 1978 she won a nationwide award for her story "The Music of the Forests." Three years later her novel *Leaden Wings* won China's Mao Dun Literary Prize.

Reader's Guide

LOVE MUST NOT BE FORGOTTEN

Background

In 1949, the Communists established the People's Republic of China under their military hero Mao Zedong (also spelled Mao Tse-tung). The new Communist regime instituted drastic social and economic changes and became increasingly oppressive. During Mao's Cultural Revolution, many moderate political figures were removed from power, imprisoned, and sometimes executed. China's writers were also silenced.

After Mao's death in 1976 China came under more moderate leadership. Encouraged by the new spirit of openness, many writers emerged and began writing of past injustices and the need for future reforms. Zhang Jie won fame for writing of the continued inequality between the sexes despite government claims to the contrary. During the 1980s the government again became more repressive and in 1989 ordered a military crackdown on prodemocracy demonstrators in Beijing's Tiananmen Square. Few writers were allowed to publish within China, and those lucky enough to escape went to live abroad.

Among Chinese readers Zhang Jie enjoys huge popularity, despite much controversy over her 1979 story "Love Must Not Be Forgotten," reprinted here. This story suggests that, for all the changes effected by the Communists, Chinese women still face centuries-old social pressures to marry and subordinate themselves to their husbands and families.

Writer's Response

Although the United States has made progress toward equality between the sexes, do you think that there is still room for improvement? Think of examples that illustrate some of the inequalities that still exist today.

Literary Focus

A **flashback** is a scene in a movie, play, or story that interrupts the present action to show or tell what happened at an earlier time. Writers often use this device to develop a character or to give additional plot information. "Love Must Not Be Forgotten" uses several flashbacks to show the narrator's growing awareness of her mother's true situation and feelings.

LOVE MUST NOT BE FORGOTTEN

Zhang Jie

translated by

GLADYS YANG

> *In the opening paragraphs of "Love Must Not Be Forgotten,"*
> *the narrator wonders if she should marry a certain man. As*
> *you read the story, decide what advice her mother would*
> *probably have given her about her dilemma.*

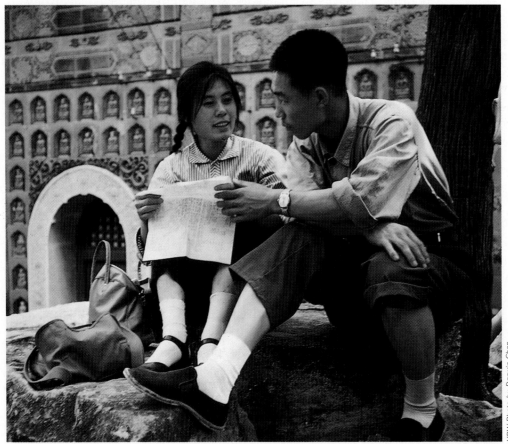

HRW Photo by Darwin Chen

I am thirty, the same age as our People's Republic. For a republic thirty is still young. But a girl of thirty is virtually on the shelf.

Actually, I have a bona fide suitor. Have you seen the Greek sculptor Myron's *Discobolus?*[1] Qiao Lin[2] is the image of that discus thrower. Even the padded clothes he wears in winter fail to hide his fine physique. Bronzed, with clear-cut features, a broad forehead and large eyes, his appearance alone attracts most girls to him.

But I can't make up my mind to marry him. I'm not clear what attracts me to him, or him to me. I know people are gossiping behind my back, "Who does she think she is, to be so choosy?" To them, I'm a nobody playing hard to get. They take offense at such preposterous behavior.

Of course, I shouldn't be captious.[3] In a society where commercial production still exists, marriage, like most other transactions, is still a form of barter.

I have known Qiao Lin for nearly two years, yet still cannot fathom whether he keeps so quiet from aversion to talking or from having nothing to say. When, by way of a small intelligence test, I demand his opinion of this or that, he says "good" or "bad" like a child in kindergarten.

Once I asked, "Qiao Lin, why do you love me?" He thought the question over seriously for what seemed an age. I could see from his normally smooth but now wrinkled forehead that the little gray cells in his handsome head were hard at work cogitating. I felt ashamed to have put him on the spot.

Finally he raised his clear childlike eyes to tell me, "Because you're good!"

Loneliness flooded my heart. "Thank you, Qiao Lin!" I couldn't help wondering, if we were to marry, whether we could discharge our duties to each other as husband and wife. Maybe, because law and morality would have bound us together. But how tragic simply to comply with law and morality! Was there no stronger bond to link us?

When such thoughts cross my mind I have the strange sensation that instead of being a girl contemplating marriage I am an elderly social scientist.

Perhaps I worry too much. We can live like most married couples, bringing up children together, strictly true to each other according to the law.... Although living in the seventies of the twentieth century, people still consider marriage the way they did millennia ago, as a means of continuing the race, a form of barter or a business transaction in which love and marriage can be separated. Since this is the common practice, why shouldn't we follow suit?

But I still can't make up my mind. As a child, I remember, I often cried all night for no rhyme or reason, unable to sleep and disturbing the whole household. My old nurse, a shrewd though uneducated woman, said an ill wind had blown through my ear. I think this judgment showed prescience, because I still have that old weakness. I upset myself over things which really present no problem, upsetting other people at the same time. One's nature is hard to change.

I think of my mother, too. If she were alive, what would she say about my attitude to Qiao Lin and my uncertainty about marrying him? My thoughts constantly turn to her, not because she was such a strict mother that her ghost is still watching over me since her death. No, she was not just my mother but my closest friend. I loved her so

1. **Myron's *Discobolus:*** famous statue of a handsome athlete by this Greek sculptor of the fifth century B.C.
2. **Qiao Lin** (chyou' lin')
3. **captious** (kap'shəs): fault-finding; critical.

much that the thought of her leaving me makes my heart ache.

She never lectured me, just told me quietly in her deep, unwomanly voice about her successes and failures, so that I could learn from her experience. She had evidently not had many successes—her life was full of failures.

During her last days she followed me with her fine, expressive eyes, as if wondering how I would manage on my own and as if she had some important advice for me but hesitated to give it. She must have been worried by my naiveté and sloppy ways. She suddenly blurted out, "Shanshan, if you aren't sure what you want, don't rush into marriage—better live on your own!"

Other people might think this strange advice from a mother to her daughter, but to me it embodied her bitter experience. I don't think she underestimated me or my knowledge of life. She loved me and didn't want me to be unhappy.

"I don't want to marry, mother!" I said, not out of bashfulness or a show of coyness. I can't think why a girl should pretend to be coy. She had long since taught me about things not generally mentioned to girls.

"If you meet the right man, then marry him. Only if he's right for you!"

"I'm afraid no such man exists!"

"That's not true. But it's hard. The world is so vast, I'm afraid you may never meet him." Whether married or not was not what concerned her, but the quality of the marriage.

"Haven't you managed fine without a husband?"

"Who says so?"

"I think you've done fine."

"I had no choice. . . ." She broke off, lost in thought, her face wistful. Her wistful lined face reminded me of a withered flower I had pressed in a book.

"Why did you have no choice?"

"You ask too many questions," she parried, not ashamed to confide in me but afraid that I might reach the wrong conclusion. Besides, everyone treasures a secret to carry to the grave. Feeling a bit put out, I demanded bluntly, "Didn't you love my dad?"

"No, I never loved him."

"Did he love you?"

"No, he didn't."

"Then why get married?"

She paused, searching for the right words to explain this mystery, then answered bitterly, "When you're young you don't always know what you're looking for, what you need, and people may talk you into getting married. As you grow older and more experienced you find out your true needs. By then, though, you've done many foolish things for which you could kick yourself. You'd give anything to be able to make a fresh start and live more wisely. Those content with their lot will always be happy, they say, but I shall never enjoy that happiness." She added self-mockingly, "A wretched idealist, that's all I am."

Did I take after her? Did we both have genes which attracted ill winds?

"Why don't you marry again?"

"I'm afraid I'm still not sure what I really want." She was obviously unwilling to tell me the truth.

I cannot remember my father. He and Mother split up when I was very small. I just recall her telling me sheepishly that he was a fine handsome fellow. I could see she was ashamed of having judged by appearances and made a futile choice. She told me, "When I can't sleep at night, I force myself to sober up by recalling all those stupid blunders I made. Of course it's so distasteful that I often hide my face in the sheet for shame,

Chinese woman.

🅺 *At what point does the narrative shift from the narrator's story to her mother's story?*

The Bettmann Archive

as if there were eyes watching me in the dark. But distasteful as it is, I take some pleasure in this form of atonement."

I was really sorry that she hadn't remarried. She was such a fascinating character, if she'd married a man she loved, what a happy household ours would surely have been. Though not beautiful, she had the simple charm of an ink landscape. She was a fine writer, too. Another author who knew her well used to say teasingly, "Just reading your

works is enough to make anyone love you!"

She would retort, "If he knew that the object of his affection was a white-haired old crone, that would frighten him away." At her age, she must have known what she really wanted, so this was obviously an evasion. I say this because she had quirks which puzzled me.

For instance, whenever she left Beijing on a trip, she always took with her one of the twenty-seven volumes of Chekhov's stories published between 1950 and 1955.[4] She also warned me, "Don't touch these books. If you want to read Chekhov, read that set I bought you." There was no need to caution me. Having a set of my own, why should I touch hers? Besides, she'd told me this over and over again. Still she was on her guard. She seemed bewitched by those books.

So we had two sets of Chekhov's stories at home. Not just because we loved Chekhov, but to parry other people like me who loved Chekhov. Whenever anyone asked to borrow a volume, she would lend one of mine. Once, in her absence, a close friend took a volume from her set. When she found out, she was frantic, and at once took a volume of mine to exchange for it.

Ever since I can remember, those books were on her bookcase. Although I admire Chekhov as a great writer, I was puzzled by the way she never tired of reading him. Why, for over twenty years, had she had to read him every single day? Sometimes, when tired of writing, she poured herself a cup of strong tea and sat down in front of the bookcase, staring raptly at that set of books. If I went into her room then it flustered her, and she either spilt her tea or blushed like

---

4. **twenty-seven volumes of Chekhov's . . . 1955:** complete stories of Russian author Anton Chekhov, published in a Chinese edition in the 1950s.

a girl discovered with her lover.

I wondered: Has she fallen in love with Chekhov? She might have if he'd still been alive.

When her mind was wandering just before her death, her last words to me were: "That set . . ." She hadn't the strength to give it its complete title. But I knew what she meant. "And my diary . . . 'Love Must Not Be Forgotten'. . . . Cremate them with me."

I carried out her last instruction regarding the works of Chekhov, but couldn't bring myself to destroy her diary. I thought, if it could be published, it would surely prove the most moving thing she had written. But naturally publication was out of the question.

At first I imagined the entries were raw material she had jotted down. They read neither like stories, essays, a diary, or letters. But after reading the whole I formed a hazy impression, helped out by my imperfect memory. Thinking it over, I finally realized that this was no lifeless manuscript I was holding, but an anguished, loving heart. For over twenty years one man had occupied her heart, but he was not for her. She used these diaries as a substitute for him, a means of pouring out her feelings to him, day after day, year after year.

No wonder she had never considered any eligible proposals, had turned a deaf ear to idle talk whether well meant or malicious. Her heart was already full, to the exclusion of anybody else. "No lake can compare with the ocean, no cloud with those on Mount Wu."[5] Remembering those lines I often reflected sadly that few people in real life could love like this. No one would love me like this.

I learned that toward the end of the thirties, when this man was doing underground work for the Party in Shanghai,[6] an old worker had given his life to cover him, leaving behind a helpless wife and daughter. Out of a sense of duty, of gratitude to the dead, and deep class feeling, he had unhesitatingly married the daughter. When he saw the endless troubles of couples who had married for "love," he may have thought, "Thank Heaven, though I didn't marry for love, we get on well, able to help each other." For years, as man and wife they lived through hard times.

He must have been my mother's colleague. Had I ever met him? He couldn't have visited our home. Who was he?

In the spring of 1962, Mother took me to a concert. We went on foot, the theater being quite near. On the way a black limousine pulled up silently by the pavement. Out stepped an elderly man with white hair in a black serge tunic suit. What a striking shock of white hair! Strict, scrupulous, distinguished, transparently honest—that was my impression of him. The cold glint of his flashing eyes reminded me of lightning or swordplay. Only ardent love for a woman really deserving his love could fill cold eyes like those with tenderness.

He walked up to Mother and said, "How are you, Comrade Zhong Yu?[7] It's been a long time."

"How are you!" Mother's hand holding mine suddenly turned icy cold and trembled a little.

They stood face to face without looking at each other, each appearing upset, even

---

5. **Mount Wu:** one of a chain of picturesque mountains in eastern China.

6. **Party in Shanghai** (shang'hī'): that is, the Communist Party in the large eastern Chinese city of Shanghai.

7. **Zhong Yu** (jong'yōo')

Exterior gate of the Forbidden City in Beijing, China. *The Forbidden City was the dwelling of the Chinese Imperial family before the era of Communism.*

stern. Mother fixed her eyes on the trees by the roadside, not yet in leaf. He looked at me. "Such a big girl already. Good, fine—you take after your mother."

Instead of shaking hands with Mother, he shook hands with me. His hand was as icy as hers and trembling a little. As if transmitting an electric current, I felt a sudden shock. Snatching my hand away I cried, "There's nothing good about that!"

"Why not?" he asked with the surprised expression grown-ups always have when children speak out frankly.

I glanced at Mother's face. I did take after her, to my disappointment. "Because she's not beautiful!"

He laughed, then said teasingly, "Too bad that there should be a child who doesn't find her own mother beautiful. Do you remember in '53, when your mother was transferred to Beijing, she came to our ministry to report for duty? She left you outside on the veranda, but like a monkey you climbed all the stairs, peeped through the cracks in doors, and caught your finger in the door of my office. You sobbed so bitterly that I carried you off to find her."

"I don't remember that." I was annoyed at his harking back to a time when I was still in open-seat pants.

"Ah, we old people have better memories." He turned abruptly and remarked to Mother, "I've read that last story of yours. Frankly speaking, there's something not quite right about it. You shouldn't have condemned the heroine. . . .There's nothing wrong with falling in love, as long as you don't spoil someone else's life. . . . In fact, the

Zhang Jie **1421**

hero might have loved her, too. Only for the sake of a third person's happiness, they had to renounce their love...."

A policeman came over to where the car was parked and ordered the driver to move on. When the driver made some excuse, the old man looked around. After a hasty "Goodbye" he strode back to the car and told the policeman, "Sorry. It's not his fault, it's mine...."

I found it amusing watching this old cadre[8] listening respectfully to the policeman's strictures. When I turned to Mother with a mischievous smile, she looked as upset as a first-form[9] primary schoolchild standing forlornly in front of the stern headmistress.[10] Anyone would have thought she was the one being lectured by the policeman. The car drove off, leaving a puff of smoke. Very soon even this smoke vanished with the wind, as if nothing at all had happened. But the incident stuck in my mind.

Analyzing it now, I realize he must have been the man whose strength of character won Mother's heart. That strength came from his firm political convictions, his narrow escapes from death in the revolution, his active brain, his drive at work, his well-cultivated mind. Besides, strange to say, he and Mother both liked the oboe. Yes, she must have worshiped him. She once told me that unless she worshiped a man, she couldn't love him even for one day.

But I could not tell whether he loved her or not. If not, why was there this entry in her diary?

"This is far too fine a present. But how did you know that Chekhov's my favorite writer?"

"You said so."

"I don't remember that."

"I remember. I heard you mention it when you were chatting with someone."

So he was the one who had given her the *Selected Stories of Chekhov*. For her that was tantamount to a love letter. Maybe this man, who didn't believe in love, realized by the time his hair was white that in his heart was something which could be called love. By the time he no longer had the right to love, he made the tragic discovery of this love for which he would have given his life. Or did it go deeper even than that?

This is all I remember about him.

Banner showing Chairman Mao, the leader of China's Communist revolution.

---

8. **old cadre** (kaʹdrē): here, former member of a cadre, or small unified group; in this case, a group of underground rebels.

9. **first-form:** first-grade.

10. **headmistress:** female school principal.

How wretched Mother must have been, deprived of the man to whom she was devoted! To catch a glimpse of his car or the back of his head through its rear window, she carefully figured out which roads he would take to work and back. Whenever he made a speech, she sat at the back of the hall watching his face rendered hazy by cigarette smoke and poor lighting. Her eyes would brim with tears, but she swallowed them back. If a fit of coughing made him break off, she wondered anxiously why no one persuaded him to give up smoking. She was afraid he would get bronchitis again. Why was he so near yet so far?

He, to catch a glimpse of her, looked out of the car window every day straining his eyes to watch the streams of cyclists, afraid that she might have an accident. On the rare evenings on which he had no meetings, he would walk by a roundabout way to our neighborhood, to pass our compound gate. However busy, he would always make time to look in papers and journals for her work. His duty had always been clear to him, even in the most difficult times. But now confronted by this love he became a weakling, quite helpless. At his age it was laughable. Why should life play this trick on him?

Yet when they happened to meet at work, each tried to avoid the other, hurrying off with a nod. Even so, this would make Mother blind and deaf to everything around her. If she met a colleague named Wang[11] she would call him Guo[12] and mutter something unintelligible.

It was a cruel ordeal for her. She wrote:

11. **Wang:** common Chinese family name.
12. **Guo** (gwō): The names "Wang" and "Guo" are written with similar characters; because she is preoccupied, she confuses the two.

We agreed to forget each other. But I deceived you, I have never forgotten. I don't think you've forgotten either. We're just deceiving each other, hiding our misery. I haven't deceived you deliberately, though; I did my best to carry out our agreement. I often stay far away from Beijing, hoping time and distance will help me to forget you. But when I return, as the train pulls into the station, my head reels. I stand on the platform looking round intently, as if someone were waiting for me. Of course there is no one. I realize then that I have forgotten nothing. Everything is unchanged. My love is like a tree the roots of which strike deeper year after year—I have no way to uproot it.

At the end of every day, I feel as if I've forgotten something important. I may wake with a start from my dreams wondering what has happened. But nothing has happened. Nothing. Then it comes home to me that you are missing! So everything seems lacking, incomplete, and there is nothing to fill up the blank. We are nearing the ends of our lives, why should we be carried away by emotion like children? Why should life submit people to such ordeals, then unfold before you your lifelong dream? Because I started off blindly, I took the wrong turning, and now there are insuperable obstacles between me and my dream.

Yes, Mother never let me go to the station to meet her when she came back from a trip, preferring to stand alone on the platform and imagine that he had met her. Poor mother with her graying hair was as infatuated as a girl.

Not much space in the diary was devoted to their romance. Most entries dealt with trivia: why one of her articles had not come off; her fear that she had no real talent; the excellent play she missed by mistaking the time on the ticket; the drenching she got by going out for a stroll without her umbrella. In spirit they were together day and night, like a devoted married couple. In fact, they spent no more than twenty-four hours together in all. Yet in that time they experienced deeper happiness than some people in a whole lifetime. Shakespeare makes Juliet say, "I cannot sum up half my sum of wealth."[13] And probably that is how Mother felt.

He must have been killed in the Cultural Revolution. Perhaps because of the conditions then, that section of the diary is ambiguous and obscure. Mother had been so fiercely attacked for her writing, it amazed me that she went on keeping a diary. From some veiled allusions I gathered that he had questioned the theories advanced by that "theoretician" then at the height of favor and had told someone, "This is sheer Rightist[14] talk." It was clear from the tear-stained pages of Mother's diary that he had been harshly denounced; but the steadfast old man never knuckled under to the authorities. His last words were, "When I go to meet Marx,[15] I shall go on fighting my case!"

That must have been in the winter of 1969, because that was when Mother's hair turned white overnight, though she was not yet fifty. And she put on a black armband.[16] Her position then was extremely difficult. She was criticized for wearing this old-style mourning and ordered to say for whom she was in mourning.

"For whom are you wearing that, Mother?" I asked anxiously.

"For my lover." Not to frighten me she explained, "Someone you never knew."

"Shall I put one on too?" She patted my cheeks, as she had when I was a child. It was years since she had shown me such affection. I often felt that as she aged, especially during these last years of persecution, all tenderness had left her, or was concealed in her heart, so that she seemed like a man.

She smiled sadly and said, "No, you needn't wear one." Her eyes were as dry as if she had no more tears to shed. I longed to comfort her or do something to please her. But she said, "Off you go."

I felt an inexplicable dread, as if dear Mother had already half left me. I blurted out, "Mother!"

Quick to sense my desolation, she said gently, "Don't be afraid. Off you go. Leave me alone for a little."

I was right. She wrote:

You have gone. Half my soul seems to have taken flight with you.

I had no means of knowing what had become of you, much less of seeing you for the last time. I had no right to ask either, not being your wife or friend. . . . So we are torn apart. If only I could have borne that inhuman treatment for you, so that you could have lived on! You should have lived to see your name cleared and take up your work again, for the sake of those who loved you. I knew you could not be a counterrevolutionary. You were one of the finest men killed. That's why I love you—I am not afraid now to avow it.

Snow is whirling down. Heavens, even God is such a hypocrite, he is using

---

13. **Shakespeare . . . wealth:** In *Romeo and Juliet* by William Shakespeare, Juliet makes this remark in describing her love for Romeo.

14. **Rightist:** in politics, conservative or reactionary; Chinese politics during the Cultural Revolution was dominated by Rightist Party members.

15. **Marx:** Karl Marx (1818–1883), German-born economic philosopher and father of modern socialism; a revered figure by Chinese and other Communists.

16. **black armband:** traditional sign of mourning in China and elsewhere.

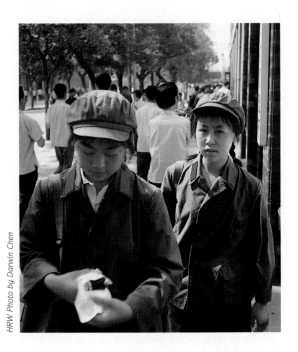

this whiteness to cover up your blood and the scandal of your murder.

I have never set store by my life. But now I keep wondering whether anything I say or do would make you contract your shaggy eyebrows in a frown. I must live a worthwhile life like you, and do some honest work for our country. Things can't go on like this—those criminals will get what's coming to them.

I used to walk alone along that small asphalt road, the only place where we once walked together, hearing my footsteps in the silent night. . . . I always paced to and fro and lingered there, but never as wretchedly as now. Then, though you were not beside me, I knew you were still in this world and felt that you were keeping me company. Now I can hardly believe that you have gone.

At the end of the road I would retrace my steps, then walk along it again. Rounding the fence I always looked back, as if you were still standing there waving goodbye. We smiled faintly, like

casual acquaintances, to conceal our undying love. That ordinary evening in early spring a chilly wind was blowing as we walked silently away from each other. You were wheezing a little because of your chronic bronchitis. That upset me. I wanted to beg you to slow down, but somehow I couldn't. We both walked very fast, as if some important business were waiting for us. How we prized that single stroll we had together, but we were afraid we might lose control of ourselves and burst out with "I love you"—those three words which had tormented us for years. Probably no one else could believe that we never once even clasped hands!

No, Mother, I believe it. I am the only one able to see into your locked heart.

Ah, that little asphalt road, so haunted by bitter memories. We shouldn't overlook the most insignificant spots on earth. For who knows how much secret grief and joy they may hide. No wonder that when tired of writing, she would pace slowly along that little road behind our window. Sometimes at dawn after a sleepless night, sometimes on a moonless, windy evening. Even in winter during howling gales which hurled sand and pebbles against the window pane. . . . I thought this was one of her eccentricities, not knowing that she had gone to meet him in spirit.

She liked to stand by the window, too, staring at the small asphalt road. Once I thought from her expression that one of our closest friends must be coming to call. I hurried to the window. It was a late autumn evening. The cold wind was stripping dead leaves from the trees and blowing them down the small empty road.

She went on pouring out her heart to him in her diary as she had when he was alive.

Zhang Jie   **1425**

Right up to the day when the pen slipped from her fingers. Her last message was:

I am a materialist, yet I wish there were a Heaven. For then, I know, I would find you there waiting for me. I am going there to join you, to be together for eternity. We need never be parted again or keep at a distance for fear of spoiling someone else's life. Wait for me, dearest, I am coming—

I do not know how, on her deathbed, Mother could still love so ardently with all her heart. To me it seemed not love but a form of madness, a passion stronger than death. If undying love really exists, she reached its extreme. She obviously died happy, because she had known true love. She had no regrets.

Now these old people's ashes have mingled with the elements. But I know that no matter what form they may take, they still love each other. Though not bound together by earthly laws or morality, though they never once clasped hands, each possessed the other completely. Nothing could part them. Centuries to come, if one white cloud trails another, two grasses grow side by side, one wave splashes another, a breeze follows another . . . believe me, that will be them.

Each time I read that diary, "Love Must Not Be Forgotten," I cannot hold back my tears. I often weep bitterly, as if I myself experienced their ill-fated love. If not a tragedy it was too laughable. No matter how beautiful or moving I find it, I have no wish to follow suit!

Thomas Hardy[17] wrote that "the call seldom produces the comer, the man to love rarely coincides with the hour for loving." I cannot judge them by conventional moral standards. What I deplore is that they did not wait for a "missing counterpart" to call them. If everyone could wait, instead of rushing into marriage, how many tragedies could be averted!

When we reach communism,[18] will there still be cases of marriage without love? Perhaps. . .since the world is so vast, two kindred spirits may never be able to answer each other's call. But how tragic! Could it be that by then we will have devised ways to escape such tragedies? But this is all conjecture.

Maybe after all we are accountable for these tragedies. Who knows? Should we take the responsibility for the old ideas handed down from the past? Because, if you choose not to marry, your behavior is considered a direct challenge to these ideas. You will be called neurotic, accused of having guilty secrets or having made political mistakes. You may be regarded as an eccentric who looks down on ordinary people, not respecting age-old customs—a heretic. In short, they will trump up endless vulgar and futile charges to ruin your reputation. Then you have to succumb to those ideas and marry regardless. But once you put the chains of an indifferent marriage around your neck, you will suffer for it for the rest of your life.

I long to shout: "Mind your own business! Let us wait patiently for our counterparts. Even waiting in vain is better than loveless marriage. To live single is not such a fearful disaster. I believe it may be a sign of a step forward in culture, education, and the quality of life."

---

17. **Thomas Hardy:** British author (1840–1928) whose fiction often challenged conventional morality and ideas about romantic love; his characters are often destroyed by love.

18. **When we reach communism:** when we reach a Communist ideal or perfect Communist state, as the teachings of communism say will one day happen.

First Thoughts

Did you find yourself sympathetic to the narrator's thoughts in the last paragraph? Explain why you agree or disagree with her point of view about marriage.

Identifying Facts

1. How old is the narrator, and why does she say she is virtually "on the shelf"? Who is Qiao Lin?
2. What is "Love Must Not Be Forgotten"? What private information does it reveal?
3. When did the mother's beloved die? What happened afterward?

Interpreting Meanings

1. What do the opening details reveal about the kind of person Qiao Lin is? Do you think the narrator will marry him? Why or why not?
2. What do the **flashbacks** involving the mother's true love reveal about the kind of person he was and the reasons the mother loved him?
3. Some readers feel that this story is very disjointed: It begins with the narrator's feelings about marriage but then veers off into a lengthy **flashback** about the narrator's mother and her love affair. Do you feel that the story is flawed and does not hold together, or do you think that it is a unified piece with a central theme? Explain your response.

Applying Meanings

Do the social pressures that affect the narrator and her mother exist in America today? Discuss.

Creative Writing Response

Writing a Diary Entry. Do you, like the narrator, feel that "If everyone could wait, instead of rushing into marriage, how many tragedies could be averted!"? Write your personal views about marriage, independence, or one of the other related ideas that Zhang Jie deals with in her story, as though you were writing a diary entry.

Language and Vocabulary

Wade-Giles and Pinyin Transliterations

Unlike English and many other **phonetic** languages written in an alphabet where letters represent sounds, Chinese is written in **characters** that represent ideas or meanings. These characters have many pronunciations, depending on the word's context and regional differences. This **ideographic** system has certain advantages: Chinese people who speak very different dialects can still understand each other by using the written characters. But Chinese can be extremely inaccessible to foreigners. For this reason, China's Communist government devised a way to use the Roman alphabet as an alternate way of writing Chinese. The system they developed, called **Pinyin**, came into standard use in the West in 1979 when the Chinese government asked English-language publications to adopt it.

Before 1979, however, the West had been using the **Wade-Giles** system to transliterate—that is, transfer into a different alphabet—Chinese words. Thus, while the names of recent Chinese writers like Zhang Jie (Chang Chieh in the Wade-Giles system) are more familiar under their Pinyin spellings, the names of earlier writers are better known by their Wade-Giles spellings. Except for Zhang Jie, the names of all Chinese writers in this book use Wade-Giles spellings. Consult a recent encyclopedia or another recent reference work to learn the Pinyin spellings of the following writers' names:

1. Li Po
2. Tu Fu
3. Chuang Tzu
4. Lao-tzu

LANGUAGE
—AND—
CULTURE

CONSCIENCE AND CONTROVERSY

Most of us think of writing, especially fiction writing, as a fairly benign process. We picture writers as a studious, slightly absent-minded breed for whom a brush with the law means, at worst, a parking ticket. But the reality for some writers has been far more harrowing. At different periods in history, writers the world over have come into conflict with repressive governments. Since the invention of the printing press, when the written word became widely available, down to the present day, there have been governments that have tried to block the writer's pen.

Aleksandr Solzhenitsyn (b. 1918)

Russian author Aleksandr Solzhenitsyn (sōl′zhə·nēt′sin) (see page 1264) moved from obscurity as a high-school teacher to international renown as a writer after the publication of his first novel, *One Day in the Life of Ivan Denisovich* (1962). The novel, based on his own experiences, delivered a scathing condemnation of Soviet prison camps. Solzhenitsyn eventually became a thorn in the side of the Soviet government, which sought to quiet all forms of criticism. In spite of the obvious danger of writing inflammatory fiction under a regime of strict censorship, Solzhenitsyn was committed to his craft and his country. When he won the Nobel Prize for literature in 1970, he did not travel to Stockholm to claim the award, fearing that the Soviet government would not allow him to re-enter his country. Solzhenitsyn was finally deported in 1974. He now lives and writes in the U.S.

In spite of the Soviet Union's official view of Solzhenitsyn as a political threat, the author's writings go beyond the sphere of politics, reaching for what he feels are the higher truths of humanity. In his novel *Cancer Ward,* he wrote, ''. . . it is not the task of the writer . . . to defend or criticize one or another form of government organization. The task of the writer is to select more universal and eternal questions, the secrets of the human heart and conscience . . . the laws of the history of mankind that were born in the depths of time immemorial and that will cease to exist only when the sun ceases to shine.''

Federico García Lorca (1878–1936)

Some writers do not write about politics or governments at all, yet still make enemies of political and military leaders. Nowhere is this point more clearly made than in the life and death of the

Spanish poet and playwright Federico García Lorca (gär·sē′ə lôr′kä) (see page 1228). García Lorca is among the best-loved Spanish-language poets of all time. Scholar Edith Helman writes, "Fervent in the love of his people, rooted in the Spanish earth, he inevitably expressed in his poetry . . . all the fears and hatred, frustration and longing of the Spaniards of his time and all times. When he voiced his own passionate love of freedom and impulse to revolt, he gave expression to the feelings of great numbers of inarticulate Spaniards who felt that he was speaking for them." In 1936, García Lorca found himself at the center of one of the great moral struggles of the twentieth century, the Spanish Civil War, which pitted the democratically elected Republic against Fascist forces backed by Hitler and Mussolini. García Lorca was already famous for his work in the theater, which he brought directly to farm workers in small Spanish villages. Early in the war, the Fascists, risking international condemnation, murdered the poet who so eloquently expressed the spirit of the Spanish people. The Fascists, lead by Franco, went on to win the war.

Ngũgĩ wa Thiong'o (b. 1938)

Even writers in nominally democratic countries have suffered imprisonment because of their words. By the 1970s, Kenyan author Ngũgĩ ('n·goo′gē), the head of the Department of Literature at the University of Nairobi (Kenya's capital), had gained international acclaim as an author. But in 1977, Ngũgĩ was arrested. The cause of his arrest was never stated. Government officials—who had already banned a play that Ngũgĩ coauthored, *Ngaahika Ndeenda (I Will Marry When I Like)*—simply felt that his writings painted the regime in an unflattering light. Although he was never charged with any crime, Ngũgĩ remained in prison for over a year. Finally, mounting pressure by groups such as Amnesty International led to his release. He recorded his experience in his 1981 novel, *Detained*. Ngũgĩ continued to criticize the increasingly repressive Kenyan government. In 1982, hearing that he was soon to be arrested again, the author exiled himself and his family to England, where he lives, writes, and lectures today.

All of these authors hold one thing in common: their writings give a voice to thousands of voiceless people. And nothing worries tyrants more than citizens who, through the words of authors, can articulate their desires.

Kenyan writer Ngũgĩ wa Thiong'o.

VARYING SENTENCES

Although it is possible to construct a seemingly endless variety of sentences in English, there are basically only four main sentence structures. When you can successfully use all four types, you can avoid monotony in your writing, create pleasing rhythms, avoid choppiness, and control the tone and impact of your words.

Simple Sentences

A **simple sentence** consists of one independent clause. An **independent clause** contains a subject and predicate and expresses a complete thought.

SIMPLE SENTENCE
The British headmistress changes Santha's name to Cynthia.

Compound Sentences

A **compound sentence** contains two or more independent clauses.

COMPOUND SENTENCE
The British headmistress changes Santha's name to Cynthia, and she changes Premila's name to Pamela.

The independent clauses may be joined with a comma and a coordinating conjunction (*and, but, or, nor*). They may also be joined with a semicolon.

Complex Sentences

A **complex sentence** contains one independent clause and one or more dependent clauses. **Dependent clauses** (also called **subordinate clauses**) begin with words like *although, because, since, when, while, who, what, which,* or *that.* A dependent clause has a subject and predicate but does not express a complete thought.

COMPLEX SENTENCE
The British headmistress, who is uncomfortable with Indian names, changes Santha's name to Cynthia.

Compound-Complex Sentences

Compound-complex sentences contain one or more independent clauses and one or more dependent clauses.

COMPOUND–COMPLEX SENTENCE
The British headmistress, who is uncomfortable with Indian names, changes Santha's name to Cynthia, and she changes Premila's name to Pamela.

Note that it is the arrangement of words, not only their meaning, that determines sentence structure.

Exercise 1: Identifying Sentence Structures

Identify which of the four structures each sentence below represents.

1. Truth is like the sun.

2. Akutagawa Ryunosuke became a famous writer in his youth, but he always doubted his artistic abilities.
3. The name of Mahfouz was placed on an Arab boycott list, although the Arab-speaking public continued to read his works.
4. Young Naguib's father urged him to go into school alone; he told him to smile because that would set a good example for the others.
5. Naguib peered around, but he found no trace of his father, who had promised to be there.

Using Complex and Compound-Complex Sentences

Complex and compound-complex sentences increase your ability to express shades of meaning. They also help you to keep your writing concise. To use these sentences effectively, you must subordinate ideas—decide which idea is more important and how the ideas are related.

LOOSE

Zhang Jie once scolded American poet Allen Ginsberg. Her concern was that he was not socially responsible.

SUBORDINATED

Zhang Jie once scolded American poet Allen Ginsberg because he was not socially responsible.

Subordinating the second sentence—making it into a subordinate clause—results in clearer and more concise writing. Subordinate clauses often begin with subordinating conjunctions. The following list provides examples of these conjunctions.

SUBORDINATING CONJUNCTIONS

after	if	unless
although	since	until
as	that	when
because	though	where
before	till	while

Exercise 2: Using Subordinate Clauses

Subordinate the second sentence in each pair, using the subordinating conjunction in parentheses. Combine the sentences to create one complex or compound-complex sentence.

1. The First World War was especially horrible. Each side used poison gas. (because)
2. The Cold War began in 1945. The U.S. and the U.S.S.R. began stockpiling nuclear weapons. (after)
3. Akutagawa Ryunosuke began writing. He was only ten years old. (when)
4. Having a long nose was an intolerable nuisance for the holy man. A disciple discovered a remedy. (until)
5. Two huge cranes fly into the air. The men crawl into the bushes. (as)
6. Raised in North Vietnam, Nguyen Thi Vinh was forced to flee to Hanoi. She endured deep homesickness and anguish over the war. (where)
7. Gregor remained secluded in his room. His family became more unsympathetic over his plight. (while)
8. The villagers' lives have changed. They work to preserve Esteban's memory. (since)
9. The narrator will never be satisfied. He escapes Borges. (until)

IDENTIFYING A THEME

Have you ever read a short story and then said, "I don't get it"? To "get it" is to understand the story's theme. Though you probably find the language of modern short stories clear, you may find their themes less so. However, you can learn to identify the theme of—and discover the insights in—any story.

Writing Assignment

In an informative essay, identify the theme of a story you've read in this unit. Your audience is a classmate who has read the work but is having trouble understanding it. In this assignment, you will draw inferences and check them for accuracy.

Background

A **theme** is an underlying truth about life or human nature. Very seldom does an author state a theme directly; rather, the events of the story reveal it. To find the theme of a story, you must make **inferences**, or intelligent guesses. Three steps can help you to identify a theme. In the example below, they are applied to a short story entitled "Pear Tree Dance," by Australian writer Elizabeth Jolley.

1. **Summarize the story's plot.** A toughened old woman, who was raised in a factory town and has always been poor,

begins wishing for land in the country. She scrimps and saves but still can't afford the land she wants. Finally, she finds a plot she can afford. To her joy, it includes flowers and a little house. There she plants a pear tree and then dances for the first time in her life.

2. **Infer what the main character learns or how he or she changes.** She learns to dream and then learns that she can attain her dream. In the process she becomes more deeply alive.

3. **Broaden your answer into a statement that could apply to people, or life, in general.** *Daring to dream, and following the dream, enriches people in ways beyond those they can foresee.* This is a statement of theme. Notice that you need at least one complete sentence to express a theme.

Prewriting

Identifying Responses. Freewrite your responses to a favorite short story in this unit. Touch on the following questions.

1. What did you like most about the story?

2. Which parts seemed most intense?

3. How did you feel as you read the story, and what did you think about?

Drawing and Checking Inferences. Summarize the story's plot. Using your summary and your personal responses, infer what the main character has learned and how he or she has changed. To check your inferences, fill out a chart like the one below with supporting facts and events from the story.

Inference	Support from Story
1.	a. _____ b. _____ c. _____
2.	a. _____ b. _____ c. _____

Then broaden your inferences into a general statement of theme.

Writing

Use the following guidelines as you draft your essay.

1. **Introductory Paragraph.** Begin by noting what originally attracted you to the story, being sure to cite the title, author, and author's country of origin. Explain how your original attraction to the story relates (or doesn't relate) to the story's theme. End the paragraph by stating the theme clearly.

2. **Body Paragraphs.** Use at least one paragraph to explain each inference on which your statement of theme is based. Referring to your prewriting chart, show how facts and details in the story support each inference. Use transitions that keep your logic clear for your readers (see page 56), and arrange paragraphs in a way that makes sense.

3. **Concluding Paragraph.** Quote a line from the story that is especially relevant to the theme. Explain briefly how it relates to the theme, perhaps touching on what the theme means to you. Leave your readers with a clear idea of the theme and the way the story reveals it.

Evaluating and Revising

Use the following checklist as you revise your essay.

1. Does your first paragraph catch the reader's attention, identify the story, and state the theme?

2. Do body paragraphs explain the inferences on which your statement of theme is based?

3. Are your inferences supported with enough facts and details from the story?

4. Are your ideas organized logically and linked with appropriate transitions?

5. Does the concluding paragraph leave the reader with one clear idea about the theme?

6. Are your sentences varied and grammatically correct?

Proofreading and Publishing

Proofread to eliminate errors in mechanics, and make a final copy of your essay. As a class, gather the essays into a booklet that next year's students can use with your literature text.

WRITING ABOUT LITERATURE

Writing Answers to Essay Questions

The following strategies will help you write answers to the essay questions following each selection in this book. Instructions on the writing process may also be found in the Exercises in Critical Thinking and Writing. A list of these exercises appears in the index on page 1494.

1. Begin by reading the essay question carefully. Make sure you understand exactly what the question is asking you to do and note how much evidence it asks you to provide.

2. Identify the key verb in the question. It will help you pinpoint your assignment. Look for these key verbs:

- **Analyze (Examine).** To *analyze* something is to take it apart and see how it works. You might be asked to analyze one element of a work and explain its effect on other elements or the work as a whole. For example, you might be asked to analyze Gregor's reaction to finding himself an insect in Franz Kafka's *The Metamorphosis* (see page 1154). Begin by identifying his reaction and then show how it affects his relationship with his employer, his relationship with his family, and his sense of self. (See **Analyzing Imagery**, page 616, and **Observing and Analyzing a Process**, page 676.)

- **Compare/Contrast.** When you *compare*, you point out similarities; when you *contrast*, you point out differences. You might, for example, be asked to compare and contrast two short stories. The best way to organize information for your essay is to use a chart like this one, which shows you similarities and differences at a glance:

	Story A	Story B
Character		
Setting		
Plot		

Vary the chart to suit the particular assignment. If you are asked to compare and contrast two poems, for example, you might use imagery, figures of speech, and tone as your points of discussion. If you are asked to compare and contrast two characters within a play, you might use personality, goals, and change. Once you have decided what points to discuss in your essay, decide on the order in which you will present your ideas. You can discuss all the elements of the first work and then all the elements of the second work (AABB order). Or you can discuss each element in turn (ABAB order), showing how it is similar or different in the two works. (See **Discovering Connections in Literature**, page 58.)

- **Describe.** To *describe* means to paint a picture in words. For example, if you were asked to describe the scene at the entrance to Hell in Dante Alighieri's *Inferno* (see page 748), you would try to convey its sights, sounds, and mood so that your readers can experience the scene. If you were asked to describe Eveline in James Joyce's story of the same name (see page 1209), you would discuss what you know about her through direct and indirect characterization—how she looks, acts, speaks, feels, and affects others. (See **Writing a Character Sketch**, page 790.)

- **Discuss.** To *discuss* means to comment about something in a general way. For example, if you were asked to discuss the point of one of Jean de La Fontaine's fables (see page 942), you might summarize the fable and comment on its moral.

- **Evaluate.** To *evaluate* something is to judge how good or bad—or how effective or ineffective—it is. In thinking about your evaluation, start with your personal reaction to the work. (Did you like it or hate it? Did you find it fascinating or boring?). Next, refine this reaction into a more specific judgment. ("Even though the play was written in the nineteenth century, it still speaks to us today," or "This poem was too rambling to hold my interest.") In the body of your essay, state the reasons for your judgment, each reason examining an element of the work and each backed up with evidence from the work. **Writing a Literary Review** provides hints on selecting criteria (see page 1132).

- **Illustrate.** To *illustrate* means to provide examples to support an idea or statement. For example, you might be asked to illustrate the principles of Japanese haiku poetry. You would first define haiku and then show how several haiku poems fit this definition.

- **Interpret.** To *interpret* something means to explain its meaning and importance. For example, if you were asked to interpret a Shakespearean sonnet, you might explain each quatrain in turn, then show how the final couplet summarizes or comments on the ideas in the quatrains. If you were asked to interpret a story's meaning, you would first identify the theme and then cite specific details from the work to support your interpretation. (See **Identifying a Theme**, page 1432.)

- **Respond.** To *respond* is to give your personal reaction to something. If you were asked to respond to Barbara Kimenye's "The Pig," for example, you would state explicitly whether you liked or disliked it, how it made you feel, and what it made you think about. Be as specific as possible as you explain the reasons for your response. (See **A Personal Response to Literature**, page 122.)

3. Write a thesis statement in which you state the main idea of your essay. Include your thesis statement in the first paragraph, along with any additional sentences that help you catch the reader's attention.

4. Gather evidence to support this thesis statement. If you can use your book, look back over the work for examples and illustrations. For a closed-book essay, make notes on all the supporting details you can remember.

5. Write one paragraph for each main point. Include a topic sentence for each paragraph, and express your ideas as clearly as you can. Don't pad your answer with unrelated details or ideas.

6. End with a concluding paragraph. Summarize or restate your main points, and if you wish, give your personal response to the work. Try to end your essay with a "clincher sentence."

Writing and Revising an Essay

You may be asked to choose your own topic for an essay on a specific work.

Prewriting

1. Choose a limited topic that you can cover adequately. If your assignment is an essay of four paragraphs, you can't possibly analyze all the characters in Ibsen's *A Doll's House*. But you do have room to analyze one character or the significance of the title. For ideas on the kinds of topics you might choose, review the list of key verbs on pages 1434–1435.

2. Write a thesis statement. Ask yourself, "What main idea about my topic do I want to discuss?" Then write one or two sentences that state this main idea. If you have trouble expressing your ideas in only one or two sentences, consider narrowing the topic.

3. List two or three main ideas that develop your thesis statement. Jot down the ideas that come to mind when you think about your thesis statement, and choose the strongest two or three. Then go back over the work to find specific points you may have overlooked. Don't rely simply on your memory.

4. Gather and arrange supporting evidence. Your essay should include quotations, specific details, and incidents from the literary work you are writing about—known as the **primary source**. You might also wish to refer to other works, letters, or interviews by the same writer. Finally, information from **secondary sources**—books, reviews, and critical essays about the work or the writer—may also provide supporting evidence for your ideas.

Before you begin writing, decide which evidence best supports your thesis statement. Then discard any weak or unrelated material. Once you've arranged your main ideas and evidence in the order that seems the most logical, you'll have an informal outline to work from.

Writing

Draft your essay following your outline and notes. Include evidence to support your thesis statement and the main idea of each paragraph. Structure your essay according to this plan:

I. INTRODUCTORY PARAGRAPH
   Catch the reader's interest.
   Tell what the essay will be about.
   Begin or end with the thesis statement.
II. BODY (Paragraphs 2, 3, etc.)
   Develop the thesis statement.
   Include a topic sentence and supporting
      evidence in each paragraph.
III. CONCLUDING PARAGRAPH
   Let the reader know that the essay is
      completed.
   Restate or summarize the thesis statement
      and main ideas.
   Include a personal response (optional).

Evaluating and Revising

Reread your first draft at least twice, checking once for content and once for style.

1. Content. Check to see that you've supported your thesis statement with at least two main ideas and that you've supported each main idea with sufficient evidence. If any part of your evidence appears weak or vague, go back over the work to find more convincing examples.

2. Style. To make your essay read smoothly, you may need to combine related sentences or break up long sentences into shorter ones. Cut unnecessary or repetitive words and phrases.

Proofreading and Publishing

The titles of poems, short stories, and essays should be enclosed in quotation marks; the titles of plays, novels, and other long works (such as epic poems) should be in italics. Sacred works like the Bible and the Koran and the individual books of these works are neither italicized nor placed in quotation marks. In handwriting and typing, italics are indicated by underlining.

Proofreader's Symbols

Symbol	Example	Meaning of Symbol
≡	"An honest thief"	Capitalize a lower-case letter.
/	"Wind And Water And Stone"	Change a capital letter to lower case.
∧	"Love Must Not Be Forgotten"	Insert a word.
∧	Lépold Sédar Senghor	Insert or change a letter.
⊙	2000 B.C.	Insert a period.
∧	"For Wei Pa In Retirement"	Insert a comma.
∨	Petrarchs sonnets	Insert an apostrophe.
∨ ∨	Half a Day	Insert quotation marks.
(underscore)	from Kaffir Boy	Set in italics.
∿	Chrétein de Troyes	Change the order of letters.
∿	"Laments on the Dead War"	Change the order of words.
#	Guy deMaupassant	Insert space.
⌒	the nine teenth century	Close up space.
ℓ	Isak Dinesen	Delete.
....	Isak Dinesen	Let it stand (stet).
⌣	Fyodor Dosstoevsky	Delete and close up space.
(SP)	"The 4 Ages"	Spell it out.
¶	¶In this story, Tolstoy	Indent to begin a new paragraph.

A Model Essay

The following essay is an interpretation of "The Two Brothers," by Leo Tolstoy. The essay shows the writer's revisions for a second draft.

TWO BROTHERS, TWO WAYS TO LIVE

To be content with what one has or to take a risk—what's [*is*] the best way to live? [*Leo*] Tolstoy deals with this question in his short parable The [*2*] Brothers. [*Although*] He seems to except [*ac—approaches to life*] both ways. [*"*] He also seems to favor [*s*] the risk-taker. In the story, [*2*] brothers come across a stone with writing on it. The stone [*message*] declares that any one who goes into the forrest, crosses the river, siezes some bear cubs away from their mother and runs up the moun-tin [*a*] without looking back will find happiness in a house there. In other words, there will be [*awaits*] a great reward for one who takes a great risk.

The older brother, the cautious one, raises many [*reasonable*] objections. The message might be a lie or a joke, or the brothers may have misunderstood it [*he says*]. They might get lost in the forrest or the river might be too wide to swim. The mother bear might kill the brothers. They might not be able to run up the mountain. And [*Finally*] even if all goes well, the older brother warns, [*that*] and they reach the house, "the happiness awaiting us there is not at all the sort of happiness we would want." Here are all the reasons why [*in brief form*] people do not take risks: they can't be sure [*aren't*], there might be danger, the result might not be worth the effort [*what to do*].

INTRODUCTORY PARAGRAPH
Catches the reader's interest.
Presents thesis statement—the story's theme.

BODY
Begins to summarize the story.

States topic sentence.

Gives details to support topic sentence.

Quotes from story.

Interprets older brother's reaction.

adventurous   *is willing to take the risks*

The younger brother ~~gives his reasons for going on~~. There

^he believes   *feel*

must be a reason for the message. He does not ~~believe~~ the

danger will be great, and if they dont try it, some one else will.

also

He points out that you can't suceed unless you try. Finally, he

says   *is*

~~said~~, he wouldn't want others to think he was afraid. He is a

casual

classic risk-taker. He is confident of the outcome, ~~unconcerned~~

about the danger, and proud of his reputation.

the brothers   adages

Now ~~they~~ trade old ~~sayings~~—and act on them. "A bird in the

says

hand is worth two in the bush," ~~said~~ the older brother, and set-

says

tles in. "Beneath a stone no water flows," ~~said~~ the younger

ing

brother. He sets out. He follow the instructions on the stone.

whose

At the top of the mountain he finds a city. ~~The~~ residents make

him their king. After ruling for (5) years, a stronger king defeats

him and he ~~is banished and~~ returns to his older brother.

brothers   their lives

~~So~~ who made the best decision? ~~Well~~, both are happy with

~~what has happened to them~~. The older brother says that he has

lived "Quietly and well" but the younger brother, while admit-

ting he has nothing now, beleives he has had wonderful experi-

however

ences. Tolstoy lets both brothers speak, but there is a hint that

he favors the younger brother. The younger brother is the one

eagerly   of the stone   also

who speaks first, accepting the challenge. ~~And~~ he is the one

who speaks last. "I shall always have something to remember,

while you have no memories at all," he says, and I can't help

States topic sentence.

Gives details to support topic sentence.

Interprets younger brother's reaction.

States topic sentence.

Supports topic sentence with quotations and details.

CONCLUDING PARAGRAPH

States topic sentence in question form.
Explains topic sentence.

Restates thesis statement.

Explains interpretation.

Quotes key passage in story.

Offers personal comment on interpretation.

agreeing with him. A quiet life can be ~~rewarding~~ satisfying, but the possibility of a big reward—and the chance for ~~memories~~ vivid memories—tempts me to aim as high as the younger brother.

Ends with clincher sentence.

Documenting Sources for a Research Paper

1. Parenthetical citations give brief information in parentheses immediately after a quotation or other reference. More detailed information about each source is given in the bibliography. This method of documenting sources is recommended by the Modern Language Association (MLA).

> **For a quotation from a prose passage by a writer who is identified in the text (page number):**
> Joyce ends the chapter with a beautiful image, ''the tide . . . flowing in fast to the land with a low whisper of her waves, islanding a few last figures in distant pools'' (173).
>
> **For a quotation by a writer whose name is not mentioned in the text (author's last name, page number):**
> In *Dubliners,* Joyce's collection of short stories, ''[T]he recurrent situation is entrapment'' (Levin, 5).
>
> **For a quotation from a play (act and scene, and line number if a poetic drama):**
> At this point Miranda rejoices, ''O brave new world/That has such people in't!'' (Act 5, Scene 1, lines 213–14).
>
> **For a quotation from a poem (line number):**
> In Paul Verlaine's ''The Sky Is Just Beyond the Roof,'' the speaker asks, ''Say, what have you done, you who are here, / With your lost youth?'' (lines 15–16).

2. Footnotes are placed at the bottom of the page on which the reference appears. A raised number at the end of the reference within the essay indicates a footnote.[1] Footnotes are generally numbered consecutively within a work.

[1] Harry Levin, ed. *The Portable James Joyce* (New York: The Viking Press, 1965) p. 5.

[2] Frank O'Connor, *A Short History of Irish Literature* (New York: G.P. Putnam's Sons, 1967) p. 57.

Check a writing handbook, or ask your teacher for the style for footnoting poems, magazine articles, interviews, and books with more than one author.

3. End notes are identical to footnotes except that they are listed on a separate page entitled "Notes" at the end of a paper. End notes are numbered consecutively.

4. A **Works Cited** section should be included at the end of your essay. This is an alphabetical list of all of the print and nonprint sources you referenced in your essay. The list may include not only books but also magazine articles and videotapes. Entries in your **Works Cited** section are listed alphabetically by the author's last name. Here is a sample **Works Cited** section.

Works Cited

Alazraki, Jaime, ed. *Critical Essays on Jorge Luis Borges.* Boston: G. K. Hall & Company, 1987.

Paz, Octavio. "In Time's Labyrinth." *The New Republic* 3 November 1986: 30–35.

A HANDBOOK OF LITERARY TERMS

ALLEGORY **A story in which the characters, settings, and events stand for abstract or moral concepts.** An allegory can be read on one level for its literal meaning and on another level for its symbolic, or allegorical, meaning. Leo Tolstoy's "How Much Land Does a Man Need?" (Unit Ten) is an example of an allegory. *See pages* 198, 421, 771, 1044.

ALLITERATION **The repetition of consonant sounds in words that are close to one another.** Alliteration occurs most often at the beginning of words, as in "broken bottle," but consonants within words may also alliterate, as in "always wide awake." The repetition of final consonant sounds in closely grouped words—as in *boasts and jests*—is called **consonance**. Poets may use alliteration and consonance to achieve special rhythmic and musical effects, to emphasize particular images and moods, or to give their poems greater unity. *See pages* 84, 519. *See also* **Assonance**.

ALLUSION **A reference to a statement, person, place, event, or thing that is known from literature, history, religion, myth, politics, or some other field of knowledge.** For example, the title of Anna Akhmatova's poem "Lot's Wife" (Unit Eleven) is an allusion to the Hebrew Bible story of the destruction of Sodom and Gomorrah. Allusions add depth of meaning to a work of literature by inviting comparisons. *See pages* 185, 436, 1308.

ANALOGY **A comparison of two things to show that they are alike in certain respects.** Writers often make analogies to show how something unfamiliar is like something well known or widely experienced. For example, people often draw an analogy between creating a work of art and giving birth. *See pages* 294, 300, 662.

ANECDOTE **A brief and sometimes witty story that focuses on a single interesting incident or event, often in order to make a point or teach a moral lesson.** Sometimes an anecdote reveals the character of a famous person. Taoists, Zen Buddhists, and Sufis, among others, use anecdotes to convey indirectly the teachings of their philosophies. *See pages* 547, 666.

ANTAGONIST *See* **Protagonist**.

ANTITHESIS **A form of parallelism in which contrasting ideas are expressed in a grammatically balanced statement.** The following proverb from the Hebrew Bible balances opposite ideas:

> Faithful are the wounds of a friend; but the kisses of an enemy are deceitful.

See pages 195, 634.

APHORISM **A concise, sometimes witty saying that expresses a principle, truth, or observation about life.** "Don't cry over spilt milk" is a well-known aphorism that points to the uselessness of regretting things that cannot be changed. *See page* 666. *See also* **Epigram, Maxim, Moral, Proverb**.

APOSTROPHE **A figure of speech in which a speaker directly addresses an absent or dead person, a deity, an abstract quality, or something nonhuman as if it were present and capable of responding.** Apostrophe is commonly used in hymns to address a divine being. *See pages* 77, 457.

ARCHETYPE **A pattern or model that serves as the basis for different, but related, versions of a character, plot, image, or theme.** For example, the basic plot of the hero's quest is a recurring pattern in myths and other types of literature from different cultures around the world. *See pages* 8–9, 54–55.

ARGUMENT *See* **Persuasion**.

ASIDE **Private words that a character in a play speaks to another character or to the audience that are not supposed to be overheard by others onstage.** Stage directions usually tell when a speech is an aside. For example, toward the end of Act I in Shakespeare's *The Tempest* (Unit Nine), Prospero makes several asides to Ariel that Miranda and Ferdinand do not hear.

ASSONANCE **The repetition of similar vowel sounds followed by different consonant sounds in words that are close together.** For example, the long *a* sounds in "It's a great day for baseball" create assonance. Certain languages, such as

Japanese, lend themselves to assonance. Like **alliteration**, assonance may be used in poetry to create special rhythmic and musical effects, to emphasize particular images or moods, or to achieve unity. *See pages* 88, 568, 1229. *See also* **Alliteration.**

ATMOSPHERE **The mood or feeling in a literary work.** Atmosphere is usually created through descriptive details and evocative imagery. For example, a story set in a grimy factory town may create a gloomy atmosphere in which characters struggle against despair. *See pages* 729, 1259. *See also* **Mood.**

AUTOBIOGRAPHY **An account of a person's own life.** *Kaffir Boy* by Mark Mathabane (Unit Eleven) is an autobiography about growing up under apartheid in South Africa. *See pages* 66, 1233, 1364.

BALLAD **A song or songlike poem that tells a story.** Most ballads have a regular pattern of **rhythm** and **rhyme** and use simple language and **refrains** as well as other kinds of **repetition**. Ballads usually tell sensational stories of tragedy, adventure, betrayal, revenge, and jealousy. Arising in the Middle Ages, **folk ballads** were composed by anonymous singers and were passed down orally from generation to generation before they were written down. **Literary ballads**, on the other hand, are composed and written down by known poets, usually in the style of the older folk ballads.

The typical ballad **stanza** is a **quatrain** with the **rhyme scheme** *abcb* (although this is by no means universal). The **meter** is often only loosely **iambic**, with four stresses in the first and third lines and three stresses in the second and fourth lines. The number of unstressed syllables in each line may vary. *See pages* 512, 687.

BIOGRAPHY **An account of a person's life written or told by another person.** For example, Tacitus' historical account of imperial Rome, the *Annals* (Unit Four), includes a biography of the emperor Nero. *See page* 552.

BLANK VERSE **Poetry written in unrhymed iambic pentameter.** *Blank* means that the poetry is unrhymed. *Iambic pentameter* means that each line contains five **iambs**, or metrical feet, each consisting of an unstressed syllable followed by a stressed syllable (˘ ´). Blank verse was the most common metrical form used in English dramatic

and epic poetry during the Renaissance. It is the verse form used, for example, in all of Shakespeare's plays, including *The Tempest* (Unit Nine), and in John Milton's epic poem *Paradise Lost*. Because blank verse lends itself easily to slight variations within the basic pattern and can mimic the natural **rhythms** of English speech, it has been used over the centuries by many poets writing in English. Here are the closing lines from *Paradise Lost*, describing Adam and Eve's departure from Paradise:

> The world was all before them, where to choose
> Their place of rest, and Providence their guide;
> They hand in hand, with wand'ring steps and
>   slow,
> Through Eden took their solitary way.

See page 932.

CANTO **A subdivision in a long poem, similar to a chapter in a book.** Dante's *Divine Comedy* (Unit Eight), for example, is divided into one hundred cantos.

CHANSON DE GESTE **A kind of epic poem composed in Old French mostly in the eleventh and twelfth centuries, focusing on the heroic deeds of Charlemagne and other feudal lords.** Literally meaning "songs of deeds," *chansons de geste* such as the *Song of Roland* (Unit Eight) share many characteristics with classical **epics**. *See pages* 687, 693.

CHARACTER **An individual in a story, play, or narrative poem.** A character always has human traits, even if the character is an animal, such as the trickster Coyote in Native American tales, or a god or monster, such as Aphrodite and the giant Sinis in the Greek myth of Theseus (Unit One). Most characters, however, are ordinary human beings, like Nora in Ibsen's *A Doll's House* (Unit Ten).

Characters can be classified as static or dynamic. A **static character** is one who does not change much in the course of a story. A **dynamic character**, on the other hand, changes in some important way as a result of the story's action. Characters can also be classified as flat or round. **Flat characters** have only one or two personality traits. They are one-dimensional—their personalities can be summed up by a single phrase. In contrast, **round characters** have more dimensions to their personalities—they are complex, solid, and multifaceted, like real people. *See pages* 599, 785, 1215. *See also* **Characterization**.

CHARACTERIZATION **The process by which the writer reveals the personality of a character.** A writer can reveal a character in the following ways:

1. By telling us directly what the character is like: humble, ambitious, impetuous, easily manipulated, and so on
2. By describing how the character looks and dresses
3. By letting us hear the character speak
4. By revealing the character's private thoughts and feelings
5. By revealing the character's effect on other people—showing how other characters feel or behave toward the character
6. By showing the character's actions

The first method of revealing character is called **direct characterization**. When a writer uses this method, we do not have to figure out what a character's personality is like—the writer tells us directly. The other five methods of revealing a character are known as **indirect characterization**. When a writer uses these methods, we have to exercise our own judgment, putting clues together to figure out what a character is like—just as we do in real life when we are getting to know someone. *See pages* 28, 1070. *See also* **Character**.

CHORUS **In classical Greek tragedies, a group of nameless onlookers who comment on and interpret the action of the play.** In most Greek tragedies, the chorus consists of twelve or fifteen performers who dance as they sing their lines. In Sophocles' *Oedipus Rex* (Unit Four), the chorus is used as a collective "actor" within the drama itself. *See page* 305.

CLIMAX **The point of greatest emotional intensity or suspense in a plot.** The climax usually marks the moment toward the end of the plot when the conflict is decided one way or the other. Following the climax, the story is usually **resolved**. Long works, such as novels, may have more than one climactic moment, though usually the greatest climax occurs last. *See pages* 17, 844, 1033. *See also* **Plot, Dramatic Structure**.

COMEDY **In general, a story that ends happily.** The hero or heroine of a comedy is usually a character who overcomes a series of obstacles and is reconciled with his or her opponents in a way that suggests the renewal of life or the formation of a harmonious society. Shakespeare's *The Tempest* (Unit Nine) contains elements of comedy, as Prospero is ultimately reconciled with Antonio and King Alonso, and the union of the children Miranda and Ferdinand implies that future generations will live in peace. In contrast, the hero or heroine in a **tragedy**, such as *Oedipus Rex,* comes to an unhappy or disastrous end, often due to some **tragic flaw** in his or her personality.

Farce is a type of comedy in which ridiculous and often stereotyped characters are involved in far-fetched, silly situations. The humor in farce is based on crude physical action, slapstick, and clowning. Many of Shakespeare's dramas, including *The Tempest,* contain elements of farce. *See pages* 221, 375, 962, 964. *See also* **Tragedy**.

CONFLICT **A struggle or clash between opposing characters, forces, or emotions.** In an **external conflict**, a character struggles against some outside force: another character, society as a whole, or some natural force. An **internal conflict**, on the other hand, is a struggle between opposing needs, desires, or emotions within a single character. Many works, especially longer ones, contain both internal and external conflicts that are often interrelated. *See pages* 40, 382, 732, 1403.

CONNOTATIONS **All the meanings, associations, or emotions that a word suggests.** For example, an expensive restaurant might prefer to advertise its excellent "cuisine" rather than its excellent "cooking." Both words have the same literal meaning, or **denotation**: "prepared food." *Cuisine,* however, has connotations of elegance and sophistication, while *cooking* does not. The same restaurant would certainly not describe its food as "great grub."

Notice the difference between the following pairs of words: young/immature, ambitious/cutthroat, uninhibited/shameless, lenient/lax. In each pair, the second word carries unfavorable connotations that the first word does not. *See page* 435.

CONVENTIONS, EPIC *See* **Epic**.

COUPLET **Two consecutive lines of poetry that rhyme.** The Persian epic poem the *Shahname*

(Unit Seven), consists of more than 60,000 couplets. When a couplet forms a complete thought, it is called a **closed couplet**. Shakespeare's **sonnets** (Unit Nine) end in closed couplets. *See pages 646, 805.*

CRISIS *See* **Dramatic Structure.**

DENOTATION **The literal, dictionary definition of a word.** *See* **Connotations.**

DESCRIPTION **Writing that is intended to recreate a person, place, thing, event, or experience.** Description uses **imagery**—language that appeals to the senses to show how something looks, sounds, smells, tastes, or feels to the touch. *See pages 721, 729.*

DICTION **A writer's or speaker's choice of words.** People use different types of words depending on the audience they're addressing, the subject they're discussing, and the effect they're trying to produce. For example, slang words that would be suitable in a casual conversation among friends ("Yo, Dude") would be unsuitable at a presidential news conference. Similarly, the language a scientist would use in a scholarly article to describe a snowflake would be different from the language used by a poet.

Diction is an essential element of a writer's **style**. It may be, for instance, simple or ornate (big rooms/commodious chambers), general or specific (fish/fantailed goldfish), modern or old-fashioned (men's store/haberdashery). An important aspect of any writer's diction is the **connotation** that the words carry. *See pages 1031, 1231.*

DIDACTIC LITERATURE **A literary work that is meant to instruct, give advice, or convey a philosophy or a moral message.** In ancient Egypt, didactic literature included **instructions**, sets of moral teachings often in the form of **proverbs**. The New Testament **parables** (Unit Three) and Rumi's "Unmarked Boxes" (Unit Seven) are examples of didactic literature that convey religious teachings. *See pages 467, 590. See also* **Fable.**

DRAMA **A story that is written to be acted out in front of an audience.** Drama is one of the major **genres**, or forms, of literature. The earliest dramas—from the Greek comedies and tragedies to the medieval European mystery, miracle, and morality plays—originally had a **sacred** or **ritual** function and were used in religious ceremonies or services. In medieval Japan, a very formal and styl-

ized mode of drama known as **Noh** also developed from religious sources.

In Europe during the Renaissance and Enlightenment, playwrights such as William Shakespeare, Molière, and William Congreve created dramas in several forms—satires, historical plays, comedies, tragedies, and tragicomedies (which combined elements of both comedy and tragedy). In the late nineteenth century, the Norwegian playwright Henrik Ibsen helped influence the direction of much modern drama by creating such **Realist** plays as *A Doll's House* (Unit Ten). *See pages* 302–305, 596–597, 786–787, 840–843, 964–965, 1127.

DRAMATIC STRUCTURE **The method of development of a play's plot.** A typical dramatic structure, especially in the plays of Shakespeare, includes **exposition**, in which relevant background information is presented; **rising action**, which accelerates and adds complications to the plot; the **climax** (sometimes called the **turning point** or **crisis**), which is the moment of greatest emotional intensity or suspense; **falling action**, which unravels the complications; and the **resolution**, which settles the play's conflicts. *See page 844.*

ELEGY **A poem that mourns the death of a person or laments something lost.** Elegies may lament the passing of life and beauty, or they may be meditations on the nature of death. A type of **lyric poetry**, an elegy is usually formal in language and structure, and solemn or even melancholy in **tone**. Modern examples include Margaret Atwood's "Elegy for the Giant Tortoises" and Aleksandr Solzhenitsyn's prose poem "A Journey Along the Oka" (Unit Eleven). *See pages 631, 1317.*

ENJAMBMENT **The running on of a thought from one line of verse to the next.** By cutting down on **end-stopped lines** (lines that conclude a thought with punctuation), enjambment enhances the flow of the poem's language and prevents a strict **rhyme scheme** or **rhythm** from sounding predictable and rigid. Here, for example, are four lines from Edward FitzGerald's translation of the *Rubáiyát* of Omar Khayyám. Notice how the thoughts spill from one line to the next.

> Myself when young did eagerly frequent
> Doctor and Saint, and heard great argument
>   About it and about: but evermore
> Came out by the same door where in I went.

See page 812.

EPIC **A long narrative poem that relates the great deeds of a larger-than-life hero who embodies the values of a particular society.** Most epics include elements of myth, legend, folklore, and history. Their tone is serious and their language grand. Most **epic heroes** undertake **quests** to achieve something of tremendous value to themselves—like Gilgamesh (Unit Three)—or to their society—like the hero of Virgil's *Aeneid* (Unit Four).

Most ancient epics began as **oral epics**, also known as **primary epics**, that were performed by generations of anonymous storytellers and changed slightly with each retelling. The African epic *Sundìata* (Unit Two), for example, was passed down orally for hundreds of years by storytellers known as **griots** before it was written down in the 1950s. **Literary epics**, on the other hand, are created by individual writers, often from earlier models. Virgil's *Aeneid* is an example of a literary epic modeled after earlier Greek epics—Homer's *Iliad* (Unit Four) and *Odyssey*.

Many epics share standard characteristics and formulas known as **epic conventions**, including:

- an **invocation**, or formal plea for aid, to a deity or some other spiritual power to inspire the poet;

- action that begins *in medias res* (literally, "in the middle of things") and then **flashes back** to events that take place before the narrative's current time setting;

- **epic similes**, or elaborately extended comparisons relating heroic events to simple, everyday events;

- a consistently predictable **metrical structure** (originally intended as a memorization aid in oral performances of the epic);

- **stock epithets**, or descriptive adjectives or phrases used repeatedly with—or in place of—a noun or proper name, such as "the wine-dark sea" in Homer's *Odyssey*. *See pages* 104, 136–137, 224–227, 458–459, 485, 646–647, 693, 703.

EPIGRAM **A brief, clever, and usually memorable statement that often contains a moral.** Fables, such as those in the *Panchatantra* (Unit Five) and by Jean de La Fontaine (Unit Nine), often end with epigrams that summarize the message of the story line. *See pages* 483, 941. *See also* **Aphorism, Maxim, Moral, Proverb**.

EPIPHANY **In a literary work, a moment of** sudden insight or revelation that a character experiences. The word *epiphany* comes from the Greek and can be translated as "manifestation" or "showing forth." The term has religious meanings that have been transferred to literature. James Joyce gave the word its literary meaning in an early draft of his novel *A Portrait of the Artist as a Young Man*. In his story "Eveline" (Unit Eleven) for example, the title character's epiphany comes when she realizes she is unable to board the ship with the sailor. *See page* 1208.

EPITHET **An adjective or other descriptive phrase that is regularly used to characterize a person, place, or thing.** Phrases such as "Ivan the Terrible" and "Jack the Giant-Killer" are epithets. Homer created so many **stock epithets** in his *Iliad* (Unit Four) and *Odyssey* that his name has been permanently associated with a particular type of epithet. The **Homeric epithet** consists of a compound adjective that is regularly used to modify a particular noun. Famous examples are "the wine-dark sea," "the gray-eyed goddess Athena," and "rosy-fingered dawn." *See pages* 72, 457. *See also* **Epic**.

EPONYM **A real or mythical person from whose name the name of a nation, institution, idea, or term has been derived.** For example, Miguel de Cervantes' character Don Quixote (Unit Nine) is the eponym for the word *quixotic*, which describes someone who is like Don Quixote—impractical, romantic, and visionary. *See pages* 436–437.

ESSAY **A short piece of nonfiction prose that examines a single subject from a limited point of view.** There are two major types of essays. **Formal essays** are usually serious and impersonal in tone. Because they are written to inform or persuade, they are expected to be factual, logical, and tightly organized. **Informal essays** (also called **personal essays**) generally reveal much about the personalities and feelings of their authors. They tend to be conversational in tone, and many, such as Santha Rama Rau's "By Any Other Name" (Unit Eleven), are autobiographical in nature. *See page* 1386.

EXISTENTIALISM **A modern European movement in philosophy, religion, and art that asserts "existence precedes essence," that is, that the universe and everything in it exists**

but has no meaning, and that people supply meaning through their actions. Some existentialists such as Albert Camus emphasize that each person is free to make moral choices that define and give meaning to his or her life. Through their choices and actions, human beings are responsible for what they make of themselves and their lives. *See pages* 1145, 1245, 1257.

FABLE   A very brief story in prose or verse that teaches a moral or a practical lesson about life. In **beast fables**, the characters are animals that behave and speak like human beings. Some of the most popular fables are those attributed to Aesop, a Greek slave who supposedly lived in the sixth century B.C. Other popular and widely influential fables include those collected in the *Panchatantra* (Unit Five). *See pages* 479, 941. *See also* **Parable**.

FAIRY TALE   A type of folktale that features supernatural elements such as spirits, talking animals, and magic. Good-hearted, common people who triumph over evil are usually the heroes of fairy tales. Many fairy tales also contain a **moral**—a message about how people ought to behave. *See pages* 46, 52–53.

FALLING ACTION *See* **Dramatic Structure**.

FANTASY   A work that takes place in an unreal world and features incredible characters. Much **science fiction** is fantasy. *See pages* 1146, 1272.

FARCE *See* **Comedy**.

FICTION *See* **Nonfiction**.

FIGURE OF SPEECH   A word or phrase that describes one thing in terms of another and is not meant to be understood on a literal level. Figures of speech (sometimes called **figurative language**) always involve some sort of imaginative comparison between seemingly unlike things. The most common figures of speech are the **simile** (a heart like a comforting fire), the **metaphor** (the dark cloak of night), and **personification** (angry winds shouting through the canyon). *See pages* 89, 370, 1149, 1295. *See also* **Hyperbole, Metaphor, Onomatopoeia, Personification, Simile, Symbol, Understatement**.

FLASHBACK   A scene in a narrative work that interrupts the present action of the plot to ''flash backward'' and tell what happened at an earlier time. The flashback is one of the **con**-

ventions of Homer's *Iliad* (Unit Four) and *Odyssey* that became a standard feature of many later epics. *See pages* 225, 228.

FOIL   A character who is used as a contrast to another character. The use of a foil emphasizes the differences between two characters, bringing out the distinctive qualities in each. For example, in the *Nibelungenlied* (Unit Eight), Hagen serves as a foil for Siegfried, thereby emphasizing Siegfried's heroic qualities. *See pages* 740, 837.

FOLKTALE   A story told by the common people. Folktales belong to the oral tradition. Most folktales are told for entertainment, although they may also teach moral values. Legends, tall tales, fables, ghost stories, and fairy tales are all forms of folktales. *See pages* 1, 7, 26–27.

FORESHADOWING   Clues that hint at what is going to happen later in the plot. Foreshadowing arouses the reader's curiosity and builds up **suspense**. In ''Life Is Sweet at Kumansenu'' (Unit Eleven), for example, Abioseh Nicol includes details in his initial description of Meji to foreshadow the story's surprise ending. *See pages* 228, 740, 1335.

FRAME STORY   A story that serves to bind together several different narratives. Both *The Thousand and One Nights* (Unit Seven) and Boccaccio's *Decameron* (Unit Nine) use frame stories as a device for unifying various shorter stories. *See pages* 478, 638, 814.

FREE VERSE   Poetry that has no regular meter or rhyme scheme. Free verse usually relies instead on the natural rhythms of ordinary speech. Poets writing in free verse may use **alliteration**, **internal rhyme**, **onomatopoeia**, **repetition**, or other devices to achieve their effects. They may also place great emphasis on **imagery**. *See pages* 1144, 1229.

GENRE   The category to which a literary work belongs. Examples of genres include **drama**, the **epic**, the **novel**, the **short story**, and **lyric poetry**. *See pages* 161, 987.

HAIKU   A brief, unrhymed, three-line poem developed in Japan in the 1600s. In the original language, the first and third lines of a haiku have five syllables each, and the middle line has seven. Haiku generally juxtapose familiar images and present them in a compressed form, forcing the reader to make an imaginative leap to understand the connection between them.

A light-hearted variation on the traditional haiku form is the **senryu**. Senryu are intended to point out the humor and irony of the human condition. *See pages* 563, 572–573, 577, 612–613.

HYMN   A lyric poem or song addressed to a divine being. Hymns praise the power and wisdom of the deity and often ask for divine help or mercy. *See pages* 66, 72, 455. *See also* **Apostrophe, Psalm**.

HYPERBOLE   A figure of speech that uses exaggeration to express a strong sentiment or create a comic effect. Also called **overstatement** and **exaggeration**, hyperbole does not express the literal truth; however, it is often used to capture a sense of intensity or to emphasize the essential nature of something. For example, when we say we are ''sweating to death'' in a stuffy room, we are using a hyperbole to express extreme discomfort. Hyperbole is often used in **satire**, such as Voltaire's *Candide* (Unit Nine), for ridiculing or exposing an opponent's vices or follies. *See pages* 410, 413.

IAMBIC PENTAMETER   A line of poetry made up of five iambs. An **iamb** is a metrical **foot**, or unit of measure, consisting of an unstressed syllable followed by a stressed syllable (ˇ ′). The word *preferred*, for example, is made up of one iamb. Pentameter is derived from the Greek words *penta* (''five'') and *meter* (''measure''). **Sonnets** and **blank verse** use iambic pentameter. It is by far the most common verse line in English poetry because of its similarity to the natural rhythms of the English language. Here, for example, are two lines of iambic pentameter from Shakespeare's *The Tempest:*

His mother was a witch, and one so strong

That could control the moon, make flows and ebbs

See pages 805, 932, 1003. *See also* **Meter**.

IMAGERY   Language that appeals to the senses. Most images are visual—that is, they appeal to the sense of sight. But imagery can also appeal to the reader's senses of hearing, touch, taste, or smell. While imagery is an element in all types of writing that involve **description**, it is especially important in poetry. Writers and poets often use figures of speech to create vivid images. *See pages* 280, 575, 1012, 1016, 1028, 1331.

IRONY   A contrast or discrepancy between expectations and reality—between what is said and what is really meant, between what is expected and what really happens, or between what appears to be true and what is really true. Irony in literature falls into three major categories:

1. Verbal irony occurs when a writer or speaker says one thing but really means the opposite. If you tell a friend who shows up an hour late for an appointment that ''you just love being kept waiting in the rain,'' you are using verbal irony.

2. Situational irony occurs when what actually happens is the opposite of what is expected or appropriate. An example of situational irony takes place in Greek mythology when Zeus falls in love with a mortal woman named Semele. Zeus promises to give Semele anything she wants. To his dismay, she begs to see him in his true form as the Lord of Heaven. Zeus reluctantly agrees, and the brilliant splendor of the god burns her to death.

3. Dramatic irony occurs when the audience or the reader knows something important that a character in a play or story does not know. Dramatic irony can heighten a comic effect or generate **suspense**. In *Oedipus Rex* (Unit Four), for example, when the Corinthian messenger tells Oedipus that the King of Corinth has died of natural causes, Oedipus believes he has been released from the prophecy that says he will murder his father. The audience, however, knows that the truth has yet to come to light. *See pages* 98, 306, 648, 705, 814, 1282, 1344.

LEGEND   A story about extraordinary deeds, based to some extent on fact. The African epic *Sundiata* (Unit Two), for example, is based on the life of a historical figure, Sundiata Keita, who reestablished the Mandingo Empire of Old Mali in 1235. Through many retellings over time, however, the facts of his life were greatly embellished, and Sundiata Keita became a legendary hero. *See pages* 102–103.

LYRIC POETRY   Songlike poetry that focuses on expressing private emotions or thoughts. Most lyric poems are short, and they usually imply rather than directly state a single strong emotion. The term *lyric* comes from the ancient Greece, where lyric poems, such as those by Sappho (Unit Four), were recited to the accompaniment of a stringed instrument called a lyre. Today lyric poets still try to make their poems melodious, but they rely only on the musical effects they can create with words (such as **rhyme**, **rhythm**, **alliteration**, and **onomatopoeia**). *See pages* 80, 218, 280, 987, 1290, 1410.

MAGICAL REALISM   A twentieth-century literary style that combines incredible events with realistic details and relates them all in a matter-of-fact tone. Magical realism originated in Latin America, where authors such as Gabriel García Márquez (Unit Eleven) drew on elements of **surrealism** and local **folklore** to create a style that was both timeless and innovative. *See pages* 1146, 1308.

MAXIM   A brief, direct statement that expresses a basic rule of human conduct or a general truth about human behavior. "It is better to give than to receive" is an example of a well-known maxim. *See pages* 415, 537, 540, 542. *See also* **Epigram, Moral, Proverb.**

METAPHOR   A figure of speech that makes a comparison between two seemingly unlike things without using the connective words *like, as, than,* or *resembles.* A **direct metaphor** states that one thing is another, such as "the stars are icy diamonds." ("Stars like icy diamonds" is a **simile**.) Often metaphors are **implied**: "Against her black formal gown, she wore a constellation of diamonds" implies a comparison between diamonds and stars and between the black gown and a night sky.

- An **extended metaphor** is a metaphor that is developed over several lines of writing or even through an entire poem or paragraph. Marie de France uses an extended metaphor that compares the love of Tristan and Iseult to a honeysuckle in "Chevrefoil" (Unit Eight).
- A type of **cliché,** a **dead metaphor** is a metaphor that has become so common that we no longer even notice that it is a figure of speech. Our everyday language is filled with dead metaphors, such as "the pinnacle of success," "a tower of strength," and "the root of the problem."
- A **mixed metaphor** is the inconsistent mixture of two or more metaphors. Mixed metaphors are usually unintentional and often conjure up ludi-

crous images: "Those snakes in the grass pulled the rug out from under us." *See pages* 89, 370, 1125, 1295.

METER   A generally regular pattern of stressed and unstressed syllables in poetry. Meter is measured in units called feet. A **foot** consists of one stressed syllable and usually one or more unstressed syllables. The standard feet used in English poetry are the **iamb** (as in convínce), the **trochee** (as in bórrow), the **anapest** (as in contradíct), the **dactyl** (as in áccurate), and the **spondee** (as in séawéed). In meters such as **iambic pentameter**—which consists of five iambs per line—other feet may be substituted occasionally. Such variations prevent the meter from sounding sing-song and monotonous.

When we want to indicate the metrical pattern of a poem, we mark the stressed syllables with the symbol ′ and the unstressed syllables with the symbol �’. Indicating the metrical pattern of a poem in this way is called **scanning** the poem, or **scansion**. Here, for example, is a passage from *The Tempest* with the scansion marked. Note how Shakespeare varies the basic iambic pentameter by substituting an anapest for one of the feet in the second line and by adding an extra unstressed syllable at the end of the third line.

This blue-eyed hag was hither brought with child
And here was left by the sailors. Thou, my slave,
As thou reportst thyself, wast then her servant

See pages 226, 805, 807, 1229. *See also* **Blank Verse, Iambic Pentameter.**

MIRACLE, MYSTERY, AND MORALITY PLAYS *See* **Drama**.

MODERNISM   A broad trend in literature and the other arts, from approximately 1890 to 1940, that reflected many artists' concern over society's loss of traditional values. In general, modernist writers sought new forms to reflect the fragmentation and uncertainty that they felt characterized modern life. Many modernist poets, for example, rejected traditional meter in favor of **free verse**. Novelists such as James Joyce employed a new technique called **stream of consciousness** to record the jagged monologue of their characters' thoughts. *See pages* 1143, 1302.

MOOD **The overall emotion created by a work of literature.** Mood can usually be described with one or two adjectives, such as eerie, dreamy, jubilant, or angry. All of the elements of literature, from **figures of speech** to to the language's **rhythm**, contribute to the work's mood. *See pages* 527, 916, 1022, 1061. *See also* **Atmosphere**.

MORAL **A lesson about life that a story teaches.** Fables often end with a moral that is clearly stated. *See pages* 46, 203, 483. *See also* **Epigram, Maxim, Proverb**.

MOTIF **In literature, a word, character, object, image, metaphor, or idea that recurs in a work or in several works.** The rose is a motif that has reccurred throughout centuries of love poetry. In the *Prose Edda* (Unit Eight), contest is a recurring motif. A literary motif always bears an important relationship to the theme of the work. *See pages* 10, 46, 713, 1193. *See also* **Symbol**.

MOTIVATION **The reasons that compel a character to act as he or she does.** A character's motivations fuel the plot of a story and set it into motion. *See pages* 22, 151.

MYTH **An anonymous, traditional story that explains a belief, a custom, or a mysterious natural phenomenon.** Most myths are related to religion in some way, and almost all of them involve the exploits of gods and heroes. Every culture has its own mythology, including **origin myths**, which explain how things came to be. *See* Unit One.

NARRATIVE **Any work of literature, written or oral, that tells a story.** Narrative literature may be fictional (such as fairy tales and short stories) or nonfictional (such as autobiographies and histories); it may be prose, such as *The Metamorphosis* (Unit Eleven), or poetry, such as the *Iliad* (Unit Four). Narrative is distinguished from drama, which acts out, rather than tells, a story.

NARRATOR **The person or character who tells a story.** *See* **Point of View**.

NATURALISM **A radical offshoot of Realism that arose in France in the 1870s.** Naturalist writers, led by Émile Zola, considered free will an illusion and often showed their characters as helpless victims of heredity, fate, and their environment. *See pages* 983, 1042. *See also* **Realism**.

NEOCLASSICISM **The revival of classical Greek and Roman standards and forms, especially during the late seventeenth and eighteenth centuries.** The neoclassicists valued the classical ideals of order, reason, balance, harmony, clarity, and restraint. In literature, in particular, they studied and tried to emulate the Roman poets Horace and Virgil. *See page* 802.

NOH **A highly stylized form of Japanese drama that originated in the Middle Ages.** Noh dramas, which are still performed in Japan today, incorporate music, dance, and rhyme. *See pages* 596–597. *See also* **Drama**.

NONFICTION **Prose writing that narrates real events.** Nonfiction is distinguished from **fiction**—writing that is basically imaginative rather than factually true. Popular forms of nonfiction are **autobiography**, **biography**, and the **essay**. Other forms of nonfiction include newspaper articles, historical and scientific writing, and even personal diaries and letters.

NOVEL **A long fictional prose narrative, usually of more than fifty thousand words.** In general, the novel uses the same basic literary elements as the short story: **plot**, **character**, **setting**, **theme**, and **point of view**. The novel's length usually permits these elements to be more fully developed than they are in the short story. However, this is not always true of the modern novel. Some are basically character studies, with only the barest plot structures. Others reveal little about their characters and concentrate instead on setting or **tone** or even on language itself.

Although some early prose narratives resemble the novel in form, the novel as a distinct literary genre is widely considered to have emerged in Japan around A.D. 1000 with Lady Murasaki Shikibu's *Tale of Genji* and in Europe with the publication of Miguel de Cervantes' *Don Quixote* in 1605 (Unit Nine). *See page* 588.

ODE **A complex, generally lengthy lyric poem on a serious subject.** The two main types of modern odes are based on classical models. One is highly formal and dignified in style and is generally written for ceremonial or public occasions. This type of ode, called the **Pindaric ode**, derives from the choral odes of the ancient Greek poet Pindar, who wrote them in honor of the victors at the Olympics and other sacred games. The **Horatian ode**, like the lyrics of the Roman poet Horace for whom it is named, tends to be more personal and reflective in style. *See page* 415.

ONOMATOPOEIA   **The use of a word whose sound imitates or suggests its meaning.** Many familiar words, such as *clap, squish, snort,* and *whine,* are examples of onomatopoeia. In poetry, onomatopoeia can reinforce meaning while creating evocative and musical effects. *See page* 1229.

OXYMORON   **A figure of speech that combines apparently contradictory or opposing ideas.** "Living death," "cruel love," and "deafening silence" are oxymorons. The classic oxymoron "wise fool" is almost a literal translation of the term from the Greek: *oxys* means "sharp" or "keen," and *moros* means "foolish." *See page* 811.

PARABLE   **A short, allegorical story that teaches a moral or religious lesson about life.** The most famous parables in Western literature are those told by Jesus in the Gospels of the New Testament. *See pages* 198, 590, 1044. *See also* **Allegory**.

PARADOX   **An apparent contradiction that is actually true.** For example, to say that "she killed him with kindness" is a paradox. The statement challenges us to find an underlying truth that resolves the apparent contradiction. *See pages* 468, 476, 542, 1413. *See also* **Oxymoron**.

PARALLELISM   **The repetition of words, phrases, or sentences that have the same grammatical structure or that restate a similar idea.** Also called **parallel structure**, parallelism is used frequently in literature that is meant to be read aloud, such as poetry and speeches, because it helps make the literature memorable. In much biblical writing, such as the Book of Psalms (Unit Three), the rhythm of parallelism helps to unify ideas, emphasize images, and heighten the emotional effect of the words. **Structural parallelism** (repetition of a word or an entire sentence pattern), **restatement** (repetition of an idea using different words), and **antithesis** (the balancing of contrasting ideas) are some of the ways writers achieve the effect of parallelism. *See pages* 94, 186, 195, 476.

PARODY   **The imitation of a serious artistic work for amusement or instruction.** Parodies use exaggeration or inappropriate subject matter to make a serious form or particular work of art

seem laughable or to highlight its flaws. In *Don Quixote* (Unit Nine), for example, Cervantes parodies the courtly tradition of chivalry and knighthood. *See page* 822.

PASTORAL POETRY   **Poetry that depicts rustic life in idealized terms.** The term *pastoral* comes from the Latin word for shepherd, and originally pastorals were about shepherds and nymphs. Today the term has a looser meaning and refers to any poem that portrays an idealized rural setting or that expresses nostalgia for an age or place of lost innocence. *See pages* 67, 379.

PERSONA   *See* **Speaker**.

PERSONIFICATION   **A kind of metaphor in which a nonhuman thing or quality is talked about as if it were human.** For example, the familiar figure of a blindfolded woman holding a sword and a pair of scales is a personification of justice. The names of many everyday objects, such as the "hands of a clock," and many ordinary expressions, such "an angry sky," involve personification. In poetry, personification invites the reader to view the world as if natural and inanimate objects possess the same feelings, qualities, and souls that people do. Li Ch'ing-chao's "Peonies" (Unit Six), provides a fine example of personification. *See pages* 370, 457, 533, 1304.

PERSUASION   **Writing that tries to convince the reader or listener to think or act in a certain way.** Examples of persuasion include political speeches, editorials, and advertisements, as well as many **essays** and longer works of literature. Persuasion may appeal to both the emotions and the intellect. When it appeals primarily to reason rather than to emotion, it is called **argument**. *See page* 285.

PLOT   **The series of related events that make up a narrative, such as a story, novel, or epic.** The plot is the underlying structure of a narrative. Most plots are built on these "bare bones": A **basic situation**, or **exposition**, introduces the characters, setting, and, usually, the narrative's major **conflict**. Out of this basic situation, **complications** develop, intensifying the conflict. **Suspense** mounts to a **climax**—the most exciting or tense part of the plot. At the climax, the outcome of the conflict is determined. Finally, all the problems or mysteries of the plot are unraveled in the **resolution**, or **dénouement**. Longer narrative works, such as novels, plays, or epics, often contain **subplots**, or minor plots interwoven with the main plot. *See pages* 17, 639, 1033. *See also* **Dramatic Structure**.

POETRY **A kind of rhythmic, compressed language that uses figures of speech and imagery designed to appeal to our emotions and imaginations.** Most of the world's poetry falls into three major types: **lyric poetry**, the **ballad**, and the **epic**. Some specialized types of poetry, however, such as the **haiku** of Japan, defy these broad categorizations. Though poetry is one of the oldest forms of human expression, it is extremely difficult to define. The English Romantic poet William Wordsworth called it ''the spontaneous overflow of powerful feelings,'' and the Japanese scholar Kamo Mabuchi claimed that it provides ''without explanation the reasons governing order and disorder in the world.'' *See page* 1290. *See also* **Ballad, Epic, Haiku, Lyric Poetry, Pastoral Poetry, Prose Poetry, Psalm, Rubá'i, Sonnet**.

POINT OF VIEW   **The vantage point from which a writer tells a story.** There are three main points of view: **omniscient**, **first-person**, and **limited third-person**.

1. In the **omniscient** (or **''all-knowing''**) **point of view**, the person telling the story—the **narrator** —knows everything that's going on in the story. This omniscient narrator is outside the story, a godlike observer who can tell us what all the characters are thinking and feeling, as well as what is happening anywhere in the story. For example, in ''The Rat Trap'' by Selma Lagerlöf (Unit Eleven), the narrator enters into the thoughts and secrets of every character.

2. In the **first-person point of view**, the narrator is a character in the story. Using the pronoun *I,* this narrator tells us his or her own experiences but cannot reveal with certainty any other character's private thoughts. When we read a story in the first person, we hear and see only what the narrator hears and sees. We may have to be skeptical and interpret what this narrator says because a first-person narrator may or may not be objective, honest, or perceptive. The short story ''Borges and Myself'' (Unit Eleven) uses a first-person narrator.

3. In the **limited third-person point of view**, the narrator is outside the story—like an omniscient

narrator—but tells the story from the vantage point of only one character. The narrator goes where this chosen character goes and reveals this character's thoughts. The reader learns the events of the narrative through the perceptions of the chosen character. Hwang Sun-won's ''Cranes'' (Unit Eleven) is an example of a story told from the limited third-person point of view. *See pages* 34, 1041, 1197.

PROSE POETRY   **Poetry written in prose form, but using poetic devices such as rhythm, imagery, and figurative language to express a single strong emotion or idea.** This form of lyric poetry developed in the nineteenth century in France and was popularized by Charles Baudelaire and Arthur Rimbaud. *See page* 1265.

PROTAGONIST   **The main character in a work of fiction, drama, or narrative poetry.** The protagonist is the character whose conflict sets the plot in motion. (The character or force that struggles against or blocks the protagonist is called the **antagonist**.) Most protagonists are **rounded**, **dynamic characters** who change in some important way by the end of the story. Whatever the protagonist's weaknesses, we usually identify with his or her conflict and care about how it is resolved. *See also* **Character**.

PROVERB   **A short saying that expresses a common truth or experience, usually about human failings and the ways that people interact with one another.** Proverbs often incorporate such literary elements as **metaphor**, **alliteration**, **parallelism**, **and rhyme**. *See page* 84. *See also* **Aphorism, Epigram, Maxim, Moral**.

PSALM   **Any sacred song or hymn.** Psalms were originally sung to the accompaniment of a harp (the word *psalm* comes from a Greek verb meaning ''to pluck''). Today the term is usually used to refer to any of the one hundred fifty poems that make up the Book of Psalms in the Old Testament. These lyric poems greatly influenced the development of **free verse** in the nineteenth and twentieth centuries. *See page* 186. *See also* **Hymn**.

QUATRAIN   **A four-line stanza or poem, or a group of four lines unified by a rhyme scheme.** *See pages* 655, 805, 1224. *See also* **Ballad, Rubá'i, Sonnet, Stanza**.

REALISM   **In literature and art, the attempt to depict people and things as they are, with-**

out idealization. Although realistic description has long been a tool of writers the world over, Realism as a movement developed during the mid-nineteenth century as a reaction against Romanticism. Realist writers believed fiction and drama should truthfully depict the harsh, gritty reality of everyday life without beautifying, sentimentalizing, or romanticizing it. Gustave Flaubert, Henrik Ibsen, and Anton Chekhov are considered Realist writers. *See pages* 982–985, 1042, 1127. *See also* **Naturalism**.

REFRAIN   A repeated word, phrase, line, or group of lines. While refrains are most common in poetry and songs, they are sometimes used in prose, particularly speeches. Refrains are used to create rhythm, build suspense, or emphasize important words or ideas. An example of a refrain occurs in Baudelaire's poem, "Invitation to the Voyage" (Unit Ten). *See pages* 88, 514, 1022.

REPETITION   The intentional repeating of a sound, word, phrase, line, or idea in order to create a musical or rhythmic effect, build suspense, add emphasis, or otherwise give unity to language. Many literary elements involve some kind of repetition. For example, **alliteration** repeats consonant sounds, **parallelism** repeats grammatical structures or ideas, **meter** repeats a regular pattern of stressed and unstressed syllables, and **refrains** repeat a line or group of lines. In **incremental repetition**, a line or section of a poem or song is repeated with some variation in wording. Usually the variation adds significant new information or expresses a significant change in meaning or attitude. Yehuda Amichai's "Laments on the War Dead" (Unit Eleven) uses incremental repetition. *See pages* 94, 162, 1382. *See also* **Alliteration, Assonance, Meter, Parallelism, Refrain, Rhyme.**

RESOLUTION   *See* **Plot.**

RHYME   The repetition of accented vowel sounds and all sounds following them in words that are close together in a poem. "Lark" and "shark" rhyme, as do "follow" and "hollow." The most common type of rhyme, **end rhymes**, occurs at the ends of lines. **Internal rhymes** occur within lines.

When words sound similar but do not rhyme exactly, they are called **approximate rhymes** (or **half rhymes**, **slant rhymes**, or **imperfect**

rhymes). "Lark" and "lurk" are approximate rhymes, as are "follow" and "halo."

The pattern of end rhymes in a poem is called its **rhyme scheme**. A rhyme scheme is indicated by assigning each new end rhyme a different letter of the alphabet. Many traditional forms of poems, such as the **Italian sonnet** and the Persian **rubá'i**, follow strict rhyme schemes. For example, most English translations of the rubá'i follow the rhyme scheme *aaba,* as the following example from Edward FitzGerald's translation of Omar Khayyám's *Rubáiyát* illustrates:

A Book of Verses underneath the Bough,	*a*
A Jug of Wine, a Loaf of Bread—and Thou	*a*
Beside me singing in the Wilderness—	*b*
Oh, Wilderness were Paradise now!	*a*

See pages 804–805, 807, 812, 1224, 1229. *See also* **Couplet, Rubá'i, Sonnet.**

RHYTHM   The alternation of stressed and unstressed syllables in language. Rhythm occurs naturally in all forms of spoken and written language. The most obvious kind of rhythm is produced by **meter**, the regular pattern of stressed and unstressed syllables found in some poetry. But writers can also create less structured rhythms by using different kinds of **repetition** (such as **rhyme**, **alliteration**, **assonance**, **parallelism**, and **refrains**), or by balancing long and short words, phrases, or lines. Such rhythms are common in **free verse**. *See pages* 88, 804, 932, 1229. *See also* **Blank Verse, Free Verse, Meter.**

RISING ACTION   *See* **Dramatic Structure.**

ROMANCE   Historically, a medieval European verse narrative chronicling the adventures of a brave knight or other hero who must overcome great danger for love of a noble lady or high ideal. The stories of King Arthur and of his chivalrous knights of the Round Table, such as Perceval and Lancelot, are examples of **courtly romances**. Today the term has come to mean any story that presents a world that is happier, more exciting, or more heroic than the real world. *See pages* 688, 822, 838.

ROMANTICISM   A literary, artistic, and philosophical movement that developed during the late eighteenth and early nineteenth centuries as a reaction against neoclassicism. While neoclassicism (and classicism) emphasize reason, order, harmony, and restraint, Romanticism emphasizes emotion, imagination, intuition, freedom, personal experience, and the beauty of nature. However, many critics feel that the traditional opposition between Romanticism and classicism is all too often forced and exaggerated. The works of the German poet and dramatist Johann Wolfgang von Goethe and the English poet William Wordsworth are closely identified with Romanticism. *See pages* 52, 979.

RUBÁ'I (*plural:* **rubáiyát) A Persian word meaning "quatrain," or four-line verse.** The rubá'i is an ancient literary form that Persian poets used to express their thoughts on diverse subjects. In English translation, the most famous example is *The Rubáiyát of Omar Khayyám* (Unit Seven), published by Edward FitzGerald in 1859. Generally faithful to the eleventh-century originals, FitzGerald's translation is widely considered a masterpiece of English poetry in its own right. *See page* 659.

SATIRE A kind of writing that ridicules human weakness, vices, or folly in order to bring about social reform. Satires often try to persuade the reader to do or believe something by showing the opposite view as absurd or—even more forcefully—vicious and inhumane. To achieve their purpose, satirists may use **exaggeration** (such as **hyperbole**), **irony**, **parody**, and **wit**. Voltaire uses all these techniques in his scathing satire of European Rationalism, *Candide* (Unit Nine). *See pages* 838, 938, 946, 962, 1272.

SCANSION *See* **Meter**.

SCIENCE FICTION A form of fantasy writing in which scientific facts, assumptions, or hypotheses form the basis of adventures in the future, on other planets, in other dimensions of space or time, or under new variants of scientific laws. Although science fiction is usually set in the future, writers often use it to comment, in the form of **satire**, on the present. *See pages* 1146, 1272.

SETTING The time and place of a story, play, or narrative poem. Usually the setting is established early in a narrative through descriptive details and **imagery**. Longer works may have more than one setting. For example, Voltaire's *Candide* (Unit Nine) begins in Europe but moves to South America and other parts of the globe.

Setting is often closely linked to the **mood** of a literary work. For example, the exotic island setting of *The Tempest* (Unit Nine) contributes to the play's mood of isolation, imprisonment, and supernatural mystery. Setting may also reveal **character** by showing whether a character is in harmony with a particular place or in **conflict** with it. In "Life Is Sweet at Kumansenu" (Unit Eleven), for example, the mother Bola accepts and ultimately gains consolation from the traditions of her village. Finally, setting may suggest a story's **theme**. In "Eveline" (Unit Eleven), for example, the main character must make a decision between remaining in the paralyzing setting of Dublin and escaping overseas with a sailor. *See pages* 1007, 1259, 1314–1315. *See also* **Atmosphere, Mood**.

SHORT STORY A short fictional prose narrative. Although some ancient prose narratives (such as the Book of Ruth, Unit Three) resemble modern short stories, as a distinct **genre** the short story developed in the nineteenth century. Short stories are more limited than **novels**, usually having only one major **character**, **plot**, **setting**, and **theme**. The short story is usually built on a plot that consists of a **basic situation** or **exposition**, **conflict**, **complications**, **climax**, and **resolution**. However, many modern short stories concentrate less on "what happens" and more on revealing a character or evoking a vivid emotional effect. *See pages* 177, 1042.

SIMILE A figure of speech that makes a comparison between two seemingly unlike things by using a connective word such as *like, as, than,* **or** *resembles.* "A full moon like an accusing face," "hail hard as B-B pellets," "an actor's hand opening more gracefully than a blossom," and "clouds resembling stuffed animals" are all examples of similes.

Like an extended metaphor, an **extended simile** is developed over several lines of writing or even through an entire poem or paragraph. An **epic** or **Homeric simile** is an elaborately extended simile that relates heroic events to simple, everyday events. Homer used many such similes in his epic poems, the *Iliad* (Unit Four) and the *Odyssey*. *See pages* 370, 1295. *See also* **Figure of Speech, Metaphor**.

SONNET A fourteen-line lyric poem, usually written in iambic pentameter, that has one of

several traditional rhyme schemes. The oldest sonnet form is the **Petrarchan** (or **Italian**) **sonnet,** which was popularized by the fourteenth-century Italian poet Francesco Petrarch. This kind of sonnet is divided into two parts: an eight-line **stanza** called the **octave**, having the rhyme scheme *abbaabba,* and a six-line stanza called the **sestet**, having the rhyme scheme *cdecde* or *cdcdcd*. The octave usually presents a problem, poses a question, or expresses an idea that leads up to the **turn** (called the **volta** in Italian), which marks a shift in the poem. The sestet then resolves, answers, or drives home the idea that was developed in the octave.

The other major sonnet form, which was widely used by Shakespeare, is known as the **Shakespearean** (or **English**) **sonnet**. It consists of three stanzas called **quatrains** followed by a concluding stanza called the **couplet**. The three quatrains often express related ideas or examples, while the couplet sums up the poet's conclusion or message. The most common rhyme scheme for the Shakespearean sonnet is *abab cdcd efef gg*. Subsequent generations of poets have developed many variations based on the Petrarchan and Shakespearean forms. *See pages* 804–805, 1003. *See also* **Couplet, Quatrain, Stanza**.

SPEAKER **In a poem, the voice that addresses us.** The speaker may be the poet or may be a **persona**, a character whose voice and concerns do not necessarily reflect those of the poet. *See page* 80.

STANZA **A group of lines in a poem that form a single unit.** A stanza in a poem is something like a paragraph in prose: It often expresses a unit of thought. A stanza may consist of one line or any number of lines beyond that. Stanzas are usually named for the number of lines they contain or for the meter and rhyme scheme that they follow. A **couplet**, for example, consists of two lines, a **tercet** of three lines, and a **quatrain** of four lines. The typical **ballad stanza** is a quatrain with the rhyme scheme *abcb* and an **iambic meter** with four stresses in the first and third lines and three stresses in the second and fourth lines. *See pages* 1224, 1226. *See also* **Rubá'i**.

STREAM OF CONSCIOUSNESS **A modern writing style that tries to depict the random flow of thoughts, emotions, memories, and as-** sociations rushing through a character's mind. The writings of both the Irish novelist James Joyce and the English novelist Virginia Woolf employ stream-of-consciousness technique. *See page* 1208.

STYLE **The way a writer expresses his or her thoughts through language.** Style may best be described as *how* an author writes rather then *what* he or she writes. **Diction**, **tone**, **figures of speech**—every choice a writer makes in deciding how to communicate his or her ideas contributes to style. Style is usually viewed separately from content, and it is often what leads critics to classify certain works as "great." *See pages* 429, 435.

SURREALISM **A twentieth-century literary and artistic movement that sought to break down the barriers between rational and irrational thoughts and situations.** Influenced by the theories of Sigmund Freud and using dreamlike imagery, surrealist writers and artists sought to portray the workings of the unconscious mind. Leading figures in the Surrealist movement, which flourished in the 1920s and 1930s, include André Breton, Guillaume Appolinaire, and Salvador Dalí. *See page* 1155.

SUSPENSE **The uncertainty or anxiety a reader feels about what will happen next in a story.** Any kind of writing that has an effective plot involves some degree of suspense. *See pages* 51, 494. *See also* **Plot**.

SYMBOL **A person, place, thing, or event that stands both for itself and for something beyond itself.** Many symbols have become widely recognized: A lion is a symbol of majesty and power; a dove is a symbol of peace. These symbols are sometimes called **public symbols**. But writers often invent new, personal symbols, whose meaning is revealed in a work of poetry or prose. In Maupassant's short story "The Jewels" (Unit Ten), for example, Madame Lantin's jewelry becomes a symbol for the deceptive nature of appearances. *See pages* 746, 1108, 1155. *See also* **Allegory**.

SYMBOLISM **A literary movement that began in France during the late nineteenth century and emphasized the use of highly personal symbols to suggest ideas, emotions, and moods.** The French Symbolists believed that emotions are fleeting, individual, and essentially inexpressible—and that therefore the poet is forced to *suggest* meaning rather than express it. The leading Symbolists, such as Paul Verlaine and Arthur Rimbaud, were reacting against **Realism** and **Naturalism** and became important influences on the **Surrealist** movement of the twentieth century. *See pages* 983, 1026, 1223. *See also* **Naturalism, Realism, Surrealism**.

TANKA   A traditional, five-line form of Japanese poetry. In the original language, the tanka follows a strict form: the first and third lines contain five syllables each, and the second, fourth, and fifth lines contain seven syllables each. *See pages* 564–565.

TERZA RIMA   An interlocking, three-line stanza form with the rhyme scheme *aba bcb cdc ded,* and so on. Terza rima is an Italian verse form (Dante used it throughout the *Divine Comedy*) that has also been used by English poets such as Percy Bysshe Shelley. *See pages* 743, 746.

THEME   The central idea or insight of a work of literature. A theme is not the same as the subject of a work, which can usually be expressed in a word or two: old age, ambition, love. The theme is the idea the writer wishes to convey about the subject—the writer's view of the world or revelation about human nature. In "Life Is Sweet at Kumansenu" (Unit Eleven), for example, Abioseh Nicol's subject is love, but his theme is that love endures despite repeated disappointment and death and ultimately makes life sweet and worth living.

While some stories, poems, and plays have themes that are **directly stated**, most themes are **implied**. It is up to the reader to piece together all the clues the writer has provided about the work's total meaning. Two of the most important clues to consider are how the main character has changed and how the conflict has been resolved. In addition, long works such as novels and plays may have more than one theme. *See pages* 116, 170, 406–407, 460, 1376, 1394, 1432.

TONE   The attitude a writer takes toward the reader, a subject, or a character. Tone is conveyed through the writer's choice of words and descriptions of **characters** and **setting**. Tone can usually be described with an adjective, such as amused, angry, indifferent, or sarcastic. *See pages* 415, 552, 1061.

TRAGEDY   A play, novel, or other narrative depicting serious and important events, in which the main character comes to an unhappy end. In the traditional tragedy, the main character is usually dignified, courageous, and often high ranking. The character's downfall may be caused by a **tragic flaw**—an error in judgment or a character weakness—or the downfall may result from forces beyond his or her control. The tragic hero or heroine usually wins some self-knowledge and wisdom, even though he or she suffers defeat, possibly even death.

Tragedy is distinct from **comedy**, in which an ordinary character overcomes obstacles to get what he or she wants. Sophocles' *Oedipus Rex* (Unit Four) is an example of a tragedy. Dramas that contain elements of both tragedy and comedy, such as Shakespeare's *The Tempest* (Unit Nine), are often called **tragicomedies**. *See pages* 302, 305, 371, 844.

TURNING POINT   See Dramatic Structure.

UNDERSTATEMENT   A figure of speech that consists of saying less than what is really meant, or saying something with less force than is appropriate. Understatement is the opposite of **hyperbole**, or **overstatement**, and is a form of **irony**. To say, "It is a bit wet out there" after coming in from a torrential downpour is to use understatement. Understatement can be used to create a kind of deadpan humor, and it can contribute to an overall satiric tone, as in Cervantes' *Don Quixote* (Unit Nine). *See page* 705.

WIT   A quality of speech or writing that combines verbal cleverness with keen perception, especially of the incongruous. Wit may be a product of **puns** and word play, **hyperbole**, or **verbal irony**. Sei Shōnagon's *The Pillow Book* offers many examples of wit in her **understated** descriptions of humorous situations, as the following example from her chapter entitled "Hateful Things" illustrates:

A man recites his own poems (not especially good ones) and tells one about the praise they have received—most embarrassing.

See page 580.

Grammar, Usage, and Mechanics: A Reference Guide

Problems of Agreement

Agreement of Subject and Verb

1. **A verb should agree with its subject in number. Singular subjects take singular verbs. Plural subjects take plural verbs.**

   He watches movies. [The singular verb *watches* agrees with the singular subject *he*.]

   They watch movies. [The plural verb *watch* agrees with the plural subject *they*.]

   Like single-word verbs, verb phrases also agree with their subjects. However, in a verb phrase, only the first auxiliary (helping) verb changes its form to agree with a singular or plural subject.

   The **train was arriving** late.
   Two **trains were arriving** late.

2. **The number of the subject is not changed by a phrase following the subject.**

   This **bag** of marbles **is** full. [*Bag* is the subject, not *marbles*.]
   These **marbles** of glass **are** blue. [*Marbles* is the subject, not *glass*.]

3. **Compound prepositions such as** *together with, in addition to, as well as,* **and** *along with* **following the subject do not affect the number of the subject.**

   Sara, along with Elena, **is going** on the trip. [The subject of the sentence is singular because it names one person, *Sara*. Therefore, the predicate of the sentence uses the singular auxiliary verb form *is*.]

4. **The following indefinite pronouns are singular:** *each, either, neither, one, everyone, everybody, no one, nobody, anyone, anybody, someone, somebody.*

   Each of the dessert-chefs **bakes** pastry. [*Each one* bakes.]
   Neither of the pastries **is** an éclair. [*Neither one* is an éclair.]

5. **The following indefinite pronouns are plural:** *several, few, both, many.*

   Several of these trails **are** dangerous for hikers who are inexperienced.

6. **The indefinite pronouns** *some, all, most, any,* **and** *none* **may be either singular or plural. These pronouns are singular when they refer to a singular word and plural when they refer to a plural word.**

   Some of the writing **is** scary. [*Some* refers to the singular noun *writing*.]
   Some of the words **are** descriptive. [*Some* refers to the plural noun *words*.]

7. **A compound subject contains two or more nouns or pronouns that are the subject of the same verb. Compound subjects joined by the word** *and* **are usually plural in form and therefore take a plural verb.**

   Dante, Boccaccio, and **Calvino are** great writers in the Italian language. [Three people *are* writers.]

8. **Compound subjects that name only one person or thing take a singular verb.**

   My **best friend and constant companion is** Kara Kern. [One person is my best friend and constant companion.]

9. **Singular subjects joined by the words** *or* **or** *nor* **take a singular verb.**

   Either **Carlos** or **Tony bikes** to school. [*Either* Carlos bikes *or* Tony bikes, not both.]

10. When a singular subject and a plural subject are joined by *or* or *nor*, the verb agrees with the subject nearer the verb.

Neither the producers nor the **director was** present at the screening.

Neither the director nor the **producers were** present at the screening.

Other Problems in Subject-Verb Agreement

11. The contractions *don't* and *doesn't* must agree with their subjects.

With the singular subjects *I* and *you* and with plural subjects, use the contraction *don't* (*do not*).

I **don't** speak.	They **don't** tell.
We **don't** care.	These **don't** work.

With all other singular subjects, use the singular *doesn't* (*does not*).

She **doesn't** study.	This **doesn't** move.
It **doesn't** run well.	Donna **doesn't** work here.

12. *Collective nouns* are singular in form, but they name a group of persons or things. Use a plural verb with a singular collective noun when you are referring to the individual parts or members of the group acting separately. Use a singular verb when you refer to the group acting together as a unit.

army	club	fleet	jury
assembly	committee	flock	panel
audience	faculty	group	swarm
class	family	herd	team

The family **have** sat down for their dinner. [*Family* is thought of as a group of individuals.]

The family **has** its meals mostly at home. [*Family* is thought of as a single unit.]

Be sure that any pronoun referring to the collective noun agrees with the noun (*their* in the first example above, *its* in the second).

13. A verb agrees with its subject, not with its predicate nominative, the noun or pronoun complement that refers to the same person or thing as the subject.

    S   PN
Cavities are my biggest problem.

          S   PN
My biggest **problem is** cavities.

14. Contractions such as *here's*, *where's*, *how's*, and *what's* include the verb *is*. Do not use one of these contractions unless a singular subject follows it.

There **are** [not *There's*] **mice** on the counter!

15. A word or a phrase stating a weight, a measurement, or an amount of money or time is usually considered one item and takes a singular verb.

Five dollars is all I can spend.

One quarter of the grain **was** sold at the market.

Sometimes, however, the amount is thought

of as individual pieces or parts. If so, a plural verb is used.

> **Ten** of the pages **were** missing.
> **Two thirds** of the apples **taste** sour.

16. **The title of a work of art, literature, or music, even when plural in form, takes a singular verb.**

> ***Dubliners*** contains "Eveline," one of my favorite short stories. [one collection]

17. ***Every*** **or** ***many a*** **before a subject calls for a singular verb.**

> Almost **every** member **was** tired.
> **Many a** student **enjoys** poetry.

18. **A few nouns that look plural in form take singular verbs.**

> The **news is** on at six and ten o'clock.
> **Physics was** Willis's best subject.

Some nouns that end in *-s* take a plural verb even though they refer to a single item.

> The **pliers are** in the toolbox.
> Your **pants are** very stylish.

See also "Maintaining Subject-Verb Agreement" on pages 438–439.

Agreement of Pronoun and Antecedent

1. **A pronoun should agree with its antecedent in number and gender.**

A pronoun usually refers to a noun or another pronoun that comes before it. The word that a pronoun refers to is called its **antecedent**.

A few singular personal pronouns have forms that indicate the gender of the antecedent. *He, him,* and *his* are masculine; *she, her,* and *hers* are feminine; *it* and *its* are neuter.

> **Sei Shōnagon** kept **her** journal in private.
> **Elie Wiesel** wrote **his** memoirs years after the war.

2. **When the antecedent of a personal pronoun is another kind of pronoun, look in a phrase following the antecedent to determine gender.**

> **Each** of the **girls** reads **her** own newspaper.
> **One** of the **boys** cooks **his** own dinner.

3. **When the antecedent may be either masculine or feminine, use both the masculine and the feminine forms.**

> **Every one** of the passengers sat in **his or her** assigned seat.

4. **Use a singular pronoun to refer to** *each, either, neither, one, everyone, everybody, no one, nobody, anyone, anybody, someone,* **or** *somebody.*

> **Every** boy in the bus fastened **his** seatbelt.
> **Each** student has **his or her** own locker.

When the meaning of *everyone* and *everybody* is clearly plural, use the plural pronoun.

> **Everyone** talked to **their** [not *his or her*] parents.

5. **Two or more singular antecedents joined by** *or* **or** *nor* **should be referred to by a singular pronoun.**

> Neither **Palmira nor Alicia** fixed **herself** any dinner.

6. **Two or more antecedents joined by** *and* **should be referred to by a plural pronoun.**

> **Tia and Reg** grew **their** own vegetables.

7. **The number of a relative pronoun is determined by the number of its antecedent.**

> **Everyone who** comes to the party will have a good time. [The relative pronoun *who* refers to the singular pronoun *everyone* and thus takes the singular verb form *comes.*]
> **All who** come will have a good time. [*Who* refers to the plural pronoun *all* and thus takes the plural verb form *come.*]

Tips for Writers

Sentences with two or more singular antecedents joined by *or* or *nor* can sound awkward if the antecedents are of different genders. If a sentence sounds awkward, revise it to avoid the problem.

AWKWARD: **Nelson** or **Liz** will bring **his** or **her** records.

REVISED: **Nelson** will bring **his** records, or **Liz** will bring **hers.**

See also "Maintaining Pronoun-Antecedent Agreement" on pages 614–615.

Using Pronouns Correctly

Case

Case is the form of a noun or pronoun that shows its use in a sentence. In English, there are three cases: *nominative*, *objective*, and *possessive*.

Choosing the correct case form for a noun is no problem, because the form remains the same in the nominative and objective cases.

> The **professor** [nominative] carpools with another **professor** [objective].

Only in the possessive case does a noun change its form, usually by adding an apostrophe and *s*.

> My **father's** [possessive] workshop is cluttered with gardening tools and broken appliances.
> **I** [nominative] forgot to mail **my** [possessive] application to **her** [objective] yesterday.

The Case Forms of Personal Pronouns

Here are the case forms of personal pronouns. Notice that all personal pronouns, except *you* and *it*, have different nominative and objective forms.

PERSONAL PRONOUNS

SINGULAR

Nominative Case	Objective Case	Possessive Case
I	me	my, mine
you	you	your, yours
he, she, it	him, her, it	his, her, hers, its

PLURAL

Nominative Case	Objective Case	Possessive Case
we	us	our, ours
you	you	your, yours
they	them	their, theirs

The Nominative Case

1. **The *subject* of a verb is in the nominative case.**

   > **He** was excited that **they** had come. [*He* is the subject of *was*; *they* is the subject of *had come*.]

2. **A *predicate nominative* is in the nominative case.**

   A pronoun used as a predicate nominative always follows a form of the verb *be* or a verb phrase ending in *be* or *been*.

   > It is **he**.
   > That could be **she**.

The Objective Case

3. **The *direct object* of a verb is in the objective case.**

   A *direct object* is a noun or pronoun that receives the action of the verb or shows the result of the action.

   > The lesson of La Fontaine's fable impressed **him** and **me**. [*The lesson* is the subject of the verb *impressed*. The lesson impressed *whom*? The answer is *him and me*.]

4. **The *indirect object* of the verb is in the objective case.**

   An *indirect object* is a noun or pronoun that tells to whom or for whom something is done. Pronouns used as indirect objects are in the objective case: *me, him, her, us, them*.

   > Prospero's magic cloak gave **him** many powers.
   > Sei Shōnagon's writing brought **her** much delight.

5. **The *object of a preposition* is in the objective case.**

   A prepositional phrase begins with a preposition and ends with a noun or pronoun, which is the *object of the preposition*. A pronoun used as an object of a preposition must be in the objective case.

   > Jared sat behind **us**.

   Errors often occur when the object of a preposition is compound. You can usually figure out the correct pronouns by trying each one separately in the prepositional phrase.

> Mike raced ahead of him and I. [*Mike raced ahead of him* is correct, but *Mike raced ahead of I* is incorrect. The correct forms of the pronouns are *him* and *me*: Mike raced ahead of **him** and **me**.]

Tips for Writers

Some mistakes in usage are more common than others. In speech, for example, people often incorrectly use the pronoun *me* in a compound subject.

INCORRECT: Faith and **me** built a bookcase.
CORRECT: Faith and **I** built a bookcase.

6. In an infinitive clause, both the subject and object of the infinitive are in the objective case.

> My baby sister wanted **me to carry her**. [*Me* is the subject of *to carry*. *Her* is the object of *to carry*. The entire infinitive clause is the direct object of *wanted*.]

Many people use incorrect pronoun forms with the preposition *between*. You have probably heard phrases such as *between you and I* and *between you and he*. These phrases are incorrect. The pronouns are objects of a preposition and should be in the objective case. The correct phrases are *between you and me* and *between you and him*.

Special Pronoun Problems

Using *Who* and *Whom* Correctly

7. *Who* is used as a subject or predicate nominative, and *whom* is used as an object.

NOMINATIVE	OBJECTIVE
who	whom
whoever	whomever

In spoken English, the use of *whom* is becoming less common. In fact, when you are speaking, you may correctly begin any question with *who*, regardless of the grammar of the sentence. In written English, however, you should make a distinction between *who* and *whom*.

8. The use of *who* or *whom* in a subordinate clause depends on how the pronoun functions in the clause.

When you choose between *who(ever)* or *whom(ever)* in a subordinate clause, follow these steps:

STEP 1: Find the subordinate clause.
STEP 2: Decide how the pronoun is used in the clause—as subject, predicate nominative, object of the verb, or object of a preposition.
STEP 3: Determine the case of the pronoun according to the rules of standard English.
STEP 4: Select the correct form of the pronoun.

(*Whoever, Whomever*) I choose will lead the group.

STEP 1: The subordinate clause is (*whoever, whomever*) I choose.
STEP 2: In this clause, the subject is *I*, the verb is *choose*, and the pronoun is the direct object of the verb *choose*; I choose (*whoever, whomever*).
STEP 3: The direct object of a verb is in the objective case.
STEP 4: The objective form is *whomever*.
ANSWER: **Whomever** I choose will lead the group.

Remember that no words outside the subordinate clause affect the case of the pronoun. In this example, the entire clause is used as the subject of *will lead*, the verb in the main clause. The pronoun *whomever* is used as the direct object (objective case) within its clause.

Frequently, in subordinate clauses *whom* is omitted because it is understood.

> The person [whom] he asked is Joyce.
> The person [whom] she talked to is from the Australian outback.

9. Pronouns used as *appositives* are in the same case as the word to which they refer.

An *appositive* is a noun or pronoun that follows another noun or pronoun to identify or explain it.

The members, **he, she,** and **I,** each read a different part. [Since *members* is the subject of the sentence, the pronouns in apposition with it (*he, she, I*) must be in the nominative case.]

10. **Use the possessive case of a noun or pronoun before a gerund. Do not confuse the gerund form with the present participle, also an *-ing* form of the verb, which is used as an adjective.**

The panel applauded **my dancing**. [The gerund *dancing* is the object of the verb *applauded*. The possessive form *my* modifies the gerund.]

Can you see **me dancing** a ballet with a professional troupe? [Here the participle *dancing* modifies *me*, the object of *see*.]

The Pronoun in an Incomplete Construction

11. **When *than* and *as* introduce an incomplete construction, use the form of the pronoun that you would use if the construction were completed.**

Notice how pronouns change the meaning of sentences with incomplete constructions.

Vicky likes Paula better than **I.**
Vicky likes Paula better than **me.**

In the first sentence, the nominative case pronoun *I* is the subject of an understood verb: *Vicky likes Paula better than I* [*like Paula*]. In the second sentence, the objective case pronoun *me* is the object of the under-

stood verb: *Vicky likes Paula better than* [*Vicky likes*] *me.*

Using Modifiers Correctly

1. **Adjectives and adverbs are modifiers; that is, they state qualities of other parts of speech. Adjectives modify nouns and pronouns. Adverbs modify verbs, adjectives, and other adverbs.**

ripe apple	**juicy** peaches	[adjectives]
talk **softly**	jump **well**	[adverbs]

2. **Use adjectives to compare one noun with another noun that has the same quality.**

That apple is **riper** than this one.
This peach is **juicier** than that one.

3. **Use adverbs to make comparisons between verbs.**

I shoveled the snow slowly, but Phoebe shoveled even **more slowly**.

4. **There are three degrees of comparison: *positive*, *comparative*, and *superlative*.**

POSITIVE	COMPARATIVE	SUPERLATIVE
cool	cooler	coolest
wet	wetter	wettest
tasty	tastier	tastiest
helpful	more helpful	most helpful
slowly	more slowly	most slowly
good	better	best
bad	worse	worst

5. **Avoid double comparisons.**

A **double comparison** is incorrect because it contains both *-er* and *more* or *-est* and *most*.

This is the **dullest** [not *most dullest*] movie I've ever seen.

6. **Be sure your comparisons are clear.**

The snowfall here this year was as much as the Rockies. [This sentence incorrectly compares snowfall to mountains.]

The snowfall here this year was as much as it was in the Rockies. [This sentence correctly compares the snowfall in two different places.]

Dangling Modifiers

See pages 206–207.

Misplaced Modifiers

7. A misplaced modifier is a phrase or clause that sounds awkward because it modifies the wrong word(s). Modifying phrases should be placed as near as possible to the words they modify.

> MISPLACED: I was awarded a scholarship after four years of study yesterday.
> CORRECTED: Yesterday, I was awarded a scholarship after four years of study.

8. Place an adjective or adverb clause as near as possible to the word it modifies.

> MISPLACED: I carried the box from school, which weighed thirty pounds.
> CORRECTED: From school, I carried the box, **which weighed thirty pounds**.

The Rules for Capitalization

First Words

1. Capitalize the first word in every sentence.

Each room of the house seemed to have its own color theme. In one room there was a host of blues—pale, slate, and midnight. In yet another we found only orange and yellow tones.

Traditionally, the first word of a line of poetry is capitalized.

> Water, water, everywhere,
> And all the boards did shrink;

> Water, water, everywhere,
> Nor any drop to drink.
> —from "The Rime of the Ancient Mariner," Samuel Taylor Coleridge

Some writers do not follow these practices. When you are quoting, be sure to use capital letters exactly as they are used in the source of the quotation.

Pronoun *I*

2. Capitalize the pronoun *I*.

Lani and **I** always walk to school.

Proper Nouns and Proper Adjectives

3. Capitalize proper nouns and proper adjectives.

Common nouns name general people, places, or things. A **proper noun** names a particular person, place, or thing. **Proper adjectives** are formed from proper nouns.

Common nouns are not capitalized unless they begin a sentence or a direct quotation or are included in a title (see page 1463). Proper nouns are always capitalized.

> COMMON NOUNS: a **p**hilosopher, a **c**ountry, a **r**uler
> PROPER NOUNS: **P**lato, **F**rance, **Q**ueen **E**lizabeth
> PROPER ADJECTIVES: **P**latonic ideas, **F**rench bread, **E**lizabethan drama

Some proper names consist of more than one word. In these names, short prepositions (generally, fewer than five letters) and articles are not capitalized.

> Joan **o**f Arc
> American Federation **o**f Labor
> Alexander **t**he Great

To find out whether a noun should be capitalized, check in a dictionary. The dictionary will tell you if a word should always be capitalized or if it should be capitalized only in certain uses.

Names of People

4. Capitalize the names of people.

> GIVEN NAMES: **L**en, **B**eth
> SURNAMES: **A**ndretti, **S**chwartz

Geographical Names

5. Capitalize geographical names.

> TOWNS, CITIES: Los Angeles, Beijing, Madrid
> COUNTIES, TOWNSHIPS: Nassau County, Township of Soweto
> STATES: Missouri, Nebraska, Connecticut, Oregon
> REGIONS: the North, the Northwest, Continental Divide

Words such as *north, west,* and *southeast* are *not* capitalized when they indicate direction, unless they begin a sentence.

> west of here, heading northeast

> COUNTRIES: the United States; Scotland, Australia
> CONTINENTS: North America, Europe, Asia, Antarctica
> ISLANDS: Ceylon, Madagascar, Hawaii
> MOUNTAINS: the Himalayas, Mount McKinley, the Urals
> BODIES OF WATER: Atlantic Ocean, Gulf of Mexico
> PARKS: Yellowstone National Park, Hyde Park
> ROADS, HIGHWAYS, STREETS: Route 45, Interstate 80, East Eleventh Street

In a hyphenated number, the second word begins with a small letter.

> Seventy-seventh Street

Organizations

6. Capitalize names of organizations, businesses, institutions, and government bodies.

> ORGANIZATIONS: American Medical Association, National Association for the Advancement of Colored People, United Nations

The word *party* is usually written without a capital letter when it follows a proper adjective: *Republican party, Democratic party, Communist party*

> BUSINESSES: General Electric, New York Telephone, Estelle's Auto Body
> INSTITUTIONS: Sloan-Kettering Hospital, Boston University, Crossroads High School

Do not capitalize words like *hotel, theater,* college, high school, and *post office* unless they begin a sentence or are part of a proper name.

> Howard University   a college course
> Trocadero Hotel   a hotel in Miami
> Shubert Theater   a theater in New York
> Seattle Post Office   a local post office
> Suffolk County Courthouse   the courthouse doors

> GOVERNMENT BODIES: Federal Bureau of Investigation, Congress, Department of Agriculture

Historical Events

7. Capitalize the names of historical events and periods, special events, and calendar items.

> HISTORICAL EVENTS AND PERIODS: French Revolution, Battle of Gettysburg, Vietnam War, Middle Ages, Great Depression
> SPECIAL EVENTS: Special Olympics, the U.S. Open
> CALENDAR ITEMS: Thursday, June, Chinese New Year

Nationalities and Races

8. Capitalize the names of nationalities, races, and peoples.

> African, Greek, Bantu, Chinese, Commanche, Korean

Brand Names

9. Capitalize the brand names of business products.

> Nylon, Skippy, Chrysler, Xerox

Do not capitalize the noun that often follows a brand name: *Skippy peanut butter.*

Tips for Writers

Do not capitalize the names of seasons unless they are personified or are part of the names of special events.

> "I saw old Autumn in the misty morn." [personification]
> Suzanne was voted Most Likely to Succeed in the annual Spring Election. [special event]

Particular Places, Things, Events

10. Capitalize the names of ships, planets, monuments, awards, and any other particular places, things, or events.

> SHIPS, TRAINS: the **U.S.S.** *Minnow*, the *Titanic*, the *Clipper*
> AIRCRAFT, SPACECRAFT, MISSILES: *Apollo 7*, *Challenger*, *Patriot*
> PLANETS, STARS: **S**aturn, **O**rion **N**ebula

Sun, moon and *earth* are not capitalized unless they begin a sentence or are listed with other heavenly bodies.

> MONUMENTS, MEMORIALS: **G**raceland, the **L**incoln **M**emorial
> BUILDINGS: **M**useum of **M**odern **A**rt, the **E**mpire **S**tate **B**uilding
> AWARDS: **M**edal of **H**onor, **N**obel **P**rize, **P**alm d'**O**r

Specific Courses, Languages

11. Do *not* capitalize names of school subjects, except for languages and for course names followed by a number.

> Chris is taking **E**nglish, **h**istory and **t**yping. I'm taking **F**rench, **d**rama, **T**rigonometry II, and **E**nglish literature.

Do *not* capitalize the name of a class (*freshman, sophomore, junior, senior*) unless it is used as part of a proper noun.

> The sophomore class is going to win the **F**reshman-**S**ophomore game.

Titles of People

12. Capitalize the title of a person when it comes before a name.

> **P**resident **B**ush   **M**r. **C**ovello
> **D**r. **V**aldez   **M**s. **W**elch

Do not capitalize a title used alone or following a person's name, especially if the title is preceded by *a* or *the*.

> Julius Caesar wanted to be **e**mperor of Rome.
> The **g**overnor will present her speech at the groundbreaking ceremony.

13. Capitalize words showing family relation-

ship when used with a person's name but *not* when preceded by a possessive or article.

> Ramon's **g**randmother visited us last year.
> For Thanksgiving, we usually go to **A**unt **C**arlene and **U**ncle **M**ax's house.
> Does **C**ousin **E**d like your cat?
> But: My **c**ousin **E**d loves my dog.

Titles of Literary and Other Creative Works

14. Capitalize the first and last words and all important words in titles of books, periodicals, poems, stories, historical documents, movies, television programs, works of art, and musical compositions.

Unimportant words in a title are articles:
a, an, the
short prepositions (fewer than five letters):
of, to, for, from
coordinating conjunctions: *and, but, so, nor, or, yet, for*

> BOOKS: *The Tale of Genji, Madame Bovary, Things Fall Apart, The Name of the Rose*
> PERIODICALS: *Time, Life, Newsweek, Field and Stream*
> POEMS: "The World Is Too Much with Us," "The Golden Mean," "Jade Flower Palace"
> STORIES: "The Handsomest Drowned Man in the World," "The Jewels," "Cranes"
> HISTORICAL DOCUMENTS: **C**onstitution, **D**eclaration of **I**ndependence, **M**agna **C**arta
> TELEVISION PROGRAMS: *Murphy Brown, Nova, Murder She Wrote, Saturday Night Live*
> WORKS OF ART: *Odalisque, Waterlilies*
> MUSICAL COMPOSITIONS: *Aida*, "Can't Touch This," **M**ozart's *Requiem, The Magic Flute*

The words *a, an,* and *the* written before a title are capitalized only when they are the first word of a title.

> the *Chicago Sun Times, For Whom the Bell Tolls, The Diary of Anne Frank, The Red and the Black*

Before the names of magazines and newspapers, *a, an,* and *the* are usually not capitalized.

Religions

15. Capitalize names of religions and their

followers, holy celebrations, holy writings, and specific deities.

> RELIGIONS AND FOLLOWERS: **C**atholicism, **Q**uaker, **J**ehovah's **W**itness, **H**indu, **P**rotestant, **J**ewish, **M**uslim, **M**ethodist, **B**uddhist, **A**nglican, **T**aoist, **P**resbyterian
> HOLY DAYS AND SEASONS: **E**aster, **Y**om **K**ippur, **Q**uamsa, **P**assover, **C**hristmas, **R**amadan
> HOLY WRITINGS: the **B**ible, the **T**almud, the **K**oran, the **V**edas, the **A**cts of the **A**postles
> SPECIFIC DEITIES: **A**llah, **G**od, **B**rahma, **J**ehovah, **B**uddha

The word *god* is not capitalized when it refers to the gods of ancient mythology.

> Zeus was the father of all **g**ods.
> The **g**oddess Athena was thought to be all-wise.
> The Greek **g**od Hermes was the messenger of the **g**ods; in Roman mythology, he is known as Mercury.

Punctuation

End Marks

End marks—*periods, question marks,* and *exclamation points*—are used to indicate the purpose of a sentence.

1. Use a period to end a statement (*or declarative sentence*).

> Your father is here.
> The child wanted to know where the toy was.

Notice in the second example that a declarative sentence containing an indirect question is followed by a period.

2. Use a question mark to end a question (*or interrogative sentence*).

> Should we buy these**?**
> Is it time yet**?**

A direct question may have the same word order as a declarative sentence. Since it is a question, however, it is followed by a question mark.

> She was a nice person**?**

3. Use a period or exclamation point to end an imperative sentence.

When an imperative sentence makes a request, it is generally followed by a period.

> Please run fast.
> Bring me a pen.

4. Use an exclamation point to end an exclamation.

> Excellent! What a great job!
> Oops!

Sometimes declarative, interrogative, and imperative sentences show such strong feeling that they are more like exclamations than statements, questions, or requests. If so, an exclamation point should be used instead of a period or question mark.

> The house is on fire!
> Won't you leave!
> Don't break that!

5. Use a period after an abbreviation.

> PERSONAL NAMES: D. H. Lawrence, N. K. Sandars
> TITLES USED WITH NAMES: Mr,, Ms., Mrs., Dr.
> STATES: Fla., Mo., Pa., Ala.
> TIME OF DAY: A.M., P.M.
> YEARS: B.C., A.D.
> ADDRESSES: Ave., St., Blvd.
> ORGANIZATIONS AND COMPANIES: Co., Corp., Inc.
> UNITS OF MEASURE: lb., oz., in., ft., yd., mi.

Abbreviations for government agencies and international organizations and some other frequently used abbreviations are written without periods. Abbreviations in the metric system are often written without the periods, especially in science books.

Commas

1. Use commas to separate two or more adjectives preceding a noun.

We explored the **hot, damp, smelly attic.**

When the last adjective in a series is thought of as part of the noun, the comma before the adjective is omitted.

We washed the **small, round glass windows.**

You can use two tests to determine whether two adjectives should be separated by a comma:

TEST 1: Insert the word *and* between the adjectives. If *and* fits sensibly between the adjectives, use a comma. In the first example sentence, *and* can be logically inserted: *hot and damp attic.* In the second sentence, *and* sounds logical between the first two adjectives (*small and round*) but not between the second and third (*round and glass*).

TEST 2: Change the order of the adjectives. If the order of the adjectives can be reversed sensibly, use a comma. *Round, small glass windows* makes sense, but *glass, small round windows* does not.

2. **Use commas before *and*, *but*, *or*, *nor*, *for*, *so*, and *yet* when they join independent clauses.**

Howard stubbed his toe, and **he screamed.**
María gets up early, yet **she is always late.**

Do not be misled by compound verbs, which often make a sentence look as though it contains two independent clauses.

COMPOUND SENTENCE: **Jean cut the vegetables,** and **Malcolm made the salad.** [two independent clauses]
SIMPLE SENTENCE: **John Milton outlined** the poem and **wrote** it. [one subject with a compound verb]

In the following correctly punctuated com-pound sentence, notice that independent clauses appear on both sides of the coordinating conjunction.

He wrote poetry, and **he loved to act.**

3. **Use commas to set off nonessential clauses and nonessential participial phrases.**

A *nonessential* (or *nonrestrictive*) clause or participial phrase adds information that is not necessary to the main idea in the sentence. Omitting such a clause or phrase will not change the basic meaning of the sentence.

NONESSENTIAL CLAUSE: The letter, **which is not stamped,** cannot be mailed.
NONESSENTIAL PHRASE: William Black, **an accomplished artist,** illustrated many of his own poems.

When a clause or phrase is necessary to the meaning of a sentence—that is, when it tells *which ones*—the clause or phrase is *essential* (or *restrictive*), and commas are *not* used.

Notice how the meaning of each sentence below changes when the essential clause or phrase is omitted.

ESSENTIAL CLAUSE: Only students **who are taller than five feet eight inches** may try out for the basketball team.
ESSENTIAL CLAUSE: The poster **that I want** has a green border.

An adjective clause beginning with *that* is usually essential.

ESSENTIAL PHRASE: The most famous speech **made by Dr. Martin Luther King, Jr.,** began "I have a dream. . . ."

4. **Use a comma after introductory words such as *well*, *yes*, *no*, and *why* when they begin a sentence.**

Yes, my hair is natural.
Well, it's always been this color.

5. **Use a comma after an introductory participial phrase.**

Resting in the shade of the tree, I felt cooler.
Disappointed with the film, Tia left the theater.

6. **Use a comma after a series of introductory prepositional phrases.**

> **Toward the end of the speech,** we started clapping.
> **By the end of the night,** we were all tired.

A short introductory prepositional phrase does not require a comma unless the comma is necessary to make the meaning clear.

> **With my car** I can get to work faster.
> **With my car,** driving is a pleasure. [The comma is necessary to avoid reading *car driving*.]

7. **Use a comma after an introductory adverb clause.**

> **When you get home,** give me a call.
> **After you figure it out,** tell me what to do.

8. **Use commas to set off elements that interrupt the sentence.**

> He is, **in fact,** my best friend.
> My brother, **of course,** scored the winning run.

If an "interrupter" comes at the beginning or at the end of a sentence, only one comma is needed.

> **After all,** he is an expert.

9. **Use commas to set off appositives and appositive phrases.**

> The Minters, **our neighbors,** were invited to the picnic.

When an appositive has no modifiers and is closely related to the word preceding it, it should not be set off by commas.

> The Polish composer **Chopin** is her favorite.
> We **students** took a poll.

10. **Use commas to set off words used in direct address.**

> **Corey,** you need a new coat.
> I need to ask your advice, **Ms. Kim.**

11. **Use commas to set off parenthetical expressions.**

> **Strictly speaking,** I don't like it.
> Yesterday, **I believe,** was her birthday.

A contrasting expression introduced by *not* is parenthetical and must be set off by commas.

> I'm sure it was Ferdowsi, **not Saadi,** who wrote the *Shahname*.

12. **Use a comma to separate items in dates and addresses.**

> My friend traveled to **Paris, France,** on **Sunday, July 14, 1991.**
> I mailed the letter to **29 West Orange Road, Teaneck, NJ 07631,** on **May 19, 1991.**

Notice that no comma separates the month and day (*May 19*) or the house number and street name (*29 West Orange Road*) because each is considered one item. Also, the ZIP code is not separated from the name of the state by a comma: *Teaneck, NJ 07631*.

13. **Use a comma after the salutation of a friendly letter and after the closing of any letter.**

> Dear Mr. Kilgannon,
> Yours truly,

14. **Use a comma after a name followed by an abbreviation such as** *Jr., Sr.,* **and** *M.D.*

> Johnny Chin, **M.D.**
> John F. Kennedy, **Jr.**

Semicolons

1. **Use a semicolon between independent clauses in a sentence if they are not joined by** *and, but, or, nor, for, so,* **or** *yet.*

Notice in the following examples that the semicolon replaces the comma and the conjunction joining the independent clauses.

> First I filled the tub, **and** then I took a bath.
> **First I filled the tub;** then I took a bath.

A semicolon can be used between two closely related independent clauses.

> Phoebe baked the bread. Then she set the table.
> **Phoebe baked the bread;** then she set the table.

2. **Use a semicolon between independent clauses joined by conjunctive adverbs or transitional expressions.**

> Gabe was tired; **however,** he couldn't fall asleep.

I made several dishes; **in addition,** several friends brought appetizers.

When conjunctive adverbs and transitional expressions appear *within* one of the clauses and not *between* clauses, they are usually punctuated as interrupters (set off by commas). The two clauses are still separated by a semicolon.

We tried to see all the Seurat paintings; the museum, **however,** closed before we could do so.

3. Use a semicolon (rather than a comma) to separate independent clauses joined by a coordinating conjunction when there are commas within the clauses.

CONFUSING: Broccoli, peppers, and lettuce are vegetables, and nectarines, peaches, and bananas are fruits.

CLEAR: Broccoli, peppers, and lettuce are vegetables; nectarines, peaches, and bananas are fruits.

4. Use a semicolon between items in a series if the items contain commas.

He visited **Brussels, Belgium; Naples, Italy; Bombay, India; and Bangkok, Thailand,** on his trip.

Auditions will be held **Tuesday, July 16; Wednesday, July 17; and Thursday, July 18.**

Colons

1. Use a colon before a list of items, especially after expressions like *the following* and *as follows.*

You will visit **the following cities:** London, Athens, and Cairo.

Other colors are **as follows:** green, yellow, blue, and white.

If a noun is followed by a list of appositives, then the colon is used to make the meaning of the sentence clear.

On the menu there were three choices: French, Italian, or blue cheese dressing.

Do *not* use a colon before a list that follows a verb or a preposition.

INCORRECT: Additional sports include: table tennis, badminton, croquet, and horseshoes.

CORRECT: Additional sports include table tennis, badminton, croquet, and horseshoes.

2. Use a colon before a long, formal statement or quotation.

Alfred North Whitehead wrote**:** "Intelligence is quickness to apprehend as distinct from ability, which is capacity to act wisely on the thing apprehended."

3. Use a colon between the hour and the minute.

4:08 A.M.   9:14 P.M.

4. Use a colon between chapter and verse when referring to passages from the Bible.

Psalms 110:2   Genesis 2:3

5. Use a colon between volume and issue number or between volume and page number of a periodical.

Life 58:4 [volume and issue number]
Life 58:102 [volume and page number]

6. Use a colon after the salutation of a business letter.

Dear Dr. Adell: To Whom It May Concern:

Italics

When writing or typing, indicate italics by underlining. If your composition were to be printed, the underlined words would be set in italics. For example, if you type:

Anton Chekhov wrote <u>The Cherry Orchard</u>.

the sentence would be printed like this:

Anton Chekhov wrote *The Cherry Orchard*.

If you use a personal computer, you can probably set words in italics yourself.

1. Use italics (underlining) for titles of books, plays, films, newspapers, periodicals, works of art, long musical compositions, long poems, television programs, ships, aircraft, and so on.

BOOKS: *Love in the Time of Cholera, Divine Comedy*
PLAYS: *The Misanthrope, Oedipus Rex*

FILMS: *Casablanca, Alien*
PERIODICALS: *Discover,* the *New Statesman*
WORKS OF ART: *Starry Night, Nightwatch*
LONG MUSICAL COMPOSITIONS: *Aida,*
The 1812 Overture
TELEVISION SERIES: *The Wonder Years, Master-*
piece Theater
SHIPS: *Titanic, Andrea Doria*
AIRCRAFT, SPACECRAFT: *Luna 7, Saturn 2, Hin-*
denburg

The words *a, an,* and *the* written before a title are italicized only when they are part of the title. Before the names of newspapers and magazines, however, they are not italicized, even if they are capitalized on the front page of the newspaper or on the cover of the magazine.

Holst composed **The Planets**.
I read the **Boston Phoenix** and **People**.

Magazine articles, chapter headings, and titles of short poems, short stories, short musical compositions, and individual episodes of TV shows should be placed in quotation marks, not italicized, when referred to in a composition. See the following section.

2. **Use italics (underlining) for foreign words and for words, letters, and figures referred to as such.**

The word **hullabaloo** comes from Scottish.
The **5** on my test looks like an **8**.

Quotation Marks

1. **Use quotation marks to enclose a direct quotation—a person's exact words.**

Cynthia asked, **"How long is the movie?"**
"It's two hours," I answered.

2. **Begin a direct quotation with a capital letter.**

When he was finished raking the yard, Mack said, "**L**et's cook out."
Amy said, "**A**bout ten minutes." [Although this quotation is not a sentence, it is Amy's complete remark.]

If the direct quotation is a fragment of the original quotation, it may begin with a small letter.

When Shakespeare's Miranda first lays eyes on Ferdinand, she remarks that "**n**othing ill can dwell in such a temple." [The quotation is only a phrase from Miranda's sentence.]

3. **When a quoted sentence is divided into two parts by an interrupting expression, begin the second part with a small letter.**

"Before yesterday," she said, "**t**here were trees here."

If the second part of a quotation is a new sentence, a period (not a comma) follows the interrupting expression; and the second part begins with a capital letter.

"The game already started," May said. "**L**et's go to the movies, instead."

An interrupting expression is not a part of a quotation and therefore should never be inside quotation marks.

INCORRECT: "If he doesn't come, he said, we won't have enough people."
CORRECT: **"If he doesn't come,"** he said, **"we won't have enough people."**

When two or more sentences by the same speaker are quoted together, use only one set of quotation marks.

Wanda said, **"Yesterday seemed warmer than today. I wonder what the temperature is?"**

Tips for Writers
Do not use quotation marks for *indirect quotations.*

DIRECT QUOTATIONS: Sasha said, "I've already read that book."
She asked him, "Have you ever been to Memphis?"
INDIRECT QUOTATIONS: Sasha said that he'd already read that book.
She asked him if he'd ever been to Memphis.

4. **Set off a direct quotation from the rest of the sentence by commas or by a question mark or an exclamation point.**

Mr. Rosenfeld said, "Please come back and visit us soon**,**" as he dropped me off at my house.
Grace asked, "Have you been able to locate Sur-

inam?" as she opened the oversized atlas on her desk.

5. **Place commas and periods inside closing quotation marks.**

   "I haven't read the book," said Janine, "but I saw the movie."
   "Mushrooms," a poem by Margaret Atwood, presents vivid images.

6. **Place semicolons and colons outside closing quotation marks.**

   Father's advice was, "Always be polite"; I wonder if his father told him that, too.
   Choose one of the following "specials of the day": pot roast, chicken, or pasta salad.

7. **If the quotation is a question or an exclamation, place question marks and exclamation points inside the closing quotation marks. Otherwise, place them outside.**

   "Are we there yet?" I asked, hoping for the best.
   What is the meaning of "censer"?

8. **When you write dialogue (a conversation), begin a new paragraph every time the speaker changes.**

   "I won't go through with it," said Adam softly.
   "Well, then," Alice said, "I guess I'll have to do it alone."
   "Yes," he said. "You will."

9. **When a quoted passage consists of more than one paragraph, put quotation marks at the beginning of each paragraph and at the end of the entire passage. Do not put quotation marks after any paragraph but the last.**

   "Today," the reporter said, "several buildings were burned to the ground in Waco, Texas.
   "Police are ruling the fires accidental, and are still searching for the cause of the blaze. Eyewitnesses speculate that it may have been caused by a gas leak."

10. **Use single quotation marks to enclose a quotation within a quotation.**

    Vernon said, "I saw Run DMC live, singing 'Rock-box.' "

Michael asked, "Who said 'Go West, young man'?"

11. **Use quotation marks to enclose titles of articles, short stories, essays, poems, songs, individual episodes of TV shows, chapters, and other parts of books or periodicals.**

    I'm going to read Flannery O'Connor's short story "A Good Man Is Hard to Find."
    He likes the song "My Way."

Italicize the title of a poem long enough to be published in a separate volume. Such poems are usually divided into titled or numbered sections, such as cantos, parts, or books. Long musical compositions include operas, symphonies, ballets, oratorios, and concertos.

   When I read *Thurber's Carnival,* I wanted to read "The Scotty Who Knew Too Much," too.
   I read "Canto 6" of the *Divine Comedy* by the Italian poet Dante.

See also "Using Quotations Effectively" on pages 120–121.

Apostrophes

With the Possessive Case

1. **Add an apostrophe and an *s* to form the possessive case of a singular noun. The *possessive* of a noun or pronoun shows ownership or relationship.**

   an **editor's** opinion   **Francine's** book

2. **Add only an apostrophe to a proper name ending in an *s*-sound if the name has two or more syllables or if the addition of *'s* would make the name awkward to pronounce.**

   Ms. Rodriguez' wallet   **Wallace Stevens'** poetry

3. **Add only an apostrophe to form the possessive case of a plural noun ending in *s.***

   countries' populations   **dentists'** bills

Although most plural nouns end in *s,* some are irregular. To form the possessive case of a plural noun that does not end in *s*, add an apostrophe and an *s*.

children's toys **women's** careers

Do not use an apostrophe to form the *plural* of a noun. Remember that the apostrophe shows ownership or relationship.

Three **runners** [not **runners'**] wore sneakers.
Three **runners'** [not **runner's**] sneakers were white.

4. Do not use an apostrophe with a possessive personal pronoun.

My, your, her, its, our, and *their* are used before a noun. *Mine, yours, hers, ours,* and *theirs,* on the other hand, are never used before a noun; they are used as subjects, complements, or objects in sentences. *His* may be used in either way.

I saw **your** jacket. I saw a jacket of **yours**.
That is **her** baby. That baby is **hers**.

The possessive form of *who* is *whose*, not *who's*. Similarly, the possessive forms for *it* and *they* are *its* and *their,* not *it's* or *they're*.

5. Add an apostrophe and an *s* to form the possessive case of an indefinite pronoun.

anyone**'s** guess neither**'s** book

6. For possessives of compound words, names of organizations and businesses, and words showing joint possession, make only the last word possessive in form.

COMPOUND WORDS:
someone else's problem
state legislature's decision
ORGANIZATIONS:
World Wildlife Conservation's plea
Greenpeace's funding
BUSINESS:
Con Edison's workers
JOINT POSSESSION:
Matt and Julie**'s** story had the fewest characters and the most dialogue. [The story belongs to both Matt and Julie.]

When one of the words showing joint possession is a pronoun, both words should be possessive in form.

Eddie's and my surfboards were in desperate need of wax. [not *Eddie and my surfboards*]
Alex's and my relationship has improved since we began to write to each other.

7. When two or more persons possess something individually, make each of their names possessive in form.

Mrs. Mackay's and **Mrs. Stone's** husbands both work in the local post office. [the husbands of two different women]
Bill's and **Leon's** backpacks have reflective strips attached to them. [individual, not joint, possession]

With Contractions

8. Use an apostrophe to show where letters or numbers have been omitted in a contraction.

who is / who's   I am / I'm
1991 / '91   you are / you're
EXCEPTIONS:
will not / won't   shall not / shan't

9. To prevent confusion, use an apostrophe and an *s* to form the plurals of lowercase letters, some uppercase letters, numerals, and some words referred to as words.

My daughter is learning her ABC**'s**.
Good writers dot their *i***'s** and cross their *t***'s**.

Hyphens

1. Use a hyphen in some compound nouns.

brand-new   great-grandmother   mother-in-law

2. Use a hyphen to divide a word at the end of a line.

One of my favorite words is the noun **an-thology**.

Divide an already hyphenated word only at a hyphen.

Yesterday at the fair he went on the **merry-go-round**.

Do not divide a word so that one letter stands alone.

The young couple rented a new **apart-ment** [not a-partment].

A dictionary will indicate the best place to divide a word.

3. Use a hyphen with compound numbers from *twenty-one* to *ninety-nine* and with fractions used as adjectives.

> twenty-four degrees
> one-third gallon [but *one third* of the paint]

4. Use a hyphen with the prefixes *ex-*, *self-*, *all-*, and with the suffix *-elect*, and with all prefixes before a proper noun or proper adjective.

> **mid-**September, **self-**taught, President-**elect**

Dashes

Use a dash to indicate an abrupt break in thought or speech or an unfinished statement or question.

Many words and phrases are used parenthetically; that is, they break into the main thought of a sentence. Most parenthetical elements are set off by commas or parentheses.

> The general, **I believe,** is a brilliant strategist.
> Radishes, **however,** do not agree with me.

Sometimes these elements demand a stronger emphasis. In such instances, a dash is used.

> She had only one desire—to flee, flee from the dull life she led—but it was too late.
> The real culprit, you see—ah, but that information must remain a secret for the moment.

Parentheses

Use parentheses to enclose material that is added to a sentence but is not considered of major importance.

> During World War I **(from 1914 to 1918)**, the airplane came into prominence in military strategy.

Punctuation marks are used within parentheses when the parenthetical matter is a full sentence. However, a punctuation mark is not placed within parentheses if the mark belongs to the sentence as a whole.

> Mark your answers clearly. (Do not use ink.)
> Senator Albert Gore (Democrat, Tennessee) has made several speeches on that subject.
> The graph shows the changes clearly (see Figure 3).

Spelling

> ### Tips for Writers
> Here are five tips for improving your spelling.
> 1. To learn the spelling of a word, pronounce it, study it, and write it.
> 2. Use a dictionary.
> 3. Spell by syllables.
> 4. Proofread for careless spelling errors.
> 5. Keep a spelling notebook.

Words with *ie* and *ei*

1. Write *ie* when the sound is long *e*, except after *c*.

> achieve niece ceiling reprieve
> conceit thief siege fiend

2. Write *ei* when the sound is not long *e*.

> neighbor weigh freight
> reign heinous height

> EXCEPTIONS: friend, conscience, financier, seize

Words with *-cede*, *-ceed*, and *-sede*.

3. Only one English word ends in *-sede*: *supersede*; only three words end in *-ceed*: *exceed*, *proceed*, and *succeed*; all other words with this sound end in *-cede*.

> precede recede secede
> intercede concede accede

Adding Prefixes

4. When a prefix is added to a word, the spelling of the original word itself remains the same.

> dis + satisfy = **dis**satisfy   im + mature = **im**mature

Adding Suffixes

5. When the suffix *-ness* or *-ly* is added to a word, the spelling of the original word remains the same.

> casual + ly = casual**ly**   habitual + ly = habitual**ly**

Grammar, Usage, and Mechanics **1471**

EXCEPTIONS:
1. Words ending in *y* usually change the *y* to *i* before *-ness* and *-ly*: *empty / emptiness; busy / busily*
2. *True, due,* and *whole* drop the final *e* before *-ly*: *truly, duly, wholly*

Most one-syllable adjectives ending in *y do* follow rule 5: *sly / slyness; dry / dryly.*

6. Drop the final silent *e* before adding a suffix that begins with a vowel.

care + ing = caring   sense + ible = sensible

EXCEPTIONS:
1. Keep the final silent *e* in words ending in *ce* or *ge* before a suffix that begins with *a* or *o*: *manageable, courageous*
2. To avoid confusion with other words, keep the final silent *e* in some words:
dye + ing = dyeing [not dying]
singe + ing = singeing [not singing]

7. Keep the final silent *e* before adding a suffix that begins with a consonant.

nine + ty = ninety   definite + ly = definitely

EXCEPTIONS:
true + ly = truly   judge + ment = judgment

8. When a word ends in *y* preceded by a consonant, change the *y* to *i* before any suffix except one beginning with *i*.

accompany + ment = accompaniment
plenty + ful = plentiful

EXCEPTIONS:
1. Some one-syllable words:
shy + ness = shyness
sky + ward = skyward
2. *lady* and *baby* with suffixes:
ladylike   ladyship   babyhood

9. When a word ends in *y* preceded by a vowel, simply add the suffix.

buoy + ant = buoyant   joy + ful = joyful

EXCEPTIONS:
day + ly = daily   pay + ed = paid

Doubling Final Consonants

10. When a word ends in a consonant, double

the final consonant before a suffix that begins with a vowel only if the word: (1) has only one syllable or is accented on the last syllable, and (2) ends in a single consonant preceded by a single vowel.

swim + ing = swimming
repel + ent = repellent

Otherwise, simply add the suffix.

wink + ed = winked
insist + ence = insistence

Plurals of Nouns

11. To form the plurals of most English nouns, add *s*.

violin / violins   night / nights

12. To form the plurals of other nouns, follow these rules.

If the noun ends in *s, x, z, ch,* or *sh,* add *es.*

dress / dresses   fox / foxes   match / matches

If the noun ends in *y* preceded by a consonant, change the *y* to *i* and *es.*

cry / cries   theory / theories   ruby / rubies

EXCEPTION: The plurals of proper nouns: the *Murphys,* the *Rileys.*

If the noun ends in *y* preceded by a vowel, add *s.*

monkey / monkeys   buoy / buoys

For some nouns ending in *f* or *fe,* change the *f* to *v* and add *s* or *es.*

Noticing how the plural is pronounced will help you remember whether to change the *f* to *v.*

kerchief / kerchiefs   safe / safes   knife / knives

If the noun ends in *o* preceded by a consonant, add *es.*

potato / potatoes   hero / heroes
tomato / tomatoes

If the noun ends in *o* preceded by a vowel, add *s.*

patio / patios   radio / radios   tattoo / tattoos

Nouns for musical terms that end in *o* preceded by a consonant form the plural by adding only *s*.

soprano / soprano**s**   solo / solo**s**
piano / piano**s**

A number of nouns that end in *o* preceded by a consonant have two plural forms.

tornado / tornado**s** *or* tornado**es**
zero / zero**s** *or* zero**es**

The best way to handle plurals of words ending in *o* preceded by a consonant is to check their spelling in a dictionary.
The plurals of some nouns are irregular.

tooth / teeth   man / men   mouse / mice

Some nouns have the same form in both the singular and the plural.

deer   moose   salmon   Swiss

Plurals of Common Nouns

13. **If a compound noun is written as one word, form the plural by adding *s* or *es*.**

cupful / cupful**s**   leftover / leftover**s**
eyelash / eyelash**es**

If a compound noun is hyphenated or written as two words, make the main noun plural. The *main noun* is the noun that is modified.

mother-in-law / mother**s**-in-law
notary public / notari**es** public

EXCEPTIONS: drive-in / drive-in**s**
lean-to / lean-to**s**

Plurals of Latin and Greek Loan Words

14. **Some nouns borrowed from Latin and Greek form the plural as in the original language.**

nucleus / nucl**ei**   crisis / cris**es**   datum / dat**a**

A few Latin and Greek loan words have two plural forms.

vortex / vorti**ces** *or* vorte**xes**
gymnasium / gymnasi**a** *or* gymnasium**s**

Check a dictionary to find the preferred spelling of such plurals.

Plurals of Numbers, Letters, Symbols, and Words Used as Words

15. **To form the plurals of numerals, most capital letters, symbols, and words used as words, add an *s*.**

Change the **N**s to **V**s.

To prevent confusion, use an apostrophe and an *s* to form the plurals of lowercase letters, certain capital letters, and some words used as words.

Your **r's** look like **z's**.

The plurals of decades and centuries may be formed by adding an *s* or an apostrophe and an *s* ('s).

During the **1900's** (*or* **1900s**) many new inventions appeared.

Spelling Numbers

16. **Always spell out a number that begins a sentence.**

Two thousand two hundred cows are kept on this farm.

17. **Within a sentence, spell out numbers that can be written in one word or two words; use numerals for other numbers.**

Over the weekend we drove **seven hundred miles**.
He has a collection of **325** different butterflies.

18. **Spell out numbers used to indicate order.**

I placed **third** [not 3rd] in the tournament.

EXCEPTION: Use numerals for dates when you include the name of the month. Always use numerals for years.

School ends on June **3** [not 3rd]. [Writing *the third of June* is also correct.]
In **1945**, Ricardo came from Italy to the United States.

GLOSSARY

The glossary below is an alphabetical list of words found in the selections in this book. Use this glossary just as you use a dictionary—to find out the meanings of unfamiliar words. (A few technical, foreign, or obscure words in this book are not listed here, but instead are defined for you in the footnotes or glosses that accompany each selection.)

Many words in the English language have more than one meaning. This glossary gives the meanings that apply to the words as they are used in the selections of this book. Words closely associated in form and meaning are usually listed together as one entry (for example, *invert* and *inverted*), and the definition is given for the first form.

The following abbreviations are used:

adj., adjective   **n.**, noun   **v.**, verb
adv., adverb   **pl.**, plural form

Unless a word is very simple to pronounce, its pronunciation is given in parentheses. A guide to the pronunciation symbols appears at the bottom of each right-hand glossary page.

For more information about words in this glossary, or about words not listed here, consult a dictionary.

▼ A ▼

abase (ə·bās′) **v.** To humble, humiliate, degrade.

abdicate (ab′di·kāt′) **v.** To formally withdraw from an office or position.

abhor (ab·hôr′) **v.** To draw back in hatred or disgust.

abjure (ab·joor′) **v.** To reject; renounce; give up.

abode (ə·bōd′) **n.** Home; dwelling place.

abominable (ə·bäm′ə·nə·bəl) **adj.** Hateful; repulsive.

abound (ə·bound′) **v.** To be abundant; exist in plentiful amounts.

abstain (ab·stān′) **v.** To do without voluntarily.

abstemious (ab·stē′mē·əs) **adj.** Moderate; temperate.

abyss (ə·bis′) **n. 1.** The void or chaos which existed before the world's creation. **2.** A bottomless pit.

accomplice (ə·käm′plis) **n.** A partner in a criminal act.

accord **v.** To give or bestow upon.

accouterments (ə·kōōt′ər·mənts) **n., pl.** Equipment issued to a soldier, excluding clothes and weapons.

acquit (ə·kwit′) **v.** To clear someone of a charge or accusation.—**acquittal** **n.**

adept (ə·dept′) **adj.** Highly skilled, expert. **n.** (ad′ept′) an expert.

adjacent (ə·jā′sənt) **adj.** Next to; near.

admonition (ad·mə·nish′ən) **n.** A warning or scolding.

adorn (ə·dôrn′) **v.** To decorate.

adversary (ad′vər·ser′·ē) **n.** An opponent; enemy.

adverse (ad·vurs′) **adj. 1.** Moving or working in an opposite direction. **2.** Unfavorable; harmful.

advocate (ad′və·kit) **n.** A person who speaks in another's cause.

aesthetic (es·thet′ik) **adj.** Relating to what is tasteful or beautiful in art, nature, and the like.—**aesthetically** **adv.**

affable (af′ə·bəl) **adj.** Easy to talk to; approachable; good-natured.

afflict (ə·flikt′) **v.** To inflict pain or suffering upon.

afford (ə·fôrd′) **v. 1.** To be able to pay for. **2.** To give.

affront (ə·frunt′) **n.** An open or intentional offense or insult.

aggrieved (ə·grēvd′) **adj.** Offended; wrongly treated; injured in legal rights.

alight **v.** To dismount; descend.

allay (ə·lā′) **v.** To relieve (fears, for example); pacify; calm.

allot (ə·lät′) **v.** To distribute or apportion by random chance.

allusion (ə·lōō′zhən) **n.** An indirect reference; casual mention.

aloof (ə·lōōf′) **adj.** Cool and distant; reserved.

amble (am′bəl) **v.** To walk in an unhurried, leisurely fashion.

amiable (ā′mē·ə·bəl) **adj.** Friendly or good-natured.

ample (am′pəl) **adj. 1.** Adequate. **2.** More than enough.

anarchy (an′ər·kē) **n. 1.** Political disorder; chaos. **2.** Breakdown of government.

ancestral (an·ses′trəl) **adj.** Coming from an ancestor or forefather.

anguish (ang′gwish) **n.** Great pain and suffering because of loss, worry, or grief.

animated (an′i·māt·id) **adj.** Lively; spirited.

annex (ə·neks′) **v.** To add on or attach, especially to a larger thing.

anticipate (an·tis′ə·pāt′) **v.** To expect.

apparition (ap·ə·rish'ən) *n.* A strange figure, like a ghost, that appears suddenly.

appeal *v.* To make an earnest request.

appease (ə·pēz') *v.* To pacify or quiet by giving what is demanded.

apprehension (ap'rē·hen'shən) *n.* A sudden anxious expectation; dread.

approbation (ap·rə·bā'shən) *n.* Official approval.

arable (ar'ə·bəl) *adj.* Able to be plowed so as to produce crops.

ardor (är'dər) *n.* Passion.

arduous (är'jōō·əs) *adj.* That which requires great care or effort.

arid (ar'id) *adj.* Dry; wasted and lifeless.

arrest (ə·rest') *v.* To stop or check the progress or course of.

arrogant (ar'ə·gənt) *adj.* Being unjustifiably proud; haughty.

asinine (as'ə·nīn) *adj.* Like an ass; stupid; silly; stubborn. **—asininely** *adv.*

assail (ə·sāl') *v.* To attack with physical violence; assault.

assent (ə·sent') *v.* To agree.

assert (ə·surt') *v.* To declare. **—assert oneself:** To insist on attention or one's rights.

assiduous (ə·sij'ōō·əs) *adj.* Performed with careful and persistent attention.

assuage (ə·swāj') *v.* To lessen, calm, or ease.

atone (ə·tōn') *v.* To make amends for.

augury (ô'gyōō·rē) *n.* Telling of the future from omens.

auspicious (ôs'pish·əs) *adj.* Of good omen; favorable.

avert (ə·vurt') *v.* 1. To turn away. 2. To prevent. **—aversion** *n.*

avid (av'id) *adj.* 1. Eager; enthusiastic. 2. Characterized by a very strong desire or craving.

avowal (ə·vou'əl) *n.* An open acknowledgment or admission.

▼ B ▼

babel (bā'bəl) *n.* Tumult; confusion.

baleful (bāl'fəl) *adj.* Of evil or harmful appearance or effect. **—balefully** *adv.*

ballast (bal'əst) *n.* Anything heavy carried in the hold of a ship to improve stability.

banal (bā'nəl) *adj.* Unoriginal; stale; commonplace.

barren (ber'ən) *adj.* Sterile; unproductive; empty.

beguile (bē·gīl') *v.* To deceive.

bemuse (bē·myōōz') *v.* To bewilder or confuse.

benevolent (bə·nev'ə·lənt) *adj.* Desiring to do good; kindly.

bereave (bē·rēv') *v.* To deprive of something or someone.

bid *v.* To command.

blandishment (blan'dish·mənt) *n.* A flattering remark, intended to coax or persuade.

blasphemy (blas'fə·mē') *n.* Any act, writing, or speech showing disrespect or irreverence for God or sacred things.

bode *v.* To predict, usually that which is evil.

boon *n.* Blessing; benefit.

boor *n.* A clumsy, ill-mannered person.

bounty *n.* 1. Reward. 2. Generosity.

brandish *v.* To wield in an exultant manner.

brood *v.* To contemplate in a troubled way.

▼ C ▼

cajole (kə·jōl') *v.* To coax with insincere flattery.

calamitous (kə·lam'ə·təs) *adj.* Causing an extreme misfortune; disastrous.

caldron (kôl'drən) *n.* A large vat or boiler.

candid (kan'did) *adj.* Honest; straightforward.

candor (kan'dər) *n.* 1. Honesty and frankness in expression. 2. A fair and unbiased attitude.

capacity (kə·pas'i·tē) *n.* Ability or talent.

capricious (kə·prish'əs, -prē'shəs) *adj.* Tending to change suddenly and impulsively; flighty.

captivate (kap'tə·vāt') *v.* To fascinate; hold the attention of.

censure (sen'shər) *v.* To condemn severely.

chide *v.* To scold mildly.

chivalry (shiv'əl·rē) *n.* The qualities of a knight: courage, honor, and willingness to help the weak and protect women.

chronicle (krän'i·kəl) *n.* A chronologically arranged historical record.

civic (siv'ik) *adj.* Of or having to do with a city, citizens, or citizenship.

clairvoyant (kler·voi'ənt) *adj.* Able to perceive things that are beyond the range of the senses.

clamber (klam'bər) **v.** To climb clumsily, especially with all fours.

clan **n.** A tribal division; extended family.

clandestine (klan·des'tin) **adj.** Kept hidden or secret because unlawful or evil.

clemency (klem'ən·sē) **n.** Mercy toward an enemy or offender.

coagulate (kō·ag'yōō·lāt') **v.** To thicken; solidify.

coddle **v.** To treat a weak person tenderly.

cogitate (käj'ə·tāt') **v.** To ponder carefully or think deeply about.

colossus (kə·läs'əs) **n.** Anything great in size or importance.

comely (kum'lē) **adj.** 1. Pleasing or attractive in appearance. 2. Seemly, decorous, proper.

commandeer (käm'ən·dir') **v.** To seize.

commend (kə·mend') **v.** 1. To praise. 2. To recommend. 3. To entrust.

commiserate (kə·miz'ər·āt') **v.** To feel pity or sympathy for.

commission (kə·mish'ən) **n.** Money paid to a salesperson or agent, usually a percentage of a sale's proceeds.

communal (käm·yōō'nəl) **adj.** Held in common; shared by all.

compatriot (kəm·pā'trē·ət) **n.** A fellow citizen or countryman.

compensation (käm'pen·sā'shən) **n.** Anything given in exchange for, especially payment for damage or loss.

complacent (kəm·plās'ənt) **adj.** Overly contented or self-satisfied.

comprise (kəm·prīz') **v.** To consist of; be composed of.

compunction (kəm·punk'shən) **n.** Remorse; feeling of guilty uneasiness.

concede (kən·sēd') **v.** 1. To grant a privilege. 2. To admit that something is true.

conceivable (kən·sēv'ə·bəl) **adj.** Able to be imagined or believed. —**conceivably** **adv.**

conciliatory (kən·sil'e·ə·tôr'ē) **adj.** That which placates or soothes the anger of.

condescend (kän'di·send') **v.** To deal with a person as if he or she were of inferior status.

conducive (kən·dōōs'iv) **adj.** That contributes.

confer (kən·fur') **v.** 1. To give or bestow. 2. To consult together.

conflagration (kän'flə·grā'shən) **n.** A large, destructive fire.

conjecture (kən·jek'chər) **n.** A guess.

conjugal (kän'jə·gəl) **adj.** Of or relating to marriage or the marital relation.

consecrate (kän'si·krāt') **v.** To set apart as holy and sacred.

consign (kən·sīn') **v.** To assign to an unfavorable, objectionable position or place; relegate.

console (kən·sōl') **v.** To comfort; ease the grief or sadness of. —**consolation** **n.**

conspicuous (kən·spik'yōō·əs) **adj.** Attracting attention because of an unusual quality or qualities; noticeable. —**conspicuously** **adv.**

conspiracy (kən·spir'ə·sē) **n.** A secret plan to do a foul deed.

consternation (kän'stər·nā'shən) **n.** Strong shock or fear that makes a person feel bewildered or helpless.

constitutional (kän'stə·tōō'shə·nəl) **adj.** Basic to the make-up of a person or thing.

consume (kən·sōōm') **v.** To destroy; burn.

contaminate (kən·tam'ə·nāt') **v.** To corrupt or defile.

contemplate (kän'təm·plāt') **v.** 1. To look at with focused and thoughtful attention. 2. To ponder deeply. —**contemplation** **n.**

contemptuous (kən·temp'chōō·əs) **adj.** Regarding another as mean or unworthy; scornful. —**contemptuously** **adv.**

contentious (kən·ten'shəs) **adj.** Argumentative; quarrelsome.

contrive **v.** (kən·trīv') To bring about; manage.

converse (kən·vurs') **v.** To speak with informally.

conviction (kən·vik'shən) **n.** 1. A deeply held belief. 2. A judgment of guilt by a court of law.

convulse (kən·vuls') **v.** To cause to tremble or shake, as with pain or laughter.

corpulent (kôr'pyōō·lənt) **adj.** Obese; excessively fat.

corrosive (kə·rōs'iv) **adj.** Causing to wear away or be eaten away.

cosmopolitan (käz'mə·päl'ə·tən) **adj.** 1. Common to or representative of all or much of the world. 2. Worldly or broad-minded in views or habits.

counsel (koun'səl) **n.** Advice.

courier (koor'ē·ər) **n.** A messenger.

courtier (kôrt'ē·ər) **n.** An attendant in a court of royalty.

covenant (kuv'ə·nənt) **n.** A solemn agreement or contract in which two or more parties promise to do or refrain from doing some specific thing.

covert (kuv′ərt, *often, as adj.,* kō′vərt) *n.* A hiding place. *adj.* Covered over; secret; disguised.

cower (kou′ər) *v.* To hunch down or shrink from, as with fear.

credulous (krej′oo·ləs) *adj.* Believing too easily.

creed *n.* **1.** A formal statement or expression of religious faith. **2.** A statement of beliefs or principles on any subject.

crestfallen (krest′fôl′ən) *adj.* Depressed; dejected.

crux *n.* The crucial or critical point.

curate (kyoo′rit; -rāt) *n.* A member of the clergy.

curt *adj.* Rudely brief.

▼ D ▼

dalliance (dal′yəns) *n.* Flirting.

debacle (di·bä′kəl) *n.* A sudden and complete failure or defeat.

decrepit (dē·krep′it) *adj.* Weak or worn out by old age or long use.

defile (dē·fīl′) *v.* To profane; show disrespect and contempt.

deft *adj.* Skillful and quick.

deign (dān) *v.* To perform some action, despite believing it to be beneath one's dignity.

dejected (di·jek′tid) *adj.* Depressed; downcast. —**dejectedly** *adv.*

deluge (del′yōōj′) *n.* A great flood.

delusion (di·lōō′zhən) *n.* A false belief; wrong notion.

denounce (di·nouns′) *v.* **1.** To inform against. **2.** To publicly censure or condemn.

deploy (dē·ploi′) *v.* To position forces systematically over an area.

depraved (dē·prāvd′, di-) *adj.* Morally corrupt; utterly wicked.

desolate (des′ə·lit) *adj.* Uninhabited; forlorn.

despicable (des′pi·kə·bəl; də·spik′ə-) *adj.* Contemptible; vile; low.

destine (des′tin) *v.* To predetermine; insure or intend by fate.

destitute (des′tə·tōōt′) *adj.* **1.** Extremely poor. **2.** (with **of**) Totally lacking.

deteriorate (dē·tir′ē·ə·rāt′) *v.* To become or cause to be worse.

detest (dē·test′) *v.* To hate. —**detestable** *adj.*

dexterous (deks′tər·əs; -trəs) *adj.* Being skillful in using the body or mind. —**dexterously** *adv.*

dictate (dik′tāt′) *n.* A guiding principle; something required by authority.

dictum *n.* A formal pronouncement or statement.

diffuse (di·fyōōs′) *adj.* Spread out.

digression (di·gresh′ən) *n.* A temporary turning aside from the main subject.

diligence (dil′ə·jəns) *n.* Careful, hard work.

din *n.* Loud, chaotic noise.

dire *adj.* Dreadful; awful.

discern (di·zurn′; -surn′) *v.* To perceive and recognize differences.

discomfiture (dis·kum′fi·chər) *n.* Frustration.

disconcert (disk′ən·surt′) *v.* To upset, fluster, or embarrass.

disconsolate (dis·kän′sə·lit) *adj.* Inconsolable; terribly unhappy.

discordant (dis·kôrd′'nt) *adj.* Not in agreement; conflicting.

disdain (dis·dān′) *n.* Scorn felt for someone considered inferior.

disheveled (di·shev′əld) *adj.* Untidy; in disorder.

disjointed (dis·joint′id) *adj.* Lacking unity; disconnected.

disown (dis·ōn′) *v.* To refuse to accept as one's own.

disparage (di·spar′ij) *v.* To speak of in a belittling way.

dispel (di·spel′) *v.* To scatter; disperse.

dispense (di·spens′) *v.* To exempt. —**dispense with** *v.* To eliminate.

disperse (di·spurs′) *v.* To break up and scatter; distribute widely.

disposed (dis·pōzd′) *adj.* Inclined; possessing a certain demeanor or tendency.

dispute (di·spyōōt′) *v.* To argue; quarrel.

dissimulate (di·sim′yōō·lat′) *v.* To conceal (one's feelings, for example) by pretense.

dissipated (dis′ə·pāt·id) *adj.* Spent or wasted by excessive pleasure-seeking, especially drinking and gambling.

dissolution (dis′ə·lōō′shən) *n.* Death; dissolving.

dissuade (di·swād′) *v.* To advise or persuade against

---

fat, āpe, cär; ten, ēven; is, bīte; gō, hôrn, tōōl, look; oil; out; up, fur; get; joy; yet; chin; she; thin, *th*en; zh, leisure; ng, ring; ə for *a* in *ago*; *e* in *agent*; *i* in *sanity*; *o* in *comply*; *u* in *focus*; ′ as in *able* (ā′b'l).

an action. **—dissuasion** *n.*

distend (dis·tend′) *v.* **1.** To extend or stretch out. **2.** To be or cause to become swollen.

diversified (də·vər′sə·fīd′) *adj.* Varied.

divination (div′ə·nā′shən) *n.* Foretelling the future by means of omens or magic.

divinity (də·vin′ə·tē) *n.* Quality of being like God or a god; a god or deity.

docile (däs′əl) *adj.* Easily managed or controlled; submissive.

doctrine (däk′trən) *n.* The body of beliefs or principles of a religion, political party, and the like.

dominion (də·min′yən) *n.* Sovereignty; power to control or rule.

dumb *adj.* Silent; mute.

duplicity (dōō·plis′ə·tē) *n.* A deception based on hypocritical actions; deceitfulness.

▼ E ▼

ebb *v.* To weaken or decline.

edict (ē′dikt′) *n.* A decree; a publicly proclaimed order.

edify (ed′i·fī′) *v.* To instruct so as to improve morally.

efface (ə·fās′) *v.* To erase.

egocentric (ē′gō·sen′trik) *adj.* Self-centered.

elated *adj.* Very happy.

elude (e·lōōd′) *v.* To evade or escape from by cleverness or quickness.

eminence (em′i·nəns) *n.* **1.** An elevated thing or place, as a mountain. **2.** Greatness.

emphatic (em·fat′ik) *adj.* Expressed with force or stress. **—emphatically** *adv.*

emulate (em′yōō·lāt′) *v.* To imitate in order to equal or surpass.

endow (en·dou′) *v.* **1.** To give some quality to. **2.** To give money or property which will provide additional income.

engender (en·jen′dər) *v.* To cause to be; produce.

enjoin (en·join′) *v.* To command someone to do or refrain from doing something.

enmity (en′mə·tē) *n.* Hostility.

ensue (en·sōō′) *v.* To follow immediately, as an event.

enterprise (ent′ər·prīz′) *n.* An undertaking.

entreat (en·trēt′) *v.* To ask sincerely and urgently; beg.

equanimity (ek′wə·nim′ə·tē) *n.* The ability to maintain composure and calmness.

eschew (es·chōō′) *v.* To stay away from; avoid.

estrange (e·strānj′) *v.* **1.** To keep apart or separate. **2.** To make hostile or unfriendly.

etiquette (et′i·kit) *n.* Established rules of behavior in society or a profession.

evasion (ē·vā′zhən) *n.* The act of evading (a consequence or responsibility, for example) through deception or cleverness.

evoke *v.* To draw forth a mental image or reaction. **—evocation** *n.*

exasperate (eg·zas′pər·āt′) *v.* To annoy; try the patience of.

excel (ek·sel′) *v.* To be better than others.

excursion (eks·kur′zhən) *n.* A short trip taken for pleasure.

execration (ek′si·krā′shən) *n.* The act of cursing or speaking abusively of a person or thing.

executor (ek′si·kyōōt·ər) *n.* A person who carries out some action.

exhilarate (eg·zil′ə·rāt′) *v.* To make lively; stimulate.

exorcise (eks′ôr·sīz′) *v.* To drive out an evil spirit by a religious or magic ritual. **—exorcist** *n.*

expanse (ek·spans′) *n.* A wide, open area.

expedient (ek·spē′dē·ənt) *n.* A thing useful to achieve an end.

extirpate (ek′stər·pāt′) *v.* To destroy; exterminate; uproot.

extort (eks·tôrt′) *v.* To get money or goods by threats or violence.

exude (eg·zyōōd′; -zōōd′) *v.* To ooze.

exult (eg·zult′) *v.* To be very happy; to feel joyful and triumphant.

▼ F ▼

faction (fak′shən) *n.* A split within an organization or country; internal conflict.

fallow *adj.* Plowed but not cultivated or planted.

falsification (fôl′sə·fi·kā′shən) *n.* A false or misleading statement.

falter (fôl′tər) *v.* To weaken or waver.

fastidious (fas·tid′ē·əs) *adj.* Overly particular and critical. **—fastidiously** *adv.*

fatuous (fach′ōō·əs) *adj.* Contentedly stupid; foolish.

feign (fān) *v.* To pretend.

felicity (fə·lis′i·tē) *n.* Joy; gladness.

fervent (fur′vənt) *adj.* Very warm or intense in feeling.

fervor (fur′vər) *n.* Strong, warm feeling.

filial (fil′ē·əl) *adj.* Of, referring to, or appropriate for one's children.

flaccid (flak′sid; flas′id) *adj.* Flabby; hanging loosely.

flail *v.* To beat with a stick or whip.

flaunt (flônt) **v.** To make a showy, impudent display; show off.

flout v. To scoff or jeer at; scorn.

forbear (fôr'bər') **v.** [past tense, *forbore*] To refrain from; to be patient.

foreboding (fôr·bōd'ing) **n.** A prediction or feeling that something harmful will take place; apprehension.

forestall (fôr·stôl') **v.** To prevent or delay by taking action ahead of time.

forfeit (fôr'fit) **v.** To lose, give up, or be deprived of because of some crime or failure.

forge v. To make a metal object by heating and hammering.

forlorn (fôr·lôrn') **adj.** Deserted; miserable; hopeless.

formidable (fôr'mə·də·bəl) **adj.** Producing fear or horror.

forswear v. (fôr·swer') To promise abstinence from; pledge to give up.

fortitude (fôr'tə·tōōd') **n.** The strength to bear misfortune or pain with patience.

foster v. To bring up or raise with care.

fraternal (frə·turn'əl) **adj.** Brotherly.

frivolity (fri·väl'ə·tē') **n.** Lack of seriousness or sense; silliness.

furtive (fur'tiv) **adj.** Secretive; done in a stealthy or sneaky way.

futile (fyōōt'l) **adj.** Useless; hopeless.

▼ G ▼

gall (gôl) **n.** 1. Feeling of bitterness. 2. Irritation, annoyance.

gambol (gam'bəl) **v.** To frolic; to play animatedly.

gaunt (gônt) **adj.** Lean and bony; emaciated; scrawny.

gentility (jen·til'i·tē) **n.** 1. The quality of being refined and polite. 2. The condition of being born into the upper classes.

glade n. An open area or space, especially in the woods.

glut n. Excessive fullness.

goad v. To urge on.

grapple (grap'əl) **v.** To struggle in hand-to-hand combat.

grizzled (griz'əld) **adj.** Gray, especially in reference to hair.

grueling (grōō'əl·ing) **adj.** Exhausting; very difficult.

guile (gīl) **n.** Deceitfulness and craftiness; cunning.

guise (gīz) **n.** 1. Manner or way of dressing. 2. Deceiving or false appearance.

gyration (jī·rā'shən) **n.** The act of moving in a circular or spiral path around a central axis or point.

▼ H ▼

haggard (hag'ərd) **adj.** Gaunt, having a wasted, wild look.

haggle v. To argue about the price of.

hapless (hap'lis) **adj.** Unlucky.

harry v. 1. To disturb or worry; harass. 2. To force or prod.

havoc (hav'ek) **n.** Vast destruction or ruin.

hectic (hek'tik) **adj.** Happening in a confused or excited rush.

heedless (hēd'lis) **adj.** Paying no attention.

homage (häm'ij; äm'-) **n.** Something given or done to show respect.

homily (häm'ə·lē) **n.** A sermon, especially on a religious or biblical subject.

hovel (huv'əl) **n.** A small, impoverished dwelling or hut.

hover (huv'ər) **v.** To float or remain suspended in the air; wait close by, especially in an annoying way.

▼ I ▼

icon (ī'kän) **n.** A picture or image, regarded as sacred, of a religious figure.

ignoble (ig·nō'bəl) **adj.** Not noble; common or low.

immaculate (im·mak'yōō·lit) **adj.** 1. Spotlessly clean. 2. Flawless. 3. Pure; innocent.

imminent (im'ə·nənt) **adj.** Likely to happen very soon.

immutable (im·myōōt'ə·bəl) **adj.** Unchangeable.

impartial (im·pär'shəl) **adj.** Unbiased; not favoring either side in a dispute or contest.

impassive (im·pas'iv) **adj.** Displaying no emotion; calm.

impediment (im·ped'ə·mənt) **n.** Hindrance.

impel (im·pel') **v.** To propel; drive forward.

impend (im·pend') **v.** To be about to occur; to loom.

impenetrable (im·pen'i·trə·bəl) **adj.** Not capable of being passed through; dense.

---

fat, āpe, cär; ten, ēven; is, bīte; gō, hôrn, tōōl, look; oil, out; up, fur; get; joy; yet; chin; she; thin, then; zh, leisure; ng, ring; ə for *a* in *ago*; *e* in *agent*; *i* in *sanity*; *o* in *comply*; *u* in *focus*; ' as in *able* (ā' b'l).

imperceptible (im′pər·sep′tə·bəl) *adj.* Not easily sensed.—**imperceptibly** *adv.*

imperial (im·pir′ē·əl) *adj.* **1.** Of or relating to an empire. **2.** Majestic.

imperious (im·pir′ē·əs) *adj.* Bossy; arrogant; domineering.

impervious (im·pur′vē·əs) *adj.* Incapable of being attacked.

implacable (im·plā′kə·bəl; -plak′-) *adj.* Not capable of being pacified or quieted.

implore (im·plôr′) *v.* To beg or plead for.

impotent (im′pə·tənt) *adj.* Powerless, ineffective. —**impotently** *adv.*

impregnable (im·preg′nə·bəl) *adj.* Not capable of being penetrated or entered by force.

improvise (im′prə·viz′) *v.* To make or do with the materials at hand in order to fill a pressing need.

impudent (im′pyoo·dənt) *adj.* Disrespectfully bold; brazen. —**impudently** *adv.*

impulsive (im·pul′siv) *adj.* Acting or likely to act without forethought or plan. —**impulsively** *adv.*

incantation (in′kan·tā′shən) *n.* The recitation of magical words to cast a spell or perform magic.

incarnate (in·kär′nit; -nāt) *adj.* Appearing as a recognizable, living example; personified.

incendiary (in·sen′dē·er′ē) *adj.* Related to the deliberate destruction of property by fire.

incense (in·sens′) *v.* To make very angry; enrage.

incessant (in·ses′ənt) *adj.* Unending; continuing or repeating endlessly. —**incessantly** *adv.*

incomprehensible (in′käm·prē·hen′sə·bəl) *adj.* Not understandable.

incongruous (in·kän′groo·əs) *adj.* Inconsistent with expectations; lacking harmony or compatibility.

incredulous (in·krej′oo·ləs) *adj.* Disbelieving or unwilling to believe; skeptical.

indefatigable (in′di·fat′i·gə·bəl) *adj.* Untiring.

indifferent (in·dif′ər·ənt) *adj.* Having or displaying no preference, bias or interest.

indignation (in′dig·nā′shən) *n.* Anger felt in reaction to unfairness.

indiscretion (in′di·skresh′ən) *n.* An unwise or careless act or comment.

indispensable (in′di·spen′sə·bəl) *adj.* Of key importance; necessary.

indisposition (in′dis·pə·zish′ən) *n.* Unwellness or slight sickness.

indulgence (in·dul′jəns) *n.* **1.** The act of giving way to another's or one's own desires. **2.** Something given as a favor.

inert (in·urt′) *adj.* Characterized by mental or physical inactivity or slowness.

inextricable (in·eks′tri·kə·bəl) *adj.* Incapable of being set free or disentangled from.

infallible (in·fal′ə·bəl) *adj.* Incapable of error; reliable.

infamy (in′fə·mē) *n.* Shameful or wicked reputation.

infatuation (in·fach·oo·ā′shən) *n.* An unreasoning or shallow love, affection, or attachment.

infer (in·fur′) *v.* To draw a conclusion from evidence or an assumption.

infuse (in·fyooz′) *v.* To put; fill. —**infused** *adj.*

ingenious (in·jēn′yəs) *adj.* Demonstrating creativity or resourcefulness.—**ingenuity** *n.*

ingrate (in′grāt) *n.* An ungrateful person.

inherent (in·hir′ənt) *adj.* Existing as an essential or natural part of the whole.

iniquity (i·nik′wi·tē) *n.* Wickedness; sinfulness; wrongdoing.

initiate (i·nish′ē·āt′) *v.* To introduce or instruct.

initiative (i·nish′ə·tiv) *n.* **1.** Responsibility for taking the first step in and following through with a project or plan. **2.** Ability to think or act for oneself, without needing encouragement or urging.

inordinate (in·ôr′də·nit) *adj.* Lacking restraint; excessive.

insensible (in·sen′sə·bəl) *adj.* Lacking sensation or consciousness; unaware.

insignificant (in′sig·nif′i·kənt) *adj.* Unimportant; of no meaning or consequence.

insolent (in′sə·lənt) *adj.* Disrespectful; rude; arrogant.

insouciant (in·soo′sē·ənt) *adj.* Calmly indifferent; carefree. —**insouciance** *n.*

instigation (in′stə·gā′shən) *n.* An urging on to some evil act.

insular (in′sə·lər) *adj.* **1.** Isolated. **2.** Narrow-minded.

insuperable (in·soo′pər·ə·bəl) *adj.* Incapable of being overcome.

intensive (in·ten′siv) *adj.* Thorough; deep; concentrated. —**intensively** *adv.*

intent (in·tent′) *adj.* Directed or fixed. —**intent on** or **upon** *adj.* Having the attention fixed; strongly directed.

intercede (in′tər·sēd′) *v.* To make an appeal on behalf of another or others. —**intercession** *n.*

interlude (in′tər·lood′) *n.* Entertainment between the acts of a play.

interminable (in·tur'mi·nə·bəl) *adj.* That which continues, or seems to continue, without end.

intermittent (in'tər·mit''nt) *adj.* Ending and beginning again at intervals.

intervene (in'tər·vēn') *v.* **1.** To occur between two points in time. **2.** To come between.

intimate (in'tə·mət) *adj.* **1.** Innermost or personal **2.** Closely acquainted; very familiar.

intimation (in'tə·mā'shən) *n.* A hint; subtle implication.

intolerable (in·täl'ər·ə·bəl) *adj.* Unbearable; too painful or severe to be endured.

intrepid (in·trep'id) *adj.* Not afraid; courageous.

intricate (in'tri·kit) *adj.* Elaborately detailed; complex.

intrigue (in·trēg'; *for n., also* in'trēg) *v.* **1.** To plot or scheme in a secret manner. **2.** To interest greatly. *n.* A secret plot or scheme.

invariable (in·ver'ē·ə·bəl) *adj.* Never changing; constant.

invert (in·vurt') *v.* To place upside down. **—inverted** *adj.*

inveterate (in·vet'ər·it) *adj.* Long-lasting; long-standing; habitual.

invoke *v.* To call on God or a god for assistance.

irreparable (ir·rep'ə·rə·bəl) *adj.* Not able to be repaired.

issue (ish'ōō; -yōō) *n.* Children; offspring.

▼ **J** ▼

jeopardy (jep'ərd·dē) *n.* Intense danger or peril.

joust *n.* A fight between two mounted knights wielding lances.

jubilation (jōō'bə·lā'shən) *n.* Triumphant joyfulness.

judicious (jōō·dish'əs) *adj.* Showing good judgment; wise and cautious.

justification (jus'tə·fi·kā'shən) *n.* A fact or argument that shows that someone is right or has acted reasonably.

juxtapose (juks'tə·pōz') *v.* To place one thing or idea close to or side by side with another.

▼ **K** ▼

kindred (kin'drid) *n.* Family; kinfolk.

knight-errant (nīt er''nt) *n.* A knight looking for ad-

ventures that will allow him to correct injustices or show his strength and skill.

knoll (nōl) *n.* Small hill.

▼ **L** ▼

laborious (lə·bôr'ē·əs) *adj.* Involving intensive work; difficult.

labyrinth (lab'ə·rinth') *n.* An complex network of winding passageways; maze.

lamentation (lam'ən·tā'shən) *n.* An outward show of grief; wailing or crying.

legitimate (lə·jit'ə·mət) *adj.* **1.** Born to married parents. **2.** Legal; lawful.

lineage (lin'ē·ij) *n.* Direct descent from an ancestor.

loath (lōth, lōth) *adj.* Reluctant.

loin *n.* [usually plural] The hips or the lower abdomen of the body, regarded as the source of strength and procreative power.

loll *v.* To lounge about.

lop *v.* To remove by chopping off.

lout *n.* An awkward, foolish person; oaf.

lucid (lōō'sid) *adj.* Easily understood.

lumber (lum'bər) *v.* To move about in a clumsy, noisy manner.

▼ **M** ▼

magnanimous (mag·nan'ə·məs) *adj.* Noble-spirited; generous. **—magnanimity** *n.*

malice (mal'is) *n.* Active ill will; desire to deliberately harm another; spite. **—malicious** *adj.*

malignant (mə·lig'nənt) *adj.* Very evil or dangerous.

manifest (man'ə·fest') *v.* To become apparent; show.

manifold (man'ə·fōld') *adj.* Many and diverse.

mannerism (man'ər·iz''m) *n.* A unique feature of behavior, speech, and so on, that has become habitual.

martyr (märt'ər) *n.* **1.** A person who prefers to suffer or die rather than deny his or her principles or beliefs. **2.** A person who undergoes immense pain or suffering for a long time.

materialize (mə·tir'ē·əl·īz') *v.* To appear suddenly, in concrete form.

mean *adj.* Of little value; inferior.

mediocre (mē'dē·ō'kər) *adj.* **1.** Average; ordinary **2.** Of inferior quality.

---

fat, āpe, cär; ten, ēven; is, bīte; gō, hôrn, tōōl, look; oil, out; up, fur; get; joy; yet; chin; she; thin, *th*en; zh, leisure; ng, ring; ə for *a* in *ago*; e in *agent*; i in *sanity*; o in *comply*; u in *focus*; ' as in *able* (ā'b'l).

meditation (med′ə·tā′shən) **n.** Solemn reflection on spiritual matters.

melancholy (mel′ən·käl′ē) **n.** Depression; gloominess; sadness.

metaphysics (met·ə·fiz′iks) **n.** A branch of philosophy dealing with the nature of being and reality.

mete **v.** To distribute or dole out: usually with *out*.

meticulous (mə·tik′yōō·ləs) **adj.** Very careful or finicky about details.

minister (min′is·tər) **n.** A person or thing serving as the agent of some higher power.

mire **n.** An area of deep mud or slush.

misalliance (mis·ə·lī′əns) **n.** A bad partnership; a marriage of incompatible partners.

misgiving (mis·giv′ing) **n.** An unsettling feeling of fear or doubt.

monotony (mə·nät′′n·ē) **n.** Boring sameness.

morose (mə·rōs′) **adj.** Gloomy; in a bad or sullen mood.

mortify (môrt′ə·fī′) **v.** To arouse great shame or humiliation.

mundane (mun·dān′) **adj.** Of the world; ordinary, day-to-day.

muster **v.** To gather or bring together.

mutiny (myōōt′′n·ē) **n.** A revolt, as by soldiers or sailors, against their officers. —**mutinous** **adj.**

▼ N ▼

nascent (nas′ənt; nās′-) **adj.** Coming into existence; in the process of being born.

nativity (nə·tiv′ə·tē) **n.** Birth and, particularly, the circumstances surrounding a birth.

nimble **adj.** Moving about in a quick or light manner. —**nimbly** **adv.**

nocturnal (näk·tʉr′nəl) **adj.** Of or occurring during the night.

nonplus (nän′plus′) **v.** To puzzle or bewilder into a state of inaction.

novice (näv′is) **n.** A beginner; amateur; newcomer.

nuptial (nup′shəl) **n.** A wedding.

nurture (nʉr′chər) **v.** To care for, especially by feeding or protecting.

▼ O ▼

obdurate (äb′door·ət) **adj.** 1. Lacking sympathy. 2. Stubborn. —**obduracy** **n.**

oblation (ə·blā′shən) **n.** 1. Gift of or offering to God or a god. 2. The bread and wine of the Eucharist.

oblige (ə·blīj′) **v.** 1. To cause to do something by moral, legal, or physical force. 2. To perform a favor.

oblivion (ə·bliv′ē·ən) **n.** The state of complete forgetfulness.

obscurity (əb·skyoor′ə·tē) **n.** Inconspicuousness; lack of fame.

obsess (əb·ses′) **v.** To haunt in mind or preoccupy to an extreme degree.

obsolete (äb′sə·lēt′) **adj.** 1. Outdated. 2. No longer used.

obstinate (äb′stə·nət) **adj.** Very stubborn.

obtuse (äb·tōōs′) **adj.** Slow to comprehend; dull-witted. —**obtuseness** **n.**

odious (ō′dē·əs) **adj.** Hateful; disgusting.

ogre (ō′gər) **n.** A monster or giant who eats people.

ominous (äm′ə·nəs) **adj.** Seeming to threaten evil or misfortune; sinister.

omnipotent (äm·nip′ə·tənt) **adj.** All-powerful.

oratory (ôr′ə·tôr′ē) **n.** Public speaking, especially in a traditional manner.

▼ P ▼

pacify (pas′ə·fī′) **v.** To make calm; to appease or make quiet.

painstaking (pānz′tāk′ing) **adj.** Taking great pains or care. —**painstakingly** **adv.**

pallid (pal′id) **adj.** Pale in color or complexion.

palpable (pal′pə·bəl) **adj.** Plainly evident to the senses.

palpitate (pal′pə·tāt′) **v.** To beat more rapidly than normal, usually referring to the heart.

paltry (pôl′trē) **adj.** Trivial; having little or no worth.

pandemonium (pan′də·mō′nē·əm) **n.** Any scene of chaotic noise or confusion.

pander **v.** To act in a way that helps satisfy the base desires or exploits the weakness of another.

paragon (par′ə·gän′) **n.** Something that is a model or example of perfection.

paternal (pə·tʉr′nəl) **adj.** Of or referring to the father's side of a family; fatherly.

pathos (pā′thäs′) **n.** The quality in something experienced or observed that moves one to feelings of pity or sorrow.

patriarch (pā′trē·ärk) **n.** 1. An elderly and honored man. 2. A man regarded as the father or founder of a family or institution.

patronize (pā′trən·īz′) **v.** To be helpful to or supportive of someone but treat as an inferior. —**patronizingly** **adv.**

pedant (ped′′nt) **n.** A teacher who places undue emphasis on minor details or rules rather than on genuine learning.

peer *n.* A person who is the equal of another.

peevish (pē'vish) *adj.* Difficult to please; easily irritated. —**peevishly** *adv.* —**peevishness** *n.*

pelt *n.* The coat or skin of a fur-bearing animal. *v.* To throw things at.

penitent (pen'i·tent) *adj.* Feeling sorry or regretful for having done wrong.

pensive *adj.* (pen'siv) Thoughtful; considering sad or serious matters.

perfidious (pər·fid'ē·əs) *adj.* Acting in betrayal of trust; treacherous.

peril (per'əl) *n.* Danger.

periphery (pə·rif'ər·ē) *n.* Outer parts or boundary, especially of a rounded object.

perish (per'ish) *v.* 1. To be destroyed, obliterated, or ruined. 2. To die suddenly and violently.

perplexed (pər·plekst') *adj.* Puzzled; confused.

persecution (pur'sə·kyōō'shən) *n.* The state of being cruelly oppressed or mistreated.

perseverance (pur'sə·vir'əns) *n.* Persistent, patient effort.

pervade (pər·vād') *v.* To exist widely.

perverse (pər·vurs') *adj.* Stubbornly persisting in error.

pestilence (pes'tə·ləns) *n.* Any disease, especially one of epidemic proportions, as bubonic plague.

pestilential (pes'tə·len'shəl) *adj.* 1. Of, causing, or likely to cause infection. 2. Deadly to a wide population.

petition (pə·tish'ən) *v.* To ask for sincerely or formally.

petrify (pe'tri·fī') *v.* To paralyze with fear.

phantasm (fan'taz'em) *n.* A ghost, specter; a vision of something that has no physical reality.

piety (pī'ə·tē) *n.* Loyalty (to God, parents, or country, for example).

pilgrimage (pil'grim·ij) *n.* 1. A trip undertaken by a pilgrim, especially to a holy place. 2. A long journey.

pitiable (pit'ē·ə·bəl) *adj.* Arousing or deserving compassion, sometimes mixed with scorn.

plunder (plun'dər) *v.* To steal, especially during a time of war.

ponder (pän'dər) *v.* To consider deeply and carefully.

ponderous (pän'dər·əs) *adj.* Heavy or massive.

portent (pôr'tent) *n.* Something that foretells or predicts a coming event, often of an unfortunate nature; an omen.

postulate (päs'chə·lāt') *v.* To assume, as the basis of an argument, the truth of something unproven or unprovable; claim.

practicable (prak'ti·kə·bəl) *adj.* That which can be accomplished or put into practice.

precarious (pri·ker'ē·əs) *adj.* Dependent upon uncertain circumstances or persons.

precedent (pres'ə·dənt) *n.* A case that may serve as an example for a later one.

precept (prē'sept) *n.* A command or direction for action or behavior.

precinct (prē'sinkt') *n.* A district of a city; neighborhood.

precipice (pres'i·pis) *n.* A high, steep cliff.

precipitate (prē·sip'ə·tit) *adj.* Acting or happening very hastily. —**precipitately** *adv.*

precursor (prē·kur'sər) *n.* A person or thing that comes before another; forerunner.

predatory (pred'ə·tôr'ē) *adj.* Living by hunting and feeding on other animals.

preeminent (prē·em'ə·nənt) *adj.* Very fine; surpassing all others.

preliminaries (prē·lim'ə·ner'ēs) *n., pl.* Procedures or steps leading up to main part or action.

premonition (prēm'ə·nish'ən) *n.* A feeling that something unfortunate is going to happen.

preoccupied (prē·äk'yə·pīd') *adj.* Wholly absorbed with one's thoughts; engrossed. —**preoccupation** *n.*

prescience (presh'əns) *n.* Knowledge of a thing or event before it exists or takes place.

presumption (prē·zump'shən) *n.* 1. An overstepping of proper limits. 2. A supposing.

pretension (prē·ten'shən) *n.* 1. A claim to nobility or some other distinction. 2. An extravagant and unjustified outward show; pretentiousness.

prevaricate (pri·var'i·kāt') *v.* To avoid the truth; lie.

primal (prī'məl) *adj.* 1. Original. 2. Of chief importance.

---

fat, āpe, cär; ten, ēven; is, bīte; gō, hôrn, tōōl, look; oil; out; up, fur; get; joy; yet; chin; she; thin, then; zh, leisure; ng, ring; ə for a in ago; e in agent; i in sanity; o in comply; u in focus; ' as in able (ā'b'l).

primordial (prī·môr′dē·əl) *adj.* Existing or occurring from the world's beginning.

pristine (pris′tēn′) *adj.* 1. Original. 2. Unspoiled.

procure (prō·kyoor′) *v.* To obtain or make happen by an effort; secure.

prodigal (präd′i·gəl) *adj.* Carelessly wasteful.

prodigy (präd′ə·jē) *n.* A person of amazing ability. —**prodigious** *adj.*

profound (prō′found′) *adj.* 1. Deeply felt. 2. Having great intellectual depth.

profuse (prō·fyoos′) *adj.* Abundant; pouring out in excess. —**profusely** *adv.*

promontory (präm′ən·tôr·ē) *n.* A high ridge of land that overlooks a body of water.

propaganda (präp′ə·gan′də) *n.* The widespread promotion of the ideas or practices of a particular group or party intended to gain support for one's own cause or to damage another's.

propitiate (prō·pish′ē·āt′) *v.* To appease or pacify.

prostrate (präs′trāt′) *adj.* Lying face down.

protract (prō·trakt′) *v.* To prolong; lengthen.

protrude (prō·trood′) *v.* To jut out.

provincial (prə·vin′shəl) *adj.* 1. Narrowminded; unsophisticated. 2. From a province, especially a rural one.

prowess (prou′is) *adj.* Bravery; courage.

prudent (prood′′nt) *adj.* Careful; cautious.

punctual (punk′choo·əl) *adj.* Timely; prompt. —**punctually** *adv.*

purge (purj) *v.* To cleanse of impurities; to clear away or out.

▼ Q ▼

quandary (kwän′drē) *n.* A state of perplexity or confusion; dilemma.

quarter (kwôrt′ər) *n.* 1. A particular district or neighborhood. 2. Lodgings. 3. Mercy granted to a surrendering enemy.

quaver (kwā′vər) *v.* To shake or quiver.

quibble (kwib′əl) *v.* To evade the truth of a point by focusing on a petty detail.

quicken (kwik′ən) *v.* To become revived.

▼ R ▼

rampart (ram′pärt′, -pərt) *n.* An embankment of earth, usually supporting a wall, that encircles a castle or fort for defense against attack.

rapture (rap′chər) *n.* A joyous, almost ecstatic condition or feeling.

ratify (rat′ə·fī) *v.* To confirm; make valid or legal.

ravage (rav′ij) *v.* To ruin; destroy.

raze *v.* To lay level with the ground; destroy.

realm (relm) *n.* Kingdom; province; region.

rebuke (ri·byook′) *v.* To reprimand or scold.

reckoning (rek′ən·ing) *n.* 1. The settlement or accounting of rewards or punishments for an action. 2. Counting or calculation.

recompense (rek′əm·pens′) *v.* To pay for; compensate.

reconciliation (rek′ən·sil′ē·ā′shən) *n.* A settling of a quarrel; restoration of harmony.

recriminate (ri·krim′ə·nāt′) *v.* To meet the charges of an accuser by accusing him or her of wrongdoing. —**recrimination** *n.*

rectify (rek′tə·fī′) *v.* To amend, correct, or make right.

redemption (ri·demp′shən) *n.* A deliverance from sin and its punishments.

redouble (rē·dub′əl) *v.* To double, as in size or degree.

reflect (ri·flekt′) *v.* To contemplate seriously; ponder. —**reflection** *n.*

relent (ri·lent′) *v.* To yield.

relic (rel′ik) *n.* 1. A thing of the past, saved for its historic interest. 2. *pl.* Those fragments surviving from the past.

relinquish (ri·ling′kwish) *v.* To abandon claim to; let go of; yield.

rend *v.* [past tense *rent*] To rip up or tear apart violently.

render *v.* To represent or reproduce in words, pictures, or performance.

renounce (ri·nouns′) *v.* To purposefully give up a claim, right, way of living, and so forth; to repudiate or disown.

renown (ri·noun′) *n.* Illustrious reputation; great fame.

repast (ri·past′) *n.* A meal; feast.

replenish (ri·plen′ish) *v.* To refill or make complete again; to renew the supply.

reprehensible (rep′ri·hen′sə·bəl) *adj.* Deserving of criticism or blame.

repress (ri·pres′) *v.* To hold back, restrain or curb. —**repression** *n.*

reprimand (rep′rə·mand) *n.* A severe scolding, especially by someone in authority.

reproach (ri·prōch′) *v.* To scold, reprimand, or censure, especially in a way that produces shame.

reprobation (rep′rə·bā′shən) *n.* Disapproval, condemnation, rejection.

reprove (ri·proov′) **v.** To scold or censure.

repulse (ri·puls′) **v. 1.** To repel or drive back; reject. **2.** To be disgusting to. —**repulsive** *adj.*; **repulsion** *n.*

reputed (ri·pyoot′id) *adj.* Recognized or supposed to be so.

requite (ri·kwīt′) **v. 1.** To repay or reward. **2.** [*Archaic*] To do something in return.

residue (rez′·ə·doo′) *n.* Left-over portion; remainder.

resin (rez′ən) *n.* A semisolid, sticky substance given off by some plants and trees.

resolute (rez′ə·loot′) *adj.* Having a decided purpose; determined.

resolve (ri·zälv′) **v.** To determine or decide; settle on.

respite (res′pit) *n.* A temporary period of rest or relief.

resplendent (ri·splen′dənt) *adj.* With much splendor; dazzling; shining brilliantly.

retaliate (ri·tal′ē·āt′) **v.** To do something to get revenge for an injury or evil. —**retaliation** *n.*

retinue (ret′′n·yoo′) *n.* A group of assistants and servants who follow an important person.

retort **v.** To reply in a quick, sharp manner.

revel (rev′əl) **v.** To be festive in a noisy manner.

reverberate (ri·vur′bə·rāt′) **v.** To resound; continue in a series of echoes.

revere (ri·vēr′) **v.** To have great respect and love for.

reverie (rev′ər·ē) *n.* Daydreaming; state of being lost in thought or imagining, especially of pleasant things.

revile (ri·vīl′) **v.** To verbally abuse someone.

rhetoric (ret′ər·ik) *n.* **1.** Language intended to persuade. **2.** Showy, elaborate language that is lacking in clarity and sincerity.

rile **v.** To prod into action by upsetting; irritate.

rout *n.* An utter and overpowering defeat.

ruse (rooz) *n.* A trick.

▼ S ▼

sacrilege (sak′rə·lij) *n.* The act of taking, using, violating, or treating disrespectfully something which is consecrated to God or religion.

sage *n.* A person greatly respected for wisdom and judgment.

salutation (sal·yoo·tā′shən) *n.* A greeting.

sanctify (sank′te·fī′) **v.** To make or set apart as holy.

sanction (sank′shən) *n.* Official approval given for an action.

sap **v.** To empty, drain, or exhaust; weaken.

scourge (skurj) *n.* A punishment; a cause of severe trouble or suffering.

scrupulous (skroo′pyə·ləs) *adj.* Giving careful attention to what is right or proper.

scrutinize (skroot′′n·īz′) **v.** To examine or inspect carefully and closely.

seduce (si·doos′) **v.** To persuade into wrongdoing or disloyalty.

sensuous (sen′shoo·əs) *adj.* Perceived by the senses, especially with pleasure or enjoyment.

sepulcher (sep′əl·kər) *n.* A vault, chamber, or grave for the dead.

sequence (sē′kwens) *n.* The following of one thing after another in some logical order.

serenity (sə·ren′ə·tē) *n.* Calmness; composure; tranquility.

sever (sev′ər) **v. 1.** To cut off by force. **2.** To separate; divide.

sheaf *n.* A quantity of cut stalks of grain, and the like, bundled together.

sheer *adj.* Very steep.

shroud **v. 1.** To wrap a corpse in burial cloth. **2.** To hide or conceal.

siege (sēj) *n.* The besetting of a fortified place by an army to compel surrender.

sinewy (sin′yoo·ē) *adj.* **1.** Strong; powerful. **2.** Marked by good muscular development.

sinister (sin′is·tər) *adj.* Ominous; indicating lurking evil or harm.

slake **v. 1.** Satisfy; quench. **2.** To cause a fire to die out.

slough (sluf) **v.** To get rid of or throw off.

sluice (sloos) *n.* A gate or valve used in opening or closing an artificial passage for water.

sojourn (sō′jurn) **v.** To stop and dwell in a place temporarily.

solder (säd′ər) **v.** To join (metal pieces) with a melted metal compound.

solicitous (sə·lis′ə·təs) *adj.* Showing care or attention; anxiously willing. —**solicitously** *adv.*

---

fat, āpe, cär; ten, ēven; is, bīte; gō, hôrn, tool, look; oil, out; up, fur; get; joy; yet; chin; she; thin, then; zh, leisure; ng, ring; ə for *a* in *ago*; *e* in *agent*; *i* in *sanity*; *o* in *comply*; *u* in *focus*; ′ as in *able* (ā′b′l).

---

soliloquy (sə·lil'ə·kwē) *n.* **1.** The act of talking to oneself. **2.** Lines in a play used to reveal a character's thoughts to the audience.

somber (säm'bər) *adj.* **1.** Dark and dismal. **2.** Melancholy; depressed.

sonorous (sə·nôr'əs; sän'ər-) *adj.* Quality of sound which is full, deep, and resonant.

sordid (sôr'did) *adj.* **1.** Dirty; squalid. **2.** Dishonorable or ignoble; mean or petty.

sovereignty (säv'rən·tē) *n.* **1.** Supreme political power or authority. **2.** Supremacy in power or position.

spit *n.* A thin, pointed rod used to hold meat over a fire.

spoils *n., pl.* Goods and land captured in war; booty.

squander (skwän'dər) *v.* To spend wastefully or extravagantly.

stamina (stam'ə·nə) *n.* Endurance; ability to stand fatigue.

statute (stach'ōōt) *n.* A law or established rule.

steadfast (sted'fast') *adj.* Firmly established; unchanging; steady.

stealthy (stel'thē) *adj.* Intentionally secretive or sly. **—stealthily** *adv.*

stifling (stī'fling) *adj.* Suffocating; oppressively lacking in fresh air.

stoic (stō'ik) *adj.* Showing no emotion; indifferent.

stratagem (strat'ə·jəm) *n.* A trick or plan to fool an enemy.

stricture (strik'chər) *n.* **1.** A condition that limits, restrains, or restricts. **2.** Harsh criticism.

stupefy (stōō'pə·fī') *v.* To deprive of sensibility; stun.

stupendous (stōō·pen'dəs) *adj.* Amazing; astonishing in magnitude or scope.

stupor (stōō'pər) *n.* Condition in which there is a partial or complete loss of sensibility, as from shock.

suave (swäv) *adj.* Smoothly pleasant and polite. **—suavely** *adv.*

subdue (sub·dōō') *v.* **1.** To conquer. **2.** To bring wild land into a cultivated state.

submissive (sub·mis'iv) *adj.* Being obedient and yielding without resistance. **—submission** *n.*

subside (səb·sīd') *v.* **1.** To descend; move to a lower level. **2.** To become tranquil, less intense.

substantiate (səb·stan'shē·āt') *v.* To establish the existence or truth of; prove.

subtle (sut'əl) *adj.* **1.** Able to see fine distinctions. **2.** Mentally acute; clever. **—subtly** *adv.*

suckle *v.* **1.** To nurse. **2.** To bring up or rear.

suffice (sə·fīs') *v.* To meet or satisfy a need; to be sufficient.

sumptuous (sump'chōō·əs) *adj.* Expensive; lavish; luxurious.

superficial (sōō'pər·fish'əl) *adj.* **1.** Concerned only with the obvious; not profound; shallow. **2.** Lying on or affecting only the surface.

superfluous (sə·pur'flōō·əs) *adj.* **1.** Not necessary or needed. **2.** More than is needed.

supplant (sə·plant') *v.* To replace, especially through force, trickery, or treachery.

supplication (sup'lə·kā'shən) *n.* A humble prayer or request to a deity or superior.

surety (shoor'ə·tē) *n.* Guarantee.

surpass (sər·pas') *v.* To excel; outdo all others.

surreptitious (sur·əp·tish'əs) *adj.* Secretive. **—surreptitiously** *adj.*

sway *n.* Influence; clout; dominant control.

syntax (sin'taks) *n.* The arrangement, organization, and relationship of words in a sentence.

▼ T ▼

taciturn (tas'ə·turn') *adj.* Usually silent; not fond of talking.

tantamount (tan'tə·mount') *adj.* Equivalent in value, meaning, or effect.

tarry *v.* To stay in a place, especially in expectation; delay; linger.

temper *v.* To bring steel to the required degree of strength and toughness by heating and sudden cooling.

temperate (tem'pər·it) *adj.* Moderate; self-restrained.

tempestuous (tem·pes'chōō·əs) *adj.* Like a storm with high winds and heavy rain; violent.

temporal (tem'pə·rəl) *adj.* **1.** Worldly; not eternal. **2.** Of, pertaining to, or limited by, time.

tenet (ten'it) *n.* Any principle or creed held to be true, especially by some organization.

tenuous (ten'yōō·əs) *adj.* **1.** Not dense, as the atmosphere at a high altitude. **2.** Insubstantial; fragile; inadequate.

tepid (tep'id) *adj.* Lukewarm.

terminate (tur'mə·nāt) *v.* To end.

theological (thē'ə·läj'i·kəl) *adj.* Having to do with the study of God.

throng *n.* A multitude of people crowded together.

thwart (thwôrt) *v.* To hinder; block.

timorous (tim'ər·es) *adj.* Fearful; timid. **—timorously** *adv.*

torrid (tôr'id) *adj.* **1.** Very hot, especially with reference to climate. **2.** Extremely passionate.

tortuous (tôr'chōō·əs) *adj.* Winding; crooked; not straight.

transact (tran·zakt') *v.* To carry on or conduct, especially business —**transaction** *n.*

transgress (trans·gres') *v.* To go beyond the limits set by laws, commandments, and so forth. —**transgression** *n.*

traverse (trə·vʉrs') *v.* To move across.

tribute (trib'yōōt) *n.* Money paid to one nation's sovereign by another, as a tax, payment for protection, and so on.

tumult (tōō'mult') *n.* Noisy commotion and uproar; violent disturbance.

turmoil (tʉr'moil) *n.* Disturbed activity; violent agitation.

▼ **U** ▼

unassailable (un'ə·sāl'ə·bəl) *adj.* Unable to be successfully attacked or challenged.

unassuming (un'ə·sōō'ming) *adj.* Modest.

unconditional (un·kən·dish'ən·əl) *adj.* Absolute; without exceptions or reservations.

undermine (un'dər·mīn') *v.* **1.** To wear away the foundations of. **2.** To cause to weaken by craft or stealth.

underpin (un'dər·pin') *v.* To prop up or support from underneath.

undeterred (un·dē·tʉrd') *adj.* Not kept from action by fear or doubt.

undulate (un'dyōō·lāt) *v.* To move in a wavelike manner.

unremitting (un'ri·mit'ing) *adj.* Persistent; persevering; not stopping. —**unremittingly** *adv.*

unshriven (un·shriv'ən) *adj.* Without forgiveness of sin through confession.

unwonted (un·wän'tid) *adj.* Uncommon; unaccustomed; unusual.

upbraid (up·brād') *v.* To scold or rebuke strongly.

usurp (yōō·zʉrp') *v.* To take power unlawfully.

▼ **V** ▼

valiant (val'yənt) *adj.* Brave.

valor (val'ər) *n.* Bravery.

vanguard (van'gärd) *n.* The leading part of an army.

vanquish (vang'kwish) *v.* To conquer.

vehement (ve'ə·ment) *adj.* With great passion —**vehemently** *adv.*

venerate (ven'ər·āt') *v.* To look upon with reverence.

vent *v.* To express feelings.

veracious (və·rā'shəs) *adj.* **1.** Telling the truth; honest. **2.** Characterized by truth and accuracy.

vermin (vʉr'mən) *n. pl.* Various insects regarded as pests.

versatile (vʉr'sə·təl) *adj.* Able to do many things.

vex *v.* To irritate; annoy. —**vexation** *n.*

vicissitudes (vi·sis'ə·tōōdz') *n. pl.* Unpredictable and irregular changes in fortune, life, and so on; ups and downs.

vile *adj.* Very bad; evil; wicked; low.

vindictive (vin·dik'tiv) *adj.* Tending to seek revenge; retaliatory. —**vindictiveness** *n.*

vivacity (vi·vas'ə·tē) *n.* Liveliness; spiritedness.

void *n.* That which is empty; vacuum. *adj.* Empty; vacant.

voluminous (və·lōōm'ə·nəs) *adj.* **1.** Filling, or capable of filling, volumes. **2.** Of great quantity.

vulnerable (vul'nər·ə·bəl) *adj.* Easily attacked, tempted, or damaged.

▼ **W** ▼

wake *n.* A watch over a dead body before burial.

wane *v.* To grow smaller gradually, said of the moon's face, after it has been fully lighted.

wanton (wän'tən) *adj.* Willfully and intentionally malicious.

wax *v.* To grow larger gradually, said of the lighted portion of the moon's face, until the full moon is visible.

wisp *n.* A slender, filmy fragment or strand.

wrangle (rang'gəl) *v.* To dispute or quarrel angrily and noisily; brawl.

wrathful (rath'fəl) *adj.* Extremely angry.

wrest (rest) *v.* To snatch or wrench forcibly.

writhe (rīth) *v.* To twist and turn in pain.

▼ **Z** ▼

zenith (zē'nith) *n.* **1.** The summit; peak. **2.** That point in the sky directly overhead.

---

fat, āpe, cär; ten, ēven; is, bīte; gō, hôrn, tōol, look; oil, out; up, fʉr; get; joy; yet; chin; she; thin, then; zh, leisure; ng, ring; ə for a in ago; e in agent; i in sanity; o in comply; u in focus; ' as in able (ā'b'l).

Glossary

INDEX OF SKILLS

Literary Skills

The boldfaced page numbers indicate an extensive treatment of the topic.

Absurdism 1145
Acmeism 1223, **1224**
Allegory 198, 421, 771, 787, 1044, 1059, 1193, **1440**
Alliteration 84, **519,** 522, 1229, 1333, **1440**
Allusion 185, 436–437, 573, 1308, **1440**
Analogy 294, 300, 662, 664, **1440**
Anecdote 547, 550, 580, 629, 666, 671, 814, 820, **1440**
Antagonist 1450
Antithesis 195, **292, 634, 1440**
Aphorism 666, 671, **1440**
Apocalyptic literature 197
Apostrophe 77, 457, 1440
Archetype 8, 9, 54–55, 137, **1440**
Argument 285, 292
Arthurian romance 688, 720
Aside 1440
Assonance 568, 570, 1229, 1333, **1440**
Atmosphere 729, **1259,** 1263, **1441**
Autobiography 66, 208, **1233,** 1241, **1364,** 1374, **1441**
Ballad 512, 514, 687, 806, **1441**
Bard 71
Beast fable 443, 448–449, 629, 687, **941,** 944
Biography 552, 557, **1441**
Blank verse 932, 1441
Call-and-response (technique) 88
Canto 743, **1441**
Carpe diem 415, 655, 659, 807

Catharsis 371
Chansons de geste 679, 687, **693,** 702, **1441**
Chant 88, 93, 118
Character 33, 115, 176, 184, 245, 466, 479, 597, **599,** 609, 644, 702, 713, 740, **773,** 785, 787, 790, 791, 837, 931, 1001, 1041, 1068, 1092, 1125, 1193, 1206, **1215,** 1222, 1328, **1441–1442**
Characterization 15, **28,** 33, 101, 184, 441, 644, 713, 790, **1070,** 1092, **1442**
Chorus 305, 597, **1442**
Chronicle 684
Cliché 82, 771
Climax 17, 20, 368, 639, 644, 702, 844, 904, 1033, 1041, 1192, **1442**
Comedy 221, 302, 375, 803, 839, 844, 964, 965, **1442**
Comedy of manners 964
Commedia dell'arte 964
Complications 639, 644, 844, 889, 1033, 1041
Conflict 40, 45, 341, **382,** 408, 458, 468, 494, 609, 639, 719, **732,** 740, 844, 1041, 1044, 1213, 1321, 1328, 1350, **1403,** 1408, **1442**
Connotation 435, 1242, **1442**
Couplet 646, 661, 731, 805, **1442–1443**
Court poetry 443, 448, 512
Courtly love 420, 627, 679, 688, 689, 716, 814
Courtly romance 822, 838
Cradle song 89
Crisis 45
Dactylic hexameter 226, 421
Denotation 435, 1242, **1442– 1443**
Description 721, 729, **1443**
Destiny *See* **Fate**

Detail 208, 209, 531, 677, 790, 1259, 1263
Detective story 367, 1042
Dialogue 33, 293, 545, 677, 790, 987, 1005, 1127, 1222, 1354
Diary 503, 579, 580, 1427
Diction 1031, 1132, 1231, **1443**
Didactic literature 467, 590, 629, 661, 941, **1443**
Digression 458
Dirges 125
Drama 302–305, 375, 443, 453, 503, **563, 596–597,** 599, 609, 786–787, 793, 803, 839, **840–843, 929– 930, 933, 964–965, 985,** 987, 1069, **1127,** 1135, 1145, **1443**
Dramatic poetry 1290, 1293
Dramatic structure 844, 1443
Dystopia *See* **Utopian literature**
Elegiac couplet 409
Elegy 630, **631,** 632, **1317,** 1319, 1384, **1443**
End-stopped lines 932
Enjambment 812, 932, **1443**
Epic 102–103, **104,** 116, **136–138, 224–227, 380– 381,** 443, **458, 459,** 467, 484, **485,** 494, **495,** 610, 619, **646–647,** 685, 692, **693,** 702, **703,** 730, 731, 743, 987, **1444**
Epic conventions 225, 440, **1444**
Epic hero 104, 136, **138,** 152, 466, 485, 688, **693,** 702, 837, **1444**
Epic simile 226, 277, 441, **1444**
Epigram 483, 941, 944, **1444**
Epigraph 1329
Epilogue 931

Epiphany 1208, 1213, **1444**
Epistle **197**, 414
Epitaph 294, 839
Epithet **72**, 77, **1444**
Eponym **436**, **1444**
Essay 793, **1386**, 1392, **1444**
Exaggeration (hyperbole) 822, 838, 946, 1354, **1446**
Existentialism 1145, **1244, 1245**, 1257, 1445
Exodos 305
Exposition 844, 867, 1033, 1041
Extended metaphor 1125, 1149, 1152
Extended simile 1384
Fable 198, 443, 478, **479**, 483, 715, 940, **941**, 944, **1445**
Fairy tale **46**, 51, 52, 689, 731, **1445**
Falling action 844, 916
Fantasy 844, 867, 1146, 1272, 1282, 1315, **1445**
Fate 302, 305
Figures of speech (figurative language) 89, 122, **370**, 457, 616, 632, 807, 811, 1132, **1149**, 1152, 1265, 1269, **1295**, 1297, **1445**
Flashback 209, 225, **228, 1415**, 1427, **1445**
Foil 740, 837, **1445**
Folk songs 512, 514, 517
Folktale 1, 2, 5, **7**, 16, 22, 25, 58, 511, 644, 672, 687, 814, 820, **1445**
Folktale hero 7, 26–27
Foreshadowing 228, 740, 1058, 1108, 1213, **1335**, 1342, **1445**
Form 341, 609, 1005
Frame narrative 478, 638, 814, 1287, **1445**
Free verse 1144, **1229**, **1445**
Genre 66, 161, **987**, **1445**
Ghazal 629
Gothic style 1128–1129
Griots **70**, 88, 103, 119, 1331
Haiku 503, 563, 564, **572–**

573, 577, 589, **612, 1445– 1446**
Hero 7, **26–27, 54–55**, 102, 103, 104, **138, 371**, 380, 408, 440, 644, 685, 686, 688, 702, 703, 730, 731, 740, 822, 837
Hexameter 409
High comedy 964
Histories 378, 428
Hubris 33, 371
Humanism **797**, 800
Humor 101, 672–673, 785, 787, 842, 962, 1401
Hymn 72, 77, 161, 443, 447, 450, 454, **455**, 457, 512, **1446**
Hyperbole 410, 413, **1446**
Iambic pentameter 805, 932, 1003, **1446**
Idiom 1194
Imagery (image) 15, 16, **21**, 122, 194, 280, 283, 457, 519, 522, 570, 572, 573, **575**, 577, 612, 616, 617, 655, 664, 793, 867, **1012**, 1014, **1016**, 1020, 1025, **1028**, 1031, 1132, 1152, 1229, 1231, 1265, 1269, 1319, **1331**, 1333, **1446**
Imagist (movement) 283
In medias res 225, 382
Incremental repetition 1382, 1384
Instruction (Egyptian genre) 66, 68
Invocation 225
Irony 98, 122, 152, 184, 300, 305, **306**, 341, 557, **648**, 653, **705**, 713, **814**, 820, 838, 1020, 1031, 1041, 1061, 1068, **1282**, 1287, **1344**, 1350, **1446**
Journal 503, 580, 587
Kabuki 563
Lais 689, 715, 806
Legend 102, 103, 485, 512, 513, 541, 684, 720, 987, 1014, 1446
Literary tradition 61, 102,

443, 449, 503, 506, 511, 565, 627
Love poetry 67, 80, 82, 409, 420, 806, 811, 1011
Lü-shih (poetic form) 527
Lyric poetry 80, 186, **218, 280**, 283, 376, 455, 511, 513, 518, 532, 564, 619, 804, 807, 1290, 1410, **1446–1447**
Magical realism 1146, 1282, 1307, **1308**, 1315, **1447**
Maxims 415, **537**, 540, 542, 547, 1447
Metamorphosis 39, 421, 1155, 1193, 1308
Metaphor 82, 84, 89, **370**, 457, 616, 655, **716**, 719, 771, 807, 811, 1020, 1125, **1149, 1295**, 1297, **1447**
Metaphysical poetry 803
Meter 226, 409, 533, 805, 807, 1229, **1447**
Miracle plays 786–787
Modernism 1143–1144, **1302**, 1375, **1447**
Monody 279
Monologue 294
Monomyth 26
Mood 194, 466, 522, **527**, 531, 535, 575, 596, 916, 1010, 1014, 1022, 1025, 1061, **1448**
Moral 46, 51, 87, 198, 203, 479, 483, 590, 671, 785, 944, 1193, **1448**
Moral tale 503
Morality plays 786, **787**
Motif 10, 46, 655, 713, 1193, **1448**
Motivation 22, 24, **1448**
Mystery plays 786
Myth 1, 2, **5–6**, 7, 16, 22, 34, 58, 427, 485, 646, 704, 713, 714, 1308, **1448**; Origin myth 8, 9, 10, 15
Mythic hero 26, 27, 1308
Narrative 160, 162, 208, 209, 421, 503, **1448**
Narrative poetry 1290, 1293

Narrator 468, 644, 1197, 1299, 1448

Naturalism 983, 1032, 1042, **1448**

Neoclassicism 802, **1448**

Noh 503, 563, 589, **596–597,** 598, 609–610, **1448**

Nonfiction 1265, 1364, 1386, **1448**

Novel 503, 588, 821, 984, 987, **1128–1129,** 1145, 1146, **1448**

Novella 1155

Négritude 1147, **1330,** 1333, 1352

Octave 804, 805, 1003

Ode 305, 341, **415,** 661, 806, **1448–1449**

Onomatopoeia 122, 1229, **1449**

Oral epic 69, **102–103**

Oral literature (oral tradition) 2, **61,** 68, 71, 84, **88,** 89, 94, 104, **118–119,** 160, 224, 225, 447, 503, 511, 626, 679, 687, 691

Oratory 375

Orature 70, **88**

Oxymoron 811, **1449**

Parable 198, 203, 511, **590,** 595, **1044,** 1058, **1449**

Parados 305, 341

Paradox 468, 476, **542,** 545, 595, 1413, **1449**

Parallelism (parallel structure) 84, 88, **94,** 97, 122, 133, **186,** 194, **195,** 476, 522, 542, 634, **1449**

Parody 822, 837, 838, **1449**

Pastoral poetry 67, 379, **1449**

Pentameter 409

Persona 280, 1453

Personification 283, **370,** 457, **533,** 535, 616, 787, 807, 1010, **1304,** 1306, **1449**

Persuasion 285, 292, **1449**

Petrarchan (Italian) sonnet 804, 807, **1003**

Plot 17, 22, 177, **639,** 644, 801, 844, 889, **1033,** 1041, 1061, **1449–1450**

Poetry 1290, 1293, 1450 *See also* **Ballad, Epic, Lyric Poetry**

Point of view 34, 39, 168, 644, 653, 1031, 1041, 1092, 1152, 1193, **1197,** 1206, 1299, **1450**

Praise song 72, 77

Problem play 985

Prologue 305

Propaganda 377, 379

Prose poetry 578, 1021, **1265,** 1269, **1450**

Protagonist 1215, **1450**

Proverb 84, 87, 537, 626, **1450**

Psalm 161, **186,** 195, **1450**

Psychological realism 588, **1282**

Pun 580, 842

Quatrain 655, 805, 944, 1224, 1450

Quest 27, 28, **54–55,** 485, 822

Rationalism 937

Realism 973, **982–983, 984,** 985, 1042, 1069, **1127, 1450–1451**

Refrain 88, **514, 1022,** 1025, **1451**

Religious literature 66, 160, 302, 619, 624, 633, 634, 786

Repeat-and-vary (technique) 88

Repetition 88, **94,** 97, 102, 122, **162,** 168, 514, 517, 693, 702, 812, 1229, 1241, **1382,** 1384, **1451**

Resolution 639, 644, 844, 930, 1033, 1041

Rhapsode 224

Rhetoric 285, 428

Rhyme 84, 568, 572, 804, 812, 932, 1224, 1226, **1451**

Rhyme scheme 533, 655, 743, 804, 805, 807, 812, 941, 1003, 1224, 1229, **1451**

Rhythm 514, 517, 519, 568, 932, 941, 1195, 1231, 1265, **1451**

Riddle 466

Rising action 639, 844, 889

Romance 679, 688, 814, 820, 821, 822, 837, 838, 839, **1451**

Romanticism 52, 973, 976, **979,** 985, 986, 1002, 1015, 1022, **1451–1452**

Rubá'i 629, 654, **655,** 659, **1452**

Run-on lines *See* **Enjambment**

Saga 679, 683, 686, 714

Saints' lives 679, **687,** 715

Satire 691, 793, 806, **838,** 938, 946, 962, 983, 1272, 1280, **1352,** 1354, **1452**

Science fiction 9, 55, **1146,** 1271, **1272,** 1280, **1452**

Senryu **612–613**

Sestet 804, 805, 1003

Setting 45, 277, 466, 531, 790, 867, **1007,** 1010, 1259, 1280, 1314, **1452**

Shakespearean (English) sonnet 805, 807

Short story 177, 184, 421, 987, 1033, **1042,** 1207, **1452**

Simile 89, 93, 370, 457, 616, 807, 811, 1149, 1151, 1269, **1295,** 1297, 1384, **1452**

Skald 704

Sonnet 527, 793, 802, **804– 805,** 806, 807, 811, **1003,** 1005, **1452–1453**

Speaker 80, 82, 1301, **1410,** 1413, **1453**

Stanza 731, 1224, 1226, 1293, **1453**

Stock epithet 227, 441

Stream of consciousness 1144, 1207, **1208,** 1213, **1453**

Structure 305, 631, 644, **844**

Sturm und Drang ("Storm and Stress") 986
Style **429**, 435, 511, 526, 659, 731, 744–745, 807, 930, 985, 1061, 1132, 1263, 1453
Surrealism 1146, 1155, **1453**
Suspense 51, 494, 812, 844, 1042, 1108, **1453**
Symbol (symbolic meaning) 198, 542, 595, 599, 639, 743, 744, **746**, 759, 770, 771, 904, 1108, 1155, 1156, 1193, 1206, 1222, 1269, 1408, **1453**
Symbolism (poetic movement) **983**, 1022, 1026, 1028, 1223, **1453–1454**
Tall tale 1
Tanka 503, 562, **564–565**, 566, 567, 568, 570, 571, **1454**
Tercet 743
Terza rima 743, 746, **1454**
Theme 33, 39, 58, 116, **170**, 176, 305, **367–368, 406–407, 460**, 466, 531, 571, 634, 689, 732, 804, 806, 814, 822, 867, 1005, 1044, 1058, 1126, 1132, 1215, 1269, 1315, 1319, 1342, 1350, **1376**, 1380, **1394, 1432–1433**, **1454**
Tonal assonance 88
Tone 82, 413, **415**, 418, 531, **552**, 557, 577, 612, 631, 916, 1001, 1014, 1058, **1061**, 1068, 1132, **1356**, 1362, **1454**
Tragedy 302, 303, **304**, 369, **371**, 803, 839, 844, 987, **1454**
Tragic flaw *(hamartia)* 302, 371
Tragic hero 302, 369, **371**
Tragicomedy 843, 844, 931
Trickster **22**, 25, 497
Troubadour 689
Trouvère 687

Turn (in a sonnet) 804, 1003, 1005
Turning point (crisis) 45, 844, 904, 916
Tz'u (poetic form) 533
Understatement **705**, 713, 946, **1454**
Utopian literature **963**
Verbal irony 705, 713
Verse 627, 715, 716, 720, 731, 812
Volta (turn) 804, 1005
Wit **580**, 586, 793, 964, 1351, **1454**

Language and Vocabulary Skills

Most of the page numbers listed below refer to discussions that appear in the Language and Vocabulary exercises. The page numbers in italic type refer to subjects covered in the Language Skills exercises found at the end of each unit. Additional page references for some terms may also be found in the Literary Skills index on page 1488.

Active voice 587, *968–969*
Adjectives (from people's names) 1194
African influences on the English language 1342
Agreement, pronoun-antecedent *614–615*
Agreement, subject-verb *438–439*
Alliteration 519
Alphabet 215
Ambiguity 535
Analogy 294, 300, 662
Antecedent *1130*
Antithesis 292, 634
Antonyms 117
Apostrophe 457
Appositive 117

Arabic influences on the English language 1380
Asian influences on the English language 1401
Assonance 568
Avoiding sentence fragments and run-on sentences *498–499*
Blank verse 932
Capitalization *1461–1464*
Chinese characters 506, 507, 523, 1427
Choosing effective diction *788–789*
Clichés 82
Connotations 435
Context clues 117
Cuneiform 79, 130–131, 204–205
Dangling modifiers *207*
Deciphering ancient texts 204–205
Definitions 117
Denotations 435
Demotic script 83
Dialogue 33
Diction *788–789*, 1031, 1231
Enjambment 812, 932
Epic simile 408
Epithet 72, 77
Eponym 436–437
Etymology 418
Figures of speech (figurative language) 370
German influences on the English language 1152
Hebrew influences on the English language 1384
Hieratic script 83
Hieroglyphics 79, 83
Iambic pentameter 932
Idioms 1194
Ideographic writing system 1427
Imagery 21
Inference 16, 1432
Keeping pronoun reference clear *1130–1131*
Latin word roots 418
Loaded language 435

Maintaining pronoun—antecedent agreement *614–615*
Maintaining subject-verb agreement *438–439*
Maintaining verb tense consistency *674–675*
Metaphor 370
Middle English influences on the modern English language 785
Modifiers 1460
Native American influences on the English language 16
Nominative case 1458
Norse influences on the English language 713
Nouns and verbs, concrete *788*
Nouns and verbs, exact *788–789*
Objective case *1458–1459*
Oxymoron 610
Pacific language influences on the English language 1401
Parallelism 94, 186, 195, 476
Passive voice 587, *968–969*
Personification 370
Phonetic languages 1427
Pinyin transliteration 1427
Portuguese influences on the English language 1288
Prefixes 418
Pronoun-antecedent agreement *614–615*, 1457
Pronoun reference *1130–1131*, *1459–1460*
Pronouns *1130*, *1459–1460*
Propaganda 377, 379
Punctuation *1464–1471*
Quotations, punctuation of *120–121*
Repetition 94, 162, 514, 1382
Restatements 117
Rhetoric 223, 285, 293, 376, 428
Romance languages 1288
Run—on sentences *499*
Sentence fragments *498*
Sentences *1430–1431*
Simile 370

Spelling *1471–1473*
Subject-verb agreement *438–439*, *1455–1457*
Summary 45
Synonyms 117
Thesis statement 59
Tonal language 88
Transitional expressions 45, *56–57*
Translations 153, 169, 278, 523, 660, *1194–1195*
Using active and passive voices effectively *968–969*
Using quotations effectively *120–121*
Using transitions for comparison and contrast *56–57*
Varying sentence beginnings and avoiding dangling modifiers *206–207*
Varying sentences *1430–1431*
Verb tense consistency *674–675*
Vernacular 691, 745, 796
Wade-Giles transliteration 1427
Words from place names 1222
Writing systems 83, 1427

Speaking and Listening Skills

Acting out a parable 595
Conducting an interview 702
Creating a news report 653
Defending a position 152
Dramatizing a scene 729
Enacting a courtroom trial 557
Interviewing to find an answer 785
Planning and performing a choral reading 522
Staging an episode of the play 932
Storytelling session, A 820
Telling an anecdote 550
Telling the story of an unlikely hero 116

Composition Skills

Writing: A Creative Response

Adding a stanza to a poem 1293
Adopting a character's point of view 1092
Analyzing a character 1125
Capturing your own stream of consciousness 1213
Changing the premise 1315
Coauthoring a tanka 571
Composing a chant 93
Composing a rap song 517
Composing and delivering a sermon 637
Continuing the narrative 729
Continuing the story 1257
Creating a dialogue 545
Creating a folktale 644
Creating a list 587
Creating a new episode of the epic 152
Creating an atmosphere 1263
Creating riddles 466
Creating your own proverbs 87
Describing a place 1328
Describing an imaginary land 1025
Describing another metamorphosis 1193
Describing visual images 1319
Dramatizing a proverb 87
Drawing a character in the poem 97
Entering the story 1068
Exchanging letters 820
Extending the myth 369
Extending the story 33
Imagining a bizarre change 1401
Imagining a character's future 1068
Inventing a board game 770
Judging Socrates 300
Letting a "double" speak 1301
Narrating a dramatic event 1241
Narrating a series of events 21
Personifying nature 1306
Recording an oral history 116

Rewriting an account 435
Updating a parable 203
Writing a character sketch 1041
Writing a description 457
Writing a dialogue 1005, 1222
Writing a diary entry 653, 1427
Writing a different conclusion 1206
Writing a dramatic scene 413
Writing a fable 483, 944
Writing a fairy tale 52
Writing a fourth act 1125
Writing a haiku 577
Writing a humorous episode 713
Writing a hymn to the sun 77
Writing a letter 184
Writing a lyric 283
Writing a new ending 45
Writing a newspaper account 1020
Writing a parable 595
Writing a parody 837
Writing a personal essay 1392
Writing a persuasive letter 740
Writing a poem 664, 811, 1010, 1031, 1413
Writing a poem based on a myth 16
Writing a poem in letter form 522
Writing a prose poem using imagery 1269
Writing a rebuttal 476
Writing a rhymed stanza 1226
Writing a rubá'i 659
Writing a satire 962
Writing a satiric dialogue 1354
Writing a saying 671
Writing a scene from a larger story 719
Writing a science-fiction story 1280
Writing a screenplay 277
Writing a script 1242
Writing a sequel 494, 1350
Writing a skit 1001
Writing a speech for a character 1001
Writing a synopsis 931
Writing a television script 25

Writing a "thing poem" about an animal 1152
Writing about a chain of events 1293
Writing about a childhood memory 1380
Writing about a familiar place 1297
Writing about a legend 1014
Writing about a moment of decision 1408
Writing about a pet 1362
Writing about heritage 1333
Writing an autobiographical episode 1374
Writing an elegy 632, 1384
Writing and acting out a dramatic sketch 176
Writing as a different speaker 82
Writing from a bird's point of view 1288
Writing from a different point of view 39, 1193
Writing from another point of view 1152
Writing from the first-person point of view 168
Writing maxims 540
Writing song lyrics 535

Writing: A Critical Response

Analyzing a character 1193
Analyzing a dynamic character 1222
Analyzing a foil 740
Analyzing a poem's theme 1269
Analyzing a story's appeal 719
Analyzing an author's use of humor 962
Analyzing an essay's purpose 1392
Analyzing an internal conflict 1328
Analyzing characterization 184
Analyzing diction 1031
Analyzing form 341
Analyzing magical realism 1315
Analyzing Oedipus as a tragic hero 369

Analyzing the narrator as a character 644
Analyzing the poem's effect 535
Analyzing the poem's meaning 664
Analyzing the sonnet form 1005
Analyzing theme 466
Comparing a Sufi saying and a Zen parable 671
Comparing allegorical interpretations of myths 427
Comparing and contrasting accounts of the flood 176
Comparing and contrasting characters 1206
Comparing and contrasting characters in two works 1059
Comparing and contrasting heroes 277
Comparing and contrasting love poems 811
Comparing and contrasting maxims 540
Comparing and contrasting two folk songs 517
Comparing and contrasting two folktales 25
Comparing and contrasting two hymns 457
Comparing and contrasting two passages 545
Comparing and contrasting two poems 531
Comparing aspects of two Indian epics 494
Comparing democracies 292
Comparing dramatic forms 609
Comparing epic heroes 702
Comparing heroes 52, 408
Comparing love poems 82
Comparing lyric poetry 283, 413
Comparing poems 97
Comparing poetic themes 418
Comparing poets' views 1020
Comparing themes in two stories 1380
Comparing translations 1025, 1231
Comparing translations of the Twenty-third Psalm 194

Comparing two poems 1010, 1014
Comparing two translations 571
Comparing viewpoints 1413
Comparing views 550
Contrasting characters 931
Editing Shakespeare 932
Establishing a theme 168
Evaluating a character's actions 1001
Evaluating a statement of theme 39
Examining paradox 476
Explicating the theme 116
Identifying a main idea 101
Identifying theme 1126
Interpreting a passage 1126
Interpreting a poem 837
Interpreting a poet's philosophy 659
Making a literary judgment 770
Making and supporting a generalization 93
Making inferences 16
Responding to a critic 1193
Responding to a story 1288
Supporting an opinion 1041

Understanding analogies 300
Writing a character sketch 587
Writing about a poem's theme 1319
Writing about a title 1242
Writing about an author's purpose 1374
Writing about an epiphany 1213
Writing about an extended simile 1384
Writing about conflict 1408
Writing about existentialism 1257
Writing about foreshadowing 1342
Writing about négritude 1333
Writing about psychological insights 1401
Writing about satire 1280
Writing about style 1263

Critical Thinking Skills

The following list refers to the two-page Critical Thinking and Writing exercises that follow each unit. Additional exercises in all of the critical thinking skills, including synthesis, will be found in the Composition Skills index on the preceding pages.

Analyzing imagery 616–617
Creating an epic adventure 440–441
Discovering connections in literature 58–59
Identifying a theme 1432–1433
Observing and analyzing a process 676–677
A personal response to literature, 122–123
Resolving a controversy 970–971
Writing a character sketch 790–791
Writing a literary review 1132–1133
Writing an autobiographical narrative 208–209
Writing to persuade 500–501

INDEX OF AUTHORS AND TITLES

Page numbers in italic type refer to the pages on which author biographies appear. Translators of selections are identified by the notation *(trans.)*.

Achebe, Chinua *1343*; selection 1345–1349
Aeneid, from the 380–381; selection 383–406
African Proverbs 85–86
After he's scolded . . . 612
Akhmatova, Anna *1223*; selection 1225–1226
Akutagawa Ryunosuke *1393*; selection 1395–1400
Aldington, Richard (trans.) 947–961
al-Khansa *630*; selection 631–632
Amichai, Yehuda *1381*; selection 1383
Analects, from the 538–539
Anchor Bible, from The 194
Ancient pond . . . , The 573
And We Shall Be Steeped 1332
Anecdotes and Sayings of Saadi 667–670
Anecdotes of Mulla Nasrudin 672–673
Annals, from the 430–434
Annie John, from 1322–1327
Apology, from the 295–299
Applegate, Bergen (trans.) 1029
Arberry, A. J. (trans.) 660
Art of Poetry, from The 419
Asatarō Miyamori (trans.) 573
Ashanti Proverbs 85
Atsumori 600–609
Atwood, Margaret *1316*; selection 1318
Auslander, Joseph (trans.) 804, 808

Baganda Proverbs 86
Bargad, Warren (trans.) 1383
Barks, Coleman (trans.) 663
Barnard, Mary (trans.) 281–282
Barnstone, Willis (trans.) 631–632
Bashō *see* Matsuo Bashō

Baudelaire, Charles *1021*; selections 1023–1024, 1025
Behn, Harry (trans.) 573; 576
Beier, Ulli (trans.) 95–96
Beilenson, Peter (trans.) 576
Benson, Rachel (trans.) 1230
Bhagavad-Gita, from the 467; selection 469–475
Bible, from the 163–167, 171–175, 178–183, 187–193, 199–202
Black Cat 1150
Blossoms on the pear 576
Bly, Robert (trans.) 1151, 1231
Boccaccio, Giovanni *813*; selection 815–820
Bondanella, Peter (trans.) 815–820
Book of Songs, from The 512–513; selections 515–516
Borges and Myself 1300–1301
Borges, Jorge Luis *1298*; selection 1300–1301
Bownas, Geoffrey (trans.) 569–570
Bowra, C. M. (trans.) 97
Brahma 477
Burgos, Julia de 1302
Burning of Rome, The 430–434
Buson *see* Taniguchi Buson
But helpless Pieces of the Game He plays 660
Butterfly, The 548
By Any Other Name 1387–1391
Bynner, Witter (trans.) 525

Calvino, Italo *1258*; selection 1259–1263
Camus, Albert *1244*; selection 1246–1256
Canary's Ideas, A 1283–1287
Candide, from 947–961
Canterbury Tales, from The 774–784
Carpe Diem 417
Catullus *409*; selection 411–412
Cech, John 2–5
Cervantes, Miguel de *821*; selection 823–836
Cessation, The 635–636
Chapter X 1329
Chaucer, Geoffrey *772*; selection 774–784

Chekhov, Anton *1060*; selection 1062–1068
Chevrefoil 717–719
Chrétien de Troyes *720*; selection 722–729
Chuang Tzu *546*; selection 548
Chyet, Stanley F. (trans.) 1383
Ciardi, John (trans.) 747–769
Cline, Ruth Harwood (trans.) 722–729
Clinton, Jerome W. (trans.) 649–652
Cock and the Fox, The 943
Coghill, Nevill (trans.) 774–784
Colet, Roger (trans.) 1034–1040
Colquhoun, Archibald (trans.) 1259–1263
Colum, Padraic 35–38
Comfort 636
Confucius *536*; selections 538–539
Cooper, Arthur (trans.) 520–521, 528–529
Corngold, Stanley (trans.) 1156–1192, 1195
Council Held by the Rats, The 942
Courlander, Harold 98–100
Cowper, William (trans.) 416–417
Coyote and the Origin of Death 23–24
Cranes 1404–1407

Dante Alighieri *741*; selection 747–769
Dawood, N. J. (trans.) 635–636, 640–643
Daylight 636
Death of Atsumori, The 610–611
Decameron, from the 815–820
Dialogues, from the 295–299
Dickinson, Emily 82
Dinesen, Isak *1214*; selection 1216–1221
Discoverers of Chile 1296–1297
Divine Comedy, from the 742–745; selections 747–769
Doll's House, A 1071–1124
Don Quixote, from 823–836
Don't Ask Me What to Wear 282
"Don't worry," he says . . . 612
Doolittle, Hilda (H. D.) 283
"Do take out your teeth . . ." 613
Do You Want to Improve the World? 544

Driberg, Jack H. (trans.) 90–92
Duke, Francis (trans.) 1025

Ecclesiastes, from the Book of 545
Eldorado 1014
Elegy for the Giant Tortoises 1318
Elephant II, from The 97
Embarrassing Things 582
Emerson, Ralph Waldo 477
Enchanted Garden, The 1259–1263
End of My Journey, The 569
Epic of Gilgamesh, from the 136–
    137; selections 139–151, 153
Erdoes, Richard 23–24
Eveline 1209–1212
Even stones in streams 576
Every Single Thing 570
Exordium, The 635
Expiation, from The 1017–1019

Fables, from 942–943
Fagles, Robert (trans.) 278
Fall of Troy, The 383–406
Faust, Part I, from 988–1000
Ferdowsi, Abol-Qasem 647; selec-
    tion 649–652
Ferrante, Joan (trans.) 717–719
Fitts, Dudley (trans.) 307–367
FitzGerald, Edward (trans.) 656–
    658, 660
Fitzgerald, Robert (trans.) 229–
    276, 307–367, 383–406
For Wei Pa, in Retirement 528
Fox, Douglas G. (trans.) 101
Freedom to Breathe 1266
Frobenius, Leo (trans.) 101
Funeral Speech of Pericles 286–291

García Lorca, Federico 1228;
    selections 1230, 1231
García Márquez, Gabriel 1307;
    selection 1309–1314
Garnett, Constance (trans.) 1062–
    1068
Gbadamosi, Bakare (trans.) 95–96
Genesis, from the Book of 163–
    167, 171–175
Giovanni, N. T. di (trans.) 1300–
    1301
Glenny, Michael (trans.) 1266–
    1268
Goethe, Johann Wolfgang von 986;
    selection 988–1000
Gold, Gold 548–549
Golden Mean, The 416–417
Goldin, Frederick (trans.) 694–701

Grail, The 722–729
Graves, Robert 29–32
Great Hymn to the Aten, The 73–76
Green Willow 41–44
Grimm, Jakob and Wilhelm 52–53;
    selection 47–51
Guest, The 1246–1256
Guitar, The 1230, 1231

Half a Day, 1377–1379
Handsomest Drowned Man in the
    World, The 1309–1314
Hanning, Robert (trans.) 717–719
Hateful Things, from 582
Hatto, A. T. (trans.) 733–739
Hawkins, Thomas (trans.) 417
Hedin, Florence and Naboth (trans.)
    1198–1205
Heine, Heinrich 1011; selection
    1013
Henderson, Harold G. (trans.) 573,
    576
He who talks doesn't know . . . 541
History of the Peloponnesian War,
    from 286–291
Hollander, Robert (trans.) 809
Home from work . . . 612
Homer 224; selections 229–276,
    278
Horace 414; selections 416–417,
    419
How Helpless My Heart! 570
How Much Land Does a Man Need?
    1045–1058
How Siegfried Was Slain 733–739
How the World Was Made 11–15
Hughes, Langston (trans.) 1290
Hugo, Victor 1015; selection
    1017–1019
Humphries, Rolfe (trans.) 422–426
Hundred Questions 461–465
Hwang Sun-won 1402; selection
    1404–1407

I Am Not Lonely 1290
I Hate and I Love 412
I Have Visited Again 1008–1009
I Waited and I 569
Ibsen, Henrik 1069; selection
    1071–1124
If Ever Anyone Anywhere 412
If to the moon 573
Iliad, from the 224–227; selections
    229–276, 278
Inferno, from the 747–769

In Spring It Is the Dawn 581–582
In the Beginning 163–167
Invitation to the Voyage 1023–
    1024
Invitation to Travel 1025
Ishimatsu, Lorie (trans.) 1283–
    1287
It's all I have to bring today— 82

Jabo Proverbs 85
Jade Flower Palace 530
Jewels, The 1034–1040
Johnson-Davies, Denys (trans.)
    1377–1379
Jordan-Smith, Paul 41–44
Journey Along the Oka, A 1267–
    1268
Jowett, Benjamin (trans.) 286–291,
    295–299
Joyce, James 1207; selection
    1209–1212
Judging from the pictures . . . 612

Kaffir Boy, from 1365–1373
Kafka, Franz 1154; selections
    1156–1192, 1195
Kandel, Michael (trans.) 1273–
    1279
Keats, John 185
Keene, Donald (trans.) 571
Khayyám, Omar 654; selections
    656–658
Kimenye, Barbara 1355; selection
    1356–1362
Kincaid, Jamaica 1320; selection
    1322–1327
King James Bible, from the 163–
    167, 178–183, 187–193, 545
Ki Tsurayuki 566; selection 569
Kobayashi Issa 574, selection 576
Koran, from the 633; selections
    635–636

La Fontaine, Jean de 940; selec-
    tions 942–943
Lagerlöf, Selma 1196; selection
    1198–1205
Laments on the War Dead, from
    1383
Lao-tzu 541; selections 543–544
Lee, Peter H. (trans.) 1404–1407
Lem, Stanislaw 1271; selection
    1273–1279
Lesbia Says She'ld Rather Marry
    Me 412

Letter to His Two Small Children 520

Letters to a Young Poet, from 1153

Lewisohn, Ludwig (trans.) 1030

Li Ch'ing-chao *532*; selection 534

Lichtheim, Miriam (trans.) 73–76

Lieh Tzu *546*; selection 548–549

Life Is Sweet at Kumansenu 1336–1341

Ling Chung (trans.) 534

Li Po *518*; selections 520–521, 523–525

Little Girl That Lost a Finger, The 1291–1292

Lorelei, The 1013

Lost Horse, The 549

Lot's Wife 1225–1226

Love Must Not Be Forgotten 1416–1426

Lowell, Robert (trans.) 1017–1019

Lui An *546*; selection 549

Machado de Assis, Joaquim Maria *1281*; selection 1283–1287

MacNeice, Louis (trans.) 988–1000

Mahabharata, from the 458–459; selection 461–465

Mahfouz, Naguib *1375*; selection 1377–1379

Marie de France *715*; selection 717–719

Marriott, Alice 11–15

Masahiro Really Is a Laughing-Stock 583–584

Masai Proverbs 86

Mason, Herbert (trans.) 153

Mathabane, Mark *1363*; selection 1365–1373

Matsuo Bashō *574*; selections 573, 576, 578

Maude, Louise and Aylmer (trans.) 1045–1058

Maupassant, Guy de *1032*; selection 1034–1040

Maxims of Benjamin Franklin 540

Metamorphoses, from 422–426

Metamorphosis, The 1156–1192, 1195

Meyer, Michael (trans.) 1071–1124

Miller, Barbara Stoler (trans.) 469–475

Milton, John 770

Missing Axe, The 549

Mistral, Gabriela *1289*; selections 1290–1292

Mitchell, Stephen (trans.) 543–544, 1150

Moonrise 283

Moon's snow falls on the plum tree . . ., The 523

morning-glory vine, A 576

Morris, Ivan (trans.) 581–586

Most Beautiful Youth Who Ever Happened 81

Moyne, John (trans.) 663

Muddy Road 591

Muir, Willa and Edwin (trans.) 1195

Muñoz Marín, Muna Lee de (trans.) 1291–1292

Musa, Mark (trans.) 815–820

Mutability 1010

Myers, Reney (trans.) 411

Nakosteen, Mehdi (trans.) 672–673

Narayan, R. K. (trans.) 461–465, 486–493

Neruda, Pablo *1294*, selection 1296–1297

New English Bible, from the 199–202

New Jewish Society Publications 171–175

New Kingdom Love Lyrics 81

Nguyen Ngoc Bich (trans.) 1411–1412

Nguyen Thi Vinh *1409*; selection 1411–1412

Niane, D. T. 105–115

Nibelungenlied, from the 730–731; selection 733–739

Nicol, Abioseh *1334*; selection 1336–1341

Nieh Cheng 553–556

Night (from the *Rig Veda*) 456

Night, from (Wiesel) 1234–1241

Night Thoughts Afloat 529

Noah and the Flood 171–175

Nobel Acceptance Speech (Solzhenitsyn) 1270

Nobel Acceptance Speech (Wiesel) 1242–1243

No rice?—In that hour 576

Nose, The 1395–1400

Now, I Cannot Tell 569

Nukada, Princess *566*; selection 569

O'Brien, Justin (trans.) 1246–1256

O'Brien, Robert (trans.) 1230

Ode to a Nightingale, from 185

Oedipus Rex 302–305; selection 307–367

Off to work . . . 612

O'Flaherty, Wendy Doniger (trans.) 456

Ogun Kills on the Right 95–96

Old pond 573

Old silent pond, An 573

On a bicycle . . . 613

On a withered branch 576

One bite . . . 612

On Her Brother 631–632

Onitsura *see* Uejima Onitsura

Ono Komachi *567*; selections 570, 571

O Oriole, Yellow Bird 515

On top of skeletons 573

Origin of Death, The 25

Ormsby, Robert J. (trans.) 411

Ortiz, Alfonso 23–24

Oshikochi Mitsune *566*; selection 569

Osiris and Isis 35–38

Ovid *420*; selections 422–426

Ozymandias 531

Panchatantra, from the 478, selection 480–483

Parable (Richard Wilbur) 837

Parable, A (Zen) 591–592

Parables (New Testament) 199–202

Paradise Lost, Book I, from 770

Pasternak, Boris 1227

Paz, Octavio *1303*; selection 1305

Peonies 534

Perceval, from 722–729

Petrarch *806*; selections 804, 808

Philosophy and Spiritual Discipline 469–475

Pickett, G. D. (trans.) 105–115

Pig, The 1356–1362

Pillow Book, from The 581–586

Plato *293*; selection 295–299

Pleasing Things 585–586

Po Chü-i 541

Poe, Edgar Allan 1014

Popol Vuh, from the 18–20

Pound, Ezra (trans.) 523, 524

Problem, A 1062–1068

Prodigal Son, The 199–200

Prose Edda, from the 706–712

Prose Poem on the Unreal Dwelling, from 578

Psalm 23 (Anchor Bible translation) 194

Psalm 23 (King James Version) 187

Psalm 104 188–191

Psalm 137 192–193

Publishing the Sutras 592–593

Pushkin, Alexander *1006*; selection 1008–1009

Putnam, Samuel (trans.) 823–836

Quiet Night Thoughts 520

Rabassa, Gregory (trans.) 1309–1314

Rachlin, Carol K. 11–15

Radin, Paul 25

Rama and Ravana in Battle 486–493

Rama Rau, Santha *1385*; selection 1387–1391

Ramayana, from the 484; selection 486–493

Ramsay, George Gilbert (trans.) 430–434

Rat Trap, The 1198–1205

Records of the Historian, from 553–556

Reed, John (trans.) 1332

Reps, Paul (trans.) 591–594

Rexroth, Kenneth (trans.) 530, 534

Rig Veda, from the 454; selection 456

Right-Mind and Wrong-Mind 480–483

Rilke, Rainer Maria *1148*; selections 1150–1151, 1153

Rimbaud, Arthur *1027*; selection 1030

Ring, The 1216–1221

River Merchant's Wife: A Letter 524

Roberts, Moss (trans.) 548–549

Rodway, Stella (trans.) 1234–1241

Ronsard, Pierre de *806*; selection 809

Rubáiyát, from the 656–658, 660

Rumi *661*; selection 663

Russia 1812 1017–1019

Ruth, the *Book of* 178–183

Ryder, Arthur William (trans.) 480–483

Saadi *665*; selections 667–670

Saigyo, Priest *567*; selection 570

Sandars, N. K. (trans.) 139–151

Sappho *279*; selections 281–282

Schmitt, Jack (trans.) 1283–1287

Schulman, Grace (trans.) 1302

Seami Motokiyo *598*; selection 600–609

Seeger, Pete 517

Sei Shōnagon . . . 613

Sei Shōnagan *579*; selections 581–586

Senghor, Léopold Sédar *1330*; selection 1332

Shah, Idries (trans.) 667–670

Shakespeare, William *806, 839*; selections 805, 810, 845–928

Shahname, from the 646–647; selection 649–652

Shelley, Percy Bysshe 531, 1010

Shukei 613

Shunu 613

Simpson, William Kelley (trans.) 81

Sky Is Just Beyond the Roof, The 1029

Sleep, Darling 281

Sleeper of the Valley, The 1030

Snorri Sturluson *704*; selection 706–712

Sokan 573

So Lonely Am I 571

Solzhenitsyn, Aleksandr *1264*; selections 1266–1268, 1270

Song of a Mother to Her Firstborn 90–92

Song of Ch'ang-Kan, A 525

Song of Roland, from the 692; selections 694–701

Sonnet 29 (Shakespeare) 810

Sonnet 42 (Petrarch) 804

Sonnet 61 (Petrarch) 808

Sonnet 64 (Shakespeare) 810

Sonnet 73 (Shakespeare) 805

Sophocles *301*; selection 307–367

Sower, The 200–201

Soyinka, Wolé *1351*; selection 1353–1354

Ssu-ma Ch'ien *551*; selection 553–556

Storytelling Stone, The 2–5

Strand, Mark (trans.) 1305

Sundiata, from 102–103; selections 105–115

Supreme Good Is Like Water 544

Swan, The 1151

Tacitus *428*; selection 430–434

Takashi Kojima (trans.) 1395–1400

Talents, The 202

Tale of the Falcon, The 815–820

Tale of the Heike, from The 610–611

Tales of the Islands, from 1329

Talk 98–100

Talking Skull, The 101

Taniguchi Buson *574*; selection 576

Taoist Anecdotes 548–549

Tao Te Ching, from the 543–544

Taste of Banzo's Sword, The 593–594

Tedlock, Dennis (trans.) 18–20

Telephone Conversation 1353–1354

Tempest, The 842–843, selection 845–928

Theseus 29–32

Thief Who Became a Disciple, The 593

Things That Cannot Be Compared 582

Third Voyage of Sindbad the Sailor, from The 640–643

This perfectly still 565

Thomas, D. M. (trans.) 1008–1009

Thor and Loki in Giantland 706–712

Thoughts of Hanoi 1411–1412

Thousand and One Nights, from The 638; selection 640–643

Thucydides *284*; selection 286–291

Thwaite, Anthony (trans.) 569–570

To an Army Wife, in Sardis 282

To Anna Akhmatova 1227

To Hélène 809

To Julia de Burgos 1302

Tolstoy, Leo *1043*; selection 1045–1058

Tonight I've Watched 282

Tragedy of Sohráb and Rostám, from The 649–652

Trurl's Machine 1273–1279

Tu Fu *526*; selections 528–530

Uejima Onitsura *574*; selections 573, 576

Unmarked Boxes 663

Untermeyer, Louis (trans.) 1013

Verlaine, Paul *1027*; selection 1029

Village where they ring, A 576

Virgil *379*; selection 383–406

Voice of the Wild Goose, The 81

Voltaire, François-Marie Arouet *945*, selections 947–961

Wagging My Tail in the Mud 548
Wake, Clive (trans.) 1332
Walcott, Derek 1329
Waley, Arthur (trans.) 515–516, 538–539, 600–609
Walk to the Jetty, A 1322–1327
Watson, Burton (trans.) 553–556
We are playthings, and heaven is the player 660
We Drink Your Health 281
What Plant Is Not Faded? 516
When people see some things as beautiful 543
When You Are Old 811
Where Have All the Flowers Gone? 517
Whigham, Peter (trans.) 412

White Snake, The 47–51
Wiesel, Elie *1232*; selections 1234–1241, 1242–1243
Wife of Bath's Tale, The 774–784
Wilbur, Richard 837; (trans.) 1023–1024, 1225–1226
Wind and Water and Stone 1305
Wooden People, The 18–20
Wordsworth, William *1002*; selection 1004
Workmen eating lunch . . . 612
World Is Too Much with Us, The 1004
Wretched Catullus, Leave Off Playing the Fool 411
Wright Jr., Elizur (trans.) 942–943
Wright, Peggy (trans.) 1259–1263

Yang, Gladys (trans.) 1416–1426
Yeats, William Butler 811
Yoruba Proverbs 85
You Are the Herdsman of Evening 281
You May Forget But 282
Young, Jean I. (trans.) 706–712

Zen Parables 589; selections 591–594
Zen priest . . . 612
Zhang Jie *1414*; selection 1416–1426
Zipes, Jack (trans.) 47–51
Zulu Proverbs 86

Index of Authors and Titles

ACKNOWLEDGMENTS
(Continued from page iv)

J. M. Dent & Sons Ltd.: Quatrain # 44 from *A New Selection from The Rubáiyát of Omar Khayyám*, literal translation by Dr. A. J. Arberry. Published by The Unicorn Press, London, 1961.

Doubleday, a division of Bantam Doubleday Dell Publishing Group, Inc.: "Marriage Is a Private Affair" from *Girls at War and Other Stories* by Chinua Achebe. Copyright © 1972, 1973 by Chinua Achebe. "Psalm 23" from *Anchor Bible*. Copyright © 1985 by Doubleday, a division of Bantam Doubleday Dell Publishing Group, Inc. From *The Iliad* by Homer, translated by Robert Fitzgerald. Copyright © 1974 by Robert Fitzgerald. "Old pond" and transliteration of "Old pond" by Bashō, comment by Harold Henderson, "A morning-glory vine" by Kobayashi Issa, "On top of skeletons" by Onitsura, and "If to the moon" by Sōkan from *An Introduction to Haiku*, translated by Harold G. Henderson. Copyright © 1958 by Harold G. Henderson. "Half a Day" from *The Time and the Place and Other Stories* by Naguib Mahfouz, translated by Denys Johnson-Davies. Translation copyright © 1978 by Denys Johnson-Davies. Six senryū from *From the Country of Eight Islands*, edited and translated by Hiroaki Sato and Burton Watson. Copyright © 1981 by Hiroaki Sato and Burton Watson.

Dutton, an imprint of New American Library, a division of Penguin Books USA Inc.: "Borges and Myself" and from "commentary" from *The Aleph and Other Stories* by Jorge Luis Borges, translated by Norman Thomas di Giovanni. Translation copyright © 1968, 1969, 1970 by Emecé Editores, S. A. and Norman Thomas di Giovanni. From "Sayings by Saadi" from *The Way of the Sufi* by Idries Shah. Copyright © 1968 by Idries Shah.

Faber and Faber Limited: From the "Introduction" from *Voices from Twentieth-Century Africa: Griots and Towncriers*, edited by Chinweizu. Copyright © 1988 by Chinweizu.

Farrar, Straus and Giroux, Inc.: "Russia 1812" by Victor Hugo from *Imitations*, translated by Robert Lowell. Copyright © 1961 by Robert Lowell; copyright renewed © 1986, 1987, 1989 by Caroline Lowell, Harriet Lowell, and Sheridan Lowell. "A Walk to the Jetty" from *Annie John* by Jamaica Kincaid. Copyright © 1983, 1984, 1985 by Jamaica Kincaid. From *Memoirs* by Pablo Neruda, translated by Hardie St. Martin. Translation copyright © 1976, 1977 by Farrar, Straus and Giroux, Inc. From the appendix to *Cancer Ward* by Alexander Solzhenitsyn. Copyright © 1969 by Farrar, Straus and Giroux, Inc. From *Nobel Lecture* by Alexander Solzhenitsyn, translated by F. D. Reeve. English translation copyright © 1972 by Farrar, Straus and Giroux, Inc. "A Journey Along the Oka" and "Freedom to Breathe" from *Stories and Prose Poems* by Alexander Solzhenitsyn. Translation copyright

© 1970, 1971 by Michael Glenny. From "Tales of the Islands" from *Collected Poems 1948–1984* by Derek Walcott. Copyright © 1962, 1986 by Derek Walcott.

Angel Flores: "The Guitar" by Federico García Lorca, translated by Rachel Benson and Robert O'Brien from *An Anthology of Spanish Poetry from Garcilaso to García Lorca in English Translation with Spanish Originals*, edited by Angel Flores. Copyright © 1961 by Angel Flores.

Foreign Languages Press: Quote by Mao Tse-tung from "On Coalition Government" (April 24, 1945) from *Selected Works*, Vol. III, pg. 257. Copyright © 1945 by Foreign Languages Press.

Grove Press, Inc.: "Atsumori" by Seami Motokiyo, translated by Arthur Waley, "This perfectly still" by Ki no Tomonori (Japanese and English version), "So lonely am I" by Ono no Komachi, from "Sotoba Komachi" by Kan'ami Kioyotsugu, from "The Tale of the Heike," from "Prose Poem on the Unreal Dwelling" by Matsuo Bashō, and from "Introduction" from *Anthology of Japanese Literature*, edited and translated by Donald Keene. Copyright © 1955 by Grove Press, Inc. From letter by Ssu-ma Ch'ien to Jen An (Shao-ch'ing), and from page 118, translated by Burton Watson, from *Anthology of Chinese Literature*, compiled by Cyril Birch. Copyright © 1965 by Grove Press, Inc. From page 61 from *Waiting for Godot* by Samuel Beckett. Copyright © 1954 by Grove Press, Inc. From page 15 from *Hiroshima Mon Amour* by Marguerite Duras, translated by Richard Seaver. Copyright © 1961 by Grove Press, Inc.

Harcourt Brace Jovanovich, Inc.: *Oedipus Rex* by Sophocles, translated by Dudley Fitts and Robert Fitzgerald. Copyright 1949 by Harcourt Brace Jovanovich, Inc. and renewed © 1977 by Cornelia Fitts and Robert Fitzgerald. CAUTION: All rights, including professional, amateur, motion picture, recitation, lecturing, performance, public reading, radio broadcasting, and television are strictly reserved. Inquiries on all rights should be addressed to Harcourt Brace Jovanovich, Inc., Orlando, FL 32887. "The Enchanted Garden" from *Difficult Loves* by Italo Calvino. Copyright 1949 by Giulio Einaudi editore, Torino. Copyright © 1958 by Giulio Einaudi editore s.p.a., Torino. English translation copyright © 1984 by Harcourt Brace Jovanovich, Inc. "Sonnet" by Pierre de Ronsard from *Western Literature II: The Middle Ages Renaissance Enlightenment* by Robert Hollander and A. B. Giamatti. Copyright © 1971 by Harcourt Brace Jovanovich, Inc. "Parable" from *Ceremony and Other Poems* by Richard Wilbur. Copyright 1950 and renewed © 1978 by Richard Wilbur. "Charles Baudelaire: L'Invitation au Voyage" from *Things of This World* by Richard Wilbur. Copyright © 1956 and renewed © 1984 by Richard Wilbur.

HarperCollins Publishers, Inc.: From "The Elephant II" from *Primitive Song*, translated by C. M. Bowra. Copyright © 1962 by C. M. Bowra. From *An Open Life: Joseph Campbell in Conversation with Michael Toms*, selected